I: HOMER TO CERVANTES

GREEK AND ROMAN CLASSICISM
HOMER: *Odyssey*
SOPHOCLES: *Œdipus the King; Antigone*
EURIPIDES: *Medea*   PLATO: *The Apology; Phædo*
VIRGIL: *The Æneid*   PLUTARCH: *Antony*   LYRIC POETRY

THE MIDDLE AGES
The Song of Roland   The Nibelungenlied
Tristan and Iseult   DANTE: *The Divine Comedy*
CHAUCER: *The Canterbury Tales*

HEBRAISM
The Bible

THE RENAISSANCE IN EUROPE
RABELAIS: *Gargantua*   MONTAIGNE: *Essays*
CERVANTES: *Don Quixote*

II: SHAKESPEARE TO ADAMS

THE RENAISSANCE IN ENGLAND
SHAKESPEARE: *Romeo and Juliet*   BACON: *Essays*
MILTON: *Paradise Lost*
LYRIC POETRY *of the Renaissance*

NEO-CLASSICISM
MOLIÈRE: *Tartuffe*   RACINE: *Phædra*
VOLTAIRE: *Candide*

ROMANTICISM AND THE MODERN WORLD
ROUSSEAU: *Confessions*   GOETHE: *Faust*
TOLSTOY: *The Death of Ivan Ilyitch*
IBSEN: *An Enemy of the People*   LYRIC POETRY

CROSS-CURRENTS
from THE EDUCATION OF HENRY ADAMS

808.8
E95
vol. 1

PN
6014
.E88
vol. 1

8834

Masterworks

OF WORLD

Literature

EDWIN M. EVERETT, Head, Dept. of English

CALVIN S. BROWN, Professor of English

JOHN D. WADE, Former Head, Dept. of English
UNIVERSITY OF GEORGIA

VOLUME ONE

THE DRYDEN PRESS · NEW YORK

Copyright, 1947, by The Dryden Press, Inc.

386 Fourth Avenue, New York 16, N. Y.

The selections reprinted in this work are used

by permission of and special arrangement with the

proprietors of their respective copyrights.

Designed by Stanley Burnshaw

Manufactured in the U. S. A.

First Printing, August 1947

Second Printing, November 1948

Third Printing, September 1949

PREFACE

LIKE most anthologies, the present work began with an ideal and ended in a practical solution. The ideal was to give the reader a grasp, and a sense of the entirety, of a limited number of masterworks of the Western World. This could best be effected by presenting complete texts—as has been done here with all the plays but *Faust*. But such broad inclusiveness is physically and pedagogically impossible, and the ideal remains only in the fact that these volumes offer more extensive selections from fewer works than any similar anthology. Furthermore, those works that are offered in abridged form convey a greater than usual impression of organic unity. The editors believe that the present anthology may justifiably be regarded as an approach to the "Great Books" plan of teaching world literature.

Abridgments have been made according to the structure of the works. Since the *Nibelungenlied*, for example, falls into two halves, it is possible to confine the readings to the story of Siegfried and merely to indicate in the introduction that the poem proceeds to the revenge of Kriemhild. But Part I of *Faust* leaves the essential problem in suspense, and it is therefore necessary to carry the reader on to the last act of Part II for the solution. *Don Quixote* and *Gargantua and Pantagruel* are both highly episodic, but the basic idea of Cervantes requires that the reader be present at the end, whereas the lack of organic structure in Rabelais makes possible the use of only the earlier part as an adequate representation of the whole. Thus the method of abridgment varies, but the purpose is always to give as great a sense of integrity as space will permit. The extent of abridgment is always clearly shown. Omissions of more than a few lines are indicated, and all considerable omissions are summarized in brackets.

The final choice of the selections represents a long and distressing process of winnowing. Few readers will question the inclusion of any of the writers who survived; many will protest the exclusion of their favorites. The tests applied, in general, were intrinsic merit, international importance, incorporation into the tradition of Western civilization, and teachability. No attempt was made to provide proportional representation to countries or languages. In the main sections there are

CONCORDIA COLLEGE LIBRARY
BRONXVILLE, N.Y. 10708

many French writers, but only one Spanish, one Italian, one Russian, and no American: for this disproportion the editors feel no sense of responsibility. Going beyond the literature of power and into the literature of knowledge would undoubtedly have altered this pattern.

The inclusion of three groups of lyrics makes it possible to extend the list of writers represented. In these groups, however, the emphasis is upon periods and tendencies rather than upon authors. Because of the insuperable difficulty of translating lyric poetry, the English lyric is intentionally stressed. Thus the use of *Paradise Lost* instead of *Der Messias* indicates an editorial evaluation of Milton and Klopstock, but the inclusion of Keats instead of Hölderlin implies no such judgment.

It is regrettable that the most popular literary form of modern times cannot be properly represented in a collection. The great novels of England, France, Russia, and the United States are simply not honestly presentable in an anthology.

The format and design of these volumes are intended to encourage reading. Boswell reports that Dr. Johnson "used to say that no man read long together with a folio on his table:—'Books,' said he, 'that you may carry to the fire, and hold readily in your hand, are the most useful after all.' He would say, such books form the man of general and easy reading." Although few of our students today have fires, it may not be entirely quixotic to hope that some of them will become men of general and easy reading. The editors wish to thank Mr. Stanley Burnshaw of The Dryden Press for designing these volumes with that end in view; they believe that the convenient size and format of the type-page—set in single, rather than double, column and omitting marginal line numbers—should add to the student's enjoyment of reading.

And they wish to thank Mr. Burnshaw and Mr. Donald Ambler, also of The Dryden Press, for their encouragement, their counsel, and their tyranny in bringing to an issue an enterprise that many times threatened to fail from either inanition or distraction. The editors' colleagues upon the staff of the English Department of the University of Georgia have patiently listened and advised, and among these Mr. Roosevelt P. Walker has participated in the planning of the work and in some of the editing. More practically than anyone else, Mrs. Calvin S. Brown has assisted this venture in the burdensome task of reading proof.

Acknowledgment of permissions to use copyrighted material, as well as indebtedness to translators, has been made in footnotes at the beginning of certain selections. In addition, the editors record the following acknowledgments:

The translation of Montaigne's *Essays*, by Charles Cotton as revised by W. C. Hazlitt, is used by permission of G. Bell & Sons, London.

The translation of Pushkin's "Message to Siberia," by Max Eastman, is used by permission of *The Nation*, New York.

The *Odyssey* is translated by S. H. Butcher and Andrew Lang; *Œdipus the King* and *Antigone*, by E. H. Plumptre; *Medea,* by M. Wodhull; the *Apology* and *Phædo*, by Benjamin Jowett; the *Æneid*, by J. W. Mackail; Plutarch's *Antony*, by John Dryden as revised by A. H. Clough; the *Divine Comedy*, by J. A. Carlyle, Thomas Okey, and P. H. Wicksteed; Rabelais' *Gargantua*, by Sir Thomas Urquhart and Peter A. Motteux; *Don Quixote,* by Peter A. Motteux; *Tartuffe,* by H. Van Laun; *Phædra,* by Robert Henderson; *An Enemy of the People,* by R. F. Sharp. Rousseau's *Confessions* is taken from John Grant's translation, published by the J. M. Dent Company, London, and by E. P. Dutton, Inc., New York. The prose versions of the *Canterbury Tales* were done by Edwin M. Everett.

The binding illustration of Volume Two, a detail of Rodin's "The Thinker," is reproduced from *Rodin*, by courtesy of the Phaidon Press, Ltd. and the Oxford University Press, New York.

E. M. E.

C. S. B.

J. D. W.

Athens, Georgia
August, 1947

TABLE OF CONTENTS

Greek and Roman Classicism

The Middle Ages

Hebraism

The Renaissance

I.   The Renaissance in Europe

LYRIC POETRY OF GREECE AND ROME

GREEK AND
ROMAN
CLASSICISM

GREEK AND ROMAN CLASSICISM

EUROPEAN HISTORY PROPER, as distinguished from purely archaeological and anthropological data, may be said to begin about a thousand years before the birth of Christ in the eastern end of the Mediterranean. On such a computation we have thirty centuries of history behind our present civilization, and exactly half of this period is entirely dominated by Greece and Rome. It is small wonder, then, that the culture of these countries has exerted a tremendous influence on the latter half of our history and is still a powerful force in our institutions and our habits of thought. Whether we consider literature, philosophy, and mathematics, or engineering, democracy, and public administration, we find that Greece and Rome not only made the crude beginnings—as the first comers they had to do that—but also established fundamental principles which are still valid. In their happiest efforts, they achieved results unsurpassed in their kind.

When we speak of Greece during classical times we mean both more and less than the name implies today: less because Greece was not a country politically until shortly before Rome conquered her, but rather a collection of independent city-states; and more, because Greece was not merely a peninsula and a few adjoining islands, but was a civilization including a considerable part of Asia Minor, Sicily and southern Italy, and ultimately northern Egypt.

In pre-Homeric times the Greeks had invaded the peninsula from the north, though the different Greek tribes did not settle down into their permanent homes until considerably later. Not too much is known about Greek history during these early times—the essential facts are given in our introduction to Homer. Epic, lyric, and didactic poetry are the chief literary remains of this pre-Athenian period.

In the early part of the fifth century before Christ, Athens took the lead in repelling an attack on Greece by the Persian Empire, and thus became the acknowledged leader of Greece. Her domination in the intellectual sphere was even more obvious than in the political, and when we think of the outstanding achievements of classical Greece, we frequently have in mind Athens in the fifth and early fourth centuries B.C. Here belong the tragic poets Aeschylus, Sophocles, and Euripides; the comic poet Aristophanes; the historian Thucydides; the philosophers Socrates and Plato; and the statesman Pericles, from whose name is taken the designation "Periclean Athens" for this climax of Greek civilization. Even after Athens declined politically, she kept her intellectual leadership, so that most Greek writers or thinkers of any importance had some close connection there. Herodotus, whom Cicero calls "the father of history," visited Athens on several occasions and gave readings of his book, and Aristotle spent his youth there as a student and returned as a teacher for his last years.

After the death of Alexander the Great (323 B.C.), Greece rapidly declined and Alexandria (in Egypt) became the center for literature and philosophy. The Alexandrian Age produced more scholarship than creative work and gave rise to few writers of any great significance, but to the labors of its scholars we owe a considerable part of our knowledge of earlier Greek culture. Finally, Constantinople (Byzantium, before it was renamed for the Roman Emperor Constantine), as the seat of the Eastern Roman Empire, became a repository for the learning and manuscripts of ancient Greece, and from there they emerged to reawaken Europe during the Renaissance.

The legendary date for the founding of Rome, 753 B.C., seems to be reasonably accurate, though the story that its founders were fugitive Trojans is pure myth. For a long time Rome was a minor settlement ruled over by a series of kings who were finally ousted in 510 B.C. During the five centuries of republican rule which followed, Rome gradually became a great power. She expanded in Italy, fought a series of desperate wars with her great rival, Carthage, from which she emerged victorious, and set out on a career of conquest which made her mistress of practically all the known world. Soon after Greece began to decline, she became a Roman colony. So did all Europe west of the Rhine (including England) and south of the Danube, as well as Asia Minor (Christ was a Roman subject), Egypt, and the whole of Mediterranean Africa. Midway in this period of conquest, during the time of Augustus, Rome evolved from a republican to an imperial form of government. For some time she ruled the world, but gradually the empire began to crumble at the edges. The Roman legions were withdrawn from England in A.D. 410 because they were needed for defence nearer home; the barbarians gradually closed in on the decaying empire. The year A.D. 476 is usually taken as the end of the Western Roman Empire.

No single reason can be assigned for its collapse. Actually, it continued to exist long after it had lost its vitality, and its rise, flourishing, and decline are the normal stages in the history of any empire. Nevertheless, its collapse has been attributed, at one time or another, to Christianity, to divorce, to malaria, to excessive growth, and to any number of other simple causes. Almost everyone who has a historical or social axe to grind proceeds to grind it on the Fall of Rome.

The best literature of Rome was produced within a relatively short period and was strongly influenced by the Greeks. It is significant that one of the first ambitious literary works in Latin was a translation of the *Odyssey,* and that its author, a Greek slave, also wrote tragedies and comedies adapted from the Greek. This was about 240 B.C., and Roman literature before that time is negligible. In fact, with the exception of the comic poets Plautus and Terence, nothing of permanent value was produced before the first century B.C., and the greatest period of Latin literature was over at the death of Augustus in A.D. 14. It is customary to divide this flowering of literature into a Ciceronian Age, beginning about 70 B.C. and including Cicero, Catullus, and Lucretius as its principal writers, and an Augustan Age, extending from 27 B.C. to A.D. 14, during which Virgil, Horace, Ovid, and Livy wrote. The later centuries never matched the literature of these periods, though they produced a number of distinguished authors in a series extending down almost to the fall of the empire.

Unlike the great Athenians, the writers of Rome were not natives of the city. A table of the birthplaces of the fifty leading writers in Latin shows only five who may possibly have been native Romans, and not a single one who is known to have been born in the capital. This fact points to an important distinction. Periclean Athens produced and stimulated its own intellects, but Rome merely attracted by extraneous means those produced elsewhere.

In a broader sense, something like this is true of Latin literature as a whole. While it makes its own contributions and has its own originality, it is largely based on that of Greece, which was one of the principal subjects taught in the schools. Virgil recognized the fact in a famous passage in the *Aeneid,* in which Anchises tells Aeneas that others may be better artists, poets, and thinkers, but the mission of Rome is to stabilize and govern the world.

In many respects the Romans resembled contemporary Americans: they had a rather narrow practicality; they worshipped size, and considered that in both architecture and institutions "bigger" necessarily meant "better", their arts were largely transplanted, and were not held in great esteem by the general populace; but they had a peculiar genius for engineering and organization, and, in the days of the Republic, they made large-scale democracy actually work over a long period of time in spite of a great amount of graft and corruption.

HOMER

The Odyssey

THE OLDEST BOOKS of Europe that have survived are the *Iliad* and the *Odyssey,* which contain the only written record of the Homeric or Achaian age of ancient Greece. The evidence of archaeologists, particularly of Heinrich Schliemann, who in the nineteenth century excavated the sites of ancient Troy, Mycenae, and Tiryns, is in substantial accord with the evidence of these poems. This civilization was not nationalized in the modern sense of the word, for it was not composed of different national stocks with different customs, institutions, and languages.

Although topography made social unity difficult, this Greek world comprised a number of states and kingdoms having a common language in spite of great dialectal variations, similar political institutions, and essentially the same gods, commonly recognized, if not always commonly worshipped. Governments were monarchies supported by patriarchal aristocracies; and though the king, who was likely to be chief soldier, judge, and priest, ruled as by divine right, he frequently had a strong sense of social responsibility, and kings and queens were not above working like the lowliest servants. Slavery was

5

a common institution, but slaves were frequently part of the family and enjoyed a comfort and security above the hired laborer. Copper and bronze were the chief metals; silver and gold were known, and iron was coming into use.

Among professional men were minstrels, sooth-sayers, and physicians. Farming, the arts, and crafts were the chief occupations. Trade was conducted usually by barter, and the ox was the chief unit of value. The position of women was in many ways better than in some later centuries; polygamy and divorce were unknown. Feasting, singing, dancing, and athletic sports were the chief forms of entertainment. Hospitality of the most generous sort was a high ideal and a common practice. As far back as this civilization the origin of European literature has been traced.

No one can say just when Greek poetry had its beginnings, but a type of verse celebrating the heroic deeds of men and gods arose among the Aeolians of Thessaly in northern Greece perhaps as early as 1000 B.C. This poetry was in the form of ballads or lays, and it was sung by minstrels, for there was then, and for many centuries after, no reading public in Greece. Although not the first poetry of Europe, it must have been the most popular of its time; and so strong was its appeal that in their migrations to the coast of Asia Minor, the Aeolians carried with them these songs of their national heroism and worship. It is generally believed today that in Asia Minor the Ionian Greeks, neighbors of the Aeolians, adopted these songs; that somehow in this part of the world and among these two Greek peoples this poetry was developed and perfected in a literary type called the epic; and that a man named Homer played a more than ordinary part in this perfecting.

Who the man Homer was, no one knows, nor is there any reliable assurance that such a person ever actually lived. According to persistent legend he was blind, he was the author of many poems, and after his death seven different cities claimed the honor of having given him birth. It is now believed that most probably he was born in Smyrna on the coast of Asia Minor and that he wrote his poetry on the Ionian island of Chios. The time of his birth has been placed as early as the twelfth century B.C. and as late as the seventh; most recent authorities have placed it in the ninth. One fact alone is certain: as far back as the obscure beginnings of European literature the name of Homer has been identified with the heroic tradition in poetry, at first as the author of many epic poems but finally as the creator of the *Iliad* and the *Odyssey* only.

   The Greek epic was a long narrative poem on an exalted subject of greater than local scope, treated with artistic elaboration and in the grand style. It dealt with characters of heroic stature; and presiding over its action, and at times taking part in it, were the gods and goddesses of Olympus. The epic poems of the Greeks seem to have grown up around several great legendary subjects, the chief of which was the Trojan War, which is thought to have occurred at some time about the twelfth century B.C. And in the literary traditions and records of the Greeks there are indications of a whole series of epic poems dealing with the genesis of that war, the ten years' siege of Troy, and the subsequent fortunes of the greatest of the heroes. The *Cypria* narrated the causes of the war and the events leading up to the *Iliad*. After the action of the *Iliad* three other poems—the *Aethiopis,* the *Little Iliad,* and the *Sack of Ilion*—carried the story to the end of the war. The *Homecomings* and the *Odyssey* recounted the return of the heroes to their own lands. Finally, one other poem, the *Telegoneia,* is said to have continued the story of Odysseus and related the circumstances of his death. Of all these the *Iliad* and the *Odyssey* are the only Greek epics that have survived.

   In their main actions the *Iliad* and the *Odyssey* give only a small part of the large legend of the Trojan War, though various diversions from their themes enlarge the account. In later Greek literature, in the tragic drama, for instance, the rest of the legend comes to light, so that pieced out from many sources, the whole story may be told, of how the god Zeus realized by somewhat devious means his desire to reduce the number of inhabitants of a world grown too populous.

   When Zeus and Poseidon, who both loved the sea-nymph Thetis, learned of a prophecy that she would bear a son greater than his father, their ardor was somewhat mitigated, and they married the nymph to a mortal, King Peleus, ruler of the Myrmidons in Phthia. During the wedding feast Eris, goddess of discord, piqued at not being invited to the ceremonies, cast among the guests a golden apple inscribed "For the Fairest," whereupon rose great commotion among the women. Hera, Pallas Athene, and Aphrodite preferred the strongest claims, and these contestants sought final judgment of a young shepherd named Paris, actually the son of Priam, king of Troy. The goddesses were not above offering Paris bribes to win his decision, and Aphrodite bore off the prize when she promised him the most beautiful woman in Greece for his wife. With Aphrodite's aid Paris assumed his princely position, sailed for Sparta to visit the court of King Menelaus, and eloped with Helen, Menelaus' wife.

Menelaus now called upon the other kings of Greece for help in regaining Helen, for before her marriage her suitors had pledged their aid to the successful man should he ever need it in protecting her. Under the leadership of Agamemnon, Menelaus' brother, the Greeks assembled at Aulis a great expeditionary force and after some difficulty and delay sailed against Troy. By emissaries they demanded the surrender of Helen; but the Trojans, though far inferior to the Greeks in numbers, refused to give her back and elected to fight. For nine years the Greeks besieged Troy, but because of the strong fortifications and the stubbornness of the defense they accomplished little besides ravaging the surrounding countryside. In the tenth year of the war, however, their persistence succeeded.

The *Iliad* narrates the events of fifty-one days of the tenth year of the Trojan War. Its central theme, which at times is blurred by other interests, is the quarrel of Agamemnon and the great Achilles, son of Peleus and Thetis, over possession of Briseis, a woman captured by Achilles in one of the Greeks' many marauding expeditions against neighboring towns. When Agamemnon takes Briseis, in bitterness and wrath Achilles withdraws from the fighting and through his mother prevails upon Zeus to give victory to the Trojans so long as the Greeks continue to disregard his worthiness. Shortly thereafter Paris challenges Menelaus to single combat to decide the issue of the war. A truce is declared; but in the fight between the two champions Menelaus wounds Paris, and Aphrodite rescues her favorite and conveys him safely to the royal palace. General fighting is resumed, in which the god Ares and the goddesses Hera, Pallas, and Aphrodite take part and in which the Greek hero Diomed distinguishes himself. In a scene of deep pathos Hector, son of Priam and pre-eminent warrior among the Trojans, bids farewell to his wife Andromache and his infant son Astyanax and returns to the fighting as the Trojans assume the offensive and storm the Greek camp. The Greeks appeal to Achilles for aid, but he is stubborn in his resolution not to fight. The plight of the Greeks growing desperate, Achilles' dearest friend, Patroclus, borrows Achilles' armor and leads Achilles' followers against the Trojans. Patroclus turns the tide of battle, but he ventures too far and is killed by Hector, who strips from him the armor of Achilles. By the most desperate fighting the Greeks barely rescue his body.

When Achilles learns of the death of Patroclus, he is overcome with grief but determines to avenge his friend. Obtaining new armor from the god Hephaestus and making up his quarrel with Agamemnon, he leads the Greeks in driving most of the Trojans back into the city. He kills Hector, abuses his dead body, and drags the corpse into the Greek camp. After the burial of Patroclus and the funeral games in his honor, Priam successfully appeals to Achilles to return his son's body. The *Iliad* ends with the funeral of Hector.

After the action of the *Iliad* the legend tells of the death of Achilles, who is killed by Paris with the aid of Apollo; the stratagem of the wooden horse devised by the Greeks to gain entrance into Troy; and the sacking and destruction of the city. Finally, the war ended, the Greeks depart for home, some of them to return to disaster, many of them never to reach their goal, and one of them to come back after ten years' wandering, alone, unknown, and beset by dangers in his own house.

Odysseus, king of Ithaca, an island off the west coast of Greece, is the hero of the *Odyssey,* a work composed possibly by the author of the *Iliad,* possibly by another hand as much as a hundred years later. Although the time taken by Odysseus in returning from Troy is ten years, the action of the *Odyssey* occupies only about six weeks. The basic pattern of the verse is dactylic hexameter; that is, the lines contain six feet called dactyls, the dactyl being a combination of a long syllable followed by two short ones. (Accentuation, or stress as observed in English poetry, is artistically irrelevant in the classical Greek and Latin poets.) There is no rhyme in either the *Iliad* or the *Odyssey.* The language is basically Ionian Greek with admixtures of the Aeolian dialect. It is a language never spoken by any one people in any one place or time; and it is in the language as much as in any other evidence that the explanation is found for the difficulty of consigning the authorship of the *Iliad* and the *Odyssey* to a particular time and a particular place. It is undoubtedly true that, though one man may have originally written either or both of the poems, their composition as they exist today in manuscripts of the tenth century of the Christian era has been affected by many hands in many times.

The *Odyssey* is a book of high adventure, sudden turns of fortune, dramatic suspense, and heroic triumphs. Though its theme, taken too literally, may seem no more exalted than the story of a husband trying against considerable odds to get home to his wife, it is the epic of man against the world—against the world of hostile men, the world of hostile nature, and the world even, at times, of hostile gods. What one man can bear and sustain, what he can escape by alertness and craft, what he can accomplish by ingenuity and a great heart—these things are shown in the character of Odysseus, who is not so much man aspiring and achieving as he is man surviving.

THE ODYSSEY

Tell me, Muse,[1] of that man, so ready at need, who wandered far and wide, after he had sacked the sacred citadel of Troy, and many were the men whose towns he saw and whose mind he learnt, yea, and many the woes he suffered in his heart upon the deep, striving to win his own life and the return of his company. Nay, but even so he saved not his company, though he desired it sore. For through the blindness of their own hearts they perished, fools, who devoured the oxen of Helios Hyperion:[2] but the god took from them their day of returning. Of these things, goddess, daughter of Zeus, whencesoever thou hast heard thereof, declare thou even unto us.

Now all the rest, as many as fled from sheer destruction, were at home, and had escaped both war and sea, but Odysseus only, craving for his wife and for his homeward path, the lady nymph Calypso held, that fair goddess, in her hollow caves, longing to have him for her lord. But when now the year had come in the courses of the seasons, wherein the gods had ordained that he should return home to Ithaca, not even there was he quit of labours, not even among his own; but all the gods had pity on him save Poseidon,[3] who raged continually against godlike Odysseus, till he came to his own country. Howbeit Poseidon had now departed for the distant Ethiopians. . . . There he made merry sitting at the feast, but the other gods were gathered

1. For aid and inspiration Homer calls upon Calliope, muse of epic poetry. The nine muses, who presided over the arts, were daughters of the supreme god Zeus and Mnemosyne (Memory). They were subordinate to Apollo, a god of many aspects including patronage of the arts.
2. Helios, god of the sun, was the son of the Titan Hyperion. Homer seems to make no distinction between the two.
3. Brother of Zeus and god of the sea.

in the halls of Olympian Zeus. Then among them the father of gods
and men began to speak, for he bethought him in his heart of noble
Aegisthus, whom the son of Agamemnon, far-famed Orestes, slew.[4]
Thinking upon him he spake out among the Immortals:

'Lo you now, how vainly mortal men do blame the gods! For
of us they say comes evil, whereas they even of themselves, through
the blindness of their own hearts, have sorrows beyond that which is
ordained. Even as of late Aegisthus, beyond that which was ordained,
took to him the wedded wife of the son of Atreus and killed her lord
on his return, and that with sheer doom before his eyes, since we had
warned him by the embassy of Hermes the keen-sighted, the slayer
of Argos,[5] that he should neither kill the man, nor woo his wife. For
the son of Atreus shall be avenged at the hand of Orestes, so soon as
he shall come to man's estate and long for his own country. So spake
Hermes, yet he prevailed not on the heart of Aegisthus, for all his
good will; but now hath he paid one price for all.'

And the goddess, grey-eyed Athene,[6] answered him, saying: 'O
father, our father Cronides,[7] throned in the highest, that man assuredly
lies in a death that is his due; so perish likewise all who work such
deeds! But my heart is rent for wise Odysseus, the hapless one, who
far from his friends this long while suffereth affliction in a sea-girt isle,
where is the navel of the sea, a woodland isle, and therein a goddess
hath her habitation, the daughter of the wizard Atlas, who knows the
depths of every sea, and himself upholds the tall pillars which keep
earth and sky asunder. His daughter it is that holds the hapless man
in sorrow: and ever with soft and guileful tales she is wooing him to
forgetfulness of Ithaca. But Odysseus yearning to see if it were but
the smoke leap upwards from his own land, hath a desire to die.
As for thee, thine heart regardeth it not at all, Olympian!'

And Zeus the cloud-gatherer answered her, and said: 'My child,
what word hath escaped the door of thy lips? Yea, how should I

4. Agamemnon, leader of the Greek expedition against Troy, was, on his return home from the war, murdered by Aegisthus, lover of Agamemnon's wife
Clytæmnestra. Orestes, son of Agamemnon, avenged his father's death by
killing his mother and Aegisthus.

5. Because Zeus was in love with Io, his wife Here turned her into a cow
and set Argos, who had a hundred eyes, to watch her. Zeus sent Hermes,
herald of the gods, to kill Argos.

6. Pallas Athene, daughter of Zeus, was a goddess of many aspects, chiefly
of war and wisdom.

7. Cronides is a name for Zeus, son of Cronos. The Greek ending "-ides"
is equivalent to "son of." The form "Cronides" is called a patronymic.

forget divine Odysseus, who in understanding is beyond mortals and beyond all men hath done sacrifice to the deathless gods, who keep the wide heaven? Nay, but it is Poseidon, the girdler of the earth, that hath been wroth continually with quenchless anger for the Cyclops' sake whom he blinded of his eye. From that day forth Poseidon the earth-shaker doth not indeed slay Odysseus, but driveth him wandering from his own country. But come, let us here one and all take good counsel as touching his returning, that he may be got home; so shall Poseidon let go his displeasure, for he will in no wise be able to strive alone against all, in despite of all the deathless gods.'

Then the goddess, grey-eyed Athene, answered him, and said: 'O father, our father Cronides, throned in the highest, if indeed this thing is now well pleasing to the blessed gods, that wise Odysseus should return to his own home, let us then speed Hermes the messenger, the slayer of Argos, to the island of Ogygia. There with all speed let him declare to the lady of the braided tresses our unerring counsel, even the return of the patient Odysseus, that so he may come to his home. But as for me I will go to Ithaca that I may rouse his son yet the more, planting might in his heart, to call an assembly of the long-haired Achaeans[8] and speak out to all the wooers who slaughter continually the sheep of his thronging flocks, and his kine with trailing feet and shambling gait. And I will guide him to Sparta and to sandy Pylos to seek tidings of his dear father's return, if peradventure he may hear thereof and that so he may be had in good report among men.'

She spake and bound beneath her feet her lovely golden sandals. And she seized her doughty spear, shod with sharp bronze, weighty and huge and strong, wherewith she quells the ranks of heroes with whomsoever she is wroth, the daughter of the mighty sire. Then from the heights of Olympus she came glancing down, and she stood in the land of Ithaca, at the entry of the gate of Odysseus, on the threshold of the courtyard, holding in her hand the spear of bronze, in the semblance of a stranger, Mentes the captain of the Taphians. And there she found the lordly wooers: now they were taking their pleasure at draughts in front of the doors, sitting on hides of oxen, which themselves had slain. And of the henchmen and the ready squires, some were mixing for them wine and water in bowls, and some again were washing the tables with porous sponges and were setting them forth, and others were carving flesh in plenty.

8. Homer's name for Greeks. He also calls them Argives and Danaans.

And godlike Telemachus was far the first to descry her, for he was sitting with a heavy heart among the wooers dreaming on his good father, if haply he might come somewhence, and make a scattering of the wooers there throughout the palace, and himself get honour and bear rule among his own possessions. Thinking thereupon, as he sat among the wooers, he saw Athene—and he went straight to the outer porch, for he thought it blame in his heart that a stranger should stand long at the gates: and halting nigh her he clasped her right hand and took from her the spear of bronze, and uttered his voice and spake unto her winged words:

'Hail, stranger, with us thou shalt be kindly entreated, and thereafter, when thou hast tasted meat, thou shalt tell us that whereof thou hast need.'

Therewith he led the way, and Pallas Athene followed. And when they were now within the lofty house, he set her spear that he bore against a tall pillar; and he led the goddess and seated her on a goodly carven chair, and spread a linen cloth thereunder, and beneath was a footstool for the feet. . . .

Then a handmaid bare water for the washing of hands and drew to their side a polished table. And a grave dame bare wheaten bread and set it by them, and laid on the board many dainties, giving freely of such things as she had by her. And a carver lifted and placed by them platters of divers kinds of flesh, and nigh them he set golden bowls, and a henchman walked to and fro pouring out to them the wine.

Then in came the lordly wooers; and they sat them down in rows on chairs and on high seats, and henchmen poured water on their hands, and maidservants piled wheaten bread by them in baskets, and pages crowned the bowls with drink; and they stretched forth their hands upon the good cheer spread before them. Now when the wooers had put from them the desire of meat and drink, they minded them of other things, even of the song and dance: for these are crown of the feast. And a henchman placed a beauteous lyre in the hands of Phemius, who was minstrel to the wooers despite his will. Yea, and as he touched the lyre he lifted up his voice in sweet song.

But Telemachus spake unto grey-eyed Athene, holding his head close to her that those others might not hear: 'Dear stranger, wilt thou of a truth be wroth at the word that I shall say? Yonder men verily care for such things as these, the lyre and song, lightly, as they that devour the livelihood of another without atonement, of that man whose white bones, it may be, lie wasting in the rain upon the mainland, or the billow rolls them in the brine. Were but these men to see him returned to Ithaca, they all would pray rather for greater speed of foot than for gain of gold and raiment. But now he hath perished, even so, an evil doom, and for us is no comfort, no, not though any of earthly men should say that he will come again. Gone is the day of his returning! But come, declare me this, and tell me all plainly: Who art thou of the sons of men, and whence? . . .'

Then the goddess, grey-eyed Athene, answered him: 'Yea now, I will plainly tell thee all. I avow me to be Mentes, son of wise Anchialus, and I bear rule among the Taphians, lovers of the oar. And now am I come to shore, as thou seest, with ship and crew, sailing over the wine-dark sea, unto men of strange speech, even to Temesa, in quest of copper, and my cargo is shining iron. And there my ship is lying toward the upland, away from the city; and we declare ourselves to be friends one of the other, and of houses friendly, from of old. Nay, if thou wouldest be assured, go ask the old man, the hero Laertes,[9] who they say no more comes to the city, but far away toward the upland suffers affliction, with an ancient woman for his handmaid. And now am I come; for verily they said that *he,* thy father, was among his people; but lo, the gods withhold him from his way. For goodly Odysseus hath not yet perished on the earth; but still, methinks, he lives and is kept on the wide deep in a sea-girt isle, and hard men constrain him, wild folk that hold him, it may be, sore against his will. But now of a truth will I utter my word of prophecy, as the Immortals bring it into my heart and as I deem it will be accomplished, though no soothsayer am I, nor skilled in the signs of birds. Henceforth indeed for no long while shall he be far from his own dear country, not though bonds of iron bind him; he will advise him of a way to return, for he is a man of many devices. But come, declare me this, and tell me all plainly, whether indeed, so tall as thou art, thou art sprung from the loins of Odysseus. Thy head surely and thy beauteous eyes are wondrous like to his, since full many a time have we held converse together ere he embarked for Troy. From that day forth neither have I seen Odysseus, nor he me.'

Then wise Telemachus answered her, and said: 'Yea, sir, now will I plainly tell thee all. My mother verily saith that I am his; for myself I know not, for never man yet knew of himself his own descent. O that I had been the son of some blessed man, whom old age overtook

9. Father of Odysseus.

among his own possessions! But now of him that is the most hapless
of mortal men, his son they say that I am, since thou dost question me
hereof.'

Then the goddess, grey-eyed Athene, spake unto him, and said:
'Surely no nameless lineage have the gods ordained for thee in days
to come, since Penelope bore thee so goodly a man. But come, declare
me this, and tell it all plainly. What feast, nay, what rout is this?
What hast thou to do therewith? . . .'

Then wise Telemachus answered her, and said: 'Sir, forasmuch as
thou questionest me of these things and inquirest thereof, our house
was once like to have been rich and honourable, while yet that man
was among his people. But now the gods willed it otherwise, in evil
purpose, who have made him pass utterly out of sight as no man ever
before. Truly I would not even for his death make so great sorrow,
had he fallen among his fellows in the land of the Trojans, or in the
arms of his friends when he had wound up the clew of war. Then
would the whole Achaean host have builded him a barrow, and even
for his son would he have won great glory in the after days. But now
the spirits of the storm have swept him away inglorious. He is gone,
lost to sight and hearsay, but for me hath he left anguish and lamentation; nor henceforth is it for him alone that I mourn and weep, since
the gods have wrought for me other sore distress. For all the noblest
that are princes in the isles woo my mother and waste my house. But
as for her she neither refuseth the hated bridal, nor hath the heart to
make an end: so they devour and minish my house, and ere long will
they make havoc likewise of myself.'

Then in heavy displeasure spake unto him Pallas Athene: 'God
help thee! thou art surely sore in need of Odysseus that is afar, to
stretch forth his hands upon the shameless wooers. If he could but
come now and stand at the entering in of the gate, with helmet and
shield and lances twain, as mighty a man as when first I marked him
in our house drinking and making merry! . . . O that Odysseus might
in such strength consort with the wooers: so should they all have swift
fate and bitter wedlock! Howbeit these things surely lie on the knees
of the gods, whether he shall return or not and take vengeance in his
halls. But I charge thee to take counsel how thou mayest thrust forth
the wooers from the hall. Come now, mark and take heed unto my
words. On the morrow call the Achaean lords to the assembly, and
declare thy saying to all, and take the gods to witness. As for the
wooers bid them scatter them each one to his own, and for thy mother,

if her heart is moved to marriage, let her go back to the hall of that mighty man her father, and her kinsfolk will furnish a wedding feast, and array the gifts of wooing exceeding many. And to thyself I will give a word of wise counsel. Fit out a ship, the best thou hast, with twenty oarsmen, and go to inquire concerning thy father that is long afar, if perchance any man shall tell thee aught, or if thou mayest hear the voice from Zeus, which chiefly brings tidings to men. Get thee first to Pylos and inquire of goodly Nestor,[10] and from thence to Sparta to Menelaus[11] of the fair hair, for he came home the last of the mail-coated Achaeans. If thou shalt hear news of the life and the returning of thy father, then verily thou mayest endure the wasting for yet a year. But if thou shalt hear that he is dead and gone, return then to thine own dear country and pile his mound, and over it pay burial rites, full many as is due, and give thy mother to a husband. But when thou hast done this and made an end, thereafter take counsel in thy mind and heart, how thou mayest slay the wooers in thy halls, whether by guile or openly; for thou shouldest not carry childish thoughts, being no longer of years thereto. . . .'

Then wise Telemachus answered her, saying: 'Sir, verily thou speakest these things out of a friendly heart, as a father to his son, and never will I forget them. But now I pray thee abide here, though eager to be gone, to the end that after thou hast bathed and had all thy heart's desire, thou mayest wend to the ship joyful in spirit, with a costly gift and very goodly, to be an heirloom of my giving, such as dear friends give to friends.'

Then the goddess, grey-eyed Athene, answered him: 'Hold me now no longer, that am eager for the way. But whatsoever gift thine heart shall bid thee give me, when I am on my way back let it be mine to carry home: bear from thy stores a gift right goodly, and it shall bring thee the worth thereof in return.'

So spake she and departed, the grey-eyed Athene, and like an eagle of the sea she flew away, but in his spirit she planted might and courage, and put him in mind of his father yet more than heretofore. And he marked the thing and was amazed, for he deemed that it was a god: and anon he went among the wooers, a godlike man.

Now the renowned minstrel was singing to the wooers, and they

10. Nestor, king of Pylos, was the oldest of the Greeks that besieged Troy. He was famous for his wisdom.

11. Menelaus, brother of Agamemnon and king of Sparta, was the husband of Helen. He and his brother, sons of Atreus, are both called Atrides.

sat listening in silence; and his song was of the pitiful return of the Achaeans, that Pallas Athene laid on them as they came forth from Troy. And from her upper chamber the daughter of Icarius, wise Penelope, caught the glorious strain, and she went down the high stairs from her chamber, not alone, for two of her handmaids bare her company. Now when the fair lady had come unto the wooers, she stood by the pillar of the well-builded roof holding glistening tire before her face; and a faithful maiden stood on either side her. Then she fell a-weeping, and spake unto the divine minstrel:

'Phemius, since thou knowest many other charms for mortals, deeds of men and gods, which bards rehearse, some one of these do thou sing as thou sittest by them, and let them drink their wine in silence; but cease from this pitiful strain, that ever wastes my heart within my breast, since to me above all women hath come a sorrow comfortless. So dear a head do I long for in constant memory, namely, that man whose fame is noised abroad from Hellas to mid Argos.'

Then wise Telemachus answered her, and said: 'O my mother, why then dost thou grudge the sweet minstrel to gladden us as his spirit moves him? It is not minstrels who are in fault, but Zeus, methinks, is in fault, who gives to men, that live by bread, to each one as he will. As for him it is no blame if he sings the ill-faring of the Danaans; for men always prize that song the most, which rings newest in their ears. But let thy heart and mind endure to listen, for not Odysseus only lost in Troy the day of his returning, but many another likewise perished. Howbeit go to thy chamber and mind thine own house-wiferies, the loom and distaff, and bid thy handmaids ply their tasks. But speech shall be for men, for all, but for me in chief; for mine is the lordship in the house.'

Then in amaze she went back to her chamber, for she laid up the wise saying of her son in her heart.

Now the wooers clamoured throughout the shadowy halls, and each one uttered a prayer to be her bedfellow. And wise Telemachus first spake among them:

'Wooers of my mother, men despiteful out of measure, let us feast now and make merry and let there be no brawling; for, lo, it is a good thing to list to a minstrel such as him, like to the gods in voice. But in the morning let us all go to the assembly and sit us down, that I may declare my saying outright, to wit that ye leave these halls: and busy yourselves with other feasts, eating your own substance, going in turn from house to house. But if ye deem this a likelier and a better thing, that one man's goods should perish without atonement, then waste ye as ye will; and I will call upon the everlasting gods, if haply Zeus may grant that acts of recompense be made: so should ye hereafter perish within the halls without atonement.'

So spake he, and all that heard him bit their lips and marvelled at Telemachus, in that he spake boldly. . . .

Now the wooers turned them to the dance and the delightsome song, and made merry, and waited till evening should come on. And as they made merry, dusk evening came upon them. Then they went each one to his own house to lie down to rest.

But Telemachus, where his chamber was builded high up in the fair court, in a place with wide prospect, thither betook him to his bed, pondering many thoughts in his mind; and with him went trusty Eurycleia, and bare for him torches burning. She was the daughter of Ops, son of Peisenor, and Laertes bought her on a time with his wealth, while as yet she was in her first youth, and gave for her the worth of twenty oxen. And he honoured her even as he honoured his dear wife in the halls, but he never lay with her, for he shunned the wrath of his lady. She went with Telemachus and bare for him the burning torches: and of all the women of the household she loved him most, and she had nursed him when a little one. Then he opened the doors of the well-builded chamber and sat down on the bed and took off his soft doublet, and put it in the wise old woman's hands. So she folded the doublet and smoothed it, and hung it on a pin by the jointed bedstead, and went forth on her way from the room, and pulled to the door with the silver handle, and drew home the bar with the thong. There, all night through, wrapt in a fleece of wool, he meditated in his heart upon the journey that Athene had showed him.

BOOK II

Now so soon as early Dawn shone forth, the rosy-fingered, the dear son of Odysseus gat him up from his bed, and put on his raiment and cast his sharp sword about his shoulder, and beneath his smooth feet he bound his goodly sandals, and stept forth from his chamber in presence like a god. And straightway he bade the clear-voiced heralds to call the long-haired Achaeans to the assembly. And the heralds called the gathering, and the Achaeans were assembled quickly. Now when they were gathered and come together, he went on his way to the assembly holding in his hand a spear of bronze,—not alone he went, for two swift hounds bare him company. Then Athene shed on him a wondrous grace, and all the people marvelled at him as he came. And he sat him in his father's seat and the elders gave place to him.

Then the lord Aegyptus spake among them first; bowed was he with age, and skilled in things past number. . . .

'Hearken now to me, ye men of Ithaca, to the word that I shall say. Never hath our assembly or session been since the day that goodly Odysseus departed in the hollow ships. And now who was minded thus to assemble us? On what man hath such sore need come, of the young men or of the elder born? Hath he heard some tidings of the host now returning, which he might plainly declare to us, for that he first learned thereof, or doth he show forth and tell some other matter of the common weal? Methinks he is a true man—good luck be with him! Zeus vouchsafe him some good thing in his turn, even all his heart's desire!'

So spake he, and the dear son of Odysseus was glad at the omen of the word; nor sat he now much longer, but he burned to speak, and he stood in mid assembly; and the herald Peisenor, skilled in sage counsels, placed the staff in his hands. Then he spake, accosting the old man first:

'Old man, he is not far off, and soon shalt thou know it for thy- self, he who called the folk together, even I: for sorrow hath come to me in chief. Neither have I heard any tidings of the host now return- ing, which I may plainly declare to you, for that I first learned thereof; neither do I show forth or tell any other matter of the common weal, but mine own need, for that evil hath befallen my house, a double woe. First, I have lost my noble sire, who sometime was king among you here, and was gentle as a father; and now is there an evil yet greater far, which surely shall soon make grievous havoc of my whole house and ruin all my livelihood. My mother did certain wooers beset sore against her will, even the sons of those men that here are the noblest. They are too craven to go to the house of her father Icarius, that he may himself set the bride-price for his daughter, and bestow her on whom he will. But they resorting to our house day by day sacrifice oxen and sheep and fat goats, and keep revel, and drink the dark wine recklessly, and lo, our great wealth is wasted, for there is no man now alive such as Odysseus was, to keep ruin from the house. . . . Resent it in your own hearts, and have regard to your neighbours who dwell!

around, and tremble ye at the anger of the gods, lest haply they turn
upon you in wrath at your evil deeds. I pray you by Olympian Zeus
and by Themis,[1] who looseth and gathereth the meetings of men, let
be, my friends, and leave me alone to waste in bitter grief;—unless
it so be that my father, the good Odysseus, out of evil heart wrought
harm to the goodly-greaved Achaeans, in quittance whereof ye now
work me harm out of evil hearts, and spur on these men. Better for me
that ye yourselves should eat up my treasures and my flocks. Were *ye*
so to devour them, ere long would some recompense be made, for we
would urge our plea throughout the town, begging back our substance,
until all should be restored. But now without remedy are the pains
that ye lay up in my heart.'

So spake he in wrath, and dashed the staff to the ground, and
brake forth in tears; and pity fell on all the people. Then all the others
held their peace, and none had the heart to answer Telemachus with
hard words, but Antinous alone made answer, saying:

'Telemachus, proud of speech and unrestrained in fury, what is this
thou hast said to put us to shame, and wouldest fasten on us reproach?
Behold the fault is not in the Achaean wooers, but in thine own mother,
for she is the craftiest of women. For it is now the third year, and the
fourth is fast going by, since she began to deceive the minds of the
Achaeans in their breasts. She gives hope to all, and makes promises
to every man, and sends them messages, but her mind is set on other
things. And she hath devised in her heart this wile besides; she set up
in her halls a mighty web, fine of woof and very wide, whereat she
would weave, and anon she spake among us:

' "Ye princely youths, my wooers, now that the goodly Odysseus
is dead, do ye abide patiently, how eager soever to speed on this marriage of mine, till I finish the robe. I would not that the threads perish
to no avail, even this shroud for the hero Laertes, against the day when
the ruinous doom shall bring him low, of death that lays men at their
length. So shall none of the Achaean women in the land count it
blame in me, as well might be, were he to lie without a winding-sheet,
a man that had gotten great possessions."

'So spake she, and our high hearts consented thereto. So then in
the day time she would weave the mighty web, and in the night
unravel the same. Thus for the space of three years she hid the thing
by craft and beguiled the minds of the Achaeans; but when the fourth

1. Goddess of order, presiding over the assemblies of men and convening
the assemblies of gods.

year arrived one of her women who knew all declared it, and we found her unravelling the splendid web. Thus she finished it perforce and sore against her will. But as for thee, the wooers make thee answer thus, that thou mayest know it in thine own heart, thou and all the Achaeans! Send away thy mother, and bid her be married to whosoever her father commands, and whoso is well pleasing unto her. But if she will continue for long to vex the sons of the Achaeans, pondering in her heart those things that Athene hath given her beyond women, knowledge of all fair handiwork, yea, and cunning wit, and wiles— so be it! . . . For in despite of her the wooers will devour thy living and thy substance, so long as she is steadfast in such purpose as the gods now put within her breast: great renown for herself she winneth, but for thee regret for thy much livelihood. But we will neither go to our own lands, nor otherwhere, till she marry that man whom she will of the Achaeans.'

Then wise Telemachus answered him, saying: 'Antinous, I may in no wise thrust forth from the house, against her will, the woman that bare me, that reared me: while as for my father he is abroad on the earth, whether he be alive or dead. Moreover it is hard for me to make heavy restitution to Icarius, as needs I must, if of mine own will I send my mother away. . . . If your own heart, even yours, is indignant, quit ye my halls, and busy yourselves with other feasts, eating your own substance, and going in turn from house to house. But if ye deem this a likelier and a better thing, that one man's goods should perish without atonement, then waste ye as ye will: and I will call upon the everlasting gods, if haply Zeus may grant that acts of recompense be made: so should ye hereafter perish in the halls without atonement.'

So spake Telemachus, and in answer to his prayer did Zeus, of the far-borne voice, send forth two eagles in flight, from on high, from the mountain-crest. Awhile they flew as fleet as the blasts of the wind, side by side, with straining of their pinions. But when they had now reached the mid assembly, the place of many voices, there they wheeled about and flapped their strong wings, and looked down upon the heads of all, and destruction was in their gaze. Then tore they with their talons each the other's cheeks and neck on every side, and so sped to the right across the dwellings and the city of the people. And the men marvelled at the birds when they had sight of them, and pondered in their hearts the things that should come to pass. Yea and the old man, the lord Halitherses, spake among them, for he excelled his peers in knowledge of birds, and in uttering words of fate. With good will he made harangue and spake among them:

'Hearken to me now, ye men of Ithaca, to the word that I shall say: and mainly to the wooers do I show forth and tell these things, seeing that a mighty woe is rolling upon them. For Odysseus shall not long be away from his friends, nay, even now, it may be, he is near, and sowing the seeds of death and fate for these men, every one; and he will be a bane to many another likewise of us who dwell in clear-seen Ithaca. But long ere that falls out let us advise us how we may make an end of their mischief; yea, let them of their own selves make an end, for this is the better way for them, as will soon be seen. For I prophesy not as one unproved, but with sure knowledge; verily, I say, that for him all things now are come to pass, even as I told him, what time the Argives embarked for Ilios, and with them went the wise Odysseus. I said that after sore affliction, with the loss of all his company, unknown to all, in the twentieth year he should come home. And behold, all these things now have an end.'

And Eurymachus, son of Polybus, answered him, saying: 'Go now, old man, get thee home and prophesy to thine own children, lest haply they suffer harm hereafter: but herein am I a far better prophet than thou. Howbeit there be many birds that fly to and fro under the sun's rays, but all are not birds of fate. Now as for Odysseus, he hath perished far away, as would that thou too with him hadst been cut off: so wouldst thou not have babbled thus much prophecy, nor wouldst thou hound on Telemachus that is already angered, expecting a gift for thy house, if perchance he may vouchsafe thee aught. But now will I speak out, and my word shall surely be accomplished. If thou, that knowest much lore from of old, shalt beguile with words a younger man, and rouse him to indignation, first it shall be a great grief to him:—and yet he can count on no aid from these who hear him;—while upon thee, old man, we will lay a fine, that thou mayest pay it and chafe at heart, and sore pain shall be thine. And I myself will give a word of counsel to Telemachus in presence of you all. Let him command his mother to return to her father's house; and her kinsfolk will furnish a wedding feast, and array the gifts of wooing, exceeding many, all that should go back with a daughter dearly beloved. For ere that, I trow, we sons of the Achaeans will not cease from our rough wooing, since, come what may, we fear not any man, no, not Telemachus, full of words though he be. His substance too shall be woefully devoured, nor shall recompense ever be made, so long as she shall put off the Achaeans in the matter of her marriage; while we in expectation, from day to day, vie one with another for the prize of her perfection, nor go we after other women whom it were meet that we should each one wed.'

Then wise Telemachus answered him, saying: 'Eurymachus, and ye others, that are lordly wooers, I entreat you no more concerning this nor speak thereof, for the gods have knowledge of it now and all the Achaeans. But come, give me a swift ship and twenty men, who shall accomplish for me my voyage to and fro. For I will go to Sparta and to sandy Pylos to inquire concerning the return of my father that is long afar. If I shall hear news of the life and the returning of my father, then verily I may endure the wasting for yet a year; but if I shall hear that he is dead and gone, let me then return to my own dear country, and pile his mound, and over it pay burial rites full many as is due, and I will give my mother to a husband.'

So with that word he sat him down; then in the midst uprose Mentor, the companion of noble Odysseus. He it was to whom Odysseus, as he departed in the fleet, had given the charge over all his house, that it should obey the old man, and that he should keep all things safe. With good will he now made harangue and spake among them:

'Hearken to me now, ye men of Ithaca, to the word that I shall say. Henceforth let not any sceptred king be kind and gentle with all his heart, nor minded to do righteousness: for behold, there is none that remembereth divine Odysseus of the people whose lord he was, and was gentle as a father. Howsoever, it is not that I grudge the lordly wooers their deeds of violence in the evil devices of their heart. For at the hazard of their own heads they violently devour the household of Odysseus, and say of him that he will come no more again. But I am indeed wroth with the rest of the people, to see how ye all sit thus speechless, and do not cry shame upon the wooers, and put them down, ye that are so many and they so few.'

And Leocritus, son of Euenor, answered him, saying: 'Mentor infatuate, with thy wandering wits, what word hast thou spoken, that callest upon them to put us down? Nay, it is a hard thing to fight about a feast, and that with men who are even more in number than you. Though Odysseus of Ithaca himself should come and were eager of heart to drive forth from the hall the lordly wooers that feast throughout his house, yet should his wife have no joy of his coming, though she yearns for him;—but even there should he meet foul doom, if he fought with those that outnumbered him; so thou hast not spoken aright. But as for the people, come now, scatter yourselves each one to his own lands, but Mentor and Halitherses will speed this man's voyage, for they are friends of his house from of old. Yet after all, methinks that long time he will abide and seek tidings in Ithaca, and never accomplish this voyage.'

Thus he spake, and in haste they broke up the assembly. So they were scattered each one to his own dwelling, while the wooers departed to the house of divine Odysseus.

Then Telemachus, going far apart to the shore of the sea, laved his hands in the grey sea water, and prayed unto Athene, saying: 'Hear me, thou who yesterday didst come in thy godhead to our house, and badest me go in a ship across the misty seas, to seek tidings of the return of my father that is long gone: but all this my purpose do the Achaeans delay, and mainly the wooers in the naughtiness of their pride.'

So spake he in prayer, and Athene drew nigh him in the likeness of Mentor, in fashion and in voice, and she spake and hailed him in winged words:

'Telemachus, even hereafter thou shalt not be craven or witless, if indeed thou hast a drop of thy father's blood and a portion of his spirit; such an one was he to fulfil both word and work. Nor, if this be so, shall thy voyage be vain or unfulfilled. . . . Wherefore now take no heed of the counsel or the purpose of the senseless wooers, for they are in no way wise or just: neither know they aught of death and of black fate, which already is close upon them, that they are all to perish in one day. But the voyage on which thy heart is set shall not long be lacking to thee—so faithful a friend of thy father am I, who will furnish thee a swift ship and myself be thy companion. But go thou to the house, and consort with the wooers, and make ready corn, and bestow all in vessels, the wine in jars and barley-flour, the marrow of men, in well-sewn skins; and I will lightly gather in the township a crew that offer themselves willingly. There are many ships, new and old, in seagirt Ithaca; of these I will choose out the best for thee, and we will quickly rig her and launch her on the broad deep.'

So spake Athene, daughter of Zeus, and Telemachus made no long tarrying, when he had heard the voice of the goddess. He went on his way towards the house, heavy at heart, and there he found the noble wooers in the halls, flaying goats and singeing swine in the court. And Antinous laughed out and went straight to Telemachus, clasped his hand and spake and hailed him:

'Telemachus, proud of speech and unrestrained in fury, let no evil word any more be in thy heart, nor evil work, but let me see thee eat and drink as of old. And the Achaeans will make thee ready all things without fail, a ship and chosen oarsmen, that thou mayest come the quicker to fair Pylos, to seek tidings of thy noble father.'

Then wise Telemachus answered him, saying: 'Antinous, in no wise in your proud company can I sup in peace, and make merry with a quiet mind. Is it a little thing, ye wooers, that in time past ye wasted many good things of my getting, while as yet I was a child? But now that I am a man grown, and learn the story from the lips of others, and my spirit waxeth within me, I will seek to let loose upon you evil fates, as I may, going either to Pylos for help or abiding here in this township.'

He spake and snatched his hand from out the hand of Antinous, lightly, and all the while the wooers were busy feasting through the house; and they mocked him and sharply taunted him. . . .

But he stepped down into the vaulted treasure-chamber of his father, a spacious room, where gold and bronze lay piled, and raiment in coffers, and fragrant olive oil in plenty. And there stood casks of sweet wine and old. And the close-fitted doors, the folding doors, were shut, and night and day there abode within a dame in charge, who guarded all the fulness of her wisdom, Eurycleia, daughter of Ops son of Peisenor. Telemachus now called her into the chamber and spake unto her, saying:

'Mother, come draw off for me sweet wine in jars, the choicest next to that thou keepest mindful ever of that ill-fated one, Odysseus, of the seed of Zeus,[2] if perchance he may come I know not whence, having avoided death and the fates. So fill twelve jars, and close each with his lid, and pour me barley-meal into well-sewn skins, and let there be twenty measures of the grain of bruised barley-meal. Let none know this but thyself! As for these things let them all be got together; for in the evening I will take them with me, at the time that my mother hath gone to her upper chamber and turned her thoughts to sleep. Lo, to Sparta I go and to sandy Pylos to seek tidings of my dear father's return, if haply I may hear thereof.'

So spake he, and the good nurse Eurycleia wailed aloud, and

2. Odysseus' maternal grandfather was Autolycus, son of Hermes, who was son of Zeus and Maia. Autolycus, according to Homer, was the sharpest thief of antiquity.

making lament spake to him winged words: 'Ah, wherefore, dear child, hath such a thought arisen in thine heart? How shouldst thou fare over wide lands, thou that art an only child and well-beloved? As for him he hath perished, Odysseus of the seed of Zeus, far from his own country in the land of strangers. And yonder men, so soon as thou art gone, will devise mischief against thee thereafter, that thou mayest perish by guile, and they will share among them all this wealth of thine. Nay, abide here, settled on thine own lands: thou hast no need upon the deep unharvested to suffer evil and go wandering.'

Then wise Telemachus answered her, saying: 'Take heart, nurse, for lo, this my purpose came not but of a god. But swear to tell no word thereof to my dear mother, till at least it shall be the eleventh or twelfth day from hence, or till she miss me of herself, and hear of my departure, that so she may not mar her fair face with her tears.'

Thus he spake, and the old woman sware a great oath by the gods not to reveal it. But when she had sworn and done that oath, straightway she drew off the wine for him in jars, and poured barley-meal into well-sewn skins, and Telemachus departed to the house and consorted with the wooers.

Then the goddess, grey-eyed Athene, turned to other thoughts. In the likeness of Telemachus she went all through the city, and stood by each one of the men and spake her saying, and bade them gather at even by the swift ship. Furthermore, she craved a swift ship of Noemon, and right gladly he promised it.

Now the sun sank and all the ways were darkened. Then at length she let drag the swift ship to the sea and stored within it all such tackling as decked ships carry. And she moored it at the far end of the harbour and the good company were gathered together, and the goddess cheered on all.

Then the goddess, grey-eyed Athene, turned to other thoughts. She went on her way to the house of divine Odysseus; and there she shed sweet sleep upon the wooers and made them distraught in their drinking, and cast the cups from their hands. And they arose up to go to rest throughout the city, nor sat they yet a long while, for slumber was falling on their eyelids. Now grey-eyed Athene spake unto Telemachus, and called him from out the fair-lying halls, taking the likeness of Mentor, both in fashion and in voice:

'Telemachus, thy goodly-greaved companions are sitting already at their oars, it is thy despatch they are awaiting. Nay then, let us go, that we delay them not long from the way.'

Therewith Pallas Athene led the way quickly, and he followed hard in the steps of the goddess. Now when they had come down to the ship and to the sea, they found the long-haired youths of the company on the shore; and the mighty prince Telemachus spake among them:

'Come hither, friends, let us carry the corn on board, for all is now together in the room, and my mother knows nought thereof, nor any of the maidens of the house: one woman only heard my saying.'

Thus he spake and led the way, and they went with him. So they brought all and stowed it in the decked ship, according to the word of the dear son of Odysseus. Then Telemachus climbed the ship, and Athene went before him, and behold, she sat her down in the stern, and near her sat Telemachus. And the men loosed the hawsers and climbed on board themselves, and sat down upon the benches.

And Telemachus called unto his company and bade them lay hands on the tackling, and they hearkened to his call. So they raised the mast of pine tree and set it in the hole of the cross plank, and made it fast with forestays, and hauled up the white sails with twisted ropes of oxhide. And the wind filled the belly of the sail, and the dark wave seethed loudly round the stem of the running ship, and she fleeted over the wave, accomplishing her path. Then they made all fast in the swift black ship, and set mixing bowls brimmed with wine, and poured drink offering to the deathless gods that are from everlasting, and in chief to the grey-eyed daughter of Zeus.[3] So all night long and through the dawn the ship cleft her way.

[BOOK III: Accompanied by Athene in the guise of Mentor, Telemachus sails to Pylos, home of Nestor, to seek news of Odysseus. Nestor tells of the quarrels among the Greeks after the fall of Troy, of his own safe return to Pylos, and of the return home and the murder of Agamemnon. He advises Telemachus to seek farther for word of Odysseus and urges him to visit Menelaus in Sparta. He offers Telemachus a chariot and his own son Peisistratus as charioteer. The two young men set out for Sparta.

[BOOK IV: Menelaus cordially welcomes his unknown guests, Telemachus and Peisistratus; and Helen recognizes Telemachus, in whom she immediately detects a likeness to Odysseus. Menelaus and Helen entertain their visitors with tales of Odysseus at Troy. The next day

3. Athene.

Telemachus describes to Menelaus the state of affairs in Ithaca and begs news of his father. Menelaus recounts to Telemachus the tale of his own adventures after the fall of Troy: how he forced Proteus, the Old Man of the Sea, to help him on his way, how he learned from Proteus of the murder of Agamemnon, and how Proteus informed him that he had last seen Odysseus held in constraint by the nymph Calypso. Meanwhile, the wooers, learning of Telemachus' absence, plan to ambush and kill him on his way home.]

BOOK V

Now the Dawn arose from her couch to bear light to the immortals and to mortal men. And lo, the gods were gathering to session. And Athene told them the tale of the many woes of Odysseus, recalling them to mind:

'Father Zeus, and all ye other blessed gods that live for ever, henceforth let not any sceptred king be kind and gentle with all his heart, nor minded to do righteously, but let him always be a hard man and work unrighteousness, for behold, there is none that remembereth divine Odysseus of the people whose lord he was, and was gentle as a father. Howbeit, as for him he lieth in an island suffering strong pains, in the halls of the nymph Calypso, who holdeth him perforce; so he may not reach his own country, for he hath no ships by him with oars, and no companions to send him on his way over the broad back of the sea. And now, again, they are set on slaying his beloved son on his homeward way, for he is gone to fair Pylos and to goodly Lacedaemon,[1] to seek tidings of his father.'

And Zeus, gatherer of the clouds, answered and spake unto her: 'My child, what word hath escaped the door of thy lips? Nay, didst thou not thyself plan this device, that Odysseus may assuredly take vengeance on those men at his coming? As for Telemachus, do thou guide him by thine art, as well thou mayest, that so he may come to his own country all unharmed.'

Therewith he spake to Hermes, his dear son: 'Hermes, forasmuch as even in all else thou art our herald, tell unto the nymph of the braided tresses my unerring counsel, even the return of the patient Odysseus, how he is to come to his home, with no furtherance of gods or of mortal men. Nay, he shall sail on a well-bound raft, in sore distress, and on the twentieth day arrive at fertile Scheria, even at the

1. Sparta.

land of the Phaeacians, who are near of kin to the gods. And they
shall give him all worship heartily as to a god, and send him on his
way in a ship to his own dear country, with gifts of bronze and gold,
and raiment in plenty, much store, such as never would Odysseus have
won for himself out of Troy, yea, though he had returned unhurt with
the share of the spoil that fell to him. On such wise is he fated to see
his friends, and come to his high-roofed home and his own country.'

So spake he, nor heedless was the messenger. Straightway he
bound beneath his feet his lovely golden sandals, that wax not old,
that bare him alike over the wet sea and over the limitless land, swift
as the breath of the wind. And he took the wand wherewith he lulls
the eyes of whomso he will, while others again he even wakes from
out of sleep. Above Pieria he passed and leapt from the upper air into
the deep. But when he had now reached that far-off isle, he went forth
from the sea of violet blue to get him up into the land, till he came to
a great cave, wherein dwelt the nymph of the braided tresses: and he
found her within. And the nymph within was singing with a sweet
voice as she fared to and fro before the loom, and wove with a shuttle
of gold. . . . And all around soft meadows bloomed of violets and
parsley, yea, even a deathless god who came thither might wonder at
the sight and be glad at heart. There the messenger, the slayer of
Argos, stood and wondered. Now when he had gazed at all with wonder, anon he went into the wide cave; nor did Calypso, that fair
goddess, fail to know him, when she saw him face to face; for the
gods use not be strange one to another, the immortals, not though one
have his habitation far away. But he found not Odysseus, the great-
hearted, within the cave, who sat weeping on the shore even as afore-
time, straining his soul with tears and groans and griefs, and as he
wept he looked wistfully over the unharvested deep. And Calypso,
that fair goddess, questioned Hermes, when she had made him sit on
a bright shining seat:

'Wherefore, I pray thee, Hermes, of the golden wand, hast thou
come hither, worshipful and welcome, whereas as of old thou wert
not wont to visit me? Tell me all thy thought; my heart is set on ful-
filling it, if fulfil it I may, and if it hath been fulfilled in the counsel
of fate. But now follow me further, that I may set before thee the
entertainment of strangers.'

Therewith the goddess spread a table with ambrosia and set it by
him, and mixed the ruddy nectar. So the messenger, the slayer of
Argos, did eat and drink. Now after he had supped and comforted

his soul with food, at the last he answered, and spake to her on this wise:

'Thou makest question of me on my coming, a goddess of a god, and I will tell thee this my saying truly, at thy command. 'Twas Zeus that bade me come hither, by no will of mine; nay, who of his free will would speed over such a wondrous space of brine, whereby is no city of mortals that do sacrifice to the gods? But surely it is in no wise possible for another god to go beyond or to make void the purpose of Zeus, lord of the aegis.[2] He saith that thou hast with thee a man most wretched beyond his fellows, beyond those men that round the burg of Priam[3] for nine years fought, and in the tenth year sacked the city and departed homeward. Yet on the way they sinned against Athene, and she raised upon them an evil blast and long waves of the sea. Then all the rest of his good company was lost, but it came to pass that the wind bare and the wave brought him hither. And now Zeus biddeth thee send him hence with what speed thou mayest, for it is not ordained that he die away from his friends, but rather it is his fate to look on them even yet, and to come to his high-roofed home and his own country.'

So spake he, and Calypso, that fair goddess, shuddered and uttered her voice, and spake unto him winged words: 'Hard are ye gods and jealous exceeding, who ever grudge goddesses openly to mate with men, if any make a mortal her dear bed-fellow. . . . Ye gods now grudge that a mortal man should dwell with me. Him I saved as he went all alone bestriding the keel of a bark, for that Zeus had crushed and cleft his swift ship with a white bolt in the midst of the wine-dark deep. And him have I loved and cherished, and I said that I would make him to know not death and age for ever. Yet forasmuch as it is in no wise possible for another god to go beyond, or make void the purpose of Zeus, lord of the aegis, let him away over the unharvested seas, if the summons and the bidding be of Zeus. But I will give him no despatch, not I, for I have no ships by me with oars, nor company to bear him on his way over the broad back of the sea. Yet will I be forward to put this in his mind, and will hide nought, that all unharmed he may come to his own country.'

Then the messenger, the slayer of Argos, answered her: 'Yea, speed

2. The mantle, or shield, of Zeus. When shaken by him, it causes thunder, lightning, and destruction.
3. King of Troy.

him now upon his path and have regard unto the wrath of Zeus, lest
haply he be angered and bear hard on thee hereafter.'

Therewith the great slayer of Argos departed, but the lady nymph
went on her way to the great-hearted Odysseus, when she had heard
the message of Zeus. And there she found him sitting on the shore,
and his eyes were never dry of tears, and his sweet life was ebbing
away as he mourned for his return; for the nymph no more found
favour in his sight. Howsoever by night he would sleep by her, as needs
he must, in the hollow caves, unwilling lover by a willing lady. And
in the day-time he would sit on the rocks and on the beach, straining
his soul with tears, and groans, and griefs, and through his tears he
would look wistfully over the unharvested deep. So standing near him
that fair goddess spake to him:

'Hapless man, sorrow no more I pray thee in this isle, nor let thy
good life waste away, for even now will I send thee hence with all
my heart. Nay, arise and cut long beams, and fashion a wide raft
with the axe, and lay deckings high thereupon, that it may bear thee
over the misty deep. And I will place therein bread and water, and
red wine to thy heart's desire, to keep hunger far away. And I will
put raiment upon thee, and send a fair gale in thy wake, that so thou
mayest come all unharmed to thine own country, if indeed it be the
good pleasure of the gods who hold wide heaven, who are stronger
than I am both to will and to do.'

So she spake, and the steadfast goodly Odysseus shuddered, and
uttering his voice spake to her winged words: 'Herein, goddess, thou
hast plainly some other thought, and in no wise my furtherance, for
that thou biddest me to cross in a raft the great gulf of the sea so dread
and difficult, which not even the swift gallant ships pass over rejoicing in the breeze of Zeus. Nor would I go aboard a raft to displeasure
thee, unless thou wilt deign, O goddess, to swear a great oath not to
plan any hidden guile to mine own hurt.'

So spake he, and Calypso, the fair goddess, smiled and caressed
him with her hand, and spake and hailed him:

'Knavish thou art, and no weakling in wit, thou that hast conceived and spoken such a word. Let earth be now witness hereto, and
the wide heaven above, and that falling water of the Styx,[4] the greatest
oath and the most terrible to the blessed gods, that I will not plan any
hidden guile to thine own hurt. Nay, but my thoughts are such, and
such will be my counsel, as I would devise for myself, if ever so sore

4. The river Styx was chief river of the lower world.

a need came over me. For I too have a righteous mind, and my
heart within me is not of iron, but pitiful even as thine.'

Therewith the fair goddess led the way quickly, and he followed
hard in the steps of the goddess. And they reached the hollow cave, the
goddess and the man; so he sat him down upon the chair whence
Hermes had arisen, and the nymph placed by him all manner of food
to eat and drink, such as is meat for men. But after they had taken their
fill of meat and drink, Calypso, the fair goddess, spake first and said:

'Son of Laertes, of the seed of Zeus, Odysseus of many devices, so it
is indeed thy wish to get thee home to thine own dear country even in
this hour? Good fortune go with thee even so! Yet didst thou know in
thine heart what a measure of suffering thou art ordained to fulfil, or
ever thou reach thine own country, here, even here, thou wouldst abide
with me and keep this house, and wouldst never taste of death, though
thou longest to see thy wife, for whom thou hast ever a desire day by
day. Not in sooth that I avow me to be less noble than she in form or
fashion, for it is in no wise meet that mortal women should match
them with immortals, in shape and comeliness.'

And Odysseus of many counsels answered, and spake unto her:
'Be not wroth with me hereat, goddess and queen. Myself I know it
well, how wise Penelope is meaner to look upon than thou, in comeliness and stature. But she is mortal and thou knowest not age nor
death. Yet even so, I wish and long day by day to fare homeward and
see the day of my returning. Yea, and if some god shall wreck me in
the wine-dark deep, even so I will endure, with a heart within me
patient of affliction. For already have I suffered full much, and much
have I toiled in perils of waves and war; let this be added to the tale of
those.'

So spake he, and the sun sank and darkness came on. Then they
twain went into the chamber of the hollow rock, and had their delight
of love, abiding each by other.

So soon as early Dawn shone forth, the rosy-fingered, anon
Odysseus put on him a mantle and doublet, and the nymph clad her in
a great shining robe, light of woof and gracious, and about her waist
she cast a fair golden girdle, and a veil withal upon her head. Then she
considered of the sending of Odysseus, the great-hearted. She gave him
a great axe, fitted to his grasp, an axe of bronze double-edged, and with
a goodly handle of olive wood fastened well. Next she gave him a
polished adze, and she led the way to the border of the isle where tall
trees grew, alder and poplar, and pine that reacheth unto heaven,

seasoned long since and sere, that might lightly float for him. Now after she had shown him where the tall trees grew, Calypso, the fair goddess, departed homeward. And he set to cutting timber, and his work went busily. Twenty trees in all he felled, and then trimmed them with the axe of bronze, and deftly smoothed them, and over them made straight the line. Meanwhile Calypso, the fair goddess, brought him augers, so he bored each piece and jointed them together, and then made all fast with trenails and dowels. Wide as is the floor of a broad ship of burden, which some man well skilled in carpentry may trace him out, of such beam did Odysseus fashion his broad raft. And thereat he wrought, and set up the deckings, fitting them to the close-set up-rights, and finished them off with long gunwales, and therein he set a mast, and a yard-arm fitted thereto, and moreover he made him a rudder to guide the craft. And he fenced it with wattled osier withies from stem to stern, to be a bulwark against the wave, and piled up wood to back them. Meanwhile Calypso, the fair goddess, brought him web of cloth to make his sails; and these too he fashioned very skil-fully. And he made fast therein braces and halyards and sheets, and at last he pushed the raft with levers down to the fair salt sea.

It was the fourth day when he had accomplished all. And, lo, on the fifth, the fair Calypso sent him on his way from the island, when she had bathed him and clad him in fragrant attire. Moreover, the goddess placed on board the ship two skins, one of dark wine, and another, a great one, of water, and corn too in a wallet, and she set therein a store of dainties to his heart's desire, and sent forth a warm and gentle wind to blow. And goodly Odysseus rejoiced as he set his sails to the breeze. So he sate and cunningly guided the craft with the helm. . . . Ten days and seven he sailed traversing the deep, and on the eighteenth day ap-peared the shadowy hills of the land of the Phaeacians, at the point where it lay nearest to him; and it showed like a shield in the misty deep.

Now the lord, the shaker of the earth,[5] on his way from the Ethiopians espied him afar off from the mountains of the Solymi: even thence he saw Odysseus as he sailed over the deep; and he was mightily angered in spirit, and shaking his head he communed with his own heart. 'Lo now, it must be that the gods at the last have changed their purposes concerning Odysseus, while I was away among the Ethiop-ians. And now he is nigh to the Phaeacian land, where it is ordained that he escape the great issues of the woe which hath come upon him.

5. Poseidon.

But methinks that even yet I will drive him far enough in the path of suffering.'

With that he gathered the clouds and troubled the waters of the deep, grasping his trident in his hands; and he roused all storms of all manner of winds, and shrouded in clouds the land and sea: and down sped night from heaven. The East Wind and the South Wind clashed, and the stormy West, and the North, that is born in the bright air, rolling onward a great wave. Then were the knees of Odysseus loosened and his heart melted, and heavily he spake to his own great spirit:

'Oh, wretched man that I am! what is to befall me at the last? I fear that indeed the goddess spake all things truly, who said that I should fill up the measure of sorrow on the deep, or ever I came to mine own country; and lo, all these things have an end. Thrice blessed those Danaans, yea, four times blessed, who perished on a time in wide Troy-land, doing a pleasure to the sons of Atreus! Would to God that I too had died, and met my fate on that day when the press of Trojans cast their bronze-shod spears upon me, fighting for the body of the son of Peleus![6] So should I have gotten my dues of burial, and the Achaeans would have spread my fame; but now it is my fate to be overtaken by a pitiful death.'

Even as he spake, the great wave smote down upon him, driving on in terrible wise, that the raft reeled again. And far therefrom he fell, and lost the helm from his hand; and the fierce blast of the jostling winds came and brake his mast in the midst, and sail and yard-arm fell afar into the deep. Long time the water kept him under, nor could he speedily rise from beneath the rush of the mighty wave: for the garments hung heavy which fair Calypso gave him. But late and at length he came up, and spat forth from his mouth the bitter salt water, which ran down in streams from his head. Yet even so forgat he not his raft, for all his wretched plight, but made a spring after it in the waves, and clutched it to him, and sat in the midst thereof, avoiding the issues of death; and the great wave swept it hither and thither along the stream. And as the North Wind in the harvest tide sweeps the thistledown along the plain, and close the tufts cling each to other, even so the winds bare the raft hither and thither along the main. Now the South would toss it to the North to carry, and now again the East would yield it to the West to chase.

But the daughter of Cadmus marked him, Ino of the fair ankles,

6. Achilles, who died from the wound of an arrow shot by Paris and guided by Apollo.

Leucothea,[7] who in time past was a maiden of mortal speech, but now in the depths of the salt sea she had gotten her share of worship from the gods. She took pity on Odysseus in his wandering and travail, and she rose, like a sea-gull on the wing, from the depth of the mere, and sat upon the well-bound raft and spake saying:

'Hapless one, wherefore was Poseidon, shaker of the earth, so wondrous wroth with thee, seeing that he soweth for thee the seeds of many evils? Yet shall he not make a full end of thee, for all his desire. But do even as I tell thee, and methinks thou art not witless. Cast off these garments, and leave the raft to drift before the winds, but do thou swim with thine hands and strive to win a footing on the coast of the Phaeacians, where it is decreed that thou escape. Here, take this veil imperishable and wind it about thy breast; so is there no fear that thou suffer aught or perish. But when thou hast laid hold of the mainland with thy hands, loose it from off thee and cast it into the wine-dark deep far from the land, and thyself turn away.'

With that the goddess gave the veil, and for her part dived back into the heaving deep, like a sea-gull: and the dark wave closed over her. But the steadfast goodly Odysseus pondered, and heavily he spake to his own brave spirit:

'Ah, woe is me! Can it be that some one of the immortals is weaving a new snare for me, that she bids me quit my raft? Nay verily, I will not yet obey, for I had sight of the shore yet a long way off, where she told me that I might escape. I am resolved what I will do;—and methinks on this wise it is best. So long as the timbers abide in the dowels, so long will I endure steadfast in affliction, but so soon as the wave hath shattered my raft asunder, I will swim, for meanwhile no better counsel may be.'

While yet he pondered these things in his heart and soul, Poseidon, shaker of the earth, stirred against him a great wave, terrible and grievous, and vaulted from the crest, and therewith smote him. And as when a great tempestuous wind tosseth a heap of parched husks, and scatters them this way and that, even so did the wave scatter the long beams of the raft. But Odysseus bestrode a single beam, as one rideth on a courser, and stript him of the garments which fair Calypso gave him. And presently he wound the veil beneath his breast, and fell prone into the sea, outstretching his hands as one eager to swim. And the lord, the shaker of the earth, saw him and shook his head, and

7. Ino, a mortal, became Leucothea, a sea goddess, when she cast herself into the sea to escape her insane husband.

communed with his own soul. 'Even so, after all thy sufferings, go wandering over the deep, till thou shalt come among a people, the fosterlings of Zeus. Yet for all that I deem not that thou shalt think thyself too lightly afflicted.' Therewith he lashed his steeds of the flowing manes, and came to Aegae, where is his lordly home.

But Athene, daughter of Zeus, turned to new thoughts. Behold, she bound up the courses of the other winds, and charged them all to cease and be still; but she roused the swift North and brake the waves before him, that so Odysseus, of the seed of Zeus, might mingle with the Phaeacians, lovers of the oar, avoiding death and the fates.

So for two nights and two days he was wandering in the swell of the sea, and much his heart boded of death. But when at last the fair-tressed Dawn brought the full light of the third day, thereafter the breeze fell, and lo, there was a breathless calm, and with a quick glance ahead (he being upborne on a great wave) he saw the land very near. . . . And he swam onward, being eager to set foot on the strand. But when he was within earshot of the shore, and heard now the thunder of the sea against the reefs—for the great wave crashed against the dry land belching in terrible wise, and all was covered with foam of the sea,—for there were no harbours for ships nor shelters, but jutting headlands and reefs and cliffs; then at last the knees of Odysseus were loosened and his heart melted, and in heaviness he spake to his own brave spirit:

'Ah me! now that beyond all hope Zeus hath given me sight of land, and withal I have cloven my way through this gulf of the sea, here there is no place to land on from out of the grey water. For without are sharp crags, and round them the wave roars surging, and sheer the smooth rock rises, and the sea is deep thereby, so that in no wise may I find firm foothold and escape my bane, for as I fain would go ashore, the great wave may haply snatch and dash me on the jagged rock—and a wretched endeavour that would be. But if I swim yet further along the coast to find, if I may, spits that take the waves aslant and havens of the sea, I fear lest the storm-winds catch me again and bear me over the teeming deep, making heavy moan; or else some god may even send forth against me a monster from out of the shore water; and many such pastureth the renowned Amphitrite.[8] For I know how wroth against me hath been the great Shaker of the Earth.'

Whilst yet he pondered these things in his heart and mind, a great wave bore him to the rugged shore. There would he have been stript

8. Wife of Poseidon and chief goddess of the sea.

of his skin and all his bones been broken, but that the goddess, grey-eyed Athene, put a thought into his heart. He rushed in, and with both his hands clutched the rock, whereto he clung till the great wave went by. So he escaped that peril, but again with backward wash it leapt on him and smote him and cast him forth into the deep. And as when the cuttlefish is dragged forth from his chamber, the many pebbles clinging to his suckers, even so was the skin stript from his strong hand against the rocks, and the great wave closed over him. There of a truth would luckless Odysseus have perished beyond that which was ordained, had not grey-eyed Athene given him sure counsel. He rose from the line of the breakers that belch upon the shore, and swam outside, ever looking landwards, to find, if he might, spits that take the waves aslant, and havens of the sea. But when he came in his swimming over against the mouth of a fair-flowing river, whereby the place seemed best in his eyes, smooth of rocks, and withal there was a covert from the wind, Odysseus felt the river running, and prayed to him in his heart. . . .

And the god straightway stayed his stream and withheld his waves, and made the water smooth before him, and brought him safely to the mouths of the river. And his knees bowed and his stout hands fell, for his heart was broken by the brine. And his flesh was all swollen and a great stream of sea water gushed up through his mouth and nostrils. So he lay without breath or speech, swooning, such terrible weariness came upon him. But when now his breath returned and his spirit came to him again, he loosed from off him the veil of the goddess, and let it fall into the salt-flowing river. And the great wave bare it back down the stream, and lightly Ino caught it in her hands. Then Odysseus turned from the river, and fell back in the reeds, and kissed earth, the grain-giver, and heavily he spake unto his own brave spirit:

'Ah, woe is me! what is to betide me? what shall happen unto me at the last? If I watch in the river bed all through the careful night, I fear that the bitter frost and fresh dew may overcome me, as I breathe forth my life for faintness, for the river breeze blows cold betimes in the morning. But if I climb the hill-side up to the shady wood, and there take rest in the thickets, though perchance the cold and weariness leave hold of me, and sweet sleep may come over me, I fear lest of wild beasts I become the spoil and prey.'

So as he thought thereon this seemed to him the better way. He went up to the wood, and found it nigh the water in a place of wide prospect. So he crept beneath twin bushes that grew from one stem. . . . And anon he heaped together with his hands a broad couch; for of fallen leaves there was great plenty, enough to cover two or three men in winter time, however hard the weather. And the steadfast goodly Odysseus beheld it and rejoiced, and he laid him in the midst thereof and flung over him the fallen leaves. . . . And Athene shed sleep upon his eyes, that so it might soon release him from his weary travail, overshadowing his eyelids.

BOOK VI

So there he lay asleep, the steadfast goodly Odysseus, fordone with toil and drowsiness. Meanwhile Athene went to the land and the city of the Phaeacians, . . . where Alcinous was reigning, with wisdom granted by the gods. To his house went the goddess, grey-eyed Athene, devising a return for the great-hearted Odysseus. She betook her to the rich-wrought bower, wherein was sleeping a maiden like to the gods in form and comeliness, Nausicaa, the daughter of Alcinous, high of heart.

The goddess, fleet as the breath of the wind, swept towards the couch of the maiden, and stood above her head, and spake to her in the semblance of the daughter of a famous seafarer, Dymas, a girl of like age with Nausicaa, who had found grace in her sight. In her shape the grey-eyed Athene spake to the princess, saying:

'Nausicaa, how hath thy mother so heedless a maiden to her daughter? Lo, thou hast shining raiment that lies by thee uncared for, and thy marriage-day is near at hand, when thou thyself must needs go beautifully clad, and have garments to give to them who shall lead thee to the house of the bridegroom! And, behold, these are the things whence a good report goes abroad among men, wherein a father and lady mother take delight. But come, let us arise and go a-washing with the breaking of the day, and I will follow with thee to be thy mate in the toil, that without delay thou mayest get thee ready, since truly thou art not long to be a maiden. Lo, already they are wooing thee, the noblest youths of all the Phaeacians, among that people whence thou thyself dost draw thy lineage. So come, beseech thy noble father betimes in the morning to furnish thee with mules and a wain to carry the men's raiment, and the robes, and the shining coverlets. Yea and for thyself it is seemlier far to go thus than on foot, for the places where we must wash are a great way off the town.'

So spake the grey-eyed Athene, and departed to Olympus, where, as they say, is the seat of the gods that standeth fast for ever. . . .

Anon came the throned Dawn, and awakened Nausicaa of the fair robes, who straightway marvelled on the dream, and went through the halls to tell her parents, her father dear and her mother. And she found them within, her mother sitting by the hearth with the women her handmaids, spinning yarn of sea-purple stain, but her father she met as he was going forth to the renowned kings in their council, whither the noble Phaeacians called him. Standing close by her dear father she spake, saying: 'Father, dear, couldst thou not lend me a high waggon with strong wheels, that I may take the goodly raiment to the river to wash, so much as I have lying soiled? Yea and it is seemly that thou thyself, when thou art with the princes in council, shouldest have fresh raiment to wear. Also, there are five dear sons of thine in the halls, two married, but three are lusty bachelors, and these are always eager for new-washen garments wherein to go to the dances: for all these things have I taken thought.'

This she said, because she was ashamed to speak of glad marriage to her father; but he saw all and answered, saying:

'Neither the mules nor aught else do I grudge thee, my child. Go thy ways, and the thralls shall get thee ready a high waggon with good wheels, and fitted with an upper frame.'

Therewith he called to his men, and they gave ear, and without the palace they made ready the smooth-running mule-wain, while the maiden brought forth from her bower the shining raiment. This she stored in the polished car, and her mother filled a basket with all manner of food to the heart's desire, dainties too she set therein, and she poured wine into a goat-skin bottle, while Nausicaa climbed into the wain. And her mother gave her soft olive oil also in a golden cruse, that she and her maidens might anoint themselves after the bath. Then Nausicaa took the whip and the shining reins, and touched the mules to start them; then there was a clatter of hoofs, and on they strained without flagging, with their load of the raiment and the maiden. Not alone did she go, for her attendants followed with her.

Now when they were come to the beautiful stream of the river, where truly were the unfailing cisterns, and bright water welled up free from beneath, and flowed past, enough to wash the foulest garments clean, there the girls unharnessed the mules from under the chariot, and turning them loose they drove them along the banks of the eddying river to graze on the honey-sweet clover. Then they took the garments from the wain, in their hands, and bore them to the black water, and briskly trod them down in the trenches, in busy rivalry.

Now when they had washed and cleansed all the stains, they spread all out in order along the shore of the deep, even where the sea, in beating on the coast, washed the pebbles clean. Then having bathed and anointed them well with olive oil, they took their mid-day meal on the river's banks, waiting till the clothes should dry in the brightness of the sun. Anon, when they were satisfied with food, the maidens and the princess, they fell to playing at ball, casting away their tires, and among them Nausicaa of the white arms began their song. . . .

But when now she was about going homewards, after yoking the mules and folding up the goodly raiment, then grey-eyed Athene turned to other thoughts, that so Odysseus might awake, and see the lovely maiden, who should be his guide to the city of the Phaeacian men. So then the princess threw the ball at one of her company; she missed the girl, and cast the ball into the deep eddying current, whereat they all raised a piercing cry. Then the goodly Odysseus awoke and sat up, pondering in his heart and spirit:

'Woe is me! to what men's land am I come now? say, are they froward, and wild, and unjust, or are they hospitable, and of God-fearing mind? How shrill a cry of maidens rings round me, of the nymphs that hold the steep hill-tops, and the river-springs, and the grassy water-meadows! It must be, methinks, that I am near men of human speech. Go to, I myself will make trial and see.'

Therewith the goodly Odysseus crept out from under the coppice, having broken with his strong hand a leafy bough from the thick wood, to hold athwart his body, that it might hide his nakedness withal. And forth he sallied, fain to draw nigh to the fair-tressed maidens, all naked as he was, such need had come upon him. But he was terrible in their eyes, being marred with the salt sea foam, and they fled cowering here and there about the jutting spits of shore. And the daughter of Alcinous alone stood firm, for Athene gave her courage of heart, and took all trembling from her limbs. So she halted and stood over against him, and Odysseus considered whether he should clasp the knees of the lovely maiden, and so make his prayer, or should stand as he was, apart, and beseech her with smooth words, if haply she might show him the town, and give him raiment. And as he thought within himself, it seemed better to stand apart, and beseech her with smooth words, lest the maiden should be angered with him if he touched her knees: so straightway he spake a sweet and cunning word:

'I supplicate thee, O queen, whether thou art a goddess or a mortal! If indeed thou art a goddess of them that keep the wide heaven; to Artemis,[1] then, the daughter of great Zeus, I mainly liken thee, for beauty and stature and shapeliness. But if thou art one of the daughters of men who dwell on earth, thrice blessed are thy father and thy lady mother, and thrice blessed thy brethren. Surely their souls ever glow with gladness for thy sake, each time they see thee entering the dance, so fair a flower of maidens. But he is of heart the most blessed beyond all other who shall prevail with gifts of wooing, and lead thee to his home. Never have mine eyes beheld such an one among mortals, neither man nor woman; great awe comes upon me as I look on thee. . . . I wonder at thee, lady, and am astonied and do greatly fear to touch thy knees, though grievous sorrow is upon me. Yesterday, on the twentieth day, I escaped from the wine-dark deep, but all that time continually the wave bare me, and the vehement winds drave, from the isle Ogygia. And now some god has cast me on this shore, that here too, methinks, some evil may betide me. But, queen, have pity on me, for after many trials and sore to thee first of all am I come, and of the other folk, who hold this city and land, I know no man. Nay show me the town, give me an old garment to cast about me, if thou hadst, when thou camest here, any wrap for the linen. And may the gods grant thee all thy heart's desire: a husband and a home, and a mind at one with his may they give—a good gift, for there is nothing mightier and nobler than when man and wife are of one heart and mind in a house, a grief to their foes, and to their friends great joy, but their own hearts know it best.'

Then Nausicaa of the white arms answered him, and said: 'Stranger, forasmuch as thou seemest no evil man nor foolish—and it is Olympian Zeus himself that giveth weal to men, to the good and to the evil, to each one as he will, and this thy lot doubtless is of him, and so thou must in anywise endure it:—and now, since thou hast come to our city and our land, thou shalt not lack raiment, nor aught else that is the due of a hapless suppliant, when he has met them who can befriend him. And I will show thee the town, and name the name of the people. The Phaeacians hold this city and land, and I am the daughter of Alcinous, great of heart, on whom all the might and force of the Phaeacians depend.'

Thus she spake, and called to her maidens of the fair tresses: 'Halt, my maidens, whither flee ye at the sight of a man? Ye surely do not take him for an enemy? . . . This man is some helpless one come hither in his wanderings, whom now we must kindly entreat, for

1. Goddess of the moon and the chase.

all strangers and beggars are from Zeus, and a little gift is dear. So, my maidens, give the stranger meat and drink, and bathe him in the river, where withal is a shelter from the winds.'

So she spake, but they had halted and called each to the other, and they brought Odysseus to the sheltered place, and made him sit down, as Nausicaa bade them, the daughter of Alcinous, high of heart. Beside him they laid a mantle, and a doublet for raiment, and gave him soft olive oil in the golden cruse, and bade him wash in the streams of the river. Then goodly Odysseus spake among the maidens, saying: 'I pray you stand thus apart, while I myself wash the brine from my shoulders, and anoint me with olive oil, for truly oil is long a stranger to my skin. But in your sight I will not bathe, for I am ashamed to make me naked in the company of fair-tressed maidens.'

Then they went apart and told all to their lady. But with the river water the goodly Odysseus washed from his skin the salt scurf that covered his back and broad shoulders, and from his head he wiped the crusted brine of the barren sea. But when he had washed his whole body, and anointed him with olive oil, and had clad himself in the raiment that the unwedded maiden gave him, then Athene, the daughter of Zeus, made him greater and more mighty to behold, and from his head caused deep curling locks to flow, like the hyacinth flower.

Then to the shore of the sea went Odysseus apart, and sat down, glowing in beauty and grace, and the princess marvelled at him, and spake among her fair-tressed maidens, saying:

'Listen, my white-armed maidens, and I will say somewhat. Not without the will of all the gods who hold Olympus hath this man come among the godlike Phaeacians. Erewhile he seemed to me uncomely, but now he is like the gods that keep the wide heaven. Would that such an one might be called my husband, dwelling here, and that it might please him here to abide! But come, my maidens, give the stranger meat and drink.'

Thus she spake, and they gave ready ear and hearkened, and set beside Odysseus meat and drink, and the steadfast goodly Odysseus did eat and drink eagerly, for it was long since he had tasted food.

Now Nausicaa of the white arms had another thought. She folded the raiment and stored it in the goodly wain, and yoked the mules strong of hoof, and herself climbed into the car. Then she called on Odysseus, and spake and hailed him: 'Up now, stranger, and rouse thee to go to the city, that I may convey thee to the house of my wise father. where, I promise thee, thou shalt get knowledge of all the noblest of the Phaeacians. But do thou even as I tell thee, and thou seemest a discreet man enough. So long as we are passing along the fields and farms of men, do thou fare quickly with the maidens behind the mules and the chariot, and I will lead the way. But when we set foot within the city,—whereby goes a high wall with towers, and there is a fair haven on either side of the town, and narrow is the entrance, and curved ships are drawn up on either hand of the mole, for all the folk have stations for their vessels, each man one for himself. And there is the place of assembly about the goodly temple of Poseidon, furnished with heavy stones, deep bedded in the earth. There men look to the gear of the black ships, hawsers and sails, and there they fine down the oars. For the Phaeacians care not for bow nor quiver, but for masts, and oars of ships, and gallant barques, wherein rejoicing they cross the grey sea. Their ungracious speech it is that I would avoid, lest some man afterward rebuke me, and there are but too many insolent folk among the people. And some one of the baser sort might meet me and say: "Who is this that goes with Nausicaa, this tall and goodly stranger? Where found she him? Her husband he will be, her very own. Either she has taken in some shipwrecked wanderer of strange men,—for no men dwell near us; or some god has come in answer to her instant prayer; from heaven has he descended, and will have her to wife for evermore. Better so, if herself she has ranged abroad and found a lord from a strange land, for verily she holds in no regard the Phaeacians here in this country, the many men and noble who are her wooers." So will they speak, and this would turn to my reproach. But, stranger, heed well what I say, that as soon as may be thou mayest gain at my father's hands an escort and a safe return. Thou shalt find a fair grove of Athene, a poplar grove near the road, and a spring wells forth therein, and a meadow lies all around. There is my father's demesne, and his fruitful close, within the sound of a man's shout from the city. Sit thee down there and wait until such time as we may have come into the city, and reached the house of my father. But when thou deemest that we are got to the palace, then go up to the city of the Phaeacians, and ask for the house of my father Alcinous, high of heart. But when thou art within the shadow of the halls and the court, pass quickly through the great chamber, till thou comest to my mother, who sits at the hearth in the light of the fire, weaving yarn of sea-purple stain, a wonder to behold. And there my father's throne leans close to hers, wherein he sits and drinks his wine, like an immortal. Pass thou by him, and cast thy hands about my mother's knees, that thou mayest see quickly and with joy the day of thy returning, even if thou art from a very far country. If but her heart be kindly disposed toward thee, then is there hope that thou shalt see thy friends, and come to thy well-builded house, and to thine own country.'

She spake, and smote the mules with the shining whip, and quickly they left behind them the streams of the river. And well they trotted and well they paced, and she took heed to drive in such wise that the maidens and Odysseus might follow on foot, and cunningly she plied the lash. Then the sun set, and they came to the famous grove, the sacred place of Athene; so there the goodly Odysseus sat him down. Then straightway he prayed to the daughter of mighty Zeus: 'Listen to me, child of Zeus, lord of the aegis, unwearied maiden; hear me even now, since before thou heardest not when I was smitten on the sea, when the renowned Earth-shaker smote me. Grant me to come to the Phaeacians as one dear, and worthy of pity.'

So he spake in prayer, and Pallas Athene heard him; but she did not yet appear to him face to face, for she had regard unto her father's brother, who furiously raged against the godlike Odysseus, till he should come to his own country.

[BOOK VII: Mindful of Nausicaa's instructions, Odysseus sets out for the city, enshrouded in a mist by Athene and led by the goddess in the form of a young girl. Like Nausicaa, Athene advises Odysseus to seek favor of Queen Arete. Still enveloped in the cloud, Odysseus enters the palace of Alcinous, finds the king and queen, and as the mist disappears throws himself at the feet of Arete and begs hospitality. He tells of his hardships after leaving Calypso; and, still unknown, he gains the promise of Alcinous to send him by ship to his home.

[BOOK VIII: On the next day Alcinous prepares a banquet for his guest, and Athene casts a glamor upon Odysseus to impress the Phaeacians. In the banquet hall the blind minstrel Demodocus sings of the Trojan War—of the great deeds of Achilles and of Odysseus. Unnoticed by all but Alcinous, Odysseus weeps at the song. Alcinous proposes games and trials of strength, in which Odysseus surpasses the rest at weight-throwing. After the games the Phaeacians shower Odysseus with rich gifts, and there is more feasting. Again Demodocus sings of Troy, this time of the wooden horse, and again Odysseus weeps. In the end Alcinous, suspicious, urges Odysseus to disclose his name and country.]

BOOK IX

And Odysseus of many counsels answered him saying: 'King Alcinous, most notable of all the people, verily it is a good thing to list to a minstrel such as this one, like to the gods in voice. Nay, as for me, I say that there is no more gracious or perfect delight than when a whole people makes merry, and the men sit orderly at feast in the halls and listen to the singer, and the tables by them are laden with bread and flesh, and a wine-bearer drawing the wine serves it round and pours it into the cups. This seems to me well-nigh the fairest thing in the world. But now thy heart was inclined to ask of my grievous troubles, that I may mourn for more exceeding sorrow. What then shall I tell of first, what last, for the gods of heaven have given me woes in plenty? Now, first, will I tell my name, that ye too may know it, and that I, when I have escaped the pitiless day, may yet be your host, though my home is in a far country. I am ODYSSEUS, SON OF LAERTES, who am in men's minds for all manner of wiles, and my fame reaches unto heaven. And I dwell in clear-seen Ithaca. . . .

'The wind that bare me from Ilios brought me nigh to the Cicones, even to Ismarus, whereupon I sacked their city and slew the people. And from out the city we took their wives and much substance, and divided them amongst us that none through me might go lacking his proper share. Howbeit, thereafter I commanded that we should flee with a swift foot, but my men in their great folly hearkened not. There was much wine still a-drinking, and still they slew many flocks of sheep by the seashore and kine with trailing feet and shambling gait. Meanwhile the Cicones went and raised a cry to other Cicones their neighbours. So they gathered in the early morning as thick as leaves and flowers that spring in their season. They set their battle in array by the swift ships, and the hosts cast at one another with their bronze-shod spears. So long as it was morn and the sacred day waxed stronger, so long we abode their assault and beat them off, albeit they outnumbered us. But when the sun was wending to the time of the loosing of cattle, then at last the Cicones drave in the Achaeans and overcame them, and six of my goodly-greaved company perished from each ship: but the remnant of us escaped death and destiny.

'Thence we sailed onward stricken at heart, yet glad as men saved from death, albeit we had lost our dear companions. Now Zeus, gatherer of the clouds, aroused the North Wind against our ships with a terrible tempest, and covered land and sea alike with clouds,

and down sped night from heaven. Thus the ships were driven headlong, and their sails were torn to shreds by the might of the wind. Sc
we lowered the sails into the hold, in fear of death, but rowed the ships
landward apace. There for two nights and two days we lay continually,
consuming our hearts with weariness and sorrow. But when the fair-
tressed Dawn had at last brought the full light of the third day, we set
up the masts and hoisted the white sails and sat us down, while the
wind and the helmsman guided the ships. And now I should have
come to mine own country all unhurt, but the wave and the stream of
the sea and the North Wind swept me from my course as I was dou-
bling Malea, and drave me wandering past Cythera.

'Thence for nine whole days was I borne by ruinous winds over the
teeming deep; but on the tenth day we set foot on the land of the
lotus-eaters, who eat a flowery food. So we stepped ashore and drew
water, and straightway my company took their midday meal by the
swift ships. Now when we had tasted meat and drink I sent forth certain of my company to go and make search what manner of men they
were who here live upon the earth by bread, and I chose out two of my
fellows, and sent a third with them as herald. Then straightway they
went and mixed with the men of the lotus-eaters, and so it was that
the lotus-eaters devised not death for our fellows, but gave them of the
lotus to taste. Now whosoever of them did eat the honey-sweet fruit of
the lotus, had no more wish to bring tidings nor to come back, but
there he chose to abide with the lotus-eating men, ever feeding on the
lotus, and forgetful of his homeward way. Therefore I led them back
to the ships weeping, and sore against their will, and dragged them
beneath the benches, and bound them in the hollow barques. But I
commanded the rest of my well-loved company to make speed and go
on board the swift ships, lest haply any should eat of the lotus and be
forgetful of returning. Right soon they embarked and sat upon the
benches, and sitting orderly they smote the grey sea water with their
oars.

'Thence we sailed onward stricken at heart. And we came to the
land of the Cyclôpes, a froward and a lawless folk, who trusting to the
deathless gods plant not aught with their hands, neither plough: but,
behold, all these things spring for them in plenty, unsown and untilled,
wheat, and barley, and vines, which bear great clusters of the juice of
the grape, and the rain of Zeus gives them increase. These have neither
gatherings for council nor oracles of law, but they dwell in hollow

caves on the crests of the high hills, and each one utters the law to his children and his wives, and they reck not one of another.

'Now there is a waste isle stretching without the harbour of the land of the Cyclôpes, neither nigh at hand nor yet afar off, a woodland isle, wherein are wild goats unnumbered. . . . Also there is a fair haven, where is no need of moorings, either to cast anchor or to fasten hawsers, but men may run the ship on the beach. Now at the head of the harbour is a well of bright water issuing from a cave, and round it are poplars growing. Thither we sailed, and some god guided us through the night, for it was dark and there was no light to see, a mist lying deep about the ships, nor did the moon show her light from heaven, but was shut in with clouds. And when our ships were beached, we took down all their sails, and ourselves too stept forth upon the strand of the sea, and there we fell into sound sleep and waited for the bright Dawn.

'So soon as early Dawn shone forth, the rosy-fingered, in wonder at the island we roamed over the length thereof: and the Nymphs, the daughters of Zeus, lord of the aegis, started the wild goats of the hills, that my company might have wherewith to sup. Anon we took to us our curved bows from out the ships and long spears, and arrayed in three bands we began shooting at the goats; and the god[1] soon gave us game in plenty. Now twelve ships bare me company, and to each ship fell nine goats for a portion, but for me alone they set ten apart.

'Thus we sat there the livelong day until the going down of the sun, feasting on abundant flesh and on sweet wine. And we looked across to the land of the Cyclôpes who dwell nigh, and to the smoke, and to the voice of the men, and of the sheep and of the goats. And when the sun had sunk and darkness had come on, then we laid us to rest upon the sea-beach. So soon as early Dawn shone forth, the rosy-fingered, then I called a gathering of my men, and spake among them all:

' "Abide here all the rest of you, my dear companions; but I will go with mine own ship and my ship's company, and make proof of these men, what manner of folk they are, whether froward, and wild, and unjust, or hospitable and of god-fearing mind."

'So I spake, and I climbed the ship's side, and bade my company themselves to mount, and to loose the hawsers. So they soon embarked and sat upon the benches, and sitting orderly smote the grey sea water with their oars. Now when we had come to the land that lies hard by, we saw a cave on the border near to the sea, lofty and roofed over with laurels, and there many flocks of sheep and goats were used to rest.

1. Apollo, the archer god, brother of Artemis.

And about it a high outer court was built with stones, deep bedded, and with tall pines and oaks with their high crown of leaves. And a man was wont to sleep therein, of monstrous size, who shepherded his flocks alone and afar, and was not conversant with others, but dwelt apart in lawlessness of mind. Yea, for he was a monstrous thing and fashioned marvellously, nor was he like to any man that lives by bread, but like a wooded peak of the towering hills, which stands out apart and alone from others.

'Then I commanded the rest of my well-loved company to tarry there by the ship, and to guard the ship, but I chose out twelve men, the best of my company, and sallied forth. Now I had with me a goat-skin of the dark wine and sweet, which Maron, son of Euanthes, had given me, the priest of Apollo, the god that watched over Ismarus. And he gave it, for that we had protected him with his wife and child reverently. . . .

'With this wine I filled a great skin, and bare it with me, and corn too I put in a wallet, for my lordly spirit straightway had a boding that a man would come to me, a strange man, clothed in mighty strength, one that knew not judgment and justice.

'Soon we came to the cave, but we found him not within; he was shepherding his fat flocks in the pastures. So we went into the cave, and gazed on all that was therein. The baskets were well laden with cheeses, and the folds were thronged with lambs and kids. Now all the vessels swam with whey, the milk-pails and the bowls, the well-wrought vessels whereinto he milked. My company then spake and besought me first of all to take of the cheeses and to return, and afterwards to make haste and drive off the kids and lambs to the swift ships from out the pens, and to sail over the salt sea water. Howbeit I hearkened not (and far better would it have been), but waited to see the giant himself, and whether he would give me gifts as a stranger's due. Yet was not his coming to be with joy to my company.

'Then we kindled a fire, and made burnt-offering, and ourselves likewise took of the cheeses, and did eat, and sat waiting for him within till he came back, shepherding his flocks. And he bore a grievous weight of dry wood, against supper time. This log he cast down with a din inside the cave, and in fear we fled to the secret place of the rock. As for him, he drave his fat flocks into the wide cavern, even all that he was wont to milk. Thereafter he lifted a huge doorstone and weighty, and set it in the mouth of the cave, such an one as two and twenty good four-wheeled wains could not raise from the ground, so

mighty a sheer rock did he set against the doorway. Then he sat down
and milked the ewes and bleating goats all orderly, and beneath each
ewe he placed her young. And anon he curdled one half of the white
milk, and massed it together, and stored it in wicker-baskets, and the
other half he let stand in pails, that he might have it to take and drink
against supper time. Now when he had done all his work busily then
he kindled the fire anew, and espied us, and made question:

' "Strangers, who are ye? Whence sail ye over the wet ways? On
some trading enterprise or at adventure do ye rove, even as sea-robbers
over the brine, for at hazard of their own lives they wander, bringing
bale to alien men."

'So spake he, but as for us our heart within us was broken for
terror of the deep voice and his own monstrous shape; yet despite all I
answered and spake unto him, saying:

' "Lo, we are Achaeans, driven wandering from Troy, by all
manner of winds over the great gulf of the sea; seeking our homes we
fare, but another path have we come, by other ways: even such, methinks, was the will and the counsel of Zeus. And we avow us to be the
men of Agamemnon, son of Atreus, whose fame is even now the
mightiest under heaven, so great a city did he sack, and destroyed
many people; but as for us we have lighted here, and come to these thy
knees, if perchance thou wilt give us a stranger's gift, or make any
present, as is the due of strangers. Nay, lord, have regard to the gods,
for we are thy suppliants; and Zeus is the avenger of suppliants and
sojourners, Zeus, the god of the stranger, who fareth in the company
of reverend strangers."

'So I spake, and anon he answered out of his pitiless heart: "Thou
art witless, my stranger, or thou hast come from afar, who biddest me
either to fear or shun the gods. For the Cyclôpes pay no heed to Zeus,
lord of the aegis, nor to the blessed gods, for verily we are better men
than they. Nor would I, to shun the enmity of Zeus, spare either thee
or thy company, unless my spirit bade me. But tell me where thou didst
stay thy well-wrought ship on thy coming? Was it perchance at the
far end of the island, or hard by, that I may know?"

'So he spake tempting me, but he cheated me not, who knew full
much, and I answered him again with words of guile:

' "As for my ship, Poseidon, the shaker of the earth, brake it to
pieces, for he cast it upon the rocks at the border of your country, and
brought it nigh the headland, and a wind bare it thither from the sea.
But I with these my men escaped from utter doom."

'So I spake, and out of his pitiless heart he answered me not a word, but sprang up, and laid his hands upon my fellows, and clutching two together dashed them, as they had been whelps, to the earth, and the brain flowed forth upon the ground and the earth was wet. Then cut he them up piecemeal, and made ready his supper. So he ate even as a mountain-bred lion, and ceased not, devouring entrails and flesh and bones with their marrow. And we wept and raised our hands to Zeus, beholding the cruel deeds; and we were at our wits' end. And after the Cyclops had filled his huge maw with human flesh and the milk he drank thereafter, he lay within the cave, stretched out among his sheep.

'So I took counsel in my great heart, whether I should draw near, and pluck my sharp sword from my thigh, and stab him in the breast, where the midriff holds the liver, feeling for the place with my hand. But my second thought withheld me, for so should we too have perished even there with utter doom. For we should not have prevailed to roll away with our hands from the lofty door the heavy stone which he set there. So for that time we made moan, awaiting the bright Dawn.

'Now when early Dawn shone forth, the rosy-fingered, again he kindled the fire and milked his goodly flocks all orderly, and beneath each ewe set her lamb. Anon when he had done all his work busily, again he seized yet other two men and made ready his mid-day meal. And after the meal, lightly he moved away the great door-stone, and drave his fat flocks forth from the cave, and afterwards he set it in its place again, as one might set the lid on a quiver. Then with a loud whoop, the Cyclops turned his fat flocks towards the hills; but I was left devising evil in the deep of my heart, if in any wise I might avenge me, and Athene grant me renown.

'And this was the counsel that showed best in my sight. There lay by a sheep-fold a great club of the Cyclops, a club of olive wood, yet green, which he had cut to carry with him when it should be seasoned. Now when we saw it we likened it in size to the mast of a black ship of twenty oars, so huge it was to view in bulk and length. I stood thereby and cut off from it a portion as it were a fathom's length, and set it by my fellows, and bade them fine it down, and they made it even, while I stood by and sharpened it to a point, and straightway I took it and hardened it in the bright fire. Then I laid it well away, and hid it beneath the dung, which was scattered in great heaps in the depths of the cave. And I bade my company cast lots among them, which of them should risk the adventure with me, and lift the bar and turn it about in his eye, when sweet sleep came upon him. And the lot fell upon those four whom I myself would have been fain to choose, and I appointed myself to be the fifth among them. In the evening he came shepherding his flocks of goodly fleece, and presently he drave his fat flocks into the cave each and all, nor left he any without in the deep court-yard, whether through some foreboding, or perchance that the god so bade him do. Thereafter he lifted the huge door-stone and set it in the mouth of the cave, and sitting down he milked the ewes and bleating goats, all orderly, and beneath each ewe he placed her young. Now when he had done all his work busily, again he seized yet other two and made ready his supper. Then I stood by the Cyclops and spake to him, holding in my hands an ivy bowl of the dark wine:

'"Cyclops, take and drink wine after thy feast of man's meat, that thou mayest know what manner of drink this was that our ship held. And lo, I was bringing it thee as a drink offering, if haply thou mayest take pity and send me on my way home, but thy mad rage is past all sufferance. O hard of heart, how may another of the many men there be come ever to thee again, seeing that thy deeds have been lawless?"

'So I spake, and he took the cup and drank it off, and found great delight in drinking the sweet draught, and asked me for it yet a second time:

'"Give it me again of thy grace, and tell me thy name straightway, that I may give thee a stranger's gift, wherein thou mayest be glad."

'So he spake, and again I handed him the dark wine. Thrice I bare and gave it him, and thrice in his folly he drank it to the lees. Now when the wine had got about the wits of the Cyclops, then did I speak to him with soft words:

'"Cyclops, thou askest me my renowned name, and I will declare it unto thee, and do thou grant me a stranger's gift, as thou didst promise. Noman is my name, and Noman they call me, my father and my mother and all my fellows."

'So I spake, and straightway he answered me out of his pitiless heart:

'"Noman will I eat last in the number of his fellows, and the others before him: that shall be thy gift."

'Therewith he sank backwards and fell with face upturned, and there he lay with his great neck bent round, and sleep, that conquers all men, overcame him. And the wine and the fragments of men's flesh issued forth from his mouth, and he vomited, being heavy with wine. Then I thrust in that stake under the deep ashes, until it should grow hot, and I spake to my companions comfortable words, lest any should hang back from me in fear. But when that bar of olive wood was just about to catch fire in the flame, green though it was, and began to glow terribly, even then I came nigh, and drew it from the coals, and my fellows gathered about me, and some god breathed great courage into us. For their part they seized the bar of olive wood, that was sharpened at the point, and thrust it into his eye, while I from my place aloft turned it about, as when a man bores a ship's beam with a drill while his fellows below spin it with a strap, which they hold at either end, and the auger runs round continually. Even so did we seize the fiery-pointed brand and whirled it round in his eye, and the blood flowed about the heated bar. And the breath of the flame singed his eyelids and brows all about, as the ball of the eye burnt away, and the roots thereof crackled in the flame. And as when a smith dips an axe or adze in chill water with a great hissing, when he would temper it— for hereby anon comes the strength of iron—even so did his eye hiss round the stake of olive. And he raised a great and terrible cry, that the rock rang around, and we fled away in fear, while he plucked forth from his eye the brand bedabbled in much blood. Then maddened with pain he cast it from him with his hands, and called with a loud voice on the Cyclôpes, who dwelt about him in the caves along the windy heights. And they heard the cry and flocked together from every side, and gathering round the cave asked him what ailed him:

' "What hath so distressed thee, Polyphemus, that thou criest thus aloud through the immortal night, and makest us sleepless? Surely no mortal driveth off thy flocks against thy will: surely none slayeth thyself by force or craft?"

'And the strong Polyphemus spake to them again from out the cave: "My friends, Noman is slaying me by guile, nor at all by force."

'And they answered and spake winged words: "If then no man is violently handling thee in thy solitude, it can in no wise be that thou shouldest escape the sickness sent by mighty Zeus. Nay, pray thou to thy father, the lord Poseidon."

'On this wise they spake and departed; and my heart within me laughed to see how my name and cunning counsel had beguiled them. But the Cyclops, groaning and travailing in pain, groped with his hands, and lifted away the stone from the door of the cave, and himself sat in the entry, with arms outstretched to catch, if he might, any one that was going forth with his sheep, so witless, methinks, did he hope to find me. But I advised me how all might be for the very best, if perchance I might find a way of escape from death for my companions and myself, and I wove all manner of craft and counsel, as a man will for his life, seeing that great mischief was nigh. And this was the counsel that showed best in my sight. The rams of the flock were well nurtured and thick of fleece, great and goodly, with wool dark as the violet. Quietly I lashed them together with twisted withies, whereon the Cyclops slept, that lawless monster. Three together I took: now the middle one of the three would bear each a man, but the other twain went on either side, saving my fellows. Thus every three sheep bare their man. But as for me I laid hold of the back of a young ram who was far the best and the goodliest of all the flock, and curled beneath his shaggy belly there I lay, and so clung face upward, grasping the wondrous fleece with a steadfast heart. So for that time making moan we awaited the bright Dawn.

'So soon as early Dawn shone forth, the rosy-fingered, then did the rams of the flock hasten forth to pasture, but the ewes bleated unmilked about the pens, for their udders were swollen to bursting. Then their lord, sore stricken with pain, felt along the backs of all the sheep as they stood up before him, and guessed not in his folly how that my men were bound beneath the breasts of his thick-fleeced flocks. Last of all the sheep came forth the ram, cumbered with his wool, and the weight of me and my cunning. And the strong Polyphemus laid his hands on him and spake to him, saying:

' "Dear ram, wherefore, I pray thee, art thou the last of all the flocks to go forth from the cave, who of old wast not wont to lag behind the sheep, but wert ever the foremost to pluck the tender blossom of the pasture, faring with long strides, and wert still the first to come to the streams of the rivers, and first didst long to return to the homestead in the evening. But now art thou the very last. Surely thou art sorrowing for the eye of thy lord, which an evil man blinded, with his accursed fellows, when he had subdued my wits with wine, even Noman, whom I say hath not yet escaped destruction. Ah, if thou couldst feel as I, and be endued with speech, to tell me where he shifts about to shun my wrath; then should he be smitten, and his brains be dashed against the floor here and there about the cave, and my heart be lightened of the sorrows which Noman, nothing worth, hath brought me!"

'Therewith he sent the ram forth from him, and when we had gone but a little way from the cave and from the yard, first I loosed myself from under the ram and then I set my fellows free. And swiftly we drave on those stiff-shanked sheep, so rich in fat, and often turned to look about, till we came to the ship. And a glad sight to our fellows were we that had fled from death, but the others they would have bemoaned with tears; howbeit I suffered it not, but with frowning brows forbade each man to weep. Rather I bade them to cast on board the many sheep with goodly fleece, and to sail over the salt sea water. So they embarked forthwith, and sate upon the benches, and sitting orderly smote the grey sea water with their oars. But when I had not gone so far, but that a man's shout might be heard, then I spoke unto the Cyclops taunting him:

' "Cyclops, so thou wert not to eat the company of a weakling by main might in thy hollow cave! Thine evil deeds were very sure to find thee out, thou cruel man, who hadst no shame to eat thy guests within thy gates, wherefore Zeus hath requited thee, and the other gods."

'So I spake, and he was mightily angered at heart, and he brake off the peak of a great hill and threw it at us, and it fell in front of the dark-prowed ship. And the sea heaved beneath the fall of the rock, and the backward flow of the wave bare the ship quickly to the dry land, with the wash from the deep sea, and drave it to the shore. Then I caught up a long pole in my hands, and thrust the ship from off the land, and roused my company, and with a motion of the head bade them dash in with their oars, that so we might escape our evil plight. So they bent to their oars and rowed on. But when we had now made twice the distance over the brine, I would fain have spoken to the Cyclops, but my company stayed me on every side with soft words, saying:

' "Foolhardy that thou art, why wouldst thou rouse a wild man to wrath, who even now hath cast so mighty a throw towards the deep and brought our ship back to land, yea and we thought that we had perished even there? If he had heard any of us utter sound or speech he would have crushed our heads and our ship timbers with a cast of a rugged stone, so mightily he hurls."

'So spake they, but they prevailed not on my lordly spirit, and I answered him again from out an angry heart:

' "Cyclops, if any one of mortal men shall ask thee of the unsightly blinding of thine eye, say that it was Odysseus that blinded it, the waster of cities, son of Laertes, whose dwelling is in Ithaca."

'So I spake, and with a moan he answered me, saying:

' "Lo now, in very truth the ancient oracles have come upon me.

There lived here a soothsayer, a noble man and a mighty, Telemus, son of Eurymus, who surpassed all men in soothsaying, and waxed old as a seer among the Cyclôpes. He told me that all these things should come to pass in the aftertime, even that I should lose my eyesight at the hand of Odysseus. But I ever looked for some tall and goodly man to come hither, clad in great might, but behold now one that is a dwarf, a man of no worth and a weakling, hath blinded me of my eye after subduing me with wine. Nay come hither, Odysseus, that I may set by thee a stranger's cheer, and speed thy parting hence, that so the Earth-shaker may vouchsafe it thee, for his son am I, and he avows him for my father. And he himself will heal me, if it be his will; and none other of the blessed gods or of mortal men."

'Even so he spake, but I answered him, and said: "Would god that I were as sure to rob thee of soul and life, and send thee within the house of Hades, as I am that not even the Earth-shaker will heal thine eye!"

'So I spake, and then he prayed to the lord Poseidon stretching forth his hands to the starry heaven: "Hear me, Poseidon, girdler of the earth, god of the dark hair, if indeed I be thine, and thou avowest thee my sire,—grant that he may never come to his home, even Odysseus, waster of cities, the son of Laertes, whose dwelling is in Ithaca; yet if he is ordained to see his friends and come unto his well-builded house, and his own country, late may he come in evil case, with the loss of all his company, in the ship of strangers, and find sorrows in his house."

'So he spake in prayer, and the god of the dark locks heard him. And once again he lifted a stone, far greater than the first, and with one swing he hurled it, and he put forth a measureless strength, and cast it but a little space behind the dark-prowed ship, and all but struck the end of the rudder. And the sea heaved beneath the fall of the rock, but the wave bare on the ship and drave it to the further shore.

'But when we had now reached that island, where all our other decked ships abode together, and our company were gathered sorrowing, expecting us nevermore, on our coming thither we ran our ship ashore upon the sand, and ourselves too stept forth upon the sea-beach. Next we took forth the sheep of the Cyclops from out the hollow ship, and divided them, that none through me might go lacking his proper share. But the ram for me alone my goodly-greaved company chose out, in the dividing of the sheep, and on the shore I offered him up to Zeus, even to the son of Cronos, who dwells in the dark clouds, and is lord of all, and I burnt the slices of the thighs. But he heeded not the sacrifice, but was devising how my decked ships and my dear company might perish utterly. Thus for that time we sat the livelong day, until the going down of the sun, feasting on abundant flesh and sweet wine. And when the sun had sunk and darkness had come on, then we laid us to rest upon the sea-beach. So soon as early Dawn shone forth, the rosy-fingered, I called to my company, and commanded them that they should themselves climb the ship and loose the hawsers. So they soon embarked and sat upon the benches, and sitting orderly smote the grey sea water with their oars.

'Thence we sailed onward stricken at heart, yet glad as men saved from death, albeit we had lost our dear companions.

BOOK X

'Then we came to the isle Aeolian, where dwelt Aeolus,[1] in a floating island. . . . And the king entreated me kindly for a whole month, and sought out each thing, Ilios[2] and the ships of the Argives, and the return of the Achaeans. So I told him all the tale in order duly. But when I in turn took the word and asked of my journey, and bade him send me on my way, he too denied me not, but furnished an escort. He gave me a wallet, made of the hide of an ox of nine seasons old, which he let flay, and therein he bound the ways of all the noisy winds; for him the son of Cronos made keeper of the winds, either to lull or to rouse what blasts he will. And he made it fast in the hold of the ship with a shining silver thong, that not the faintest breath might escape. Then he sent forth the blast of the West Wind to blow for me, to bear our ships and ourselves upon our way; but this he was never to bring to pass, for we were undone through our own heedlessness.

'For nine whole days we sailed by night and day continually, and now on the tenth day my native land came in sight, and already we were so near that we beheld the folk tending the beacon fires. Then over me there came sweet slumber in my weariness. Meanwhile my company held converse together, and said that I was bringing home for myself gold and silver, gifts from Aeolus. And thus would they speak looking each man to his neighbour:

' "Many are the goodly treasures he taketh with him out of the spoil from Troy, while we who have fulfilled like journeying with him return homeward bringing with us but empty hands. And now Aeolus

1. God of the winds.   2. Troy.

hath given unto him these things freely in his love. Nay come, let us quickly see what they are, even what wealth of gold and silver is in the wallet."

'So they spake, and the evil counsel of my company prevailed. They loosed the wallet, and all the winds brake forth. And the violent blast seized my men, and bare them towards the high seas weeping, away from their own country; but as for me, I awoke and communed with my great heart, whether I should cast myself from the ship and perish in the deep, or endure in silence and abide yet among the living. Howbeit I hardened my heart to endure, and muffling my head I lay still in the ship. But the vessels were driven by the evil storm-wind back to the isle Aeolian, and my company made moan.

'Now when we had tasted bread and wine, I took with me a herald and one of my company, and went to the famous dwelling of Aeolus: and I found him feasting with his wife and children. So we went in and sat by the pillars of the door on the threshold, and they all marvelled and asked us:

' "How hast thou come hither, Odysseus? What evil god assailed thee? Surely we sent thee on thy way with all diligence, that thou mightest get thee to thine own country and thy home, and whithersoever thou wouldest."

'Even so they said, but I spake among them heavy at heart: "My evil company hath been my bane, and sleep thereto remorseless. Come, my friends, do ye heal the harm, for yours is the power."

'So I spake, beseeching them in soft words, but they held their peace. And the father answered, saying: "Get thee forth from the island straightway, thou that art the most reprobate of living men. Far be it from me to help or to further that man whom the blessed gods abhor! Get thee forth, for lo, thy coming marks thee hated by the deathless gods."

'Therewith he sent me forth from the house making heavy moan. So for the space of six days we sailed by night and day continually, and on the seventh we came to the steep stronghold of the Laestrygons. . . . Now the vessels were bound within the hollow harbour each hard by other. But I alone moored my dark ship without the harbour, at the uttermost point thereof, and made fast the hawser to a rock. And I went up a craggy hill, a place of outlook, and stood thereon. Then I sent forth certain of my company to go and search out what manner of men they were who here live upon the earth by bread, choosing out two of my company and sending a third with them as herald. Now when they had gone ashore, they went along a level road whereby wains were wont to draw down wood from the high hills to the town. And without the town they fell in with a damsel drawing water, the noble daughter of Laestrygonian Antiphates. So they stood by her and spake unto her, and asked who was king of that land, and who they were he ruled over. Then at once she showed them the high-roofed hall of her father. Now when they had entered the renowned house, they found his wife therein: she was huge of bulk as a mountain peak and was loathly in their sight. Straightway she called the renowned Antiphates, her lord, from the assembly-place, and he contrived a pitiful destruction for my men. Forthwith he clutched up one of my company and made ready his mid-day meal, but the other twain sprang up and came in flight to the ships. Then he raised the war-cry through the town, and the valiant Laestrygonians at the sound thereof flocked together from every side, a host past number, not like men but like the Giants. They cast at us from the cliffs with great rocks, each of them a man's burden, and anon there arose from the fleet an evil din of men dying and ships shattered withal. And like folks spearing fishes they bare home their hideous meal. While as yet they were slaying my friends within the deep harbour, I drew my sharp sword from my thigh, and with it cut the hawsers of my dark-prowed ship. Quickly then I called to my company, and bade them dash in with the oars, that we might clean escape this evil plight. And all with one accord they tossed the sea water with the oar-blade, in dread of death, and to my delight my barque flew forth to the high seas away from the beetling rocks, but those other ships were lost there, one and all.

'Thence we sailed onward stricken at heart, yet glad as men saved from death, albeit we had lost our dear companions. And we came to the isle Aeaean, where dwelt Circé of the braided tresses, an awful goddess of mortal speech. There on the shore we put in with our ship into the sheltering haven silently, and some god was our guide. Then we stept ashore, and for two days and two nights lay there, consuming our own hearts for weariness and pain. But when now the fair-tressed Dawn had brought the full light of the third day, then did I seize my spear and my sharp sword, and quickly departing from the ship I went up unto a place of wide prospect, and I saw the smoke rising from the broad-wayed earth in the halls of Circé. Then I mused in my mind and heart whether I should go and make discovery, for that I had seen the smoke and flame. And as I thought thereon this seemed to me the better counsel, to go first to the swift ship and to the sea-banks, and give my company their midday meal, and then send them to make search. But as I came and drew nigh to the curved ship, some god even then took pity on me in my loneliness, and sent a tall antlered stag across my very path. I smote him on the spine in the middle of the back, and the brazen shaft went clean through him, and with a moan he fell in the dust, and his life passed from him. Then I set my foot on him and drew forth the brazen shaft from the wound, and laid it hard by upon the ground and let it lie. Next I broke withies and willow twigs, and wove me a rope a fathom in length, well twisted from end to end, and bound together the feet of the huge beast, and went to the black ship bearing him across my neck, and leaning on a spear, for it was in no wise possible to carry him on my shoulder with the one hand, for he was a mighty quarry. And I threw him down before the ship and roused my company with soft words, standing by each man in turn:

‘ "Friends, for all our sorrows we shall not yet a while go down to the house of Hades, ere the coming of the day of destiny; go to then, while as yet there is meat and drink in the swift ship, let us take thought thereof, that we be not famished for hunger."

‘Even so I spake, and they speedily hearkened to my words. So for that time we sat the livelong day till the going down of the sun, feasting on abundant flesh and sweet wine. But when the sun sank and darkness had come on, then we laid us to rest upon the sea beach. So soon as early Dawn shone forth, the rosy-fingered, I called a gathering of my men and spake in the ears of them all:

‘ "Hear my words, my fellows, despite your evil case. My friends, lo, now we know not where is the place of darkness or of dawning, nor where the Sun, that gives light to men, goes beneath the earth, nor where he rises; therefore let us advise us speedily if any counsel yet may be: as for me, I deem there is none. . . ."

‘Then I numbered my goodly-greaved company in two bands, and appointed a leader for each, and I myself took the command of the one part, and godlike Eurylochus of the other. And anon we shook the lots in a brazen-fitted helmet, and out leapt the lot of proud Eurylochus. So he went on his way, and with him two and twenty of my fellowship all weeping; and we were left behind making lament. In the forest glades they found the halls of Circé builded. And all around the palace mountain-bred wolves and lions were roaming, whom she herself had bewitched with evil drugs that she gave them. Yet the beasts

did not set on my men, but lo, they ramped about them and fawned
on them, wagging their long tails. And as when dogs fawn about their
lord when he comes from the feast, for he always brings them the
fragments that soothe their mood, even so the strong-clawed wolves
and the lions fawned around them; but they were affrighted when
they saw the strange and terrible creatures. So they stood at the outer
gate of the fair-tressed goddess, and within they heard Circé singing
in a sweet voice. Then Polites, a leader of men, the dearest to me and
the trustiest of all my company, first spake to them:

'"Friends, forasmuch as there is one within—a goddess she is or
a woman—come quickly and cry aloud to her."

'He spake the word and they cried aloud and called to her. And
straightway she came forth and opened the shining doors and bade
them in, and all went with her in their heedlessness. But Eurylochus
tarried behind, for he guessed that there was some treason. So she led
them in and set them upon the chairs and high seats, and made them
a mess of cheese and barley-meal and yellow honey with Pramnian
wine, and mixed harmful drugs with the food to make them utterly
forget their own country. Now when she had given them the cup and
they had drunk it off, presently she smote them with a wand, and in
the styes of the swine she penned them. So they had the head and
voice, the bristles and the shape of swine, but their mind abode even
as of old. Thus were they penned there weeping, and Circé flung them
acorns and mast and fruit of the cornel tree to eat, whereon
wallowing swine do always batten.

'Now Eurylochus came back to the swift black ship to bring tidings
of his fellows, and of their unseemly doom. Not a word could he utter,
for all his desire, so deeply smitten was he to the heart with grief, and
his eyes were filled with tears and his soul was fain of lamentation.
But when we all had pressed him with our questions in amazement,
even then he told the fate of the remnant of our company. . . .

'Whereon I cast about my shoulder my silver-studded sword, a
great blade of bronze, and slung my bow about me and bade him
lead me again by the way that he came. But he caught me with both
hands, and by my knees he besought me, and bewailing him spake to
me winged words:

'"Lead me not thither against my will, oh fosterling of Zeus, but
leave me here! For well I know thou shalt thyself return no more,
nor bring any one of all thy fellowship; nay, let us flee the swifter
with those that be here, for even yet may we escape the evil day."

'On this wise he spake, but I answered him, saying: "Eurylochus, abide for thy part here in this place, eating and drinking by the black hollow ship: but I will go forth, for a strong constraint is laid on me."

'With that I went up from the ship and the sea-shore. But lo, when in my faring through the sacred glades I was now drawing near to the great hall of the enchantress Circé, then did Hermes, of the golden wand, meet me as I approached the house, in the likeness of a young man with the first down on his lip, the time when youth is most gracious. So he clasped my hand and spake and hailed me:

' "Ah, hapless man, whither away again, all alone through the wolds, thou that knowest not this country? And thy company yonder in the hall of Circé are penned in the guise of swine, in their deep lairs abiding. Is it in hope to free them that thou art come hither? Nay, methinks, thou thyself shalt never return but remain there with the others. Come then, I will redeem thee from thy distress, and bring deliverance. Lo, take this herb of virtue, and go to the dwelling of Circé, that it may keep from thy head the evil day. And I will tell thee all the magic sleight of Circé. She will mix thee a potion and cast drugs into the mess; but not even so shall she be able to enchant thee; so helpful is this charmed herb that I shall give thee, and I will tell thee all. When it shall be that Circé smites thee with her long wand, even then draw thou thy sharp sword from thy thigh, and spring on her, as one eager to slay her. And she will shrink away and be instant with thee to lie with her. Thenceforth disdain not thou the bed of the goddess, that she may deliver thy company and kindly entertain thee. But command her to swear a mighty oath by the blessed gods, that she will plan nought else of mischief to thine own hurt, lest she make thee a dastard and unmanned, when she hath thee naked."

'Therewith the slayer of Argos gave me the plant that he had plucked from the ground. Moly the gods call it, but it is hard for mortal men to dig; howbeit with the gods all things are possible.

'Then Hermes departed toward high Olympus, up through the woodland isle, but as for me I held on my way to the house of Circé, and my heart was darkly troubled as I went. So I halted in the portals of the fair-tressed goddess; there I stood and called aloud and the goddess heard my voice, who presently came forth and opened the shining doors and bade me in, and I went with her heavy at heart. So she led me in and set me on a chair with studs of silver. And she made me a potion in a golden cup, that I might drink, and she also

put a charm therein, in the evil counsel of her heart. Now when she
had given it and I had drunk it off and was not bewitched, she smote
me with her wand and spake and hailed me:

'"Go thy way now to the stye, couch thee there with the rest of
thy company."

'So spake she, but I drew my sharp sword from my thigh and
sprang upon Circé, as one eager to slay her. But with a great cry she
slipped under, and clasped my knees, and bewailing herself spake to
me winged words:

'"Who art thou of the sons of men, and whence? Where is thy
city? Where are they that begat thee? I marvel to see how thou hast
drunk of this charm, and wast nowise subdued. Nay, for there lives
no man else that is proof against this charm, whoso hath drunk
thereof, and once it hath passed his lips. But thou hast, methinks, a
mind within thee that may not be enchanted. Verily thou art Odysseus, ready at need, whom he of the golden wand, the slayer of Argos,
full often told me was to come hither, on his way from Troy with his
swift black ship. Nay come, put thy sword into the sheath, and thereafter let us go up into my bed, that meeting in love and sleep we may
trust each the other."

'So spake she, but I answered her, saying: "Nay, Circé, how canst
thou bid me be gentle to thee, who hast turned my company into
swine within thy halls, and holding me here with a guileful heart requirest me to pass within thy chamber and go up into thy bed, that so
thou mayest make me a dastard and unmanned when thou hast me
naked? Nay, never will I consent to go up into thy bed, except thou
wilt deign, goddess, to swear a mighty oath, that thou wilt plan
nought else of mischief to mine own hurt."

'So I spake, and she straightway swore the oath not to harm me,
as I bade her. But when she had sworn and had done that oath, then
at last I went up into the beautiful bed of Circé.

'Now all this while her handmaids busied them in the halls. . . .
And a handmaid bare water for the hands in a goodly golden ewer,
and poured it forth over a silver basin to wash withal; and to my side
she drew a polished table, and a grave dame bare wheaten bread and
set it by me, and laid on the board many dainties. And she bade me
eat, but my soul found no pleasure therein. I sat with other thoughts,
and my heart had a boding of ill.

'Now when Circé saw that I sat thus, and that I put not forth my hands to the meat, and that I was mightily afflicted, she drew near to me and spake to me winged words:

'"Wherefore thus, Odysseus, dost thou sit there like a speechless man, consuming thine own soul, and dost not touch meat nor drink?"

'So spake she, but I answered her, saying: "Oh, Circé, what righteous man would have the heart to taste meat and drink ere he had redeemed his company, and beheld them face to face?"

'So I spake, and Circé passed out through the hall with the wand in her hand, and opened the doors of the stye, and drave them forth in the shape of swine of nine seasons old. There they stood before her, and she went through their midst, and anointed each one of them with another charm. And lo, from their limbs the bristles dropped away. And they became men again, younger than before they were, and goodlier far, and taller to behold. And they all knew me again and each one took my hands, and wistful was the lament that sank into their souls, and the roof around rang wondrously. And even the goddess herself was moved with compassion.

'Then standing nigh me the fair goddess spake unto me: "Son of Laertes, of the seed of Zeus, Odysseus of many devices, depart now to thy swift ship and the sea banks. And first of all, draw ye up the ship ashore, and bestow the goods in the caves and all the gear. And thyself return again, and bring with thee thy dear companions."

'So spake she, and my lordly spirit consented thereto. So I went on my way to the swift ship and the sea-banks, and there I found my dear company on the swift ship lamenting piteously, shedding big tears. And as when calves of the homestead gather round the droves of kine that have returned to the yard, when they have had their fill of pasture, and all with one accord frisk before them, and the folds may no more contain them, but with a ceaseless lowing they skip about their dams, so flocked they all about me weeping, when their eyes beheld me.

'Then making lament they spake to me winged words: "O fosterling of Zeus, we were none otherwise glad at thy returning, than if we had come to Ithaca, our own country. Nay come, of our other companions tell us the tale of their ruin."

'So spake they, but I answered them with soft words: "Behold, let us first of all draw up the ship ashore, and bestow our goods in the caves and all our gear. And do ye bestir you, one and all, to go with me, that ye may see your fellows in the sacred dwelling of Circé, eating and drinking, for they have continual store."

'So spake I, and at once they hearkened to my words, but Eurylochus alone would have holden all my companions, and uttering his voice he spake to them winged words:

'"Wretched men that we are! whither are we going? Why are your hearts so set on sorrow that ye should go down to the hall of Circé, who will surely change us all to swine, or wolves, or lions, to guard her great house perforce."

'So spake he, but I mused in my heart whether to draw my long hanger from my stout thigh, and therewith smite off his head and bring it to the dust, albeit he was very near of kin to me; but the men of my company stayed me on every side with soothing words:

'"Prince of the seed of Zeus, as for this man, we will suffer him, if thou wilt have it so, to abide here by the ship and guard the ship; but as for us, be our guide to the sacred house of Circé."

'So they spake and went up from the ship and the sea. Nay, nor yet was Eurylochus left by the hollow ship, but he went with us, for he feared my terrible rebuke.

'Meanwhile Circé bathed the rest of my company in her halls with all care, and anointed them well with olive oil; and cast thick mantles and doublets about them. And we found them all feasting nobly in the halls. And when they saw and knew each other face to face, they wept and mourned, and the house rang around. Then she stood near me, that fair goddess, and spake saying:

'"Son of Laertes, of the seed of Zeus, Odysseus of many devices, no more now wake this plenteous weeping: myself I know of all the pains ye endured upon the teeming deep, and the great despite done you by unkindly men upon the land. Nay come, eat ye meat and drink wine, till your spirit shall return to you again, as it was when first ye left your own country of rugged Ithaca."

'So spake she, and our lordly spirit consented thereto. So there we sat day by day for the full circle of a year. Then did my dear company call me forth, and say:

'"Good sir, now is it high time to mind thee of thy native land, if it is ordained that thou shalt be saved, and come to thy lofty house and thine own country."

'So spake they and my lordly spirit consented thereto. But when I had gone up into the fair bed of Circé, I besought her by her knees, and the goddess heard my speech, and uttering my voice I spake to her winged words: "Circé, fulfil for me the promise which thou madest me to send me on my homeward way. Now is my spirit eager to be gone, and the spirit of my company."

'So spake I, and the fair goddess answered me anon: "Son of Laertes, of the seed of Zeus, Odysseus of many devices, tarry ye now no longer in my house against your will; but first must ye perform another journey, and reach the dwelling of Hades and of dread Persephone[3] to seek to the spirit of Theban Teiresias, the blind soothsayer, whose wits abide steadfast. To him Persephone hath given judgment, even in death, that he alone should have understanding; but the other souls sweep shadow-like around."

'Thus spake she, but as for me, my heart was broken, and I wept as I sat upon the bed, and my soul had no more care to live and see the sunlight. But when I had my fill of weeping and grovelling, then at the last I answered and spake unto her saying: "And who, Circé, will guide us on this way? for no man ever yet sailed to hell in a black ship."

'So spake I, and the fair goddess answered me anon: "Son of Laertes, nay, trouble not thyself for want of a guide, by thy ship abiding, but set up the mast and spread abroad the white sails and sit thee down; and the breeze of the North Wind will bear thy vessel on her way. But when thou hast now sailed in thy ship across the stream Oceanus,[4] where is a waste shore and the groves of Persephone, even tall poplar trees and willows that shed their fruit before the season, there beach thy ship by deep eddying Oceanus, but go thyself to the dank house of Hades. Thereby into Acheron flows Pyriphlegethon, and Cocytus, a branch of the water of the Styx, and there is a rock, and the meeting of the two roaring waters. So, hero, draw nigh thereto, and dig a trench as it were a cubit in length and breadth, and about it pour a drink-offering to all the dead, first with mead and thereafter with sweet wine, and for the third time with water, and sprinkle white meal thereon; and entreat with many prayers the strengthless heads of the dead, and promise that on thy return to Ithaca thou wilt offer in thy halls a barren heifer, the best thou hast, and wilt fill the pyre with treasure, and wilt sacrifice apart, to Teiresias alone, a black ram without spot, the fairest of your flock. But when thou hast with prayers made supplication to the lordly races of the dead, then offer up a ram and a black ewe, and thyself turn thy back, with thy face

3. Queen of the lower world.
4. The great stream believed by the ancients to encircle the plane surface of the earth.

set for the shore of the river. Then will many spirits come to thee of the dead that be departed. Thereafter thou shalt call to thy company and command them to flay the sheep which even now lie slain by the pitiless sword, and to consume them with fire, and to make prayer to the gods, to mighty Hades and to dread Persephone. And thyself draw the sharp sword from thy thigh and sit there, suffering not the strengthless heads of the dead to draw nigh to the blood, ere thou hast word of Teiresias. Then the seer will come to thee quickly, leader of the people; he will surely declare to thee the way and the measure of thy path, and as touching thy returning, how thou mayst go over the teeming deep."

'So spake she, and anon came the golden throned Dawn. Then she put on me a mantle and a doublet for raiment, and the nymph clad herself in a great shining robe, and put a veil upon her head. But I passed through the halls and roused my men with smooth words, standing by each one in turn:

' "Sleep ye now no more nor breathe the sweet slumber; but let us go on our way, for surely she hath shown me all, the lady Circé."

'So spake I, and their lordly soul consented thereto. Yet even thence I led not my company safe away. There was one, Elpenor, the youngest of us all, not very valiant in war, neither steadfast in mind. He was lying apart from the rest of my men on the housetop of Circé's sacred dwelling, very fain of the cool air, as one heavy with wine. Now when he heard the noise of the voices and of the feet of my fellows as they moved to and fro, he leaped up of a sudden and minded him not to descend again by the way of the tall ladder, but fell right down from the roof, and his neck was broken from the bones of the spine, and his spirit went down to the house of Hades.

'Then I spake among my men as they went on their way, saying: "Ye deem now, I see, that ye are going to your own dear country; but Circé hath showed us another way, even to the dwelling of Hades and of dread Persephone, to seek to the spirit of Theban Teiresias."

'Even so I spake, but their heart within them was broken, and they sat them down even where they were, and made lament and tore their hair. Howbeit no help came of their weeping.

'But as we were now wending sorrowful to the swift ship and the sea-banks, shedding big tears, Circé meanwhile had gone her ways and made fast a ram and a black ewe by the dark ship, lightly passing us by: who may behold a god against his will, whether going to or fro?

BOOK XI

'Now when we had gone down to the ship and to the sea, first of all we drew the ship unto the fair salt water, and placed the mast and sails in the black ship, and took those sheep and put them therein, and ourselves too climbed on board, sorrowing, and shedding big tears. And in the wake of our dark-prowed ship she sent a favouring wind that filled the sails, a kindly escort,—even Circé of the braided tresses, a dread goddess of human speech. And we set in order all the gear throughout the ship and sat us down; and the wind and the helmsman guided our barque. And all day long her sails were stretched in her seafaring; and the sun sank and all the ways were darkened.

'She came to the limits of the world, to the deep flowing Oceanus. There is the land and the city of the Cimmerians, shrouded in mist and cloud, and never does the shining sun look down on them with his rays. Thither we came and ran the ship ashore and took out the sheep; but for our part we held on our way along the stream of Oceanus, till we came to the place which Circé had declared to us.

'I drew my sharp sword from my thigh, and dug a pit, as it were a cubit in length and breadth, and about it poured a drink-offering to all the dead. And I sprinkled white meal thereon, and entreated with many prayers the strengthless heads of the dead, and promised that on my return to Ithaca I would offer in my halls a barren heifer, the best I had, and fill the pyre with treasure, and apart unto Teiresias alone sacrifice a black ram without spot, the fairest of my flock. But when I had besought the tribes of the dead with vows and prayers, I took the sheep and cut their throats over the trench, and the dark blood flowed forth, and lo, the spirits of the dead that be departed gathered them from out of Erebus.[1] And these many ghosts flocked together from every side about the trench with a wondrous cry, and pale fear gat hold on me. Then did I speak to my company and command them to flay the sheep that lay slain by the pitiless sword, and to consume them with fire, and to make prayer to the gods, to mighty Hades and to dread Persephone, and myself I drew the sharp sword from my thigh and sat there, suffering not the strengthless heads of the dead to draw nigh to the blood, ere I had word of Teiresias.

'And first came the soul of Elpenor, my companion, that had not yet been buried beneath the wide-wayed earth; for we left the corpse behind us in the hall of Circé, unwept and unburied, seeing that an-

1. The dark subterranean space through which souls journey to Hades.

other task was instant on us. At the sight of him I wept and had com-
passion on him, and uttering my voice spake to him winged words:
"Elpenor, how hast thou come beneath the darkness and the shadow?
Thou hast come fleeter on foot than I in my black ship."

'So spake I, and with a moan he answered me, saying: "Son of
Laertes, of the seed of Zeus, Odysseus of many devices, an evil doom
of some god was my bane and wine out of measure. When I laid me
down on the house-top of Circé I minded me not to descend again by
way of the tall ladder, but fell right down from the roof, and my neck
was broken off from the bones of the spine, and my spirit went down
to the house of Hades. And now I pray thee in the name of those
whom we left; forasmuch as I know that on thy way hence from out
the dwelling of Hades, thou wilt stay thy well-wrought ship at the
isle Aeaean, even then, my lord, I charge thee to think on me. Leave
me not unwept and unburied as thou goest hence, nor turn thy back
upon me, lest haply I bring on thee the anger of the gods. Nay, burn
me there with mine armour, all that is mine, and pile me a barrow
on the shore of the grey sea, the grave of a luckless man, that even
men unborn may hear my story. . . ."

'Anon came the soul of Theban Teiresias, with a golden sceptre
in his hand, and he knew me and spake unto me: "Son of Laertes,
of the seed of Zeus, Odysseus of many devices, what seekest thou *now*,
wretched man, wherefore hast thou left the sunlight and come hither
to behold the dead and a land desolate of joy? Nay, hold off from the
ditch and draw back thy sharp sword, that I may drink of the blood
and tell thee sooth."

'So spake he and I put my silver-studded sword into the sheath,
and when he had drunk the dark blood, even then did the noble seer
speak unto me, saying: "Thou art asking of thy sweet returning, great
Odysseus, but that will the god make hard for thee; for methinks
thou shalt not pass unheeded by the Shaker of the Earth, who hath
laid up wrath in his heart against thee, for rage at the blinding of his
dear son. Yet even so, through many troubles, ye may come home, if
thou wilt restrain thy spirit and the spirit of thy men so soon as thou
shalt bring thy well-wrought ship nigh to the isle Thrinacia, when
ye find the herds of Helios grazing and his brave flocks. If thou doest
these no hurt, being heedful of thy return, so may ye reach Ithaca,
albeit in evil case. But if thou hurtest them, I foreshow ruin for thy
ship and for thy men, and even though thou shalt thyself escape, late
shalt thou return in evil plight, with the loss of all thy company, on

board the ship of strangers, and thou shalt find sorrows in thy house, even proud men that devour thy living, while they woo thy godlike wife and offer the gifts of wooing. Yet I tell thee, on thy coming thou shalt avenge their violence. But when thou hast slain the wooers in thy halls, whether by guile, or openly with the edge of the sword, thereafter go thy way, taking with thee a shapen oar, till thou shalt come to such men as know not the sea, neither eat meat savoured with salt; yea, nor have they knowledge of ships of purple cheek, nor shapen oars which serve for wings to ships. And I will give thee a most manifest token, which cannot escape thee. In the day when another wayfarer shall meet thee and say that thou hast a winnowing fan on thy stout shoulder, even then make fast thy shapen oar in the earth and do goodly sacrifice to the lord Poseidon, even with a ram and a bull and a boar, the mate of swine, and depart for home and offer holy hecatombs to the deathless gods that keep the wide heaven, to each in order due. And from the sea shall thine own death come, the gentlest death that may be, which shall end thee foredone with smooth old age, and the folk shall dwell happily around thee. This that I say is sooth."

'So spake he, and I answered him, saying: "Teiresias, all these threads, methinks, the gods themselves have spun. But come, declare me this and plainly tell me all. I see here the spirit of Anticleia, my mother dead; lo, she sits in silence near the blood, nor deigns to look her son in the face nor speak to him! Tell me, prince, how may she know me again that I am he?"

'So spake I, and anon he answered me, and said: "I will tell thee an easy saying, and will put it in thy heart. Whomsoever of the dead that be departed thou shalt suffer to draw nigh to the blood, he shall tell thee sooth; but if thou shalt grudge any, that one shall go to his own place again." Therewith the spirit of the prince Teiresias went back within the house of Hades, when he had told all his oracles. But I abode there steadfastly, till my mother drew nigh and drank the dark blood; and at once she knew me, and bewailing herself spake to me winged words:

' "Dear child, how didst thou come beneath the darkness and the shadow, thou that art a living man? Art thou but now come hither with thy ship and thy company in thy long wanderings from Troy? and hast thou not yet reached Ithaca, nor seen thy wife in thy halls?"

'Even so she spake, and I answered her, and said: "O my mother, necessity was on me to come down to the house of Hades to seek to the spirit of Theban Teiresias. For not yet have I drawn near to the Achaean shore, nor yet have I set foot on mine own country. But come, declare me this and plainly tell it all. What doom overcame thee of death that lays men at their length? And tell me of my father and my son, that I left behind me; doth my honour yet abide with them, or hath another already taken it, while they say that I shall come home no more? And tell me of my wedded wife, of her counsel and her purpose, doth she abide with her son and keep all secure, or hath she already wedded the best of the Achaeans?"

'Even so I spake, and anon my lady mother answered me: "Yea verily, she abideth with steadfast spirit in thy halls; and wearily for her the nights wane always and the days in shedding of tears. But the fair honour that is thine no man hath yet taken; but Telemachus sits at peace on his demesne, and feasts at equal banquets. And thy father abides there in the field, and goes not down to the town, nor lies he on bedding or rugs or shining blankets, but all the winter he sleeps, where sleep the thralls in the house, in the ashes by the fire, and is clad in sorry raiment. But when the summer comes and the rich harvest-tide, his beds of fallen leaves are strewn lowly all about the knoll of his vineyard plot. There he lies sorrowing and nurses his mighty grief, for long desire of thy return, and old age withal comes heavy upon him. Yea and even so did I too perish and meet my doom. It was my sore longing for thee, and for thy counsels, great Odysseus, and for thy loving-kindness, that reft me of sweet life."...

'Thus we twain held discourse together; and lo, the women came up, for the high goddess Persephone sent them forth, all they that had been the wives and daughters of mighty men. And they gathered and flocked about the black blood, and I took counsel how I might question them each one. And this was the counsel that showed best in my sight. I drew my long hanger from my stalwart thigh, and suffered them not all at one time to drink of the dark blood. So they drew nigh one by one, and each declared her lineage, and I made question of all. . . .

'Now when holy Persephone had scattered this way and that the spirits of the women folk, thereafter came the soul of Agamemnon, son of Atreus, sorrowing; and round him others were gathered, the ghosts of them who had died with him in the house of Aegisthus and met their doom. And he knew me straightway when he had drunk the dark blood, yea, and he wept aloud, and shed big tears as he stretched forth his hands in his longing to reach me.

'At the sight of him I wept and was moved with compassion, and uttering my voice, spake to him winged words: "Most renowned son of Atreus, Agamemnon, king of men, say what doom overcame thee of death that lays men at their length? Did Poseidon smite thee in thy ships, or did unfriendly men do thee hurt upon the land, whilst thou wert cutting off their oxen and fair flocks of sheep, or fighting to win a city and the women thereof?"

'So spake I, and straightway he answered, and said unto me: "Son of Laertes, of the seed of Zeus, Odysseus of many devices, it was not Poseidon that smote me in my ships, nor did unfriendly men do me hurt upon the land, but Aegisthus it was that wrought me death and doom and slew me, with the aid of my accursed wife, as one slays an ox at the stall, after he had bidden me to his house, and entertained me at a feast. Even so I died by a death most pitiful, and round me my company likewise were slain without ceasing, like swine with glittering tusks which are slaughtered in the house of a rich and mighty man. . . . And most pitiful of all that I heard was the voice of the daughter of Priam, of Cassandra,[2] whom hard by me the crafty Clytemnestra slew. Then I strove to raise my hands as I was dying upon the sword, but to earth they fell. And that shameless one turned her back upon me, and had not the heart to draw down my eyelids with her fingers nor to close my mouth. Verily I had thought to come home most welcome to my children and my thralls; but she, out of the depth of her evil knowledge, hath shed shame on herself and on all womankind, which shall be for ever, even on the upright."

'Even so he spake, but I answered him, saying: "Lo now, in very sooth, hath Zeus of the far-borne voice wreaked wondrous hatred on the seed of Atreus through the counsels of woman from of old. For Helen's sake so many of us perished, and now Clytemnestra hath practised treason against thee, while yet thou wast afar off."

'Even so I spake, and anon he answered me, saying: "Wherefore do thou too, never henceforth be soft even to thy wife, neither show her all the counsel that thou knowest, but a part declare and let part be hid. . . . And yet another thing will I tell thee, and do thou ponder it in thy heart. Put thy ship to land in secret, and not openly, on the shore of thy dear country; for there is no more faith in woman. . . ."

'Thus we twain stood sorrowing, holding sad discourse, while the big tears fell fast: and therewithal came the soul of Achilles, son

2. After the fall of Troy the Trojan princess Cassandra became the prize of Agamemnon.

of Peleus, and of Patroclus and of noble Antilochus and of Aias,[3] who in face and form was goodliest of all the Danaans, after the noble son of Peleus. And the spirit of the son of Aeacus,[4] fleet of foot, knew me again, and making lament spake to me winged words:

'"Son of Laertes, of the seed of Zeus, Odysseus of many devices, man overbold, what new deed and hardier than this wilt thou devise in thy heart? How durst thou come down to the house of Hades, where dwell the senseless dead, the phantoms of men outworn?"

'So he spake, but I answered him: "Achilles, son of Peleus, mightiest far of the Achaeans, I am come hither to seek to Teiresias, if he may tell me any counsel, how I may come to rugged Ithaca. For not yet have I come nigh the Achaean land, nor set foot on mine own soil, but am still in evil case; while as for thee, Achilles, none other than thou wast heretofore the most blessed of men, nor shall any be hereafter. For of old, in the days of thy life, we Argives gave thee one honour with the gods, and now thou art a great prince here among the dead. Wherefore let not thy death be any grief to thee, Achilles."

'Even so I spake, and he straightway answered me, and said: "Nay, speak not comfortably to me of death, oh great Odysseus. Rather would I live on ground as the hireling of another, with a landless man who had no great livelihood, than bear sway among all the dead that be departed. But come, tell me tidings of that lordly son of mine—did he follow to the war to be a leader or not? And tell me of noble Peleus, if thou hast heard aught,—is he yet held in worship among the Myrmidons,[5] or do they dishonour him from Hellas to Phthia, for that old age binds him hand and foot? For I am no longer his champion under the sun, so mighty a man as once I was, when in wide Troy I slew the best of the host, and succoured the Argives. Ah! could I but come for an hour to my father's house as then I was, so would I make my might and hands invincible, to be hateful to many an one of those who do him despite and keep him from his honour."

'Even so he spake, but I answered him saying: "As for noble Peleus, verily I have heard nought of him; but concerning thy dear son Neoptolemus, I will tell thee all the truth, according to thy word. Now oft as we took counsel around Troy town, he was ever the first to speak, and no word missed the mark; the godlike Nestor and I

3. All these were famous Greek warriors.
4. Achilles, grandson of Aeacus.
5. Peleus was king of the Myrmidons.

alone surpassed him. But whensoever we Achaeans did battle on the plain of Troy, he never tarried behind in the throng or the press of men, but ran out far before us all, yielding to none in that might of his. And many men he slew in warfare dread; but I could not tell of all or name their names. . . . And again when we, the best of the Argives, were about to go down into the horse which Epeus wrought, and the charge of all was laid on me, both to open the door of our good ambush and to shut the same, then did the other princes and counsellors of the Danaans wipe away the tears, and the limbs of each one trembled beneath him, but never once did I see thy son's fair face wax pale, nor did he wipe the tears from his cheeks: but he besought me often to let him go forth from the horse, and kept handling his sword-hilt, and his heavy bronze-shod spear, and he was set on mischief against the Trojans. But after we had sacked the steep city of Priam, he embarked unscathed with his share of the spoil, and with a noble prize; he was not smitten with the sharp spear, and got no wound in close fight: and many such chances there be in war, for Ares[6] rageth confusedly."

'So I spake, and the spirit of the son of Aeacus, fleet of foot, passed with great strides along the mead of asphodel, rejoicing in that I had told him of his son's renown.

'But lo, other spirits of the dead that be departed stood sorrowing, and each one asked of those that were dear to them. . . .

'There then I saw Minos, glorious son of Zeus, wielding a golden sceptre, giving sentence from his throne to the dead, while they sat and stood around the prince, asking his dooms through the wide-gated house of Hades. . . .

'Moreover I beheld Tantalus[7] in grievous torment, standing in a mere and the water came nigh unto his chin. And he stood straining as one athirst, but he might not attain to the water to drink of it. For often as that old man stooped down in his eagerness to drink, so often the water was swallowed up and it vanished away, and the black earth still showed at his feet, for some god parched it evermore. And tall trees flowering shed their fruit overhead, pears and pomegranates and apple trees with bright fruit, and sweet figs and olives in their

6. God of war.
7. Tantalus, a legendary king, had offended the gods; but as to how, the accounts vary (by serving them his son's flesh as food, by stealing from them nectar and ambrosia, or by revealing divine secrets). The punishment described by Homer has added a word, "to tantalize," to the English vocabulary.

bloom, whereat when that old man reached out his hands to clutch them, the wind would toss them to the shadowy clouds.

'Yea and I beheld Sisyphus[8] in strong torment, grasping a monstrous stone with both his hands. He was pressing thereat with hands and feet, and trying to roll the stone upward toward the brow of the hill. But oft as he was about to hurl it over the top, the weight would drive him back, so once again to the plain rolled the stone, the shameless thing. And he once more kept heaving and straining, and the sweat the while was pouring down his limbs, and the dust rose upwards from his head.

'And after him I descried the mighty Heracles,[9] his phantom, I say; but as for himself he hath joy at the banquet among the deathless gods, and hath to wife Hebe of the fair ankles, child of great Zeus, and of Here of the golden sandals. And all about him there was a clamour of the dead, as it were fowls flying every way in fear, and he like black Night, with bow uncased, and shaft upon the string, fiercely glancing around, like one in the act to shoot. . . . And anon he knew me when his eyes beheld me, and making lament he spake unto me winged words:

' "Son of Laertes, of the seed of Zeus, Odysseus of many devices: ah! wretched one, dost thou too lead such a life of evil doom, as I endured beneath the rays of the sun? I was the son of Zeus Cronion, yet had I trouble beyond measure, for I was subdued unto a man far worse than I. And he enjoined on me hard adventures, yea and on a time he sent me hither to bring back the hound of hell; for he devised no harder task for me than this. I lifted the hound and brought him forth from out of the house of Hades; and Hermes sped me on my way and the grey-eyed Athene."

'Therewith he departed again into the house of Hades, but I abode there still, if perchance some one of the hero folk besides might come, who died in old time. Yea and I should have seen the men of old, whom I was fain to look on, Theseus and Peirithous,[10] renowned

8. Sisyphus was a legendary king of Corinth whose numerous and varied misdeeds usually involved insolence towards the gods.

9. As penance for the murder of his own wife and children during a fit of madness, Hercules had to serve Eurystheus, king of Tiryns, for twelve years. By order of Eurystheus he performed his famous twelve labors, including the capture of Cerberus, watchdog of Hades.

10. Theseus was a legendary king of Athens whose exploits somewhat parallel those of Hercules. Peirithous, his dearest friend, shared with him his most outrageous escapades.

children of the gods. But ere that might be the myriad tribes of the dead thronged up together with wondrous clamour: and pale fear gat hold of me, lest the high goddess Persephone should send me the head of the Gorgon,[11] that dread monster, from out of Hades.

'Straightway then I went to the ship, and bade my men mount the vessel, and loose the hawsers. So speedily they went on board, and sat upon the benches. And the wave of the flood bore the barque down the stream of Oceanus, we rowing first, and afterwards the fair wind was our convoy.'

BOOK XII

[Returned to the palace of Circé, Odysseus tells of his descent into Hades. Circé warns him of bitter trials to come: of the seductions of the Sirens, of the dangerous cliffs called the Skurries, of the ravenous, six-headed monster Scylla, and of the whirlpool Charybdis. She instructs Odysseus how best to avoid each danger, and she warns him against harming any of the cattle of Helios on the island of Thrinacia.]

'. . . So spake she, and anon came the golden-throned Dawn. Then the fair goddess took her way up the island. But I departed to my ship and roused my men themselves to mount the vessel and loose the hawsers. And speedily they went aboard and sat upon the benches, and sitting orderly smote the grey sea water with their oars. And in the wake of our dark-prowed ship she sent a favouring wind that filled the sails, a kindly escort.

'Then I spake among my company with a heavy heart: "Friends, forasmuch as it is not well that one or two alone should know of the oracles that Circé, the fair goddess, spake unto me, therefore will I declare them, that with foreknowledge we may die, or haply shunning death and destiny escape. First she bade us avoid the sound of the voice of the wondrous Sirens, and their field of flowers, and me only she bade listen to their voices. So bind ye me in a hard bond, that I may abide unmoved in my place, upright in the mast-stead, and if I beseech and bid you to set me free, then do ye straiten me with yet more bonds."

'Thus I rehearsed these things one and all, and declared them to my company. Meanwhile our good ship quickly came to the island of

11. The Gorgon Medusa, whose gaze even after her death would turn one to stone.

the Sirens twain, for a gentle breeze sped her on her way. Then straightway the wind ceased, and lo, there was a windless calm, and some god lulled the waves. Then my company rose up and drew in the ship's sails, and stowed them in the hold of the ship, while they sat at the oars and whitened the water with their polished pine blades. But I with my sharp sword cleft in pieces a great circle of wax, and with my strong hands kneaded it. And I anointed therewith the ears of all my men in their order, and in the ship they bound me hand and foot upright in the mast-stead, and from the mast they fastened rope-ends and themselves sat down, and smote the grey sea water with their oars. But when the ship was within the sound of a man's shout from the land, we fleeing swiftly on our way, the Sirens espied the swift ship speeding toward them, and they raised their clear-toned song:

' "Hither, come hither, renowned Odysseus, great glory of the Achaeans, here stay thy barque, that thou mayest listen to the voice of us twain. For none hath ever driven by this way in his black ship, till he hath heard from our lips the voice sweet as the honeycomb, and hath had joy thereof and gone on his way the wiser. For lo, we know all things, all the travail that in wide Troy-land the Argives and Trojans bare by the gods' designs, yea, and we know all that shall hereafter be upon the fruitful earth."

'So spake they uttering a sweet voice, and my heart was fain to listen, and I bade my company unbind me, nodding at them with a frown, but they bent to their oars and rowed on. Then straight uprose Perimedes and Eurylochus and bound me with more cords and strait-ened me yet the more. Now when we had driven past them, nor heard we any longer the sound of the Sirens or their song, forthwith my dear company took away the wax wherewith I had anointed their ears and loosed me from my bonds.

'But so soon as we left that isle, thereafter presently I saw smoke and a great wave, and heard the sea roaring. Then for very fear the oars flew from their hands, and down the stream they all splashed, and the ship was holden there, for my company no longer plied with their hands the tapering oars. But I paced the ship and cheered on my men, as I stood by each one and spake smooth words:

' "Friends, forasmuch as in sorrow we are not all unlearned, truly this is no greater woe that is upon us, than when the Cyclops penned us by main might in his hollow cave; yet even thence we made escape by my manfulness, even by my counsel and my wit, and some day I think that this adventure too we shall remember. Come now, there-

fore, let us all give ear to do according to my word. Do ye smite the
deep surf of the sea with your oars, as ye sit on the benches, if peradventure Zeus may grant us to escape from and shun this death. And
as for thee, helmsman, thus I charge thee, and ponder it in thine heart
seeing that thou wieldest the helm of the hollow ship. Keep the ship
well away from this smoke and from the wave and hug the rocks,
lest the ship, ere thou art aware, start from her course to the other side,
and so thou hurl us into ruin."

'So I spake, and quickly they hearkened to my words. But of Scylla
I told them nothing more, a bane none might deal with, lest haply
my company should cease from rowing for fear, and hide them in the
hold. In that same hour I suffered myself to forget the hard behest of
Circé in that she bade me in no wise be armed; but I did on my glorious harness and caught up two long lances in my hands, and went on
to the decking of the prow, for thence methought that Scylla of the
rock would first be seen, who was to bring woe on my company. Yet
could I not spy her anywhere, and my eyes waxed weary for gazing all
about toward the darkness of the rock.

'Next we began to sail up the narrow strait lamenting. For on
the one hand lay Scylla, and on the other mighty Charybdis in terrible
wise sucked down the salt sea water. As often as she belched it forth,
like a cauldron on a great fire she would seethe up through all her
troubled deeps, and overhead the spray fell on the tops of either cliff.
Toward her, then, we looked fearing destruction; but Scylla meanwhile caught from out my hollow ship six of my company, the hardiest
of their hands and the chief in might. And looking into the swift ship
to find my men, even then I marked their feet and hands as they were
lifted on high, and they cried aloud in their agony, and called me by
my name for that last time of all. Even as when a fisher on some headland lets down with a long rod his baits for a snare to the little fishes
below, casting into the deep the horn of an ox of the homestead, and
as he catches each flings it writhing ashore, so writhing were they borne
upward to the cliff. And there she devoured them shrieking in her
gates, they stretching forth their hands to me in the dread death-
struggle. And the most pitiful thing was this that mine eyes have seen
of all my travail in searching out the paths of the sea.

'Now when we had escaped the Rocks and dread Charybdis and
Scylla, thereafter we soon came to the fair island of the god; where
were the goodly kine, broad of brow, and the many brave flocks of
Helios Hyperion. Then while as yet I was in my black ship upon the

deep, I heard the lowing of the cattle being stalled and the bleating of the sheep. Then I spake out among my company in sorrow of heart:

'"Hear my words, my men, albeit in evil plight, that I may declare unto you the oracles of Teiresias and of Circé, who very straitly charged me to shun the isle of Helios, the gladdener of the world. For there she said the most dreadful mischief would befall us. Nay, drive ye then the black ship beyond and past that isle."

'So spake I, and their heart was broken within them. And Eurylochus straightway answered me sadly, saying:

'"Hardy art thou, Odysseus, of might beyond measure, and thy limbs are never weary; verily thou art fashioned all of iron, that sufferest not thy fellows, foredone with toil and drowsiness, to set foot on shore, where we might presently prepare us a good supper in this sea-girt island. But even as we are thou biddest us fare blindly through the sudden night, and from the isle go wandering on the misty deep. Howbeit for this present let us yield to the black night, and we will make ready our supper abiding by the swift ship, and in the morning we will climb on board, and put out into the broad deep."

'So spake Eurylochus, and the rest of my company consented thereto. Then at the last I knew that some god was indeed imagining evil, and I uttered my voice and spake unto him winged words:

'"Eurylochus, verily ye put force upon me, being but one among you all. But come, swear me now a mighty oath, one and all, to the intent that if we light on a herd of kine or a great flock of sheep, none in the evil folly of his heart may slay any sheep or ox; but in quiet eat ye the meat which the deathless Circé gave."

'So I spake, and straightway they swore to refrain as I commanded them. Now after they had sworn and done that oath, we stayed our well-built ship in the hollow harbour near to a well of sweet water, and my company went forth from out the ship and deftly got ready supper. But when they had put from them the desire of meat and drink, thereafter they fell a weeping as they thought upon their dear companions whom Scylla had snatched from out the hollow ship and so devoured. And deep sleep came upon them amid their weeping. Now when early Dawn shone forth, the rosy-fingered, we beached the ship, and dragged it up within a hollow cave. Thereupon I ordered a gathering of my men and spake in their midst, saying:

'"Friends, forasmuch as there is yet meat and drink in the swift ship, let us keep our hands off those kine, lest some evil thing befall us. For these are the kine and the brave flocks of a dread god, even of Helios, who overseeth all and overheareth all things."

'So I spake, and their lordly spirit hearkened thereto. Then for a whole month the South Wind blew without ceasing, and no other wind arose, save only the East and the South.

'Now so long as my company still had corn and red wine, they refrained them from the kine, for they were fain of life. But when the corn was now all spent from out the ship, and they went wandering with barbed hooks in quest of game, as needs they must, fishes and fowls, whatsoever might come to their hand, for hunger gnawed at their belly, then at last I departed up the isle, that I might pray to the gods, if perchance some one of them might show me a way of returning. And now when I had avoided my company on my way through the island, I laved my hands where was a shelter from the wind, and prayed to all the gods that hold Olympus. But they shed sweet sleep upon my eyelids. And Eurylochus the while set forth an evil counsel to my company:

'"Hear my words, my friends, though ye be in evil case. Truly every shape of death is hateful to wretched mortals, but to die of hunger and so meet doom is most pitiful of all. Nay come, we will drive off the best of the kine of Helios and will do sacrifice to the deathless gods who keep wide heaven. . . ."

'So spake Eurylochus, and the rest of the company consented thereto. Forthwith they drave off the best of the kine of Helios that were nigh at hand, for the fair kine of shambling gait and broad of brow were feeding no great way from the dark-prowed ship. Now after they had prayed and cut the throats of the kine and flayed them, they cut out slices of the thighs and wrapped them in the fat, making a double fold, and thereon they laid raw flesh. Yet had they no pure wine to pour over the flaming sacrifices, but they made libation with water and roasted the entrails over the fire. Now after the thighs were quite consumed and they had tasted the inner parts, they cut the rest up small and spitted it on spits. In the same hour deep sleep sped from my eyelids and I sallied forth to the swift ship and the sea-banks. But on my way as I drew near to the curved ship, the sweet savour of the fat came all about me; and I groaned and spake out before the deathless gods:

'"Father Zeus, and all ye other blessed gods that live for ever, verily to my undoing ye have lulled me with a ruthless sleep, and my company abiding behind have imagined a monstrous deed."

'But when I had come down to the ship and to the sea, I went up to my companions and rebuked them one by one; but we could find no remedy, the cattle were dead and gone. And soon thereafter the gods showed forth signs and wonders to my company. The skins were creeping, and the flesh bellowing upon the spits, both the roast and raw, and there was a sound as the voice of kine.

'Then for six days my dear company feasted on the best of the kine of Helios which they had driven off. But when Zeus, son of Cronos, had added the seventh day thereto, thereafter the wind ceased to blow with a rushing storm, and at once we climbed the ship and launched into the broad deep.

'But now when we left that isle nor any other land appeared, but sky and sea only, even then the son of Cronos stayed a dark cloud above the hollow ship, and beneath it the deep darkened. And the ship ran on her way for no long while, for of a sudden came the shrilling West, with the rushing of a great tempest, and the blast of wind snapped the two forestays of the mast, and the mast fell backward and all the gear dropped into the bilge. And behold, on the hind part of the ship the mast struck the head of the pilot and brake all the bones of his skull together, and like a diver he dropt down from the deck, and his brave spirit left his bones. In that same hour Zeus thundered and cast his bolt upon the ship, and she reeled all over being stricken by the bolt of Zeus, and was filled with sulphur, and lo, my company fell from out the vessel. Like sea-gulls they were borne round the black ship upon the billows, and the god reft them of returning.

'But I kept pacing through my ship, till the surge loosened the sides from the keel, and the wave swept her along stript of her tackling, and brake her mast clean off at the keel. Now the backstay fashioned of an oxhide had been flung thereon; therewith I lashed together both keel and mast and sitting thereon I was borne by the ruinous winds.

'Then verily the West Wind ceased to blow with a rushing storm, and swiftly withal the South Wind came, bringing sorrow to my soul, that so I might again measure back that space of sea, the way to deadly Charybdis. All the night was I borne, but with the rising of the sun I came to the rock of Scylla, and to dread Charybdis. Now she had sucked down her salt sea water, when I was swung up on high to the tall fig tree whereto I clung like a bat, and could find no sure rest for my feet nor place to stand, for the roots spread far below and the branches hung aloft out of reach, long and large, and overshadowed Charybdis. Steadfast I clung till she should spew forth mast and keel again; and late they came to my desire. And I let myself drop down hands and feet, and plunged heavily in the midst of the waters beyond the long timbers, and sitting on these I rowed hard with my hands. But the father of gods and of men suffered me no more to behold Scylla, else I should never have escaped from utter doom.

'Thence for nine days was I borne, and on the tenth night the gods brought me nigh to the isle of Ogygia, where dwells Calypso of the braided tresses, an awful goddess of mortal speech, who took me in and entreated me kindly. But why rehearse all this tale? For even yesterday I told it to thee and to thy noble wife in thy house; and it liketh me not twice to tell a plain-told tale.'

[BOOK XIII: With rich gifts and with prayers to Zeus, the Phaeacians set Odysseus upon his journey home in one of their swift ships. In short time, while he is sleeping, the sailors land him upon the shore of Ithaca, pile his treasures beside him, and speed away. On awakening, he does not recognize his surroundings, but he is overjoyed when he sees Athene standing before him. She tells him that he is in his own land, warns him against further hardships, and advises him against making himself known in Ithaca, whatever his pride may suffer. After concealing the gifts of the Phaeacians, Odysseus and Athene consider the problem of the wooers. Disguising Odysseus as an aged beggar, Athene instructs him to join company with the swineherd Eumaeus. She leaves to summon home Telemachus from Sparta.]

BOOK XIV

But Odysseus fared forth from the haven by the rough track, up the wooded country and through the heights, where Athene had showed him that he should find the goodly swineherd, who cared most for his substance of all the thralls that goodly Odysseus had gotten.

Now he found him sitting at the vestibule of the house, where his courtyard was builded high, in a place with wide prospect; a great court it was and a fair, with free range round it. . . .

And of a sudden the baying dogs saw Odysseus, and they ran at him yelping, but Odysseus in his wariness sat him down, and let the staff fall from his hand. There by his own homestead would he have suffered foul hurt, but the swineherd with quick feet hasted after them, and sped through the outer door. And the hounds he chid and drave them this way and that, with a shower of stones, and he spake unto his lord, saying:

'Old man, truly the dogs went nigh to be the death of thee all of a sudden, so shouldest thou have brought shame on me. Yea, and the gods have given me other pains and griefs enough. Here I sit, mourning and sorrowing for my godlike lord, and foster the fat swine for others to eat, while he craving, perchance, for food, wanders over some land and city of men of a strange speech, if haply he yet lives and beholds the sunlight. But come with me, let us to the inner steading, old man, that when thy heart is satisfied with bread and wine, thou too mayest tell thy tale and declare whence thou art, and how many woes thou hast endured.'

Therewith the goodly swineherd led him to the steading, and took him in and set him down, and strewed beneath him thick brushwood, and spread thereon the hide of a shaggy wild goat, wide and soft, which served himself for a mattress. And Odysseus rejoiced that he had given him such welcome, and spake and hailed him:

'May Zeus, O stranger, and all the other deathless gods grant thee thy dearest wish, since thou hast received me heartily!'

Then, O swineherd Eumaeus, didst thou answer him, saying: 'Guest of mine, it were an impious thing for me to slight a stranger, even if there came a meaner man than thou; for from Zeus are all strangers and beggars. Surely the gods have stayed the returning of my master, who would have loved me diligently, and given me somewhat of my own, a house and a parcel of ground, and a comely wife, such as a kind lord gives to his man, who hath laboured much for him. Therefore would my lord have rewarded me greatly, had he grown old at home. But he hath perished, as I would that all the stock of Helen had perished utterly, forasmuch as she hath caused the loosening of many a man's knees. For he too departed to Ilios of the goodly steeds, to get atonement for Agamemnon, that so he might war with the Trojans.'

Therewith he quickly bound up his doublet with his girdle, and went his way to the styes, where the tribes of the swine were penned. Thence he took and brought forth two, and sacrificed them both, and singed them and cut them small, and spitted them. And when he had roasted all, he bare and set it by Odysseus, all hot as it was upon the spits, and he sprinkled thereupon white barley-meal. Then in a bowl of ivywood he mixed the honey-sweet wine, and himself sat over against him and bade him fall to:

'Eat now, stranger, such fare as thralls have to hand, even flesh of sucking pigs; but the fatted hogs the wooers devour, for they know not the wrath of the gods nor any pity. . . . For every day and every night that comes from Zeus, they make sacrifice not of one victim only, nor of two, and wine they draw and waste it riotously. For surely his livelihood was great past telling, no lord in the dark mainland had so much, nor any in Ithaca itself; nay, not twenty men together have wealth so great. . . . And day by day each man of these ever drives one of the flock to the wooers, whichsoever seems the best of the fatted goats. But as for me I guard and keep these swine and I choose out for them, as well as I may, the best of the swine and send it hence.'

So spake he, but Odysseus ceased not to eat flesh and drink wine right eagerly and in silence, and the while was sowing the seeds of evil for the wooers. Now when he had well eaten and comforted his heart with food, then the herdsman filled him the bowl out of which he was wont himself to drink, and he gave it him brimming with wine, and he took it and was glad at heart, and uttering his voice spake to him winged words:

'My friend, who was it then that bought thee with his wealth, a man so exceeding rich and mighty as thou declarest? Thou saidest that he perished to get atonement for Agamemnon; tell me, if perchance I may know him, being such an one as thou sayest. For Zeus, methinks, and the other deathless gods know whether I may bring tidings of having seen him; for I have wandered far.'

Then the swineherd, a master of men, answered him: 'Old man, no wanderer who may come hither and bring tidings of him can win the ear of his wife and his dear son; but lightly do vagrants lie when they need entertainment, and care not to tell truth. Whosoever comes straying to the land of Ithaca, goes to my mistress and speaks words of guile. And she receives him kindly and lovingly and inquires of all things, and the tears fall from her eyelids for weeping, as is meet for a woman when her lord hath died afar. And quickly enough wouldst thou too, old man, forge a tale, if any would but give thee a mantle and a doublet for raiment. But as for him, dogs and swift fowls are like already to have torn his skin from the bones, and his spirit hath left him. Or the fishes have eaten him in the deep, and there lie his bones swathed in sand-drift on the shore. . . . But desire comes over me for Odysseus who is afar. His name, stranger, even though he is not here, it shameth me to speak.'

Then the steadfast goodly Odysseus spake to him again: 'My

friend, forasmuch as thou gainsayest utterly, and sayest that henceforth he will not come again, and thine heart is ever slow to believe, therefore will I tell thee not lightly but with an oath, that Odysseus shall return. And let me have the wages of good tidings as soon as ever he in his journeying shall come hither to his home. Then clothe me in a mantle and a doublet, goodly raiment. . . . All these things shall surely be accomplished even as I tell thee. In this same year Odysseus shall come hither; as the old moon wanes and the new is born shall he return to his home, and shall take vengeance on all who here dishonour his wife and noble son.'

Then didst thou make answer, swineherd Eumaeus: 'Old man, it is not I then, that shall ever pay thee these wages of good tidings, nor henceforth shall Odysseus ever come to his home. Nay drink in peace, and let us turn our thoughts to other matters, and bring not these to my remembrance, for surely my heart within me is sorrowful whenever any man puts me in mind of my true lord. But as for thine oath, we will let it go by; yet, oh that Odysseus may come according to my desire, and the desire of Penelope and of that old man Laertes and godlike Telemachus! . . . But come, old man, do thou tell me of thine own troubles. And herein tell me true, that I may surely know. Who art thou of the sons of men, and whence? Where is thy city, where are they that begat thee? Say on what manner of ship didst thou come, and how did sailors bring thee to Ithaca, and who did they avow them to be? For in no wise do I deem that thou camest hither by land.'

And Odysseus of many counsels answered him saying: 'Yea now, I will tell thee all most plainly. Might we have food and sweet wine enough to last for long, while we abide within thy hut to feast thereon in quiet, and others betake them to their work; then could I easily speak for a whole year, nor yet make a full end of telling all the troubles of my spirit, all the travail I have wrought by the will of the gods.

'I avow that I come by lineage from wide Crete, and am the son of a wealthy man. And many other sons he had born and bred in the halls, lawful-born of a wedded wife; but the mother that bare me was a concubine bought with a price. The fates of death bare him away to the house of Hades, and his gallant sons divided among them his living and cast lots for it. But to me they gave a very small gift and assigned me a dwelling, and I took unto me a wife. . . . Ere ever the sons of the Achaeans had set foot on the land of Troy, I had nine times been a leader of men and of swift-faring ships against a strange people, and wealth fell ever to my hands. Of the booty I would choose out for me all that I craved, and much thereafter I won by lot. So my house got increase speedily, and thus I waxed dread and honourable among the Cretans. But when Zeus, of the far-borne voice, devised at the last that hateful path which loosened the knees of many a man in death, then the people called on me and on renowned Idomeneus to lead the ship to Ilios, nor was there any way whereby to refuse, for the people's voice bore hard upon us. There we sons of the Achaeans warred for nine whole years, and then in the tenth year we sacked the city of Priam, and departed homeward with our ships, and a god scattered the Achaeans. But Zeus, the counsellor, devised mischief against me, wretched man that I was! For one month only I abode and had joy in my children and my wedded wife, and all that I had; and thereafter my spirit bade me fit out ships in the best manner and sail to Egypt with my godlike company. . . . And on the fifth day we came to the fair-flowing Aegyptus, and in the river Aegyptus I stayed my curved ships. Then verily I bade my dear companions to abide there by the ships and to guard them, and I sent forth scouts to range the points of outlook. But my men gave place to wantonness, being the fools of their own force, and soon they fell to wasting the fields of the Egyptians, exceeding fair, and led away their wives and infant children and slew the men. And the cry came quickly to the city, and the people hearing the shout came forth at the breaking of the day. And Zeus, whose joy is in the thunder, sent an evil panic upon my company, and none durst stand and face the foe, for danger encompassed us on every side. There they slew many of us with the edge of the sword, and others they led up with them alive to work for them perforce. But as for me, Zeus himself put a thought into my heart; would to God that I had rather died, and met my fate there in Egypt, for sorrow was still mine host! Straightway I put off my well-wrought helmet from my head, and the shield from off my shoulders, and I cast away my spear from my hand, and I came over against the chariots of the king, and clasped and kissed his knees, and he saved me and delivered me, and setting me on his own chariot took me weeping to his home. So for seven whole years I abode with their king, and gathered much substance among the Egyptians, for they all gave me gifts. But when the eighth year came in due season, there arrived a Phoenician practised in deceit, a greedy knave, who had already done much mischief among men. He wrought on me with his cunning, and took me with him until he came to Phoenicia, where was his house and where his treasures lay. There I abode with him for the space of a full year. But when now the months and days were fulfilled, as the year came round and the seasons returned, he set me aboard a seafaring ship for Libya under colour as though I was to convey a cargo thither with him, but his purpose was to sell me in Libya, and get a great price. So I went with him on board, perforce, yet boding evil. And the ship ran before a North Wind fresh and fair, through the mid sea over above Crete, and Zeus contrived the destruction of the crew. But when we left Crete, and no land showed in sight but sky and sea only, even then the son of Cronos stayed a dark cloud over the hollow ship, and the deep grew dark beneath it. And in the same moment Zeus thundered and smote his bolt into the ship, and she reeled all over being stricken by the bolt of Zeus, and was filled with fire and brimstone, and all the crew fell overboard. But in this hour of my affliction Zeus himself put into my hands the huge mast of the dark-prowed ship, that even yet I might escape from harm. So I clung round the mast and was borne by the ruinous winds. For nine days was I borne, and on the tenth black night the great rolling wave brought me nigh to the land of the Thesprotians. . . .

'There I heard tidings of Odysseus, for the king told me that he had entertained him, and kindly entreated him on his way to his own country; and he showed me all the wealth that Odysseus had gathered, bronze and gold and well-wrought iron; yea it would suffice for his children after him even to the tenth generation, so great were the treasures he had stored in the chambers of the king. He had gone, he said, to Dodona[1] to hear the counsel of Zeus, from the high leafy oak tree of the god, how he should return to the fat land of Ithaca after long absence, whether openly or by stealth. Moreover, he sware, in mine own presence, as he poured the drink offering in his house, that the ship was drawn down to the sea and his company were ready, who were to convey him to his own dear country. But ere that, he sent me off, for it chanced that a ship of the Thesprotians was starting for Dulichium. Thither he bade them bring me with all diligence to the king Acastus. When the seafaring ship had sailed a great way from the land, anon they sought how they might compass for me the day of slavery. They stript me of my garments, my mantle and a doublet, and changed my raiment to a vile wrap and doublet, tattered garments, even those thou seest now before thee; and in the evening they reached the fields of clear-seen Ithaca. There in the decked ship they bound me closely with a twisted rope, and themselves went ashore, and hasted to take supper by the sea-banks. Meanwhile the gods themselves lightly un-

1. Seat of the oldest oracle in Greece, dedicated to Zeus.

clasped my bands, and muffling my head with the wrap I slid down the smooth lading-plank, and set my breast to the sea and rowed hard with both hands as I swam, and very soon I was out of the water and beyond their reach. And they went hither and thither making great moan; but when now it seemed to them little avail to go further on their quest, they departed back again aboard their hollow ship. And the gods themselves hid me easily and brought me nigh to the homestead of a wise man; for still, methinks, I am ordained to live on.'

Then didst thou make answer to him, swineherd Eumaeus: 'Ah! wretched guest, verily thou hast stirred my heart with the tale of all these things, of thy sufferings and thy wanderings. Yet herein, methinks, thou speakest not aright, and never shalt thou persuade me with the tale about Odysseus; why should one in thy plight lie vainly? . . .'

And Odysseus of many counsels answered him saying: 'Verily thy heart within thee is slow to believe, seeing that even with an oath I have not won thee, nor find credence with thee. But come now, let us make a covenant; and we will each one have for witnesses the gods above, who hold Olympus. If thy lord shall return to this house, put on me a mantle and doublet for raiment, and send me on my way to Dulichium, whither I had a desire to go. But if thy lord return not according to my word, set thy thralls upon me, and cast me down from a mighty rock, that another beggar in his turn may beware of deceiving.'

And the goodly swineherd answered him, saying: 'Yea stranger, even so should I get much honour and good luck among men both now and ever hereafter, if after bringing thee to my hut and giving thee a stranger's cheer, I should turn again and slay thee and take away thy dear life.'

Thus they spake one to the other. And lo, the swine and the swineherds drew nigh. And the swine they shut up to sleep in their lairs, and a mighty din arose as the swine were being stalled. Then the goodly swineherd called to his fellows, saying:

'Bring the best of the swine, that I may sacrifice it for a guest of mine from a far land: and we too will have good cheer therewith.'

Therewithal he cleft logs with the pitiless axe, and the others brought in a well-fatted boar of five years old; and they set him by the hearth, nor did the swineherd forget the deathless gods, for he was of an understanding heart. But for a beginning of sacrifice he cast bristles from the head of the white-tusked boar upon the fire, and prayed to all the gods that wise Odysseus might return to his own house. Then he stood erect, and smote the boar with a billet of oak which he had left in the cleaving, and the boar yielded up his life. Then they cut the throat and singed the carcase and quickly cut it up, and the swineherd took a first portion from all the limbs, and laid the raw flesh on the rich fat. And some pieces he cast into the fire after sprinkling them with bruised barley-meal, and they cut the rest up small, and pierced it, and spitted and roasted it carefully, and drew it all off from the spits, and put the whole mess together on trenchers. Then the swineherd stood up to carve, for well he knew what was fair, and he cut up the whole and divided it into seven portions. One, when he had prayed, he set aside for the nymphs and for Hermes son of Maia, and the rest he distributed to each. And he gave Odysseus the portion of honour, the long back of the white-tusked boar, and the soul of his lord rejoiced at this renown, and Odysseus of many counsels hailed him saying:

'Eumaeus, oh that thou mayest so surely be dear to father Zeus, as thou art to me, seeing that thou honourest me with a good portion, such an one as I am!'

Then didst thou make answer, swineherd Eumaeus:

'Eat, luckless stranger, and make merry with such fare as is here. And one thing the god will give and another withhold, even as he will, for with him all things are possible.'

So he spake, and made burnt offering of the hallowed parts to the everlasting gods, and poured the dark wine for a drink offering, and set the cup in the hands of Odysseus, the waster of cities, and sat down by his own mess. So they stretched forth their hands upon the good cheer spread before them. Now after they had put from them the desire of meat and drink, they were moved to go to rest.

[BOOK XV: Meanwhile Athene has gone to Sparta to speed Telemachus back home. She warns him of the wooers' ambush, instructs him how to escape this danger, and advises him to take shelter with the swineherd Eumaeus. With royal gifts from their hosts, Telemachus and Peisistratus leave Sparta for Pylos, whence Telemachus embarks hastily and without ceremony. Still at the swineherd's retreat, Odysseus probes for news of his wife Penelope and his father Laertes. Telemachus eludes the wooers, lands in Ithaca, and makes his way to the house of Eumaeus.]

BOOK XVI

Now these twain, Odysseus and the goodly swineherd, within the hut had kindled a fire, and were making ready breakfast at the dawn,

and had sent forth the herdsmen with the droves of swine. And round
Telemachus the hounds, that love to bark, fawned and barked not, as
he drew nigh. And goodly Odysseus took note of the fawning of the
dogs, and the noise of footsteps fell upon his ears. Then straight he
spake to Eumaeus winged words:

'Eumaeus, verily some friend or some other of thy familiars will
soon be here, for the dogs do not bark but fawn around, and I catch the
sound of footsteps.'

While the word was yet on his lips, his own dear son stood at the
entering in of the gate. Then the swineherd sprang up in amazement,
and out of his hands fell the vessels wherewith he was busied in mingling the dark wine. And he came over against his master and kissed
his head and both his beautiful eyes and both his hands, and he let a
great tear fall. .... And he wept aloud and spake to him winged words:

'Thou art come, Telemachus, a sweet light in the dark; methought
I should see thee never again, after thou hadst gone in thy ship to
Pylos. Nay now enter, dear child, that my heart may be glad at the
sight of thee in mine house, who hast newly come from afar.'

Then wise Telemachus answered him, saying: 'So be it, father, as
thou sayest; and for thy sake am I come hither to see thee with mine
eyes, and to hear from thy lips whether my mother yet abides in the
halls or another has already wedded her, and the couch of Odysseus,
perchance, lies in lack of bedding and deep in foul spider-webs.'

Then the swineherd, a master of men, answered him: 'Yea verily,
she abides with patient spirit in thy halls, and wearily for her the
nights wane always and the days, in shedding of tears.'

So he spake and took from him the spear of bronze. Then Telemachus passed within and crossed the threshold of stone. As he came
near, his father Odysseus arose from his seat to give him place; but
Telemachus, on his part, stayed him and spake saying:

'Be seated, stranger, and we will find a seat some other where in
our steading, and there is a man here to set it for us.'

So he spake, and Odysseus went back and sat him down again.
And the swineherd strewed for Telemachus green brushwood below,
and a fleece thereupon, and there presently the dear son of Odysseus
sat him down. Next the swineherd set by them platters of roast flesh,
the fragments that were left from the meal of yesterday. And wheaten
bread he briskly heaped up in baskets, and mixed the honeysweet wine
in a goblet of ivy wood, and himself sat down over against divine
Odysseus. So they stretched forth their hands upon the good cheer set

before them. Now when they had put from them the desire of meat and drink, Telemachus spake to the goodly swineherd, saying:

'Father, whence came this stranger to thee? How did sailors bring him to Ithaca? and who did they avow them to be? For in no wise, I deem, did he come hither by land.'

Then didst thou make answer, swineherd Eumaeus: 'Yea now, my son, I will tell thee all the truth. Of wide Crete he avows him to be by lineage, and he says that round many cities of mortals he has wandered at adventure; even so has some god spun for him the thread of fate. But now, as a runaway from the ship of the Thesprotians, has he come to my steading, and I will give him to thee for thy man; do with him as thou wilt; he avows him for thy suppliant.'

Then wise Telemachus answered him, saying: 'Eumaeus, verily a bitter word is this that thou speakest. How indeed shall I receive this guest in my house? Myself I am young, and trust not yet to my strength of hands to defend me against the man who does violence without a cause. . . . But behold, as for this guest of thine, now that he has come to thy house, I will clothe him in a mantle and a doublet, goodly raiment, and I will give him a two-edged sword, and shoes for his feet, and send him on his way, whithersoever his heart and his spirit bid him go. Or, if thou wilt, hold him here in the steading and take care of him, and raiment I will send hither, and all manner of food to eat, that he be not ruinous to thee and to thy fellows. But thither into the company of the wooers would I not suffer him to go, for they are exceedingly full of infatuate insolence, lest they mock at him, and that would be a sore grief to me. And hard it is for one man, how valiant soever, to achieve aught among a multitude, for verily they are far the stronger.'

Then the steadfast goodly Odysseus answered him: 'My friend, since it is indeed my right to answer thee withal, of a truth my heart is rent as I hear your words, such infatuate deeds ye say the wooers devise in the halls, in despite of thee, a man so noble. Say, dost thou willingly submit thee to oppression, or do the people through the township hate thee, obedient to the voice of a god? Or hast thou cause to blame thy brethren, in whose battle a man puts trust, even if a great feud arise? Ah, would that I had the youth, as now I have the spirit, and were either the son of noble Odysseus or Odysseus' very self, straightway then might a stranger sever my head from off my neck, if I went not to the halls of Odysseus, son of Laertes, and made myself the bane of every man among them! But if they should overcome me by numbers, being but one man against so many, far rather would I die slain in mine own halls, than witness for ever these unseemly deeds, strangers shamefully entreated, and men haling the handmaidens in foul wise through the fair house, and wine drawn wastefully, and the wooers devouring food all recklessly without avail, at a work that knows no ending.'

Then wise Telemachus answered him, saying: 'Yea now, stranger, I will plainly tell thee all. There is no grudge and hatred borne me by the whole people, neither have I cause to blame my brethren, in whose battle a man puts trust, even if a great feud arise. For thus, as thou seest, Cronion has made us a house of but one heir. . . . But as for my mother she neither refuseth the hated bridal, nor hath the heart to make an end; so they devour and minish my house; and ere long will they make havoc likewise of myself. Howbeit these things surely lie on the knees of the gods. Nay, father, but do thou go with haste and tell the constant Penelope that she hath got me safe and that I am come up out of Pylos. As for me, I will tarry here, and do thou return hither when thou hast told the tidings to her alone; but of the other Achaeans let no man learn it, for there be many that devise mischief against me.' . . .

With that word he roused the swineherd, who took his sandals in his hands and bound them beneath his feet and departed for the city. Now Athene noted Eumaeus the swineherd pass from the steading, and she drew nigh in the semblance of a woman fair and tall. And she stood in presence manifest to Odysseus over against the doorway of the hut; but it was so that Telemachus saw her not before him and marked her not; for the gods in no wise appear visibly to all. But Odysseus was ware of her and the dogs likewise, which barked not, but with a low whine shrank cowering to the far side of the steading. Then she nodded at him with bent brows, and goodly Odysseus perceived it, and came forth from the room, past the great wall of the yard, and stood before her, and Athene spake to him, saying:

'Son of Laertes, of the seed of Zeus, Odysseus of many devices, now is the hour to reveal thy word to thy son, and hide it not, that ye twain having framed death and doom for the wooers, may fare to the famous town. Nor will I, even I, be long away from you, being right eager for battle.'

Therewith Athene touched him with her golden wand. First she cast about his breast a fresh linen robe and a doublet, and she increased his bulk and bloom. Dark his colour grew again, and his cheeks filled out, and the black beard spread thick around his chin.

Now she, when she had so wrought, withdrew again, but Odysseus went into the hut, and his dear son marvelled at him and looked away for very fear lest it should be a god, and he uttered his voice and spake to him winged words:

'Even now, stranger, thou art other in my sight than that thou wert a moment since, and other garments thou hast, and the colour of thy skin is no longer the same. Surely thou art a god of those that keep the wide heaven. Nay then, be gracious, that we may offer to thee well-pleasing sacrifices and golden gifts, beautifully wrought; and spare us I pray thee.'

Then the steadfast goodly Odysseus answered him, saying: 'Behold, no god am I; why likenest thou me to the immortals? nay, thy father am I, for whose sake thou sufferest many pains and groanest sore, and submittest thee to the despite of men.'

At the word he kissed his son, and from his cheeks let a tear fall to earth: before, he had stayed the tears continually. But Telemachus answered in turn and spake, saying:

'Thou art not Odysseus my father, but some god beguiles me, that I may groan for more exceeding sorrow. For it cannot be that a mortal man should contrive this by the aid of his own wit, unless a god were himself to visit him, and lightly of his own will to make him young or old. For truly, but a moment gone, thou wert old and foully clad, but now thou art like the gods who keep the wide heaven.'

Then Odysseus of many counsels answered him saying:

'Telemachus, it fits thee not to marvel overmuch that thy father is come home, or to be amazed. Nay for thou shalt find no other Odysseus come hither any more; but lo, I, all as I am, after sufferings and much wandering have come in the twentieth year to mine own country. Behold, this is the work of Athene, who makes me such manner of man as she will.'

With this word then he sat down again; but Telemachus, flinging himself upon his noble father's neck, mourned and shed tears, and in both their hearts arose the desire of lamentation. And they wailed aloud, more ceaselessly than birds, sea-eagles or vultures of crooked claws, whose younglings the country folk have taken from the nest, ere yet they are fledged. Even so pitifully fell the tears beneath their brows. And now would the sunlight have gone down upon their sorrowing, had not Telemachus spoken to his father suddenly:

'And in what manner of ship, father dear, did sailors at length bring thee hither to Ithaca?'

And the steadfast goodly Odysseus answered him: 'Yea now, my child, I will tell thee all the truth. The Phaeacians brought me hither, mariners renowned, who speed other men too upon their way, whosoever comes to them. Asleep in the swift ship they bore me over the seas and set me down in Ithaca, and gave me splendid gifts, bronze and gold in plenty and woven raiment. And these treasures are lying by the gods' grace in the caves. But now I am come hither by the promptings of Athene, that we may take counsel for the slaughter of the foemen. But come, tell me all the tale of the wooers and their number, that I may know how many and what men they be, and that so I may commune with my good heart and advise me, whether we twain shall be able alone to make head against them without aid, or whether we should even seek succour of others.'

Then wise Telemachus answered him, saying: 'Verily, father, I have ever heard of thy great fame, for a warrior hardy of thy hands, and sage in counsel. But this is a hard saying of thine: awe comes over me; for it may not be that two men should do battle with many men and stalwart. For of the wooers there are not barely ten nor twice ten only, but many a decade more: and straight shalt thou learn the tale of them ere we part. From Dulichium there be two and fifty chosen lords, and six serving men go with them; and out of Same four and twenty men; and from Zacynthus there are twenty lords of the Achaeans; and from Ithaca itself full twelve men of the best, and with them Medon the henchman, and the divine minstrel, and two squires skilled in carving viands. If we shall encounter all these within the halls, see thou to it, lest bitter and baneful for us be the vengeance thou takest on their violence at thy coming. But do thou, if thou canst think of some champion, advise thee of any that may help us with all his heart.'

Then the steadfast goodly Odysseus answered him, saying:

'Yea now, I will tell thee, and do thou mark and listen to me, and consider whether Athene with Father Zeus will suffice for us twain, or whether I shall cast about for some other champion.'

Then wise Telemachus answered him, saying: 'Valiant helpers, in sooth, are these two thou namest, whose seat is aloft in the clouds, and they rule among all men and among the deathless gods!'

Then the steadfast goodly Odysseus answered him: 'Yet will the twain not long keep aloof from the strong tumult of war, when between the wooers and us in my halls is held the trial of the might of Ares. But as now, do thou go homeward at the breaking of the day, and consort with the proud wooers. As for me, the swineherd will lead me to the town later in the day, in the likeness of a beggar, a wretched man and an old. And if they shall evil entreat me in the house, let thy heart harden itself to endure while I am shamefully handled, yea even if they drag me by the feet through the house to the doors, or cast at me and smite me: still do thou bear the sight. Howbeit thou shalt surely bid them cease from their folly, exhorting them with smooth words; yet no whit will they hearken, nay for the day of their doom is at hand. Yet another thing will I tell thee, and do thou ponder in thy heart. When Athene, of deep counsel, shall put it into my heart, I will nod to thee with my head and do thou note it, and carry away all thy weapons of war that lie in the halls, and lay them down every one in the secret place of the lofty chamber. . . . But for us twain alone leave two swords and two spears and two shields of oxhide to grasp, that we may rush upon the arms and seize them; and then shall Pallas Athene and Zeus the counsellor enchant the wooers to their ruin. Yet another thing will I tell thee, and do thou ponder it in thy heart. If in very truth thou art my son and of our blood, then let no man hear that Odysseus is come home; neither let Laertes know it, nor the swineherd nor any of the household nor Penelope herself, but let me and thee alone discover the intent of the women. Yea, and we would moreover make trial of certain of the men among the thralls, and learn who of them chances to honour us and to fear us heartily, and who regards us not at all and holds even thee in no esteem, so noble a man as thou art.' . . .

Thus they spake one to the other. And now the well-built ship was being brought to land at Ithaca, the ship that bare Telemachus from Pylos with all his company. When they were now come within the deep harbour, the men drew up the black ship on the shore, while squires, haughty of heart, bare away their weapons, and straightway carried the glorious gifts to the house of Clytius. Anon they sent forward a herald to the house of Odysseus to bear the tidings to prudent Penelope, namely, how Telemachus was in the field, and had bidden the ship sail to the city, lest the noble queen should be afraid, and let the round tears fall. So these two met, the herald and the goodly swineherd, come on the same errand to tell all to the lady. . . .

Now the wooers were troubled and downcast in spirit, and forth they went from the hall past the great wall of the court, and there in front of the gates they held their session. . . . Then Antinous spake among them, the son of Eupeithes:

'Lo now, how the gods have delivered this man from his evil case! All day long did scouts sit along the windy headlands, ever in quick succession, and at the going down of the sun we never rested for a night upon the shore, but sailing with our swift ship on the high seas we awaited the bright Dawn, as we lay in wait for Telemachus, that we might take and slay the man himself; but meanwhile some god has brought him home. But even here let us devise an evil end for him, even for Telemachus, and let him not escape out of our hands, for methinks that while he lives we shall never achieve this task of ours. . . . Let us be beforehand and take him in the field far from the city, or by the way; and let us ourselves keep his livelihood and his possessions, making fair division among us, but the house we would give to his mother to keep and to whomsoever marries her. But if this saying likes you not, but ye chose rather that he should live and keep the heritage of his father, no longer then let us gather here and eat all his store of pleasant substance, but let each one from his own hall woo her with his bridal gifts and seek to win her; so should she wed the man that gives the most and comes as the chosen of fate.'

So he spake, and they all held their peace. Then Amphinomus made harangue and spake out among them. . . .

'Friends, I for one would not choose to kill Telemachus; it is a fearful thing to slay one of the stock of kings! Nay, first let us seek to the counsel of the gods, and if the oracles of great Zeus approve, myself I will slay him and bid all the rest to aid. But if the gods are disposed to avert it, I bid you to refrain.'

So spake Amphinomus, and his saying pleased them well. Then straightway they arose and went to the house of Odysseus, and entering in sat down on the polished seats.

Then the wise Penelope had a new thought, namely, to show herself to the wooers, so despiteful in their insolence; for she had heard of the death of her son that was to be in the halls, seeing that Medon the henchman had told her of it, who heard their counsels. So she went on her way to the hall, with the women her handmaids. Now when that fair lady had come unto the wooers, she stood by the pillar of the well-builded roof, holding up her glistening tire before her face, and rebuked Antinous and spake and hailed him:

'Antinous, full of all insolence, deviser of mischief! and yet they say that in the land of Ithaca thou art chiefest among thy peers in counsel and in speech. Nay, no such man dost thou show thyself. Fool! why indeed dost thou contrive death and doom for Telemachus, and hast no regard unto suppliants who have Zeus to witness? Nay but it is an impious thing to contrive evil one against another. What! knowest thou not of the day when thy father fled to this house in fear of the people, for verily they were exceeding wroth against him, but Odysseus stayed and withheld them, for all their desire. His house thou now consumest without atonement, and his wife thou wooest, and wouldst slay his son, and dost greatly grieve me. But I bid thee cease, and command the others to do likewise.'

Then Eurymachus, son of Polybus, answered her saying: 'Daughter of Icarius, wise Penelope, take courage, and let not thy heart be careful for these things. The man is not, nor shall be, nor ever shall be born, that shall stretch forth his hands against Telemachus, thy son, while I live and am on earth and see the light. . . .'

Thus he spake comforting her, but was himself the while framing death for her son.

Now she ascended to her shining upper chamber, and there was bewailing Odysseus, her dear lord, till grey-eyed Athene cast sweet sleep upon her eyelids.

And in the evening the goodly swineherd came back to Odysseus and his son, and they made ready and served the supper, when they had sacrificed a swine of a year old. Then Athene drew near Odysseus, son of Laertes, and smote him with her wand, and made him into an old man again. In sorry raiment she clad him about his body, lest the swineherd should look on him and know him, and depart to tell the constant Penelope, and not keep the matter in his heart.

Then Telemachus spake first to the swineherd, saying: 'Thou hast come, goodly Eumaeus. What news is there in the town? Are the lordly wooers now come in from their ambush, or do they still watch for me as before on my homeward way?'

Then didst thou make answer, swineherd Eumaeus: 'I had no mind to go down the city asking and inquiring hereof; my heart bade me get me home again, as quick as might be, when once I had told the tidings. And the swift messenger from thy company joined himself unto me, the henchman, who was the first to tell the news to thy mother.'

So spake he, and the mighty prince Telemachus smiled, and glanced at his father, while he shunned the eye of the swineherd.

Now when they had ceased from the work and got supper ready, they fell to feasting, and their hearts lacked not ought of the equal banquet. But when they had put from them the desire of meat and drink, they bethought them of rest, and took the boon of sleep.

BOOK XVII

[After ordering Eumaeus to bring their visitor to the city, Telemachus goes to the palace to greet his mother and the wooers.]

Now all this while Odysseus and the goodly swineherd were bestirring them to go from the field to the city; and the swineherd, a master of men, spake first saying:

'Well, my friend, forasmuch as I see thou art eager to be going to the city to-day, even as my master gave command; come then, let us go on our way, for lo, the day is far spent, and soon wilt thou find it colder toward evening.'

Then Odysseus of many counsels answered him saying: 'Let us be going, and be thou my guide withal to the end. And if thou hast anywhere a staff ready cut, give it me to lean upon, for truly ye said that slippery was the way.'

Therewith he cast about his shoulders a mean scrip, all tattered, and a cord withal to hang it, and Eumaeus gave him a staff to his mind. And the swineherd led his lord to the city in the guise of a beggar. But as they fared along the rugged path they drew near to the town, and came to the fair flowing spring, with a basin fashioned, whence the people of the city drew water. . . . In that place Melanthius, son of Dolius, met them, leading his goats to feast the wooers, the best goats that were in all the herds; and two herdsmen bare him company. Now when he saw them he reviled them, and spake and hailed them, in terrible and evil fashion, and stirred the heart of Odysseus, saying:

'Now in very truth the vile is leading the vile, for God brings ever like to like! Say, whither art thou leading this glutton,—thou wretched swineherd,—this plaguy beggar, a kill-joy of the feast? . . . If ever he fares to the house of divine Odysseus, many a stool that men's hands hurl shall fly about his head, and break upon his ribs, as they pelt him through the house.'

Therewith, as he went past, he kicked Odysseus on the hip, in his witlessness, yet he drave him not from the path, but he abode steadfast. And Odysseus pondered whether he should rush upon him and take away his life with the staff, or lift him in his grasp and smite his head to the earth. Yet he hardened his heart to endure and refrained himself. And the swineherd looked at the other and rebuked him, and lifting up his hands prayed aloud:

'Nymphs of the well-water, daughters of Zeus, if ever Odysseus burned on your altars pieces of the thighs of rams or kids, in their covering of rich fat, fulfil for me this wish:—oh that he, even he, may come home, and that some god may bring him!'

Then Melanthius, the goatherd, answered: 'Lo now, what a word has this evil-witted dog been saying! Some day I will take him in a black decked ship far from Ithaca, that he may bring me in much live-lihood.'[1]

So he spake and left them there as they walked slowly on. . . .

Now Odysseus and the goodly swineherd drew near and stood by, and the sound of the hollow lyre rang around them, for Phemius was lifting up his voice amid the company in song, and Odysseus caught the swineherd by the hand, and spake, saying:

'Eumaeus, verily this is the fair house of Odysseus, and right easily might it be known and marked even among many. And I see that many men keep revel within, for the savour of the fat rises upward, and the voice of the lyre is heard there, which the gods have made to be the mate of the feast.'

Then didst thou make answer, swineherd Eumaeus: 'Easily thou knowest it, for indeed thou never lackest understanding. But come, let us advise us, how things shall fall out here. Either do thou go first within the fair-lying halls, and join the company of the wooers, so will I remain here, or if thou wilt, abide here, and I will go before thy face, and tarry not long, lest one see thee without, and hurl at thee or strike thee. Look well to this, I bid thee.'

Then the steadfast goodly Odysseus answered him, saying: 'I mark, I heed, all this thou speakest to one with understanding. Do thou then go before me, and I will remain here, for well I know what it is to be smitten and hurled at. My heart is full of hardiness, for much evil have I suffered in perils of waves and war; let this be added to the tale of those. But a ravening belly may none conceal, a thing accursed, that works much ill for men.'

Thus they spake one to the other. And lo, a hound raised up his head and pricked his ears, even where he lay, Argos, the hound of Odysseus, of the hardy heart, which of old himself had bred, but had got no joy of him, for ere that, he went to sacred Ilios. Now in time

1. That is, sell him into slavery.

past the young men used to lead the hound against wild goats and deer and hares; but as then, despised he lay (his master being afar) in the deep dung of mules and kine, whereof an ample bed was spread before the doors, till the thralls of Odysseus should carry it away to dung therewith his wide demesne. There lay the dog Argos, full of vermin. Yet even now when he was ware of Odysseus standing by, he wagged his tail and dropped both his ears, but nearer to his master he had not now the strength to draw. But Odysseus looked aside and wiped away a tear that he easily hid from Eumaeus, and straightway he asked him, saying:

'Eumaeus, verily this is a great marvel, this hound lying here in the dung. Truly he is goodly of growth, but I know not certainly if he have speed with this beauty, or if he be comely only, like as are men's trencher dogs that their lords keep for the pleasure of the eye.'

Then didst thou make answer, swineherd Eumaeus: 'In very truth this is the dog of a man that has died in a far land. If he were what once he was in limb and in the feats of the chase, when Odysseus left him to go to Troy, soon wouldst thou marvel at the sight of his swiftness and his strength. There was no beast that could flee from him in the deep places of the wood, when he was in pursuit; for even on a track he was the keenest hound. But now he is holden in an evil case, and his lord hath perished far from his own country, and the careless women take no charge of him.'

Therewith he passed within the fair-lying house, and went straight to the hall, to the company of the proud wooers. But upon Argos came the fate of black death even in the hour that he beheld Odysseus again, in the twentieth year.

Now godlike Telemachus was far the first to behold the swineherd as he came into the hall, and straightway then he beckoned and called him to his side. . . .

And close behind him Odysseus entered the house in the guise of a beggar, a wretched man and an old, leaning on his staff, and clothed on with sorry raiment. And he sat down on the ashen threshold within the doorway, leaning against a pillar of cypress wood. And Telemachus called the swineherd to him, and took a whole loaf out of the fair basket, and of flesh so much as his hands could hold in their grasp, saying:

'Take and give this to the stranger, and bid him go about and beg himself of all the wooers in their turn, for shame is an ill mate of a needy man.'

So he spake, and the swineherd went when he heard that saying, and stood by and spake to him winged words:

'Stranger, Telemachus gives thee these and bids thee go about and beg of all the wooers in their turn, for, he says, "shame ill becomes a beggar man."'

Then Odysseus of many counsels answered him and said: 'King Zeus, grant me that Telemachus may be happy among men, and may he have all his heart's desire!'

Therewith he took the gift in both hands, and set it there before his feet on his unsightly scrip. Then he ate meat so long as the minstrel was singing in the halls. When he had done supper, and the divine minstrel was ending his song, then the wooers raised a clamour through the halls; but Athene stood by Odysseus, son of Laertes, and moved him to go gathering morsels of bread among the wooers, and learn which were righteous and which unjust. Yet not even so was she fated to redeem one man of them from an evil doom. So he set out, beginning on the right, to ask of each man, stretching out his hand on every side, as though he were a beggar from of old. And they in pity gave him somewhat, and were amazed at the man, asking one another who he was and whence he came.

Then Melanthius, the goatherd, spake among them:

'Listen, ye wooers of the renowned queen, concerning this stranger, for verily I have seen him before. The swineherd truly was his guide hither, but of him I have no certain knowledge, whence he avows him to be born.'

So spake he, but Antinous rebuked the swineherd, saying: 'Oh notorious swineherd, wherefore, I pray thee, didst thou bring this man to the city? Have we not vagrants enough besides, plaguy beggars, kill-joys of the feast?'

Then didst thou make answer, swineherd Eumaeus: 'Antinous, no fair words are these of thine, noble though thou art. . . . But thou art ever hard above all the other wooers to the servants of Odysseus, and, beyond all, to me; but behold, I care not, so long as my mistress, the constant Penelope, lives in the halls and godlike Telemachus.'

Then wise Telemachus answered him, saying: 'Be silent, answer him not, I pray thee, with many words, for Antinous is wont ever to chide us shamefully with bitter speech, yea, and urges the others thereto.'

Therewithal he spake winged words to Antinous: 'Antinous, verily thou hast a good care for me, as it were a father for his son, thou that biddest me drive our guest from the hall with a harsh command. God forbid that such a thing should be! Take somewhat and give it him: lo, I grudge it not; nay, I charge thee to do it. But thou hast no such thought in thy heart, for thou art far more fain to eat thyself than to give to another.'

Then Antinous answered him and spake, saying: 'Telemachus, proud of speech, and unrestrained in fury, what word hast thou spoken? If all the wooers should vouchsafe him as much as I, this house would keep him far enough aloof even for three months' space.'

So he spake, and seized the footstool whereon he rested his sleek feet as he sat at the feast, and showed it from beneath the table where it lay. But all the others gave somewhat and filled the wallet with bread and flesh; yea, and even now, Odysseus as he returned to the threshold, was like to escape scot free, making trial of the Achaeans, but he halted by Antinous, and spake to him, saying:

'Friend, give me somewhat; for methinks thou art not the basest of the Achaeans, but the best man of them all, for thou art like a king. . . .'

Then Antinous answered, and spake, saying: 'What god hath brought this plague hither to trouble the feast? Stand forth thus in the midst, away from my table; for a bold beggar art thou and a shameless. Thou standest by all in turn and recklessly they give to thee, for they hold not their hand nor feel any ruth in giving freely of others' goods, for that each man has plenty by him.'

Then Odysseus of many counsels drew back and answered him: 'Lo now, I see thou hast not wisdom with thy beauty! From out of thine own house thou wouldest not give even so much as a grain of salt to thy suppliant, thou who now even at another's board dost sit, and canst not find it in thy heart to take of the bread and give it me, where there is plenty to thy hand.'

He spake, and Antinous was mightily angered at heart, and looked fiercely on him and spake winged words:

'Henceforth, methinks, thou shalt not get thee out with honour from the hall, seeing thou dost even rail upon me.'

Therewith he caught up the footstool and smote Odysseus at the base of the right shoulder by the back. But he stood firm as a rock, nor reeled he beneath the blow of Antinous, but shook his head in silence, brooding evil in the deep of his heart. Then he went back to the threshold, and sat him there, and laid down his well-filled scrip, and spake among the wooers:

'Hear me, ye wooers of the renowned queen, and I will say what my spirit within me bids me. Verily there is neither pain nor grief of heart, when a man is smitten in battle fighting for his own possessions, whether cattle or white sheep. But now Antinous hath stricken me for my wretched belly's sake, a thing accursed, that works much ill for men. Ah, if indeed there be gods and Avengers of beggars, may the issues of death come upon Antinous before his wedding!'

Then Antinous, son of Eupeithes, answered him: 'Sit and eat thy meat in quiet, stranger, or get thee elsewhere, lest the young men drag thee by hand or foot through the house for thy evil words, and strip all thy flesh from off thee.'

Even so he spake, and they were all exceedingly wroth at his word. And on this wise would one of the lordly young men speak:

'Antinous, thou didst ill to strike the hapless wanderer, doomed man that thou art,—if indeed there be a god in heaven. Yea and the gods, in the likeness of strangers from far countries, put on all manner of shapes, and wander through the cities, beholding the violence and the righteousness of men.'

So the wooers spake, but he heeded not their words. Now Telemachus nursed in his heart a mighty grief at the smiting of Odysseus, yet he let no tear fall from his eyelids to the ground, but shook his head in silence, brooding evil in the deep of his heart.

Now when wise Penelope heard of the stranger being smitten in the halls, she spake among her maidens, saying:

'Oh that Apollo, the famed archer, may so smite thee thyself, Antinous!'

. . . So she spake among her maidens, sitting in her chamber, while goodly Odysseus was at meat. Then she called to her the goodly swineherd and spake, saying:

'Go thy way, goodly Eumaeus, and bid the stranger come hither, that I may speak him a word of greeting, and ask him if haply he has heard tidings of Odysseus of the hardy heart, or seen him with his eyes; for he seems like one that has wandered far.'

Then didst thou make answer, swineherd Eumaeus: 'Queen, oh that the Achaeans would hold their peace! so would he charm thy very heart, such things doth he say. For I kept him three nights, and three days I held him in the steading, for to me he came first when he fled from the ship, yet he had not made an end of the tale of his affliction. He says that he is a friend of Odysseus and of his house, one that dwells in Crete, where is the race of Minos. Thence he has come hither even now, with sorrow by the way, onward and yet onward wandering; and he stands to it that he has heard tidings of Odysseus nigh at hand and yet alive in the fat land of the men of Thesprotia; and he is bringing many treasures to his home.'

Then wise Penelope answered him, saying: 'Go, call him hither, that he may speak to me face to face. But let these men sit in the doorway and take their pleasure, or even here in the house, since their heart is glad. For their own wealth lies unspoiled at home, bread and sweet wine, and thereon do their servants feed. But they resorting to our house day by day sacrifice oxen and sheep and fat goats, and keep revel and drink the dark wine recklessly; and, lo, our great wealth is wasted, for there is no man now alive, such as Odysseus was, to keep ruin from the house. Oh, if Odysseus might come again to his own country; soon would he and his son avenge the violence of these men!'

Even so she spake, and Telemachus sneezed loudly, and around the roof rang wondrously. And Penelope laughed, and straightway spake to Eumaeus winged words:

'Go, call me the stranger, even so, into my presence. Dost thou not mark how my son has sneezed a blessing on all my words? Wherefore no half-wrought doom shall befall the wooers every one, nor shall any avoid death and the fates. Yet another thing will I say, and do thou ponder it in thy heart. If I shall find that he himself speaks nought but truth, I will clothe him with a mantle and a doublet, goodly raiment.'

So she spake, and the swineherd departed when he heard that saying, and stood by the stranger and spake winged words:

'Father and stranger, wise Penelope, the mother of Telemachus, is calling for thee, and her mind bids her inquire as touching her lord, albeit she has sorrowed much already.'

Then the steadfast goodly Odysseus answered him, saying: 'Eumaeus, soon would I tell all the truth to the daughter of Icarius, wise Penelope, for well I know his story, and we have borne our travail together. But I tremble before the throng of the froward wooers, whose outrage and violence reach even to the iron heaven. Wherefore now, bid Penelope tarry in the chambers, for all her eagerness, till the going down of the sun, and then let her ask me concerning her lord, as touching the day of his returning.'

Even so he spake, and the swineherd departed when he heard that saying. And as he crossed the threshold Penelope spake to him: 'Thou bringest him not, Eumaeus: what means the wanderer hereby?'

Then didst thou make answer, swineherd Eumaeus: 'He speaks aright, and but as another would deem, in that he shuns the outrage of overweening men. Rather would he have thee wait till the going down of the sun. Yea, and it is far meeter for thyself, O queen, to utter thy word to the stranger alone, and to listen to his speech.'

Then the wise Penelope answered: 'Not witless is the stranger; even as he deems, so it well may be. For there are no mortal men, methinks, so wanton as these, and none that devise such infatuate deeds.'

So she spake, and the goodly swineherd departed into the throng of the wooers, when he had showed her all his message. . . .

[BOOK XVIII: A beggar named Irus arrives in the hall and threatens to turn out Odysseus. The two abuse each other until, urged on by the crowd, they come to blows. Odysseus beats Irus to the ground and drags him from the hall. Inspired by Athene, Penelope makes her appearance to inflame the wooers' hearts and to encourage Telemachus. From those that would marry her she solicits rich gifts and then returns to her room. Odysseus is further reviled by both servants and wooers, whom Telemachus reproves with great forthrightness. The wooers then leave the hall.]

BOOK XIX

Now the goodly Odysseus was left behind in the hall, devising with Athene's aid the slaying of the wooers, and straightway he spake winged words to Telemachus:

'Telemachus, we must needs lay by the weapons of war within, every one; and when the wooers miss them and ask thee concerning them, thou shalt beguile them with soft words, saying:

' "Out of the smoke I laid them by, since they were no longer like those that Odysseus left behind him of old, when he went to Troy, but they are wholly marred, so mightily hath passed upon them the vapour of fire. Moreover some god hath put into my heart this other and greater care, that perchance when ye are heated with wine, ye set a quarrel between you and wound one the other, and thereby shame the feast and the wooing; for iron of itself draws a man thereto.'

Thus he spake, and Telemachus hearkened to his dear father, and called forth to him the nurse Eurycleia and spake to her, saying:

'Nurse, come now I pray thee, shut up the women in their chambers till I shall have laid by in the armoury the goodly weapons of my father, which all uncared for the smoke dims in the hall." '

. . . Thus he spake, and she closed the doors of the fair-lying chambers. Then they twain sprang up, Odysseus and his renowned son, and set to carry within the helmets and the bossy shields, and the sharp-pointed spears; and before them Pallas Athene bare a golden cresset and cast a most lovely light. Thereon Telemachus spake to his father suddenly:

'Father, surely a great marvel is this that I behold with mine eyes; meseems, at least, that the walls of the hall and the fair main-beams of the roof and the cross-beams of pine, and the pillars that run aloft, are bright as it were with flaming fire. Verily some god is within, of those that hold the wide heaven.'

And Odysseus of many counsels answered him and said: 'Hold thy peace and keep thy thoughts in check and ask not hereof. Lo, this is the wont of the gods that hold Olympus. But do thou go and lay thee down, and I will abide here, that I may yet further provoke the maids and thy mother to answer; and she in her sorrow will ask me concerning each thing, one by one.'

So he spake, and Telemachus passed out through the hall to his chamber to lie down, by the light of the flaming torches, even to the chamber where of old he took his rest. There now too he lay down and awaited the bright Dawn. But goodly Odysseus was left behind in the hall, devising with Athene's aid the slaying of the wooers.

Now forth from her chamber came the wise Penelope, like Artemis or golden Aphrodite,[1] and they set a chair for her hard by before the fire, where she was wont to sit. Here, then, the wise Penelope sat her down, and next came white-armed handmaids from the women's chamber, and began to take away the many fragments of food, and the tables and the cups whence the proud lords had been drinking, and they raked out the fire from the braziers on to the floor, and piled many fresh logs upon them, to give light and warmth.

Then the serving maid Melantho began to revile Odysseus, saying: 'Stranger, wilt thou still be a plague to us here, circling round the house in the night, and spying the women? Nay, get thee forth, thou wretched thing, and be thankful for thy supper, or straightway shalt thou even be smitten with a torch and so fare out of the doors.'

Then Odysseus of many counsels looked fiercely on her, and said: 'Good woman, what possesses thee to assail me thus out of an angry

1. Goddess of Love.

heart? Is it because I go filthy and am clothed about in sorry raiment, and beg through the land, for necessity is laid on me? This is the manner of beggars and of wandering men. For I too once had a house of mine own among men, a rich man with a wealthy house, and many a time would I give to a wanderer, what manner of man soever he might be, and in whatsoever need he came. . . .'

Thus he spake, and the wise Penelope heard him, and rebuked the handmaid, and spake and hailed her:

'Thou reckless thing and unabashed, be sure thy great sin is not hidden from me, and thy blood shall be on thine own head for the same! For thou knewest right well, in that thou hadst heard it from my lips, how that I was minded to ask the stranger in my halls for tidings of my lord; for I am grievously afflicted.'

Therewith she spake likewise to the housedame, Eurynome, saying:

'Eurynome, bring hither a settle with a fleece thereon, that the stranger may sit and speak with me and hear my words, for I would ask him all his story.'

So she spake, and the nurse made haste and brought a polished settle, and cast a fleece thereon; and then the steadfast goodly Odysseus sat him down there, and the wise Penelope spake first, saying:

'Stranger, I will make bold first to ask thee this: who art thou of the sons of men, and whence? Where is thy city, and where are they that begat thee?'

And Odysseus of many counsels answered her and said: 'Lady, no one of mortal men in the wide world could find fault with thee, for lo, thy fame goes up to the wide heaven, as doth the fame of a blameless king. . . . Wherefore do thou ask me now in thy house all else that thou wilt, but inquire not concerning my race and mine own country, lest as I think thereupon thou fill my heart the more with pains, for I am a man of many sorrows.'

Then wise Penelope answered him, and said: 'Stranger, surely my excellence, both of face and form, the gods destroyed in the day when the Argives embarked for Ilios, and with them went my lord Odysseus. If but he might come and watch over this my life, greater and fairer thus would be my fame! But now am I in sorrow, such a host of ills some god has sent against me. For all the noblest that are princes in the isles, in Dulichium and Same and wooded Zacynthus, and they that dwell around even in clear-seen Ithaca, these are wooing me against my will, and devouring the house. Wherefore I take no heed of strangers, nor suppliants, nor at all of heralds, the craftsmen of the people. But I waste my heart away in longing for Odysseus; so they speed on my marriage and I weave a web of wiles. First some god put it into my heart to set up a great web in the halls, and thereat to weave a robe fine of woof and very wide; and anon I spake among them, saying: "Ye princely youths, my wooers, now that goodly Odysseus is dead, do ye abide patiently, how eager soever to speed on this marriage of mine, till I finish the robe. I would not that the threads perish to no avail, even this shroud for the hero Laertes, against the day when the ruinous doom shall bring him low, of death that lays men at their length. So shall none of the Achaean women in the land count it blame in me, as well might be, were he to lie without a winding sheet, a man that had gotten great possessions."

'So spake I, and their high hearts consented thereto. So then in the daytime I would weave the mighty web, and in the night unravel the same, when I had let place the torches by me. Thus for the space of three years I hid the thing by craft and beguiled the minds of the Achaeans. But when the fourth year arrived, and the seasons came round as the months waned, and many days were accomplished, then it was that by help of the handmaids, shameless things and reckless, the wooers came and trapped me, and chid me loudly. Thus did I finish the web by no will of mine, for so I must. And now I can neither escape the marriage nor devise any further counsel, and my parents are instant with me to marry, and my son chafes that these men devour his livelihood, as he takes note of all; for by this time he has come to man's estate, and is full able to care for a household, for one to which Zeus vouchsafes honour. But even so tell me of thine own stock, whence thou art, for thou art not sprung of oak or rock, whereof old tales tell.'

And Odysseus of many counsels answered her and said:

'O wife revered of Odysseus, son of Laertes, wilt thou never have done asking me about mine own race? Yet even so I will tell thee what thou askest and inquirest. There is a land called Crete in the midst of the wine-dark sea, a fair land and a rich, begirt with water, and therein are many men innumerable, and ninety cities. And among these cities is the mighty city Cnosus, wherein Minos when he was nine years old began to rule, he who held converse with great Zeus,[2] and

2. Minos, king of Crete, is said to have retired periodically to a cave sacred to Zeus, where he conversed with the god and received from him laws of the realm.

was the father of my father, even of Deucalion, high of heart. Now
Deucalion begat me and Idomeneus the prince. But my famed name is
Aethon, being the younger of the twain. There I saw Odysseus, and
gave him guest-gifts, for the might of the wind bare him too to Crete,
as he was making for Troy-land, and had driven him wandering past
Malea. Anon he came up to the city and asked for Idomeneus, saying
that he was his friend and held by him in love and honour. But it was
now the tenth or the eleventh dawn since Idomeneus had gone in his
beaked ships up into Ilios. Then I led him to the house, and gave him
good entertainment with all loving-kindness out of the plenty in my
house. There the goodly Achaeans abode twelve days, for the strong
North Wind penned them there. On the thirteenth day the wind fell,
and then they lifted anchor.'

So he told many a false tale in the likeness of truth, and her tears
flowed as she listened, and her flesh melted. And even as the snow
melts in the high places of the hills, the snow that the South-East wind
has thawed, even so her fair cheeks melted beneath her tears, as she
wept her own lord, who even then was sitting by her. Now Odysseus
had compassion of heart upon his wife in her lamenting, but his eyes
kept steadfast between his eyelids as it were horn or iron, and craftily
he hid his tears. But she, when she had taken her fill of tearful lamentation, answered him in turn and spake, saying:

'Friend as thou art, even now I think to make trial of thee, and
learn whether in very truth thou didst entertain my lord there in thy
halls with his godlike company, as thou sayest. Tell me what manner
of raiment he was clothed in about his body, and what manner of man
he was himself, and tell me of his fellows that went with him.'

Then Odysseus of many counsels answered her saying: 'Lady, it
is hard for one so long parted from him to tell thee all this, for it is
now the twentieth year since he went thither and left my country.
Yet even so I will tell thee as I see him in spirit. Goodly Odysseus wore
a thick purple mantle, twofold, which had a brooch fashioned in gold,
with two sheaths for the pins, and on the face of it was a curious
device: a hound in his forepaws held a dappled fawn and gazed on it
as it writhed. Moreover, I marked the shining doublet about his body,
like the gleam over the skin of a dried onion, so smooth it was, and
glistening as the sun; truly many women looked thereon and wondered. Yet another thing will I tell thee, and do thou ponder it in thy
heart. I know not if Odysseus was thus clothed upon at home, or if
one of his fellows gave him the raiment as he went on board the swift

ship. Moreover, a henchman bare him company, somewhat older than he, and I will tell thee of him too, what manner of man he was. He was round-shouldered, black-skinned, and curly-headed, his name Eurybates; and Odysseus honoured him above all his company, because in all things he was like-minded with himself.'

So he spake, and in her heart he stirred yet more the desire of weeping, as she knew the certain tokens that Odysseus showed her. So when she had taken her fill of tearful lament, then she answered him, and spake saying:

'Now verily, stranger, thou that even before wert held in pity, shalt be dear and honourable in my halls, for it was I who gave him these garments, as judging from thy words, and folded them myself, and brought them from the chamber, and added besides the shining brooch to be his jewel. But him I shall never welcome back, returned home to his own dear country. Wherefore with an evil fate it was that Odysseus went hence in the hollow ship to see that evil Ilios, never to be named!'

And Odysseus of many counsels answered her saying: 'Wife revered of Odysseus, son of Laertes, destroy not now thy fair flesh any more, nor waste thy heart with weeping for thy lord. Nay, cease from thy lamenting, and lay up my word in thy heart; for I will tell thee without fail, and will hide nought, how but lately I heard tell of the return of Odysseus, that he is nigh at hand, and yet alive in the fat land of the men of Thesprotia, and is bringing with him many choice treasures, as he begs through the land. But he has lost his dear companions and his hollow ship on the wine-dark sea, for Zeus and Helios had a grudge against him, because his company had slain the kine of Helios. They for their part all perished in the wash of the sea, but the wave cast him on the keel of the ship out upon the coast, on the land of the Phaeacians that are near of kin to the gods, and they did him all honour heartily as unto a god, and gave him many gifts, and themselves would fain have sent him scatheless home. Yea and Odysseus would have been here long since, but he thought it more profitable to gather wealth, as he journeyed over wide lands. So Pheidon king of the Thesprotians told me. Moreover he sware, in mine own presence, that the ship was drawn down to the sea and his company were ready, who were to convey him to his own dear country. But me he first sent off, for it chanced that a ship of the Thesprotians was on her way to Dulichium, a land rich in grain. And he showed me all the wealth that Odysseus had gathered, yea, it would suffice for his children after him, even to the tenth generation, so great were the treasures he had stored in the chambers of the king. As for him he had gone, he said, to Dodona to hear the counsel of Zeus, from the high leafy oak tree of the god, how he should return to his own dear country, having now been long afar, whether openly or by stealth.

'In this wise, as I tell thee, he is safe and will come shortly, and very near he is and will not much longer be far from his friends and his own country; yet withal I will give thee my oath on it. Zeus be my witness first, of gods the highest and best, and the hearth of noble Odysseus whereunto I am come, that all these things shall surely be accomplished even as I tell thee. In this same year Odysseus shall come hither, as the old moon wanes and the new is born.'

Then wise Penelope answered him: 'Ah! stranger, would that this word may be accomplished. Soon shouldst thou be aware of kindness and many a gift at my hands. But on this wise my heart has a boding, and so it shall be. Neither shall Odysseus come home any more, nor shalt thou gain an escort hence. But do ye, my handmaids, wash this man's feet and strew a couch for him, bedding and mantles and shining blankets, that well and warmly he may come to the time of golden-throned Dawn. . . .'

Then Odysseus of many counsels answered her and said: 'O wife revered of Odysseus, son of Laertes, mantles verily and shining blankets are hateful to me, since first I left behind me the snowy hills of Crete, voyaging in the long-oared galley; nay, I will lie as in time past I was used to rest through the sleepless nights. For full many a night I have lain on an unsightly bed, and awaited the bright-throned Dawn. And baths for the feet are no longer my delight, nor shall any women of those who are serving maidens in thy house touch my foot, unless there chance to be some old wife, true of heart, one that has borne as much trouble as myself; I would not grudge such an one to touch my feet.'

Then wise Penelope answered him: 'Dear stranger, for never yet has there come to my house, of strangers from afar, a dearer man or so discreet as thou, uttering so heedfully the words of wisdom. I have an ancient woman of an understanding heart, that diligently nursed and tended that hapless man my lord, she took him in her arms in the hour when his mother bare him. She will wash thy feet, albeit her strength is frail. Up now, wise Eurycleia, and wash this man, whose years are the same as thy master's. Yea and perchance such even now are the feet of Odysseus, and such too his hands, for quickly men age in misery.'

So she spake, and the old woman covered her face with her hands and shed hot tears, and spake a word of lamentation, saying:

'Ah, woe is me, Odysseus, my child, for thy sake, all helpless that I am! Surely Zeus hated thee above all men, though thou hadst a god-fearing spirit! . . . But come, mark the word that I shall speak. Many strangers travel-worn have ere now come hither, but I say that I have never seen any so like another, as thou art like Odysseus, in fashion, in voice, and in feet.'

Then Odysseus of many counsels answered her saying: 'Old wife, even so all men declare, that have beheld us twain, that we favour each other exceedingly, even as thou dost mark and say.'

Thereupon the crone took the shining cauldron, wherefrom she set to wash his feet, and poured in much cold water and next mingled therewith the warm. Now Odysseus sat aloof from the hearth, and of a sudden he turned his face to the darkness, for anon he had a misgiving of heart lest when she handled him she might know the scar again, and all should be revealed. Now she drew near her lord to wash him, and straightway she knew the scar of the wound that the boar had dealt him with his white tusk long ago. . . . The old woman took the scarred limb and passed her hands down it, and knew it by the touch and let the foot drop suddenly, so that the knee fell into the bath, and the brazen vessel rang, being turned over on the other side, and behold, the water was spilled on the ground. Then joy and anguish came on her in one moment, and both her eyes filled up with tears, and the voice of her utterance was stayed, and touching the chin of Odysseus she spake to him, saying:

'Yea verily, thou art Odysseus my dear child, and I knew thee nor before, till I had handled all the body of my lord.'

Therewithal she looked towards Penelope, as minded to make a sign that her husband was now home. But Penelope could not meet her eyes nor take note of her, for Athene had bent her thoughts to other things. But Odysseus feeling for the old woman's throat gript it with his right hand and with the other drew her closer to him and spake saying:

'Woman, why wouldest thou indeed destroy me? It was thou that didst nurse me there at thine own breast, and now after travail and much pain I am come in the twentieth year to mine own country. But since thou art ware of me, and the god has put this in thy heart, be silent, lest another learn the matter in the halls. For on this wise I will declare it, and it shall surely be accomplished:—if the gods subdue the lordly wooers unto me, I will not hold my hand from thee, my nurse though thou art, when I slay the other handmaids in my halls.'

Then wise Eurycleia answered, saying: 'My child, what word hath escaped the door of thy lips? Thou knowest how firm is my spirit and unyielding, and I will keep me fast as stubborn stone or iron. Yet another thing will I tell thee, and do thou ponder it in thine heart. If the gods subdue the lordly wooers to thy hand, then will I tell thee all the tale of the women in the halls, which of them dishonour thee and which be guiltless.'

Then Odysseus of many counsels answered her saying: 'Nurse, wherefore I pray thee wilt thou speak of these? Thou needest not, for even I myself will mark them well and take knowledge of each. Nay, do thou keep thy saying to thyself, and leave the rest to the gods.'

Even so he spake, and the old woman passed forth from the hall to bring water for his feet, for the first water was all spilled. So when she had washed him and anointed him well with olive-oil, Odysseus again drew up his settle nearer to the fire to warm himself, and covered up the scar with his rags: Then the wise Penelope spake first, saying:

'Stranger, there is yet a little thing I will make bold to ask thee, for soon will it be the hour for pleasant rest, for him on whomsoever sweet sleep falls, though he be heavy with care. But to me has the god given sorrow, yea sorrow measureless, for all the day I have my fill of wailing and lamenting, as I look to mine own housewiferies and to the tasks of the maidens in the house. . . . Shall I abide with my son, and keep all secure, all the things of my getting, my thralls and great high-roofed home, having respect unto the bed of my lord and the voice of the people, or even now follow with the best of the Achaeans that woos me in the halls, and gives a bride-price beyond reckoning? Now my son, so long as he was a child and light of heart, suffered me not to marry and leave the house of my husband; but now that he is great of growth, and is come to the full measure of manhood, lo now he prays me to go back home from these walls, being vexed for his possessions that the Achaeans devour before his eyes. But come now, hear a dream of mine and tell me the interpretation thereof. Twenty geese I have in the house, that eat wheat, coming forth from the water, and I am gladdened at the sight. Now a great eagle of crooked beak swooped from the mountain, and brake all their necks and slew them; and they lay strewn in a heap in the halls, while he was borne aloft to the bright air. Thereupon I wept and wailed, in a dream though it was, and around me were gathered the fair-tressed Achaean women as I made piteous lament, for that the eagle had slain my geese. But he came back and sat him down on a jutting point of the roof-beam, and with the voice of a man he spake, and stayed my weeping:

'"Take heart, O daughter of renowned Icarius; this is no dream but a true vision, that shall be accomplished for thee. The geese are the wooers, and I that before was the eagle am now thy husband come again, who will let slip unsightly death upon all the wooers." With that word sweet slumber let me go, and I looked about, and beheld the geese in the court pecking their wheat at the trough, where they were wont before.'

Then Odysseus of many counsels answered her and said: 'Lady, none may turn aside the dream to interpret it otherwise, seeing that Odysseus himself hath showed thee how he will fulfil it. For the wooers destruction is clearly boded, for all and every one; not a man shall avoid death and the fates.'

Then wise Penelope answered him: 'Stranger, verily dreams are hard, and hard to be discerned; nor are all things therein fulfilled for men. . . . But another thing will I tell thee, and do thou ponder it in thy heart. Lo, even now draws nigh the morn of evil name, that is to sever me from the house of Odysseus, for now I am about to ordain for a trial those axes that he would set up in a row in his halls, like stays of oak in ship-building, twelve in all, and he would stand far apart and shoot his arrow through them all. And now I will offer this contest to the wooers: whoso shall most easily string the bow in his hands, and shoot through all twelve axes, with him will I go and forsake this house, this house of my wedlock, so fair and filled with all livelihood, which me-thinks I shall yet remember, aye, in a dream.'

Then Odysseus of many counsels answered her and said: 'Wife revered of Odysseus, son of Laertes, no longer delay this contest in thy halls; for, lo, Odysseus of many counsels will be here, before these men, for all their handling of this polished bow, shall have strung it, and shot the arrow through the iron.'

Then the wise Penelope answered him: 'Stranger, if only thou wert willing still to sit beside me in the halls and to delight me, not upon my eyelids would sleep be shed. But men may in no wise abide sleepless ever, for the immortals have made a time for all things for mortals on the grain-giving earth. Howbeit I will go aloft to my upper chamber, and lay me on my bed, the place of my groanings, that is ever watered by my tears, since the day that Odysseus went to see that evil Ilios, never to be named. There will I lay me down, but do thou lie in this house; either strew thee somewhat on the floor, or let them lay bedding for thee.'

Therewith she ascended to her shining upper chamber, not alone, for with her likewise went her handmaids. So she went aloft to her upper chamber with the women her handmaids, and there was bewailing Odysseus, her dear lord, till grey-eyed Athene cast sweet sleep upon her eyelids.

[BOOK XX: Odysseus spends the night upon the floor of the entrance hall, planning evil for the wooers and the loose women of his household. Passionate and impatient for action, he is unable to rest until Athene comes to him with comforting words and sleep. In the morning he goes to the great hall, where food and drink are being prepared. The wooers gather, with insults for both Odysseus and Telemachus; and as Telemachus grows bolder in dealing with them, they become more insistent that Penelope arrive at a choice. It is a day of public festival in honor of the archer god Apollo, and an air of strain and suspense prevails.]

BOOK XXI

Now the goddess, grey-eyed Athene, put it into the heart of wise Penelope to set the bow and the axes of grey iron, for the wooers in the halls of Odysseus, to be the weapons of the contest, and the beginning of death. So she descended the tall staircase of her chamber, and took the well-bent key in her strong hand. And she betook her, with her handmaidens, to the treasure-chamber in the uttermost part of the house, where lay the treasures of her lord, bronze and gold and wellwrought iron. And there lay the back-bent bow and the quiver for the arrows, and many shafts were therein, winged for death. . . .

Now when the fair lady had come even to the treasure-chamber, and had stept upon the threshold of oak, which the carpenter had on a time planed cunningly, anon she quickly loosed the strap from the handle of the door, and thrust in the key, and with a straight aim shot back the bolts. And even as a bull roars that is grazing in a meadow, so mightily roared the fair doors smitten by the key; and speedily they flew open before her. Then she stept on to the high floor, where the coffers stood, wherein the fragrant raiment was stored. Thence she stretched forth her hand, and took the bow from off the pin, all in the bright case which sheathed it around. And there she sat down, and set the case upon her knees, and cried aloud and wept, and took out the bow of her lord. Now when she had her fill of tearful lament, she set forth to go to the hall to the company of the proud wooers, with the back-bent bow in her hands, and the quiver for the arrows, and many shafts were therein winged for death. And her maidens along with her bare a chest, wherein lay much store of iron and bronze, the gear of combat of their lord. Now when the fair lady had come unto the wooers, she stood by the pillar of the well-builded roof, holding up her glistening tire before her face; and a faithful maiden stood on either side of her, and straightway she spake out among the wooers and declared her word, saying:

'Hear me, ye lordly wooers, who have vexed this house, that ye might eat and drink here evermore, forasmuch as the master is long gone, nor could ye find any other mark for your speech, but all your desire was to wed me and take me to wife. Nay come now, ye wooers, seeing that this is the prize that is put before you. I will set forth for you the great bow of divine Odysseus, and whoso shall most easily string the bow in his hands, and shoot through all twelve axes, with him will I go and forsake this house, this house of my wedlock, so fair and filled with all livelihood, which methinks I shall yet remember, aye, in a dream.'

So spake she, and commanded Eumaeus, the goodly swineherd, to set the bow for the wooers and the axes of grey iron. And Eumaeus took them with tears, and laid them down; and otherwhere the neatherd wept, when he beheld the bow of his lord. Then Antinous rebuked them, and spake and hailed them:

'Foolish boors, whose thoughts look not beyond the day, ah, wretched pair, wherefore now do ye shed tears, and stir the soul of the lady within her, when her heart already lies low in pain, for that she has lost her dear lord? Nay sit, and feast in silence, or else get ye forth and weep, and leave the bow here behind, to be a terrible contest for the wooers, for methinks that this polished bow does not lightly yield itself to be strung. For there is no man among all these present such as Odysseus was, and I myself saw him, yea I remember it well, though I was still but a child.'

So spake he, but his heart within him hoped that he would string the bow, and shoot through the iron. Yet verily, he was to be the first that should taste the arrow at the hands of the noble Odysseus, whom but late he was dishonouring as he sat in the halls, and was inciting all his fellows to do likewise.

Then the mighty prince Telemachus spake among them, saying: 'Lo now, in very truth, Cronion has robbed me of my wits! My dear mother, wise as she is, declares that she will go with a stranger and forsake this house; yet I laugh and in my silly heart I am glad. Nay come now, ye wooers, seeing that this is the prize which is set before you, a lady, the like of whom there is not now in the Achaean land. Come therefore, delay not the issue with excuses, nor hold much longer aloof from the drawing of the bow, that we may see the thing that is to be. Yea and I myself would make trial of this bow. If I shall string it, and shoot through the iron, then should I not sorrow if my lady mother were to quit these halls and go with a stranger, seeing that I should be left behind, well able now to lift my father's goodly gear of combat.'

Therewith he cast from off his neck his cloak of scarlet, and sprang to his full height, and put away the sword from his shoulders. First he dug a good trench and set up the axes, one long trench for them all, and over it he made straight the line and round about stamped in the earth. And amazement fell on all that beheld how orderly he set the axes, though never before had he seen it so. Then he went and stood by the threshold and began to prove the bow. Thrice he made it to tremble in his great desire to draw it, and thrice he rested from his effort, though still he hoped in his heart to string the bow, and shoot through the iron. And now at last he might have strung it, mightily straining thereat for the fourth time, but Odysseus nodded frowning and stayed him, for all his eagerness. Then the strong prince Telemachus spake among them again:

'Lo you now, even to the end of my days I shall be a coward and a weakling, or it may be I am too young, and have as yet no trust in my hands to defend me from such an one as does violence without a cause. But come now, ye who are mightier men than I, essay the bow and let us make an end of the contest.'

Therewith he put the bow from him on the ground, leaning it against the smooth and well-compacted doors, and the swift shaft he propped hard by against the fair bow-tip, and then he sat down once more on the high seat, whence he had risen.

Then Antinous, son of Eupeithes, spake among them, saying: 'Rise up in order, all my friends, beginning from the left, even from the place whence the wine is poured.'

So spake Antinous, and the saying pleased them well. Then first stood up Leiodes, son of Oenops, who was their soothsayer and ever sat by the fair mixing bowl at the extremity of the hall; he alone hated their infatuate deeds and was indignant with all the wooers. He now first took the bow and the swift shaft, and he went and stood by the threshold, and began to prove the bow; but he could not bend it; so he spake among the wooers, saying:

'Friends, of a truth I cannot bend it, let some other take it. Ah, many of our bravest shall this bow rob of spirit and of life, since truly it is far better for us to die, than to live on and to fail of that for which we assemble evermore in this place, day by day expecting the prize.' So he spake, and put from him the bow.

But Antinous rebuked him, and spake and hailed him: 'Leiodes, what word hath escaped the door of thy lips; a hard word, and a grievous? Nay, it angers me to hear it, and to think that a bow such as this shall rob our bravest of spirit and of life, and all because thou canst not draw it.'

So he spake, and commanded Melanthius, the goatherd, saying: 'Up now, light a fire in the halls, Melanthius; and place a great settle by the fire and a fleece thereon, and bring forth a great ball of lard that is within, that we young men may warm and anoint the bow therewith and prove it, and make an end of the contest.'

So he spake, and Melanthius soon kindled the never-resting fire, and drew up a settle and placed it near, and put a fleece thereon, and he brought forth a great ball of lard that was within. Therewith the young men warmed the bow, and made essay, but could not string it, for they were greatly lacking of such might. And Antinous still held to the task and godlike Eurymachus, chief men among the wooers, who were far the most excellent of all.

But those other twain went forth both together from the house, the neatherd and the swineherd of godlike Odysseus; and Odysseus passed out after them. But when they were now gotten without the gates and the courtyard, he uttered his voice and spake to them in gentle words:

'Neatherd and thou swineherd, shall I say somewhat or keep it to myself? Nay, my spirit bids me declare it. What manner of men would ye be to help Odysseus, if he should come thus suddenly, I know not whence, and some god were to bring him? Would ye stand on the side of the wooers or of Odysseus? Tell me even as your heart and spirit bid you.'

Then the neatherd answered him, saying: 'Father Zeus, if but thou wouldst fulfil this wish:—oh, that that man might come, and some god lead him hither! So shouldest thou know what my might is, and how my hands follow to obey.'

In like manner Eumaeus prayed to all the gods that wise Odysseus might return to his own home.

Now when he knew for a surety what spirit they were of, once more he answered and spake to them, saying:

'Behold, home am I come, even I; after much travail and sore am I come in the twentieth year to mine own country. And I know how that my coming is desired by you alone of all my thralls, for from none besides have I heard a prayer that I might return once more to my home. And now I will tell you all the truth, even as it shall come to pass. If the god shall subdue the proud wooers to my hands, I will bring you each one a wife, and will give you a heritage of your own and a house builded near to me, and ye twain shall be thereafter in mine eyes as the brethren and companions of Telemachus. But behold, I will likewise show you a most manifest token, that ye may know me well and be certified in heart, even the wound that the boar dealt me with his white tusk long ago, when I went to Parnassus with the sons of Autolycus.'

Therewith he drew aside the rags from the great scar. And when the twain had beheld it and marked it well, they cast their arms about the wise Odysseus, and fell a-weeping; and kissed him lovingly on head and shoulders. And in like manner Odysseus too kissed their heads and hands. And now would the sunlight have gone down upon their sorrowing, had not Odysseus himself stayed them saying:

'Cease ye from weeping and lamentation, lest some one come forth from the hall and see us, and tell it likewise in the house. Nay, go ye within one by one and not both together, I first and you following, and let this be the token between us. All the rest, as many as are proud wooers, will not suffer that I should be given the bow and quiver; do thou then, goodly Eumaeus, as thou bearest the bow through the hall, set it in my hands and speak to the women that they bar the well-fitting doors of their chamber. And if any of them hear the sound of groaning or the din of men within our walls, let them not run forth but abide where they are in silence at their work. But on thee, goodly Philoetius, I lay this charge, to bolt and bar the outer gate of the court and swiftly to tie the knot.'

Therewith he passed within the fair-lying halls, and went and sat upon the settle whence he had risen. And likewise the two thralls of divine Odysseus went within.

And now Eurymachus was handling the bow, warming it on this side and on that at the light of the fire; yet even so he could not string it, and in his great heart he groaned mightily; and in heaviness of spirit he spake and called aloud, saying:

'Lo you now, truly am I grieved for myself and for you all! Not for the marriage do I mourn so greatly, afflicted though I be; but I grieve, if indeed we are so far worse than god-like Odysseus in might, seeing that we cannot bend the bow. It will be a shame even for men unborn to hear thereof.'

Then Antinous, son of Eupeithes, answered him: 'Eurymachus, this shall not be so, and thou thyself too knowest it. For to-day the feast of the archer god is held in the land, a holy feast. Who at such a time would be bending bows? Nay, set it quietly by; what and if we should let the axes all stand as they are? None methinks will come to the hall of Odysseus, son of Laertes, and carry them away. Go to now, let the wine-bearer pour for libation into each cup in turn, that after the drink-offering we may set down the curved bow. And in the morning bid Melanthius, the goatherd, to lead hither the very best goats in all his herds, that we may lay pieces of the thighs on the altar of Apollo the archer, and essay the bow and make an end of the contest.'

So spake Antinous, and the saying pleased them well. But when they had poured forth and had drunken to their hearts' desire, Odysseus of many counsels spake among them out of a crafty heart, saying:

'Hear me, ye wooers of the renowned queen, that I may say that which my heart within me bids. And mainly to Eurymachus I make my prayer and to the godlike Antinous. Come, give me the polished bow, that in your presence I may prove my hands and strength, whether I have yet any force such as once was in my supple limbs, or whether my wanderings and needy fare have even now destroyed it.'

So spake he and they all were exceeding wroth, for fear lest he should string the polished bow. And Antinous rebuked him, and spake and hailed him:

'Wretched stranger, thou hast no wit, nay never so little. Art thou not content to feast at ease in our high company, and to lack not thy share of the banquet, but to listen to our speech and our discourse, while no guest and beggar beside thee hears our speech? Wine it is that wounds thee, honey-sweet wine, that is the bane of others too. . . .

Even so I declare great mischief unto thee if thou shalt string the bow, for thou shalt find no courtesy at the hand of any one in our land, and anon we will send thee in a black ship to Echetus, the maimer of all men, and thence thou shalt not be saved alive. Nay then, drink at thine ease, and strive not still with men that are younger than thou.'

Then wise Penelope answered him: 'Antinous, truly it is not fair nor just to rob the guests of Telemachus of their due, whosoever he may be that comes to this house. Dost thou think if yonder stranger strings the great bow of Odysseus, in the pride of his might and of his strength of arm, that he will lead me to his home and make me his wife? Nay he himself, methinks, has no such hope in his breast; so, as for that, let not any of you fret himself while feasting in this place; that were indeed unmeet.'

Then Eurymachus, son of Polybus, answered her, saying: 'Daughter of Icarius, wise Penelope, it is not that we deem that he will lead thee to his home,—far be such a thought from us,—but we dread the speech of men and women, lest some day one of the baser sort among the Achaeans say: "Truly men far too mean are wooing the wife of one that is noble, nor can they string the polished bow. But a stranger and a beggar came in his wanderings, and lightly strung the bow, and shot through the iron." Thus will they speak, and this will turn to our reproach.'

Then wise Penelope answered him: 'Eurymachus, never can there be fair fame in the land for those that devour and dishonour the house of a prince, but why make ye this thing into a reproach? But, behold, our guest is great of growth and well-knit, and avows him to be born the son of a good father. Come then, give ye him the polished bow, that we may see that which is to be. . . .'

Then wise Telemachus answered her, saying: 'My mother, as for the bow, no Achaean is mightier than I to give or to deny it to whomso I will. But do thou go to thine own chamber and mind thine own housewiferies, the loom and distaff, and bid thine handmaids ply their tasks. But the bow shall be for men, for all, but for me in chief, for mine is the lordship in the house.'

Then in amaze she went back to her chamber, for she laid up the wise saying of her son in her heart. . . . Then the swineherd bare the bow through the hall, and went up to wise Odysseus, and set it in his hands. And he called forth the nurse Eurycleia from the chamber and spake to her:

'Wise Eurycleia, Telemachus bids thee bar the well-fitting doors of thy chamber, and if any of the women hear the sound of groaning or the din of men within our walls, let them not go forth, but abide where they are in silence at their work.'

So he spake, and wingless her speech remained, and she barred the doors of the fair-lying chambers.

Then Philoetius hasted forth silently from the house, and barred the outer gates of the fenced court. Now there lay beneath the gallery the cable of a curved ship, fashioned of the byblus plant, wherewith he made fast the gates, and then himself passed within. Then he went and sat on the settle whence he had risen, and gazed upon Odysseus. He already was handling the bow, turning it every way about, and proving it on this side and on that, lest the worms might have eaten the horns when the lord of the bow was away. And thus men spake looking each one to his neighbour:

'Verily he has a good eye, and a shrewd turn for a bow! Either, methinks, he himself has such a bow lying by at home or else he is set on making one, in such wise does he turn it hither and thither in his hands, this evil-witted beggar.'

But Odysseus of many counsels had lifted the great bow and viewed it on every side, and even as when a man that is skilled in the lyre and in minstrelsy, easily stretches a cord about a new peg, after tying at either end the twisted sheep-gut, even so Odysseus straightway bent the great bow, all without effort, and took it in his right hand and proved the bow-string, which rang sweetly at the touch, in tone like a swallow. Then great grief came upon the wooers, and the colour of their countenance was changed, and Zeus thundered loud showing forth his tokens. And the steadfast goodly Odysseus was glad thereat, in that the son of deep-counselling Cronos had sent him a sign. Then he caught up a swift arrow which lay by his table, bare, but the other shafts were stored within the hollow quiver, those whereof the Achaeans were soon to taste. He took and laid it on the bridge of the bow, and held the notch and drew the string, even from the settle whereon he sat, and with straight aim shot the shaft and missed not one of the axes, beginning from the first axe-handle, and the bronze-weighted shaft passed clean through and out at the last. Then he spake to Telemachus saying:

'Telemachus, thy guest that sits in the halls does thee no shame. In no wise did I miss my mark, nor was I wearied with long bending of the bow. Still is my might steadfast—not as the wooers say scornfully to slight me. But now is it time that supper too be got ready for the

Achaeans, while it is yet light, and thereafter must we make other sport
with the dance and the lyre, for these are the crown of the feast.'

Therewith he nodded with bent brows, and Telemachus, the dear
son of divine Odysseus, girt his sharp sword about him and took the
spear in his grasp, and stood by his high seat at his father's side, armed
with the gleaming bronze.

BOOK XXII

Then Odysseus of many counsels stripped him of his rags and
leaped on to the great threshold with his bow and quiver full of arrows,
and poured forth all the swift shafts there before his feet, and spake
among the wooers:

'Lo, now is this terrible trial ended at last; and now will I know
of another mark, which never yet man has smitten, if perchance I may
hit it and Apollo grant me renown.'

With that he pointed the bitter arrow at Antinous. Now he was
about raising to his lips a fair twy-eared chalice of gold, and behold, he
was handling it to drink of the wine, and death was far from his
thoughts. For who among men at feast would deem that one man
amongst so many, how hardy soever he were, would bring on him foul
death and black fate? But Odysseus aimed and smote him with the
arrow in the throat, and the point passed clean out through his delicate
neck, and he fell sidelong and the cup dropped from his hand as he
was smitten, and at once through his nostrils there came up a thick jet
of slain man's blood, and quickly he spurned the table from him with
his foot, and spilt the food on the ground, and the bread and the roast
flesh were defiled. Then the wooers raised a clamour through the halls
when they saw the man fallen, and they leaped from their high seats,
as men stirred by fear, all through the hall, peering everywhere along
the well-builded walls, and nowhere was there a shield or mighty spear
to lay hold on. Then they reviled Odysseus with angry words:

'Stranger, thou shootest at men to thy hurt. Never again shalt thou
enter other lists, now is utter doom assured thee. Yea, for now hast
thou slain the man that was far the best of all the noble youths in
Ithaca; wherefore vultures shall devour thee here.'

So each one spake, for indeed they thought that Odysseus had not
slain him wilfully; but they knew not in their folly that on their own
heads, each and all them, the bands of death had been made fast. Then
Odysseus of many counsels looked fiercely on them, and spake:

'Ye dogs, ye said in your hearts that I should never more come
home from the land of the Trojans, in that ye wasted my house, and
lay with the maidservants by force, and traitorously wooed my wife
while I was yet alive, and ye had no fear of the gods, that hold the
wide heaven, nor of the indignation of men hereafter. But now the
bands of death have been made fast upon you one and all.'

Even so he spake, and pale fear gat hold on the limbs of all, and
each man looked about, where he might shun utter doom. And Eurymachus alone answered him, and spake: 'If thou art indeed Odysseus
of Ithaca, come home again, with right thou speakest thus, of all that
the Achaeans have wrought, many infatuate deeds in thy halls and
many in the field. Howbeit, he now lies dead that is to blame for all,
Antinous; for he brought all these things upon us, not as longing very
greatly for the marriage nor needing it sore, but with another purpose,
that Cronion has not fulfilled for him, namely, that he might himself
be king over all the land of stablished Ithaca, and he was to have lain
in wait for thy son and killed him. But now he is slain after his deserving, and do thou spare thy people, even thine own; and we will
hereafter go about the township and yield thee amends for all that has
been eaten and drunken in thy halls, each for himself bringing atonement of twenty oxen worth, and requiting thee in gold and bronze till
thy heart is softened, but till then none may blame thee that thou art
angry.'

Then Odysseus of many counsels looked fiercely on him, and said:
'Eurymachus, not even if ye gave me all your heritage, all that ye now
have, and whatsoever else ye might in any wise add thereto, not even
so would I henceforth hold my hands from slaying, ere the wooers had
paid for all their transgressions. And now the choice lies before you,
whether to fight in fair battle or to fly, if any may avoid death and the
fates. But there be some, methinks, that shall not escape from utter
doom.'

He spake, and their knees were straightway loosened and their
hearts melted within them. And Eurymachus spake among them yet
again:

'Friends, it is plain that this man will not hold his unconquerable
hands, but now that he has caught up the polished bow and quiver, he
will shoot from the smooth threshold, till he has slain us all; wherefore
let us take thought for the delight of battle. Draw your blades, and hold
up the tables to ward off the arrows of swift death, and let us all have
at him with one accord, and drive him, if it may be, from the threshold

and the doorway and then go through the city, and quickly would the cry be raised. Thereby should this man soon have shot his latest bolt.'

Therewith he drew his sharp two-edged sword of bronze, and leapt on Odysseus with a terrible cry, but in the same moment goodly Odysseus shot the arrow forth and struck him on the breast by the pap, and drave the swift shaft into his liver. So he let the sword fall from his hand, and grovelling over the table he bowed and fell, and spilt the food and the two-handled cup on the floor. And in his agony he smote the ground with his brow, and spurning with both his feet he overthrew the high seat, and the mist of death was shed upon his eyes.

Then Amphinomus made at renowned Odysseus, setting straight at him, and drew his sharp sword, if perchance he might make him give ground from the door. But Telemachus was beforehand with him, and cast and smote him from behind with a bronze-shod spear between the shoulders, and drave it out through the breast, and he fell with a crash and struck the ground full with his forehead. Then Telemachus sprang away, leaving the long spear fixed in Amphinomus, for he greatly dreaded lest one of the Achaeans might run upon him with his blade, and stab him as he drew forth the spear, or smite him with a down stroke of the sword. So he started and ran and came quickly to his father, and stood by him, and spake winged words:

'Father, lo, now I will bring thee a shield and two spears and a helmet all of bronze, close fitting on the temples, and when I return I will arm myself, and likewise give arms to the swineherd and to the neatherd yonder: for it is better to be clad in full armour.'

And Odysseus of many counsels answered him saying: 'Run and bring them while I have arrows to defend me, lest they thrust me from the doorway, one man against them all.'

So he spake, and Telemachus obeyed his dear father, and went forth to the chamber, where his famous weapons were lying. Thence he took out four shields and eight spears, and four helmets of bronze, with thick plumes of horse hair, and he started to bring them and came quickly to his father. Now he girded the gear of bronze about his own body first, and in like manner the two thralls did on the goodly armour, and stood beside the wise and crafty Odysseus. Now he, so long as he had arrows to defend him, kept aiming and smote the wooers one by one in his house, and they fell thick one upon another. But when the arrows failed the prince in his archery, he leaned his bow against the doorpost of the stablished hall, against the shining faces of the entrance. As for him he girt his fourfold shield about his shoulders and bound on his mighty head a well-wrought helmet, with horse hair crest, and terribly the plume waved aloft. And he grasped two mighty spears tipped with bronze.

Now there was in the well-builded wall a certain postern raised above the floor, and there by the topmost level of the threshold of the stablished hall, was a way into an open passage, closed by well-fitted folding doors. So Odysseus bade the goodly swineherd stand near thereto and watch the way, for thither was there but one approach. Then Agelaus spake among them, and declared his word to all:

'Friends, will not some man climb up to the postern, and give word to the people, and a cry would be raised straightway; so should this man soon have shot his latest bolt?'

Then Melanthius, the goatherd, answered him, saying: 'It may in no wise be, prince Agelaus; for the fair gate of the courtyard is terribly nigh, and perilous is the entrance to the passage, and one man, if he were valiant, might keep back a host. But come, let me bring you armour from the inner chamber, that ye may be clad in hauberks, for, methinks, within that room and not elsewhere did Odysseus and his renowned son lay by the arms.'

Therewith Melanthius, the goatherd, climbed up by the clerestory of the hall to the inner chambers of Odysseus, whence he took twelve shields and as many spears, and as many helmets of bronze with thick plumes of horse hair, and he came forth and brought them speedily, and gave them to the wooers. Then the knees of Odysseus were loosened and his heart melted within him, when he saw them girding on the armour and brandishing the long spears in their hands, and great, he saw, was the adventure. Quickly he spake to Telemachus winged words:

'Telemachus, sure I am that one of the women in the halls is stirring up an evil battle against us, or perchance it is Melanthius.'

Then wise Telemachus answered him: 'My father, it is I that have erred herein and none other is to blame, for I left the well-fitted door of the chamber open, and there has been one of them but too quick to spy it. Go now, goodly Eumaeus, and close the door of the chamber, and mark if it be indeed one of the women that does this mischief, or Melanthius, son of Dolius, as methinks it is.'

Even so they spake one to the other. And Melanthius, the goatherd, went yet again to the chamber to bring the fair armour. But the goodly swineherd was ware thereof, and quickly he spake to Odysseus who stood nigh him:

'Son of Laertes, of the seed of Zeus, Odysseus, of many devices, lo, there again is that baleful man, whom we ourselves suspect, going to the chamber; do thou tell me truly, shall I slay him if I prove the better man, or bring him hither to thee, that he may pay for the many transgressions that he has devised in thy house?'

Then Odysseus of many counsels answered saying: 'Verily, I and Telemachus will keep the proud wooers within the halls, for all their fury, but do ye twain tie his feet and arms behind his back and cast him into the chamber, and close the doors after you, and make fast to his body a twisted rope, and drag him up the lofty pillar till he be near the roof-beams, that he may hang there and live for long, and suffer grievous torment.'

So he spake, and they gave good heed and hearkened. So they went forth to the chamber, but the goatherd who was within knew not of their coming. Now he was seeking for the armour in the secret place of the chamber, but they twain stood in waiting on either side the doorposts. And when Melanthius, the goatherd, was crossing the threshold with a goodly helm in one hand, and in the other a wide shield and an old, then the twain rushed on him and caught him, and dragged him in by the hair, and cast him on the floor in sorrowful plight, and bound him hand and foot in a bitter bond, tightly winding each limb behind his back, even as the son of Laertes bade them, the steadfast goodly Odysseus. And they made fast to his body a twisted rope, and dragged him up the lofty pillar till he came near the roof-beams. . . .

So he was left there, stretched tight in the deadly bond. But they twain got into their harness, and closed the shining door, and went to Odysseus, wise and crafty chief. There they stood breathing fury, four men by the threshold, while those others within the halls were many and good warriors. Then Athene, daughter of Zeus, drew nigh them, like Mentor in fashion and in voice, and Odysseus was glad when he saw her and spake, saying:

'Mentor, ward from us hurt, and remember me thy dear companion, that befriended thee often, and thou art of like age with me.'

So he spake, deeming the while that it was Athene, summoner of the host. But the wooers on the other side shouted in the halls, and first Agelaus son of Damastor rebuked Athene, saying:

'Mentor, let not the speech of Odysseus beguile thee to fight against the wooers, and to succour him. For methinks that on this wise we shall work our will. When we shall have slain these men, father and son, thereafter shalt thou perish with them, such deeds thou art set on doing in these halls; nay, with thine own head shalt thou pay the price. . . .'

So spake he, and Athene was mightily angered at heart, and chid Odysseus in wrathful words: 'Odysseus, thou hast no more steadfast might nor any prowess, as when for nine whole years continually thou didst battle with the Trojans for high-born Helen, of the white arms, and many men thou slewest in terrible warfare, and by thy device[1] the wide-wayed city of Priam was taken. How then, now that thou art come to thy house and thine own possessions, dost thou bewail thee and art of feeble courage to stand before the wooers? Nay, come hither, friend, and stand by me, and I will show thee a thing, that thou mayest know what manner of man is Mentor, son of Alcimus, to repay good deeds in the ranks of foemen.'

She spake, and gave him not yet clear victory in full, but still for a while made trial of the might and prowess of Odysseus and his renowned son. As for her she flew up to the roof timber of the murky hall, in such fashion as a swallow flies, and there sat down. . . .

Then Agelaus spake among the wooers, and made known his word to all:

'Friends, now at last will this man hold his unconquerable hands. Lo, now has Mentor left him and spoken but vain boasts, and these remain alone at the entrance of the doors. Wherefore now, throw not your long spears all together, but come, do ye six cast first, if perchance Zeus may grant us to smite Odysseus and win renown. Of the rest will we take no heed, so soon as that man shall have fallen.'

So he spake and they all cast their javelins, as he bade them, eagerly; but behold, Athene so wrought that they were all in vain. So when they had avoided all the spears of the wooers, the steadfast goodly Odysseus began first to speak among them:

'Friends, now my word is that we too cast and hurl into the press of the wooers, that are mad to slay and strip us beyond the measure of their former iniquities.'

So he spake, and they all took good aim and threw their sharp spears, and Odysseus smote Demoptolemus, and Telemachus Euryades, and the swineherd slew Elatus, and the neatherd Peisandrus. Thus they all bit the wide floor with their teeth, and the wooers fell back into the

---

1. Odysseus devised the stratagem of entering Troy by means of the wooden horse.

inmost part of the hall. But the others dashed upon them, and drew forth the shafts from the bodies of the dead.

Then once more the wooers threw their sharp spears eagerly; but behold, Athene so wrought that many of them were in vain. Yet Amphimedon hit Telemachus on the hand by the wrist lightly, and the shaft of bronze wounded the surface of the skin. And Ctesippus grazed the shoulder of Eumaeus with a long spear high above the shield, and the spear flew over and fell to the ground. Then again Odysseus, the wise and crafty, he and his men cast their swift spears into the press of the wooers, and now once more Odysseus, waster of cities, smote Eurydamas, and Telemachus Amphimedon, and the swineherd slew Polybus, and last, the neatherd struck Ctesippus in the breast. . . .

Next Odysseus wounded the son of Damastor in close fight with his long spear, and Telemachus wounded Leocritus son of Euenor, right in the flank with his lance, and drave the bronze point clean through, that he fell prone and struck the ground full with his forehead. Then Athene held up her destroying aegis[2] on high from the roof, and their minds were scared, and they fled through the hall, like a drove of kine that the flitting gadfly falls upon and scatters hither and thither in spring time, when the long days begin. But the others set on like vultures of crooked claws and curved beak, that come forth from the mountains and dash upon smaller birds; even so did the company of Odysseus set upon the wooers and smite them right and left through the hall; and there rose a hideous moaning as their heads were smitten, and the floor all ran with blood.

Now Leiodes took hold of the knees of Odysseus eagerly, and besought him and spake winged words: 'I entreat thee by thy knees, Odysseus, and do thou show mercy on me and have pity. For never yet, I say, have I wronged a maiden in thy halls by froward word or deed, nay I bade the other wooers refrain, whoso of them wrought thus. But they hearkened not unto me to keep their hands from evil. Yet I, the soothsayer among them, that have wrought no evil, shall fall even as they, for no grace abides for good deeds done.'

Then Odysseus of many counsels looked askance at him, and said: 'If indeed thou dost avow thee to be the soothsayer of these men, thou art like to have often prayed in the halls that the issue of a glad return might be far from me, and that my dear wife should follow thee and bear thee children; wherefore thou shalt not escape the bitterness of death.'

2. The aegis of Zeus, employed on occasion by Athene and Apollo.

Therewith he caught up a sword in his strong hand, that lay where Agelaus had let it fall to the ground when he was slain, and drave it clean through his neck, and as he yet spake his head fell even to the dust.

But the son of Terpes, the minstrel, still sought how he might shun black fate, Phemius, who sang among the wooers of necessity. He stood with the loud lyre in his hand hard by the postern gate, and his heart was divided within him, whether he should slip forth from the hall and sit down by the well-wrought altar of great Zeus of the household court, or should spring forward and beseech Odysseus by his knees. And as he thought thereupon this seemed to him the better way, to embrace the knees of Odysseus, son of Laertes. So he laid the hollow lyre on the ground and sprang forward and seized Odysseus by the knees, and besought him and spake winged words:

'I entreat thee by thy knees, Odysseus, and do thou show mercy on me and have pity. It will be a sorrow to thyself in the aftertime if thou slayest me who am a minstrel, and sing before gods and men. And Telemachus will testify of this, thine own dear son, that not by mine own will or desire did I resort to thy house to sing to the wooers at their feasts; but being so many and stronger than I they led me by constraint.'

So he spake, and the mighty prince Telemachus heard him and quickly spake to his father at his side: 'Hold thy hand, and wound not this blameless man with the sword; and let us save also the henchman Medon, that ever had charge of me in our house when I was a child, unless perchance Philoetius or the swineherd have already slain him, or he hath met thee in thy raging through the house.'

So he spake, and Medon, wise of heart, heard him. For he lay crouching beneath a high seat, clad about in the new-flayed hide of an ox and shunned black fate. So he rose up quickly from under the seat, and cast off the oxhide, and sprang forth and caught Telemachus by the knees, and besought him and spake winged words:

'Friend, here am I; prithee stay thy hand and speak to thy father, lest he harm me with the sharp sword in the greatness of his strength, out of his anger for the wooers that wasted his possessions in the halls, and in their folly held thee in no honour.'

And Odysseus of many counsels smiled on him and said: 'Take courage, for lo, he has saved thee and delivered thee, that thou mayst know in thy heart, and tell it even to another, how far more excellent are good deeds than evil.'

Therewith the two went forth and gat them from the hall. And Odysseus peered all through the house, to see if any man was yet alive and hiding away to shun black fate. But he found all the sort of them fallen in their blood in the dust, like fishes that the fishermen have drawn forth in the meshes of the net into a hollow of the beach from out the grey sea, and all the fish, sore longing for the salt sea waves, are heaped upon the sand, and the sun shines forth and takes their life away; so now the wooers lay heaped upon each other. Then Odysseus of many counsels spake to Telemachus:

'Telemachus, go, call me the nurse Eurycleia, that I may tell her a word that is on my mind.'

So he spake, and Telemachus obeyed his dear father, and smote at the door, and spake to the nurse Eurycleia: 'Up now, aged wife, that overlookest all the women servants in our halls, come hither, my father calls thee and has somewhat to say to thee.'

Even so he spake, and wingless her speech remained, and she opened the doors of the fair-lying halls, and came forth, and Telemachus led the way before her. So she found Odysseus among the bodies of the dead, stained with blood and soil of battle, like a lion that has eaten of an ox of the homestead and goes on his way, and all his breast and his cheeks on either side are flecked with blood, and he is terrible to behold; even so was Odysseus stained, both hands and feet. Now the nurse, when she saw the bodies of the dead and the great gore of blood, made ready to cry aloud for joy, beholding so great an adventure. But Odysseus checked and held her in her eagerness, and uttering his voice spake to her winged words:

'Within thine own heart rejoice, old nurse, and be still, and cry not aloud; for it is an unholy thing to boast over slain men. Now these hath the destiny of the gods overcome, and their own cruel deeds, for they honoured none of earthly men, neither the bad nor yet the good, that came among them. Wherefore they have met a shameful death through their own infatuate deeds. But come, tell me the tale of the women in my halls, which of them dishonour me, and which be guiltless.'

Then the good nurse Eurycleia answered him: 'Yea now, my child, I will tell thee all the truth. Thou hast fifty women-servants in thy halls, that we have taught the ways of housewifery, how to card wool and to bear bondage. Of these twelve in all have gone the way of shame, and honour not me, nor their lady Penelope. And Telemachus hath but newly come to his strength, and his mother suffered him not to take command over the women in this house. But now, let me go aloft to the shining upper chamber, and tell all to thy wife, on whom some god hath sent a sleep.'

And Odysseus of many counsels answered her, saying: 'Wake her not yet, but bid the women come hither, who in time past behaved themselves unseemly.'

So he spake, and the old wife passed through the hall, to tell the women and to hasten their coming. Then Odysseus called to him Telemachus, and the neatherd, and the swineherd, and spake to them winged words:

'Begin ye now to carry out the dead, and bid the women help you, and thereafter cleanse the fair high seats and the tables with water and porous sponges. And when ye have set all the house in order, lead the maidens without the stablished hall, between the vaulted room and the goodly fence of the court, and there slay them with your long blades, till they shall have all given up the ghost and forgotten the love that of old they had at the bidding of the wooers, in secret dalliance.'

Even so he spake, and the women came all in a crowd together, making a terrible lament and shedding big tears. So first they carried forth the bodies of the slain, and set them beneath the gallery of the fenced court, and propped them one on another; and Odysseus himself hasted the women and directed them, and they carried forth the dead perforce. Thereafter they cleansed the fair high seats and the tables with water and porous sponges. And Telemachus, and the neatherd, and the swineherd, scraped with spades the floor of the well-builded house, and, behold, the maidens carried all forth and laid it without the doors.

Now when they had made an end of setting the hall in order, they led the maidens forth from the stablished hall, and drove them up in a narrow space between the vaulted room and the goodly fence of the court, whence none might avoid; and wise Telemachus began to speak to his fellows, saying:

'God forbid that I should take these women's lives by a clean death, these that have poured dishonour on my head and on my mother, and have lain with the wooers.'

With that word he tied the cable of a dark-prowed ship to a great pillar and flung it round the vaulted room, and fastened it aloft, that none might touch the ground with her feet. And even as when thrushes, long of wing, or doves fall into a net that is set in a thicket, as they seek to their roosting-place, and a loathly bed harbours them, even so the women held their heads all in a row, and about all their necks nooses were cast, that they might die by the most pitiful death. And they writhed with their feet for a little space, but for no long while.

Then they led out Melanthius through the doorway and the court, and cut off his nostrils and his ears with the pitiless sword, and drew forth his vitals for the dogs to devour raw, and cut off his hands and feet in their cruel anger.

Thereafter they washed their hands and feet, and went into the house to Odysseus, and all the adventure was over. So Odysseus called to the good nurse Eurycleia: 'Bring sulphur, old nurse, that cleanses all pollution and bring me fire, that I may purify the house with sulphur, and do thou bid Penelope come here with her handmaidens, and tell all the women to hasten into the hall.'

Then the good nurse Eurycleia made answer: 'Yea, my child, herein thou hast spoken aright. But go to, let me bring thee a mantle and a doublet for raiment, and stand not thus in the halls with thy broad shoulders wrapped in rags; it were blame in thee so to do.'

And Odysseus of many counsels answered her saying: 'First let a fire now be made me in the hall.'

So he spake, and the good nurse Eurycleia was not slow to obey, but brought fire and brimstone; and Odysseus thoroughly purged the women's chamber and the great hall and the court.

Then the old wife went through the fair halls of Odysseus to tell the women, and to hasten their coming. So they came forth from their chamber with torches in their hands, and fell about Odysseus, and embraced him and kissed and clasped his head and shoulders and his hands lovingly, and a sweet longing came on him to weep and moan, for he remembered them every one.

BOOK XXIII

Then the ancient woman went up into the upper chamber laughing aloud, to tell her mistress how her dear lord was within, and her knees moved fast for joy, and her feet stumbled one over the other; and she stood above the lady's head and spake to her, saying:

'Awake, Penelope, dear child, that thou mayest see with thine own eyes that which thou desirest day by day. Odysseus hath come, and hath got him to his own house, though late hath he come, and hath slain the proud wooers that troubled his house, and devoured his substance and oppressed his child.'

Then wise Penelope answered her: 'Dear nurse, the gods have made thee distraught. They it is that have marred thy reason, though heretofore thou hadst a prudent heart. Why dost thou mock me, who have a spirit full of sorrow, to speak these wild words, and rousest me out of sweet slumber, that had bound me and overshadowed mine eyelids? Never yet have I slept so sound since the day that Odysseus went forth to see that evil Ilios, never to be named. Go to now, get thee down and back to the women's chamber.'

Then the good nurse Eurycleia answered her: 'I mock thee not, dear child, but in very deed Odysseus is here, and hath come home, even as I tell thee. He is that guest on whom all men wrought such dishonour in the halls. But long ago Telemachus was ware of him, that he was within the house, yet in his prudence he hid the counsels of his father, that he might take vengeance on the violence of the haughty wooers.'

Thus she spake, and then was Penelope glad, and leaping from her bed she fell on the old woman's neck, and let fall the tears from her eyelids, and uttering her voice spake to her winged words: 'Come, dear nurse, I pray thee, tell me all truly—if indeed he hath come home as thou sayest—how he hath laid his hands on the shameless wooers, he being but one man, while they abode ever in their companies within the house.'

Then the good nurse Eurycleia answered her: 'I saw not, I wist not, only I heard the groaning of men slain. And we in an inmost place of the well-built chambers sat all amazed, and the close-fitted doors shut in the room, till thy son called me from the chamber, for his father sent him out to that end. Then I found Odysseus standing among the slain, who around him, stretched on the hard floor, lay one upon the other; it would have comforted thy heart to see him, all stained like a lion with blood and soil of battle. And now are all the wooers gathered in an heap by the gates of the court, while he is purifying his fair house with brimstone, and hath kindled a great fire, and hath sent me forth to call thee. . . .'

Then wise Penelope answered her: 'Thou knowest how welcome the sight of him would be in the halls to all, and to me in chief, and to his son that we got between us. But this is no true tale, as thou declarest it, nay but it is one of the deathless gods that hath slain the proud wooers, in wrath at their bitter insolence and evil deeds. But Odysseus, far away hath lost his homeward path to the Achaean land, and himself is lost.'

Then the good nurse Eurycleia made answer to her: 'My child, what word hath escaped the door of thy lips, in that thou saidest that thy lord, who is even now within, and by his own hearthstone, would return no more? Nay, thy heart is ever hard of belief. Go to now, and I will tell thee besides a most manifest token, even the scar of the wound that the boar on a time dealt him with his white tusk. This I spied while washing his feet, and fain I would have told it even to thee, but he laid his hand on my mouth, and in the fulness of his wisdom suffered me not to speak. But come with me and I will stake my life on it; and, if I play thee false, do thou slay me by a death most pitiful.'

Then wise Penelope made answer to her: 'Dear nurse, it is hard for thee, how wise soever, to observe the purposes of the everlasting gods. None the less let us go to my child, that I may see the wooers dead, and him that slew them.'

With that word she went down from the upper chamber, and much her heart debated, whether she should stand apart, and question her dear lord or draw nigh, and clasp and kiss his head and hands. But when she had come within and had crossed the threshold of stone, she sat down over against Odysseus, in the light of the fire, by the further wall. Now he was sitting by the tall pillar, looking down and waiting to know if perchance his noble wife would speak to him, when her eyes beheld him. But she sat long in silence, and amazement came upon her soul, and now she would look upon him steadfastly with her eyes, and now again she knew him not, for that he was clad in vile raiment. And Telemachus rebuked her, and spake and hailed her:

'Mother mine, ill mother, of an ungentle heart, why turnest thou thus away from my father, and dost not sit by him and question him and ask him all? No other woman in the world would harden her heart to stand thus aloof from her lord, who after much travail and sore had come to her in the twentieth year to his own country. But thy heart is ever harder than stone.'

Then wise Penelope answered him, saying: 'Child, my mind is amazed within me, and I have no strength to speak, nor to ask him aught, nay nor to look on him face to face. But if in truth this be Odysseus, and he hath indeed come home, verily we shall be ware of each other the more surely, for we have tokens that we twain know, even we, secret from all others.'

So she spake, and the steadfast goodly Odysseus smiled, and quickly he spake to Telemachus winged words: 'Telemachus, leave now thy mother to make trial of me within the chambers; so shall she soon come to a better knowledge than heretofore. But now I go filthy, and am clad in vile raiment, wherefore she has me in dishonour, and as yet will not allow that I am he. Let us then advise us how all may be for the very best. For whoso has slain but one man in a land, even one that leaves not many behind him to take up the feud for him, turns outlaw and leaves his kindred and his own country; but we have slain the very stay of the city, the men who were far the best of all the noble youths in Ithaca. So this I bid thee consider.'

Then wise Telemachus answered him, saying: 'Father, see thou to this, for they say that thy counsel is far the best among men, nor might any other of mortal men contend with thee.'

And Odysseus of many counsels answered him saying: 'Yea now, I will tell on what wise methinks it is best. First, go ye to the bath and array you in your doublets, and bid the maidens in the chambers to take to them their garments. Then let the divine minstrel, with his loud lyre in hand, lead off for us the measure of the mirthful dance. So shall any man that hears the sound from without, whether a way-farer or one of those that dwell around, say that it is a wedding feast. And thus the slaughter of the wooers shall not be noised abroad through the town before we go forth to our well-wooded farm-land. Thereafter shall we consider what gainful counsel the Olympian may vouchsafe us.'

So he spake, and they gave good ear and hearkened to him. So first they went to the bath, and arrayed them in doublets, and the women were apparelled, and the divine minstrel took the hollow harp, and aroused in them the desire of sweet song and of the happy dance. Then the great hall rang round them with the sound of the feet of dancing men and of fair-girdled women.

Meanwhile, the house-dame Eurynome had bathed the great-hearted Odysseus within his house, and anointed him with olive-oil, and cast about him a goodly mantle and a doublet. Moreover, Athene shed great beauty from his head downwards, and made him greater and more mighty to behold, and from his head caused deep curling locks to flow, like the hyacinth flower. . . . Then he sat down again on the high seat, whence he had arisen, over against his wife, and spake to her, saying:

'Strange lady, surely to thee above all womankind the Olympians have given a heart that cannot be softened. No other woman in the world would harden her heart to stand thus aloof from her husband, who after much travail and sore had come to her, in the twentieth year, to his own country. Nay come, nurse, strew a bed for me to lie all alone, for assuredly her spirit within her is as iron.'

Then wise Penelope answered him again: 'Strange man, I have no proud thoughts nor do I think scorn of thee, nor am I too greatly astonied, but I know right well what manner of man thou wert, when thou wentest forth out of Ithaca, on the long-oared galley. But come, Eurycleia, spread for him the good bedstead outside the stablished bridal chamber that he built himself. Thither bring ye forth the good bedstead and cast bedding thereon, even fleeces and rugs and shining blankets.'

So she spake and made trial of her lord, but Odysseus in sore displeasure spake to his true wife, saying: 'Verily a bitter word is this, lady, that thou hast spoken. Who has set my bed otherwhere? Hard it would be for one, how skilled soever, unless a god were to come that might easily set it in another place, if so he would. But of men there is none living, howsoever strong in his youth, that could lightly upheave it, for a great token is wrought in the fashioning of the bed, and it was I that made it and none other. There was growing a bush of olive, long of leaf, and most goodly of growth, within the inner court, and the stem as large as a pillar. Round about this I built the chamber. Next I sheared off all the light wood of the long-leaved olive, and rough-hewed the trunk upwards from the root, and smoothed it around with the adze, and so fashioned it into the bed-post, and I bored it all with the auger. Beginning from this bed-post, I wrought at the bedstead till I had finished it, and made it fair with inlaid work of gold and of silver and of ivory. Even so I declare to thee this token, and I know not, lady, if the bedstead be yet fast in his place, or if some man has cut away the stem of the olive tree, and set the bedstead otherwhere.'

So he spake, and at once her knees were loosened, and her heart melted within her, as she knew the sure tokens that Odysseus showed her. Then she fell a-weeping, and ran straight toward him and cast her hands about his neck, and kissed his head and spake, saying:

'Be not angry with me, Odysseus, for thou wert ever at other times the wisest of men. It is the gods that gave us sorrow, the gods who begrudged us that we should abide together and have joy of our youth, and come to the threshold of old age. So now be not wroth with me hereat nor full of indignation, because at the first, when I saw thee, I did not welcome thee straightway. For always my heart within my breast shuddered, for fear lest some man should come and deceive me with his words, for many they be that devise gainful schemes and evil. . . . But now that thou hast told all the sure tokens of our bed, which never was seen by mortal man, save by thee and me and one maiden only, that my father gave me ere yet I had come hither, she who kept the doors of our strong bridal chamber, even now dost thou bend my soul, all ungentle as it is.'

Thus she spake, and in his heart she stirred yet a greater longing to lament, and he wept as he embraced his beloved wife and true. And even as when the sight of land is welcome to swimmers, whose well-wrought ship Poseidon hath smitten on the deep, so welcome to her was the sight of her lord, and her white arms she would never quite let go from his neck. And now would the rosy-fingered Dawn have risen upon their weeping, but the goddess, grey-eyed Athene, had other thoughts. The night she held long in the utmost West, and on the other side she stayed the golden-throned Dawn by the stream Oceanus, and suffered her not to harness the swift-footed steeds that bear light to men.

Then at the last, Odysseus of many counsels spake to his wife, saying: 'Lady, we have not yet come to the issue of all our labours; but still there will be toil unmeasured, long and difficult, that I must needs bring to a full end. Even so the spirit of Teiresias foretold to me, on that day when I went down into the house of Hades, to inquire after a returning for myself and my company. Wherefore come, lady, let us to bed, that forthwith we may take our joy of rest beneath the spell of sweet sleep.'

Then wise Penelope answered him: 'Thy bed verily shall be ready whensoever thy soul desires it, forasmuch as the gods have indeed caused thee to come back to thy stablished home and thine own country. But now that thou hast noted it and the god has put it into thy heart, come, tell me of this ordeal, for methinks the day will come when I must learn it, and timely knowledge is no hurt.'

And Odysseus of many counsels answered her saying: 'Ah, why now art thou so instant with me to declare it? Yet I will tell thee all and hide nought. Howbeit thy heart shall have no joy of it, as even I myself have no pleasure therein. For Teiresias bade me fare to many cities of men, carrying a shapen oar in my hands, till I should come to such men as know not the sea, neither eat meat savoured with salt, nor have they knowledge of ships of purple cheek nor of shapen oars, which serve for wings to ships. And he told me this with manifest token, which I will not hide from thee. In the day when another way-farer should meet me and say that I had a winnowing fan on my stout shoulder, even then he bade me make fast my shapen oar in the earth, and do goodly sacrifice to the lord Poseidon, even with a ram and a bull and a boar, the mate of swine, and depart for home, and offer holy hecatombs to the deathless gods, that keep the wide heaven, to each in order due. And from the sea shall mine own death come, the gentlest death that may be, which shall end me, foredone with smooth old age, and the folk shall dwell happily around. All this, he said, was to be fulfilled.'

Then wise Penelope answered him saying: 'If indeed the gods will bring about for thee a happier old age at the last, then is there hope that thou mayest yet have an escape from evil.'

Thus they spake one to the other. Meanwhile, Eurynome and the nurse spread the bed with soft coverlets, by the light of the torches burning. But when they had busied them and spread the good bed, the ancient nurse went back to her chamber to lie down, and Eurynome, the bower-maiden, guided them on their way to the couch, with torches in her hands, and when she had led them to the bridal-chamber she departed. And so they came gladly to the rites of their bed, as of old.

Now when the twain had taken their fill of sweet love, they had delight in the tales, which they told one to the other. The fair lady spoke of all that she had endured in the halls at the sight of the ruinous throng of wooers. And in turn, Odysseus, of the seed of Zeus, recounted all the griefs he had wrought on men, and all his own travail and sorrow and she was delighted with the story, and sweet sleep fell not upon her eyelids till the tale was ended. . . . Then sweet sleep came speedily upon him, sleep that loosens the limbs of men, un-knitting the cares of his soul.

Then the goddess, grey-eyed Athene, turned to new thoughts. When she deemed that Odysseus had taken his fill of love and sleep, straightway she aroused from out Oceanus the golden throned Dawn, to bear light to men. Then Odysseus gat him up from his soft bed, and laid this charge on his wife, saying:

'Lady, already have we had enough of labours, thou and I; thou, in weeping here, and longing for my troublous return, I, while Zeus and the other gods bound me fast in pain, despite my yearning after home, away from mine own country. But now that we both have come to the bed of our desire, take thou thought for the care of my wealth within the halls. But as for the sheep that the proud wooers have slain,

I myself will lift many more as spoil, and others the Achaeans will give, till they fill all my folds. But now, behold, I go to the well-wooded farm-land, to see my good father, who for love of me has been in sorrow continually. And this charge I lay on thee, lady, too wise though thou art to need it. Quickly will the bruit go forth with the rising sun, the bruit concerning the wooers whom I slew in the halls. Wherefore ascend with the women thy handmaids into the upper chamber, and sit there and look on no man, nor ask any question.'

Therewith he girded on his shoulder his goodly armour, and roused Telemachus and the neatherd and the swineherd, and bade them all take weapons of war in their hands. So they were not disobedient to his word, but clad themselves in mail, and opened the doors and went forth, and Odysseus led the way. And now there was light over all the earth; but them Athene hid in night, and quickly conducted out of the town.

BOOK XXIV

. . . Now when those others had gone down from the city, quickly they came to the rich and well-ordered farm-land of Laertes, that he had won for himself of old, as the prize of great toil in war. There was his house, and all about it ran the huts wherein the thralls were wont to eat and dwell and sleep, bondsmen that worked his will. And in the house there was an old Sicilian woman, who diligently cared for the old man, in the upland far from the city. There Odysseus spake to his thralls and to his son, saying:

'Do ye now get you within the well-builded house, and quickly sacrifice the best of the swine for the midday meal, but I will make trial of my father, whether he will know me again and be aware of me when he sees me, or know me not, so long have I been away.'

Therewith he gave the thralls his weapons of war. Then they went speedily to the house, while Odysseus drew near to the fruitful vineyard to make trial of his father. Now he found not Dolius there, as he went down into the great garden, nor any of the thralls nor of their sons. It chanced that they had all gone to gather stones for a garden fence, and the old man at their head. So he found his father alone in the terraced vineyard, digging about a plant. He was clothed in a filthy doublet, patched and unseemly, with clouted leggings of oxhide bound about his legs, against the scratches of the thorns, and long sleeves over his hands by reason of the brambles, and on his head he wore a goatskin cap, and so he nursed his sorrow. Now when the steadfast goodly Odysseus saw his father thus wasted with age and in great grief of heart, he stood still beneath a tall pear tree and let fall a tear. Then he communed with his heart and soul, whether he should fall on his father's neck and kiss him, and tell him all, how he had returned and come to his own country, or whether he should first question him and prove him in every word. And as he thought within himself, this seemed to him the better way, namely, first to prove his father and speak to him sharply. So with this intent the goodly Odysseus went up to him. Now he was holding his head down and kept digging about the plant, while his renowned son stood by him and spake saying:

'Old man, thou hast no lack of skill in tending a garden; lo, thou carest well for all, nor is there aught whatsoever, either plant or fig tree, or vine, yea, or olive, or pear, or garden-bed in all the close, that is not well seen to. Yet another thing will I tell thee and lay not up wrath thereat in thy heart. Thyself art scarce so well cared for, but a pitiful old age is on thee, and withal thou art withered and unkempt, and clad ·unseemly. It cannot be to punish thy sloth that thy master cares not for thee; there shows nothing of the slave about thy face and stature, for thou art like a kingly man. Whose thrall art thou, and whose garden dost thou tend? Tell me moreover truly, that I may surely know, if it be indeed to Ithaca that I am now come, as one yonder told me who met with me but now on the way hither. He was but of little understanding, for he deigned not to tell me all nor to heed my saying, when I questioned him concerning my friend, whether indeed he is yet alive or is even now dead and within the house of Hades. For I will declare it and do thou mark and listen: once did I kindly entreat a man in mine own dear country, who came to our home, and never yet has any mortal been dearer of all the strangers that have drawn to my house from afar. He declared him to be by lineage from out of Ithaca, and said that his own father was Laertes son of Arceisius. So I led him to our halls and gave him good entertainment, with all loving-kindness, out of the plenty that was within. Such gifts too I gave him as are the due of guests; of well-wrought gold I gave him seven talents, and a mixing bowl of flowered work, all of silver, and twelve cloaks of single fold, and as many coverlets, and as many goodly mantles and doublets to boot, and besides all these, four women skilled in all fair works and most comely, the women of his choice.'

Then his father answered him, weeping: 'Stranger, thou art verily come to that country whereof thou askest, but outrageous men and froward hold it. And these thy gifts, thy countless gifts, thou didst bestow in vain. For if thou hadst found that man yet living in the land of Ithaca he would have sent thee on thy way with good return of thy presents, and with all hospitality, as is due to the man that begins the kindness. But come, declare me this and plainly tell me all; how many years are passed since thou didst entertain him, thy guest ill-fated and my child,—if ever such an one there was,—hapless man, whom far from his friends and his country's soil, the fishes, it may be, have devoured in the deep sea, or on the shore he has fallen the prey of birds and beasts. His mother wept not over him nor clad him for burial, nor his father, we that begat him. Nor did his bride, whom men sought with rich gifts, the constant Penelope, bewail her lord upon the bier, as was meet, nor closed his eyes, as is the due of the departed. Moreover, tell me this truly, that I may surely know, who art thou and whence of the sons of men? Where is thy city and where are they that begat thee? Where now is thy swift ship moored, that brought thee thither with thy godlike company? Hast thou come as a passenger on another's ship, while they set thee ashore and went away?'

Then Odysseus of many counsels answered him, saying: 'Yea now, I will tell thee all most plainly. From out of Alybas I come, where I dwell in a house renowned, and am the son of Apheidas the son of Polypemon, the prince, and my own name is Eperitus. But some god drave me wandering hither from Sicania against my will, and yonder my ship is moored toward the upland away from the city. But for Odysseus, this is now the fifth year since he went thence and departed out of my country. . . .'

So he spake, and on the old man fell a black cloud of sorrow. With both his hands he clutched the dust and ashes and showered them on his grey head, with ceaseless groaning. Then the heart of Odysseus was moved, and up through his nostrils throbbed anon the keen sting of sorrow at the sight of his dear father. And he sprang towards him and fell on his neck and kissed him, saying:

'Behold, I here, even I, my father, am the man of whom thou askest; in the twentieth year am I come to mine own country. But stay thy weeping and tearful lamentation, for I will tell thee all clearly, though great need there is of haste. I have slain the wooers in our halls and avenged their bitter scorn and evil deeds.'

Then Laertes answered him and spake, saying: 'If thou art indeed

Odysseus, mine own child, that art come hither, show me now a manifest token, that I may be assured.'

Then Odysseus of many counsels answered him saying: 'Look first on this scar and consider it, that the boar dealt me with his white tusk on Parnassus, whither I had gone, and thou didst send me forth, thou and my lady mother, to Autolycus my mother's father, to get the gifts which when he came hither he promised and covenanted to give me. But come, and I will even tell thee the trees through all the terraced garden, which thou gavest me once for mine own, and I was begging of thee this and that, being but a little child, and following thee through the garden. Through these very trees we were going, and thou didst tell me the names of each of them. Pear trees thirteen thou gavest me and ten apple trees and figs two-score, and, as we went, thou didst name the fifty rows of vines thou wouldest give me.'

So he spake, and straightway his knees were loosened, and his heart melted within him, as he knew the sure tokens that Odysseus showed him. About his dear son he cast his arms, and the steadfast goodly Odysseus caught him fainting to his breast. Now when he had got breath and his spirit came to him again, once more he answered and spake, saying:

'Father Zeus, verily ye gods yet bear sway on high Olympus, if indeed the wooers have paid for their infatuate pride! But now my heart is terribly afraid, lest straightway all the men of Ithaca come up against us here.'

Then Odysseus of many counsels answered him saying: 'Take courage, and let not thy heart be careful about these matters. But come, let us go to the house that lies near the garden, for thither I sent forward Telemachus and the neatherd and the swineherd to get ready the meal as speedily as may be.'

After these words the twain set out to the goodly halls. Now when they had come to the fair-lying house, they found Telemachus and the neatherd and the swineherd carving much flesh, and mixing the dark wine. Meanwhile the Sicilian handmaid bathed high-hearted Laertes in his house, and anointed him with olive-oil, and cast a fair mantle about him. Then Athene drew nigh, and made greater the limbs of the shepherd of the people, taller she made him than before and mightier to behold. Then he went forth from the bath, and his dear son marvelled at him, beholding him like to the deathless gods in presence. And uttering his voice he spake to him winged words:

'Father, surely one of the gods that are from everlasting hath made thee goodlier and greater to behold.'

Then wise Laertes answered him, saying: 'Ah, would to father Zeus and Athene and Apollo, that such as I was when I took Nericus, the stablished castle on the foreland of the continent, would that in such might, and with mail about my shoulders, I had stood to aid thee yesterday in our house, and to beat back the wooers; so should I have loosened the knees of many an one of them in the halls, and thou shouldest have been gladdened in thine inmost heart!'

So they spake each with the other. But when the others had ceased from their task and made ready the feast, they sat down all orderly on chairs and on high seats. Then they began to put forth their hands on the meat, and the old man Dolius drew nigh, and the old man's sons withal came tired from their labour in the fields. So soon as they looked on Odysseus and took knowledge of him they stood still in the halls in great amazement. But Odysseus addressed them in gentle words, saying:

'Old man, sit down to meat and do ye forget your marvelling, for long have we been eager to put forth our hands on the food, as we abode in the hall always expecting your coming.'

. . . So they were busy with the meal in the halls. Now Rumour the messenger went swiftly all about the city, telling the tale of the dire death and fate of the wooers. And the people heard it, and all at once gathered together from every side with sighing and groaning before the house of Odysseus. And each brought forth his dead from the halls, and buried them; but those that came out of other cities they placed on swift ships and sent with fisherfolk, each to be carried to his own home. As for them they all fared together to the assembly-place, in sorrow of heart. When they were all gathered and come together, Eupeithes arose and spake among them, for a comfortless grief lay heavy on his heart for his son Antinous, the first man that goodly Odysseus had slain. Weeping for him he made harangue and spake among them:

'Friends, a great deed truly hath this man devised against the Achaeans. Some with his ships he led away, many men and noble, and his hollow ships hath he lost, and utterly lost of his company, and others again he hath slain on his coming home. Up now, before ever he gets him swiftly either to Pylos or to fair Elis, let us go forth; else even hereafter shall we have shame of face for ever. For a scorn this is even for the ears of men unborn to hear, if we avenge not ourselves on the slayers of our sons and of our brethren.'

Thus he spake weeping, and pity fell on all the Achaeans. Then came near to them Medon and the divine minstrel, forth from the halls of Odysseus, for that sleep had let them go. They stood in the midst of the gathering, and amazement seized every man. Then Medon, wise of heart, spake among them, saying:

'Hearken to me now, ye men of Ithaca, for surely Odysseus planned not these deeds without the will of the gods. Nay I myself beheld a god immortal, who stood hard by Odysseus, in the perfect semblance of Mentor; now as a deathless god was he manifest in front of Odysseus, cheering him, and yet again scaring the wooers he stormed through the hall, and they fell thick one on another.'

Thus he spake, and pale fear gat hold of the limbs of all. Then the old man, the lord Halitherses, spake among them. Out of his good will he made harangue and spake among them, saying:

'Hearken to me now, ye men of Ithaca, to the word that I will say. Through your own cowardice, my friends, have these deeds come to pass. For ye obeyed not me, nor Mentor, the shepherd of the people, to make your sons cease from their foolish ways. A great villainy they wrought in their evil infatuation, wasting the wealth and holding in no regard the wife of a prince, while they deemed that he would never more come home. And now let things be on this wise, and obey my counsel. Let us not go forth against him, lest haply some may find a bane of their own bringing.'

So he spake, but they leapt up with a great cry, the more part of them, while the rest abode there together; for his counsel was not to the mind of the more part, but they gave ear to Eupeithes, and swiftly thereafter they rushed for their armour. So when they had arrayed them in shining mail, they assembled together in front of the spacious town. And Eupeithes led them in his witlessness, for he thought to avenge the slaying of his son, yet himself was never to return, but then and there to meet his doom.

Now Athene spake to Zeus, the son of Cronos, saying: 'O Father, our father Cronides, throned in the highest, answer and tell me what is now the hidden counsel of thy heart? Wilt thou yet further rouse up evil war and the terrible din of battle, or art thou minded to set them at one again in friendship?'

Then Zeus, the gatherer of the clouds, answered her saying: 'My child, why dost thou thus straitly question me, and ask me this? Nay, didst not thou thyself devise this very thought, namely, that Odysseus should indeed take vengeance on these men at his coming? Do as thou wilt, but I will tell thee of the better way. Now that goodly Odysseus hath wreaked vengeance on the wooers, let them make a firm covenant together with sacrifice, and let him be king all his days, and let us bring about oblivion of the slaying of their children and their brethren; so may both sides love one another as of old, and let peace and wealth abundant be their portion.'

Therewith he roused Athene to yet greater eagerness, and from the peaks of Olympus she came glancing down.

Now when they had put from them the desire of honey-sweet food, the steadfast goodly Odysseus began to speak among them, saying:

'Let one go forth and see, lest the people be already drawing near against us.'

So he spake, and the son of Dolius went forth at his bidding, and stood on the outer threshold and saw them all close at hand. Then straightway he spake to Odysseus winged words:

'Here they be, close upon us! Quick, let us to arms!'

Thereon they rose up and arrayed them in their harness, Odysseus and his men being four, and the six sons of Dolius, and likewise Laertes and Dolius did on their armour, grey-headed as they were, warriors through stress of need. Now when they had clad them in shining mail, they opened the gates and went forth and Odysseus led them.

Then Athene, daughter of Zeus, drew near them in the likeness of Mentor, in fashion and in voice. And the steadfast goodly Odysseus beheld her and was glad, and straightway he spake to Telemachus his dear son:

'Telemachus, soon shalt thou learn this, when thou thyself art got to the place of the battle where the best men try the issue,—namely, not to bring shame on thy father's house, on us who in time past have been eminent for might and hardihood over all the world.'

Then wise Telemachus answered him, saying: 'Thou shalt see me, if thou wilt, dear father, in this my mood no whit disgracing thy line, according to thy word.'

So spake he, and Laertes was glad and spake, saying: 'What a day has dawned for me, kind gods; yea, a glad man am I! My son and my son's son are vying with one another in valour.'

Then grey-eyed Athene stood beside Laertes, and spake to him: 'O son of Arceisius that art far the dearest of all my friends, pray first to the grey-eyed maid and to father Zeus, then swing thy long spear aloft and hurl it straightway.'

Therewith Pallas Athene breathed into him great strength. Then he prayed to the daughter of mighty Zeus, and straightway swung his long spear aloft and hurled it, and smote Eupeithes through his casque with the cheekpiece of bronze. The armour kept not out the spear that went clean through, and he fell with a crash, and his arms rattled about his body. Then Odysseus and his renowned son fell on the fore-fighters, and smote them with swords and two-headed spears. And now would they have slain them all and cut off their return, had not Athene called aloud, the daughter of Zeus lord of the aegis, and stayed all the host of the enemy, saying:

'Hold your hands from fierce fighting, ye men of Ithaca, that so ye may be parted quickly, without bloodshed.'

So spake Athene, and pale fear gat hold of them all. The arms flew from their hands in their terror and fell all upon the ground, as the goddess uttered her voice. To the city they turned their steps, as men fain of life, and the steadfast goodly Odysseus with a terrible cry gathered himself together and hurled in on them, like an eagle of lofty flight. Then in that hour the son of Cronos cast forth a flaming bolt, and it fell at the feet of the grey-eyed goddess, the daughter of the mighty Sire. Then grey-eyed Athene spake to Odysseus, saying:

'Son of Laertes, of the seed of Zeus, Odysseus of many devices, re-frain thee now and stay the strife of even-handed war, lest perchance the son of Cronos be angry with thee, even Zeus of the far-borne voice.'

So spake Athene, and he obeyed and was glad at heart. And there-after Pallas Athene set a covenant between them with sacrifice, she, the daughter of Zeus lord of the aegis, in the likeness of Mentor, both in fashion and in voice.

SOPHOCLES

Oedipus the King

GREEK TRAGEDY was practically a monopoly of Athens, and its history closely parallels the rise, power, and decline of that city-state. Thus its course is largely run in the fifth century B.C.

At the beginning of this period, the mighty Persian Empire undertook the conquest of Greece, and Athens bore the brunt of the onslaught. When the Persians made a landing at Marathon in 490 B.C., they were repulsed by the Athenians alone—Sparta had refused to send aid because the phase of the moon was not propitious. Later, the Persians crossed the Hellespont and, in spite of the heroic stand made by the Spartans and Thespians at Thermopylae, marched on into Greece, and burned Athens; but in the same year (480 B.C.) they suffered a naval defeat at Salamis which destroyed their last real hope of conquering Greece. Athens had a large share in this victory, and was able to organize a league for mutual defense and build her prestige into real power. During the next seventy years this little democracy of slightly more than a hundred thousand inhabitants produced a flowering of the human spirit unique in history. The latter years of the century, however, were clouded by the Peloponnesian War, which arose from the rivalry of Athens and Sparta, and ended with the Athenian surrender in 404 B.C.

The three great writers of Greek tragedy were all connected in one way or another with the Persian War. Aeschylus (525-456 B.C.), already a recognized playwright, fought with distinction at Marathon; Sophocles (c.496-406 B.C.) was chosen by his city to lead the band of Athenian youths who danced in celebration of the victory at Salamis; and, if legend is to be trusted, Euripides (c.480-406 B.C.) was born on the island of Salamis on the day of the great battle. When we note that both Sophocles and Euripides died two years before the disastrous end of the Peloponnesian War, we see how exactly the lives of the great tragedians cover the period of Athens' greatness.

Sophocles is a fine example of the type of genius which involves a perfect balance of all faculties, and though few significant details of his life are known, the general picture comes out clearly. He won more victories in dramatic competitions than any other writer, and was so popular that the Athenians bestowed on him various military and political offices, among them one of the ten elective generalships of the city, the highest honor in their gift. But when we consider that he wrote more than a hundred and twenty plays (only seven of which survive), we must realize that the major part of his life was devoted to poetry. So it continued to the end. There is an interesting story to the effect that Sophocles' son, fearing to be disinherited in favor of a grandson, haled the old man (now nearly ninety) into court and sought to get possession of the property on the ground that his father was mentally incompetent. Sophocles' only defense was to read a chorus from the *Oedipus at Colonus,* which he had just written. The judges promptly threw the case out of court: no man in his dotage could write such poetry. Happily, Sophocles died shortly before the Peloponnesian War closed the greatest period of Athenian culture. A year after his death, and just before the surrender to Sparta, Sophocles' friend, the comic poet Aristophanes, described him as "happy among the living, happy among the dead." And twenty-three centuries later Matthew Arnold paid his famous tribute to Sophocles as a man "who saw life steadily and saw it whole."

In his plays, as in his life, he gains his effects without straining or eccentricity. When he began to write, the general form of tragedy was already well established, though he made some innovations such as increasing the standard chorus from twelve to fifteen, and introducing a third actor so that the scenes between characters of the play were not literally confined to dialogue. These, however, were simply technical improvements designed to help in producing the effects already established as proper to tragedy.

Euripides differs from Sophocles in almost every respect. He was unsociable and unpopular. Though he wrote some ninety plays (only eighteen of which survive), he won the first prize only five times. He was a rebel against the conventions of his age, and a freethinker in matters of religion and morality. He began his career as a successful athlete, but abandoned this calling for the theater, and later declared that "of all the million plagues of Greece none is worse than the tribe of athletes." His plays were a constant target for the ridicule of the comic poets, though the high esteem in which Socrates held them may have gone far to balance accounts. His doctrines were often considered dangerous, and he finally left Athens and went to the court of King Archelaus of Macedonia, shortly before his death.

In his plays, the traditional legends are freely handled and frequently altered to suit his own purposes. He is not so much interested in man's struggle against fate, or even against other men, as in his struggle against himself. And it may be added that, for him, man usually turns out to be woman—almost all his great characterizations are of women. His particular type of interest is readily visible in the *Medea,* a study of raging jealousy finally triumphing over maternal affection. Here the struggle is not that of a man like Oedipus enmeshed in his fate, or a woman like Antigone unswervingly following her principles to her death, but rather the battle of opposing impulses in his heroine's mind. There is only one real character in this play, because actually the play takes place within her. Euripides takes nothing for granted—the gods are not necessarily just or respectable; women may be higher and more interesting characters than men; small farmers are likely to be better men than kings. In a word, he invented what we have come to call the "problem play," and it is characteristic of this type of drama that its audience is not certain just what to make of it.

The plays of Sophocles and Euripides will be much more accessible to the modern reader if he has some knowledge of the conditions which produced them. Greek drama, like that of India, of Japan, and of Europe in the Middle Ages, developed from religious ritual. The festival of Dionysus, or Bacchus, god of fertility and of wine, was early celebrated by a chorus of revelers, who soon began singing some of the adventures of the god. The goat (Greek *tragos*) was sacred to Dionysus, and his worshipers wore goat skins to chant the ode (Greek *ōdē*) in his honor; from the two Greek words comes *tragedy.* Dialogue was used between leader and chorus, and a certain amount of mimicry and acting soon entered in. Aeschylus created real drama by introducing a second actor, so that it was possible to have dialogue plus a chorus. While technical improvements were going on, the scope of drama was also being extended from the life of Dionysus to any historical or legendary material (and it would have been impossible sharply to distinguish history from legend) which had dramatic possibilities. Frequently the subject had some specific local significance, such as the good fortune to follow the burial of Oedipus at Athens in the *Oedipus at Colonus.*

In the earlier period, tragedies were written in groups of three, each complete in itself, but the entire trilogy dealing with one large subject. One such trilogy survives, Aeschylus' *Agamemnon, Libation-Bearers,* and *Eumenides,* tracing the results to the house of Atreus of Agamemnon's return from Troy. (Eugene O'Neill's *Mourning Becomes Electra* is a modernization of this group of plays.) To the three tragedies was attached a satyr-play, a licentious burlesque of one of the myths or legends. The group of four plays (three tragedies and a satyr-play) remained standard, but Sophocles led the way in allowing the tragedies to be entirely independent of each other. Though the following selections consider three of his plays tracing the history of the House of Oedipus, they are not a trilogy. In the order of events the first of the series is *Oedipus the King,* probably written about 430 B.C.; the second is *Oedipus at Colonus,* written about 406 B.C. and performed posthumously in 401 B.C.; and the third, *Antigone,* was the first one to be written, about 441 B.C. The differing characterizations of Creon in these plays are explained by the fact that they were not written as a connected series.

The group of four plays was the standard entry in the dramatic competitions at which all Athenian dramas were produced. There were two of these festivals annually, the more important one being the Great Dionysia in the spring. This was, as the name indicates, a festival in honor of Dionysus, and it included various processions and celebrations, but the climax of the festival was the three days' dramatic contest held in the outdoor Theater of Dionysus, which seated about

17,000 spectators. It is hard for the modern reader to appreciate the exact atmosphere of such performances. The combination of religious and artistic event is duplicated by a present-day performance of Bach's *St. Matthew Passion* or Handel's *Messiah,* but the dramatic competition had also the community spirit of a civic undertaking and the interest (and partisanship) of a contest. There was no commercial element whatsoever: the city furnished the actors, wealthy citizens trained the choruses at their own expense, there was no charge for admission,[1] and the only prizes were laurel wreaths and honor.

Like all drama, that of the Greeks was conditioned by the theater for which it was written. This was an outdoor semicircle somewhat like the closed end of a modern stadium, with a large level *orchestra* ("place for dancing") in the center. This space contained the altar of Dionysus. Behind it, from the point of view of the audience, was a slightly raised porch or entrance-platform to a façade of the general type familiar in Greek temples. The principal action took place here, in the open, with characters entering or leaving through one of the three doors of the façade, which might represent a palace, a temple, or any other type of building demanded by the play. Since the action of a drama was continuous and the chorus was always present, verisimilitude required that the plot be confined to one place and a single day, though there were occasional exceptions to this "rule." The vast size of the theater made facial expression useless in acting, and hence all actors wore symbolical masks indicating their status and dominant characteristics. They were built up to superhuman size by thick-soled shoes and high head-dress. Thus the whole performance was stylized rather than realistic, and this effect was heightened by the music used for the choral odes and the stately dancing of the chorus.

The reader who comes to classical tragedy will probably have the Shakespearean type as his standard of comparison. The methods of these two dramatic forms are different, as are the effects achieved. The small cast and limited time of Greek tragedy prevent it from attaining the breadth and sweep of Elizabethan drama, but in return they give a speed, a concentration, and an inevitability which the larger form cannot produce.

Greek drama was borrowed and imitated by the Romans, who

1. At first there was no charge; later the price was two *obols* (that is, less than a nickel), and this was refunded by the state to anyone unable to afford it.

made no real contribution of their own. After the fall of the Roman Empire a few Latin plays continued to be read throughout the Middle Ages, but they had no effect on the independent rediscovery of drama during this period. With the Renaissance, however, the Greco-Roman dramatic tradition was revived as an important influence on Shakespeare and the other Elizabethans, and as the foundation of the Neo-Classical drama which reached its highest point in France with the works of Corneille, Racine, and Molière.

ŒDIPUS THE KING

Persons of the Drama

ŒDIPUS, *king of Thebes*
PRIEST *of Zeus*
CREON, *brother of Jocasta, the queen*
TEIRESIAS, *a prophet, with the title of king*
A MESSENGER *from Corinth*
AN OLD SHEPHERD
A SECOND MESSENGER, *servant to Œdipus' household*
JOCASTA, *queen, wife of Œdipus, formerly married to Laios, the last king*
ANTIGONE ⎫
                 ⎬ *daughters of Œdipus and Jocasta*
ISMENE   ⎭
CHORUS OF SENATORS OF THEBES
INHABITANTS *of Thebes*
ATTENDANTS
A BOY *leading Teiresias*

SCENE.—THEBES. *In the background, the palace of ŒDIPUS; in front, the altar of ZEUS, Priests and Boys round it in the attitude of suppliants, with olive and laurel branches in their hands, entwined with woollen threads.*

[*Enter ŒDIPUS.*]

ŒDIPUS. Why sit ye here, my children, youngest brood
Of Cadmos[1] famed of old, in solemn state,
Your hands thus wreathèd with suppliants' boughs?
And all the city reeks with incense smoke,
And all re-echoes with your hymns and groans;
And I, my children, counting it unmeet
To hear report from others, I have come
Myself, whom all name Œdipus the Great.—
Do thou, then, agèd Sire, since thine the right
To speak for these, tell clearly how you stand,
In terror or submission; speak to me
As willing helper. Heartless should I be
To see you prostrate, thus, and feel no ruth.
    PRIEST. Yea, Œdipus, thou ruler of my land,
Thou seest our age, who sit as suppliants, bowed
Around thine altars; some as yet too weak
For distant flight, and some weighed down with age,
Priest, I, of Zeus, and these the chosen youth:
And in the market-places of the town
The people sit and wail, with wreath in hand,
By the two shrines of Pallas, or the grave,
Where still the seer Ismenos prophesies,
For this our city, as thine eyes may see,
Is sorely tempest-tossed, nor lifts its head
From out the surging sea of blood-flecked waves,
All smitten in the ripening blooms of earth,
All smitten in the herds that graze the fields,
Yea, and in timeless births of woman's fruit;
And still the God, fire-darting Pestilence,
As deadliest foe, upon our city swoops,
And desolates the home where Cadmos dwelt,
And Hades dark grows rich in sighs and groans.
It is not that we deem of thee as one
Equaled with gods in power, that we sit here,
These little ones and I, as suppliants prone;
But, judging thee, in all life's shifting scenes,
Chiefest of men, yea, and of chiefest skill
In communings with Heaven. For thou did'st come
And freed'st the city, named of Cadmos old,

  1. *Cadmos*, legendary founder of Thebes.

From the sad tribute which of yore we paid
To that stern songstress,[2] all untaught of us,
And all unprompted; but by gift of God,
Men think and say, thou did'st our life upraise,
And now, dear Œdipus, most honored lord,
We pray thee, we thy suppliants, find for us
Some succor, whether voice of any God,
Or any man brings knowledge to thy soul;
For still I see, with those whom life has trained
To long-tried skill, the issues of their thoughts
Live and are mighty. Come then, noblest one,
Raise up our city; come, take heed to it;
As yet this land, for all thy former zeal,
Calls thee its savior: do not give us cause
So to remember this thy reign, as men
Who having risen, then fall low again;
But raise our state to safety. Omens good
Were then with thee; thou did'st thy work, and now
Be equal to thyself! If thou wilt rule,
As thou dost sway, this land wherein we dwell,
'Twere better far to rule o'er living men
Than o'er a realm dispeopled. Nought avails,
Or tower or ship, when men are not within.

    ŒDIPUS. O children, wailing loud, ye come with wish
Well-known, not unknown; well I know that ye
Are smitten, one and all, with taint of plague,
And yet though smitten, none that taint of plague
Feels, as I feel it. Each his burden bears,
His own and not another's; but my heart
Mourns for the state, for you, and for myself;
And, lo, ye wake me not as plunged in sleep,
But find me weeping, weeping many tears,
And treading many paths in wandering thought;
And that one way of health I, seeking, found,
This have I acted on. Menœkeus' son,

2. *songstress*, the Sphinx. She was a monster who had plagued Thebes, asking
people a riddle and killing those who could not answer it. Creon offered the
kingdom of Thebes and his sister Jocasta's hand in marriage to whoever would
rid the city of this pest. Œdipus answered the riddle, and the Sphinx thereupon
killed herself. It was in this way that Œdipus came to marry Jocasta and
become King of Thebes.

Creon, my kinsman, have I sent to seek
The Pythian home of Phœbos, there to learn
The words or deeds wherewith to save the state;
And even now I measure o'er the time,
And ask, "How fares he?" grieving, for he stays,
Most strangely, far beyond the appointed day;
But when he comes, I should be base indeed,
Failing to do whate'er the God declares.

PRIEST. Well hast thou spoken! And these bring me word,
That Creon comes advancing on his way.

ŒDIPUS. O king Apollo, may he come with chance
That brings deliverance, as his looks are bright.

PRIEST. If one may guess, he's glad. He had not come
Crowned with rich wreaths of fruitful laurel else.

ŒDIPUS. Soon we shall know. Our voice can reach him now.
Say, prince, our well-beloved, Menœkeus' son,
What sacred answer bring'st thou from the God?

[*Enter* CREON.]

CREON. A right good answer! E'en our evil plight,
If all goes well, may end in highest good.

ŒDIPUS. What were the words? Nor full of eager hope,
Nor trembling panic, list I to thy speech.

CREON. I, if thou wish, am ready, these being by,
To tell thee all, or go within the gates.

ŒDIPUS. Speak out to all. I sorrow more for them
Than for the woe which touches me alone.

CREON. I then will speak what from the god I heard:
King Phœbos bids us chase the plague away
(The words were plain) now cleaving to our land,
Nor cherish guilt which still remains unhealed.

ŒDIPUS. But with what rites? And what the deed itself?

CREON. Or drive far off or blood for blood repay;
That guilt of blood is blasting all the state.

ŒDIPUS. But whose fate is it that He pointeth to?

CREON. Once, O my king, ere thou did'st guide our state,
Our sovereign Laios ruled o'er all the land.

ŒDIPUS. So have I heard, for him I never saw.

CREON. Now the God clearly bids us, he being dead,
To take revenge on those who shed his blood.

ŒDIPUS. Yes; but where are they? How to track the course
Of guilt all shrouded in the doubtful past?

CREON. In this our land, so said He; those who seek
Shall find; unsought, we lose it utterly.

ŒDIPUS. Was it at home, or in the field, or else
In some strange land that Laios met his doom?

CREON. He went, so spake he, pilgrim-wise afar,
And never more came back as forth he went.

ŒDIPUS. Was there no courier, none who shared his road,
Who knew what, learning, one might turn to good?

CREON. Dead were they all, save one who fled for fear,
And he knew nought to tell but one small fact.

ŒDIPUS. [Interrupting.] And what was that? One fact might
    teach us much,
Had we but one small starting-point of hope.

CREON. He used to tell that robbers fell on him,
Not man for man, but with outnumbering force.

ŒDIPUS. How could the robber e'er have dared this deed,
Unless some bribe from hence had tempted him?

CREON. So men might think; but Laios having died,
There was no helper for us in our ills.

ŒDIPUS. What ill then hindered, when your sovereignty
Had fallen thus, from searching out the truth?

CREON. The Sphinx, with her dark riddle, bade us look
At nearer facts, and leave the dim obscure.

ŒDIPUS. Well, be it mine to track them to their source.
Right well hath Phœbos, and right well hast thou,
Shown for the dead your care, and ye shall find,
As is most meet, in me a helper true,
Aiding at once my country and the God.
It is not for the sake of friends remote,
But for mine own, that I dispel this pest;
For he that slew him, whosoe'er he be,
Will wish, perchance, with such a blow to smite
Me also. Helping him, I help myself.
And now, my children, rise with utmost speed
From off these steps, and raise your suppliant boughs;
And let another call my people here,
The race of Cadmos, and make known that I
Will do my taskwork to the uttermost;

So, as God wills, we prosper, or we fail.

PRIEST. Rise then, my children, 'twas for this we came,
For these good tidings which those lips have brought,
And Phœbos, who hath sent these oracles,
Pray that He come to save, and heal our plague.

> [*Exeunt* CREON, *Priest, and Suppliants, the latter taking
> their boughs from the altar and bearing them as
> they march in procession.*]

> [*Enter* CHORUS OF THEBAN CITIZENS.]

STROPHE I

CHORUS. O word of Zeus,[3] glad-voiced, with what intent
> From Pytho, bright with gold,
Cam'st thou to Thebes, our city of high fame?
> For lo! I faint for fear,
Through all my soul I quiver in suspense,
(Hear, Io Pæan! God of Delos,[4] hear!)
In brooding dread, what doom, of present growth,
Or as the months roll on, thy hand will work;
Tell me, O deathless Voice, thou child of golden hope!

ANTISTROPHE I

Thee first, Zeus-born Athena, thee I call,
> Divine and deathless One,
And next thy sister, Goddess of our land,
> Our Artemis, who sits,
Queen of our market, on encircled throne;
And Phœbos, the far-darter! O ye Three,
Shine on us, and deliver us from ill!
If e'er before, when storms of woe oppressed,
Ye stayed the fiery tide, O come and help us now!

STROPHE II

Ah me, ah me, for sorrows numberless
> Press on my soul;

3. Apollo's oracle is considered as voicing the will of Zeus.
4. *God of Delos*, Apollo.

And all the host is smitten, and our thoughts
    Lack weapons to resist.
For increase fails of fruits of goodly earth,
And women sink in childbirth's wailing pangs,
    And one by one, as flit
    The swift-winged birds through air,
So, flitting to the shore of Him[5] who dwells
    Down in the darkling West,
    Fleeter than mightiest fire,
    Thou see'st them passing on.

ANTISTROPHE II

Yea, numberless are they who perish thus;
    And on the earth,
Still breeding plague, unpitied infants lie,
    Cast out all ruthlessly;
And wives and mothers, gray with hoary age,
Some here, some there, by every altar mourn,
    With woe and sorrow crushed,
    And chant their wailing plaint.
Clear thrills the sense their solemn Pæan cry,
    And the sad anthem song;
    Hear, golden child of Zeus,
    And send us bright-eyed help.

STROPHE III

And Ares the destroyer drive away!
    Who now, though hushed the din
    Of brazen shield and spear,
    With fiercest battle-cry
    Wars on me mightily.
    Bid him go back in flight,
    Retreat from this our land,
    Or to the ocean bed,
    Where Amphitrite sleeps,
Or to that haven of the homeless sea
    Which sweeps the Thracian shore.

5. *Him*, Hades.

If waning night spares aught,
That doth the day assail:
Do thou, then, Sire almighty,
Wielding the lightning's strength,
Blast him with thy dread fiery thunderbolts.

ANTISTROPHE III

And thou, Lykeian king, the wolf's dread foe,
Fain would I see thy darts
From out thy golden bow
Go forth invincible,
Helping and bringing aid;
And with them, winged with fire,
The rays of Artemis,
With which on Lykian hills,
She moveth on her course.
And last, O golden-crowned, I call on thee,
Named after this our land,
Bacchos, all flushed with wine,
With clamor loud and long,
Wandering with Mænads wild,
Flashing with blazing torch,
Draw near against the God[6] whom all the Gods disown.

ŒDIPUS.   Thou prayest, and for thy prayers, if thou wilt hear
My words, and treat the dire disease with skill,
Thou shalt find help and respite from thy pain,—
My words, which I, a stranger to report,
A stranger to the deed, will now declare:
For I myself should fail to track it far,
Finding no trace to guide my steps aright.
But now, as I have joined you since the deed,
A citizen with citizens, I speak
To all the sons of Cadmos. Lives there one
Who knows of Laios, son of Labdacos,
The hand that slew him; him I bid to tell
His tale to me; and should it chance he shrinks
From raking up the charge against himself,

6. *God*, Ares, the cause of the pestilence.

Still let him speak; no heavier doom is his
Than to depart uninjured from the land;
Or, if there be that knows an alien arm
As guilty, let him hold his peace no more;
I will secure his gain and thanks beside.
But if ye hold your peace, if one through fear,
Or for himself, or friend, shall hide this thing,
What then I purpose let him hear from me.
That man I banish, whosoe'er he be,
From out this land whose power and throne are mine;
And none may give him shelter, none speak to him,
Nor join with him in prayers and sacrifice,
Nor give him share in holy lustral stream;
But all shall thrust him from their homes, declared
Our curse and our pollution, as but now
The Pythian God's prophetic word has shown:
With acts like this, I stand before you here,
A helper to the God and to the dead.
All this I charge you do, for mine own sake,
And for the God's, and for this land that pines,
Barren and god-deserted. Wrong 'twould be
E'en if no voice from heaven had urged us on,
That ye should leave the stain of guilt uncleansed,
Your noblest chief, your king himself, being slain.
Yea, rather, seek and find. And since I reign,
Wielding the might his hand did wield before,
Filling his couch, and calling his wife mine,
Yea, and our offspring too, but for the fate
That fell on his, had grown in brotherhood;
But now an evil chance on his head swooped;
And therefore will I strive my best for him,
As for my father, and will go all lengths
To seek and find the murderer, him who slew
The son of Labdacos, and Polydore,
And earlier Cadmos, and Agenor old;
And for all those who hearken not, I pray
The Gods to give them neither fruit of earth,
Nor seed of woman, but consume their lives
With this dire plague, or evil worse than this.
And for the man who did the guilty deed,

Whether alone he lurks, or leagued with more,
I pray that he may waste his life away,
For vile deeds, vilely dying; and for me,
If in my house, I knowing it, he dwells,
May every curse I spake on my head fall.
And you, the rest, the men from Cadmos sprung,
To whom these words approve themselves as good,
May Righteousness befriend you, and the Gods,
In full accord, dwell with you evermore.

CHORUS. Since thou hast bound me by a curse, O king,
I will speak thus. I neither slew the man,
Nor know who slew. To say who did the deed
Is quest for Him who sent us on the search.

ŒDIPUS. Right well thou speak'st, man's best strength must fail
To force the Gods to do the things they will not.

CHORUS. Fain would I speak the thoughts that second stand.

ŒDIPUS. Though there be third, shrink not from speaking out.

CHORUS. One man I know, a prince, whose insight deep
Sees clear as princely Phœbos, and from him,
Teiresias, one might learn, O king, the truth.

ŒDIPUS. That too is done. No loiterer I in this,
For I, on Creon's hint, two couriers sent
To summon him, and wonder that he comes not.

CHORUS. Old rumors are there also, dark and dumb.

ŒDIPUS. And what are they? I weigh the slightest word.

CHORUS. 'Twas said he died by some chance traveler's hand.

ŒDIPUS. I, too, heard that. But none the eye-witness sees.

CHORUS. If yet his soul be capable of awe,
Hearing thy curses, he will shrink from them.

ŒDIPUS. Words fright not him, who doing, knows no fear.

CHORUS. Well, here is one who'll put him to the proof.
For lo! they bring the seer inspired of God,
With whom alone of all men, truth abides.

[*Enter* TEIRESIAS, *blind and guided by a boy.*]

ŒDIPUS. Teiresias! thou whose mind embraceth all,
Told or untold, of heaven or paths of earth;
Thou knowest, although thou see'st not, what a pest
Dwells on us, and we find in thee, O prince,
Our one deliverer, yea, our only help.

For Phœbos (if the couriers told thee not)
Sent back this word to us, who sent to ask,
That this one way was open to escape
From this fell plague,—if those who Laios slew,
We in our turn discovering should slay,
Or drive them forth as exiles from the land.
Thou, therefore, grudge not either sign from birds,
Or any other path of prophecy;
But save the city, save thyself, save me;
Save from the curse the dead has left behind;
On thee we hang. To use our means, our power,
In doing good, is noblest service owned.

TEIRESIAS. Ah me! ah me! how dread is wisdom's gift,
When no good issue waiteth on the wise!
I knew it all too well, and then forgot,
Or else I had not on this journey come.

ŒDIPUS. What means this? How despondingly thou com'st!

TEIRESIAS. Let me go home! for thus thy lot shalt thou,
And I mine own, bear easiest, if thou yield.

ŒDIPUS. No loyal words thou speak'st, nor true to Thebes
Who reared thee, holding back this oracle.

TEIRESIAS. I see thy lips speak words that profit not:
And lest I too a like fault should commit—

ŒDIPUS. Now, by the Gods, unless thy reason fails,
Refuse us not, who all implore thy help.

TEIRESIAS. Ah! Reason fails you all, but ne'er will I
Say what thou bidd'st, lest I thy troubles show.

ŒDIPUS. What mean'st thou, then? Thou know'st and wilt not
            tell,
But wilt betray us, and the state destroy?

TEIRESIAS. I will not pain myself nor thee. Why, then,
All vainly question? Thou shalt never know.

ŒDIPUS. Oh, basest of the base! (for thou would'st stir
A heart of stone); and wilt thou never tell,
But still abide relentless and unmoved?

TEIRESIAS. My mood thou blamest, but thou dost not know
What dwelleth with thee while thou chidest me.

ŒDIPUS. And who would not feel anger, hearing words
Like those with which thou dost the state insult?

TEIRESIAS. Well! come they will, though I should hold my peace.

ŒDIPUS. If come they must, thy duty is to speak.

TEIRESIAS. I speak no more. So, if thou wilt, rage on,
With every mood of wrath most desperate.

ŒDIPUS. Yes; I will not refrain, so fierce my wrath,
From speaking all my thought. I think that thou
Did'st plot the deed, and do it, though the blow
Thy hands, it may be, dealt not. Had'st thou seen,
I would have said it was thy deed alone.

TEIRESIAS. And has it come to this? I charge thee, hold
To thy late edict, and from this day forth
Speak not to me, nor yet to these, for thou,
Thou art the accursèd plague-spot of the land.

ŒDIPUS. Art thou so shameless as to vent such words,
And dost thou think to 'scape scot-free for this?

TEIRESIAS. I have escaped. The strength of truth is mine.

ŒDIPUS. Who prompted thee? This comes not from thine art.

TEIRESIAS. 'Twas thou. Thou mad'st me speak against my will.

ŒDIPUS. What say'st thou? Speak again, that I may know.

TEIRESIAS. Did'st thou not know before? Or dost thou try me?

ŒDIPUS. I could not say I knew it. Speak again.

TEIRESIAS. I say thou art the murderer whom thou seek'st.

ŒDIPUS. Thou shalt not twice revile, and go unharmed.

TEIRESIAS. And shall I tell thee more to stir thy rage?

ŒDIPUS. Say what thou pleasest. 'Twill be said in vain.

TEIRESIAS. I say that thou, in vilest intercourse
With those that dearest are, dost blindly live,
Nor see'st the depth of evil thou hast reached.

ŒDIPUS. And dost thou think to say these things unscathed?

TEIRESIAS. I doubt it not, if truth retain her might.

ŒDIPUS. That might is not for thee; thou can'st not claim it,
Blind in thine ears, thy reason, and thine eyes.

TEIRESIAS. How wretched thou, thus hurling this reproach!
Such, all too soon, will all men hurl at thee.

ŒDIPUS. In one long night thou liv'st, and can'st not hurt,
Or me, or any man who sees the light.

TEIRESIAS. 'Tis not thy doom to owe thy fall to me;
Apollo is enough, be His the task.

ŒDIPUS. Are these devices Creon's, or thine own?

TEIRESIAS. It is not Creon harms thee, but thyself.

ŒDIPUS. O wealth, and sovereignty, and noblest skill

Surpassing skill in life so envy-fraught,
How great the ill-will dogging all your steps!
If for the sake of kingship, which the state
Hath given, unasked for, freely in mine hands,
Creon the faithful, found my friend throughout,
Now seeks with masked attack to drive me forth,
And hires this wizard, plotter of foul schemes,
A vagrant mountebank, whose sight is clear
For pay alone, but in his art stone-blind.
Is it not so? When wast thou true seer found?
Why, when the monster with her song was here,
Spak'st thou no word our countrymen to help?
And yet the riddle lay above the ken
Of common men, and called for prophet's skill.
And this thou show'dst thou had'st not, nor by bird,
Nor any God made known; but then I came,
I, Œdipus, who nothing know, and slew her,
With mine own counsel winning, all untaught
By flight of birds. And now thou would'st expel me,
And think'st to take thy stand by Creon's throne.
But, as I think, both thou and he that plans
With thee, will hunt this mischief to your cost;
And but that I must think of thee as old,
Thou had'st learnt wisdom, suffering what thou plann'st.

   CHORUS. Far as we dare to guess, we think his words,
And thine, O Œdipus, in wrath are said.
Not such as these we need, but this to see,
How best to solve the God's great oracles.

   TEIRESIAS. King though thou be, I claim an equal right
To make reply. That power, at least, is mine:
For I am not thy slave, but Loxias';[7]
Nor shall I stand on Creon's patronage:
And this I say, since thou my blindness mock'st,
That thou, though seeing, failest to perceive
Thy evil plight, nor where thou liv'st, nor yet
With whom thou dwellest. Know'st thou even this,
Whence thou art sprung? All ignorant thou sinn'st
Against thine own, beneath, and on the earth:
And soon a two-edged Curse from sire and mother,

  7. *Loxias'*, Apollo's.

With foot of fear, shall chase thee forth from us,
Now seeing all things clear, then all things dark.
And will not then each creek repeat thy wail,
Each valley of Kithæron echoing ring,
When thou discern'st the marriage, fatal port,
To which thy prosp'rous voyage brought thy bark?
And other ills, in countless multitude,
Thou see'st not yet, shall make thy lot as one
With sire's and child's. Vent forth thy wrath then loud,
On Creon, and my speech. There lives not man
Whose life shall waste more wretchedly than thine.

 Œdipus. Can this be longer borne! Away with thee!
A curse light on thee! Wilt thou not depart?
Wilt thou not turn and from this house go back?

 Teiresias. I had not come, had'st thou not called me here.

 Œdipus. I knew not thou would'st speak so foolishly;
Else I had hardly fetched thee to my house.

 Teiresias. We then, so seems it thee, are fools from birth,
But, unto those who gave thee birth, seem wise.

              [Turns to go.]

 Œdipus. [*Starting forward.*] What? Stay thy foot. What mortal
   gave me birth?

 Teiresias. This day shall give thy birth, and work thy doom.

 Œdipus. What riddles dark and dim thou lov'st to speak.

 Teiresias. Yes. But thy skill excels in solving such.

 Œdipus. Scoff thou at that in which thou'lt find me strong.

 Teiresias. And yet this same success has worked thy fall.

 Œdipus. I little care, if I have saved the state.

 Teiresias. Well, then, I go. Do thou, boy, lead me on!

 Œdipus. Let him lead on. Most hateful art thou near;
Thou can'st not pain me more when thou art gone.

 Teiresias. I go then, having said the things I came
To say. No fear of thee compels me. Thine
Is not the power to hurt me. And I say,
This man whom thou dost seek with hue-and-cry,
As murderer of Laios, he is here,
In show an alien sojourner, but in truth
A homeborn Theban. No delight to him
Will that discovery bring. Blind, having seen,
Poor, having rolled in wealth,—he, with a staff

Feeling his way, to a strange land shall go!
And to his sons shall he be seen at once
Father and brother, and of her who bore him
Husband and son, sharing his father's bed,
His father's murd'rer. Go thou then within,
And brood o'er this, and, if thou find'st me fail,
Say that my skill in prophecy is gone.

[*Exeunt* ŒDIPUS *and* TEIRESIAS.]

STROPHE I

CHORUS. Who was it that the rock oracular
          Of Delphi spake of, working
With bloody hands of all dread deeds most dread?
          Time is it now for him,
Swifter than fastest steed to bend his flight;
          For, in full armor clad,
          Upon him darts, with fire
And lightning flash, the radiant Son of Zeus,
          And with Him come in train
          The dread and awful Powers,
The Destinies that fail not of their aim.

ANTISTROPHE I

For from Parnassos' heights, enwreathed with snow,
          Gleaming, but now there shone
The oracle that bade us, one and all,
          Track the unnamed, unknown;
For, lo! he wanders through the forest wild,
          In caves and over rocks,
          As strays the mountain bull,

In dreary loneliness with dreary tread,
          Seeking in vain to shun
          Dread words from central shrine;[8]
Yet they around him hover, full of life.

---

8. *central shrine*, Delphi, thought to be the center of the earth.

Strophe II

Fearfully, fearfully the augur moves me.
　　Nor answering, aye nor no!
And what to say I know not, but float on,
　　And hover still in hopes,
And fail to scan things present or to come.
　　For not of old, nor now,
Learnt I what cause of strife at variance set
　　The old Labdakid race[9]
With him, the child and heir of Polybos,
　　Nor can I test the tale,
And take my stand against the well-earned fame,
　　Of Œdipus, my lord,
As champion of the old Labdakid race,
　　For deaths obscure and dark!

Antistrophe II

For Zeus and King Apollo, they are wise,
　　And know the hearts of men:
But that a seer excelleth me in skill,
　　This is no judgment true;
And one man may another's wisdom pass,
　　By wisdom higher still.
I, for my part, before the word is plain,
　　Will ne'er assent in blame.
Full clear, the wingèd Maiden-monster came
　　Against him, and he proved,
By sharpest test, that he was wise indeed,
　　By all the land beloved,
And never, from my heart at least, shall come
　　Words that accuse of guilt.

[*Enter* Creon.]

Creon. I come, ye citizens, as having learnt
Our sovereign, Œdipus, accuses me
Of dreadful things I cannot bear to hear.

q. *Labdakid race*, the family of Œdipus.

For if, in these calamities of ours,
He thinks he suffers wrongly at my hands,
In word or deed, aught tending to his hurt,
I set no value on a life prolonged,
While this reproach hangs on me; for its harm
Affects not slightly, but is direst shame,
If through the town my name as villain rings,
By thee and by my friends a villain called.

CHORUS. But this reproach, it may be, came from wrath
All hasty, rather than from calm, clear mind.

CREON. And who informed him that the seer, seduced
By my devices, spoke his lying words?

CHORUS. The words were said, but with what mind I know not.

CREON. And was it with calm eyes and judgment calm,
This charge was brought against my name and fame?

CHORUS. I cannot say. To what our rulers do
I close my eyes. But here he comes himself.

[Enter ŒDIPUS.]

ŒDIPUS. Ho, there! is't thou? And does thy boldness soar
So shameless as to come beneath my roof,
When thou, 'tis clear, dost plot against my life,
And seek'st to rob me of my sovereignty?
Is it, by all the gods, that thou hast seen
Or cowardice or folly in my soul,
That thou hast laid thy plans? Or thoughtest thou
That I should neither see thy sinuous wiles,
Nor, knowing, ward them off? This scheme of thine,
Is it not wild, backed nor by force nor friends,
To seek the power which force and wealth must grasp?

CREON. Dost know what thou wilt do? For words of thine
Hear like words back, and as thou hearest, judge.

ŒDIPUS. Cunning of speech art thou. But I am slow
Of thee to learn, whom I have found my foe.

CREON. Of this, then, first, hear what I have to speak.

ŒDIPUS. But this, then, say not, that thou art not vile.

CREON. If that thou thinkest self-willed pride avails,
Apart from judgment, know thou art not wise.

ŒDIPUS. If that thou think'st, thy kinsman injuring,
To do it unchastised, thou art not wise.

CREON. In this, I grant, thou speakest right; but tell,
What form of injury hast thou to endure?

ŒDIPUS. Did'st thou, or did'st thou not, thy counsel give,
Some one to send to fetch this reverend seer?

CREON. And even now by that advice I hold!

ŒDIPUS. How long a time has passed since Laios chanced—
[*Pauses.*]

CREON. Chanced to do what? I understand not yet.

ŒDIPUS. Since he was smitten with the deadly blow?

CREON. The years would measure out a long, long tale.

ŒDIPUS. And was this seer then practicing his art?

CREON. Full wise as now, and equal in repute.

ŒDIPUS. Did he at that time say a word of me?

CREON. Not one, while I, at any rate, was by.

ŒDIPUS. What? Held ye not your quest upon the dead?

CREON. Of course we held it, but we nothing heard.

ŒDIPUS. How was it he, this wise one, spoke not then?

CREON. I know not, and, not knowing, hold my peace.

ŒDIPUS. Thy deed thou know'st, and with clear mind could'st
speak!

CREON. What is't! I'll not deny it, if I know.

ŒDIPUS. Were he not leagued with thee he ne'er had talked
Of felon deed by me on Laios done.

CREON. If he says this, thou know'st it. I of thee
Desire to learn, as thou hast learnt of me.

ŒDIPUS. Learn then; on me no guilt of blood shall rest.

CREON. Well, then,—my sister? dost thou own her wife?

ŒDIPUS. I cannot meet this question with denial.

CREON. Rul'st thou this land in equal right with her?

ŒDIPUS. Her every wish she doth from me receive.

CREON. And am not I co-equal with you twain?

ŒDIPUS. Yes; and just here thou show'st thyself false friend.

CREON. Not so, if thou would'st reason with thyself,
As I will reason. First reflect on this;
Supposest thou that one would rather choose
To reign with fears than sleep untroubled sleep,
His power being equal? I, for one, prize less
The name of king than deeds of kingly power;
And so would all who learn in wisdom's school.
Now without fear I have what I desire,

At thy hand given. Did I rule, myself,
I might do much unwillingly. Why then
Should sovereignty exert a softer charm,
Than power and might unchequered by a care?
I am not yet so cheated by myself,
As to desire aught else but honest gain.
Now all men hail me, every one salutes,
Now they who seek thy favor court my smiles,
For on this hinge does all their fortune turn.
Why then should I leave this to hunt for that?
My mind, retaining reason, ne'er could act
The villain's part. I was not born to love
Such thoughts, nor join another in the act;
And as a proof of this, go thou thyself,
And ask at Pytho whether I brought back,
In very deed, the oracles I heard.
And if thou find me plotting with the seer,
In common concert, not by one decree,
But two, thine own and mine, put me to death.
But charge me not with crime on shadowy proof;
For neither is it just, in random thought,
The bad to count as good, nor good as bad;
For to thrust out a friend of noble heart,
Is like the parting with the life we love.
And this in time thou'lt know, for time alone
Makes manifest the righteous. Of the vile
Thou may'st detect the vileness in a day.

    CHORUS. To one who fears to fall, his words seem good;
O king, swift counsels are not always safe.

    ŒDIPUS. But when a man is swift in wily schemes,
Swift must I be to baffle plot with plot;
And if I stand and wait, he wins the day,
And all my state to rack and ruin goes.

    CREON. What seek'st thou, then? to drive me from the land?

    ŒDIPUS. Not so. I seek thy death, not banishment.

    CREON. When thou show'st first what grudge I bear to thee.

    ŒDIPUS. And say'st thou this defying, yielding not?

    CREON. I see your mind is gone.

    ŒDIPUS.   My right I mind.

    CREON. Mine has an equal claim.

ŒDIPUS. Nay, thou art vile.

CREON. And if thy mind is darkened—?

ŒDIPUS. Still obey!

CREON. Nay, not a tyrant king.

ŒDIPUS. O country mine!

CREON. That country, too, is mine, not thine alone.

CHORUS. Cease, O my princes! In good time I see
Jocasta coming hither from the house;
And it were well with her to hush this brawl.

[*Enter* JOCASTA.]

JOCASTA. Why, O ye wretched ones, this strife of tongues
Raise ye in your unwisdom, nor are shamed,
Our country suffering, private griefs to stir?
Come thou within; and thou, O Creon, go;
Bring not a trifling sore to mischief great!

CREON. My sister! Œdipus thy husband claims
The right to do me one of two great wrongs,
To thrust me from my fatherland, or slay me.

ŒDIPUS. 'Tis even so, for I have found him, wife,
Against my life his evil wiles devising.

CREON. May I ne'er prosper, but accursèd die,
If I have done the things he says I did!

JOCASTA. Oh, by the Gods, believe him, Œdipus!
Respect his oath, which calls the Gods to hear;
And reverence me, and these who stand by thee.

CHORUS. Hearken, my king! Be calmer, I implore!

ŒDIPUS. What wilt thou that I yield?

CHORUS. Oh, have respect
To one not weak before, who now is strong
In this his oath.

ŒDIPUS. And know'st thou what thou ask'st?

CHORUS. I know right well.

ŒDIPUS. Say on, then, what thou wilt.

CHORUS. Hurl not to shame, on grounds of mere mistrust,
The friend on whom no taint of evil hangs.

ŒDIPUS. Know then that, seeking this, thou seek'st, in truth,
To work my death, or else my banishment.

CHORUS. Nay, by the Sun-God, Helios, chief of Gods!
May I, too, die, of God and man accursed,

If I wish aught like this! But on my soul,
Our wasting land dwells heavily; ills on ills
Still coming, new upon the heels of old.

  ŒDIPUS. Let him depart then, even though I die,
Or from my country be thrust forth in shame:
Thy face, not his, I view with pitying eye;
For him, where'er he be, is nought but hate.

  CREON. Thou'rt loth to yield, 'twould seem, and wilt be vexed
When this thy wrath is over: moods like thine
Are fitly to themselves most hard to bear.

  ŒDIPUS. Wilt thou not go, and leave me?

  CREON.   I will go,
By thee misjudged, but known as just by these. [*Exit.*]

  CHORUS. Why, lady, art thou slow to lead him in?

  JOCASTA. I fain would learn how this sad chance arose.

  CHORUS. Blind haste of speech there was, and wrong will sting.

  JOCASTA. From both of them?

  CHORUS.   Yea, both.

  JOCASTA.   And what said each?

  CHORUS. Enough for me, enough, our land laid low,
It seems, to leave the quarrel where it stopped.

  ŒDIPUS. See'st thou, thou good in counsel, what thou dost,
Slighting my cause, and toning down thy zeal?

  CHORUS. My chief, not once alone I spoke,
Unwise, unapt for wisdom should I seem,
Were I to turn from thee aside,
Who, when my country rocked in storm,
Did'st right her course. Ah! if thou can'st,
Steer her well onward now.

  JOCASTA. Tell me, my king, what cause of fell debate
Has bred this discord, and provoked thy soul.

  ŒDIPUS. Thee will I tell, for thee I honor more
Than these. 'Twas Creon and his plots against me.

  JOCASTA. Say then, if clearly thou can'st tell the strife.

  ŒDIPUS. He says that I am Laios' murderer.

  JOCASTA. Of his own knowledge, or by some one taught?

  ŒDIPUS. A scoundrel seer suborning. For himself,
He takes good care to free his lips from blame.

  JOCASTA. Leave now thyself, and all thy thoughts of this,
And list to me, and learn how little skill

In art prophetic mortal man may claim;
And of this truth, I'll give thee one short proof.
There came to Laios once an oracle,
(I say not that it came from Phœbos' self,
But from his servants,) that his fate was fixed
By his son's hand to fall—his own and mine;
And him, so rumor runs, a robber band
Of aliens slay, where meet the three great roads.
Nor did three days succeed the infant's birth,
Before, by other hands, he cast him forth,
Piercing his ankles, on a lonely hill.
Here, then, Apollo failed to make the boy
His father's murderer; nor by his son's hands,
Doom that he dreaded, did our Laios die;
Such things divining oracles proclaimed;
Therefore regard them not. Whate'er the God
Desires to search he will himself declare.

    Œdipus. [*Trembling.*] Ah, as but now I heard thee speak, my
        queen,
Strange whirl of soul, and rush of thoughts o'ercome me.

    Jocasta. What vexing care bespeaks this sudden change?

    Œdipus. I thought I heard thee say that Laios fell,
Smitten to death where meet the three great roads.

    Jocasta. So was it said, and still the rumors hold.

    Œdipus. Where was the spot in which this matter passed?

    Jocasta. They call the country Phocis, and the roads
From Delphi and from Daulia there converge.

    Œdipus. And what the interval of time since then?

    Jocasta. But just before thou camest to possess
And rule this land the tidings reached our city.

    Œdipus. Great Zeus! what fate hast thou decreed for me?

    Jocasta. What thought is this, my Œdipus, of thine?

    Œdipus. Ask me not yet, but Laios,—tell of him,
His build, his features, and his years of life.

    Jocasta. Tall was he, and the white hairs snowed his head,
And in his form not much unlike to thee.

    Œdipus. Woe, woe is me! so seems it I have plunged
All blindly into curses terrible.

    Jocasta. What sayest thou? I fear to look at thee.

ŒDIPUS. I tremble lest the seer has seen indeed:
But thou can'st clear it, answering yet once more.
JOCASTA. And I too fear, yet what thou ask'st I'll tell.
ŒDIPUS. Went he in humble guise, or with a troop
Of spearmen, as becomes a man that rules?
JOCASTA. Five were they altogether, and of them
One was a herald, and one chariot bore him.
ŒDIPUS. Woe! woe! 'tis all too clear. And who was he
That told these tidings to thee, O my queen?
JOCASTA. A servant who alone escaped with life.
ŒDIPUS. And does he chance to dwell among us now?
JOCASTA. Not so; for from the time when he returned,
And found thee bearing sway, and Laios dead,
He, at my hand, a suppliant, implored
This boon, to send him to the distant fields
To feed his flocks, as far as possible
From this our city. And I sent him forth;
For though a slave, he might have claimed yet more.
ŒDIPUS. Ah! could we fetch him quickly back again!
JOCASTA. That may well be. But why dost thou wish this?
ŒDIPUS. I fear, O queen, that words best left unsaid
Have passed these lips, and therefore wish to see him.
JOCASTA. Well, he shall come. But some small claim have I,
O king, to learn what touches thee with woe.
ŒDIPUS. Thou shalt not fail to learn it, now that I
Have gone so far in bodings. Whom should I
More than to thee tell all the passing chance?
I had a father, Polybos of Corinth,
And Merope of Doris was my mother,
And I was held in honor by the rest
Who dwelt there, till this accident befell,
Worthy of wonder, of the heat unworthy
It roused within me. Thus it chanced: A man
At supper, in his cups, with wine o'ertaken,
Reviles me as a spurious changeling boy;
And I, sore vexèd, hardly for that day
Restrained myself. And when the morrow came
I went and charged my father and my mother
With what I thus had heard. They heaped reproach
On him who stirred the matter, and I soothed

My soul with what they told me; yet it teased,
Still vexing more and more, and so I went,
Unknown to them, to Pytho, and the god
Sent me forth shamed, unanswered in my quest;
And other things he spake, dread, dire, and dark,
That I should join in wedlock with my mother,
Beget a brood that men should loathe to look at,
Be murderer of the father that begot me.
And, hearing this, I straight from Corinth fled,
The stars henceforth the land-marks of my way,
And fled where never more mine eyes might see
The shame of those dire oracles fulfilled;
And as I went I reached the spot where he,
This king, thou tell'st me, met the fatal blow.
And now, O lady, I will tell the truth.
Wending my steps that way where three roads meet,
There met me first a herald, and a man
Like him thou told'st of, riding on his car,
Drawn by young colts. With rough and hasty force
They drove me from the road,—the driver first,
And that old man himself; and then in rage
I strike the driver, who had turned me back,
And when the old man sees it, watching me
As by the chariot side I passed, he struck
My forehead with a double-pointed goad.
But we were more than quits, for in a trice
With this right hand I struck him with my staff,
And he rolls backward from his chariot's seat.
And then I slay them all. And if it chance
That Laios and this stranger are akin,
What man more wretched than this man who speaks?
What man more harassed by the vexing gods?
He whom none now, or alien, or of Thebes,
May welcome to their house, or speak to him,
But thrust him forth an exile. And 'twas I,
None other, who against myself proclaimed
These curses. And the bed of him that died
I with my hands, by which he fell, defile.
Am I not born to evil, all unclean?
If I must flee, yet still in flight my doom

Is never more to see the friends I love,
Nor tread my country's soil; or else to bear
The guilt of incest, and my father slay,
Yea, Polybos, who begat and brought me up.
Would not a man say right who said that here
Some cruel God was pressing hard on me?
Not that, not that, at least, thou Presence, pure
And awful, of the Gods; may I ne'er look
On such a day as that, but far away
Depart unseen from all the haunts of men,
Before such great pollution comes on me.

    CHORUS. We, too, O king, are grieved, yet hope thou on,
Till thou hast asked the man who then was by.

    ŒDIPUS. And this indeed is all the hope I have,
Waiting until that shepherd-slave appear.

    JOCASTA. And when he comes, what ground for hope is there?

    ŒDIPUS. I'll tell thee. Should he now repeat the tale
Thou told'st me, I, at least, stand free from guilt.

    JOCASTA. What special word was that thou heard'st from me?

    ŒDIPUS. Thou said'st he told that robbers slew his lord,
And should he give their number as the same
Now as before, it was not I who slew him,
For one man could not be the same as many,
But if he speak of one man, all alone,
Then, all too plain, the deed cleaves fast to me.

    JOCASTA. But know, the thing was said, and clearly said,
And now he cannot from his word draw back.
Not I alone, but the whole city, heard it;
And should he now retract his former tale,
Not then, my husband, will he rightly show
The death of Laios, who, as Loxias told,
By my son's hands should die; and yet, poor boy,
He killed him not, but perished long ago,
So I, at least, for all their oracles,
Will never more cast glance or here, or there.

    ŒDIPUS. Thou reasonest well. Yet send a messenger
To fetch that peasant. Be not slack in this.

    JOCASTA. I will make haste. But let us now go in;
I would do nothing that displeaseth thee.   [*Exeunt.*]

CHORUS. O that 'twere mine to keep
        An awful purity,
    In words and deeds whose laws on high are set
        Through heaven's clear æther spread,
        Whose birth Olympos boasts,
        Their one, their only sire,
        Whom man's frail flesh begat not,
        Nor in forgetfulness
        Shall lull to sleep of death;
        In them our God is great,
    In them He grows not old for evermore.

        But pride begets the mood
        Of wanton, tyrant power;
    Pride filled with many thoughts, yet filled in vain,
        Untimely, ill-advised,
        Scaling the topmost height,
        Falls to the abyss of woe,
        Where step that profiteth
        It seeks in vain to take.
        I ask our God to stay
        The labours never more
        That work our country's good;
    I will not cease to call on God for aid.

    But if there be who walketh haughtily,
        In action or in speech,
    Whom Righteousness herself has ceased to awe,
    Who shrines of Gods reveres not,
        An evil fate be his,
    (Fit meed for all his evil boastfulness;)
    Unless he gain his gains more righteously,
    And draweth back from deeds of sacrilege,
    Nor lays rash hand upon the holy things,

By man inviolable:
Who now, if such things be,
Will boast that he can guard
His soul from darts of wrath?
If deeds like these are held in high repute,
What profit is't for me
To raise my choral strain?

ANTISTROPHE II

No longer will I go in pilgrim's guise,
To yon all holy place,
Earth's central shrine, nor Abæ's temple old,
Nor to Olympia's fane,
Unless these things shall stand
In sight of all men, tokens clear from God.
But, O thou sovereign Ruler! if that name,
O Zeus, belongs to thee, who reign'st o'er all,
Let not this trespass hide itself from thee,
Or thine undying sway;
For now they set at nought
The worn-out oracles,
That Laios heard of old,
And king Apollo's wonted worship flags,
And all to wreck is gone
The homage due to God.

[*Enter* JOCASTA, *followed by Attendants.*]

JOCASTA. Princes of this our land, across my soul
There comes the thought to go from shrine to shrine
Of all the Gods, these garlands in my hand,
And waving incense; for our Œdipus
Vexes his soul too wildly with all woes,
And speaks not as a man should speak who scans
New issues by experience of the old,
But hangs on every breath that tells of fear.
And since I find that my advice avails not,
To thee, Lykeian King, Apollo, first
I come,—for thou art nearest,—suppliant
With these devotions, trusting thou wilt work

Some way of healing for us, free from guilt;
For now we shudder, all of us, seeing him,
The good ship's pilot, stricken down with fear.

[Enter MESSENGER.]

MESSENGER.   May I inquire of you, O strangers, where
To find the house of Œdipus the king,
And, above all, where he is, if ye know?
CHORUS.   This is the house, and he, good sir, within,
And here stands she, the mother of his children.
MESSENGER.   Good fortune be with her and all her kin,
Being, as she is, his true and honoured wife.
JOCASTA.   Like fortune be with thee, my friend. Thy speech,
So kind, deserves no less. But tell me why
Thou comest, what thou hast to ask or tell.
MESSENGER.   Good news to thee, and to thy husband, lady.
JOCASTA.   What is it, then? and who has sent thee here?
MESSENGER.   I come from Corinth, and the news I'll tell
May give thee joy. How else? Yet thou may'st grieve.
JOCASTA.   What is the news that has this twofold power?
MESSENGER.   The citizens that on the Isthmus dwell
Will make him sovereign. So the rumour ran,
JOCASTA.   What! Does old Polybos hold his own no more?
MESSENGER.   Nay, nay. Death holds him in his sepulchre.
JOCASTA.   What say'st thou? Polybos, thy king, is dead?
MESSENGER.   If I speak false, I bid you take my life.
JOCASTA.   Go, maiden, at thy topmost speed, and tell
Thy master this. Now, oracles of Gods,
Where are ye now? Long since my Œdipus
Fled, fearing lest his hand should slay the man;
And now he dies by fate, and not by him.

[Enter ŒDIPUS.]

ŒDIPUS.   Mine own Jocasta, why, O dearest one,
Why hast thou sent to fetch me from the house?
JOCASTA.   List this man's tale, and, when thou hearest, see
The plight of those the God's dread oracles.
ŒDIPUS.   Who then is this, and what has he to tell?
JOCASTA.   He comes from Corinth, and he brings thee word
That Polybos thy father lives no more.

Œdipus. What say'st thou, friend? Tell me thy tale thyself.

Messenger. If I must needs report the story clear,
Know well that he has gone the way of death.

Œdipus. Was it by plot, or chance of some disease?

Messenger. An old man's frame a little stroke lays low.

Œdipus. By some disease, 'twould seem, he met his death?

Messenger. Yes, that, and partly worn by lingering age.

Œdipus. Ha! ha! Why now, my queen, should we regard
The Pythian hearth oracular, or birds
In mid-air crying? By their auguries,
I was to slay my father. And he dies,
And the grave hides him; and I find myself
Handling no sword; unless for love of me
He pined away, and so I caused his death.
So Polybos is gone, and bears with him,
In Hades 'whelmed, those worthless oracles.

Jocasta. Did I not tell thee this long time ago?

Œdipus. Thou did'st, but I was led away by fears.

Jocasta. Dismiss them, then, for ever from thy thoughts!

Œdipus. And yet that "incest"; must I not fear that?

Jocasta. Why should we fear, when chance rules everything,
And foresight of the future there is none;
'Tis best to live at random, as one can.
But thou, fear not that marriage with thy mother:
Many ere now have dreamt of things like this,
But who cares least about them bears life best.

Œdipus. Right well thou speakest all things, save that she
Still lives that bore me, and I can but fear,
Seeing that she lives, although thou speakest well.

Jocasta. And yet great light comes from thy father's grave.

Œdipus. Great light I own; yet while she lives I fear.

Messenger. Who is this woman about whom ye fear?

Œdipus. 'Tis Merope, old sir, who lived with Polybos.

Messenger. And what leads you to think of her with fear?

Œdipus. A fearful oracle, my friend, from God.

Messenger. Can'st tell it? or must others ask in vain?

Œdipus. Most readily: for Loxias said of old
That I should with my mother wed, and then
With mine own hands should spill my father's blood.
And therefore Corinth long ago I left.

And journeyed far, right prosperously I own;—
And yet 'tis sweet to see one's parents' face.

MESSENGER. And did this fear thy steps to exile lead?

ŒDIPUS. I did not wish to take my father's life.

MESSENGER. Why, then, O king, did I, with good-will come,
Not free thee from this fear that haunts thy soul?

ŒDIPUS. Yes, and for this thou shalt have worthy thanks.

MESSENGER. For this, indeed, I chiefly came to thee:
That I on thy return might prosper well.

ŒDIPUS. And yet I will not with a parent meet.

MESSENGER. 'Tis clear, my son, thou know'st not what thou dost.

ŒDIPUS. What is't? By all the Gods, old man, speak out.

MESSENGER. If 'tis for them thou fearest to return—

ŒDIPUS. I fear lest Phœbos prove himself too true.

MESSENGER. Is it lest thou should'st stain thy soul through them?

ŒDIPUS. This self-same fear, old man, for ever haunts me.

MESSENGER. And know'st thou not there is no cause for fear?

ŒDIPUS. Is there no cause if I was born their son?

MESSENGER. None is there. Polybos was nought to thee.

ŒDIPUS. What say'st thou? Did not Polybos beget me?

MESSENGER. No more than he thou speak'st to; just as much.

ŒDIPUS. How could a father's claim become as nought?

MESSENGER. Well, neither he begat thee nor did I.

ŒDIPUS. Why then did he acknowledge me as his?

MESSENGER. He at my hands received thee as a gift.

ŒDIPUS. And could he love another's child so much?

MESSENGER. Yes; for his former childlessness wrought on him.

ŒDIPUS. And gav'st thou me as foundling or as bought?

MESSENGER. I found thee in Kithæron's shrub-grown hollow.

ŒDIPUS. And for what cause did'st travel thitherwards?

MESSENGER. I had the charge to tend the mountain flocks.

ŒDIPUS. Wast thou a shepherd, then, and seeking hire?

MESSENGER. E'en so, my son, and so I saved thee then.

ŒDIPUS. What evil plight then did'st thou find me in?

MESSENGER. The sinews of thy feet would tell that tale.

ŒDIPUS. Ah, me! why speak'st thou of that ancient wrong?

MESSENGER. I freed thee when thy insteps both were pierced.

ŒDIPUS. A foul disgrace I had in swaddling-clothes.

MESSENGER. Thus from this chance there came the name thou
      bearest.[10]

10. *Œdipus* means "Swell-Foot."

ŒDIPUS. [*Starting.*] Who gave the name, my father or my
   mother?

MESSENGER. I know not. He who gave thee better knows.

ŒDIPUS. Did'st thou then take me from another's hand,
Not finding me thyself?

MESSENGER.   Not I, indeed;
Another shepherd made a gift of thee.

ŒDIPUS. Who was he? Know'st thou how to point him out?

MESSENGER. They called him one of those that Laios owned.

ŒDIPUS. Mean'st thou the former sovereign of this land?

MESSENGER. E'en so. He fed the flocks of him thou nam'st.

ŒDIPUS. And is he living still that I might see him?

MESSENGER. You, his own countryman, should know that best.

ŒDIPUS. Is there of you who stand and listen here
One who has known the shepherd that he tells of,
Or seeing him upon the hills or here?
If so, declare it; 'tis full time to know.

CHORUS. I think that this is he whom from the fields
But now thou soughtest. But Jocasta here
Could tell thee this with surer word than I.

ŒDIPUS. Think'st thou, my queen, the man whom late we sent
   for
Is one with him of whom this stranger speaks?

JOCASTA [*With forced calmness*]. Whom did he speak of? Care
   not thou for it,
Nor even wish to keep his words in mind.

ŒDIPUS. I cannot fail, once getting on the scent,
To track at last the secret of my birth.

JOCASTA. Ah, by the Gods, if that thou valuest life
Inquire no more. My misery is enough.

ŒDIPUS. Take heart; though I should prove thrice base-born
   slave,
Born of thrice base-born mother, thou art still
Free from all stain.

JOCASTA.   Yet, I implore thee, pause!
Yield to my counsels, do not do this deed.

ŒDIPUS. I may not yield, nor fail to search it out.

JOCASTA. And yet best counsels give I, for thy good.

ŒDIPUS. What thou call'st best has long been grief to me.

JOCASTA. May'st thou ne'er know, ill-starred one, who thou art!

ŒDIPUS. Will some one bring that shepherd to me here?
Leave her to glory in her high descent.
      JOCASTA. Woe! woe! ill-fated one! my last word this,
This only, and no more for evermore   [*Rushes out.*]
      CHORUS. Why has thy queen, O Œdipus, gone forth
In her wild sorrow rushing? Much I fear
Lest from such silence evil deeds burst out.
      ŒDIPUS. Burst out what will; I seek to know my birth,
Low though it be, and she perhaps is shamed
(For, like a woman, she is proud of heart)
At thoughts of my low birth; but I, who count
Myself the child of Fortune, fear no shame;
My mother she, and she has prospered me.
And so the months that span my life have made me
Both low and high; but whatsoe'er I be,
Such as I am I am, and needs must on
To fathom all the secret of my birth.

                    STROPHE

      CHORUS. If the seer's gift be mine,
            Or skill in counsel wise,
      Thou, O Kithæron, by Olympos high,
            When next our full moon comes,
            Shall fail not to resound
      With cry that greets thee, fellow-citizen,
            Mother and nurse of Œdipus;
      And we will on thee weave our choral dance,
      As bringing to our princes glad good news,
      Hail, hail, O Phœbos, grant that what we do
            May meet thy favouring smile.

                  ANTISTROPHE

      Who was it bore thee, child,[11]
      Of Nymphs whose years are long,
      Or drawing near the mighty Father, Pan,

11. *child*, Œdipus. The Chorus, not realizing the implications of the mystery
of his birth, goes on to conjecture that he is the child of one of the gods.

> Who wanders o'er the hills,
> Or Loxias' paramour,
> Who loves the high lawns of the pasturing flocks?
> Or was it He who rules
> Kyllene's height; or did the Bacchic god,
> Whose dwelling is upon the mountain peaks,
> Receive thee, gift of Heliconian nymphs,
> With whom He loves to sport?

ŒDIPUS.   If I must needs conjecture, who as yet
Ne'er met the man, I think I see the shepherd,
Whom this long while we sought for. In his age
He this man matches. And I see besides,
My servants bring him. Thou perchance can'st speak
From former knowledge yet more certainly.

    CHORUS.   I know him, king, be sure; for this man stood,
If any, known as Laios' herdsman true.

[*Enter* SHEPHERD.]

    ŒDIPUS.   Thee first I ask, Corinthian stranger, say,
Is this the man?

    MESSENGER.   The very man thou seek'st.

    ŒDIPUS.   Ho there! old man. Come hither, look on me,
And tell me all. Did Laios own thee once?

    SHEPHERD.   His slave I was, not bought, but reared at home.

    ŒDIPUS.   What was thy work, or what thy mode of life?

    SHEPHERD.   Near all my life I followed with the flock.

    ŒDIPUS.   And in what region did'st thou chiefly dwell?

    SHEPHERD.   Now 'twas Kithæron, now on neighbouring fields.

    ŒDIPUS.   Know'st thou this man? Did'st ever see him there?

    SHEPHERD.   What did he do? Of what man speakest thou?

    ŒDIPUS.   This man now present. Did ye ever meet?

    SHEPHERD.   I cannot say off-hand from memory.

    MESSENGER.   No wonder that, my lord. But I'll remind him
Right well of things forgotten. Well I know
He needs must know when on Kithæron's fields,
He with a double flock, and I with one,
I was his neighbour during three half years,
From springtide till Arcturos rose; and I
In winter to mine own fold drove my flocks,

And he to those of Laios. [*To* SHEPHERD.] Answer me,
Speak I, or speak I not, the thing that was?

    SHEPHERD. Thou speak'st the truth, although long years
        have passed.

    MESSENGER. Come, then, say on. Dost know thou gav'st me once
A boy, that I might rear him as my child?

    SHEPHERD. What means this? Wherefore askest thou of that?

    MESSENGER. Here stands he, fellow! that same tiny boy.

    SHEPHERD. A curse befall thee! Wilt not hold thy tongue?

    ŒDIPUS. Rebuke him not, old man; thy words need more
The language of rebuker than do his.

    SHEPHERD. Say, good my lord, what fault do I commit?

    ŒDIPUS. This, that thou tell'st not of the child he asks for.

    SHEPHERD. Yes, for he nothing knows, and wastes his pains.

    ŒDIPUS. For favour thou speak'st not, but shalt for
        pain.   [*Strikes him.*]

    SHEPHERD. By all the Gods, hurt not an old man weak.

    ŒDIPUS. Will no one bind his hands behind his back?

    SHEPHERD. Oh wretched me! And what then wilt thou learn?

    ŒDIPUS. Gav'st thou this man the boy of whom he asks?

    SHEPHERD. I gave him. Would that I that day had died.

    ŒDIPUS. Soon thou wilt come to that if thou speak'st wrong.

    SHEPHERD. Nay, much more shall I perish if I speak.

    ŒDIPUS. This fellow, as it seems, would tire us out.

    SHEPHERD. Not so. I said long since I gave it him.

    ŒDIPUS. Whence came it? Was the child thine own or not?

    SHEPHERD. Mine own 'twas not, from some one else I had it.

    ŒDIPUS. Which of our people, or from out what home?

    SHEPHERD. Oh, by the Gods, my master, ask no more!

    ŒDIPUS. Thou diest if I question this again.

    SHEPHERD. Some one it was of Laios' household born.

    ŒDIPUS. Was it a slave, or some one kin to him?

    SHEPHERD. Ah me, I stand upon the very brink
Where most I dread to speak.

    ŒDIPUS.   And I to hear:
And yet I needs must hear it, come what may.

    SHEPHERD. The boy was said to be his son; but she,
Thy queen within, could tell the whole truth best.

    ŒDIPUS. What! was it she who gave it?

SHEPHERD. Yea, O king!

ŒDIPUS. And to what end ?

SHEPHERD. To make away with it.

ŒDIPUS. And dared a mother—?

SHEPHERD. Auguries dark she feared.

ŒDIPUS. What were they?

SHEPHERD. E'en that he his sire should kill.

ŒDIPUS. Why then did'st thou to this old man resign him?

SHEPHERD. I pitied him, O master, and I thought
That he would bear him to another land,
Whence he himself had come. But him he saved
For direst evil. For if thou be he
Whom this man speaks of, thou art evil-starred.

ŒDIPUS. Woe! woe! woe! woe! all cometh clear at last.
O light, may this my last glance be on thee,
Who now am seen owing my birth to those
To whom I ought not, and with whom I ought not
In wedlock living, whom I ought not slaying. [*Exit.*]

STROPHE I

CHORUS. Ah, race of mortal men,
How as a thing of nought
I count ye, though ye live;
For who is there of men
That more of blessing knows,
Than just a little while
To seem to prosper well,
And, having seemed, to fall?
With thee as pattern given,
Thy destiny, e'en thine,
Ill-fated Œdipus,
I count nought human blest.

ANTISTROPHE I

For he, with wondrous skill,
Taking his aim, did hit
Success, in all things blest;
And did, O Zeus! destroy

The Virgin with claws bent,
And sayings wild and dark;
And against many deaths
A tower and strong defence
Did for my country rise:
And so thou king art named,
With highest glory crowned,
Ruling in mighty Thebes.

STROPHE II

And now, who lives than thou more miserable?
Who equals thee in wild woes manifold,
   In shifting turns of life?
   Ah, noble one, our Œdipus!
For whom the same wide harbour
Sufficed for sire and son,
   In marriage rites to enter:
   Ah, how, ah, wretched one,
   How could thy father's bed
   Receive thee, and so long,
   Even till now, be dumb?

ANTISTROPHE II

Time, who sees all things, he hath found thee out,
Against thy will, and long ago condemned
The wedlock none may wed,
   Begetter and begotten.
   Ah, child of Laios! would
   I ne'er had seen thy face!
   I mourn with wailing lips,
   Mourn sore exceedingly.
   'Tis simplest truth to say,
   By thee from death I rose,
   By thee in death I sleep.

[*Enter* SECOND MESSENGER]

SECOND MESSENGER. Ye chieftains, honoured most in this our
land

What deeds ye now will hear of, what will see,
How great a wailing will ye raise, if still
Ye truly love the house of Labdacos!
For sure I think that neither Istros' stream
Nor Phasis' floods could purify this house,
Such horrors does it hold. But soon 'twill show
Evils self-chosen, not without free choice:
These self-sought sorrows ever pain men most.

  CHORUS. The ills we knew before lacked nothing meet
For plaint and moaning. Now, what add'st thou more?

  SECOND MESSENGER. Quickest for me to speak, and thee to learn;
Our sacred queen Jocasta,—she is dead.

  CHORUS. Ah, crushed with many sorrows! How and why?

  SECOND MESSENGER. Herself she slew. The worst of all that
    passed
I must omit, for none were there to see.
Yet, far as memory suffers me to speak,
That sorrow-stricken woman's end I'll tell;
For when to passion yielding, on she passed
Within the porch, straight to the couch she rushed,
Her bridal bed, with both hands tore her hair,
And as she entered, dashing through the doors,
Calls on her Laios, dead long years ago,
Remembering that embrace of long ago,
Which brought him death, and left to her who bore,
With his own son a hateful motherhood.
And o'er her bed she wailed, where she had borne
Spouse to her spouse, and children to her child;
And how she perished after this I know not;
For Œdipus struck in with woeful cry,
And we no longer looked upon her fate,
But gazed on him as to and fro he rushed.
For so he raves, and asks us for a sword,
Wherewith to smite the wife that wife was none,
The womb polluted with accursèd births,
Himself, his children,—so, as thus he raves,
Some spirit shows her to him, (none of us,
Who stood hard by had done so): with a shout
Most terrible, as some one led him on,
Through the two gates he leapt, and from the wards

He slid the hollow bolt, and rushes in;
And there we saw his wife had hung herself,
By twisted cords suspended. When her form
He saw, poor wretch! with one wild, fearful cry,
The twisted rope he loosens, and she fell,
Ill-starred one, on the ground. Then came a sight
Most fearful. Tearing from her robe the clasps,
All chased with gold, with which she decked herself,
He with them struck the pupils of his eyes,
With words like these—"Because they had not seen
What ills he suffered and what ills he did,
They in the dark should look, in time to come,
On those whom they ought never to have seen,
Nor know the dear ones whom he fain had known."
With such like wails, not once or twice alone,
Raising his eyes, he smote them, and the balls,
All bleeding, stained his cheek, nor poured they forth
Gore drops slow trickling, but the purple shower
Fell fast and full, a pelting storm of blood,
Such were the ills that sprang from both of them,
Not on one only, wife and husband both.
His ancient fortune, which he held of old,
Was truly fortune: but for this day's doom
Wailing and woe, and death and shame, all forms
That man can name of evil, none have failed.
    CHORUS. What rest from suffering hath the poor wretch now?
    SECOND MESSENGER. He calls to us to ope the bolts, and show
To all in Thebes his father's murderer,
His mother's— Foul and fearful were the words
He spoke; I dare not speak them. Then he said
That he would cast himself adrift, nor stay
At home accursèd, as himself had cursed.
Some stay he surely needs, or guiding hand,
For greater is the ill than he can bear,
For this he soon will show thee, for the bolts
Of the two gates are opening, and thou'lt see
A sight to touch e'en hatred's self with pity.

[*The doors of the Palace are thrown open, and* ŒDIPUS *is seen within.*]

Chorus. Oh, fearful sight for men to look upon!
        Most fearful of all woes
I hitherto have known! What madness strange
Has come on thee, thou wretched one?
        What Power with one fell swoop,
        Ills heaping upon ills,
        Than greatest greater yet,
        Has marked thee for its prey?
Woe! woe! thou doomed one, wishing much to ask,
And much to learn, and much to gaze into,
        I cannot look on thee,
        So horrible the sight!
Œdipus. Ah, woe! ah, woe! ah, woe!
        Woe for my misery!
Where am I wandering in my utter woe?
        Where floats my voice in air?
Dread Power, with crushing might
        Thou leapèd'st on my head.
Chorus. Yea, with dread doom nor sight nor speech may bear.
Œdipus. O cloud of darkness, causing one to shrink,
That onward sweeps with dread ineffable,
Resistless, borne along by evil blast,
        Woe, woe, and woe again!
How through me darts the throb these clasps have caused,
And memory of my ills.
Chorus. And who can wonder that in such dire woes
Thou mournest doubly, bearing twofold ills?
Œdipus. Ah, friend,
Thou only keepest by me, faithful found,
Nor dost the blind one slight.
        Woe, woe,
For thou escap'st me not; I clearly know,
Though all is dark, at least that voice of thine.
Chorus. O man of fearful deeds, how could'st thou bear
Thine eyes to outrage? What Power stirred thee to it?
Œdipus. Apollo, oh, my friends, the God, Apollo,
Who worketh out all these, my bitter woes:
Yet no man's hand but mine has smitten them.
        What need for me to see,
When nothing's left that's sweet to look upon?

CHORUS. Too truly dost thou speak the thing that is.
ŒDIPUS. Yea, what remains to see,
  Or what to love, or hear,
  With any touch of joy?
Lead me away, my friends, with utmost speed
Lead me away, the foul polluted one,
  Of all men most accursed,
  Most hateful to the Gods.
CHORUS. Ah, wretched one, alike in soul and doom.
I fain could wish that I had never known thee.
ŒDIPUS. Ill fate be his who from the fetters freed
  The child upon the hills,
And rescued me from death,
  And saved me,—thankless boon!
  Ah! had I died but then,
Nor to my friends nor me had been such woe.
CHORUS. I, too, could fain wish that.
ŒDIPUS. Yes; then I had not been
  My father's murderer:
Nor had men pointed to me as the man
  Wedded with her who bore him.
But now all godless, born of impious stock,
In incest joined with her who gave me birth;—
Yea, if there be an evil worse than all,
It falls on Œdipus!
CHORUS. I may not say that thou art well-advised,
For better wert thou dead than living blind.
ŒDIPUS. Persuade me not, nor counsel give to show
That what I did was not the best to do.
I know not with what eyes, in Hades dark,
To look on mine own father or my mother,
When I against them both, alas! have done
Deeds for which strangling were too light a doom.
My children's face, forsooth, was sweet to see,
Their birth being what it was; nay, nay, not so
To these mine eyes, nor yet this town, nor tower,
Nor sacred shrines of Gods whence I, who stood
Most honoured one in Thebes, myself have banished,
Commanding all to thrust the godless forth,
Him whom the Gods do show accursed, the stock

Of Laios old. And could I dare to look,
Such dire pollution fixing on myself,
And meet these face to face? Not so, not so.
Yea, if I could but stop the stream of sound,
And dam mine ears against it, I would do it,
Sealing my carcase vile, that I might live
Both blind, and hearing nothing. Sweet 'twould be
To keep my soul beyond the reach of ills.
Why, O Kithæron, did'st thou shelter me,
Nor kill me out of hand? I had not shown,
In that case, all men whence I drew my birth.
O Polybos, and Corinth, and the home
Of old called mine, how strange a growth ye reared,
All fair outside, all rotten at the core;
For vile I stand, descended from the vile.
Ye threefold roads and thickets half concealed,
The copse, the narrow pass where three ways meet,
Which at my hands did drink my father's blood,
Remember ye, what deeds I did in you,
What, hither come, I did?—O marriage rites
That gave me birth, and, having borne me, gave
To me in turn an offspring, and ye showed
Fathers, and sons, and brothers, all in one,
Mothers, and wives, and daughters, hateful names,
All foulest deeds that men have ever done.
But, since, where deeds are evil, speech is wrong,
With utmost speed, by all the Gods, or slay me,
Or drive me forth, or hide me in the sea,
Where never more your eyes may look on me,
Come, scorn ye not to touch a wretch like me,
But hearken; fear ye not; no soul save me
Can bear the burden of my countless ills.
But ye, if ye have lost your sense of shame
For mortal men, yet reverence the light
Of him, our King, the Sun-God, source of life,
Nor sight so foul expose unveiled to view,
Which neither earth, nor shower from heaven, nor light,
Can see and welcome. But with utmost speed
Convey me in; for nearest kin alone
Can meetly see and hear their kindred's ills.

CHORUS. The man for what thou need'st is come in time,
Creon, to counsel, and to act, for now
He in thy stead is left our state's one guide.[12]

ŒDIPUS. Ah, me! what language shall I hold to him,
What trust at his hands claim? In all the past
I showed myself to him most vile and base.

[Enter CREON.*]*

CREON. I have not come, O Œdipus, to scorn,
Nor to reproach thee for thy former crimes.

ŒDIPUS. Oh, by the Gods! since thou, beyond my hopes.
Dost come all noble unto me all base,
One favour grant. I seek thy good, not mine.

CREON. And what request seek'st thou so wistfully?

ŒDIPUS. Cast me with all thy speed from out this land,
Where nevermore a man may speak to me!

CREON. Be sure, I would have done so, but I wished
To learn what now the God will bid us do.

ŒDIPUS. The oracle was surely clear enough
That I the parricide, the pest, should die.

CREON. So ran the words. But in our present need
'Tis better to learn surely what to do.

ŒDIPUS. And will ye ask for one so vile as I?

CREON. Yea, thou, too, now would'st trust the voice of God.

ŒDIPUS. And this I charge thee, yea, and supplicate;
For her within, provide what tomb thou wilt,
For for thine own most meetly thou wilt care;
But never let this city of my fathers
Be sentenced to receive me as its guest;
But suffer me on yon lone hills to dwell,
On my Kithæron, destined for my tomb,
While still I lived, by mother and by sire,
That I may die by those who sought to kill.
And yet this much I know, that no disease,
Nor aught else could have killed me; ne'er from death
Had I been saved but for some evil dread.
As for our fate, let it go where it will;
But for my children, of my boys, O Creon,
Take thou no thought; as men they will not feel,

12. Œdipus' two sons, Polyneikes and Eteocles, are not old enough to rule.

Where'er they be, the lack of means to live.
But for my two poor girls,[13] all desolate,
To whom my table never brought a meal
Without my presence, but whate'er I touched
They still partook of with me;—care for these;
Yea, let me touch them with my hands, and weep
With them my sorrows. Grant it, O my prince,
O born of noble nature!
Could I but touch them with my hands, I feel
Still I should have them mine, as when I saw.

[*Enter* ANTIGONE *and* ISMENE.]

What say I? What is this?
Do I not hear, ye Gods, their dear, loved tones,
Broken with sobs, and Creon, pitying me,
Hath sent the dearest of my children to me?
Is it not so?
     CREON. It is so. I am he who gives thee this,
Knowing the joy thou had'st in them of old.
     ŒDIPUS. A blessing on thee! May the Powers on high
Guard thy path better than they guarded mine!
Where are ye, O my children? Come, oh, come
To these your brother's hands, that now have brought
Your father's once bright eyes to this fell pass,
Who, O my children, blind and knowing nought,
Became your father e'en by her who bore me.
I weep for you, (for sight is mine no more,)
Picturing in mind the sad and dreary life
Which waits you at men's hands in years to come;
For to what friendly gatherings will ye go,
Or solemn feasts, from whence, for all the joy
And pride, ye shall not home return in tears?
And when ye come to marriageable age,
Who is there, O my children, rash enough
To make his own the shame that then will fall,
Reproaches on my parents, and on yours?
What evil fails us here? Your father killed
His father, and was wed in incest foul
With her who bore him, and you twain begat

13. *girls,* Antigone and Ismene.

Of her who gave him birth. Such shame as this
Will men lay on you, and who then will dare
To make you his in marriage? None, not one,
My children! but ye needs must waste away,
Unwedded, childless. Thou, Menœkeus' son,
Since thou alone art left a father to them,
(For we their parents perish utterly,)
Suffer them not to wander husbandless,
Nor let thy kindred beg their daily bread,
Nor make them sharers with me in my woe;
But look on them with pity, seeing them
At their age, but for thee, deprived of all.
O noble soul, I pray thee, touch my hand
In token of consent. And ye, my girls,
Had ye the minds to hearken I would fain
Give ye much counsel. As it is, pray for me
To live where'er is meet; and for yourselves
A brighter life than his ye call your sire.

    CREON. Enough of tears. Go thou within the house.
    ŒDIPUS. I needs must yield, however hard it be.
    CREON. In their right season all things prosper best.
    ŒDIPUS. Know'st thou my wish?
    CREON.   Speak and I then shall know.
    ŒDIPUS. That thou should'st send me far away from home.
    CREON. Thou askest what the Gods alone can give.
    ŒDIPUS. As for the Gods, above all men they hate me.
    CREON. And therefore it may chance thou gain'st thy wish.
    ŒDIPUS. And dost thou promise?
    CREON.   When I mean them not,
I am not wont to utter idle words.
    ŒDIPUS. Lead me, then, hence.
    CREON.   Go thou, but leave the girls.
    ŒDIPUS. Ah, take them not from me!
    CREON.   Thou must not think
To hold the sway in all things all thy life:
The sway thou had'st did not abide with thee.
    CHORUS. Ye men of Thebes, behold this Œdipus,
Who knew the famous riddle and was noblest,
Whose fortune who saw not with envious glances!
And, lo! in what a sea of direst trouble

He now is plunged. From hence the lesson learn ye,
To reckon no man happy till ye witness
The closing day; until he pass the border
Which severs life from death, unscathed by sorrow.

THE END

[*What happens between the end of* ŒDIPUS THE KING *and the beginning of* ANTIGONE:

Œdipus, blinded and broken, begs to be sent into exile; but Creon, Jocasta's brother, forbids his departure. So Œdipus, with his four young children—two boys, Eteocles and Polyneikes, and two girls, Antigone and Ismene—remains in Thebes. Creon, during the minority of the boys, acts as regent.

After many years some of the Thebans feel that Œdipus' presence is a pollution and will bring evil upon the city. Creon drives Œdipus into exile and the two sons, now about grown, concur in his pitiless decree. The old man, accompanied only by his devoted daughter Antigone, sets out on his wanderings. He is the most pathetic of all creatures to the ancient Greek—a cityless man. Soon after, Eteocles and Polyneikes contend for the throne. Eteocles, having won over the support of most of the citizens, becomes king, and Polyneikes flies for his life. Eventually he reaches Argos, where he is hospitably received and later marries the daughter of the king.

Meanwhile, the blind Œdipus, led by faithful Antigone, reaches the sacred grove of Colonus, just outside Athens, where the hero Theseus is king. Father and daughter, ragged and exhausted after their long wanderings, stop to rest. It is now twenty years since the events described in *Œdipus the King*. There, resting in the grove, they are found by Œdipus' younger daughter Ismene, who has come to bring them important news from Thebes. An oracle has just declared that, when he dies, Œdipus will bring great blessing to whatever country his body is buried in. Ismene warns him that Creon is coming hard on her heels, intent upon inducing the old exile to return to Thebes so that the prosperity promised by the oracle may be enjoyed by that city.

By this time Theseus, who has learned of Œdipus' arrival, comes out to the grove and warmly offers him hospitality and protection. In return, Œdipus tells the king about the oracle, and declares that at his death he wishes his body to be buried in Theseus' dominion so that the promised blessing may come to Athens.

The compact has hardly been made before Creon and a band of armed men appear in hot pursuit of Œdipus. After an attempt at wheedling, which Œdipus rebuffs, Creon threatens to drag him willy-nilly back to Thebes. He does actually seize the two girls, but Theseus rescues them and expels Creon and his men from the grove.

Polyneikes, the son who has been expelled from Thebes by his brother Eteocles, raises an army in Argos and marches on Thebes. Passing Athens on his way, he visits Œdipus. He has heard, he says, that still another oracle has announced that whichever brother Œdipus favors will win the approaching battle. And so, far from helping either brother, Œdipus places a curse on both of them and prophesies that they will kill each other. Polyneikes, believing that everything will come to pass just as his father has said, fatalistically goes away to meet his doom. As he leaves, he exacts a promise from Antigone that she will see to it that his body is buried with all the essential rites.

Now a heavy peal of supernatural thunder is heard. Œdipus recognizes that it is the signal that the time has come for his departure from this world. Solemnly he bids farewell to his daughters, who cling to him, weeping, as though they would never let him go. The old man, in a mood of exaltation and peace, walks slowly away, miraculously guided by an inner light. Only Theseus goes with him, for the place of his entombment is to be a secret known only to the king of Athens.

Antigone, with Ismene, sets out for Thebes, where she means to prevent the battle if she can, and inter the body of Polyneikes if she must. At the beginning of the play *Antigone*, the battle has taken place, and, just as Œdipus foretold, both brothers have been killed, each by the other's hand. Only one thing now remains to be done to complete the story of the House of Œdipus. Antigone must keep her promise to Polyneikes, knowing that the penalty for so doing will be her own death.]

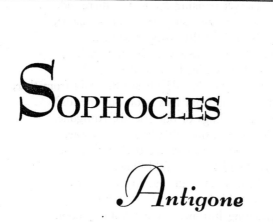

SOPHOCLES
Antigone

Persons of the Drama

CREON, *king of Thebes*
HÆMON, *son of Creon*
TEIRESIAS, *a seer*
GUARD
FIRST MESSENGER
SECOND MESSENGER
EURYDIKE, *wife of Creon*
ANTIGONE, } *daughters of Œdipus*
ISMENE,
CHORUS OF THEBAN ELDERS

SCENE: *Thebes, in front of the Palace. Early morning. Hills in the distance on the left; on the right the city.*

[*Enter* ANTIGONE *and* ISMENE.]

ANTIG. Ismene, mine own sister, darling one!
Is there, of ills that sprang from Œdipus,

199

One left that Zeus will fail to bring on us,
The two who yet remain? Nought is there sad,
Nought full of sorrow, steeped in sin or shame,
But I have seen it in thy woes and mine.
And now, what new decree is this they tell,
Our captain has enjoined on all the State?
Know'st thou? Hast heard? Or are they hid from thee,
The ills that come from foes upon our friends?

    IsME. No tidings of our friends, Antigone,
Pleasant or painful, since that hour have come,
When we, two sisters, lost our brothers twain,
In one day dying by a twofold blow.
And since in this last night the Argive[1] host
Has left the field, I nothing further know,
Nor brightening fortune, nor increasing gloom.

    ANTIG. That knew I well, and therefore sent for thee
Beyond the gates, that thou may'st hear alone.

    IsME. What meanest thou? It is but all too clear
Thou broodest darkly o'er some tale of woe.

    ANTIG. And does not Creon treat our brothers twain
One with the rites of burial, one with shame?
Eteocles, so say they, he interred
Fitly, with wonted rites, as one held meet
To pass with honor to the dead below.
But for the corpse of Polyneikes, slain
So piteously, they say, he has proclaimed
To all the citizens, that none should give
His body burial, or bewail his fate,
But leave it still unwept, unsepulchered,
A prize full rich for birds that scent afar
Their sweet repast. So Creon bids, they say,
Creon the good, commanding thee and me,—
Yes, me, I say,—and now is coming here,
To make it clear to those who know it not,
And counts the matter not a trivial thing;
But whoso does the things that he forbids,
For him there waits within the city's walls
The death of stoning. Thus, then, stands thy case;
And quickly thou wilt show, if thou art born

    1. The forces that joined with Polyneikes in his attack on Thebes came from
Argos.

Of noble nature, or degenerate liv'st,
Base child of honored parents.

ISME.   How could I,
O daring in thy mood, in this our plight,
Or breaking law or keeping, aught avail?

ANTIG. Wilt thou with me share risk and toil?
Look to it.

ISME. What risk is this? What purpose fills thy mind?

ANTIG. Wilt thou help this my hand to lift the dead?

ISME. Mean'st thou to bury him, when law forbids?

ANTIG. He is my brother; yes, and thine, though thou
Would'st fain he were not. I desert him not.

ISME. O daring one, when Creon bids thee not?

ANTIG. He has no right to keep me from mine own.

ISME. Ah me! remember, sister, how our sire
Perished, with hate o'erwhelmed and infamy,
From evils that himself did bring to light,
With his own hand himself of eyes bereaving,
And how his wife and mother, both in one,
With twisted cordage, cast away her life;
And thirdly, how our brothers in one day
In suicidal conflict wrought the doom,
Each of the other. And we twain are left;
And think, how much more wretchedly than all
We twain shall perish, if, against the law,
We brave our sovereign's edict and his power.
This first we need remember, we were born
Women; as such, not made to strive with men.
And next, that they who reign surpass in strength,
And we must bow to this, and worse than this.
I then, entreating those that dwell below,
To judge me leniently, as forced to yield,
Will hearken to our rulers. Over-zeal
That still will meddle, little wisdom shows.

ANTIG. I will not ask thee, nor though thou should'st wish
To do it, should'st thou join with my consent.
Do what thou wilt, I go to bury him;
And good it were, in doing this, to die.
Loved I shall be with him whom I have loved,
Guilty of holiest crime. More time is mine

In which to share the favor of the dead,
Than that of those who live; for I shall rest
For ever there. But thou, if thus thou please,
Count as dishonored what the Gods approve.

ISME. I do them no dishonor, but I find
Myself too weak to war against the State.

ANTIG. Make what excuse thou wilt, I go to rear
A grave above the brother whom I love.

ISME. Ah, wretched me! how much I fear for thee!

ANTIG. Fear not for me. Thine own fate raise to safety.

ISME. At any rate, disclose this deed to none;
Keep it close hidden: I will hide it too.

ANTIG. Speak out! I bid thee. Silent, thou wilt be
More hateful to me, if thou fail to tell
My deed to all men.

ISME.   Fiery is thy mood,
Although thy deeds the very blood might chill.

ANTIG. I know I please the souls I ought to please.

ISME. Yes, if thou canst; thou seek'st the impossible.

ANTIG. When strength shall fail me, then I'll cease to strive.

ISME. We should not hunt the impossible at all.

ANTIG. If thou speak thus, my hatred wilt thou gain,
And rightly wilt be hated of the dead.
Leave me and my ill counsel to endure
This dreadful doom. I shall not suffer aught
So evil as a death dishonorable.

ISME. Go then, if so thou wilt. Of this be sure,
Wild as thou art, thy friends must love thee still.

                                              [*Exeunt.*]

[*Enter* CHORUS OF THEBAN ELDERS.]

STROPHE I

CHORUS. O light of yon bright sun,
Fairest of all that ever shone on Thebes,
        Thebes with her seven high gates,
        Thou didst appear that day,
        Eye of the golden dawn,
        O'er Dirké's[2] streams advancing,

2. *Dirké*, a small stream rising from several springs near Thebes.

Driving with quickened curb,
In haste of headlong flight,
The warrior[3] who, in panoply of proof,
From Argos came, with shield of glittering white;
Whom Polyneikes brought,
Roused by the strife of tongues
Against our fatherland,
As eagle shrieking shrill,
He hovered o'er our land,
With snow-white wing bedecked,
Begirt with myriad arms,
And flowing horsehair crests.

Antistrophe I

He stood above our towers,
Encircling, with his spears all blood-bestained,
The portals of our gates;
He went, before he filled
His jaws with blood of men,
Ere the pine-fed Hephæstos[4]
Had seized our crown of towers.
So loud the battle din
That Ares loves was raised around his rear,
A conflict hard e'en for his dragon foe.
For breath of haughty speech
Zeus hateth evermore;
And seeing them advance,
With mighty rushing stream,
And clang of golden arms,
With brandished fire he hurls
One who rushed eagerly
From topmost battlement
To shout out, "Victory!"

Strophe II

Crashing to earth he fell,
Down-smitten, with his torch,

3. *warrior*, the entire enemy army is here personified as a single warrior.
4. *Hephæstos*, poetically used for "fire."

Who came, with madman's haste,
Drunken, with frenzied soul,
And swept o'er us with blasts,
The whirlwind blasts of hate.
Thus on one side they fare,
And Ares great, like war-horse in his strength,
Smiting now here, now there,
Brought each his several fate.
For seven chief warriors at the seven gates met,
Equals with equals matched,
To Zeus, the Lord of War,
Left tribute, arms of bronze;
All but the hateful ones,
Who, from one father and mother sprung,
Stood wielding, hand to hand,
Their two victorious spears,
And had their doom of death as common lot.

ANTISTROPHE II

But now, since Victory,
Of mightiest name, hath come
To Thebes, of chariots proud,
Joying and giving joy,
After these wars just past,
Learn ye forgetfulness,
And all night long, with dance and voice of hymns,
Let us go round in state
To all the shrines of Gods,
While Bacchos, making Thebes resound with dance,
Begins the strain of joy.
But, lo! our country's king,
Creon, Menœkeus' son,
New ruler, by new change,
And providence of God,
Comes to us steering on some new device;
For, lo! he hath convened,
By herald's loud command,
This council of the elders of our land.

[*Enter* CREON.]

CREON. My friends, for what concerns our commonwealth,
The Gods who vexed it with the billowing storms
Have righted it again; and I have sent,
By special summons, calling you to come
Apart from all the others. This, in part,
As knowing ye did all along uphold
The might of Laios' throne, in part again,
Because when Œdipus our country ruled,
And, when he perished, then towards his sons
Ye still were faithful in your steadfast mind.
And since they fell, as by a double death,
Both on the selfsame day with murderous blow,
Smiting and being smitten, now I hold
Their thrones and all their power of sov'reignty
By nearness of my kindred to the dead.
And hard it is to learn what each man is,
In heart and mind and judgment, till he gain
Experience in princedom and in laws.
For me, whoe'er is called to guide a State,
And does not catch at counsels wise and good,
But holds his peace through any fear of man,
I deem him basest of all men that are,
And so have deemed long since; and whosoe'er
As worthier than his country counts his friend,
I utterly despise him. I myself,
Zeus be my witness, who beholdeth all,
Would not keep silence, seeing danger come,
Instead of safety, to my subjects true.
Nor could I take as friend my country's foe;
For this I know, that there our safety lies,
And sailing while the good ship holds her course,
We gather friends around us. By these rules
And such as these do I maintain the State.
And now I come, with edicts, close allied
To these in spirit, for my citizens,
Concerning those two sons of Œdipus.
Eteocles, who died in deeds of might
Illustrious, fighting for our fatherland,
To honor him with sepulture, all rites
Duly performed that to the noblest dead

Of right belong. Not so his brother; him
I speak of, Polyneikes, who, returned
From exile, sought with fire to desolate
His father's city and the shrines of Gods,
Yes, sought to glut his rage with blood of men,
And lead them captives to the bondslave's doom;
Him I decree that none shall dare entomb,
That none shall utter wail or loud lament,
But leave his corpse unburied, by the dogs
And vultures mangled, foul to look upon.
Such is my purpose. Ne'er, if I can help,
Shall the vile have more honor than the just;
But whoso shows himself my country's friend,
Living or dead, from me shall honor gain.
CHORUS. This is thy pleasure, O Menœkeus' son,
For him who hated, him who loved our State;
And thou hast power to make what laws thou wilt,
Both for the dead and for all us who live.
CREON. Be ye then guardians of the things I speak.
CHORUS. Commit this task to one of younger years.
CREON. Nay, watchmen are appointed for the corpse.
CHORUS. What other task then dost thou lay on us?
CREON. Not to consent with those that disobey.
CHORUS. None are so foolish as to seek for death.
CREON. Yet that shall be the doom; but love of gain
Hath oft with false hopes lured men to their death.

[*Enter* GUARD.]

GUARD. I will not say, O king, that I have come
Panting with speed, and plying nimble feet,
For I had many halting-points of thought,
Backwards and forwards turning, round and round:
For now my mind would give me sage advice;
"Poor wretch, why go where thou must bear the blame?
Or wilt thou tarry, fool? Shall Creon know
These things from others? How wilt thou 'scape grief?"
Revolving thus, I came in haste, yet slow,
And thus a short way finds itself prolonged;
But, last of all, to come to thee prevailed.
And though I tell of nought, yet I will speak;

For this one hope I cling to, might and main,
That I shall suffer nought but destiny.
    CREON. What is it then that causes such dismay?
    GUARD. First, for mine own share in it, this I say,
The deed I did not, do not know who did,
Nor should I rightly come to ill for it.
    CREON. Thou feel'st thy way and fencest up thy deed
All round and round. 'Twould seem thou hast some news.
    GUARD. Yea, news of fear engenders long delay.
    CREON. Wilt thou not speak, and then depart in peace?
    GUARD. Well, speak I will. The corpse— Some one has been
But now and buried it, a little dust
O'er the skin scattering, with the wonted rites.
    CREON. What say'st thou? What man dared this deed of guilt?
    GUARD. I know not. Neither was there stroke of axe,
Nor earth cast up by mattock. All the soil
Was dry and hard, no track of chariot wheel;
But he who did it went and left no sign.
And when the first day-watchman showed it us,
The sight caused wonder and sore grief to all;
For he had disappeared: no tomb indeed
Was over him, but dust all lightly strown,
As by some hand that shunned defiling guilt;
And no sign was there of wild beast or dog
Having come and torn him. Evil words arose
Among us, guard to guard imputing blame,
Which might have come to blows, and none was there
To check its course, for each to each appeared
The man whose hand had done it. Yet not one
Had it brought home, but each disclaimed all knowledge;
And we were ready in our hands to take
Bars of hot iron, and to walk through fire,
And call the Gods to witness none of us
Were privy to his schemes who planned the deed,
Nor his who wrought it. Then at last, when nought
Was gained by all our searching, some one speaks,
Who made us bend our gaze upon the ground
In fear and trembling: for we neither saw
How to oppose it, nor, accepting it,
How we might prosper in it. And his speech

Was this, that all our tale should go to thee,
Not hushed up anywise. This gained the day;
And me, ill-starred, the lot condemns to win
This precious prize. So here I come to thee
Against my will; and surely do I trow
Thou dost not wish to see me. Still 'tis true
That no man loves the messenger of ill.

    CHORUS. For me, my prince, my mind some time has thought
If this perchance has some divine intent.

    CREON. Cease then, before thou fillest me with wrath,
Lest thou be found, though full of years, a fool.
For what thou say'st is most intolerable,
That for this corpse the providence of Gods
Has any care. What! have they buried him,
As to their patron paying honors high,
Who came to waste their columned shrines with fire,
To desecrate their offerings and their lands,
And all their wonted customs? Dost thou see
The Gods approving men of evil deeds?
It is not so; but men of rebel mood,
Lifting their head in secret long ago,
Still murmured thus against me. Never yet
Had they their neck beneath the yoke, content
To bear it with submission. They, I know,
Have bribed these men to let the deed be done.
No thing in use by man, for power of ill,
Can equal money. This lays cities low,
This drives men forth from quiet dwelling-place,
This warps and changes minds of worthiest stamp,
To turn to deeds of baseness, teaching men
All shifts of cunning, and to know the guilt
Of every impious deed. But they who, hired,
Have wrought this crime, have labored to their cost,
Or soon or late to pay the penalty.
But if Zeus still claims any awe from me,
Know this, and with an oath I tell it thee,
Unless ye find the very man whose hand
Has wrought this burial, and before mine eyes
Present him captive, death shall not suffice,
Till first, hung up still living, ye shall show

The story of this outrage, that henceforth,
Knowing what gain is lawful, ye may grasp
At that, and learn it is not meet to love
Gain from all quarters. By base profit won
You will see more destroyed than prospering.
    GUARD. May I then speak? Or shall I turn and go?
    CREON. See'st not e'en yet how vexing are thy words?
    GUARD. Is it thine ears they trouble, or thy soul?
    CREON. Why dost thou gauge my trouble where it is?
    GUARD. The doer grieves thy heart, but I thine ears.
    CREON. Pshaw! what a babbler, born to prate art thou!
    GUARD. May be; yet I this deed, at least, did not.
    CREON. Yes, and for money; selling e'en thy soul.
    GUARD. Ah me!
How dire it is, in thinking, false to think!
    CREON. Prate about thinking: but unless ye show
To me the doers, ye shall say ere long
That scoundrel gains still work their punishment.   [*Exit.*]
    GUARD. God send we find him! Should we find him not,
As well may be (for this must chance decide),
You will not see me coming here again;
For now, being safe beyond all hope of mine,
Beyond all thought, I owe the Gods much thanks.   [*Exit.*]

STROPHE I

    CHORUS. Many the forms of life,
    Wondrous and strange to see,
    But nought than man appears
    More wondrous and more strange.
    He, with the wintry gales,
    O'er the white foaming sea,
    'Mid wild waves surging round,
    Wendeth his way across:
Earth, of all Gods, from ancient days the first,
    Unworn and undecayed,
He, with his ploughs that travel o'er and o'er,
    Furrowing with horse and mule,
    Wears ever year by year.

ANTISTROPHE I

The thoughtless tribe of birds,
The beasts that roam the fields,
The brood in sea-depths born,
He takes them all in nets
Knotted in snaring mesh,
Man, wonderful in skill.
And by his subtle arts
He holds in sway the beasts
That roam the fields, or tread the mountain's height;
And brings the binding yoke
Upon the neck of horse with shaggy mane,
Or bull on mountain crest,
Untamable in strength.

STROPHE II

And speech, and thought as swift as wind,
And tempered mood for higher life of states,
These he has learnt, and how to flee
Or the clear cold of frost unkind,
Or darts of storm and shower,
Man all-providing. Unprovided, he
Meeteth no chance the coming days may bring;
Only from Hades, still
He fails to find escape,
Though skill of art may teach him how to flee
From depths of fell disease incurable.

ANTISTROPHE II

So, gifted with a wondrous might,
Above all fancy's dreams, with skill to plan,
Now unto evil, now to good,
He turns. While holding fast the laws,
His country's sacred rights,
That rest upon the oath of Gods on high,
High in the State: an outlaw from the State,

When loving, in his pride,
The thing that is not good;
Ne'er may he share my hearth, nor yet my thoughts,
Who worketh deeds of evil like to this.

[*Enter* GUARDS, *bringing in* ANTIGONE.]

As to this portent which the Gods have sent,
I stand in doubt. Can I, who know her, say
That this is not the maid Antigone?
O wretched one of wretched father born,
Thou child of Œdipus,
What means this? Surely 'tis not that they bring
Thee as a rebel 'gainst the king's decree,
And taken in the folly of thine act?
    GUARD. Yes! She it was by whom the deed was done.
We found her burying. Where is Creon, pray?
    CHORUS. Back from his palace comes he just in time.

[*Enter* CREON.]

    CREON. What chance is this, with which my coming fits?
    GUARD. Men, O my king, should pledge themselves to nought;
For cool reflection makes their purpose.void.
I surely thought I should be slow to come here,
Cowed by thy threats, which then fell thick on me;
But now persuaded by the sweet delight
Which comes unlooked for, and beyond our hopes,
I come, although I swore the contrary,
Bringing this maiden, whom in act we found
Decking the grave. No need for lots was now;
The prize was mine, and not another man's.
And now, O king, take her, and as thou wilt,
Judge and convict her. I can claim a right
To wash my hands of all this troublous coil.
    CREON. How and where was it that ye seized and brought her?
    GUARD. She was in act of burying. Thou knowest all.
    CREON. Dost know and rightly speak the tale thou tell'st?
    GUARD. I saw her burying that self-same corpse
Thou bad'st us not to bury. Speak I clear?
    CREON. How was she seen, and taken in the act?
    GUARD. The matter passed as follows:—When we came,

With all those dreadful threats of thine upon us,
Sweeping away the dust which, lightly spread,
Covered the corpse, and laying stript and bare
The tainted carcase, on the hill we sat
To windward, shunning the infected air,
Each stirring up his fellow with strong words,
If any shirked his duty. This went on
Some time, until the glowing orb of day
Stood in mid heaven, and the scorching heat
Fell on us. Then a sudden whirlwind rose,
A scourge from heaven, raising squalls on earth,
And filled the plain, the leafage stripping bare
Of all the forest, and the air's vast space
Was thick and troubled, and we closed our eyes,
Until the plague the Gods had sent was past;
And when it ceased, a weary time being gone,
The girl is seen, and with a bitter cry,
Shrill as a bird's, when it beholds its nest
All emptied of its infant brood, she wails;
Thus she, when she beholds the corpse all stript,
Groaned loud with many moanings, and she called
Fierce curses down on those who did the deed.
And in her hand she brings some fine, dry dust,
And from a vase of bronze, well wrought, upraised,
She pours the three libations o'er the dead.
And we, beholding, give her chase forthwith,
And run her down, nought terrified at us.
And then we charged her with the former deed,
As well as this. And nothing she denied.
But this to me both bitter is and sweet,
For to escape one's-self from ill is sweet,
But to bring friends to trouble, this is hard
And painful. Yet my nature bids me count
Above all these things safety for myself.

     CREON (*to* ANTIGONE). Thou, then—yes, thou, who bend'st thy
        face to earth—
Confessest thou, or dost deny the deed?

     ANTIG. I own I did it, and will not deny.

     CREON (*to* GUARD). Go thou thy way, where'er thy will may
        choose,

Freed from a weighty charge.   [*Exit* GUARD.]
[*To* ANTIGONE.]   And now for thee.
Say in few words, not lengthening out thy speech,
Knew'st thou the edicts which forbade these things?
    ANTIG. I knew them. Could I fail? Full clear were they.
    CREON. And thou did'st dare to disobey these laws?
    ANTIG. Yes, for it was not Zeus who gave them forth,
Nor justice, dwelling with the Gods below,
Who traced these laws for all the sons of men;
Nor did I deem thy edicts strong enough,
That thou, a mortal man, should'st overpass
The unwritten laws of God that know not change.
They are not of to-day nor yesterday,
But live for ever, nor can man assign
When first they sprang to being. Not through fear
Of any man's resolve was I prepared
Before the Gods to bear the penalty
Of sinning against these. That I should die
I knew (how should I not?) though thy decree
Had never spoken. And, before my time
If I shall die, I reckon this a gain;
For whoso lives, as I, in many woes,
How can it be but he shall gain by death?
And so for me to bear this doom of thine
Has nothing painful. But, if I had left
My mother's son unburied on his death,
In that I should have suffered; but in this
I suffer not. And should I seem to thee
To do a foolish deed, 'tis simply this,—
I bear the charge of folly from a fool.
    CHORUS. The maiden's stubborn will, of stubborn sire
The offspring shows itself. She knows not yet
To yield to evils.
    CREON.   Know then, minds too stiff
Most often stumble, and the rigid steel
Baked in the furnace, made exceeding hard,
Thou see'st most often split and shivered lie;
And I have known the steeds of fiery mood
With a small curb subdued. It is not meet
That one who lives in bondage to his neighbors

Should think too proudly. Wanton outrage then
This girl first learnt, transgressing these my laws;
But this, when she has done it, is again
A second outrage, over it to boast,
And laugh as having done it. Surely, then,
She is the man, not I, if, all unscathed,
Such deeds of might are hers. But be she child
Of mine own sister, or of one more near
Than all the kith and kin of Household Zeus,
She and her sister shall not 'scape a doom
Most foul and shameful; for I charge her, too,
With having planned this deed of sepulture.
Go ye and call her. 'Twas but now within
I saw her raving, losing self-command.
And still the mind of those who in the dark
Plan deeds of evil is the first to fail,
And so convicts itself of secret guilt.
But most I hate when one found out in guilt
Will seek to gloze and brave it to the end.

ANTIG.   And dost thou seek aught else beyond my death?

CREON.   Nought else for me. That gaining, I gain all.

ANTIG.   Why then delay? Of all thy words not one
Pleases me now (and may it never please!),
And so all mine must grate upon thine ears.
And yet how could I higher glory gain
Than placing my true brother in his tomb?
There is not one of these but would confess
It pleases them, did fear not seal their lips.
The tyrant's might in much besides excels,
And it may do and say whate'er it will.

CREON.   Of all the race of Cadmos thou alone
Look'st thus upon the deed.

ANTIG.   They see it too
As I do, but their tongue is tied for thee.

CREON.   Art not ashamed against their thoughts to think?

ANTIG.   There is nought base in honoring our own blood.

CREON.   And was he not thy kin who fought against him?

ANTIG.   Yea, brother, of one father and one mother.

CREON.   Why then give honor which dishonors him?

ANTIG.   The dead below will not repeat thy words.

CREON. Yes, if thou give like honor to the godless.
ANTIG. It was his brother, not his slave that died.
CREON. Wasting this land, while *he* died fighting for it.
ANTIG. Yet Hades still craves equal rites for all.
CREON. The good craves not the portion of the bad.
ANTIG. Who knows if this be holy deemed below?
CREON. Not even when he dies can foe be friend.
ANTIG. My nature leads to sharing love, not hate.
CREON. Go then below; and if thou must have love,
Love them. While I live, women shall not rule.

[*Enter* ISMENE, *led in by Attendants.*]

CHORUS. And, lo! Ismene at the gate
Comes shedding tears of sisterly regard,
And o'er her brow a gathering cloud
      Mars the deep roseate blush,
      Bedewing her fair cheek.
CREON [*to* ISMENE]. And thou who, creeping as a viper creeps,
Did'st drain my life in secret, and I knew not
That I was rearing two accursèd ones,
Subverters of my throne,—come, tell me, then,
Wilt thou confess thou took'st thy part in this,
Or wilt thou swear thou did'st not know of it?
ISME. I did the deed, if she did, go with her;
Yes, share the guilt, and bear an equal blame.
ANTIG. Nay, justice will not suffer this, for thou
Did'st not consent, nor did I let thee join.
ISME. Nay, in thy troubles, I am not ashamed
In the same boat with thee to share thy fate.
ANTIG. Who did it, Hades knows, and those below:
I do not love a friend who loves in words.
ISME. Do not, my sister, put me to such shame,
As not to let me join in death with thee,
And so to pay due reverence to the dead.
ANTIG. Share not my death, nor make thine own this deed
Thou had'st no hand in. My death shall suffice.
ISME. What life to me is sweet, bereaved of thee?
ANTIG. Ask Creon there, since thou o'er him dost watch.
ISME. Why vex me so, in nothing bettered by it?
ANTIG. 'Tis pain indeed, to laugh my laugh at thee.

Isme. But now, at least, how may I profit thee?

Antig. Save thou thyself. I grudge not thy escape.

Isme. Ah, woe is me! and must I miss thy fate?

Antig. Thou mad'st thy choice to live, and I to die.

Isme. 'Twas not because I failed to speak my thoughts.

Antig. To these did'st thou, to those did I seem wise.

Isme. And yet the offense is equal in us both.

Antig. Take courage. Thou dost live. My soul long since
Hath died to render service to the dead.

Creon. Of these two girls, the one goes mad but now,
The other ever since her life began.

Isme. E'en so, O king; no mind that ever lived
Stands firm in evil days, but goes astray.

Creon. Thine did, when, with the vile, vile deeds thou chosest.

Isme. How could I live without her presence here?

Creon. Speak not of presence. She is here no more.

Isme. And wilt thou slay thy son's betrothèd bride?

Creon. Full many a field there is which he may plough.

Isme. None like that plighted troth 'twixt him and her.

Creon. Wives that are vile I love not for my sons.

Isme. Ah, dearest Hæmon, how thy father shames thee!

Creon. Thou with that marriage dost but vex my soul.

Chorus. And wilt thou rob thy son of her he loved?

Creon. 'Tis Death, not I, shall break the marriage off.

Chorus. Her doom is fixed, it seems, then. She must die.

Creon. Fixed, yes, by me and thee. No more delay,
Lead them within, ye slaves. These must be kept
Henceforth as women, suffered not to roam;
For even boldest natures shrink in fear
When they see Hades overshadowing life.

[*Exeunt* Guards *with* Antigone *and* Ismene.]

Strophe I

Chorus. Blessed are those whose life no woe doth taste!
For unto those whose house
The Gods have shaken, nothing fails of curse
Or woe, that creeps to generations far.
E'en thus a wave (when spreads,
With blasts from Thracian coasts,

The darkness of the deep)
Up from the sea's abyss
Hither and thither rolls the black sand on,
And every jutting peak,
Swept by the storm-wind's strength,
Lashed by the fierce wild waves,
Re-echoes with the far-resounding roar.

ANTISTROPHE I

I see the woes that smote, in ancient days,
The seed of Labdacos,
Who perished long ago, with grief on grief
Still falling, nor does this age rescue that;
Some God still smites it down,
Nor have they any end:
For now there rose a gleam,
Over the last weak shoots,
That sprang from out the race of Œdipus;
Yet this the blood-stained scythe
Of those that reign below
Cuts off relentlessly,
And maddened speech, and frenzied rage of heart.

STROPHE II

Thy power, O Zeus, what haughtiness of man,
Yea, what can hold in check?
Which neither sleep, that maketh all things old,
Nor the long months of Gods that never fail,
Can for a moment seize.
But still as Lord supreme,
Waxing not old with time,
Thou dwellest in Thy sheen of radiancy
On far Olympus' height.
Through future near or far as through the past,
One law holds ever good,
Nought comes to life of man unscathed throughout by woe.

ANTISTROPHE II

For hope to many comes in wanderings wild,
    A solace and support;
To many as a cheat of fond desires,
And creepeth still on him who knows it not,
    Until he burn his foot
    Within the scorching flame.
Full well spake one of old,
That evil ever seems to be as good
    To those whose thoughts of heart
    God leadeth unto woe,
And without woe, he spends but shortest space of time.

And here comes Hæmon, last of all thy sons:
    Comes he bewailing sore
The fate of her who should have been his bride,
    The maid Antigone,
    Grieving o'er vanished joys?

[*Enter* HÆMON.]

CREON. Soon we shall know much more than seers can tell.
Surely thou dost not come, my son, to rage
Against thy father, hearing his decree,
Fixing her doom who should have been thy bride;
Or dost thou love us still, whate'er we do?
    HÆMON. My father, I am thine; and thou dost guide
With thy wise counsels, which I gladly follow.
No marriage weighs one moment in the scales
With me, while thou dost guide my steps aright.
    CREON. This thought, my son, should dwell within thy breast,
That all things stand below a father's will;
For so men pray that they may rear and keep
Obedient offspring by their hearths and homes,
That they may both requite their father's foes,
And pay with him like honors to his friend.
But he who reareth sons that profit not,
What could one say of him but this, that he
Breeds his own sorrow, laughter to his foes?
Lose not thy reason, then, my son, o'ercome

By pleasure, for a woman's sake, but know,
A cold embrace is that to have at home
A worthless wife, the partner of thy bed.
What ulcerous sore is worse than one we love
Who proves all worthless? No! with loathing scorn,
As hateful to thee, let that girl go wed
A spouse in Hades. Taken in the act
I found her, her alone of all the State,
Rebellious. And I will not make myself
False to the State. She dies. So let her call
On Zeus, the lord of kindred. If I rear
Of mine own stock things foul and orderless,
I shall have work enough with those without.
For he who in the life of home is good
Will still be seen as just in things of state;
I should be sure that man would govern well,
And know well to be governed, and would stand
In war's wild storm, on his appointed post,
A just and good defender. But the man
Who by transgressions violates the laws,
Or thinks to bid the powers that be obey,
He must not hope to gather praise from me.
No! we must follow whom the State appoints,
In things or just and trivial, or, may be,
The opposite of these. For anarchy
Is our worst evil, brings our commonwealth
To utter ruin, lays whole houses low,
In a battle strife hurls firm allies in flight;
But they who yield to guidance—these shall find
Obedience saves most men. Thus health should come
To what our rulers order; least of all
Ought men to bow before a woman's sway.
Far better, if it must be so, to fall
By a man's hand, than thus to bear reproach,
By woman conquered.
    CHORUS.   Unto us, O king,
Unless our years have robbed us of our wit,
Thou seemest to say wisely what thou say'st.
    HÆMON.   The Gods, my father, have bestowed on man
His reason, noblest of all earthly gifts;

And that thou speakest wrongly these thy words
I cannot say (God grant I ne'er know how
Such things to utter!) yet another's thoughts
May have some reason. 'Tis my lot to watch
What each man says or does, or blames in thee,
For dread thy face to one of low estate,
Who speaks what thou wilt not rejoice to hear.
But I can hear the things in darkness said,
How the whole city wails this maiden's fate,
As one "who of all women most unjustly,
For noblest deed must die the foulest death,
Who her own brother, fallen in the fray,
Would neither leave unburied, nor expose
To carrion dogs, or any bird of prey,
May she not claim the meed of golden praise?"
Such is the whisper that in secret runs
All darkling. And for me, my father, nought
Is dearer than thy welfare. What can be
A nobler prize of honor for the son
Than a sire's glory, or for sire than son's?
I pray thee, then, wear not one mood alone,
That what thou say'st is right, and nought but that;
For he who thinks that he alone is wise,
His mind and speech above what others have,
Such men when searched are mostly empty found.
But for a man to learn, though he be wise,
Yea to learn much, and know the time to yield,
Brings no disgrace. When winter floods the streams,
Thou see'st the trees that bend before the storm
Save their last twigs, while those that will not yield
Perish with root and branch. And when one hauls
Too tight the mainsail rope, and will not slack,
He has to end his voyage with deck o'erturned.
Do thou then yield; permit thyself to change.
Young though I be, if any prudent thought
Be with me, I at least will dare assert
The higher worth of one, who, come what will,
Is full of knowledge. If that may not be
(For nature is not wont to take that bent),
'Tis good to learn from those who counsel well.

CHORUS. My king! 'tis fit that thou should'st learn from him,
If he speaks words in season; and, in turn,
That thou [*to* HÆMON] should'st learn of him, for both speak well.
CREON. Shall we at our age stoop to learn from him,
Young as he is, the lesson to be wise?
HÆMON. Learn nought thou should'st not learn, and if I'm
            young,
Thou should'st my deeds and not my years consider.
CREON. Is that thy deed to reverence rebel souls?
HÆMON. I would bid none waste reverence on the base.
CREON. Has not that girl been seized with that disease?
HÆMON. The men of Thebes with one accord say, No.
CREON. And will my subjects tell us how to rule?
HÆMON. Dost thou not see thou speakest like a boy?
CREON. Must I then rule for others than myself?
HÆMON. That is no State which hangs on one man's will.
CREON. Is not the State deemed his who governs it?
HÆMON. Brave rule! Alone, and o'er an empty land!
CREON. This boy, it seems, will be his bride's ally.
HÆMON. If thou art she, for thou art all my care.
CREON. Basest of base, against thy father pleading!
HÆMON. Yea, for I see thee sin a grievous sin.
CREON. And do I sin revering mine own sway?
HÆMON. Thou show'st no reverence, trampling on God's laws.
CREON. O guilty soul, by woman's craft beguiled!
HÆMON. Thou wilt not find me slave unto the base.
CREON. Thy every word is still on her behalf.
HÆMON. Yea, and on thine and mine, and theirs below.
CREON. Be sure thou shalt not wed her while she lives.
HÆMON. Then she must die, and, dying, others slay.
CREON. And dost thou dare to come to me with threats?
HÆMON. Is it a threat against vain thoughts to speak?
CREON. Thou to thy cost shalt teach me wisdom's ways,
Thyself in wisdom wanting.
HÆMON.   I would say
Thou wast unwise, if thou wert not my father.
CREON. Thou woman's slave, I say, prate on no more.
HÆMON. Wilt thou then speak, and, speaking, listen not?
CREON. Nay, by Olympus! Thou shalt not go free
To flout me with reproaches. Lead her out

Whom my soul hates, that she may die forthwith
Before mine eyes, and near her bridegroom here.
    HÆMON. No! Think it not! Near me she shall not die,
And thou shalt never see my face alive,
That thou may'st storm at those who like to yield.   [*Exit.*]
    CHORUS. The man has gone, O king, in hasty mood.
A mind distressed in youth is hard to bear.
    CREON. Let him do what he will, and bear himself
As more than man, he shall not save those girls.
    CHORUS. What! Dost thou mean to slay them both alike?
    CREON. Not her who touched it not; there thou say'st well.
    CHORUS. What form of death mean'st thou to slay her with?
    CREON. Leading her on to where the desert path
Is loneliest, there alive, in rocky cave
Will I immure her, just so much of food
Before her set as may avert pollution,
And save the city from the guilt of blood;
And there, invoking Hades, whom alone
Of all the Gods she worships, she, perchance,
Shall gain escape from death, or then shall know
That Hades-worship is but labor lost.   [*Exit.*]

STROPHE

    CHORUS. O Love, in every battle victor owned;
      Love, rushing on thy prey,
Now on a maiden's soft and blooming cheek,
    In secret ambush hid;
Now o'er the broad sea wandering at will,
    And now in shepherd's folds;
Of all the Undying Ones none 'scape from thee,
    Nor yet of mortal men
Whose lives are measured as a fleeting day;
And who has thee is frenzied in his soul.

ANTISTROPHE

Thou makest vile the purpose of the just,
    To his own fatal harm;
Thou hast stirred up this fierce and deadly strife,
    Of men of nearest kin;

The charm of eyes of bride beloved and fair
    Is crowned with victory,
And dwells on high among the powers that rule.
    Equal with holiest laws;
For Aphrodite, she whom none subdues,
Sports in her might and majesty divine.
    I, even I, am borne
    Beyond the appointed laws;
    I look on this, and cannot stay
    The fountain of my tears.
    For, lo! I see her, see Antigone
    Wend her sad, lonely way
To that bride-chamber where we all must lie.

[*Enter* ANTIGONE.]

ANTIG. Behold, O men of this my fatherland,
    I wend my last lone way,
Seeing the last sunbeam, now and nevermore;
    He leads me yet alive,
    Hades that welcomes all,
    To Acheron's dark shore,
    With neither part nor lot
    In marriage festival,
    Nor hath the marriage hymn
    Been sung for me as bride,
But I shall be the bride of Acheron.
    CHORUS. And hast thou not all honor, worthiest praise,
Who goest to the home that hides the dead,
Not smitten by the sickness that decays,
    Nor by the sharp sword's meed,
But of thy own free will, in fullest life,
    Alone of mortals, thus
    To Hades tak'st thy way?
    ANTIG. I heard of old her pitiable end,
    On Sipylos' high crag,
The Phrygian stranger[5] from a far land come,

---

5. *Phrygian stranger*. Niobe. She boasted of her seven sons and seven daughters,
and scorned Leto, who had only one of each. To punish her, Leto's children,
Apollo and Artemis, killed all Niobe's children with their arrows. Niobe
mourned for them until she was turned into a pillar of stone, from which
tears continued to flow.

Whom Tantalus begat;
Whom growth of rugged rock,
Clinging as ivy clings,
Subdued, and made its own:
And now, so runs the tale,
There, as she melts in shower,
The snow abideth aye,
And still bedews yon cliffs that lie below
Those brows that ever weep.
With fate like hers God brings me to my rest.
 CHORUS. A Goddess she, and of the high Gods born;
And we are mortals, born of mortal seed.
And lo! for one who liveth but to die,
To gain like doom with those of heavenly race,
 Is great and strange to hear.
 ANTIG. Ye mock me then. Alas! Why wait ye not,
By all our fathers' Gods, I ask of you,
 Till I have passed away,
 But flout me while I live?
 O city that I love,
 O men that claim as yours
 That city stored with wealth,
 O Dirkè, fairest fount,
O grove of Thebes, that boasts her chariot host,
 I bid you witness all,
 How, with no friends to weep,
 By what stern laws condemned,
I go to that strong dungeon of the tomb,
 For burial strange, ah me!
Nor dwelling with the living, nor the dead.
 CHORUS. Forward and forward still to farthest verge
Of daring hast thou gone,
And now, O child, thou hast rushed violently
 Where Right erects her throne;
Surely thou payest to the uttermost
 Thy father's debt of guilt.
 ANTIG. Ah! Thou hast touched the quick of all my grief,
The thrice-told tale of all my father's woe,
 The fate which dogs us all,
The old Labdakid race of ancient fame.

Woe for the curses dire
Of that defilèd bed,
With foulest incest stained,
My mother's with my sire,
Whence I myself have sprung, most miserable.
    And now, I go to them,
    To sojourn in the grave,
    Accursèd, and unwed;
    Ah, brother, thou didst find
    Thy marriage fraught with ill,
And thou, though dead, hast smitten down my life.
    CHORUS. Acts reverent and devout
    May claim devotion's name,
But power, in one to whom power comes as trust,
    May never be defied;
    And thee, thy stubborn mood,
    Self-chosen, layeth low.
    ANTIG. Unwept, without a friend,
    Unwed, and whelmed in woe,
I journey on this road that open lies.
No more shall it be mine (O misery!)
To look upon yon daylight's holy eye;
    And yet, of all my friends,
    Not one bewails my fate,
    No kindly tear is shed.

                    [*Enter* CREON.]

    CREON. And know ye not, if men have leave to speak
Their songs and wailings thus to stave off death,
That they will never stop? Lead, lead her on,
Without delay, and, as I said, immure
In yon cavernous tomb, and then depart.
Leave her to choose, or drear and lonely death,
Or, living, in the tomb to find her home.
Our hands are clean in all that touches her;
But she no more shall dwell on earth with us.
    ANTIG. (*turning towards the cavern*). O tomb, my bridal
            chamber, vaulted home.
Guarded right well for ever, where I go

To join mine own, of whom the greater part
Among the dead doth Persephassa[6] hold;
And I, of all the last and saddest, wend
My way below, life's little span unfilled.
And yet I go, and feed myself with hopes
That I shall meet them, by my father loved,
Dear to my mother, well-beloved of thee,
Thou darling brother: I, with these hands,
Washed each dear corpse, arrayed you, poured libations,
In rites of burial; and in care for thee,
Thy body, Polyneikes, honoring,
I gain this recompense. (And yet in sight
Of all that rightly judge the deed was good;
I had not done it had I come to be
A mother with her children,—had not dared,
Though 'twere a husband dead that moldered there,
Against my country's will to bear this toil.
And am I asked what law constrained me thus?
I answer, had I lost a husband dear,
I might have had another; other sons
By other spouse, if one were lost to me;
But when my father and my mother sleep
In Hades, then no brother more can come.
And therefore, giving thee the foremost place,
I seemed in Creon's eyes, O brother dear,
To sin in boldest daring. Therefore now
He leads me, having taken me by force,
Cut off from marriage bed and marriage song,
Untasting wife's true joy, or mother's bliss,
With infant at her breast, but all forlorn,
Bereaved of friends, in utter misery,
Alive, I tread the chambers of the dead.)
What law of Heaven have I transgressed against?
What use for me, ill-starred one, still to look
To any God for succor, or to call
On any friend for aid? For holiest deed
I bear this charge of rank unholiness.
If acts like these the Gods on high approve,
We, taught by pain, shall own that we have sinned;

6. *Persephassa*, Persephone.

But if these sin [*looking at* CREON] I pray they suffer not
Worse evils than the wrongs they do to me.
    CHORUS. Still do the same wild blasts
    Vex her who standeth there.
    CREON. Therefore shall these her guards
    Weep sore for this delay.
    ANTIG. Ah me! this word of thine
    Tells of death drawing nigh.
    CHORUS. I cannot bid thee hope
      For other end than this.
    ANTIG. O citadel of Thebes, my native land,
      Ye Gods of ancient days,
      I go, and linger not.
Behold me, O ye senators of Thebes,
The last, lone scion of the kingly race,
What things I suffer, and from whom they come,
Revering still the laws of reverence.
                [GUARDS *lead* ANTIGONE *away*.]

STROPHE I

    CHORUS. So did the form of Danaë[7] bear of old,
    In brazen palace hid,
    To lose the light of heaven,
And in her tomb-like chamber was enclosed:
Yet she, O child, was noble in her race,
And well she stored the golden shower of Zeus.
But great and dread the might of Destiny:
    Nor kingly wealth, nor war,
    Nor tower, nor dark-hulled ships
Beaten by waves, escape.

ANTISTROPHE I

So too was shut, enclosed in dungeon cave,
    Bitter and fierce in mood,
    The son of Dryas,[8] king

7. *Danaë*, though locked up by her father, was visited by Zeus in the form of a shower of gold.
8. *son of Dryas*, Lycurgus. He tried to root out the worship of Dionysos in Thrace, and was punished bv the gods as here stated.

Of yon Edonian tribes, for vile reproach,
By Dionysos' hands, and so his strength
And soul o'ermad wastes drop by drop away,
And so he learnt that he, against the God,
  Spake his mad words of scorn;
  For he the Mænad throng
  And bright fire fain had stopped,
  And roused the Muses' wrath.

Strophe II

And by the double sea of those Dark Rocks
  Are shores of Bosporos,
And Thracian isle, as Salmydessos known,
  Where Ares, whom they serve,
  God of the region round,
  Saw the dire, blinding wound,
  That smote the twin-born sons
Of Phineus[9] by relentless step-dame's hand,—
  Dark wound, on dark-doomed eyes,
  Not with the stroke of sword,
But blood-stained hands, and point of spindle sharp.

Antistrophe II

And they in misery, miserable fate,
  Wasting away, wept sore,
Born of a mother wedded with a curse.
  And she[10] who claimed descent
  From men of ancient fame,
  The old Erechtheid race,
  Amid her father's winds,
Daughter of Boreas, in far distant caves
  Was reared, a child of Gods,
  Swift moving as the steed

9. *Phineus*, King of Salmydessos, blinded his two sons because of false accusations made against them by their stepmother.

10. *She*, Phineus' first wife, daughter of Boreas and mother of the blinded children.

O'er lofty crag, and yet
The ever-living Fates bore hard on her.

[*Enter* Teiresias, *guided by a Boy.*]

   Teir. Princes of Thebes, we come as travellers joined,
One seeing for both, for still the blind must use
A guide's assistance to direct his steps.
   Creon. And what new thing, Teiresias, brings thee here?
   Teir. I'll tell thee, and do thou the seer obey.
   Creon. Of old I was not wont to slight thy thoughts.
   Teir. So did'st thou steer our city's course full well.
   Creon. I bear my witness from good profit gained.
   Teir. Know then, thou walk'st on fortune's razor-edge.
   Creon. What means this? How I shudder at thy speech!
   Teir. Soon shalt thou know, as thou dost hear the signs
Of my dread art. For sitting, as of old,
Upon my ancient seat of augury,
Where every bird finds haven, lo! I hear
Strange cry of wingèd creatures, shouting shrill,
With inarticulate passion, and I knew
That they were tearing each the other's flesh
With bloody talons, for their whirring wings
Made that quite clear: and straightway I, in fear,
Made trial of the sacrifice that lay
On fiery altar. And Hephæstos' flame
Shone not from out the offering; but there oozed
Upon the ashes, trickling from the bones,
A moisture, and it smouldered, and it spat,
And, lo! the gall was scattered to the air,
And forth from out the fat that wrapped them round
The thigh-bones fell. Such omens of decay
From holy sacrifice I learnt from him,
This boy, who now stands here, for he is still
A guide to me, as I to others am.
And all this evil falls upon the State,
From out thy counsels; for our altars all,
Our sacred hearths are full of food for dogs
And birds unclean, the flesh of that poor wretch
Who fell, the son of Œdipus. And so
The Gods no more hear prayers of sacrifice,

Nor own the flame that burns the victim's limbs;
Nor do the birds give cry of omen good,
But feed on carrion of a slaughtered corpse.
Think thou on this, my son: to err, indeed,
Is common unto all, but having erred,
He is no longer reckless or unblest,
Who, having fallen into evil, seeks
For healing, nor continues still unmoved.
Self-will must bear the charge of stubbornness:
Yield to the dead, and outrage not a corpse.
What prowess is it fallen foes to slay?
Good counsel give I, planning good for thee,
And of all joys the sweetest is to learn
From one who speaketh well, should that bring gain.

    CREON. Old man, as archers aiming at their mark,
So ye shoot forth your venomed darts at me;
I know your augur's tricks, and by your tribe
Long since am tricked and sold. Yes, gain your gains,
Get Sardis' amber metal, Indian gold;
That corpse ye shall not hide in any tomb.
Not though the eagles, birds of Zeus, should bear
Their carrion morsels to the throne of God,
Not even fearing this pollution dire,
Will I consent to burial. Well I know
That man is powerless to pollute the Gods.
But many fall, Teiresias, dotard old,
A shameful fall, who gloze their shameful words
For lucre's sake, with surface show of good.

      TEIR. Ah me! Does no man know, does none consider—?
    CREON. Consider what? What trite poor saw comes now?
      TEIR. How far good counsel is of all things best?
    CREON. So far, I trow, as folly is worst ill.
      TEIR. Of that disease thy soul, alas! is full.
    CREON. I will not meet a seer with evil words.
      TEIR. Thou dost so, saying I divine with lies.
    CREON. The race of seers is ever fond of gold.
      TEIR. And that of tyrants still loves lucre foul.
    CREON. Dost know thou speak'st thy words of those that rule?
      TEIR. I know. Through me thou rul'st a city saved.
    CREON. Wise seer art thou, yet given o'ermuch to wrong.

TEIR. Thou'lt stir me to speak out my soul's dread secrets.
CREON. Out with them; only speak them not for gain.
TEIR. So is't, I trow, in all that touches thee.
CREON. Know that thou shalt not bargain with my will.
TEIR. Know, then, and know it well, that thou shalt see
Not many winding circuits of the sun,
Before thou giv'st as quittance for the dead,
A corpse by thee begotten; for that thou
Hast to the ground cast one that walked on earth,
And foully placed within a sepulchre
A living soul; and now thou keep'st from them,
The Gods below, the corpse of one unblest,
Unwept, unhallowed, and in these things thou
Canst claim no part, nor yet the Gods above;
But they by thee are outraged; and they wait,
The sure though slow avengers of the grave,
The dread Erinnyes[11] of the mighty Gods,
For thee in these same evils to be snared.
Search well if I say this as one who sells
His soul for money. Yet a little while,
And in thy house the wail of men and women
Shall make it plain. And every city stirs
Itself in arms against thee, owning those
Whose limbs the dogs have buried, or fierce wolves,
Or wingèd birds have brought the accursèd taint
To region consecrate. Doom like to this,
Sure darting as an arrow to its mark,
I launch at thee (for thou dost vex me sore),
An archer aiming at the very heart,
And thou shalt not escape its fiery sting.
And now, O boy, lead thou me home again,
That he may vent his spleen on younger men,
And learn to keep his tongue more orderly,
With better thoughts than this his present mood.   [*Exit.*]
CHORUS. The man has gone, O king, predicting woe,
And well we know, since first our raven hair
Was mixed with gray, that never yet his words
Were uttered to our State and failed of truth.
CREON. I know it too, 'tis that that troubles me.

11. *Erinnyes*, the Furies, avengers of crime, especially crime against kindred.

To yield is hard, but, holding out, to smite
One's soul with sorrow, this is harder still.
CHORUS. We need wise counsel, O Menœkeus' son.
CREON. What shall I do? Speak thou, and I'll obey.
CHORUS. Go then, and free the maiden from her tomb,
And give a grave to him who lies exposed.
CREON. Is this thy counsel? Dost thou bid me yield?
CHORUS. Without delay, O king, for lo! they come,
The God's swift-footed ministers of ill,
And in an instant lay the self-willed low.
CREON. Ah me! 'tis hard; and yet I bend my will
To do thy bidding. With necessity
We must not fight at such o'erwhelming odds.
CHORUS. Go then and act! Commit it not to others.
CREON. E'en as I am I'll go. Come, come my men,
Present or absent, come, and in your hands
Bring axes: come to yonder eminence.
And I, since now my judgment leans that way,
Who myself bound her, now myself will loose,
Too much I fear lest it should wisest prove
Maintaining ancient laws to end my life. [*Exit.*]

STROPHE I

CHORUS. O Thou of many names,
Of that Cadmeian maid[12]
The glory and the joy,
Whom Zeus as offspring owns,
Zeus, thundering deep and loud,
Who watchest over famed Italia,
And reign'st o'er all the bays that Deo claims
On fair Eleusis' coast.
Bacchos, who dwell'st in Thebes, the mother-town
Of all thy Bacchant train,
Along Ismenus' stream,
And with the dragon's brood;[13]

12. *maid*, Semele, mother of Dionysos, and wife of Zeus.
13. *Cadmus*, after killing a dragon, sowed the dragon's teeth, which turned into armed men. They all killed each other except for five, who became the ancestors of the Thebans.

ANTISTROPHE I

Thee, o'er the double peak
Of yonder height the blaze
Of flashing fire beholds,
Where nymphs of Corycos
Go forth in Bacchic dance,
And by the flowery stream of Castaly,
And Thee, the ivied slopes of Nysa's hills,
And vine-clad promontory,
(While words of more than mortal melody
Shout out the well-known name,)
Send forth, the guardian lord
Of the wide streets of Thebes.

STROPHE II

Above all cities Thou,
With her, thy mother whom the thunder slew,
Dost look on it with love;
And now, since all the city bendeth low
Beneath the sullen plague,
Come Thou with cleansing tread
O'er the Parnassian slopes,
Or o'er the moaning straits.

ANTISTROPHE II

O Thou, who lead'st the band,
The choral band of stars still breathing fire,
Lord of the hymns of night,
The child of highest Zeus; appear, O king,
With Thyian maidens wild,
Who all night long in dance,
With frenzied chorus sing
Thy praise, their lord, Iacchos.[14]

[Enter MESSENGER.]

14. Iacchos, Bacchos.

MESS.   Ye men of Cadmos and Amphion's house,
I know no life of mortal man which I
Would either praise or blame. 'Tis Fortune's chance
That raiseth up, and Fortune bringeth low,
The man who lives in good or evil plight;
And prophet of men's future there is none.
For Creon, so I deemed, deserved to be
At once admired and envied, having saved
This land of Cadmos from the hands of foes;
And, having ruled with fullest sovereignty,
He lived and prospered, joyous in a race
Of goodly offspring. Now, all this is gone;
For when men lose the joys that sweeten life,
I cannot deem they live, but rather count
As if a breathing corpse. His heaped-up stores
Of wealth are large, so be it, and he lives
With all a sovereign's state; and yet, if joy
Be absent, all the rest I count as nought,
And would not weigh them against pleasure's charm,
More than a vapor's shadow.

CHORUS.   What is this?
What new disaster tell'st thou of our chiefs?

MESS.   Dead are they, and the living cause of their death.

CHORUS.   Who slays, and who is slaughtered? Tell thy tale.

MESS.   Hæmon is dead, slain, weltering in his blood.

CHORUS.   By his own act, or by his father's hand?

MESS.   His own, in wrath against his father's crime.

CHORUS.   O prophet! true, most true, those words of thine.

MESS.   Since things stand thus, we well may counsel take.

CHORUS.   Lo! Creon's wife comes, sad Eurydike.
She from the house approaches, hearing speech
About her son, or else by accident.

[*Enter* EURYDIKE.]

EURYD.   I on my way, my friends, as suppliant bound,
To pay my vows at Pallas' shrine, have heard
Your words, and so I chanced to draw the bolt
Of the half-opened door, when lo! a sound
Falls on my ears, of evil striking home,
And terror-struck I fall in deadly swoon

Back in my handmaids' arms; yet tell it me,
Tell the tale once again, for I shall hear,
By long experience disciplined to grief.
   Mess. Dear lady, I will tell thee: I was by,
And will not leave one word of truth untold.
Why should we smooth and gloze, where all too soon
We should be found as liars? Truth is still
The only safety. Lo! I went with him,
Thy husband, in attendance, to the edge
Of yonder plain, where still all ruthlessly
The corpse of Polyneikes lay exposed,
Mangled by dogs. And, having prayed to her,
The Goddess of all pathways, and to Pluto,
To temper wrath with pity, him they washed
With holy washing; and what yet was left
We burnt in branches freshly cut, and heaped
A high-raised grave from out his native soil,
And then we entered on the stone-paved home,
Death's marriage-chamber for the ill-starred maid.
And some one hears, while standing yet afar,
Shrill voice of wailing near the bridal bower,
By funeral rites unhallowed, and he comes
And tells my master, Creon. On his ears,
Advancing nearer, falls a shriek confused
Of bitter sorrow, and with groaning loud,
He utters one sad cry, "Me miserable!
And am I then a prophet? Do I wend
This day the dreariest way of all my life?
My son's voice greets me. Go, my servants, go,
Quickly draw near, and standing by the tomb,
Search ye and see; and where the stone torn out
Shall make an opening, look ye in, and say
If I hear Hæmon's voice, or if my soul
Is cheated by the Gods." And then we searched,
As he, our master, in his frenzy bade us;
And, in the furthest corner of the vault,
We saw her hanging by her neck, with cord
Of linen threads entwined, and him we found
Clasping her form in passionate embrace,
And mourning o'er the doom that robbed him of her,

His father's deed, and that his marriage bed,
So full of woe. When Creon saw him there,
Groaning aloud in bitterness of heart,
He goes to him, and calls in wailing voice,
"Poor boy! what hast thou done? Hast thou then lost
Thy reason? In what evil sinkest thou?
Come forth, my child, on bended knee I ask thee."
And then the boy, with fierce, wild-gleaming eyes,
Glared at him, spat upon his face, and draws,
Still answering nought, the sharp two-handled sword.
Missing his aim (his father from the blow
Turning aside), in anger with himself,
The poor ill-doomed one, even as he was,
Fell on his sword, and drove it through his breast,
Full half its length, and clasping, yet alive,
The maiden's arm, still soft, he there breathes out
In broken gasps, upon her fair white cheek,
Swift stream of bloody shower. So they lie,
Dead bridegroom with dead bride, and he has gained,
Poor boy, his marriage rites in Hades home,
And left to all men witness terrible,
That man's worst ill is want of counsel wise.   [*Exit* EURYDIKE.]
    CHORUS. What dost thou make of this?
        She turneth back,
Before one word, or good or ill, she speaks.
    MESS. I too am full of wonder. Yet with hopes
I feed myself, she will not think it meet,
Hearing her son's woes, openly to wail
Out in the town, but to her handmaids there
Will give command to wail her woe at home.
Too trained a judgment has she so to err.
    CHORUS. I know not. To my mind, or silence hard,
Or vain wild cries, are signs of bitter woe.
    MESS. Soon we shall know, within the house advancing,
If, in the passion of her heart, she hides
A secret purpose. Truly dost thou speak;
There is a terror in that silence hard.
    CHORUS [*seeing* CREON *approaching with the corpse of* HÆMON
       in his arms].
And lo! the king himself is drawing nigh,

And in his hands he bears a record clear,
No woe (if I may speak) by others caused,
    Himself the great offender.

[*Enter* CREON, *bearing* HÆMON's *body.*]

    CREON.   Woe! for the sins of souls of evil mood,
Stern, mighty to destroy!
O ye who look on those of kindred race,
    The slayers and the slain,
Woe for mine own rash plans that prosper not!
Woe for thee, son; but new in life's career,
    And by a new fate dying!
        Woe! woe!
    Thou diest, thou art gone,
Not by thine evil counsel, but by mine.
    CHORUS.   Ah me! Too late thou seem'st to see the right.
    CREON.   Ah me!
I learn the grievous lesson. On my head,
God, pressing sore, hath smitten me and vexed,
In ways most rough and terrible (Ah me!),
Shattering my joy, as trampled under foot.
Woe! woe! Man's labors are but labor lost.

    [*Enter* SECOND MESSENGER.]

    SEC. MESS.   My master! thou, as one who hast full store,
One source of sorrow bearest in thine arms,
And others in thy house, too soon, it seems,
Thou need'st must come and see.
    CREON.   And what remains
Worse evil than the evils that we bear?
    SEC. MESS.   Thy wife is dead, that corpse's mother true,
Ill starred one, smitten with a blow just dealt.
    CREON.   O agony!
Haven of Death, that none may pacify,
    Why dost thou thus destroy me?
[*Turning to* MESSENGER.]   O thou who comest, bringing in thy train
    Woes horrible to tell,
Thou tramplest on a man already slain.
What say'st thou? What new tidings bring'st to me?
        Ah me! ah me!

Is it that now there waits in store for me
My own wife's death to crown my misery?
    CHORUS. Full clearly thou may'st see. No longer now
Does yon recess conceal her.

    [*The gates open and show the dead body of* EURYDIKE.]

    CREON.   Woe is me!
This second ill I gaze on, miserable,
What fate, yea, what still lies in wait for me?
Here in my arms I bear what was my son;
And there, O misery! look upon the dead.
Ah, wretched mother! ah, my son! my son!
    SEC. MESS. In frenzy wild she round the altar clung,
And closed her darkening eyelids, and bewailed
The noble fate of Megareus,[15] who died
Before, and then again that corpse thou hast;
And last of all she cried a bitter cry
Against thy deeds, the murderer of thy sons.
    CREON. Woe! woe! alas!
I shudder in my fear. Will no one strike
A deadly blow with sharp two-edgèd sword?
    Fearful my fate, alas!
And with a fearful woe full sore beset.
    SEC. MESS. She in her death charged thee with being the cause
Of all their sorrows, these and those of old.
    CREON. And in what way struck she the murderous blow?
    SEC. MESS. With her own hand below her heart she stabbed,
Hearing her son's most pitiable fate.
    CREON. Ah me! The fault is mine. On no one else,
Of all that live, the fearful guilt can come;
I, even I, did slay thee, woe is me!
I, yes, I speak the truth. Lead me, ye guards,
Lead me forth quickly; lead me out of sight,
More crushed to nothing than is nothing's self.
    CHORUS. Thou counsellest gain, if gain there be in ills,
For present ills when shortest then are best.
    CREON. Oh, come thou then, come thou,
The last of all my dooms, that brings to me

    15. *Megareus*, Eurydike's other son, who had defended one of the seven
gates of Thebes.

Best boon, my life's last day. Come then, oh come,
That never more I look upon the light.
    CHORUS. These things are in the future. What is near,
That we must do. O'er what is yet to come
They watch, to Whom that work of right belongs.
    CREON. I did but pray for what I most desire.
    CHORUS. Pray thou for nothing then: for mortal man
There is no issue from a doom decreed.
    CREON [*looking at the two corpses*]. Lead me then forth, vain
        shadow that I am,
Who slew thee, O my son, unwillingly,
And thee too—(O my sorrow!)—and I know not
Which way to look or turn. All near at hand
Is turned to evil; and upon my head
There falls a doom far worse than I can bear.
    CHORUS. Man's highest blessedness,
    In wisdom chiefly stands;
And in the things that touch upon the Gods,
    'Tis best in word or deed
    To shun unholy pride;
Great words of boasting bring great punishments,
    And so to gray-haired age
    Teach wisdom at the last.

EURIPIDES
Medea

AESON had been wrongfully deprived of his kingdom of Iolchos, in Thessaly, by his half-brother Pelias. Aeson's son, Jason, set out to regain the kingdom. Pelias promised to restore it to him if he would go to Colchis, at the eastern end of the Black Sea, and bring back the golden fleece kept there by King Aeëtes, for Pelias felt sure that Jason would perish in the attempt. Jason set out in the ship *Argo* with some fifty companions (the Argonauts), and reached Colchis after various adventures. King Aeëtes promised to give him the fleece if he would yoke a pair of fire-breathing bulls, plow the field of Ares, sow a dragon's teeth there, and kill all the armed warriors who would spring up.

Medea, the king's daughter, had fallen in love with Jason, and by her sorcery she enabled him to perform these tasks. When Aeëtes still refused to give up the fleece, Medea fled to the *Argo*, and, after making Jason swear eternal faith to her, told him how to get the fleece by killing the dragon that guarded it. Jason did this, but the *Argo* was pursued and Medea had to kill her brother (the details differ in various versions of the legend) to make good their escape.

They went to Iolchos, where they found that Pelias had killed Jason's entire family. To gain revenge, Medea disguised herself and went to Pelias' daughters, to whom she explained that she could restore their father's youth. As proof of her ability she had them kill and dismember a ram, and then made a magic stew of the pieces and produced a lamb from it. After this demonstration Pelias' daughters readily killed and cut up their father—and Medea refused to act further in the matter.

She and Jason fled to Corinth, and after some years there Jason decided to put aside Medea and marry the daughter of King Creon of Corinth (not to be confused with Creon of Thebes). It is at this point that the action of the play begins.

Persons of the Drama

NURSE OF MEDEA
ATTENDANT OF THE CHILDREN
MEDEA
CHORUS OF CORINTHIAN WOMEN
CREON, *king of Corinth*
JASON
ÆGEUS, *king of Athens*
MESSENGER
THE TWO SONS OF JASON AND MEDEA

SCENE: *Before the Palace of Creon at Corinth.*

NURSE

Ah! would to heaven the *Argo* ne'er had urged
Its rapid voyage to the Colchian strand
'Twixt the Cyanean rocks,[1] nor had the pine
Been felled in Pelion's forests, nor the hands
Of those illustrious chiefs, who that famed bark
Ascended to obtain the golden fleece
For royal Pelias, plied the stubborn oar;
So to Iolchos' turrets had my Queen
Medea never sailed, her soul with love

---

1. *Cyanean rocks,* two rocks which rushed together and crushed ships between them, and which the *Argo* barely escaped.

For Jason smitten, nor, as since her arts
Prevailed on Pelias' daughters to destroy
Their father, in this realm of Corinth dwelt
An exile with her husband and her sons;
Thus to the citizens whose land received her
Had she grown pleasing, and in all his schemes
Assisted Jason: to the wedded pair,
Hence bliss supreme arises, when the bond
Of concord joins them: now their souls are filled
With ruthless hate, and all affection's lost:
For false to his own sons, and her I serve,
With a new consort of imperial birth
Sleeps the perfidious Jason, to the daughter
Of Creon wedded, lord of these domains.
The wretched scorned Medea oft exclaims,
"O by those oaths, by that right hand thou gav'st
The pledge of faith!" She then invokes the gods
To witness what requital she hath found
From Jason. On a couch she lies, no food
Receiving, her whole frame subdued by grief;
And since she marked the treachery of her lord
Melts into tears incessant, from the ground
Her eyes she never raises, never turns
Her face aside, but steadfast as a rock,
Or as the ocean's rising billows, hears
The counsels of her friends, save when she weeps
In silent anguish, with her snowy neck
Averted, for her sire, her native land,
And home, which she forsaking hither came
With him who scorns her now. She from her woes
Too late hath learnt how enviable the lot
Of those who leave not their paternal roof.
She even hates her children, nor with joy
Beholds them: much I dread lest she contrive
Some enterprise unheard of, for her soul
Is vehement, nor will she tamely brook
Injurious treatment; well, full well I know
Her temper, which alarms me, lest she steal
Into their chamber, where the genial couch
Is spread, and with the sword their vitals pierce,

Or to the slaughter of the bridegroom add
That of the monarch, and in some mischance,
Yet more severe than death, herself involve:
For dreadful is her wrath, nor will the object
Of her aversion gain an easy triumph.
But lo, returning from the race, her sons
Draw near: they think not of their mother's woes,
For youthful souls are strangers to affliction.

ATTENDANT, *with the* SONS *of* JASON
and MEDEA, NURSE

ATTEND. O thou, who for a length of time hast dwelt
Beneath the roofs of that illustrious dame
I serve, why stand'st thou at these gates alone
Repeating to thyself a doleful tale:
Or wherefore by Medea from her presence
Art thou dismissed?
NURSE.   Old man, O you who tend
On Jason's sons, to faithful servants aught
Of evil fortune that befalls their lords
Is a calamity: but such a pitch
Of grief am I arrived at, that I felt
An impulse which constrained me to come forth
From these abodes, and to the conscious earth
And heaven proclaim the lost Medea's fate.
ATTEND. Cease not the plaints of that unhappy dame?
NURSE. Your ignorance I envy: for her woes
Are but beginning, nor have yet attained
Their mid career.
ATTEND.   O how devoid of reason,
If we with terms thus harsh may brand our lords,
Of ills more recent nothing yet she knows.
NURSE. Old man, what mean you? Scruple not to speak.
ATTEND. Nought. What I have already said repents me.
NURSE. I by that beard conjure you not to hide
The secret from your faithful fellow-servant.
For I the strictest silence will observe
If it be needful.
ATTEND.   Some one I o'erheard
(Appearing not to listen, as I came

Where aged men sit near Pirene's fount
And hurl their dice) say that from Corinth's land
Creon, the lord of these domains, will banish
The children with their mother; but I know not
Whether th' intelligence be true, and wish
It may prove otherwise.
      NURSE.   Will Jason brook
Such an injurious treatment of his sons,
Although he be at variance with their mother?
      ATTEND. By new connections are all former ties
Dissolved, and he no longer is a friend
To this neglected race.
      NURSE.   We shall be plunged
In utter ruin, if to our old woes,
Yet unexhausted, any fresh we add.
      ATTEND. Be silent, and suppress the dismal tale,
For 'tis unfit our royal mistress know.
      NURSE. Hear, O ye children, how your father's soul
Is turned against you: still, that he may perish
I do not pray, because he is my lord;
Yet treacherous to his friends hath he been found.
      ATTEND. Who is not treacherous? Hast thou lived so long
Without discerning how self-love prevails
O'er social? Some by glory, some by gain,
Are prompted. Then what wonder, for the sake
Of a new consort, if the father slight
These children?
      NURSE.   Go, all will be well, go in.
Keep them as far as possible away,
Nor suffer them to come into the presence
Of their afflicted mother; for her eyes
Have I just seen with wild distraction fired,
As if some horrid purpose against them
She meant to execute; her wrath I know
Will not be pacified, till on some victim
It like a thunderbolt from Heaven descends;
May she assail her foes alone, nor aim
The stroke at those she ought to hold most dear.
      MEDEA [*within*]. Ah me! how grievous are my woes!
         What means
Can I devise to end this hated life?

NURSE. 'Tis as I said: strong agitations seize
Your mother's heart, her choler's raised. Dear children,
Beneath these roofs hie instantly, nor come
Into her sight, accost her not, beware
Of these ferocious manners and the rage
Which boils in that ungovernable spirit.
Go with the utmost speed, for I perceive
Too clearly that her plaints, which in thick clouds
Arise at first, will kindle ere 'tis long
With tenfold violence. What deeds of horror
From that high-soaring, that remorseless soul,
May we expect, when goaded by despair!

                                      [*Exeunt* ATTENDANT *and* SONS.]

MEDEA [*within*]. I have endured, alas! I have endured—
Wretch that I am!—such agonies as call
For loudest plaints. Ye execrable sons
Of a devoted mother, perish ye
With your false sire, and perish his whole house!

NURSE. Why should the sons—ah, wretched me!—partake
Their father's guilt? Why hat'st thou them? Ah me!
How greatly, O ye children, do I fear
Lest mischief should befall you: for the souls
Of kings are prone to cruelty, so seldom
Subdued, and over others wont to rule,
That it is difficult for such to change
Their angry purpose. Happier I esteem
The lot of those who still are wont to live
Among their equals. May I thus grow old,
If not in splendor, yet with safety blest!
For first of all, renown attends the name
Of mediocrity, and to mankind
Such station is more useful: but not long
Can the extremes of grandeur ever last;
And heavier are the curses which it brings
When Fortune visits us in all her wrath.

CHORUS, NURSE

CHORUS. The voice of Colchos' hapless dame I heard—
A clamorous voice, nor yet is she appeased.
Speak, O thou aged matron, for her cries

I from the innermost apartment heard;
Nor can I triumph in the woes with which
This house is visited; for to my soul
Dear are its interests.

NURSE.   This whole house is plunged
In ruin, and its interests are no more.
While Corinth's palace to our lord affords
A residence, within her chamber pines
My mistress, and the counsels of her friends
Afford no comfort to her tortured soul.

MEDEA [*within*]. O that a flaming thunderbolt from Heaven
Would pierce this brain! for what can longer life
To me avail? Fain would I seek repose
In death, and cast away this hated being.

CHORUS. Heard'st thou, all-righteous Jove, thou fostering earth,
And thou, O radiant lamp of day, what plaints,
What clamorous plaints this miserable wife
Hath uttered? Through insatiable desire,
Ah why would you precipitate your death?
O most unwise! These imprecations spare.
What if your lord's affections are engaged
By a new bride, reproach him not, for Jove
Will be the dread avenger of your wrongs;
Nor melt away with unavailing grief,
Weeping for the lost partner of your bed.

MEDEA [*within*]. Great Themis[2] and Diana, awful queen,
Do ye behold the insults I endure,
Though by each oath most holy I have bound
That execrable husband. May I see
Him and his bride, torn limb from limb, bestrew
The palace; me have they presumed to wrong,
Although I ne'er provoked them. O my sire,
And thou my native land, whence I with shame
Departed when my brother I had slain.

NURSE. Heard ye not all she said, with a loud voice
Invoking Themis, who fulfils the vow,
And Jove, to whom the tribes of men look up
As guardian of their oaths? Medea's rage
Can by no trivial vengeance be appeased.

2. *Themis*, a goddess of order and justice.

CHORUS. Could we but draw her hither, and prevail
On her to hear the counsels we suggest,
Then haply might she check that bitter wrath,
That vehemence of temper; for my zeal
Shall not be spared to aid my friends. But go,
And say, "O hasten, ere to those within
Thou do some mischief, for these sorrows rush
With an impetuous tempest on thy soul."
NURSE. This will I do; though there is cause to fear
That on my mistress I shall ne'er prevail:
Yet I my labor gladly will bestow.
Though such a look she on her servants casts
As the ferocious lioness who guards
Her tender young, when anyone draws near
To speak to her. Thou wouldst not judge amiss,
In charging folly and a total want
Of wisdom on the men of ancient days,
Who for their festivals invented hymns,
And to the banquet and the genial board
Confined those actions which o'er human life
Diffuse ecstatic pleasures: but no artist
Hath yet discovered, by the tuneful song,
And varied modulations of the lyre,
How we those piercing sorrows may assuage
Whence slaughters and such horrid mischief spring
As many a prosperous mansion have o'erthrown.
Could music interpose her healing aid
In these inveterate maladies, such gift
Had been the first of blessings to mankind:
But, 'midst choice viands and the circling bowl,
Why should those minstrels strain their useless throat?
To cheer the drooping heart, convivial joys
Are in themselves sufficient.   [Exit NURSE.]
CHORUS.   Mingled groans
And lamentations burst upon mine ear:
She in the bitterness of soul exclaims
Against her impious husband, who betrayed
His plighted faith. By grievous wrongs opprest,
She the vindictive gods invokes, and Themis,

Jove's daughter, guardian of the sacred oath,
Who o'er the waves to Greece benignly steered
Their bark adventurous, launched in midnight gloom,
Through ocean's gates which never can be closed![3]

Medea, Chorus

Medea. From my apartment, ye Corinthian dames,
Lest ye my conduct censure, I come forth:
For I have known full many who obtained
Fame and high rank; some to the public gaze
Stood ever forth, while others, in a sphere
More distant, chose their merits to display:
Nor yet a few, who, studious of repose,
Have with malignant obloquy been called
Devoid of spirit: for no human eyes
Can form a just discernment; at one glance,
Before the inmost secrets of the heart
Are clearly known, a bitter hate 'gainst him
Who never wronged us they too oft inspire.
But 'tis a stranger's duty to adopt
The manners of the land in which he dwells;
Nor can I praise that native, led astray
By mere perverseness and o'erweening folly,
Who bitter enmity incurs from those
Of his own city. But, alas! my friends,
This unforeseen calamity hath withered
The vigor of my soul. I am undone,
Bereft of every joy that life can yield,
And therefore wish to die. For as to him,
My husband, whom it did import me most
To have a thorough knowledge of, he proves
The worst of men. But sure among all those
Who have with breath and reason been endued,
We women are the most unhappy race.
First, with abundant gold are we constrained
To buy a husband, and in him receive

3. The *Argo* was the first ship to escape the Cyanean rocks, or **Symplegades,** and it was fated that, after one ship had passed safely between them, they should never clash together again.

A haughty master. Still doth there remain
One mischief than this mischief yet more grievous,
The hazard whether we procure a mate
Worthless or virtuous: for divorces bring
Reproach to woman, nor must she renounce
The man she wedded; as for her who comes
Where usages and edicts, which at home
She learnt not, are established, she the gift
Of divination needs to teach her how
A husband must be chosen: if aright
These duties we perform, and he the yoke
Of wedlock with complacency sustains,
Ours is a happy life; but if we fail
In this great object, better 'twere to die.
For, when afflicted by domestic ills,
A man goes forth, his choler to appease,
And to some friend or comrade can reveal
What he endures; but we to him alone
For succor must look up. They still contend
That we, at home remaining, lead a life
Exempt from danger, while they launch the spear:
False are these judgments; rather would I thrice,
Armed with a target, in th' embattled field
Maintain my stand, than suffer once the throes
Of childbirth. But this language suits not you:
This is your native city, the abode
Of your loved parents, every comfort life
Can furnish is at hand, and with your friends
You here converse: but I, forlorn, and left
Without a home, am by that husband scorned
Who carried me from a Barbarian realm.
Nor mother, brother, or relation now
Have I, to whom I 'midst these storms of woe,
Like an auspicious haven, can repair.
Thus far I therefore crave ye will espouse
My interests, as if haply any means
Or any stratagem can be devised
For me with justice to avenge these wrongs
On my perfidious husband, on the king
Who to that husband's arms his daughter gave,

And the new-wedded princess; to observe
Strict silence. For although at other times
A woman, filled with terror, is unfit
For battle, or to face the lifted sword,
She when her soul by marriage wrongs is fired,
Thirsts with a rage unparalleled for blood.
    CHORUS. The silence you request I will observe,
For justly on your lord may you inflict
Severest vengeance: still I wonder not
If your disastrous fortunes you bewail:
But Creon I behold who wields the sceptre
Of these domains; the monarch hither comes
His fresh resolves in person to declare.

CREON, MEDEA, CHORUS

    CREON. Thee, O Medea, who, beneath those looks
Stern and forbidding, harbor'st 'gainst thy lord
Resentment, I command to leave these realms
An exile; for companions of thy flight
Take both thy children with thee, nor delay.
Myself pronounce this edict: I my home
Will not revisit, from the utmost bounds
Of this domain, till I have cast thee forth.
    MEDEA. Ah, wretched me! I utterly am ruined:
For in the swift pursuit, my ruthless foes,
Each cable loosing, have unfurled their sails,
Nor can I land on any friendly shore
To save myself, yet am resolved to speak,
Though punishment impend. What cause, O Creon
Have you for banishing me?
    CREON.   Thee I dread
(No longer is it needful to disguise
My thoughts) lest 'gainst my daughter thou contrive
Some evil such as medicine cannot reach.
Full many incidents conspire to raise
This apprehension: with a deep-laid craft
Art thou endued, expert in the device
Of mischiefs numberless; thou also griev'st
Since thou art severed from thy husband's bed.

I am informed, too, thou hast menaced vengeance
'Gainst me, because my daughter I bestowed
In marriage, and the bridegroom, and his bride.
Against these threats I therefore ought to guard
Before they take effect; and better far
Is it for me, O woman, to incur
Thy hatred now, than, soothed by thy mild words,
Hereafter my forbearance to bewail.

     MEDEA. Not now, alas! for the first time, but oft
To me, O Creon, hath opinion proved
Most baleful, and the source of grievous woes.
Nor ever ought the man, who is possest
Of a sound judgment, to train up his children
To be too wise: for they who live exempt
From war and all its toils, the odious name
Among their fellow-citizens acquire
Of abject sluggards. If to the unwise
You some fresh doctrine broach, you are esteemed
Not sapient, but a trifler: when to those
Who in their own conceit possess each branch
Of knowledge, you in state affairs obtain
Superior fame, to them you grow obnoxious.
I also feel the grievance I lament;
Some envy my attainments, others think
My temper uncomplying, though my wisdom
Is not transcendent. But from me it seems
You apprehend some violence; dismiss
Those fears; my situation now is such,
O Creon, that to monarchs I can give
No umbrage: and in what respect have you
Treated me with injustice? You bestowed
Your daughter where your inclination led.
Though I abhor my husband, I suppose
That you have acted wisely, nor repine
At your prosperity. Conclude the match;
Be happy: but allow me in this land
Yet to reside; for I my wrongs will bear
In silence, and to my superiors yield.

     CREON. Soft is the sound of thy persuasive words,
But in my soul I feel the strongest dread

Lest thou devise some mischief, and now less
Than ever can I trust thee; for 'gainst those
Of hasty tempers with more ease we guard,
Or men or women, than the silent foe
Who acts with prudence. Therefore be thou gone
With speed, no answer make: it is decreed,
Nor hast thou art sufficient to avert
Thy doom of banishment; for well aware
Am I thou hat'st me.

  MEDEA.   Spare me, by those knees
And your new-wedded daughter, I implore.

   CREON. Lavish of words, thou never shalt persuade me.

   MEDEA. Will you then drive me hence, and to my prayers
No reverence yield?

   CREON.   I do not love thee more
Than those of my own house.

   MEDEA.   With what regret
Do I remember thee, my native land.

   CREON. Except my children, I hold nought so dear.

   MEDEA. To mortals what a dreadful scourge is love.

   CREON. As fortune dictates, love becomes, I ween,
Either a curse or blessing.

   MEDEA.   Righteous Jove,
Let not the author of my woes escape thee.

   CREON. Away vain woman, free me from my cares.

   MEDEA. No lack of cares have I.

   CREON.   Thou from this spot
Shalt by my servants' hands ere long be torn.

   MEDEA. Not thus, O Creon, I your mercy crave.

   CREON. To trouble me, it seems, thou art resolved.

   MEDEA. I will depart, nor urge this fond request.

   CREON. Why dost thou struggle then, nor from our realm
Withdraw thyself?

   MEDEA.   Allow me this one day
Here to remain, till my maturer thoughts
Instruct me to what region I can fly,
Where for my sons find shelter, since their sire
Attends not to the welfare of his race.
Take pity on them, for you also know
What 'tis to be a parent, and must feel

Parental love: as for myself, I heed not
The being doomed to exile, but lament
Their hapless fortunes.

    CREON.   No tyrannic rage
Within this bosom dwells, but pity oft
Hath warped my better judgment, and though now
My error I perceive, shall thy request
Be granted. Yet of this must I forewarn thee:
If when to-morrow with his orient beams
Phœbus the world revisits, he shall view
Thee and thy children still within the bounds
Of these domains, thou certainly shalt die—
Th' irrevocable sentence is pronounced.
But if thou needs must tarry, tarry here
This single day, for in so short a space
Thou canst not execute the ills I dread.   [*Exit* CREON.]

    CHORUS. Alas! thou wretched woman, overpowered
By thy afflictions, whither wilt thou turn?
What hospitable board, what mansion, find,
Or country to protect thee from these ills?
Into what storms of misery have the gods
Caused thee to rush!

    MEDEA.   On every side distress
Assails me: who can contradict this truth?
Yet think not that my sorrows thus shall end.
By yon new-wedded pair must be sustained
Dire conflicts, and no light or trivial woes
By them who in affinity are joined
With this devoted house. Can ye suppose
That I would e'er have soothed him, had no gain
Or stratagem induced me? Else to him
Never would I have spoken, nor once raised
My suppliant hands. But now is he so lost
In folly, that, when all my schemes with ease
He might have baffled, if he from this land
Had cast me forth, he grants me to remain
For this one day, and ere the setting sun
Three of my foes will I destroy—the sire,
The daughter, and my husband: various means
Have I of slaying them, and, O my friends,

Am at a loss to fix on which I first
Shall undertake, or to consume with flames
The bridal mansion, or a dagger plunge
Into their bosoms, entering unperceived
The chamber where they sleep. But there remains
One danger to obstruct my path: if caught
Stealing into the palace, and intent
On such emprise, in death shall I afford
A subject of derision to my foes,
This obvious method were the best, in which
I am most skilled, to take their lives away
By sorceries. Be it so; suppose them dead.
What city will receive me as its guest,
What hospitable foreigner afford
A shelter in his land, or to his hearth
Admit, or snatch me from impending fate?
Alas! I have no friend. I will delay
A little longer therefore; if perchance,
To screen me from destruction, I can find
Some fortress, then I in this deed of blood
With artifice and silence will engage;
But, if by woes inextricable urged
Too closely, snatching up the dagger them
Am I resolved to slay, although myself
Must perish too; for courage unappalled
This bosom animates. By that dread queen,
By her whom first of all th' immortal powers
I worship, and to aid my bold emprise
Have chosen, the thrice awful Hecaté,[4]
Who in my innermost apartment dwells,
Not one of them shall triumph in the pangs
With which they wound my heart; for I will render
This spousal rite to them a plenteous source
Of bitterness and mourning—they shall rue
Their union, rue my exile from this land.
But now come on, nor, O Medea, spare
Thy utmost science to devise and frame
Deep stratagems, with swift career advance

4. *Hecaté,* a goddess of the underworld, and hence of witchcraft and sorcery.
Medea had been a priestess of Hecaté in Colchis, and still kept an image of her.

To deeds of horror. Such a strife demands
Thy utmost courage. Hast thou any sense
Of these indignities? Nor is it fit
That thou, who spring'st from an illustrious sire,
And from that great progenitor the sun,
Shouldst be derided by the impious brood
Of Sisyphus,[5] at Jason's nuptial feast
Exposed to scorn: for thou hast ample skill
To right thyself. Although by Nature formed
Without a genius apt for virtuous deeds,
We women are in mischiefs most expert.

CHORUS

ODE

I. 1

Now upward to their source the rivers flow,
 And in a retrograde career
Justice and all the baffled virtues go.
  The views of man are insincere,
  Nor to the gods though he appeal,
  And with an oath each promise seal,
Can he be trusted. Yet doth veering fame
  Loudly assert the female claim,
  Causing our sex to be renowned,
  And our whole lives with glory crowned.
  No longer shall we mourn the wrongs
  Of slanderous and inhuman tongues.

I. 2

Nor shall the Muses, as in ancient days,
 Make the deceit of womankind
The constant theme of their malignant lays.
  For ne'er on our uncultured mind
  Hath Phœbus, god of verse, bestowed
  Genius to frame the lofty ode;
Else had we waked the lyre, and in reply
  With descants on man's infamy

 5. *Sisyphus*, founder of Corinth.

Oft lengthened out th' opprobrious page.
Yet may we from each distant age
Collect such records as disgrace
Both us and man's imperious race.

II.   I

By love distracted, from thy native strand,
Thou 'twixt the ocean's clashing rocks didst sail
But now, loathed inmate of a foreign land,
Thy treacherous husband's loss art doomed to wail.
O hapless matron, overwhelmed with woe,
From this unpitying realm dishonored must thou go.

II.   2

No longer sacred oaths their credit bear,
And virtuous shame hath left the Grecian plain,
She mounts to Heaven, and breathes a purer air.
For thee doth no paternal house remain
The sheltering haven from affliction's tides;
Over these hostile roofs a mightier queen presides.

JASON, MEDEA, CHORUS

JASON.   Not now for the first time, but oft, full oft
Have I observed that anger is a pest
The most unruly. For when in this land,
These mansions, you in peace might have abode,
By patiently submitting to the will
Of your superiors, you, for empty words,
Are doomed to exile. Not that I regard
Your calling Jason with incessant rage
The worst of men; but for those bitter taunts
With which you have reviled a mighty king,
Too mild a penalty may you esteem
Such banishment. I still have soothed the wrath
Of the offended monarch, still have wished
That you might here continue; but no bounds
Your folly knows, nor can that tongue e'er cease
To utter menaces against your lords;
Hence from these regions justly are you doomed

To be cast forth. But with unwearied love
Attentive to your interest am I come,
Lest with your children you by cruel want
Should be encompassed; exile with it brings
Full many evils. Me though you abhor,
To you I harbor no unfriendly thought.

    MEDEA. Thou worst of villains (for this bitter charge
Against thy abject cowardice my tongue
May justly urge), com'st thou to me, O wretch,
Who to the gods art odious, and to me
And all the human race? It is no proof
Of courage, or of steadfastness, to face
Thy injured friends, but impudence, the worst
Of all diseases. Yet hast thou done well
In coming: I by uttering the reproaches
Which thou deservest shall ease my burdened soul,
And thou wilt grieve to hear them. With th' events
Which happened first will I begin my charge.
Each Grecian chief who in the *Argo* sailed
Knows how from death I saved thee, when to yoke
The raging bulls whose nostrils poured forth flames,
And sow the baleful harvest, thou wert sent:
Then having slain the dragon, who preserved
With many a scaly fold the golden fleece,
Nor ever closed in sleep his watchful eyes,
I caused the morn with its auspicious beams
To shine on thy deliverance; but, my sire
And native land betraying, came with thee
To Pelion, and Iolchos' gates: for love
Prevailed o'er reason. Pelias next I slew—
Most wretched death—by his own daughters' hands
And thus delivered thee from all thy fears.
Yet though to me, O most ungrateful man,
Thus much indebted, hast thou proved a traitor,
And to the arms of this new consort fled,
Although a rising progeny is thine.
Hadst thou been childless, 'twere a venial fault
In thee to court another for thy bride.
But vanished is the faith which oaths erst bore,
Nor can I judge whether thou think'st the gods

Who ruled the world have lost their ancient power
Or that fresh laws at present are in force
Among mankind, because thou to thyself
Art conscious, thou thy plighted faith hast broken.
O my right hand, which thou didst oft embrace,
Oft to these knees a suppliant cling! How vainly
Did I my virgin purity yield up
To a perfidious husband, led astray
By flattering hopes! Yet I to thee will speak
As if thou wert a friend, and I expected
From thee some mighty favor to obtain:
Yet thou, if strictly questioned, must appear
More odious. Whither shall I turn me now?
To those deserted mansions of my father,
Which, with my country, I to thee betrayed,
And hither came; or to the wretched daughters
Of Pelias? They forsooth, whose sire I slew,
Beneath their roofs with kindness would receive me!
'Tis even thus: by those of my own house
Am I detested, and, to serve thy cause,
Those very friends, whom least of all I ought
To have unkindly treated, have I made
My enemies. But eager to repay
Such favors, 'mongst unnumbered Grecian dames
On me superior bliss hast thou bestowed,
And I, unhappy woman, find in thee
A husband who deserves to be admired
For his fidelity. But from this realm
When I am exiled, and by every friend
Deserted, with my children left forlorn,
A glorious triumph, in thy bridal hour,
To thee will it afford, if those thy sons,
And I who saved thee, should like vagrants roam.
Wherefore, O Jove, didst thou instruct mankind
How to distinguish by undoubted marks
Counterfeit gold, yet in the front of vice
Impress no brand to show the tainted heart?
    CHORUS. How sharp their wrath, how hard to be appeased,
When friends with friends begin the cruel strife.
    JASON. I ought not to be rash, it seems, in speech,

But like the skillful pilot, who, with sails
Scarce half unfurled, his bark more surely guides,
Escape, O woman, your ungoverned tongue.
Since you the benefits on me conferred
Exaggerate in so proud a strain, I deem
That I to Venus only, and no god
Or man beside, my prosperous voyage owe.
Although a wondrous subtlety of soul
To you belong, 'twere an invidious speech
For me to make should I relate how Love
By his inevitable shafts constrained you
To save my life. I will not therefore state
This argument too nicely, but allow,
As you did aid me, it was kindly done.
But by preserving me have you gained more
Than you bestowed, as I shall prove: and first,
Transplanted from barbaric shores, you dwell
In Grecian regions, and have here been taught
To act as justice and the laws ordain,
Nor follow the caprice of brutal strength.
By all the Greeks your wisdom is perceived,
And you acquire renown; but had you still
Inhabited that distant spot of earth,
You never had been named. I would not wish
For mansions heaped with gold, or to exceed
The sweetest notes of Orpheus' magic lyre,
Were those unfading wreaths which fame bestows
From me withheld by fortune. I thus far
On my own labors only have discoursed.
For you this odious strife of words began.
But in espousing Creon's royal daughter,
With which you have reproached me, I will prove
That I in acting thus am wise and chaste,
That I to you have been the best of friends,
And to our children. But make no reply.
Since hither from Iolchos' land I came,
Accompanied by many woes, and such
As could not be avoided, what device
More advantageous could an exile frame
Than wedding the king's daughter? Not through hate

To you, which you reproach me with, not smitten
With love for a new consort, or a wish
The number of my children to augment:
For those we have already might suffice,
And I complain not. But to me it seemed
Of great importance that we both might live
As suits our rank, nor suffer abject need,
Well knowing that each friend avoids the poor.
I also wished to educate our sons
In such a manner as befits my race
And with their noble brothers yet unborn,
Make them one family, that thus, my house
Cementing, I might prosper. In some measure
Is it your interest too that by my bride
I should have sons, and me it much imports,
By future children, to provide for those
Who are in being. Have I judged amiss?
You would not censure me, unless your soul
Were by a rival stung. But your whole sex
Hath these ideas; if in marriage blest
Ye deem nought wanting, but if some reverse
Of fortune e'er betide the nuptial couch,
All that was good and lovely ye abhor.
Far better were it for the human race
Had children been produced by other means,
No females e'er existing: hence might man
Exempt from every evil have remained.

    CHORUS. Thy words hast thou with specious art adorned,
Yet thou to me (it is against my will
That I such language hold), O Jason, seem'st
Not to have acted justly in betraying
Thy consort.

    MEDEA.   From the many I dissent
In many points: for, in my judgment, he
Who tramples on the laws, but can express
His thoughts with plausibility, deserves
Severest punishment: for that injustice
On which he glories, with his artful tongue,
That he a fair appearance can bestow,
He dares to practise, nor is truly wise.

No longer then this specious language hold
To me, who by one word can strike thee dumb.
Hadst thou not acted with a base design,
It was thy duty first to have prevailed
On me to give consent, ere these espousals
Thou hadst contracted, nor kept such design
A secret from thy friends.

JASON.   You would have served
My cause most gloriously, had I disclosed
To you my purposed nuptials, when the rage
Of that proud heart still unsubdued remains.

MEDEA.   Thy real motive was not what thou sayst,
But a Barbarian wife, in thy old age,
Might have appeared to tarnish thy renown.

JASON.   Be well assured, love urged me not to take
The daughter of the monarch to my bed.
But 'twas my wish to save you from distress,
As I already have declared, and raise
Some royal brothers to our former sons,
Strengthening with fresh supports our shattered house.

MEDEA.   May that prosperity which brings remorse
Be never mine, nor riches such as sting
The soul with anguish.

JASON.   Are you not aware
You soon will change your mind and grow more wise?
Forbear to spurn the blessings you possess,
Nor droop beneath imaginary woes,
When you are happy.

MEDEA.   Scoff at my distress,
For thou hast an asylum to receive thee:
But from this land am I constrained to roam
A lonely exile.

JASON.   This was your own choice:
Accuse none else.

MEDEA.   What have I done—betrayed
My plighted faith and sought a foreign bed?

JASON.   You uttered impious curses 'gainst the king.

MEDEA.   I also in thy mansions am accursed.

JASON.   With you I on these subjects will contend

No longer. But speak freely, what relief,
Or for the children or your exiled state,
You from my prosperous fortunes would receive:
For with a liberal hand am I inclined
My bounties to confer, and hence despatch
Such tokens, as to hospitable kindness
Will recommend you. Woman, to refuse
These offers were mere folly; from your soul
Banish resentment, and no trifling gain
Will hence ensue.

    MEDEA.   No use I of thy friends
Will make, nor aught accept; thy presents spare,
For nothing which the wicked man can give
Proves beneficial.

    JASON.   I invoke the gods
To witness that I gladly would supply
You and your children with whate'er ye need:
But you these favors loathe, and with disdain
Repel your friends: hence an increase of woe
Shall be your lot.

    MEDEA.   Be gone; for thou, with love
For thy young bride inflamed, too long remain'st
Without the palace. Wed her; though perhaps
(Yet with submission to the righteous gods,
This I announce) such marriage thou mayst rue.   [*Exit* JASON.]

CHORUS

ODE

I. I

Th' immoderate loves in their career,
Nor glory nor esteem attends,
But when the Cyprian queen[6] descends
Benignant from her starry sphere,
No goddess can more justly claim
    From man the grateful prayer.
Thy wrath, O Venus, still forbear,
Nor at my tender bosom aim

6. *Cyprian queen*, Venus.

That venomed arrow, ever wont t' inspire
Winged from thy golden bow, the pangs of keen desire.

I. 2

May I in modesty delight,
Best present which the gods can give,
Nor torn by jarring passions live
A prey to wrath and cankered spite,
Still envious of a rival's charms,
    Nor rouse the endless strife
While on my soul another wife
Impresses vehement alarms:
On us, dread queen, thy mildest influence shed
Thou who discern'st each crime that stains the nuptial bed.

II. 1

My native land, and dearest home!
May I ne'er know an exiled state,
Nor be it ever my sad fate
While from thy well-known bourn I roam,
My hopeless anguish to bemoan.
    Rather let death, let death
Take at that hour my forfeit breath,
For surely never was there known
On earth a curse so great as to exceed,
From his loved country torn, the wretched exile's need.

II. 2

These eyes attest thy piteous tale,
Which not from fame alone we know;
But, O thou royal dame, thy woe
No generous city doth bewail,
Nor one among thy former friends.
    Abhorred by Heaven and earth,
Perish the wretch devoid of worth,
Engrossed by mean and selfish ends,
Whose heart expands not those he loved to aid;
Never may I lament attachments thus repaid.

ÆGEUS, MEDEA, CHORUS

ÆGEUS. Medea, hail! for no man can devise
Terms more auspicious to accost his friends.
MEDEA. And you, O son of wise Pandion, hail
Illustrious Ægeus. But to these domains
Whence came you?
ÆGEUS.   From Apollo's ancient shrine.
MEDEA. But to that centre of the world, whence sounds
Prophetic issue, why did you repair?
ÆGEUS. To question by what means I may obtain
A race of children.
MEDEA.   By the gods, inform me,
Are you still doomed to drag a childless life?
ÆGEUS. Such is the influence of some adverse demon.
MEDEA. Have you a wife, or did you never try
The nuptial yoke?
ÆGEUS.   With wedlock's sacred bonds
I am not unacquainted.
MEDEA.   On the subject
Of children, what did Phœbus say?
ÆGEUS.   His words
Were such as mortals cannot comprehend.
MEDEA. Am I allowed to know the god's reply?
ÆGEUS. Thou surely art: such mystery to expound
There needs the help of thy sagacious soul.
MEDEA. Inform me what the oracle pronounced,
If I may hear it.
ÆGEUS.   "The projecting foot,
Thou, of the vessel must not dare to loose"—
MEDEA. Till you do what, or to what region come?
ÆGEUS. "Till thou return to thy paternal lares."
MEDEA. But what are you in need of, that you steer
Your bark to Corinth's shores?
ÆGEUS.   A king, whose name
Is Pittheus, o'er Trœzene's realm presides.
MEDEA. That most religious man, they say, is son
Of Pelops.
ÆGEUS. I with him would fain discuss
The god's prophetic voice.

MEDEA.   For he is wise,
And in this science long hath been expert.
ÆGEUS. Dearest to me of those with whom I formed
A league of friendship in the embattled field.
MEDEA. But, O may you be happy, and obtain
All that you wish for.
ÆGEUS.   Why those downcast eyes,
That wasted form?
MEDEA.   O Ægeus, he I wedded
To me hath proved of all mankind most base.
ÆGEUS. What mean'st thou? In plain terms thy grief declare.
MEDEA. Jason hath wronged me, though without a cause.
ÆGEUS. Be more explicit, what injurious treatment
Complain'st thou of?
MEDEA.   To me hath he preferred
Another wife, the mistress of this house.
ÆGEUS. Dared he to act so basely?
MEDEA.   Be assured
That I, whom erst he loved, am now forsaken.
ÆGEUS. What amorous passion triumphs o'er his soul?
Or doth he loathe thy bed?
MEDEA.   'Tis mighty love,
That to his first attachment makes him false.
ÆGEUS. Let him depart then, if he be so void
Of honor as thou sayst.
MEDEA.   He sought to form
Alliance with a monarch.
ÆGEUS.   Who bestows
On him a royal bride? Conclude thy tale.
MEDEA. Creon, the ruler of this land.
ÆGEUS.   Thy sorrows
Are then excusable.
MEDEA.   I am undone,
And banished hence.
ÆGEUS.   By whom? There's not a word
Thou utter'st but unfolds fresh scenes of woe.
MEDEA. Me from this realm to exile Creon drives.
ÆGEUS. Doth Jason suffer this? I cannot praise
Such conduct.
MEDEA.   Not in words: though he submits

Without reluctance. But I by that beard,
And by those knees, a wretched suppliant, crave
Your pity; see me not cast forth forlorn,
But to your realms and to your social hearth
Receive me as a guest; so may your desire
For children be accomplished by the gods,
And happiness your close of life attend.
But how important a discovery Fortune
To you here makes you are not yet apprised:
For destitute of heirs will I permit you
No longer to remain, but through my aid
Shall you have sons, such potent drugs I know.

    ÆGEUS. Various inducements urge me to comply
With this request, O woman; first an awe
For the immortal gods, and then the hope
That I the promised issue shall obtain.
On what my senses scarce can comprehend
I will rely. O that thy arts may prove
Effectual! Thee, if haply thou arriv'st
In my domain, with hospitable rites
Shall it be my endeavor to receive,
As justice dictates: but to thee, thus much
It previously behoves me to announce:
I will not take thee with me from this realm,
But to my house if of thyself thou come
Thou a secure asylum there shalt find,
Nor will I yield thee up to any foe.
But hence without my aid must thou depart,
For I, from those who in this neighboring land
Of Corinth entertain me as their guest,
Wish to incur no censure.

    MEDEA.   Your commands
Shall be obeyed: but would you plight your faith
That you this promise will to me perform,
A noble friend in you shall I have found.

    ÆGEUS. Believ'st thou not? Whence rise these anxious doubts?

    MEDEA. In you I trust; though Pelias' hostile race
And Creon's hate pursue me: but, if bound
By the firm sanction of a solemn oath,
You will not suffer them with brutal force

To drag me from your realm, but having entered
Into such compact, and by every god
Sworn to protect me, still remain a friend,
Nor hearken to their embassies. My fortune
Is in its wane, but wealth to them belongs,
And an imperial mansion.

ÆGEUS.   In these words
Hast thou expressed great forethought: but if thus
Thou art disposed to act, I my consent
Will not refuse; for I shall be more safe
If to thy foes some plausible excuse
I can allege, and thee more firmly stablish.
But say thou first what gods I shall invoke.

MEDEA. Swear by the earth on which we tread, the sun
My grandsire, and by all the race of gods.

ÆGEUS. What action, or to do or to forbear?

MEDEA. That from your land you never will expel,
Nor while you live consent that any foe
Shall tear me thence.

ÆGEUS.   By earth, the radiant sun,
And every god I swear, I to the terms
Thou hast proposed will steadfastly adhere.

MEDEA. This may suffice. But what if you infringe
Your oath, what punishment will you endure?

ÆGEUS. Each curse that can befall the impious man.

MEDEA. Depart, and prosper: all things now advance
In their right track, and with the utmost speed
I to your city will direct my course,
When I have executed those designs
I meditate, and compassed what I wish.   [Exit ÆGEUS.]

CHORUS. But thee, O king, may Maia's wingéd son[7]
Lead to thy Athens; there mayst thou attain
All that thy soul desires, for thou to me,
O Ægeus, seem'st most generous.

MEDEA.   Awful Jove,
Thou too, O Justice, who art ever joined
With thundering Jove, and bright Hyperion's beams,
You I invoke. Now, O my friends, o'er those
I hate shall we prevail: 'tis the career

7. Hermes.

Of victory that we tread, and I at length
Have hopes the strictest vengeance on my foes
To execute: for where we most in need
Of a protector stood, appeared this stranger,
The haven of my counsels: we shall fix
Our cables to this poop, soon as we reach
That hallowed city where Minerva[8] reigns.
But now to you the whole of my designs
Will I relate; look not for such a tale
As yields delight: some servant will I send
An interview with Jason to request,
And on his coming, in the softest words
Address him; say these matters are well pleasing
To me, and in the strongest terms applaud
That marriage with the daughter of the king,
Which now the traitor celebrates; then add,
" 'Tis for our mutual good, 'tis rightly done."
But the request which I intend to make
Is that he here will let my children stay;
Not that I mean to leave them thus behind,
Exposed to insults in a hostile realm
From those I hate; but that my arts may slay
The royal maid: with presents in their hands,
A vesture finely wrought and golden crown,
Will I despatch them; these they to the bride
Shall bear, that she their exile may reverse:
If these destructive ornaments she take
And put them on, both she, and every one
Who touches her, shall miserably perish—
My presents with such drugs I will anoint.
Far as to this relates, here ends my speech.
But I with anguish think upon a deed
Of more than common horror, which remains
By me to be accomplished: for my sons
Am I resolved to slay, them from this arm
Shall no man rescue. When I thus have filled
With dire confusion Jason's wretched house,
I, from this land, yet reeking with the gore
Of my dear sons, will fly, and having dared

8. Athens is named for and sacred to Athene (Minerva).

A deed most impious. For the scornful taunts
Of those we hate are not to be endured,
Happen what may. Can life be any gain
To me who have no country left, no home,
No place of refuge? Greatly did I err
When I forsook the mansions of my sire,
Persuaded by the flattery of that Greek
Whom I will punish, if just Heaven permit.
For he shall not again behold the children
I bore him while yet living. From his bride
Nor shall there issue any second race,
Since that vile woman by my baleful drugs
Vilely to perish have the Fates ordained.
None shall think lightly of me, as if weak,
Of courage void, or with a soul too tame,
But formed by Heaven in a far different mould,
The terror of my foes, and to my friends
Benignant: for most glorious are the lives
Of those who act with such determined zeal.

    CHORUS. Since thy design thus freely thou to us
Communicat'st, I, through a wish to serve
Thy interests, and a reverence for those laws
Which all mankind hold sacred, from thy purpose
Exhort thee to desist.

    MEDEA.   This cannot be:
Yet I from you, because ye have not felt
Distress like mine, such language can excuse.

    CHORUS. Thy guiltless children wilt thou dare to slay?

    MEDEA. My husband hence more deeply shall I wound.

    CHORUS. But thou wilt of all women be most wretched.

    MEDEA. No matter: all the counsels ye can give
Are now superfluous. But this instant go
And Jason hither bring; for on your faith,
In all things I depend; nor these resolves
Will you divulge if you your mistress love,
And feel a woman's interest in my wrongs.

CHORUS

ODE

I. 1

Heroes of Erectheus' race[9]
To the gods who owe your birth,
And in a long succession trace
Your sacred origin from earth,
Who on wisdom's fruit regale,
Purest breezes still inhale,
And behold skies ever bright,
   Wandering through those haunted glades
Where fame relates that the Pierian maids,[10]
Soothing the soul of man with chaste delight,
Taught Harmony to breathe her first enchanting tale.

I. 2

From Cephisus'[11] amber tide,
At the Cyprian queen's command,
As sing the Muses, are supplied
To refresh the thirsty land,
Fragrant gales of temperate air;
While around her auburn hair,
In a vivid chaplet twined
   Never-fading roses bloom
And scent the champaign with their rich perfume,
Love comes in unison with wisdom joined,
Each virtue thrives if Beauty lend her fostering care.

II. 1

For its holy streams renowned
Can that city, can that state
Where friendship's generous train are found
Shelter thee from public hate,
When, defiled with horrid guilt,
Thou thy children's blood hast spilt?

9. *Erectheus' race*, the Athenians.
10. *Pierian maids*, the Muses.
11. *Cephisus*, a river about a mile from Athens.

Think on this atrocious deed
Ere the dagger aim the blow:
Around thy knees our suppliant arms we throw,
O doom not, doom them not to bleed.

II. 2

How can thy relentless heart
All humanity disclaim,
Thy lifted arm perform its part?
Lost to a sense of honest shame,
Canst thou take their lives away
And these guiltless children slay?
Soon as thou thy sons shalt view,
How wilt thou the tear restrain,
Or with their blood thy ruthless hands distain,
When prostrate they for mercy sue?

JASON, MEDEA, CHORUS

JASON. I at your call am come; for though such hate
To me you bear, you shall not be denied
In this request; but let me hear what else
You would solicit.
MEDEA.   Jason, I of thee
Crave pardon for the hasty words I spoke;
Since just it were that thou shouldst bear my wrath,
When by such mutual proofs of love our union
Hath been cemented. For I reasoned thus,
And in these terms reproached myself: "O wretch,
Wretch that I am, what madness fires my breast?
Or why 'gainst those who counsel me aright
Such fierce resentment harbor? What just cause
Have I to hate the rulers of this land,
My husband too, who acts but for my good
In his espousals with the royal maid,
That to my sons he hence may add a race
Of noble brothers? Shall not I appease
The tempest of my soul? Why, when the gods
Confer their choicest blessings, should I grieve?
Have not I helpless children? Well I know

That we are banished from Thessalia's realm
And left without a friend." When I these thoughts
Maturely had revolved, I saw how great
My folly and how groundless was my wrath.
Now therefore I commend, now deem thee wise
In forming this connection for my sake:
But I was void of wisdom, or had borne
A part in these designs, the genial bed
Obsequiously attended, and with joy
Performed each menial office for the bride.
I will not speak in too reproachful terms
Of my own sex; but we, weak women, are
What nature formed us; therefore our defects
Thou must not imitate, nor yet return
Folly for folly. I submit and own
My judgment was erroneous, but at length
Have I formed better counsels. O my sons,
Come hither, leave the palace, from those doors
Advance, and in a soft persuasive strain
With me unite your father to accost,
Forget past enmity, and to your friends
Be reconciled, for 'twixt us is a league
Of peace established, and my wrath subsides.

[*The* Sons *of* Jason *and* Medea *enter.*]

Take hold of his right hand. Ah me, how great
Are my afflictions oft as I revolve
A deed of darkness in my laboring soul!
How long, alas! my sons, are ye ordained
To live, how long to stretch forth those dear arms?
Wretch that I am! how much am I disposed
To weep! how subject to each fresh alarm!
For I at length desisting from that strife,
Which with your sire I rashly did maintain,
Feel gushing tears bedew my tender cheek.
    Chorus. Fresh tears too from these eyes have forced their way;
And may no greater ill than that which now
We suffer, overtake us!
    Jason.   I applaud
Your present conduct, and your former rage

Condemn not; for 'tis natural that the race
Of women should be angry when their lord
For a new consort trucks them. But your heart
Is for the better changed, and you, though late,
At length acknowledge the resistless power
Of reason; this is acting like a dame
Endued with prudence. But for you, my sons,
Abundant safety your considerate sire
Hath with the favor of the gods procured,
For ye, I trust, shall with my future race
Bear the first rank in this Corinthian realm,
Advance to full maturity; the rest,
Aided by each benignant god, your father
Shall soon accomplish. Virtuously trained up
May I behold you at a riper age
Obtain pre-eminence o'er those I hate.
But, ha! Why with fresh tears do you thus keep
Those eyelids moist? From your averted cheeks
Why is the color fled, or why these words
Receive you not with a complacent ear?

    MEDEA. Nothing: my thoughts were busied for these children.
    JASON. Be of good courage, and for them depend
On my protecting care.
    MEDEA.   I will obey,
Nor disbelieve the promise thou hast made:
But woman, ever frail, is prone to shed
Involuntary tears.
    JASON.   But why bewail
With such deep groans these children?
    MEDEA.   Them I bore;
And that our sons might live, while to the gods
Thou didst address thy vows, a pitying thought
Entered my soul; 'twas whether this could be.
But of th' affairs on which thou com'st to hold
This conference with me, have I told a part
Already, and to thee will now disclose
The sequel: since the rulers of this land
Resolve to banish me, as well I know
That it were best for me to give no umbrage,
Or to the king of Corinth, or to thee,

EURIPIDES
275

By dwelling here: because I to this house
Seem to bear enmity, from these domains
Will I depart: but urge thy suit to Creon,
That under thy paternal care our sons
May be trained up, nor from this realm expelled.

JASON. Though doubtful of success, I yet am bound
To make th' attempt.

MEDEA.   Thou rather shouldst enjoin
Thy bride her royal father to entreat,
That he these children's exile may reverse.

JASON. With pleasure; and I doubt not but on her,
If like her sex humane, I shall prevail.

MEDEA. To aid thee in this difficult emprise
Shall be my care, for I to her will send
Gifts that I know in beauty far exceed
The gorgeous works of man; a tissued vest
And golden crown the children shall present,
But with the utmost speed these ornaments
One of thy menial train must hither bring,
For not with one, but with ten thousand blessings
Shall she be gratified; thee, best of men,
Obtaining for the partner of her bed,
And in possession of those splendid robes
Which erst the sun my grandsire did bestow
On his descendants: take them in your hands,
My children, to the happy royal bride
Instantly bear them, and in dower bestow,
For such a gift as ought not to be scorned
Shall she receive.

JASON.   Why rashly part with these?
Of tissued robes or gold can you suppose
The palace destitute? These trappings keep,
Nor to another give: for if the dame
On me place real value, well I know
My love she to all treasures will prefer.

MEDEA. Speak not so hastily: the gods themselves
By gifts are swayed, as fame relates; and gold
Hath a far greater influence o'er the souls
Of mortals than the most persuasive words:
With fortune, the propitious heavens conspire

To add fresh glories to thy youthful bride,
All here submits to her despotic sway.
But I my children's exile would redeem,
Though at the cost of life, not gold alone.
But these adjacent mansions of the king
Soon as ye enter, O ye little ones,
Your sire's new consort and my queen entreat
That ye may not be banished from this land:
At the same time these ornaments present,
For most important is it that these gifts
With her own hands the royal dame receive.
Go forth, delay not, and, if ye succeed,
Your mother with the welcome tidings greet.

[*Exeunt* JASON *and* SONS.]

CHORUS

ODE

I. 1

Now from my soul each hope is fled,
I deem those hapless children dead,
    They rush to meet the wound:
    Mistrustful of no latent pest
Th' exulting bride will seize the gorgeous vest,
    Her auburn tresses crowned
    By baleful Pluto,[12] shall she stand,
And take the presents with an eager hand.

I. 2

The splendid robe of thousand dyes
Will fascinate her raptured eyes,
    And tempt her till she wear
    The golden diadem, arrayed
To meet her bridegroom in th' infernal shade
    She thus into the snare
    Of death shall be surprised by fate,
Nor 'scape remorseless Atè's[13] direful hate.

12. *Pluto*, god of Hades.
13. *Atè*, an avenging goddess.

II. 1

But as for thee whose nuptials bring
The proud alliance of a king,
  'Midst dangers unespied
Thou madly rushing, aid'st the blow
Ordained by Heaven to lay thy children low,
  And thy lamented bride:
  O man, how little dost thou know
That o'er thy head impends severest woe!

II. 2

Thy anguish I no less bemoan,
  No less for thee, O mother, groan,
    Bent on a horrid deed,
  Thy children who resolv'st to slay,
Nor fear'st to take their guiltless lives away.
    Those innocents must bleed,
  Because, disdainful of thy charms,
The husband flies to a new consort's arms.

Attendant, Sons, Medea, Chorus

Attend. Your sons, my honored mistress, are set free
From banishment; in her own hands those gifts
With courtesy the royal bride received;
Hence have your sons obtained their peace.
Medea.   No matter.
Attend. Why stand you in confusion, when befriended
By prosperous fortune?
Medea.   Ah!
Attend.   This harsh reception
Accords not with the tidings which I bring.
Medea. Alas! and yet again I say, alas!
Attend. Have I related with unconscious tongue
Some great calamity, by the fond hope
Of bearing glad intelligence misled?
Medea. For having told what thou hast told, no blame
To thee do I impute.
Attend.   But on the ground
Why fix those eyes, and shed abundant tears?

MEDEA.   Necessity constrains me: for the gods
Of Erebus[14] and I in evil hour
Our baleful machinations have devised.
    ATTEND. Be of good cheer; for in your children still
Are you successful.
    MEDEA.   'Midst the realms of night
Others I first will plunge. Ah, wretched me!
    ATTEND. Not you alone are from your children torn,
Mortal you are, and therefore must endure
Calamity with patience.
    MEDEA.   I these counsels
Will practise: but go thou into the palace,
And for the children whatsoe'er to-day
Is requisite, make ready.   [*Exit* ATTENDANT.]
                         O my sons!
My sons! ye have a city and a house
Where, leaving hapless me behind, without
A mother ye for ever shall reside.
But I to other realms an exile go,
Ere any help from you I could derive,
Or see you blest; the hymeneal pomp,
The bride, the genial couch, for you adorn,
And in these hands the kindled torch sustain.
How wretched am I through my own perverseness!
You, O my sons, I then in vain have nurtured,
In vain have toiled, and, wasted with fatigue,
Suffered the pregnant matron's grievous throes.
On you, in my afflictions, many hopes
I founded erst: that ye with pious care
Would foster my old age, and on the bier
Extend me after death—much envied lot
Of mortals; but these pleasing anxious thoughts
Are vanished now; for, losing you, a life
Of bitterness and anguish shall I lead.
But as for you, my sons, with those dear eyes
Fated no more your mother to behold,
Hence are ye hastening to a world unknown.
Why do ye gaze on me with such a look
Of tenderness, or wherefore smile? for these

14. *Erebus*, Darkness, son of Chaos.

Are your last smiles. Ah wretched, wretched me!
What shall I do? My resolution fails.
Sparkling with joy now I their looks have seen,
My friends, I can no more. To those past schemes
I bid adieu, and with me from this land
My children will convey. Why should I cause
A twofold portion of distress to fall
On my own head, that I may grieve the sire
By punishing his sons? This shall not be:
Such counsels I dismiss. But in my purpose
What means this change? Can I prefer derision,
And with impunity permit the foe
To 'scape? My utmost courage I must rouse:
For the suggestion of these tender thoughts
Proceeds from an enervate heart. My sons,
Enter the regal mansion.   [*Exeunt* Sons.]
                     As for those
Who deem that to be present were unholy
While I the destined victims offer up,
Let them see to it. This uplifted arm
Shall never shrink. Alas! alas! my soul,
Commit not such a deed. Unhappy woman,
Desist and spare thy children; we will live
Together, they in foreign realms shall cheer
Thy exile. No, by those avenging fiends
Who dwell with Pluto in the realms beneath,
This shall not be, nor will I ever leave
My sons to be insulted by their foes.
They certainly must die; since then they must,
I bore and I will slay them: 'tis a deed
Resolved on, nor my purpose will I change.
Full well I know that now the royal bride
Wears on her head the magic diadem,
And in the variegated robe expires:
But, hurried on by fate, I tread a path
Of utter wretchedness, and them will plunge
Into one yet more wretched. To my sons
Fain would I say: "O stretch forth your right hands,
Ye children, for your mother to embrace.
O dearest hands, ye lips to me most dear,

Engaging features and ingenuous looks,
May ye be blest, but in another world;
For by the treacherous conduct of your sire
Are ye bereft of all this earth bestowed.
Farewell, sweet kisses—tender limbs, farewell!
And fragrant breath! I never more can bear
To look on you, my children." My afflictions
Have conquered me; I now am well aware
What crimes I venture on: but rage, the cause
Of woes most grievous to the human race,
Over my better reason hath prevailed.

      CHORUS. In subtle questions I full many a time
Have heretofore engaged, and this great point
Debated, whether woman should extend
Her search into abstruse and hidden truths.
But we too have a Muse, who with our sex
Associates to expound the mystic lore
Of wisdom, though she dwell not with us all.
Yet haply a small number may be found,
Among the multitude of females, dear
To the celestial Muses. I maintain,
They who in total inexperience live,
Nor ever have been parents, are more happy
Than they to whom much progeny belongs,
Because the childless, having never tried
Whether more pain or pleasure from their offspring
To mortals rises, 'scape unnumbered toils.
But I observe that they, whose fruitful house
Is with a lovely race of infants filled,
Are harassed with perpetual cares; how first
To train them up in virtue, and whence leave
Fit portions for their sons; but on the good
Or worthless, whether they these toils bestow
Remains involved in doubt. I yet must name
One evil the most grievous, to which all
The human race is subject; some there are
Who for their sons have gained sufficient wealth,
Seen them to full maturity advance,
And decked with every virtue, when, by fate
If thus it be ordained, comes death unseen

And hurries them to Pluto's gloomy realm.
Can it be any profit to the gods
To heap the loss of children, that one ill
Than all the rest more bitter, on mankind?
    MEDEA. My friends, with anxious expectation long
Here have I waited, from within to learn
How fortune will dispose the dread event.
But one of Jason's servants I behold
With breathless speed advancing: his looks show
That he some recent mischief would relate.

MESSENGER, MEDEA, CHORUS

    MESS. O thou, who impiously hast wrought a deed
Of horror, fly, Medea, from this land,
Fly with such haste as not to leave the bark
Or from the car alight.
    MEDEA.   What crime, to merit
A banishment like this, have I committed?
    MESS. By thy enchantments is the royal maid
This instant dead, and Creon, too, her sire.
    MEDEA. Most glorious are the tidings you relate:
Henceforth shall you be numbered with my friends
And benefactors.
    MESS.   Ha! what words are these?
Dost thou preserve thy senses yet entire?
O woman, hath not madness fired thy brain?
The wrongs thou to the royal house hast done
Hear'st thou with joy, nor shudder'st at the tale?
    MEDEA. Somewhat I have in answer to your speech:
But be not too precipitate, my friend;
Inform me how they died, for twofold joy
Wilt thou afford, if wretchedly they perished.
    MESS. When with their father thy two sons arrived
And went into the mansion of the bride,
We servants, who had shared thy griefs, rejoiced;
For a loud rumor instantly prevailed
That all past strife betwixt thy lord and thee
Was reconciled. Some kissed the children's hands,
And some their auburn tresses. I with joy

To those apartments where the women dwell
Attended them. Our mistress, the new object
Of homage such as erst to thee was paid,
Ere she beheld thy sons on Jason cast
A look of fond desire: but then she veiled
Her eyes, and turned her pallid cheeks away
Disgusted at their coming, till his voice
Appeased her anger with these gentle words:
"O be not thou inveterate 'gainst thy friends,
But lay aside disdain, thy beauteous face
Turn hither, and let amity for those
Thy husband loves still warm that generous breast.
Accept these gifts, and to thy father sue,
That, for my sake, the exile of my sons
He will remit." Soon as the princess saw
Thy glittering ornaments, she could resist
No longer, but to all her lord's requests
Assented, and before thy sons were gone
Far from the regal mansion with their sire,
The vest, resplendent with a thousand dyes,
Put on, and o'er her loosely floating hair
Placing the golden crown, before the mirror
Her tresses braided, and with smiles surveyed
Th' inanimated semblance of her charms:
Then rising from her seat across the palace
Walked with a delicate and graceful step,
In the rich gifts exulting, and oft turned
Enraptured eyes on her own stately neck,
Reflected to her view: but now a scene
Of horror followed; her complexion changed,
And she reeled backward, trembling every limb;
Scarce did her chair receive her as she sunk
In time to save her falling to the ground.
One of her menial train, an aged dame,
Possest with an idea that the wrath
Either of Pan[15] or of some god unknown
Her mistress had invaded, in shrill tone
Poured forth a vow to Heaven, till from her mouth

15. *Pan,* a pastoral deity, who was sometimes the cause of sudden attacks of groundless fear—hence *panic.*

She saw foam issue, in their sockets roll
Her wildly glaring eyeballs, and the blood
Leave her whole frame; a shriek, that differed far
From her first plaints, then gave she. In an instant
This to her father's house, and that to tell
The bridegroom the mischance which had befallen
His consort, rushed impetuous; through the dome
The frequent steps of those who to and fro
Ran in confusion did resound. But soon
As the fleet courser at the goal arrives,
She who was silent, and had closed her eyes,
Roused from her swoon, and burst forth into groans
Most dreadful, for 'gainst her two evils warred:
Placed on her head the golden crown poured forth
A wondrous torrent of devouring flames,
And the embroidered robes, thy children's gifts,
Preyed on the hapless virgin's tender flesh;
Covered with fire she started from her seat
Shaking her hair, and from her head the crown
With violence attempting to remove,
But still more firmly did the heated gold
Adhere, and the fanned blaze with double lustre
Burst forth as she her streaming tresses shook:
Subdued by fate, at length she to the ground
Fell prostrate: scarce could anyone have known her
Except her father; for those radiant eyes
Dropped from their sockets, that majestic face
Its wonted features lost, and blood with fire
Ran down her head in intermingled streams,
While from her bones the flesh, like weeping pitch,
Melted away, through the consuming power
Of those unseen enchantments, 'twas a sight
Most horrible: all feared to touch the corpse,
For her disastrous end had taught us caution.
Meanwhile her hapless sire, who knew not aught
Of this calamity, as he with haste
Entered the palace, stumbled o'er her body;
Instantly shrieking out, then with his arms
Infolded, kissed it oft, and, "O my child,
My wretched child," exclaimed; "what envious god,

Author of thy dishonorable fall,
Of thee bereaves an old decrepit man
Whom the grave claims? With thee I wish to die,
My daughter." Scarcely had the hoary father
These lamentations ended; to uplift
His feeble body striving, he adhered
(As ivy with its pliant tendrils clings
Around the laurel) to the tissued vest.
Dire was the conflict; he to raise his knee
From earth attempted, but his daughter's corse
Still held him down, or if with greater force
He dragged it onward, from his bones he tore
The aged flesh: at length he sunk, and breathed
In agonizing pangs his soul away:
For he against such evil could bear up
No longer. To each other close in death
The daughter and her father lie: their fate
Demands our tears. Warned by my words, with haste
From this domain convey thyself, or vengeance
Will overtake thee for this impious deed.
Not now for the first time do I esteem
Human affairs a shadow. Without fear
Can I pronounce, they who appear endued
With wisdom, and most plausibly trick out
Specious harangues, deserve to be accounted
The worst of fools. The man completely blest
Exists not. Some in overflowing wealth
May be more fortunate, but none are happy.

    CHORUS. Heaven its collected store of evil seems
This day resolved with justice to pour down
On perjured Jason. Thy untimely fate
How do we pity, O thou wretched daughter
Of Creon, who in Pluto's mansions go'st
To celebrate thy nuptial feast.

    MEDEA.   My friends,
I am resolved, as soon as I have slain
My children, from these regions to depart,
Nor through inglorious sloth will I abandon
My sons to perish by detested hands;
They certainly must die: since then they must,

I bore and I will slay them. O my heart!
Be armed with tenfold firmness. What avails it
To loiter, when inevitable ills
Remain to be accomplished? Take the sword,
And, O my hand, on to the goal that ends
Their life, nor let one intervening thought
Of pity or maternal tenderness
Suspend thy purpose: for this one short day
Forget how fondly thou didst love thy sons,
How bring them forth, and after that lament
Their cruel fate: although thou art resolved
To slay, yet hast thou ever held them dear.
But I am of all women the most wretched.   [*Exit* MEDEA.]

CHORUS

ODE

I

Earth, and thou sun, whose fervid blaze
From pole to pole illumes each distant land,
View this abandoned woman, ere she raise
Against her children's lives a ruthless hand;
    For from thy race, divinely bright,
They spring, and should the sons of gods be slain
    By man, 'twere dreadful. O restrain
Her fury, thou celestial source of light,
    Ere she with blood pollute your regal dome,
Chased by the demons hence let this Erinnys[16] roam.

II

The pregnant matron's throes in vain
Hast thou endured, and borne a lovely race,
    O thou, who o'er th' inhospitable main,
    Where the Cyanean rocks scarce leave a space,
        Thy daring voyage didst pursue.
Why, O thou wretch, thy soul doth anger rend,
        Such as in murder soon must end?
They who with kindred gore are stained shall rue

16. *Erinnys,* Fury.

Their guilt inexpiable: full well I know
The gods will on this house inflict severest woe.

      1ST SON [*within*].   Ah me! what can I do, or whither fly
To 'scape a mother's arm?
      2ND SON [*within*].   I cannot tell:
For, O my dearest brother, we are lost.
      CHORUS.   Heard you the children's shrieks? I (O thou dame,
Whom woes and evil fortune still attend)
Will rush into the regal dome, from death
Resolved to snatch thy sons.
      1ST SON [*within*].   We by the gods
Conjure you to protect us in this hour
Of utmost peril, for the treacherous snare
Hath caught us, and we perish by the sword.
      CHORUS.   Art thou a rock, O wretch, or steel, to slay
With thine own hand that generous race of sons
Whom you didst bear? I hitherto have heard
But of one woman, who in ancient days
Smote her dear children, Ino,[17] by the gods
With frenzy stung, when Jove's malignant queen
Distracted from her mansion drove her forth.
But she, yet reeking with the impious gore
Of her own progeny, into the waves
Plunged headlong from the ocean's craggy beach,
And shared with her two sons one common fate.
Can there be deeds more horrible than these
Left for succeeding ages to produce?
Disastrous union with the female sex,
How great a source of woes art thou to man!

JASON, CHORUS

JASON.   Ye dames who near the portals stand, is she
Who hath committed these atrocious crimes,
Medea, in the palace, or by flight
Hath she retreated? For beneath the ground
Must she conceal herself, or, borne on wings,
Ascend the heights of Ether, to avoid

17. Ino nursed Dionysus as an infant, and in punishment for this Hera drove
her mad. She killed her two sons and threw herself into the sea.

The vengeance due for Corinth's royal house.
Having destroyed the rulers of the land,
Can she presume she shall escape unhurt
From these abodes? But less am I concerned
On her account, than for my sons; since they
Whom she hath injured will on her inflict
Due punishment: but hither am I come
To save my children's lives, lest on their heads
The noble Creon's kindred should retaliate
That impious murder by their mother wrought.

    CHORUS. Thou know'st not yet, O thou unhappy man,
What ills thou art involved in, or these words
Had not escaped thee.

    JASON.   Ha, what ills are these
Thou speak'st of? Would she also murder me?

    CHORUS. By their own mother's hand thy sons are slain.

    JASON. What can you mean? How utterly, O woman,
Have you undone me!

    CHORUS.   Be assured thy children
Are now no more.

    JASON.   Where was it, or within
Those mansions or without, that she destroyed
Our progeny?

    CHORUS.   As soon as thou these doors
Hast oped, their weltering corses wilt thou view.

    JASON. Loose the firm bars and bolts of yonder gates
With speed, ye servants, that I may behold
This scene of twofold misery, the remains
Of the deceased, and punish her who slew them.

    MEDEA, *in a chariot drawn by dragons,* JASON, CHORUS

    MEDEA. With levers wherefore dost thou shake those doors
In quest of them who are no more, and me
Who dared to perpetrate the bloody deed?
Desist from such unprofitable toil:
But if there yet be aught that thou with me
Canst want, speak freely whatsoe'er thou wilt:
For with that hand me never shalt thou reach,
Such steeds the sun my grandsire gives to whirl
This chariot and protect me from my foes.

    JASON. O most abandoned woman, by the gods,

By me and all the human race abhorred,
Who with the sword could pierce the sons you bore,
And ruin me, a childless wretched man,
Yet after you this impious deed have dared
To perpetrate, still view the radiant sun
And fostering earth; may vengeance overtake you!
For I that reason have regained which erst
Forsook me, when to the abodes of Greece
I from your home, from a barbarian realm,
Conveyed you, to your sire a grievous bane,
And the corrupt betrayer of that land
Which nurtured you. Some envious god first roused
Your evil genius from the shades of hell
For my undoing: after you had slain
Your brother at the altar, you embarked
In the famed *Argo*. Deeds like these a life
Of guilt commenced; with me in wedlock joined,
You bore those sons, whom you have now destroyed
Because I left your bed. No Grecian dame
Would e'er have ventured on a deed so impious;
Yet I to them preferred you for my bride:
This was a hostile union, and to me
The most destructive; for my arms received
No woman, but a lioness more fell
Than Tuscan Scylla. Vainly should I strive
To wound you with reproaches numberless,
For you are grown insensible of shame!
Vile sorceress, and polluted with the blood
Of your own children, perish—my hard fate
While I lament, for I shall ne'er enjoy
My lovely bride, nor with those sons, who owe
To me their birth and nurture, ever hold
Sweet converse. They, alas! can live no more,
Utterly lost to their desponding sire.

    MEDEA. Much could I say in answer to this charge,
Were not the benefits from me received,
And thy abhorred ingratitude, well known
To Jove, dread sire. Yet was it not ordained,
Scorning my bed, that thou shouldst lead a life
Of fond delight, and ridicule my griefs;

Nor that the royal virgin thou didst wed,
Or Creon, who to thee his daughter gave,
Should drive me from these regions unavenged.
A lioness then call me if thou wilt,
Or by the name of Scylla, whose abode
Was in Etrurian caverns. For thy heart,
As justice prompted, in my turn I wounded.

JASON.   You grieve, and are the partner of my woes.

MEDEA.   Be well assured I am: but what assuages
My grief is this, that thou no more canst scoff.

JASON.   How vile a mother, O my sons, was yours!

MEDEA.   How did ye perish through your father's lust!

JASON.   But my right hand was guiltless of their death.

MEDEA.   Not so thy cruel taunts, and that new marriage.

JASON.   Was my new marriage a sufficient cause
For thee to murder them?

MEDEA.   Canst thou suppose
Such wrongs sit light upon the female breast?

JASON.   On a chaste woman's; but your soul abounds
With wickedness.

MEDEA.   Thy sons are now no more,
This will afflict thee.

JASON.   O'er your head, alas!
They now two evil geniuses impend.

MEDEA.   The gods know who these ruthless deeds began.

JASON.   They know the hateful temper of your soul.

MEDEA.   In detestation thee I hold, and loathe
Thy conversation.

JASON.   Yours too I abhor;
But we with ease may settle on what terms
To part for ever.

MEDEA.   Name those terms. Say how
Shall I proceed? For such my ardent wish.

JASON.   Let me inter the dead, and o'er them weep.

MEDEA.   Thou shalt not. For their corses with this hand
Am I resolved to bury in the grove
Sacred to awful Juno, who protects
The citadel of Corinth, lest their foes
Insult them, and with impious rage pluck up
The monumental stone. I in this realm

Of Sisyphus moreover will ordain
A solemn festival and mystic rites,
To make a due atonement for my guilt
In having slain them. To Erectheus' land
I now am on my road, where I shall dwell
With Ægeus, great Pandion's son; but thou
Shalt vilely perish as thy crimes deserve,
Beneath the shattered relics of thy bark,
The *Argo,* crushed;[18] such is the bitter end
Of our espousals and thy faith betrayed.

    JASON.   May the Erinnys of our slaughtered sons
And justice, who requites each murderous deed,
Destroy you utterly!

    MEDEA.   Will any god
Or demon hear thy curses, O thou wretch,
False to thy oath, and to the sacred laws
Of hospitality?

    JASON.   Most impious woman,
Those hands yet reeking with your children's gore—

    MEDEA.   Go to the palace, and inter thy bride.

    JASON.   Bereft of both my sons, I thither go.

    MEDEA.   Not yet enough lament'st thou: to increase
Thy sorrows, mayst thou live till thou art old!

    JASON.   Ye dearest children.

    MEDEA.   To their mother dear,
But not to thee.

    JASON.   Yet them have you destroyed.

    MEDEA.   That I might punish thee.

    JASON.   One more fond kiss
On their loved lips, ah me! would I imprint.

    MEDEA.   Now wouldst thou speak to them, and in thine arms
Clasp those whom living thou didst banish hence.

    JASON.   Allow me, I conjure you by the gods,
My children's tender bodies to embrace.

    MEDEA.   Thou shalt not: these presumptuous words in vain
By thee were hazarded.

    JASON.   Jove, hear'st thou this,
How I with scorn am driven away, how wronged
By that detested lioness, whose fangs

18. According to the legend, this prophecy was fulfilled.

Have slain her children? Yet shall my loud plaints,
While here I fix my seat, if 'tis allowed,
And this be possible, call down the gods
To witness that you hinder me from touching
My murdered sons, and paying the deceased
Funereal honors. Would to Heaven I ne'er
Had seen them born to perish by your hand!
  CHORUS. Throned on Olympus, with his sovereign nod,
Jove unexpectedly performs the schemes
Divine foreknowledge planned; our firmest hopes
Oft fail us: but the god still finds the means
Of compassing what man could ne'er have looked for;
And thus doth this important business end.

PLATO

The Apology

AFTER THE AGE of Pericles, Athenian fortunes and Greek literature declined, for the Peloponnesian War between Athens and Sparta was long and exhausting and left the Athenians defeated, dispirited, and cynical. The high times of Pericles had passed, and Athenian democracy had decayed; but in this ebb of Athenian prestige two names emerged that have since exerted on man's thought an intellectual and spiritual influence hardly to be estimated. These were Socrates and Plato.

Plato (428? B.C.-348? B.C.) was born in Athens of an aristocratic family about the time of the death of Pericles, probably in 428 B.C. His education, which included letters, music, and athletics, was proper to his high station in life, and he might well have gone into politics like a number of his associates. Instead he is said to have written poetry in his youth and to have given himself eagerly to the study of philosophy. The most important fact of his life occurred in his twentieth year, when he became the friend and pupil of the philosopher Socrates, then about sixty years old and one of the most active and effective teachers of all time. But if the debt of Plato to Socrates was great, Plato has amply repaid it by preserving in his works the personality and thought of his master, who, so far as is known, left not a single literary production of his own.

What is known of Socrates today is found almost entirely in the writings of his disciples, principally in the dialogues of Plato and in the *Memorabilia* of Xenophon. Socrates, the son of a stone-mason and a midwife, was one of the strangest of mortals. He is said to have practiced for a while the profession of sculpture, but if he ever did so he very early gave up that particular interest. He was ugly, poor, badly clothed, uneducated in any formal sense of the word, not well-read, untraveled, and wholly unprepossessing—until he began to talk. On the streets of Athens, in the market-place, in the gymnasia—wherever, in fact, he met men who would converse with him—he exercised his passion for inquiry and discussion. Although he seems to have been familiar with the various philosophic systems current in his time, he was an adherent of none of them; yet by the force of his own ideas he attracted followers of the greatest diversity of belief. Many young Athenians who were to become prominent in the affairs of their city became his pupils, among them the statesman Alcibiades, who, although he rose to great political heights, was in some regards no great credit to his teacher. With these young men Socrates talked fluently and volubly of justice, piety, love, and goodness. He believed that no man consciously does evil, that knowledge is virtue, and that doing right is the way to happiness. His style of reasoning, called the Socratic method, was based upon persistent questioning in an effort to arrive inductively at definitions of essential qualities. His peculiar dialectic and his intense concern for ethical values were his greatest contributions to philosophy.

But because of his disconcerting questions, his distressing skepticism, and his unconventional monotheism Socrates made many enemies among the Athenians. Charged with impiety and corruption of the young, he was brought to trial, declared guilty, and sentenced to death. He could have saved himself by promising to abandon his teaching, but this he refused to do. Attended by his friends, he died in the year 399 B.C. by drinking hemlock.

After the death of Socrates, Plato left Athens for about ten years, and during this time he is said to have visited Egypt and Cyrene, traveling and studying. Some accounts of his life say that he traveled as far as southern Italy and Sicily, where he visited Syracuse and was sold into slavery by the tyrant Dionysius I. He returned to Athens around

389 B.C. and established a school known as the Academy (so called for the surrounding grove sacred to the memory of an Athenian hero named Academus). Except for two more visits to Syracuse, he spent the rest of his life teaching in the Academy, which was perhaps the first European university and which was attended by young men from all over the Greek world. Among these his greatest pupil was Aristotle, who studied with him for twenty years.

The writings of Plato, which have been preserved in their entirety, are almost all in the form of philosophical dialogue, a type of literature that may owe something to the great Greek drama of the fifth century and which undoubtedly owes much to the fact that in an age of disillusionment such as Plato's time, sensitive and intelligent human beings turned naturally to philosophical inquiry. In these dialogues the character of Socrates as presented by Plato is a masterpiece of dramatic characterization, while the literary style and the philosophical content are among the highest achievements of the human mind.

Four of Plato's dialogues are related to the trial and death of Socrates. In the *Euthyphro* Socrates first makes known the fact that he has been indicted for impious actions and seeks to arrive at a definition of piety. In the *Apology,* actually an oration rather than a dialogue, Socrates defends himself before his accusers. The *Crito,* in which Socrates in prison explains his reasons for refusing to avail himself of the opportunity made by his friends for him to escape, examines the obligations of the good citizen. Finally the *Phaedo,* in which the chief subject of discourse is the immortality of the soul, describes movingly the last hours and the death of a wise and good man.

Though Plato had no great confidence in the ultimate effectiveness of writing, he resorted to the written word to popularize the teaching of Socrates and his own philosophical concepts. In this literary form he attacked the shams and pretensions of his age, and he explored the realms of virtue and truth. Among the most influential of the dialogues is the *Symposium,* in which Plato develops his conception of love—his belief that human love can rise above the physical to the intellectual, that it can become the supreme love of spiritual beauty. But the most elaborate and comprehensive of the dialogues is the *Republic,* in which Plato presents Socrates probing the question of justice. The definition of the just man, Plato believes, may best be found by first defining the just state. Primarily, the *Republic* offers such a definition; perhaps more than any other dialogue, it presents the basic doctrines of Plato.

In his construction of the ideal state Plato finds room to examine such subjects as education, the quality of true knowledge, the rewards of virtue, the immortality of the soul, and the nature of the future life. Among these speculations he presents his theory of Ideas, or Forms, already considered in some of his earlier dialogues and forming the basis of his philosophic idealism. The *idea* or *form* of any physical entity is, for Plato, a concept existing independently of the material substance of that entity; it is the persistent reality, of which the material substance is merely the transient manifestation. Matter as man conceives it does not exist in Plato's philosophy, any more than it exists in the speculations of modern physics.

In his allegory of the cave in Book VII of the *Republic,* Plato shows how man may take the shadow for the reality. Socrates is speaking to his friend Glaucon:

"And now, I said, let me show in a figure how far our nature is enlightened or unenlightened:—Behold! human beings living in an underground den, which has a mouth open toward the light and reaching all along the den; here they have been from their childhood, and have their legs and necks chained so that they cannot move, and can only see before them, being prevented by the chains from turning round their heads. Above and behind them a fire is blazing at a distance, and between the fire and the prisoners there is a raised way; and you will see, if you look, a low wall built along the way, like the screen which marionette players have in front of them, over which they show the puppets. . . .

"And do you see, I said, men passing along the wall carrying all sorts of vessels, and statues and figures of animals made of wood and stone and various materials, which appear over the wall? Some of them are talking, others silent. . . .

"And they [the men in the cave] see only their own shadows, or the shadows of one another, which the fire throws on the opposite wall of the cave? . . .

"And of the objects which are being carried in like manner they would only see the shadows? . . .

"And if they were able to converse with one another, would they not suppose that they were naming what was actually before them? . . .

"And suppose further that the prison had an echo which came from the other side, would they not be sure to fancy when one of the passers-by spoke that the voice which they heard came from the passing shadow? . . .

"To them, I said, the truth would be nothing but the shadows of the images."

The philosophic idealism of Plato—that is, his belief that the world of mind and spirit is the real world of which the physical world is the mere shadow—has had immense effect upon the philosophical and religious thinking of Western man. In the age following his own the Aristotelians and the Stoics were indebted to Plato, and somewhat later his influence is seen among the founders of Christianity. Both Cicero and Virgil felt the influence of his doctrines, and in Alexandria in the third century of the Christian era arose an active school of Neo-Platonists. He affected the thinking of Dante, Spenser, and Milton; and in more recent times his doctrines are found in the works of Wordsworth, Shelley, and Carlyle. And almost continuously, from his own day to the present, his influence has been felt in liberal education, for in the Socrates of the dialogues the world has seen the model of the great teacher, seeking and eliciting the truth without benefit of equipment or statistics, while the doctrine of philosophic idealism has transported the growing mind beyond the restraints of the material world.

THE APOLOGY

How you, O Athenians, have been affected by my accusers, I cannot tell; but I know that they almost made me forget who I was—so persuasively did they speak; and yet they have hardly uttered a word of truth. But of the many falsehoods told by them, there was one which quite amazed me;—I mean when they said that you should be upon your guard and not allow yourselves to be deceived by the force of my eloquence. To say this, when they were certain to be detected as soon as I opened my lips and proved myself to be anything but a great speaker, did indeed appear to me most shameless—unless by the force of eloquence they mean the force of truth; for if such is their meaning, I admit that I am eloquent. But in how different a way from theirs! Well, as I was saying, they have scarcely spoken the truth at all; but from me you shall hear the whole truth: not, however, delivered after their manner in a set oration duly ornamented with words and phrases. No, by heaven! but I shall use the words and arguments which occur to me at the moment; for I am confident in the justice of my cause. . . .

And first, I have to reply to the older charges and to my first accusers, and then I will go on to the later ones. For of old I have had many accusers, who have accused me falsely to you during many years; and I am more afraid of them than of Anytus and his associates, who are dangerous, too, in their own way. But far more dangerous are the others, who began when you were children, and took possession of your minds with their falsehoods, telling of one Socrates, a wise man, who speculated about the heaven above, and searched into the earth beneath, and made the worse appear the better cause. The disseminators of this tale are the accusers whom I dread; for their hearers are apt to fancy that such enquirers do not believe in the existence of the gods. And they are many, and their charges against me are of ancient date, and they were made by them in the days when you were more impressible than you are now—in childhood, or it may have been in youth—and the cause when heard went by default, for there was none to answer. And hardest of all, I do not know and cannot tell the names of my accusers; unless in the chance case of a comic poet.[1] All who from envy and malice have persuaded you— some of them having first convinced themselves—all this class of men are most difficult to deal with; for I cannot have them up here, and cross-examine them, and therefore I must simply fight with shadows in my own defence, and argue when there is no one who answers. I will ask you then to assume with me, as I was saying, that my opponents are of two kinds; one recent, the other ancient: and I hope that you will see the propriety of my answering the latter first, for these accusations you heard long before the others, and much oftener . . .

I will begin at the beginning, and ask what is the accusation which has given rise to the slander of me, and in fact has encouraged Meletus to prefer this charge against me. Well, what do the slanderers say? They shall be my prosecutors, and I will sum up their words in an affidavit: "Socrates is an evildoer, and a curious person, who searches into things under the earth and in heaven, and he makes the worse appear the better cause; and he teaches the aforesaid doctrines to others." Such is the nature of the accusation: it is just what you have yourselves seen in the comedy of Aristophanes, who has intro-

---

1. Probably a reference to the dramatist Aristophanes, who had satirized Socrates in his comedy *The Clouds*.

duced a man whom he calls Socrates, going about and saying that
he walks in air, and talking a deal of nonsense concerning matters
of which I do not pretend to know either much or little—not that I
mean to speak disparagingly of any one who is a student of natural
philosophy. I should be very sorry if Meletus could bring so grave a
charge against me. But the simple truth is, O Athenians, that I have
nothing to do with physical speculations. Very many of those here
present are witnesses to the truth of this, and to them I appeal. Speak
then, you who have heard me, and tell your neighbours whether any
of you have ever known me hold forth in few words or in many upon
such matters. . . . You hear their answer. And from what they say
of this part of the charge you will be able to judge of the truth of the
rest.

As little foundation is there for the report that I am a teacher,
and take money; this accusation has no more truth in it than the
other. Although, if a man were really able to instruct mankind, to
receive money for giving instruction would, in my opinion, be an
honour to him. . . . There is at this time a Parian philosopher resid-
ing in Athens, of whom I have heard; and I came to hear of him in
this way:—I came across a man who has spent a world of money on
the Sophists, Callias, the son of Hipponicus, and knowing that he
had sons, I asked him: "Callias," I said, "if your two sons were foals
or calves, there would be no difficulty in finding some one to put over
them; we should hire a trainer of horses, or a farmer, probably, who
would improve and perfect them in their own proper virtue and excellence; but as they are human beings, whom are you thinking of
placing over them? Is there any one who understands human and
political virtue? You must have thought about the matter, for you
have sons; is there any one?" "There is," he said. "Who is he?" said
I; "and of what country? and what does he charge?" "Evenus the
Parian," he replied; "he is the man, and his charge is five minae."[2]
Happy is Evenus, I said to myself, if he really has this wisdom, and
teaches at such a moderate charge. Had I the same, I should have
been very proud and conceited; but the truth is that I have no knowledge of the kind.

I dare say, Athenians, that some one among you will reply, "Yes,
Socrates, but what is the origin of these accusations which are brought
against you; there must have been something strange which you have
been doing? All these rumours and this talk about you would never

2. A mina was about fifteen dollars.

have arisen if you had been like other men: tell us, then, what is the cause of them, for we should be sorry to judge hastily of you." Now, I regard this as a fair challenge, and I will endeavour to explain to you the reason why I am called wise and have such an evil fame. Please to attend then. And although some of you may think that I am joking, I declare that I will tell you the entire truth. Men of Athens, this reputation of mine has come of a certain sort of wisdom which I possess. If you ask me what kind of wisdom, I reply, wisdom such as may perhaps be attained by man, for to that extent I am inclined to believe that I am wise; whereas the persons of whom I was speaking have a superhuman wisdom, which I may fail to describe, because I have it not myself; and he who says that I have, speaks falsely, and is taking away my character. And here, O men of Athens, I must beg you not to interrupt me, even if I seem to say something extravagant. For the word which I will speak is not mine. I will refer you to a witness who is worthy of credit; that witness shall be the god of Delphi[3]—he will tell you about my wisdom, if I have any, and of what sort it is. You must have known Chaerephon; he was early a friend of mine, and also a friend of yours. Well, Chaerephon, as you know, was very impetuous in all his doings, and he went to Delphi and boldly asked the oracle to tell him whether—as I was saying, I must beg you not to interrupt—he asked the oracle to tell him whether any one was wiser than I was, and the Pythian prophetess answered, that there was no man wiser.

Why do I mention this? Because I am going to explain to you why I have such an evil name. When I heard the answer, I said to myself, What can the god mean? and what is the interpretation of his riddle? for I know that I have no wisdom, small or great. What then can he mean when he says that I am the wisest of men? And yet he is a god, and cannot lie; that would be against his nature. After long consideration, I thought of a method of trying the question. I reflected that if I could only find a man wiser than myself, then I might go to the god with a refutation in my hand. I should say to him, "Here is a man who is wiser than I am; but you said that I was the wisest." Accordingly I went to one who had the reputation of wisdom, and observed him—his name I need not mention; he was a politician whom I selected for examination—and the result was as

3. There was a famous shrine, or oracle, of Apollo at Delphi (formerly called Pytho), where a priestess, sitting upon a tripod and inhaling the fumes from an opening beneath, uttered the advice and prophecies of the oracle.

follows: When I began to talk with him, I could not help thinking that he was not really wise, although he was thought wise by many, and still wiser by himself; and thereupon I tried to explain to him that he thought himself wise, but was not really wise; and the consequence was that he hated me, and his enmity was shared by several who were present and heard me. So I left him, saying to myself, as I went away: Well, although I do not suppose that either of us knows anything really beautiful and good, I am better off than he is,—for he knows nothing, and thinks that he knows; I neither know nor think that I know. In this latter particular, then, I seem to have slightly the advantage of him. Then I went to another who had still higher pretensions to wisdom, and my conclusion was exactly the same. Whereupon I made another enemy of him, and of many others besides him.

Then I went to one man after another, being not unconscious of the enmity which I provoked, and I lamented and feared this: but necessity was laid upon me—the word of God, I thought, ought to be considered first. And I said to myself, Go I must to all who appear to know, and find out the meaning of the oracle. And I swear to you, Athenians, by the dog I swear![4]—for I must tell you the truth—the result of my mission was just this: I found that the men most in repute were all but the most foolish; and that others less esteemed were really wiser and better. After the politicians, I went to the poets. And there, I said to myself, you will be instantly detected; now you will find out that you are more ignorant than they are. Accordingly I took them some of the most elaborate passages in their own writings, and asked what was the meaning of them—thinking that they would teach me something. Will you believe me? I am almost ashamed to confess the truth, but I must say that there is hardly a person present who would not have talked better about their poetry than they did themselves. Then I knew that not by wisdom do poets write poetry, but by a sort of genius and inspiration; they are like diviners or soothsayers who also say many fine things, but do not understand the meaning of them. The poets appeared to me to be much in the same case; and I further observed that upon the strength of their poetry they believed themselves to be the wisest of men in other things in which they were not wise. So I departed, conceiving myself to be

4. There are many explanations of this oath, none of them very satisfactory. Socrates may be swearing by the dog as an emblem of fidelity or by Anubis, the Egyptian dog-god. He may simply be avoiding swearing by the gods.

superior to them for the same reason that I was superior to the politicians.

At last I went to the artisans. I was conscious that I knew nothing at all, as I may say, and I was sure that they knew many fine things; and here I was not mistaken, for they did know many things of which I was ignorant, and in this they certainly were wiser than I was. But I observed that even the good artisans fell into the same error as the poets;—because they were good workmen they thought that they also knew all sorts of high matters, and this defect in them over-shadowed their wisdom; and therefore I asked myself on behalf of the oracle, whether I would like to be as I was, neither having their knowledge nor their ignorance, or like them in both; and I made answer to myself and to the oracle that I was better off as I was.

This inquisition has led to my having many enemies of the worst and most dangerous kind, and has given occasion also to many calumnies. And I am called wise, for my hearers always imagine that I myself possess the wisdom which I find wanting in others: but the truth is, O men of Athens, that God only is wise; and by his answer he intends to show that the wisdom of men is worth little or nothing; he is not speaking of Socrates, he is only using my name by way of illustration, as if he said, He, O men, is the wisest, who, like Socrates, knows that his wisdom is in truth worth nothing. And so I go about the world obedient to the god, and search and make enquiry into the wisdom of any one, whether citizen or stranger, who appears to be wise; and if he is not wise, then in vindication of the oracle I show him that he is not wise; and my occupation quite absorbs me, and I have no time to give either to any public matter of interest or to any concern of my own, but I am in utter poverty by reason of my devotion to the god.

There is another thing:—young men of the richer classes, who have not much to do, come about me of their own accord; they like to hear the pretenders examined, and they often imitate me, and proceed to examine others; there are plenty of persons, as they quickly discover, who think that they know something, but really know little or nothing; and then those who are examined by them instead of being angry with themselves are angry with me: This confounded Socrates, they say; this villainous misleader of youth!—and then if somebody asks them, Why, what evil does he practice or teach? they do not know, and cannot tell; but in order that they may not appear to be at a loss, they repeat the ready-made charges which are used against all philosophers about teaching things up in the clouds and under the earth, and having no gods, and making the worse appear the better cause; for they do not like to confess that their pretence of knowledge has been detected—which is the truth; and as they are numerous and ambitious and energetic, and are drawn up in battle array and have persuasive tongues, they have filled your ears with their loud and inveterate calumnies. And this is the reason why my three accusers, Meletus and Anytus and Lycon, have set upon me; Meletus, who has a quarrel with me on behalf of the poets; Anytus, on behalf of the craftsmen and politicians; Lycon, on behalf of the rhetoricians: and, as I said at the beginning, I cannot expect to get rid of such a mass of calumny all in a moment. . . .

I have said enough in my defence against the first class of my accusers; I turn to the second class. They are headed by Meletus, that good man and true lover of his country, as he calls himself. Against these, too, I must try to make a defence:—Let their affidavit be read: it contains something of this kind: It says that Socrates is a doer of evil, who corrupts the youth; and who does not believe in the gods of the State, but has other new divinities of his own. Such is the charge; and now let us examine the particular counts. He says that I am a doer of evil, and corrupt the youth; but I say, O men of Athens, that Meletus is a doer of evil, in that he pretends to be in earnest when he is only in jest, and is so eager to bring men to trial from a pretended zeal and interest about matters in which he really never had the smallest interest. And the truth of this I will endeavour to prove to you.

Come hither, Meletus, and let me ask a question of you. You think a great deal about the improvement of youth?

Yes, I do.

Tell the judges, then, who is their improver; for you must know, as you have taken the pains to discover their corrupter, and are citing and accusing me before them. Speak, then, and tell the judges who their improver is.—Observe, Meletus, that you are silent, and have nothing to say. But is not this rather disgraceful, and a very considerable proof of what I was saying, that you have no interest in the matter? Speak up, friend, and tell us who their improver is.

The laws.

But that, my good sir, is not my meaning. I want to know who the person is, who, in the first place, knows the laws.

The judges, Socrates, who are present in court.

What, do you mean to say, Meletus, that they are able to instruct and improve youth?

Certainly they are.

What, all of them, or some only and not others?

All of them.

By the goddess Here, that is good news! There are plenty of improvers, then. And what do you say of the audience,—do they improve them?

Yes, they do.

And the senators?

Yes, the senators improve them.

But perhaps the members of the assembly corrupt them?—or do they improve them?

They improve them.

Then every Athenian improves and elevates them; all with the exception of myself; and I alone am their corrupter? Is that what you affirm?

That is what I stoutly affirm.

I am very unfortunate if you are right. But suppose I ask you a question: How about horses? Does one man do them harm and all the world good? Is not the exact opposite the truth? One man is able to do them good, or at least not many;—the trainer of horses, that is to say, does them good, and others who have to do with them rather injure them? Is not that true, Meletus, of horses, or of any other animals? Most assuredly it is; whether you and Anytus say yes or no. Happy indeed would be the condition of youth if they had one corrupter only, and all the rest of the world were their improvers. But you, Meletus, have sufficiently shown that you never had a thought about the young: your carelessness is seen in your not caring about the very things which you bring against me.

And now, Meletus, I will ask you another question—by Zeus I will: Which is better, to live among bad citizens, or among good ones? Answer, friend, I say; the question is one which may be easily answered. Do not the good do their neighbours good, and the bad do them evil?

Certainly.

And is there any one who would rather be injured than benefited by those who live with him? Answer, my good friend, the law requires you to answer—does any one like to be injured?

Certainly not.

And when you accuse me of corrupting and deteriorating the youth, do you allege that I corrupt them intentionally or unintentionally?

Intentionally, I say.

But you have just admitted that the good do their neighbours good, and the evil do them evil. Now, is that a truth which your superior wisdom has recognized thus early in life, and am I, at my age, in such darkness and ignorance as not to know that if a man with whom I have to live is corrupted by me, I am very likely to be harmed by him; and yet I corrupt him, and intentionally, too—so you say, although neither I nor any other human being is ever likely to be convinced by you. But either I do not corrupt them, or I corrupt them unintentionally; and on either view of the case you lie. If my offence is unintentional, the law has no cognizance of unintentional offences: you ought to have taken me privately, and warned and admonished me; for if I had been better advised, I should have left off doing what I only did unintentionally—no doubt I should; but you would have nothing to say to me and refused to teach me. And now you bring me up in this court, which is a place not of instruction, but of punishment.

It will be very clear to you, Athenians, as I was saying, that Meletus has no care at all, great or small, about the matter. But still I should like to know, Meletus, in what I am affirmed to corrupt the young. I suppose you mean, as I infer from your indictment, that I teach them not to acknowledge the gods which the State acknowledges, but some other new divinities or spiritual agencies in their stead. These are the lessons by which I corrupt the youth, as you say.

Yes, that I say emphatically.

Then, by the gods, Meletus, of whom we are speaking, tell me and the court, in somewhat plainer terms, what you mean! For I do not as yet understand whether you affirm that I teach other men to acknowledge some gods, and therefore that I do believe in gods, and am not an entire atheist—this you do not lay to my charge,—but only you say that they are not the same gods which the city recognizes—the charge is that they are different gods. Or, do you mean that I am an atheist simply, and a teacher of atheism?

I mean the latter—that you are a complete atheist.

What an extraordinary statement! Why do you think so, Meletus? Do you mean that I do not believe in the godhead of the sun or moon, like other men?

I assure you, judges, that he does not: for he says that the sun is stone, and the moon earth. . . . And so, Meletus, you really think that I do not believe in any god?

I swear by Zeus that you believe absolutely in none at all.

Nobody will believe you, Meletus, and I am pretty sure that you do not believe yourself. I cannot help thinking, men of Athens, that Meletus is reckless and impudent, and that he has written this indictment in a spirit of mere wantonness and youthful bravado. . . . For he certainly does appear to me to contradict himself in the indictment as much as if he said that Socrates is guilty of not believing in the gods, and yet of believing in them—but this is not like a person who is in earnest.

I should like you, O men of Athens, to join me in examining what I conceive to be his inconsistency; and do you, Meletus, answer. And I must remind the audience of my request that they would not make a disturbance if I speak in my accustomed manner:

Did ever man, Meletus, believe in the existence of human things, and not of human beings? . . . I wish, men of Athens, that he would answer, and not be always trying to get up an interruption. Did ever any man believe in horsemanship, and not in horses? or in flute-playing, and not in flute-players? No, my friend; I will answer to you and to the court, as you refuse to answer for yourself. There is no man who ever did. But now please to answer the next question: Can a man believe in spiritual and divine agencies, and not in spirits or demigods?

He cannot.

How lucky I am to have extracted that answer, by the assistance of the court! But then you swear in the indictment that I teach and believe in divine or spiritual agencies (new or old, no matter for that); at any rate, I believe in spiritual agencies,—so you say and swear in the affidavit; and yet if I believe in divine beings, how can I help believing in spirits or demigods;—must I not? To be sure I must; and therefore I may assume that your silence gives consent. Now what are spirits or demigods? are they not either gods or the sons of gods?

Certainly they are.

But this is what I call the facetious riddle invented by you: the demigods or spirits are gods, and you say first that I do not believe in gods, and then again that I do believe in gods; that is, if I believe in demigods. For if the demigods are the illegitimate sons of gods, whether by the nymphs or by any other mothers, of whom they are said to be the sons—what human being will ever believe that there

are no gods if they are the sons of gods? You might as well affirm
the existence of mules, and deny that of horses and asses. Such nonsense, Meletus, could only have been intended by you to make trial
of me. You have put this into the indictment because you had nothing real of which to accuse me. But no one who has a particle of
understanding will ever be convinced by you that the same men can
believe in divine and superhuman things, and yet not believe that
there are gods and demigods and heroes.

I have said enough in answer to the charge of Meletus: any
elaborate defence is unnecessary; but I know only too well how
many are the enmities which I have incurred, and this is what will
be my destruction if I am destroyed;—not Meletus, nor yet Anytus,
but the envy and detraction of the world, which has been the death
of many good men, and will probably be the death of many more;
there is no danger of my being the last of them.

Some one will say: And are you not ashamed, Socrates, of a course
of life which is likely to bring you to an untimely end? To him I
may fairly answer: There you are mistaken: a man who is good for
anything ought not to calculate the chance of living or dying; he
ought only to consider whether in doing anything he is doing right
or wrong—acting the part of a good man or of a bad. Whereas, upon
your view, the heroes who fell at Troy were not good for much, and
the son of Thetis above all, who altogether despised danger in comparison with disgrace; and when he was so eager to slay Hector, his
goddess mother said to him, that if he avenged his companion Patroclus, and slew Hector, he would die himself—"Fate," she said, in these
or the like words, "waits for you next after Hector;" he, receiving this
warning, utterly despised danger and death, and instead of fearing
them, feared rather to live in dishonour, and not to avenge his friend.
"Let me die forthwith," he replies, "and be avenged of my enemy,
rather than abide here by the beaked ships, a laughing stock and a
burden of the earth." Had Achilles any thought of death and danger?
For wherever a man's place is, whether the place which he has chosen
or that in which he has been placed by a commander, there he ought
to remain in the hour of danger; he should not think of death or of
anything but of disgrace. And this, O men of Athens, is a true saying.

Strange, indeed, would be my conduct, O men of Athens, if I,
who, when I was ordered by the generals whom you chose to command me at Potidaea and Amphipolis and Delium, remained where
they placed me, like any other man, facing death—if now, when, as I

conceive and imagine, God orders me to fulfil the philosopher's mission of searching into myself and other men, I were to desert my post through fear of death, or any other fear; that would indeed be strange, and I might justly be arraigned in court for denying the existence of the gods, if I disobeyed the oracle because I was afraid of death, fancying that I was wise when I was not wise. For the fear of death is indeed the pretence of wisdom, and not real wisdom, being a pretence of knowing the unknown; and no one knows whether death, which men in their fear apprehend to be the greatest evil, may not be the greatest good. Is not this ignorance of a disgraceful sort, the ignorance which is the conceit that a man knows what he does not know? And in this respect only I believe myself to differ from men in general, and may perhaps claim to be wiser than they are:—that whereas I know but little of the world below, I do not suppose that I know: but I do know that injustice and disobedience to a better, whether God or man, is evil and dishonourable, and I will never fear or avoid a possible good rather than a certain evil. And therefore if you let me go now, and are not convinced by Anytus, who said that since I had been prosecuted I must be put to death (or if not that I ought never to have been prosecuted at all); and that if I escape now, your sons will all be utterly ruined by listening to my words—if you say to me, Socrates, this time we will not mind Anytus, and you shall be let off, but upon one condition, that you are not to inquire and speculate in this way any more, and that if you are caught doing so again you shall die;—if this was the condition on which you let me go, I should reply: Men of Athens, I honour and love you; but I shall obey God rather than you, and while I have life and strength I shall never cease from the practice and teaching of philosophy, exhorting any one whom I meet and saying to him after my manner: You, my friend,—a citizen of the great and mighty and wise city of Athens,— are you not ashamed of heaping up the greatest amount of money and honour and reputation, and caring so little about wisdom and truth and the greatest improvement of the soul, which you never regard or heed at all? And if the person with whom I am arguing says: Yes, but I do care; then I do not leave him or let him go at once; but I proceed to interrogate and examine and cross-examine him, and if I think that he has no virtue in him, but only says that he has, I reproach him with undervaluing the greater, and overvaluing the less. And I shall repeat the same words to every one whom I meet, young and old, citizen and alien, but especially to the citizens, inasmuch as they are my brethren. For know that this is the command of God; and I believe that no greater good has ever happened in the State than my service to the God. For I do nothing but go about persuading you all, old and young alike, not to take thought for your persons or your properties, but first and chiefly to care about the greatest improvement of the soul. I tell you that virtue is not given by money, but that from virtue comes money and every other good of man, public as well as private. This is my teaching, and if this is the doctrine which corrupts the youth, I am a mischievous person. But if any one says that this is not my teaching, he is speaking an untruth. Wherefore, O men of Athens, I say to you, do as Anytus bids or not as Anytus bids, and either acquit me or not; but whichever you do, understand that I shall never alter my ways, not even if I have to die many times.

Men of Athens, do not interrupt, but hear me; there was an understanding between us that you should hear me to the end: I have something more to say, at which you may be inclined to cry out; but I believe that to hear me will be good for you, and therefore I beg that you will not cry out. I would have you know, that if you kill such an one as I am, you will injure yourselves more than you will injure me. Nothing will injure me, not Meletus nor yet Anytus—they cannot, for a bad man is not permitted to injure a better than himself. I do not deny that Anytus may, perhaps, kill him, or drive him into exile, or deprive him of civil rights; and he may imagine, and others may imagine, that he is inflicting a great injury upon him: but there I do not agree. For the evil of doing as he is doing—the evil of unjustly taking away the life of another—is greater far.

And now, Athenians, I am not going to argue for my own sake, as you may think, but for yours, that you may not sin against the God by condemning me, who am his gift to you. For if you kill me you will not easily find a successor to me, who, if I may use such a ludicrous figure of speech, am a sort of gadfly, given to the State by God; and the State is a great and noble steed who is tardy in his motions owing to his very size, and requires to be stirred into life. I am that gadfly which God has attached to the State, and all day long and in all places am always fastening upon you, arousing and persuading and reproaching you. You will not easily find another like me, and therefore I would advise you to spare me. I dare say that you may feel out of temper (like a person who is suddenly awakened from sleep), and you think that you might easily strike me dead as Anytus advises, and then you would sleep on for the remainder of your lives, unless God in his care of you send you another gadfly. When I say that I am given to you by God, the proof of my mission is this:—if I had been like other men, I should not have neglected all my own concerns or patiently seen the neglect of them during all these years, and have been doing yours, coming to you individually like a father or elder brother, exhorting you to regard virtue; such conduct, I say, would be unlike human nature. If I had gained anything, or if my exhortations had been paid, there would have been some sense in my doing so; but now, as you will perceive, not even the impudence of my accusers dares to say that I have ever exacted or sought pay of any one; of that they have no witness. And I have a sufficient witness to the truth of what I say—my poverty.

Some one may wonder why I go about in private giving advice and busying myself with the concerns of others, but do not venture to come forward in public and advise the State. I will tell you why. You have heard me speak at sundry times and in divers places of an oracle[5] or sign which comes to me, and is the divinity which Meletus ridicules in the indictment. This sign, which is a kind of voice, first began to come to me when I was a child; it always forbids but never commands me to do anything which I am going to do. This is what deters me from being a politician. And rightly, as I think. For I am certain, O men of Athens, that if I had engaged in politics, I should have perished long ago, and done no good either to you or to myself. And do not be offended at my telling you the truth: for the truth is, that no man who goes to war with you or any other multitude, honestly striving against the many lawless and unrighteous deeds which are done in a State, will save his life; he who will fight for the right, if he would live even for a brief space, must have a private station and not a public one. . . .

Now, do you really imagine that I could have survived all these years, if I had led a public life, supposing that like a good man I had always maintained the right and had made justice, as I ought, the first thing? No, indeed, men of Athens, neither I nor any other man. But I have been always the same in all my actions, public as well as private, and never have I yielded any base compliance to those who are slanderously termed my disciples, or to any other. Not that I have any regular disciples. But if any one likes to come and hear me

5. Not to be confused with the oracle of Delphi, mentioned previously by Socrates.

while I am pursuing my mission, whether he be young or old, he is not excluded. Nor do I converse only with those who pay; but any one, whether he be rich or poor, may ask and answer me and listen to my words; and whether he turns out to be a bad man or a good one, neither result can be justly imputed to me; for I never taught or professed to teach him anything. And if any one says that he has ever learned or heard anything from me in private which all the world has not heard, let me tell you that he is lying.

But I shall be asked, Why do people delight in continually conversing with you? I have told you already, Athenians, the whole truth about this matter: they like to hear the cross-examination of the pretenders to wisdom; there is amusement in it. Now, this duty of cross-examining other men has been imposed upon me by God; and has been signified to me by oracles, visions, and in every way in which the will of divine power was ever intimated to any one. This is true, O Athenians; or, if not true, would be soon refuted. If I am or have been corrupting the youth, those of them who are now grown up and have become sensible that I gave them bad advice in the days of their youth should come forward as accusers, and take their revenge; or if they do not like to come themselves, some of their relatives, fathers, brothers, or other kinsmen, should say what evil their families have suffered at my hands. Now is their time. Many of them I see in the court. . . . Nay, Athenians, the very opposite is the truth. For all these are ready to witness on behalf of the corrupter, of the injurer of their kindred, as Meletus and Anytus call me; not the corrupted youth only—there might have been a motive for that—but their uncorrupted elder relatives. Why should they too support me with their testimony? Why, indeed, except for the sake of truth and justice, and because they know that I am speaking the truth, and that Meletus is a liar.

Well, Athenians, this and the like of this is all the defence which I have to offer. Yet a word more. Perhaps there may be some one who is offended at me, when he calls to mind how he himself on a similar, or even a less serious occasion, prayed and entreated the judges with many tears, and how he produced his children in court, which was a moving spectacle, together with a host of relations and friends; whereas I, who am probably in danger of my life, will do none of these things. The contrast may occur to his mind, and he may be set against me, and vote in anger because he is displeased at me on this account. Now, if there be such a person among you,—mind, I do not say that there is,—to him I may fairly reply: My friend, I am a man, and like other men, a creature of flesh and blood, and not "of wood or stone," as Homer says; and I have a family, yes, and sons, O Athenians, three in number, one almost a man, and two others who are still young; and yet I will not bring any of them hither in order to petition you for an acquittal. And why not? Not from any self-assertion or want of respect for you. Whether I am or am not afraid of death is another question, of which I will not now speak. But, having regard to public opinion, I feel that such conduct would be discreditable to myself, and to you, and to the whole State. One who has reached my years, and who has a name for wisdom, ought not to demean himself. Whether this opinion of me is deserved or not, at any rate the world has decided that Socrates is in some way superior to other men. And if those among you who are said to be superior in wisdom and courage, and any other virtue, demean themselves in this way, how shameful is their conduct! I have seen men of reputation, when they have been condemned, behaving in the strangest manner: they seemed to fancy that they were going to suffer something dreadful if they died, and that they could be immortal if you only allowed them to live; and I think that such are a dishonour to the State, and that any stranger coming in would have said of them that the most eminent men of Athens, to whom the Athenians themselves give honour and command, are no better than women. And I say that these things ought not to be done by those of us who have a reputation; and if they are done, you ought not to permit them; you ought rather to show that you are far more disposed to condemn the man who gets up a doleful scene and makes the city ridiculous, than him who holds his peace. . . .

Do not then require me to do what I consider dishonourable and impious and wrong, especially now, when I am being tried for impiety on the indictment of Meletus. For if, O men of Athens, by force of persuasion and entreaty I could overpower your oaths, then I should be teaching you to believe that there are no gods, and in defending should simply convict myself of the charge of not believing in them. But that is not so—far otherwise. For I do believe that there are gods, and in a sense higher than that in which any of my accusers believe in them. And to you and to God I commit my cause, to be determined by you as is best for you and me.

There are many reasons why I am not grieved, O men of Athens, at the vote of condemnation. I expected it, and am only surprised

that the votes are so nearly equal; for I had thought that the majority
against me would have been far larger; but now, had thirty votes
gone over to the other side, I should have been acquitted. And I may
say, I think, that I have escaped Meletus. I may say more; for without
the assistance of Anytus and Lycon, any one may see that he would
not have had a fifth part of the votes, as the law requires, in which
case he would have incurred a fine of a thousand drachmae.[6]

And so he proposes death as the penalty. And what shall
I propose on my part, O men of Athens? Clearly that which is my
due. And what is my due? What returns shall be made to the man
who has never had the wit to be idle during his whole life; but has
been careless of what the many care for—wealth, and family interests,
and military offices, and speaking in the assembly, and magistracies,
and plots, and parties. Reflecting that I was really too honest a man to
be a politician and live, I did not go where I could do no good to you
or to myself; but where I could do the greatest good privately to every
one of you, thither I went, and sought to persuade every man among
you that he must look to himself, and seek virtue and wisdom before
he looks to his private interests, and look to the State before he looks
to the interests of the State; and that this should be the order which
he observes in all his actions. What shall be done to such an one?
Doubtless some good thing, O men of Athens, if he has his reward;
and the good should be of a kind suitable to him. What would be a
reward suitable to a poor man who is your benefactor, and who desires
leisure that he may instruct you? There can be no reward so fitting as
maintenance in the Prytaneum,[7] O men of Athens, a reward which
he deserves far more than the citizen who has won the prize at Olympia
in the horse or chariot race, whether the chariots were drawn by two
horses or by many. For I am in want, and he has enough; and he only
gives you the appearance of happiness, and I give you the reality.
And if I am to estimate the penalty fairly, I should say that maintenance in the Prytaneum is the just return.

Perhaps you think that I am braving you in what I am saying
now, as in what I said before about the tears and prayers. But this is
not so. I speak rather because I am convinced that I never intentionally
wronged any one, although I cannot convince you—the time has been
too short; if there were a law at Athens, as there is in other cities, that

6. A drachma was about fifteen cents.
7. A kind of city-hall, where guests of the state and public benefactors were
entertained.

a capital cause should not be decided in one day, then I believe that
I should have convinced you. But I cannot in a moment refute great
slanders; and, as I am convinced that I never wronged another, I will
assuredly not wrong myself. I will not say of myself that I deserve any
evil, or propose any penalty. Why should I? Because I am afraid
of the penalty of death which Meletus proposes? When I do not know
whether death is a good or an evil, why should I propose a penalty
which would certainly be an evil? Shall I say imprisonment? And
why should I live in prison, and be the slave of the magistrate of the
year—of the Eleven?[8] Or shall the penalty be a fine, and imprisonment until the fine is paid? There is the same objection. I should have
to lie in prison, for money I have none, and cannot pay. And if I say
exile (and this may possibly be the penalty which you will affix), I
must indeed be blinded by the love of life if I am so irrational as to
expect that when you, who are my own citizens, cannot endure my
discourses and words, and have found them so grievous and odious
that you will have no more of them, others are likely to endure me.
No, indeed, men of Athens, that is not very likely. And what a life
should I lead, at my age, wandering from city to city, ever changing
my place of exile, and always being driven out! For I am quite sure
that wherever I go, there, as here, the young men will flock to
me; and if I drive them away, their elders will drive me out at their
request; and if I let them come, their fathers and friends will drive me
out for their sakes.

Some one will say: Yes, Socrates, but cannot you hold your
tongue, and then you may go into a foreign city, and no one will
interfere with you? Now, I have great difficulty in making you understand my answer to this. For if I tell you that to do as you say would
be a disobedience to the God, and therefore that I cannot hold my
tongue, you will not believe that I am serious; and if I say again that
daily to discourse about virtue, and of those other things about which
you hear me examining myself and others, is the greatest good of man,
and that the unexamined life is not worth living, you are still less
likely to believe me. Yet I say what is true, although a thing of which
it is hard for me to persuade you. Also, I have never been accustomed
to think that I deserve to suffer any harm. Had I money I might have
estimated the offence at what I was able to pay, and not have been
much the worse. But I have none, and therefore I must ask you to
proportion the fine to my means. Well, perhaps I could afford a mina,

8. Police magistrates who had charge of prisons and the execution of sentences.

and therefore I propose that penalty: Plato, Crito, Critobulus, and Apollodorus, my friends here, bid me say thirty minæ, and they will be the sureties. Let thirty minæ be the penalty; for which sum they will be ample security to you.

Not much time will be gained, O Athenians, in return for the evil name which you will get from the detractors of the city, who will say that you killed Socrates, a wise man; for they will call me wise, even although I am not wise, when they want to reproach you. If you had waited a little while, your desire would have been fulfilled in the course of nature. For I am far advanced in years, as you may perceive, and not far from death. I am speaking now not to all of you, but only to those who have condemned me to death. And I have another thing to say to them: You think that I was convicted because I had no words of the sort which would have procured my acquittal— I mean, if I had thought fit to leave nothing undone or unsaid. Not so; the deficiency which led to my conviction was not of words—certainly not. But I had not the boldness or impudence or inclination to address you as you would have liked me to do, weeping and wailing and lamenting, and saying and doing many things which you have been accustomed to hear from others, and which, as I maintain, are unworthy of me. I thought at the time that I ought not to do anything common or mean when in danger: nor do I now repent of the style of my defence; I would rather die having spoken after my manner, than speak in your manner and live. For neither in war nor yet at law ought I or any man to use every way of escaping death. Often in battle there can be no doubt that if a man will throw away his arms, and fall on his knees before his pursuers, he may escape death; and in other dangers there are other ways of escaping death, if a man is willing to say and do anything. The difficulty, my friends, is not to avoid death, but to avoid unrighteousness; for that runs faster than death. I am old and move slowly, and the slower runner has overtaken me, and my accusers are keen and quick, and the faster runner, who is unrighteousness, has overtaken them. And now I depart hence condemned by you to suffer the penalty of death,—they too go their ways condemned by the truth to suffer the penalty of villainy and wrong; and I must abide by my award—let them abide by theirs. I suppose that these things may be regarded as fated—and I think that they are well.

And now, O men who have condemned me, I would fain prophesy to you; for I am about to die, and in the hour of death men are gifted with prophetic power. And I prophesy to you who are my murderers, that immediately after my departure punishment far heavier than you have inflicted on me will surely await you. Me you have killed because you wanted to escape the accuser, and not to give an account of your lives. But that will not be as you suppose: far otherwise. For I say that there will be more accusers of you than there are now; accusers whom hitherto I have restrained: and as they are younger they will be more inconsiderate with you, and you will be more offended at them. If you think that by killing men you can prevent some one from censuring your evil lives, you are mistaken; that is not a way of escape which is either possible or honourable; the easiest and the noblest way is not to be disabling others, but to be improving yourselves. This is the prophecy which I utter before my departure to the judges who have condemned me.

Friends, who would have acquitted me, I would like also to talk with you about the thing which has come to pass, while the magistrates are busy, and before I go to the place at which I must die. Stay then a little, for we may as well talk with one another while there is time. You are my friends, and I should like to show you the meaning of this event which has happened to me. O my judges—for you I may truly call judges—I should like to tell you of a wonderful circumstance. Hitherto the divine faculty of which the internal oracle is the source has constantly been in the habit of opposing me even about trifles, if I was going to make a slip or error in any manner; and now as you see there has come upon me that which may be thought, and is generally believed to be, the last and worst evil. But the oracle made no sign of opposition, either when I was leaving my house in the morning, or when I was on my way to the court, or while I was speaking, at anything which I was going to say; and yet I have often been stopped in the middle of a speech, but now in nothing I either said or did touching the matter in hand has the oracle opposed me. What do I take to be the explanation of this silence? I will tell you. It is an intimation that what has happened to me is a good, and that those of us who think that death is an evil are in error. For the customary sign would surely have opposed me had I been going to evil and not to good.

Let us reflect in another way, and we shall see that there is great reason to hope that death is a good; for one of two things—either death is a state of nothingness and utter unconsciousness, or, as men say, there is a change and migration of the soul from this world to another. Now, if you suppose that there is no consciousness, but a sleep like the sleep of him who is undisturbed even by dreams, death will be an unspeakable gain. For if a person were to select the night in which his sleep was undisturbed even by dreams, and were to compare with this the other days and nights of his life, and then were to tell us how many days and nights he had passed in the course of his life better and more pleasantly than this one, I think that any man, I will not say a private man, but even the great king will not find many such days or nights, when compared with the others. Now, if death be of such a nature, I say that to die is gain; for eternity is then only a single night. But if death is the journey to another place, and there, as men say, all the dead abide, what good, O my friends and judges, can be greater than this? If, indeed, when the pilgrim arrives in the world below, he is delivered from the professors of justice in this world, and finds the true judges who are said to give judgment there, Minos and Rhadamanthus and Aeacus and Triptolemus, and other sons of God who were righteous in their own life, that pilgrimage will be worth making. What would not a man give if he might converse with Orpheus and Musaeus and Hesiod and Homer? Nay, if this be true, let me die again and again. I myself, too, shall have a wonderful interest in there meeting and conversing with Palamedes, and Ajax the son of Telamon, and any other ancient hero who has suffered death through an unjust judgment; and there will be no small pleasure, as I think, in comparing my own sufferings with theirs. Above all, I shall then be able to continue my search into true and false knowledge; as in this world, so also in the next; and I shall find out who is wise, and who pretends to be wise, and is not. What would not a man give, O judges, to be able to examine the leader of the great Trojan expedition; or Odysseus or Sisyphus, or numberless others, men and women too! What infinite delight would there be in conversing with them and asking them questions! In another world they do not put a man to death for asking questions: assuredly not. For besides being happier than we are, they will be immortal, if what is said is true.

Wherefore, O judges, be of good cheer about death, and know of a certainty, that no evil can happen to a good man, either in life or after death. He and his are not neglected by the gods; nor has my own approaching end happened by mere chance. But I see clearly that the time had arrived when it was better for me to die and be released from trouble; wherefore the oracle gave no sign. For which reason, also, I am not angry with my condemners, or with my accusers; they have done me no harm, although they did not mean to do me any good; and for this I may gently blame them.

Still, I have a favour to ask of them. When my sons are grown up, I would ask you, O my friends, to punish them; and I would have you trouble them, as I have troubled you, if they seem to care about riches, or anything, more than about virtue; or if they pretend to be something when they are really nothing,—then reprove them, as I have reproved you, for not caring about that for which they ought to care, and thinking that they are something when they are really nothing. And if you do this, both I and my sons will have received justice at your hands.

The hour of departure has arrived, and we go our ways—I to die, and you to live. Which is better God only knows.

PLATO

Phaedo

ECHECRATES. Were you yourself, Phaedo, in the prison with Socrates on the day when he drank the poison?

PHAEDO. Yes, Echecrates, I was.

ECH. I should so like to hear about his death. What did he say in his last hours? We were informed that he died by taking poison, but no one knew anything more; for no Phliasian ever goes to Athens now, and it is a long time since any stranger from Athens has found his way hither; so that we had no clear account.[1]

PHAED. Did you not hear of the proceedings at the trial?

ECH. Yes; some one told us about the trial, and we could not understand why, having been condemned, he should have been put to death, not at the time, but long afterwards. What was the reason of this?

PHAED. An accident, Echecrates: the stern of the ship which the Athenians sent to Delos happened to have been crowned on the day before he was tried.

ECH. What is this ship?

1. Phaedo's narrative takes place at Phlius.

319

PHAED. It is the ship in which, according to Athenian tradition, Theseus went to Crete when he took with him the fourteen youths, and was the saviour of them and of himself.[2] And they are said to have vowed to Apollo at the time, that if they were saved they would send a yearly mission to Delos.[3] Now this custom still continues, and the whole period of the voyage to and from Delos, beginning when the priest of Apollo crowns the stern of the ship, is a holy season, during which the city is not allowed to be polluted by public executions; and when the vessel is detained by contrary winds, the time spent in going and returning is very considerable. As I was saying, the ship was crowned on the day before the trial, and this was the reason why Socrates lay in prison and was not put to death until long after he was condemned.

ECH. What was the manner of his death, Phaedo? What was said or done? And which of his friends were with him? Or did the authorities forbid them to be present—so that he had no friends near him when he died?

PHAED. No; there were several of them with him.

ECH. If you have nothing to do, I wish that you would tell me what passed, as exactly as you can.

PHAED. I have nothing at all to do, and will try to gratify your wish. To be reminded of Socrates is always the greatest delight to me, whether I speak myself or hear another speak of him.

ECH. You will have listeners who are of the same mind with you, and I hope that you will be as exact as you can.

PHAED. I had a singular feeling at being in his company. For I could hardly believe that I was present at the death of a friend, and therefore I did not pity him, Echecrates; he died so fearlessly, and his words and bearing were so noble and gracious, that to me he appeared blessed. I thought that in going to the other world he could not be without a divine call, and that he would be happy, if any man ever was, when he arrived there; and therefore I did not pity him as might have seemed natural at such an hour. But I had not the pleasure which I usually feel in philosophical discourse (for philosophy was the theme of which we spoke). I was pleased, but in the pleasure there was also a strange admixture of pain; for I reflected that he was soon to die,

2. Athens had paid to Crete an annual tribute of fourteen young men and women to be killed by the Minotaur, a monster half man and half bull kept by King Minos in the Labyrinth.

3. Birthplace of Apollo.

and this double feeling was shared by us all; we were laughing and
weeping by turns, especially the excitable Apollodorus—you know the
sort of man?

ECH. Yes.

PHAED. He was quite beside himself; and I and all of us were
greatly moved. . . .

ECH. Well, and what did you talk about?

PHAED. I will begin at the beginning, and endeavour to repeat
the entire conversation. On the previous days we had been in the habit
of assembling early in the morning at the court in which the trial
took place, and which is not far from the prison. There we used to
wait talking with one another until the opening of the doors (for they
were not opened very early); then we went in and generally passed the
day with Socrates. On the last morning we assembled sooner than
usual, having heard on the day before when we quitted the prison
in the evening that the sacred ship had come from Delos; and so we
arranged to meet very early at the accustomed place. On our arrival
the jailer who answered the door, instead of admitting us, came out
and told us to stay until he called us. "For the Eleven," he said
"are now with Socrates, they are taking off his chains, and giving
orders that he is to die to-day." He soon returned and said that we
might come in. On entering we found Socrates just released from
chains, and Xanthippe,[4] whom you know, sitting by him, and holding
his child in her arms. When she saw us she uttered a cry and said, as
women will: "O Socrates, this is the last time that either you will
converse with your friends, or they with you." Socrates turned to Crito
and said: "Crito, let some one take her home." Some of Crito's people
accordingly led her away, crying out and beating herself. And when
she was gone, Socrates, sitting up on the couch, bent and rubbed
his leg, saying, as he was rubbing: How singular is the thing called
pleasure, and how curiously related to pain, which might be thought
to be the opposite of it; for they are never present to a man at the
same instant, and yet he who pursues either is generally compelled
to take the other; their bodies are two, but they are joined by a single
head. And I cannot help thinking that if Aesop had remembered
them, he would have made a fable about God trying to reconcile their
strife, and how, when he could not, he fastened their heads together;
and this is the reason why when one comes the other follows: as I

4. Wife of Socrates.

PLATO

know by my own experience now, when after the pain in my leg which was caused by the chain pleasure appears to succeed.

Upon this Cebes said: I am glad, Socrates, that you have mentioned the name of Aesop. For it reminds me of a question which has been asked by many, and was asked of me only the day before yesterday by Evenus the poet—he will be sure to ask it again, and therefore if you would like me to have an answer ready for him, you may as well tell me what I should say to him:—he wanted to know why you, who never before wrote a line of poetry, now that you are in prison are turning Aesop's fables into verse, and also composing that hymn in honour of Apollo.

Tell him, Cebes, he replied, what is the truth—that I had no idea of rivalling him or his poems; to do so, as I knew, would be no easy task. But I wanted to see whether I could purge away a scruple which I felt about the meaning of certain dreams. In the course of my life I have often had intimations in dreams "that I should compose music." The same dream came to me sometimes in one form, and sometimes in another, but always saying the same or nearly the same words: "Cultivate and make music," said the dream. And hitherto I had imagined that this was only intended to exhort and encourage me in the study of philosophy, which has been the pursuit of my life, and is the noblest and best of music. The dream was bidding me do what I was already doing, in the same way that the competitor in a race is bidden by the spectators to run when he is already running. But I was not certain of this; for the dream might have meant music in the popular sense of the word, and being under sentence of death, and the festival giving me a respite, I thought that it would be safer for me to satisfy the scruple, and, in obedience to the dream, to compose a few verses before I departed. And first I made a hymn in honour of the god of the festival, and then considering that a poet, if he is really to be a poet, should not only put together words, but should invent stories, and that I have no invention, I took some fables of Aesop, which I had ready at hand and which I knew—they were the first I came upon—and turned them into verse. Tell this to Evenus, Cebes, and bid him be of good cheer; say that I would have him come after me if he be a wise man, and not tarry; and that to-day I am likely to be going, for the Athenians say that I must. . . .

And now, O my judges, I desire to prove to you that the real philosopher has reason to be of good cheer when he is about to die, and that after death he may hope to obtain the greatest good in the other world. And how this may be, Simmias and Cebes, I will endeavour to explain. For I deem that the true votary of philosophy is likely to be misunderstood by other men; they do not perceive that he is always pursuing death and dying; and if this be so, and he has had the desire of death all his life long, why when his time comes should he repine at that which he had been always pursuing and desiring?

Simmias said laughingly: Though not in a laughing humour, you have made me laugh, Socrates; for I cannot help thinking that the many when they hear your words will say how truly you have described philosophers, and our people at home will likewise say that the life which philosophers desire is in reality death, and that they have found them out to be deserving of the death which they desire.

And they are right, Simmias, in thinking so, with the exception of the words "they have found them out"; for they have not found out either what is the nature of that death which the true philosopher deserves, or how he deserves or desires death. But enough of them:— let us discuss the matter among ourselves. Do we believe that there is such a thing as death?

To be sure, replied Simmias.

Is it not the separation of soul and body? And to be dead is the completion of this; when the soul exists in herself, and is released from the body and the body is released from the soul, what is this but death?

Just so, he replied.

There is another question, which will probably throw light on our present enquiry if you and I can agree about it:—Ought the philosopher to care about the pleasures—if they are to be called pleasures— of eating and drinking?

Certainly not, answered Simmias.

And what about the pleasures of love—should he care for them? By no means.

And will he think much of the other ways of indulging the body, for example, the acquisition of costly raiment, or sandals, or other adornments of the body? Instead of caring about them, does he not rather despise anything more than nature needs? What do you say?

I should say that the true philosopher would despise them.

Would you not say that he is entirely concerned with the soul and not with the body? He would like, as far as he can, to get away from the body and to turn to the soul.

Quite true.

In matters of this sort philosophers, above all other men, may be observed in every sort of way to dissever the soul from the communion of the body.

Very true.

Whereas, Simmias, the rest of the world are of opinion that to him who has no sense of pleasure and no part in bodily pleasure, life is not worth having; and that he who is indifferent about them is as good as dead.

That is also true.

What again shall we say of the actual acquirement of knowledge? —is the body, if invited to share in the enquiry, a hinderer or a helper? I mean to say, have sight and hearing any truth in them? Are they not, as the poets are always telling us, inaccurate witnesses? and yet, if even they are inaccurate and indistinct, what is to be said of the other senses?—for you will allow that they are the best of them?

Certainly, he replied.

Then when does the soul attain truth?—for in attempting to consider anything in company with the body she is obviously deceived.

True.

Then must not true existence be revealed to her in thought, if at all?

Yes.

And thought is best when the mind is gathered into herself and none of these things trouble her—neither sounds nor sights nor pain nor any pleasure,—when she takes leave of the body, and has as little as possible to do with it, when she has no bodily sense or desire, but is aspiring after true being?

Certainly.

And in this the philosopher dishonours the body; his soul runs away from his body and desires to be alone and by herself?

That is true.

Well, but there is another thing, Simmias: Is there or is there not an absolute justice?

Assuredly there is.

And an absolute beauty and absolute good?

Of course.

But did you ever behold any of them with your eyes?

Certainly not.

Or did you ever reach them with any other bodily sense?—and I speak not of these alone, but of absolute greatness, and health, and strength, and of the essence or true nature of everything. Has the reality of them ever been perceived by you through the bodily organs? or rather, is not the nearest approach to the knowledge of their several natures made by him who so orders his intellectual vision as to have the most exact conception of the essence of each thing which he considers?

Certainly.

And he attains to the purest knowledge of them who goes to each with the mind alone, not introducing or intruding in the act of thought sight or any other sense together with reason, but with the very light of the mind in her own clearness searches into the very truth of each; he who has got rid, as far as he can, of eyes and ears and, so to speak, of the whole body, these being in his opinion distracting elements which when they infect the soul hinder her from acquiring truth and knowledge—who, if not he, is likely to attain to the knowledge of true being?

What you say has a wonderful truth in it, Socrates, replied Simmias.

And when real philosophers consider all these things, will they not be led to make a reflection which they will express in words something like the following? "Have we not found," they will say, "a path of thought which seems to bring us and our argument to the conclusion, that while we are in the body, and while the soul is infected with the evils of the body, our desire will not be satisfied, and our desire is of the truth? For the body is a source of endless trouble to us by reason of the mere requirement of food; and is liable also to diseases which overtake and impede us in the search after true being: it fills us full of loves, and lusts, and fears, and fancies of all kinds, and endless foolery, and, in fact, as men say, takes away from us the power of thinking at all. Whence come wars, and fightings, and factions? whence but from the body and the lusts of the body? Wars are occasioned by the love of money, and money has to be acquired for the sake and service of the body; and by reason of all these impediments we have no time to give to philosophy; and, last and worst of all, even if we are at leisure and betake ourselves to some speculation, the body is always breaking in upon us, causing turmoil and confusion in our enquiries, and so amazing us that we are prevented from seeing the truth. It has been proved to us by experience that if we would have pure knowledge of anything we must be quit of the body—the soul in herself must behold things in themselves: and then we shall attain the

wisdom which we desire, and of which we say that we are lovers; not
while we live, but after death; for if while in company with the body,
the soul cannot have pure knowledge, one of two things follows—
either knowledge is not to be attained at all, or, if at all, after death.
For then, and not till then, the soul will be parted from the body and
exist in herself alone. In this present life, I reckon that we make
the nearest approach to knowledge when we have the least possible
intercourse or communion with the body, and are not surfeited with
the bodily nature, but keep ourselves pure until the hour when God
himself is pleased to release us. And thus having got rid of the foolishness of the body we shall be pure and hold converse with the pure, and
know of ourselves the clear light everywhere, which is no other than
the light of truth." For the impure are not permitted to approach the
pure. These are the sort of words, Simmias, which the true lovers of
knowledge cannot help saying to one another, and thinking. You
would agree; would you not?

Undoubtedly, Socrates.

But, O my friend, if this be true, there is great reason to hope
that, going whither I go, when I have come to the end of my journey,
I shall attain that which has been the pursuit of my life. And therefore I go on my way rejoicing, and not I only, but every other man
who believes that his mind has been made ready and that he is in a
manner purified.

[By demonstrating that all knowledge is but recollection, Socrates
proves to the satisfaction of Simmias and Cebes the existence of the
soul before birth. But they are unconvinced that the soul is therefore
immortal. Socrates then examines the doctrine of the transmigration
of souls and concludes that the souls of the good, freed in the end from
human ills, enjoy immortal life. But Simmias and Cebes are still
skeptical and, though reluctant to express their doubts at this particular
time, present to Socrates their rather forceful objections. He rallies
several new arguments, as much to convince himself as his friends.
He finally convinces them and ends his long discourse with a visionary
account of the regions of the earth and of the unseen world.]

Wherefore, Simmias, seeing all these things, what ought not we
to do that we may obtain virtue and wisdom in this life? Fair is the
prize, and the hope great!

A man of sense ought not to say, nor will I be very confident, that the description which I have given of the soul and her mansions is exactly true. But I do say that, inasmuch as the soul is shown to be immortal, he may venture to think, not improperly or unworthily, that something of the kind is true. The venture is a glorious one, and he ought to comfort himself with words like these, which is the reason why I lengthen out the tale. Wherefore, I say, let a man be of good cheer about his soul, who having cast away the pleasures and ornaments of the body as alien to him and working harm rather than good, has sought after the pleasures of knowledge; and has arrayed the soul, not in some foreign attire, but in her own proper jewels, temperance, and justice, and courage, and nobility, and truth—in these adorned she is ready to go on her journey to the world below, when her hour comes. You, Simmias and Cebes, and all other men, will depart at some time or other. Me already, as a tragic poet would say, the voice of fate calls. Soon I must drink the poison; and I think that I had better repair to the bath first, in order that the women may not have the trouble of washing my body after I am dead.

When he had done speaking, Crito said: And have you any commands for us, Socrates—anything to say about your children, or any other matter in which we can serve you?

Nothing particular, Crito, he replied: only, as I have always told you, take care of yourselves; that is a service which you may be ever rendering to me and mine and to all of us, whether you promise to do so or not. But if you have no thought for yourselves, and care not to walk according to the rule which I have prescribed for you, not now for the first time, however much you may profess or promise at the moment, it will be of no avail.

We will do our best, said Crito: And in what way shall we bury you?

In any way that you like; but you must get hold of me, and take care that I do not run away from you. Then he turned to us, and added with a smile:—I cannot make Crito believe that I am the same Socrates who have been talking and conducting the argument; he fancies that I am the other Socrates whom he will soon see, a dead body—and he asks, How shall he bury me? And though I have spoken many words in the endeavour to show that when I have drunk the poison I shall leave you and go to the joys of the blessed,—these words of mine, with which I was comforting you and myself, have had, as I perceive, no effect upon Crito. And therefore I want you to be surety for me to him now, as at the trial he was surety to the judges for me:

but let the promise be of another sort; for he was surety for me to the judges that I would remain, and you must be my surety to him that I shall not remain, but go away and depart; and then he will suffer less at my death, and not be grieved when he sees my body being burned or buried. I would not have him sorrow at my hard lot, or say at the burial, Thus we lay out Socrates, or, Thus we follow him to the grave or bury him; for false words are not only evil in themselves, but they inflict the soul with evil. Be of good cheer then, my dear Crito, and say that you are burying my body only, and do with that whatever is usual, and what you think best.

When he had spoken these words, he arose and went into a chamber to bathe; Crito followed him and told us to wait. So we remained behind, talking and thinking of the subject of discourse, and also of the greatness of our sorrow; he was like a father of whom we were being bereaved, and we were about to pass the rest of our lives as orphans. When he had taken the bath his children were brought to him (he had two young sons and an elder one); and the women of his family also came, and he talked to them and gave them a few directions in the presence of Crito; then he dismissed them and returned to us.

Now the hour of sunset was near, for a good deal of time had passed while he was within. When he came out, he sat down with us again after his bath, but not much was said. Soon the jailer, who was the servant of the Eleven, entered and stood by him, saying:—To you, Socrates, whom I know to be noblest and gentlest and best of all who ever came to this place, I will not impute the angry feeling of other men, who rage and swear at me, when, in obedience to the authorities, I bid them drink the poison—indeed, I am sure that you will not be angry with me; for others, as you are aware, and not I, are to blame. And so fare you well, and try to bear lightly what must needs be—you know my errand. Then bursting into tears he turned away and went out.

Socrates looked at him and said: I return your good wishes, and will do as you bid. Then turning to us, he said, How charming the man is: since I have been in prison he has always been coming to see me, and at times he would talk to me, and was as good to me as could be, and now see how generously he sorrows on my account. We must do as he says, Crito; and therefore let the cup be brought, if the poison is prepared: if not, let the attendant prepare some.

Yet, said Crito, the sun is still upon the hill-tops, and I know that

many a one has taken the draught late, and after the announcement
has been made to him, he has eaten and drunk, and enjoyed the
society of his beloved: do not hurry—there is time enough.

Socrates said: Yes, Crito, and they of whom you speak are right
in so acting, for they think that they will be gainers by the delay;
but I am right in not following their example, for I do not think
that I should gain anything by drinking the poison a little later; I
should only be ridiculous in my own eyes for sparing and saving a
life which is already forfeit. Please then to do as I say, and not to
refuse me.

Crito made a sign to the servant, who was standing by; and he
went out, and having been absent for some time, returned with the
jailer carrying the cup of poison. Socrates said: You, my good friend,
who are experienced in these matters, shall give me directions how I
am to proceed. The man answered: You have only to walk about
until your legs are heavy, and then to lie down, and the poison will
act. At the same time he handed the cup to Socrates, who in the
easiest and gentlest manner, without the least fear or change of colour
or feature, looking at the man with all his eyes, Echecrates, as his
manner was, took the cup and said: What do you say about making
a libation out of this cup to any god? May I, or not? The man
answered: We only prepare, Socrates, just so much as we deem
enough. I understand, he said: but I may and must ask the gods to
prosper my journey from this to the other world—even so—and so
be it according to my prayer. Then raising the cup to his lips, quite
readily and cheerfully he drank off the poison. And hitherto most
of us had been able to control our sorrow; but now when we saw
him drinking, and saw too that he had finished the draught, we could
no longer forbear, and in spite of myself my own tears were flowing
fast; so that I covered my face and wept, not for him, but at the
thought of my own calamity in having to part from such a friend.
Nor was I the first; for Crito, when he found himself unable to restrain his tears, had got up, and I followed; and at that moment,
Apollodorus, who had been weeping all the time, broke out in a loud
and passionate cry which made cowards of us all. Socrates alone retained his calmness: What is this strange outcry? he said. I sent away
the women mainly in order that they might not misbehave in this
way, for I have been told that a man should die in peace. Be quiet
then, and have patience. When we heard his words we were ashamed,
and refrained our tears; and he walked about until, as he said, his

legs began to fail, and then he lay on his back, according to directions, and the man who gave him the poison now and then looked at his feet and legs; and after a while he pressed his foot hard, and asked him if he could feel; and he said, No; and then his leg, and so upwards and upwards, and showed us that he was cold and stiff. And he felt them himself, and said: When the poison reaches the heart, that will be the end. He was beginning to grow cold about the groin, when he uncovered his face, for he had covered himself up, and said—they were his last words—he said: Crito, I owe a cock to Asclepius;[5] will you remember to pay the debt? The debt shall be paid, said Crito; is there anything else? There was no answer to this question; but in a minute or two a movement was heard, and the attendants uncovered him; his eyes were set, and Crito closed his eyes and mouth.

Such was the end, Echecrates, of our friend; concerning whom I may truly say, that of all men of his time whom I have known, he was the wisest and justest and best.

5. A cock was the prescribed sacrifice to Asclepius, god of medicine, for recovery from illness.

VIRGIL

The Aeneid

PUBLIUS VERGILIUS MARO (70-19 B.C.) grew up where he was born, on the farm of his well-to-do father, near Mantua, Italy, about two hundred and fifty miles north of Rome. For the seven or eight years before he was twenty, he was in one or another of the Italian cities in pursuit of his education, which was mainly an immersion in the lore and learning of ancient Greece. In Rome he studied under the man who was at the same time teaching the boy, seven years Virgil's junior, who was later to become Emperor. When he returned home, where he remained during most of his twenties, he was engaged chiefly in farming, and in studying and writing as opportunity offered. When he was about thirty, his family farm was confiscated by the returning veterans of the Civil Wars, to whom Octavian (the later Augustus) gave, as a reward for their services, a number of districts that had been on the side of his defeated enemy, Brutus. It is possible that Virgil was twice dispossessed in this way, but at any rate he finally received relief from Octavian himself.

The *First Eclogue* reflects Virgil's gratitude. The *Eclogues,* or *Bucolics,* written in the years about 40 B.C., are ten poems totalling about a thousand lines. They followed and revitalized the pastoral tradition as it had been employed over two hundred years earlier by the Greek Theocritus. This means that they treat of rural life in a romantic and idealized fashion, suppressing all that is disagreeable and embellishing all that is pleasant. The theme and the mood of the *Bucolics* brought Virgil to immediate fame with his contemporaries who felt that their world was overurbanized and in need of a renewed interest in country living. And the *Fourth Eclogue,* particularly, kept him famous with his successors who became Christian. In this poem, written a year after the Battle of Philippi, Virgil hopes that the dissidence and turmoil of the Civil Wars is over, and that a new, glorious, and stable order is to be established under Octavian and his expected child. It was not only reasonable, but almost inevitable, that the early Christians should have taken this poem as a prophecy of the birth of Christ, particularly since its language and imagery owe a considerable debt to the Jewish Messianic ideas which achieved some currency in Rome during Virgil's lifetime.

A fellow-countryman of Virgil's, Cornelius Gallus, high in the favor of Octavian, now brought the poet to the attention of many exalted personages in Rome. Among these was Maecenas, a rich and worthy man, a sort of "home-secretary" for Octavian, who took it as his privilege to foster and promote prodigally the best writers of his time and country. Virgil's next work, the *Georgics,* which he completed after seven years of meticulous labor, when he was forty, is a 2000-line poem, in four books, so scrupulously wrought that it is often esteemed the greatest of his performances. Dedicated to Maecenas, it is a charming, patriotic, nobly earnest, and detailed "textbook" on Italian farming. It was above all, consciously, propaganda for the back-to-the-soil, faithful-work-and-simple-living ideal that Virgil, along with the government of his time, believed it mandatory to assert if the Roman hegemony, or any hegemony, were to survive.

At last an exalted personage himself, a friend of the mighty, sponsor of the poet Horace, the wise, simple, and serious Virgil now bent himself to an assignment in propaganda not theretofore achieved in prose or rhyme. What resulted was the long epic poem, *The Aeneid.* It is said that the task was set directly by the emperor-god, Augustus. It is certain that, while away in Spain some three years later, he was asking to see a draft of the poem, and that, a little later still, back in Rome, he listened with his sister, Octavia, while the author read aloud to them a large part of it. The propaganda was to be nationalistic, in that it was to justify and make clear, for that time and all time to come, Rome's destiny to rule the world. But it was to be more than that only, whether or not so intended, because of the mind and the character of its maker, who was too exalted by then not to over-reach (in his implications, at least) any impulse less than cosmic.

The Aeneid was written in twelve books of approximately equal length, as nearly in the meter and the mood of Homer as the nature of the case made possible. That meter, habitual with Virgil, was exquisitely artful with him rather than ruggedly strong as with Homer; and that mood, more disciplined and purposeful and piteous than with Homer, had become at bottom one as determined to make the gods glorify man as to make man glorify the gods. The subject, the divinely ordained founding of Rome by fugitives from Troy, had been current for two centuries before Virgil used it, but he gave the story its definitive form. This fact is typical, for Virgil's mind was not original in the usual sense of the word. He took his legend from popular tradition; he modeled the first half of his poem on the *Odyssey* and the last half on the *Iliad;* he borrowed extensive passages and episodes from Homer, from the later Greeks, and from the earlier Latin writers—but the result is distinctive and unique. Particularly notable is his feeling for the tragedy of life, for "the tears of things"; though he sincerely glorifies the foundation of Rome, he has a touching pity for Dido, for Pallas, for Turnus, for all the innocent human beings who must be sacrificed on the altars of the future empire. *The Aeneid* remains for future ages as the literary monument of one of the superlative episodes of human history, the Roman Empire of Virgil's day.

Virgil spent his later years near Naples working on *The Aeneid.* When he estimated that three years more were needed for the final revision, he set sail for Greece to visit some of the scenes of the poem. On the return trip with Augustus, he fell ill, and died soon after landing in Italy. *The Aeneid* needed so much more work to bring it up to Virgil's standard that, on his deathbed, he ordered the manuscript destroyed; but Augustus, who knew the poem well, countermanded the order.

Virgil's subsequent reputation is one of the strangest chapters in literary history. He immediately became a literary classic on the strength of his own merits, but he soon became much more. By the second century he already had magic powers, and the future could be foretold by the *sortes Virgilianae*—by opening his works at random and reading whatever passage appeared. By virtue of the *Fourth Eclogue,* Virgil escaped the sweeping anathemas of early Christian zealots against pagan poetry. His magic powers increased, and spells and incantations were extracted from his works. Entire poems were put together out of quotations from Virgil, and these religious *centos* became so important that a papal proclamation was necessary to point out to the credulous that such works had no religious authority. Because of the association of purity with *virgo* ("virgin") and of magic with *virga* ("wand"), the *e* of the poet's name was changed to *i*. And *The Aeneid* made Trojan origins so desirable that barbarians to the north and west *yearned* into being for themselves a kindred myth, so that atavistically they too could be stimulated by the thought of Ilium's once-lofty towers.

The superstitions have passed, but the poems remain as the inspiration of great men as diverse as St. Augustine, Dante, Chaucer, and Dryden. It is nearly twenty centuries since Virgil first rose to fame, and he is one of the few ancient writers who suffered no eclipse in the Dark Ages—whose shaping of human thought extends unbroken from his own time to us, and beyond.

THE ÆNEID

I sing of arms and the man who came of old, a fated wanderer, from the coasts of Troy to Italy and the shore of Lavinium;[1] hard driven on land and on the deep by the violence of heaven, by reason of cruel Juno's[2] unforgetful anger, and hard bestead in war also, ere he might found a city and carry his gods into Latium; from whom is the Latin race, the lords of Alba,[3] and high-embattled Rome.

Muse, tell me why, for what attaint of her deity, or in what vexation, did the queen of heaven urge on a man excellent in goodness to circle through all those afflictions, to face all those toils? Is anger so fierce in celestial spirits?

There was a city of ancient days that Tyrian settlers dwelt in, Carthage, over against Italy and the Tiber mouths afar; plenteous of

1. Lavinium is a city which Aeneas is to name for his Latin wife, Lavinia. It is in Latium, the district now containing Rome.
2. Juno is equivalent to Hera, and is the daughter of Saturn.
3. Alba Longa, the early settlement from which Rome originated.

wealth, and most grim in the arts of war; wherein, they say, alone beyond all other lands had Juno her seat. Here was her armour, here her chariot; even now, if fate permit, the goddess strives to nurture it for dominion over the nations. Nevertheless she had heard that a race was issuing of the blood of Troy, which sometime should overthrow her Tyrian fortress; from it should come a people, lord of lands and tyrannous in war, the destroyer of Libya: thus the Fates unrolled their volume. Fearful of that, the daughter of Saturn, the old war in her remembrance that she fought at Troy for her beloved Argos long ago, —nor had the springs of her anger nor that bitter pain yet gone out of mind: deep stored in her soul lies the judgment of Paris,[4] the insult of her slighted beauty, the hated race and the dignities of ravished Ganymede;[5] fired by these also, she drove all over ocean the Trojan remnant left of the Greek host and merciless Achilles, and held them afar from Latium; and many a year were they wandering driven of fate around all the seas. Such work was it to found the Roman people.

Hardly out of sight of the land of Sicily did they set their sails joyously to sea, and upturned the salt foam with brazen prow, when Juno, the undying wound still deep in her heart, thus broke out alone:

'Am I then to abandon my baffled purpose, powerless to keep the Teucrian[6] king from Italy? and because fate forbids me? Could Pallas lay the Argive fleet in ashes, and sink the Argives in the sea, for the guilt and madness of Oilean Ajax[7] alone? Her hand darted Jove's flying fire from the clouds, scattered their ships, upturned the seas in tempest; him, his pierced breast yet breathing forth the flame, she caught in a whirlwind and impaled on a spike of rock. But I, who move queen among immortals, I sister and wife of Jove, wage warfare all these years with a single people; and is there any who still adores Juno's divinity, or will lay sacrifice with prayer on her altars?'

Such thoughts inly revolving in her fiery heart, the goddess reaches

---

4. Paris had passed over Juno and Minerva to award the prize of beauty to Venus, who in return had given him Menelaos' wife, Helen. Paris carried her off to Troy, and the Greek expedition to recover her developed into the Trojan War. The position of Venus as protector of the Trojans and Juno as their enemy comes from these events.

5. Ganymede, a Trojan, had been snatched by an eagle to heaven to become cup-bearer to the gods, and had replaced Juno's daughter, Hebe, in this office.

6. Teucer was the first king of Troy; hence *Teucrian* is frequently used for *Trojan*.

7. Oilean Ajax violated the sanctuary of Athene's temple during the sack of Troy. In punishment for this crime, she wrecked his fleet on the return voyage and killed him with a thunderbolt.

Aeolia, the home of storm-clouds, the land teeming with furious southern gales. Here in a dreary cavern Aeolus keeps under royal dominion and yokes in dungeon fetters the struggling winds and re-sounding storms. They with mighty moan rage indignant round their mountain barriers. In his lofty citadel Aeolus sits sceptred, assuages their temper and soothes their rage; else would they carry with them seas and lands, and the depth of heaven, and sweep them through space in their flying course. But, fearful of this, the Lord omnipotent has hidden them in caverned gloom, and laid mountains high over them, and appointed them a ruler, who under a fixed covenant should know to strain and slacken the reins at command. To him now Juno spoke thus in suppliant accents:

'Aeolus—for to thee has the father of gods and king of men given to lull and to lift the wind-blown waves—the race I hate sails the Tyrrhene sea, carrying Ilium and her conquered household-gods[8] into Italy. Rouse thy winds to fury, and overwhelm and sink their hulls, or drive them asunder and strew ocean with their corpses. Mine are twice seven nymphs of passing loveliness, and Deïopea is most ex-cellent in beauty of them all; her will I unite to thee in wedlock to be thine for ever; that for this thy service she may fulfil all her years at thy side, and make thee father of a beautiful race.'

Aeolus thus returned: 'Thine, O queen, the task to search out what thou wilt; for me it is right to do thy bidding. From thee I hold all this my realm, from thee my sceptre and Jove's grace; thou dost grant me to take my seat at the feasts of the gods, and makest me sovereign over clouds and storms.'

Even with these words, turning his spear, he struck the side of the hollow hill, and the winds, as in banded array, pour where passage is given them, and cover earth with eddying blasts. East wind and south wind together, and the gusty south-wester, falling prone on the sea, stir it up from its lowest chambers, and roll vast billows to the shore. Behind rises shouting of men and creaking of cordage. In a moment clouds blot sky and daylight from the Teucrians' eyes; black night broods over the deep. The heavens crash with thunder, and the air quivers with incessant flashes; all menaces them with instant death. Straightway Aeneas' frame grows unnerved and chill, and stretching either hand to heaven, he cries thus aloud: 'Ah, thrice and four times

8. The household-gods (Penates) were the guardian spirits of the Roman home. There were also Penates of the state, and Aeneas is bringing those of Troy to preside over the new empire.

happy they who found their doom in high-embattled Troy before their fathers' faces! Ah, son of Tydeus,[9] bravest of the Grecian race, that I could not have fallen on the Ilian plains, and gasped out this my life beneath thine hand! where under the spear of Aeacides[10] lies fierce Hector, lies mighty Sarpedon; where Simoïs[11] so often caught and whirled beneath his wave shields and helmets and brave bodies of men.'

As the cry leaves his lips, a gust of the shrill north strikes full on the sail and raises the waves up to heaven. The oars are snapped; the prow swings away and gives her side to the waves; down in a heap comes a broken mountain of water. These hang on the wave's ridge; to these the yawning billow shows ground amid the surge, where the tide churns with sand. Three ships the south wind catches and hurls on hidden rocks, rocks amid the waves which Italians call the Altars, a vast reef banking the sea. Three the east forces from the deep into shallows and quicksands, piteous to see, dashes on shoals and girdles with a sandbank. One, wherein loyal Orontes and his Lycians rode, before his very eyes a huge sea descending strikes astern. The helmsman is dashed away and rolled forward headlong; her as she lies the billow sends spinning thrice round with it, and engulfs in the swift whirl. Scattered swimmers appear in the dreary eddy, armour of men, timbers and Trojan treasure amid the water. Ere now the stout ship of Ilioneus, ere now of brave Achates, and she wherein Abas rode, and she wherein aged Aletes, have yielded to the storm; the framework of their sides is started, and they all let in the deadly stream through gaping leaks.

Meanwhile Neptune discerned with astonishment the loud roaring of the vexed sea, the tempest let loose from prison, and the still water boiling up from its depths, and looking forth over the deep, raised his head serene above the waves. He sees Aeneas' fleet scattered all over ocean, the Trojans overwhelmed by the waves and the tempest of heaven. Juno's guile and wrath lay clear to her brother's eye; East wind and West he calls before him, and thereon speaks thus:

'Stand you then so sure in your confidence of birth? Dare you without my warrant, O winds, confound sky and earth, and raise so huge coil? you whom I— But better to still the vexed waves; for a second transgression you shall pay me another penalty. Speed your flight, and say this to your king: not to him but to me was allotted the empire of ocean and the stern trident. His fastness is on the monstrous

9. *son of Tydeus,* Diomedes. Venus had saved Aeneas from him in the *Iliad.*
10. *Aeacides,* Achilles.
11. *Simoïs,* a river flowing by Troy.

rocks where thou and thine, East wind, dwell: there let Aeolus glory in his court and reign over the barred prison of his winds.'

Thus he speaks, and quicker than the word he soothes the swollen seas, chases away the gathered clouds, and restores the sunlight. Cymothoë and Triton[12] together push the ships strongly off the sharp reef; himself he eases them with his trident, channels the vast quicksands, and assuages the sea, gliding on light wheels along the watery floor. Even as when oft in a throng of people strife has risen, and the base multitude rage in their minds, and now brands and stones are flying; madness lends arms; then if perchance they catch sight of one reverend for goodness and worth, they are silent and stand by with attentive ear; he with speech sways their temper and soothes their breasts; even so has fallen all the thunder of ocean, when riding with forward gaze beneath a cloudless sky the lord of the sea wheels his coursers and lets his gliding chariot fly with loosened rein.

The outworn Aeneadae hasten to run for the nearest shore, and steer for the coast of Libya. There a place lies deep withdrawn; an island forms a harbour, thrusting forth its sides, whereon all the waves break from the open sea and part into the hollows of the bay. On this side and that enormous cliffs rise threatening heaven, and twin crags beneath whose crest the sheltered water lies wide and calm; above is a background of waving forest, and a woodland overhangs dark with rustling shade. Beneath the seaward brow is a rock-hung cavern, within it fresh springs and seats in the living stone, a haunt of nymphs; here tired ships need no fetters to hold nor anchor to fasten them with crooked fang. Hither with seven sail gathered of all his company Aeneas glides in; and disembarking on the land so sorely desired the Trojans gain the chosen beach, and fling their limbs dripping with brine upon the shore. Forthwith Achates has struck a spark from the flint and caught the fire on leaves, and laying dry fuel round kindled the touchwood into flame. Then, in their weary case, they fetch out sea-soaked corn and weapons of corn-dressing, and set to parch over the fire and bruise with stones the grain that they have rescued.

Meanwhile Aeneas scales the cliff, and scans the whole view wide over ocean, if he may see aught of Antheus and his storm-tossed Phrygian galleys, aught of Capys or of the lofty hulls that bear the arms of Caïcus. Ship in sight is none; three stags he espies straying on the shore; behind whole herds follow, and graze in long train across the valleys. Stopping short, he snatched up a bow and swift arrows, the

12. Cymothoë is a sea-nymph, and Triton a sea-god.

arms that trusty Achates was carrying; and first the leaders, their
stately heads high with branching antlers, then the common herd he
lays low, as he drives them with his shafts in a broken crowd through
the leafy woods. Nor stays he till seven great victims are stretched on
the sod, and the number of his ships is equalled. Thence he seeks the
harbour and parts them among all his company; next the wine-casks
that good Acestes had loaded on the Trinacrian beach, the hero's gift
at their departure, he shares, and assuages their sorrowing hearts with
speech:

'O comrades, for not ere now are we ignorant of ill, O tried by
heavier fortunes, to these also God will appoint an end. The fury of
Scylla and the roaring recesses of her crags you have come nigh, and
known the rocks of the Cyclops. Recall your courage, put sorrow and
fear away. This too sometime we shall haply remember with delight.
Through chequered fortunes, through many perilous ways, we steer for
Latium, where destiny points us a quiet home. There the realm of
Troy may rise again unforbidden. Keep heart, and endure till prosperous fortune come.'

Such words he utters, and sick with deep distress he feigns hope
on his face, and keeps his anguish hidden deep in his breast. The others
set to the spoil that is to be their banquet, sever chine from ribs and
lay bare the flesh; some cut it into pieces and pierce it still quivering
with spits; others plant caldrons on the beach and feed them with
flame. Then they repair their strength with food, and lying along the
grass take their fill of old wine and fat venison. After hunger is driven
away by feasting, and the board cleared, they talk with lingering regret
of their lost companions, swaying between hope and fear, whether
they may believe them yet alive, or now meeting the last enemy and
deaf to mortal call.

And now they ceased; when Jupiter looked through the height of
air on the sail-winged sea and outspread lands, the shores and broad
countries, and looking stood on the cope of heaven, and cast down his
eyes on the realm of Libya. To him thus troubled at heart Venus, her
bright eyes brimming with tears, sorrowfully speaks:

'O thou who dost sway mortal and immortal things in eternal
lordship with the terror of thy thunderbolt, how can mv Aeneas have
transgressed so grievously against thee? how his Trojans? on whom,
after so many deaths borne, all the world is barred for Italy's sake.
From them sometime in the rolling years the Romans were to arise
indeed; from them were to be rulers who, renewing the blood of

Teucer, should hold sea and all lands in dominion. This thou didst promise: why, O father, is thy decree reversed? This was my solace for the wretched ruin of sunken Troy, doom balanced against doom. Now so many woes are spent, and the same fortune still pursues them; Lord and King, what limit dost thou set to their distresses? We, thy children, we whom thou beckonest to the heights of heaven, our fleet miserably cast away for a single enemy's anger, are betrayed and severed far from the Italian coasts. Is this the reward of goodness? is it thus thou dost restore our throne?'

Smiling on her with that look which clears sky and storms, the parent of men and gods lightly kissed his daughter's lips; then answered thus:

'Spare thy fear, Cytherean;[13] thy people's destiny abides unshaken. Thine eyes shall see the city Lavinium, their promised fortress; thou shalt exalt to the starry heaven thy noble Aeneas; nor is my decree reversed. He whom thou lovest (for I will speak, since this care keeps torturing thee, and will unroll further the secret records of fate) shall wage a great war in Italy, and crush warrior nations; he shall appoint his people a law and a city; till the third summer see him reigning in Latium, and three winters' camps are overpast among the conquered Rutulians. But the boy Ascanius,[14] whose surname is now Iülus—Ilus he was while the Ilian state stood sovereign—thirty great circles of rolling months shall he fulfil in government; he shall carry the kingdom from its seat in Lavinium, and make a strong fortress of Alba the Long. Here the full space of thrice an hundred years shall the kingdom endure under the race of Hector's kin, till the royal priestess Ilia[15] from Mars' embrace shall give birth to a twin progeny. Thence shall Romulus, gay in the tawny hide of the she-wolf that nursed him, take up their line, and name them Romans after his own name. To these I ordain neither period nor boundary of empire: I have given them dominion without end. Nay, harsh Juno, who in her fear now troubles earth and sea and sky, shall change to better counsels, and with me shall cherish the lords of the world, the gowned race of Rome. Thus is it willed. A day will come in the lapse of cycles, when the house of Assaracus[16] shall lay Phthia and famed Mycenae in bondage,

13. *Cytherean*, Venus, who was born from the sea near the island of Cythera.
14. Ascanius, or Iülus, is Aeneas' son.
15. Romulus and Remus, sons of the vestal virgin Ilia by Mars, were suckled by a she-wolf.
16. *Assaracus*, great-grandfather of Aeneas. His descendants are to even the score by conquering Greece.

and reign over conquered Argos. From the fair line of Troy a Caesar shall arise, who shall limit his empire with ocean, his glory with the firmament, Julius,[17] inheritor of great Iülus' name. Him one day, thy care done, thou shalt welcome to heaven loaded with Eastern spoils; to him too shall vows be addressed. Then shall war cease, and the iron ages soften. The dreadful steel-clenched gates of War shall be shut fast;[18] inhuman Fury, his hands bound behind him with an hundred rivets of brass, shall sit within on murderous weapons, shrieking with ghastly blood-stained lips.'

So speaking, he sends Maia's son[19] down from above, that the lands and towers of Carthage, the new town, may receive the Trojans with open welcome; lest Dido, ignorant of doom, might debar them her land. Flying through the depth of air on winged oarage, the fleet messenger alights on the Libyan coasts. At once he does his bidding; at once, for a god willed it, the Phoenicians allay their haughty temper; the queen above all takes to herself grace and compassion towards the Teucrians.

But good Aeneas, nightlong revolving many and many a thing, issues forth, so soon as bountiful light is given, to explore the strange country; to what coasts the wind has borne him, who are their habitants, men or wild beasts, for all he sees is wilderness—this he resolves to search, and bring back the certainty to his comrades. The fleet he hides close in embosoming groves beneath a caverned rock, amid rustling shadow of the woodland; himself, Achates alone following, he strides forward, clenching in his hand two broad-headed spears. And amid the forest his mother crossed his way, wearing the face and raiment of a maiden, the arms of a maiden of Sparta. For in huntress fashion had she slung the ready bow from her shoulder, and left her blown tresses free, bared her knee, and knotted together her garments' flowing folds. 'Ho, gallants,' she begins, 'shew me if haply you have seen a sister of mine straying here girt with quiver and dappled lynx-pelt, or pressing with shouts on the track of a foaming boar.'

Thus Venus, and Venus' son answering thus began:

'Sound nor sight have I had of sister of thine, O maiden, how

17. This refers, not to Julius Caesar, but to Augustus. *Augustus* was actually a title, and his name was C. Julius Caesar Octavianus. He was worshipped even during his lifetime.

18. One gate of the Temple of Janus was closed whenever Rome was at peace. At the time of Virgil's death it had been closed only four times.

19. *Maia's son*, Mercury, equivalent to Hermes.

may I name thee? for thy face is not mortal, nor thy voice of human tone; O goddess assuredly! sister of Phoebus perchance, or one of the nymphs' blood? Be thou gracious, whoso thou art, and lighten our distress; deign to instruct us beneath what skies, on what coast of the world, we are thrown. Driven hither by wind and desolate waves, we wander in a strange land among unknown men. Many a sacrifice shall fall by our hand before thine altars.'

Then Venus: 'Nay, to no such offerings do I aspire. Tyrian maidens are wont ever to wear the quiver, to tie the purple buskin high above their ankle. Punic is the realm thou seest, Tyrian the people, and the city of Agenor's kin; but their borders are Libyan, a race untameable in war. Dido sways the sceptre, who flying her brother set sail from the Tyrian town. Long is the tale of crime, long and intricate; but I will follow its argument in brief. Her husband was Sychaeus, wealthiest in lands of the Phoenicians, and loved of her with all-fated passion; to whom with virgin rites her father had given her maidenhood in wedlock. But the kingdom of Tyre was in her brother Pygmalion's hands, a monster of guilt unparalleled. Between these madness came; the unnatural brother, blind with lust of gold, and reckless of his sister's love, lays Sychaeus low before the altars with stealthy unsuspected weapon; and for long he hid the deed, and by many a crafty pretence cheated her love-sickness with hollow hope. But in slumber came the very ghost of her unburied husband, lifting up a face pale in wonderful wise; he exposed the cruel altars and his breast stabbed through with steel, and unwove all the blind web of household guilt. Then he counsels hasty flight and abandonment of her country, and to aid her passage discloses treasures long hidden underground, an untold mass of silver and gold. Stirred thereby, Dido gathered a company for flight. All assemble in whom hatred of the tyrant was relentless or terror keen; they seize on ships that chanced to lie ready, and load them with the gold. Pygmalion's hoarded wealth is borne overseas; a woman guides the enterprise. They came at last to the land where thou wilt descry a city now great, New Carthage, and her rising citadel, and bought ground, as much as a bull's hide would encircle. But who, I pray, are you, or from what coasts come, or whither hold you your way?'

At her question he, sighing and drawing speech deep from his breast, thus replied:

'Ah goddess, should I go on retracing from the fountain head, were time free to hear the history of our woes, sooner will the evening star lay day asleep in the closed gates of heaven. Us, as from ancient Troy (if the name of Troy has haply passed through your ears) we sailed over distant seas, the tempest at his own wild will has driven on the Libyan coast. I am Aeneas the good, who carry in my fleet the household gods I rescued from the enemy; my fame is known high in heaven. I seek Italy my country, and my kin of Jove's supreme blood. With twenty sail did I climb the Phrygian sea; oracular tokens led me on; my goddess mother pointed the way; scarce seven survive the shattering of wave and wind. Myself unknown, destitute, driven from Europe and Asia, I wander over the Libyan wilderness.'

But staying longer complaint, Venus thus broke in on his half-told sorrows:

'Whoso thou art, not hated I think of the immortals dost thou draw the breath of life, who hast reached the Tyrian city. Only go on, and betake thee hence to the courts of the queen. For I declare to thee thy comrades are restored, thy fleet driven back into safety by the shifted northern gales. . . . Only go on, and point thy steps where the pathway leads thee.'

Speaking she turned away, and her neck shone roseate, the immortal tresses on her head breathed the fragrance of deity; her raiment fell flowing down to her feet, and a very goddess was manifest in her tread. He knew her for his mother, and with this cry pursued her flight: 'Thou also merciless! why mockest thou thy son so often in feigned likeness? Why is it forbidden to clasp hand in hand, to hear and to reply in true speech?' Thus reproaching her he bends his steps towards the city.

[Venus makes Aeneas and Achates invisible with a cloud of mist. They enter Carthage and see a temple on which are carved scenes from the Trojan War. Dido appears, and men from Aeneas' lost ships come to request her protection and permission to land. (Only one ship has been destroyed in the storm.) Dido welcomes the Trojans and, as the cloud dissolves, Aeneas reveals himself to them. He sends for Ascanius, but Venus substitutes Cupid in Ascanius' form, in order to inflame Dido with love for Aeneas—thus protecting him from any possible treachery. At a banquet given for the Trojan leaders that night, Dido asks Aeneas to describe the fall of Troy and the intervening seven years.]

BOOK II

All were hushed, and sate with steadfast countenance; thereon, from his cushioned high seat, lord Aeneas thus began:

'Dreadful, O Queen, is the woe thou bidst me recall, how the Grecians pitiably overthrew the wealth and lordship of Troy; and I myself saw these things in all their horror, and I bore great part in them. What Myrmidon or Dolopian,[1] or soldier of stern Ulysses,[2] could in such a tale restrain his tears! and now night falls dewy from the steep of heaven, and the setting stars counsel to slumber. Yet if thy desire be such to know our calamities, and briefly to hear Troy's last agony, though my spirit shudders at the remembrance and recoils in pain, I will essay.

'Broken in war, beaten back by fate, and so many years now slid away, the Grecian captains build by Pallas' divine craft a horse of mountain bulk, and frame its ribs with sawn fir; they feign it vowed for their return, and this rumour goes about. Within the blind sides they stealthily imprison chosen men picked out one by one, and fill the vast cavern of its womb full with armed soldiery.

'There lies in sight an island well known in fame, Tenedos, rich of store while the realm of Priam endured, now but a bay and road-stead treacherous to ships. Hither they launch forth, and hide on the solitary shore: we fancied they were gone, and had run down the wind for Mycenae. So all the Teucrian land put her long grief away. The gates are flung open; men go rejoicingly to see the Doric camp, the deserted stations and abandoned shore. Here the Dolopian troops were tented, here cruel Achilles; here their squadrons lay; here they were wont to meet in battle-line. Some gaze astonished at the deadly gift of Minerva[3] the Virgin, and wonder at the horse's bulk; and Thymoetes begins to advise that it be drawn within our walls and set in the citadel, whether in guile,[4] or that the doom of Troy was even now setting thus. But Capys, and they whose mind was of better counsel, bid us either hurl sheer into the sea the guileful and sinister gift of Greece, and heap flames beneath to consume it, or pierce and explore the hollow hiding-

1. The Myrmidons and Dolopians were the soldiers of Achilles.
2. *Ulysses*, Odysseus.
3. *Minerva*, equivalent to Athene.
4. There had been a prophecy that a child born on a certain day would be the destruction of Troy. Both Paris and a child of Thymoetes were born on that day, and Priam had the latter and his mother put to death. Thus Thymoetes had a grudge against Priam which might well have led to his betraying Troy.

place of its womb. The wavering crowd is torn apart in eager dispute.

'At that, foremost of all and with a great throng about him, Laoc-oön afire runs down from the fortress height, and cries from far: "Ah, wretched citizens, what height of madness is this? Believe you the foe is gone? or think you any Grecian gift is free of treachery? is it thus we know Ulysses? Either Achaeans are hid in this cage of wood, or the engine is fashioned against our walls to overlook the houses and descend upon the city; or some delusion lurks in it: trust not the horse, O Trojans. Be it what it may, I fear the Grecians even when they offer gifts." Thus speaking, he hurled his huge spear with mighty strength at the creature's side and the curved framework of the belly: the spear stood quivering, and the jarred cavern of the womb sounded hollow and uttered a groan. And had divine ordinance been thus and our soul not infatuate he had moved us to lay violent steel on the Argolic hiding place; and Troy would now stand, and you, tall towers of Priam, yet abide.

'Lo, Dardanian[5] shepherds meanwhile dragged clamorously before the King a man with hands tied behind his back, who to compass this very thing, to lay Troy open to the Achaeans, had gone to meet their ignorant approach, confident of his courage, and doubly prepared to spin his snares or to meet assured death. From all sides, in eagerness to see, the people of Troy run streaming in, and vie in jeers at their prisoner. Know now the treachery of the Grecians, and from a single crime learn them all. For as he stood amid our gaze confounded, dis-armed, and cast his eyes around the Phrygian columns, "Alas!" he cried, "what land now, what seas may receive me? or what is the last doom that yet awaits a wretch like me? who have neither any place among the Grecians, and likewise the Dardanians clamour in wrath for the forfeit of my blood." At that lament our spirit was changed, and all assault stayed: we encourage him to speak, and tell of what blood he is sprung, or what assurance he brings his captors.

' "In all things assuredly," says he, "O King, befall what may, I will confess to thee the truth; nor will I deny myself of Argolic birth —this first—nor, if Fortune has made Sinon unhappy, shall her malice mould him to a cheat and a liar. If the tale of the name of Palamedes, son of Belus, has haply reached thine ears, and of his glorious rumour and renown; whom under false evidence the Pelasgians, because he forbade the war, sent innocent to death by wicked witness; now they bewail him when his light is quenched;—in his company, being near

5. *Dardanian*, Trojan.

of blood, my father, poor as he was, sent me hither to arms from mine earliest years. While he stood unshaken in royalty and potent in the councils of the kings, we too wore a name and honour. When by subtle Ulysses' malice (no unknown tale do I tell) he left the upper regions,[6] my shattered life crept on in darkness and grief, inly indignant at the fate of my innocent friend. Nor in my madness was I silent: and, should any chance offer, did I ever return a conqueror to my native Argos, I vowed myself his avenger, and with my words I stirred bitter hatred. From this came the first taint of ill; from this did Ulysses ever threaten me with fresh charges, from this flung dark sayings among the crowd and sought confederate arms. Nay, nor did he rest, till by Calchas'[7] service—but yet why do I vainly unroll the unavailing tale, or why hold you in delay? If all Achaeans are ranked together in your mind, and it is enough that I bear the name, take your vengeance none too soon; this the Ithacan would desire, and the sons of Atreus buy at a great ransom."

'Then indeed we press on to ask and inquire the cause, witless of wickedness so great and Pelasgian craft. Tremblingly the false-hearted one pursues his speech:

'"Often would the Grecians have taken to flight, leaving Troy behind, and disbanded in weariness of the long war; and would God they had! as often the fierce sea-tempest barred their way, and the south wind frightened them from going. Most of all when this horse already stood framed with beams of maple, stormclouds roared over all the sky. In perplexity we send Eurypylus to inquire of Phoebus' oracle; and he brings back from the sanctuary these words of terror: *With blood of a slain maiden, O Grecians, you appeased the winds when first you came to the Ilian coasts;*[8] *with blood must you seek your return, and an Argive life be the accepted sacrifice.* When that utterance reached the ears of the crowd, their hearts stood still, and a cold shudder ran through their inmost sense: for whom is doom purposed? whom does Apollo demand? At this the Ithacan with loud clamour drags Calchas the soothsayer forth amidst them, and demands of him what is this the

6. When Ulysses feigned madness to avoid joining the Trojan expedition, it was Palamedes who discovered the trick. In revenge, Ulysses "framed" him: he had a forged letter (purporting to be from Priam) and a large quantity of gold hidden in Palamedes' tent; then he accused Palamedes of treason, searched his tent, found the planted evidence, and had him stoned to death by the Greeks.

7. Calchas was the chief soothsayer of the Greeks.

8. Agamemnon's daughter, Iphigenia, had been sacrificed at Aulis in order to obtain favorable winds for the voyage to Troy.

gods signify. And now many and one foretold me the villain's craft and cruelty, and silently saw what was to come. Twice five days he is speechless in his tent, and will not have any one denounced by his lips, or given up to death. Scarcely at last, at the loud urgence of the Ithacan, he breaks into speech as was planned, and appoints me for the altar. All consented; and each one's particular fear was turned, ah me! to my single destruction. And now the dreadful day was at hand; the rites were being ordered for me, the salted corn, and the chaplets to wreathe my temples. I broke away, I confess it, from death; I burst my bonds, and lurked all night darkling in the sedge of the marshy pool, till they might set their sails, if haply they should set them. Nor have I any hope more of seeing my old home nor my darling children and the father whom I desire. Of them will they even haply claim vengeance for my flight, and wash away this crime in their wretched death. By the heavenly powers I beseech thee, the deities to whom truth is known, by all the faith yet unsullied that is anywhere left among mortals, pity woes so great, pity a soul that bears intolerable wrong."

'At these his tears we grant him life, and accord our pity. Priam himself at once commands his shackles and strait bonds to be undone, and thus speaks with kindly words: "Whoso thou art, now and henceforth dismiss and forget the Greeks: thou shalt be ours. And unfold the truth to this my question: wherefore have they reared the bulk of this monstrous steed? who is their counsellor? or what their aim? what propitiation, or what engine of war is this?" He ended; the other, stored with the treacherous craft of Pelasgia, lifts to heaven his freed hands. "You, everlasting fires," he cries, "and your inviolable sanctity be my witness; you, O altars and accursed swords I fled, and chaplets of the gods I wore as victim! unblamed may I break the oath of Greek allegiance, unblamed hate them and bring all to light that they conceal; nor am I bound by any laws of country. Do thou only keep by thy promise, O Troy, and preserve faith with thy preserver, as my news shall be true, as my recompense ample.

'"All the hope of Greece, and the confidence in which the war began, ever centred in Pallas' aid. But since the wicked son of Tydeus, and Ulysses, forger of crime, made bold to tear the fated Palladium from her sanctuary, and cut down the sentries on the towered height; since they grasped the holy image, and dared with bloody hands to touch the maiden chaplets of the goddess; since then the hope of Greece ebbed and slid away backwards, their strength was broken, and the

mind of the goddess estranged. Whereof the Tritonian[9] gave token by
no uncertain signs. Scarcely was the image set in the camp; flame shot
sparkling from its lifted eyes, and salt sweat started over its body;
thrice, wonderful to tell, it leapt from the ground with shield and spear
quivering. Immediately Calchas prophesies that the seas must be explored in flight, nor may Troy towers be overthrown by Argive weapons, except they repeat their auspices at Argos, and bring back that
divine presence they have borne away with them in the curved ships
overseas. And now they have run down the wind for their native
Mycenae, to gather arms and gods to attend them; they will remeasure
ocean and be on you unawares. So Calchas expounds the omens. This
image at his warning they reared in recompense for the Palladium and
the injured deity, to expiate the horror of sacrilege. Yet Calchas bade
them raise it to this vast size with oaken crossbeams, and build it up to
heaven, that it might not find entry at the gates nor be drawn within
the city, nor protect your people beneath the consecration of old. For
if hand of yours should violate Minerva's offering, then utter destruction (the gods turn rather on himself his augury!) should be upon
Priam's empire and the Phrygian people. But if under your hands it
climbed into your city, Asia should advance in mighty war to the walls
of Pelops,[10] and a like fate awaited our children's children."

'So by Sinon's wiles and craft and perjury the thing gained belief;
and we were ensnared by treachery and forced tears, we whom neither
the son of Tydeus nor Achilles of Larissa, whom not ten years nor a
thousand ships brought down.

'Hereon another sight, greater, alas! and far more terrible meets
us, and alarms our thoughtless senses. Laocoön, allotted priest for Neptune, was slaying a great bull at the accustomed altars. And lo! from
Tenedos, over the placid depths (I shudder as I recall) two snakes in
enormous coils press down the sea and advance together to the shore;
their breasts rise through the surge, and their blood-red crests overtop
the waves; the rest trails through the main behind and wreathes back
in voluminous curves; the brine gurgles and foams. And now they
gained the fields, while their bloodshot eyes blazed with fire, and their
tongues lapped and flickered in their hissing mouths. We scatter,
blanched at the sight. They in unfaltering train make towards Laocoön.
And first the serpents twine in their double embrace his two little
children, and bite deep in their wretched limbs; then him likewise, as

9. *the Tritonian,* Minerva.
10. *Pelops* is used here for Greece in general.

he comes up to help with arms in his hand, they seize and fasten in
their enormous coils; and now twice clasping his waist, twice encircling
his neck with their scaly bodies, they tower head and neck above him.
He at once strains his hands to tear their knots apart, his fillets spattered with foul black venom; at once raises to heaven awful cries; as
when, bellowing, a bull shakes the wavering axe from his neck and
rushes wounded from the altar. But the two snakes glide away to the
high sanctuary and seek the fierce Tritonian's citadel, and take shelter
under the goddess' feet beneath the circle of her shield. Then indeed
a strange terror thrills in all our amazed breasts; and Laocoön, men
say, has fulfilled his crime's desert, in piercing the consecrated wood
and hurling his guilty spear into its body. All cry out that the image
must be drawn to its home and supplication made to her deity. We
breach the walls, and lay open the ramparts of the city. All set to the
work; they fix sliding rollers under its feet, and tie hempen bands on
its neck. The fated engine climbs our walls, big with arms. Around it
boys and unwedded girls chant hymns and joyfully lay their hand on
the rope. It moves up, and glides menacing into the middle of the
town. O native land! O Ilium, house of gods, and Dardanian ramparts
renowned in war! four times in the very gateway did it come to a
stand, and four times armour rang in its womb. Yet we urge it on,
mindless and infatuate, and plant the ill-omened portent in our hallowed citadel. Even then Cassandra[11] opens her lips to the coming
doom, lips at a god's bidding never believed by the Trojans. We, the
wretched people to whom that day was our last, hang the shrines of the
gods with festal boughs throughout the city. Meanwhile the heavens
wheel on, and night rises from the sea, wrapping in her vast shadow
earth and sky and the wiles of the Myrmidons; about the town the
Teucrians are stretched in silence; slumber laps their tired limbs.

'And now the Argive squadron was sailing in order from Tenedos,
and in the favouring stillness of the quiet moon sought the shores it
knew; when the royal galley ran out a flame, and, protected by the
gods' malign decrees, Sinon stealthily lets loose the imprisoned Grecians from their barriers of pine; the horse opens and restores them to
the air; and joyfully issuing from the hollow wood, Thessander and
Sthenelus the captains, and terrible Ulysses, slide down the dangling

11. Cassandra was a daughter of Priam. Apollo, who loved her, gave her the
gift of prophecy in return for her favors. When she refused to carry out her
part of the bargain, he added to his gift the qualification that no one would
believe her prophecies.

rope, with Acamas and Thoas and Neoptolemus[12] son of Peleus, and
Machaon first of all, and Menelaus, and Epeüs himself the artificer of
the snare. They rush upon a city buried in drunken sleep; the watchmen are cut down, and at the open gates they welcome all their comrades, and unite their confederate bands.

'It was the time when by the gift of God rest comes stealing first
and sweetest on unhappy men. In slumber, lo! before mine eyes Hector
seemed to stand by, deep in grief and shedding abundant tears; torn
by the chariot, as once of old, and black with gory dust, his swoln feet
pierced with the thongs. Ah me! in what guise was he! how changed
from the Hector who returns from putting on Achilles' spoils, or
launching the fires of Phrygia on the Grecian ships! with ragged beard
and tresses clotted with blood, and all the many wounds upon him
that he received around his ancestral walls. Myself too weeping I
seemed to accost him ere he spoke, and utter forth mournful accents:
"O light of Dardania, O surest hope of the Trojans, what long delays
have withheld thee? from what borders comest thou, Hector our desire? with what weary eyes we see thee, after many deaths of thy kin,
after divers woes of people and city! What indignity has marred thy
serene visage? or why discern I these wounds?" He replies naught, nor
regards my idle questioning; but heavily drawing a heart-deep groan,
"Ah, fly, goddess-born," he says, "and rescue thyself from these flames.
The foe holds our walls; from her high ridges Troy is toppling down.
Thy country and Priam ask no more. If our towers might be defended
by strength of hand, this hand too had been their defence. Troy com-
mends to thee her holy things and household gods; take them to accompany thy fate; seek for them a city, which, after all the seas have
known thy wanderings, thou shalt at last establish in might." So speaks
he, and carries forth in his hands from their inner shrine the chaplets
and strength of Vesta, and the everlasting fire.[13]

'Meanwhile the city is stirred with mingled agony; and more and
more, though my father Anchises' house lay deep withdrawn and
screened by trees, the noises grow clearer and the clash of armour
swells. I shake myself from sleep and mount over the sloping roof,
and stand there with ears attent: even as when flame catches a cornfield while south winds are furious, or the racing torrent of a mountain

12. Neoptolemus (also called Pyrrhus) is a descendant of Peleus, but is
actually the son of Achilles.
13. Vesta was goddess of the hearth. In her temple in Rome the fire (tended
by the Vestal virgins) was never allowed to go out.

stream sweeps the fields, sweeps the smiling crops and labours of the oxen, and hurls the forest with it headlong; the shepherd in ignorant amaze hears the roar from the cliff-top. Then indeed proof is clear, and the treachery of the Grecians opens out. Already the house of Deïphobus has crashed down in wide ruin amid the overpowering flames; already Ucalegon[14] is ablaze hard by: the broad Sigean bay it lit with the fire. Cries of men and blare of trumpets rise up. Madly I seize my arms, nor is there much purpose in arms; but my spirit is on fire to gather a band for fighting and charge for the citadel with my comrades. Fury and wrath drive me headlong, and I think how noble is death in arms.

'And lo! Panthus, eluding the Achaean weapons, Panthus son of Othrys, priest of Phoebus in the citadel, comes hurrying with the sacred vessels and conquered gods and his little grandchild in his hand, and runs distractedly towards my gates. "How stands the state, O Panthus? what stronghold are we to occupy?" Scarcely had I said so, when groaning he thus returns: "The crowning day is come, the irreversible time of the Dardanian land. No more are we a Trojan people; Ilium and the great glory of the Teucrians is no more. Angry Jupiter has cast all into the scale of Argos. The Grecians are lords of the burning town. The horse, standing high amid the city, pours forth armed men, and Sinon scatters fire, insolent in victory. Some are at the wide-flung gates, all the thousands that ever came from populous Mycenae. Others have beset the narrow streets with lowered weapons; edge and glittering point of steel stand drawn, ready for the slaughter; scarcely at the entry do the guards of the gates essay battle, and hold out in the blind fight."

[Aeneas collects a band of Trojans. After killing some Greeks in a surprise attack, they put on their victims' armour and, being thus mistaken for Greeks, do great damage to the enemy. But they are also attacked by other Trojans. They are finally detected by the Greeks and overwhelmed by superior numbers. Aeneas and a few other survivors go on to Priam's palace.]

'Here indeed the fight is fiercest, as if all the rest of the warfare were nowhere, and no slaughter but here throughout the city, so do we descry the battle in full fury, the Grecians rushing on the building, and their shielded column driving up against the beleaguered threshold.

14. *Ucalegon*, i.e., the house of Ucalegon, one of the Trojan leaders.

Ladders cling to the walls; and hard by the doors and planted on the rungs they hold up their shields in the left hand to ward off our weapons, and with their right clutch the battlements. The Dardanians tear down turrets and whole pinnacles of the palace against them; with these for weapons, since they see the end is come, they prepare to defend themselves even in death's extremity: and hurl down gilded beams, the stately decorations of their fathers of old. Others with drawn swords have beset the doorway below and keep it in crowded column. We renew our courage, to aid the royal dwelling, to support them with our succour, and swell the force of the conquered.

'There was a blind doorway giving passage through the range of Priam's halls by a solitary postern, whereby, while our realm endured, hapless Andromache[15] would often and often glide unattended to her father-in-law's house, and carry the boy Astyanax to his grandsire. I issue out on the sloping height of the ridge, whence wretched Teucrian hands were hurling their ineffectual weapons. A tower stood on the sheer brink, its roof ascending high into heaven, whence was wont to be seen all Troy and the Grecian ships and Achaean camp: attacking it with iron round about, where the joints of the lofty flooring yielded, we wrench it from its high foundations and shake it free; it gives way, and suddenly falls thundering in ruin, crashing wide over the Grecian ranks. But others swarm up; nor meanwhile do stones nor any sort of missile slacken. Right before the vestibule and in the front doorway Pyrrhus moves rejoicingly in the sparkle of arms and gleaming brass: like as when a snake fed on poisonous herbs, whom chill winter kept hid and swollen underground, now fresh from his weeds outworn and shining in youth wreathes his slippery body into the daylight, his upreared breast meets the sun, and his triple-cloven tongue flickers in his mouth. With him huge Periphas, and Automedon the armour-bearer, driver of Achilles' horses, with him all his Scyrian men climb the roof and hurl flames on the housetop. Himself among the foremost he grasps a poleaxe, bursts through the hard doorway, and wrenches the brazen-plated doors from the hinge; and now he has cut out a plank from the solid oak and pierced a vast gaping hole. The house within is open to sight, and the long halls lie plain; open to sight are the secret chambers of Priam and the kings of old, and they see armed men standing in front of the doorway.

'But the inner house is stirred with shrieks and misery and confusion, and the court echoes deep with women's wailing; the din strikes

15. *Andromache,* daughter-in-law of Priam and wife of Hector.

up to the golden stars. Affrighted mothers stray about the vast house, and cling fast to the doors and print them with kisses. With his father's might Pyrrhus presses on; nor guards nor barriers can hold out. The gate totters under the hard-driven ram, and the doors fall flat, rent from the hinge. The passage is forced; the Greeks burst through the entrance and pour in, slaughtering the foremost, and filling the space with a wide stream of soldiers. Not so furiously when a foaming river bursts his banks and overflows, beating down the opposing dykes with whirling water, is he borne mounded over the fields, and sweeps herds and pens all about the plains. Myself I saw in the gateway Neoptolemus mad with carnage, and the two sons of Atreus, saw Hecuba[16] and the hundred daughters of her house, and Priam polluting with his blood the altar fires of his own consecration. The fifty bridal chambers, the abundant hope of his children's children, their doors magnificent with spoils of barbaric gold, have sunk in ruin; where the fire fails the Greeks are in possession.

'Perchance too thou mayest inquire what was Priam's fate. When he saw the ruin of his captured city, the gates of his house burst open, and the enemy amid his innermost chambers, the old man idly fastens round his aged trembling shoulders his long disused armour, girds on the unavailing sword, and advances on his death among the thronging foe.

'Within the palace and under the bare cope of sky was a massive altar, and hard on the altar an ancient bay tree leaned clasping the household gods in its shadow. Here Hecuba and her daughters crowded vainly about the altar-stones, like doves driven headlong by a black tempest, and crouched clasping the gods' images. And when she saw Priam her lord with the armour of youth on him, "What spirit of madness, my poor husband," she cries, "has moved thee to gird on these weapons? or whither dost thou run? Not such the succour nor these the defenders the time requires: no, were mine own Hector now beside us. Retire, I beseech thee, hither; this altar will protect us all, or thou wilt share our death." With these words on her lips she drew the aged man to her, and set him on the holy seat.

'And lo, escaped from slaughtering Pyrrhus through the weapons of the enemy, Polites, one of Priam's children, flies wounded down the long colonnades and circles the empty halls. Pyrrhus pursues him fiercely with aimed wound, just catching at him, and follows hard on him with his spear. As at last he issued before his parents' eyes and

16. *Hecuba*, wife of Priam.

faces, he fell, and shed his life in a pool of blood. At this Priam, although even now fast in the toils of death, yet withheld not nor spared
a wrathful cry: "Ah, for thy crime, for this thy hardihood, may the
gods, if there is goodness in heaven to care for aught such, pay thee in
full thy worthy meed, and return thee the reward that is due! who hast
made me look face to face on my child's murder, and polluted a father's
countenance with death. Ah, not such to a foe was the Achilles whose
parentage thou beliest; but he revered a suppliant's right and trust,
restored to the tomb Hector's blood-drained corpse, and sent me back
to my own realm." Thus the old man spoke, and launched his weak
and unwounding spear, which, recoiling straight from the jarring
brass, hung idly from his shield above the boss. Thereat Pyrrhus:
"Thou then shalt tell this, and go with the message to my sire the son
of Peleus: remember to tell him of my baleful deeds, and the degen-
eracy of Neoptolemus. Now die." So saying, he drew him quivering
to the very altar, slipping in the pool of his child's blood, and wound
his hair in the left hand, while in the right the sword flashed out and
plunged to the hilt in his side. This was the end of Priam's fortunes;
thus did allotted fate find him, with burning Troy and her sunken
towers before his eyes, once magnificent lord over so many peoples
and lands of Asia. The great corpse lies along the shore, a head severed
from the shoulders and a body without a name.

'But then an awful terror began to encircle me; I stood in amaze;
there rose before me the sight of my loved father, as I saw the king,
old as he, sobbing out his life under the ghastly wound; there rose
Creüsa[17] forlorn, my plundered house, and little Iülus' peril. I look
back and survey what force is around me. All, outwearied, have given
up and leapt headlong to the ground, or flung themselves wretchedly
into the fire.

'Yes, and now I only was left; when I espy the daughter of Tyndarus[18] close in the courts of Vesta, crouching silently in the fane's
recesses; the bright glow of the fires lights my wandering, as my eyes
stray all about. Fearing Teucrian anger for the overthrown towers of
Troy, and the Grecians' vengeance and the wrath of the husband she
had abandoned, she, the common Fury of Troy and her native country, had hidden herself and cowered unseen by the altars. My spirit
kindles to fire, and rises in wrath to avenge my dying land and take
repayment for her crimes. Shall she verily see Sparta and her native

17. *Creüsa,* Aeneas' wife.
18. *daughter of Tyndarus,* Helen of Troy.

Mycenae unscathed, and depart a queen and triumphant? Shall she see her spousal and her father's house and children, attended by a crowd of Trojan women and Phrygians to serve her? and Priam have fallen under the sword? Troy blazed in fire? the shore of Dardania so often soaked with blood? Not so. For though there is no name or fame in a woman's punishment, nor honour in the victory, yet shall I have praise in quenching a guilty life and exacting a just recompense; and it will be good to fill my soul with the flame of vengeance, and satisfy the ashes of my people. Thus broke I forth, and advanced infuriate; when my mother came visibly before me, clear to sight as never till then, and shone forth in pure radiance through the night, gracious, evident in godhead, in shape and stature such as she is wont to appear to the heavenly people; she caught me by the hand and stayed me, and pursued thus with roseate lips:

' "Son, what overmastering pain thus wakes thy wrath? Why ravest thou? or whither is thy care for us fled? Wilt thou not first look to it, where thou hast left Anchises, thine aged worn father; or if Creüsa thy wife and the child Ascanius survive? round about whom all the Greek battalions range; and without my preventing care, the flames ere this had consumed them, and the hostile sword drunk their blood. Not the hated face of the Laconian woman, Tyndarus' daughter; not Paris is to blame; the gods, the gods in anger overturn this magnificence, and make Troy topple down. Look, for all the cloud that now veils thy gaze and dulls mortal vision with damp encircling mist, I will rend from before thee. Fear thou no commands of thy mother, nor refuse to obey her counsels. Here, where thou seest sundered piles of masonry and rocks violently torn from rocks, and smoke eddying mixed with dust, Neptune with his great trident shakes wall and foundation out of their places, and upturns all the city from her base. Here Juno in all her terror holds the Scaean gates at the entry, and, girt with steel, calls her allied army furiously from their ships. Even now on the citadel's height, look back! Tritonian Pallas is planted with glittering bordure and awful Gorgon head. Their lord himself pours courage and prosperous strength on the Grecians, himself stirs the gods against the arms of Dardania. Haste away, O son, and put an end to the struggle. Nowhere will I desert thee; I will set thee safe in the courts of thy father's house."

'She ended, and plunged in the dense blackness of the night. Awful faces shine forth, and, set against Troy, divine majesties.

'Then indeed I saw all Ilium sinking in flame, and Neptunian

Troy uprooted from her base: even as an ancient ash on the mountain heights, hacked all about with steel and fast-glancing axes, when husbandmen emulously strain to cut it down: it nods to the fall, with shaken top and quivering tresses asway; till gradually overmastered with wounds, it utters one last groan, and rending itself away, falls in ruin along the ridge. I descend, and under a god's guidance clear my way between foe and flame; weapons give ground before me, and flames retire.

'And now, when I have reached the courts of my ancestral dwelling, our home of old, my father, whom it was my first desire to carry high into the hills, and whom first I sought, refuses wholly, now Troy is rooted out, to prolong his life through the pains of exile.

'"Ah, you," he cries, "whose blood is at the prime, whose strength stands firm in native vigour, do you take your flight. Had the lords of heaven willed to prolong life for me, they should have preserved this my home. Enough and more is the one desolation we have seen, survivors of a captured city.[19] Thus, oh thus salute me and depart, as a body laid out for burial. Mine own hand shall find me death: the foe will be merciful and seek my spoils: light is the loss of a tomb. This long time hated of heaven, I uselessly delay the years, since the father of gods and king of men blasted me with wind of thunder and scathe of flame."[20]

'Thus held he on in utterance, and remained unstirred. We press him, dissolved in tears, my wife Creüsa, Ascanius, all our household, that our father involve us not all in his ruin, and add his weight to the sinking scale of doom. He refuses, and keeps seated steadfast in his purpose. Again I rush to battle, and choose death in my misery. For what had counsel or chance yet to give? Thoughtest thou my feet, O father, could retire and abandon thee? and fell so unnatural words from a parent's lips? "If heaven wills that naught be left of our mighty city, if this be thy planted purpose, thy pleasure to cast in thyself and thine to the doom of Troy; for this death indeed the gate is wide, and even now Pyrrhus will be here newly bathed in Priam's blood, Pyrrhus who slaughters the son before the father's face, the father at his altars. For this was it, bountiful mother, that thou snatchedst me from amid fire and sword, to see the foe in my inmost chambers, and Ascanius and my father, Creüsa by their side, butchered in one another's blood?

19. Anchises had survived an earlier sack of Troy by Hercules.
20. Jupiter struck Anchises with a thunderbolt to punish him for boasting to other mortals about his relationship with Venus.

To arms, my men, to arms! the last day calls on the conquered. Return me to the Greeks; let me revisit and renew the fight. Never today shall we all perish unavenged."

'Thereat I again gird on my sword, and fitting my left arm into the clasps of the shield, strode forth of the palace. But lo! my wife clung round my feet on the threshold, and held little Iülus up to his father's sight. "If thou goest to die, let us too hurry with thee to the end. But if thou knowest any hope to place in arms, be this household thy first defence. To what is little Iülus and thy father, to what am I left who once was called thy wife?"

'So she shrieked, and filled all the house with her weeping; when a sign arises sudden and marvellous to tell. For, between the hands and before the faces of his sorrowing parents, lo! above Iülus' head there seemed to stream a light luminous cone, and a flame whose touch hurt not to flicker in his soft hair and play round his brows. We in hurrying affright shook out the blazing hair and quenched the holy fires with spring water. But lord Anchises joyfully upraised his eyes; and stretching his hands to heaven: "Jupiter omnipotent," he cries, "if thou dost relent at any prayers, look on us this once alone; and if our goodness deserve it, give a sign hereafter, O lord, and confirm this thine omen."

'Scarcely had the aged man spoken thus, when with sudden crash it thundered on the left, and a star gliding through the dusk shot from heaven drawing a bright trail of light. We watch it slide over the palace roof, leaving the mark of its pathway, and bury its brilliance in the wood of Ida; the long-drawn track shines, and the region all about reeks with sulphur. Then conquered indeed my father rises to address the gods and worship the holy star. "Now, now delay is done with: I follow, and where you lead, I come, gods of my fathers; save my house, save my grandchild. Yours is this omen, and in your deity Troy stands. I yield, O my son, and refuse not to pass forth beside thee."

'He ended; and now more loudly the fire roars along the city, and nearer roll the burning tides. "Up then, beloved father, and place thyself on my neck; these shoulders of mine will sustain thee, nor will a burden so dear weigh me down. Howsoever fortune fall, one and undivided shall be our peril, one the escape of us twain. Little Iülus shall go along with me, and my wife follow our steps afar. You of my household, give heed to what I say. On a mound as you leave the city an ancient temple of Ceres stands lonely, and hard by an aged cypress, guarded many years in ancestral observance: to this gathering-place we will come from diverse quarters. Thou, O father, take the sacred things and the household gods of our ancestors in thine hand. For me, just parted from the desperate battle, with slaughter fresh upon me, to handle them were guilt, until I have washed me in a living stream." So spoke I, and spread over my neck and broad shoulders a tawny lion-skin for covering, and stoop to my burden. Little Iülus, with his hand fast in mine, keeps uneven pace after his father. Behind my wife follows. We pass on in the shadows. And I, lately moved by no weapons launched against me, nor by the thronging bands of my Grecian foes, am now terrified at every breath, startled by every noise, thrilling with fear alike for my companion and my burden.

'And now I was nearing the gates, and thought I had outsped all the way; when suddenly the crowded trampling of feet came to our ears, and my father, looking forth into the darkness, cries: "My son, my son, fly; they draw near. I espy gleaming shields and the flicker of brass." At this, in my flurry and confusion, some hostile god bereft me of my senses. For while I plunge down byways, and swerve from where the familiar streets ran, Creüsa, alas! whether, torn by fate from her unhappy husband, she stood still, or did she mistake the way, or sink down outwearied? I know not; and never again was she given back to our eyes; nor did I turn to look for my lost one, or cast back a thought, ere we were come to ancient Ceres' mound and hallowed seat; here at last, when all gathered, one was missing, vanished from her child's and her husband's company. What man or god did I spare in frantic reproaches? or what crueller sight did I see in our city's overthrow? I charge my comrades with Ascanius and lord Anchises, and the gods of Teucria, hiding them in the winding vale. Myself I regain the city, girding on my shining armour; fixed to renew every danger, to retrace my way throughout Troy, and fling myself again on its perils. First of all I regain the walls and the dim gateway whence my steps had issued; I scan and follow back my footprints with search-ing gaze in the night. Everywhere my spirit shudders, dismayed at the very silence. Thence I pass on home, if haply her feet (if haply!) had led her thither. The Grecians had poured in, and filled the palace. The devouring fire goes rolling before the wind high as the roof; the flames tower over it, and the heat surges up into the air. I move on, and revisit the citadel and Priam's dwelling; where now in the spa-cious porticoes of Juno's sanctuary Phoenix and accursed Ulysses, chosen sentries, were guarding the spoil. Hither from all quarters is flung in masses the treasure of Troy torn from burning shrines, tables of the gods, bowls of solid gold, and captive raiment. Boys and cowering mothers in long file stand round. Yes, and I dared to cry abroad through the darkness; I filled the streets with calling, and again and yet again with vain reiterance cried piteously on Creüsa. As I sought her and rushed endlessly among the houses of the town, there rose before mine eyes a melancholy phantom, the ghost of very Creüsa, in likeness larger than her wont. I was motionless; my hair stood up, and the voice choked in my throat. Then she thus addressed me, and with this speech allayed my distresses: "What help is there in this mad passion of grief, sweet my husband? not without divine influence does this come to pass: nor may it be, nor does the high lord of Olympus allow, that thou shouldest carry Creüsa hence in thy company. Long shall be thine exile, and weary spaces of sea must thou plough; yet thou shalt come to the land Hesperia, where Lydian Tiber flows with soft current through rich and populous fields. There prosperity awaits thee, and a kingdom, and a king's daughter for thy wife. Dispel these tears for thy beloved Creüsa. Never will I look on the proud homes of the Myrmidons or Dolopians, or go to be the slave of Greek matrons, I a daughter of Dardania, a daughter-in-law of Venus the goddess. But the mighty mother of the gods keeps me in these her borders. And now farewell, and still love thy child and mine." This speech uttered, while I wept and would have said many a thing, she left me and retreated into thin air. Thrice there was I fain to lay mine arms round her neck; thrice the vision I vainly clasped fled out of my hands, even as the light breezes, or most like to fluttering sleep. So at last, when night is spent, I revisit my comrades.

'And here I find a marvellous great company, newly flocked in, mothers and men, a people gathered for exile, a pitiable crowd. From all quarters they are assembled, ready in heart and fortune, to whatsoever land I will conduct them overseas. And now the morning star rose over the high ridges of Ida, and led on the day; and the Grecians held the gateways in leaguer, nor was any hope of help given. I withdrew, and raising my father up, I sought the mountains.'

[BOOK III: Aeneas takes up the tale of his adventures since the fall of Troy, and describes his attempts to reach the land promised as the seat of the new Trojan empire. At first this was thought to be Crete, but later prophecies showed that it was Italy. During their wanderings the Trojans experienced many adventures (imitated, for the most part, from those of Odysseus), involving pestilence, Greeks, harpies, the

Cyclops, Scylla, etc. They reached Sicily, where Anchises died, and had set sail for the mainland when the storm described at the beginning of the poem broke upon them.]

BOOK IV

But Queen Dido, long ere now pierced sore with passion, feeds the wound with her life-blood, and wastes in a hidden fire. Again and again his own valiance and his line's renown flood back upon her spirit; look and accent cling fast in her bosom, and the pain allows not her limbs rest or calm. The morrow's dawn bore the torch of Phoebus across the earth, and had rolled away the dewy darkness from the sky, when, scarce herself, she thus addresses the sister of her heart:

'Anna, my sister, such dreams of terror thrill me through! What guest unknown is this who has entered our dwelling? How high his mien! how great in heart as in arms! I believe it well, with no vain assurance, his blood is divine. Fear proves the vulgar spirit. Alas, by what destinies is he driven! of what wars fought out he told! Were my mind not planted fixed and immovable, to ally myself to none in wedlock since my first love of old played me false in death; were I not sick to the heart of bridal torch and chamber, to this temptation alone I might haply yield. Anna, I will confess it; since Sychaeus mine husband met his piteous doom, and our household was shattered by a brother's murder, he only has touched mine heart and shaken my soul from its balance. I know the prints of the ancient flame. But rather, I pray, may earth first yawn deep for me, or the Lord omnipotent hurl me with his thunderbolt into gloom, the pallid gloom and profound night of Erebus, ere I soil thee, mine honour, or undo thy laws. He took my love away who made me one with him at first; he shall keep it with him, and guard it in the tomb.' She spoke, and filled her bosom with welling tears.

Anna replies: 'O dearer than the daylight to thy sister, wilt thou waste, sad and alone, all thy length of youth, and know not the sweetness of motherhood, nor love's bounty? Deemest thou the ashes care for that, or the ghost within the tomb? Be it so: in days gone by no wooers bent thy sorrow, not in Libya, nor ere then in Tyre; Iarbas was slighted and other princes nurtured by the triumphal land of Africa; wilt thou contend even with a love to thy liking? nor does it cross thy mind whose are these fields about thy dwelling? On this side are the Gaetulian towns, a race unconquerable in war; the reinless Numidian riders and the grim Syrtis hem thee in; on this lies a thirsty tract of desert, swept by the raiders of Barca. Why speak of the war gathering from Tyre, and thy brother's menaces? Under gods' control to my thinking, and with Juno's favour, has the Ilian fleet held on hither before the gale. What a city wilt thou discern here, O sister! what a realm will rise on such a union! the arms of Troy ranged with ours, what glory will exalt the Punic state! Do thou only, asking divine favour with peace-offerings, be bounteous in welcome and multiply reasons for delay, while the storm rages out at sea and Orion is rainy, and his ships are shattered and the sky unvoyageable.' With these words she fired her spirit with resolved love, put hope in her wavering soul, and undid her shame.

First they visit the shrines, and desire grace from altar to altar; they sacrifice sheep fitly chosen to Ceres the Lawgiver, to Phoebus and lord Lyaeus,[1] to Juno before all, guardian of the marriage bond. Dido herself, excellent in beauty, holds the cup in her hand, and pours libation between the horns of a milk-white cow, or moves in state to the rich altars before the gods' presences, day by day renewing her gifts, and plunges her gaze into the breasts of cattle laid open to take counsel from the throbbing entrails. Ah, witless souls of soothsayers! how may cows or shrines help her madness? all the while the subtle flame consumes her inly, and deep in her breast the wound is silent and alive. Stung to misery, Dido wanders in frenzy all down the city, even as an arrow-stricken deer, whom, far and heedless amid the Cretan woodland, a shepherd archer has pierced and left the flying steel in her unaware; she ranges in flight the Dictaean forest lawns; fast in her side clings the deadly reed. Now she leads Aeneas with her through the town, and displays her Sidonian treasure and ordered city; she essays to speak, and breaks off half-way in utterance. Now, as day wanes, she seeks the repeated banquet, and again in her madness pleads to hear the agonies of Ilium, and again hangs on the teller's lips. Thereafter, when all are gone their ways, and the dim moon in turn quenches her light, and the setting stars counsel to sleep, alone in the empty house she mourns, and flings herself on the couch he left: distant she hears and sees him in the distance; or enthralled by some look of his father, she holds Ascanius on her lap, if so she may steal her love unuttered. No more do the unfinished towers rise, no more do the people exercise in arms, nor work for safety in war on harbour or bastion; the works hang broken off, vast looming walls and engines towering into the sky.

1. *Lyaeus*, Bacchus.

So soon as she perceives her thus fast in the toils, and madly care-less of her name, Jove's beloved wife, daughter of Saturn, accosts Venus thus:

'Noble indeed is the fame and splendid the spoils you win, thou and that boy of thine, and mighty the renown of your deity, if two gods have vanquished one woman by treachery. Nor am I so blind to thy terror of our town, thine old jealousy of the high house of Car-thage. But what shall be the end? or why all this contest now? Nay, rather let us work an enduring peace and a bridal compact. Thou hast what all thy soul desired; Dido is on fire with love, and has caught the madness through and through. Then rule we this people jointly in equal lordship; allow her to be a Phrygian husband's slave, and to lay her Tyrians for dowry in thine hand.'

To her—for she knew the dissembled purpose in her words, to turn the kingdom of Italy away to the coasts of Libya—Venus thus began in answer: 'Who so mad as to reject these terms, or choose rather to try the fortune of war with thee? if only when done, as thou sayest, fortune follow. But I move uncertain of Jove's ordinance, whether he will that Tyrians and wanderers from Troy be one city, or approve the mingling of peoples or the treaty of union. Thou art his wife, and thy prayers may put his mind to proof. Go on; I will follow.'

Then Queen Juno thus rejoined: 'That task shall be mine. Now, by what means the present need may be fulfilled, attend and I will explain in brief. Aeneas and lovelorn Dido are to go hunting together in the woodland when to-morrow's rising sun goes forth and his rays unveil the world. On them, while the beaters run up and down, and encircle the lawns with toils, will I pour down a blackening rain-cloud mingled with hail, and wake all the sky with thunder. Their com-pany will scatter for shelter in the dim darkness; Dido and the Trojan captain will take covert in the same cavern. I will be there, and if thy goodwill is assured me, I will unite them in wedlock, and make her wholly his; here shall Hymen[2] be present.' The Cytherean gave ready assent to her request, and laughed at the guileful device.

Meanwhile Dawn has arisen forth of ocean. A chosen company issue from the gates while the morning star is high; they pour forth with meshed nets, toils, broad-headed hunting spears, Massylian horse-men and hounds of scent. At her doorway the Punic princes await their queen, who yet lingers in her chamber, and her horse stands

2. *Hymen*, god of marriage.

splendid in gold and purple with clattering feet and jaws champing
on the foamy bit. At last she comes forth amid a great thronging train,
girt in a Sidonian mantle, broidered with needlework; her quiver is of
gold, her tresses gathered into gold, a golden buckle clasps up her
crimson gown. Therewithal the Phrygian train advances with joyous
Iülus. Himself first and foremost of all, Aeneas joins her company and
mingles his train with hers. . . . But the boy Ascanius is in the valleys,
exultant on his fiery horse, and gallops past one and another, praying
that among the unwarlike herds a foaming boar may issue or a tawny
lion descend the hill.

Meanwhile the sky begins to thicken and roar aloud. A rain-cloud
comes down mingled with hail; the Tyrian train and the men of Troy,
and Venus' Dardanian grandchild, scatter in fear and seek shelter far
over the fields. Streams pour from the hills. Dido and the Trojan captain take covert in the same cavern. Primeval Earth and Juno the
bridesmaid give the sign; fires flash out high in air, witnessing the
union, and Nymphs cry aloud on the mountain-top. That day opened
the gate of death and the springs of ill. For now Dido recks not of eye
or tongue, nor sets her heart on love in secret: she calls it marriage,
and with this word shrouds her blame.

Straightway Rumour runs through the great cities of Libya,—
Rumour, than whom none other is more swift to mischief; she thrives
on restlessness and gains strength by going: at first small and timorous; soon she lifts herself on high and paces the ground with head
hidden among the clouds. Her, as they tell, Mother Earth, when stung
by wrath against the gods,[3] bore last sister to Coeus and Enceladus,
fleet-footed and swift of wing, ominous, awful, vast; for every feather
on her body is a waking eye beneath, wonderful to tell, and a tongue,
and as many loud lips and straining ears. By night she flits between
sky and land, shrilling through the dusk, and droops not her lids in
sweet slumber; in daylight she sits on guard upon tall towers or the
ridge of the house-roof, and makes great cities afraid; obstinate in
perverseness and forgery no less than messenger of truth. She then
exultingly filled the countries with manifold talk, and blazoned alike
what was done and undone: one Aeneas is come, born of Trojan blood;
on him beautiful Dido thinks no shame to fling herself; now they pass
the long winter-tide together in revelry, regardless of their realms and
enthralled by dishonouring passion. This the pestilent goddess spreads

3. Earth, angry at the gods because they had overthrown her children, the
Titans, bore Rumour as the last of these giants.

abroad in the mouths of men, and bends her course right on to King Iarbas, and with her words fires his spirit and swells his wrath.

He, the seed of Ammon[4] by a ravished Garamantian Nymph, had built to Jove in his wide realms an hundred great temples, an hundred altars, and consecrated the wakeful fire that keeps watch by night before the gods perpetually, where the soil is fat with blood of beasts and the courts blossom with pied garlands. And he, distraught at heart and on fire at the bitter tidings, before his altars, amid the divine presences often, it is said, bowed in prayer to Jove with uplifted hands:

'Jupiter omnipotent, to whom from the broidered cushions of their banqueting halls the Maurusian[5] people now pour offering of the wine-vat, lookest thou on this? or do we shudder vainly when our father hurls the thunderbolt, and do blind fires in the clouds and idle rumblings appal our soul? The woman wanderer who in our coasts planted a small town on purchased ground, to whom we gave fields by the shore and laws of settlement, has spurned our alliance and taken Aeneas for lord of her realm. And now that Paris,[6] with his effeminate crew, his chin and oozy hair swathed in the turban of Maeonia, takes and keeps her; since to thy temples we bear oblation, and hallow an empty name.'

In such words he pleaded, clasping the altars; the Lord omnipotent heard, and cast his eye on the royal city and the lovers forgetful of their fairer fame. Then he addresses this charge to Mercury:

'Up and away, O son! call the breezes and slide down them on thy wings: accost the Dardanian captain who now loiters in Tyrian Carthage and casts not a look on the cities destined for him; carry down my words through the fleet air. Not such an one did his mother most beautiful vouch him to us, nor for this twice rescue him from Grecian arms; but he was to rule an Italy teeming with empire and loud with war, to transmit the line of Teucer's royal blood, and lay all the world beneath his law. If such glories kindle him in no wise, and he take no trouble for his own honour, does a father grudge his Ascanius the towers of Rome? with what device or in what hope loiters he among a hostile race, and casts not a glance on his Ausonian children and the fields of Lavinium? Let him set sail: this is the sum: thereof be thou our messenger.'

4. Jupiter Ammon, a North African god.
5. *Maurusian*, Moorish.
6. From Iarbas' point of view, Aeneas is like Paris in two ways: (1) he is effeminate, with his Asiatic dress and anointed hair, and (2) he is a woman-stealer.

He ended: the other made ready to obey his father's high command. . . . So soon as his winged feet touched at the hut-villages, he espies Aeneas founding towers and ordering new dwellings; his sword twinkled with yellow jasper, and a cloak hung from his shoulders ablaze with Tyrian sea-purple, a gift that Dido had made costly and shot the warp with threads of gold. Straightway he breaks in: 'Layest thou now the foundations of high Carthage, and buildest up a fair city in dalliance? ah, forgetful of thine own kingdom and state! From bright Olympus I descend to thee at express command of heaven's sovereign, whose deity sways sky and earth; expressly he bids me carry this charge through the fleet air: with what device or in what hope dost thou loiter idly on Libyan lands? if such glories kindle thee in no wise, yet cast an eye on growing Ascanius, on Iülus thine hope and heir, to whom the kingdom of Italy and the Roman land is due.' As these words left his lips the Cyllenian,[7] yet speaking, quitted mortal sight and vanished into thin air away out of his eyes.

But Aeneas in truth gazed in dumb amazement, his hair thrilled up, and the voice choked in his throat. He burns to flee away and leave the pleasant land, aghast at the high warning and divine ordinance. Alas, what shall he do? how venture now to smooth the tale to the frenzied queen? what prologue shall he find? and this way and that he rapidly throws his mind, and turns it on all hands in swift change of thought. In his perplexity this seemed the better counsel; he calls Mnestheus and Sergestus, and brave Serestus, and bids them silently equip the fleet, gather their crews to the shore, and prepare their armament, keeping the cause of the commotion hid; himself meanwhile, since Dido in her kindness knows not and looks not for severance to so strong a love, will essay to approach her when she may be told most gently, and the way for it be fair. All at once gladly do as bidden, and obey his command.

But the Queen—who may delude a lover?—foreknew his devices, and at once caught the presaging stir, fearing even where no fear was. To her likewise had evil Rumour borne the maddening news of the fleet in equipment and the voyage prepared. Helpless at heart, she reels aflame with rage throughout the city. Thus at last she breaks out upon Aeneas:

'And thou didst hope, traitor, to mask such infamy, and slip away silently from my land? Our love holds thee not, nor the hand thou once gavest, nor the bitter death that is left for Dido's portion? Nay, even in

7. *the Cyllenian*, Mercury, who was born on Mt. Cyllene.

winter weather thou labourest on thy fleet, and hastenest to launch
into the deep amid northern gales; ah, cruel! Why, were thy quest
not of alien fields and unknown dwellings, did thine ancient Troy
remain, should Troy be sought in voyages over tempestuous seas?
Fliest thou from me? me who by these tears and thine own hand beseech thee, since naught else, alas! have I kept mine own—by our union
and the marriage rites begun; if I have done thee any grace, or aught
of mine was once sweet to thee,—pity our sinking house, and if there
yet be room for prayers, put off this purpose of thine. For thy sake
Libyan tribes and Nomad kings are hostile; my Tyrians are estranged; for thy sake, thine, is mine honour perished, and the former
fame, my one title to the skies. How leavest thou me to die, O my
guest? since of the name of husband all that is left is this. For what do
I wait? till Pygmalion overthrow his sister's city, or Gaetulian Iarbas
lead me to captivity? At least if before thy flight a child of thine had
been clasped in my arms, if a tiny Aeneas were playing in my hall,
whose face might yet image thine, I would not think myself ensnared
and deserted utterly.'

She ended; he by counsel of Jove held his gaze unstirred, and kept
his anguish hard down in his heart. At last he briefly answers:

'Never, O Queen, will I deny that thy goodness has gone high as
thy words can swell the reckoning; nor will I grudge a memory to
Elissa[8] while I remember myself, and breath sways this body. Little will
I say where little is to be said. I never hoped to slip away in stealthy
flight; fancy not that; nor did I ever hold out the marriage torch
or enter thus into alliance. Did fate allow me to guide my life by mine
own government, and calm my sorrows as I would, my first duty were
to the Trojan city and the dear remnant of my kindred; the high house
of Priam should abide, and my hand had set up Troy towers anew
for a conquered people. But now for broad Italy has Apollo[9] of Grynos
bidden me steer, for Italy the oracles of Lycia. Here is my desire; this
is my native country. If thy Phoenician eyes are stayed on the fortress
of Carthage and thy Libyan city, what wrong is it, I pray, that we Trojans should find rest on Ausonian land? We too may seek a foreign
realm unforbidden. In my sleep, often as the dank shades of night
veil the earth, often as the stars lift their fires, the troubled phantom of

8. *Elissa*, Dido.

9. The reference here is to the various prophecies and oracles (presided over
by Apollo as god of prophecy) which have ordered Aeneas to found a new
realm in Italy, not to the reminder of this destiny which Mercury has just
brought.

my father Anchises comes in warning and dread; my boy Ascanius comes and the wrong done to one so dear in cheating him of an Hesperian kingdom and destined fields. Now even the gods' interpreter, sent straight from Jove—I call both to witness—has borne down his commands through the fleet air. Myself in broad daylight I saw the deity passing within the walls, and these ears drank his utterance. Cease to madden me and thyself alike with plaints. Not of my will do I follow Italy.'

Long ere he ended she gazes on him askance, turning her eyes from side to side and perusing him with silent glances; then thus wrathfully speaks:

'No goddess was thy mother, nor Dardanus founder of thy line, traitor! but rough Caucasus bore thee on his iron crags, and Hyrcanian tigresses gave thee suck. For why do I conceal it? For what further outrage do I wait? Has our weeping cost him a sigh, or a lowered glance? Has he broken into tears, or had pity on his lover? Where, where shall I begin? Now neither doth Queen Juno nor our Saturnian lord regard us with righteous eyes. Nowhere is trust safe. Cast ashore and destitute I welcomed him, and madly gave him place and portion in my kingdom; I found him his lost fleet and drew his comrades from death. Alas, the fire of madness speeds me on. Now prophetic Apollo, now oracles of Lycia, now the very gods' interpreter sent straight from Jove through the air carries these rude commands! Truly that is work for the gods, that a care to vex their peace! I detain thee not, nor gainsay thy words: go, follow thine Italy down the wind; seek thy realm overseas. Yet midway my hope is, if righteous gods can do aught at all, thou wilt drain the cup of vengeance on the rocks, and re-echo calls on Dido's name. In murky fires I will follow far away, and when chill death has severed body from soul, my ghost will haunt thee in every region. Wretch, thou shalt repay! I will hear; and the rumor of it shall reach me deep in the under world.'

Even on these words she breaks off her speech unfinished, and, sick at heart, escapes out of the air and sweeps round and away out of sight, leaving him in fear and much hesitance, and with much on his mind to say. Her women catch her in their arms, and carry her swooning limbs to her marble chamber and lay her on her bed.

But good Aeneas, though he would fain soothe and comfort her grief, and quell her passion by speech, with many a sigh, and melted in soul by his great love, yet fulfils the divine commands and returns to his fleet. Then indeed the Teucrians set to work, and haul down their tall ships all along the shore. The hulls are oiled and afloat; they carry from the woodland green boughs for oars and massy logs unhewn, in hot haste to go. One might descry them shifting their quarters and pouring out of all the town: even as ants, mindful of winter, plunder a great heap of wheat and store it in their house; a black column advances on the plain as they carry home their spoil on a narrow track through the grass. Some shove and strain with their shoulders at big grains, some marshal the ranks and chastise delay; all the path is aswarm with work. What then were thy thoughts, O Dido, as thou sawest it? What sighs didst thou utter, viewing from the fortress roof the broad beach aswarm, and seeing before thine eyes the whole sea stirred with their noisy din? Injurious Love, to what dost thou not compel mortal hearts! Again she must needs break into tears, again essay entreaty, and bow her spirit down to love, not to leave aught untried and go to death in vain.

'Anna, thou seest the bustle that fills the circle of the shore. They have gathered from every quarter; already their canvas woos the breezes, and the joyous sailors have garlanded the sterns. This great pain, my sister, I shall have strength to bear, as I have had strength to foresee. Yet this one thing, Anna, for love and pity's sake—for of thee alone was the traitor fain, to thee even his secret thoughts were confided, alone thou knewest his moods and tender fits—go, my sister, and humbly accost the haughty stranger: I did not take the Grecian oath in Aulis to root out the race of Troy; I sent no fleet against her fortresses, neither have I disentombed his father Anchises' ashes and ghost. Why does he refuse my words entrance to his stubborn ears? Whither does he run? let him grant this grace—alas, the last!—to his lover, and await fair winds and an easy passage. No more do I pray for the old delusive marriage, nor that he give up fair Latium and abandon a kingdom. A breathing-space I ask, to give my madness rest and room, till my very fortune teach my grief submission. This last grace I implore—sister, be pitiful—let him but grant me this and I will repay it weighted with my death.'

So she pleaded, and so her sister carries and recarries the piteous tale of weeping. But by no weeping is he stirred, and no words that he hears may bend him. Fate withstands, and lays divine bars on unmoved mortal ears. Even as when the eddying blasts of northern Alpine winds are emulous to uproot the secular strength of a mighty oak, it wails on, and the trunk quivers and the high foliage strews the ground; the tree clings fast on the rocks, and high as her top soars into the aëry sky, so deep strike her roots to hell; even thus is the hero buffeted with changeful perpetual accents, and distress thrills his mighty breast, while his purpose stays unstirred, and her tears are shed in vain.

Then indeed, hapless and dismayed by doom, Dido prays for death, and is weary of looking on the arch of heaven. The more to make her fulfil her purpose and quit the light, she saw, when she laid her gifts on the altars alight with incense, awful to tell, the holy streams blacken, and the wine turn as it poured into ghastly blood. Of this sight she spoke to none—no, not to her sister. Likewise there was within the house a marble temple of her ancient lord, kept of her in marvellous honour, and fastened with snowy fleeces and festal boughs. Forth of it she seemed to hear her husband's voice crying and calling when night was dim upon earth, and alone on the house-tops the screech-owl often made moan with funeral note and long-drawn sobbing cry. Therewithal many a warning of wizards of old terrifies her with appalling presage. In her sleep fierce Aeneas drives her wildly, and ever she seems being left by herself alone, ever going un-companioned on a weary way, and seeking her Tyrians in a solitary land.

So when, overcome by her pangs, she has caught the madness and resolved to die, she works out secretly the time and fashion, and accosts her sorrowing sister with mien hiding her design and hope calm on her brow.

'I have found a way, mine own—wish me joy, sisterlike—to restore him to me or release me of my love for him. Hard by the ocean limit and the set of sun is the extreme Aethiopian land, where ancient Atlas turns on his shoulders the starred burning axletree of heaven. Out of it has been shown to me a priestess of Massylian race, warder of the temple of the Hesperides,[10] even she who gave the dragon his food, and kept the holy boughs on the tree, sprinkling clammy honey and slumberous poppy-seed. She vouches with her spells to relax the pur-poses of whom she will, but on others to bring passion and pain; to stay the river-waters and turn the stars backward: she calls up ghosts by night; thou shalt see earth moaning under foot and mountain-ashes descending from the hills. I take heaven, sweet, to witness, and thee, mine own darling sister, I do not willingly arm myself with the arts of magic. Do thou secretly raise a pyre in the inner court, and lay upon

10. In the fabulous gardens of Hesperides, far in the West, trees bearing golden apples were guarded by a dragon.

it the arms of the man that he cruelly left hanging in our chamber, and all the dress he wore, and the bridal bed where I fell. It is good to wipe out all traces of the accursed one, and the priestess orders thus.' So speaks she, and is silent, while pallor overruns her face. Yet Anna deems not her sister drapes death in these strange rites, and grasps not her wild purpose, nor fears aught deeper than at Sychaeus' death. So she makes ready as bidden.

But the Queen, when the pyre is built up of piled faggots and cleft ilex in the inmost of her dwelling, hangs the room with chaplets and garlands it with funeral boughs: on the pillow she lays the dress he wore, the sword he left, and an image of him, knowing what was to come. Altars are reared around, and the priestess, with hair undone, thrice peals from her lips the hundred gods of Erebus and Chaos, and the triform Hecate, the triple-faced maidenhood of Diana. Likewise she had sprinkled pretended waters of Avernus' spring, and rank herbs are sought mown by moonlight with brazen sickles, dark with milky venom, and sought is the talisman torn from a horse's forehead at birth ere the dam could snatch it. Herself, the holy cake in her pure hands, hard by the altars, with one foot unshod and garments flowing loose, she invokes the gods ere she die, and the stars that know of doom; then prays to whatsoever deity looks in righteousness and re- membrance on lovers ill allied.

Night fell; weary creatures took quiet slumber all over earth, and woodland and wild waters had sunk to rest; now the stars wheel mid- way on their gliding path, now all the country is silent, and beasts and gay birds that haunt liquid levels of lake or •thorny rustic thicket lay couched asleep under the still night. But not so the distressed Phoeni- cian, nor does she ever sink asleep or take the night upon eyes or breast; her pain redoubles, and her love swells to renewed madness, as she tosses on the strong tide of wrath. Even so she begins, and thus revolves with her heart alone:

'Lo, what do I? Shall I again make trial of mine old wooers that will scorn me? and stoop to sue for a Numidian marriage among those whom already over and over I have disdained for husbands? Then shall I follow the Ilian fleets and the uttermost bidding of the Teucrians? because they are glad to have been once raised up by my succour, or the grace of mine old kindness is fresh in their remem- brance? And who will permit me, if I would? or take a hated woman on their proud fleet? art thou ignorant, ah me, even in ruin, and knowest not yet the forsworn race of Laomedon?[11] And then? shall I accompany the triumphant sailors, a lonely fugitive? or plunge forth girt with all my Tyrian train? so hardly severed from Sidon city, shall I again drive them seaward, and bid them spread their sails to the tempest? Nay die thou, as thou deservest, and let the steel end thy pain. With thee it began; overborne by my tears, thou, O my sister, dost load me with this madness and agony, and cast me to the enemy. It was not mine to spend a wild life without stain, far from a bridal chamber, and untouched by this passion. O faith ill kept, that was plighted to Sychaeus' ashes!' Thus her heart broke in long lamentation.

Now Aeneas was fixed to go, and now, with all set duly in order, was taking hasty sleep on his high quarterdeck. To him as he slept the god appeared once again in the same fashion of countenance, and thus seemed to renew his warning, in all points like to Mercury, voice and hue and golden hair and limbs gracious in youth. 'Goddess-born, canst thou sleep on in such danger? and seest not the coming perils that hem thee in, madman! nor hearest the breezes blowing fair? She, fixed on death, is revolving craft and crime grimly in her bosom, and swells the changing surge of wrath. Fliest thou not hence headlong, while headlong flight is yet possible? Even now wilt thou see ocean weltering with broken timbers, see the fierce glare of torches and the beach in a riot of flame, if dawn break on thee yet dallying in this land. Up ho! linger no more! Woman is ever a fickle and changing thing.' So spoke he, and melted in the black night.

Then indeed Aeneas, startled by the sudden phantom, leaps out of slumber and bestirs his crew to headlong haste. 'Awake, O men, and sit down to the thwarts; shake out sail speedily. A god sent from high heaven, lo! again spurs us to speed our flight and cut the twisted cables. We follow thee, holy one of heaven, whoso thou art, and again joyfully obey thy command. O be favourable; give gracious aid and bring fair sky and weather.' He spoke, and snatching his sword like lightning from the sheath, strikes at the hawser with the drawn steel. The same zeal catches all at once; rushing and tearing they quit the shore; the sea is hidden under their fleets; strongly they toss up the foam and sweep the blue water.

11. Laomedon, father of Priam, broke his word on one bargain with Neptune and Apollo, and another with Hercules. Thus Dido's opinion of the Trojans as hereditary liars parallels Aeneas' opinion of the Greeks—and the standard Roman opinion of the Carthaginians. In Latin, "Punic faith" means *duplicity*.

And now Dawn broke, and, leaving the saffron bed of Tithonus,[12] shed her radiance anew over the world; when the Queen saw from her watch-tower the first light whitening, and the fleet standing out under squared sail, and discerned shore and haven empty of all their oarsmen. Thrice and four times she struck her hand on her lovely breast and rent her yellow hair: 'God!' she cries, 'shall he go? shall an alien make mock of our realm? Will they not issue in armed pursuit from all the city, and some launch ships from the dockyards? Go; bring fire in haste, serve out weapons, ply the oars! What do I talk? or where am I? what mad change is on my purpose? Alas, Dido! now evil deeds touch thee; that had been fitting once, when thou gavest away thy crown. Behold the faith and hand of him! who, they say, carries his household's ancestral gods about with him! who stooped his shoulders to a father outworn with age! Could I not have riven his body in sunder and strewn it on the waves? and slain with the sword his comrades and his dear Ascanius, and served him for the banquet at his father's table? But the chance of battle had been dubious. If it had! whom did I fear in the death-agony? I should have borne firebrands into his camp and filled his decks with flame, blotted out father and son and race together, and flung myself atop of all. Sun, whose fires lighten all the works of the world, and thou, Juno, mediatress and witness of these my distresses, and Hecate, cried on by night in crossways of cities, and you, fatal avenging sisters and gods of dying Elissa, hear me now; bend your just deity to my woes, and listen to our prayers. If it must needs be that the accursed one touch his haven and float up to land, if thus Jove's decrees demand, and this is the appointed term,—yet, distressed in war by an armed and gallant nation, driven homeless from his borders, rent from Iülus' embrace, let him sue for succour and see death on death untimely on his people; nor when he has yielded him to the terms of a harsh peace, may he have joy of his kingdom or the pleasant light; but let him fall before his day and without burial amid its soil. This I pray; this and my blood with it I pour for the last utterance. Then do you, O Tyrians, pursue his seed with your hatred for all ages to come; send this guerdon to our ashes. Let no kindness nor truce be between the nations. Arise, some avenger, out of our dust, to follow the Dardanian settlers with firebrand and steel. Now, then, whensoever strength shall be given, I invoke the enmity of shore to

12. Dawn (Eos) loved Tithonus and prayed to the higher gods to make him immortal. They gave him immortality, but not perpetual youth.

shore, wave to water, sword to sword; let their battles go down to their children's children.'[13]

So speaks she as she kept turning her mind round about, seeking how soonest to break away from the hateful light. Thereon she speaks briefly to Barce, nurse of Sychaeus; for a heap of dusky ashes held her own, in her country of long ago:

'Sweet nurse, bring Anna my sister hither to me. Bid her haste and sprinkle river water over her body, and bring with her the beasts ordained for expiation: so let her come: and thou likewise veil thy brows with a pure chaplet. I would fulfil the rites of Stygian Jove[14] that I have fitly ordered and begun, so to set the limit to my distresses and give over to flame the pyre of the Dardanian chief.'

So speaks she; the old woman went eagerly with quickened pace. But Dido, panting and fierce in her awful purpose, with bloodshot restless gaze, and spots on her quivering cheeks burning through the pallor of imminent death, bursts into the inner courts of the house, and mounts in madness the lofty stairs, and unsheathes the sword of Dardania, a gift sought for other use than this. Then after her eyes fell on the Ilian raiment and the bed she knew, dallying a little with her purpose through her tears, she sank on the pillow and spoke the last words of all:

'Dress he wore, sweet while doom and deity allowed! receive my spirit now, and release me from my distresses. I have lived and fulfilled Fortune's allotted course; and now shall I go a queenly phantom under the earth. I have built a renowned city; I have seen my ramparts rise; by my brother's punishment I have avenged my husband of his enemy; happy, ah me! and over happy, had but the keels of Dardania never touched our shores!' She spoke; and burying her face in the pillow, 'Death it will be,' she cries, 'and unavenged; but death be it. Thus, thus is it good to pass into the dark. Let the pitiless Dardanian's gaze drink in this fire out at sea, and my death be the omen he carries on his way.'

She ceased; and even as she spoke her people see her sunk on the steel, and blood reeking on the sword and spattered on her hands. A cry rises in the high halls; Rumour riots down the quaking city. The house resounds with lamentation and sobbing and bitter crying of women;

13. Dido's curse is designed by Virgil as an explanation of the rivalry and hatred between Rome and Carthage which led to the three Punic Wars (265-146 B.C.) and the final destruction of Carthage. The specific avenger demanded by Dido is Hannibal, who in the Second Punic War annihilated two Roman armies and maintained his own forces in Italy for years.

14. *Stygian Jove*, Pluto.

heaven echoes their loud wails; even as though all Carthage or ancient Tyre went down as the foe poured in, and the flames rolled furious over the roofs of house and temple. Death-stricken her sister heard, and in swift hurrying dismay, with torn face and smitten bosom, darts through them all, and calls the dying woman by her name. 'Was it this, mine own? Was my summons a snare? Was it this thy pyre, ah me, this thine altar fires meant? How shall I begin my desolate moan? Didst thou disdain a sister's company in death? Thou shouldst have called me to share thy doom; in the self-same hour, the self-same pang of steel had been our portion. Did these very hands build it, did my voice call on our father's gods, that with thee lying thus I should be away, O merciless? Thou hast destroyed thyself and me together, O my sister, and the Sidonian lords and people, and this thy city. Give her wounds water: I will bathe them and catch on my lips the last breath that haply yet lingers.'[15] So speaking she had climbed the high steps, and, wailing, clasped and caressed her half-lifeless sister in her bosom, and stanched the dark streams of blood with her gown. She, essaying to lift her heavy eyes, swoons back; the deep-driven wound gurgles in her breast. Thrice she rose, and strained to lift herself on her elbow; thrice she rolled back on the pillow, and with wandering eyes sought the light of high heaven, and moaned as she found it.

Then Juno omnipotent, pitying her long pain and difficult decease, sent Iris down from heaven to unloose the struggling life from the body where it clung. For since neither by fate did she perish, nor as one who had earned her death, but woefully before her day, and fired by sudden madness, not yet had Proserpine taken her tress from the golden head, nor sentenced her to the nether Stygian world. So Iris on dewy saffron pinions flits down through the sky athwart the sun in a trail of a thousand changing dyes, and stopping over her head: 'This lock, sacred to Dis, I take as bidden, and release thee from that body of thine.' So speaks she, and cuts it with her hand.[16] And therewith all the warmth ebbed forth from her, and the life passed away upon the winds.

[BOOK V: As the fleet stands out to sea, the Trojans look back and see the glow of Dido's funeral pyre. They are not sure what it is, "but the

15. This was the duty of the nearest relative present at the time of death.
16. The dead were considered as an offering to Pluto (Dis) and Proserpine, and a lock of hair was cut from the dying in the same way as hair was cut from the foreheads of sacrificial animals and thrown on the fire of the altar. Since Dido's death is sudden and wilful (not fated), her life lingers, Proserpine delays, and Juno sends Iris to release Dido from life.

bitter pain of a great love trampled, and the knowledge of what woman can do in madness draw the Teucrians' hearts to gloomy guesses." They steer for Italy, but threatening weather makes them stop off in Sicily at the friendly Trojan colony headed by Acestes. Here they celebrate the first anniversary of Anchises' death by holding the traditional funeral games in his honor: a boat-race, a foot-race, a boxing-match, an archery contest, and cavalry maneuvers.

While this is going on, Juno leads some of the women of Aeneas' fleet, weary of wandering, to set the ships on fire. Jupiter sends rain to save the ships. Aeneas decides to leave the "souls that are content to have none of glory" to settle in Sicily. Venus gets a promise of Neptune that he will protect the Trojans on their voyage to Italy—only one man (the pilot Palinurus) will be lost.]

BOOK VI

[The Trojans land in Italy, and Aeneas seeks out the Cumaean Sibyl in order to hear her prophecies and to gain instructions for visiting Anchises in Hades. Before he can enter Hades, he must secure a golden bough as a talisman and propitiate the shade of an unburied Trojan. When these things have been done, the Sibyl leads him to the Styx, where he sees the shades of the unburied (including Palinurus) refused passage. After crossing the Styx and getting past Cerberus, they see the children who died in infancy, and the suicides.]

And not far from here are shewn stretching on every side the Wailing Fields; so they call them by name. Here they whom pitiless love has wasted in cruel decay hide among untrodden ways, shrouded in embosoming myrtle thickets; not death itself ends their distresses. In this region he discerns Phaedra and Procris and woeful Eriphyle, shewing on her the wounds of her merciless son, and Evadne and Pasiphaë; Laodamia goes in their company, and she who was once Caeneus and a man, now woman, and again returned by fate into her shape of old. Among whom Dido the Phoenician, fresh from her death-wound, wandered into the vast forest; by her the Trojan hero stood, and knew the dim form through the darkness, even as the moon at the month's beginning to him who sees or thinks he sees her rising through the vapours; he let tears fall, and spoke to her lovingly and sweet:

'Alas, Dido! so the news was true that reached me; thou didst perish, and the sword sealed thy doom! Ah me, was I cause of thy death? By the stars I swear, by the heavenly powers and all that is sacred beneath the earth, unwillingly, O queen, I left thy shore. But the gods' commands, which now compel me to pass through this shadowy place, this land of mouldering overgrowth and deep night, drove me imperiously forth; nor could I deem my departure would bring thee pain so great. Stay thy footstep, and withdraw not from our gaze. From whom fliest thou? the last speech of thee fate ordains me is this.'

In such words and with starting tears Aeneas soothed the burning and fierce-eyed spirit. She turned away with looks fixed fast on the ground, stirred no more in countenance by the speech he essays than if she stood in iron flint or Marpesian stone.[1] At length she started, and fled wrathfully into the shadowy woodland, where Sychaeus, in responsive passion and equal love, is her husband as long ago. Yet Aeneas, dismayed by her cruel doom, follows her far on her way with pitying tears.

Thence he pursues his appointed path. And now they trod those utmost fields where the renowned in war have their haunt apart. Here Tydeus meets him; here Parthenopaeus, glorious in arms, and the pallid phantom of Adrastus; here the Dardanians long wept on earth and fallen in the war; sighing he discerns all their long array, Glaucus and Medon and Thersilochus, the three sons of Antenor, and Polyboetes, Ceres' priest, and Idaeus yet charioted, yet grasping his arms. The souls throng round him to right and left; nor is one look enough; it delights them to linger on, to pace by his side and learn wherefore he is come. But the princes of the Grecians and Agamemnon's armies, when they see him glittering in arms through the gloom, hurry terror-stricken away; some turn backward, as when of old they fled to the ships; some raise their voice faintly, and gasp out a broken ineffectual cry. . . .

[Aeneas talks with Deiphobus, a Trojan who had married Helen after the death of Paris, and who had been horribly mutilated and killed by Menelaos after the fall of Troy.

The Sibyl interrupts this conversation, and they pass on by the walls of Tartarus. Aeneas inquires about the horrible sounds that issue from Tartarus, and the Sibyl explains the punishments which the wicked endure there.]

Now at length they came to the happy place, the green pleasances and blissful seats of the Fortunate Woodlands. Here an ampler air

1. *Marpesian stone*, marble.

clothes the meadows in lustrous sheen, and they know their own sun
and a starlight of their own. Some exercise their limbs in tournament
on the greensward, contend in games, and wrestle on the yellow sand.
Some dance with beating footfall and lips that sing; with them is the
Thracian priest[2] in sweeping robe, and makes music to their measures
with the notes' sevenfold interval, the notes struck now with his
fingers, now with his ivory rod. Here is Teucer's ancient brood, a
generation excellent in beauty, heroic souls born in happier years, Ilus
and Assaracus, and Dardanus, founder of Troy. Afar he marvels at the
armour and chariots empty of their lords: their spears stand fixed in
the ground, and their unyoked horses pasture at large over the plain:
their life's delight in chariot and armour, their care in pasturing their
sleek horses, follows them in like wise to their place under earth.
Others, lo! he beholds feasting on the sward to right and left, and
singing in chorus the glad Paean-cry, within a scented laurel-grove
whence Eridanus river surges upward full-volumed through the wood.
Here is the band of them who bore wounds in fighting for their
country, and they who were pure in priesthood while life endured, and
the good poets whose speech abased not Apollo; and they who made
life beautiful by the arts of their invention, and who won by service a
memory among others. . . .

But lord Anchises, deep in the green valley, was musing in earnest
survey over the imprisoned souls destined to the daylight above, and
haply reviewing his beloved children and all the tale of his people,
them and their fates and fortunes, their works and ways. And he, when
he saw Aeneas advancing to meet him over the greensward, stretched
forth both hands eagerly, while tears rolled over his cheeks, and his lips
parted in a cry: 'Art thou come at last, and has thy love, child of my
desire, conquered the difficult road? Is it granted, O my son, to gaze on
thy face, to hear and to answer in the speech we know? Thus indeed
did I forecast in spirit, counting the days between; nor has my care
misled me. What lands, what space of seas hast thou traversed to reach
me, through what surge of perils, O my son! How I dreaded lest the
realm of Libya might work thee harm!'

And he: 'Thy melancholy phantom, thine, O my father, came
before me often and often, and moved me to steer to these portals. My
fleet is anchored on the Tyrrhenian brine. Give thine hand to clasp, O
my father, give it, and withdraw not from our embrace.'

So spoke he, his face wet the while with abundant weeping. Thrice
there did he essay to fling his arms about his neck; thrice the phantom

2. *the Thracian priest*, Orpheus.

vainly grasped fled out of his hands even as light wind, and most like to fluttering sleep.

Meanwhile Aeneas sees deep withdrawn in the covert of the vale a woodland and rustling forest thickets, and the river of Lethe that floats past the peaceful dwellings. Around it flittered nations and peoples innumerable; even as in the meadows when in clear summer weather bees settle on the variegated flowers and stream round the snow-white lilies, all the plain is murmurous with their humming. Aeneas starts at the sudden view, and asks the reason he knows not; what are those spreading streams, or who are they whose endless train fills the banks? Then lord Anchises: 'Souls, for whom second bodies are destined and due, drink at the wave of the Lethean stream the heedless water of long forgetfulness. These of a truth have I long desired to tell thee and show thee face to face, and number all the generation of thy children, that so thou mayest the more rejoice with me in finding Italy.'—'O father, must we think that any souls travel hence into upper air, and return again to bodily fetters? why this strange sad longing for the light?' 'I will tell,' rejoins Anchises, 'nor will I hold thee in suspense, O my son.' And he unfolds all things in order one by one.

'First of all, heaven and earth and the liquid fields, the shining orb of the moon and the Titanian star,[3] doth a spirit sustain inly, and a soul shed abroad in them sways all their members and mingles in the mighty frame. Thence is the generation of man and beast, the life of winged things, and the monstrous forms that ocean breeds under his glittering floor. Those seeds have fiery force and divine birth, so far as they are not clogged by sinful bodies and dulled by earthy frames and limbs ready to die. From these is it that they fear and desire, sorrow and rejoice; nor do their eyes pierce the air while barred in the blind darkness of their prison-house. Nay, even when the last ray of life is gone, nor yet, alas! does all their woe, nor do all the plagues of the body wholly leave them free; and needs must be that many a long-hardened evil should take root marvellously deep. Therefore they are schooled in punishment, and pay all the forfeit of a lifelong ill; some are hung stretched to the viewless winds; some have the taint of guilt washed away beneath the dreary deep, or burned out in fire. We suffer, each in his own ghost; thereafter we are sent to the broad spaces of Elysium, some few of us to possess the happy fields; till length of days

3. *Titanian star*, probably the sun, though there is some question as to the exact meaning.

completing time's circle takes out the clotted soilure and leaves un-
tainted the ethereal sense and pure spiritual flame. All these before
thee, when the wheel of a thousand years has come fully round, a God
summons in vast train to the river of Lethe, that so they may regain in
forgetfulness the slopes of upper earth again, and begin to desire to
return into the body.'

Anchises ceased, and leads his son and the Sibyl likewise amid the
assembled murmurous throng, and mounts a hillock whence he might
scan all the long ranks and learn their countenances as they came.

'Now come, the glory hereafter to follow our Dardanian progeny,
the posterity to abide in our Italian people, illustrious souls and in-
heritors of our name to be, these will I rehearse, and instruct thee of
thy destinies. He yonder, seest thou? the warrior who leans on his
pointless spear, holds the place allotted nearest to daylight, and shall
rise first into the air of heaven from the mingling blood of Italy,
Silvius[4] of Alban name, the child of thine age, whom late in thy length
of days thy wife Lavinia shall nurture in the woodland, king and
father of kings; from him in Alba the Long shall our house have
dominion. He next him is Procas, glory of the Trojan race; and Capys
and Numitor; and he who shall renew thy name, Silvius Aeneas,
eminent alike in goodness or in arms, if ever he shall receive his
kingdom in Alba.[5] Nay, Romulus likewise, seed of Mavors, shall join
his grandsire's company, from his mother Ilia's nurture and Assaracus'
blood. Seest thou how the twin plumes stand upright on his crest, and
his father's own emblazonment already marks him for upper air?
Behold, O son! in his auspices shall Rome the renowned fill earth with
her empire and heaven with her pride, and gird about seven fortresses
with her single wall, prosperous mother of men. Hither now bend thy
twin-eyed gaze; behold this people, the Romans that are thine. Here is
Caesar and all Iülus' posterity that shall arise under the mighty cope of
heaven. Here is he, he of whose promise thou hearest so often, Caesar
Augustus, a god's son,[6] who shall again establish the ages of gold in
Latium over the fields that once were the realm of Saturn, and carry
his empire afar to Garamant and Indian, to the land that lies beyond

---

4. Ascanius founded Alba Longa, but the Alban royal house was descended
from Silvius—from the union of Trojan and Latin blood. The headless spear
is a symbol of royalty.

5. Silvius Aeneas, son of the Silvius mentioned above, was kept from the
throne by an uncle who had been his guardian until he was fifty-three years old.

6. This is a bit strained. Julius Caesar was deified after his death, and
Augustus was his adopted son.

our stars, beyond the sun's yearlong ways, where Atlas the sky-bearer wheels on his shoulder the glittering star-spangled pole. Before his coming even now the kingdoms of the Caspian shudder at oracular answers, and the Maeotic land and the mouths of sevenfold Nile shudder in alarm. Wilt thou see also the Tarquin kings, and the haughty soul of Brutus the Avenger,[7] and the fasces regained? He shall first receive a consul's power and the merciless axes, and when his children would stir fresh war, the father, for fair freedom's sake, shall summon them to doom. Unhappy! yet howsoever posterity shall take the deed, love of country and limitless passion for honour shall prevail. Yonder souls[8] likewise, whom thou discernest gleaming in equal arms, at one now, while shut in Night, ah me! what mutual war, what battle-lines and bloodshed shall they summon forth, so they attain the light of the living! father-in-law descending from the Alpine barriers and the fortress of the Dweller Alone, son-in-law facing him with the embattled East. Nay, O my children, harden not your hearts to such warfare, neither turn upon her own heart the mastering might of your country; and thou, be thou first to forgive, who drawest thy descent from heaven; cast down the weapons from thy hand, O blood of mine. He[9] shall drive his conquering chariot to the Capitoline height triumphant over Corinth, glorious in Achaean slaughter. He shall uproot Argos and Agamemnonian Mycenae, and the Aeacid's own heir, the seed of Achilles mighty in arms, avenging his ancestors in Troy and Minerva's polluted temple. Others shall beat out the breathing bronze to softer lines, I believe it well; shall draw living lineaments from the marble; the cause shall be more eloquent on their lips; their pencil shall portray the pathways of heaven, and tell the stars in their arising: be thy charge, O Roman, to rule the nations in thine empire; this shall be thine art, to ordain the law of peace, to be merciful to the conquered and beat the haughty down.' . . .

Thus they wander up and down over the whole region of broad vaporous plains, and scan all the scene. And when Anchises had led his son over it, each point by each, and kindled his spirit with passion for the glories on their way, he tells him thereafter of the war he next

7. Brutus the Avenger expelled the tyrannous Tarquin kings from Rome, thus avenging the rape of Lucretia and the wrongs of the populace, and recovering popular control of the government, symbolized by the fasces. His two sons joined a conspiracy to restore the Tarquins, and Brutus, as consul, presided over their trial, flogging, and beheading.

8. Caesar and his son-in-law, Pompey.

9. This shade and the one described in the next sentence are Mummius and Paulus, Roman conquerors of Greece.

must wage, and instructs him of the Laurentine peoples and the city of Latinus, and in what wise he may avoid or endure every burden.

There are twin portals of Sleep, whereof the one is fabled of horn, and by it real shadows are given easy outlet; the other shining white of polished ivory, but false visions issue upward from the ghostly world. With these words then Anchises follows forth his son and the Sibyl together there, and dismisses them by the ivory gate. He pursues his way to the ships and revisits his comrades; then bears on to Caieta's haven straight along the shore. The anchor is cast from the prow; the sterns lie aground on the beach.

BOOK VII

[Aeneas and his men land at the mouth of the Tiber. There King Latinus rules, with Amata, his wife, and Lavinia, his daughter. Turnus is a suitor for Lavinia's hand, and is encouraged by Amata, but the omens are against the match: Latinus has received prophecies telling him to marry his daughter to the strangers who will arrive. Aeneas sends an embassy to Latinus, who welcomes the Trojans as the promised strangers.]

And lo! the fierce consort of Jove was returning from Inachian Argos, and held her way along the air, when out of the distant sky, far as from Sicilian Pachynus, she espied the rejoicing of Aeneas and the Dardanian fleet. She sees them already building homes, already trusting in the land, their ships left empty. She stops, shot with sharp pain; then shaking her head, she pours forth these words:

'Ah, hated brood, and doom of the Phrygians that thwarts our doom! Could they perish on the Sigean plains? Could they be ensnared when taken? Did the fires of Troy consume her people? Through the midst of armies and through the midst of flames they have found their way. But, I think, my deity lies at last outwearied, or my hatred is fed full and satisfied? Nay, it is I who have been fierce to follow them over the waves when hurled from their country, and on all the seas to cross their flight. Against the Teucrians the forces of sky and sea are spent. What have availed me Syrtes or Scylla, what desolate Charybdis? they find shelter in their desired Tiber-bed, careless of ocean and of me. Mars availed to destroy the giant race of the Lapithae;[1] the very father of the

---

1. After the king of the Lapithae omitted Mars from the invitation list for his wedding feast, Mars engineered a war between the Centaurs and the Lapithae.

gods gave over ancient Calydon to Diana's wrath:[2] for forfeit of what crime in the Lapithae, what in Calydon? But I, Jove's imperial consort, who have borne, ah me! to leave naught undared, who have shifted to every device, I am vanquished by Aeneas. If my deity is not great enough, I will not assuredly falter to seek succour where it may be found; if I cannot bend the gods, I will stir up Acheron. It may not be to debar him of a Latin realm; be it so; and Lavinia is destined his bride unalterably. But it may be yet to draw out and breed delay in these high affairs; but it may be yet to waste away the nation of either king; at such forfeit of their people may son-in-law and father-in-law enter into union. Blood of Troy and Rutulia[3] shall be thy dower, O maiden, and Bellona[4] is the bridesmaid who awaits thee. Nor did Cisseus' daughter[5] alone conceive a firebrand and travail of bridal flames. Nay, even such a birth has Venus of her own, a second Paris, another balefire for Troy towers reborn.'

These words uttered, she descends to earth in all her terrors, and calls dolorous Allecto[6] from the home of the awful goddesses in nether gloom, whose delight is in woeful wars, in wrath and treachery and evil feuds: hateful to Lord Pluto himself, hateful and horrible to her hell-born sisters; into so many faces does she turn, so savage the guise of each, so thick her black viper-growth. With these words Juno spurs her on, saying thus:

'Grant me, virgin born of Night, this thy proper task and service, that our renown may not be broken or our fame dwindle, nor the Aeneadae have power to win Latinus by marriage or beset the borders of Italy. Thou canst set in armed conflict brothers once united, and overturn families with hatreds; thou canst launch into houses thy whips and deadly brands; thine are a thousand names, a thousand devices of injury. Stir up thy teeming breast, sunder the peace they have joined, and sow seeds of quarrel; let their warriors at once desire and demand and fly to arms.'

Thereon Allecto, steeped in Gorgonian venom, first seeks Latium and the high house of the Laurentine monarch, and silently sits down

2. When the king of Calydon neglected the worship of Diana, she sent a huge wild boar to lay waste the country.
3. *Rutulia*, a district of Latium, south of the Tiber.
4. *Bellona*, a goddess of war, sister of Mars.
5. Before the birth of Paris, Hecuba dreamed that she would give birth to a firebrand which would burn Troy. Juno intends Aeneas to bring destruction to his new Troy by a quarrel over a woman, just as Paris had to the old.
6. *Allecto*, a Fury.

before Amata's doors, whom a woman's distress and anger heated to frenzy over the Teucrians' coming and the marriage of Turnus. At her the goddess flings a snake out of her dusky tresses,[7] and slips it into her bosom to her very inmost heart, that she may embroil all her house under its maddening magic. Sliding between her raiment and smooth breasts, it coils without touch, and instils its viperous breath unseen; the great serpent turns into the twisted gold about her neck, turns into the long ribbon of her chaplet, inweaves her hair, and winds slippery over her body. And while the gliding infection of the clammy poison begins to penetrate her sense and run in fire through her frame, nor as yet has all her breast caught the fire, softly she spoke and in mothers' wonted wise, with many a tear over her daughter's Phrygian bridal:

'Is it to exiles, to Teucrians, that Lavinia is proffered in marriage, O father? and hast thou no compassion on thy daughter and on thyself? no compassion on her mother, whom with the first northern wind the treacherous rover will abandon, steering to sea with his maiden prize? But is it not thus the Phrygian herdsman,[8] winding his way to Lacedaemon, carried Leda's Helen to the Trojan towns? What of thy plighted faith? What of thine ancient care for thy people, and the hand Turnus thy kinsman has clasped so often? If one of alien race from the Latins is sought to be our son, if this stands fixed, and thy father Faunus' commands are heavy upon thee, all the land whose freedom severs it from our sway is to my mind alien, and of this is the divine word. And Turnus, if one retrace the earliest source of his line, is born of Inachus and Acrisius, and of the midmost of Mycenae.'

When in this vain essay of words she sees Latinus fixed against her, and the serpent's maddening poison is sunk deep in her vitals and runs through and through her, then indeed, stung by infinite horrors, hapless and frenzied, she rages wildly through the endless city. Nay, she flies intó the woodland under feigned Bacchic influence, assumes a greater guilt, arouses a greater frenzy, and hides her daughter in the mountain coverts to rob the Teucrians of their bridal and stay the marriage torches. 'Hail, Bacchus!' she shrieks and clamours; 'thou only art worthy of the maiden; for to thee she takes up the lissom wands, about thee she circles in the dance, to thee she trains and consecrates her tresses.' Rumour flies abroad; and the matrons, their breasts kindled with madness, run at once with a single ardour to seek out

7. The hair of Furies is composed of snakes.
8. *Phrygian herdsman*. Paris was a shepherd on Mt. Ida when the goddesses came to him for judgment.

strange dwellings. They have left their homes empty, they throw neck and hair free to the winds; while others fill the air with ringing cries, girt about with fawnskins, and carrying spears of vine. Amid them the infuriate queen holds her blazing pine-torch on high, and chants the wedding of Turnus and her daughter; and rolling her bloodshot gaze, cries sudden and harsh: 'Hear, O mothers of Latium, wheresoever you be; if unhappy Amata has yet any favour in your affection, if care for a mother's right pierces you, untie the fillets from your hair, begin the orgies with me.' Thus, amid woods and wild beasts' solitary places, does Allecto drive the queen on and on with the Bacchic sting.

When their frenzy seemed heightened and her first task complete, the purpose and all the house of Latinus turned upside down, the dolorous goddess next flies onward, soaring on dusky wing, to the walls of the gallant Rutulian. The place was called Ardea once of old; and still Ardea remains a mighty name; but its fortune is past. Here in his high house Turnus now took rest in the black midnight. Allecto puts off her grim feature and the body of a Fury; she transforms her face to an aged woman's, and furrows her brow with ugly wrinkles; she puts on white tresses fillet-bound, and entwines them with an olive spray; she becomes aged Calybe, priestess of Juno's temple, and presents herself before his eyes, uttering thus:

'Turnus, wilt thou brook all these toils poured out in vain, and the conveyance of thy crown to Dardanian settlers? The King denies thee thy bride and the dower thy blood had earned; and a foreigner is sought for heir to the kingdom. Forth now, dupe, and face thankless perils; forth, mow down the Tyrrhenian lines; give the Latins peace in thy protection. This Saturn's omnipotent daughter in very presence commanded me to pronounce to thee, as thou wert lying in the still night. Wherefore arise, and make ready with good cheer to arm thy people and march through thy gates to battle; consume those Phrygian captains that lie with their painted hulls in the beautiful river. All the force of heaven orders thee on. Let King Latinus himself, unless he consents to give thee thy bridal, and abide by his words, be aware and at last make proof of Turnus' arms.'

But he, deriding her inspiration, with the words of his mouth thus answers her again:

'The fleets ride on the Tiber wave; that news has not, as thou deemest, escaped mine ears. Frame not such terrors before me. Neither is Queen Juno forgetful of us. But thee, O mother, overworn old age, exhausted and untrue, frets with vain distress, and amid embattled kings mocks thy presage with false dismay. Thy charge it is to keep the divine images and temples; war and peace shall be in the hands of men whose task is warfare.'

At such words Allecto's wrath blazed out. But amid his utterance a quick shudder overruns his limbs; his eyes are fixed in horror; so thickly hiss the snakes of the Fury, so vast her form expands. Then rolling her fiery eyes, she thrust him back as he would stammer out more, raised two serpents in her hair, and, sounding her whip, resumed with furious tone:

'Behold me the overworn! me whom old age, exhausted and untrue, mocks with false dismay amid embattled kings! Look on this! I am come from the home of the Dread Sisters: war and death are in my hand.'

So speaking, she hurled her torch at him, and pierced his breast with the lurid smoking brand. He breaks from sleep in overpowering fear, his limbs and frame bathed in sweat that starts out all over his body; he shrieks madly for arms, searches for arms on his bed and in his palace. The passion of the sword rages high, the accursed fury of war, and wrath over all: even as when flaming sticks are heaped roaring loud under the sides of a seething caldron, and the boiling tides leap up; the river of water within smokes furiously and swells high in overflowing foam, and now the wave contains itself no longer; the dark steam flies aloft. So, in breach of peace, he orders his chief warriors to march on King Latinus, and bids prepare for battle, to defend Italy and drive the foe from their borders; himself will suffice for Trojans and Latins together. When he uttered these words and called the gods to hear his vows, the Rutulians stir one another up to arms. One the splendour of his youthful beauty, one his royal ancestry fires, another the noble deeds of his hand.

[Allecto now goes to the Trojan camp, where she puts Ascanius' hounds on the trail of a pet stag belonging to a powerful family. Ascanius gives it a mortal wound, and when it staggers back to its owner to die, Allecto manages to bring the two sides to blows, and the first blood is shed. Juno congratulates Allecto on her work, and dismisses her. The Latins now prepare for a general war, and Virgil gives an account of their chief warriors.]

BOOK VIII

[Aeneas is worried by the Latin preparations for war. In a dream, the Tiber appears to him, confirms the earlier prophecies of his success, and tells him that upstream from his camp lives Evander, an Arcadian, who has long been an enemy of the Latins and who will be willing to ally himself with the Trojans. The Tiber will arrest its current and stand stagnant for the night to enable Aeneas to make the voyage to Evander quickly. Aeneas, encouraged by favourable omens, sets out.]

It chanced on that day the Arcadian king paid his accustomed sacrifice to the great son of Amphitryon[1] and all the gods in a grove before the city. With him his son Pallas, with him all the chief of his people and his poor senate were offering incense, and the blood steamed warm at their altars. When they saw the high ships gliding up between the shady woodlands and resting on their silent oars, the sudden sight appals them, and all at once they rise and stop the banquet. Pallas courageously forbids them to break off the rites; snatching up a spear, he flies forward, and from a hillock cries afar: 'O men, what cause has driven you to explore these unknown ways? or whither do you steer? What is your kin, whence your habitation? Is it peace or arms you carry hither?' Then from the lofty stern lord Aeneas thus speaks, stretching forth in his hand a peace-bearing olive bough:

'Thou seest men born of Troy and arms hostile to the Latins, who have driven us to flight in insolent warfare. We seek Evander; carry this message, and tell him that chosen men of the Dardanian captains are come pleading for an armed alliance.'

Pallas stood amazed at the august name. 'Descend,' he cries, whoso thou art, and speak with my father face to face, and enter our home and hospitality.' And giving him the grasp of welcome, he caught and clung to his hand. Advancing, they enter the grove and leave the river. Then Aeneas in courteous words addresses the King:

'Best of the Grecian race, thou whom by fortune's decree I supplicate, holding before me boughs dressed in fillets, no fear stayed me because thou wert a Grecian chief and an Arcadian, or allied by descent to the twin sons of Atreus. Nay, mine own prowess and the sanctity of divine oracles, our ancestral kinship, and the fame of thee that is spread abroad over the earth, have allied me to thee and led me willingly on the path of fate. Dardanus, who sailed to the Teucrian land, the first

1. Hercules is meant, though he was actually the son of Jove.

father and founder of the Ilian city, was born, as Greeks relate, of Electra the Atlantid; Electra's sire is ancient Atlas, whose shoulder sustains the heavenly spheres. Your father is Mercury, whom white Maia conceived and bore on the cold summit of Cyllene; but Maia, if we give any credence to report, is daughter of Atlas, that same Atlas who bears up the starry heavens; so both our families branch from a single blood. In this confidence I sent no embassy, I framed no crafty overtures; myself I have presented mine own person, and come a suppliant to thy courts. The same Daunian[2] race pursues us and thee in merciless warfare; we once expelled, they trust nothing will withhold them from laying all Hesperia wholly beneath their yoke, and holding the two seas that wash it above and below. Accept and return our friendship. We can give brave hearts in war, high souls and men approved in deeds.'

Aeneas ended. The other ere now scanned in a long gaze the face and eyes and all the form of the speaker; then thus briefly returns:

'How gladly, bravest of the Teucrians, do I hail and own thee! how I recall thy father's words and the very tone and glance of great Anchises! For I remember how Priam son of Laomedon, when he sought Salamis on his way to the realm of his sister Hesione, went on to visit the cold borders of Arcadia. Then early youth clad my cheeks with bloom: I admired the Teucrian captains, admired their lord, the son of Laomedon; but Anchises moved high above them all. My heart burned with youthful passion to accost him and clasp hand in hand; I made my way to him, and led him eagerly to Pheneus' high town. Departing he gave me an adorned quiver and Lycian arrows, a scarf interwoven with gold, and a pair of golden bits that now my Pallas possesses. Therefore my hand is already joined in the alliance you seek, and soon as to-morrow's dawn rises again over earth, I will send you away rejoicing in mine aid, and supply you from my store. Meanwhile, since you are come hither in friendship, solemnise with us these yearly rites which we may not defer, and even now learn to be familiar at your comrades' board.'

[After dinner Evander tells of Hercules' killing of the giant Cacus in that vicinity. The next morning he and Aeneas discuss military matters. Evander opens the conversation.]

'Princely chief of the Teucrians, in whose lifetime I will never allow the state or realm of Troy vanquished, our strength is scant to

2. Daunius was an ancestor of Turnus.

succour in war for so great a name. On this side the Tuscan river shuts us in; on that the Rutulian drives us hard, and thunders in arms about our walls. But I purpose to unite to thee mighty peoples and the camp of a wealthy realm; an unforeseen chance offers this for thy salvation. Thou comest at Fate's call. Not far from here stands fast Agylla city, an ancient pile of stone, where of old the Lydian race, eminent in war, settled on the Etruscan ridges. For many years it flourished, till King Mezentius ruled it with insolent sway and armed terror. Why should I relate the horrible murders, the savage deeds of the monarch? May the gods keep them in store for himself and his line! Nay, he would even link dead bodies to living, fitting hand to hand and face to face (the torture!), and in the oozy foulness and corruption of the dreadful embrace so slay them by a lingering death. But at last his citizens, out-wearied by his mad excesses, surround him and his house in arms, cut down his comrades, and hurl fire in his roof. Amid the massacre he escaped to the refuge of Rutulian land and the armed defence of Turnus' friendship. So all Etruria has risen in righteous fury, and in immediate battle claim their king for punishment. Over these thou-sands will I make thee chief, O Aeneas; for their noisy ships crowd all the shore, and they bid the standards advance, while the aged diviner stays them with prophecies: "O chosen men of Maeonia, flower and strength of them of old time, whom righteous anger urges on the enemy, and Mezentius inflames with just wrath, to no Italian is it per-mitted to hold this great nation in control: choose foreigners to lead you." At that, terrified by the divine warning, the Etruscan lines have encamped on the plain; Tarchon himself has sent ambassadors to me with the crown and sceptre of the kingdom, and offers the royal attire will I but enter their camp and accept the Tyrrhene realm. But old age, frozen to dulness, and exhausted with length of life, denies me the load of empire, and my prowess is past its day. I would urge it on my son, did not the mixture of blood by his Sabellian mother make him half a native here. Thou, to whose years and race alike the fates extend their favour, on whom fortune calls, enter thou in, a leader supreme in bravery over Teucrians and Italians. Mine own Pallas like-wise, our hope and comfort, I will send with thee; let him grow used to endure warfare and the stern work of battle under thy teaching, to regard thine actions, and from his earliest years look up to thee. To him will I give two hundred Arcadian cavalry, the choice of our war-like strength, and Pallas as many more to thee in his own name.'

Scarce had he ended; Aeneas, son of Anchises, and trusty Achates

gazed with steadfast face, and, sad at heart, were revolving inly many
a labour, had not the Cytherean sent a sign from the clear sky. For
suddenly a flash and peal come quivering from heaven, and all seemed
in a moment to totter, and the Tyrrhene trumpet-blast to roar along
the sky. They look up; again and yet again the heavy crash re-echoes.
They see in a serene space of sky armour gleam red through a cloud
in the clear air, and ring clashing out. The others stood in amaze; but
the Trojan hero knew the sound and the promise of his goddess
mother; then he speaks: 'Ask not, O friend, ask not in any wise what
fortune this presage announces; it is I who am summoned. This sign
the goddess who bore me foretold she would send from heaven if war
were gathering, and would bring through the air to my succour
armour from Vulcan's hands. . . . Ah, what slaughter awaits the
wretched Laurentines! what a price, O Turnus, wilt thou pay me! how
many shields and helmets and brave bodies of men shalt thou, Lord
Tiber, roll under thy waves! Let them call for armed array and break
the treaty!' . . .

Rumour flies suddenly, spreading over the little town, that they
ride in haste to the courts of the Tyrrhene king. Mothers redouble
their prayers in terror, as fear treads closer on peril and the likeness of
the War God looms larger in sight. Then Evander, clasping the hand
of his departing son, clings to him weeping unsated, and speaks thus:

'Oh, if Jupiter would restore me the years that are past, as I was
when, close under Praeneste, I cut down their foremost ranks and
burned the piled shields of the conquered! then this right hand sent
King Erulus down to hell, though to him at his birth his mother Fero-
nia (awful to tell) had given three lives and triple arms to wield; thrice
must he be laid low in death; yet then this hand took all his lives and
as often stripped him of his arms: in nowise should I now, O son, be
severed from thy dear embrace; never had the insolent sword of
Mezentius on my borders dealt so many cruel deaths, widowed the
city of so many citizens. But you, O heavenly powers, and thou, Jupiter,
Lord and Governor of Heaven, have compassion, I pray, on the Arcadian king, and hear a father's prayers. If your deity and decrees keep
my Pallas safe for me, if I live that I may see him and meet him yet,
I pray for life; any burden soever I have patience to endure. But if, O
Fortune, thou threatenest some dread calamity, now, ah now, may I
break off a cruel life, while anxiety still wavers and expectation is in
doubt, while thou, dear boy, the one delight of my age, art yet clasped

in my embrace; let no bitterer message wound mine ear.' These words the father poured forth at the final parting; his servants bore him swooning within.

[Venus has divine armour made for Aeneas by Vulcan. On the shield are depicted scenes from the future of Rome.]

[BOOK IX: Turnus, being informed by Iris of Aeneas' absence, attacks the Trojan camp. The Trojans stay behind their fortifications and fight a defensive action. Turnus sets out to burn the Trojan fleet, but it has now served its purpose: the ships are turned into mermaids, and set out to sea. Two boys, Nisus and Euryalus, want to accomplish something notable, and volunteer to try to get through the enemy lines to notify Aeneas of their plight. They make a gallant effort, but fail—because they put their friendship above the military objective. Both are killed. Turnus breaks into the Trojan camp, and fights his way out again.]

[BOOK X: Jupiter's question as to the origin of the war in Italy precipitates a violent quarrel between Juno and Venus. Jupiter outlaws any further interference by the gods: "Each as he has begun shall work out his destiny. Jupiter is one and king over all; the fates will find their way."

Aeneas, following Evander's suggestion, has made an alliance with the Etrurians, and is on his way back with an Etrurian fleet when his transformed ships meet him, and one of them tells him of the desperate situation of the Trojan camp. Turnus opposes the landing, and a furious battle develops on the beach. Pallas makes a heroic showing, and is engaged in combat with Lausus, son of Mezentius.]

Meanwhile Turnus' gracious sister[1] bids him come to Lausus' aid, and his fleet chariot parts the ranks. When he saw his comrades, 'It is time,' he cried, 'to stay from battle. I alone must assail Pallas; to me and none other Pallas is due; I would his father himself were here to see.' So speaks he, and his Rutulians draw back from a level space at his bidding. But then as they withdrew, he, wondering at the haughty command, stands in amaze at Turnus, his eyes scanning the vast frame, and his fierce glance perusing him from afar. And with these words he returns the words of the monarch: 'For me, my praise shall even now be in the lordly spoils I win, or in illustrious death: my father will bear

1. Juturna, a nymph.

calmly either lot: away with menaces.' He speaks, and advances into
the level ring. The Arcadians' blood gathers chill about their hearts.
Turnus leaps from his chariot and prepares to close with him. And as
a lion sees from some lofty outlook a bull stand far off on the plain
revolving battle, and flies at him, even such to see is Turnus' coming.
When Pallas deemed him within reach of a spear-throw, he advances,
if so chance may assist the daring of his overmatched strength, and
thus cries into the depth of sky: 'By my father's hospitality and the
board whereto thou camest a wanderer, on thee I call, Alcides;[2] be
favourable to my high emprise; let Turnus even in death discern me
stripping his blood-stained armour, and his swooning eyes endure the
sight of his conqueror.' Alcides heard him, and deep in his heart he
stifled a heavy sigh, and let idle tears fall. Then with kindly words the
father accosts his son:[3] 'Each has his own appointed day; short and
irrecoverable is the span of life for all: but to spread renown by deeds
is the task of valour. Under high Troy town many and many a god's
son fell; nay, mine own child Sarpedon likewise perished. Turnus too
his own fate summons, and his allotted period has reached the goal.'
So speaks he, and turns his eyes away from the Rutulian fields. But
Pallas hurls his spear with all his strength, and pulls his sword flashing
out of the hollow scabbard. The flying spear lights where the armour
rises high above the shoulder, and, forcing a way through the shield's
rim, stayed not till it drew blood from mighty Turnus. At this Turnus
long poises the spear-shaft with its sharp steel head, and hurls it on
Pallas with these words: 'See thou if our weapon have not a keener
point.' He ended; but for all the shield's plating of iron and brass, for
all the bull-hide that covers it round about, the quivering spear-head
smashes it fair through and through, passes the guard of the corslet,
and pierces the breast with a gaping hole. He tears the warm weapon
from the wound; in vain; together and at once life-blood and sense
follow it. He falls heavily on the ground, his armour clashes over him,
and his bloodstained face sinks in death on the hostile soil. And
Turnus standing over him, 'Arcadians,' he cries, 'remember these my
words, and bear them to Evander. I send him back his Pallas as was
due. All the meed of the tomb, all the solace of sepulture, I give freely.
Dearly must he pay his welcome to Aeneas.' And with these words,
planting his left foot on the dead, he tore away the broad heavy sword-

2. *Alcides*, Hercules.
3. Jupiter speaks to Hercules, comforting him for the impending death of
Pallas.

belt engraven with a tale of crime, the array of grooms foully slain together on their bridal night, and the nuptial chambers dabbled with blood,[4] which Clonus, son of Eurytus, had wrought richly in gold. Now Turnus exults in spoiling him of it, and rejoices at his prize. Ah spirit of man, ignorant of fate and the allotted future, or to keep bounds when elate with prosperity!—the day will come when Turnus shall desire to have bought Pallas' safety at a great ransom, and curse the spoils of this fatal day. But with many moans and tears Pallas' comrades lay him on his shield and bear him away amid their ranks. O grief and glory and grace of the father to whom thou shalt return! This one day sent thee first to war, this one day takes thee away, while yet thou leavest heaped high thy Rutulian dead.

[Turnus is hard pressed, and Jove allows Juno to withdraw him from battle temporarily. Mezentius works havoc among the Trojans until he meets Aeneas, who wounds him with a spear. Lausus intervenes to save his father, and Mezentius withdraws under his and others' protection; but Aeneas kills Lausus.]

Meanwhile his father, by the wave of the Tiber river, stanched his wound with water, and rested his body against a tree-trunk. Hard by his brazen helmet hangs from the boughs, and the heavy armour lies quietly on the meadow. Chosen men stand round; he, sick and panting, leans his neck and lets his beard spread down over his chest. Many a time he asks for Lausus, and sends many an one to call him back and carry a grieving parent's commands. But Lausus his weeping comrades were bearing lifeless on his armour, mighty and mightily wounded to death. Afar the soul prophetic of ill knew their lamentation: he soils his grey hairs plenteously with dust, and stretches both hands on high, and clings on the dead. 'Was life's hold on me so sweet, O my son, that I let him I bore receive the hostile stroke in my room? Am I, thy father, saved by these wounds of thine, and living by thy death? Alas and woe! now at last death is bitter! now the wound is driven deep! And I, even I, O my son, stained thy name with crime, driven in hatred from the throne and sceptre of my fathers. I owed vengeance to my country and my people's resentment; might mine own guilty life but have paid it by every form of death! Now I live,

4. The fifty daughters of Danaus, acting on their father's instructions, murdered their husbands (who were also their first cousins) on their wedding night. Only one was spared.

and leave not yet man and day; but I will.' As he speaks thus he raises himself painfully on his thigh, and though the violence of the deep wound cripples him, yet unbroken he bids his horse be brought, his beauty, his comfort, that ever had carried him victorious out of war, and says these words to the grieving beast: 'Rhoebus, we have lived long, if aught at all lasts long with mortals. This day either shalt thou bring back in triumph the gory spoils and head of Aeneas, and we will avenge Lausus' agonies; or if no force opens a way, thou wilt die with me: for I deem not, bravest, thou wilt deign to bear an alien rule and a Teucrian lord.' He spoke, and took his welcome seat on the back he knew, loading both hands with keen javelins, his head sheathed in glittering brass and shaggy horse-hair plumes. Thus he galloped in. Through his heart sweep together the vast tides of shame and mingling madness and grief. And with that he thrice loudly calls Aeneas. Aeneas knew the call, and makes glad invocation: 'So the father of gods speed me, so Apollo on high: do thou essay to close hand to hand.' Thus much he utters, and moves up to meet him with levelled spear. And he: 'Why seek to frighten me, fierce man, now my son is gone? this was thy one road to my ruin. We shrink not from death, nor relent before any of thy gods. Cease; for I come to my death, first carrying these gifts for thee.' He spoke, and hurled a weapon at his enemy; then plants another and yet another as he darts round in a wide circle; but they are stayed on the boss of gold. Thrice he rode wheeling close round him by the left, and sent his weapons strongly in; thrice the Trojan hero turns round, taking the grim forest on his brazen guard. Then, weary of lingering in delay on delay, and plucking out spear-head after spear-head, and hard pressed in the uneven match of battle, with much counselling of spirit now at last he bursts forth, and sends his spear at the war-horse between the hollows of the temples. The creature raises itself erect, beating the air with its feet, throws its rider, and coming down after him in an entangled mass, slips its shoulder as it tumbles forward. The cries of Trojans and Latins kindle the sky. Aeneas rushes up, drawing his sword from the scabbard, and thus above him: 'Where now is fierce Mezentius and all that wild courage of his?' Thereto the Tyrrhenian, as he came to himself and gazing up drank the air of heaven: 'Bitter foe, why these taunts and menaces of death? Naught forbids my slaughter; neither on such terms came I to battle, nor did my Lausus make treaty for this between me and thee. This one thing I beseech thee, by whatsoever grace a vanquished enemy may claim: allow my body sepulture. I know I am girt by the

bitter hatred of my people. Stay, I implore, their fury, and grant me
and my son union in the tomb.' So speaks he, and takes the sword in
his throat unfalteringly, and the lifeblood spreads in a wave over his
armour.

BOOK XI

[Aeneas prepares to send the body of Pallas home, but first he
makes his own lament over it.]

'Did Fortune in her joyous coming,' he cries, 'O luckless boy,
grudge thee to see our realm, and ride victorious to thy father's dwelling? Not this promise of thee had I given to Evander thy sire at my
departure, when he embraced me as I went and bade me speed to a
wide empire, and yet warned me in fear that the men were valiant,
the people obstinate in battle. And now he, fast ensnared by empty
hope, perchance offers vows and heaps gifts on his altars; we, a mourning train, go in hollow honour by his corpse, who now owes no more
to aught in heaven. Unhappy! thou wilt see thy son cruelly slain; is this
the triumphal return we awaited? is this my strong assurance? Yet
thou shalt not see him, Evander, with the shameful wounds of flight,
nor shall death's terrors be welcome to the father because the son lives.
Ah me, what a shield is lost, Iülus, to Ausonia and to thee!'

This lament done, he bids raise the piteous body, and sends a
thousand men chosen from all his army for the last honour of escort,
to mingle in the father's tears; a small comfort in a great sorrow, yet
the unhappy parent's due. Others quickly plait a soft wicker bier of
arbutus rods and oak shoots, and shadow the heaped pillows with a
leafy covering. Here they lay him, high on their rustic strewing; even
as some tender violet or drooping hyacinth-blossom plucked by a
maiden's finger, whose sheen and whose grace is not yet departed,
but no more does Earth the mother feed it or lend it strength. Then
Aeneas bore forth two purple garments stiff with gold, that Sidonian
Dido's own hands, happy over their work, had once wrought for him,
and shot the warp with thread of gold. One of these he sadly folds
round him, a last honour, and veils in its covering the tresses destined
to the fire; and heaps up besides many a Laurentine battle-prize, and
bids his spoils be led forth in long train; with them the horses and
arms whereof he had stripped the enemy, and those, with hands tied
behind their back, whom he would send as nether offering to his ghost,

and sprinkle the blood of their slaying on the flame and bids his captains carry stems dressed in the armour of the foe, with the hostile names fixed on them.[1] Unhappy Acoetes[2] is led along, outworn with age; he smites his breast and rends his face, and flings himself forward all along the ground. Likewise they lead forth the chariot bathed in Rutulian blood; behind goes weeping Aethon the war-horse, his trappings removed, and big drops wet his face. Others bear his spear and helmet, for all else is Turnus' prize. Then follow in mourning array the Teucrians and all the Tyrrhenians, and the Arcadians with arms reversed. When the whole long escorting file had advanced, Aeneas stopped, and sighing deep, pursued thus: 'Once again war's dreadful destiny calls us hence to other tears: hail thou for evermore, O princely Pallas, and for evermore farewell.' And without more words he bent his way to the high walls and advanced towards his camp. . . .

And now flying Rumour, harbinger of the heavy woe, fills Evander and Evander's house and city with the same voice that but now told of Pallas victorious over Latium. The Arcadians stream to the gates, snatching funeral torches after their ancient use; the road gleams with the long line of flame, and parts the fields with a broad pathway of light; the arriving crowd of Phrygians meets them and mingles in mourning array. When the matrons saw all the train approach their dwellings they kindle the town with loud wailing. But no force may withhold Evander; he comes amid them; the bier is set down; he flings himself on Pallas, and clasps him with tears and sighs, and scarcely at last does grief let loose his utterance. 'Not this, O Pallas! was the promise that thou hadst given thy father. Hadst thou been content to plunge less recklessly into the fury of battle! I knew well how strong was the fresh pride of arms and the sweetness of honour in a first battle. Ah, unhappy first-fruits of his youth and bitter prelude of the war upon our borders! ah, vows and prayers of mine that no god heard! and thou, holiest of wives, happy that thou art dead and not spared for this sorrow! But I have outgone my destiny in living, to stay here the survivor of my child. Would I had followed the allied arms of Troy, to be overwhelmed by Rutulian weapons! Would my life had been given, and I and not my Pallas were borne home in this procession! I would not blame you, O Teucrians, nor our treaty and

---

1. The arms stripped from the victims of Pallas are hung on the lopped branches of trees, and to each tree is attached a sign bearing the name of the warrior whose arms are displayed on it.
2. *Acoetes*, Evander's armour-bearer.

the friendly hands we clasped: our old age had that appointed debt to pay. Yet if untimely death awaited my son, we will be glad that he perished leading the Teucrians into Latium, and slew his Volscian thousands before he fell. Nay, no other funeral would I deem thy due, my Pallas, than good Aeneas does, than the mighty Phrygians, than the Tyrrhene captains and all the army of Tyrrhenia. Great are the trophies they bring on whom thine hand deals death; thou also, Turnus, wert standing now a great trunk dressed in arms, had his age and his strength of years equalled thine. But why does my misery keep back the Trojans from arms? Go, and forget not to carry this message to your king: Thine hand keeps me lingering in a life that is hateful since Pallas fell, and Turnus is the debt thou seest son and father claim: for thy virtue and thy fortune this scope alone is left. I ask not joy in life; I may not; but to carry this to my son deep in the under world.'

[A truce has been made to allow for burial of the dead. During this period the Latins learn that a hoped alliance has fallen through. A council deliberates on offers of peace, but Turnus blocks any such move. The life and death of the warrior-maiden Camilla are described. Finally, the Latins are driven within their walls.]

BOOK XII

[In spite of the protests of Latinus and Amata, Turnus challenges Aeneas to a single combat to decide the issues of the war. Aeneas accepts, and the terms are drawn up; but Juno sends Turnus' sister, Juturna, to egg the Latins on to break the agreement and resume the general fighting. Aeneas, in trying to stop it, is wounded by an arrow, but is healed by Venus. Juturna, assuming the form of Turnus' charioteer, tries to protect him by leading him out of the press of the battle. Aeneas attacks the city, and Amata hangs herself. Finally Turnus recognizes the fact that only his sister has protected him, and that the city is doomed.]

As the scene shifted before him Turnus froze in horror and stood in dumb gaze; together in his heart sweep the vast mingling tides of shame and maddened grief, and love stung to frenzy and resolved valour. So soon as the darkness cleared and light returned to his soul, he fiercely turned his blazing eyeballs towards the ramparts, and gazed

back from his wheels on the great city. And lo! a spire of flame wreath-
ing through the floors wavered up skyward and held a turret fast, a
turret that he himself had reared of mortised planks and set on rollers
and laid with high gangways. 'Now, O my sisters, now fate prevails:
cease to hinder; let us follow where deity and stern fortune call. I am
resolved to face Aeneas, resolved to bear what bitterness there is in
death; nor shalt thou longer see me shamed, sister of mine. Let me be
mad, I pray thee, with this madness before the end.' He spoke, and
leapt swiftly from his chariot to the field, and darting through weapons
and through enemies, leaves his sorrowing sister, and bursts in rapid
course amid their columns. And as when a rock rushes headlong from
some mountain peak, torn away by the blast, or if the rushing rain
washes it away, or the stealing years loosen its ancient hold; the reckless mountain mass goes sheer and impetuous, and leaps along the
ground, hurling with it forests and herds and men; thus through the
scattering columns Turnus rushes to the city walls, where the earth is
wettest with bloodshed and the air sings with spears; and beckons with
his hand, and thus begins aloud: 'Forbear now, O Rutulians, and you,
Latins, stay your weapons. Whatsoever fortune is left is mine: I singly
must expiate the treaty for you all, and make decision with the sword.'
All drew aside and left him room.

But lord Aeneas, hearing Turnus' name, abandons the walls,
abandons the fortress height, and in exultant joy flings aside all
hindrance, breaks off all work, and clashes his armour terribly, vast as
Athos,[1] or as Eryx, or as the lord of Apennine when he roars with his
tossing ilex woods and rears his snowy crest rejoicing into air. Now
indeed Rutulians and Trojans and all Italy turned in emulous gaze,
both they who held the high city, and they whose ram was battering
the wall below, and took off the armour from their shoulders. Latinus
himself stands in amaze at the mighty men, born in distant quarters
of the world, met and making decision with the sword. And they, in
the empty level field that cleared for them, darting swiftly forward,
and hurling their spears from far, close in battle shock with clangour of
brazen shields. Earth utters a moan; the sword-strokes fall thick and
fast, chance and valour joining in one. And as in broad Sila or high
on Taburnus, when two bulls rush to deadly battle forehead to forehead, the herdsmen retire in terror, all the cattle stand dumb in dismay, and the heifers murmur in doubt which shall be lord in the
woodland, which the whole herd must follow; they violently deal

1. Athos, Eryx, and "the lord of Apennine" are mountains.

many a mutual wound, and gore with their stubborn horns, bathing
their necks and shoulders in abundant blood; all the woodland echoes
back their bellowing with a moan: even thus Aeneas of Troy and the
Daunian hero rush together shield to shield; the mighty crash fills
the sky, Jupiter himself holds up the two scales in even balance, and
lays in them the different fates of both, trying which shall pay forfeit
of the strife, whose weight shall sink in death. Turnus darts out,
thinking it secure, and rises with his whole reach of body on his uplifted sword; then strikes; Trojans and Latins cry out in alarm, and
both armies strain their gaze. But the treacherous sword shivers, and
in mid-stroke deserts its eager lord. If flight aid him not now! He
flies swifter than the wind, when once he descries a strange hilt in his
weaponless hand. Rumour is that in his headlong haste, when mounting behind his yoked horses to begin the battle, he left his father's
sword behind and caught up his charioteer Metiscus' weapon; and that
served him long, while Teucrian stragglers turned their backs; when
it met the divine Vulcanian armour, the mortal blade like brittle ice
snapped in the stroke; the shards lie glittering upon the yellow
sand. So in distracted flight Turnus darts afar over the plain, and now
this way and now that crosses in wavering circles; for on all hands
the Teucrians locked him in crowded ring, and the waste marsh on
this side, on this the steep city ramparts hem him in.

Therewith Aeneas pursues, though ever and anon his knees, dis-
abled by the arrow, hinder him and refuse to run; and foot hard on
foot presses hotly on his hurrying enemy. Then indeed a cry goes up,
and banks and pools answer round about, and all the sky echoes the
din. He, even as he flies, chides all his Rutulians, calling each by name,
and shrieks for the sword he knows. But Aeneas denounces death and
instant doom if one of them draw nigh, and doubles their terror with
threats of their city's destruction, and though wounded presses on.
Five circles they cover at full speed and unwind as many, this way and
that; for not light nor slight is the prize they seek, but Turnus' very
lifeblood is at issue. Here had stood a bitter-leaved wild olive, sacred
to Faunus; but the Teucrians, unregarding, had cleared away the
sacred stem, that they might meet on unimpeded lists. Here was
lodged Aeneas' spear; hither borne by its own speed it was held fast
stuck in the tough root. The Dardanian stooped over it, and would
wrench away the steel, to follow with the weapon him whom he could
not catch in running. Then indeed Turnus cries in frantic terror:
'Faunus, have pity, I beseech thee! and thou, most gracious Earth, keep

thy hold on the steel, if I alway have kept your worship, and the Aeneadae contrariwise have profaned it in war.' He spoke, and called the god to aid in vows that fell not fruitless. For all Aeneas' strength, his long struggling and delay over the tough stem availed not to unclose the hard grip of the wood. While he strains and pulls hard, the Daunian goddess,[2] changing once more into the charioteer Metiscus' likeness, runs forward and passes her brother his sword. But Venus, indignant that the Nymph might be so bold, drew nigh and wrenched away the spear where it stuck deep in the root. Erect in fresh courage and arms, he with his faithful sword, he towering fierce over his spear, they face one another panting in the battle shock.

Meanwhile the King of Heaven's omnipotence accosts Juno as she gazes on the battle from a sunlit cloud. 'What yet shall be the end, O wife? what remains at the last? Aeneas is claimed by Heaven as his country's god, thou thyself knowest and avowest to know, and is lifted by fate to the stars. With what device or in what hope hangest thou chill in cloudland? Was it well that a deity should be sullied by a mortal's wound? or that the lost sword—for what without thee could Juturna avail?—should be restored to Turnus and swell the force of the vanquished? Forbear now, I pray, and bend to our entreaties; let not all this pain devour thee in silence, and distress so often flood back on me from thy sweet lips. The end is come. Thou hast had power to hunt the Trojans on land or wave, to kindle accursed war, to put the house in mourning, and plunge the bridal in grief: further attempt I forbid thee.' Thus Jupiter began: thus the goddess, daughter of Saturn, returned with humbled aspect:

'Even because this thy will, great Jupiter, is known to me for thine, have I left, though loth, Turnus and earth; nor else wouldst thou see me now, alone on this skyey seat, enduring even past endurance; but girt in flame I were standing by their very lines, and dragging the Teucrians into the deadly battle. I counselled Juturna, I confess it, to succour her hapless brother, and for his life's sake favoured a greater daring; yet not the arrow-shot,[3] not the bending of the bow, I swear by the merciless well-head of the Stygian spring, the single ordained dread of the gods in heaven. And now I retire, and leave the battle in loathing. This thing I beseech thee, that is bound by no fatal law, for Latium and for the majesty of thy kindred. When now they shall plight peace with prosperous marriages (be it so!), when now they

2. Juturna.
3. The shot which had wounded Aeneas.

shall join in laws and treaties, bid thou not the native Latins change
their name of old, nor become Trojans and take the Teucrian name,
or change their language, or alter their attire: let Latium be, let Alban
kings endure through ages, let Italian valour be potent in the race of
Rome. Troy is fallen; let her and her name lie where they fell.'

To her smilingly the designer of men and things:

'Jove's own sister thou art, and second offspring of Saturn, such
surge of wrath tosses within thy breast! But come, allay this madness
so vainly stirred. I give thee thy will, and yield thee ungrudged victory. Ausonia shall keep her native speech and usage, and as her name
is, it shall be. The Trojans shall sink incorporate with them; I will add
their sacred law and ritual, and make all Latins and of a single speech.
Hence shall spring a race of tempered Ausonian blood, whom thou
shalt see outdo men and gods in duty; nor shall any nation so observe
thy worship.' To this Juno assented, and in gladness withdrew her
purpose; meanwhile she quits her cloud, and retires out of the sky.

This done, the Father revolves inly another counsel, and prepares
to separate Juturna from her brother's arms. Twin monsters there are
called the Awful Ones by name, whom with infernal Megaera⁴ the
dead of night bore at one single birth, and wreathed them in like
serpent coils, and clothed them in windy wings. They appear at Jove's
throne and in the courts of the grim king, and quicken the terrors of
wretched men whensoever the lord of heaven deals sicknesses and
dreadful death, or sends terror of war upon guilty cities. One of these
Jupiter sent swiftly down from the height of heaven, and bade her meet
Juturna for an omen. She wings her way, and darts in a whirlwind to
earth. Even as an arrow through a cloud darting from the string,
which Parthian has poisoned with bitter gall, Parthian or Cydonian,
and sped the immedicable shaft, leaps through the swift shadow whistling and unknown; so sprang and swept to earth the daughter of
Night. When she espies the Ilian ranks and Turnus' columns, suddenly shrinking to the shape of a small bird that often sits late by night
on tombs or ruinous roofs, and vexes the darkness with her cry, in
such change of likeness the monster shrilly passes and repasses before
Turnus' face, and her wings beat restlessly on his shield. A strange
numbing terror unnerves his limbs, his hair thrills up, and the voice in
his throat was choked. But when Juturna his hapless sister knew afar
the whistling wings of the Fury, she unbinds and tears her tresses,
with rent face and smitten bosom. 'How, O Turnus, can thine own

4. *Megaera*, one of the Furies, daughters of Night.

sister help thee now? or what more is there if I break not under this?
By what device may I lengthen out thy day? can I contend with this
ominous thing? Now, now I quit the field. . . .

So spoke she, and wrapping her head in her grey vesture, the
goddess moaning sore sank in the river depth.

But Aeneas presses on, brandishing his vast tree-like spear, and
fiercely speaks thus: 'What more delay is there now? or why, Turnus,
dost thou yet shrink away? Not in speed of foot, in grim arms, hand
to hand, must be the conflict. Transform thyself as thou wilt, and
collect what strength of courage or skill is thine; pray that thou mayest
wing thy flight to the stars on high, or that sheltering earth may shut
thee in.' The other, shaking his head: 'Thy fierce words dismay me
not, insolent! the gods dismay me, and Jupiter's enmity.' And no
more said, his eyes light on a vast stone, a stone ancient and vast that
haply lay upon the plain, set for a landmark to divide contested
fields: scarcely might twelve chosen men lift it on their shoulders, of
such frame as now earth breeds mankind: then the hero caught it up
with shaking hand and whirled it at the enemy, rising higher and
quickening his speed. But he knows not his own self running nor going nor lifting his hands or moving the mighty stone; his knees totter,
his blood freezes cold; the very stone he hurls, spinning through the
empty void, neither wholly reached its distance nor carried its blow
home. And as in sleep, when rest at night weighs down our tired eyes,
we seem vainly to will to run eagerly on, and sink faint amidst our
struggles; the tongue is powerless, the familiar strength fails the body,
nor do words or utterance follow: so the awful goddess brings to
naught all the valour of Turnus where he seeks a way. Shifting thoughts
pass through his breast; he gazes on his Rutulians and on the city, and
falters in terror, and shudders at the imminent death; neither sees he
whither he may escape nor what force is his to meet the foe, and nowhere his chariot, nowhere his sister at the reins. As he wavers Aeneas
poises the deadly weapon, and, marking his chance, hurls it in from
afar with all his strength of body. Never with such a roar are stones
hurled from some engine on ramparts, nor does the thunder burst in
so loud a peal. Carrying grim death with it, the spear flies in fashion
of some dark whirlwind, and opens the rim of the corslet and 'the
utmost circles of the sevenfold shield. Right through the thigh it
passes hurtling on; under the blow Turnus falls huge to earth with
his leg doubled under him. The Rutulians start up with a groan, and
all the hill echoes round about, and the width of high woodland re-

turns their cry. Lifting up beseechingly his humbled eyes and suppliant hand: 'I have deserved it,' he says, 'nor do I ask for mercy; use
thy fortune. If an unhappy parent's distress may at all touch thee, this
I pray; even such a father was Anchises to thee; pity Daunus' old
age, and restore to my kindred which thou wilt, me or my body bereft
of day. Thou art conqueror, and the Ausonians have seen me stretch
conquered hands. Lavinia is thine in marriage; press not hatred
farther.'

Aeneas stood wrathful in arms, with rolling eyes, and lowered his
hand; and now and now yet more the speech began to bend him to
waver: when high on his shoulder appeared the sword-belt with the
shining bosses that he knew, the luckless belt of the boy Pallas, whom
Turnus had struck down with mastering wound, and wore on his
shoulders the fatal ornament. The other, as his eyes drank in the
plundered record of his fierce grief, kindles to fury, and cries terrible in
anger: 'Mayest thou, clad in the spoils of my dearest, be snatched from
me now? Pallas it is, Pallas who strikes the deathblow, and exacts
vengeance in thy guilty blood.' So saying, he fiercely plunges the steel
full in his breast. But his limbs grow slack and chill, and the life with
a moan flies indignant into the dark.

PLUTARCH

Antony

CONCERNING the life of the Greek biographer Plutarch (*c.* 50 A.D.—*c.* 120 A.D.) very little is accurately known. He was born in Chaeronea in Greece, probably about 50 A.D., during the reign of the Roman Emperor Claudius. As his family was distinguished and wealthy, Plutarch studied in Athens and traveled widely, visiting Alexandria and various parts of Greece and Italy. He went to Rome, possibly on public business, and it is believed that he stayed there for a long time. In Rome, under the reign of Domitian, he gave lectures on learned subjects, seemed to enjoy considerable popularity, and is said to have conducted the education of the future emperor Hadrian. But he returned to Chaeronea, whose population he said he was loth "to make less by the withdrawal of even one inhabitant," and there he remained the rest of his life. In Chaeronea he held political offices, he occupied a priesthood of Apollo, and he completed his literary works.

Eighty-three separate treatises of Plutarch have been collected in a volume rather inaccurately entitled *Moralia*. These discussions are concerned with the greatest variety of subjects: manners and conduct, the opinions of the philosophers, the natural sciences, literature, and religion. Some of the titles are indicative of Plutarch's homely interests: "On Restraint of Anger," "On Busybodies," "Advice to Married Couples." Some of the treatises are in the form of Platonic dialogues; others show the influence of Aristotle; throughout, the considerations are largely ethical. Though this work has never been admired as a great literary achievement, it has been generally prized for the light that it sheds upon the manners of Plutarch's time.

Far better known than the *Moralia* and far more influential upon subsequent writers is Plutarch's *Lives,* a collection of parallel biographies beginning as early as the legendary Theseus and ending with the Roman Emperor Otho, who died when Plutarch was a young man. These biographies are arranged in pairs, a Greek soldier or statesman paired with a Roman; and each pair of biographies is followed by a short comparison of the two men. In all, Plutarch completed twenty-three pairs of lives and four lives that appear singly. The book as it exists today seems to have neither its original arrangement nor all the lives that Plutarch wrote. Furthermore he seems to have contemplated writing a number of others.

As history Plutarch's *Lives* has certain defects, for it contains mistakes and inaccuracies and does not seem to indicate a sufficiently careful weighing of sources; but the work fills many gaps in the long range of ancient history, and it manifests a lack of prejudice that is a great credit to its author. Plutarch, however, a man of great moral earnestness, was not primarily interested in history, or rather he was much more the moralist than the historian. His first concern is human character and the moral lessons to be derived from its study. The subjects of his biographies are either models of virtue or victims of personal weakness. The great amount of anecdotal material of the *Lives* is used primarily as revelation of character.

Plutarch himself seems to have been a man of cheerful disposition, natural simplicity, and great amiability, for his literary works reflect these traits. Concerning his *Lives* it has been said, "This is what, in the second century of our era, Greeks and Romans loved to believe about their warriors and statesmen of the past." Whether this judgment be taken as praise or blame, the fact remains that Plutarch has strongly appealed to a great diversity of men in many ages. Three of Shakespeare's plays—*Julius Caesar, Antony and Cleopatra,* and *Coriolanus*—are based upon accounts in the *Lives.* The writings of Francis Bacon are filled with quotations from Plutarch. Montaigne modeled his essays upon the *Moralia*. The not-too-classical Rousseau, in his boyhood, eagerly read Plutarch. And American statesmen have found in the lives of Plutarch's Greeks and Romans the material of practical politics.

ANTONY
[c. 82 B.C.–30 B.C.]

The grandfather of Antony was the famous pleader, whom Marius put to death for having taken part with Sylla. His father was Antony, surnamed of Crete, not very famous or distinguished in public life, but a worthy good man, and particularly remarkable for his liberality. . . .

His wife was Julia, of the family of the Cæsars, who, for her discretion and fair behaviour, was not inferior to any of her time. Under her, Antony received his education. . . . Antony grew up a very beautiful youth, but by the worst of misfortunes, he fell into the acquaintance and friendship of Curio, a man abandoned to his pleasures, who, to make Antony's dependence upon him a matter of greater necessity, plunged him into a life of drinking and dissipation, and led him through a course of such extravagance that he ran, at that early age, into debt to the amount of two hundred and fifty talents.[1] For this sum Curio became his surety; on hearing which, the elder Curio, his father, drove Antony out of his house. After this, for some short time he took part with Clodius, the most insolent and outrageous demagogue of the time, in his course of violence and disorder; but getting weary, before long, of his madness, and apprehensive of the powerful party forming against him, he left Italy and travelled into Greece, where he spent his time in military exercises and in the study of eloquence. He took most to what was called the Asiatic taste in speaking, which was then at its height, and was, in many ways, suitable to his ostentations, vaunting temper, full of empty flourishes and unsteady efforts for glory. . . .

1. The talent was a Greek measure of weight as well as a monetary unit, varying with time and place. In the Attic system the talent was equivalent to about 58 pounds; a talent of silver was worth about $1,000.

His first service was against Aristobulus, who had prevailed with
the Jews to rebel. Here he was himself the first man to scale the
largest of the works, and beat Aristobulus out of all of them; after
which he routed, in a pitched battle, an army many times over the
number of his, killed almost all of them and took Aristobulus and
his son prisoners. . . . In all the great and frequent skirmishes and
battles he gave continual proofs of his personal valour and military
conduct. . . . The consequence was that he left behind him a great
name, and all who were serving in the Roman army looked upon him
as a most gallant soldier.

He had also a very good and noble appearance; his beard was
well grown, his forehead large, and his nose aquiline, giving him
altogether a bold, masculine look that reminded people of the faces
of Hercules in paintings and sculptures. It was, moreover, an ancient
tradition, that the Antonys were descended from Hercules, by a son
of his called Anton; and this opinion he thought to give credit to by
the similarity of his person just mentioned, and also by the fashion of
his dress. For, whenever he had to appear before large numbers, he
wore his tunic girt low about the hips, a broadsword on his side, and
over all a large coarse mantle. What might seem to some very insup-
portable, his vaunting, his raillery, his drinking in public, sitting
down by the men as they were taking their food, and eating, as he
stood, off the common soldiers' tables, made him the delight and
pleasure of the army. In love affairs, also, he was very agreeable: he
gained many friends by the assistance he gave them in theirs, and took
other people's raillery upon his own with good-humour. And his
generous ways, his open and lavish hand in gifts and favours to his
friends and fellow-soldiers, did a great deal for him in his first advance to power, and after he had become great, long maintained his
fortunes, when a thousand follies were hastening their overthrow. . . .

When the Roman state finally broke up into two hostile factions,
the aristocratical party joining Pompey, who was in the city, and the
popular side seeking help from Cæsar, who was at the head of an
army in Gaul, Curio, the friend of Antony, having changed his party
and devoted himself to Cæsar, brought over Antony also to his service.
And the influence which he gained with the people by his eloquence
and by the money which was supplied by Cæsar, enabled him to make
Antony, first, tribune of the people, and then, augur. And Antony's
accession to office was at once of the greatest advantage to Cæsar. . . .
At length, two questions being put in the senate, the one, whether

Pompey should dismiss his army, the other, if Cæsar his, some were for the former, for the latter all, except some few, when Antony stood up and put the question, if it would be agreeable to them that both Pompey and Cæsar should dismiss their armies. This proposal met with the greatest approval, they gave him loud acclamations, and called for it to be put to the vote. But when the consuls would not have it so, Cæsar's friends again made some few offers, very fair and equitable, but were strongly opposed by Cato, and Antony himself was commanded to leave the senate. So, leaving them with execrations, and disguising himself in a servant's dress, hiring a carriage, he went straight away to Cæsar, declaring at once, when they reached the camp, that affairs at Rome were conducted without any order or justice, that the privilege of speaking in the senate was denied the tribunes, and that he who spoke for common fair dealing was driven out and in danger of his life.

Upon this, Cæsar set his army in motion, and marched into Italy; and for this reason it is that Cicero writes in his Philippics[2] that Antony was as much the cause of the civil war as Helen was of the Trojan. But this is but a calumny. . . . So soon, then, as Cæsar had advanced and occupied Rome, and driven Pompey out of Italy, he proposed first to go against the legions that Pompey had in Spain, and then cross over and follow him with the fleet that should be prepared during his absence, in the meantime leaving the government of Rome to Lepidus, as prætor, and the command of the troops and of Italy to Antony, as tribune of the people. Antony was not long in getting the hearts of the soldiers, joining with them in their exercises, and for the most part living amongst them and making them presents to the utmost of his abilities; but with all others he was unpopular enough. He was too lazy to pay attention to the complaints of persons who were injured; he listened impatiently to petitions; and he had an ill name for familiarity with other people's wives. In short, the government of Cæsar got a bad repute through his friends. And of these friends, Antony, as he had the largest trust, and committed the greatest errors, was thought the most deeply in fault.

Cæsar, however, at his return from Spain, overlooked the charges against him, and had no reason ever to complain, in the employments he gave him in the war, of any want of courage, energy, or military skill. . . .

2. A series of speeches directed against Antony during the civil confusion following the death of Cæsar.

There was not one of the many engagements that now took place
one after another in which Antony did not signalise himself; twice
he stopped the army in its full flight, led them back to a charge, and
gained the victory. So that not without reason his reputation, next to
Cæsar's, was greatest in the army. And what opinion Cæsar himself
had of him well appeared when, for the final battle in Pharsalia,[3]
which was to determine everything, he himself chose to lead the right
wing, committing the charge of the left to Antony, as to the best
officer of all that served under him. After the battle, Cæsar, being
created dictator, went in pursuit of Pompey, and sent Antony to Rome,
with the character of Master of the Horse, who is in office and power
next to the dictator, when present, and in his absence the first, and
pretty nearly indeed the sole magistrate.

Dolabella, however, who was tribune, being a young man and
eager for change, was now for bringing in a general measure for
cancelling debts, and wanted Antony, who was his friend, and forward
enough to promote any popular project, to take part with him in this
step. Asinius and Trebellius were of the contrary opinion, and it so
happened, at the same time, Antony was crossed by a terrible suspicion that Dolabella was too familiar with his wife; and in great
trouble at this, he parted with her, and, taking part with Asinius,
came to open hostilities with Dolabella, who had seized on the forum,
intending to pass his law by force. Antony, backed by a vote of the
senate that Dolabella should be put down by force of arms, went
down and attacked him, killing some of his, and losing some of his
own men; and by this action lost his favour with the commonalty,
while with the better class and with all well-conducted people his
general course of life made him, as Cicero says, absolutely odious,
utter disgust being excited by his drinking bouts at all hours, his wild
expenses, his gross amours, the day spent in sleeping or walking off
his debauches, and the night in banquets and at theatres, and in
celebrating the nuptials of some comedian or buffoon. It is related
that, drinking all night at the wedding of Hippias, the comedian, on
the morning, having to harangue the people, he came forward, over-
charged as he was, and vomited before them all, one of his friends
holding his gown for him. . . .

However, Cæsar, by dealing gently with his errors, seems to
have succeeded in curing him of a good deal of his folly and extravagance. He gave up his former courses, and took a wife, Fulvia,

3. The decisive battle against Pompey, 48 B.C.

a woman not born for spinning or housewifery, nor one that could be content with ruling a private husband, but prepared to govern a first magistrate, or give orders to a commander-in-chief. So that Cleopatra had great obligations to her for having taught Antony to be so good a servant, he coming to her hands tame and broken into entire obedience to the commands of a mistress. He used to play all sorts of sportive, boyish tricks, to keep Fulvia in good humour. As, for example, when Cæsar, after his victory in Spain, was on his return, Antony, among the rest, went out to meet him; and, a rumour being spread that Cæsar was killed, and the enemy marching into Italy, he returned to Rome, and, disguising himself, came to her by night muffled up as a servant that brought letters from Antony. She, with great impatience, before she received the letter, asks if Antony were well, and instead of an answer he gives her the letter; and, as she was opening it, took her about the neck and kissed her. This little story, of many of the same nature, I give as a specimen.

There was nobody of any rank in Rome that did not go some days' journey to meet Cæsar on his return from Spain; but Antony was the best received of any, admitted to ride the whole journey with him in his carriage. Cæsar being created, the fifth time, consul, without delay chose Antony for his colleague, but designing himself to give up his own consulate to Dolabella, he acquainted the senate with his resolution. But Antony opposed it with all his might, saying much that was bad against Dolabella, and receiving the like language in return, till Cæsar could bear with the indecency no longer, and deferred the matter to another time. And it is credible that Cæsar was about as much disgusted with the one as the other. When some one was accusing them both to him, "It is not," said he, "these well-fed, long-haired men that I fear, but the pale and the hungry-looking;" meaning Brutus and Cassius, by whose conspiracy he afterwards fell.

And the fairest pretext for that conspiracy was furnished, without his meaning it, by Antony himself. The Romans were celebrating their festival, called the Lupercalia,[4] when Cæsar, in his triumphal habit, and seated above the rostra in the market-place, was a spectator of the sports. The custom is, that many young noblemen and of the magistracy, anointed with oil and having straps of hide in their hands, run about and strike, in sport, at every one they meet. Antony was running with the rest; but, omitting the old ceremony, twining

4. A religious festival, celebrated annually on February 15, for the purpose of securing fertility of fields, flocks, and populace.

a garland of bay round a diadem, he ran up to the rostra, and, being lifted up by his companions, would have put it upon the head of Cæsar, as if by that ceremony he were declared king. Cæsar seemingly refused, and drew aside to avoid it, and was applauded by the people with great shouts. Again Antony pressed it, and again he declined its acceptance. And so the dispute between them went on for some time, Antony's solicitations receiving but little encouragement from the shouts of a few friends, and Cæsar's refusal being accompanied with the general applause of the people; a curious thing enough, that they should submit with patience to the fact, and yet at the same time dread the name as the destruction of their liberty. Cæsar, very much discomposed at what had passed, got up from his seat, and, laying bare his neck, said he was ready to receive a stroke, if any one of them desired to give it. The crown was at last put on one of his statues, but was taken down by some of the tribunes, who were followed home by the people with shouts of applause. Cæsar, however, resented it, and deposed them.

These passages gave great encouragement to Brutus and Cassius, who, in making choice of trusty friends for such an enterprise, were thinking to engage Antony. The rest approved, except Trebonius, who told them that Antony and he had lodged and travelled together in the last journey they took to meet Cæsar, and that he had let fall several words, in a cautious way, on purpose to sound him; that Antony very well understood him, but did not encourage it; however, he had said nothing of it to Cæsar, but had kept the secret faithfully. The conspirators then proposed that Antony should die with him, which Brutus would not consent to, insisting that an action undertaken in defence of right and the laws must be maintained unsullied, and pure of injustice. It was settled that Antony, whose bodily strength and high office made him formidable, should, at Cæsar's entrance into the senate, when the deed was to be done, be amused outside by some of the party in a conversation about some pretended business.

So when all was proceeded with, according to their plan, and Cæsar had fallen in the senate-house, Antony, at the first moment, took a servant's dress, and hid himself. But, understanding that the conspirators had assembled in the Capitol, and had no further design upon any one, he persuaded them to come down, giving them his son as a hostage. That night Cassius supped at Antony's house, and Brutus with Lepidus. Antony then convened the senate, and spoke in favour of an act of oblivion, and the appointment of Brutus and Cassius to provinces. These measures the senate passed; and resolved that all Cæsar's acts should remain in force. Thus Antony went out of the senate with the highest possible reputation and esteem; for it was apparent that he had prevented a civil war, and had composed, in the wisest and most statesmanlike way, questions of the greatest difficulty and embarrassment. But these temperate counsels were soon swept away by the tide of popular applause, and the prospect, if Brutus were overthrown, of being without doubt the ruler-in-chief. As Cæsar's body was conveying to the tomb, Antony, according to the custom, was making his funeral oration in the market-place, and perceiving the people to be infinitely affected with what he had said, he began to mingle with his praises language of commiseration, and horror at what had happened, and, as he was ending his speech, he took the underclothes of the dead, and held them up, showing them stains of blood and the holes of the many stabs, calling those that had done this act villains and bloody murderers. All which excited the people to such indignation, that they would not defer the funeral, but, making a pile of tables and forms in the very market-place, set fire to it; and every one, taking a brand, ran to the conspirators' houses, to attack them. Upon this, Brutus and his whole party left the city, and Cæsar's friends joined themselves to Antony. Calpurnia, Cæsar's wife, lodged with him the best part of the property, to the value of four thousand talents. . . .

While matters went thus in Rome, the young Cæsar, Cæsar's niece's son, and by testament left his heir, arrived at Rome from Apollonia, where he was when his uncle was killed. The first thing he did was to visit Antony, as his father's friend.[5] He spoke to him concerning the money that was in his hands, and reminded him of the legacy Cæsar had made of seventy-five drachmas[6] to every Roman citizen. Antony, at first, laughing at such discourse from so young a man, told him he wished he were in his health, and that he wanted good counsel and good friends to tell him the burden of being executor to Cæsar would sit very uneasy upon his young shoulders. This was no answer to him; and, when he persisted in demanding the property, Antony went on treating him injuriously both in word and deed, opposed him when he stood for the tribune's office, and, when he was taking steps for the dedication of his father's golden chair, as

5. Julius Cæsar had legally adopted Octavius as a son.
6. A drachma was about fifteen cents.

had been enacted, he threatened to send him to prison if he did not give over soliciting the people. This made the young Cæsar apply himself to Cicero, and all those that hated Antony; by them he was recommended to the senate, while he himself courted the people, and drew together the soldiers from their settlements, till Antony got alarmed, and gave him a meeting in the Capitol, where, after some words, they came to an accommodation. . . . Cicero was at this time the man of greatest influence in Rome. He made use of all his art to exasperate the people against Antony, and at length persuaded the senate to declare him a public enemy, to send Cæsar the rods and axes[7] and other marks of honour usually given to prætors, and to issue orders to Hirtius and Pansa, who were the consuls, to drive Antony out of Italy. The armies engaged near Modena, and Cæsar himself was present and took part in the battle. Antony was defeated, but both the consuls were slain. Antony, in his flight, was overtaken by distresses of every kind, and the worst of all of them was famine. But it was his character in calamities to be better than at any other time. Antony, in misfortune, was most nearly a virtuous man. . . . On this occasion, he was a most wonderful example to his soldiers. He, who had just quitted so much luxury and sumptuous living, made no difficulty now of drinking foul water and feeding on wild fruits and roots. Nay, it is related they ate the very bark of trees, and, in passing over the Alps, lived upon creatures that no one before had ever been willing to touch.

The design was to join the army on the other side the Alps, commanded by Lepidus, who he imagined would stand his friend. On coming up and encamping near at hand, finding he had no sort of encouragement offered him, he resolved to push his fortune and venture all. His hair was long and disordered, nor had he shaved his beard since his defeat; in this guise, and with a dark coloured cloak flung over him, he came into the trenches of Lepidus, and began to address the army. Some were moved at his habit, others at his words, so that Lepidus, not liking it, ordered the trumpets to sound, that he might be heard no longer. This raised in the soldiers yet a greater pity, so that they resolved to confer secretly with him. They advised him without delay to attack Lepidus's trenches, assuring him that a strong party would receive him, and, if he wished it, would kill Lepidus. Antony, however, had no wish for this, but next morning marched

7. The *Fasces*, bundles of wooden rods enclosing an axe, were originally the symbol of the king's authority. The modern term *fascist* is derived from *Fasces*.

his army to pass over the river that parted the two camps. He was himself the first man that stepped in, and, as he went through towards the other bank, he saw Lepidus's soldiers in great numbers reaching out their hands to help him, and beating down the works to make him way. Being entered into the camp, and finding himself absolute master, he nevertheless treated Lepidus with the greatest civility. In great strength he repassed the Alps, leading with him into Italy seventeen legions and ten thousand horse.

Cæsar, perceiving that Cicero's wishes were for liberty, had ceased to pay any further regard to him, and was now employing the mediation of his friends to come to a good understanding with Antony. They both met together with Lepidus in a small island, where the conference lasted three days. The empire was soon determined of, it being divided amongst them as if it had been their paternal inheritance. That which gave them all the trouble was to agree who should be put to death, each of them desiring to destroy his enemies and to save his friends. But, in the end, animosity to those they hated carried the day against respect for relations and affection for friends; and Cæsar sacrificed Cicero to Antony, Antony gave up his uncle Lucius Cæsar, and Lepidus received permission to murder his brother Paulus, or, as others say, yielded his brother to them. I do not believe anything ever took place more truly savage or barbarous than this composition, for, in this exchange of blood for blood, they were equally guilty of the lives they surrendered and of those they took; or, indeed, more guilty in the case of their friends, for whose deaths they had not even the justification of hatred. Three hundred persons were put to death by proscription. Antony gave orders to those that were to kill Cicero to cut off his head and right hand, with which he had written his invectives against him; and, when they were brought before him, he regarded them joyfully, actually bursting out more than once into laughter, and, when he had satiated himself with the sight of them, ordered them to be hung up above the speaker's place in the forum, thinking thus to insult the dead, while in fact he only exposed his own wanton arrogance, and his unworthiness to hold the power that fortune had given him. His uncle, Lucius Cæsar, being closely pursued, took refuge with his sister, who, when the murderers had broken into her house and were pressing into her chamber, met them at the door, and spreading out her hands, cried out several times. "You shall not kill Lucius Cæsar till you first despatch me, who gave your general his birth;" and in this manner she succeeded in getting her brother out of the way, and saving his life.

This triumvirate was very hateful to the Romans, and Antony most of all bore the blame, because he was older than Cæsar, and had greater authority than Lepidus, and withal he was no sooner settled in his affairs, but he turned to his luxurious and dissolute way of living. . . . They did not limit themselves to the forfeiture of the estates of such as were proscribed, defrauding the widows and families, nor were they contented with laying on every possible kind of tax and imposition; but hearing that several sums of money were, as well by strangers as citizens of Rome, deposited in the hands of the vestal virgins,[8] they went and took the money away by force. When it was manifest that nothing would ever be enough for Antony, Cæsar at last called for a division of property. The army was also divided between them, upon their march into Macedonia to make war with Brutus and Cassius, Lepidus being left with the command of the city.

However, after they had crossed the sea and engaged in operations of war, encamping in front of the enemy, Antony opposite Cassius, and Cæsar opposite Brutus, Cæsar did nothing worth relating, and all the success and victory were Antony's.[9] In the first battle, Cæsar was completely routed by Brutus, his camp taken, he himself very narrowly escaping by flight. As he himself writes in his Memoirs, he retired before the battle, on account of a dream which one of his friends had. But Antony, on the other hand, defeated Cassius; though some have written that he was not actually present in the engagement, and only joined afterwards in the pursuit. Cassius was killed, at his own entreaty and order, by one of his most trusted freedmen, Pindarus, not being aware of Brutus's victory. After a few days' interval, they fought another battle, in which Brutus lost the day, and slew himself; and Cæsar being sick, Antony had almost all the honour of the victory. Standing over Brutus's dead body, he uttered a few words of reproach upon him for the death of his brother Caius, who had been executed by Brutus's order in Macedonia in revenge of Cicero; but, throwing his own scarlet mantle, which was of great value, upon the body of Brutus, he gave charge to one of his own freedmen to take care of his funeral.

But Cæsar was conveyed to Rome, no one expecting that he would

8. Four (later six) virgins, entrusted with keeping the sacred fire of the state in the temple of Vesta, goddess of the Hearth.

9. The campaign of Philippi, 42 B.C.

long survive. Antony, purposing to go to the eastern provinces to lay them under contribution, entered Greece with a large force. The promise had been made that every common soldier should receive for his pay five thousand drachmas; so it was likely there would be need of pretty severe taxing and levying to raise money. However, to the Greeks he showed at first reason and moderation enough; he gratified his love of amusement by hearing the learned men dispute, by seeing the games, and undergoing initiation; and in judicial matters he was equitable, taking pleasure in being styled a lover of Greece, but, above all, being called a lover of Athens, to which city he made very considerable presents. . . .

He crossed over into Asia, and there laid his hands on the stores of accumulated wealth, while kings waited at his door, and queens were rivalling one another, who should make him the greatest presents or appear most charming in his eyes. Thus, whilst Cæsar in Rome was wearing out his strength amidst seditions and wars, Antony, with nothing to do amidst the enjoyments of peace, let his passions carry him easily back to the old course of life that was familiar to him. . . .

When he made his entry into Ephesus, the women met him dressed up like Bacchantes, and the men and boys like satyrs and fauns, and throughout the town nothing was to be seen but spears wreathed about with ivy, harps, flutes, and psalteries, while Antony in their songs was Bacchus, the Giver of Joy, and the Gentle. And so indeed he was to some, but to far more the Devourer and the Savage; for he would deprive persons of worth and quality of their fortunes to gratify villains and flatterers, who would sometimes beg the estates of men yet living, pretending they were dead, and, obtaining a grant, take possession. He gave his cook the house of a Magnesian citizen, as a reward for a single highly successful supper. . . .
There was much simplicity in his character; he was slow to see his faults, but when he did see them, was extremely repentant, and ready to ask pardon of those he had injured; prodigal in his acts of reparation, and severe in his punishments, but his generosity was much more extravagant than his severity; his raillery was sharp and insulting, but the edge of it was taken off by his readiness to submit to any kind of repartee; for he was as well contented to be rallied, as he was pleased to rally others. And this freedom of speech was, indeed, the cause of many of his disasters. He never imagined those who used so much liberty in their mirth would flatter or deceive him in business of consequence, not knowing how common it is with parasites to mix

their flattery with boldness, as confectioners do their sweetmeats with
something biting, to prevent the sense of satiety. Their freedoms and
impertinences at table were designed expressly to give to their ob-
sequiousness in council the air of being not complaisance, but conviction.

Such being his temper, the last and crowning mischief that could
befall him came in the love of Cleopatra, to awaken and kindle to
fury passions that as yet lay still and dormant in his nature, and to
stifle and finally corrupt any elements that yet made resistance in him
of goodness and a sound judgment. He fell into the snare thus. When
making preparation for the Parthian war, he sent to command her
to make her personal appearance in Cilicia, to answer an accusation,
that she had given great assistance, in the late wars, to Cassius. Dellius,
who was sent on this message, had no sooner seen her face, and remarked her adroitness and subtlety in speech, but he felt convinced
that Antony would not so much as think of giving any molestation
to a woman like this; on the contrary, she would be the first in favour
with him. So he set himself at once to pay his court to the Egyptian,
and gave her his advice, "to go," in the Homeric style, to Cilicia, "in
her best attire," and bade her fear nothing from Antony, the gentlest
and kindest of soldiers. She had some faith in the words of Dellius,
but more in her own attractions; which, having formerly recommended her to Cæsar and the young Cænus Pompey, she did not doubt
might prove yet more successful with Antony. . . . Their acquaintance
was with her when a girl, young and ignorant of the world, but she
was to meet Antony in the time of life when women's beauty is most
splendid, and their intellects are in full maturity. She made great
preparation for her journey, of money, gifts, and ornaments of value,
such as so wealthy a kingdom might afford, but she brought with her
her surest hopes in her own magic arts and charms.

She received several letters, both from Antony and from his
friends, to summon her, but she took no account of these orders; and
at last, as if in mockery of them, she came sailing up the river Cydnus,
in a barge with gilded stern and outspread sails of purple, while oars
of silver beat time to the music of flutes and fifes and harps. She herself lay all along under a canopy of cloth of gold, dressed as Venus
in a picture, and beautiful young boys, like painted Cupids, stood on
each side to fan her. Her maids were dressed like sea nymphs and
graces, some steering at the rudder, some working at the ropes. The
perfumes diffused themselves from the vessel to the shore, which was

covered with multitudes, part following the galley up the river on
either bank, part running out of the city to see the sight. The market-
place was quite emptied, and Antony at last was left alone sitting
upon the tribunal; while the word went through all the multitude,
that Venus was come to feast with Bacchus, for the common good
of Asia. On her arrival, Antony sent to invite her to supper. She
thought it fitter he should come to her; so, willing to show his good-
humour and courtesy, he complied, and went. He found the preparations to receive him magnificent beyond expression. . . .

The next day, Antony invited her to supper, and was very desirous to outdo her as well in magnificence as contrivance; but he found
he was altogether beaten in both, and was so well convinced of it that
he was himself the first to jest and mock at his poverty of wit and
his rustic awkwardness. She, perceiving that his raillery was broad
and gross, and savoured more of the soldier than the courtier, rejoined
in the same taste, and fell into it at once, without any sort of reluctance
or reserve. For her actual beauty, it is said, was not in itself so remarkable that none could be compared with her, or that no one could
see her without being struck by it, but the contact of her presence, if
you lived with her, was irresistible; the attraction of her person, joining with the charm of her conversation, and the character that attended
all she said or did, was something bewitching. It was a pleasure merely
to hear the sound of her voice, with which, like an instrument of many
strings, she could pass from one language to another; so that there
were few of the barbarian nations that she answered by an interpreter. . . .

Antony was so captivated by her that, while Fulvia his wife maintained his quarrels in Rome against Cæsar by actual force of arms,
and the Parthian troops were assembled in Mesopotamia, and ready
to enter Syria, he could yet suffer himself to be carried away by her
to Alexandria, there to keep holiday, like a boy, in play and diversion,
squandering and fooling away in enjoyments that most costly of all
valuables, time. They had a sort of company, to which they gave a
particular name, calling it that of the Inimitable Livers. The members
entertained one another daily in turn, with an extravagance of expendi-
ture beyond measure or belief. Philotas, a physician of Amphissa, who
was at that time a student of medicine in Alexandria, used to tell my
grandfather Lamprias that, having some acquaintance with one of
the royal cooks, he was invited by him, being a young man, to come
and see the sumptuous preparations for supper. So he was taken into

the kitchen, where he admired the prodigious variety of all things; but particularly, seeing eight wild boars roasting whole, says he, "Surely you have a great number of guests." The cook laughed at his simplicity, and told him there were not above twelve to sup, but that every dish was to be served up just roasted to a turn, and if anything was but one minute ill-timed, it was spoiled; "And," said he, "maybe Antony will sup just now, maybe not this hour, maybe he will call for wine, or begin to talk, and will put it off. So that," he continued, "it is not one, but many suppers must be had in readiness, as it is impossible to guess at his hour." . . .

To return to Cleopatra; Plato admits four sorts of flattery, but she had a thousand. Were Antony serious or disposed to mirth, she had at any moment some new delight or charm to meet his wishes; at every turn she was upon him, and let him escape her neither by day nor by night. She played at dice with him, drank with him, hunted with him; and when he exercised in arms, she was there to see. At night she would go rambling with him to disturb and torment people at their doors and windows, dressed like a servant-woman, for Antony also went in servant's disguise, and from these expeditions he often came home very scurvily answered, and sometimes even beaten severely, though most people guessed who it was. It would be trifling without end to be particular in his follies, but his fishing must not be forgotten. He went out one day to angle with Cleopatra, and, being so unfortunate as to catch nothing in the presence of his mistress, he gave secret orders to the fishermen to dive under water, and put fishes that had been already taken upon his hooks; and these he drew so fast that the Egyptian perceived it. But, feigning great admiration, she told everybody how dexterous Antony was, and invited them next day to come and see him again. So, when a number of them had come on board the fishing-boats, as soon as he had let down his hook, one of her servants was beforehand with his divers, and fixed upon his hook a salted fish from Pontus. Antony, feeling his line give, drew up the prey, and when, as may be imagined, great laughter ensued, "Leave," said Cleopatra, "the fishing-rod, general, to us poor sovereigns of Pharos and Canopus;[10] your game is cities, provinces, and kingdoms."

Whilst he was thus diverting himself and engaged in this boy's play, two despatches arrived; one from Rome, that his brother Lucius

10. Pharos was an island in the harbor of Alexandria, noted for its lighthouse, one of the seven wonders of the ancient world. Canopus was a mouth of the Nile.

and his wife Fulvia, after many quarrels among themselves, had joined in war against Cæsar, and having lost all, had fled out of Italy; the other bringing little better news, that Labienus, at the head of the Parthians, was overrunning Asia, from Euphrates and Syria as far as Lydia and Ionia. So, scarcely at last rousing himself from sleep, and shaking off the fumes of wine, he set out to attack the Parthians, and went as far as Phœnicia; but, upon the receipt of lamentable letters from Fulvia, turned his course with two hundred ships to Italy. And, in his way, receiving such of his friends as fled from Italy, he was given to understand that Fulvia was the sole cause of the war, a woman of a restless spirit and very bold, and withal her hopes were that commotions in Italy would force Antony from Cleopatra. But it happened that Fulvia, as she was coming to meet her husband, fell sick by the way, and died at Sicyon, so that an accommodation was the more easily made. For when he reached Italy, and Cæsar showed no intention of laying anything to his charge, and he on his part shifted the blame of everything on Fulvia, those that were friends to them would not suffer that the time should be spent in looking narrowly into the plea, but made a reconciliation first, and then a partition of the empire between them, taking as their boundary the Ionian Sea, the eastern provinces falling to Antony, to Cæsar the western, and Africa being left to Lepidus.

These terms were well approved of, but yet it was thought some closer tie would be desirable; and for this, fortune offered occasion. Cæsar had an elder sister, not of the whole blood.[11] This sister, Octavia, he was extremely attached to, as indeed she was, it is said, quite a wonder of a woman. Her husband had died not long before, and Antony was now a widower by the death of Fulvia; for, though he did not disavow the passion he had for Cleopatra, yet he disowned anything of marriage, reason as yet, upon this point, still maintaining the debate against the charms of the Egyptian. Everybody concurred in promoting this new alliance, fully expecting that with the beauty, honour, and prudence of Octavia, when her company should, as it was certain it would, have engaged his affections, all would be kept in the safe and happy course of friendship. So, both parties being agreed, they went to Rome to celebrate the nuptials. . . .

Antony despatched Ventidius into Asia to check the advance of the Parthians, while he, as a compliment to Cæsar, accepted the office

11. That is, a half-sister.

of priest to the deceased Cæsar.[12] And in any state affair and matter of consequence, they both behaved themselves with much consideration and friendliness for each other. But it annoyed Antony that in all their amusements, on any trial of skill or fortune, Cæsar should be constantly victorious. He had with him an Egyptian diviner, one of those who calculate nativities, who, either to make his court to Cleopatra, or that by the rules of his art he found it to be so, openly declared to him that though the fortune that attended him was bright and glorious, yet it was overshadowed by Cæsar's; and advised him to keep himself as far distant as he could from that young man; "for your Genius,"[13] said he, "dreads his; when absent from him yours is proud and brave, but in his presence unmanly and dejected;" and incidents that occurred appeared to show that the Egyptian spoke truth. For whenever they cast lots for any playful purpose, or threw dice, Antony was still the loser; and repeatedly, when they fought game-cocks or quails, Cæsar's had the victory. This gave Antony a secret displeasure, and made him put the more confidence in the skill of his Egyptian. So, leaving the management of his home affairs to Cæsar, he left Italy, and took Octavia, who had lately borne him a daughter, along with him into Greece. . . .

Antony, however, once more, upon some unfavourable stories, taking offence against Cæsar, set sail with three hundred ships for Italy, and, being refused admittance to the port of Brundusium, made for Tarentum. There his wife Octavia, who came from Greece with him, obtained leave to visit her brother, she being then great with child, having already borne her husband a second daughter; and as she was on her way she met Cæsar, with his two friends Agrippa and Mæcenas, and, taking these two aside, with great entreaties and lamentations she told them, that of the most fortunate woman upon earth, she was in danger of becoming the most unhappy; for as yet every one's eyes were fixed upon her as the wife and sister of the two great commanders, but, if rash counsels should prevail, and war ensue, "I shall be miserable," said she, "without redress; for on what side soever victory falls, I shall be sure to be a loser." Cæsar was overcome by these entreaties, and advanced in a peaceable temper to Tarentum, where those that were present beheld a most stately spectacle; a vast army drawn up by the shore, and as great a fleet in the harbour, all without

12. Roman gods, including the deified rulers, had special priests called flamens.
13. The spirit of a man, dwelling within him, representing all his powers of manhood, and presiding over his destiny.

the occurrence of any act of hostility; nothing but the salutations of friends, and other expressions of joy and kindness, passing from one armament to the other. Antony first entertained Cæsar, this also being a concession on Cæsar's part to his sister; and when at length an agreement was made between them, that Cæsar should give Antony two of his legions to serve him in the Parthian war, and that Antony should in return leave with him a hundred armed galleys, Octavia further obtained of her husband, besides this, twenty light ships for her brother, and of her brother, a thousand foot for her husband. So, having parted good friends, Cæsar went immediately to make war with Pompey to conquer Sicily. And Antony, leaving in Cæsar's charge his wife and children, and his children by his former wife Fulvia, set sail for Asia.

But the mischief that thus long had lain still, the passion for Cleopatra, which better thoughts had seemed to have lulled and charmed into oblivion, upon his approach to Syria gathered strength again, and broke out into a flame. And, in fine, like Plato's restive and rebellious horse of the human soul, flinging off all good and wholesome counsel, and breaking fairly loose, he sends Fonteius Capito to bring Cleopatra into Syria. To whom at her arrival he made no small or trifling present, Phœnicia, Cœle-Syria, Cyprus, great part of Cilicia, that side of Judæa which produces balm, that part of Arabia where the Nabathæans extend to the outer sea; profuse gifts which much displeased the Romans. For although he had invested several private persons in great governments and kingdoms, and bereaved many kings of theirs, yet nothing stung the Romans like the shame of these honours paid to Cleopatra. Their dissatisfaction was augmented also by his acknowledging as his own the twin children he had by her, giving them the name of Alexander and Cleopatra, and adding, as their surnames, the titles of Sun and Moon. But he, who knew how to put a good colour on the most dishonest action, would say that the greatness of the Roman empire consisted more in giving than in taking kingdoms, and that the way to carry noble blood through the world was by begetting in every place a new line and series of kings; his own ancestor had thus been born of Hercules; Hercules had not limited his hopes of progeny to a single womb, but had freely let nature take her will in the foundation and first commencement of many families.

After Phraates had killed his father Hyrodes, and taken possession of his kingdom, many of the Parthians left their country; among the rest Monæses, a man of great distinction and authority, sought refuge with Antony. But when the King of Parthia soon recalled him, giving him his word and honour for his safety, Antony was not unwilling to give him leave to return, hoping thereby to surprise Phraates, who would believe that peace would continue; for he only made the demand of him that he should send back the Roman ensigns which were taken when Crassus was slain, and the prisoners that remained yet alive. This done, he sent Cleopatra to Egypt, and marched through Arabia and Armenia; and, when his forces came together, and were joined by those of his confederate kings he made a general muster. There appeared sixty thousand Roman foot, ten thousand horse, Spaniards and Gauls, who counted as Romans; and, of other nations, horse and foot thirty thousand. And these great preparations, that put the Indians beyond Bactria into alarm, and made all Asia shake, were all we are told rendered useless to him because of Cleopatra. For, in order to pass the winter with her, the war was pushed on before its due time; and all he did was done without perfect consideration, as by a man who had no power of control over his faculties, who, under the effect of some drug or magic, was still looking back elsewhere, and whose object was much more to hasten his return than to conquer his enemies.

For, first of all, when he should have taken up his winter-quarters in Armenia, to refresh his men, and then having taken the advantage in the beginning of the spring to invade Media, before the Parthians were out of winter-quarters, he had not patience to expect his time, but marched into the province of Atropatene, leaving Armenia on the left hand, and laid waste all that country. Secondly, his haste was so great that he left behind the engines absolutely required for any siege, which followed the camp in three hundred waggons, and, among the rest, a ram eighty feet long; none of which was it possible, if lost or damaged, to repair or to make the like. Nevertheless, he left them all behind, as a mere impediment to his speed, in the charge of a detachment under the command of Statianus, the waggon officer. He himself laid siege to Phraata, a principal city of the King of Media. And when actual need proved the greatness of his error, in leaving the siege-train behind him, he had nothing for it but to come up and raise a mound against the walls, with infinite labour and great loss of time. Meantime Phraates, coming down with a large army, and hearing that the waggons were left behind with the battering engines, sent a strong party of horse, by which Statianus was surprised, he himself and ten thousand of his men slain, the engines all broken in pieces, and many taken prisoners.

This great miscarriage in the opening of the campaign much discouraged Antony's army, and Artavasdes, King of Armenia, deciding that the Roman prospects were bad, withdrew with all his forces from the camp, although he had been the chief promoter of the war. The Parthians, encouraged by their success, came up to the Romans at the siege, and gave them many affronts; upon which Antony, fearing that the despondency and alarm of his soldiers would only grow worse if he let them lie idle, taking all the horse, ten legions, and three prætorian cohorts of heavy infantry, resolved to go out and forage, designing by this means to draw the enemy with more advantage to a battle. To effect this, he marched a day's journey from his camp, and finding the Parthians hovering about, in readiness to attack him while he was in motion, he gave orders for the signal of battle to be hung out in the encampment, but, at the same time, pulled down the tents, as if he meant not to fight, but to lead his men home again; and so he proceeded to lead them past the enemy, who were drawn up in a half-moon, his orders being that the horse should charge as soon as the legions were come up near enough to second them. The Parthians, standing still while the Romans marched by them, were in great admiration of their army, and of the exact discipline it observed, rank after rank passing on at equal distances in perfect order and silence, their pikes all ready in their hands. But when the signal was given, and the horse turned short upon the Parthians, and with loud cries charged them, they bravely received them, though they were at once too near for bowshot; but the legions coming up with loud shouts and rattling of their arms so frightened their horses and indeed the men themselves, that they kept their ground no longer. Antony pressed them hard, in great hopes that this victory should put an end to the war; the foot had them in pursuit for fifty furlongs, and the horse for thrice that distance, and yet, the advantage summed up, they had but thirty prisoners, and there were but fourscore slain. So that they were all filled with dejection and discouragement, to consider that when they were victorious, their advantages were so small, and that when they were beaten, they lost so great a number of men as they had done when the carriages were taken. . . .

The war was now become grievous to both parties, and the prospect of its continuance yet more fearful to Antony, in respect that he was threatened with famine; for he could no longer forage without wounds and slaughter.

Marching his army in great haste in the depth of winter through continual storms of snow, he lost eight thousand of his men, and came with much diminished numbers to a place called the White Village, between Sidon and Berytus, on the sea-coast, where he waited for the arrival of Cleopatra. And, being impatient of the delay she made, he bethought himself of shortening the time in wine and drunkenness, and yet could not endure the tediousness of a meal, but would start from table and run to see if she were coming. Till at last she came into port, and brought with her clothes and money for the soldiers. Though some say that Antony only received the clothes from her and distributed his own money in her name. . . . But Octavia, in Rome, being desirous to see Antony, asked Cæsar's leave to go to him; which he gave her, not so much, say most authors, to gratify his sister, as to obtain a fair pretence to begin the war upon her dishonourable reception. She no sooner arrived at Athens, but by letters from Antony she was informed of his will that she should await him there. And, though she were much displeased, not being ignorant of the real reason of this usage, yet she wrote to him to know to what place he would be pleased she should send the things she had brought with her for his use; for she had brought clothes for his soldiers, baggage, cattle, money, and presents for his friends and officers, and two thousand chosen soldiers sumptuously armed. Cleopatra, feeling her rival already, as it were, at hand, was seized with fear, lest if to her noble life and her high alliance, she once could add the charm of daily habit and affectionate intercourse, she should become irresistible, and be his absolute mistress forever. So she feigned to be dying for love of Antony, bringing her body down by slender diet; when he entered the room, she fixed her eyes upon him in a rapture, and when he left, seemed to languish and half faint away. She took great pains that he should see her in tears, and, as soon as he noticed it, hastily dried them up and turned away, as if it were her wish that he should know nothing of it. All this was acting while he prepared for Media; and Cleopatra's creatures were not slow to forward the design, upbraiding Antony with his unfeeling, hard-hearted temper, thus letting a woman perish whose soul depended upon him and him alone. . . . In fine, they so melted and unmanned him that, fully believing she would die if he forsook her, he put off the war and returned to Alexandria.

When Octavia returned from Athens, Cæsar, who considered she

had been injuriously treated, commanded her to live in a separate
house; but she refused to leave the house of her husband, and entreated him, unless he had already resolved, upon other motives, to
make war with Antony, that he would on her account let it alone; it
would be intolerable to have it said of the two greatest commanders
in the world that they had involved the Roman people in a civil war,
the one out of passion for, the other out of resentment about, a woman.
And her behaviour proved her words to be sincere. She remained in
Antony's house as if he were at home in it, and took the noblest and
most generous care, not only of his children by her, but of those by
Fulvia also. She received all the friends of Antony that came to
Rome to seek office or upon any business, and did her utmost to prefer
their requests to Cæsar; yet this her honourable deportment did but,
without her meaning it, damage the reputation of Antony; the wrong
he did to such a woman made him hated. Nor was the division he
made among his sons at Alexandria less unpopular; it seemed a
theatrical piece of insolence and contempt of his country. For assembling the people in the exercise ground, and causing two golden
thrones to be placed on a platform of silver, the one for him and the
other for Cleopatra, and at their feet lower thrones for their children,
he proclaimed Cleopatra Queen of Egypt, Cyprus, Libya, and Cœle-
Syria, and with her conjointly Cæsarion, the reputed son of the former
Cæsar, who left Cleopatra with child. His own sons by Cleopatra were
to have the style of kings of kings; to Alexander he gave Armenia and
Media, with Parthia, so soon as it should be overcome; to Ptolemy,
Phœnicia, Syria, and Cilicia. . . . Cleopatra was then, as at other times
when she appeared in public, dressed in the habit of the goddess Isis,[14]
and gave audience to the people under the name of the New Isis.

   Cæsar, relating these things in the senate, and often complaining
to the people, excited men's minds against Antony, and Antony also
sent messages of accusation against Cæsar. The principal of his charges
were these: first, that he had not made any division with him of Sicily,
which was lately taken from Pompey; secondly, that he had retained
the ships he had lent him for the war; thirdly, that, after deposing
Lepidus, their colleague, he had taken for himself the army, governments, and revenues formerly appropriated to him; and lastly, that
he had parcelled out almost all Italy amongst his own soldiers, and left

   14. Isis, sister and wife of Osiris, was a goddess representing the principle of
fruitfulness. The Greeks identified her with Demeter, goddess of agriculture
and harvests. In Rome her worship was popular during the time of the empire.

nothing for his. Cæsar's answer was as follows: that he had put
Lepidus out of government because of his own misconduct; that
what he had got in war he would divide with Antony, so soon as
Antony gave him a share of Armenia; that Antony's soldiers had no
claims in Italy, being in possession of Media and Parthia.

Antony was in Armenia when this answer came to him, and immediately sent Canidius with sixteen legions towards the sea; but he,
in the company of Cleopatra, went to Ephesus, whither ships were
coming in from all quarters to form the navy, consisting, vessels of
burden included, of eight hundred vessels, of which Cleopatra furnished two hundred, together with twenty thousand talents, and provision for the whole army during the war. . . .

The speed and extent of Antony's preparations alarmed Cæsar,
who feared he might be forced to fight the decisive battle that summer.
For he wanted many necessaries, and the people grudged very much
to pay the taxes; freemen being called upon to pay a fourth part of
their incomes, and freed slaves an eighth of their property, so that
there were loud outcries against him, and disturbances throughout
all Italy. And this is looked upon as one of the greatest of Antony's
oversights, that he did not then press the war. For he allowed time at
once for Cæsar to make his preparations and for the commotions to
pass over. . . .

As soon as Cæsar had completed his preparations, he had a decree
made declaring war on Cleopatra, and depriving Antony of the
authority which he had let a woman exercise in his place. . . .

So wholly was Antony now the mere appendage to the person of
Cleopatra that, although he was much superior to the enemy in land-
forces, yet, out of complaisance to his mistress, he wished the victory
to be gained by sea, and that, too, when he could not but see how, for
want of sailors, his captains, all through unhappy Greece, were pressing every description of men, common travellers and ass-drivers, harvest labourers and boys, and for all this the vessels had not their
complements, but remained, most of them, ill-manned and badly rowed.
Cæsar, on the other side, had ships that were built not for size or
show, but for service, not pompous galleys, but light, swift, and perfectly manned; and from his headquarters at Tarentum and Brundusium he sent messages to Antony not to protract the war, but come
out with his forces. Antony, on the other side, with the like bold language, challenged him to a single combat, though he were much the
older; and, that being refused, proposed to meet him in the Pharsalian

fields, where Cæsar and Pompey had fought before. But whilst Antony
lay with his fleet near Actium, Cæsar seized his opportunity and
crossed the Ionian sea. . . .

When it was resolved to stand to a fight at sea, Antony set fire
to all the Egyptian ships except sixty; and of these the best and largest,
from ten banks down to three, he manned with twenty thousand full-
armed men and two thousand archers. Here it is related that a foot
captain, one that had fought often under Antony, and had his body all
mangled with wounds, exclaimed, "O my general, what have our
wounds and swords done to displease you, that you should give your
confidence to rotten timbers? Let Egyptians and Phœnicians contend
at sea, give us the land, where we know well how to die upon the
spot or gain the victory." . . .

That day and the three following the sea was so rough they could
not engage. But on the fifth there was a calm, and they fought. . . .[15]
Antony in a small boat went from one ship to another, encouraging
his soldiers, and bidding them stand firm and fight as steadily on their
large ships as if they were on land. The masters he ordered that they
should receive the enemy lying still as if they were at anchor, and
maintain the entrance of the port, which was a narrow and difficult
passage. . . . But about noon a breeze sprang up from the sea, and
Antony's men, weary of expecting the enemy so long, and trusting to
their large tall vessels, as if they had been invincible, began to advance
the left squadron. Cæsar was overjoyed to see them move, and ordered
his own right squadron to retire, that he might entice them out to
sea as far as he could, his design being to sail round and round, and
so with his light and well-manned galleys to attack these huge vessels,
which their size and their want of men made slow to move and difficult to manage.

When they engaged, there was no charging or striking of one
ship by another, because Antony's, by reason of their great bulk, were
incapable of the rapidity required to make the stroke effectual, and
on the other side, Cæsar's durst not charge head to head on Antony's,
which were all armed with solid masses and spikes of brass; nor did
they like even to run in on their sides, which were so strongly built
with great squared pieces of timber, fastened together with iron bolts,
that their vessels' beaks would easily have been shattered upon them.
So that the engagement resembled a land fight, or, to speak yet more
properly, the attack and defence of a fortified place; for there were

15. The battle of Actium, 31 B.C.

always three or four vessels of Cæsar's about one of Antony's, pressing them with spears, javelins, poles, and several inventions of fire, which they flung among them, Antony's men using catapults also, to pour down missiles from wooden towers ... The fortune of the day was still undecided, and the battle equal, when on a sudden Cleopatra's sixty ships were seen hoisting sail and making out to sea in full flight, right through the ships that were engaged. For they were placed behind the great ships, which, in breaking through, they put into disorder. The enemy was astonished to see them sailing off with a fair wind towards Peloponnesus. Here it was that Antony showed to all the world that he was no longer actuated by the thoughts and motives of a commander or a man, or indeed by his own judgment at all, and what was once said as a jest, that the soul of a lover lives in some one else's body, he proved to be a serious truth. For, as if he had been born part of her, and must move with her wheresoever she went, as soon as he saw her ship sailing away, he abandoned all that were fighting and spending their lives for him, and put himself aboard a galley of five banks of oars to follow her that had so well begun his ruin and would hereafter accomplish it.

She, perceiving him to follow, gave the signal to come aboard. So, as soon as he came up with them, he was taken into the ship. But without seeing her or letting himself be seen by her, he went forward by himself, and sat alone, without a word, in the ship's prow, covering his face with his two hands. In the meanwhile, some of Cæsar's light Liburnian ships, that were in pursuit, came in sight. But on Antony's commanding to face about, they all gave back except Eurycles the Laconian, who pressed on, shaking a lance from the deck, as if he meant to hurl it at him. Antony, standing at the prow, demanded of him, "Who is this that pursues Antony?" "I am," said he, "Eurycles, the son of Lachares, armed with Cæsar's fortune to revenge my father's death." Lachares had been condemned for a robbery, and beheaded by Antony's orders. However, Eurycles did not attack Antony, but ran with his full force upon the other admiral-galley (for there were two of them), and with the blow turned her round, and took both her and another ship, in which was a quantity of rich plate and furniture. So soon as Eurycles was gone, Antony returned to his posture and sate silent, and thus he remained for three days, either in anger with Cleopatra, or wishing not to upbraid her, at the end of which they touched at Tænarus. Here the women of their company succeeded first in bringing them to speak, and afterwards to eat and sleep to-

gether. And, by this time, several of the ships of burden and some
of his friends began to come in to him from the rout, bringing news
of his fleet's being quite destroyed, but that the land forces, they
thought, still stood firm. So that he sent messengers to Canidius to
march the army with all speed through Macedonia into Asia. And,
designing himself to go from Tænarus into Africa, he gave one of the
merchant ships, laden with a large sum of money, and vessels of
silver and gold of great value, belonging to the royal collections, to
his friends, desiring them to share it amongst them, and provide for
their own safety. . . .

But at Actium, his fleet, after a long resistance to Cæsar, and
suffering the most damage from a heavy sea that set in right ahead,
scarcely at four in the afternoon, gave up the contest, with the loss of
not more than five thousand men killed, but of three hundred ships
taken, as Cæsar himself has recorded. Only a few had known of
Antony's flight; and those who were told of it could not at first give
any belief to so incredible a thing as that a general who had nineteen
entire legions and twelve thousand horse upon the seashore, could
abandon all and fly away; and he, above all, who had so often
experienced both good and evil fortune, and had in a thousand wars
and battles been inured to changes. His soldiers, however, would not
give up their desires and expectations, still fancying he would appear
from some part or other, and showed such a generous fidelity to his
service that, when they were thoroughly assured that he was fled in
earnest, they kept themselves in a body seven days, making no account
of the messages that Cæsar sent to them. But at last, seeing that
Canidius himself, who commanded them, was fled from the camp
by night, and that all their officers had quite abandoned them, they
gave way, and made their submission to the conqueror. . . .

When Antony came into Africa, he sent on Cleopatra into Egypt,
and stayed himself in the most entire solitude that he could desire,
roaming and wandering about with only two friends. . . .

But when the officer who commanded for him in Africa, to whose
care he had committed all his forces there, took them over to Cæsar, he
resolved to kill himself, but was hindered by his friends. And coming to
Alexandria, he found Cleopatra busied in a most bold and wonderful
enterprise. Over the small space of land which divides the Red Sea
from the sea near Egypt, Cleopatra had formed a project of dragging
her fleet and setting it afloat in the Arabian Gulf, thus with her soldiers
and her treasure to secure herself a home on the other side, where she

might live in peace far away from war and slavery. But the first galleys which were carried over being burnt by the Arabians of Petra, and Antony not knowing but that the army before Actium still held together, she desisted from her enterprise, and gave orders for the fortifying all the approaches to Egypt. But Antony, leaving the city and the conversation of his friends, built him a dwelling-place in the water, near Pharos, upon a little mole which he cast up in the sea, and there, secluding himself from the company of mankind, said he desired nothing but to live the life of Timon;[16] as indeed, his case was the same, and the ingratitude and injuries which he suffered from those he had esteemed his friends made him hate and distrust all mankind. . . .

Canidius now came, bringing word in person of the loss of the army before Actium. Then he received news that Herod of Judæa was gone over to Cæsar with some legions and cohorts, and that the other kings and princes were in like manner deserting him, and that, out of Egypt, nothing stood by him. All this, however, seemed not to disturb him, but, as if he were glad to put away all hope, that with it he might be rid of all care, and leaving his habitation by the sea, which he called the Timoneum, he was received by Cleopatra in the palace, and set the whole city into a course of feasting, drinking, and presents. . . . But Cleopatra was busied in making a collection of all varieties of poisonous drugs, and, in order to see which of them were the least painful in the operation, she had them tried upon prisoners condemned to die. But, finding that the quick poisons always worked with sharp pains, and that the less painful were slow, she next tried venomous animals, and watching with her own eyes whilst they were applied, one creature to the body of another. This was her daily practice, and she pretty well satisfied herself that nothing was comparable to the bite of the asp, which, without convulsion or groaning, brought on a heavy drowsiness and lethargy, with a gentle sweat on the face, the senses being stupefied by degrees; the patient, in appearance, being sensible of no pain, but rather troubled to be disturbed or awakened like those that are in a profound natural sleep.

At the same time, they sent ambassadors to Cæsar into Asia, Cleopatra asking for the kingdom of Egypt for her children, and Antony, that he might have leave to live as a private man in Egypt,

16. An Athenian misanthrope of the 5th century B.C., who, after disillusionment with mankind, retired into almost complete seclusion—the hero of Shakespeare's *Timon of Athens*.

or, if that were thought too much, that he might retire to Athens. . . .

Cæsar would not listen to any proposals for Antony, but he made answer to Cleopatra, that there was no reasonable favour which she might not expect, if she put Antony to death, or expelled him from Egypt. He sent back with the ambassadors his own freedman, Thyrsus, a man of understanding, and not at all ill-qualified for conveying the messages of a youthful general to a woman so proud of her charms and possessed with the opinion of the power of her beauty. But by the long audiences he received from her, and the special honours which she paid him, Antony's jealousy began to be awakened; he had him seized, whipped, and sent back; writing Cæsar word that the man's busy, impertinent ways had provoked him; in his circumstances he could not be expected to be very patient: "But if it offend you," he added, "you have got my freedman, Hipparchus, with you; hang him up and scourge him to make us even." But Cleopatra, after this, to clear herself, and to allay his jealousies, paid him all the attentions imaginable. When her own birthday came, she kept it as was suitable to their fallen fortunes; but his was observed with the utmost prodigality of splendour and magnificence, so that many of the guests sat down in want, and went home wealthy men. Meantime, continual letters came to Cæsar, telling him his presence was extremely required at Rome.

And so the war was deferred for a season. But, the winter being over, he began his march; he himself by Syria, and his captains through Africa. . . . Cleopatra had caused to be built, joining to the temple of Isis, several tombs and monuments of wonderful height, and very remarkable for the workmanship; thither she removed her treasure, her gold, silver, emeralds, pearls, ebony, ivory, cinnamon, and, after all, a great quantity of torchwood and tow. Upon which Cæsar began to fear lest she should, in a desperate fit, set all these riches on fire; and, therefore, while he was marching towards the city with his army, he omitted no occasion of giving her new assurances of his good intentions. He took up his position in the Hippodrome, where Antony made a fierce sally upon him, routed the horse, and beat them back into their trenches, and so returned with great satisfaction to the palace. . . .

After this, Antony sent a new challenge to Cæsar to fight him hand-to-hand; who made him answer that he might find several other ways to end his life; and he, considering with himself that he could not die more honourably than in battle, resolved to make an effort both by land and sea. At supper, it is said, he bade his servants help him freely, and pour him out wine plentifully, since to-morrow, perhaps, they should not do the same, but be servants to a new master, whilst he should lie on the ground a dead corpse, and nothing. His friends that were about him wept to hear him talk so; which he perceiving, told that he would not lead them to a battle in which he expected rather an honourable death than either safety or victory. That night, it is related, about the middle of it, when the whole city was in a deep silence and general sadness, expecting the event of the next day, on a sudden was heard the sound of all sorts of instruments, and voices singing in tune, and the cry of a crowd of people shouting and dancing, like a troop of bacchanals on its way. This tumultuous procession seemed to take its course right through the middle of the city to the gate nearest the enemy; here it became the loudest, and suddenly passed out. People who reflected considered this to signify that Bacchus, the God whom Antony had always made it his study to copy and imitate, had now forsaken him.

As soon as it was light, he marched his infantry out of the city, and posted them upon a rising ground, from whence he saw his fleet make up to the enemy. There he stood in expectation of the event; but as soon as the fleets came near to one another, his men saluted Cæsar's with their oars; and on their responding, the whole body of the ships, forming into a single fleet, rowed up direct to the city. Antony had no sooner seen this, but the horse deserted him, and went over to Cæsar; and his foot being defeated, he retired into the city, crying out that Cleopatra had betrayed him to the enemies he had made for her sake. She, being afraid lest in his fury and despair he might do her a mischief, fled to her monument, and letting down the falling doors, which were strong with bars and bolts, she sent messengers who should tell Antony she was dead. He, believing it, cried out, "Now, Antony, why delay longer? Fate has snatched away the only pretext for which you could say you desired yet to live." Going into his chamber, and there loosening and opening his coat of armour, "I am not," said he, "troubled, Cleopatra, to be at present bereaved of you, for I shall soon be with you; but it distresses me that so great a general should be found of a tardier courage than a woman." He had a faithful servant, whose name was Eros; he had engaged him formerly to kill him when he should think it necessary, and now he put him to his promise. Eros drew his sword, as designing to kill him, but, suddenly turning round, he slew himself. And as he fell dead at his feet, "It is well done, Eros," said Antony; "you show your master how to do what you had not the heart to do yourself; and so he ran himself into the belly, and laid himself upon the couch. The wound however, was not immediately mortal; and the flow of blood ceasing when he lay down, presently he came to himself, and entreated those that were about him to put him out of his pain; but they all fled out of the chamber, and left him crying out and struggling, until Cleopatra's secretary came to him, having orders from her to bring him into the monument.

When he understood she was alive, he eagerly gave order to the servants to take him up, and in their arms was carried to the door of the building. Cleopatra would not open the door, but, looking from a sort of window, she let down ropes and cords, to which Antony was fastened; and she and her two women, the only persons she had allowed to enter the monument, drew him up. . . . When she had got him up, she laid him on the bed, tearing all her clothes, which she spread upon him; and, beating her breast with her hands, lacerating herself, and disfiguring her own face with the blood from his wounds, she called him her lord, her husband, her emperor, and seemed to have pretty nearly forgotten all her own evils, she was so intent upon his misfortunes. Antony, stopping her lamentations as well as he could, called for wine to drink, either that he was thirsty, or that he imagined that it might put him the sooner out of pain. When he had drunk, he advised her to bring her own affairs, so far as might be honourably done, to a safe conclusion, and that, among all the friends of Cæsar, she should rely on Proculeius; that she should not pity him in his last turn of fate, but rather rejoice for him in remembrance of his past happiness, who had been of all men the most illustrious and powerful, and in the end had fallen not ignobly, a Roman by a Roman overcome.

Just as he breathed his last, Proculeius arrived from Cæsar; for when Antony gave himself his wound, and was carried in to Cleopatra, one of his guards took up Antony's sword and hid it; and, when he saw his opportunity, stole away to Cæsar, and brought him the first news of Antony's death, and withal showed him the bloody sword. Cæsar, upon this, retired into the inner part of his tent, and giving some tears to the death of one that had been nearly allied to him in marriage, his colleague in empire, and companion in so many wars and dangers, he came out to his friends, and, bringing with him many letters, he read to them with how much reason and moderation

he had always addressed himself to Antony, and in return what over-
bearing and arrogant answers he received. Then he sent Proculeius to
use his utmost endeavours to get Cleopatra alive into his power; for
he was afraid of losing a great treasure, and, besides, she would be no
small addition to the glory of his triumph. She, however, was careful
not to put herself in Proculeius's power. . . .

Having taken particular notice of the place, he returned to Cæsar,
and Gallus was sent to parley with her the second time; who, being
come to the door, on purpose prolonged the conference, while Proculeius fixed his scaling-ladders in the window through which the
women had pulled Antony. And so entering, with two men to follow
him, he went straight down to the door where Cleopatra was discoursing with Gallus. One of the two women who were shut up
in the monument with her cried out, "Miserable Cleopatra, you are
taken prisoner!" Upon which she turned quick, and, looking at
Proculeius, drew out her dagger which she had with her to stab
herself. But Proculeius ran up quickly, and seizing her with both his
hands, "For shame," said he, "Cleopatra; you wrong yourself and
Cæsar much, who would rob him of so fair an occasion of showing
his clemency, and would make the world believe the most gentle
of commanders to be a faithless and implacable enemy." And so, taking the dagger out of her hand, he also shook her dress to see if
there were any poison hid in it. After this, Cæsar sent one of his
freedmen with orders to treat her with all gentleness and civility
possible, but to take the strictest precautions to keep her alive. . . .

Of Antony's children, Antyllus, his son by Fulvia, being betrayed
by his tutor, Theodorus, was put to death; and while the soldiers
were cutting off his head, his tutor contrived to steal a precious jewel
which he wore about his neck, and put it in his pocket, and afterwards denied the fact, but was convicted and crucified. Cleopatra's
children, with their attendants, had a guard set on them, and were
treated very honourably. Cæsarion, who was reputed to be the son of
Cæsar the Dictator, was sent by his mother, with a great sum of
money, through Æthiopia, to pass into India; but his tutor persuaded
him to turn back, for that Cæsar designed to make him king. Afterwards, when Cleopatra was dead he was killed.

Many kings and great commanders made petition to Cæsar for
the body of Antony, to give him his funeral rites; but he would
not take away his corpse from Cleopatra, by whose hands he was
buried with royal splendour and magnificence, it being granted to her

to employ what she pleased on his funeral. In this extremity of grief and sorrow, and having inflamed and ulcerated her breasts with beating them, she fell into a high fever, and was very glad of the occasion, hoping, under this pretext, to abstain from food, and so to die in quiet without interference. She had her own physician, Olympus, to whom she told the truth, and asked his advice and help to put an end to herself. But Cæsar, suspecting her purpose, took to menacing language about her children, and excited her fears for them, before which engines her purpose shook and gave way, so that she suffered those about her to give her what meat or medicine they pleased.

Some few days after, Cæsar himself came to make her a visit and comfort her. She lay then upon her pallet-bed in undress, and, on his entering, sprang up from off her bed, having nothing on but the one garment next her body, and flung herself at his feet, her hair and face looking wild and disfigured, her voice quivering, and her eyes sunk in her head. The marks of the blows she had given herself were visible about her bosom, and altogether her whole person seemed no less afflicted than her soul. But, for all this, her old charm, and the boldness of her youthful beauty, had not wholly left her, and, in spite of her present condition, still sparkled from within, and let itself appear in all the movements of her countenance. Cæsar, desiring her to repose herself, sat down by her; and, on this opportunity, she said something to justify her actions, attributing what she had done to the necessity she was under, and to her fear of Antony; and when Cæsar, on each point, made his objections, and she found herself confuted, she broke off at once into language of entreaty and deprecation, as if she desired nothing more than to prolong her life. . . . Cæsar was pleased to hear her talk thus. And, therefore, he went away, well satisfied that he had overreached her, but, in fact, was himself deceived.

There was a young man of distinction among Cæsar's companions named Cornelius Dolabella. He was not without a certain tenderness for Cleopatra, and sent her word privately, as she had besought him to do, that Cæsar was about to return through Syria, and that she and her children were to be sent on within three days. When she understood this, she made her request to Cæsar that he would be pleased to permit her to make oblations to the departed Antony; which being granted, she ordered herself to be carried to the place where he was buried, and there, accompanied by her women, she embraced his tomb with tears in her eyes, and spoke in this manner; "O, dearest Antony," said she, "it is not long since that with these hands I buried you; then they were free, now I am a captive, and pay these last duties to you with a guard upon me, for fear that my just griefs and sorrows should impair my servile body, and make it less fit to appear in their triumph over you. No further offerings or libations expect from me; these are the last honours that Cleopatra can pay your memory, for she is to be hurried away far from you. Nothing could part us whilst we lived, but death seems to threaten to divide us. You, a Roman born, have found a grave in Egypt; I, an Egyptian, am to seek that favour, and none but that, in your country. But if the gods below, with whom you now are, either can or will do anything (since those above have betrayed us), suffer not your living wife to be abandoned; let me not be led in triumph to your shame, but hide me and bury me here with you, since, amongst all my bitter misfortunes, nothing has afflicted me like this brief time that I have lived away from you."

Having made these lamentations, crowning the tomb with garlands and kissing it, she gave orders to prepare her a bath, and, coming out of the bath, she lay down and made a sumptuous meal. And a country fellow brought her a little basket, which the guards intercepting and asking what it was, the fellow put the leaves which lay uppermost aside, and showed them it was full of figs; and on their admiring the largeness and beauty of the figs, he laughed, and invited them to take some, which they refused, and, suspecting nothing, bade him carry them in. After her repast, Cleopatra sent to Cæsar a letter which she had written and sealed; and, putting everybody out of the monument but her two women, she shut the doors. Cæsar, opening her letter, and finding pathetic prayers and entreaties that she might be buried in the same tomb with Antony, soon guessed what was doing. At first he was going himself in all haste, but, changing his mind, he sent others to see. The thing had been quickly done. The messengers came at full speed, and found the guards apprehensive of nothing; but on opening the doors they saw her stone-dead, lying upon a bed of gold, set out in all her royal ornaments. Iras, one of her women, lay dying at her feet, and Charmion, just ready to fall, scarce able to hold up her head, was adjusting her mistress's diadem. And when one that came in said angrily, "Was this well done of your lady, Charmion?" "Extremely well,"

she answered, "and as became the descendant of so many kings";
and as she said this, she fell down dead by the bedside.

Some relate that an asp was brought in amongst those figs and
covered with the leaves, and that Cleopatra had arranged that it
might settle on her before she knew, but, when she took away some
of the figs and saw it, she said, "So here it is," and held out her bare
arm to be bitten. Others say that it was kept in a vase, and that she
vexed and pricked it with a golden spindle till it seized her arm.
But what really took place is known to no one, since it was also said
that she carried poison in a hollow bodkin, about which she wound
her hair: yet there was not so much as a spot found, or any symptom
of poison upon her body, nor was the asp seen within the monument;
only something like the trail of it was said to have been noticed
on the sand by the sea, on the part towards which the building faced
and where the windows were. Some relate that two faint puncture-
marks were found on Cleopatra's arm, and to this account Cæsar
seems to have given credit; for in his triumph there was carried a
figure of Cleopatra, with an asp clinging to her. Such are the various
accounts. But Cæsar, though much disappointed by her death, yet
could not but admire the greatness of her spirit, and gave order that
her body should be buried by Antony with royal splendour and magnificence. Her women, also, received honourable burial by his
directions. Cleopatra had lived nine-and-thirty years, during twenty-
two of which she had reigned as queen, and for fourteen had been
Antony's partner in his empire. Antony, according to some authorities, was fifty-three, according to others, fifty-six years old. His
statues were all thrown down, but those of Cleopatra were left untouched; for one of her friends gave Cæsar two thousand talents to
save them from the fate of Antony's.

LYRIC POETRY

of Greece and Rome

AS THE NAME indicates, a lyric was at one time the text of a song—a poem to be sung to the accompaniment of the lyre. But men sang before they invented instruments, and the literary type is older than its name. In fact, philology and anthropology agree in supposing that the "spontaneous overflow of powerful feelings" into the war song, the hunting song, the incantation, the pæan of victory, and the hymns of thanksgiving was the simultaneous origin of music and of literature. These primitive songs later furnished the starting points for epic, drama, and other literary types, but the purely lyrical impulse was never lost. The folksong has always kept the original relationship between the two arts, and even the literary lyric has never entirely forgot its origins. Sometimes, as in early Greece, medieval Provence and Germany, and Elizabethan England, the union between lyric and song has been close; but since the beginning of the eighteenth century they have been drifting apart, and at present the lyric is seldom intended as a song.

Nevertheless, the idea of song still determines the nature of the lyric. It must be relatively brief. Its rhythms and patterns of sound

439

must be highly organized and eminently satisfying. And, above all, it must communicate the personal feeling of the author, for the lyric may or may not have "ideas," but if it lacks feeling it is not a lyric. In fact, the personal element is so strong that the quality and status of lyric poetry at any given time are a safe index to the value placed on the individual. Thus both the Renaissance and the Romantic Period stressed the full development of each person, the right and duty of a man to be himself; and they consequently produced splendid outbursts of lyric poetry. But the Neo-Classical Period emphasized the general and objective point of view, and made conformity one of the great objectives of civilized man; and consequently the lyric poetry of this period is both slight and inferior by comparison with that of the preceding and following ages.

The concentration in style, the importance of sound, and the personal expression make adequate translation of Greek and Roman lyric poetry impossible. In a way, no translation is entirely satisfactory, but with lyrics the difficulty is particularly acute. A competent craftsman can produce a translation which may adequately imitate sound and reproduce meaning, but the poetry will disappear in the process. And a good poet often writes an excellent version which can stand on its own merits, but is simply a different poem from the original. The translator of lyric poetry is really faced with three tasks, all impossible: he must approximate the rhythms and sounds of an alien tongue; he must say in one language exactly what has been said in another; and he must *feel* his subject just as a totally different person felt it. Anyone who does not read the original languages must simply take it on faith that the lyrics of foreign literatures are really much better poems than they seem to be in English translations.

The following selection presents some of the dominant types of the lyric poetry of civilized Europe for a period of over a thousand years. Naturally, not all good poets, or even all types, can be represented. Thus the odes of Pindar are not attempted, and the elegiac poem is shown only slightly in Catullus. However, the nature of the lyrics of the Greek and Roman worlds can be seen even in a brief collection. In Sappho, Catullus, and Horace we have a clear picture of three very different persons, and of life—and particularly love—as seen through their eyes. The deep and splendid passion of Sappho is far removed from the intense but unstable emotions of Catullus; and the urbane good-nature of Horace probably regarded both these children of feeling rather quizzically.

Anacreon devoted his life to singing the praises of love and wine with an elegance that sometimes conceals his sincerity. He realized his limitations and stayed within them, but so well did he cultivate his small garden that it still bears his name. Since his Greek and Roman imitators, Anacreontic poetry has been recognized as a fixed literary form, and in the modern world it has attracted men as diverse as Ronsard, Ben Jonson, Goethe, and Keats.

Theocritus also developed and fixed for centuries one particular type of poetry, the pastoral idyll. He describes the life and amusements of the simple folk of his native Sicily—the songs and loves of the shepherds, the toil of the fishermen, the gossip of the women—but casts over the rustic scene a spell of poetic idealization that transforms Sicily of the third century before Christ into a land of dreams. The pastoral tradition which he established was followed by Bion and Moschus in Greek, and by Virgil in Latin. With the Renaissance it was adapted to dramatic use in innumerable pastoral plays, and was continued in much its original form in Spenser's *Shepherd's Calendar*. This pastoral tradition is perhaps best known to English readers through Milton's use of it in *Lycidas*.

The *Greek Anthology* is a vast collection of short poems covering the whole range of Greek lyric poetry for seventeen hundred years. It is one of the things preserved for the world at Constantinople during the Dark Ages. About 900 A.D., Constantinus Cephalas, using a number of earlier collections, put together an anthology of Greek poetry representing 320 authors and containing about six thousand poems. This collection was long known in the form of a later abridgement, but in the seventeenth century the complete manuscript was discovered in the Palatine library in Heidelberg. Hence the work is sometimes known as the *Palatine Anthology*. Its contents include love-poems, epitaphs, inscriptions, rhetorical exercises—almost everything that can be dealt with in short verses.

Since Latin poetry derived its metrics, its forms, and its inspiration from Greece, it is perfectly proper to consider the classical lyric as one body of literature, and in spite of a wide variety of subjects, forms, and moods, this poetry has rather definite general characteristics. Particularly notable is the combination of flawless workmanship and perfection of form down to the last detail with a sense of genuine and often powerful emotion. This nice balance of forces has served as a constant inspiration and model for poets of later ages, and the modern reader may possibly get a better idea of the original effect of the classical lyric by reading some of the lyrics of Ben Jonson, Walter Savage Landor, and A. E. Housman than he can gain by a study of any of the translations from Greek and Latin.

SAPPHO
(7TH CENTURY B. C.)

ODE TO APHRODITE
(1)

Splendor-throned Queen, immortal Aphrodite,
Daughter of Jove, Enchantress, I implore thee
Vex not my soul with agonies and anguish;
    Slay me not, Goddess!

Come in thy pity—come, if I have prayed thee;
Come at the cry of my sorrow; in the old times
Oft thou hast heard, and left thy father's heaven,
    Left the gold houses,

Yoking thy chariot. Swiftly did the doves fly,
Swiftly they brought thee, waving plumes of wonder—
Waving their dark plumes all across the aether,
    All down the azure.

Very soon they lighted. Then didst thou, Divine one,
Laugh a bright laugh from lips and eyes immortal,
Ask me what ailed me, wherefore out of heaven
    Thus I had called thee;

What it was made me madden in my heart so;
Question me, smiling—say to me, "My Sappho,
Who is it wrongs thee? Tell me who refuses
    Thee, vainly sighing.

"Be it who it may be, he that flies shall follow;
He that rejects gifts, he shall bring thee many;
He that hates now shall love thee dearly, madly—
    Aye, though thou wouldst not."

So once again come, Mistress; and, releasing
Me from my sadness, give me what I sue for,
Grant me my prayer, and be as heretofore now
    Friend and protectress.

(Edwin Arnold)

ODE TO ANACTORIA
(2)

Peer of gods he seemeth to me, the blissful
Man who sits and gazes at thee before him,
Close beside thee sits, and in silence hears thee
    Silverly speaking,

Laughing love's low laughter. Oh this, this only
Stirs the troubled heart in my breast to tremble!
For should I but see thee a little moment,
    Straight is my voice hushed;

Yea, my tongue is broken, and through and through me
'Neath the flesh impalpable fire runs tingling;
Nothing see mine eyes, and a noise of roaring
    Waves in my ear sounds;

Sweat runs down in rivers, a tremor seizes
All my limbs, and paler than grass in autumn,
Caught by pains of menacing death, I falter,
    Lost in the love-trance.

(J. Addington Symonds)

LONGING
(52)

The silver moon is set;
 The Pleiades are gone;
Half the long night is spent, and yet
 I lie alone.

(J. H. Merivale)

ONE GIRL
(93, 94)

I

Like the sweet apple which reddens upon the topmost bough,
A-top on the topmost twig,—which the pluckers forgot, somehow,—
Forgot it not, nay, but got it not, for none could get it till now.

II

Like the wild hyacinth flower which on the hills is found,
Which the passing feet of the shepherds forever tear and wound,
Until the purple blossom is trodden into the ground.

(D. G. Rossetti)

EVENING
(95)

Evening, all things thou bringest
 Which dawn spread apart from each other;
The lamb and the kid thou bringest,
 Thou bringest the boy to his mother.

(J. Addington Symonds)

DEATH
(137)

Death is an evil. This the gods on high
Know well: if it were good, the gods would die.

(C. S. Brown)

ANACREON
(6TH CENTURY B. C.)

THE STUBBORN LYRE
(Ode 1)

While I sweep the sounding string,
While th' Atridae's praise I sing,
Victors on the Trojan plain,
Or to Cadmus raise the strain,
Hark! in soft and whispered sighs
Love's sweet notes the shell replies.
Late I strung my harp anew,
Changed the strings—the subject too;—
Loud I sang Alcides' toils;
Still the lyre my labor foils,
Still with love's sweet silver sounds
Every martial theme confounds.
Farewell, heroes, chiefs, and kings:
Naught but love will suit my strings.

(C. A. Wheelwright)

DEFIANCE OF AGE
(Ode 11)

The women tell me every day
That all my bloom has passed away.
"Behold," the pretty wantons cry,
"Behold this mirror with a sigh;
The locks upon thy brow are few,
And, like the rest, they're withering too!"
Whether decline has thinned my hair
I'm sure I neither know nor care;
But this I know, and this I feel,
As onward to the tomb I steal,
That still, as death approaches nearer,
The joys of life are sweeter, dearer;
And had I but an hour to live,
That little hour to bliss I'd give!

(Thomas Moore)

THE NECESSITY OF DRINKING
(Ode 19)

Observe when mother earth is dry
She drinks the droppings of the sky;
And then the dewy cordial gives
To every thirsty plant that lives.
The vapors, which at evening weep,
Are beverage to the swelling deep;
And when the rosy sun appears
He drinks the ocean's misty tears.
The moon, too, quaffs her paly stream
Of lustre from the solar beam.
Then hence with all your sober thinking!
Since Nature's holy law is drinking,
I'll make the laws of Nature mine,
And pledge the universe in wine!

(Thomas Moore)

THE ONE CONSOLATION
(Ode 25)

Within this goblet, rich and deep,
I cradle all my woes to sleep.
Why should we breathe the sigh of fear,
Or pour the unavailing tear?
For Death will never heed the sigh,
Nor soften at the tearful eye;
And eyes that sparkle, eyes that weep,
Must all alike be sealed in sleep.
Then let us never vainly stray,
In search of thorns, from pleasure's way;
Oh! let us quaff the rosy wave
Which Bacchus loves, which Bacchus gave;
And in the goblet, rich and deep,
Cradle our crying woes to sleep!

(Thomas Moore)

FAREWELL TO TRIFLES
(Ode 36)

Away, away, you men of rules,
What have I to do with schools?
They'd make me learn, they'd make me think,
But would they make me love and drink?
Teach me this, and let me swim
My soul upon the goblet's brim;
Teach me this, and let me twine
My arms around the nymph divine!
Age begins to blanch my brow,
I've time for naught but pleasure now.
Fly, and cool my goblet's glow
At yonder fountain's gelid flow;
I'll quaff, my boy, and calmly sink
This soul to slumber as I drink!
Soon, too soon, my jocund slave,
You'll deck your master's grassy grave,
And there's an end—for ah! you know
They drink but little wine below.

(Thomas Moore)

CUPID AND THE BEE
(Ode 40)

Cupid once upon a bed
Of roses laid his weary head;
Luckless urchin not to see
Within the leaves a slumbering bee!
The bee awaked—with anger wild
The bee awaked and stung the child.
Loud and piteous are his cries;
To Venus quick he runs, he flies!
"Oh mother!—I am wounded through—
I die with pain—in sooth I do!
Stung by some angry little thing,
Some serpent on a tiny wing—
A bee it was—for once, I know,
I heard a rustic call it so."

Thus he spoke, and she the while
Heard him with a soothing smile;
Then said, "My infant, if so much
Thou feel the little wild bee's touch,
How must the heart, ah, Cupid! be,
The hapless heart that's stung by thee!"

(Thomas Moore)

THEOCRITUS
(FL. 270 B. C.)

THE CYCLOPS IN LOVE
(Idyl 6)

Damoetas, and Daphnis the herdsman, once on a time, Aratus,[1] led the flock together into one place. Golden was the down on the chin of one, the beard of the other was half-grown, and by a well-head the twain sat them down, in the summer noon, and thus they sang. 'Twas Daphnis that began the singing, for the challenge had come from Daphnis.

Daphnis's Song of the Cyclops

Galatea[2] is pelting thy flock with apples, Polyphemus, she says the goatherd is a laggard lover! And thou dost not glance at her, oh hard, hard that thou art, but still thou sittest at thy sweet piping. Ah see, again, she is pelting thy dog, that follows thee to watch thy sheep. He barks, as he looks into the brine, and now the beautiful waves that softly plash reveal him as he runs upon the shore. Take heed that he leap not on the maiden's limbs as she rises from the salt water; see that he rend not her lovely body! Ah, thence again, see, she is wantoning, light as dry thistle-down in the scorching summer weather. She flies when thou art wooing her; when thou woo'st not she pursues thee, she plays out all her game and leaves her king unguarded. For truly, to Love, Polyphemus, many a time doth foul seem fair!

*He ended, and Damoetas touched a prelude to
his sweet song.*

1. A friend of Theocritus, to whom the poem is addressed.
2. *Galatea*, a sea-nymph.

I saw her, by Pan, I saw her when she was pelting my flock. Nay, she escaped not my one dear eye,—wherewith I shall see to my life's end,—let Telemus[3] the soothsayer, that prophesies hateful things, hateful things take home, to keep them for his children! But it is all to torment her, that I, in my turn, give not back her glances, pretending that I have another love. To hear this makes her jealous of me, by Paean, and she wastes with pain, and springs madly from the sea, gazing at my caves and at my herds. And I hiss on my dog to bark at her, for when I loved Galatea he would whine with joy, and lay his muzzle on her lap. Perchance when she marks how I use her she will send me many a messenger, but on her envoys I will shut my door till she promises that herself will make a glorious bridal-bed on this island for me. For in truth, I am not so hideous as they say! But lately I was looking into the sea, when all was calm; beautiful seemed my beard, beautiful my one eye—as I count beauty—and the sea reflected the gleam of my teeth whiter than the Parian stone. Then, all to shun the evil eye, did I spit thrice in my breast; for this spell was taught me by the crone, Cottytaris, that piped of yore to the reapers in Hippocoon's field.

Then Damoetas kissed Daphnis, as he ended his song, and he gave Daphnis a pipe, and Daphnis gave him a beautiful flute. Damoetas fluted, and Daphnis piped, the herdsmen,—and anon the calves were dancing in the soft green grass. Neither won the victory, but both were invincible.

(Andrew Lang)

3. Telemus had predicted that Polyphemus would be blinded by Odysseus.

THE GREEK ANTHOLOGY*
(490 B.C.–A.D. 1000)

A WOMAN'S VOW
(V, 7)

In holy night we made the vow;
And the same night, that long before

*The translations by F. A. Wright are taken from *Poets of the Greek Anthology,* by F. A. Wright, translated by F. A. Wright, published by E. P. Dutton & Co., Inc., N. Y.

Had seen our early passion grow,
  Was witness to the faith we swore.
Did I not swear to love her ever?
  And have I ever dared to rove?
Did she not vow a rival never
  Should shake her faith, or steal her love?
Yet now she says those words are air;
  Those vows were written in the water;
And, by the lamp that heard her swear,
  Hath yielded to the first who sought her.

MELEAGER *(C. Merivale)*

HERACLITUS
(VII, 80)

They told me, Heraclitus, they told me you were dead,
They brought me bitter news to hear and bitter tears to shed.
I wept as I remembered how often you and I
Had tired the sun with talking and sent him down the sky.
And now that you are lying, my dear old Carian[1] guest,
A handful of gray ashes, long, long ago at rest,
Still are thy pleasant voices, thy Nightingales,[2] awake;
For Death, he taketh all away, but them he cannot take.

CALLIMACHUS *(William Cory)*

LOT'S WIFE
(VII, 311)

No corpse doth lie within this stone,
No tomb without this corpse doth own;
For corpse and tomb here both are one.

AGATHIAS *(F. A. Wright)*

1. Caria was a province on the coast of Asia Minor. Its capital, Halicarnassus, was the home of the Heraclitus here commemorated, who is not the philosopher of that name.
2. Reference to the title of a volume of poems by Heraclitus.

EPITAPH
(VII, 307)

My name, my country, what are they to thee?
What, whether proud or base my pedigree?
Perhaps I far surpassed all other men;
Perhaps I fell below them all. What then?
Suffice it, stranger, that thou seest a tomb.
Thou knowst its use. It hides—no matter whom.
PAULUS SILENTIARIUS (William Cowper)

HIS OWN EPITAPH
(VII, 715)

Far, far away is Italy,
   And far Tarentum dear;
O thought more sad than death itself,
   I lie a stranger here.

Such is the life of wanderers,
   A life of toil and strain;
And yet the Muses' love has brought
   Some sweetness to my pain.

"Leonidas—Leonidas"—
   That name they'll ne'er forget;
The Muses' gift shall spread my fame
   Till every sun be set.
LEONIDAS OF TARENTUM (F. A. Wright)

A BOXER'S STATUE
(IX, 80)

He never hurt a living thing,
   His hands with blood were never wet;
So we who fought him in the ring
   His statue here have set.
LUCILIUS (F. A. Wright)

TO XANTHO SINGING
(IX, 570)

White waxen cheeks, soft scented breast,
    Deep eyes wherein the Muses nest;
Sweet lips that perfect pleasure bring,
    Sing me your song: pale Xantho, sing.

"Close shut within a bed of stone
    Soon shall I rest in sleep alone
And there for ever sleeping lie
    For ever and eternity."

Too soon the music ends. Again,
    Again, repeat the sad sweet strain.
With perfumed fingers touch the string;
    O Love's delight, pale Xantho, sing.
          PHILODEMUS THE EPICUREAN *(F. A. Wright)*

THE BUTCHER
(X, 85)

Death is the butcher, men his herd of swine;
    To him we owe our life.
He picks at random from the squealing line;
    Then draws his knife.
          PALLADAS OF ALEXANDRIA *(F. A. Wright)*

REPROACH TO DIONYSUS
(XI, 26)

See, I am drunk with wine, my body reels—
O save me from this spell that on me steals.
Nay, 'tis not just: I bear the god divine
And he won't even guide these legs of mine.
          MARCUS ARGENTARIUS *(F. A. Wright)*

MORNING AND EVENING STAR
(XII, 114)

Hail and farewell, bright star,
  Glad harbinger of morn,
  Thou leavest me forlorn,
Oh, cruel morning star.

As light of eve return,
  And through the darkness guide
  My darling to my side,
Let her to me return.

MELEAGER (F. A. Wright)

CATULLUS
(c. 84–c. 54 B. c.)

DEDICATION
(1)

My little volume is complete,
  With all the care and polish neat
    That makes it fair to see;
To whom shall I then—to whose praise—
Inscribe my lively, graceful lays?
    Cornelius,[1] friend, to thee.

Thou only of th' Italian race
Hast dared in three small books to trace
    All time's remotest flight.
O Jove, how labor'd, learn'd, and wise!
Yet still thou ne'er wouldst quite despise
    The trifles that I write.

Then take the book I now address;
Though small its size—its merit less—
    'Tis all thy friend can give;

1. Cornelius Nepos, Roman historian.

And let me, guardian Muse, implore
That when at least one age is o'er,
    This volume yet may live.

(Charles Lamb)

LOVE BEYOND RECKONING
(5)

Let us, Lesbia darling, still
Live our life, and love our fill;
Heeding not a jot, howe'er
Churlish dotards chide or stare!
Suns go down, but 'tis to rise
Brighter in the morning skies;
But when sets our little light,
We must sleep in endless night.
A thousand kisses grant me, sweet;
With a hundred these complete;
Lip me a thousand more, and then
Another hundred give again.
A thousand add to these, anon
A hundred more, then hurry on
Kiss after kiss without cessation,
Until we lose all calculation;
So envy shall not mar our blisses
By numbering up our tale of kisses.

(T. Martin)

ADVICE TO HIMSELF
(8)

Cease from this idle fooling trade—
    Cease, wretch Catullus, all is o'er;
And what thou seest has long decayed,
    E'en think it lost for evermore.

Of old thy suns were bright and clear,
    When thou, where'er her path has lain,
Wouldst chase the damsel, loved so dear
    As none will e'er be loved again.

Then were the sports of amorous jest
    Still urged by thee with new delight;
While she scarce chid and not repressed—
    Oh, then thy suns were truly bright!

She now rejects thee—cast her off,
    Nor weakly chase a flying fair;
Nor grieving live to be her scoff,
    But coldly steel thy mind to bear.

Damsel, farewell! Catullus stern
    Thy scorn disdains, thy love will shun;
And soon thy pride to grief shall turn,
    When left by him, and wooed by none.

Think, wanton, what remains for thee:
    Who will pursue thy lonely way?
Who in thy form will beauty see?
    Whose fervent love shalt thou repay?

Whose fondling care shalt thou avow?
    Whose kisses now shalt thou return?
Whose lip in rapture bite?—But thou—
    Hold! hold! Catullus, cold and stern.

                              (Charles Lamb)

LAST WORD TO LESBIA
(11)

O Furius and Aurelius, comrades sweet!
    Who to Ind's farthest shore with me would roam,
Where the far-sounding Orient billows beat
    Their fury into foam;

Or to Hyrcania,[2] balm-breathed Araby,
    The Sacian's or the quivered Parthian's land,
Or where seven-mantled Nile's swoll'n waters dye
    The sea with yellow sand;

2. Hyrcania (southeast of the Caspian Sea) and all the other districts listed here are used simply as examples of remote and outlandish places.

Or cross the lofty Alpine fells, to view
   Great Caesar's trophied fields, the Gallic Rhine,
The paint-smeared Briton race, grim-visaged crew,
   Placed by earth's limit-line.

To all prepared with me to brave the way,
   To dare whate'er the eternal gods decree—
These few unwelcome words to her convey
   Who once was all to me.

Still let her revel with her godless train,
   Still clasp her hundred slaves to passion's thrall,
Still truly love not one, but ever drain
   The life-blood of them all.

Nor let her more my once fond passion heed,
   For by her faithlessness 'tis blighted now,
Like floweret on the verge of grassy mead
   Crushed by the passing plow.

                           (J. Cranstoun)

THE PROOF
(92)

Lesbia forever on me rails;
To talk of me she never fails.
Now, hang me, but for all her art,
I find that I have gained her heart.

My proof is this: I plainly see
The case is just the same with me.
I curse her every hour sincerely;
Yet, hang me, but I love her dearly!

                          (Jonathan Swift)

TO A BEREAVED FRIEND*
(96)

Friend, if the mute and shrouded dead
   Are touched at all by tears,
By love long fled and friendship sped
   And the unreturning years,

O then, to her that early died,
   O doubt not, bridegroom, to thy bride
Thy love is sweet and sweeteneth
   The very bitterness of death.

(H. W. Garrod)

AT HIS BROTHER'S GRAVE*
(101)

Over the mighty world's highway,
   City by city, sea by sea,
Brother, thy brother comes to pay
   Pitiful offerings unto thee.

I only ask to grace thy bier
   With gifts that only give farewell,
To tell to ears that cannot hear
   The things that it is vain to tell,

And, idly communing with dust,
   To know thy presence still denied,
And ever mourn forever lost
   A soul that never should have died.

Yet think not wholly vain today
   The fashion that our fathers gave
That hither brings me, here to lay
   Some gift of sorrow on thy grave.

* Taken from *The Oxford Book of Latin Verse* and used by permission of
The Clarendon Press, Oxford.

Take, brother, gifts a brother's tears
Bedewed with sorrow as they fell,
And 'Greeting' to the end of years,
And to the end of years 'Farewell.'

(H. W. Garrod)

HORACE
(65–8 B. C.)

THE SCHOOL OF EXPERIENCE
(Odes, I, 5)

What slender youth, bedew'd with liquid odors,
Courts thee on roses in some pleasant cave,
 Pyrrha? For whom bind'st thou
 In wreaths thy golden hair,

Plain in thy neatness? O how oft shall he
Of faith and changed gods complain, and seas
 Rough with black winds, and storms
 Unwonted shall admire!

Who now enjoys thee credulous, all gold,
Who, always vacant, always amiable
 Hopes thee, of flattering gales
 Unmindful. Hapless they

To whom thou untried seem'st fair. Me in my vow'd
Picture, the sacred wall declares to have hung
 My dank and dropping weeds
 To the stern god of sea.[1]

(John Milton)

THE DEATH OF CLEOPATRA
(Odes, I, 37)

Drink, comrades, drink; give loose to mirth!
With joyous footstep beat the earth,

1. Shipwrecked sailors frequently hung up their brine-soaked clothes in Neptune's temple as an offering of thanks for their deliverance.

And spread before the War-God's shrine
The Salian[2] feast, the sacrificial wine.

Bring forth from each ancestral hoard
Strong draughts of Caecuban[3] long stored,
Till now forbidden. Fill the bowl!
For she is fallen, that great Egyptian Queen,
With all her crew contaminate and obscene,
Who, mad with triumph, in her pride,
The manly might of Rome defied,
And vowed destruction to the Capitol.

As the swift falcon stooping from above
With beak unerring strikes the dove,
Or as the hunter tracks the deer
Over Haemonian plains[4] of snow,
Thus Caesar came. Then on her royal State
With Mareotic[5] fumes inebriate,
A shadow fell of fate and fear,
And through the lurid glow
From all her burning galleys shed
She turned her last surviving bark, and fled.[6]
She sought no refuge on a foreign shore.
She sought her doom: far nobler 't was to die
Than like a panther caged in Roman bonds to lie.
The sword she feared not. In her realm once more,
Serene amongst deserted fanes,
Unmoved 'mid vacant halls she stood;
Then to the aspic gave her darkening veins,
And sucked the death into her blood.

Deliberately she died: fiercely disdained
To bow her haughty head to Roman scorn,

2. The luxury of the banquets of the Salian priests was proverbial.
3. A fine wine.
4. The snowfields of the Balkan mountains.
5. *Mareotic*, Egyptian, here meaning Egyptian wine.
6. Horace (apparently writing just after the event) confuses Antony's fleet with Cleopatra's.

Discrowned, and yet a Queen; a captive chained;
A woman desolate and forlorn.

(Stephen E. de Vere)

THE RECONCILIATION
(Odes, III, 9)

HORACE

Whilst I was dear and thou wert kind,
  And I, and I alone, might lie
Upon thy snowy breast reclined,
  Not Persia's king so blest as I.

LYDIA

Whilst I to thee was all in all,
  Nor Chloe might with Lydia vie,
Renowned in ode or madrigal,
  Not Roman Ilia famed as I.

HORACE

I now am Thracian Chloe's slave,
  With hand and voice that charms the air,
For whom even death itself I'd brave,
  So fate the darling girl would spare!

LYDIA

I dote on Calais—and I
  Am all his passion, all his care,
For whom a double death I'd die,
  So fate the darling boy would spare!

HORACE

What if our ancient love return,
  And bind us with a closer tie,
If I the fair-haired Chloe spurn,
  And as of old for Lydia sigh?

LYDIA

Though lovelier than yon star is he,
   Thou fickle as an April sky,
More churlish, too, than Adria's sea,
   With thee I'd live, with thee I'd die!

(T. Martin)

LAST PRAYER TO VENUS
(Odes, III, 26)

I once was all that girls desire
   And fought with glory at Love's call;
But now my arms and worn-out lyre
   I hang up, idle, on the wall,

And pray that sea-born Venus show
   One final kindness. Here, O here,
Hang up the crowbar, torch, and bow
   That stubborn doors have learned to fear.

Goddess of blessed Cyprus' land
   And Memphis' clime (too warm for snow)—
Queen, with the lash raised in your hand
   Strike haughty Chloe just one blow.

(C. S. Brown)

MORTALITY
(Odes IV, 7)

The snow, dissolv'd, no more is seen,
The fields and woods, behold, are green;
The changing year renews the plain,
The rivers know their banks again;
The sprightly Nymph and naked Grace
The mazy dance together trace;
The changing year's successive plan
Proclaims mortality to Man.
Rough winter's blasts to spring give way,
Spring yields to summer's sovran ray;

Then summer sinks in autumn's reign,
And winter holds the world again.
Her losses soon the moon supplies,
But wretched Man, when once he lies
Where Priam and his sons are laid,
Is naught but ashes and a shade.
Who knows if Jove, who counts our score,
Will toss us in a morning more?
What with your friend you nobly share
At least you rescue from your heir.
Nor you, Torquatus, boast of Rome,
When Minos once has fixed your doom,
Or eloquence or splendid birth
Or virtue shall restore to earth.
Hippolytus,[7] unjustly slain,
Diana calls to life in vain,
Nor can the might of Theseus rend
The chains of hell that hold his friend.[8]

(Samuel Johnson)

7. Hippolytus, a worshipper of Diana, was killed because of false accusations made by his stepmother, Phaedra. Racine's play on the subject appears later in this anthology.

8. Theseus went to Hades to help his friend Pirithous carry off Persephone. The two men were caught there and imprisoned until Hercules rescued Theseus, but Pirithous was left behind.

THE
MIDDLE
AGES

THE MIDDLE AGES

THE PERIOD OF HISTORY between ancient and modern times is called the Middle Ages. Although historians are agreed in fixing its beginning at the disintegration of the western Roman Empire, about the middle of the fifth century of the Christian era, they are not so well agreed in fixing its termination. The fall of Constantinople, the revival of ancient classical learning, the invention of printing, the voyages of Columbus have all been proposed as marking the end of medieval times; but it is fairly safe to say that all the extraordinary activity in the fifteenth century in expanding man's intellectual and geographical worlds was the true beginning of modern times.

The first thing to remember about the Middle Ages is that the term itself is one of historical convenience rather than accuracy, for the Middle Ages manifested no continuous or prevalent unity in thought or institutions. The Middle Ages were many ages and not one. In reality the thousand or more years of this era constitute the period of gestation of the modern world.

The official end of Roman authority in western Europe came with the termination of the reign of the young emperor Romulus Augustulus in A.D. 476. From that time until the year 800 there was no emperor of Rome in the West. In these years innumerable political and economic changes took place, chief among them the decreasing importance of the culture of cities and the accompanying spread of agrarian life. There were constant migrations of the Germanic tribes that had overthrown the Romans; and from the fifth to the tenth centuries, while these Germanic peoples were learning the essentials of civilization, very little social progress as conceived of by modern man was apparent. But the eleventh century saw the rise to power of the Papal Monarchy and the Holy Roman Empire, and in the twelfth century national states began to take shape.

In one form or another, feudalism, a system of land tenure and social organization, was dominant in part of Europe for centuries. In the feudal state the king was supreme, theoretically owning all the land and deriving his power from God. Under him and holding their land at his pleasure were nobles of varying degree, who owed him service and who, ranking one below another, constituted a kind of pyramid of vassalage. At the base of this structure was the agricultural worker or serf, who lived and labored in complete subjugation to his overlord. The feudal aristocracy inhabited castles located strategically

464

and designed more for military defence than for the comforts of life. Small wars between great lords occurred constantly, and wars on a national scale depended upon feudal loyalties for the raising of armed forces. At its best this feudal society offered to king and overlord the stable service of those below them and to the serf a degree of protection and social security. At its worst it provided the same excellent opportunity for exploitation of the weak by the strong that has been afforded by many systems in many ages.

Poet and priest combined to hold up to the feudal lord the ideal of chivalry, an ideal that embraced obligation to the weak and the needy, unswerving devotion to God, to the Church, and to the Virgin (and hence to womanhood in general), and stout enmity toward heretic and heathen. Although the ideal knight existed only in medieval literature, the conventions of chivalry were strongly inherent in feudalism and influenced the lives of the feudal aristocracy. There may never have been in fact a Sir Lancelot of the Lake, but there were in fact a Richard the Lion-Hearted and a Chevalier Bayard. The education and training of the young noble comprised in the positions of page and squire certain genteel accomplishments, religious devotion, and expertness at arms. The rank of knighthood, bestowed at times with elaborate ceremony, was the reward of valor. In combining religious zeal and military action, the campaigns against the Saracens in Spain, and the crusades to recover from the Seljuk Turks the holy sepulchre of Christ offered the best medieval opportunities for the exploitation of the chivalric ideal.

The Christian Church was the one institution that exerted continuous force and effectiveness throughout the Middle Ages. During the early fourth century, Christianity had been established as the official religion of Rome, and from that time until the sixteenth century its rites and doctrines under the administration of the Roman Catholic Church held sway in western Europe without successful questioning.

The influence of the Church was manifested in many ways. In addition to the secular clergy, who dealt directly with the people, there were innumerable religious organizations. Among these the most active were the monks and the friars. The greatest monastic order was the Benedictine, founded by St. Benedict in Italy in the sixth century and effectively established at Monte Cassino through the energy of Pope Gregory the Great. Its elaborate organization and its rule of conduct exerted an influence that has continued to the present day.

Organized much later were the orders of friars, which rose as a protest against the increasing worldliness of the monasteries. In the thirteenth century the Franciscans were founded in Italy and the Dominicans in Spain. The friars were dedicated to a life of poverty and devotion and in their early years were forbidden to own property of any kind. They were preachers and scholars and counted among their number such great names as Thomas Aquinas, Roger Bacon, and Martin Luther.

The influence of the Church and its various religious orders in fostering education, in accumulating great libraries, and in preserving the learning of the past is immeasurable. And whatever the greed and brutality of individual priest and pope, the fact remains that the Christian Church was probably the greatest civilizing influence of the Middle Ages.

In art, scholarship, philosophy, and literature the late medieval centuries were rich in accomplishment. Through the work of Arabic scholars certain writers of antiquity, translated from Greek into Arabic and then into Latin, became a force in medieval science, theology, and philosophy. In the thirteenth century Albertus Magnus and Thomas Aquinas, by their translations and commentaries, made available to Western scholars most of the works of Aristotle and attempted to reconcile classical philosophy with medieval theology. In his *Summa Theologiae* Thomas Aquinas (*c.* 1225-1274) attempted to harmonize human reason and Christian faith. One of the great monuments of scholastic philosophy, his work was perhaps the greatest intellectual product of the medieval mind.

In art and literature the highest medieval achievement is seen during the four hundred years beginning with the tenth century. Romanesque architecture, derived from the Romans as its name indicates, was the first great medieval style of building; and its distinctive square towers and round arches are characteristic of many famous cathedrals scattered from Italy to England. The Gothic style, originating in northern France in the twelfth century, ultimately supplanted the Romanesque and is one of the supreme artistic achievements of the Middle Ages. Among its best-known examples are the cathedral of Notre Dame in Paris and Westminster Abbey in London. The pointed arch, the flying buttress, brilliant stained glass, and elaborate religious sculpture integrated with architectural form and structure are typical of the Gothic style. They are a tribute to the genius and ingenuity of countless unknown artists.

As with medieval art, much medieval literature is anonymous. The

Anglo-Saxon epic of *Beowulf,* the great mass of popular ballads, the early dramas that sprang from the ceremonies of the Church, the many satires in the form of beast-epic and *fabliau,* and some of the best French, English, and German verse romances have survived without known authorship. Because there was no inexpensive method of reproducing books—and consequently no real reading public—authors did not have the prominence that they were to enjoy in later days; and besides, the oral circulation of much medieval literature tended to obscure the importance of the individual writer. Ballad and drama were the chief literature of the people, while at the courts of kings and nobles a more sophisticated product was purveyed by trouvère and minnesinger, who established distinctive forms of romance and lyric. Rhyme and accentual rhythm, as well as new forms, characterized the literary art of the late Middle Ages. Great legends arose in England, France, Spain, and Germany and were given wide currency in both ballad and romance. Arthur, Roland, the Cid, Siegfried, and Robin Hood are typical legendary heroes of the Middle Ages. Among known literary artists two great names are outstanding in medieval literature: Dante Alighieri (1265-1321) and Geoffrey Chaucer (1340?-1400). *The Divine Comedy* and the *Canterbury Tales* are among the great works of Western World literature.

Exact historical knowledge of the Middle Ages is relatively new, for only in the last hundred years has the historian been able to overcome the prejudice of the Renaissance humanists and the unbounded and equally partial enthusiasm of the nineteenth-century romanticists. In the minds of many persons today the terms "medieval" and "feudal" are readily available to characterize anything barbarous or reactionary. It is more than likely true, as has been observed before, that the phrase "the Dark Ages" is frequently not nearly so accurate in describing a historical period as in betraying our condition of historical ignorance.

The Song

of Roland

IN THE YEAR 778 at Roncesvaux, a mountain pass of the Pyrenees, a force of Gascon mountaineers set upon and and destroyed to the last man the rearguard of the Emperor Charlemagne, who was returning to France after a successful campaign against the Saracens in Spain. Upon this slight historical foundation the force of legend and the passion of religion very soon set to work.

As the years passed, and the centuries, the emperor of the Franks evolved in men's minds into the great champion of Christianity and the symbol of Christian opposition to heathendom, a patriarchal figure surrounded by twelve great warriors and intimate with the angel Gabriel. In the legend Charlemagne grew into an old man with a white beard; his age was reputed to have been about two hundred; and many persons believed that he would return before too long a time, the further to make right prevail.

Meanwhile the historically undistinguished leader of the emperor's rearguard became the great peer Roland, nephew of the emperor and exemplary vassal to his sovereign and to his God; he had conquered whole kingdoms for his emperor, and when he blew his horn of ivory he could be heard for thirty leagues. Furthermore, other figures emerged in this legend: Roland's companion-in-arms Oliver, the fighting archbishop Turpin, and the traitor Ganelon. The small force of Gascons metamorphosed into whole armies of Saracens, and the annihilation of the rearguard of the Franks became a sacrifice and a martyrdom and ultimately a complete triumph of Christian heroism over the utmost strength of the world of Islam. Finally, out of this material and possibly from an earlier poetic source, an unknown poet, probably of northern France, around the year 1100 created *The Song of Roland,* to make memorably vital the whole Christian repudiation of Islam and the whole commitment of strong and sure men to their God and king and to all of France.

The Song of Roland is of the literary type called the *chanson de geste,* that is, a song of history or of heroic deeds. It is the best example of this type, and it is the first great work of French literature. One of a cycle of heroic poems sung about the deeds of Charlemagne and his great vassals, it is a picture of idealized feudalism in vivid action.

The best narrative literature of Christian Europe in the Middle Ages was at first generally sung or recited rather than written down for readers. Brief and unrelated as the stories may have been, they were always likely to be unified or transmuted into a great epic, and fairly naturally they fell into three large divisions of subject material, or "matter," as it was called by the thirteenth-century French poet Jehan Bodel.

Bodel pointed out that there were three great themes, or "matters," for treatment in heroic narrative: the matter of Britain, which meant the stories of King Arthur and his knights; the matter of "Rome the great," which dealt with the stories of antiquity, of Rome, Thebes, Troy, and the Orient; and the matter of France, which was essentially the tales of Charlemagne and his warriors, and of which *The Song of Roland* was a part.

The text that is the basis of study of *The Song of Roland* is the manuscript in the Bodleian Library of Oxford University. It is a poem of about 4,000 ten-syllabled lines grouped in short sections or stanzas of varying length called *laisses.* These *laisses,* which may be lyrical in origin, have no rhyme but are technically unified by assonance; that is, all the lines of a *laisse* end with the same vowel sound, without regard to neighboring consonants. For example, one *laisse* contains lines, among others, ending with the words *flors, proz,* and *baron,* the sound of the vowel "o" being common to all final syllables of the lines. The language of the poem is Old French.

The origins of *The Song of Roland,* like the origins of Homer, are obscure. Its motivations are strongly religious, and some scholars believe that its author's purpose was primarily propagandist, that he composed the poem to arouse Christian Europe against the Moslems, not only in Spain but in the Holy Land, and to encourage enthusiasm for the crusades.

The author of *The Song of Roland,* a man of considerable literary skill, was concerned with the characters and the tragedies of men. His delineation of Roland, Oliver, Charlemagne, and Ganelon has less artificiality than some of the later narrative poems. The quarrel of Roland and Oliver, their reconciliation, and their final parting to die among the dead are handled with a good sense of pathos and the tragic. Charlemagne, like Roland, is of heroic stature, but as the poem progresses his plain humanity becomes more and more evident. In one regard the poem is perhaps unique among the *chansons de geste:* the part played in it by woman is practically negligible. Except for its implications of joyous salvation for the faithful, *The Song of Roland* is essentially tragic, and its tragic consequences spring from the weaknesses of mankind, from jealousy and hatred and from stubbornness and pride.

At least parts of the legend of Roland were put into song as early as 1066, for it is reported that a Norman warrior at the Battle of Hastings sang of Roland and of Charlemagne, of Oliver and of Roncesvaux. *The Song of Roland* is only one of a number of versions of the story of Roland; but perhaps more than any other version this poem inspired imitations and adaptations and influenced other works among the medieval poets. Dante was familiar with Roland's fame, and poets retold the story in Latin, Provençal, Spanish, and Italian. In Germany in the twelfth century appeared Conrad's *Rolandslied,* and in Iceland the story of Roland became a part of the *Karlamagnus Saga.* The last great use of the legend was in the year 1516, when the Italian poet Ariosto published his *Orlando Furioso.*

Roland and his fame have survived the centuries. Today, in Italian puppet theaters, Christian and Saracen contend upon the stage in puppet plays that run almost interminably. And in the French cathedral of Chartres, shining in stained glass, Count Roland, surrounded by heaps of the dead, blows his ivory horn and strikes with his sword Durendal upon the rock.

THE SONG OF ROLAND*

PART I

GANELON'S TREACHERY

Charles the King, our great Emperor, has been for seven long years in Spain; he has conquered all the high land down to the sea; not a castle holds out against him, not a wall or city is left unshattered, save Saragossa, which stands high on a mountain. King Marsila holds it, who loves not God, but serves Mahound, and worships Apollon[1]; ill hap must in sooth befall him.

King Marsila abides in Saragossa. And on a day he passes into the shade of his orchard; there he sits on a terrace of blue marble, and around him his men are gathered to the number of twenty thousand. He speaks to his dukes and his counts, saying: "Hear, lords, what evil overwhelms us; Charles the Emperor of fair France has come into this land to confound us. I have no host to do battle against him, nor any folk to discomfort his. Counsel me, lords, as wise men and save me from death and shame." But not a man has any word in answer, save Blancandrin of the castle of Val-Fonde.

Blancandrin was among the wisest of the paynims, a good knight of much prowess, discreet and valiant in the service of his lord. He saith to the King: "Be not out of all comfort. Send to Charles the proud, the terrible, proffer of faithful service and goodly friendship; give him bears and lions and dogs, seven hundred camels and a thousand falcons past the moulting time, four hundred mules laden with gold and silver, that he may send before him fifty full wains. And therewith shall he richly reward his followers. Long has he waged war in this land, it is meet he return again to Aix in France. And do thou pledge thy word to follow him at the feast of Saint Michael, to receive the faith of the Christians, and to become his man in all honour and loyalty. If he would have hostages, send them to him, or ten or twenty, to make good the compact. We will send him the sons of our wives; yea, though it be to death, I will send mine own. Better it were that

---

* Translated by Isabel Butler. The selections from *The Song of Roland* are used by permission of the publishers, Houghton Mifflin Company.

1. Mahound is Mohammed; Apollon seems to be a corruption of Apollo. The Mohammedans did not worship Mohammed as a god, nor were they polytheistic. The poet of Roland had little knowledge of Arabic culture.

they lose their lives than that we be spoiled of lands and lordship, and be brought to beg our bread.

"By this my right hand," saith Blancandrin, "and by the beard that the wind blows about my breast, ye shall see the Frankish host straight-way scatter abroad, and the Franks return again to their land of France. When each is in his own home, and Charles is in his chapel at Aix, he will hold high festival on the day of Saint Michael. The day will come, and the term appointed will pass, but of us he will have no word nor tidings. The King is proud and cruel of heart, he will let smite off the heads of our hostages, but better it is that they lose their lives than that we be spoiled of bright Spain, the fair, or suffer so great dole and sorrow." And the paynims cry: "Let it be as he saith."

So King Marsila hath ended his council; he then called Clarin de Balaguer, Estramarin, and Endropin, his fellow, and Priamon, and Garlan the Bearded, Machiner, and Maheu his uncle, Joïmer, and Malbien from oversea, and Blancandrin; ten of the fiercest he hath called, to make known his will unto them. "Lords, barons," he saith, "go ye to Charlemagne, who is at the siege of the city of Cordova, bearing olive branches in your hands in token of peace and submission. If by your wit ye can make me a covenant with Charles, I will give you great store of gold and silver, and lands and fiefs as much as ye may desire." "Nay," say the paynims, "of these things we have and to spare."

King Marsila has ended his council. And again he saith to his men: "Go ye forth, lords, and bear in your hands branches of olive; bid Charles the King that he have mercy on me for the love of his God; say before this first month ends, I will follow him with a thousand of my true liege people, to receive the Christian faith and become his man in all love and truth. If he would have hostages, they shall be given him." Then said Blancandrin: "We will make thee a fair covenant."

And King Marsila let bring[2] the ten white mules the which had been sent him by the King of Suatilie; their bridles are of gold and their saddles wrought of silver. They who are to do the King's message set forth, bearing in their hands branches of olive. Anon there-after they come before Charles, who holds France as his domain; alack, he cannot but be beguiled by them.

The Emperor is joyous and glad at heart; he has taken Cordova and overthrown its walls; and with his mangonels he has beaten down

2. Ordered brought.

its towers. Great was the plunder which fell to his knights in gold and silver and goodly armour. Not a heathen is left in the city; all are either slain or brought to Christianity. The Emperor is in a wide orchard, and with him are Roland, and Oliver, Samson the Duke, and Anseïs the Proud, Geoffrey of Anjou, the King's standard bearer, and thereto are Gerin, and Gerier, and with them is many another man of France to the number of fifteen thousand. Upon the grass are spread cloths of white silk whereon the knights may sit; and some of these play at tables[3] for their delight, but the old and wise play at chess, and the young lords practise the sword-play. Under a pine, beside an eglantine, stands a throne made all of beaten gold; there sits the King who rules sweet France; white is his beard and his head is hoary, his body is well fashioned and his countenance noble; those who seek him have no need to ask which is the King. And the messengers lighted down from their mules and saluted him in all love and friendship.

Blancandrin was the first to speak, and said to the King: "Greeting in the name of God the Glorious whom ye adore. Thus saith to you King Marsila the valiant: much has he enquired into the faith which brings salvation; and now he would fain give you good store of his substance, bears and lions, and greyhounds in leash, seven hundred camels and a thousand falcons past the moulting time, four hundred mules laden with gold and silver, that ye may carry away fifty full wains of treasure; so many bezants of fine gold shall there be that well may ye reward your men of arms therewith. Long have you tarried in this land, it is meet that ye return again to Aix in France; there my lord will follow you, he gives you his word, and will receive the faith that you hold; with joined hands he will become your man,[4] and will hold from you the kingdom of Spain." At these words the Emperor stretches his two hands towards heaven, and then bows his head and begins to think.

The Emperor sat with bowed head, for he was in no wise hasty of his words, but was ever wont to speak at his leisure. When again he raised his head, proud was his face, and he said to the messengers: "Fairly have ye spoken. Yet King Marsila is much mine enemy. By what token may I set my trust in the words that ye have said?" "By hostages," the Saracen made answer, "of which you shall have or ten or fifteen or twenty. Though it be to death I will send mine own son, and you shall have others, methinks, of yet gentler birth. When you

3. A game similar to backgammon.
4. That is, liege man or vassal to you.

are in your kingly palace at the high feast of Saint Michael of the Peril, my lord will come to you, he gives you his word, and there in the springs that God made flow for you, he would be baptized a Christian." "Yea, even yet he may be saved," Charles made answer.

Fair was the evening and bright the sun. Charles has let stable the ten mules, and in a wide orchard has let pitch a tent wherein the ten messengers are lodged. Ten sergeants make them right good cheer; and there they abide the night through, till the clear dawn. The Emperor has risen early, and heard mass and matins; and now he sits under a pine tree, and calls his barons into council, for he would act in all matters by the advice of those of France.

[At the great council called by Charles, Roland warns against trusting the paynims and advises continuing the war. Ganelon and Duke Naymes advise accepting Marsila's proposal of peace. Charles agrees with these and turns to the appointment of an emissary.

Roland and others offer to carry the terms to Marsila, but Charles is not pleased to send any of them. At Roland's suggestion Ganelon is chosen for the dangerous mission. With hatred toward Roland and despair of returning, Ganelon departs for Saragossa.

As they travel, Ganelon and Blancandrin plot together. At Saragossa Ganelon delivers a false message in order to stir the anger of Marsila against Roland. Ganelon advises Marsila to send hostages to Charles and upon the withdrawal of Charles from Spain to set upon the Franks' rearguard, which, he promises, Roland will command.

With the hostages and with rich gifts for himself and for Charles, Ganelon departs for the camp of the Franks. There he reports that Marsila will come that month to swear fealty to Charles and to receive the Christian faith. At Ganelon's suggestion Roland is chosen captain of the rearguard. Charles has a dream ominous of tragedy and reluctantly departs for France.

The paynims gather their forces and plan to fall upon Roland in the valley of Roncevals. They move into position, four hundred thousand strong, blowing a thousand trumpets. Far away the Franks hear them. "Sir comrade," says Oliver to Roland, "methinks we shall have ado with the Saracens."]

PART II

THE BATTLE AT RONCEVALS

Then Oliver goes up into a high mountain, and looks away to the right, all down a grassy valley, and sees the host of the heathen coming on, and he called to Roland, his comrade, saying: "From the side of Spain I see a great light coming, thousands of white hauberks and thousands of gleaming helms. They will fall upon our Franks with great wrath. Ganelon the felon has done this treason, and he it was adjudged us to the rearguard, before the Emperor." "Peace Oliver," saith Count Roland, "he is my mother's husband, speak thou no ill of him.". . . .

"I have seen the paynims," said Oliver; "never was so great a multitude seen of living men. Those of the vanguard are upon a hundred thousand, all armed with shields and helmets, and clad in white hauberks; right straight are the shafts of their lances, and bright the points thereof. Such a battle we shall have as was never before seen of man. Ye lords of France, may God give you might! and stand ye firm that we be not overcome." "Foul fall him who flees!" then say the Franks, "for no peril of death will we fail thee."

"Great is the host of the heathen," saith Oliver, "and few is our fellowship. Roland, fair comrade, I pray thee sound thy horn of ivory that Charles may hear it and return again with all his host." "That were but folly," quoth Roland, "and thereby would I lose all fame in sweet France. Rather will I strike good blows and great with Durendal, that the blade thereof shall be blooded even unto the hilt. . . ."

Saith Oliver, "I see no shame herein. I have seen the Saracens of Spain, they cover the hills and the valleys, the heaths and the plains. Great are the hosts of this hostile folk, and ours is but a little fellowship." And Roland makes answer: "My desire is the greater thereby. May God and His most holy angels forfend that France should lose aught of worship[5] through me. Liefer had I die than bring dishonour upon me. The Emperor loves us for dealing stout blows."

Roland is brave, and Oliver is wise, and both are good men of their hands; once armed and a-horseback, rather would they die than flee the battle. Hardy are the Counts and high their speech. The felon paynims ride on in great wrath. Saith Oliver: "Roland, prithee look. They are close upon us, but Charles is afar off. Thou wouldst not

5. Honor.

deign to sound thy horn of ivory; but were the King here we should suffer no hurt. Look up towards the passes of Aspre and thou shalt see the woeful rearguard; they who are of it will do no more service henceforth." But Roland answers him: "Speak not so cowardly. Cursed be the heart that turns coward in the breast! Hold we the field, and ours be the buffets and the slaughter."

. . . Nigh at hand is Archbishop Turpin; he now spurs his horse to the crest of a knoll, and speaks to the Franks, and this is his sermon: "Lords, barons, Charles left us here, and it is a man's devoir[6] to die for his King. Now help ye to uphold Christianity. Certes, ye shall have a battle, for here before you are the Saracens. Confess your sins and pray God's mercy, and that your souls may be saved I will absolve you. If ye are slain ye will be holy martyrs, and ye shall have seats in the higher Paradise." The Franks light off their horses and kneel down, and the Archbishop blesses them, and for a penance bids them that they lay on with their swords.

The Franks get upon their feet, freed and absolved from sin; and the Archbishop blesses them in the name of God. Then they mounted their swift horses, and armed themselves after the manner of knights, and made them ready for battle. . . .

Roland rides through the passes of Spain on Veillantif, his good horse and swift. He is clad in his harness, right well it becomes him, and as he rides he brandishes his spear, turning its point towards heaven; and to its top is bound a gonfanon of pure white, whereof the golden fringes fall down even unto his hands. Well fashioned is his body, and his face fair and laughing; close behind him rides his comrade; and all the Franks claim him as their champion. . . .

The nephew of Marsila, who was called Ælroth, rides before all his host, and foul are his words to our Franks: "Ye Frankish felons, today ye shall do battle with us. He who should have been your surety has betrayed you; mad is the King who left you behind in the passes. Today shall fair France lose her fame, and the right arm of Charles[7] shall be smitten off from his body." When Roland hears this, God! how great is his wrath. He spurs as fast as his horse may run, and with all the might he hath he smites Ælroth, and breaks his shield, and rends apart his hauberk, that he cleaves his breast and breaks the bone, and severs the spine from the back; with his lance he drives out the soul from the body, for so fierce is the blow Ælroth wavers, and with all the force of his lance Roland hurls him from his horse dead, his

6. Duty.   7. Roland is "the right arm of Charles."

neck broken in two parts. Yet Roland still chides him, saying: "Out, coward! Charles is not mad, nor loves he treason. He did well and knightly to leave us in the passes. Today shall France lose naught of her fame. Franks, lay on! Our is the first blow. Right is with us, and these swine are in the wrong."

Among the paynims is a Duke, Falsaron by name, who was brother to King Marsila; there is no more shameless felon on all the earth; so wide is his forehead that the space between his eyes measures a full half foot. When he sees his nephew slain, he is full of dole, and he drives through the press as swift as he may, and cries aloud the paynim war-cry. Great is his hatred of the Franks. "Today shall fair France lose her fame!" Oliver hears him and is passing wroth; with his golden spurs he pricks on his horse and rides upon him like a true baron; he breaks the shield, tears asunder the hauberk, and drives his lance into the body up to the flaps of his pennon, and with the might of his blow hurls him dead from the saddle. He looks to earth where lies the felon, and speaks him haughtily: "Coward, naught care I for thy threats. Lay on, Franks, certes, we shall overcome them." And he cries out Montjoy, the war-cry of Charles. . . .

Now the battle waxes passing great on both parties. Count Roland spares himself no whit, but smites with his lance as long as the shaft holds, but by fifteen blows it is broken and lost; thereupon he draws out Durendal his good sword, all naked, spurs his horse and rides on Chernuble, breaks his helm whereon the carbuncles[8] blaze, cleaves his mail-coif and the hair of his head that the sword cuts through eyes and face, and the white hauberk of fine mail, and all the body to the fork of the legs, sheer into the saddle of beaten gold, nor did the sword stint till it had entered the horse and cleft the backbone, never staying for joint, that man and horse fell dead upon the thick grass. . . .

Oliver drives through the stour; his lance is broken and naught is left him but the truncheon; yet he smites the paynim Malsaron that his shield patterned with gold and flowers is broken, and his two eyes fly out from his head, and his brains fall at his feet; among seven hundred of his fellows Oliver smites him dead. Then he slew Turgin and Esturgus, and thereby broke his lance that it splintered even unto the pommel. . . .

But now the lord Oliver hath drawn his good sword, even as his comrade had besought him, and hath shown it to him in knightly

8. Precious stones, which, it was thought, not only shone by reflection but also gave off a light of their own.

wise; and therewith he smites the paynim Justin de Val Ferrée that he severs his head in twain, cuts through his broidered hauberk and his body, through his good saddle set with gold, and severs the backbone of his steed, that man and horse fall dead on the field before him. Then said Roland: "Now I hold you as my brother, and 't is for such buffets the Emperor loves us." And on all sides they cry out Montjoy. . . .

Meantime, in France, a wondrous tempest broke forth, a mighty storm of wind and lightning, with rain and hail out of all measure, and bolts of thunder that fell ever and again; and verily therewith came a quaking of the earth that ran through all the land from Saint Michael of the Peril, even unto Xanten, and from Besançon to the port of Guitsand; and there was not a dwelling whose walls were not rent asunder. And at noon fell a shadow of great darkness, nor was there any light save as the heavens opened. They that saw these things were sore afraid, and many a one said: "This is the day of judgment and the end of the world is at hand." But they were deceived, and knew not whereof they spoke; it was the great mourning for the death of Roland.

Meantime the Franks smote manfully and with good courage, and the paynims were slain by thousands and by multitudes; of a hundred thousand not two may survive. . . . And the Franks fare through the field seeking their fellows, and weeping from dole and pity for their kin, in all love and kindness. But even now King Marsila is upon them with his great host. . . .

Marsila comes on down the valley with the mighty host that he has assembled; full twenty battles[9] the King has arrayed. There is a great shining of helmets, set with gold and precious stones, and of shields and of broidered hauberks. Trumpets to the number of seven thousand sound the onset, and the din thereof runs far and wide. . . .

Wily and cunning is King Marsila, and he saith to the paynims: "Now set your trust in me; this Roland is of wondrous might, and he who would overcome him must strive his uttermost; in two encounters he will not be vanquished methinks, and if not, we will give him three. Then Charles the King shall lose his glory, and shall see France fall into dishonour. Ten battles shall abide here with me, and the remaining ten shall set upon the Franks." Then to Grandonie he gave a broidered banner that it might be a sign unto the rest, and gave over to him the commandment.

Among the paynims is a Saracen of Saragossa, lord he is of half the

9. Battalions.

city, and Climborin, he hight[10]; never will he flee from any living man. He it was who swore fellowship with Count Ganelon, kissed him in all friendship upon the lips, and gave him his helm and his carbuncle. And he hath sworn to bring the Great Land[11] to shame, and to strip the Emperor of his crown. He rides his horse whom he calls Barbamusche, that is swifter than falcon or swallow; and slackening his rein, he spurs mightily, and rides upon Engelier of Gascony that neither shield nor byrnie may save him, but he drives the head of his lance into his body, thrusting so manfully that the point thereof passes through to the other side, and with all the might of his lance hurls him in the field dead. Thereafter he cries: "These folk are good to slay!" But the Franks say: "Alack, that so good a knight should take his end."

And Count Roland speaks to Oliver, saying: "Sir comrade, now is Engelier slain, nor have we any knight of more valour." And the Count answers him, saying: "Now God grant me to avenge him." He pricks on his horse with spurs of pure gold, and he grasps Halteclere—already is the blade thereof reddened—and with all his strength he smites the paynim; he drives the blow home that the Saracen falls; and the devils carry away his soul. . . .

Wondrous and fierce is the battle; the Franks lay on in their wrath and their might, that hands and sides and bones fall to earth, and garments are rent off to the very flesh, and the blood runs down to the green grass. The paynims cry: "We may not longer endure. May the curse of Mahound fall upon the Great Land, for its folk have not their fellows for hardiness." And there was not a man but cried out: "Marsila! haste, O King, for we are in sore need of thy help."

. . . Marsila sees the slaughter of his people, and lets sound his horns and bussynes,[12] and gets to horse with all his vassal host. In the foremost front rides the Saracen Abisme, the falsest knight of his fellowship, all compact of evil and villainy. He believes not in God the son of Mary; and he is black as melted pitch. . . . But he is a good man of arms, and bold to rashness, wherefor he is well beloved of the felon King Marsila, and to him it is given to bear the Dragon,[13] around which the paynims gather. The Archbishop hath small love for Abisme, and so soon as he sees him he is all desirous to smite him, and quietly, within himself, he saith: "This Saracen seems a misbelieving

10. Was named.   12. Trumpets.
11. The empire of Charlemagne.   13. The standard of the paynims.

felon, I had liefer die than not set upon him to slay him; never shall I love coward or cowardice."

Whereupon the Archbishop begins the battle. He rides the horse that he won from Grossaille, a King whom he slew in Denmark; the good steed is swift and keen, featly fashioned of foot, and flat of leg; short in the thigh and large of croupe, long of flank and high of back; his tail is white and yellow his mane, his head is the colour of the fawn, and small are his ears; of all four-footed beasts none may outstrip him. The Archbishop spurs mightily, and will not fail to meet with Abisme and smite him on his shield, a very marvel, set with gems. ... Now Turpin smites it and spares it not, that after his buffet it has not the worth of a doit. And he pierces Abisme through the body, and hurls him dead in the open field. . . .

And Count Roland speaks to Oliver, saying: "Sir comrade, what say ye, is not the Archbishop a right good knight, that there is no better under heaven? for well he knows how to smite with lance and spear." "Now let us aid him," the Count makes answer. And at these words the Franks go into battle again; great are the blows and grievous the slaughter, and great is the dolour of the Christians.

The Franks have lost much of their arms, yet still there are a good four hundred of naked swords with which they smite and hew on shining helmets. God, how many a head is cleft in twain; and there is great rending of hauberks and unmailing of byrnies; and they smite off feet and hands and heads. The paynims cry: "These Franks sore mishandle us, whoso doth not defend himself hath no care for his life.". . .

The felon paynims again smite with their lances upon shields and bright helmets; so great is the shock of iron and steel that the flame springs out toward heaven; and lo, how the blood and the brains run down! Great is the dolour and grief of Roland when he sees so many good knights take their end; he calls to remembrance the land of France, and his uncle, Charlemagne the good King, and he cannot help but be heavy. . . .

Would ye had seen Roland and Oliver hack and hew with their swords, and the Archbishop smite with his lance. We can reckon those that fell by their hands for the number thereof is written in charter and record; the Geste says more than four thousand.[14] In four en-counters all went well with the Franks, but the fifth was sore and

14. The author asserts that the histories will confirm him; the "Geste" is one of his sources.

grievous to them, for in this all their knights were slain save only sixty, spared by God's mercy. Before they die they will sell their lives dear.

When Count Roland is ware of the great slaughter of his men, he turns to Oliver, saying: "Sir comrade, as God may save thee, see how many a good man of arms lies on the ground; we may well have pity on sweet France, the fair, that must now be desolate of such barons. Ah, King and friend, would thou wert here! Oliver, my brother, what shall we do? How shall we send him tidings?" "Nay, I know not how to seek him," saith Oliver; "but liefer had I die than bring dishonour upon me."

Then saith Roland: "I will sound my horn of ivory, and Charles, as he passes the mountains, will hear it; and I pledge thee my faith the Franks will return again." Then saith Oliver: "Therein would be great shame for thee, and dishonour for all thy kindred, a reproach that would last all the days of their life. Thou wouldst not sound it when I bid thee, and now thou shalt not by my counsel. . . ."

Then saith Roland: "Sore is our battle, I will blow a blast, and Charles the King will hear it." "That would not be knightly," saith Oliver; "when I bid thee, comrade, thou didst disdain it. Had the King been here, we had not suffered this damage; but they who are afar off are free from all reproach. By this my beard, an I see again my sister, Aude the Fair, never shalt thou lie in her arms."

Then saith Roland: "Wherefore art thou wroth with me?" And Oliver answers him, saying: "Comrade, thou thyself art to blame. Wise courage is not madness, and measure is better than rashness. Through thy folly these Franks have come to their death; nevermore shall Charles the King have service at our hands. Hadst thou taken my counsel, my liege lord had been here, and this battle had been ended, and King Marsila had been or taken or slain. Woe worth thy prowess, Roland! Henceforth Charles shall get no help of thee; never till God's Judgment Day shall there be such another man; but thou must die, and France shall be shamed thereby. And this day our loyal fellowship shall have an end; before this evening grievously shall we be parted."

The Archbishop, hearing them dispute together, spurs his horse with his spurs of pure gold, and comes unto them, and rebukes them, saying: "Sir Roland, and thou, Sir Oliver, in God's name I pray ye, let be this strife. Little help shall we now have of thy horn; and yet it were better to sound it; if the King come, he will revenge us, and the paynims shall not go hence rejoicing. . . ." "Sir, thou speakest well and truly," quoth Roland.

And therewith he sets his ivory horn to his lips, grasps it well and blows it with all the might he hath. High are the hills, and the sound echoes far, and for thirty full leagues they hear it resound. Charles and all his host hear it, and the King saith: "Our men are at battle." But Count Ganelon denies it, saying: "Had any other said so, we had deemed it great falsehood."

With dolour and pain, and in sore torment, Count Roland blows his horn of ivory, that the bright blood springs out of his mouth, and the temples of his brain are broken. . . .

[Ganelon persists in denying the urgency of Roland's signal, but the Franks now recognize his treason. They arm themselves and prepare to turn back to the aid of Roland. Charles gives Ganelon into the custody of his cooks, who pluck out his beard and mustache, beat him, and guard him till the return of Charles.]

Roland looks abroad over hill and heath and sees the great multitude of the Frankish dead, and he weeps for them as beseems a gentle knight, saying: "Lords and barons now may God have mercy upon you, and grant Paradise to all your souls, that ye may rest among the blessed flowers. Man never saw better men of arms than ye were. . . . Oliver, brother, I must not fail thee; yet I shall die of grief, and I be not slain by the sword. Sir comrade, let us get us into battle."

So Count Roland falls a-smiting again. He holds Durendal in his hand, and lays on right valiantly, and slays four and twenty of the most worshipful of the paynims. Never shall ye see man more desirous to revenge himself. And even as the hart flies before the hounds, so flee the heathen from before Roland. . . .

That man who knows he shall get no mercy defends him savagely in battle. Wherefore the Franks are fierce as lions. Marsila like a true baron sits his horse Gaignon; he spurs him well and rides on Bevon and breaks his shield and rends his hauberk, that without other hurt he smites him dead to ground. And thereafter he slew Ivon and Ivory, and with them Gerard the Old of Roussillon. Now nigh at hand is Count Roland, and he saith to the paynim: "May the Lord God bring thee to mishap! And because thou hast wrongfully slain my comrades thou shalt thyself get a buffet before we twain dispart, and this day thou shalt learn the name of my sword." And therewith he rides upon him like a true baron, and smites off his right hand, and thereafter he takes off the head of Jurfaleu the Fair, the son of King Marsila. Thereat the paynims cry: "Now help us, Mahound! O ye, our gods, revenge us upon Charles! He has sent out against us into our marches[15] men so fierce that though they die they will not give back." And one saith to another: "Let us fly." At these words a hundred thousand turn and flee, and let whosoever will call them, they will not return again. . . .

But alack, what avails it? for though Marsila be fled his uncle the Caliph[16] yet abides, he who ruled Aferne, Carthage, Garmalie, and Ethiopia, a cursed land; under his lordship he has the black folk, great are their noses and large their ears, and they are with him to the number of fifty thousand. And now they come up in pride and wrath, and cry aloud the war-cry of the paynims. Then saith Roland: "Now must we needs be slain, and well I know we have but a little space to live; but cursed be he who doth not sell himself right dear. Lay on, lords, with your burnished swords, and debate both life and death; let not sweet France be brought to shame through us. When Charles, my liege lord, shall come into this field, he will see such slaughter of the Saracens, that he shall find fifteen of them dead over against each man of ours, and he will not fail to bless us."

. . . Now when the paynims see how few are the Franks, they have great pride and joy thereof; and one saith to another: "Certes, the Emperor is in the wrong." The Caliph bestrides a sorrel horse, he pricks him on with his spurs of gold, and smites Oliver from behind, amid the back, that he drives the mails of his white hauberk into his body, and his lance passes out through his breast: "Now hast thou got a good buffet," quoth the Caliph. "On an ill day Charles the Great left thee in the passes. . . ."

Oliver feels that he is wounded unto death; in his hand he holds Halteclere, bright was its blade, and with it he smites the Caliph on his golden pointed helmet, that its flowers and gems fall to earth, and he cleaves the head even unto the teeth, and with the force of the blow smote him dead to earth, and said: "Foul fall thee, paynim! Say not that I am come to my death through Charles; and neither to thy wife, nor any other dame, shalt thou ever boast in the land from which thou art come, that thou hast taken from me so much as one farthing's

15. Borders.
16. According to legend, the caliphs were successors to Mohammed.

worth, or hast done any hurt to me or to others." And thereafter he called to Roland for succour.

Oliver feels that he is wounded unto death; never will he have his fill of vengeance. In the thick of the press he smites valiantly, cleaving lances and embossed shields, and feet and hands and flanks and shoulders. Whosoever saw him thus dismember the Saracens, and hurl one dead upon another, must call to mind true valiance; nor did he forget the war-cry of Charles, but loud and clear he cries out Montjoy! And he calls to Roland, his friend and peer: "Sir comrade, come stand thou beside me. In great dolour shall we twain soon be disparted."

Roland looks Oliver in the face, pale it is and livid and all discoloured; the bright blood flows down from amid his body and falls in streams to the ground. "God," saith the Count, "now I know not what to do. Sir comrade, woe worth thy valour! Never shall the world see again a man of thy might. Alas, fair France, today art thou stripped of goodly vassals, and fallen and undone. The Emperor will suffer great loss thereby." And so speaking he swoons upon his horse.

Lo, Roland has swooned as he sits his horse, and Oliver is wounded unto death, so much has he bled that his sight is darkened, and he can no longer distinguish any living man whether far off or near at hand; and now, as he meets his comrade, he smites him upon the helm set with gold and gems, and cleaves it down to the nasal,[17] but does not come unto the head. At the blow Roland looks up at him, and asks him fully softly and gently: "Comrade, dost thou this wittingly? I am Roland who so loves thee. Never yet hast thou mistrusted me." Then saith Oliver: "Now I hear thee speak, but I cannot see thee, may the Lord God guard thee. I have struck thee, but I pray thy pardon." "Thou hast done me no hurt," Roland answers him; "I pardon thee before God, as here and now." So speaking each leans forward towards other, and lo, in such friendship they are disparted.

Oliver feels the anguish of death come upon him; his two eyes turn in his head; and his hearing goes from him, and all sight. He lights down from his horse and lies upon the ground, and again and again he confesses his sins; he holds out his clasped hands toward heaven and prays God that he grant him Paradise, and he blesses Charles and sweet France, and Roland, his comrade, above all men. Then his heart fails him, and his head sinks upon his breast, and he lies stretched at all his length upon the ground. Dead is the Count and

17. Part of the helmet that protects the nose.

gone from hence. Roland weeps for him and is sore troubled; never on the earth shall ye see a man so sorrowful.

When Count Roland sees his friend lie prone and dead, facing the East, gently he begins to lament him: "Sir comrade, woe worth thy hardiness! We twain have held together for years and days, never didst thou me wrong or I thee. Since thou art dead, alack that I yet live." So speaking, the Count swoons as he sits Veillantif his horse, but his golden spurs hold him firm, and let him go where he will, he cannot fall.

So soon as Roland comes to his senses, and is restored from his swoon, he is ware of the great slaughter about him. Slain are the Franks, he has lost them all save only Gualter del Hum and the Archbishop. . . .

Full sorrowful is Roland and of great wrath; he falls a-smiting in the thick of the press, and of those of Spain he cast twenty to the ground dead, and Gualter slew six, and the Archbishop five. Then say the paynims: "Fierce and fell are these men. Take ye heed, lords, that they go not hence alive. He who doth not set upon them is traitor, and recreant he who lets them go hence."

. . . A thousand Saracens get them to foot, and there are still forty thousand on horseback, yet in sooth they dare not come nigh unto the three, but they hurl upon them lances and spears, arrows and darts and sharp javelins. In the first storm they slew Gualter, and sundered the shield of Turpin of Rheims, broke his helmet and wounded him in his head and rent and tore his hauberk that he was pierced in the body by four spears; and his horse was slain under him. The Archbishop falls; great is the pity thereof.

But so soon as Turpin of Rheims finds himself beaten down to earth with the wounds of four lances in his body, he right speedily gets him afoot again; he looks toward Roland, and hastes to him, and saith: "I am nowise vanquished; no good vassal yields him so long as he is a living man." And he draws Almace, his sword of brown steel, and in the thick of the press he deals well more than a thousand buffets. Afterwards Charles bore witness that Turpin spared himself no whit, for around him they found four hundred dead. . . .

Count Roland fights right nobly, but all his body is a-sweat and burning hot, and in his head he hath great pain and torment, for when he sounded his horn he rent his temples. But he would fain know that Charles were coming, and he takes his horn of ivory, and feebly he sounds it. The Emperor stops to listen: "Lords," he saith, "now has

great woe come upon us, this day shall we lose Roland my nephew, I
wot from the blast of his horn that he is nigh to death. Let him who
would reach the field ride fast. Now sound ye all the trumpets of the
host." Then they blew sixty thousand, so loud that the mountains
resound and the valleys give answer. The paynims hear them and have
no will to laugh, but one saith to another: "We shall have ado with
Charles anon."

Say the paynims: "The Emperor is returning, we hear the trumpets of France; if Charles come hither, we shall suffer sore loss. Yet if
Roland live, our war will begin again, and we shall lose Spain our
land." Then four hundred armed in their helmets, and of the best of
those on the field, gather together, and on Roland they make onset
fierce and sore. Now is the Count hard bestead.

When Count Roland sees them draw near he waxes hardy and
fierce and terrible; never will he yield as long as he is a living man.
He sits his horse Veillantif, and spurs him well with his spurs of fine
gold, and rides into the stour upon them all; and at his side is Archbishop Turpin. And the Saracens say one to another: "Now save yourselves, friends. We have heard the trumpets of France; Charles the
mighty King is returning."

Count Roland never loved the cowardly, or the proud, or the
wicked, or any knight who was not a good vassal, and now he calls to
Archbishop Turpin, saying: "Lord, thou art on foot and I am a-horseback, for thy love I would make halt, and together we will take the
good and the ill; I will not leave thee for any living man; the blows
of Almace and of Durendal shall give back this assault to the paynims."
Then saith the Archbishop: "A traitor is he who doth not smite;
Charles is returning, and well will he revenge us."

"In an evil hour," say the paynims, "were we born; woeful is the
day that has dawned for us! We have lost our lords and our peers.
Charles the valiant cometh hither again with his great host, we hear
the clear trumpets of those of France, and great is the noise of their
cry of Montjoy. Count Roland is of such might he cannot be vanquished by any mortal man. Let us hurl our missiles upon him, and
then leave him." Even so they did; and cast upon him many a dart and
javelin, and spears and lances and feathered arrows. They broke and
rent the shield of Roland, tore open and unmailed his hauberk, but did
not pierce his body: but Veillantif was wounded in thirty places, and
fell from under the Count, dead. Then the paynims flee, and leave
him: Count Roland is left alone and on foot.

The paynims flee in anger and wrath, and in all haste they fare toward Spain. Count Roland did not pursue after them, for he has lost his horse Veillantif, and whether he will or no, is left on foot. He went to the help of Archbishop Turpin, and unlaced his golden helm from his head, and took off his white hauberk of fine mail, and he tore his tunic into strips and with the pieces bound his great wounds. Then he gathers him in his arms, and lays him down full softly upon the green grass, and gently he beseeches him: "O gracious baron, I pray thy leave. Our comrades whom we so loved are slain, and it is not meet to leave them thus. I would go seek and find them, and range them before thee." "Go and return again," quoth the Archbishop. "Thank God, this field is thine and mine."

Roland turns away and fares on alone through the field; he searches the valleys and the hills; and there he found Ivon and Ivory, and Gerin, and Gerier his comrade, and he found Engelier the Gascon, and Berengier, and Oton, and he found Anseïs and Samson, and Gerard the Old of Rousillon.[18] One by one he hath taken up the barons, and hath come with them unto the Archbishop, and places them in rank before him. The Archbishop cannot help but weep; he raises his hand and gives them benediction, and thereafter saith: "Alas for ye, lords! May God the Glorious receive your souls, and bring them into Paradise among the blessed flowers. And now my death torments me sore; never again shall I see the great Emperor."

Again Roland turned away to search the field; and when he found Oliver his comrade, he gathered him close against his breast, and as best he might returned again unto the Archbishop, and laid his comrade upon a shield beside the others; and the Archbishop absolved and blessed him. Then their sorrow and pity broke forth again. . . .

When Roland sees the peers, and Oliver whom he so loved, lying dead, pity takes him and he begins to weep; and his face is all discoloured; so great is his grief he cannot stand upright, but will he, nill he,[19] falls to the ground in a swoon. Saith the Archbishop: "Alack for thee, good baron."

When the Archbishop sees Roland swoon, he has such dole as he has never known before. He stretches out his hand and takes the horn of ivory, for in Roncevals there is a swift streamlet, and he would go to it to bring of its water to Roland. Slowly and falteringly he sets forth, but so weak he is he cannot walk, his strength has gone from

18. Roland, Oliver, and these ten are the twelve peers of France.
19. In spite of himself.

him, too much blood has he lost, and before a man might cross an acre his heart faileth, and he falls forward upon his face, and the anguish of death comes upon him.

When Count Roland recovers from his swoon he gets upon his feet with great torment; he looks up and he looks down, and beyond his comrades, on the green grass, he sees that goodly baron, the Archbishop, appointed of God in His stead. Turpin saith his *mea culpa*,[20] and looks up, and stretches out his two hands towards heaven, and prays God that he grant him Paradise. And so he dies, the warrior of Charles. . . .

Count Roland sees the Archbishop upon the ground; his bowels have fallen out of his body, and his brains are oozing out of his forehead; Roland takes his fair, white hands and crosses them upon his breast between his two collar bones: and lifting up his voice, he mourns for him, after the manner of his people: "Ah gentle man, knight of high parentage, now I commend thee to the heavenly Glory; never will there be a man who shall serve Him more willingly; never since the days of the apostles hath there been such a prophet to uphold the law, and win the hearts of men; may thy soul suffer no dole or torment, but may the doors of Paradise be opened to thee."

Now Roland feels that death is near him, and his brains flow out at his ears; he prays to the Lord God for his peers that He will receive them, and he prays to the Angel Gabriel for himself. That he may be free from all reproach, he takes his horn of ivory in the one hand, and Durendal, his sword, in the other, and farther than a cross-bow can cast an arrow, through a cornfield he goeth on towards Spain. At the crest of a hill, beneath two fair trees, are four stairs of marble; there he falls down on the green grass in a swoon, for death is close upon him.

High are the hills and very tall are the trees; the four stones are of shining marble; and there Count Roland swoons upon the green grass. Meantime a Saracen is watching him; he has stained his face and body with blood, and feigning death, he lies still among his fellows; but now he springs to his feet and hastens forward. Fair he was, and strong, and of good courage; and in his pride he breaks out into mighty wrath, and seizes upon Roland, both him and his arms, and he cries: "Now is the nephew of Charles overthrown. This his sword will I carry into Arabia." But at his touch the Count recovered his senses.

Roland feels that his sword hath been taken from him, he opens his eyes, and saith: "Certes, thou are not one of our men." He holds his

20. Literally "my sin," part of the formula of the confessional.

horn of ivory which he never lets out of his grasp, and he smites the
Saracen upon the helm which was studded with gold and gems, and he
breaks steel and head and bones that his two eyes start out, and he falls
down dead at his feet. Then saith Roland: "Coward, what made thee
so bold to lay hands upon me, whether right or wrong? No man shall
hear it but shall hold thee a fool. Now is my horn of ivory broken in
the bell, and its gold and its crystals have fallen."

Now Roland feels that his sight is gone from him. With much
striving he gets upon his feet; the colour has gone from his face; before
him lies a brown stone, and in his sorrow and wrath he smites ten
blows upon it. The sword grates upon the rock, but neither breaks nor
splinters; and the Count saith: "Holy Mary, help me now! Ah Durendal, alas for your goodness! Now am I near to death, and have no
more need of you. Many a fight in the field have I won with you, many
a wide land have I conquered with you, lands now ruled by Charles
with the white beard. May the man who would flee before another
never possess you. For many a day have you been held by a right good
lord, never will there be such another in France the free."

Roland smote upon the block of hard stone, and the steel grates,
but neither breaks nor splinters. And when he sees that he can in nowise break it, he laments, saying: "O Durendal, how fair and bright
thou art, in the sunlight how thou flashest and shinest! Charles was
once in the valley of Moriane, when God commanded him by one of
his angels that he should give thee to a chieftain Count; then the great
and noble King girded thee upon me; and with thee I won for him
Anjou and Bretagne, and I conquered Poitou and Maine for him, and
for him I conquered Normandy the free, and Provence, and Acqui-
taine; and Lombardy, and all of Romagna; and I conquered for him
Bavaria, and Flanders, and Bulgaria, and all of Poland; Constantinople
which now pays him fealty, and Saxony, where he may work his will.
And I conquered for him Wales, and Scotland, and Ireland, and
England which he holds as his demesne. Many lands and countries
have I won with thee, lands which Charles of the white beard rules.
And now am I heavy of heart because of this my sword: rather would
I die than that it should fall into the hands of the paynims. Lord God
our Father, let not this shame fall upon France."

And again Roland smote upon the brown stone and beyond all
telling shattered it; the sword grates, but springs back again into the
air and is neither dinted nor broken. And when the Count sees he may
in no wise break it, he laments, saying: "O Durendal, how fair and

holy a thing thou art! In thy golden hilt is many a relic,—a tooth of Saint Peter, and some of the blood of Saint Basil, and hairs from the head of my lord, Saint Denis, and a bit of the raiment of the Virgin Mary. It is not meet that thou fall into the hands of the paynims; only Christians should wield thee. May no coward ever possess thee! Many wide lands have I conquered with thee, lands which Charles of the white beard rules; and thereby is the Emperor great and mighty."

Now Roland feels that death has come upon him, and that it creeps down from his head to his heart. In all haste he fares under a pine tree, and hath cast himself down upon his face on the green grass. Under him he laid his sword and his horn of ivory; and he turned his face towards the paynim folk, for he would that Charles and all his men should say that the gentle Count had died a conqueror. Speedily and full often he confesses his sins, and in atonement he offers his glove to God.[21]

Roland lies on a high peak looking towards Spain; he feels that his time is spent, and with one hand he beats upon his breast: "O God, I have sinned; forgive me through thy might the wrongs, both great and small, which I have done from the day I was born even to this day on which I was smitten." With his right hand he holds out his glove to God; and lo, the angels of heaven come down to him.

Count Roland lay under the pine tree; he has turned his face towards Spain, and he begins to call many things to remembrance,— all the lands he had won by his valour, and sweet France, and the men of his lineage, and Charles, his liege lord, who had brought him up in his household; and he cannot help but weep. But he would not wholly forget himself, and again he confesses his sins and begs forgiveness of God: "Our Father, who art truth, who raised up Lazarus from the dead, and who defended Daniel from the lions, save thou my soul from the perils to which it is brought through the sins I wrought in my life days." With his right hand he offers his glove to God, and Saint Gabriel has taken it from his hand. Then his head sinks on his arm, and with clasped hands he hath gone to his end. And God sent him his cherubim, and Saint Michael of the Seas, and with them went Saint Gabriel, and they carried the soul of the Count into Paradise.

21. As a sign of his vassalage to the Almighty.

PART III

THE VENGEANCE OF CHARLES

[Charles returns to Roncevals and laments the dead. He pursues and destroys the remnant of the paynim force, but Marsila escapes to Saragossa. Meanwhile the Amiral Baligant, Prince of Cairo and overlord of Marsila, has gathered at Alexandria a great host and set sail for Spain.

After harrying the heathen, Charles returns to Roncevals, laments anew for Roland, whose body he sends with those of Oliver and Turpin to France, and buries the dead. The Franks then prepare for the imminent battle with Baligant; they go forward, and the battle is joined.

The slaughter on both sides is great, and Charles, like Roland at Roncevals, fights with high heroism. Finally he meets Baligant and kills him in single combat. The paynims—for it is God's will—flee the field, pursued as far as Saragossa. Overwhelmed by the defeat, Marsila dies of sorrow, and eager devils bear away his soul. The Franks batter down the gate of Saragossa and invest the city. Then leaving a garrison, Charles and his force turn homewards, "in all joy and mirth."]

The Emperor has returned from Spain, and come again to Aix, the fairest seat in France; he has gone up into his palace and has passed into the hall. To him comes Aude, that fair damsel, and saith to the King: "Where is Roland, the captain, who pledged him to take me as his wife?" Thereat Charles is filled with dolour and grief, he weeps and plucks his white beard, saying: "Sister, sweet friend, thou askest me of one who is dead. But I will make good thy loss to thee, and will give thee Louis—a better I cannot name—my son he is, and will hold my marches." "Lord, thy words are strange to me," Aude makes answer. "May it not please God or his saints or his angels that after Roland's death I should yet live." She loses her colour and falls at the feet of Charles, and lo, she is dead. God have mercy upon her soul. The barons of France weep and lament her.

Aude the Fair has gone to her end. But the King thinks her in a swoon, he is full of pity for her, and he weeps; he takes her by the hands and raises her up, but her head falls back upon her shoulders. When Charles sees that she is dead, he straightway calls four countesses; Aude is borne to a convent of nuns hard by, and they watch by

492

her the night through till dawn. Richly and fairly they bury her beside
an altar, and the King does her great honour.

The Emperor is come again to Aix. And Ganelon the felon, in
chains of iron, is in the city, before the palace; serving-men bound him
to a stake, and made fast his hands with strips of deer's hide; well they
beat him with staves and leathern thongs, for he hath deserved no other
bounty. Thus in sore torment he awaits his trial.

It is written in the ancient Geste that Charles did summon men
from many lands, and assemble them in the chapel at Aix. Proud is the
day and high the festival, that of Saint Silvestre the baron, some men
say. And now begins the trial, and ye shall hear of Ganelon who did
the treason. The Emperor has commanded that he be brought before
him.

"Lords and barons," then saith Charles the King, "now judge me
the right concerning Ganelon. He went among my host into Spain
with me, and he reft me of twenty thousand of my Franks, and of my
nephew whom ye shall see no more, and of Oliver, the courteous, the
valiant; and the Twelve Peers likewise he betrayed for money." Then
quoth Ganelon: "I were a felon should I deny it. Roland spoiled me of
money and goods, for this I sought his death and destruction. But that
it was treason I deny." "Now let us take counsel," say the Franks in
answer.

So Ganelon stood before the King; he is strong of body and his
face is fresh of hue, if he were true hearted he were a goodly baron. He
looks on the men of France, and all the judges, and on his own kin,
thirty of whom are with him, and he cries with a loud voice: "For the
love of God now hear me, ye barons! Yea, I was in the host with the
Emperor, and I did him service in all faith and love. Then Roland, his
nephew, conceived a hatred against me, and condemned me to dolour
and death. Messenger I was to King Marsila, and if I returned unhurt
it was by mine own wit. . . . Revenged me I have, but in that is no
treason." "Let us go into council," the Franks make answer.

Now that Ganelon sees that his trial is opened, he calls about him
thirty of his kinsmen. One there is among them to whom all the rest
give ear, and he is Pinabel of the castle of Sorence. Ready of speech he
is, and he can plead full well, and if it be a question of arms he is a
goodly warrior. Then saith Ganelon: "In you I set my trust; save me
now from calumny and death." "Thou shalt be saved, and that
speedily," saith Pinabel. "If any Frank condemn thee to hang I will
give him the lie with the point of my sword wheresoever the Emperor

shall summon us to do battle man to man." And Ganelon the Count throws himself at his kinsman's feet.

Bavarians and Saxons have gone into council, Poitevins and Normans and Franks, and with them is many a German and Teuton. The men of Auvergne were the most inclined to grace, and the most friendly towards Pinabel. They said one to another: "Best let be. Let us leave the trial, and pray the King that he pardon Ganelon for this time, if he will henceforth serve him in all faith and love. Dead is Roland, ye shall see him no more, nor can ye bring him back with gold or goods; folly it were to hold trial by combat." And there was none who did not agree to this and yea-say it, save only Thierry, the brother of Lord Geoffrey. . . .

When Charles sees that they have all failed him, his face and his countenance darken, and "Woe is me!" he cried in his grief. But before him is a good knight, Thierry, brother to the Angevin Duke, Geoffrey. Lean he is of body, nimble and slender; black-haired, and brown of face he is, not tall, and yet not overshort. Courteously he bespeaks the Emperor: "Fair Sir King, make not such sorrow; thou knowest that I have served thee well, and by my lineage I have a right to a share in this trial. Howsoever Roland may have wronged Ganelon thy service should have been his protection; Ganelon is a felon in that he betrayed him, for thereby he has broken his oath to thee and transgressed. And for this I condemn him to hanging and death, and that his body be cast out to the dogs as that of a traitor, since he did traitorously. If he hath any kinsman who will give me the lie, I will uphold my judgment by the sword I have girded here at my side." "That is well said," the Franks make answer.

Then came Pinabel before the King; tall he is, and strong and hardy and swift; short is the term of the man who gets a stroke at his hands. And he saith to the King: "Lord, thine is the quarrel; I pray thee put an end to this clamour. Lo, Thierry has pronounced his judgment, I give him the lie and would do him battle." Thereupon the thirty kinsmen of Ganelon offer themselves as surety.[22] Then saith the King: "I likewise will give thee pledges; and let these be guarded till the right be made manifest."[23]

. . . By the rest the combat was pronounced lawful; and Ogier of Denmark declared the terms. Then the combatants call for their horses and arms.

22. Surety for Pinabel's appearance at the combat.
23. These are surety for the appearance of Thierry.

In that they are near to battle they confess their sins, and are shriven and blessed; they hear mass and receive the communion, and rich offerings they make to the churches. Then the twain come again before Charles. They have fastened on their spurs, and donned their shining hauberks which are both strong and light, made fast upon their heads their bright helmets, and girt on their swords hilted with pure gold, hung their quartered shields about their necks, and now in their right hands they grip their sharp spears, and mount their swift coursers. Thereupon a hundred thousand knights fell a-weeping, for they had pity upon Thierry for Roland's sake. But God knows what the end will be.

Below Aix is a wide meadow, and there the two barons are to do battle. They are men of good prowess and valour, and their horses are swift and keen. The two knights slacken rein, and spurring hard, ride each at other with all the might they have, that their shields are cleft and shattered, their hauberks rent, and thereto their girths are broken that their saddles turn and fall to earth. And the hundred thousand men who watch them weep.

Both knights are on the ground, but lightly they spring to their feet. Pinabel is strong and swift and nimble; and each runs upon other, for both now are unhorsed, and with their swords, whereof the pommels are all of gold, they hack and hew their helms of steel; and strong are the blows for the breaking of helms. The Frankish knights make great sorrow; and "O God, make clear the right," cried Charles. . . .

Right valiant is Pinabel of Sorence; he smites Thierry on his helm of Provence, that the fire sprang out therefrom and kindled the grass; he thrusts at him with the point of his sword, cleaves his helmet above his forehead, that the stroke carries to the middle of the face, and the right cheek bursts out a-bleeding; his hauberk is rent down to his belly, but God so guards him that he is not slain.

Thierry sees that he is wounded in the face, and the bright blood flows down upon the grass of the field; he smites Pinabel upon his helm of brown steel, rends it asunder even to the nasal that the brains run out; and he drives the blow home that Pinabel falls dead. So with this stroke the battle is won. And the Franks cry: "God has made manifest his might. It is meet that Ganelon be hung, and likewise his kinsmen, who answered for him."

. . . Charles calls his dukes and his counts, saying: "What counsel ye me concerning those I have in my prison, they who came to the trial to uphold Ganelon, and gave themselves as hostages for Pinabel." And

the Franks make answer: "It were ill done an one were let to live."
Then the King commands one of his wardens, Basbrun, saying: "Go
thou and hang them all to yon blasted tree; by this my beard whereof
the hairs are hoary, and if thou let one escape, thou shalt be given over
to death and destruction." And Basbrun answered him: "How else
should I do?" And by the help of a hundred sergeants he led them
away by force; and they were all hung to the number of thirty. For the
traitor brings death to both himself and to others.

Thereafter the Bavarians and Germans returned home again, and
thereto the Poitevins and Bretons and Normans. Above all the rest the
Franks agreed that Ganelon should die by great torture. They let
bring four chargers, and then they bind the traitor hand and foot;
wild and fleet are the horses, and four sergeants urge them on towards
a meadow wherein is a mare. So Ganelon is come to sore punishment,
all his sinews are put to the rack, and all his limbs are torn out from
his body, and the bright blood flows out on the green grass. Thus
Ganelon dies the death of a felon. It is not meet that he who betrays
others should boast thereof. . . .

So the Emperor has done justice and appeased his great wrath.
The day passes and night darkens, and as the King lies in his vaulted
chamber, Saint Gabriel comes to him from God, saying: "Charles, now
call together the hosts of thy empire, and go in thy might into the land
of Bire, and give succour to King Vivien at Imph, for the paynims have
laid a siege about his city, and the Christians cry out to thee and entreat thee." Little will had the Emperor to go. "Ah God," he saith,
"how is my life oppressed with burdens." And he weeps and plucks
his white beard.

Here ends the geste which Turoldus tells.[24]

24. There is doubt not only about the meaning of the original French of this
line but also about the identity of Turoldus. He may be the minstrel singing
the song, the scribe who copied it, or the author.

The NIBELUNGENLIED

THE NIBELUNGENLIED tells of the deeds of the German hero Siegfried, of his death through betrayal by his friends, and of the awful vengeance of his wife upon his betrayers. The story seems to have originated in the low country of the Rhine, for the geography of the tale and its few historical references prescribe this view. But the story somehow made its way, perhaps as early as the sixth century, into Scandinavia, subsequently even as far away as Iceland; and in these places it became a part of the varied literary traditions of the North. It is found in the *Elder Edda* of Iceland, the earliest parts of which go back as far as the ninth century; in the *Volsungasaga,* a prose version of the *Elder Edda,* perhaps of the twelfth century; and somewhat later in the *Prose Edda,* a book of instructions for poets. In the middle of the thirteenth century the story appeared in a Norwegian account of the hero Dietrich of Bern, the *Thidreksaga,* whose author says that he got the tale from Germany.

All these northern versions differ from the *Nibelungenlied,* particularly in the ancestry and early life of the hero and in the identity and names of the chief women characters. In the Norse versions the hero, Sigurd, descended from the god Wotan, is reared by the dwarf Regin. He forges himself a sword and kills a dragon that is really Regin's brother Fafnir transformed for the purpose of guarding a great treasure. By Fafnir's death Sigurd gains possession of the treasure, which from its earliest history has carried a curse upon its possessors. Learning of Regin's evil designs upon him for the sake of the treasure, Siegfried kills the dwarf. He then penetrates the wall of fire surrounding the sleeping valkyrie Brunhild and gains her promise of marriage. But leaving his betrothed, he comes to the Rhine kingdom of King Giuki and Queen Grimhild, who have three sons, Gunnar, Högni, and Gutthorm, and a daughter, Gudrun. Under the influence of a magic spell, Sigurd forgets his betrothal to Brunhild and marries the princess Gudrun. Still enchanted, he assists Gunnar in winning Brunhild as his bride. After the marriage Gudrun and Brunhild quarrel, and Gudrun discloses the secret that through Sigurd's heroism and not his own, Gunnar had won Brunhild.

Brooding over the embarrassment of her position, Brunhild demands the death of Sigurd, and Gutthorm is chosen to perform the deed. After two vain attempts Gutthorm stabs Sigurd as he lies sleeping but is himself killed by Sigurd as Sigurd expires. In sorrow for what she has done, Brunhild kills herself and is burned upon the funeral pyre of Sigurd. Some time later Gudrun marries Atli, king of the Huns, and goes to his court to live. Hoping to gain the treasure, which Gunnar now possesses, Atli invites Gunnar and Högni to his court. He demands the treasure of them, and upon Gunnar's refusal a battle ensues, in which Gudrun fights upon the side of her brothers. Gunnar and Högni are overpowered and finally killed, but Gunnar carries with him in death his secret knowledge of the place where the treasure is concealed. Finally Gudrun kills Atli, and the tragedy comes to its end. This, briefly, is the tale of the sagas and the eddas.

Although the *Nibelungenlied* does not differ in its large design from the Norse version, in the details there is consistent diversity between the two. The *Nibelungenlied* barely regards the ancestry of Siegfried and his boyhood and youth. It recounts only indirectly his fight with the dragon, his winning the treasure, and his relations with the first owners of the treasure, whom it calls the Nibelungs. There is only the slightest suggestion that Siegfried has ever before known Brunhild. And finally in the *Nibelungenlied* the whole second part of the story occupies much greater space and is of greater importance and

dramatic intensity than in the Norse version. Kriemhild marries Etzel
(Atli) and uses him to effect her vengeance upon her Burgundian kin
for the death of Siegfried. The legendary Dietrich of Bern, famous
in history and lore, is introduced into the narrative, and he and his
old retainer Hildebrand are instrumental in the destruction of the
Burgundians. After the great fight and the burning of the hall, Kriemhild herself orders the death of her brother Gunther, and with the
sword of Siegfried she herself kills Hagen as he stands defenseless
before her. She meets her own death when she is cut down by Hildebrand, who is enraged at the death of the mighty Hagen by the hand
of a woman.

The title *Nibelungenlied* means Song of the Nibelungs, and the
name Nibelung is ordinarily taken to mean "children of the mist." It
is applied first to the people from whom Siegfried has won the treasure
and who serve him at his need as liegemen. In the second part of the
story it is used to denote the Burgundians, who have taken the treasure
from Kriemhild. Some scholars consider it likely that the name originally denoted the Burgundians, that it came later to denote any posses-
sor of the treasure, and that finally it was carried back into the legends
of Siegfried's youth.

The origins of the *Nibelungenlied* are obscured in the mist of folk-
lore and myth. The composition of the poem as it is known today has
been traced to a time about the year 1200, roughly a hundred years after
The Song of Roland. It is written in the Austrian dialect of what is
called Middle High German. Nothing is known about its author.

The poem is cast in strophes, or stanzas, of four lines each, with
seven stresses in each of the first three lines and eight in the fourth.
In each line there is a caesura, or pause, after the fourth stress, which
is usually lighter than the other stresses. The first and second lines
rhyme in each strophe, as do the third and fourth. The metrical effect
is much the same as in many of the old English ballads still sung today.

The *Nibelungenlied* is a tale of heroic loyalties—of the loyalty of
vassal to lord, as of Hagen to his king; and of wife to husband, as in
the vengeance of Kriemhild for the death of her lord Siegfried. The
poem is a fusion of refinement and barbarism, of the chivalry of the
best medieval times and the brutality of the so-called Dark Ages. Like
the Anglo Saxon *Beowulf*, the *Nibelungenlied* is a pagan legend upon
which its author has imposed a veneer of Christianity. Unlike *The
Song of Roland*, it is Christian by accident and by afterthought. Its

hero is an idealization of freshness and generosity, a champion of the light against darkness. Its greatest character is Hagen of Troneg, dark and unscrupulous in his feudal loyalty, and courageous beyond mortality in fronting foreseen disaster.

THE NIBELUNGENLIED*

OF KRIEMHILD

Full many a wonder is told us in stories old, of heroes worthy of praise, of hardships dire, of joy and feasting, of the fighting of bold warriors, of weeping and of wailing; now ye may hear wonders told.

In Burgundy there grew so noble a maid that in all the lands none fairer might there be. Kriemhild was she called; a comely woman she became, for whose sake many a knight must needs lose his life. Well worth the loving was this winsome maid. Bold knights strove for her, none bare her hate. Her peerless body was beautiful beyond degree; the courtly virtues of this maid of noble birth would have adorned many another woman too.

Three kings, noble and puissant, did nurture her, Gunther[1] and Gernot, warriors worthy of praise, and Giselher, the youth, a chosen knight. This lady was their sister, the princes had her in their care. The lordings were free in giving, of race high-born, passing bold of strength were they, these chosen knights. Their realm hight Burgundy. Great marvels they wrought hereafter in Etzel's[2] land. At Worms upon the Rhine they dwelt with all their power. Proud knights from out their lands served them with honor, until their end was come. Thereafter they died grievously, through the hate of two noble dames.

Their mother, a mighty queen, was called the Lady Uta, their father, Dankrat, who left them the heritage after his life was over; a mighty man of valor that he was, who won thereto in youth worship full great. These kings, as I have said, were of high prowess. To them

---

* Translated by Daniel B. Shumway. The selections from the *Nibelungenlied* are used by permission of the publishers, Houghton Mifflin Company.
1. An actual historical character, Gundahari, king of the Burgundians in the 5th century.
2. German form for Atilla (the Hun).

owed allegiance the best of warriors, of whom tales were ever told, strong and brave, fearless in the sharp strife. Hagen there was of Troneg, thereto his brother Dankwart, the doughty; Ortwin of Metz; Gere and Eckewart, the margraves twain; Folker of Alzei, endued with fullness of strength. Rumolt was master of the kitchen, a chosen knight; the lords Sindolt and Hunolt, liegemen of these three kings, had rule of the court and of its honors. Thereto had they many a warrior whose name I cannot tell. . . .

In the midst of these high honors Kriemhild dreamed a dream, of how she trained a falcon, strong, fair, and wild, which, before her very eyes, two eagles rent to pieces. No greater sorrow might chance to her in all this world. This dream then she told to Uta her mother, who could not unfold it to the dutiful maid in better wise than thus: "The falcon which thou trainest, that is a noble man, but thou must needs lose him soon, unless so be that God preserve him."

"Why speakest thou to me of men, dear mother mine? I would fain ever be without a warrior's love. So fair will I remain until my death, that I shall never gain woe from love of man."

"Now forswear this not too roundly," spake the mother in reply. "If ever thou shalt wax glad of heart in this world, that will chance through the love of man. Passing fair wilt thou become, if God grant thee a right worthy knight."

"I pray you leave this speech," spake she, "my lady. Full oft hath it been seen in many a wife, how joy may at last end in sorrow. I shall avoid them both, then can it ne'er go ill with me."

Thus in her heart Kriemhild forsware all love. Many a happy day thereafter the maiden lived without that she wist[3] any whom she would care to love. In after days she became with worship[4] a valiant hero's bride. He was the selfsame falcon which she beheld in her dream that her mother unfolded to her. How sorely did she avenge this upon her nearest kin, who slew him after! Through his dying alone there fell full many a mother's son.

OF SIEGFRIED

In the Netherlands[5] there grew the child of a noble king (his father had for name Siegmund, his mother Siegelind), in a mighty castle, known far and wide, in the lowlands of the Rhine: Xanten,

3. Without knowing.   4. Honor.
5. Not modern Holland, but as the text has it, "the lowlands of the Rhine."

men called it. Of this hero I sing, how fair he grew. Free he was of
every blemish. Strong and famous he later became, this valiant man.
Ho! what great worship he won in this world! Siegfried hight this
good and doughty knight. Full many kingdoms did he put to the test
through his warlike mood. Through his strength of body he rode into
many lands. Ho! what bold warriors he after found in the Burgundian
land! Mickle wonders might one tell of Siegfried in his prime, in
youthful days; what honors he received and how fair of body he.
The most stately women held him in their love; with the zeal which
was his due men trained him. But of himself what virtues he attained!
Truly his father's lands were honored, that he was found in all things
of such right lordly mind. Now was he become of the age that he
might ride to court. Gladly the people saw him, many a maid wished
that his desire might ever bear him hither. Enow gazed on him with
favor; of this the prince was well aware. Full seldom was the youth
allowed to ride without a guard of knights. Siegmund and Siegelind
bade deck him out in brave attire. The older knights who were acquaint
with courtly custom had him in their care. Well therefore might he
win both folk and land.

Now he was of the strength that he bare weapons well. Whatever
he needed thereto, of this he had enow. With purpose he began to woo
fair ladies; these bold Siegfried courted well in proper wise. Then bade
Siegmund have cried to all his men, that he would hold a feasting
with his loving kindred. The tidings thereof men brought into the
lands of other kings. To the strangers and the home-folk he gave steeds
and armor. Wheresoever any was found who, because of his birth,
should become a knight, these noble youths were summoned to the
land for the feasting. Here with the youthful prince they gained the
knightly sword. . . .

The host bade make benches for the many valiant men, for the
midsummer[6] festival, at which Siegfried should gain the name of
knight. Then full many a noble knight and many a high-born squire
did hie them to the minster. Right were the elders in that they served
the young, as had been done to them afore. Pastimes they had and
hope of much good cheer. To the honor of God a mass was sung; then
there rose from the people full great a press, as the youths were made
knights in courtly wise, with such great honors as might not ever
lightly be again. Then they ran to where they found saddled many a

6. This festival has survived as St. John's Eve.

steed. In Siegmund's court the hurtling[7] waxed so fierce that both palace[8] and hall were heard to ring; the high-mettled warriors clashed with mighty sound. From young and old one heard many a shock, so that the splintering of the shafts reëchoed to the clouds. Truncheons were seen flying out before the palace from the hand of many a knight. This was done with zeal. At length the host bade cease the tourney and the steeds were led away. Upon the turf one saw all to-shivered[9] many a mighty buckler and great store of precious stones from the bright spangles of the shields. Through the hurtling this did hap.

Then the guests of the host betook them to where men bade them sit. With good cheer they refreshed them and with the very best of wine, of which one bare full plenty. To the strangers and the home-folk was shown worship enow. Though much pastime they had throughout the day, many of the strolling folk forsware all rest. They served for the largess, which men found there richly, whereby Siegmund's whole land was decked with praise. Then bade the king enfeoff Siegfried, the youth, with land and castles, as he himself had done. Much his hand bestowed upon the sword-companions. The journey liked them well, that to this land they were come. The feasting lasted until the seventh day. Siegelind, the noble queen, for the love of her son, dealt out ruddy gold in time-honored wise. Full well she wot how to make him beloved of the folk. Scarce could a poor man be found among the strolling mimes. Steeds and raiment were scattered by their hand, as if they were to live not one more day. I trow that never did serving folk use such great bounty. With worshipful honors the company departed hence. . . .

HOW SIEGFRIED CAME TO WORMS

It was seldom that sorrow of heart perturbed the prince. He heard tales told of how there lived in Burgundy a comely maid, fashioned wondrous fair, from whom he thereafter gained much of joy, but suffering, too. Her beauty out of measure was known far and wide. So many a hero heard of her noble mind, that it alone brought many a guest to Gunther's land. But however many were seen wooing for her love, Kriemhild never confessed within her heart that she listed[10] any for a lover. He was still a stranger to her, whose rule she later owned. Then did the son of Siegelind aspire to lofty love; the wooing of all

7. The clashing together of many knights.   9. Broken to pieces.
8. Reception hall.   10. Wished.

others was to his but as the wind, for well he wot how to gain a lady fair. . . .

Tidings of this reached Siegmund's ear; through the talk of the courtiers he was made ware of the wish of his son. Full loth it was to the king, that his child would woo the glorious maid. Siegelind heard it too, the wife of the noble king. Greatly she feared for her child, for full well she knew Gunther and his men. Therefore they sought to turn the hero from this venture. Up spake then the daring Siegfried: "Dear father mine, I would fain ever be without the love of noble dames, if I may not woo her in whom my heart hath great delight; whatsoever any may aver, it will avail but naught."

"And thou wilt not turn back," spake the king, "then am I in sooth glad of thy will and will help thee bring it to pass, as best I may. Yet hath this King Gunther full many a haughty man. If there were none else but Hagen, the doughty knight, he can use such arrogance that I fear me it will repent us sore, if we woo this high-born maid."

Then Siegfried made reply: "Wherefore need that hinder us? What I may not obtain from them in friendly wise, that my hand and its strength can gain. I trow that I can wrest from him both folk and land."

To this Prince Siegmund replied: "Thy speech liketh me not, for if this tale were told upon the Rhine, then durst thou never ride unto that land. Long time have Gunther and Gernot been known to me. By force may none win the maid, of this have I been well assured; but wilt thou ride with warriors unto this land, and we still have aught of friends, they shall be summoned soon."

"It is not to my mind," spake again Siegfried, "that warriors should follow me to the Rhine, as if for battle, that I constrain thereby the noble maid. My single hand can win her well—with eleven comrades I will fare to Gunther's land; thereto shalt thou help me, Father Siegmund."

Now his mother Siegelind also heard the tale. She began to make dole for her loved child, whom she feared to lose through Gunther's men. Sorely the noble queen gan weep. Lord Siegfried hied him straightway to where he saw her; to his mother he spake in gentle wise: "Lady, ye must not weep for me; naught have I to fear from all his fighting men. I pray you, speed me on my journey to the Burgundian land, that I and my warriors may have array such as proud heroes can wear with honor; for this I will say you gramercy i' faith."

"Since naught will turn thee," spake then the Lady Siegelind, "so will I speed thee on thy journey, mine only child, with the best of weeds that ever knight did wear, thee and thy comrades. Ye shall have enow."

Siegfried, the youth, then made low obeisance to the queen. He spake: "None but twelve warriors will I have upon the way. Let raiment be made ready for them, I pray, for I would fain see how it standeth with Kriemhild."

Then sate fair ladies night and day. Few enow of them, I trow, did ease them, till Siegfried's weeds had all been wrought. Nor would he desist from faring forth. His father bade adorn the knightly garb in which his son should ride forth from Siegmund's land. The shining breastplates, too, were put in trim, also the stanch helmets and their shields both fair and broad. . . .

. . . Upon the seventh morning, forth upon the river sand at Worms the brave warriors pricked. Their armor was of ruddy gold and their trappings fashioned fair. Smoothly trotted the steeds of bold Siegfried's men. Their shields were new; gleaming and broad and fair their helmets, as Siegfried, the bold, rode to court in Gunther's land. Never had such princely attire been seen on heroes; their sword-points hung down to their spurs. Sharp javelins were borne by these chosen knights. Siegfried wielded one full two spans broad, which upon its edges cut most dangerously. In their hands they held gold-colored bridles; their martingales were silken: so they came into the land. Everywhere the folk began to gape amazed and many of Gunther's men fared forth to meet them. High-mettled warriors, both knight and squire, betook them to the lords (as was but right), and received into the land of their lords these guests and took from their hands the black sumpters which bore the shields. The steeds, too, they wished to lead away for easement. How boldly then brave Siegfried spake: "Let stand the mounts of me and of my men. We will soon hence again, of this have I great desire. Whosoever knoweth rightly where I can find the king, Gunther, the mighty, of Burgundian land, let him not keep his peace but tell me."

. . . To the king now the word was brought, that full lusty knights were come, who wore white breastplates and princely garb. None knew them in the Burgundian land. Much it wondered the king whence came these lordly warriors in such shining array, with such good shields, both new and broad. . . .

Then bade the king that Hagen and his men be brought. One saw him with his warriors striding in lordly wise unto the court.

"What would the king of me?" asked Hagen.

"There be come to my house strange warriors, whom here none knoweth. If ye have ever seen them, I pray you, Hagen, tell me now the truth."

"That will I," spake then Hagen. He hied him to a window and over the guests he let his glances roam. Well liked him their trappings and their array, but full strange were they to him in the Burgundian land. He spake: "From wheresoever these warriors be come unto the Rhine, they may well be princes or envoys of kings, for their steeds are fair and their garments passing good. Whencesoever they bear these, forsooth high-mettled warriors be they."

"I dare well say," so spake Hagen, "though I never have seen Siegfried, yet can I well believe, however this may be, that he is the warrior that strideth yonder in such lordly wise. He bringeth new tidings hither to this land. By this hero's hand were slain the bold Nibelungs,[11] Schilbung and Nibelung, sons of a mighty king. Since then he hath wrought great marvels with his huge strength. Once as the hero rode alone without all aid, he found before a mountain, as I have in sooth been told, by Nibelung's hoard full many a daring man. Strangers they were to him, till he gained knowledge of them there.

"The hoard of Nibelung was borne entire from out a hollow hill. Now hear a wondrous tale, of how the liegemen of Nibelung wished to divide it there. This the hero Siegfried saw and much it gan wonder him. So near was he now come to them, that he beheld the heroes, and the knights espied him, too. One among them spake: 'Here cometh the mighty Siegfried, the hero of Netherland.' Passing strange were the tidings that he found among the Nibelungs. Schilbung and Nibelung greeted well the knight; with one accord these young and noble lordings bade the stately man divide the hoard. Eagerly they asked it, and the lord in turn gan vow[12] it to them.

"He beheld such store of gems, as we have heard said, that a hundred wains might not bear the load; still more was there of ruddy gold from the Nibelung land. All this the hand of the daring Siegfried should divide. As a guerdon they gave him the sword of Nibelung, but they were served full ill by the service which the good knight Siegfried should render them. Nor could he end it for them; angry of mood they grew. Twelve bold men of their kith were there, mighty

11. Although this poem is called *The Song of the Nibelungs*, the Nibelungs, vassals of Siegfried, do not play in it the important rôle that they play in the earlier legends.

12. Promise.

giants these. What might that avail them! Siegfried's hand slew them soon in wrath, and seven hundred warriors from the Nibelung land he vanquished with the good sword Balmung. Because of the great fear that many a young warrior had of the sword and of the valiant man, they made the land and its castles subject to his hand. Likewise both the mighty kings he slew, but soon he himself was sorely pressed by Alberich. The latter weened to venge straightway his masters, till he then discovered Siegfried's mighty strength; for no match for him was the sturdy dwarf. Like wild lions they ran to the hill, where from Alberich he won the Cloak of Darkness.[13] Thus did Siegfried, the terrible, become master of the hoard; those who had dared the combat, all lay there slain. Soon bade he cart and bear the treasure to the place from whence the men of Nibelung had borne it forth. He made Alberich, the strong, warden of the hoard and bade him swear an oath to serve him as his knave;[14] and fit he was for work of every sort."

So spake Hagen of Troneg: "This he hath done. Nevermore did warrior win such mighty strength. I wot yet more of him: it is known to me that the hero slew a dragon and bathed him in the blood, so that his skin became like horn. Therefore no weapons will cut him, as hath full oft been seen. All the better must we greet this lord, that we may not earn the youthful warrior's hate. So bold is he that we should hold him as a friend, for he hath wrought full many a wonder by his strength."

. . . The host and his warriors received the guest in such wise that full little was there lack of worship. Low bowed the stately man, that they had greeted him so fair. "It wondereth me," spake the king straightway, "whence ye, noble Siegfried, be come unto this land, or what ye seek at Worms upon the Rhine."

Then the stranger made answer to the king: "This will I not conceal from you. Tales were told me in my father's land, that here with you were the boldest warriors that ever king did gain. This I have often heard, and that I might know it of a truth, therefore am I come. Likewise do I hear boasting of your valor, that no bolder king hath ever been seen. This the folk relate much through all these lands. Therefore will I not turn back, till it be known to me. I also am a warrior and was to wear a crown. Fain would I bring it to pass that it may be said of me: Rightly doth he rule both folk and land. Of this

13. The *tarnkappe*, which made its wearer invisible and gave him superhuman strength.
14. Servant.

shall my head and honor be a pledge. Now be ye so bold, as hath been told me, I reck not be it lief or loth to any man, I will gain from you whatso ye have—land and castles shall be subject to my hand."

The king and likewise his men had marvel at the tidings they here heard, that he was willed to take from them their land. The knights waxed wroth, as they heard this word. "How have I earned this," spake Gunther, the knight, "that we should lose by the force of any man that which my father hath ruled so long with honor? We should let it ill appear that we, too, are used in knightly ways."

"In no wise will I desist," spake again the valiant man. "Unless it be that through thy strength thy land have peace, I will rule it all. And shouldst thou gain, by thy strength, my ancestral lands, they shall be subject to thy sway. Thy lands, and mine as well, shall lie alike; whether of us twain can triumph over the other, him shall both land and people serve."

Hagen and Gernot, too, straightway gainsaid this. "We have no wish," spake Gernot, "that we should conquer aught of lands, or that any man lie dead at hero's hands. We have rich lands, which serve us, as is meet, nor hath any a better claim to them than we."

There stood his kinsmen, grim of mood; among them, too, Ortwin of Metz. "It doth irk me much to hear these words of peace," spake he; "the mighty Siegfried hath defied you for no just cause. Had ye and your brothers no meet defense, and even if he led a kingly troop, I trow well so to fight that the daring man have good cause to leave this haughty mien."

At this the hero of Netherland grew wonderly wroth. He spake: "Thy hand shall not presume against me. I am a mighty king, a king's vassal thou. Twelve of thy ilk durst not match me in strife."

Then Ortwin of Metz called loudly for swords. Well was he fit to be Hagen of Troneg's sister's son. It rued the king that he had held his peace so long. Then Gernot, the bold and lusty knight, came in between. He spake to Ortwin: "Now give over thy anger. Lord Siegfried hath done us no such wrong, but that we may still part the strife in courteous wise. Be advised of me and hold him still as friend; far better will this beseem us."

Then spake the doughty Hagen: "It may well grieve us and all thy knights that he ever rode for battle to the Rhine. He should have given it over; my lordings never would have done such ill to him."

To this Siegfried, the mighty man, made answer: "Doth this irk you, Sir Hagen, which I spake, then will I let you see that my hands shall have dominion here in the Burgundian land."

"I alone will hinder this," answered Gernot, and he forbade his knights speak aught with haughtiness that might cause rue. Siegfried, too, then bethought him of the noble maid.

"How might it beseem us to fight with you?" spake Gernot anew. "However many heroes should lie dead because of this, we should have scant honor therefrom and ye but little gain."

To this Siegfried, the son of Siegmund, made reply: "Why waiteth Hagen, and Ortwin, too, that he hasteth not to fight with his kin, of whom he hath so many here in Burgundy?"

At this all held their peace; such was Gernot's counsel. Then spake Queen Uta's son: "Ye shall be welcome to us with all your warmates, who are come with you. We shall gladly serve you, I and all my kin."

Then for the guests they bade pour out King Gunther's wine. The master of the land then spake: "All that we have, if ye desire it in honorable wise, shall owe fealty to you; with you shall both life and goods be shared."

. . . Whenever the lordings and their liegemen did play at knightly games, Siegfried was aye the best, whatever they began. Herein could no one match him, so mighty was his strength, whether they threw the stone or hurled the shaft. When through courtesie the full lusty knights made merry with the ladies, there were they glad to see the hero of Netherland, for upon high love his heart was bent. . . .

Whenever the mighty kings fared forth into their land, the warriors all must needs accompany them at hand, and Siegfried, too. This the lady rued, and he, too, suffered many pangs for love of her. Thus he dwelt with the lordings, of a truth, full a year in Gunther's land, and in all this time he saw not once the lovely maid, from whom in later days there happed to him much joy and eke much woe.

[When Siegfried has been a year among the Burgundians, news comes to Worms that the Saxon Prince Liudeger and his brother Liudegast, King of Denmark, are preparing war against Burgundy. At Hagen's suggestion, Gunther seeks aid of Siegfried, who offers to lead a thousand men against the enemy. He overcomes Liudegast in single combat, forces the surrender of Liudeger, and triumphantly returns to Burgundy with many hostages. In Worms the victors are richly rewarded, and a great feast of victory is planned.]

HOW SIEGFRIED FIRST SAW KRIEMHILD

One saw daily riding to the Rhine those who would fain be at the feasting. Full many of these who for the king's sake were come into the land, were given steeds and lordly harness. Seats were prepared for all, for the highest and the best, as we are told, for two and thirty princes at the feast. For this, too, the fair ladies vied in their attire. Giselher, the youth, was aught but idle; he and Gernot and all their men received the friends and strangers. In truth, they gave the knights right courtly greetings. These brought into the land many a saddle of golden red, dainty shields and lordly armor to the feasting on the Rhine. . . .

Upon a Whitsun morning five thousand or more brave men, clad in glad attire, were seen going forth to the high festal tide. On all sides they vied with each other in knightly sports. The host marked well, what he already wot, how from his very heart the hero of Netherland did love his sister, albeit he had never seen her, whose comeliness men praised above all maids. Then spake the knight Ortwin to the king: "Would ye have full honor at your feast, so should ye let be seen the charming maids, who live in such high honors here in Burgundy. What were the joy of man, what else could give him pleasure, but pretty maids and noble dames? Pray let your sister go forth before the guests." To the joy of many a hero was this counsel given.

"This will I glady do," spake then the king, and all who heard it were merry at the thought. Then bade he say to the Lady Uta and her comely daughter, that with their maidens they should come to court. From the presses they took fair raiment and whatso of rich attire was laid away. Of rings and ribbons, too, enow they had. Thus each stately maiden decked herself with zeal. . . . Soon one saw the noble Uta coming with her child. Full hundred or more fair ladies had she taken for her train, who wore rich robes. Likewise there followed her daughter many a stately maid. When from out a bower men saw them come, there rose a mighty press of knights who had the hope, if that might be, to gaze with joy upon the noble maid. Now came she forth, the lovely fair, as doth the red of dawn from out the lowering clouds. He then was reft of many woes who bore her in his heart so long a time, when he saw the lovely maid stand forth so glorious. How shone full many a precious stone upon her robes! In lovely wise her rose-red hue appeared. Whatever one might wish, he could not but confess that never in the world had he beheld a fairer maid. As the radiant moon,

whose sheen is thrown so brightly on the clouds, doth stand before the
stars, so stood she now before full many a stately dame. . . .

Then went the kinsmen of the host to fetch the hero. To the champion from Netherland they spake: "You hath the king permitted to go
to court; his sister is to greet you. This hath he decreed to do you
honor."

At this the lord grew blithe of mood, for in his heart he bare joy
without alloy, that he thus should see fair Uta's child. With lovely grace
she greeted Siegfried then, but when she saw the haughty[15] knight
stand thus before her, her cheeks flamed bright. "Be welcome, Sir Siegfried, most good and noble knight," the fair maid spake, and at this
greeting his spirits mounted high. Courteously he made obeisance; she
took him by the hand. How gallantly he walked by the lady's side!
Upon each other this lord and lady gazed with kindling eyes. Full
secretly this happed. Was perchance a white hand there fervently
pressed by heart-felt love? That know I not; yet I cannot believe that
this was left undone, for soon had she betrayed to him her love. Nevermore in summertide nor in the days of May bare he within his heart
such lofty joy as now he gained, when hand in hand he walked with
her whom he fain would call his love. . . .

From whatever land the guests were come, all gazed alike upon
this pair alone. She then was bidden kiss the stately man, to whom no
such delight had ever happened in this world. . . .

On all sides they bade make way for Kriemhild, as thus to church
one saw her go with many a valiant knight in courtly wise. Then soon
the stately knight was parted from her side. Thus went she to the
minster, followed by many a dame. . . .

When she came forth from out the minster, they begged the
gallant knight again to bear her company, as he had done afore. Then
first the lovely maid began to thank him that he had fought so gloriously before so many knights. "Now God requite you, Sir Siegfried,"
spake the comely maid, "that ye have brought to pass with your
service, that the warriors do love you with such fealty as I hear them
say."

Then upon Dame Kriemhild he began to gaze in loving wise. "I
will serve them ever," spake then the knight, "and while life shall last,
never will I lay my head to rest till I have done their will; and this I do,
my Lady Kriemhild, to win your love."

. . . So the valiant knight stayed on to please his friends, nor could

15. Noble, exalted.

he have fared more gentilly in any land. This happed because he daily
saw Kriemhild, the fair; for the sake of her unmeasured beauty the
lording stayed. With many a pastime they whiled the hours away, but
still her love constrained him and often gave him dole. Because of this
same love in later days the valiant knight lay pitiful in death.

[Word now comes to the Rhine country of a queen of peerless
beauty and heroic strength. Brunhild, ruler of Isenland, lives in her
castle of Isenstein, where she entertains suitors and contends with them
in martial exercises. She invariably defeats them and puts them to
death. Gunther is determined to woo her, but when Siegfried warns
him of Brunhild's might he grows apprehensive of the outcome. At
Hagen's suggestion Gunther enlists Siegfried's aid in the wooing, and
Siegfried consents upon condition that if their wooing is successful
Gunther will reward him with the hand of Kriemhild. With Hagen
and his brother Dankwart they set out for Isenland and after a voyage
of twelve days come within sight of Brunhild's castle.]

HOW GUNTHER WON BRUNHILD

Meanwhile their bark had come so near the castle that the king
saw many a comely maiden standing at the casements. Much it irked
King Gunther that he knew them not. He asked his comrade Siegfried: "Hast thou no knowledge of these maidens, who yonder are
gazing downward towards us on the flood? Whoever be their lord,
they are of lofty mood."

At this Sir Siegfried spake: "I pray you, spy secretly among the
high-born maids and tell me then whom ye would choose, and ye had
the power."

"That will I," spake Gunther, the bold and valiant knight. "In
yonder window do I see one stand in snow-white weeds. She is fashioned so fair that mine eyes would choose her for her comeliness. Had
I power, she should become my wife."

"Right well thine eyes have chosen for thee. It is the noble Brunhild, the comely maid, for whom thy heart doth strive and eke thy
mind and mood." All her bearing seemed to Gunther good.

Then bade the queen her high-born maids go from the windows,
for it behooved them not to be the mark of strangers' eyes. Each one
obeyed. They decked their persons out to meet the unknown knights, a
way fair maids have ever had. To the narrow casements they came

again, where they had seen the knights. Through love of gazing this was done.

But four there were that were come to land. Through the windows the stately women saw how Siegfried led a horse out on the sand, whereby King Gunther felt himself much honored. By the bridle he held the steed, so stately, good and fair, and large and strong, until King Gunther had sat him in the saddle. Thus Siegfried served him, the which he later quite forgot. Such service he had seldom done afore, that he should stand at any hero's stirrup. Then he led his own steed from the ship. All this the comely dames of noble birth saw through the casements. The steeds and garments, too, of the lusty knights, of snow-white hue, were right well matched and all alike; the bucklers, fashioned well, gleamed in the hands of the stately men. In lordly wise they rode to Brunhild's hall, their saddles set with precious stones, with narrow martingales, from which hung bells of bright and ruddy gold. So they came to the land, as well befit their prowess, with newly sharpened spears, with well-wrought swords, the which hung down to the spurs of these stately men. The swords the bold men bore were sharp and broad. All this Brunhild, the high-born maid, espied. . . .

Thus the brave knights and good rode to the castle. Six and eighty towers they saw within, three broad palaces, and one hall well wrought of costly marble, green as grass, wherein Brunhild herself sate with her courtiers. The castle was unlocked and the gates flung wide. Then ran Brunhild's men to meet them and welcomed the strangers into their mistress' land. One bade relieve them of their steeds and shields.

Then spake a chamberlain: "Pray give us now your swords and your shining breastplates, too."

"That we may not grant you," said Hagen of Troneg; "we ourselves will bear them."

Then gan Siegfried tell aright the tale. "The usage of the castle, let me say, is such that no guests may here bear arms. Let them now be taken hence, then will all be well."

Unwillingly Hagen, Gunther's man, obeyed. For the strangers men bade pour out wine and make their lodgings ready. Many doughty knights were seen walking everywhere at court in lordly weeds. Mickle and oft were these heroes gazed upon.

Then the tidings were told to Lady Brunhild, that unknown warriors were come in lordly raiment, sailing on the flood. The fair and worthy maid gan ask concerning this. "Pray let me hear," spake the queen, "who be these unknown knights, who stand so lordly in my castle, and for whose sake the heroes have journeyed hither?"

Then spake one of the courtiers: "My lady, I can well say that never have I set eyes on any of them, but one like Siegfried doth stand among them. Him ye should give fair greetings; that is my rede, in truth. . . ."

Then spake the queen: "Now bring me my attire. If the mighty Siegfried be come unto this land through love of mine, he doth risk his life. I fear him not so sore, that I should become his wife."

Brunhild, the fair, was soon well clad. Then went there with her many a comely maid, full hundred or more, decked out in gay attire. The stately dames would gaze upon the strangers. With them there walked good knights from Isenland, Brunhild's men-at-arms, five hundred or more, who bore swords in hand. This the strangers rued. From their seats then the brave and lusty heroes rose. When that the queen spied Siegfried, now hear what the maid did speak.

"Be ye welcome, Siegfried, here in this our land! What doth your journey mean? That I fain would know."

"Gramercy, my Lady Brunhild, that ye have deigned to greet me, most generous queen, in the presence of this noble knight who standeth here before me, for he is my liege lord. This honor I must needs forswear. By birth he's from the Rhine; what more need I to say? For thy sake are we come hither. Fain would he woo thee, however he fare. Bethink thee now betimes, my lord will not let thee go. He is hight Gunther and is a lordly king. An' he win thy love, he doth crave naught more. Forsooth this knight, so well beseen, did bid me journey hither. I would fain have given it over, could I have said him nay."

She spake: "Is he thy liege and thou his man, dare he assay the games which I mete out and gain the mastery, then I'll become his wife; but should I win, 't will cost you all your lives."

Then up spake Hagen of Troneg: "My lady, let us see your mighty games. It must indeed go hard, or ever Gunther, my lord, give you the palm. He troweth well to win so fair a maid."

"He must hurl the stone and after spring and cast the spear with me. Be ye not too hasty. Ye are like to lose here your honor and your life as well. Bethink you therefore rightly," spake the lovely maid.

Siegfried, the bold, went to the king and bade him tell the queen all that he had in mind, he should have no fear. "I'll guard you well against her with my arts."

Then spake King Gunther: "Most noble queen, now mete out

whatso ye list, and were it more, that would I all endure for your sweet
sake. I'll gladly lose my head, and ye become not my wife."

When the queen heard this speech, she begged them hasten to the
games, as was but meet. She bade purvey her with good armor for the
strife: a breastplate of ruddy gold and a right good shield. A silken
surcoat, too, the maid put on, which sword had never cut in any fray,
of silken cloth of Libya. . . .

Meanwhile Siegfried, the stately man, or ever any marked it, had
hied him to the ship, where he found his magic cloak concealed. Into
it he quickly slipped and so was seen of none. He hurried back and
there he found a great press of knights, where the queen dealt out her
lofty games. Thither he went in secret wise (by his arts it happed), nor
was he seen of any that were there. The ring had been marked out,
where the games should be, afore many valiant warriors, who were to
view them there. More than seven hundred were seen bearing arms,
who were to say who won the game.

Then was come Brunhild, armed as though she would battle for
all royal lands. Above her silken coat she wore many a bar of gold;
gloriously her lovely color shone beneath the armor. Then came her
courtiers, who bare along a shield of ruddy gold with large broad strips
as hard as steel, beneath the which the lovely maid would fight. . . .
Rich enow it was, of steel and eke of gold, the which four chamberlains
could scarcely carry.

When the stalwart Hagen saw the shield borne forth, the knight of
Troneg spake full grim of mood: "How now, King Gunther? How
we shall lose our lives! She you would make your love is the devil's
bride, in truth."

. . . Then was brought forth for the lady a spear, sharp, heavy, and
large, the which she cast all time, stout and unwieldy, mickle and
broad, which on its edges cut most fearfully. Of the spear's great
weight hear wonders told. Three and one half weights of iron were
wrought therein, the which scarce three of Brunhild's men could bear.
The noble Gunther gan be sore afraid. Within his heart he thought:
"What doth this mean? How could the devil from hell himself escape
alive? Were I safe and sound in Burgundy, long might she live here
free of any love of mine."

Then spake Hagen's brother, the valiant Dankwart: "The journey
to this court doth rue me sore. We who have ever borne the name of
knights, how must we lose our lives! Shall we now perish at the hands
of women in these lands? It doth irk me much, that ever I came unto

this country. Had but my brother Hagen his sword in hand, and I mine, too, then should Brunhild's men go softly in their overweening pride. . . ."

"We might leave this land unscathed," spake then his brother Hagen, "had we the harness which we sorely need and our good swords as well; then would the pride of this strong dame become a deal more soft."

What the warrior spake the noble maid heard well. Over her shoulders she gazed with smiling mouth. "Now sith he thinketh himself so brave, bring them forth their coats-of-mail; put in the warriors' hands their sharp-edged swords."

When they received their weapons as the maiden bade, bold Dankwart blushed for very joy. "Now let them play whatso they list," spake the doughty man. "Gunther is unconquered, since now we have our arms."

Mightily now did Brunhild's strength appear. Into the ring men bare a heavy stone, huge and great, mickle and round. Twelve brave and valiant men-at-arms could scarcely bear it. This she threw at all times, when she had shot the spear. The Burgundian's fear now grew amain.

"Woe is me," cried Hagen. "Whom hath King Gunther chosen for a love? Certes she should be the foul fiend's bride in hell."

Upon her fair white arm the maid turned back her sleeves; with her hands she grasped the shield and poised the spear on high. Thus the strife began. Gunther and Siegfried feared Brunhild's hate, and had Siegfried not come to Gunther's aid, she would have bereft the king of life. Secretly Siegfried went and touched his hand; with great fear Gunther marked his wiles. "Who hath touched me?" thought the valiant man. Then he gazed around on every side, but saw none standing there.

" 'T is I, Siegfried, the dear friend of thine. Thou must not fear the queen. Give me the shield from off thy hand and let me bear it and mark aright what thou dost hear me say. Make thou the motions, I will do the deeds."

When Gunther knew that it was Siegfried, he was overjoyed. . . .

Then with might and main the noble maiden hurled the spear at a shield, mickle, new, and broad, which the son of Siegelind bore upon his arm. The sparks sprang from the steel, as if the wind did blow. The edge of the mighty spear broke fully through the shield, so that men saw the fire flame forth from the armor rings. The stalwart men both staggered at the blow; but for the Cloak of Darkness they had lain there dead. From the mouth of Siegfried, the brave, gushed forth the blood. Quickly the good knight sprang back again and snatched the spear that she had driven through his shield. Stout Siegfried's hand now sent it back again. He thought: "I will not pierce the comely maid." So he reversed the point and cast it at her armor with the butt, that it rang out loudly from his mighty hand. The sparks flew from the armor rings, as though driven by the wind. Siegmund's son had made the throw with might. With all her strength she could not stand before the blow. In faith King Gunther never could have done the deed.

Brunhild, the fair, how quickly up she sprang! "Gunther, noble knight, I cry you mercy for the shot." She weened that he had done it with his strength. To her had crept a far more powerful man. Then went she quickly, angry was her mood. The noble maid and good raised high the stone and hurled it mightily far from her hand. After the cast she sprang, that all her armor rang, in truth. The stone had fallen twelve fathoms hence, but with her leap the comely maid outsprang the throw. Then went Sir Siegfried to where lay the stone. Gunther poised it, while the hero made the throw. Siegfried was bold, strong, and tall; he threw the stone still further and made a broader jump. Through his fair arts he had strength enow to bear King Gunther with him as he sprang. The leap was made, the stone lay on the ground; men saw none other save Gunther, the knight, alone. Siegfried had banished the fear of King Gunther's death. Brunhild, the fair, waxed red with wrath. To her courtiers she spake a deal too loud, when she spied the hero safe and sound at the border of the ring: "Come nearer quickly, ye kinsmen and liegemen of mine, ye must now be subject to Gunther, the king."

Then the brave knights laid aside their arms and paid their homage at the feet of mighty Gunther from the Burgundian land. They weened that he had won the games by his own strength alone. He greeted them in loving wise; in sooth he was most rich in virtues.

Then the lovely maiden took him by the hand; full power she granted him within the land. At this Hagen, the bold and doughty knight, rejoiced him. She bade the noble knight go with her hence to the spacious palace. When this was done, they gave the warriors with their service better cheer. With good grace Hagen and Dankwart now must needs submit. The doughty Siegfried was wise enow and bare away his magic cloak. Then he repaired to where the ladies sate. To the king he spake and shrewdly did he this: "Why wait ye, good my lord? Why begin ye not the games, of which the queen doth deal so great a store? Let us soon see how they be played." The crafty man did act as though he wist not a whit thereof.

Then spake the queen: "How hath it chanced that ye, Sir Siegfried, have seen naught of the games which the hand of Gunther here hath won?"

To this Hagen of the Burgundian land made answer. He spake: "Ye have made us sad of mind, my lady. Siegfried, the good knight, was by the ship when the lord of the Rhineland won from you the games. He knoweth naught thereof."

"Well is me of this tale," spake Siegfried, the knight, "that your pride hath been brought thus low, and that there doth live a wight who hath the power to be your master. Now, O noble maiden, must ye follow us hence to the Rhine."

[Brunhild refuses to leave Isenland until she has called to her castle all her retainers to tell them of her departure to Burgundy. Upon the arrival of thousands of warriors, a threatening atmosphere develops at court, and the Burgundians become apprehensive of Brunhild's good faith and of their own safety. Siegfried, however, offers to help them further. Under concealment of his Cloak of Darkness he goes to the land of the Nibelungs, of which he is sovereign and where his great treasure is stored. Here he enlists the service of a thousand Nibelung knights, with whom he returns to the court of Brunhild. Intimidated by this force, Brunhild prepares at once to leave for Burgundy. Still playing the part of vassal to Gunther, Siegfried precedes the party to carry the great news to Worms.]

HOW BRUNHILD WAS RECEIVED AT WORMS

Across the Rhine men saw the king with his guests in many bands pricking to the shore. One saw the horse of many a maiden, too, led by the bridle. All those who should give them welcome were ready now. . . . Then many a knight and maid became acquaint. Duke Gere led Kriemhild's palfrey by the bridle till just outside the castle gate. Siegfried, the valiant knight, must needs attend her further. A fair maid was she! . . . The lovely fair stood by the shore as Gunther and his guests alighted from the boats; he himself led Brunhild by the hand. Bright gems and gleaming armor shone forth in rivalry. Lady Kriemhild walked with courtly breeding to meet Dame Brunhild and her train. White hands removed the chaplets, as these twain kissed each other; through deference this was done.

Then in courteous wise the maiden Kriemhild spake: "Be ye welcome in these lands of ours, to me and to my mother and to all the loyal kin we have."

. . . Maids and ladies now drew near each other. Many a comely dame was seen arrayed full well. Silken tents and many rich pavilions stood hard by, the which quite filled the plain of Worms. The kinsmen of the king came crowding around, when Brunhild and Kriemhild and with them all the dames were bidden go to where shade was found. Thither the knights from the Burgundian land escorted them.

Now were the strangers come to horse, and shields were pierced in many royal jousts. From the plain the dust gan rise, as though the whole land had burst forth into flames. There many a knight became well known as champion. Many a maiden saw what there the warriors plied. . . .

When now over all the plain the jousts had ceased, the knights, on pastime bent, hied them to the ladies under many a high pavilion in the hope of lofty joys. There they passed the hours until they were minded to ride away. . . .

The seats were now made ready, for the king would go to table with his guests. At his side men saw fair Brunhild stand, wearing the crown in the king's domain. Royal enow she was in sooth. Good broad tables, with full many benches for the men, were set with vitaille, as we are told. Little they lacked that they should have! At the king's table many a lordly guest was seen. The chamberlains of the host bare water forth in basins of ruddy gold. . . .

Before the lord of the Rhineland took the water to wash his hands, Siegfried did as was but meet, he minded him by his troth of what he had promised, or ever he had seen Brunhild at home in Isenland. He spake: "Ye must remember how ye swore me by your hand, that when Lady Brunhild came to this land, ye would give me your sister to wife. Where be now these oaths? I have suffered mickle hardship on our trip."

Then spake the king to his guest: "Rightly have ye minded me. Certes my hand shall not be perjured. I'll bring it to pass as best I can."

. . . Then they brought Kriemhild to where the king was found. There stood noble knights from many princes' lands; throughout the broad hall one bade them stand quite still. By this time Lady Brunhild had stepped to the table, too. Then spake King Gunther: "Sweet sister mine, by thy courtesie redeem my oath. I swore to give thee to a knight, and if he become thy husband, then hast thou done my will most loyally."

Quoth the noble maid: "Dear brother mine, ye must not thus entreat me. Certes I'll be ever so, that whatever ye command, that shall be done. I'll gladly pledge my troth to him whom ye, my lord, do give me to husband."

Siegfried here grew red at the glance of friendly eyes. The knight then proffered his service to Lady Kriemhild. Men bade them take their stand at each other's side within the ring and asked if she would take the stately man. In maidenly modesty she was a deal abashed, yet such was Siegfried's luck and fortune, that she would not refuse him out of hand. The noble king of Netherland vowed to take her, too, to wife. When he and the maid had pledged their troths, Siegfried's arm embraced eftsoon the winsome maid. Then the fair queen was kissed before the knights. The courtiers parted, when that had happed; on the bench over against the king Siegfried was seen to take his seat with Kriemhild. Thither many a man accompanied him as servitor; men saw the Nibelungs walk at Siegfried's side.

The king had seated him with Brunhild, the maid, when she espied Kriemhild (naught had ever irked her so) sitting at Siegfried's side. She began to weep and hot tears coursed down fair cheeks. Quoth the lord of the land: "What aileth you, my lady, that ye let bright eyes grow dim? Ye may well rejoice; my castles and my land and many a stately vassal own your sway."

"I have good cause to weep," spake the comely maid; "my heart is sore because of thy sister, whom I see sitting so near thy vassal's side. I must ever weep that she be so demeaned."

Then spake the King Gunther: "Ye would do well to hold your peace. At another time I will tell you the tale of why I gave Siegfried my sister unto wife. Certes she may well live ever happily with the knight."

She spake: "I sorrow ever for her beauty and her courtesie. I fain would flee, and I wist whither I might go, for never will I lie close by your side, unless ye tell me through what cause Kriemhild be Siegfried's bride."

Then spake the noble king: "I'll do it you to wit;[16] he hath castles and broad domains, as well as I. Know of a truth, he is a mighty king, therefore did I give him the peerless maid to love."

16. Let you know.

But whatsoever the king might say, she remained full sad of mood.

Now many a good knight hastened from the board. Their hurtling waxed so passing hard, that the whole castle rang. But the host was weary of his guests. Him thought[17] that he might lie more soft at his fair lady's side. As yet he had not lost at all the hope that much of joy might hap to him through her. Lovingly he began to gaze on Lady Brunhild. Men bade the guests leave off their knightly games, for the king and his wife would go to bed. Brunhild and Kriemhild then met before the stairway of the hall, as yet without the hate of either. Then came their retinue. Noble chamberlains delayed not, but brought them lights. The warriors, the liegemen of the two kings, then parted on either side and many of the knights were seen to walk with Siegfried.

The lords were now come to the rooms where they should lie. Each of the twain thought to conquer by love his winsome dame. This made them blithe of mood. Siegfried's pleasure on that night was passing great. When Lord Siegfried lay at Kriemhild's side and with his noble love caressed the high-born maid so tenderly, she grew as dear to him as life, so that not for a thousand other women would he have given her alone. No more I'll tell how Siegfried wooed his wife; hear now the tale of how King Gunther lay by Lady Brunhild's side. The stately knight had often lain more soft by other dames. The courtiers now had left, both maid and man. The chamber soon was locked; he thought to caress the lovely maid. Forsooth the time was still far off, ere she became his wife. In a smock of snowy linen she went to bed. Then thought the noble knight: "Now have I here all that I have ever craved in all my days." By rights she must needs please him through her comeliness. The noble king gan shroud the lights and then the bold knight hied him to where the lady lay. He laid him at her side, and great was his joy when in his arms he clasped the lovely fair. Many loving caresses he might have given, had but the noble dame allowed it. She waxed so wroth that he was sore a-troubled; he weened that they were lovers, but he found here hostile hate. She spake: "Sir Knight, pray give this over, which now ye hope. Forsooth this may not hap, for I will still remain a maid, until I hear the tale; now mark ye that."

Then Gunther grew wroth; he struggled for her love and rumpled all her clothes. The high-born maid then seized her girdle, the which was a stout band she wore around her waist, and with it she wrought the king great wrong enow. She bound him hand and foot and bare

17. It seemed to him.

him to a nail and hung him on the wall. She forbade him love, sith he disturbed her sleep. Of a truth he came full nigh to death through her great strength.

Then he who had weened to be the master, began to plead. "Now loose my bands, most noble queen. I no longer trow to conquer you, fair lady, and full seldom will I lie so near your side."

She recked not how he felt, for she lay full soft. There he had to hang all night till break of day, until the bright morn shone through the casements. Had he ever had great strength, it was little seen upon him now.

"Now tell me, Sir Gunther, would that irk you aught," the fair maid spake, "and your servants found you bound by a woman's hand?"

Then spake the noble knight: "That would serve you ill; nor would it gain me honor," spake the doughty man. "By your courtesie, pray let me lie now by your side. Sith that my love mislike you so, I will not touch your garment with my hands."

Then she loosed him soon and let him rise. To the bed again, to the lady he went and laid him down so far away, that thereafter he full seldom touched her comely weeds. Nor would she have allowed it.

Then their servants came and brought them new attire, of which great store was ready for them against the morn. However merry men made, the lord of the land was sad enow, albeit he wore a crown that day. As was the usage which they had and which they kept by right, Gunther and Brunhild no longer tarried, but hied them to the minster, where mass was sung. Thither, too, Sir Siegfried came and a great press arose among the crowd. In keeping with their royal rank, there was ready for them all that they did need, their crowns and robes as well. Then they were consecrated. When this was done, all four were seen to stand joyful 'neath their crowns. Many young squires, six hundred or better, were now girt with sword in honor of the kings, as ye must know. Great joy rose then in the Burgundian land; one heard spear-shafts clashing in the hands of the sworded knights. There at the windows the fair maids sat; they saw shining afore them the gleam of many a shield. But the king had sundered him from his liegemen; whatso others plied, men saw him stand full sad. Unlike stood his and Siegfried's mood. The noble knight and good would fain have known what ailed the king. He hasted to him and gan ask: "Pray let me know how ye have fared this night, Sir King."

Then spake the king to his guest: "Shame and disgrace have I won; I have brought a fell devil to my house and home. When I weened to love her, she bound me sore; she bare me to a nail and hung me high upon a wall. There I hung affrighted all night until the day, or ever she unbound me. How softly she lay bedded there! In hope of thy pity do I make plaint to thee as friend to friend."

Then spake stout Siegfried: "That rueth me in truth. I'll do you this to wit; and ye allow me without distrust, I'll contrive that she lie by you so near this night, that she'll nevermore withhold from you her love."

After all his hardships Gunther liked well this speech. Sir Siegfried spake again: "Thou mayst well be of good cheer. I ween we fared unlike last night. Thy sister Kriemhild is dearer to me than life; the Lady Brunhild must become thy wife to-night. I'll come to thy chamber this night, so secretly in my Cloud Cloak, that none may note at all my arts. Then let the chamberlains betake them to their lodgings and I'll put out the lights in the pages' hands, whereby thou mayst know that I be within and that I'll gladly serve thee. I'll tame for thee thy wife, that thou mayst have her love to-night, or else I'll lose my life."

"Unless be thou embrace my dear lady," spake then the king, "I shall be glad, if thou do to her as thou dost list. I could endure it well, an' thou didst take her life. In sooth she is a fearful wife."

"I pledge upon my troth," quoth Siegfried, "that I will not embrace her. The fair sister of thine, she is to me above all maids that I have ever seen."

Gunther believed full well what Siegfried spake. . . . In fair hope the king sate now full merrily; well he thought on that which Siegfried had vowed to do. This one day thought him as long as thirty days, for all his thoughts were bent upon his lady's love. He could scarce abide the time to leave the board.

The Lord Siegfried sate in loving wise by his fair wife, in bliss without alloy. With her snow-white hands she fondled his, till that he vanished from before her eyes, she wist not when. . . . He was gone to where he found many grooms of the chamber stand with lights. These he gan snuff out in the pages' hands. Thus Gunther knew that it was Siegfried. Well wist he what he would; he bade the maids and ladies now withdraw. When that was done, the mighty king himself made fast the door and nimbly shoved in place two sturdy bolts. Quickly then he hid the lights behind the hangings of the bed. Stout Siegfried and the maiden now began a play (for this there was no help) which was both lief and loth to Gunther. Siegfried laid him close by the high-born maid. She spake: "Now, Gunther, let that be, and it be lief to you, that ye suffer not hardship as afore."

Then the lady hurt bold Siegfried sore. He held his peace and answered not a whit. Gunther heard well, though he could not see his friend a bit, that they plied not secret things, for little ease they had upon the bed. Siegfried bare him as though he were Gunther, the mighty king. In his arms he clasped the lovely maid. She cast him from the bed upon a bench near by, so that his head struck loudly against the stool. Up sprang the valiant man with all his might; fain would he try again. When he thought now to subdue her she hurt him sore. Such defense, I ween, might nevermore be made by any wife.

When he would not desist, up sprang the maid. "Ye shall not rumple thus my shift so white. Ye are a clumsy churl and it shall rue you sore, I'll have you to know full well," spake the comely maid. In her arms she grasped the peerless knight; she weened to bind him, as she had done the king, that she might have her ease upon the bed. The lady avenged full sore, that he had rumpled thus her clothes. What availed his mickle force and his giant strength? She showed the knight her masterly strength of limb; she carried him by force (and that must needs be) and pressed him rudely 'twixt a clothes-press and the wall.

"Alas," so thought the knight, "if now I lose my life at a maiden's hands, then may all wives hereafter bear towards their husbands haughty mien, who would never do it else."

The king heard it well and feared him for his liegeman's life. Siegfried was sore ashamed; wrathful he waxed and with surpassing strength he set himself against her and tried it again with Lady Brunhild in fearful wise. It thought the king[18] full long, before he conquered her. She pressed his hands, till from her strength the blood gushed forth from out the nails: this irked the hero. Therefore he brought the high-born maiden to the pass that she gave over her unruly will, which she asserted there afore. The king heard all, albeit not a word he spake. Siegfried pressed her against the bed, so that she shrieked aloud. Passing sore his strength did hurt her. She grasped the girdle around her waist and would fain have bound him, but his hand prevented it in such a wise that her limbs and all her body cracked. Thus the strife was parted and she became King Gunther's wife.

She spake: "Most noble king, pray spare my life. I'll do thee remedy for whatso I have done thee. I'll no longer struggle against thy

18. It seemed to the king.

noble love, for I have learned full well that thou canst make thee
master over women."

Siegfried let the maiden lie and stepped away, as though he would
do off his clothes. From her hand he drew a golden finger ring, without that she wist it, the noble queen. Thereto he took her girdle, a good
stout band. I know not if he did that for very haughtiness. He gave it
to his wife and rued it sore in after time.

Then lay Gunther and the fair maid side by side. He played the
lover, as beseemed him, and thus she must needs give over wrath and
shame. From his embrace a little pale she grew. Ho, how her great
strength failed through love! Now was she no stronger than any other
wife.

[With Brunhild changed into a loving wife and with the double
wedding-feast ended, Siegfried and his bride prepare to leave Burgundy. Siegfried declines to accept the rich dowry of Kriemhild; but
Kriemhild asks, for herself, a large retinue of Burgundian knights.
Preceded by messengers, the party journeys to the court of Siegmund
and Siegelind, where they are joyfully received. Siegmund relinquishes
his crown and rule to Siegfried, and peace and quiet ensue for a
number of years. Kriemhild bears a son, named for Gunther, and
Brunhild bears a son, named for Siegfried.

After a time Brunhild yearns to see Siegfried and Kriemhild again,
and Gunther sends messengers inviting them to visit Worms. Accompanied by the old King Siegmund and a thousand Nibelung knights,
Siegfried and his wife make the long journey to the court of the
Burgundians, where they are welcomed with great joy. With feasting,
jousting, and giving of gifts the days pass peacefully, for a while.]

HOW THE QUEENS REVILED EACH OTHER

On a day before the vesper tide a great turmoil arose, which many
knights made in the court, where they plied their knightly sports for
pastime's sake, and a great throng of men and women hasted there to
gaze. The royal queens had sat them down together and talked of two
worshipful knights.

Then spake the fair Kriemhild: "I have a husband who by right
should rule over all these kingdoms."

Quoth Lady Brunhild: "How might that be? If none other lived

but he and thou, then might these kingdoms own his sway, but the
while Gunther liveth, this may never hap."

Kriemhild replied: "Now dost thou see, how he standeth, how
right royally he walketh before the knights, as the moon doth before
the stars? Therefore must I needs be merry of mood."

Said Lady Brunhild: "However stately be thy husband, howso
worthy and fair, yet must thou grant the palm to Knight Gunther, the
noble brother of thine. Know of a truth, he must be placed above all
kings."

Then Kriemhild spake again: "So doughty is my husband, that I
have not lauded him without good cause. His worship is great in many
things. Dost thou believe it, Brunhild, he is easily Gunther's peer."

"Forsooth thou must not take it amiss of me, Kriemhild, for I
have not spoken thus without good reason. I heard them both aver,
when I saw them first of all, and the king was victor against me in the
games, and when he won my love in such knightly wise, that he was
liegeman to the king, and Siegfried himself declared the same. I hold
him therefore as my vassal, sith I heard him speak thus himself."

Then spake fair Kriemhild: "Ill had I then sped. How could my
noble brothers have so wrought, that I should be a mere vassal's bride?
Therefore I do beseech thee, Brunhild, in friendly wise, that for my
sake thou kindly leave off this speech."

"I'll not leave it off," quoth the king's wife. "Why should I give
up so many a knight, who with the warrior doth owe us service?"

Kriemhild, the passing fair, waxed wroth out of wit. "Thou must
forego that he ever do you a vassal's service; he is worthier than my
brother Gunther, the full noble man. Thou must retract what I have
heard thee say. Certes, it wondereth me, sith he be thy vassal and thou
hast so much power over us twain, why he hath rendered thee no
tribute so long a time. By right I should be spared thy overweening
pride."

"Thou bearest thee too high," spake the king's wife. "I would fain
see whether men will hold thee in such high honor as they do me."

The ladies both grew wonderly wroth of mood. Then spake the
Lady Kriemhild: "This must now hap. Sith thou hast declared my
husband for thy liegeman, now must the men of the two kings perceive to-day whether I durst walk before the queen to church. Thou
must see to-day that I am noble and free and that my husband is
worthier than thine; nor will I myself be taxed therewith. Thou shalt
mark to-day how thy liegewoman goeth to court before the knights of

the Burgundian land. I myself shall be more worshipful than any queen was known to be, who ever wore a crown." Great hate enow rose then betwixt the ladies.

. Then Brunhild answered: "Wilt thou not be a liegewoman of mine, so must thou sunder thee with thy ladies from my train when that we go to church."

To this Kriemhild replied: "In faith that shall be done."

. . . Then the wife of the noble king went forth with her train. Fair Kriemhild, too, was well arrayed and three and forty maidens with her, whom she had brought hither to the Rhine. They wore bright vesture wrought in Araby, and thus the fair-fashioned maids betook them to the minster. All Siegfried's men awaited them before the house. The folk had marvel whence it chanced that the queens were seen thus sundered, so that they did not walk together as afore. From this did many a warrior later suffer dire distress. Here before the minster stood Gunther's wife, while many a good knight had pastime with the comely dames whom they there espied.

Then came the Lady Kriemhild with a large and noble train. Whatever kind of clothes the daughters of noble knights have ever worn, these were but the wind against her retinue. She was so rich in goods, that what the wives of thirty kings could not purvey, that Kriemhild did. An' one would wish to, yet he could not aver that men had ever seen such costly dresses as at this time her fair-fashioned maidens wore. Kriemhild had not done it, save to anger Brunhild. They met before the spacious minster. Through her great hate the mistress of the house in evil wise bade Kriemhild stand: "Forsooth no vassaless should ever walk before the queen."

Then spake fair Kriemhild (angry was her mood): "Couldst thou have held thy peace, 't were well for thee. Thou hast disgraced thee and the fair body of thine. How might a vassal's leman ever be the wife of any king?"

"Whom callest thou here leman?" spake the queen.

"That call I thee," quoth Kriemhild. "Thy fair person was first caressed by Siegfried, my dear husband. Certes, it was not my brother who won thy maidhood. Whither could thy wits have wandered? It was an evil trick. Wherefore didst thou let him love thee, sith he be thy vassal? I hear thee make plaint without good cause," quoth Kriemhild.

"I' faith," spake then Brunhild, "Gunther shall hear of this."

"What is that to me?" said Kriemhild. "Thy pride hath bewrayed thee. With words thus hast claimed me for thy service. Know, by my troth, it will ever grieve me, for I shall be no more thy faithful friend."

Then Brunhild wept. Kriemhild delayed no longer, but entered the minster with her train before the queen. Thus there rose great hatred, from which bright eyes grew dim and moist.

Whatso men did or sang to God's service there, the time seemed far too long for Brunhild, for she was sad of heart and mood. Many a brave knight and a good must later rue this day. Brunhild with her ladies now went forth and stopped before the minster. Her thought: "Kriemhild must tell me more of what this word-shrewd woman hath so loudly charged me. Hath Siegfried made boast of this, 't will cost his life."

Now the noble Kriemhild came with many a valiant liegeman. Lady Brunhild spake: "Stand still a while. Ye have declared me for a leman; that must ye let be seen. Know, that through thy speech, I have fared full ill."

Then spake the Lady Kriemhild: "Ye should have let me pass. I'll prove it by the ring of gold I have upon my hand, and which my lover brought me when he first lay at your side."

Brunhild had never seen so ill a day. She spake: "This costly hoop of gold was stolen from me, and hath been hid full long a time from me in evil wise. I'll find out yet who hath ta'en it from me."

Both ladies now had fallen into grievous wrath.

Kriemhild replied: "I'll not be called a thief. Thou hadst done better to have held thy peace, an' thou hold thine honor dear. I'll prove it by the girdle which I wear about my waist, that I lie not. Certes, my Siegfried became thy lord."

She wore the cord of silk of Nineveh, set with precious stones; in sooth 't was fair enow. When Brunhild spied it, she began to weep. Gunther and all the Burgundian men must needs now learn of this.

Then spake the queen: "Bid the prince of the Rhineland come hither. I will let him hear how his sister hath mocked me. She saith here openly that I be Siegfried's wife."

The king came with knights, and when he saw his love a-weeping, how gently he spake: "Pray tell me, dear lady, who hath done you aught?"

She answered to the king: "I must stand unhappy; thy sister would fain part me from all mine honors. I make here plaint to thee, she doth aver that Siegfried, her husband, hath had me as his leman."

Quoth King Gunther: "Then hath she done ill."

"She weareth here my girdle, which I have lost, and my ring of ruddy gold. It doth repent me sore that I was ever born, unless be thou clearest me of this passing great shame; for that I'll serve thee ever."

King Gunther spake: "Have him come hither. He must let us hear if he hath made boast of this, or he must make denial, the hero of Netherland." One bade fetch at once Kriemhild's love.

When Siegfried saw the angry dames (he wist not of the tale), how quickly then he spake: "I fain would know why these ladies weep, or for what cause the king hath had me fetched."

Then King Gunther spake: "It doth rue me sore, forsooth. My Lady Brunhild hath told me here a tale, that thou hast boasted thou wast the first to clasp her lovely body in thine arms; this Lady Kriemhild, thy wife, doth say."

Then spake Lord Siegfried: "And she hath told this tale, she shall rue it sore, or ever I turn back, and I'll clear me with solemn oaths in front of all thy men, that I have not told her this."

Quoth the king of the Rhineland: "Let that be seen. The oath thou dost offer, and let it now be given, shall free thee of all false charges."

They bade the proud Burgundians form a ring. Siegfried, the bold, stretched out his hand for the oath; then spake the mighty king: "Thy great innocence is so well known to me, that I will free thee of that of which my sister doth accuse thee and say, thou hast never done this thing."

Siegfried replied: "If it boot my lady aught to have thus saddened Brunhild, that will surely cause me boundless grief."

Then the lusty knights and good gazed one upon the other. "One should so train women," spake again Siegfried, the knight, "that they leave haughty words unsaid. Forbid it to thy wife, and I'll do the same to mine. In truth, I do shame me of her great discourtesie."

Many fair ladies were parted by the speech. Brunhild mourned so sore, that it moved King Gunther's men to pity. Then came Hagen of Troneg to his sovran lady. He found her weeping, and asked what grief she had. She told him then the tale. On the spot he vowed that Kriemhild's lord should rue it sore, or he would nevermore be glad.

[Skilfully Hagen plans the betrayal and murder of Siegfried. First he has strangers ride to court with false news that Liudegast and Liudeger are riding against Burgundy to avenge their old defeat. As Hagen has anticipated, Siegfried generously offers his services to Gunther. Hagen then tricks Kriemhild into sewing a small golden

cross upon Siegfried's shirt directly over the one vulnerable spot where
the linden leaf stuck upon the hero's back when he bathed in the
dragon's blood. This mark, explains Hagen, will enable Siegfried's
friends to protect him from behind in the press of battle. With this
fatal secret in his possession, Hagen then has word given out that
Liudegast and Liudeger have abandoned their war against Burgundy.
In place of the activity of battle the Burgundians plan a great hunt in
the forests beyond the Rhine.]

HOW SIEGFRIED WAS SLAIN

Gunther and Hagen, the passing bold knights, faithlessly let cry
a-hunting in the woods, that with sharp spears they would hunt boars
and bears and bison. . . . Siegfried then went to where he found
Kriemhild. His costly hunting garb and those of his fellowship were
already bound upon the sumpters, for they would cross the Rhine.
Never could Kriemhild have been more sorrowful. He kissed his love
upon her mouth. "God let me see thee, lady, still in health and grant
that thine eyes may see me too. Thou shalt have pastime with thy loving kinsmen. I may not stay at home."

Then she thought of the tale she had told to Hagen,[19] though she
durst not say a whit. The noble queen began to rue that she was ever
born. Lord Siegfried's wife wept out of measure. She spake to the
knight: "Let be your hunting. I had an evil dream last night, how two
wild boars did chase you across the heath; then flowers grew red. I
have in truth great cause to weep so sore. I be much adread of sundry
plans and whether we have not misserved some who might bear us
hostile hate. Tarry here, dear my lord, that I counsel by my troth."

He spake: "Dear love, I'll come back in a few short days. I wot
not here of people who bear me aught of hate. Each and all of thy
kinsmen be my friends, nor have I deserved it other of the knights."

"No, no, Sir Siegfried, in truth I fear thy fall. I had last night an
evil dream, how two mountains fell upon thee. I saw thee nevermore.
It doth cut me to the heart, that thou wilt part from me."

In his arms he clasped his courteous wife and kissed her tenderly.
Then in a short space he took his leave and parted hence. Alas, she
never saw him in health again.

Then they rode from thence into a deep wood for pastime's sake.
Many bold knights did follow Gunther and his men, but Gernot and

19. Concerning Siegfried's vulnerability.

Giselher stayed at home. Many laden sumpters were sent before them across the Rhine, the which bare for the hunting fellowship bread and wine, meat and fish, and great store of other things, which so mighty a king might rightly have. . . .

"Let us part," spake Hagen, "ere we begin the chase. Thereby my lords and I may know who be the best hunter on this woodland journey. Let us divide the folk and hounds and let each turn whithersoever he list. He who doth hunt the best shall have our thanks." Short time the huntsmen bided by another after that.

Then spake Lord Siegfried: "I need no dogs save one brach that hath been trained that he can tell the track of the beasts through the pine woods." Quoth Kriemhild's husband: "We'll find the game."

Then an old huntsman took a good sleuth-hound and in a short space brought the lord to where many beasts were found. Whatso rose from its lair the comrades hunted as good hunters still are wont to do. Whatever the brach started, bold Siegfried, the hero of Netherland, slew with his hand. His horse did run so hard that none escaped him. In the chase he gained the prize above them all. Doughty enow he was in all things. The beast which he slew with his hands was the first, a mighty boar; after which he found full soon a monstrous lion. When the brach started this from its lair, he shot it with his bow, in which he had placed a full sharp arrow. After the shot the lion ran the space of but three bounds. The hunting fellowship gave Siegfried thanks. Thereafter he speedily slew a bison and an elk, four strong ure-oxen,[20] and a savage shelk.[21] His horse bare him so swiftly that naught escaped him, nor could hart or hind avoid him. Then the sleuth-hound found a mighty boar; when he began to flee, at once there came the master of the hunt and encountered him upon his path. Wrathfully the boar did run against the valiant hero, but Kriemhild's husband slew him with his sword. Another huntsman might not have done this deed so lightly.

Then spake his huntsman: "Sir Siegfried, if might so be, let us leave a deal of the beasts alive. Ye'll empty both our hill and woods to-day."

At this the brave knight and a bold gan smile. Then the calls of men and the baying of hounds were heard on every side; so great was the noise that both hill and pine woods echoed with the sound. The huntsmen had let loose full four and twenty packs. Then passing many

20. The aurochs, a European bison now extinct.
21. Perhaps a deer.

beasts must needs lose their lives. Each man weened to bring it to pass that men should give him the prize of the hunt; that might not be, for the stalwart Siegfried was already standing by the fire. The chase was over, and yet not quite. Those who would to the camp-fire brought with them thither hides of many beasts and game in plenty. Ho, how much the king's meiny bare then to the kitchen!

Then bade the king announce to the huntsmen that he would dismount. A horn was blown full loud just once, that all might know that one might find the noble prince in camp. Spake then one of Siegfried's huntsmen: "My lord, I heard by the blast of a horn that we must now hie us to the quarters; I'll now give answer."

Thus by many blasts of horns they asked about the hunters. Then spake Sir Siegfried: "Now let us leave the pine wood!" His steed bare him smoothly and with him they hasted hence. With their rout they started up a savage beast; a wild bear it was. Quoth then the knight to those behind: "I'll give our fellowship a little pastime. Let loose the brach. Forsooth I spy a bear which shall journey with us to the camp. Flee he never so fast, he shall not escape us."

The brach was loosed, the bear sprang hence; Kriemhild's husband would fain overtake him. He reached a thicket, where none could follow. The mighty beast weened now to escape from the hunter with his life, but the proud knight and a good leaped from his steed and began to chase him. The bear was helpless and could not flee away. At once the hero caught it and bound it quickly with not a wound, so that it might neither scratch nor bite the men. The doughty knight then tied it to his saddle and horsed him quickly. Through his overweening mood the bold warrior and a good brought it to the camp-fire as a pastime. . . .

Gunther's men espied him coming and ran out to meet him and took his horse in charge. On his saddle he carried a large bear and a strong. When he had dismounted, he loosed the bonds from feet and snout. Those of the pack bayed loudly, that spied the bear. The beast would to the woods; the serving folk had fear. Dazed by the din, the bear made for the kitchen. Ho, how he drove the scullions from the fire! Many a kettle was upset and many a firebrand scattered. Ho, what good victual men found lying in the ashes! Then the lordings and their liegemen sprang from their seats. The bear grew furious and the king bade loose the pack that lay enleashed. Had all sped well, they would have had a merry day. No longer the doughty men delayed, but ran for the bear with bows and pikes. There was such press of dogs that none might shoot, but from the people's shouts the whole hill rang. The bear began to flee before the dogs; none could follow him but Kriemhild's husband, who caught and slew him with his sword. Then they bore the bear again to the fire. Those that saw it, averred he was a mighty man.

Men bade now the proud hunting fellowship seat them at the tables. Upon a fair mead there sate a goodly company. Ho, what rich viands they bare there to the noble huntsmen! The butlers who should bring the wine delayed; else might never heroes have been better served. Had they not been so falsely minded, then had the knights been free of every blame.

Now the Lord Siegfried spake: "Me-wondereth,[22] since men do give us such great store from the kitchen, why the butlers bring us not the wine. Unless men purvey the hunters better, I'll be no more your hunting-fellow. I have well deserved that they regard me, too."

The king addressed him from his seat with guile: "We fain would do you remedy of what we lack. It is Hagen's fault, who is willed to let us die of thirst."

Then spake Hagen: "Dear my lord, I weened that the hunt should be in the Spessart wood, therefore sent I thither the wine. Though we may not drink to-day, how well will I avoid this in the future!"

At this Lord Siegfried spake: "Small thanks ye'll get for that. One should have brought me hither seven sumpter loads of mead and mulled wine. If that might not be, then men should have placed our benches nearer to the Rhine."

Then spake Hagen of Troneg: "Ye noble knights and bold, I wot near by a good cold spring. Let us go thither, that ye wax not wroth."

. . . Hagen of Troneg now foully broke his troth to Siegfried. When they would hence to the broad linden, he spake: "It hath oft been told me, that none can keep pace with Kriemhild's husband when he be minded for to race. Ho, if he would only let us see it here!"

Bold Siegfried from Netherland then answered: "Ye can well test that, and ye will run a race with me to the spring. When that is done, we can give the prize to him who winneth."

"So let us try it then," quoth Hagen, the knight.

Spake the sturdy Siegfried: "Then will I lay me down on the green sward at your feet."[23]

How lief it was to Gunther, when he heard these words! Then

22. It is surprising to me.
23. Siegfried handicaps himself by starting from a lying position.

the bold knight spake again: "I'll tell you more. I'll take with me all my trappings, my spear and shield and all my hunting garb." Around him he quickly girded his quiver and his sword.

Then they drew the clothes from off their limbs; men saw them stand in two white shifts. Like two wild panthers through the clover they ran, but men spied bold Siegfried first at the spring. In all things he bare away the prize from many a man. Quickly he ungirt his sword and laid aside his quiver and leaned the stout spear against a linden bough. The lordly stranger stood now by the flowing spring. Passing great was Siegfried's courtesie. He laid down his shield where the spring gushed forth, but the hero drank not, albeit he thirsted sore, until the king had drunk, who gave him evil thanks. Cool, clear, and good was the spring. Gunther stooped down then to the flowing stream, and when he had drunken straightened up again. Bold Siegfried would fain also have done the same, but now he paid for his courtesie. Hagen bare quite away from him both bow and sword and bounded then to where he found the spear; then he looked for the mark on bold Siegfried's coat. As Lord Siegfried drank above the spring, he pierced him through the cross, so that his heart's blood spurted from the wounds almost on Hagen's clothes. Nevermore will hero do so foul a deed. Hagen left the spear a-sticking in his heart and fled more madly than he ever in the world had run from any man.

When Lord Siegfried felt the mighty wound, up from the spring he started in a rage. From betwixt his shoulder blades a long spearshaft towered. He weened to find his bow or his sword, and then had Hagen been repaid as he deserved. But when the sorely wounded hero found no trace of his sword, then had he naught else but his shield. This he snatched from the spring and ran at Hagen; nor could King Gunther's man escape him. Albeit he was wounded unto death, yet he smote so mightily that a plenty of precious stones were shaken from the shield. The shield itself burst quite apart. Fain would the lordly stranger have avenged him. Now was Hagen fallen to the ground at his hands, and from the force of the blow the glade rang loudly. Had he had a sword in hand, then had it been Hagen's death, so sore enraged was the wounded man. Forsooth he had good cause thereof. His hue grew pale, he could not stand; his strength of body melted quite away, for in bright colors he bore the signs of death. Thereafter he was bewailed by fair dames enow.

Kriemhild's husband fell now among the flowers. Fast from his wounds his blood was seen to gush. He began to rail, as indeed he had great cause, at those who had planned this treacherous death. The deadly wounded spake: "Forsooth, ye evil cowards, what avail my services now that ye have slain me? This is my reward that I was always faithful to you. Alas, ye have acted ill against your kinsmen. Those of them who are born in after days will be disgraced. Ye have avenged your wrath too sore upon me. With shame shall ye be parted from all good warriors."

The knights all ran to where he lay slain. For enow of them it was a hapless day. He was bewailed by those who had aught of loyalty, and this the brave and lusty knight had well deserved. The king of the Burgundians bemoaned his death. Quoth the deadly wounded: "There is no need that he should weep who hath done the damage; he doth merit mickle blame. It had been better left undone."

Then spake the fierce Hagen: "Forsooth I wot not what ye now bewail. All our fear and all our woe have now an end. We shall find scant few who dare withstand us now. Well is me, that to his rule I have put an end."

"Ye may lightly boast you," Siegfried then replied. "Had I wist your murderous bent, I had well guarded my life against you. None doth rue me so sore as Lady Kriemhild, my wife. Now may God have pity that I ever had a son to whom the reproach will be made in after days, that his kindred have slain a man with murderous intent. If I might," so spake Siegfried, "I should rightly make complaint of this." Piteously the deadly wounded spake again: "Noble king, if ye will keep your troth to any in the world, then let my dear love be commended to your grace and let it avail her that she be your sister. For the sake of your princely courtesie protect her faithfully. My father and my men must wait long time for me. Never was woman sorer wounded in a loving friend."

The flowers on every side were wet with blood. With death he struggled, but not for long, sith the sword of death had cut him all too sorely. Then the lusty warrior and a brave could speak no more.

When the lordings saw that the knight was dead, they laid him on a shield of ruddy gold and took counsel how they might conceal that Hagen had done the deed. Enow of them spake: "Ill hath it gone with us. Ye must all hide it and aver alike that robbers slew Kriemhild's husband as he rode alone a-hunting through the pine wood."

Then Hagen of Troneg spake: "I'll bring him home; I care not if it be known to her, for she hath saddened Brunhild's heart. Little doth it trouble me however much she weep."

[With the body of Siegfried, the Burgundians return to Worms. Kriemhild is grief-stricken, and Siegmund and the Nibelung warriors clamor for vengeance. Incredulous that Siegfried has been slain by robbers, Kriemhild demands that the Burgundians file past the bier of the dead man, and as Hagen passes the body the wounds of Siegfried open and flow with blood. Kriemhild is convinced that Hagen is the murderer of her husband. After the elaborate burial rites for Siegfried, Siegmund and the Nibelungs return to their home. Kriemhild, with grief and vengeance in her heart, chooses to remain at Worms.]

HOW THE NIBELUNG HOARD
WAS BROUGHT TO WORMS

When the noble Kriemhild thus was widowed, the Margrave Eckewart with his vassals stayed with her in the land, and served her alway. He also often helped his mistress mourn his lord. At Worms, hard by the minster, they built for her a dwelling, broad and passing large, costly and great, where, with her maids, she since dwelt joyless. She liked for to go to church and did this willingly. Where her love lay buried, thither she went all time in mournful mood (how seldom she gave that over). She prayed the good God to have mercy on her soul. With great fidelity she bewept the knight full oft. Uta and her meiny comforted her all time, but so sorely wounded was her heart, that it booted naught, whatever comfort men did offer her. She had the greatest longing for her dear love, that ever wife did have for loving husband. One might see thereby her passing virtue; until her end she mourned, the while life lasted. In after days brave Siegfried's wife avenged herself with might.

Thus she dwelt after her sorrow, after her husband's death, and this is true, well three and one half years, that she spake no word to Gunther, nor did she see her foeman Hagen in all this time.

Then spake Hagen of Troneg: "If ye could compass it to make your sister friendly, then might come to these lands the gold of Nibelung. Of this might ye win great store, an' the queen would be our friend."

The king made answer: "Let us try. My brothers bide with her; we will beg them to bring it to pass that she be our friend, if perchance she might gladly see us win the hoard."

"I trow not," spake Hagen, "that it will ever hap."

Then he bade Ortwin and the Margrave Gere go to court. When that was done, Gernot and Giselher, the youth, were also brought. They tried it with the Lady Kriemhild in friendly wise. Brave Gernot of Burgundy spake: "Lady, ye mourn too long for Siegfried's death. The king will give you proof that he hath not slain him. We hear you mourn all time so greatly."

She spake: "None chargeth him with this. 'T was Hagen's hand that struck him, where he could be wounded. When he learned this of me, how could I think that he did bear him hate? Else had I guarded against this full well," spake the queen, "so that I had not betrayed his life; then would I, poor wife, leave off my weeping. I'll never be a friend of him that did the deed." Then Giselher, the full stately man, began implore.

When at last she spake: "I will greet the king," men saw him stand before her with his nearest kin, but Hagen durst not come before her. Well he wot his guilt; 't was he had caused her dole. When now she would forego her hate of Gunther, so that he might kiss her, it had befitted him better had she not been wronged by his advice; then might he have gone boldly unto Kriemhild. Nevermore was peace between kindred brought to pass with so many tears; her loss still gave her woe. All, save the one man alone, she pardoned. None had slain him, had not Hagen done the deed.

Not long thereafter they brought it to pass that Lady Kriemhild gained the hoard from the Nibelung land and brought it to the Rhine. It was her marriage morning gift[24] and was hers by right. Giselher and Gernot rode to fetch it. Kriemhild ordered eighty hundred men, that they should bring it from where it lay hid, where it was guarded by the knight Alberich and his nearest kin. . . .

Then went the warder to where he found the keys. Before the castle stood Kriemhild's liegemen and a deal of her kinsfolk. Men bade carry the treasure hence to the sea, down to the boats; one bare it then upon the waves to the mountains on the Rhine. Now may ye hear marvels of the hoard, the which twelve huge wains, packed full, were just able to bear away from the hill in four days and nights and each must make the trip three times a day. There was naught else but gems and gold, and had men paid therewith the wage of all the world, not a mark less had it been in worth. Forsooth Hagen did not crave it so without good cause. The greatest prize of all was a wishing-rod[25]

24. Gift from the groom on the morning after the bridal night.
25. A divining rod for finding treasure.

of gold. He who knew its nature, might well be master over any man in all the world.

Many of Alberich's kinsmen journeyed with Gernot hence. When they stored away the hoard in Gunther's land and the queen took charge of everything, chambers and towers were filled therewith. Never did men hear tales told of such wondrous store of goods. And had it been a thousand times as much, if the Lord Siegfried were but alive again, Kriemhild would fain have stood empty-handed at his side. No more faithful wife did hero ever win. Now that she had the hoard, she brought many unknown warriors to the land. In truth the lady's hand gave in such wise that men have never seen such bounty more. She used great courtesie; men owned this of the queen. To the rich and the poor she began to give so greatly that Hagen said, should she live yet a while, she would gain so many a man for her service that they would fare full ill.

Then spake King Gunther: "Her life and her goods be hers. How shall I hinder that she do with them as she will? Forsooth I hardly compassed it, that she became thus much my friend. Let us not reck to whom she deal out her silver and her gold."

Spake Hagen to the king: "No doughty man should leave to any wife aught of the hoard. With her gifts she'll bring about the day when it well may rue the brave Burgundians sore."

Then spake King Gunther: "I swore an oath, that nevermore would I do her harm, and will keep it further, for she is my sister."

Spake then Hagen: "Let me be the guilty one."

Few of their oaths were kept. From the widow they took the mighty store and Hagen made him master of all the keys. This vexed her brother Gernot, when he heard the tale aright. Lord Giselher spake: "Hagen hath done my sister much of harm; I should prevent it. It would cost him his life, were he not my kin."

Siegfried's wife shed tears anew. Then spake the Lord Gernot: "Or ever we be imperiled by the gold, we should have it sunk entirely in the Rhine, that it belong to none."

Full pitifully she went before her brother Giselher. She spake: "Dear brother, thou shouldst think of me and be the guardian of both my life and goods."

Quoth he then to the lady: "That shall be done when we return again, for now we think to ride."

The king and his kindred voided then the land, the very best among them that one might find. Only Hagen alone remained at home, through the hatred he bare to Kriemhild, and did so willingly. Before the king was come again, Hagen had taken the treasure quite and sunk it all at Loche in the Rhine. He weened to use it, but that might not be. The lordings came again and with them many men. With her maids and ladies Kriemhild gan bewail her passing loss, for sore it grieved them. Gladly would Giselher have helped in all good faith. All spake alike: "He hath done wrong."

Hagen avoided the princes' wrath, until he gained their favor. They did him naught, but Kriemhild might never have borne him greater hate. Before Hagen of Troneg thus hid the treasure, they had sworn with mighty oaths that it should lie concealed as long as any one of them might live. Later they could not give it to themselves or any other.

Kriemhild's mind was heavy with fresh sorrow over her husband's end, and because they had taken from her all her wealth. Her plaints ceased not in all her life, down to her latest day. After Siegfried's death, and this is true, she dwelt with many a grief full thirteen years, that she could not forget the warrior's death. She was true to him, as most folk owned.

TRISTAN

AND ISEULT

ARTHURIAN LEGEND, or "the matter of Britain," forms one of the great cycles of medieval romance, but for its sources, as with the *Nibelungenlied,* one must seek in the shadows of myth and history. When the Roman legions abandoned Britain to return home to bolster the imperial defenses against the northern barbarians, the native Britons were left without assistance in repelling the invasions of those same barbarians in their western expansions. Native historians have written of the struggle that ensued, and in the writings of the British Nennius in the ninth century there appeared for the first time in historical record the name of Arthur, who, it seems, was a kind of leader of the native defenses against the Germanic invaders and who distinguished himself in at least one great victory. But legend and the human imagination did their work with this Arthur, until the "leader of the wars" of Nennius became a warrior king made up of large parts of heathen god and actual man with a substantial coloring of Christianity—witness chiefly his mysterious birth, his strong bent to do good, his mysterious death, and the promise of his beneficent return to this earth.

For more than three hundred years after Nennius the records have little or nothing to say of Arthur, until the appearance of Geoffrey of Monmouth's *History of the Kings of Britain,* written in Latin about the year 1137. Here for the first time Arthur appears as King of Britain in all the imaginative magnificence of a hero of romance. In the reign of Henry II the poet Wace translated Geoffrey into Norman French, adding the concept of the Round Table. And then about fifty years later, around 1200, an English priest named Layamon translated Wace into English verse. In ballad and romance, in all the lands where the traditions of the native Britons had persisted, legends of Arthur and his knights sprang up, in English, in Welsh, and in French. On the continent perhaps the greatest Arthurian romancer was the French Chrétien de Troies, who wrote during the last half of the twelfth century six long poems on the subject of Arthur's knights. Other writers from all Western Europe contributed to the great name of Arthur their roster of traits and exploits, and other legendary heroes were irresistibly drawn to this legend. In the tales of individual knights many incidents from fairy tale and myth were introduced into the large body of Arthurian material, the most wonderful of these having their sources in Wales and Ireland. Among these the story of Tristan appears relatively late, but it has been one of the most persistently popular of all these romances.

The love story of Tristan and Iseult, although it became a part of the Arthurian tradition, had an entirely independent beginning. Its origin goes back to the myths and legends of the early inhabitants of Britain. The original Tristan, it is believed, was one of several Pictish kings named Drostan, and his early reputation was not entirely savory. In early Welsh literature he was a sly fellow, a trickster and a liar, but a great lover withal. Originally Mark, his uncle and the husband of Iseult, was a legendary king of Cornwall of the eighth century. And then somehow the two legends, northern and southern, met and merged in Wales, and the story, somewhat as it now occurs, was the product of the union.

The earliest known versions of the legend of Tristan are those that exist now only in fragments, one by the Norman poet Béroul, who wrote about the middle of the twelfth century, and one by Thomas of Britain, more than likely a Norman living in England, who composed his poem towards the end of the twelfth century, probably under the patronage of Eleanor of Aquitaine, Queen of Henry II. It is now believed that both Béroul and Thomas worked from a single earlier source that has been lost. But the greatest of all the romances of Tristan is that by the German poet Gottfried von Strassburg, who sometime early in the thirteenth century, using Thomas' version as the basis of his work, composed in Middle High German one of the great narrative poems of the Middle Ages. Gottfried's work was left unfinished, but it was continued by two other German poets, who followed Béroul's version rather than Thomas's. Other accounts of the tale were written by Eilhart von Oberge in the twelfth century, by a certain "Brother Robert" in 1226, who made for King Haakon of Norway a translation of Thomas of Britain, and an Englishman who wrote in the thirteenth century and whose poem was first published by Sir Walter Scott.

The story of Tristan and Iseult is the first great love story in the literature of the Western world. In Greek literature nothing is comparable to it. In Roman literature only the story of Dido's fatal love of Aeneas can be thought of as dealing on a high level with the same subject, and that story is only an incident in a larger work. Undoubtedly the whole code of courtly love, that practical formulation of a system of lovers' conduct established by the Troubadours of Provençal France, imposed upon a pagan tale an elevation and a sophistication that made this story what it is.

Among the late medieval Arthurian legends its appeal was offset by the more spiritual force of the story of the Holy Grail, in which Galahad and Percival supplanted the more robust and less proper early Arthurian heroes. In Malory's *Morte D'Arthur* of the fifteenth century the beauty and fire of the early versions are lost. And after the long eclipse of things medieval, Alfred Tennyson in the nineteenth century was concerned with Tristan and Iseult only as evidence of the worldly corruption of a great spiritual ideal—though Tennyson's contemporaries Arnold and Swinburne both wrote excellent versions of the legend with greater aesthetic appreciation than Tennyson's. In 1900 Joseph Bédier, the French medieval scholar, published his *Tristan and Iseult,* based chiefly upon the poems of Béroul, Thomas, and Gottfried. His version of the story appears below. More recently, in the not too poetic twentieth century, an American poet, Edwin Arlington Robinson, made of the Tristan story a prize-winner and a best-seller. And since 1865 the opera *Tristan und Isolde* by Richard Wagner, a music drama based upon the poem of Gottfried, has kept the legend impressively alive. Of all the Arthurian tales it has been the most popular in modern times.

TRISTAN AND ISEULT*

THE CHILDHOOD OF TRISTAN

My lords, if you would hear a high tale of love and of death, here is that of Tristan and Queen Iseult; how to their full joy, but to their sorrow also, they loved each other, and how at last they died of that love together upon one day; she by him and he by her.

Long ago, when Mark was King over Cornwall, Rivalen, king of Lyonesse,[1] heard that Mark's enemies waged war on him; so he crossed the sea to bring him aid; and so faithfully did he serve him with counsel and sword that Mark gave him his sister Blanchefleur, whom King Rivalen loved most marvellously.

He wedded her in Tintagel Minster, but hardly was she wed when the news came to him that his old enemy Duke Morgan had fallen on Lyonesse and was wasting town and field. Then Rivalen manned his ships in haste, and took Blanchefleur with him to his far land; but she was with child. He landed below his castle of Kanoël and gave the Queen in ward to his Marshal Rohalt, and after that set off to wage his war.

Blanchefleur waited for him continually, but he did not come home, till she learnt upon a day that Duke Morgan had killed him in foul ambush. . . . Three days she awaited re-union with her lord, and on the fourth she brought forth a son; and taking him in her arms she said:

"Little son, I have longed a while to see you, and now I see you the fairest thing ever a woman bore. In sadness came I hither, in sadness did I bring forth, and in sadness has your first feast day gone. And as by sadness you came into the world, your name shall be called Tristan; that is the child of sadness."

After she had said these words she kissed him, and immediately when she had kissed him she died. . . .

When seven years were passed and the time had come to take the child from the women, Rohalt put Tristan under a good master, the

* Translated from the French of Bédier by Hilaire Belloc and used by permission of Albert & Charles Boni, N. Y.

1. Cornwall is the southwesternmost county of England. Lyonesse, a fabulous land, is believed to have been off the Cornish coast, but if it ever existed it is now submerged.

Squire Gorvenal, and Gorvenal taught him in a few years the arts that go with barony. He taught him the use of lance and sword and 'scutcheon and bow, and how to cast stone quoits and to leap wide dykes also: and he taught him to hate every lie and felony and to keep his given word; and he taught him the various kinds of song and harp-playing, and the hunter's craft; and when the child rode among the young squires you would have said that he and his horse and his armour were all one thing. To see him so noble and so proud, broad in the shoulders, loyal, strong and right, all men glorified Rohalt in such a son. But Rohalt remembering Rivalen and Blanchefleur (of whose youth and grace all this was a resurrection) loved him indeed as a son, but in his heart revered him as his lord.

Now all his joy was snatched from him on a day when certain merchants of Norway, having lured Tristan to their ship, bore him off as a rich prize, though Tristan fought hard, as a young wolf struggles, caught in a gin.[2] But it is a truth well proved, and every sailor knows it, that the sea will hardly bear a felon ship, and gives no aid to rapine. The sea rose and cast a dark storm round the ship and drove it eight days and eight nights at random; then they did penance, knowing that the anger of the sea came of the lad, whom they had stolen in an evil hour, and they vowed his deliverance and got ready a boat to put him, if it might be, ashore: then the wind and sea fell and the sky shone, and as the Norway ship grew small in the offing, a quiet tide cast Tristan and the boat upon a beach of sand.

Painfully he climbed the cliff and saw, beyond, a lonely rolling heath and a forest stretching out and endless. And he wept, remembering Gorvenal, his father, and the land of Lyonesse. Then the distant cry of a hunt, with horse and hound, came suddenly and lifted his heart, and a tall stag broke cover at the forest edge. The pack and the hunt streamed after it with a tumult of cries and winding horns, but just as the hounds were racing clustered at the haunch, the quarry turned to bay at a stone's throw from Tristan; a huntsman gave him the thrust, while all around the hunt had gathered and was winding the kill. But Tristan, seeing by the gesture of the huntsman that he made to cut the neck of the stag, cried out:

"My lord, what would you do? Is it fitting to cut up so noble a beast like any farm-yard hog? Is that the custom of this country?"

And the huntsman answered:

2. Trap.

"Fair friend, what startles you? Why yes, first I take off the head of a stag, and then I cut it into four quarters and we carry it on our saddle bows to King Mark, our lord. . . . If, however, you know of some nobler custom, teach it us: take this knife and we will learn it willingly."

Then Tristan kneeled and skinned the stag before he cut it up, and quartered it all in order; and the huntsmen and the kennel hinds stood over him with delight, and the Master Huntsman said:

"Friend, these are good ways. In what land learnt you them? Tell us your country and your name."

"Good lord, my name is Tristan, and I learnt these ways in my country of Lyonesse."

"Tristan," said the Master Huntsman, "God reward the father that brought you up so nobly; doubtless he is a baron, rich and strong."

Now Tristan knew both speech and silence, and he answered:

"No, lord; my father is a burgess.[3] . . ."

"Fair Tristan, I marvel there should be a land where a burgess's son can know what a knight's son knows not elsewhere, but come with us since you will it; and welcome: we will bring you to King Mark, our lord." . . .

So they took the road and spoke together, till they came on a great castle and round it fields and orchards, and living waters and fish ponds and plough lands, and many ships were in its haven, for that castle stood above the sea. . . .

And when Tristan asked its name:

"Good liege," they said, "we call it Tintagel."

And Tristan cried:

"Tintagel! Blessed be thou of God, and blessed be they that dwell within thee.". . .

When they came before the keep the horns brought the barons to the gates and King Mark himself. And when the Master Huntsman had told him all the story, and King Mark had marvelled at the good order of the cavalcade, and the cutting of the stag, and the high art of venery in all, yet most he wondered at the stranger boy, and still gazed at him, troubled and wondering whence came his tenderness, and his heart would answer him nothing. . . .

3. A substantial citizen (bourgeois), as opposed to the landed aristocracy.

That evening, when the boards were cleared, a singer out of Wales, a master, came forward among the barons in Hall and sang a harper's song. . . .

Then Tristan took the harp and sang so well that the barons softened as they heard, and King Mark marvelled at the harper from Lyonesse whither so long ago Rivalen had taken Blanchefleur away.

When the song ended, the King was silent a long space, but he said at last:

"Son, blessed be the master that taught thee, and blessed be thou of God: for God loves good singers. . . . Stay near us a long time, friend."

And Tristan answered:

"Very willingly will I serve you, sire, as your harper, your huntsman and your liege."

So did he, and for three years a mutual love grew up in their hearts. . . .

My lords, a teller that would please, should not stretch his tale too long, and truly this tale is so various and so high that it needs no straining. Then let me shortly tell how Rohalt himself, after long wandering by sea and land, came into Cornwall, and found Tristan, and showing the King the carbuncle that once was Blanchefleur's, said:

"King Mark, here is your nephew Tristan, son of your sister Blanchefleur and of King Rivalen. Duke Morgan holds his land most wrongfully; it is time such land came back to its lord."

And Tristan (in a word) when his uncle had armed him knight, crossed the sea, and was hailed of his father's vassals, and killed Rivalen's slayer and was reseized of his land.

Then remembering how King Mark could no longer live in joy without him, he summoned his council and his barons and said this:

"Lords of the Lyonesse, I have retaken this place and I have avenged King Rivalen by the help of God and of you. But two men, Rohalt and King Mark of Cornwall, nourished me, an orphan, and a wandering boy. So should I call them also fathers. Now a free man has two things thoroughly his own, his body and his land. To Rohalt then, here, I will release my land. Do you hold it, father, and your son shall hold it after you. But my body I give up to King Mark. I will leave this country, dear though it be, and in Cornwall I will serve King Mark as my lord. . . ."

All the barons praised him, though they wept; and taking with him Gorvenal only, Tristan set sail for King Mark's land.

[Returning to Cornwall, Tristan finds King Mark threatened by the Irish, to whom Cornwall has long owed tribute. A great fleet and a giant champion, brother of the Irish queen, are pressing the Irish demands. In single combat Tristan kills the giant Morholt and sends back his body to Ireland with a splinter of Tristan's sword in his head —Cornwall's tribute to Ireland. The Irish princess Iseult the Fair mourns for her uncle, saves the splinter of the sword, and vows hatred of Tristan.

But in the fight with Morholt, Tristan is wounded by a poisoned barb and lies languishing, awaiting his death. In despair he takes his harp, enters a boat without sail or oar, and resigns himself to the sea. Seven days and seven nights he drifts, playing his harp, until fishermen off the Irish coast come upon him and take him to Iseult the Fair, who is skilled in healing. Not knowing him for her enemy, Iseult heals Tristan's wound. Then Tristan, realizing his danger, flees the land and comes again to Cornwall.

Here arises fresh trouble, for Tristan's successes have inspired the jealousy of four vassals of Mark—Andret, Guenelon, Gondoïne, and Denoalen. Fearful of seeing Tristan as successor to Mark, these barons urge Mark to take a wife. But only because Tristan entreats him to do so does Mark accede. He will marry, he says, the woman of the same hair of gold as one hair brought to his window by nesting swallows. Tristan recognizes the hair as Iseult's and promises to bring Mark his bride. He and a hundred retainers sail as merchants to Ireland.

There they learn that a dragon is wasting the land and that the king has offered his daughter Iseult to the man that will kill it. Tristan destroys the monster but, wounded by its poison, falls unconscious into the high grass of a marsh. He is rescued by Iseult and her handmaid Brangien, and Iseult undertakes his cure. She observes his splintered sword, fits into the sword the piece of steel from the head of Morholt, and threatens Tristan with death. He tells her his story and finally placates her. He offers peace to Ireland and wins Iseult for Mark.]

THE PHILTRE

When the day of Iseult's livery to the Lords of Cornwall drew near, her mother gathered herbs and flowers and roots and steeped them in wine, and brewed a potion of might, and having done so, said apart to Brangien:

"Child, it is yours to go with Iseult to King Mark's country, for you love her with a faithful love. Take them this pitcher and remember well my words. Hide it so that no eye shall see nor no lip go near it: but when the wedding night has come and that moment in which the wedded are left alone, pour this essenced wine into a cup and offer it to King Mark and to Iseult his queen. Oh! Take all care, my child, that they alone shall taste this brew. For this is its power: they who drink of it together love each other with their every single sense and with their every thought, forever, in life and in death."

And Brangien promised the Queen that she would do her bidding.

On the bark that bore her to Tintagel Iseult the Fair was weeping as she remembered her own land, and mourning swelled her heart, and she said, "Who am I that I should leave you to follow unknown men, my mother and my land? Accursed be the sea that bears me, for rather would I lie dead on the earth where I was born than live out there, beyond. . . ."

One day when the wind had fallen and the sails hung slack Tristan dropped anchor by an Island and the hundred knights of Cornwall and the sailors, weary of the sea, landed all. Iseult alone remained aboard and a little serving maid, when Tristan came near the Queen to calm her sorrow. The sun was hot above them and they were athirst and, as they called, the little maid looked about for drink for them and found that pitcher which the mother of Iseult had given into Brangien's keeping. And when she came on it, the child cried, "I have found you wine!" Now she had found not wine—but Passion and Joy most sharp, and Anguish without end, and Death.

The Queen drank deep of that draught and gave it to Tristan and he drank also long and emptied it all.

Brangien came in upon them; she saw them gazing at each other in silence as though ravished and apart; she saw before them the pitcher standing there; she snatched it up and cast it into the shuddering sea and cried aloud: "Cursed be the day I was born and cursed the day that first I trod this deck. Iseult, my friend, and Tristan, you, you have drunk death together."

And once more the bark ran free for Tintagel. But it seemed to Tristan as though an ardent briar, sharp-thorned but with flower most sweet smelling, drave roots into his blood and laced the lovely body of

Iseult all round about it and bound it to his own and to his every thought and desire. . . .

And Iseult loved him, though she would have hated. She could not hate, for a tenderness more sharp than hatred tore her.

And Brangien watched them in anguish, suffering more cruelly because she alone knew the depth of evil done.

Two days she watched them, seeing them refuse all food or comfort and seeking each other as blind men seek, wretched apart and together more wretched still, for then they trembled each for the first avowal.

On the third day, as Tristan neared the tent on deck where Iseult sat, she saw him coming and she said to him, very humbly, "Come in, my lord."

"Queen," said Tristan, "why do you call me lord? Am I not your liege and vassal, to revere and serve and cherish you as my lady and Queen?"

But Iseult answered, "No, you know that you are my lord and my master, and I your slave. Ah, why did I not sharpen those wounds of the wounded singer, or let die that dragon-slayer in the grasses of the marsh? But then I did not know what now I know!"

"And what is it that you know, Iseult?"

She laid her arm upon Tristan's shoulder, the light of her eyes was drowned and her lips trembled.

"The love of you," she said. Whereat he put his lips to hers. . . .

And as evening fell, upon the bark that heeled and ran to King Mark's land, they gave themselves up utterly to love.

[In great pomp Mark receives Iseult, and they marry. But the queen lives in sadness, for she and Tristan are strained to dissemble their love. Grown suspicious, the barons of Mark warn him of the treason of his nephew with the queen, but their charges only turn Mark's rage upon them. Suspicion, however, grows in the king's mind until finally in great agony he forbids Tristan the court.

Tristan remains in Tintagel and with the help of Brangien finds his way to Iseult each night in an orchard behind the castle. Seeing the queen joyful, the barons know that she is somehow meeting Tristan. They seek counsel from the dwarf Frocin, a great magician, who promises to enable Mark to surprise the lovers. Advised by Frocin, Mark hides in a tall pine-tree in the orchard, but before betraying any sign of guilt, Tristan and Iseult observe his reflection in a stream. As though innocent, Tristan begs Iseult to intercede for him with Mark, and Iseult turns her words to throw off suspicion. Mark is convinced of their innocence.]

THE DISCOVERY

King Mark made peace with Tristan. Tristan returned to the castle as of old. Tristan slept in the King's chamber with his peers. He could come or go, the King thought no more of it. . . .

But his goodness did not feed the ire of the barons, who swore this oath: If the King kept Tristan in the land they would withdraw to their strongholds as for war, and they called the King to parley.

"Lord," said they, "Drive you Tristan forth. He loves the Queen as all who choose can see, but as for us we will bear it no longer."

And the King sighed, looking down in silence.

"King," they went on, "we will not bear it, for we know now that this is known to you and that yet you will not move. . . ."

"My lords," said he, "once I hearkened to the evil words you spoke of Tristan, yet was I wrong in the end. But you are my lieges and I would not lose the service of my men. Counsel me therefore, I charge you, you that owe me counsel. You know me for a man neither proud nor overstepping."

"Lord," said they, "call then Frocin hither. You mistrust him for that orchard night. Still, was it not he that read in the stars of the Queen's coming there and to the very pine-tree too? He is very wise, take counsel of him."

And he came, did that hunchback of Hell: the felons greeted him and he planned this evil.

"Sire," said he, "let your nephew ride hard to-morrow at dawn with a brief drawn up on parchment and well sealed with a seal: bid him ride to King Arthur at Carduel.[4] Sire, he sleeps with the peers in your chamber; go you out when the first sleep falls on men, and if he love Iseult so madly, why, then I swear by God and by the laws of Rome,[5] he will try to speak with her before he rides. But if he do so unknown to you or to me, then slay me. As for the trap, let me lay it, but do you say nothing of his ride to him until the time for sleep."

And when King Mark had agreed, this dwarf did a vile thing. He

4. One of the courts of Arthur, perhaps Carlisle in northern England, perhaps a place in Wales.
5. Laws of the Roman Catholic Church.

bought of a baker four farthings' worth of flour, and hid it in the turn of his coat. That night, when the King had supped and the men-at-arms lay down to sleep in hall, Tristan came to the King as custom was, and the King said:

"Fair nephew, do my will: ride to-morrow night to King Arthur at Carduel, and give him this brief, with my greeting, that he may open it: and stay you with him but one day."

And when Tristan said: "I will take it on the morrow;"

The King added: "Aye, and before day dawn."

But, as the peers slept all round the King their lord, that night, a mad thought took Tristan that, before he rode, he knew not for how long, before dawn he would say a last word to the Queen. And there was a spear length in the darkness between them. Now the dwarf slept with the rest in the King's chamber, and when he thought that all slept he rose and scattered the flour silently in the spear length that lay between Tristan and the Queen; but Tristan watched and saw him, and said to himself:

"It is to mark my footsteps, but there shall be no marks to show."

At midnight, when all was dark in the room, no candle nor any lamp glimmering, the King went out silently by the door and with him the dwarf. Then Tristan rose in the darkness and judged the spear length and leapt the space between, for his farewell. But that day in the hunt a boar had wounded him in the leg, and in this effort the wound bled. He did not feel it or see it in the darkness, but the blood dripped upon the couches and the flour strewn between; and outside in the moonlight the dwarf read the heavens and knew what had been done and he cried:

"Enter, my King, and if you do not hold[6] them, hang me high."

Then the King and the dwarf and the four felons ran in with lights and noise, and though Tristan had regained his place there was the blood for witness. . . .

And the four barons held Tristan down upon his bed and mocked the Queen also, promising her full justice; and they bared and showed the wound whence the blood flowed.

Then the King said:

"Tristan, now nothing longer holds.[7] To-morrow you shall die."

And Tristan answered:

"Have mercy, Lord, in the name of God that suffered the Cross!"

But the felons called on the King to take vengeance, saying:

6. Catch.   7. Restrains (me).

"Do justice, King: take vengeance."

And Tristan went on, "Have mercy, not on me—for why should I stand at dying?—Truly, but for you, I would have sold my honour high to cowards who, under your peace, have put hands on my body— but in homage to you I have yielded and you may do with me what you will. But, lord, remember the Queen!"

And as he knelt at the King's feet he still complained:

"Remember the Queen; for if any man of your household make so bold as to maintain the lie that I loved her unlawfully, I will stand up armed to him in a ring. Sire, in the name of God the Lord, have mercy on her."

Then the barons bound him with ropes, and the Queen also. But had Tristan known that trial by combat was to be denied him, certainly he would not have suffered it.

For he trusted in God and knew no man dared draw sword against him in the lists. . . .

[Without trial Mark condemns Tristan and Iseult to death by fire. On the way to the place of execution Tristan entreats his guards to let him pray in a chapel by a roadside high above the sea. Bent upon death, he leaps from a window to the rocks far below but is miraculously saved.

Iseult is dragged to the fire, but the leader of a passing band of lepers prevails upon Mark to commit her to slow death in their company. Taking her away, they pass the spot where Tristan lies hiding and where Gorvenal has joined him. Tristan rescues Iseult from the lepers, and the three seek refuge in the depths of a wild wood.]

THE WOOD OF MOROIS

. . . One day, as they were wandering in these high woods that had never yet been felled or ordered, they came upon the hermitage of Ogrin.

The old man limped in the sunlight under a light growth of maples near his chapel: he leant upon his crutch, and cried:

"Lord Tristan, hear the great oath which the Cornish men have sworn. The King has published a ban in every parish: Whosoever may seize you shall receive a hundred marks of gold for his guerdon, and all the barons have sworn to give you up alive or dead. Do penance, Tristan! God pardons the sinner who turns to repentance."

"And of what should I repent, Ogrin, my lord? Or of what crime? . . ."

"God aid you, Lord Tristan; for you have lost both this world and the next. A man that is traitor to his lord is worthy to be torn by horses and burnt upon the faggot. . . . Lord Tristan, give back the Queen to the man who espoused her lawfully according to the laws of Rome."

"He gave her to his lepers. From these lepers I myself conquered her with my own hand; and henceforth she is altogether mine. She cannot pass from me nor I from her."

Ogrin sat down; but at his feet Iseult, her head upon the knees of that man of God, wept silently. . . .

"Ah me," said Ogrin then, "what comfort can one give the dead? Do penance, Tristan, for a man who lives in sin without repenting is a man quite dead."

"Oh no," said Tristan, "I live and I do no penance. We will go back into the high wood which comforts and wards us all round about. Come with me, Iseult, my friend."

Iseult rose up; they held each other's hands. They passed into the high grass and the underwood: the trees hid them with their branches. They disappeared beyond the curtain of the leaves.

The summer passed and the winter came: the two lovers lived, all hidden in the hollow of a rock, and on the frozen earth the cold crisped their couch with dead leaves. In the strength of their love neither one nor the other felt these mortal things. But when the open skies had come back with the springtime, they built a hut of green branches under the great trees. . . .

The lovers had ceased to wander through the forest, for none of the barons ran the risk of their pursuit knowing well that Tristan would have hanged them to the branches of a tree. . . .

My lords, upon a summer day, when mowing is, a little after Whitsuntide,[8] as the birds sang dawn Tristan left his hut and girt his sword on him, and took his bow "Failnaught" and went off to hunt in the wood; but before evening, great evil was to fall on him, for no lovers ever loved so much or paid their love so dear.

When Tristan came back, broken by the heat, the Queen said: "Friend, where have you been?"

"Hunting a hart," he said, "that wearied me. I would lie down and sleep."

So she lay down, and he, and between them Tristan put his naked

8. The seventh Sunday after Easter.

sword, and on the Queen's finger was that ring of gold with emeralds set therein, which Mark had given her on her bridal day; but her hand was so wasted that the ring hardly held. . . . Now a woodman found in the wood a place where the leaves were crushed, where the lovers had halted and slept, and he followed their track and found the hut, and saw them sleeping and fled off, fearing the terrible awakening of that lord. He fled to Tintagel, and going up the stairs of the palace, found the King as he held his pleas in hall amid the vassals assembled.

"Friend," said the King, "what came you hither to seek in haste and breathless, like a huntsman that has followed the dogs afoot? Have you some wrong to right, or has any man driven you?"

But the woodman took him aside and said low down:

"I have seen the Queen and Tristan, and I feared and fled."

"Where saw you them?"

"In a hut in Morois, they slept side by side. Come swiftly and take your vengeance."

"Go," said the King, "and await me at the forest edge where the red cross stands, and tell no man what you have seen. You shall have gold and silver at your will."

The King had saddled his horse and girt his sword and left the city alone, and as he rode alone he minded him of the night when he had seen Tristan under the great pine-tree, and Iseult with her clear face, and he thought:

"If I find them I will avenge this awful wrong."

At the foot of the red cross he came to the woodman and said:

"Go first, and lead me straight and quickly."

The dark shade of the great trees wrapt them round. . . . Then the woodman said:

"King, we are near."

He held the stirrup, and tied the rein to a green apple-tree, and saw in a sunlit glade the hut with its flowers and leaves. Then the King cast his cloak with its fine buckle of gold and drew his sword from its sheath and said again in his heart that they or he should die. And he signed to the woodman to be gone.

He came alone into the hut, sword bare, and watched them as they lay: but he saw that they were apart, and he wondered because between them was the naked blade.

Then he said to himself: "My God, I may not kill them. For all the time they have lived together in this wood, these two lovers, yet is the sword here between them, and throughout Christendom men know that sign. Therefore I will not slay, for that would be treason and wrong, but I will do so that when they wake they may know that I found them here, asleep, and spared them and that God had pity on them both.". . .

Then in her sleep a vision came to Iseult. She seemed to be in a great wood and two lions near her fought for her, and she gave a cry and woke; and at the cry Tristan woke, and made to seize his sword, and saw by the golden hilt that it was the King's. And the Queen saw on her finger the King's ring, and she cried:

"O, my lord, the King has found us here!"

And Tristan said:

"He has taken my sword; he was alone, but he will return, and will burn us before the people. Let us fly."

So by great marches with Gorvenal alone they fled towards Wales.

[As Tristan ponders the action of Mark, he comes to believe that the king was moved by tenderness and pity. He would return as Mark's vassal, but then he must yield up Iseult; he prays God for strength to do right. Meanwhile Iseult sorrows for the fate she has brought Tristan. They go to the hermit Ogrin for help, and Tristan offers to yield Iseult and to go into far lands. He offers also to yield himself to trial by combat. Ogrin writes out the offer; Tristan delivers the writ to Mark and flees. Since no man of Cornwall will challenge Tristan, the barons advise Mark to receive Iseult but not to keep Tristan as liege. Iseult begs of Tristan his dog for remembrance and she gives Tristan her ring of green jasper. In anguish the lovers prepare to separate at the ford of a river; and there Iseult returns to the king amidst his assembled barons. For a while Tristan tarries in secret in Cornwall to assure himself that no harm will befall Iseult.]

THE ORDEAL BY IRON

Denoalen, Andret, and Gondoïne held themselves safe; Tristan was far over sea, far away in service of a distant king, and they beyond his power. Therefore, during a hunt one day, as the King rode apart in a glade where the pack would pass, and hearkening to the hounds, they all three rode towards him, and said:

"O King, we have somewhat to say. Once you condemned the Queen without judgment, and that was wrong; now you acquit her without judgment, and that is wrong. She is not quit by trial, and the barons of your land blame you both. Counsel her, then, to claim the ordeal in God's judgment, for since she is innocent, she may swear on the relics of the saints and hot iron will not hurt her. For so custom runs, and in this easy way are doubts dissolved.". . .

But Mark stood up in the stirrup and cried:

"Out of my land, and out of my peace, all of you! Tristan I exiled for you, and now go you in turn, out of my land!"

But they answered:

"Sire, it is well. Our keeps are strong and fenced, and stand on rocks not easy for men to climb."

And they rode off without a salutation.

But the King spurred his horse to Tintagel; and as he sprang up the stairs the Queen heard the jangle of his spurs upon the stones.

She rose to meet him and took his sword as she was wont, and bowed before him, as it was also her wont to do; but Mark raised her, holding her hands; and when Iseult looked up she saw his noble face in just that wrath she had seen before the faggot fire.

She thought that Tristan was found, and her heart grew cold, and without a word she fell at the King's feet.

He took her in his arms and kissed her gently till she could speak again, and then he said:

"Friend, friend, what evil tries you?"

"Sire, I am afraid, for I have seen your anger."

"Yes, I was angered at the hunt."

"My lord, should one take so deeply the mischances of a game?"[9]

Mark smiled and said:

"No, friend; no chance of hunting vexed me, but those three felons whom you know; and I have driven them forth from my land."

"Sire, what did they say, or dare to say of me?"

"What matter? I have driven them forth."

"Sire, all living have this right: to say the word they have conceived. And I would ask a question, but from whom shall I learn save from you? I am alone in a foreign land, and have no one else to defend me."

"They would have it that you should quit yourself by solemn oath and by the ordeal of iron, saying 'that God was a true judge, and that as the Queen was innocent, she herself should seek such judgment as would clear her for ever.' This was their clamour and their demand incessantly. But let us leave it. I tell you, I have driven them forth."

9. Sport.

Iseult trembled, but looking straight at the King, she said:

"Sire, call them back; I will clear myself by oath. But I bargain this: that on the appointed day you call King Arthur and Lord Gawain, Girflet, Kay the Seneschal, and a hundred of his knights to ride to the Sandy Heath where your land marches[10] with his, and a river flows between; for I will not swear before your barons alone...."

But as the heralds rode to Carduel, Iseult sent to Tristan secretly her squire Perinis: and he ran through the underwood, avoiding paths, till he found the hut of Orri, the woodman, where Tristan for many days had awaited news. Perinis told him all: the ordeal, the place, and the time, and added:

"My lord, the Queen would have you on that day and place come dressed as a pilgrim, so that none may know you—unarmed, so that none may challenge—to the Sandy Heath. She must cross the river to the place appointed. Beyond it, where Arthur and his hundred knights will stand, be you also; for my lady fears the judgment, but she trusts in God."

Then Tristan answered:

"Go back, friend Perinis, return you to the Queen, and say that I will do her bidding."

On the appointed day King Mark and Iseult, and the barons of Cornwall, stood by the river; and the knights of Arthur and all their host were arrayed beyond.

And just before them, sitting on the shore, was a poor pilgrim, wrapped in cloak and hood, who held his wooden platter and begged alms.

Now as the Cornish boats came to the shoal of the further bank, Iseult said to the knights:

"My lords, how shall I land without befouling my clothes in the river-mud? Fetch me a ferryman."

And one of the knights hailed the pilgrim, and said:

"Friend, truss your coat, and try the water; carry you the Queen to shore, unless you fear the burden."

But as he took the Queen in his arms she whispered to him:

"Friend."

And then she whispered to him, lower still:

"Stumble you upon the sand."

And as he touched shore, he stumbled, holding the Queen in his

10. Borders.

arms; and the squires and boatmen with their oars and boat-hooks drove the poor pilgrim away.

But the Queen said:

"Let him be; some great travail and journey has weakened him."

And she threw to the pilgrim a little clasp of gold.

Before the tent of King Arthur was spread a rich Nicean cloth upon the grass, and the holy relics were set on it, taken out of their covers and their shrines. . . .

The Queen having prayed God, took off the jewels from her neck and hands, and gave them to the beggars around; she took off her purple mantle, and her overdress, and her shoes with their precious stones, and gave them also to the poor that loved her.

She kept upon her only the sleeveless tunic, and then with arms and feet quite bare she came between the two kings, and all around the barons watched her in silence, and some wept, for near the holy relics was a brazier burning.

And trembling a little she stretched her right hand towards the bones and said: "Kings of Logres and of Cornwall; my lords Gawain, and Kay, and Girflet, and all of you that are my warrantors, by these holy things and all the holy things of earth, I swear that no man has held me in his arms saving King Mark, my lord, and that poor pilgrim. King Mark, will that oath stand?"

"Yes, Queen," he said, "and God see to it."

"Amen," said Iseult, and then she went near the brazier, pale and stumbling, and all were silent. The iron was red, but she thrust her bare arms among the coals and seized it, and bearing it took nine steps.

Then as she cast it from her, she stretched her arms out in a cross, with the palms of her hands wide open, and all men saw them fresh and clean and cold. Seeing that great sight the kings and the barons and the people stood for a moment silent, then they stirred together and they praised God loudly all around.

[Suffering greatly, Tristan goes into Wales as guest of Duke Gilain. A faery dog with a tinkling bell about its neck brings him comfort; but when he thinks how this dog might take away Iseult's sorrow, he wishes it for her. He defeats Gilain's enemy, the hairy giant Urgan, and gains the dog for reward. He sends it to Iseult, who is greatly comforted. But when she knows the cause of her comfort, she casts the bell into the sea and returns to her sorrow, not wishing to be carefree while Tristan is sad.

For two years Tristan wanders, serving many lords, and no word of Iseult comes to him. He believes that the dog and bell have done their work and that Iseult has forgotten. He comes to the land of the Bretons, where, in the castle of Carhaix, Duke Hoël is besieged by his vassal Duke Riol, who would marry Hoël's daughter, Iseult of the White Hands. Hoël and Kaherdin, his son, welcome Tristan with honor, and Tristan and Kaherdin become brothers in arms. Tristan defeats Riol, and Hoël offers Tristan his daughter. At the door of the church Tristan weds Iseult of the White Hands. On Tristan's marriage night a ring of green jasper falls from his finger upon the stones of the floor. Tristan knows he has done wrong.]

THE MADNESS OF TRISTAN

Within her room at Tintagel, Iseult the Fair sighed for the sake of Tristan, and named him, her desire, of whom for two years she had had no word, whether he lived or no. . . .

Now far from Iseult, Tristan languished, till on a day he must needs see her again. Far from her, death came surely; and he had rather die at once than day by day. And he desired some death, but that the Queen might know it was in finding her; then would death come easily.

So he left Carhaix secretly, telling no man, neither his kindred nor even Kaherdin, his brother in arms. He went in rags afoot (for no one marks the beggar on the high road) till he came to the shore of the sea.

He found in a haven a great ship ready, the sail was up and the anchor-chain short at the bow. . . .

And he went aboard, and a fair wind filled the sail, and she ran five days and nights for Cornwall, till, on the sixth day, they dropped anchor in Tintagel Haven. So Tristan went ashore and sat upon the beach, and a man told him that Mark was there and had just held his court.

"But where," said he, "is Iseult, the Queen, and her fair maid, Brangien?"

"In Tintagel too," said the other, "and I saw them lately; the Queen sad, as she always is."

At the hearing of the name, Tristan suffered, and he thought that neither by guile nor courage could he see that friend, for Mark would kill him. . . .

And he thought, "I will try guile. I will seem mad, but with a madness that shall be great wisdom. And many shall think me a fool that have less wit than I."

Just then a fisherman passed in a rough cloak and cape, and Tristan seeing him, took him aside, and said:

"Friend, will you not change clothes?"

And as the fisherman found it a very good bargain, he said in answer:

"Yes, friend, gladly."

And he changed and ran off at once for fear of losing his gain. Then Tristan shaved his wonderful hair; he shaved it close to his head and left a cross all bald, and he rubbed his face with magic herbs distilled in his own country, and it changed in colour and skin so that none could know him, and he made him a club from a young tree torn from a hedgerow and hung it to his neck, and went bare-foot towards the castle.

The porter made sure that he had to do with a fool and said:

"Come in, lord fool; the Hairy Urgan's son, I know, and like your father."

And when he was within the courts the serving men ran after him and cried:

"The fool! the fool!"

But he made play with them though they cast stones and struck him as they laughed, and in the midst of laughter and their cries, as the rout followed him, he came to that hall where, at the Queen's side, King Mark sat under his canopy.

And as he neared the door with his club at his neck, the King said:

"Here is a merry fellow, let him in."

And they brought him in, his club at his neck. And the King said:

"Friend, well come; what seek you here?"

"Iseult," said he, "whom I love so well; I bring my sister with me, Brunehild, the beautiful. Come, take her, you are weary of the Queen. Take you my sister and give me here Iseult, and I will hold her and serve you for her love."

The King said laughing:

"Fool, if I gave you the Queen, where would you take her, pray?"

"Oh, very high," he said, "between the clouds and heaven, into a fair chamber glazed. The beams of the sun shine through it, yet the winds do not trouble it at all. There would I bear the Queen into that crystal chamber of mine all compact of roses and the morning."

The King and his barons laughed and said:

"Here is a good fool at no loss for words."

But the fool as he sat at their feet gazed at Iseult most fixedly.

"Friend," said King Mark, "what warrant have you that the Queen would heed so foul a fool as you?"

"O! Sire," he answered gravely, "many deeds have I done for her, and my madness is from her alone."

"What is your name?" they said, and laughed.

"Tristan," said he, "that loved the Queen so well, and still till death will love her."

But at the name the Queen angered and weakened together, and said: "Get hence for an evil fool!"

But the fool, marking her anger, went on:

"Queen Iseult, do you mind the day, when, poisoned by the Morholt's spear, I took my harp to sea and fell upon your shore? Your mother healed me with strange drugs. Have you no memory, Queen?"

But Iseult answered:

"Out, fool, out! Your folly and you have passed the bounds!"

But the fool, still playing, pushed the barons out, crying:

"Out! madmen, out! Leave me to counsel with Iseult, since I come here for the love of her!"

And as the King laughed, Iseult blushed and said:

"King, drive me forth this fool!"

But the fool still laughed and cried:

"Queen, do you mind you of the dragon I slew in your land? I hid its tongue in my hose, and, burnt of its venom, I fell by the roadside. Ah! what a knight was I then, and it was you that succoured me."

Iseult replied:

"Silence! You wrong all knighthood by your words, for you are a fool from birth. Cursed be the seamen that brought you hither; rather should they have cast you into the sea!"

"Queen Iseult," he still said on, "do you mind you of your haste when you would have slain me with my own sword? And of the Hair of Gold? . . ."

"Silence!" she said, "you drunkard. You were drunk last night, and so you dreamt these dreams."

"Drunk, and still so am I," said he, "but of such a draught that never can the influence fade. Queen Iseult, do you mind you of that hot and open day on the high seas? We thirsted and we drank together from the same cup, and since that day have I been drunk with an awful wine."

When the Queen heard these words which she alone could understand, she rose and would have gone.

But the King held her by her ermine cloak, and she sat down again.

And as the King had his fill of the fool he called for his falcons and went to hunt; and Iseult said to him:

"Sire, I am weak and sad; let me go rest in my room; I am tired of these follies."

And she went to her room in thought and sat upon her bed and mourned, calling herself a slave and saying:

"Why was I born? Brangien, dear sister, life is so hard to me that death were better! There is a fool without, shaven criss-cross, and come in an evil hour, and he is warlock,[11] for he knows in every part myself and my whole life; he knows what you and I and Tristan only know."

Then Brangien said: "It may be Tristan."

But—"No," said the Queen, "for he was the first of knights, but this fool is foul and made awry. Curse me his hour and the ship that brought him hither."

"My lady!" said Brangien, "soothe you. You curse over much these days. May be he comes from Tristan?"

"I cannot tell. I know him not. But go find him, friend, and see if you know him."

So Brangien went to the hall where the fool still sat alone. Tristan knew her and let fall his club and said:

"Brangien, dear Brangien, before God! have pity on me!"

"Foul fool," she answered, "what devil taught you my name?"

"Lady," he said, "I have known it long. By my head, that once was fair, if I am mad the blame is yours, for it was yours to watch over the wine we drank on the high seas. The cup was of silver and I held it to Iseult and she drank. Do you remember, lady?"

"No," she said, and as she trembled and left he called out: "Pity me!"

He followed and saw Iseult. He stretched out his arms, but in her shame, sweating agony she drew back, and Tristan angered and said:

"I have lived too long, for I have seen the day that Iseult will nothing of me. Iseult, how hard love dies! Iseult, a welling water that floods and runs large is a mighty thing; on the day that it fails it is nothing; so love that turns."

11. Wizard.

But she said:

"Brother, I look at you and doubt and tremble, and I know you not for Tristan."

"Queen Iseult, I am Tristan indeed that do love you; mind you for the last time of the dwarf, and of the flour, and of the blood I shed in my leap. Oh! and of that ring I took in kisses and in tears on the day we parted. I have kept that jasper ring and asked it counsel."

Then Iseult knew Tristan for what he was, and she said:

"Heart, you should have broken of sorrow not to have known the man who has suffered so much for you. Pardon, my master and my friend."

And her eyes darkened and she fell; but when the light returned she was held by him who kissed her eyes and her face.

So passed they three full days. But, on the third, two maids that watched them told the traitor Andret, and he put spies well-armed before the women's rooms. And when Tristan would enter they cried:

"Back, fool!"

But he brandished his club laughing, and said:

"What! May I not kiss the Queen who loves me and awaits me now?"

And they feared him for a mad fool, and he passed in through the door.

Then, being with the Queen for the last time, he held her in his arms and said:

"Friend, I must fly, for they are wondering. I must fly, and perhaps shall never see you more. My death is near, and far from you my death will come of desire."

"Oh friend," she said, "fold your arms round me close and strain me so that our hearts may break and our souls go free at last. Take me to that happy place of which you told me long ago. The fields whence none return, but where great singers sing their songs for ever. Take me now."

"I will take you to the Happy Palace of the living, Queen! The time is near. We have drunk all joy and sorrow. The time is near. When it is finished, if I call you, will you come, my friend?"

"Friend," said she, "call me and you know that I shall come."

"Friend," said he, "God send you His reward."

As he went out the spies would have held him; but he laughed aloud, and flourished his club, and cried:

Peace, gentlemen, I go and will not stay. My lady sends me to prepare that shining house I vowed her, of crystal, and of rose shot through with morning."

And as they cursed and drave him, the fool went leaping on his way.

THE DEATH OF TRISTAN

When he was come back to Brittany, to Carhaix, it happened that Tristan, riding to the aid of Kaherdin his brother in arms, fell into ambush and was wounded by a poisoned spear; and many doctors came, but none could cure him of the ill. And Tristan weakened and paled, and his bones showed.

Then he knew that his life was going, and that he must die, and he had a desire to see once more Iseult the Fair, but he could not seek her, for the sea would have killed him in his weakness, and how could Iseult come to him? And sad, and suffering the poison, he awaited death.

He called Kaherdin secretly to tell him his pain, for they loved each other with a loyal love; and as he would have no one in the room save Kaherdin, nor even in the neighbouring rooms, Iseult of the White Hands began to wonder. She was afraid and wished to hear, and she came back and listened at the wall by Tristan's bed; and as she listened one of her maids kept watch for her.

Now, within, Tristan had gathered up his strength, and had half risen, leaning against the wall, and Kaherdin wept beside him. They wept their good comradeship, broken so soon, and their friendship: then Tristan told Kaherdin of his love for that other Iseult, and of the sorrow of his life.

"Fair friend and gentle," said Tristan, "I am in a foreign land where I have neither friend nor cousin, save you; and you alone in this place have given me comfort. My life is going, and I wish to see once more Iseult the Fair. Ah, did I but know of a messenger who would go to her! For now I know that she will come to me. Kaherdin, my brother in arms, I beg it of your friendship; try this thing for me, and if you carry my word, I will become your liege, and I will cherish you beyond all other men."

And as Kaherdin saw Tristan broken down, his heart reproached him and he said:

"Fair comrade, do not weep; I will do what you desire, even if it were risk of death I would do it for you. . . ."

And Tristan answered:

"Thank you, friend; this is my prayer: take this ring, it is a sign between her and me; and when you come to her land pass yourself at court for a merchant, and show her silk and stuffs, but make so that she sees the ring, for then she will find some ruse by which to speak to you in secret. Then tell her that my heart salutes her; tell her that she alone can bring me comfort; tell her that if she does not come I shall die. Tell her to remember our past time, and our great sorrows, and all the joy there was in our loyal and tender love. And tell her to remember that draught we drank together on the high seas. For we drank our death together. Tell her to remember the oath I swore to serve a single love, for I have kept that oath."

But behind the wall, Iseult of the White Hands heard all these things; and Tristan continued:

"Hasten, my friend, and come back quickly, or you will not see me again. Take forty days for your term, but come back with Iseult the Fair. And tell your sister nothing, or tell her that you seek some doctor. Take my fine ship, and two sails with you, one white, one black. And as you return, if you bring Iseult, hoist the white sail; but if you bring her not, the black. . . ."

With the first fair wind Kaherdin took the open, weighed anchor and hoisted sail, and ran with a light air and broke the seas. . . .

Now a woman's wrath is a fearful thing, and all men fear it, for according to her love, so will her vengeance be; and their love and their hate come quickly, but their hate lives longer than their love; and they will make play with love, but not with hate. So Iseult of the White Hands, who had heard every word, and who had so loved Tristan, waited her vengeance upon what she loved most in the world. . . .

And Kaherdin sailed and sailed till he dropped anchor in the haven of Tintagel. He landed and took with him a cloth of rare dye and a cup well chiselled and worked, and made a present of them to King Mark, and courteously begged of him his peace and safeguard that he might traffick in his land; and the King gave him his peace before all the men of his palace.

Then Kaherdin offered the Queen a buckle of fine gold; and "Queen," said he, "the gold is good."

Then taking from his finger Tristan's ring, he put it side by side with the jewel and said:

"See, O Queen, the gold of the buckle is the finer gold; yet that ring also has its worth."

When Iseult saw what ring that was, her heart trembled and her colour changed, and fearing what might next be said she drew Kaherdin apart near a window, as if to see and bargain the better; and Kaherdin said to her, low down:

"Lady, Tristan is wounded of a poisoned spear and is about to die. He sends you word that you alone can bring him comfort, and recalls to you the great sorrows that you bore together. Keep you the ring—it is yours."

But Iseult answered, weakening:

"Friend, I will follow you; get ready your ship to-morrow at dawn."

And on the morrow at dawn they raised anchor, stepped mast, and hoisted sail, and happily the barque left land.

But at Carhaix Tristan lay and longed for Iseult's coming. Nothing now filled him any more, and if he lived it was only as awaiting her; and day by day he sent watchers to the shore to see if some ship came, and to learn the colour of her sail. There was no other thing left in his heart.

He had himself carried to the cliff of the Penmarks, where it over-looks the sea, and all the daylight long he gazed far off over the water.

Hear now a tale most sad and pitiful to all who love. Already was Iseult near; already the cliff of the Penmarks showed far away, and the ship ran heartily, when a storm wind rose on a sudden and grew, and struck the sail, and turned the ship all round about, and the sailors bore away and sore against their will they ran before the wind. . . .

Then Iseult cried out: "God does not will that I should live to see him, my love, once—even one time more. God wills my drowning in this sea. O, Tristan, had I spoken to you but once again, it is little I should have cared for a death come afterwards. But now, my love, I cannot come to you; for God so wills it, and that is the core of my grief."

And thus the Queen complained so long as the storm endured; but after five days it died down. Kaherdin hoisted the sail, the white sail, right up to the very masthead with great joy; the white sail, that Tristan might know its colour from afar: and already Kaherdin saw Brittany far off like a cloud. Hardly were these things seen and done when a calm came, and the sea lay even and untroubled. The sail bellied no longer, and the sailors held the ship now up, now down, the tide, beating backwards and forwards in vain. They saw the shore afar off, but the storm had carried their boat away and they could not land. On the third night Iseult dreamt this dream: that she held in her lap a boar's head which befouled her skirts with blood; then she knew that she would never see her lover again alive.

Tristan was now too weak to keep his watch from the cliff of the Penmarks, and for many long days, within walls, far from the shore, he had mourned for Iseult because she did not come. Dolorous and alone, he mourned and sighed in restlessness: he was near death from desire.

At last the wind freshened and the white sail showed. Then it was that Iseult of the White Hands took her vengeance.

She came to where Tristan lay, and she said:

"Friend, Kaherdin is here. I have seen his ship upon the sea. She comes up hardly—yet I know her; may he bring that which shall heal thee, friend."

And Tristan trembled and said:

"Beautiful friend, you are sure that the ship is his indeed? Then tell me what is the manner of the sail?"

"I saw it plain and well. They have shaken it out and hoisted it very high, for they have little wind. For its colour, why, it is black."

And Tristan turned him to the wall, and said:

"I cannot keep this life of mine any longer." He said three times: "Iseult, my friend." And in saying it the fourth time, he died.

Then throughout the house, the knights and the comrades of Tristan wept out loud, and they took him from his bed and laid him on a rich cloth, and they covered his body with a shroud. But at sea the wind had risen; it struck the sail fair and full and drove the ship to shore, and Iseult the Fair set foot upon the land. She heard loud mourning in the streets, and the tolling of bells in the minsters and the chapel towers; she asked the people the meaning of the knell and of their tears. An old man said to her:

"Lady, we suffer a great grief. Tristan, that was so loyal and so right, is dead. He was open to the poor; he ministered to the suffering. It is the chief evil that has ever fallen on this land."

But Iseult, hearing them, could not answer them a word. She went up to the palace, following the way, and her cloak was random and wild. The Bretons marvelled as she went; nor had they ever seen woman of such a beauty, and they said:

"Who is she, or whence does she come?"

Near Tristan, Iseult of the White Hands crouched, maddened at the evil she had done, and calling and lamenting over the dead man. The other Iseult came in and said to her:

"Lady, rise and let me come by him; I have more right to mourn him than have you—believe me. I loved him more."

And when she had turned to the east and prayed God, she moved the body a little and lay down by the dead man, beside her friend. She kissed his mouth and his face, and clasped him closely; and so gave up her soul, and died beside him of grief for her lover.

When King Mark heard of the death of these lovers, he crossed the sea and came into Brittany; and he had two coffins hewn, for Tristan and Iseult, one of chalcedony for Iseult, and one of beryl for Tristan. And he took their beloved bodies away with him upon his ship to Tintagel, and by a chantry to the left and right of the apse he had their tombs built round. But in one night there sprang from the tomb of Tristan a green and leafy briar, strong in its branches and in the scent of its flowers. It climbed the chantry and fell to root again by Iseult's tomb. Thrice did the peasants cut it down, but thrice it grew again as flowered and as strong. They told the marvel to King Mark, and he forbade them to cut the briar any more.

The good singers of old time, Béroul and Thomas of Built, Gilbert and Gottfried told this tale for lovers and none other, and, by my pen, they beg you for your prayers. They greet those who are cast down, and those in heart, those troubled and those filled with desire. May all herein find strength against inconstancy and despite and loss and pain and all the bitterness of loving.

Dante

Divine Comedy

IN THE THIRTEENTH CENTURY Italy was an unsettled and turbulent region. It cannot be called a country, for in spite of the theoretical rule of the Holy Roman Empire, it was actually an aggregation of city states carrying on constant political maneuvering, alliances, and wars among themselves. In general, there were the two factions of the Guelphs and Ghibellines, the former theoretically supporting the Pope and the latter the Emperor in their constant struggle for power; but in practice the policies of either party at any specific time and place were determined by political opportunism as much as fixed principles. In Florence the struggle between Guelphs and Ghibellines was brief. After some preliminary skirmishing, the Guelphs were defeated in battle and expelled from the city in 1260, but six years later they reinstated themselves, drove out their enemies, and established permanently the more democratic rule of the Guelphs.

Dante Alighieri (1265-1321) was born of an old, but not wealthy, Guelph family. He seems to have had the best possible education, and he early showed interest and ability in soldiering, poetry, scholarship, philosophy, and politics. His first sonnet attracted the attention of

Guido Cavalcanti, then the leading poet of Italy, and the two formed a close friendship. In his ninth year Dante had first met Beatrice Portinari, and he developed a mystical love for her which was only deepened by her death in 1290. Shortly thereafter he collected his poems to her, setting them in a prose narrative and commentary under the title of *The New Life*. At the close of this work he gives a promise of the great poem to come: "Just after I wrote this last sonnet there came to me a marvelous vision in which I saw things that determined me to say no more of this blessed one until I should be able to treat of her more worthily. . . . So that, if it be the pleasure of Him in whom all things live that my life continue for some years, I hope to say of her what has never been said of any woman."

At some time during the next few years Dante married Gemma Donati, by whom he had four children. But there was little time for family life, for the Guelphs of Florence were now split into two factions, the "Blacks" and the "Whites." The basis of the division is not entirely clear, but in general the Blacks were the old feudal aristocracy and the Whites were the rising middle-class—often wealthier than the nobles. Dante supported the Whites in rejecting the Pope's attempts to restrict the liberties of Florence. In May, 1300, the factions came to blows. Shortly thereafter Dante, serving as one of the group of six Priors who had the highest executive power in Florence, joined in banishing the leaders of both factions in an attempt to keep peace. The Whites gained temporary control, but, with outside aid, the Blacks returned, seized the government, and began their reprisals. In 1302 Dante was one of a group sentenced to fines and banishment.

He never saw Florence again. The Florentines pursued him with a relentless hatred that fully justified his later description of them as wolves. A few months after his banishment he was sentenced to be burned to death if he ever came into the power of Florence. In 1311 he was specifically excluded from amnesty, and in 1315 the sentence of death at the stake was renewed against him, and extended to apply to his two sons as well. At first he banded with the other exiles, but soon he went his own way, hoping to the last that he might eventually go home. An extant letter shows that he once had the opportunity of returning on degrading terms, but rejected it. He finally hoped that his great poem might win over Florence, as it did, but too late. Florence entreated Ravenna to send his remains to his native city, but Ravenna refused, and he lies today in this last of his refuges.

The full details of his nineteen years of banishment are not known.

We hear of him at Padua, at Lucca, at Verona, and finally spending his last four years at Ravenna with a nephew of Francesca da Rimini. It was during these years of misery and wandering that Dante's real work was done. He wrote Latin treatises on the problem of producing literature in the vernacular language and on the nature and mission of monarchy (*De Vulgari Eloquentia* and *De Monarchia*). *The Banquet* (*Il Convivio*) is an attempt to make the fruits of philosophy more generally available. There are letters on political and literary subjects as well, but the main labor of the years of banishment is his *Commedia*.

This is his own name for the poem—*The Comedy of Dante Alighieri, a Florentine by Birth, but not in Character*. It is a comedy in the regular sense of the word during the Middle Ages, a progress from misery to bliss. This progress takes the poet through the world after death. First he descends with Virgil through the various levels of Hell, an inverted cone lying under Jerusalem and descending by successive terraces to the nethermost pit at the center of the earth. Then he ascends by a narrow passage to the mountain of Purgatory, on the opposite side of the earth, on the successive terraces of which the various sins are purged, and at whose summit lies the Garden of Eden. Here he finds Beatrice, who conducts him through the various concentric spheres of the planets and fixed stars (for the earth is the center of his universe), until at last Saint Bernard leads him to the final blaze of glory in which God Himself is made manifest.

The structure of the poem is based on symbolic numbers. The verse form of the original is an interlocking scheme of rhymes in threes. The first Canto is a general introduction, and following it there are three divisions of thirty-three cantos each—a hundred in all. A similar scheme is followed in the subdivision of each of the three main sections of the poem. "Dante's number-scheme is always based on *three* subdivided into *seven*, raised by additions of a character differing from the rest to *nine*, and by a last addition on an entirely different plane to *ten*" (Wicksteed). Thus in Purgatory there are the three divisions of excessive love, defective love, and perverted love. The first and last of these are subdivided: excessive love into carnality, gluttony, and avarice; and perverted love into anger, envy, and pride. Thus we get the seven deadly sins. To these are added the two groups in the Antepurgatory, the late-repentant and the excommunicated. Finally, the divisions are raised to ten by the Garden of Eden—an addition on an entirely different plane.

So far, all this might be mere ingenuity. But the thought of the poem is as coherent and logical as the structure, and each reinforces the other. The thought itself is, as Dante explained, plural. There is first of all an account of an imaginary journey through Hell, Purgatory, and Heaven; but along with this there is a multiple allegory, often theological, political, and moral at the same time. A single example will suffice to illustrate this simultaneous presentation of different meanings. In the opening lines Dante came to himself in "a dark wood." Literally, then, we have a picture of a man lost in a forest; but there are also three different allegorical meanings: theologically, the dark wood is a state of spiritual separation from God; politically, it is the anarchy in Dante's Italy; and morally, it is an unworthy or evil way of life. Thus Dante is speaking primarily of this world rather than another, as we can see in the carnal sinners who are swept along together on the whirling winds of the second circle of Hell. They have each other, but, in this life also, they are swept ever onward by their own uncontrolled passions, and they have nothing else. Dante himself said that his purpose was "to remove those living in this life from a state of misery and to lead them to a state of happiness."

The creation of an entire universe coherently and consistently organized on so many levels of human experience, together with its presentation in language infused with pity for man's suffering and high hopes for his destiny, is one of the supreme feats of the human imagination.

This fact was realized almost as soon as the poem appeared. (The last thirteen Cantos of the *Heaven* were found by Dante's son after his death and forwarded to his protector and patron, Can Grande della Scala, who had the rest of the manuscript.) In 1373 the city of Florence invited Boccaccio to deliver a series of public lectures on Dante. At about the same time Chaucer came under his influence, and since that time Dante has been a part of the thought of Western civilization. The value which the world has set on his poem is best shown by its usual name. Today it is generally known as *The Divine Comedy:* the adjective was so frequently applied to the work, because of both its excellence and its theme, that it gradually came to be considered a part of the title.

THE DIVINE COMEDY

HELL

CANTO I

In the middle of the journey of our life[1] I came to myself in a dark wood where the straight way was lost. Ah! how hard a thing it is to tell what a wild, and rough, and stubborn wood this was, which in my thought renews the fear! So bitter is it, that scarcely more is death: but to treat of the good that I there found, I will relate the other things that I discerned. I cannot rightly tell how I entered it, so full of sleep was I about the moment that I left the true way. But after I had reached the foot of a Hill there, where that valley ended, which had pierced my heart with fear, I looked up and saw its shoulders already clothed with the rays of the Planet[2] that leads men straight on every road. Then the fear was somewhat calmed, which had continued in the lake of my heart the night that I passed so piteously. And as he, who with panting breath has escaped from the deep sea to the shore, turns to the dangerous water and gazes: so my mind, which still was fleeing, turned back to see the pass that no one ever left alive.

After I had rested my wearied body a short while, I took the way again along the desert strand, so that the right foot always was the lower. And behold, almost at the commencement of the steep, a Leopard,[3] light and very nimble, which was covered with spotted hair. And it went not from before my face; nay, so impeded my way, that I had often turned to go back. The time was at the beginning of the morning; and the sun was mounting up with those stars,[4] which were with him when Divine Love first moved those fair things: so that the hour of time and the sweet season caused me to have good hope of that animal with the gay skin; yet not so, but that I feared at the sight,

1. The Biblical "threescore years and ten" is accepted as the span of human life, and the action of the poem begins at sunrise on Good Friday, 1300, when Dante was nearing the end of his thirty-fifth year.
2. *Planet*, the sun, which was a planet in the astronomy of Dante's time.
3. The leopard, the lion, and the she-wolf mentioned below symbolize lust, pride, and avarice respectively.
4. According to medieval tradition, the Creation occurred in the spring.

which appeared to me, of a Lion. He seemed coming upon me with head erect, and furious hunger; so that the air seemed to have fear thereat; and a She-wolf, that looked full of all cravings in her leanness; and has ere now made many live in sorrow. She brought such heaviness upon me with the terror of her aspect, that I lost the hope of ascending. And as one who is eager in gaining, and, when the time arrives that makes him lose, weeps and afflicts himself in all his thoughts: such that restless beast made me, which coming against me, by little and little drove me back to where the Sun is silent.

Whilst I was rushing downwards, there appeared before my eyes one who seemed hoarse from long silence. When I saw him in the great desert, I cried: "Have pity on me, whate'er thou be, whether shade or veritable man!"

He answered me: "Not man, a man I once was; and my parents were Lombards, and both of Mantua by country. I was born *sub Julio*,[5] though it was late; and lived at Rome under the good Augustus, in the time of the false and lying Gods. A poet I was; and sang of that just son of Anchises, who came from Troy after proud Ilium was burnt. But thou, why returnest thou to such disquiet? why ascendest not the delectable mountain, which is the beginning and the cause of all gladness?" "Art thou then that Virgil, and that fountain which pours abroad so rich a stream of speech?" I answered him, with bashful front. "O glory, and light of other poets! May the long zeal avail me, and the great love, that made me search thy volume. Thou art my master and my author; thou alone art he from whom I took the good style that hath done me honour. See the beast from which I turned back; help me from her, thou famous sage; for she makes my veins and pulses tremble."

"Thou must take another road," he answered, when he saw me weeping, "if thou desirest to escape from this wild place: because this beast, for which thou criest, lets not men pass her way; but so entangles that she slays them; and has a nature so perverse and vicious, that she never satiates her craving appetite; and after feeding, she is hungrier than before. The animals to which she weds herself are many; and will yet be more, until the Greyhound[6] comes, that will make her die with pain. He will not feed on land or pelf, but on wisdom, and love, and

---

5. Julius Caesar was murdered before Virgil rose to prominence.
6. The exact signification of the Greyhound is an insoluble problem. None of the numerous explanations which have been proposed is really satisfactory.

manfulness; and his nation shall be between Feltro and Feltro. He shall be the salvation of that low Italy, for which Camilla the virgin, Euryalus, and Turnus, and Nisus,[7] died of wounds; he shall chase her through every city, till he have put her into Hell again; from which envy first set her loose. Wherefore I think and discern this for thy best, that thou follow me; and I will be thy guide, and lead thee hence through an eternal place, where thou shalt hear the hopeless shrieks, shalt see the ancient spirits in pain, so that each calls for a second death; and then thou shalt see those who are contented in the fire: for they hope to come, whensoever it be, amongst the blessed; then to these, if thou desirest to ascend, there shall be a spirit[8] worthier than I to guide thee; with her will I leave thee at my parting: for that Emperor who reigns above, because I was rebellious to his law, wills not that I come into his city. In all parts he rules and there holds sway; there is his city, and his high seat: O happy whom he chooses for it!"

And I to him: "Poet, I beseech thee by that God whom thou knowest not: in order that I may escape this ill and worse, lead me where thou now hast said, so that I may see the Gate of St. Peter,[9] and those whom thou makest so sad." Then he moved; and I kept on behind him.

CANTO II

The day was departing, and the brown air taking the animals, that are on earth, from their toils; and I, one alone, was preparing myself to bear the war both of the journey and the pity, which memory, that errs not, shall relate. O Muses, O high Genius, now help me! O Memory, that hast inscribed what I saw, here will be shown thy nobleness.

I began: "Poet, who guidest me, look if there be worth in me sufficient, before thou trust me to the arduous passage. Thou sayest that the father of Sylvius,[1] while subject to corruption, went to the immortal world, and was there in body. But if the Adversary of all evil was propitious to him, considering the high effect, and who and what should come from him, it seems not unfitting to an understanding mind: for in the empyreal heaven, he was chosen to be the father of

7. These are all characters in the latter part of the *Aeneid*.
8. *spirit*, Beatrice.
9. *Gate of Saint Peter*, Gate of Purgatory.
1. The father of Sylvius was Aeneas.

generous Rome, and of her Empire; both these, to say the truth, were established for the holy place, where the Successor of the greatest Peter sits. By this journey, for which thou honourest him, he learned things that were the causes of his victory, and of the Papal Mantle. Afterwards, the Chosen Vessel[2] went thither, to bring confirmation of that Faith which is the entrance of the way of salvation. But I, why go? or who permits it? I am not Æneas, am not Paul; neither myself nor others deem me worthy of it. Wherefore, if I resign myself to go, I fear my going may prove foolish; thou art wise, and understandest better than I speak." And as one who unwills what he willed, and with new thoughts changes his purpose, so that he wholly quits the thing commenced, such I made myself on that dim coast: for with thinking I wasted the enterprise, that had been so quick in its commencement.

"If I have rightly understood thy words," replied that shade of the Magnanimous, "thy soul is smit with coward fear, which oftentimes encumbers men, so that it turns them back from honoured enterprise; as false seeing does a startled beast. To free thee from this dread, I will tell thee why I came, and what I heard in the first moment when I took pity of thee. I was amongst them who are in suspense[3]; and a Lady, so fair and blessed that I prayed her to command, called me. Her eyes shone brighter than the stars; and she began soft and gentle to tell me with angelic voice, in her language: 'O courteous Mantuan Spirit, whose fame still lasts in the world, and will last as long as Time! my friend, and not the friend of fortune, is so impeded in his way upon the desert shore, that he has turned back for terror; and I fear he may already be so far astray, that I have risen too late for his relief, from what I heard of him in Heaven. Now go, and with thy ornate speech, and with what is necessary for his escape, help him so, that I may be consoled thereby. I am Beatrice who send thee; I come from a place where I desire to return; love moved me, that makes me speak. When I shall be before my Lord, I oft will praise thee to him.' She was silent then, and I began: 'O Lady of virtue, through whom alone mankind excels all that is contained within the heaven which has the smallest circles! so grateful to me is thy command, that my obeying, were it done already, seems tardy; it needs not that thou more explain to me thy wish. But tell me the cause, why thou forbearest not to descend into this centre here below from the spacious place, to which thou burnest

2. *Chosen Vessel*, Saint Paul. There is a medieval story of his visit to Hell.
3. As is explained later, Virgil's place is in Limbo.

to return.' 'Since thou desirest to know thus far, I will tell thee briefly,' she replied, 'why I fear not to come within this place. Those things alone are to be feared that have the power of hurting; the others not, which are not fearful. I am made such by God, in his grace, that your misery does not touch me; nor the flame of this burning assail me. There is a noble Lady in Heaven[4] who has such pity of this hindrance, for which I send thee, that she breaks the sharp judgment there on high. She called Lucia,[5] in her request, and said: "Now thy faithful one has need of thee; and I commend him to thee." Lucia, enemy of all cruelty, arose and came to the place where I was sitting with the ancient Rachel.[6] She said: "Beatrice, true praise of God; why helpest thou not him who loved thee so, that for thee he left the vulgar crowd? Hearest not thou the misery of his plaint? Seest thou not the death which combats him?" . . . None on earth were ever swift to seek their good, or flee their hurt, as I, after these words were uttered, to come down from my blessed seat; confiding in thy noble speech, which honours thee, and them who have heard it.'

"After saying this to me, she turned away her bright eyes weeping; by which she made me hasten more to come; and thus I came to thee, as she desired; took thee from before that savage beast, which bereft thee of the short way to the beautiful mountain. What is it then? why, why haltest thou? why lodgest in thy heart such coward fear? why art thou not bold and free, when three such blessed Ladies care for thee in the court of Heaven, and my words promise thee so much good?" As flowerets, by the nightly chillness bended down and closed, erect themselves all open on their stems when the sun whitens them: thus I did, with my fainting courage; and so much good daring ran into my heart, that I began as one set free: "O compassionate she, who succoured me! and courteous thou, who quickly didst obey the true words that she gave thee! Thou hast disposed my heart with such desire to go, by what thou sayest, that I have returned to my first purpose. Now go, for both have one will; thou guide, thou lord and master." Thus I spake to him; and he moving, I entered on the arduous and savage way.

4. The Virgin, symbol of Divine Mercy.
5. St. Lucy (Dante's patron saint), symbol of Illuminating Grace.
6. Rachel, symbol of Contemplation.

CANTO III

"Through me is the way into the doleful city; through me the
way into the eternal pain; through me the way among the people lost.
Justice moved my High Maker; Divine Power made me, Wisdom
Supreme, and Primal Love.[1] Before me were no things created, but
eternal; and eternal I endure: leave all hope, ye that enter."

These words, of colour obscure, saw I written above a gate;
whereat I: "Master, their meaning to me is hard."

And he to me, as one experienced: "Here must all distrust be left;
all cowardice must here be dead. We are come to the place where I told
thee thou shouldst see the wretched people, who have lost the good of
the intellect." And placing his hand on mine, with a cheerful countenance that comforted me, he led me into the secret things.

Here sighs, plaints, and deep wailings resounded through the star-
less air: it made me weep at first. Strange tongues, horrible outcries,
words of pain, tones of anger, voices deep and hoarse, and sounds of
hands amongst them, made a tumult, which turns itself unceasing in
that air for ever dyed, as sand when it eddies in a whirlwind. And I,
my head begirt with horror, said: "Master, what is this that I hear?
and who are these that seem so overcome with pain?"

And he to me: "This miserable mode the dreary souls of those
sustain, who lived without blame, and without praise. They are mixed
with that caitiff choir of the angels, who were not rebellious, nor were
faithful to God; but were for themselves. Heaven chased them forth
to keep its beauty from impair; and the deep Hell receives them not,
for the wicked would have some glory over them."

And I: "Master, what is so grievous to them, that makes them
lament thus bitterly?"

He answered: "I will tell it to thee very briefly. These have no
hope of death; and their blind life is so mean, that they are envious
of every other lot. Report of them the world permits not to exist; Mercy
and Justice disdains them: let us not speak of them; but look, and
pass."

And I, who looked, saw an ensign, which whirling ran so quickly
that it seemed to scorn all pause; and behind it came so long a train
of people, that I should never have believed death had undone so
many. After I had recognized some amongst them, I saw and knew

1. Power, Wisdom, and Love are the attributes of the Father, Son, and Holy
Ghost, respectively.

the shadow of him² who from cowardice made the great refusal. Forthwith I understood and felt assured, that this was the crew of caitiffs, hateful to God and to his enemies. These unfortunate, who never were alive, were naked, and sorely goaded by hornets and by wasps that were there. These made their faces stream with blood, which mixed with tears was gathered at their feet by loathsome worms.

And then, as I looked onwards, I saw people on the Shore of a great River: whereat I said: "Master, now grant that I may know who these are; and what usage makes them seem so ready to pass over, as I discern by the faint light."

And he to me: "The things shall be known to thee, when we stay our steps upon the joyless strand of Acheron."

Then, with eyes ashamed and downcast, fearing my words might have offended him, I kept myself from speaking till we reached the stream. And lo! an old man, white with ancient hair, comes towards us in a bark, shouting: "Woe to you, depraved spirits! hope not ever to see Heaven: I come to lead you to the other shore; into the eternal darkness; into fire and into ice. And thou who art there, alive, depart thee from these who are dead." But when he saw that I departed not, he said: "By other ways, by other ferries, not here, shalt thou pass over: a lighter boat must carry thee."

And my guide to him: "Charon, vex not thyself: thus it is willed there, where what is willed can be done; and ask no more." Then the woolly cheeks were quiet of the steersman on the livid marsh, who round his eyes had wheels of flame. But those spirits, who were foreworn and naked, changed colour and chattered with their teeth, soon as they heard the bitter words. They blasphemed God and their parents; the human kind; the place, the time, and origin of their seed, and of their birth. Then all of them together, sorely weeping, drew to the accursed shore, which awaits every man that fears not God. Charon the demon, with eyes of glowing coal, beckoning them, collects them all; smites with his oar whoever lingers. As the leaves of autumn fall off one after the other, till the branch sees all its spoils upon the ground: so one by one the evil seed of Adam cast themselves from that shore at signals, as the bird at its call. Thus they depart on the brown water; and ere they have landed on the other shore, again a fresh crowd collects on this.

"My son," said the courteous Master, "those who die under God's

2. Probably Pope Celestine V, elected Pope in 1294 at the age of eighty. He resigned after five months in office.

wrath, all assemble here from every country; and they are prompt
to pass the river, for Divine Justice spurs them so, that fear is changed
into desire. By this way no good spirit ever passes; and hence, if Charon
complains of thee, thou easily now mayest know the import of his
words." When he had ended, the dusky champaign trembled so violently, that the remembrance of my terror bathes me still with sweat.
The tearful ground gave out wind, which flashed forth a crimson light
that conquered all my senses; and I fell, like one who is seized with
sleep.

CANTO IV

A heavy thunder broke the deep sleep in my head; so that I started
like one who is awaked by force; and, having risen erect, I moved my
rested eyes around, and looked steadfastly to know the place in which
I was. True is it, that I found myself upon the brink of the dolorous
Valley of the Abyss, which gathers thunder of endless wailings. It was
so dark, profound, and cloudy, that, with fixing my look upon the bottom, I there discerned nothing.

"Now let us descend into the blind world here below," began the
Poet all pale; "I will be first, and thou shalt be second."

And I, who had remarked his colour, said: "How shall I come,
when thou fearest, who art wont to be my strength in doubt?"

And he to me: "The anguish of the people who are here below, on
my face depaints that pity, which thou takest for fear. Let us go; for
the length of way impels us." Thus he entered, and made me enter,
into the first circle that girds the abyss.

Here there was no plaint, that could be heard, except of sighs,
which caused the eternal air to tremble; and this arose from the sadness, without torment, of the crowds that were many and great, both of
children, and of women and men.

The good Master to me: "Thou askest not what spirits are these
thou seest? I wish thee to know, before thou goest farther, that they
sinned not; and though they have merit, it suffices not: for they had not
Baptism, which is the portal of the faith that thou believest; and seeing
they were before Christianity, they worshipped not God aright; and of
these am I myself. For such defects, and for no other fault, are we lost;
and only in so far afflicted, that without hope we live in desire."

Great sadness took me at the heart on hearing this; because I knew
men of much worth, who in that Limbo were suspense. "Tell me,

Master; tell me, Sir," I began, desiring to be assured of that Faith which conquers every error; "did ever any, by his own merit, or by others', go out from hence, that afterwards was blessed?"

And he, understanding my covert speech, replied: "I was new in this condition, when I saw a Mighty One[1] come to us, crowned with sign of victory. He took away from us the shade of our First Parent, of Abel his son, and that of Noah; of Moses the Legislator and obedient; Abraham the Patriarch; David the King; Israel with his father and his children, and with Rachel, for whom he did so much; and many others, and made them blessed; and I wish thee to know, that, before these, no human souls were saved."

We ceased not to go, though he was speaking; but passed the wood meanwhile, the wood, I say, of crowded spirits. Our way was not yet far since my slumber, when I saw a fire, which conquered a hemisphere of the darkness. We were still a little distant from it; yet not so distant, that I did not in part discern what honourable people occupied that place. "O thou, that honourest every science and art; who are these, who have such honour, that it separates them from the manner of the rest?"

And he to me: "The honoured name, which sounds of them, up in that life of thine, gains favours in heaven which thus advances them."

Meanwhile a voice was heard by me: "Honour the great Poet! His shade returns that was departed." After the voice had paused, and was silent, I saw four great shadows come to us; they had an aspect neither sad nor joyful.

The good Master began to speak: "Mark him with that sword in hand, who comes before the three as their lord: that is Homer, the sovereign Poet; the next who comes is Horace the satirist; Ovid is the third, and the last is Lucan.[2] Because each agrees with me in the name, which the one voice sounded, they do me honour: and therein they do well." Thus I saw assembled the goodly school of those lords of highest song, which, like an eagle, soars above the rest. After they had talked a space together, they turned to me with a sign of salutation; and my Master smiled thereat. And greatly more besides they honoured me, for they made me of their number, so that I was a sixth amid such intelligences. Thus we went onwards to the light, speaking things which it is well to pass in silence, as it was well to speak there where I was.

1. *a Mighty One,* Christ. The names of Christ and Mary are never uttered in Hell.

2. Lucan (A.D. 39-65) wrote an epic poem on the civil war between Caesar and Pompey.

We came to the foot of a Noble Castle, seven times circled with lofty Walls, defended round by a fair Rivulet. This we passed as solid land; through seven gates I entered with those sages; we reached a meadow of fresh verdure. On it were people with eyes slow and grave, of great authority in their appearance; they spoke seldom, with mild voices. Thus we retired on one of the sides, into a place open, luminous, and high, so that they could all be seen. There direct, upon the green enamel, were shown to me the great spirits, so that I glory within myself for having seen them. I saw Electra[3] with many companions: amongst whom I knew both Hector and Æneas; Cæsar armed, with the falcon eyes. I saw Camilla and Penthesilea on the other hand, and saw the Latian King, sitting with Lavinia his daughter. I saw that Brutus who expelled the Tarquin; Lucretia, Julia, Marcia, and Cornelia; and by himself apart, I saw the Saladin.[4] When I raised my eyelids a little higher, I saw the Master of those that know,[5] sitting amid a philosophic family. All regard him; all do him honour; here I saw Socrates and Plato, who before the rest stand nearest to him; Democritus, who ascribes the world to chance; Diogenes, Anaxagoras, and Thales; Empedocles, Heraclitus, and Zeno; and I saw the good collector of the qualities, Dioscorides[6] I mean; and saw Orpheus, Tully, Linus, and Seneca the moralist; Euclid the geometer, and Ptolemæus[7]; Hippocrates,[8] Avicenna, and Galen; Averroës, who made the great comment. I may not paint them all in full: for the long theme so chases me, that many times the word comes short of the reality.

The company of six diminishes to two; by another road the sage guide leads me, out of the quiet, into the trembling air; and I come to a part where there is naught that shines.

CANTO V

Thus I descended from the first circle down into the second, which encompasses less space, and so much greater pain, that it stings to

3. Electra and all those named in the following list are characters in classical legend, literature, and history.

4. Saladin (1137-1193) fought against the Crusaders and was defeated by Richard the Lion-Hearted. He was greatly admired by his enemies.

5. Aristotle. Names of other Greek philosophers follow.

6. *Dioscorides*, author of a medical work on the qualities of plants. *Tully*, Cicero. *Orpheus and Linus*, legendary Greek poets.

7. *Ptolemy*, the astronomer whose system of the universe was accepted by the Middle Ages and used by Dante.

8. Hippocrates and Galen are Greek physicians; Avicenna and Averroës are Arabic ones.

wailing. There Minos[1] sits horrific, and grins: examines the crimes
upon the entrance; judges, and sends according as he girds himself. I
say, that when the ill-born spirit comes before him, it confesses all; and
that sin-discerner sees what place in hell is for it, and with his tail
makes as many circles round himself as the degrees he will have it to
descend. Always before him stands a crowd of them; they go each in
its turn to judgment; they tell, and hear; and then are whirled
down.

"O thou who comest to the abode of pain!" said Minos to me, when
he saw me leaving the act of that great office; "look how thou enterest,
and in whom thou trustest; let not the wideness of the entrancy deceive
thee."

And my guide to him: "Why criest thou too? Hinder not his fated
going; thus it is willed there where what is willed can be done: and
ask no more."

Now begin the doleful notes to reach me; now am I come where
much lamenting strikes me. I came into a place void of all light, which
bellows like the sea in tempest, when it is combated by warring winds.
The hellish storm, which never rests, leads the spirits with its sweep;
whirling, and smiting it vexes them. When they arrive before the
ruin, there the shrieks, the moanings, and the lamentation; there they
blaspheme the divine power. I learnt that to such torment are doomed
the carnal sinners, who subject reason to lust. And as their wings bear
along the starlings, at the cold season, in large and crowded troop: so
that blast, the evil spirits; hither, thither, down, up, it leads them. No
hope ever comforts them, not of rest but even of less pain. And as the
cranes go chanting their lays, making a long streak of themselves in the
air: so I saw the shadows come, uttering wails, borne by that strife of
winds; whereat I said: "Master, who are those people, whom the black
air thus lashes?"

"The first of these concerning whom thou seekest to know," he
then replied, "was Empress of many tongues. With the vice of luxury
she was so broken, that she made lust and law alike in her decree, to
take away the blame she had incurred. She is Semiramis,[2] of whom we
read that she succeeded Ninus, and was his spouse; she held the land
which the Soldan rules. That other is she who slew herself in love, and
broke faith to the ashes of Sichæus; next comes luxurious Cleopatra.
Helena see, for whom so long a time of ill revolved; and see the great

1. *Minos*, a mythical judge of Crete, whom Virgil had already represented
as a judge in Hades.
2. *Semiramis*, Queen of Babylonia, which Dante confuses with Babylon in
Egypt.

Achilles, who fought at last with love[3]; see Paris, Tristan"; and more than a thousand shades he showed to me, and pointing with his finger, named to me those whom love had parted from our life.

After I had heard my teacher name the olden dames and cavaliers, pity came over me, and I was as if bewildered. I began: "Poet, willingly would I speak with those two that go together, and seem so light upon the wind." And he to me: "Thou shalt see when they are nearer to us; and do thou then entreat them by that love, which leads them; and they will come."

Soon as the wind bends them to us, I raised my voice: "O wearied souls! come to speak with us, if none denies it."

As doves called by desire, with raised and steady wings come through the air to their loved nest, borne by their will: so those spirits issued from the band where Dido is, coming to us through the malignant air; such was the force of my affectuous cry.

"O living creature, gracious and benign! that goest through the black air, visiting us who stained the earth with blood: if the King of the Universe were our friend, we would pray him for thy peace; seeing that thou hast pity of our perverse misfortune. Of that which it pleases thee to hear and to speak, we will hear and speak with you, whilst the wind, as now, is silent for us. The town,[4] where I was born, sits on the shore, where Po descends to rest with his attendant streams. Love, which is quickly caught in gentle heart, took him with the fair body of which I was bereft; and the manner still afflicts me. Love, which to no loved one permits excuse for loving, took me so strongly with delight in him, that, as thou seest, even now it leaves me not. Love led us to one death; Caïna[5] waits for him who quenched our life." These words from them were offered to us.

After I had heard those wounded souls, I bowed my face, and held it low until the Poet said to me: "What art thou thinking of?"

When I answered, I began: "Ah me! what sweet thoughts, what longing led them to the woeful pass!" Then I turned again to them;

3. Medieval legend told of a love-affair between Achilles and Polyxena, Paris' sister.

4. Ravenna, birthplace of Francesca da Rimini. She was married to Gianciotto Malatesta, and, according to one tale, was duped into believing that she was marrying his brother, Paolo, who acted as his proxy. An illicit affair between Paolo and Francesca was ended when Gianciotto found them together and killed them.

5. Caïna (named from Cain) is in the ninth circle of Hell, and is the place of those who have treacherously murdered their relatives. It "waits" because Gianciotto did not die until 1304, four years after the date of Dante's vision.

and I spoke, and began: "Francesca, thy torments make me weep with grief and pity. But tell me: in the time of the sweet sighs, by what and how love granted you to know the dubious desires?"

And she to me: "There is no greater pain than to recall a happy time in wretchedness; and this thy teacher knows. But if thou hast such desire to learn the first root of our love, I will do like one who weeps and tells. One day, for pastime, we read of Lancelot,[6] how love constrained him; we were alone, and without all suspicion. Several times that reading urged our eyes to meet, and changed the colour of our faces; but one moment alone it was that overcame us. When we read how the fond smile was kissed by such a lover, he, who shall never be divided from me, kissed my mouth all trembling: the book, and he who wrote it, was a Galeotto; that day we read in it no farther." Whilst the one spirit thus spake, the other wept so, that I fainted with pity, as if I had been dying; and fell, as a dead body falls.

CANTOS VI-IX

[Dante comes to himself in the third circle, where gluttons are punished by lying in a mire under a continual storm of hail and snow while Cerberus rends them. In the fourth circle the avaricious and the prodigal are identically punished by their own mutual hatred. The fifth circle contains the Stygian Lake, where the wrathful and the sullen punish one another. The voyagers are ferried across it to the City of Dis, but at its gates a host of fallen angels refuse them admittance. Dante is afraid, and Virgil worried, until an angel comes to rout the demons and open the gate. In the sixth circle the heretics are enclosed in burning tombs, and Dante and his guide walk between these tombs and the walls of the city.]

CANTO X

Now by a secret path, between the city-wall and the torments, my Master goes on, and I behind him. "O Virtue supreme! who through the impious circles thus wheelest me, as it pleases thee," I began; "speak to me, and satisfy my wishes. Might those people, who lie within the

6. The incident described is in an Old French romance telling the story of Lancelot's love for Guenivere, King Arthur's queen. Galeotto was the knight who served them as a go-between; thus the use of his name below is exactly parallel to *pander*, from Pandarus, who performed a similar office for Troilus and Cressida.

sepulchres, be seen? the covers are all raised, and none keeps guard."

And he to me: "All shall be closed up, when they return here with the bodies which they have left above. In this part are entombed with Epicurus all his followers, who make the soul die with the body. Therefore to the question, which thou askest me, thou shalt soon have satisfaction here within; and also to the wish which thou holdest from me."[1]

And I: "Kind Guide, I do not keep my heart concealed from thee, except for brevity of speech, to which thou hast ere now disposed me."

"O Tuscan! who through the city of fire goest alive, speaking thus decorously; may it please thee to stop in this place. Thy speech clearly shows thee a native of that noble country, which perhaps I vexed too much." Suddenly this sound issued from one of the chests; whereat in fear I drew a little closer to my Guide.

And he said to me: "Turn thee round; what art thou doing? lo there Farinata![2] who has raised himself erect; from the girdle upwards thou shalt see him all."

Already I had fixed my look on his; and he rose upright with breast and countenance, as if he entertained great scorn of Hell; and the bold and ready hands of my Guide pushed me amongst the sepultures to him, saying: "Let thy words be numbered."

When I was at the foot of his tomb, he looked at me a little; and then, almost contemptuously, he asked me: "Who were thy ancestors?"

I, being desirous to obey, concealed it not; but opened the whole to him: whereupon he raised his brows a little; then he said: "Fiercely adverse were they to me, and to my progenitors, and to my party; so that twice I scattered them."

"If they were driven forth, they returned from every quarter, both times," I answered him; "but yours have not rightly learnt that art."

Then, beside him, there rose a shadow, visible to the chin; it had raised itself, I think, upon its knees. It looked around me, as if it had a wish to see whether some one were with me; but when all its expectation was quenched, it said, weeping: "If through this blind prison thou

1. Dante is thinking of Farinata, who appears a moment later, but he does not make his request specific.
2. Farinata degli Uberti was the father-in-law of Guido Cavalcanti, Dante's closest friend, whose father, Cavalcante de' Cavalcanti, is imprisoned in the same tomb with him. Farinata was the head of one of the most important Ghibelline families of Florence, and was sufficiently hated by the Guelfs that, after their final victory, he was specifically excluded from all amnesties.

goest by height of genius, where is my son and why is he not with thee?"

And I to him: "Of myself I come not: he, that waits yonder, leads me through this place; whom perhaps thy Guido held in disdain."[3] Already his words and the manner of his punishment had read his name to me: hence my answer was so full. Rising instantly erect, he cried: "How saidst thou: he had? lives he not still? does not the sweet light strike his eyes?" When he perceived that I made some delay in answering, supine he fell again, and showed himself no more.

But that other, magnanimous, at whose desire I had stopped, changed not his aspect, nor moved his neck, nor bent his side. "And if," continuing his former words, he said, "they have learnt that art badly, it more torments me than this bed. But the face of the Queen, who reigns here, shall not be fifty times[4] rekindled ere thou shalt know the hardness of that art. And so mayest thou once return to the sweet world, tell me why that people is so fierce against my kindred in all its laws?"

Whereat I to him: "The havoc, and the great slaughter, which dyed the Arbia red, causes such orations in our temple."

And sighing, he shook his head; then said: "In that I was not single; nor without cause, assuredly, should I have stirred with the others; but I was single there, where all consented to extirpate Florence, I alone with open face defended her."[5]

"Ah! so may thy seed sometime have rest," I prayed him, "solve the knot which has here involved my judgment. It seems that you see beforehand what time brings with it, if I rightly hear; and have a different manner with the present."

"Like one who has imperfect vision, we see the things," he said, "which are remote from us; so much light the Supreme Ruler still gives to us; when they draw nigh, or are, our intellect is altogether void; and except what others bring us, we know nothing of your human state. Therefore thou mayest understand that all our knowledge shall be dead, from that moment when the portal of the Future shall be closed."

Then, as compunctious for my fault, I said: "Now will you there-

---

3. Guido's disdain for Virgil has never been satisfactorily explained.

4. In Hell, "the sun is silent." Thus the time before Dante's exile is measured in lunar months.

5. These lines refer to the factional strife in Florence. Farinata's party had routed their enemies at a battle on the Arbia River. It actually was proposed that Florence be razed to the ground, and only the intercession of Farinata defeated this plan.

fore tell that fallen one, that his child is still joined to the living. And if
I was mute before, at the response, let him know, it was because my
thoughts already were in that error which you have resolved for me."...
Therewith he hid himself; and I towards the ancient Poet turned my
steps, revolving that saying which seemed hostile to me.

He moved on; and then, as we were going, he said to me: "Why
art thou so bewildered?" And I satisfied him in his question. "Let thy
memory retain what thou hast heard against thee," that Sage exhorted
me; "and now mark here"; and he raised his finger. "When thou shalt
stand before the sweet ray of that Lady, whose bright eye seeth all, from
her shalt thou know the journey of thy life." Then to the sinister hand
he turned his feet; we left the wall, and went towards the middle, by a
path that strikes into a valley, which even up there annoyed us with its
fetor.

CANTO XI

Upon the edge of a high bank, formed by large broken stones in a
circle, we came above a still more cruel throng; and here, because of
the horrible excess of stench which the deep abyss throws out, we approached it under cover of a great monument. . . . "Our descent we
must delay, till sense be somewhat used to the dismal blast, and then
we shall not heed it."

Thus the Master; and I said to him: "Find some compensation,
that the time may not be lost." And he: "Thou seest that I intend it.
My Son, within these stones," he then began to say, "are three circlets
in gradation, like those thou leavest. They all are filled with spirits
accurst; but, that the sight of these hereafter may of itself suffice thee,
hearken how and wherefore they are pent up. Of all malice, which
gains hatred in Heaven, the end is injury; and every such end, either
by force or by fraud, aggrieveth others. But because fraud is a vice
peculiar to man, it more displeases God; and therefore the fraudulent
are placed beneath, and more pain assails them. All the first circle[1] is
for the violent; but as violence may be done to three persons, it is
formed and distinguished into three rounds. To God, to one's self, and
to one's neighbour, may violence be done; I say in them and in their
things, as thou shalt hear with evident discourse. By force, death and
painful wounds may be inflicted upon one's neighbour; and upon his

1. The first circle of the three remaining, and therefore the seventh circle of
Hell. The "rounds" mentioned below are subdivisions of this circle.

substance, devastations, burnings, and injurious extortions: wherefore
the first round torments all homicides and every one who strikes
maliciously, all plunderers and robbers, in different bands. A man may
lay violent hand upon himself, and upon his property: and therefore in
the second round must every one repent in vain who deprives himself
of your world, gambles away and dissipates his wealth, and weeps there
where he should be joyous. Violence may be done against the Deity, in
the heart denying and blaspheming Him; and disdaining Nature and
her bounty: and hence the smallest round seals with its mark both
Sodom and Cahors,[2] and all who speak with disparagement of God in
their hearts.

"Fraud, which gnaws every conscience, a man may practise upon
one who confides in him; and upon him who reposes no confidence.
This latter mode seems only to cut off the bond of love which Nature
makes: hence in the second circle nests hypocrisy, flattery, sorcerers,
cheating, theft and simony, panders, barrators, and like filth. In the
other mode is forgotten that love which Nature makes, and also that
which afterwards is added, giving birth to special trust: hence in the
smallest circle, at the centre of the universe and seat of Dis, every
traitor is eternally consumed."

And I: "Master, thy discourse proceeds most clearly, and ex-
cellently distinguishes this gulf, and the people that possess it. But tell
me: Those of the fat marsh; those whom the wind leads, and whom
the rain beats; and those who meet with tongues so sharp,—why are
they not punished in the red city,[3] if God's anger be upon them? and
if not, why are they in such a plight?" And he said to me: "Wherefore
errs thy mind so much beyond its wont? or are thy thoughts turned
somewhere else? Rememberest thou not the words wherewith thy
Ethics[4] treat of the three dispositions which Heaven wills not, incontinence, malice, and mad bestiality? and how incontinence less offends
God, and receives less blame? If thou rightly considerest this doctrine,
and recallest to thy memory who they are that suffer punishment above,
without, thou easily wilt see who they are separated from these fell
spirits, and why, with less anger, Divine Justice strikes them." "O Sun!
who healest all troubled vision, thou makest so glad when thou re-
solvest me, that to doubt is not less grateful than to know. . . ."

2. Sodom and Cahors represent unnatural vice and usury.
3. Why are the sinners whom we have already seen not punished in the
City of Dis?
4. Aristotle's *Nichomachean Ethics*.

CANTOS XII-XXV

[Dante and Virgil proceed through the three divisions of the seventh circle, in the last of which Dante talks with his old and re-spected teacher, Brunetto Latini. A vast precipice separates this circle from the eighth, and they descend it on the back of the monster Geryon.

In the eighth circle, or Malebolge, simple fraud is punished—that is, fraud which does not involve a violation of trust. Malebolge con-tains ten concentric divisions in which, in descending order, seducers and panders, flatterers, simonists, diviners, peculators in public office, hypocrites, thieves, evil counsellors, sowers of dissension, and falsifiers are given various punishments. For example, the peculators are kept submerged in boiling pitch and are torn by demons if they appear at the surface (Dante and Virgil have a narrow escape from these demons); and the hypocrites drag themselves along eternally burdened with mantles of gilded lead. After leaving the thieves, but before ar-riving at the end of Malebolge, the poet comes to the evil counsellors.]

CANTO XXVI

Joy, Florence, since thou art so great that over sea and land thou beatest thy wings, and thy name through Hell expands itself! Among the thieves I found five such, thy citizens; whereat shame comes on me, and thou to great honour mountest not thereby. But if the truth is dreamed of near the morning, thou shalt feel ere long what Prato,[1] not to speak of others, craves for thee. And if it were already come, it would not be too early; so were it! since indeed it must be: for it will weigh the heavier on me as I grow older.

We departed thence; and, by the stairs which the curbstones had made for us to descend before, my Guide remounted and drew me up; and pursuing our solitary way among the jags and branches of the cliff, the foot without the hand sped not. I sorrowed then, and sorrow now again when I direct my memory to what I saw; and curb my genius more than I am wont, lest it run where Virtue guides it not; so that, if kindly star or something better have given to me the good, I may not grudge myself that gift.

1. *Prato*, a cardinal sent to Florence by the Pope in a vain effort to reconcile the warring factions. He placed the city under an interdict, and several disasters occurring shortly thereafter were taken to be the results of the curse of the Church.

As many fireflies as the peasant who is resting on the hill—at the time that he who lights the world least hides his face from us,[2] when the fly yields to the gnat—sees down along the valley, there perchance where he gathers grapes and tills: with flames thus numerous the eighth chasm was all gleaming, as I perceived, so soon as I came to where the bottom showed itself. And as he,[3] who was avenged by the bears, saw Elijah's chariot at its departure, when the horses rose erect to heaven,—for he could not so follow it with his eyes as to see other than the flame alone, like a little cloud, ascending up: thus moved each of those flames along the gullet of the fosse, for none of them shows the theft, and every flame steals a sinner.

I stood upon the bridge, having risen so to look, that, if I had not caught a rock, I should have fallen down without being pushed. And the Guide, who saw me thus attent, said: "Within those fires are the spirits; each swathes himself with that which burns him."

"Master," I replied, "from hearing thee I feel more certain; but had already discerned it to be so, and already wished to say to thee: who is in that fire, which comes so parted at the top, as if it rose from the pyre where Eteocles with his brother was placed?"[4] He answered me: "Within it there Ulysses is tortured, and Diomed[5]; and thus they run together in punishment, as erst in wrath; and in their flame they groan for the ambush of the horse, that made the door by which the noble seed of the Romans came forth; within it they lament the artifice, whereby Deidamia[6] in death still sorrows for Achilles; and there for the Palladium[7] they suffer punishment."

"If they within those sparks can speak," said I, "Master! I pray thee much, and repray that my prayer may equal a thousand, deny me not to wait until the horned flame comes hither; thou seest how with desire I bend me towards it."

And he to me: "Thy request is worthy of much praise, and therefore I accept it; but do thou refrain thy tongue. Let me speak: for I

2. In the summer, when the sun is visible longest.
3. *he*, Elisha. The children who made fun of his baldness were eaten by bears.
4. According to a late version of the story, recorded by Statius, their hatred continued after death, so that even the flames of their funeral pyre were divided.
5. *Diomed*, one of the Greek heroes of the Trojan War.
6. In order to keep Achilles from going to Troy, his mother hid him, disguised as a woman, at the court of King Lycomedes, whose daughter, Deidamia, bore him a son. Ulysses found him there and persuaded him to go to Troy. Deidamia, thus abandoned, died of grief.
7. The Palladium was an image of Pallas Athene which protected Troy. It was stolen by Ulysses and Diomed.

have conceived what thou wishest; and they, perhaps, because they were Greeks, might disdain thy words."

After the flame had come where time and place seemed fitting to my Guide, I heard him speak in this manner: "O ye, two in one fire! if I merited of you whilst I lived, if I merited of you much or little, when on earth I wrote the High Verses, move ye not; but let the one of you tell where he, having lost himself, went to die."

The greater horn of the ancient flame began to shake itself, murmuring, just like a flame that struggles with the wind. Then carrying to and fro the top, as if it were the tongue that spake, threw forth a voice, and said: "When I departed from Circe, who beyond a year detained me there near Gaeta, ere Æneas thus had named it, neither fondness for my son, nor reverence for my aged father, nor the due love that should have cheered Penelope, could conquer in me the ardour that I had to gain experience of the world, and of human vice and worth; I put forth on the deep open sea, with but one ship, and with that small company, which had not deserted me. Both the shores I saw as far as Spain, far as Morocco; and saw Sardinia and the other isles which that sea bathes round. I and my companions were old and tardy, when we came to that narrow pass, where Hercules assigned his landmarks to hinder man from venturing farther; on the right hand, I left Seville; on the other, had already left Ceuta. 'O brothers!' I said, 'who through a hundred thousand dangers have reached the West, deny not, to this the brief vigil of your senses that remains, experience of the unpeopled world behind the Sun. Consider your origin: ye were not formed to live like brutes, but to follow virtue and knowledge.' With this brief speech I made my companions so eager for the voyage, that I could hardly then have checked them; and, turning the poop towards morning, we of our oars made wings for the foolish flight, always gaining on the left. Night already saw the other pole, with all its stars; and ours so low, that it rose not from the ocean floor. Five times the light beneath the Moon had been rekindled and quenched as oft, since we had entered on the arduous passage, when there appeared to us a Mountain,[8] dim with distance; and to me it seemed the highest I had ever seen. We joyed, and soon our joy was turned to grief: for a tempest rose from the new land, and struck the forepart of our ship. Three times it made her whirl round with all the waters; at the fourth, made the poop rise up and prow go down, as pleased Another, till the sea was closed above us."

8. *Mountain*, Purgatory.

CANTOS XXVII - XXXII

[The travelers complete the eighth circle by visiting the sowers of dissension and the falsifiers. Then they come to the ninth and deepest circle of hell, which is surrounded by giants and reserved for traitors —that is, for fraud involving a breach of trust. Four descending classes are distinguished: traitors against kindred, against country, against hospitality, and against lords and benefactors. All traitors are frozen in ice, and after seeing those who betrayed their kindred, Dante and his guide come upon two frozen into the same hole. One of them is furiously gnawing at the base of the other's skull, and the poet asks him to explain his hatred.]

CANTO XXXIII

From the fell repast that sinner raised his mouth, wiping it upon the hair of the head he had laid waste behind. Then he began: "Thou willest that I renew desperate grief, which wrings my heart, even at the very thought, before I tell thereof. But if my words are to be a seed, that may bear fruit of infamy to the traitor whom I gnaw, thou shalt see me speak and weep at the same time. I know not who thou mayest be, nor by what mode thou hast come down here; but, when I hear thee, in truth thou seemest to me a Florentine. Thou hast to know that I was Count Ugolino,[1] and this the Archbishop Ruggieri; now I will tell thee why I am such a neighbour to him. That by the effect of his ill devices I, confiding in him, was taken and thereafter put to death, it is not necessary to say. But that which thou canst not have learnt, that is, how cruel was my death, thou shalt hear—and know if he has offended me. A narrow hole within the mew, which from me has the title of Famine, and in which others yet must be shut up, had through its opening already shown me several moons, when I slept the evil sleep that rent for me the curtain of the future. This man seemed to me lord and master, chasing the wolf and his whelps, upon the mountain for which the Pisans cannot see Lucca.

1. In 1288, Pisa was divided into three factions, one of which was led by Count Ugolino, and another by Archbishop Ruggieri. These two combined forces to oust the third faction, and then Ugolino took over the city, with Ruggieri as a mere puppet. The latter stirred up public resentment about Ugolino's earlier (apparently treasonable) surrender of some castles to the Florentines; and then, with popular support, seized Ugolino, his two sons, and his two grandsons, and dealt with them as here described. In telling the story, Ugolino does not distinguish between his sons and his grandsons.

With hounds meagre, keen, and dexterous, he had put in front of him
Gualandi with Sismondi, and with Lanfranchi.[2] After short course,
the father and his sons seemed to me weary; and methought I saw their
flanks torn by the sharp teeth. When I awoke before the dawn, I
heard my sons who were with me, weeping in their sleep, and asking
for bread. Thou art right cruel, if thou dost not grieve already at the
thought of what my heart foreboded; and if thou weepest not, at what
art thou used to weep? They were now awake, and the hour approaching at which our food used to be brought us, and each was anxious
from his dream, and below I heard the outlet of the horrible tower
locked up: whereat I looked into the faces of my sons, without uttering
a word. I did not weep: so stony grew I within; they wept; and my
little Anselm said: 'Thou lookest so, father, what ails thee?' But I shed
no tear, nor answered all that day, nor the next night, till another sun
came forth upon the world. When a small ray was sent into the doleful
prison, and I discerned in their four faces the aspect of my own, I
bit on both my hands for grief. And they, thinking that I did it from
desire of eating, of a sudden rose up, and said: 'Father, it will give us
much less pain, if thou wilt eat of us: thou didst put upon us this
miserable flesh, and do thou strip it off.' Then I calmed myself, in
order not to make them more unhappy; that day and the next we all
were mute. Ah, hard earth! why didst thou not open? When we had
come to the fourth day, Gaddo threw himself stretched out at my feet,
saying: 'My father! why don't you help me?' There he died; and
even as thou seest me, saw I the three fall one by one, between the
fifth day and the sixth: whence I betook me, already blind, to groping
over each, and for three days called them, after they were dead; then
fasting had more power than grief."[3] When he had spoken this, with
eyes distorted he seized the miserable skull again with his teeth, which
as a dog's were strong upon the bone. . . .

   We went farther on, where the frost ruggedly inwraps another
people, not bent downwards, but all reversed. The very weeping there
allows them not to weep; and the grief, which finds impediment upon
their eyes, turns inward to increase the agony: for their first tears form
a knot, and, like crystal vizors, fill up all the cavity beneath their eye-
brows. And although, as from a callus, through the cold all feeling
had departed from my face, it now seemed to me as if I felt some

   2. Families supporting Archbishop Ruggieri.
   3. Grief could not kill Ugolino, but starvation could.

wind; whereat I: "Master, who moves this? Is not all heat extinguished here below?"

Whence he to me: "Soon shalt thou be where thine eye itself, seeing the cause which rains the blast, shall answer thee in this."

And one of the wretched shadows of the icy crust cried out to us: "O souls, so cruel that the last post of all is given to you! Remove the hard veils from my face, that I may vent the grief, which stuffs my heart, a little, ere the weeping freeze again."

Wherefore I to him: "If thou wouldst have me aid thee, tell me who thou art; and if I do not extricate thee, may I have to go to the bottom of the ice."

He answered therefore: "I am Friar Alberigo,[4] I am he of the fruits from the ill garden, who here receive dates for my figs." "Ha!" said I to him, "then art thou dead already?" And he to me: "How my body stands in the world above, I have no knowledge. Such privilege has this Ptolomæa,[5] that oftentimes the soul falls down hither, ere Atropos[6] impels it. And that thou more willingly mayest rid the glazen tears from off my face, know that forthwith, when the soul betrays, as I did, her body is taken from her by a Demon who thereafter rules it, till its time has all revolved. She falls rushing to this cistern; and perhaps the body of this other shade, which winters here behind me, is still apparent on the earth above. Thou must know it, if thou art but now come down: it is Ser Branca d'Oria[7]; and many years have passed since he was thus shut up."

"I believe," said I to him, "that thou deceivest me: for Branca d'Oria never died; and eats, and drinks, and sleeps, and puts on clothes."

"In the ditch above, of the Malebranche," said he, "there where the tenacious pitch is boiling, Michael Zanche had not yet arrived, when this man left a Devil in his stead in the body of himself, and of one of his kindred who did the treachery along with him. But reach

---

4. To avenge a blow given him by his brother Manfred, Friar Alberigo invited Manfred and his son to a banquet, and at the prearranged signal of the order, "Bring in the fruit," had them killed by hired murderers. The "evil fruit" of Friar Alberigo became proverbial.

5. *Ptolomaea*, the section of Hell reserved for traitors to their friends and guests. The name is derived from the biblical Ptolemy, a captain of Jericho, who invited guests into his castle and murdered them there.

6. *Atropos*, the Fate that cuts the thread of human life.

7. With the aid of a relative, Branca d'Oria murdered his father-in-law, Michel Zanche, at a banquet. Zanche is higher up in hell, boiling in pitch with the other barrators in Malebranche.

hither thy hand: open my eyes"; and I opened them not for him: and to be rude to him was courtesy. . . .

CANTO XXXIV

"*Vexilla Regis prodeunt inferni*[1] towards us: therefore look in front of thee," my Master said, "if thou discernest him." As, when a thick mist breathes, or when the night comes on our hemisphere, a mill, which the wind turns, appears at distance: such an edifice did I now seem to see; and, for the wind, shrunk back behind my Guide, because no other shed was there. Already I had come (and with fear I put it into verse) where the souls were wholly covered, and shone through like straw in glass. Some are lying; some stand upright, this on its head, and that upon its soles; another, like a bow, bends face to feet. When we had proceeded on so far, that it pleased my Guide to show to me the Creature which was once so fair, he took himself from before me, and made me stop, saying: "Lo Dis!"[2] and lo the place where it behooves thee arm thyself with fortitude." How icy chill and hoarse I then became, ask not, O Reader! for I write it not, because all speech would fail to tell. I did not die, and did not remain alive: now think for thyself, if thou hast any grain of ingenuity, what I became, deprived of both death and life.

The Emperor of the dolorous realm, from mid breast stood forth out of the ice; and I in size am liker to a giant, than the giants are to his arms: mark now how great that whole must be, which corresponds to such a part. If he was once as beautiful as he is ugly now, and lifted up his brows against his Maker, well may all affliction come from him. Oh how great a marvel seemed it to me, when I saw three faces on his head! The one in front, and it was fiery red; the others were two, that were adjoined to this, above the very middle of each shoulder; and they were joined at his crest; and the right seemed between white and yellow; the left was such to look on, as they who come from where the Nile descends.[3] Under each there issued forth two mighty wings, of size befitting such a bird: sea-sails I never saw so broad. No plumes had they; but were in form and texture like a bat's: and he was flap-

1. "The banners of the King of Hell advance" (Latin). This is a parody of the first line of a medieval hymn used for the Easter procession.
2. *Dis*, properly a part of Hell, is here used as a name for Satan.
3. The three faces of Satan represent, respectively, impotence, ignorance, and hatred; thus they are the infernal antithesis of the attributes of the Trinity —power, wisdom, and love.

ping them, so that three winds went forth from him. Thereby Cocytus all was frozen; with six eyes he wept, and down three chins gushed tears and bloody foam. In every mouth he champed a sinner with his teeth, like a brake; so that he thus kept three of them in torment. To the one in front, the biting was nought, compared with the tearing: for at times the back of him remained quite stript of skin. "That soul up there, which suffers greatest punishment," said the Master, "is Judas Iscariot, he who has his head within, and outside plies his legs. Of the other two, who have their heads beneath, that one, who hangs from the black visage, is Brutus: see how he writhes himself, and utters not a word; and the other is Cassius, who seems so stark of limb. But night is reascending; and now must we depart: for we have seen the whole."

As he desired, I clasped his neck; and he took opportunity of time and place; and when the wings were opened far, applied him to the shaggy sides, and then from shag to shag descended down, between the tangled hair and frozen crusts. When we had come to where the thigh revolves just on the swelling of the haunch, my Guide with labour and with difficulty turned his head where he had had his feet before, and grappled on the hair, as one who mounts; so that I thought we were returning into Hell again. "Hold thee fast! for by such stairs," said my Guide, panting like a man forspent, "must we depart from so much ill." Thereafter through the opening of a rock he issued forth, and put me on its brim to sit; then towards me he stretched his wary step. I raised my eyes, and thought to see Lucifer as I had left him; and saw him with the legs turned upwards; and the gross people who see not what that point is which I had passed, let them judge if I grew perplexed then. "Rise up!" said the Master, "upon thy feet: the way is long, and difficult the road. . . ." It was no palace-hall, there where we stood, but natural dungeon with an evil floor and want of light.

"Before I pluck myself from the Abyss," said I when risen up, "O Master! speak to me a little, to draw me out of error. Where is the ice? and this, how is he fixed thus upside down? and how, in so short a time, has the Sun from eve to morn made transit?"

And he to me: "Thou imaginest that thou art still upon the other side of the centre, where I caught hold on the hair of the evil Worm which pierces through the world. Thou wast on that side, so long as I descended; when I turned myself, thou then didst pass the point to which all gravities from every part are drawn; and now thou art arrived beneath the hemisphere opposed to that which canopies the great dry land, and underneath whose summit was consumed the Man, who without sin was born and lived; thou hast thy feet upon a little sphere, which forms the other face of the Judecca.[4] Here it is morn, when it is evening there; and this Fiend, who made a ladder for us with his hair, is still fixed as he was before. On this side fell he down from Heaven; and the land, which erst stood out here, through fear of him veiled itself with sea, and came to our hemisphere; and perhaps, in order to escape from him, that which on this side appears left here the empty space, and upwards rushed."

Down there, from Beelzebub as far removed as his tomb extends, is a space, not known by sight but by the sound of a rivulet[5] descending in it, along the hollow of a rock which it has eaten out with tortuous course and slow declivity. The Guide and I entered by that hidden road, to return into the bright world; and, without caring for any rest, we mounted up, he first and I second, so far that I distinguished through a round opening the beauteous things which Heaven bears; and thence we issued out, again to see the Stars.

PURGATORY

CANTO I

To course o'er better waters now hoists sail the little bark of my wit, leaving behind her a sea so cruel. And I will sing of that second realm, where the human spirit is purged and becomes worthy to ascend to Heaven. But here let dead poesy rise up again, O holy Muses, since yours am I, and here let Calliope[1] rise somewhat, accompanying my song with that strain whose stroke the wretched Pies felt so that they despaired of pardon.

Sweet hue of orient sapphire which was gathering on the clear forehead of the sky, pure even to the first circle, to mine eyes restored delight, soon as I issued forth from the dead air which had afflicted eyes and heart. . . . I turned me to the right hand, and set my mind

4. *Judecca*, the pit of Hell, named for Judas.
5. *rivulet*, the River of Lethe, which bears the memory of sin from Purgatory to Hell.
1. *Calliope*, the Muse of epic poetry. The nine daughters of King Pierus challenged the nine Muses to a contest and were defeated; they were changed into magpies as a punishment.

on the other pole, and saw four stars[2] never yet seen save by the first people. The heavens seemed to rejoice in their flames. O Northern widowed clime, since thou art bereft of beholding them! When I was parted from gazing at them, turning me a little to the other pole, there whence the Wain[3] had already disappeared, I saw near me an old man[4] solitary, worthy of such great reverence in his mien, that no son owes more to a father. Long he wore his beard and mingled with white hair, like unto his locks of which a double list fell on his breast. The rays of the four holy lights adorned his face so with brightness, that I beheld him as were the sun before him.

"Who are ye that against the dark stream have fled the eternal prison?" said he, moving those venerable plumes. "Who hath guided you? or who was a lamp unto you issuing forth from the deep night that ever maketh black the infernal vale? Are the laws of the pit thus broken, or is there some new counsel changed in Heaven that being damned ye come to my rocks?"

Then did my Leader lay hold on me, and with words, and with hand, and with signs, made reverent my knees and brow. Then answered him: "Of myself I came not. A lady came down from Heaven through whose prayers I succoured this man with my company. But since it is thy will that more be unfolded of our state, how it truly is, my will it cannot be that thou be denied. He hath ne'er seen the last hour,[5] but by his madness was so near to it, that very short time there was to turn. Even as I said, I was sent to him to rescue him, and no other way there was but this along which I have set me. I have shown him all the guilty people, and now do purpose showing those spirits that purge them under thy charge. How I have brought him, 'twere long to tell thee: Virtue descends from on high which aids me to guide him to see thee and to hear thee. Now may it please thee to be gracious unto his coming: he seeketh freedom, which is so precious, as he knows who giveth up life for her. Thou knowest it; since for her sake death was not bitter to thee in Utica, where thou leftest the raiment which at the great day shall be so bright. The eternal laws by us are not vio-

2. These stars represent the virtues of prudence, justice, fortitude, and temperance. Dante either invented them or had heard of the Southern Cross. The Southern Hemisphere is supposed to have been uninhabited since the expulsion of Adam and Eve from the Garden of Eden.

3. the Wain, Ursa Major, the Great Bear, or Big Dipper.

4. Cato of Utica, who committed suicide rather than surrender himself and his principles, is praised by Virgil, Lucan, and Dante (in other writings) as a type of moral liberty and unswerving virtue.

5. last hour, both bodily and spiritual death.

lated, for he doth live and Minos binds me not; but I am of the circle where are the chaste eyes of thy Marcia,[6] who visibly yet doth pray thee, O holy breast, that thou hold her for thine own: for love of her then incline thee unto us. Let us go through thy seven kingdoms: thanks of thee I will bear back to her, if thou deign to be mentioned there below."

"Marcia was so pleasing to mine eyes while I was yonder," said he then, "that every grace she willed of me I did. Now that she dwells beyond the evil stream, no more may she move me, by that law which was made when I thence came forth. But if a heavenly lady moves and directs thee, as thou sayest, no need is there for flattery: let it suffice thee that in her name thou askest me. Go then, and look that thou gird this man with a smooth rush,[7] and that thou bathe his face so that all filth may thence be wiped away: for 'twere not meet with eye obscured by any mist to go before the first minister of those that are of Paradise. This little isle all round about the very base, there, where the wave beats it, bears rushes on the soft mud. No other plant that would put forth leaf or harden can live there, because it yields not to the buffetings. Then be not this way your return; the sun, which now is rising, will show you how to take the mount at an easier ascent."

So he vanished; and I uplifted me without speaking, and drew me all back to my Leader, and directed mine eyes to him. He began: "Son, follow thou my steps: turn we back, for this way the plain slopes down to its low bounds." The dawn was vanquishing the breath of morn which fled before her, so that from afar I recognized the trembling of the sea. We paced along the lonely plain, as one who returns to his lost road, and, till he reach it, seems to go in vain. When we came there where the dew is striving with the sun, being at a place where, in the cool air, slowly it is scattered; both hands outspread, gently my Master laid upon the sweet grass; wherefore I who was ware of his purpose, raised towards him my tear-stained cheeks: there made he all revealed my hue which Hell had hidden. We came then on to the desert shore, that never saw man navigate its waters who thereafter knew return. There he girded me even as it pleased Another: O marvel! that such as he plucked the lowly plant, even such did it forthwith spring up again, there whence he tore it.

6. Marcia was Cato's second wife, whom he yielded to a friend and remarried after the friend's death. Elsewhere Dante makes of Marcia's return to Cato an allegory of the righteous soul's return to God.
7. The rush is a symbol of humility.

CANTOS II - VIII

[A boat piloted by an angel arrives, bearing souls to Purgatory. Among them is Dante's friend, the musician Casella, who, at Dante's request, begins a song for the group; but Cato rebukes them for losing time. They start up the steep slope of the base of the mountain of purgatory, stopping on the way to talk to Manfred, Sordello, and other spirits. Here wander those who died excommunicate or who delayed repentance until death, and they must wait long before leaving the ante-purgatory and being admitted to the mountain itself. Learning that Dante is still living, they entreat his prayers and those of their friends as a means of shortening their period of exclusion. In his sleep Dante is borne to the gate of Purgatory proper.]

CANTO IX

. . . Alone beside me was my Comfort, and the sun was already more than two hours high, and mine eyes were turned to the sea. "Have no fear," said my Lord, "make thee secure, for we are at a good spot: hold not back, but put out all thy strength. Thou art now arrived at Purgatory; see there the rampart that compasseth it around; see the entrance there where it seems cleft. Erewhile, in the dawn which precedes the day, when thy soul was sleeping within thee upon the flowers wherewith down below is adorned, came a lady and said: 'I am Lucy, let me take this man who sleepeth, so will I prosper him on his way.' . . . She took thee, and as day was bright, came on upward, and I followed in her track. Here she placed thee; and first her fair eyes did show to me that open entrance; then she and sleep together went away." As doth a man who in dread is reassured, and who changes his fear to comfort after the truth is revealed to him, I changed me; and when my Leader saw me freed from care, he moved up by the rampart, and I following, towards the height.

Reader, well thou seest how I exalt my subject; therefore marvel thou not if with greater art I sustain it. We drew nigh, and were at a place, whence there where first appeared to me a break just like a fissure which divides a wall, I espied a gate, and three steps beneath to go to it, of divers colours, and a warder[1] who as yet spake no word. And as more I opened mine eyes there, I saw him seated upon the top-

---

1. The warder represents the priest hearing confession, and he holds in his hand the sword of divine justice, which is inscrutable to human eyes.

most step, such in his countenance that I endured him not; and in his hand he held a naked sword which reflected the rays so towards us, that I directed mine eyes to it oft in vain.

"Tell, there where ye stand, what would ye?" he began to say; "where is the escort? Beware lest coming upward be to your hurt!"

"A heavenly lady who well knows these things," my Master answered him, "even now did say to us: 'Go ye thither, there is the gate.'"

"And may she speed your steps to good," again began the courteous door-keeper; "come then forward to our stairs." There where we came, at the first step, was white marble so polished and smooth that I mirrored me therein as I appear. The second darker was than perse, of a stone, rugged and calcined, cracked in its length and in its breadth. The third, which is massy above, seemed to me of porphyry so flaming red as blood that spurts from a vein. Upon this God's angel held both his feet, sitting upon the threshold, which seemed to me adamantine stone.[2]

Up by the three steps, with my good will, my Leader brought me, saying: "Humbly ask that the bolt be loosed." Devoutly I flung me at the holy feet; for mercy I craved that he would open to me; but first on my breast thrice I smote me. Seven P's[3] upon my forehead he described with the point of his sword and: "Do thou wash these wounds when thou art within," he said. Ashes, or earth which is dug out dry, would be of one colour with his vesture, and from beneath it he drew forth two keys.[4] One was of gold and the other was of silver; first with the white and then with the yellow he did so to the gate that I was satisfied. "Whensoever one of these keys fails so that it turns not aright in the lock," said he to us, "this passage opens not. More precious is one, but the other requires exceeding art and wit ere it unlocks, because it is the one which unties the knot. From Peter I hold them; and he told me to err rather in opening, than in keeping it locked, if only the people fell prostrate at my feet."

Then he pushed the door of the sacred portal, saying: "Enter, but

2. The three steps represent the three parts of the Sacrament of Penance: Contrition, Confession, and Satisfaction. The adamantine stone signifies the firm basis of power of the Church to grant absolution.

3. The P's are for the seven capital sins (Latin *peccata*). As Dante ascends Purgatory they disappear one at a time, as he ascends from one terrace to the next.

4. The silver key is the knowledge and wisdom which enable the confessor to judge the penitent's sincerity and worthiness. The golden key is the absolution which he grants.

I make you ware that he who looketh behind returns outside again."...
I turned me intent for the first sound, and *Te Deum laudamus*[5]
meseemed to hear in a voice mingled with sweet music. Just such impression gave me that which I heard, as we are wont to receive when
people are singing with an organ, and now the words are clear, and
now are not.

CANTO X

When we were within the threshold of the gate, which the evil
love of souls disuses, because it makes the crooked way seem straight,
by the ringing sound I heard it was shut again; and had I turned mine
eyes to it what would have been a fitting excuse for the fault? We
climbed through a cleft rock, which was moving on one side and on
the other, even as a wave that recedes and approaches. "Here we must
use a little skill," began my Leader, "in keeping close, now hither now
thither, to the side that is receding." And this made our steps so scant,
that the waning orb of the moon regained its bed to sink again to rest
ere we were forth from that needle's eye.

But when we were free and on the open above, where the mount is
set back, I wearied and both uncertain of our way, we stood still on a
level place more solitary than roads through deserts. From its edge
where it borders on the void, to the foot of the high bank which sheer
ascends, a human body would measure in thrice; and so far as mine
eye could wing its flight, now on the left now on the right side, such
this cornice appeared to me. Thereon our feet had not yet moved,
when I discerned that circling bank (which, being upright, lacked
means of ascent) to be of pure white marble, and adorned with
sculptures so that not only Polycletus,[1] but Nature there would be put
to shame. The angel[2] that came to earth with the decree of peace wept
for since many a year, which opened heaven from its long ban, before
us appeared so vividly graven there in gentle mien, that it seemed not
an image which is dumb. One would have sworn that he was saying:
Ave; for there she was fashioned who turned the key to open the

5. "We praise Thee, O God," the opening lines of a hymn used on solemn
occasions, especially of triumph.
    1. *Polycletus*, Greek sculptor.
    2. The Angel of the Annunciation. On each terrace are sculptures representing
the virtue opposed to the sin which is being purged. Here, on the terrace
where atonement for *pride* is made, the sculptures show examples of *humility*.
The first example is always taken from the life of the Virgin Mary.

supreme love. And in her attitude were imprinted these words, *Ecce ancilla Dei*,[3] as expressly as a figure is stamped on wax.

"Keep not thy mind only on one place," said the sweet Master, who had me on that side where folk have the heart. . . . I moved my feet from the place where I stood, to scan closely another story which shone white before me. There was storied the high glory of the Roman prince whose worth moved Gregory to his great victory[4]; of Trajan the emperor I speak; and a poor widow was at his bridle in the attitude of tears and of grief. Round about him appeared a trampling and throng of horsemen and the eagles in gold above him moved visibly to the wind. The poor creature among all these seemed to say: "Lord, do me vengeance for my son who is slain, whereby my heart is pierced." And he to answer her: "Now wait until I return." And she, like a person in whom grief is urgent: "My Lord, if thou do not return?" And he: "One who shall be in my place will do it for thee." And she: "What to thee will be another's good deed if thou forget thine own?" Wherefore he: "Now comfort thee, for needs must I fulfil my duty ere I stir; justice wills and pity holds me back."

He, who ne'er beheld a new thing, wrought this visible speech, new to us because here it is not found.

While I was rejoicing to look on the images of humilities so great and for their Craftsman's sake precious to see, "Lo here," murmured the Poet, "much people, but few they make their steps; these will send us on to the high stairs." Mine eyes, that were intent on gazing to see new things whereof they are fain, were not slow in turning towards him. I would not, reader, that thou be scared from a good purpose through hearing how God wills that the debt be paid. Heed not the form of the pain; think what followeth, think that at worst beyond the great judgment it cannot go.

I began: "Master, that which I see moving towards us seems not persons to me, yet I know not what, so wanders my sight."

And he to me: "The grievous state of their torment doubles them down to earth so that mine eyes at first thereat were at strife. But look steadily there and disentwine with thy sight what is coming beneath those stones; already thou canst discern how each one beats his breast."

O ye proud Christians, wretched and weary, who, sick in mental vision, put trust in backward steps, perceive ye not that we are worms,

3. "Behold the handmaid of the Lord."
4. The story depicted here is supposed to have moved Pope Gregory to redeem Trajan from Hell by his prayers.

born to form the angelic butterfly that flieth to judgment without defence? Why doth your mind soar on high, since ye are as t'were imperfect insects, even as the grub in which full form is wanting? As to support ceiling or roof is sometimes seen for corbel a figure joining knees to breast, which of unreality begetteth real discomfort in him who beholds it; in such wise saw I these when I gave good heed. True it is that more and less were they contracted, according as they had more or less upon them, and he who had most patience in his bearing, weeping seemed to say: "I can no more."

CANTO XI

[Dante speaks with various formerly proud spirits, who now realize that earthly reputation is worthless and fleeting. Among them is a miniature-painter who once boasted of his superiority over his rivals. There is also a ruler of Siena who was proud of his exploits, but is hardly remembered in his own city.]

CANTO XII

Even in step, like oxen which go in the yoke, I went beside that burdened spirit, so long as the sweet pedagogue suffered it. But when he said: "Leave him, and press on, for here 'tis well that with sail and with oars, each one urge his bark along with all his might"; erect, even as is required for walking I made me again with my body, albeit my thoughts remained bowed down and shrunken.

I had moved me, and willingly was following my master's steps, and both of us already were showing how light of foot we were, when he said to me: "Turn thine eyes downward: good will it be, for solace of thy way, to see the bed of the soles of thy feet." As in order that there be memory of them, the tombs on the ground over the buried bear figured what they were before; wherefore there, many a time men weep for them, because of the prick of remembrance which only to the pitiful gives spur; so saw I sculptured there, but of better similitude according to the craftsmanship, all that which for road projects from the mount. I saw him[1] who was created nobler far than other creature, on one side descending like lightning from heaven. I saw

---

1. *him*, Satan. The following list gives examples of pride in parallel pairs, each of which consists of one figure from Hebraic mythology or history and one from classical.

Briareus, transfixed by the celestial bolt, on the other side, lying on
the earth heavy with the death chill. I saw Thymbræus, I saw Pallas
and Mars, armed yet, around their father, gazing on the scattered
limbs of the giants. I saw Nimrod at the foot of his great labour,
as though bewildered, and looking at the people who were proud
with him in Shinar. O Niobe, with what sorrowing eyes I saw thee
graven upon the road between seven and seven thy children slain!
O Saul, how upon thine own sword there didst thou appear dead
on Gilboa, which thereafter felt nor rain nor dew! O mad Arachne,
so saw I thee already half spider, sad upon the shreds of the work
which to thy hurt was wrought by thee! O Rehoboam, now thine
image there seems no more to threaten; but full of terror a chariot
beareth it away ere chase be given! It showed—the hard pavement
—again how Alcmæon made the luckless ornament seem costly to
his mother. It showed how his sons flung themselves upon Sennach-
erib within the temple, and how, him slain, there they left him.
It showed the destruction and the cruel slaughter which Tomyris
wrought when she said to Cyrus: "For blood thou didst thirst and
with blood I fill thee!" It showed how in a rout the Assyrians fled,
after Holofernes was slain, and also the relics of the assassination.
I saw Troy in ashes and in ruins: O Ilion, thee how base and vile it
showed—the sculpture which there is discerned! What master were
he of brush or of graver, who drew the shades and the lineaments,
which there would make every subtle wit stare? Dead seemed the dead,
and the living, living. He saw not better than I who saw the reality of
all that I trod upon while I was going bent down. Now wax proud and
on with haughty visage, ye children of Eve, and bow not down your
faces, so that ye may see your evil path!

Already more of the mount was circled by us, and of the sun's
path much more spent, than the mind, not set free, esteemed; when
he, who ever in front of me alert was going, began; "Lift up thy head,
this is no time to go thus engrossed. See there an angel who is making
ready to come towards us; look how the sixth handmaiden is returning
from the day's service.[2] Adorn with reverence thy bearing and thy
face, so that it may delight him to send us upward; think that this
day never dawns again." Right well was I used to his monitions never
to lose time so that in that matter he could not speak to me darkly.

To us came the beauteous creature, robed in white, and in his
countenance, such as a tremulous star at morn appears. His arms he

2. The hours are considered as handmaidens of the day.

opened and then outspread his wings; he said: "Come; here nigh are
the steps, and easily now is ascent made." To this announcement few
be they who come. O human folk, born to fly upward, why at a
breath of wind thus fall ye down? He led us where the rock was cut;
there he beat his wings upon my forehead, then did promise me my
journey secure. Here the bold scarp of the ascent is broken by the
steps. Even so is the bank made easier, which here right steeply falls
from the other cornice, but on this side and on that the high rock
grazes. While we were turning there our persons, *"Beati pauperes
spiritu"*[3] voices so sweetly sang, that no speech would tell it. Ah! how
different are these openings from those in Hell! for here we enter
through songs, and down there through fierce wailings.

Now were we mounting up by the sacred steps, and meseemed I
was exceeding lighter, than meseemed before on the flat; wherefore I:
"Master, say, what heavy thing has been lifted from me, that scarce
any toil is perceived by me in journeying?"

He answered: "When the P's which have remained still nearly
extinguished on thy face, shall, like the one, be wholly rased out, thy
feet shall be so vanquished by good will, that not only will they feel
it no toil, but it shall be a delight to them to be urged upward." Then
did I, like those who go with something on their head unknown to
them, save that another's signs make them suspect; wherefore the
hand lends its aid to make certain, and searches, and finds, and fulfils
that office which cannot be furnished by the sight; and with the
fingers of my right hand outspread, I found but six the letters, which
he with the keys had cut upon me over the temples: whereat my
Leader looking did smile.

CANTOS XIII-XXIX

[The circles for the purgation of the seven deadly sins are all
similar in their general plan, though not in the form taken by the
atonement. At the end of the preceding canto, Dante and Virgil rose
from the circle of pride to that of envy. From there they go on through
those of anger, sloth, avarice, gluttony, and lechery, speaking with
various notable spirits and settling various problems along the way.
In the circle of avarice they are joined by the Latin poet Statius, who
has completed his purgation and now accompanies Dante to Heaven.

On top of the mountain is the Terrestrial Paradise, in which

3. "Blessed are the poor in spirit, (for theirs is the kingdom of heaven)."

Virgil gives Dante leave to go his own way until he meets Beatrice. He comes to a stream, on the opposite side of which is a lady later identified as Matilda, and she explains to him the streams of Lethe and Eunoë. She and Dante move along opposite sides of the river, and Dante sees an elaborate religious pageant, which continues into the next canto.]

CANTO XXX

. . . As the saints at the last trump shall rise ready each one from his tomb, with re-clad voice singing Halleluiah, such rose up a hundred ministers and messengers of life eternal. All were saying: *"Benedictus qui venis"*[1]*;* and, strewing flowers above and around, *"Manibus o date lilia plenis."*[2]

Ere now have I seen, at dawn of day, the eastern part all rosy red, and the rest of heaven adorned with fair clear sky, and the face of the sun rise shadowed, so that by the tempering of the mists the eye long time endured him: so within a cloud of flowers, which rose from the angelic hands and fell down again within and without, olive-crowned over a white veil, a lady appeared to me, clad, under a green mantle, with hue of living flame.[3] And my spirit, that now so long a time had passed, since, trembling in her presence, it had been broken down with awe, without having further knowledge by mine eyes through hidden virtue which went out from her, felt the mighty power of ancient love. Soon as on my sight the lofty virtue smote, which already had pierced me ere I was out of my boyhood, I turned me to the left with the trust with which the little child runs to his mother when he is frightened or when he is afflicted, to say to Virgil: "Less than a drachm of blood is left in me that trembleth not; I recognize the tokens of the ancient flame."[4] But Virgil had left us bereft of himself, Virgil sweetest Father, Virgil to whom for my weal I gave me up; nor did all that our ancient mother lost,[5] avail to keep my dew-washed cheeks from turning dark again with tears.

1. "Blessed art thou that comest (in the name of the Lord)."
2. "Oh, with full hands give lilies." It is interesting to note that Dante here combines the *Aeneid* (VI, 884) with the New Testament in angelic song.
3. Beatrice is wearing the colors of Faith, Hope, and Charity.
4. Dante's *Conosco i segni dell' antica fiamma* is a translation of Virgil's *Agnosco veteris vestigia flammae*; from Dido's confession to Anna when she begins to feel love for Aeneas.
5. Eve lost the Earthly Paradise.

"Dante, for that Virgil goeth away, weep not yet, weep not yet, for thou must weep for other sword." Even as an admiral, who at stern and at bow, comes to see the folk that man the other ships, and heartens them to brave deeds, so, when I turned me at sound of my name, which of necessity here is recorded, I saw the lady, who first appeared to me veiled beneath the angelic festival, directing her eyes to me on this side the stream. Albeit the veil which fell from her head, crowned with Minerva's leaves,[6] did not let her appear manifest, queenlike in bearing yet stern, she continued, like one who speaks and holdeth back the hottest words till the last: "Look at me well; verily am I, verily am I Beatrice. How didst thou deign to draw nigh the mount? knewest thou not that here man is happy?" Mine eyes drooped down to the clear fount; but beholding me therein, I drew them back to the grass, so great a shame weighed down my brow. So doth the mother seem stern to her child, as she seemed to me; for the savour of harsh pity tasteth of bitterness.

She was silent, and straightway the angels sang: *In te, Domine, speravi.*[7] As the snow amid the living rafters along Italia's back is frozen under blast and stress of Slavonian winds, then melted trickles down through itself, if but the land that loseth shade do breathe, so that it seems fire melting the candle, so without tears or sighs was I before the song of those who ever accord their notes after the melodies of the eternal spheres. But when I heard in their sweet harmonies their compassion on me, more than if they had said "Lady, why dost thou so shame him?" the ice which had closed about my heart became breath and water, and with anguish through mouth and eyes issued from my breast.

She then turned her words to the pitying angels thus: "Ye watch in the everlasting day, so that nor night nor sleep stealeth from you one step which the world may take along its ways; wherefore my answer is with greater care, that he who yon side[8] doth weep may understand me, so that sin and sorrow be of one measure. Not only by operation of the mighty spheres that direct each seed to some end, according as the stars are its companions, but by the bounty of graces divine, which have for their rain vapours so high that our eyes reach not nigh them, this man was such in his new life potentially, that every good talent would have made wondrous increase in him. But so much the

6. The olive is sacred to Minerva.
7. "In thee, O Lord, have I trusted."
8. The stream of Lethe is between Dante and Beatrice.

more rank and wild the ground becomes with evil seed and untilled, the more it hath of good strength of soil. Some time I sustained him with my countenance; showing my youthful eyes to him I led him with me turned to the right goal. So soon as I was on the threshold of my second age, and I changed life, he forsook me, and gave him to others. When I was risen from flesh to spirit, and beauty and virtue were increased within me, I was less precious and less pleasing to him; and he did turn his steps by a way not true, pursuing false visions of good, that pay back no promise entire. Nor did it avail me to gain inspirations, with which in dream and otherwise, I called him back; so little recked he of them. So low sank he, that all means for his salvation were already short, save showing him the lost people. For this I visited the portal of the dead, and to him who has guided him up hither, weeping my prayers were borne. God's high decree would be broken, if Lethe were passed, and such viands were tasted, without some scot of penitence that may shed tears."

CANTO XXXI

"O thou that are yon side the sacred stream," her speech directing with the point towards me, which even with the edge had seemed sharp to me, she began again, continuing without delay, "say, say, if this is true; to such accusation thy confession must be joined." My virtue was so confounded that the voice stirred and was spent ere it was free from its organs. Short time she forbore, then said: "What thinkest thou? Answer me, for the sad memories in thee are not yet destroyed by the water."[1]

Confusion and fear, together mingled, drove forth from my mouth a "Yea" such that to understand it the eyes were needed. As a crossbow breaks, when shot at too great tension, both its string and bow, and with less force the bolt hits the mark, so burst I under this heavy charge, pouring forth a torrent of tears and sighs, and my voice died away in its passage.

Wherefore she to me: "Within thy desires of me which led thee to love the good beyond which is nought that may be aspired to, what pits didst find athwart thy path, or what claims that thou needs must strip thee of the hope of passing onward? And what allurements or

1. When Dante drinks the water of Lethe, it will obliterate all memory of sin. Later, the water of Eunoë will fix all memory of good, including any good which, being involved with sin, has been forgotten by the action of Lethe.

what advantages were displayed to thee in the aspect of the others, that thou must needs wander before them?"

After the heaving of a bitter sigh, scarce had I voice that answered, and my lips with labour gave it form. Weeping I said: "Present things with their false pleasure turned away my steps soon as your face was hidden."

And she: "If thou wert silent, or if thou hadst denied what thou confessest, not less noted were thy fault; by such a judge 'tis known. But when self-accusation of sin bursts from the cheeks in our Court, the grindstone is turned back against the edge.[2] Howbeit in order that now thou mayst bear shame for thy transgression, and that other time hearing the Sirens thou be of stouter heart, put away the seed of weeping, and hearken; so shalt thou hear how my buried flesh should have moved thee towards a contrary goal. Ne'er did nature and art present to thee pleasure so great as the fair members wherein I was enclosed, and are scattered to dust; and if the highest pleasure thus failed thee by my death, what mortal thing ought then to have drawn thee to desire it? Truly oughtest thou, at the first arrow of deceitful things, to rise up after me who was such no longer. Young damsel or other vain thing with so brief enjoyment, should not have weighed down thy wings to await more shots. The young bird waits two or three, but before the eyes of the full-fledged in vain the net is spread or arrow shot."

As children, dumb with shame, stand listening with eyes to earth, self-confessing, and repentant, such stood I. And she said: "Since through hearing thou art grieving, lift up thy beard and more grief shalt thou receive by looking."

With less resistance is uprooted the sturdy oak, whether by winds of ours, or that which blows from Iarbas' land, than at her command I lifted up my chin; and when by the beard she asked for my face, well I knew the venom of the argument. And when my face was stretched forth, my sight perceived those primal creatures resting from their strewing, and mine eyes, as yet hardly steadfast, saw Beatrice turned towards the beast, which is one sole person in two natures. Under her veil and beyond the stream, to me she seemed to surpass more her ancient self, than she surpassed the others here when she was with us. The nettle of repentance here so did sting me, that of all other things, that which turned me most to love of it became most hateful to me. So much remorse gnawed at my heart that I fell vanquished, and what I then became, she knoweth who gave me the cause.

2. Confession blunts the edge of the sword of justice.

Then when my heart restored to me the sense of outward things, the lady[3] whom I had found alone I saw above me; and she said: "Hold me! Hold me!" She had drawn me into the river up to my neck, and, pulling me after her, went along over the water light as a shuttle. When I was nigh unto the blessed bank *"Asperges me"*[4] so sweetly I heard that I cannot remember it much less describe it. The fair lady opened her arms, clasped my head, and dipped me where I must needs swallow of the water; then drew me forth, and led me bathed within the dance of the four fair ones, and each did cover me with her arm.

"Here we are nymphs and in heaven are stars[5]; ere Beatrice descended to the world we were ordained to her for her handmaids. We will lead thee to her eyes; but the three[6] on the other side who deeper gaze, will sharpen thine eyes to the joyous light that is within." Thus singing they began; and then did lead me with them up to the breast of the griffin, where Beatrice stood turned towards us. They said: "Look that thou spare not thine eyes; we have placed thee before the emeralds whence Love once drew his shafts at thee." A thousand desires hotter than flame held mine eyes bound to the shining eyes, which remained ever fixed upon the griffin. As the sun in a mirror, not otherwise the twofold beast was beaming within them, now with the attributes of one, now of the other nature.[7] Think, reader, if I marvelled within me when I saw the thing itself remain motionless, and in its image it was changing.

While my soul, filled with wonderment and glad, was tasting of that food which, satisfying of itself, causes thirst of itself, the other three, showing them to be of the chiefest order in their bearing, drew forward, dancing to their angelic roundelay. "Turn, Beatrice, turn thy holy eyes," was their song, "to thy faithful one, who to see thee hath moved so many steps. Of thy grace do us the grace that thou unveil thy mouth to him, that he may discern the second beauty[8] which thou hidest." O glory of living eternal, who that so pale hath grown be-

3. *lady*, Matilda, representing the active life. She was the first person whom Dante saw in the Terrestrial Paradise.
4. "Purge me (with hyssop, and I shall be clean; wash me, and I shall be whiter than snow)." The Latin is literally "sprinkle me."
5. *stars*, the four stars seen in Canto I of *Purgatory*.
6. *the three*, Faith, Hope, and Charity.
7. The griffin, a mythological animal, part eagle and part lion, represents Christ as a combination of his divine and human attributes.
8. Beatrice's eyes have already been seen; the second beauty is her smile.

neath the shade of Parnassus, or hath drunk at its well, that would not seem to have mind encumbered, on trying to render thee as thou appearedst, when in the free air thou didst disclose thee, where heaven in its harmony shadows thee forth?

CANTO XXXII

[Dante is warned not to look too fixedly on Beatrice. The procession goes on to the tree of the knowledge of good and evil. Dante falls asleep here, and when he awakes only the seven Virtues still accompany Beatrice. Soon, however, another allegorical pageant appears and portrays the false relationship between Church and State, as well as the corruptions and perils of the Church.]

CANTO XXXIII

"Deus, venerunt gentes":[1] now three, now four, alternately and weeping, a sweet psalmody the ladies began; and Beatrice sighing and compassionate was hearkening to them so altered, that little more did Mary change at the cross.

But when the other virgins gave place to her to speak, uprisen erect on her feet, she answered in hue of fire: *"Modicum, et non videbitis me, et iterum,* my beloved sisters, *modicum, et vos videbitis me."*[2] Then she placed them all seven in front of her, and, merely by her nod, motioned behind her, me and the Lady and the Sage who had stayed.[3] Thus she went on, and I believe not that her tenth step was put on the ground, when with her eyes mine eyes she smote; and with tranquil mien did say to me: "Come more quickly so that if I speak with thee, thou be well placed to listen to me." Soon as I was with her, as 'twas my duty to be, she said to me: "Brother, wherefore coming now with me, venturest thou not to ask of me?"

As to those, who in presence of their betters are too lowly in speech so that they bring not their voice whole to the lips, it happened to me and without full utterance I began: "My Lady, my need you know, and that which is good for it."

And she to me: "From fear and from shame I would that now

1. *Psalm* 79: "O God, the heathen are come (into thine inheritance)." The psalm is sung by the seven Virtues.
2. Christ, speaking to His disciples: "A little while, and ye shall not see me: and again, a little while and ye shall see (because I go to the Father)."
3. The lady is Matilda, and the Sage who had stayed is Statius.

thou unbind thee, so that thou speak no more like one that is dreaming. . . . But because I see thy mind turned to stone and, stonelike, such in hue that the light of my word dazes thee, I also will that thou bear it away within thee, and if not written at least outlined, for the reason that the pilgrim's staff is brought back wreathed with palm."[4]

And I: "Even as wax under the seal, that the imprinted figure changeth not, my brain is now stamped by you. But why doth your longed-for word soar so far beyond my sight, that the more it straineth the more it loses it?"

"That thou mayst know," she said, "that School which thou hast followed, and see how its teaching can keep pace with my word; and mayst see your way so far distant from the divine way, as the heaven which highest speeds is removed from earth."

Wherefore I answered her: "I remember not that I e'er estranged me from you, nor have I conscience thereof that gnaws me."

"And if thou canst not remember it," smiling she answered, "now bethink thee how thou didst drink of Lethe this very day; and if from smoke fire is argued, this forgetfulness clearly proves fault in thy desire otherwhere intent. But now my words shall be naked, so far as shall be meet to discover them to thy rude vision."

Both more refulgent, and with slower steps, the sun was holding the meridian circle, which varies hither and thither as positions vary, when did halt, even as he halts who goes for escort before folk, if he finds aught that is strange or the traces thereof, those seven ladies at the margin of a pale shadow, such as beneath green leaves and dark boughs, the Alp casts over its cool streams. In front of them I seemed to behold Euphrates and Tigris welling up from one spring, and parting like friends that linger. "O light, O glory of human kind, what water is this that here pours forth from one source, and self from self doth wend away?"

At such prayer was said to me: "Pray Matilda that she tell it thee"; and here made answer, as he doth who frees him from blame, the fair Lady: "This and other things have been told him by me, and sure am I that Lethe's water hid them not from him."

And Beatrice: "Haply a greater care that oft bereaves of memory hath dimmed his mind's eyes. But behold Eunoë, which there flows

4. Pilgrims brought back a branch of palm to show that they had been in the Holy Land. Similarly, Dante is to bring back Beatrice's prophecies (incomprehensible to him at this point, and omitted in this text) as evidence of his visit to the Terrestrial Paradise.

on; lead him to it, and as thou art wont, requicken his fainting virtue."

As a gentle soul that maketh no excuse, but makes her will of the will of another, soon as it is disclosed by outward sign, so the fair Lady, after I was taken by her, set forth, and to Statius with queenly mien did say: "Come with him."

If, reader, I had greater space for writing, I would sing, at least in part, of the sweet draught which never would have sated me; but forasmuch as all the pages ordained for this second canticle are filled, the curb of art no further lets me go. I came back from the most holy waves, born again, even as new trees renewed with new foliage, pure and ready to mount to the stars.

HEAVEN

CANTOS I-II

[Dante and Beatrice ascend through the sphere of fire and enter heaven. She explains to him that he is not conscious of the ascent because it is natural for man to rise to God. They enter the first of the heavenly spheres, that of the moon, where those souls who were inconstant in their vows are manifested. (All the spirits of the redeemed *abide* in the Empyrean, where they are seen with God and his angels in the final vision; but they are *manifested* to Dante in the various spheres of heaven, according to their virtues, as he ascends.)]

CANTO III

That sun which first warmed my bosom with love had thus unveiled for me, by proof and refutation, fair truth's sweet aspect; and I, to confess me corrected and assured, in measure as was meet, sloped up my head to speak. But there appeared to me a sight which so straitly held me to itself, to look upon it, that I bethought me not of my confession. In such guise as, from glasses transparent and polished, or from waters clear and tranquil, not so deep that the bottom is darkened, come back the notes of our faces, so faint that a pearl on a white brow cometh not slowlier upon our pupils; so did I behold many a countenance, eager to speak; wherefore I fell into the counter error

of that which kindled love between the man and fountain.[1] No sooner
was I aware of them, than, thinking them reflected images, I turned
round my eyes to see of whom they were; and I saw naught, and
turned them forward again straight on the light of my sweet guide,
whose sacred eyes glowed as she smiled.

"Wonder not that I smile," she said, "in presence of thy child-
like thought, since it trusts not its foot upon the truth, but turneth
thee after its wont, to vacancy. True substances are they which thou
beholdest, relegated here for failure of their vows. Wherefore speak
with them, and listen and believe; for the true light which satisfieth
them, suffereth them not to turn their feet aside from it."

And I to the shade who seemed most to long for converse turned
me and began, as one whom too great longing doth confound: "O
well-created spirit, who in the rays of eternal life dost feel the sweetness which, save tasted, may ne'er be understood; it were acceptable
to me, wouldst thou content me with thy name and with your lot."

Whereat she, eager and with smiling eyes: "Our love doth no
more bar the gate to a just wish, than doth that love which would have
all its court like to itself. In the world I was a virgin sister; and if thy
memory be rightly searched, my greater beauty will not hide me from
thee, but thou wilt know me again for Piccarda,[2] who, placed here
with these other blessed ones, am blessed in the sphere that moveth
slowest. Our affections, which are aflame only in the pleasure of the
Holy Spirit, rejoice to be informed after his order. And this lot, which
seemeth so far down, therefore is given us because our vows were
slighted, and on some certain side were not filled in."

Whereon I to her: "In your wondrous aspects a divine somewhat
regloweth that doth transmute you from conceits of former times.
Wherefore I lagged in calling thee to mind; now what thou tellest me
giveth such help that more articulately I retrace thee. But tell me, ye
whose blessedness is here, do you desire a more lofty place, to see more,
or to make yourselves more dear?"

With those other shades first she smiled a little, then answered me
so joyous that she seemed to burn in love's first flame: "Brother, the
quality of love stilleth our will, and maketh us long only for what we

1. Narcissus fell in love with his image in a fountain, thus taking a reflection
for a reality. Dante makes the opposite error here.

2. Piccarda Donati, as a girl, joined the Franciscan order of "Poor Clares,"
which had been founded by St. Clare, a friend and follower of St. Francis of
Assisi. Piccarda was forcibly abducted by her brother and forced into a political
marriage.

have, and giveth us no other thirst. Did we desire to be more aloft, our longings were discordant from his will who here assorteth us, and for that, thou wilt see, there is no room within these circles, if of necessity we have our being here in love, and if thou think again what is love's nature. Nay, 'tis the essence of this blessed being to hold ourselves within the divine will, whereby our own wills are themselves made one. So that our being thus, from threshold unto threshold throughout the realm, is a joy to all the realm as to the king, who draweth our wills to what he willeth; and his will is our peace; it is that sea to which all moves that it createth and that nature maketh."

Clear was it then to me how everywhere in heaven is Paradise, e'en though the grace of the chief Good doth not rain there after one only fashion. But even as it chanceth, should one food sate us while for another the appetite remaineth, that returning thanks for that, we ask for this; so with gesture and with word did I, to learn from her what was that web through which she had not drawn the shuttle to the end. "Perfected life and high desert enheaveneth a lady more aloft," she[3] said, "by whose rule down in your world there are who clothe and veil themselves, that they, even till death, may wake and sleep with that Spouse who accepteth every vow that love hath made conform with his good pleasure. From the world, to follow her, I fled while yet a girl, and in her habit I enclosed myself, and promised the way of her company. Thereafter men more used to ill than good tore me away from the sweet cloister; and God doth know what my life then became. And this other splendour who revealeth herself to thee on my right side, and who kindleth herself with all the light of our sphere, doth understand of her that which I tell of me. She was a sister, and from her head was taken in like manner the shadow of the sacred veil. Yet, turned back as she was into the world, against her pleasure and against good usage, from her heart's veil never was she loosened. This is the light of the great Constance.[4] . . .

Thus did she speak to me, and then began to sing *Ave Maria,* and vanished as she sang, like to a heavy thing through the deep water. . . .

3. *she,* St. Clare.
4. Constance, wife of Henry VI, is supposed by one tradition to have been a nun who was taken from her convent to make a marriage for reasons of state.

CANTOS IV-XVI

[After settling some doubts in Dante's mind, Beatrice conducts him into the sphere of Mercury (ambition), where they talk with the Emperor Justinian. From here they pass through the sphere of Venus (earthly love), talking with the spirits whom they encounter and discussing various matters along the way, and enter the sphere of the sun (prudence), where they speak with Thomas Aquinas and Solomon. When they enter the sphere of Mars (fortitude), Dante's great-great-grandfather, Cacciaguida, appears to them, and contrasts the virtuous simplicity of the Florentines in his day with their luxury and corruption since his time. In the opening lines of Canto XVII, Dante, with Beatrice's encouragement, determines to ask his ancestor to explain the various dark prophecies about his own future which he has heard during his journey.]

CANTO XVII

". . . Whilst I was companioned by Virgil along the mount which cureth souls, and down-going through the world defunct, heavy words were said to me anent my future life; albeit I feel me squarely set against the blows of fortune; wherefore my will were well content to hear what the disaster drawing nigh to me; for the arrow seen before cometh less rudely."

So spake I unto that same light which had before addressed me, and, as Beatrice willed, was my wish confessed. In no dark sayings, such as limed the foolish folk of old, before the Lamb of God who taketh sins away, was slain, but in clear words, and with precise discourse, answered that love paternal, hidden and revealed by his own smile: "Contingency, which beyond the sheet of your material stretcheth not, is all limned in the eternal aspect; albeit it deriveth not necessity from this. . . . Thence, as cometh to the ear sweet harmony from an organ, cometh to my sight the time that is in store for thee. As Hippolytus was severed from Athens by machination of his cruel and perfidious stepmother, so must thou needs sever thee from Florence.[1] So it is willed, so already plotted, and so shall be accomplished soon, by him who pondereth upon it in the place[2] where Christ, day in day out, is put to sale. The blame shall cleave unto the injured side in fame, as is the wont; but vengeance shall bear witness to the

1. Phædra (the stepmother) accused Hippolytus of the sin which actually was hers.
2. *place*, the court of Pope Boniface.

truth which doth dispense it. Thou shalt abandon everything beloved
most dearly; this is the arrow which the bow of exile shall first shoot.
Thou shalt make trial of how salt doth taste another's bread, and how
hard the path to descend and mount upon another's stair. And that
which most shall weigh thy shoulders down, shall be the vicious and
ill company with which thou shalt fall down into this vale, for all ungrateful, all mad and impious shall they become against thee; but, soon
after, their temples and not thine shall redden for it. Of their brutish-
ness their progress shall make proof, so that it shall be for thy fair
fame to have made a party for thyself. Thy first refuge and first
hostelry shall be the courtesy of the great Lombard, who on the ladder
beareth the sacred bird,[3] for he shall cast so benign regard on thee that
of doing and demanding, that shall be first betwixt you two, which
betwixt others most doth lag. With him shalt thou see the one[4] who
so at his birth was stamped by this strong star, that notable shall be his
deeds. Not yet have folk taken due note of him, because of his young
age, for only nine years have these wheels rolled round him. But
sparkles of his virtue shall appear in carelessness of silver and of toils.
His deeds munificent shall yet be known so that concerning them his
very foes shall not be able to keep silent tongues. Look to him and to
his benefits; by him shall many folk be changed, altering state, the
wealthy and the beggars; and thou shalt bear it written in thy mind
of him, but shalt not tell it";—and he told me things past the belief
even of who shall see them. Then he added: "Son, these are the notes
on what hath been said to thee; behold the snares that behind but few
circlings are hidden. Yet would I not have thee envious of thy neighbours, since thy life shall be prolonged far beyond falling of the penalty
upon their perfidies."

When by his silence the sacred soul showed he had finished setting
of the woof across the warp I had held out in readiness to him, I began,
as he who longeth in doubt for counsel from one who seeth and
willeth straight, and loveth: "Well do I see, my father, how time
cometh spurring toward me to give me such a buffet as is heaviest to
whoso most abandoneth himself; wherefore with foresight it were well
to arm me, that if the dearest place be reft from me, I lose not all the
rest by reason of my songs. Down in the world endlessly bitter, and

3. Some time between 1302 and 1304, Dante took refuge with Bartolommeo
della Scala, whose coat of arms was an imperial eagle on a *ladder* (Italian
scala).

4. Can Grande della Scala, Bartolommeo's younger brother, became the
great soldier of Italy and a strong defender of the imperial cause. He was
nine years old at the time of the vision.

along the mount from whose fair summit my Lady's eyes uplifted me, and after, through the heaven from light to light, I have learnt that which if I tell again, will have strong-bitter flavour unto many; and if to truth I am a shrinking friend, I fear to lose life amongst those who shall call this time ancient."

The light wherein was smiling my treasure which I there had found, first coruscated as at the sun's rays doth a golden mirror; then answered: "Conscience darkened, or by its own or by another's shame, will in truth feel thy utterance grating. But none the less, every lie set aside, make thy entire vision manifest, and let them scratch wherever is the scab; for if thy voice be grievous at first taste, yet vital nutriment shall it leave thereafter when digested. This cry of thine shall do as doth the wind, which smiteth most upon the loftiest summits; and this shall be no little argument of honour. Therefore have been displayed to thee, in these wheels, upon the mount, and in the dolorous vale, only souls known to fame; for the soul of him who heareth resteth not nor fixeth faith by an example which hath its root unknown and hidden, nor other unconspicuous argument."

CANTOS XVIII-XXX

[The journey continues into the sphere of Jupiter (justice), where a vast number of souls, grouped in the shape of an eagle, discourse on divine justice. Passing thence through the sphere of Saturn (temperance), Dante and Beatrice enter the sphere of the fixed stars, where Dante is examined by Saints Peter, James, and John on the subjects of faith, hope, and charity, respectively. Here also the spirit of Adam appears and tells various matters concerning his earthly life.

Leaving the spheres of the visible heavens, the voyagers go through the Primum Mobile, or crystal sphere, and finally arrive in the Empyrean, the abiding-place of God, his angels, and his redeemed. Here Dante's sight is strengthened to prepare him for the blaze of glory which constitutes the final vision.]

CANTO XXXI

In form, then, of a white rose displayed itself to me that sacred soldiery[1] which in his blood Christ made his spouse; but the other,[2]

---

1. *sacred soldiery*, the redeemed.
2. *other*, the angels.

which as it flieth seeth and doth sing his glory who enamoureth it, and the excellence which hath made it what it is, like to a swarm of bees which doth one while plunge into the flowers and another while wend back to where its toil is turned to sweetness, ever descended into the great flower adorned with so many leaves, and reascended thence to where its love doth ceaseless make sojourn. They had their faces all of living flame, and wings of gold, and the rest so white that never snow reacheth such limit.[3] When they descended into the flower, from rank to rank they proffered of the peace and of the ardour which they acquired as they fanned their sides, nor did the interposing of so great a flying multitude, betwixt the flower and that which was above, impede the vision nor the splendour; for the divine light so penetrateth through the universe, in measure of its worthiness, that nought hath power to oppose it.

This realm, secure and gladsome, thronged with ancient folk and new, had look and love all turned unto one mark. O threefold light, which in a single star, glinting upon their sight doth so content them, look down upon our storm!

If the Barbarians, on seeing Rome and her mighty works,—what time the Lateran[4] transcended mortal things—were stupefied; what then of me, who to the divine from the human, to the eternal from time had passed, and from Florence to a people just and sane, with what stupor must I needs be filled! verily, what with it and what with joy, my will was to hear nought and to be dumb myself. As the pilgrim who doth draw fresh life in the temple of his vow as he gazeth, and already hopeth to tell again how it be placed, so, traversing the living light, I led mine eyes along the ranks, now up, now down, and now round circling. I saw countenances suasive of love, adorned by another's light and their own smile, and gestures graced with every dignity.

The general form of Paradise my glance had already taken in, in its entirety, and on no part as yet had my sight paused; and I turned me with rekindled will to question my Lady concerning things whereanent my mind was in suspense. One thing I purposed, and another answered me; I thought to see Beatrice, and I saw an elder[5] clad like the folk in glory. His eyes and cheeks were overpoured with benign gladness, in kindly gesture as befits a tender father. And: "Where

3. Love, knowledge, and purity are indicated by these colors.
4. The Lateran Palace is here used for the splendor of Rome in general.
5. Bernard of Clairvaux (1091-1153), representative of contemplation, presides over Dante's final vision.

is she?" all sudden I exclaimed; whereunto he: "To bring thy desire
to its goal Beatrice moved me from my place; and if thou look up to
the circle third from the highest rank, thou shalt re-behold her, on the
throne her merits have assigned to her."

Without answering I lifted up mine eyes and saw her, making to
herself a crown as she reflected from her the eternal rays. From that
region which thundereth most high, no mortal eye is so far distant,
though plunged most deep within the sea, as there from Beatrice was
my sight; but that wrought not upon me, for her image descended not
to me mingled with any medium. "O Lady, in whom my hope hath
vigour, and who for my salvation didst endure to leave in Hell thy
footprints; of all the things which I have seen I recognize the grace
and might, by thy power and by thine excellence. Thou hast drawn me
from a slave to liberty by all those paths, by all those methods by which
thou hadst the power so to do. Preserve thy munificence in me, so that
my soul which thou hast made sound, may unloose it from the body,
pleasing unto thee."

So did I pray; and she, so distant as she seemed, smiled and looked
on me, then turned her to the eternal fountain. And the holy elder
said: "That thou mayest consummate thy journey perfectly—whereto
prayer and holy love dispatched me,—fly with thine eyes throughout
this garden; for gazing on it will equip thy glance better to mount
through the divine ray. And the Queen of heaven for whom I am all
burning with love, will grant us every grace, because I am her faithful
Bernard."

As is he who perchance from Croatia cometh to look on our
Veronica[6] and because of ancient fame is sated not, but saith in
thought, so long as it be shown; "My Lord Jesus Christ, true God, and
was this, then, the fashion of thy semblance?" such was I, gazing upon
the living love of him who in this world by contemplation tasted of
that peace.

"Son of grace! this joyous being," he began, "will not become
known to thee by holding thine eyes only here down at the base; but
look upon the circles even to the remotest, until thou seest enthroned
the Queen to whom this realm is subject and devoted."

I lifted up mine eyes, and as at morn the oriental regions of the
horizon overcome that where the sun declineth, so, as from the valley

6. While Christ was bearing his cross, St. Veronica lent him a handkerchief
to wipe his face, and his features were imprinted on it. At New Year and Easter
it was exhibited at Rome.

rising to the mountain; with mine eyes I saw a region at the boundary surpass all the remaining ridge in light. And as with us that place where we await the chariot pole that Phaëton[7] guided ill, is most aglow, and on this side and on that the light is shorn away; so was that pacific oriflamme[8] quickened in the midst, on either side in equal measure tempering its flame. And at that mid point, with out-stretched wings, I saw more than a thousand Angels making festival, each one distinct in glow and art. I saw there, smiling to their sports and to their songs, a beauty[9] which was gladness in the eyes of all the other saints. And had I equal wealth in speech as in conception, yet dared I not attempt the smallest part of her delightsomeness. Bernard, when he saw mine eyes fixed and eager towards the glowing source of his own glow, turned his eyes to her, with so much love that he made mine more ardent to re-gaze.

CANTO XXXII

[St. Bernard indicates to Dante the great figures of heaven, beginning with Mary. He further explains the division between the Hebrews who believed in Christ before his advent and the Christians who believed in him afterwards. Between them are the infants who died before they could exercise any moral choice, and were saved by the faith of their parents. Finally, Bernard tells him to turn to Mary in prayer, that she may grant him the grace to raise his sight to the Primal Love.]

CANTO XXXIII

"Virgin mother, daughter of thy son, lowly and uplifted more than any creature, fixed goal of the eternal counsel, thou art she who didst human nature so ennoble that its own Maker scorned not to become its making. In thy womb was lit again the love under whose warmth in the eternal peace this flower hath thus unfolded. Here art thou unto us the meridian torch of love and there below with mortals art a living

7. Phaëton made a disastrous attempt to drive the horses of the sun; hence "that place" referred to here is the point at which the sun is about to rise.
8. The Oriflamme ("golden flame") was a standard given to the ancient kings of France by the Angel Gabriel. Those who fought under it were invincible. The "pacific oriflamme" is the glow of heaven representing invincible peace.
9. *beauty*, Mary.

spring of hope. Lady, thou art so great and hast such worth, that if there be who would have grace yet betaketh not himself to thee, his longing seeketh to fly without wings. Thy kindliness not only succoureth whoso requesteth, but doth oftentimes freely forerun request. In thee is tenderness, in thee is pity, in thee munificence, in thee united whatever in created being is of excellence. Now he who from the deepest pool of the universe even to here hath seen the spirit lives one after one imploreth thee, of grace, for so much power as to be able to uplift his eyes more high towards final bliss; and I, who never burned for my own vision more than I do for his, proffer thee all my prayers and pray they be not scant that thou do scatter for him every cloud of his mortality with prayers of thine, so that the joy supreme may be unfolded to him. And further do I pray thee, Queen who canst all that thou wilt, that thou keep sound for him, after so great a vision, his affections. Let thy protection vanquish human ferments; see Beatrice, with how many Saints, for my prayers folding hands."

Those eyes, of God beloved and venerated, fixed upon him who prayed, showed us how greatly devout prayers please her. Then to the eternal light they bent themselves, wherein we may not ween that any creature's eye findeth its way so clear. And I, who to the goal of all my longings was drawing nigh, even as was meet the ardour of the yearning quenched within me. Bernard gave me the sign and smiled to me that I should look on high, but I already of myself was such as he would have me; because my sight, becoming purged, now more and more was entering through the ray of the deep light which in itself is true. Thence forward was my vision mightier than our discourse, which faileth at such sight, and faileth memory at so great outrage. As is he who dreaming seeth, and when the dream is gone the passion stamped remaineth, and nought else cometh to the mind again; even such am I; for almost wholly faileth me my vision, yet doth the sweetness that was born of it still drop within my heart. So doth the snow unstamp it to the sun, so to the wind on the light leaves was lost the Sybil's wisdom.[1]

O light supreme who so far dost uplift thee o'er mortal thoughts, re-lend unto my mind a little of what then thou didst seem, and give my tongue such power that it may leave only a single sparkle of thy glory unto the folk to come; for by returning to my memory some-

---

1. The prophecies of the Cumaean Sybil were written on leaves and scattered by the wind.

what, and by a little sounding in these verses, more of thy victory
will be conceived. I hold that by the keenness of the living ray which I
endured I had been lost, had mine eyes turned aside from it. And so I
was the bolder, as I mind me, so long to sustain it as to unite my glance
with the Worth infinite. O grace abounding, wherein I presumed to
fix my look on the eternal light so long that I consumed my sight
thereon! Within its depths I saw ingathered, bound by love in one
volume, the scattered leaves of all the universe; substance and accidents
and their relations, as though together fused, after such fashion that
what I tell of is one simple flame. The universal form of this complex
I think that I beheld, because more largely, as I say this, I feel that I
rejoice. A single moment maketh a deeper lethargy for me than
twenty and five centuries have wrought on the emprise that erst threw
Neptune in amaze at Argo's shadow.[2] Thus all suspended did my
mind gaze fixed, immovable, intent, ever enkindled by its gazing. Such
at that light doth man become that to turn thence to any other sight
could not by possibility be ever yielded. For the good, which is the
object of the will, is therein wholly gathered, and outside it that same
thing is defective which therein is perfect.

Now shall my speech fall farther short even of what I can remember than an infant's who still bathes his tongue at breast. Not that
more than a single semblance was in the living light whereon I looked,
which ever is such as it was before; but by the sight that gathered
strength in me one sole appearance even as I changed worked on my
gaze. In the profound and shining being of the deep light appeared to
me three circles, of three colours and one magnitude; one by the
second as Iris[3] by Iris seemed reflected, and the third seemed a fire
breathed equally from one and from the other. Oh but how scant the
utterance, and how faint, to my conceit! and it, to what I saw, is such
that it sufficeth not to call it little. O Light eternal who only in thyself
abidest, only thyself dost understand, and to thyself, self-understood
self-understanding, turnest love on and smilest at thyself! That circling
which appeared in thee to be conceived as a reflected light, by mine eyes
scanned some little, in itself, of its own colour, seemed to be painted with
our effigy, and thereat my sight was all committed to it. As the geometer
who all sets himself to measure the circle and who findeth not, think as

2. After the end of the vision, a single moment made the things seen less
recoverable than twenty-five centuries had made the voyage of the Argonauts.
Since the *Argus* was the first ship, it astonished Neptune.
  3. *Iris*, the rainbow.

he may, the principle he lacketh[4]; such was I at this new-seen spectacle;
I would perceive how the image consorteth with the circle, and how it
settleth there; but not for this were my proper wings, save that my
mind was smitten by a flash wherein its will came to it. To the high
fantasy here power failed; but already my desire and will were rolled
—even as a wheel that moveth equally—by the Love that moves the
sun and the other stars.

4. As the diameter and circumference of a circle are incommensurable, so are
deity and humanity.

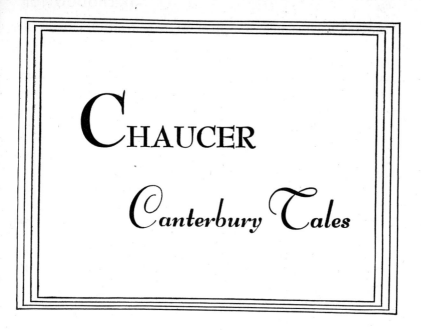

CHAUCER

Canterbury Tales

GEOFFREY CHAUCER (*c.* 1340-1400) lived at the time when England was beginning to establish its identity as a European nation. That spasmodic struggle with France called the Hundred Years War continued throughout Chaucer's lifetime, and in his boyhood the great battle names of Crécy and Poictiers rang in his ears. He lived through the Black Death, which devastated Europe in 1348, and he must have witnessed the Peasants' Revolt in 1381. Among his most distinguished contemporaries were William Langland, author of *Piers Plowman,* and the reformer John Wyclif, who, in his religious and theological activities, anticipated the Protestant Reformation.

Chaucer, the son of a London wine merchant, served during his boyhood, probably as a page, in the household of the Countess of Ulster, wife of Lionel, Duke of Clarence, third son of Edward III. As a young man he fought on the continent, was taken prisoner near Rheims, and was ransomed by the King. During a long and active public career he held many positions under the Crown. He was comptroller of the customs in the wool trade; he was a clerk of the King's works and a deputy forester; he served on diplomatic missions to

France and Italy; and down in Kent, where he retired late in life, he was a justice of the peace by the King's appointment and one of two knights elected to represent the county in Parliament. A year before his death he leased a house in the garden of Westminster Abbey, where he died in 1400, in the city in which he had spent most of his life. He was buried in that part of the Abbey that subsequently became known as the Poets' Corner.

Among Chaucer's early poems the best is *The Book of the Duchess,* written about 1369 and believed to commemorate the death of Blanche, Duchess of Lancaster and first wife of John of Gaunt. This work, in the form of a dream-allegory, a fashionable type of medieval story-telling, was influenced by the Latin poet Ovid and by the thirteenth-century French *Romance of the Rose,* a long allegorical poem which influenced much of Chaucer's early writing, and a part of which Chaucer himself translated into English. Among his other early poems *The Parliament of Fowls* and *The House of Fame* are further examples of the dream-allegory.

The House of Fame, which has some of the characteristics of Dante's *Divine Comedy,* marks prominently the beginning of the Italian influence upon Chaucer; but to the modern reader this influence is more profitably apparent in the long narrative poem *Troilus and Criseyde,* completed probably about 1385. The immediate source of this poem is Boccaccio's *Filostrato,* which Chaucer did not hesitate to trans-late and to paraphrase at will. *Troilus and Criseyde* is perhaps the earliest manifestation of the psychological method in English litera-ture. However this may be, at least one of its characters, some of its dialogue, and much of its humor show that Chaucer was moving firmly and fruitfully away from his early obsession with complaints and dreams and allegories. *Troilus and Criseyde* is the first important appearance of the story of Troy in English literature.

For all its excellence and novelty, however, *Troilus and Criseyde* does not reveal Chaucer at his best. Leaving unfinished *The Legend of Good Women,* a collection of tales about famous saints of the god Cupid, Chaucer turned, sometime about the year 1387, to the work with which his name is most frequently associated. Medieval story-tellers, following an Oriental example, collected groups of tales in a unifying framework, as, for example, Chaucer himself did in *The Legend of Good Women.* Boccaccio's *Decameron,* Gower's *Confessio Amantis,* Sercambi's *Novelle,* and *The Thousand and One Nights* are other examples of this literary convention. In adopting this style in *The Canterbury Tales,* Chaucer was not imitating any contemporary author; his work owes no more to the *Decameron,* for instance, than to any other particular frame-story. The design of *The Canterbury Tales* was purely conventional; what is distinctive about it is Chaucer's execution of the design. His introductory prologue, which is a kind of gallery of fourteenth-century English portraits, the various smaller prologues and connecting links that hold the tales together, the side-lights upon the characters and the times—these are the work of a great literary artist.

The tales themselves are of almost every variety of medieval narrative: romance, *fabliau, exemplum,* sermon, saint's legend, virtue story, fairy tale, and fable. In tone they range from the chivalric romanticism of the Knight's Tale and the solemn devoutness of the Parson's sermon to the realism and obscenities in the tales of the Summoner and the Miller. Usually Chaucer adapts the story to the character of the narrator, the coarsest personages telling the coarsest stories, the most respectable adhering to romance, religion, and the virtues. According to Chaucer's plan, there were to be one hundred and twenty tales; actually he completed only twenty. Two tales are broken off by interruptions by the pilgrims themselves; two more were left unfinished.

For the modern reader the language of Chaucer is difficult. It is an East Midland dialect of late Middle-English—the language of London at the end of the fourteenth century. Pronounced as it was in Chaucer's time, it sounds today like a foreign tongue, although on the printed page it looks not unlike present English. The vowel sounds are similar to those of modern French or German. Many of the final e's that represented case endings in the original Anglo-Saxon were still pronounced in the fourteenth century. Many plural and possessive forms of nouns are now unrecognizable as such. And many words identical in form with modern English had meanings that have long been lost. For many years ignorance of Chaucer's language led critics to assert that his poetry was rough and uneven, but since the eighteenth century, scholars have gradually come to realize that Chaucer's lines, when properly read, flow as smoothly as those of Swinburne or Keats.

It may be true, as Matthew Arnold contended, that Chaucer's poetry does not contain the "high seriousness" of the *Iliad* or of *Paradise Lost*—that question is debatable. But like the work of Shakespeare and

Fielding and others of more recent time, the poetry of Chaucer is suffused with a prevailing humor, an enduring humanity, a charitable understanding of man's frailty, and a hardy reluctance to cast the first stone at any manner of sinner taken in any manner of sin.

THE CANTERBURY TALES

THE PROLOGUE

WHAN THAT APRILLE with his shoures soote[1]
The droghte of Marche hath percèd to the roote,
And bathèd every veyne in swich licour,
Of which vertu engendrèd is the flour;
Whan Zephirus[2] eek with his swete breeth
Inspirèd hath in every holt[3] and heeth
The tendre croppes,[4] and the yonge sonne
Hath in the Ram his halfe cours y-ronne,
And smale fowles maken melodye,
That slepen al the night with open yë,
(So priketh hem nature in hir corages[5]):
Than longen folk to goon on pilgrimages,
And palmers[6] for to seken straunge strondes,
To ferne halwes,[7] couthe[8] in sondry londes;
And specially, from every shires ende
Of Engelond, to Caunterbury they wende,
The holy blisful martir[9] for to seke,
That hem hath holpen, whan that they were seke.
    Bifel that, in that sesoun on a day,
In Southwerk at the Tabard as I lay
Redy to wenden on my pilgrimage
To Caunterbury with ful devout corage,
At night was come in-to that hostelrye

1. *soote*, sweet. 2. *Zephirus*, the west wind. 3. *holt*, wood. 4. *croppes*, young shoots. 5. *corages*, feelings. 6. *palmers*, professional pilgrims. 7. *ferne halwes*, distant shrines. 8. *couthe*, well known. 9. *martir*, St. Thomas à Beckett.

Wel nyne and twenty in a compaignye,
Of sondry folk, by aventure[10] y-falle
In felawshipe, and pilgrims were they alle,
That toward Caunterbury wolden ryde;
The chambres and the stables weren wyde,
And wel we weren esèd atte beste.[11]
And shortly, whan the sonne was to reste,
So hadde I spoken with hem everichon,
That I was of hir felawshipe anon,
And made forward[12] erly for to ryse,
To take our wey, ther as I yow devyse.[13]
        But natheles,[14] whyl I have tyme and space,
Er that I ferther in this tale pace,
Me thinketh it acordaunt to resoun,
To telle yow al the condicioun
Of ech of hem, so as it semèd me,
And whiche they weren, and of what degree;[15]
And eek[16] in what array that they were inne:
And at a knight than wol I first biginne.
        A KNIGHT ther was, and that a worthy man,
That fro the tyme that he first bigan
To ryden out, he lovèd chivalrye,
Trouthe and honour, fredom[17] and curteisye.
Ful worthy was he in his lordes werre,
And thereto hadde he riden (no man ferre)[18]
As wel in cristendom as hethenesse,
And evere honourèd for his worthinesse.
At Alisaundre he was, whan it was wonne;
Ful ofte tyme he hadde the bord bigonne[19]
Aboven alle naciouns in Pruce.
In Lettow hadde he reysèd[20] and in Ruce,
No cristen man so ofte of his degree.
In Gernade at the sege eek hadde he be
Of Algezir, and riden in Belmarye.
At Lyeys was he, and at Satalye,
Whan they were wonne; and in the Grete See
At many a noble aryve[21] hadde he be.

---

10. *aventure*, chance. 11. *atte beste*, in the best manner. 12. *forward*, agreement. 13. *devyse*, describe. 14. *natheles*, nevertheless. 15. *degree*, social rank. 16. *eek*, also. 17. *fredom*, generosity. 18. *ferre*, farther. 19. *the bord bigonne*, sat at the head of the table. 20. *reysed*, campaigned. 21. *aryve*, landing.

At mortal batailles hadde he been fiftene,
And foughten for our feith at Tramissene
In listes thryes, and ay slayn his foo.
This ilke[22] worthy knight hadde been also
Somtyme with the lord of Palatye,
Ageyn another hethen in Turkye:
And everemore he hadde a sovereyn prys.[23]
And though that he were worthy, he was wys,
And of his port as meek as is a mayde.
He nevere yet no vileinye[24] ne sayde
In al his lyf, un-to no maner wight.
He was a verray[25] parfit gentil[26] knight.
But for to tellen yow of his array,
His hors were goode, but he was nat gay.
Of fustian he werèd a gipoun[27]
Al bismotered[28] with his habergeoun.[29]
For he was late y-come from his viage,
And wente for to doon his pilgrimage.
        With him there was his sone, a yong SQUYER,
A lovyer, and a lusty bacheler,[30]
With lokkes crulle,[31] as they were leyd in presse.
Of twenty yeer of age he was, I gesse.
Of his stature he was of evene lengthe,[32]
And wonderly delivere,[33] and greet of strengthe.
And he hadde been somtyme in chivachye,[34]
In Flaundres, in Artoys, and Picardye,
And born him wel, as of so litel space,
In hope to stonden in his lady grace.
Embrouded[35] was he, as it were a mede
Al ful of fresshe floures, whyte and rede.
Singinge he was, or floytinge,[36] al the day;
He was as fresh as is the month of May.
Short was his goune, with sleves longe and wyde.
Wel coude he sitte on hors, and faire ryde.
He coude songes make[37] and wel endyte,[38]

22. *ilke*, same.   23. *prys*, reputation.   24. *vileinye*, rudeness.   25. *verray*, true.
26. *gentil*, noble.   27. *gipoun*, jacket.   28. *bismotered*, soiled.   29. *habergeoun*,
armor.   30. *lusty bacheler*, eager candidate for knighthood.   31. *crulle*, curly.
32. *evene lengthe*, medium height.   33. *delivere*, active.   34. *chivachye*, expeditions.   35. *embrouded*, embroidered.   36. *floytinge*, whistling (fluting?).
37. *songes make*, compose the music of songs.   38. *endyte*, write the words of
songs.

Juste and eek daunce, and wel purtreye[39] and wryte.
So hote he lovede, that by nightertale[40]
He sleep namore than doth a nightingale.
Curteys he was, lowly, and servisable,
And carf biforn his fader at the table.

A YEMAN[41] hadde he, and servaunts namo
At that tyme, for him liste ryde so;
And he was clad in cote and hood of grene;
A sheef of pecok arwes brighte and kene
Under his belt he bar ful thriftily,[42]
(Wel coude he dresse his takel[43] yemanly:
His arwes droupèd noght with fetheres lowe),
And in his hand he bar a mighty bowe.
A not-heed[44] hadde he, with a broun visage.
O wode-craft wel coude he al the usage.
Upon his arm he bar a gay bracer,[45]
And by his syde a swerd and a bokeler,[46]
And on that other syde a gay daggere,
Harneisèd[47] wel, and sharp as point of spere;
A Cristofre[48] on his brest of silver shene.
An horn he bar, the bawdrik[49] was of grene;
A forster was he, soothly, as I gesse.

Ther was also a Nonne, a PRIORESSE,
That of hir smyling was ful simple and coy;[50]
Hir gretteste ooth was but by sëynt Loy;
And she was clepèd[51] madame Eglentyne.
Ful wel she song the service divyne,
Entunèd in hir nose ful semely;
And Frensh she spak ful fair and fetisly,[52]
After the scole of Stratford atte Bowe,
For Frensh of Paris was to hir unknowe.
At mete wel y-taught was she with-alle;
She leet no morsel from hir lippes falle,
Ne wette hir fingres in hir sauce depe.
Wel coude she carie a morsel, and wel kepe,
That no drope ne fille up-on hir brest,

39. *purtreye*, draw. 40. *by nightertale*, at night. 41. *Yeman*, Yeoman.
42. *thriftily*, carefully. 43. *dresse his takel*, care for his bow and arrows. 44.
not-heed, head with hair cut short. 45. *bracer*, arm guard. 46. *bokeler*, shield.
47. *Harneised*, mounted. 48. *Cristofre*, image of St. Christopher, patron of travelers. 49. *bawdrik*, shoulder belt. 50. *coy*, modest. 51. *cleped*, called. 52.
fetisly, gracefully.

In curteisye was set ful moche hir lest.[53]
Hir over lippe wypèd she so clene,
That in hir coppe was no ferthing[54] sene
Of grece, whan she dronken hadde hir draughte.
Ful semely[55] after hir mete she raughte,[56]
And sikerly[57] she was of greet disport,[58]
And ful plesaunt, and amiable of port,
And peynèd hir[59] to countrefete chere
Of court, and been estatlich of manere,
And to ben holden digne[60] of reverence.
But, for to speken of hir conscience,
She was so charitable and so pitous,
She wolde wepe, if that she sawe a mous
Caught in a trappe, if it were deed or bledde.
Of smale houndes had she, that she fedde
With rostèd flesh, or milk and wastel breed.[61]
But sore wepte she if oon of hem were deed,
Or if men smoot it with a yerde[62] smerte:[63]
And al was conscience and tendre herte.
Ful semely hir wimpel[64] pinchèd[65] was;
Hir nose tretys;[66] hir eyen greye as glas;
Hir mouth ful smal, and therto softe and reed;
But sikerly she hadde a fair forheed.
It was almost a spanne brood, I trowe;
For, hardily, she was nat undergrowe.
Ful fetis was hir cloke, as I was war.
Of smal coral aboute hir arm she bar
A peire of bedes,[67] gauded al with grene;[68]
And ther-on heng a broche of gold ful shene,
On which ther was first write a crownèd A,
And after, *Amor vincit omnia.*[69]

    Another NONNE with hir hadde she,
That was hir chapeleyne and PREESTES thre.

---

53. *lest,* desire. 54. *ferthing,* bit. 55. *semely,* properly. 56. *raughte,* reached.
57. *sikerly,* surely. 58. *disport,* merriment. 59. *peyned hir,* took pains. 60.
digne, worthy. 61. *wastel breed,* fine white bread. 62. *yerde,* stick. 63. *smerte,*
painfully. 64. *wimpel,* head-dress. 65. *pinched,* pleated. 66. *tretys,* well
formed. 67. *peire of bedes,* rosary. 68. *gauded al with grene,* with green
beads at regular intervals. 69. *"Amor vincit omnia,"* "Love conquers all."

A Monk ther was, a fair for the maistrye,[70]
An out-rydere,[71] that lovede venerye;[72]
A manly man, to been an abbot able.
Ful many a deyntee hors hadde he in stable:
And, whan he rood, men mighte his brydel here
Ginglen in a whistling wynd as clere,
And eek as loude as doth the chapel-belle,
Ther as this lord was keper of the celle.[73]
The reule of seint Maure or of seint Beneit,
By-cause that it was old and som-del streit,[74]
This ilke monk leet olde thinges pace,[75]
And held after the newe world the space.[76]
He yaf nat of that text a pullèd[77] hen,
That seith, that hunters been nat holy men;
Ne that a monk, whan he is cloisterlees,
Is liknèd til a fish that is waterlees;
This is to seyn, a monk out of his cloistre.
But thilke[78] text held he nat worth an oistre.
And I seyde his opinioun was good.
What[79] sholde he studie, and make him-selven wood.[80]
Upon a book in cloistre alwey to poure,
Or swinken[81] with his handes, and laboure,
As Austin bit?[82] How shal the world be servèd?
Lat Austin have his swink to him reservèd.
Therfor he was a pricasour[83] aright;
Grehoundes he hadde, as swifte as fowel in flight;
Of priking[84] and of hunting for the hare
Was al his lust,[85] for no cost wolde he spare.
I seigh[86] his sleves purfiled[87] at the hond
With grys,[88] and that the fyneste of a lond;
And, for to festne his hood under his chin,
He hadde of gold y-wroght a curious[89] pin:
A love-knot in the gretter ende ther was.
His heed was balled, that shoon as any glas,
And eek his face, as he hadde been anoint.

70. *a fair for the maistrye,* a very grand one. 71. *out-rydere,* inspector. 72.
venerye, hunting. 73. *celle,* monastery. 74. *som-del streit,* somewhat strict. 75.
pace, go by. 76. *the space,* meanwhile. 77. *pulled,* picked. 78. *thilke,* that.
79. *What,* why. 80. *wood,* crazy. 81. *swinken,* work. 82. *bit,* ordered. 83.
pricasour, hard rider. 84. *priking,* riding. 85. *lust,* pleasure. 86. *seigh,* saw.
87. *purfiled,* trimmed. 88. *grys,* gray fur. 89. *curious,* elaborate.

He was a lord ful fat and in good point;
His eyen stepe,⁹⁰ and rollinge in his heed,
That stemèd ⁹¹ as a forneys of a leed;⁹²
His botes souple, his hors in greet estat.
Now certeinly he was a fair prelat;
He was nat pale as a for-pynèd⁹³ goost.
A fat swan loved he best of any roost.
His palfrey was as broun as is a berye.

    A FRERE ther was, a wantown and a merye,
A limitour,⁹⁴ a ful solempne⁹⁵ man.
In alle the ordres foure is noon that can⁹⁶
So moche of daliaunce and fair langage.
He hadde maad ful many a mariage
Of yonge wommen, at his owne cost.
Un-to his ordre he was a noble post.
Ful wel biloved and famulier was he
With frankeleyns⁹⁷ over-al in his contree,
And eek with worthy wommen of the toun:
For he had power of confessioun,
As seyde him-self, more than a curat,
For of his ordre he was licentiat.
Ful swetely herde he confessioun,
And plesaunt was his absolucioun;
He was an esy man to yeve penaunce
Ther as he wiste⁹⁸ to han a good pitaunce;
For unto a povre ordre for to yive
Is signe that a man is wel y-shrive.⁹⁹
For if he yaf, he dorste make avaunt,
He wiste that a man was repentaunt.
For many a man so hard is of his herte,
He may nat wepe al-thogh him sore smerte.
Therfore, in stede of weping and preyeres,
Men moot¹⁰⁰ yeve silver to the povre freres.
His tipet¹⁰¹ was ay farsèd¹⁰² ful of knyves
And pinnes, for to yeven faire wyves.
And certeinly he hadde a mery note;

90. *stepe*, protruding. 91. *stemed*, gleamed. 92. *leed*, cauldron. 93. *for-pyned*, tormented. 94. *limitour*, licensed beggar. 95. *solempne*, pompous. 96. *can*, knows. 97. *frankeleyns*, untitled landowners. 98. *wiste*, was sure. 99. *y-shrive*, shriven. 100. *moot*, must. 101. *tipet*, part of a cape. 102. *farsed*, stuffed.

Wel coude he singe and pleyen on a rote;[103]
Of yeddinges[104] he bar utterly the prys.
His nekke whyt was as the flour-de-lys.
There-to he strong was as a champioun.
He knew the tavernes wel in every toun,
And everich hostiler and tappestere[105]
Bet than a lazar or a beggestere;[106]
For un-to swich a worthy man as he
Acorded nat, as by his facultee,[107]
To have with seke lazars aqueyntaunce.
It is nat honest,[108] it may nat avaunce
For to delen with no swich poraille,[109]
But al with riche and sellers of vitaille.
And over-al,[110] ther as profit sholde aryse,
Curteys he was, and lowly in servyse.
There nas no wan nowher so vertuous.[111]
He was the beste beggere in his hous;
For thogh a widwe hadde noght a sho,
So plesaunt was his *In principio*,[112]
Yet wolde he have a ferthing, er he wente.
His purchas[113] was wel bettre than his rente.[114]
And rage[115] he coude as it were right a whelpe.
In love-dayes[116] ther coude he mochel helpe.
For ther he was nat lyk a cloisterer,
With a thredbare cope,[117] as is a povre scoler,
But he was lyk a maister or a pope.
Of double worsted was his semi-cope,[118]
That rounded as a belle out of the presse.
Somwhat he lipsèd[119] for his wantownesse,[120]
To make his English swete up-on his tonge;
And in his harping, whan that he had songe,
His eyen twinklèd in his heed aright,
As doon the sterres in the frosty night.
This worthy limitour was cleped Huberd.

---

103. *rote*, stringed instrument. 104. *yeddinges*, songs. 105. *tappestere*, barmaid.
106. *beggestere*, woman beggar. 107. *facultee*, position. 108. *honest*, becoming.
109. *poraille*, poor people. 110. *over-al*, everywhere. 111. *vertuous*, efficient.
112. *In principio*, "In the beginning [was the Word] . . ." 113. *purchas*, profits
from begging. 114. *rente*, allowed income. 115. *rage*, act lecherously. 116.
love-dayes, days for arbitration of disputes. 117. *cope*, mantle. 118. *semi-cope*,
outer cloak. 119. *lipsed*, lisped. 120. *for his wantownesse*, in affectation.

A Marchant was ther with a forkèd berd,
In mottelee,[121] and hye on horse he sat,
Up-on his heed a Flaundrish bever hat;
His botes claspèd faire and fetisly.
His resons[122] he spak ful solempnely,[123]
Sowninge[124] always thencrees[125] of his winning.
He wolde the see were kept for any thing[126]
Bitwixe Middelburgh and Orewelle.
Wel coude he in eschaunge sheeldes[127] selle.
This worthy man ful wel his wit bisette;[128]
Ther wiste no wight that he was in dette,
So estatly was he of his governaunce,
With his bargaynes, and with his chevisaunce,[129]
For sothe he was a worthy man with-alle,
But sooth to seyn, I noot[130] how men him calle.

A Clerk ther was of Oxenford also,
That un-to logik hadde longe y-go.
As lene was his hors as is a rake,
And he nas nat right fat, I undertake;
But lokèd holwe, and ther-to soberly.
Ful thredbar was his overest courtepy;[131]
For he had geten him yet no benefice,
Ne was so worldly for to have office.
For him was levere[132] have at his beddes heed
Twenty bokes, clad in blak or reed
Of Aristotle and his philosophye,
Than robes riche, or fithele,[133] or gay sautrye.[134]
But al be that he was a philosophre,
Yet hadde he but litel gold in cofre;
But al that he mighte of his frendes hente,[135]
On bokes and on lerninge he it spente,
And bisily gan for the soules preye
Of hem that yaf him wher-with to scoleye.
Of studie took he most cure and most hede.
Noght o word spak he more than was nede,
And that was seyd in forme and reverence,

121. *mottelee*, figured cloth. 122. *resons*, opinions. 123. *solempnely*, impressively. 124. *Sowninge*, proclaiming. 125. *thencrees*, the increase. 126. *kept for anything*, kept open at any cost. 127. *sheeldes*, French coins worth about 3 shillings. 128. *bisette*, employed. 129. *chevisaunce*, profitable dealing. 130. *noot*, know not. 131. *overest courtepy*, outer coat. 132. *levere*, more desirable. 133. *fithele*, fiddle. 134. *sautrye*, harp-like instrument. 135. *hente*, get.

And short and quik, and ful of hy sentence.[136]
Sowninge in[137] moral vertu was his speche,
And gladly wolde he lerne, and gladly teche.

    A SERGEANT[138] OF THE LAWE, war[139] and wys,
That often hadde been at the parvys,[140]
Ther was also, ful riche of excellence.
Discreet he was, and of greet reverence:
He semèd swich, his wordes weren so wyse,
Justice he was ful often in assyse,
By patente, and by pleyn commissioun;
For his science,[141] and for his heigh renoun
Of fees and robes hadde he many oon.
So greet a purchasour was nowher noon.
Al was fee simple to him in effect,
His purchasing mighte nat been infect.[142]
Nowher so bisy a man as he ther nas,
And yet he semed bisier than he was.
In termes[143] hadde he caas and domes[144] alle,
That from the tyme of king William were falle.
Thereto he coude endyte, and make a thing,[145]
Ther coude no wight pinche[146] at his wryting;
And every statut coude[147] he pleyn by rote.
He rood but hoomly in a medlee[148] cote
Girt with a ceint[149] of silk, with barres smale;
Of his array telle I no lenger tale.

    A FRANKELEYN was in his compaignye;
Whyt was his berd, as is the dayesye.
Of his complexioun[150] he was sangwyn.
Wel loved he by the morwe a sop in wyn.
To liven in delyt was evere his wone,[151]
For he was Epicurus owne sone,
The heeld opinioun that pleyn delyt
Was verraily felicitee parfyt.
An housholdere, and that a greet, was he;

136. *sentence*, meaning. 137. *Sowninge in*, conducive to. 138. *Sergeant*, lawyer for the king. 139. *war*, prudent. 140. *parvys*, Court of the Exchequer (or porch of St. Paul's Cathedral where lawyers consulted with clients?). 141. *science*, legal knowledge. 142. *infect*, invalidated. 143. *In termes*, accurately. 144. *domes*, judgments. 145. *endyte, and make a thing*, draw up a legal document. 146. *pinche*, find fault. 147. *coude*, knew. 148. *medlee*, cloth of mixed weave. 149. *ceint*, girdle. 150. *complexioun*, disposition. 151. *wone*, practice.

Seynt Julian he was in his contree.
His breed, his ale, was alwey after oon;[152]
A bettre envyned[153] man was nevere noon.
With-oute bake mete was nevere his hous,
Of fish and flesh, and that so plentevous,
It snewèd in his hous of mete and drinke,
Of alle deyntees that men coude thinke.
After the sondry sesons of the yeer,
So chaungèd he his mete and his soper.
Ful many a fat partrich hadde he in mewe,[154]
And many a breem and many a luce in stewe.[155]
Wo was his cook, but-if[156] his sauce were
Poynaunt and sharp, and redy al his gere.
His table dormant in his halle alway
Stood redy covered al the longe day.
At sessiouns[157] ther was he lord and sire.
Ful ofte tyme he was knight of the shire.
An anlas[158] and a gipser[159] al of silk
Heng at his girdel, whyt as morne milk.
A shirreve[160] hadde he been, and a countour;[161]
Was nowher such a worthy vavasour.[162]

    An HABERDASSHER and a CARPENTER,
A WEBBE,[163] a DYERE, and a TAPICER,[164]
And they were clothèd alle in o[165] liveree,
Of a solempne and greet fraternitee.
Ful fresh and newe hir gere apykèd[166] was;
Hir knyves were y-chapèd[167] noght with bras,
But al with silver, wroght ful clene and weel
Hir girdles and hir pouches everydeel.[168]
Wel semèd ech of hem a fair burgeys,
To sitten in a yeldhalle[169] on a deys.[170]
Everich, for the wisdom that he can,
Was shaply[171] for to been an alderman.
For catel[172] hadde they ynogh and rente,

---

152. *after oon*, of constant high quality. 153. *envyned*, supplied with wine.
154. *mewe*, pen. 155. *stewe*, fish pond. 156. *but-if*, unless. 157. *sessiouns*, local
courts. 158. *anlas*, dagger. 159. *gipser*, purse. 160. *shirreve*, sheriff. 161.
countour, accountant. 162. *vavasour*, untitled landholder. 163. *Webbe*, Weaver.
164. *Tapicer*, Tapestry maker. 165. *o*, one. 166. *apykèd*, ornamented. 167.
y-chaped, mounted. 168. *everydeel*, entirely. 169. *yeldhalle*, guildhall. 170.
deys, platform. 171. *shaply*, fit. 172. *catel*, property.

And eek hir wyves wolde it wel assente;
And elles certein were they to blame.
It is ful fair to been y-clept *ma dame*,
And goon to vigilyës[173] al bifore,
And have a mantel roialliche y-bore.
    A Cook they hadde with hem for the nones,[174]
To boille chiknes with the mary-bones,
And poudre-marchant[175] tart, and galingale.[176]
Wel coude he knowe a draughte of London ale.
He coude roste, and sethe, and broille, and frye,
Maken mortreux[177] and wel bake a pye.
But greet harm was it, as it thoughte me,
That on his shine a mormal[178] hadde he;
For blankmanger,[179] that made he with the beste.
    A SHIPMAN was ther, woning[180] fer by weste:
For aught I woot, he was of Dertemouthe.
He rood up-on a rouncy,[181] as he couthe,[182]
In a gowne of falding[183] to the knee.
A daggere hanging on a laas hadde he
Aboute his nekke under his arm adoun.
The hote somer had maad his hewe al broun;
And, certeinly, he was a good felawe.[184]
Ful many a draughte of wyn had he y-drawe
From Burdeux-ward, whyl that the chapman[185] sleep.
Of nyce[186] conscience took he no keep.
If that he faught, and hadde the hyer hond,
By water he sente hem hoom to every lond.
But of his craft to rekene wel his tydes,
His stremes and his daungers him bisydes,
His herberwe[187] and his mone, his lodemenage,[188]
Ther nas noon swich from Hulle to Cartage.
Hardy he was, and wys to undertake;
With many a tempest hadde his berd been shake.
He knew wel alle the havenes, as they were,
From Gootlond to the cape of Finistere,

173. *vigilyës*, celebrations. 174. *for the nones*, for the occasion. 175. *poudre-marchant*, flavoring powder. 176. *galingale*, spice. 177. *mortreux*, stews. 178. *mormal*, sore. 179. *blankmanger*, chicken stew. 180 *woning*, living. 181. *rouncy*, dray horse. 182. *as he couthe*, as well as he could. 183. *falding*, coarse cloth. 184. *good fellawe*, rascal. 185. *chapman*, merchant. 186. *nyce*, scrupulous. 187. *herberwe*, anchorage. 188. *lodemenage*, piloting.

And every cryke in Britayne and in Spayne;
His barge y-clepèd was the Maudelayne.

    With us ther was a Doctour of Phisyk,
In al this world ne was ther noon him lyk
To speke of phisik and of surgerye;
For he was grounded in astronomye.
He kepte[189] his pacient a ful greet del
In houres,[190] by his magik naturel.[191]
Wel coude he fortunen the ascendent
Of his images[192] for his pacient.
He knew the cause of everich maladye,
Were it of hoot or cold, or moiste, or drye,
And where engendrèd, and of what humour;
He was a verray parfit practisour.
The cause y-knowe, and of his harm the rote,
Anon he yaf the seke man his bote.[193]
Ful redy hadde he his apothecaries,
To sende him drogges, and his letuaries,[194]
For ech of hem made other for to winne;
Hir frendschipe nas nat newe to biginne.
Wel knew he the olde Esculapius,
And Deiscorides, and eek Rufus;
Old Ypocras, Haly, and Galien;
Serapion, Razis, and Avicen;
Averrois, Damascien, and Constantyn;
Bernard, and Gatesden, and Gilbertyn.
Of his diete mesurable[195] was he,
For it was of no superfluitee,
But of greet norissing and digestible.
His studie was but litel on the Bible.
In sangwin[196] and in pers[197] he clad was al,
Lynèd with taffata and with sendal;[198]
And yet he was but esy of dispence;
He kepte that he wan in pestilence.
For gold in phisik is a cordial,
Therfor he lovede gold in special.

189. *kepte,* watched. 190. *in houres,* times propitious for treatment. 191.
magik naturel, knowledge based upon astrology. 192. *fortunen . . . images,* interpret the favorable position of the stars for the effective use of his talismans. 193.
bote, remedy. 194. *letuaries,* medicinal syrups. 195. *mesurable,* temperate. 196.
sangwin, red. 197. *pers,* blue. 198. *sendal,* silk.

A good W<small>YF</small> was ther of bisyde Bathe,
But she was som-del[199] deef, and that was scathe.[200]
Of cloth-making she hadde swiche an haunt,[201]
She passèd hem of Ypres and of Gaunt.
In al the parisshe wyf ne was there noon
That to the offring bifore hir sholde goon;
And if ther dide, certeyn, so wrooth was she,
That she was out of alle charitee.
Hir coverchiefs ful fyne were of ground;[202]
I dorste swere they weyeden ten pound
That on a Sonday were upon hir heed.
Hir hosen weren of fyn scarlet reed,
Ful streite y-teyd,[203] and shoos ful moiste and newe.
Bold was hir face, and fair, and reed of hewe.
She was a worthy womman al hir lyve,
Housbondes at chirche-dore she hadde fyve,
Withouten other compaignye in youthe;
But thereof nedeth nat to speke as nouthe.[204]
And thryes hadde she been at Jerusalem;
She hadde passèd many a straunge streem;
At Rome she hadde been, and at Boloigne,
In Galice at seint Jame, and at Coloigne.
She coude moche of wandring by the weye.
Gat-tothèd[205] was she, soothly for to seye.
Up-on an amblere[206] esily she sat,
Y-wimplèd wel, and on hir heed an hat
As brood as is a bokeler or a targe;[207]
A foot-mantel[208] aboute hir hipes large,
And on hir feet a paire of spores sharpe.
In felaweschip wel coude she laughe and carpe.[209]
Of remedies of love she knew per-chaunce,
For she coude of that art the olde daunce.
  A good man was ther of religioun,
And was a povre P<small>ERSOUN</small>[210] of a toun;
But riche he was of holy thoght and werk.
He was also a lernèd man, a clerk,

199. *som-del*, somewhat. 200. *scathe*, a pity. 201. *haunt*, skill. 202. *ground*,
texture. 203. *streite y-teyd*, tightly laced. 204. *as nouthe*, right now. 205. *Gat-
tothed*, with teeth set apart. 206. *amblere*, ambling horse. 207. *targe*, shield.
208. *foot-mantel*, riding skirt. 209. *carpe*, talk. 210. *Persoun*, Parson.

That Cristes gospel trewely wolde preche;
His parisshens[211] devoutly wolde he teche.
Benigne he was, and wonder diligent,
And in adversitee ful pacient;
And swich he was y-prevèd ofte sythes.
Ful looth were him to cursen[212] for his tythes,
But rather wolde he yeven, out of doute,
Un-to his povre parisshens aboute
Of his offring, and eek of his substaunce.
He coude in litel thing han suffisaunce.
Wyd was his parisshe, and houses fer a-sonder,
But he ne lafte nat, for reyn ne thonder,
In siknes nor in meschief to visyte
The ferreste in his parisshe, moche and lyte,[213]
Up-on his feet, and in his hand a staf.
This noble ensample to his sheep he yaf,
That first he wroghte, and afterward he taughte;
Out of the gospel he tho wordes caughte;
And this figure he added eek ther-to,
That if gold ruste, what shal yren do?
For if a preest be foul, on whom we truste,
No wonder is a lewèd man[214] to ruste;
And shame it is, if a preest take keep,[215]
A shiten shepherde and a clene sheep.
Wel oghte a preest ensample for to yive,
By his clennesse, how that his sheep shold live.
He sette nat his benefice to hyre,[216]
And leet his sheep encombrèd in the myre,
And ran to London, un-to sëynt Poules,
To seken him a chaunterie for soules,[217]
Or with a bretherhed to been withholde;[218]
But dwelte at hoom, and kepte wel his folde
So that the wolf ne made it nat miscarie;
He was a shepherde and no mercenarie.
And though he holy were, and vertuous,
He was to sinful man nat despitous,[219]

211. *parisshens*, parishioners. 212. *cursen*, excommunicate. 213. *moche and lyte*, high society and low. 214. *lewed man*, layman. 215. *keep*, heed. 216. *sette . . . hyre*, did not rent out his position. 217. *chaunterie for soules*, position saying masses for the dead. 218. *with a bretherhed . . . withholde*, to become chaplain of a guild. 219. *despitous*, spiteful.

Ne of his speche daungerous[220] ne digne,[221]
But in his teching discreet and benigne.
To drawen folk to heven by fairnesse
By good ensample, this was his bisynesse:
But it were any persone obstinat,
What so he were, of heigh or lowe estat,
Him wolde he snibben[222] sharply for the nones.
A bettre preest, I trowe that nowhere non is.
He wayted after no pompe and reverence,
Ne makèd him a spycèd[223] conscience,
But Cristes lore, and his apostles twelve,
He taughte, but first he folwèd it him-selve.

    With him ther was a PLOWMAN, was his brother,
That hadde y-lad[224] of dong ful many a fother,[225]
A trewe swinkere[226] and a good was he,
Living in pees and parfit charitee.
God loved he best with al his hole herte
At alle tymes, thogh him gamed or smerte,[227]
And thanne his neighebour right as himselve.
He wolde thresshe, and ther-to dyke[228] and delve,
For Cristes sake, for every povre wight,
Withouten hyre,[229] if it lay in his might.
His tythes payèd he ful faire and wel,
Bothe of his propre swink[230] and his catel.
In a tabard[231] he rood upon a mere.

    Ther was also a Reve[232] and a Millere,
A Somnour[233] and a Pardoner also,
A Maunciple,[234] and my-self; ther were namo.

    The MILLER was a stout carl,[235] for the nones,
Ful big he was of braun, and eek of bones;
That provèd[236] wel, for over-al ther he cam,
At wrastling he wolde have alwey the ram.
He was short-sholdrèd, brood, a thikke knarre[237]
Ther nas no dore that he nolde heve of harre,[238]

---

220. *daungerous*, reserved. 221. *digne*, haughty. 222. *snibben*, rebuke. 223. *spyced*, too fastidious. 224. *y-lad*, hauled. 225. *fother*, load. 226. *swinkere*, worker. 227. *gamed or smerte*, pleased or pained. 228. *dyke*, dig ditches. 229. *hyre*, pay. 230. *propre swink*, personal labor. 231. *tabard*, sleeveless coat. 232. *Reve*, steward of an estate. 233. *Somnour*, subpoena-server for the ecclesiastical court. 234. *Maunciple*, steward of a college. 235. *carl*, fellow. 236. *proved*, turned out. 237. *knarre*, knotty fellow. 238. *of harre*, off its hinges.

Or breke it, at a renning, with his heed.
His berd as any sowe or fox was reed,
And ther-to brood, as though it were a spade.
Up-on the cop[239] right of his nose he hade
A werte, and ther-on stood a tuft of heres,
Reed as the bristles of a sowes eres;
His nose-thirles[240] blake were and wyde.
A swerd and bokeler bar he by his syde;
His mouth as greet was as a greet forneys.
He was a janglere[241] and a goliardeys,[242]
And that was most of sinne and harlotryes.
Wel coude he stelen corn, and tollen thryes;[243]
And ye he hadde a thombe of gold, pardee.
A whyt cote and blew hood werèd he.
A baggepype wel coude he blowe and sowne,
And therwithal he broghte us out of towne.
    A gentil MAUNCIPLE was ther of a temple,[244]
Of which achatours[245] mighte take exemple
For to be wyse in bying of vitaille.
For whether that he payde, or took by taille,[246]
Algate[247] he wayted so in his achat,[248]
That he was ay biforn and in good stat.
Now is nat that of God a ful fair grace,
That swich a lewèd[249] mannes wit shal pace
The wisdom of an heep of lernèd men?
Of maistres hadde he mo than thryes ten,
That were of lawe expert and curious;[250]
Of which ther were a doseyn in that hous,
Worthy to been stiwardes of rente and lond
Of any lord that is in Engelond,
To make him live by his propre good,
In honour dettelees, but he were wood,[251]
Or live as scarsly as him list desire;
And able for to helpen al a shire
In any cas that mighte falle or happe;

---

239. *cop*, top. 240. *nose-thirles*, nostrils. 241. *janglere*, big talker. 242. *goliardeys*, teller of dirty stories. 243. *tollen thryes*, take toll three times. 244. *temple*, law college. 245. *achatours*, buyers. 246. *by taille*, on credit. 247. *Algate*, in any case. 248. *achat*, buying. 249. *lewed*, uneducated. 250. *curious*, skilful. 251. *but he were wood*, unless he were crazy.

And yit this maunciple sette hir aller cappe.[252]
    The REVE was a sclendre colerik man,
His berd was shave as ny as ever he can.
His heer was by his eres round y-shorn.
His top was dokkèd[253] lyk a preest biforn.
Ful longe were his legges, and ful lene,
Y-lak a staf, ther was no calf y-sene.
Wel coude he kepe a gerner[254] and a binne;
Ther was noon auditour coude on him winne.
Wel wiste he, by the droghte, and by the reyn,
The yeldyng of his seed, and of his greyn.
His lordes sheep, his neet,[255] his dayerye,
His swyn, his hors, his stoor, and his pultrye,
Was hoolly in this reves governing,
And by his covenaunt yaf the rekening,
Sin that his lord was twenty yeer of age;
Ther coude no man bringe him in arrerage.[256]
Ther nas baillif, ne herde, ne other hyne[257]
That he ne knew his sleighte and his covyne;[258]
They were adrad[259] of him, as of the deeth.
His woning[260] was ful fair up-on an heeth,
With grene treës shadwèd was his place.
He coude bettre than his lord purchace.
Ful riche he was astorèd prively,
His lord wel coude he plesen subtilly,
To yeve and lene[261] him of his owne good,
And have a thank, and yet a cote, and hood.
In youthe he lernèd hadde a good mister;[262]
He was a wel good wrighte, a carpenter.
This reve sat up-on a ful good stot,[263]
That was al pomely[264] grey, and highte[265] Scot.
A long surcote of pers up-on he hade,
And by his syde he bar a rusty blade.
Of Northfolk was this reve, of which I telle,
Bisyde a toun men clepen Baldeswelle.
Tukkèd[266] he was, as is a frere, aboute,

252. *sette hir aller cappe*, made fools of them all.   253. *dokked*, cut short.   254. *gerner*, granary.   255. *neet*, cattle.   256. *bringe him in arrerage*, catch him in arrears.   257. *hyne*, servant.   258. *covyne*, duplicity.   259. *adrad*, afraid.   260. *woning*, dwelling.   261. *lene*, lend.   262. *mister*, trade.   263. *stot*, stallion.   264. *pomely*, dappled.   265. *highte*, named.   266. *Tukked*, with coat hitched up.

And evere he rood the hindreste of our route.

    A SOMNOUR was ther with us in that place,
That hadde a fyr-reed cherubinnes face,
For sawceflem[267] he was, with eyen narwe.
As hoot he was, and lecherous as a sparwe.
With scallèd[268] browes blake, and pilèd[269] berd;
Of his visage children were aferd.
Ther nas quik-silver, litarge, ne brimstoon,
Boras, ceruce, ne oille of tartre noon,
Ne oynement that wolde clense and byte,
That him mighte helpen of his whelkes whyte,
Ne of the knobbes sittinge on his chekes.
Wel loved he garleek, oynons, and eek lekes,
And for to drinken strong wyn, reed as blood.
Thanne wolde he speke, and crye as he were wood.
And whan that he wel dronken hadde the wyn,
Than wolde he speke no word but Latyn.
A fewe termes hadde he, two or thre,
That he had lernèd out of som decree;
No wonder is, he herde it al the day;
And eek ye knowen wel, how that a jay
Can clepen 'Watte,' as well as can the pope.
But who-so coude in other thing him grope,[270]
Thanne hadde he spent al his philosophye;
Ay 'Questio quid iuris'[271] wolde he crye.
He was a gentil harlot and a kynde;
A bettre felawe sholde men noght fynde.
He wolde suffre for a quart of wyn
A good felawe to have his concubyn
A twelf-month, and excuse him atte fulle:
And prively a finch eek coude he pulle.
And if he fond owher[272] a good felawe,
He wolde techen him to have non awe,
In swich cas, of the erchedeknes curs,
But-if a mannes soule were in his purs;
For in his purs he sholde y-punisshed be.
'Purs is the erchedeknes helle,' seyde he.

---

267. *sawceflem*, pimpled. 268. *scalled*, scabby. 269. *piled*, sparse. 270. *grope*, examine. 271. *'Questio quid iuris.'* 'The question is what [part] of the law . . .' 272. *owher*, anywhere.

But wel I woot he lyèd right in dede;
Of cursing oghte ech gilty man him drede—
For curs wol slee right as assoilling[273] saveth—
And also war him[274] of a *significavit*.[275]
In daunger[276] hadde he at his owne gyse[277]
The yonge girles[278] of the diocyse,
And knew hir counseil,[279] and was al hir reed.[280]
A gerland hadde he set up-on his heed,
As greet as it were for an ale-stake;[281]
A bokeler hadde he maad him of a cake.

    With him ther rood a gentil PARDONER
Of Rouncivale, his frend and his compeer,
That streight was comen fro the court of Rome.
Ful loude he song, 'Come hider, love, to me.'
This somnour bar to him a stif burdoun,[282]
Was nevere trompe of half so greet a soun.
This pardoner hadde heer as yelow as wex,
But smothe it heng, as doth a strike[283] of flex;
By ounces[284] heng his lokkes that he hadde,
And there-with he his shuldres overspradde;
But thinne it lay, by colpons[285] oon and oon;
But hood, for jolitee, ne wered he noon,
For it was trussèd up in his walet.
Him thoughte he rood al of the newe jet,[286]
Dischevele, save his cappe, he rood al bare.
Swiche glaringe eyen hadde he as an hare.
A vernicle[287] hadde he sowed on his cappe.
His walet lay biforn him in his lappe,
Bret-ful of pardoun come from Rome al hoot.
A voys he hadde as smal as hath a goot.
No berd hadde he, ne nevere sholde have.
As smothe it was as it were late y-shave;
I trowe he were a gelding or a mare.
But of his craft, fro Berwik into Ware,

273. *assoiling*, absolution. 274. *war him*, let him beware. 275. *"significavit"*, writ of arrest of an excommunicated person. 276. *In daunger*, at his mercy. 277. *at his owne gyse*, in his own manner. 278. *girles*, persons of both sexes. 279. *counseil*, secrets. 280. *reed*, counsel. 281. *ale-stake*, pole from which the sign of an ale house hung. 282. *stif burdoun*, stout bass. 283. *strike*, hank. 284. *by ounces*, in bunches. 285. *colpons*, shreds. 286. *jet*, style. 287. *vernicle*, handkerchief imprinted with the face of Christ.

Ne was ther swich another pardoner.
For in his male[288] he hadde a pilwe-beer,[289]
Which that, he seyde, was our lady veyl:
He seyde he hadde a gobet[290] of the seyl
That sëynt Peter hadde, whan that he wente
Up-on the see, til Jesu Crist him hente.
He hadde a croys of latoun,[291] ful of stones,
And in a glas he hadde pigges bones.
But with thise relikes, whan that he fond
A povre person dwelling up-on lond,
Up-on a day he gat him more moneye
Than that the person gat in monthes tweye.
And thus with feynèd flaterye and japes,[292]
He made the person and the peple his apes.
But trewely to tellen, atte laste,
He was in chirche a noble ecclesiaste.
Wel coude he rede a lessoun or a storie,
But alderbest[293] he song an offertorie;
For wel he wiste, whan that song was songe,
He moste preche, and wel affyle[294] his tonge.
To winne silver, as he ful wel coude;
Therefore he song so meriely and loude.
        Now have I told you shortly, in a clause,
Thestat,[295] tharray,[296] the nombre, and eek the cause
Why that assemblèd was this compaignye
In Southwerk, at this gentil hostelrye,
That highte the Tabard, faste by the Belle.
But now is tyme to yow for to telle
How that we baren us that ilke night,
Whan we were in that hostelrye alight.
And after wol I telle of our viage,
And al the remenaunt of our pilgrimage.
But first I pray yow of your curteisye,
That ye narette it nat my vileinye,[297]
Thogh that I pleynly speke in this matere,
To telle yow hir wordes and hir chere;

---

288. *male*, bag. 289. *pilwe-beer*, pillow case. 290. *gobet*, scrap. 291. *latoun*, alloy. 292. *japes*, tricks. 293. *alderbest*, best of all. 294. *affyle*, smooth. 295. *Thestat*, the rank. 296. *tharray*, the dress. 297. *narette . . . vileinye*, not attribute it to coarseness in me.

Ne thogh I speke hir wordes proprely.
For this ye knowen al-so wel as I,
Who-so shal telle a tale after a man,
He moot reherce, as ny as evere he can,
Everich a word, if it be in his charge,
Al[298] speke he never so rudeliche and large;[299]
Or elles he moot telle his tale untrewe.
Or feyne thing, or fynde wordes newe.
He may nat spare, al-thogh he were his brother;
He moot as wel seye o word as another.
Crist spake him-self ful brode in holy writ,
And wel ye woot, no vileinye is it.
Eek Plato seith, who-so that can him rede,
The wordes mote be cosin to the dede.
Also I prey yow to foryeve it me ,
Al have I nat set folk in hir degree[300]
Here in this tale, as that they sholde stonde;
My wit is short, ye may wel understonde.

      Greet chere made our hoste us everichon,
And to the soper sette he us anon;
And served us with vitaille at the beste.
Strong was the wyn, and wel to drinke us leste.
A semely man our hoste was with-alle
For to han been a marshal in an halle;
A large man he was with eyen stepe,
A fairer burgeys was ther noon in Chepe:
Bold of his speche, and wys, and wel y-taught,
And of manhood him lakkede right naught.
Eek thereto he was right a mery man,
And after soper pleyen he bigan,
And spak of mirthe amonges othere thinges,
Whan that we hadde maad our reckeninges;
And seyde thus: 'Now, lordinges, trewely
Ye ben to me right welcome hertely:
For by my trouthe, if that I shal nat lye,
I ne saugh this yeer so mery a compaignye
At ones in this herberwe[301] as is now.
Fayn wolde I doon yow mirthe, wiste I how.

298. *Al*, although. 299. *large*, frankly. 300. *in hir degree*, in the order of their social rank. 301. *herberwe*, inn.

And of a mirthe I am right now bithoght,
To doon yow ese, and it shal coste noght.
    Ye goon to Caunterbury; God yow spede,
The blisful martir quyte yow your mede.[302]
And wel I woot, as ye goon by the weye,
Ye shapen yow[303] to talen and to pleye;
For trewely, confort ne mirthe is noon
To ryde by the weye doumb as a stoon;
And therfore wol I maken yow disport,
As I seyde erst, and doon yow som confort.
And if yow lyketh alle, by oon assent,
Now for to stonden at my jugement,
And for to werken as I shal yow seye,
To-morwe, whan ye ryden by the weye,
Now, by my fader soule, that is deed,
But ye be merye, I wol yeve yow myn heed.
Hold up your hond, withoute more speche.'
Our counseil was nat longe for to seche;
Us thoughte[304] it was noght worth to make it wys,[305]
And grauntèd him with-outen more avys,
And bad him seye his verdit, as him leste.
    'Lordinges,' quod he, 'now herkneth for the beste:
But tak it not, I prey yow, in desdeyn;
This is the poynt, to speken short and pleyn,
That ech of yow, to shorte with our weye,
In this viage, shal telle tales tweye,
To Caunterbury-ward, I mene it so,
And hom-ward he shal tellen othere two,
Of aventures that whylom[306] han bifalle.
And which of yow that bereth him best of alle,
That is to seyn, that telleth in this cas
Tales of best sentence and most solas,
Shal han a soper at our aller cost[307]
Here in this place, sitting by this post,
Whan that we come agayn fro Caunterbury.
And for to make yow the more mery,
I wol my-selven gladly with yow ryde,

---

302. *quyte yow your mede,* reward you. 303. *shapen yow,* plan. 304. *Us thoughte,* it seemed to us. 305. *to make it wys,* to deliberate. 306. *whylom,* formerly. 307. *at our aller cost,* at the expense of all.

Right at myn owne cost, and be your gyde.
And who-so wol my jugement withseye
Shal paye al that we spenden by the weye.
And if ye vouche-sauf that it be so,
Tel me anon, with-outen wordes mo,
And I wol erly shape me therfore.'
          This thing was graunted, and our othes swore
With ful glad herte, and preyden him also
That he wold vouche-sauf for to do so,
And that he wolde been our governour,
And of our tales juge and reportour,
And sette a soper at a certeyn prys;
And we wold reulèd been at his devys,
In heigh and lowe; and thus, by oon assent,
We been accorded to his jugement.
And ther-up-on the wyn was fet[308] anoon;
We dronken, and to reste wente echoon,
With-outen any lenger taryinge.
A-morwe, whan that day bigan to springe,
Up roos our host, and was our aller cok,[309]
And gadrede us togidre, alle in a flok,
And forth we riden, a litel more than pas[310]
Un-to the watering of seint Thomas.
And there our host bigan his hors areste,
And seyde; 'Lordinges, herkneth if yow leste.
Ye woot your forward, and I it yow recorde,[311]
If even-song and morwe-song acorde,
Lat se now who shal telle the firste tale.
As evere mote I drinke wyn or ale,
Who-so be rebel to my jugement
Shall paye for al that by the weye is spent.
Now draweth cut,[312] er that we ferrer twinne,[313]
He which that hath the shortest shal beginne.'
'Sire knight,' quod he, 'my maister and my lord,
Now draweth cut, for that is myn acord.
Cometh neer,' quod he, 'my lady prioresse;
And ye, sir clerk, lat be your shamfastnesse,

308. *fet*, fetched. 309. *our aller cok*, the cock for all of us. 310. *litel more than pas*, little faster than a walk. 311. *it yow recorde*, remind you of it. 312. *draweth cut*, draw straws. 313. *twinne*, depart.

Ne studieth noght; ley hond to, every man.'
    Anon to drawen every wight bigan,
And shortly for to tellen, as it was,
Were it by aventure, or sort, or cas,[314]
The sothe is this, the cut fil to the knight,
Of which ful blythe and glad was every wight;
And telle he moste his tale, as was resoun,
By forward and by composicioun,[315]
As ye han herd; what nedeth wordes mo?
And whan this goode man saugh it was so,
As he that wys was and obedient
To kepe his forward by his free assent,
He seyde: 'Sin I shal beginne the game,
What, welcome be the cut, a Goddes name!
Now lat us ryde, and herkneth what I seye.'
    And with that word we riden forth our weye;
And he bigan with right a mery chere
His tale anon, and seyde in this mannere.

THE FRIAR'S TALE

Prologue

THE NOBLE FRIAR, that worthy beggar, kept frowning at the Summoner, but for good manners' sake he had not yet said anything rude to him. But at last he said to the Wife [of Bath], "Madame," said he, "God pleasure you! As I live, you have touched here upon one of the hard problems of the scholars. I dare say you have said many a thing right well; but, Madame, as we ride here on our way, we must talk only for fun, and leave matters of authority, in God's name, for the preachers and theologians. And if it please this company I shall tell you a funny story about a summoner. Surely you know that no good may be said about summoners. I pray that none of you be ill-pleased—a summoner is a runner up and down with summonses for vice, and is beaten at every town's end."

314. *aventure, or sort, or cas,* chance (the words all mean essentially the same thing).   315. *composicioun,* arrangement.

Our Host then spoke: "Ah, sir, you should be polite and courteous, as becomes a man of your position. We'll have no quarrel in this company. Tell your story, and leave the Summoner alone."

"No," said the Summoner, "let him say what he pleases to me. When my time comes, by God, I'll get even with him. I shall tell him what a great honor it is to be a flattering beggar—and of all sorts of other crimes that we needn't go into here. And, indeed, I shall tell him just what his business is."

Our Host answered, "Peace, no more of this!" And then he said to the Friar, "Go on, dear Master, and tell your story."

THE FRIAR'S TALE

Once upon a time there dwelt in my part of the country an archdeacon, a man of high rank, who bravely executed the punishments for fornication, witchcraft, and pandering, for slander and adultery; the punishments of church-wardens, and the punishments for breach of wills and contracts, and also for failure to observe the sacraments, for usury and for simony. But lechers, really, he punished the hardest; they would howl, if they were caught. And those shirking their tithes were foully punished, if any priest complained against them. No fine, however small, did the archdeacon overlook. For tithes and offerings that were too little he made the people howl in anguish. For before the bishop got his hook on them they were down in the archdeacon's book, and then through his jurisdiction he had the privilege of punishing them.

Ready at hand, he had a summoner. In all England there was no slyer boy, for under cover he had his spies that advised him where he might profit. He could afford to spare a lecher or two to find his way to dozens more. For though this summoner were mad as a hare, I'll not spare to tell of his villainy; for we friars are out of his power; they have no jurisdiction over us—nor ever will have to the end of their lives.

"St. Peter!" broke in the Summoner. "So are the women in the brothels out of my power."

"Peace, curse you!" cried our Host; "and let him tell his story. Now, go on, even if the Summoner does cry out. And, my dear Master, don't spare him!"

This dishonest thief, this summoner—continued the Friar—always

had his bawds at hand, like hawks returning to the lure, to tell him
what they secretly knew; for their friendship was not new—they
were his private informers. By this connection he made himself a big
profit, and his archdeacon did not always know what he made. Even
without a summons he could threaten a sinner with excommunication. And they were glad to fill his purse and give great feasts for
him at the ale house. And just as Judas had his own small purses and
was a thief, just such a thief was he; his master gained but half of
what was coming to him. He was, to give him his due, a thief and
also a summoner and a bawd.

Among his spies he also had wenches, who, whether Sir Robert or
Sir Hugh, or Jack or Ralph or whoever it was that lay with them,
whispered it in his ear. Thus were the wench and he in business together; and he would fetch a false summons and hale them before
the chapter, both of them, and plunder the man and let the woman
go.

Then he would say, "Friend, for your sake I shall have your case
stricken from our records. You will have no more trouble with this
case. I am your friend wherever I can help you." Surely he knew
more sorts of bribery than I could tell you about in two years; for
there is not a hunting dog in this world that can tell a hurt deer from
a whole one better than this summoner could tell a sly lecher or an
adulterer or a paramour. And since that was the substance of all his
income, he set his whole mind upon it.

And it so happened that one day this summoner, always watching for a victim, rode to summon an old widow, an old hag of a
woman—feigning charges against her, for he wanted a bribe—and it
happened that he saw a gay yeoman riding before him beside a forest.
He carried a longbow and bright, sharp arrows; he had on a green
jacket and on his head a hat with black fringe. "Sir," said the summoner, "hail and well met!"

"Welcome," said the other, "and every other fellow! Where do
you ride in this greenwood thicket? Are you going far today?"

The summoner answered him and said, "No. My purpose is to
ride nearby here to pick up a payment on a debt to my lord."

"Are you a bailiff, then?" asked the yeoman.

"Yes," said the summoner. He dared not, for the very shame and
filth of the name, say that he was a summoner.

"Well, well, dear brother," said the yeoman; "you are a bailiff,
and I am one too. As I am unknown in this part of the country I

would, if you please, be friends with you and swear brotherhood. I have gold and silver in my chest; and if you happen to come to our shire, it shall all be yours, just as you wish."

"Many thanks to you, indeed," said the summoner. They shook hands upon it and swore eternal brotherhood. With gay talk they rode on their way.

This summoner was as full of jabber as a butcherbird is of spite and was always asking about everything. "Brother," said he, "where is this dwelling of yours—if I should look you up some day?" The yeoman answered him softly. "Far in the north country, brother," said he, "where I hope I shall see you sometime. Before we part I shall show you the way to my house so well that you can never miss it."

"Now, brother," said the summoner, "while we are riding along, I pray you—since you are a bailiff like me—teach me some of your tricks, and tell me faithfully how I may make the most out of my business. And spare not for conscience or sin, but as my brother tell me how you manage."

"Now, on my word, dear brother," said the yeoman, "I shall tell you the truth. My wages are very small and limited. My lord is hard on me and hard to please; and my work is most laborious; therefore I live by extortions. Indeed, I take all that anyone will give me. Always, from year to year, whatever I have to spend I make by trickery or violence. Really, I can tell you no better than this."

"Well, now," said the summoner, "I fare the same. God knows I never hesitate to take things—unless they are too heavy or too hot. I have no sort of conscience about whatever I get secretly. If it weren't for my extortions, I couldn't live. Nor do I confess to the priest these tricks of mine; I have no feeling or conscience about them. Damn these father-confessors, all of them. By God and St. James, it's good that we've met! But meanwhile tell me, dear brother, what then is your name?"

The yeoman began to smile a little. "Brother," said he, "do you really want to know? I am a devil; my home is in Hell. And here I ride about my business to see whether anybody will give me anything. What I get that way is the sum of my income. See, you go about it for the same purpose—to make something, you don't care how; I do the same, for right now I could ride to the end of the world for a victim."

"Ah, bless us," said the summoner, "what did you say? I thought you were really a yeoman; you have a man's shape like me. Have you then a particular shape when you are in your regular place in Hell?"

"Not at all," said he; "there we have none; but we can take one when we please, or else make it seem to you that we have a shape. Sometimes I go about like a man, or like an ape, or like an angel. It is not such a wonderful thing after all; even a lousy juggler can deceive you, and surely I know more tricks than he."

"Why then," said the summoner, "do you go about in different shapes instead of always in the same one?"

"Because," said he, "we assume such forms as make it easiest for us to catch our victims."

"Why," said the summoner, "do you take all this trouble?"

"For many reasons, my dear Sir Summoner," said the devil. "But everything has its time; it is already past nine, and the day is short, and still I haven't gained a thing today. I intend to gain something if I can, instead of telling all our secrets. For even though I told you, my brother, your mind is too slight to understand. But since you ask why we labor so—in different ways and forms we are sometimes God's means and instruments of executing his commandments, when it pleases him, upon his creatures. For surely we have no power if it pleases him to oppose us. And sometimes we have leave, at our request, to injure only man's body and not his soul; witness Job, whom we brought great anguish. But sometimes we have power over both— that is, over body and soul. And sometimes we are allowed to seek out a man and do mischief to his soul and not to his body. And it is all for the best. When he withstands our temptations, it is a cause of his salvation, although it was not our intention that he should be saved but that we should seize him. And sometimes we are the servants of men, as of Saint Dunstan the archbishop, and as I also was the servant of the apostles."

"Yet tell me," said the summoner, "truly; do you always thus make you a new body from the elements?"

"No," answered the devil; "sometimes we deceive, and sometimes we rise in different ways with dead bodies and speak as fluently and fairly and well as Samuel did to the Witch—and yet some say it was not he. I take no stock in your theology. But of one thing I warn you, and I'm not joking: if you go on trying to find out how we are shaped, you shall come hereafter, my dear brother, where you won't have to learn it from me, for you shall be able from your own experience to deliver a lecture on that subject better than Virgil when he was alive, or even Dante. Now let us ride on quickly, for I shall keep company with you till you decide to leave me."

"No," said the summoner, "that will never happen. I am a yeoman, well enough known; and I shall keep my word in this deal; for though you were the devil Satan, I shall keep my word to my brother, because I have sworn it—and each to the other. And we both go about our business. You take your share, whatever anyone gives you, and I'll take mine; thus we may both prosper. And if one of us has more than the other, let him be fair about it."

"On my word," said the devil, "I agree to it."

And with that they rode on their way. And right at the entrance to the town to which the summoner planned to go they saw a cart loaded with hay, which a carter was driving on his way. The mud was deep, and the cart was stuck. The carter struck and shouted like a crazy man, "Get up, Brock! Get up, Scot! What are you holding back for? The devil take you, body and bones! As sure as you were born, I've stood enough from you; the devil take all, both horses and cart, and hay!"

The summoner said, "Here we'll have some fun!" and drew near the devil as though nothing were the matter and whispered in his ear: "Listen to that, my brother! Listen! Don't you hear what the carter says? Seize it now, for he has given it to you—both hay and cart, and his three horses besides."

"No," said the devil; "God knows, not at all. He doesn't mean it, trust me for that. Ask him yourself if you don't believe me, or else wait a minute and you will see."

The carter patted his horses on the cruppers, and they began to lean into it and pull. "Get up, now!" he said, "Jesus bless you there, and all his handiwork both great and small! That was well pulled, my own grey boy! God and St. Loy save you! Now indeed my cart is out of the mud."

"See what I told you, my own dear brother?" said the devil. "Here you may see that the fellow said one thing but he meant another. Let us go on our way. I make nothing at all out of this."

When they had come a little way out of town the summoner began whispering to his brother: "Brother," said he, "here lives an old dame that had almost as lief lose her neck as to give away a penny. But I will have twelve pence of her though it drive her mad, or I will summon her to our court. And yet God knows I know no evil of her. But since you don't seem to be able to make a living out of this part of the country, watch how I do it."

The summoner knocked at the widow's gate. "Come out, old woman!" he said. "I believe you have some friar or priest with you."

"Who is knocking?" asked the woman. "God bless us! God save you, sir; what is your sweet will?"

"I have here," he said, "a summons. On pain of excommunication, see that you be at the knee of the archdeacon tomorrow to answer to the court for certain charges."

"Now, Lord," said she, "Christ Jesus, King of Kings, do help me, for I can't help myself. I have been sick, and that for many a day. I cannot walk so far, or ride, without its killing me, I have such a stitch in my side. May I not ask a bill of charges, Sir Summoner, and answer there through my lawyer to such charges as anyone brings against me?"

"Yes," said the summoner; "you may pay now—let's see—twelve pence to me, and I will acquit you. I shall make but a little profit by it; my master makes the profit, not I. Come on, and let me hurry off; give me twelve pence; I can't wait any longer."

"Twelve pence!" said she; "now Lady Mary help me out of trouble and sin. Even if I could buy the wide world for it, I haven't twelve pence to my name. You know well that I am poor and old. Show your mercy on me, a poor wretched woman!"

"Not at all," said he, "the foul fiend take me if I let you off, even though you die for it!"

"Alas!" said she; "God knows I am not guilty."

"Pay me," he said, "or by sweet Saint Anne I will take away your new pan for that old debt that you owe me. That time you were unfaithful to your husband I paid the fine for you."

"You lie," she said; "by my salvation, never before now in all my life, wife or widow, was I summoned to your court. Never was I anything but faithful to my husband. To the black devil with you—and the pan too."

And when the devil heard her on her knees cursing this way, he spoke thus: "Now, Mabel, my own mother dear, is what you say your real wish?"

"May the devil take him," she said, "before he die, and the pan and all, unless he change his mind!"

"No, old jade, it is not my purpose to repent of anything I've got from you. I wish really that I had your smock and all your clothes."

"Now, brother," said the devil, "don't be angry. Your body and this pan are mine by my rights; tonight you shall go with me to Hell, where you shall learn more about our secrets than a master of divinity."

And with that word the foul fiend seized him; body and soul he went down with the devil to the place where summoners have their heritage. And God, who made man in his own image, save and guide us all, and permit these summoners to become good men!

"My lords," said the Friar, "If this summoner here would give me the time, I could have told you, according to the words of Christ and Paul and John, and many another of our learned ones, such punishments that your heart would shudder, although no tongue may actually describe them, even if I told for a thousand years about the pains of that accursed house of Hell. But to keep out of that cursed place, beware and pray to Jesus for his grace to keep us from Satan the tempter. Listen to my words! and take care—for this example: the lion lies always in ambush to slay the innocent if he can. Ever dispose your hearts to withstand the devil, who would make you his slaves. He cannot tempt you beyond your power to resist, for Christ will be your knight and champion. And pray that these summoners repent of their misdeeds before the devil seizes them!"

THE WIFE OF BATH'S TALE

IN THE OLD DAYS of King Arthur, about which the Britons tell glorious things, this land was all filled with enchantment; the fairy queen with her carefree company often danced in many a green meadow. This, as I have read, was the old belief—for I speak of a time many hundred years ago. But today no one can see the fairies any more, for now the great charity and prayers of beggars and other holy friars, who search every land and every stream as thick as motes in the sunbeam, blessing halls, chambers, kitchens, bowers, cities, towns, castles, high towers, villages, barns, ships, dairies—all this has brought about the end of the fairies, for where the fairy used to walk, there now walks morning and afternoon the friar himself, saying his matins and his holy services as he goes about his begging. Women may nowadays go up and down, for through all the thickets there is no incubus but him, and he will do them only dishonor.

And it so happened that this King Arthur had at his court a gay young knight that one day came riding from hawking on the river-bank; and it happened that, alone as he was born, he saw a maiden walking before him, and in spite of all that she could do he forcefully ravished her. For this crime there were such petitions and clamor made to King Arthur that by course of law the knight was condemned to death and would have lost his head—such was the statute then—but that the queen and some other ladies begged the king so long for mercy that he thereupon granted the young knight his life and gave him to the queen, to choose, at her pleasure, whether she would save or destroy him.

With all her power the queen thanked the king, and afterwards, when she saw her opportunity one day, she spoke thus to the knight: "You stand yet in such state that you have still no sureness of your life. But I grant you your life if you can tell me what thing it is that women most desire. Look to it, now, and keep your neck from the axe. And if you cannot tell it right now, I shall give you leave to go for a year and a day to seek and learn a satisfactory answer to this question. But before you go I must have a guarantee that you will yield your body in this place."

Sorrowful was the knight and sorrowfully he sighed, but alas! he was in no position to do as he pleased. And finally he chose to go and to return at the year's end with such answer as God would provide him; and he took his leave and went his way.

He sought every house and every place where he hoped to find favor, to learn what thing women love most; but by no sort of effort could he succeed in finding two persons together agreeing on this question. Some said women love riches best; some said honor; some said gaity; some, rich array; some said pleasure abed and to be a widow often and to marry again. Some said that our hearts are most comforted when we are flattered and pleased. That answer, believe me, goes pretty near the truth; a man will win us best with flattery; and, both high and low, we are caught by attention and by desire to please.

And some say that we love best to be free and to do just as we please, and that no one reprove us for our sins, but say that we are wise and in no way foolish; for truly there is no one of us all who will not kick if anyone scratches a sore place of ours in telling us the truth. Let him try, and he will find out; for however vicious we are within, we like to be thought wise and pure.

And some say we take great delight in being thought constant, and also faithful to a secret, and to hold fast to one purpose and not to disclose what anyone tells us. But indeed all that is not worth a rake handle; why, we women can't conceal a thing—witness Midas, if you would hear the story.

Ovid tells, amongst lesser matters, how Midas had growing upon his head under his long hair two ass's ears, which defect he hid as best he could, very subtly, from all men's sight, so that no one knew of it but his wife. He loved her best of all, and also he trusted her. He begged her to tell no one of his deformity. She swore that, for all this world, she would not do such a low-down, shameful thing as to bring disgrace to her husband's name. For her own shame she would not tell it. She felt, nevertheless, that she would die from keeping a secret so long. It swelled so sorely about her heart that surely, it seemed, some word must escape her. And since she dare not tell a human soul, down to a nearby marsh she ran—her heart was afire till she got there—and as a bittern booms in the swamp, she laid her mouth to the water, "Betray me not, thou sounding water," she said; "I tell it to thee and to no other. My husband hath two long ass's ears! Now is my heart all whole, now it is out. No longer, really, could I keep it." Here you may see that, although we endure for a time, yet a secret must out. We cannot keep one. If you would hear the rest of the tale, read Ovid, and there you will learn about it.

This knight, of whom I speak particularly, when he saw that he might not come at it—that is, what women love most—felt within his breast most sorrowful in spirit. But home he goes, for he might not delay. The day was come when homeward he must turn. And on his way he chanced, in his sorrow, to ride beside a forest, where he saw some four-and-twenty ladies dancing. Hoping to learn some wisdom, he eagerly drew toward them. But before he came up to them, they vanished, he knew not where. He saw no living thing but an old woman sitting on the green—a fouler creature no man could imagine. As the knight came up, the old woman rose and said, "Sir Knight, there is no way out of here. Tell me, on your word, what you seek. Perhaps it may be the better for you. Old folks know many a thing."

"My dear mother," said the knight, "I am indeed a dead man

unless I can find out what thing it is that women most desire. If you could teach me this, I'd make it worth your while."

"Give me your word," she said, "and join hands upon it that the first thing I ask of you, you will do if you can. And I shall give you your answer before night."

"My word on it," said the knight; "I grant it."

"Then," said she, "I dare boast that you are saved; for I will stand by it on my life that the queen will say as I say. Let us see what proudest of ladies in fine headdress will dare deny what I shall tell you! Without more talk let us go forth." Then she whispered a word in his ear and bade him be cheerful and carefree.

When they had come to the court, the knight announced that he had kept his day as he had promised, and that his answer was ready. Many a noble lady and many a maid and many a widow—and they are wise ones—were gathered to hear his answer, the queen herself sitting as judge. And then the knight was ordered to appear. Silence was commanded of all, that the knight might tell in their hearing what thing women love best in this world. The knight did not stand there like a dumb beast, but with a manly voice gave his answer to the question that all the court might hear.

"My sovereign lady," said he, "women everywhere throughout the world desire to have sovereignty as well over their husband as over their lover, and to have the mastery of him. Though you may kill me, this is your greatest desire; do as you please with me; I am here at your will."

In all the court there was no wife or maid or widow that contradicted what he had said, but all of them held that he deserved to have his life.

And with that word up sprang the old woman whom the knight had found sitting on the green. "A favor," cried she, "my sovereign lady queen! Before your court departs, do justice to me! I taught this answer to the knight, for which he gave me his word he would do, if it lay in his power, the first thing that I asked of him. Before the court then I pray you, sir knight, that you take me for your wife; for you know well enough that I have saved you. If I speak falsely, upon your word say me nay."

"Alas and woe is me!" the knight answered. "I know well enough that such was my promise. But for God's love, make some other request. Take all my worldly goods, but let my body go!"

"No, then," said she; "I curse the two of us! For though I am ugly and old and poor, I should not wish all the metal or ore buried under the earth or lying above it unless I were thy wife and thy love."

"My love?" said he; "no, damn me! Oh, that one of my birth should ever be so foully degraded!"

But all for naught; the result was that he was forced to marry her, and take his old wife and go off to bed.

Now, perhaps some would say that I neglect to tell you all the array and joy of the feast that day, to which I shall answer briefly. There was no joy or feast at all, I say; there was but heaviness and much sorrow. For he wedded her privately the next day and afterwards hid himself like an owl, so sorrowful was he at the ugliness of his wife.

Great was the woe that the knight had in his mind when he was brought to bed with his wife; to and fro he tossed and he turned. But all the while his old wife lay smiling and said, "Bless us, dear husband, does every knight fare thus with his wife as you do? Is this the law of King Arthur's court? Is every knight of his so bashful? I am your own love and your wife; I am she that has saved you. And surely I have never done you any wrong. Why do you deal thus with me this first night? You act like a man that had lost his wits. What is my guilt? For God's love tell it, and it shall be changed if I can."

"Changed?" said the knight, "No, no! It will nevermore be changed! You are so loathsome and so old too, and such a low person besides, little wonder I toss and turn. Would to God that my heart would break!"

"Is this," said she, "the cause of your unrest?"

"Yes, certainly," said he, "and no wonder."

"Now, sir," she said, "if I wished, I could change all this before three days had passed, were you to bear yourself well toward me. But since you mention the kind of gentility that comes from ancient wealth, and that you are a gentleman for that—such arrogance is not worth a hen. Whoever is most virtuous at all times, both privately and openly, consider him the greatest gentleman. Christ wishes us to claim from Him our gentility, not from our ancestors for their ancient riches. For though they give us their whole bequest from which we claim our high lineage, still they cannot for nothing bequeath to any of us their virtuous practices that caused them to be called gentlemen, nor can they bid us follow those practices.

"Well can Dante, the wise poet of Florence, speak on this theme.

Listen to the way Dante says it: 'Very seldom does the prowess of man spring from his own weak roots; for God in his goodness wills that of Him we claim our nobility; from our ancestors we may claim nothing but the mortal powers that hurt and injure man.'

"Also, everybody knows this as well as I: if gentility were implanted by nature all down the line of a certain family, then neither openly nor privately would they ever cease to do the duties of nobility. They would be incapable of coarseness or sin.

"Take fire and bear it into the darkest house between here and the Caucasus, and then shut the doors and go thence, still will the fire burn and blaze for twenty thousand to see. On my life it will show its natural property until it dies.

"In this you may see well enough how gentility is not dependent upon wealth, because it is not constant in man as is the natural property of fire. For God knows you may often see a noble's son do an ignoble and shameful thing. And any man who prizes his nobility because he was born of a good family and had noble and virtuous ancestors, but who at the same time will not do noble acts or follow in his dead ancestors' steps—such a man is not noble, be he earl or duke, because churlish, sinful deeds make only a churl. Your kind of gentility is but the renown of your ancestors for their great worth, which is lacking in you—one's real gentility comes from God alone. From His grace comes our true nobility; it is not a thing granted through position in this world.

"Think how noble, as Valerius says, was that Tullius Hostillius who rose from poverty to high nobility. Read Seneca, and also read Boethius! There you will see it stated that there is no doubt that he is noble who does noble deeds. And therefore, dear husband, I conclude thus: although my ancestors were humble people, still I hope the all-high God will grant me the grace to live virtuously. When I begin to live virtuously and to abandon evil, then I am noble.

"And since you reproach me for my poverty, the high God in Whom we believe chose voluntarily to live his life in poverty. And surely every man, maid, or wife can understand that Jesus, the King of Heaven, could not choose an evil life. 'Cheerful poverty is an honest thing indeed.' So says Seneca—and other scholars. Whoever holds himself satisfied with his poverty, him I call rich though he hasn't a shirt to his back. Whoever covets is a poor man, for he would have what is not in his power. But he that has nothing and covets nothing is rich, though you may consider him but a servant.

"True poverty—it literally sings. Juvenal speaks gayly of poverty: 'When the poor man goes down the road among thieves, he may dance and sing.' Poverty is a hateful good, and, as I guess, a very great relief from care; to him that bears it patiently, an aid to wisdom. Though it seem wearisome, poverty is this: a possession that none will dispute. Very often, when a man is low, poverty leads him to know both himself and God. Poverty is an eye-glass, it seems to me, by which one may see his true friends. And therefore, sir, if it does not grieve you, reproach me no more for my poverty.

"Now, sir, you reproach me for my age. And surely, sir, though there were no text in the books, you gentlefolk say that your gentility obliges you to show kindness to an old man and to call him father. And I guess I could find authority for that.

"Now since you say that I am old and ugly, then you needn't fear that I shall be unfaithful to you. For old age and ugliness are, as I live, great guardians of chastity. Nevertheless, since I know your pleasure, I shall satisfy your worldly desire.

"Choose now," she said, "one of these two things: to have me old and ugly until I die, but a true, humble wife, never in my life displeasing you, or to have me young and fair and to take your chance on what happens in your house—or maybe elsewhere—because of me. Now you yourself choose whichever you please."

The knight thought about it and sighed heavily. But finally he spoke thus: "My lady and my love and my so dear wife, I put myself under your wise control. Choose yourself which may be the greatest pleasure and honor to you and also to me. It makes no difference to me whichever you choose; for if it pleases you I am satisfied."

"Then have I got the mastery of you," said she, "since I may choose and rule as I please."

"Yes, indeed, my wife," said he, "I consider that best."

"Kiss me!" she said; "we are no longer at odds; for, on my word, I shall be both to you—that is, yes, both good and fair. I pray God I may die raving mad if I am not as good and true to you as wife ever was since the world began; and if in the morning I am not as fair to look upon as any lady, empress or queen, from east to west, then do with my life and death just as you please. Throw back the curtain; see how it is!"

And when the knight indeed saw all this, that she was so beautiful and so young besides, for joy he seized her in his two arms, his heart bathed in a bath of bliss. He began to kiss her, over and over, a thousand times; and she obeyed him in all his pleasure and desire. And thus in perfect joy they lived to the end of their lives. And Jesus Christ send us meek husbands, young and fresh abed, and the grace to rule over those that we marry! And also, I pray, may Jesus shorten the lives of those that will not be governed by their wives; and old and angry misers—God send them soon a very pestilence.

THE NUN'S PRIEST'S TALE

ONCE UPON A TIME there was a poor old widow living in a little cottage near a grove in a valley. Since the day she was last a wife this widow I speak of had lived patiently her very simple life, for she had little enough of this world's goods. By great care of such things as God had granted her she provided for herself and her two daughters. She had three large sows, no more, and three cows, and a sheep named Mollie. Her bedroom was sooty, and also the hall where she ate many a slender meal. She never needed any spicy sauces, nor did any fine food pass her throat; her diet was in keeping with her house. But at least she was never sick from overeating. Simple diet, hard work, and heart's content were her only medicine. The gout never kept her from dancing, nor was she ever seized with apoplexy. She drank no wine, either white or red; her table was served mostly with white and black—that is, milk and black bread, which she never lacked—broiled bacon, and sometimes an egg or two, for she was, as it were, a kind of farm-woman.

She had a yard enclosed with palings and a dry ditch all round, in which she kept a cock named Chanticleer. In the whole crowing world he had no equal: his voice was more cheering than the merry organ that plays in church on mass days; much surer than a clock, even a great abbey clock, was his crowing in his shed. By instinct he crowed the ascension of the equinox in that town; also right upon the hour he crowed in a way you couldn't improve on. His comb was redder than fine coral and crested like a castle wall; his bill was black and shone like jet, his legs and toes like azure, his nails whiter than the fleur-de-lys; and his whole color was like burnished gold.

For his pleasure this noble cock had under his rule seven hens that were his sisters and his mistresses, wonderfully like him in color, of which the fairest was called Damoiselle Pertelote. She was courteous, discreet, gracious, and companionable, and she had borne herself so prettily since the time when she was seven nights old that truly she had the heart of Chanticleer locked in her possession. And that suited him well, he loved her so. But when the bright sun began to rise it was a great joy to hear them sing in sweet harmony "My Love Has Gone Afar." For in those days, I understand, birds and beasts could both speak and sing.

And one morning at daybreak it happened that Chanticleer—as he sat among all his wives upon the perch in the hall, with Pertelote next to him—began to groan in his throat like a man sorely tormented in a nightmare. And when Pertelote heard him groaning so, she was terrified and said, "O dear heart, what ails you, groaning this way? This is no way to sleep! Shame on you!"

And he answered her thus: "Madame, I beg you don't take it so hard. God save me, it seemed just now that I was in such danger that even yet I am terrified.

"Now," said he, "God interpret my dream right and keep my body out of foul prison. I dreamed how I roamed up and down inside our yard, where I saw a beast like a dog, which would have seized and killed me. His color was between yellow and red, and his tail and both his ears were tipped with black, unlike the rest of his hair. His snout was small, with two glowing eyes. Right now I almost die of fear at his looks. Undoubtedly this caused my groaning."

"Shame!" said Pertelote. "Shame on you, coward! For by God in Heaven, now you have lost my heart and all my love! Really now, I can't love a coward; for whatever any woman may say, surely we all desire if we can to have husbands that are brave, wise, generous, and trustworthy, and no miser or fool, nor one that is afraid of every weapon, nor a boaster—by God above! How dare you, for shame, say to your love that anything in the world might make you afraid? Haven't you the heart of a man, and yet a beard? And can you be afraid even of dreams? Why God knows there's nothing in dreams but folly. Dreams come from overeating, often from gas on the stomach, and from the condition of a man's humors. Surely this dream that you had tonight comes from an excess of red bile, which is the very thing that causes folks to fear in their dreams arrows, fire with red flames, great beasts that would bite them, all sorts of strife, and dogs both great and small—just as black bile causes many a man to cry out in his sleep for fear of black bears or black bulls, or else that black devils will get them. I could tell you also of other

humors that terrify many a man asleep, but I'll just hit the high
spots of all this. Now, you take Cato, who was so wise a man; didn't
he say, 'Take no stock in dreams'?

"Now, sir," she said, "when you fly down from the roost, for God's
love take a laxative. On my soul and life I give you the very best
advice—and I don't lie to you—that you purge yourself of both your
red bile and your black bile; and in order to lose no time, since there's
no druggist in this town, I myself shall advise you what will be best
for your health and benefit. And in our yard I shall find those herbs
that have the natural property of purging you. Don't forget, for God's
own love, that you are very bilious. Avoid the rising sun lest it cause
excess of the hot humors. For if it does, I'll lay a penny that you'll
have a fever or a chill that will be the death of you. For a day or two
you shall take a tonic of worms before you take your laxative of
laurel, centaury, and fumitory, or of hellebore that grows there, caper-
spurge, goat-tree berries, or herb-ive growing in our yard. Peck them
up just as they grow, and swallow them. Be cheerful, my husband;
don't be afraid of dreams. I can tell you no more."

"Madame," said he, "many thanks for your lore! But as to Master
Cato, who has such a great reputation for wisdom, though he said to
have no fear of dreams, by God you may read in old books by men of
greater authority than Cato, God save us, just the opposite of all this,
and they have found well enough by experience that dreams do have
significance, as well of joy as of tribulations that we must bear in
this life. There's no use arguing about it: the proof is seen in the
fact.

"Cicero, one of the greatest authors that we read, says this—that
once two men went in all innocence upon a pilgrimage, and it
happened that they came to a town where there were such crowds
of people and so little room at the inns that they found not so much
as one cottage in which they might lodge together. So of necessity
they had to part company for that night. And each of them went and
took lodging where he could get it. One of them was lodged with
plough-oxen in a stall back in a yard; the other was lodged well
enough, as was his fate or good fortune—which governs all our lives.

"And it so happened that this man dreamed, as he lay in his bed,
how his companion began to call upon him and said, 'Alas! this
night I shall be murdered where I lie in an ox-stall. Now help me,
dear brother, or I die! In all haste come to me!' This man started from
fear out of his sleep, but when he was awake he only turned over and

took no heed. It seemed to him that his dream was mere folly. Thus he dreamed twice in his sleep; and the third time it seemed that his companion came to him and said, 'I am now slain; look at my bloody wounds, deep and wide! Get up early in the morning,' said he, 'and you shall see at the west gate of the town a cart full of dung, in which my body is secretly hidden. Boldly have that cart seized. To tell the truth, my gold was the cause of my murder.' His face pale and piteous, he told in detail how he was slain.

"And depend upon it, this dream was found to be true, for on the morrow as soon as it was day, this man took his way to his companion, and when he came to the ox-stall he began to call out to him. Presently the inn-keeper answered him and said, 'Sir, your companion is gone; he went out of the town at daybreak.'

"Remembering then his dreams, this man grew suspicious, and, waiting no longer, he went forth to the west gate of the town and found a dung cart, as it were prepared to dung the land, which was exactly as you have heard the dead man describe. And with a bold heart he began to cry out vengeance and justice for this crime. 'My companion is this night murdered,' he cried, 'and in this cart here he lies flat on his back, gaping! I cry out upon the officials of this town,' he said, 'that should keep and rule it. Help! Oh, here lies my friend slain.'

"Why should I tell more of this story? The people started up and overturned the cart, and in the middle of the dung they found the dead man, just murdered.

"O blissful God, that art so just and true, lo how thou revealest murder always! 'Murder will out,' we see that every day. Murder is so loathsome and abominable to God, Who is so just and reasonable, that He will not suffer it to be concealed, though it wait for years. 'Murder will out.' That is my conviction!

"And immediately the officials of that town seized the carter and so sorely tortured him and the innkeeper upon the rack that they finally confessed their crime and were hanged by the neck.

"By this men may see that dreams are things to fear. And indeed in the same book I read, right in the next chapter after this—on my salvation, I do not speak idly—that two men would have crossed the sea for certain business in a far country, if it had not been for a contrary wind that caused them to stop in a certain city that stood fair upon a harbor-side. But one day toward evening the wind began to change and blow just right for them. Cheerful and glad, they went to bed, planning to rise very early and sail away.

"But to one of the men a marvelous thing happened. As he lay sleeping, he dreamed toward day a wonderful dream. It seemed to him that a man stood by his bedside and commanded him to delay his voyage and spoke to him thus: 'If you travel tomorrow you shall be drowned; I have warned you.'

"The man woke and told his companion what he had dreamed, and prayed him to delay his voyage, if only for that one day. His companion, who lay by his bedside, began to laugh him to scorn. 'No dream,' said he, 'may so terrify my heart that I will put off my business. I don't give a hang for your dreaming, for dreams are only jests and folly. Men dream every day of owls or apes, and of many a confused matter besides. They dream of things that never were nor will be. But since I see that you will remain here and thus wilfully and lazily waste your time, God knows, it saddens me; so good day to you!'

And thus he took his leave and went his way. But before he had sailed half his course—I don't know why nor what was the trouble— by chance the bottom of the ship gave way, and ship and men went under the water in sight of the other ships nearby that had sailed with them on the same tide. And therefore, fair Pertelote so dear, by such old examples you may yet learn that no man should be too heedless of dreams, for I say to you that without a doubt many a woeful dream is a dream to dread.

"Now look—I have read in the life of Saint Kenelm, who was son of Kenulph, the noble king of Mercia, how Kenelm had a dream! One day a little before he was murdered, he saw in a vision his own murder. His nurse interpreted to him his whole dream and advised him to guard himself against treason; but he was only seven years old, and his heart was so pure that he took little heed of any dream. By Heaven! I'd give my shirt if you had read his legend as I have.

"Dame Pertelote, I tell you truly, Macrobeus, who wrote about the vision of the famous Scipio in Africa—he believed in dreams and says that they are a warning of things to come.

"And furthermore, I pray you, look well in the Old Testament— at Daniel, whether he considered dreams foolishness.

"Read also of Joseph, and there you shall see whether dreams are sometimes—I don't say always—a warning of things to come.

"Look at Lord Pharaoh of Egypt, also at his baker and butler—

whether they felt no effect of dreams. Whoever will look into the history of various countries may read many a wonderful thing about dreams.

"Take Croesus, who was king of Lydia—didn't he dream that he sat upon a tree, which meant that he was going to be hanged?

"And there was Andromache, Hector's wife—on the very eve of the day that Hector was going to lose his life she dreamed how he would die if he went that day into battle. She warned him, but to no purpose; he went to battle anyway. But he was slain at once by Achilles.

"But that story is much too long to tell, and also it is nearly day; I mustn't draw it out. To make a long story short and to end the matter, I say that I shall have misfortune from this dream. And I say furthermore that I take no stock in laxatives. For they are poisons. I know it well. I defy them. I love them never a bit!

"Now let us speak of pleasant things and stop all this. Madame Pertelote, on my life God has sent me grace enough in one respect! For when I see the beauty of your face—you are so scarlet red about the eyes—it puts an end to all my fears. For as sure as *In principio, mulier est hominis confusio*; Madame, the meaning of this Latin is 'Woman is man's joy and all his bliss.' For when I feel you nestle softly beside me at night (even though for the narrowness of our perch I may not ride upon you) I am so filled with comfort and joy that I defy both vision and dream."

And with that word he flew down from the roost—for it was day—and also all his hens. And with a cluck he began to call them, for he had found some grain lying in the yard. Now he was royal looking; he was no more afraid. He trod Pertelote twenty times, and before mid-morning twenty times more. He looked as though he were a grim lion, and he roamed up and down on his toes—he hardly deigned to set foot to the ground. He clucked when he had found a grain, and all his wives ran then to him. Thus, royal, like a prince in his hall, I leave this Chanticleer in his yard. And now I shall relate his adventure.

When the month was past called March, when the world began and God first made man, and when thirty-two more days had gone, it happened that Chanticleer in all his pride, his seven wives walking beside him, cast up his eyes to the bright sun, which had run some twenty-one degrees in the sign of Taurus, and knew by instinct that it was nine o'clock, and crowed with blissful voice. "The sun," he said "has climbed up to heaven forty-one degrees and more. Madame Pertelote, bliss of my world, listen to the singing of these joyful birds! And see how the fresh flowers spring up! How full is my heart of comfort and delight."

But there came to him all of a sudden a woeful misfortune; for always the end of joy is woe. God knows that worldly joy is soon past. And if an orator could write, he would be the one to chronicle it most effectively.

Now let every wise man listen to me: this story, I swear, is every bit as true as the book of Lancelot of the Lake, which women hold in such esteem. Now to my theme again.

A certain fox, marked with black, sly and evil, who had lived in the grove for three years, as God had predestined, had that same night broken through the fence into the yard where Chanticleer and his wives were accustomed to repair, and he lay quiet in a bed of herbs till past mid-morning, biding his time to fall upon Chanticleer, as all these murderers gladly do that lie in wait to murder men.

O false murderer, lurking in thy den! O new Iscariot! New Ganelon! O Greek Sinon, thou false deceiver that broughtest Troy finally to grief! O Chanticleer, accursed be that morning when thou flewest into the yard from thy roost! Thou wert well warned by thy dreams that that day was perilous to thee.

But what God foreknows must needs be, that is, according to certain scholars; and let the scholars be witness that in the schools there is great altercation and dispute over this very question—and always has been, by a hundred thousand men. But unlike the learned and holy Augustine or Boethius or Bishop Bradwardine, I am not one to thresh out this matter: whether God's foreknowing constrains me necessarily to do a thing—"necessarily" I call "simple necessity"— or whether free will is granted me to do that thing or not do it, though God foreknow it before it were done; or whether his knowing constrains me only by "conditional necessity."

I'll have nothing to do with such a question; after all, my tale is of a cock, as you may hear, that took the advice of his wife (confound her!) to walk in the yard on that morning after he had had that dream that I told you about.

Women's advice is very often disastrous; women's advice first brought us to grief and made Adam leave Paradise, where he had been joyful and well at ease. But as I know not whom it might displeasure if I should blame the counsels of women, just let it go, for I only speak

jokingly. Read the authors who deal with such matters and you may
see what they say of women. These words, after all, are the cock's
words and not mine. I myself can see no harm in any woman.

Fair in the sand, merrily bathing in the sun, lay Pertelote, and
all her sisters nearby; and the carefree Chanticleer sang more blithely
than the mermaid in the sea—for indeed Physiologus tells us how
they sing merrily and well.

And it so happened that as he cast his sight upon a butterfly
among the herbs he was aware of this fox lying low. He was in no
humor then to crow, but immediately cried "cok, cok" and started up
like a man terrified. For by instinct a beast will flee from his natural
enemy when he meets it, even though he has never laid eyes on it
before.

This Chanticleer, when he first saw the fox, would have fled,
but right away the fox said, "Alas, gentle sir, where are you going?
Are you afraid of me, who am your friend? Now surely I were a
devil of a fellow if I should wish you any harm or injury. I have not
come to spy upon your privacy; but truly the cause of my coming
was only to hear how you sing. For indeed you have as merry a voice as
any angel in heaven. Besides, you have more feeling for music than
had Boethius or any that can sing. My lord your father—God bless
his soul!—and also your mother have both, by their courtesy, been in
my house to my great pleasure. And indeed, sir, most gladly would I
please you. But when it comes to the question of singing, I'd lay my
eyes on the statement that, except you yourself, I've never heard a man
sing as your father used to in the mornings. Indeed, it was from the
heart, all that he sang. And to make his voice stronger he would take
special pains to shut his eyes; so he would cry loudly, standing on tiptoe
besides and stretching his neck out long and small. And also he was of
such discretion that there was no man anywhere that might surpass
him in either song or wisdom. I have in fact read in the verses of *Bur-
nellus the Ass* how there was a cock that caused a priest's son to lose
his benefice because the man had struck him upon his leg when he
was a foolish young chicken. But that certainly doesn't compare with
the wisdom and discretion of your father, or with his subtlety. Please
sing, sir; for holy charity, let's see if you can imitate your father."

This Chanticleer began to flap his wings, like a man unable to
detect deception, he was so ravished by the fox's flattery.

Alas! you noble lords, many a false flatterer is in your courts,
and many a deceiver, who pleases you better indeed than he that

speaks the truth to you. Read *Ecclesiasticus* on flattery, and beware, my lords, of such treachery!

This Chanticleer stood high upon his toes, stretched out his neck and kept his two eyes closed, and began to crow loudly. And Master Russell the fox sprang up immediately and seized Chanticleer by the throat and bore him on his back toward the wood, for even yet there was none who had seen him.

O destiny, that may not be escaped! Alas that Chanticleer ever flew down from his roost! Alas that his wife took no heed of dreams! And on a Friday happened all this tragedy. O Venus, who art goddess of joy, since this Chanticleer was thy servant and in thy service did all in his power, more for delight than to multiply the world, why wouldst thou suffer him to die on thy day?

O Geoffrey of Vinsauf, dear sovereign master, who when Richard, thy worthy king, was slain by an arrow, lamented his death so sorely, why have I not now thy feeling and thy love to chide the Friday in your style? For indeed it was on a Friday he was slain. Then would I show you how I could lament for the terror of Chanticleer and for his anguish.

Indeed, no such cry or lamentation was ever made by the women when Troy was won and Pyrrhus with his drawn sword had seized King Priam by the beard and slain him—as the *Aeneid* tells—as all the hens made in the yard when they saw the plight of Chanticleer. But suddenly Dame Pertelote shrieked even louder than did Hasdrubal's wife when her husband had lost his life and the Romans had burned Carthage. She was so full of passion and torment that she sprang into the fire and burned herself with a steadfast heart.

O woeful hens, just so you cried out as did the senators' wives when Nero had burned the city of Rome and their husbands all lost their lives—innocent, they were slain by this Nero. But now to my tale again.

This good widow and her two daughters heard the hens cry and lament; and they immediately ran outdoors and saw the fox going toward the wood carrying off the cock on his back; and they cried "Help! Thief!" and "God help us!" and "Ho, the fox!" and they ran after him and also many a man with sticks. Our dog Collie ran, and Talbot, and Garland and Malkin with a distaff in her hand. The cow ran and the calf and even the hogs. So frightened were they by the barking of the dogs and the shouting of the men and women that they ran as though their hearts would burst. They yelled as the devils do in Hell; the ducks cried out as though someone were trying to kill them; the frightened geese flew over the trees; out of the hive came the swarm of bees. God bless you, so hideous was the noise made that day after the fox that, indeed, Jack Straw himself and his crowd never made shouts half so shrill when they were trying to kill the Flemings. They brought trumpets of brass and of boxwood, of horn and of bone, in which they puffed and blew; and at the same time they whooped and they shrieked. It seemed as though the heavens would fall.

Now, good people, pray hear it all. See how Fortune suddenly upsets the hope and pride of her enemy!

This cock that lay upon the fox's back spoke in all fearfulness to the fox, saying, "Sir, if I were you, God bless me, I would say to them, 'Turn back, all you proud churls! A pestilence on you! Now that I've got to the woodside, in spite of all you can do the cock shall stay here; I will eat him, in faith, and that at once.'"

The fox answered, "Indeed, it shall be done."

And as he spoke that word, all of a sudden the cock broke quickly from his mouth and flew high into a tree.

And when the fox saw that the cock was gone, "Alas," said he, "O Chanticleer, alas! I have done an injury to you by scaring you when I seized and brought you out of the yard. But, sir, I didn't mean any harm. Come on down, and I'll tell you what I meant. God help me, I'll tell you the truth!"

"No indeed," said the cock; "a curse on both of us—on me first of all, both blood and bones—if you deceive me any more than once. By your flattery you will never again get me to shut my eyes and sing; God never prosper a man that willingly shuts his eye when he ought to see!"

"No," said the fox, "But God give him bad luck who is so careless of self-control that he chatters when he ought to hold his peace."

And that is the way it is to be careless and negligent and to trust in flattery.

But you that take this tale for foolishness, as about a fox or a cock and hen, consider the moral of it, good people. For Saint Paul says that all that is written is indeed written for our enlightenment. Take the fruit of it, and let the chaff go!

Now, O God, if it be Thy will, as my lord always says, make us all good men, and bring us all to Thy high bliss, *Amen!*

HEBRAISM

HEBRAISM

THE WORD *Bible* comes through Latin from a Greek word meaning *little books,* and, further back, from a Greek word (borrowed from Egyptian) designating the material on which the books were written. Really a sort of anthology, a collection of separate works introduced somewhat at random, the *Bible* comprises most of the literature of the Jewish people for over a thousand years before Christ and for over a hundred years after Christ. The earliest parts were written several centuries before Homer, and the latest about a century after Virgil. Naturally a work composed under such conditions will reflect different civilizations and varying points of view. Thus it begins with nomadic Semitic herdsmen and ends with the Roman Empire; it begins with a God of vengeance who lays down the principle of "an eye for an eye and a tooth for a tooth," and ends with a God of infinite compassion.

In literary forms the range is equally wide. The *Bible* includes the account of creation and the flood, which was the common property of the Semitic peoples; the elaborate rules for religious ritual among the early Hebrews; annals and chronicles of later history; the poetry of the prophets; the lyrics of the *Psalms;* the folk-wisdom of the *Proverbs;* simple, direct narrative in the stories of Joseph and of Ruth; the philosophic dialogue of *Job;* and the poetry of disillusionment in *Ecclesiastes.* All this is in the *Old Testament,* originally written in Hebrew, but translated, about 250 B.C., into a Greek version known as the *Septuagint* because it was supposedly made by seventy-two men in seventy-two days.

The *New Testament* is devoted to the story of Christ and his disciples, and consequently shows no such diversity, but it ranges from the narrative of the Gospels and the history of the first Christians through correspondence on religious matters to the mystical vision of *Revelation.* Since Greek was the popular tongue of many of the Mediterranean countries in the time of Christ, it was only natural that it should have been the original language of the *New Testament.*

As Latin came to be the dominant Mediterranean language, more and more of the *Bible* was translated accordingly. In the year 383, Saint Jerome undertook a complete Latin text, called the *Vulgate,* which he translated largely from the original Hebrew for the *Old Testament,* and revised mainly from a number of earlier Latin versions for the *New Testament.* This work was the principal means of European acquaintance with the *Bible* for a thousand years, and it has continued up to the present—sometimes translated, as in the English *Douai Bible*—to be the Scripture of the Roman Catholic Church.

The spread of the *Bible* outside Mediterranean civilization began even before the *Vulgate* was undertaken. The earliest surviving texts in any Germanic language are parts of the *Bible* translated by Bishop Wulfila (about 350) into Gothic. In England, parts were translated into Anglo-Saxon, or Old English, and some five centuries later Chaucer's contemporary, the reformer Wyclif, finished the first complete English version in 1388.

Throughout the Middle Ages the *Bible* was a powerful force in thought and literature, but it was seldom the possession of the common man. The Christian influence in the *Nibelungenlied* and the *Song of Roland* is plain enough, but the specific influence of the *Bible* is negligible. This is true for most literature of the period except that composed by such learned men as Dante and Chaucer. With the Renaissance, all this was changed. Since one of the primary beliefs of Protestantism was that man—any man—had a direct relationship to God which did not require the intermediary of priest or Church, one of the first concerns of the Reformation was to put the *Bible* into the hands of the common man in a language he could understand. This fact explains why in this volume the *Bible* is placed between the Middle Ages and the Renaissance.

Martin Luther, most notable of Protestants, in 1534 finished translating the *Bible* from Hebrew and Greek into German. He excluded from his translation, as unauthentic, certain "books" which had till then been regarded as part of the *Bible,* in spite of their having been recognized, from a time earlier than the *Septuagint,* as less venerable than the other books, and somehow less important. These books, called the *Apocrypha,* have, since Luther, tended to be more and more disregarded by non-Catholics. Many other scholars of about Luther's time, fired as he was by the Renaissance zeal for full knowledge, translated the *Bible* from the ancient tongues into various other languages. Among these scholars was William Tyndale, who made a superlative version in English. This, after many other Englishmen had tried their hand at domesticating the *Bible,* became, with the Hebrew and Greek versions, the basis of the great joint-translation completed in 1611 by the group of forty-seven scholars whom King James I had appointed to the task.

From the first it was evident that this Authorized or King James

Version was one of the great literary monuments of all time. So adequate was it as a translation that the *Bible* became from then on, in a special sense, a great English book. From the time of the Authorized Version to the present, new translations of the *Bible* into English are apparently being always either inaugurated or completed, always with proper justification and bright promise, but rarely to great practical effect. For the very archaisms of the King James Version have come to seem delectable.

This great book has been inexhaustibly and uniquely rich in its bearing upon most of the yearnings and perplexities of good men, with only two of the better impulses of such men not prodigally ministered to—those for humor and for precise information. It would hardly have needed, then, to set it into the highest reaches of man's esteem, the pious veneration immemorially accorded it. But it has had that veneration, pressed down and running over. It has become part and parcel of nearly every item whatever in the lives of all English-speaking people, a unifying, common basis-of-reference for them, which, with hope of its edifying other people too, they have disseminated by unnumbered millions of copies, in most languages and dialects over the entire world.

It may be that this zeal has worked on the principle that to spread far is to spread thin. In any case, it is plain that the *Bible* is not now as imperious a consideration with proportionately as many English-speaking people as it was formerly. Countless things less ominous than this could have come to pass. For even the fanatical devotees of the *Bible,* who have been numerous, would likely have manifested a graver fanaticism had their devotion been focussed elsewhere. And as for the general run of earth's children, it can hardly be doubted that the promised rewards for knowing the *Bible,* and penalties for not knowing it, brought many to the feast, people who came, perhaps hardly men at all, and left strong with the bread of life, people who came for cash only, big and quick, and who left rapt with a vision of the prophet's paradise to come.

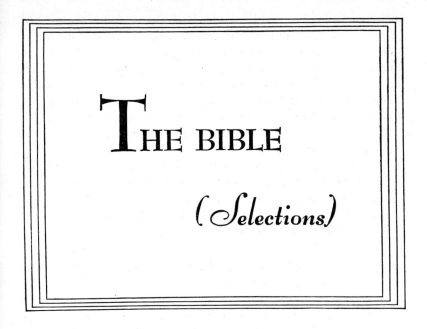

THE BIBLE

(Selections)

THE OLD TESTAMENT

CREATION
(*Genesis, 1-2*)

In the beginning God created the heaven and the earth. And the earth was without form, and void; and darkness was upon the face of the deep. And the Spirit of God moved upon the face of the waters. And God said, Let there be light: and there was light. And God saw the light, that it was good; and God divided the light from the darkness. And God called the light Day, and the darkness he called Night. And the evening and the morning were the first day.

And God said, Let there be a firmament in the midst of the waters, and let it divide the waters from the waters. And God made the firmament, and divided the waters which were under the firmament from the waters which were above the firmament; and it was so. And God called the firmament Heaven. And the evening and the morning were the second day.

And God said, Let the waters under the heaven be gathered together unto one place, and let the dry land appear; and it was so. And God called the dry land Earth; and the gathering together of the waters called he Seas; and God saw that it was good. And God said, Let the earth bring forth grass, the herb yielding seed, and the fruit tree yielding fruit after his kind, whose seed is in itself, upon the earth; and it was so. And the earth brought forth grass, and herb yielding seed after his kind, and the tree yielding fruit, whose seed was in itself, after his kind; and God saw that it was good. And the evening and the morning were the third day.

And God said, Let there be lights in the firmament of the heaven to divide the day from the night; and let them be for signs, and for seasons, and for days, and years: and let them be for lights in the firmament of the heaven to give light upon the earth; and it was so. And God made two great lights; the greater light to rule the day, and the lesser light to rule the night; he made the stars also. And God set them in the firmament of the heaven to give light upon the earth, and to rule over the day and over the night, and to divide the light from the darkness; and God saw that it was good. And the evening and the morning were the fourth day. And God said, Let the waters bring forth abundantly the moving creature that hath life, and fowl that may fly above the earth in the open firmament of heaven. And God created great whales, and every living creature that moveth, which the waters brought forth abundantly, after their kind, and every winged fowl after his kind; and God saw that it was good. And God blessed them, saying, Be fruitful, and multiply, and fill the waters in the seas, and let fowl multiply in the earth. And the evening and the morning were the fifth day.

And God said, Let the earth bring forth the living creature after his kind, cattle, and creeping thing, and beast of the earth after his kind; and it was so. And God made the beast of the earth after his kind, and cattle after their kind, and every thing that creepeth upon the earth after his kind; and God saw that it was good.

And God said, Let us make man in our image, after our likeness; and let them have dominion over the fish of the sea, and over the fowl of the air, and over the cattle, and over all the earth, and over every creeping thing that creepeth upon the earth. So God created man in his own image, in the image of God created he him; male and female created he them. And God blessed them, and God said unto them, Be fruitful, and multiply, and replenish the earth, and subdue it, and have dominion over the fish of the sea, and over the fowl of the air, and over every living thing that moveth upon the earth.

And God said, Behold, I have given you every herb bearing seed, which is upon the face of all the earth, and every tree, in the which is the fruit of a tree yielding seed; to you it shall be for meat. And to every beast of the earth, and to every fowl of the air, and to every thing that creepeth upon the earth, wherein there is life, I have given every green herb for meat: and it was so. And God saw every thing that he had made, and, behold, it was very good. And the evening and the morning were the sixth day.

Thus the heavens and the earth were finished, and all the host of them. And on the seventh day God ended his work which he had made; and he rested on the seventh day from all his work which he had made. And God blessed the seventh day, and sanctified it, because that in it he had rested from all his work which God created and made. . . .

And the Lord God planted a garden eastward in Eden; and there he put the man whom he had formed. And out of the ground made the Lord God to grow every tree that is pleasant to the sight, and good for food; the tree of life also in the midst of the garden, and the tree of knowledge of good and evil. And a river went out of Eden to water the garden; and from thence it was parted, and became into four heads. . . . And the Lord God took the man, and put him into the garden of Eden to dress it and to keep it. And the Lord God commanded the man, saying, Of every tree of the garden thou mayest freely eat; but of the tree of the knowledge of good and evil, thou shalt not eat of it, for in the day that thou eatest thereof thou shalt surely die.

And the Lord God said, It is not good that the man should be alone; I will make him an help meet for him. And out of the ground the Lord God formed every beast of the field, and every fowl of the air, and brought them unto Adam to see what he would call them; and whatsoever Adam called every living creature, that was the name thereof. And Adam gave names to all cattle, and to the fowl of the air, and to every beast of the field; but for Adam there was not found an help meet for him. And the Lord God caused a deep sleep to fall upon Adam, and he slept; and he took one of his ribs, and closed up the flesh instead thereof; and the rib, which the Lord God had taken from man, made he a woman, and brought her unto the man. And Adam said, This is now bone of my bones, and flesh of my flesh; she shall be called Woman, because she was taken out of Man. Therefore shall a man leave his father and his mother, and shall cleave unto his wife; and they shall be one flesh. And they were both naked, the man and his wife, and were not ashamed.

THE FALL OF MAN
(*Genesis, 3*)

Now the serpent was more subtil than any beast of the field which the LORD God had made. And he said unto the woman, Yea, hath God said, Ye shall not eat of every tree of the garden? And the woman said unto the serpent, We may eat of the fruit of the trees of the garden; but of the fruit of the tree which is in the midst of the garden, God hath said, Ye shall not eat of it, neither shall ye touch it, lest ye die. And the serpent said unto the woman, Ye shall not surely die; for God doth know that in the day ye eat thereof, then your eyes shall be opened, and ye shall be as gods, knowing good and evil. And when the woman saw that the tree was good for food, and that it was pleasant to the eyes, and a tree to be desired to make one wise, she took of the fruit thereof, and did eat, and gave also unto her husband with her; and he did eat. And the eyes of them both were opened, and they knew that they were naked; and they sewed fig leaves together, and made themselves aprons. And they heard the voice of the LORD God walking in the garden in the cool of the day; and Adam and his wife hid themselves from the presence of the LORD God amongst the trees of the garden. And the LORD God called unto Adam, and said unto him, Where art thou? And he said, I heard thy voice in the garden, and I was afraid, because I was naked; and I hid myself. And he said, Who told thee that thou wast naked? Hast thou eaten of the tree, whereof I commanded thee that thou shouldest not eat? And the man said, The woman whom thou gavest to be with me, she gave me of the tree, and I did eat. And the LORD God said unto the woman, What is this that thou hast done? And the woman said, The serpent beguiled me, and I did eat. And the LORD God said unto the serpent, Because thou hast done this, thou art cursed above all cattle, and above every beast of the field; upon thy belly shalt thou go, and dust shalt thou eat all the days of thy life; and I will put enmity between thee and the woman, and between thy seed and her seed; it shall bruise thy head, and thou shalt bruise his heel. Unto the woman he said, I will greatly multiply thy sorrow and thy conception; in sorrow thou shalt bring forth children;

and thy desire shall be to thy husband, and he shall rule over thee. And unto Adam he said, Because thou hast hearkened unto the voice of thy wife, and hast eaten of the tree, of which I commanded thee, saying, Thou shalt not eat of it, cursed is the ground for thy sake; in sorrow shalt thou eat of it all the days of thy life; thorns also and thistles shall it bring forth to thee; and thou shalt eat the herb of the field; in the sweat of thy face shalt thou eat bread, till thou return unto the ground; for out of it wast thou taken: for dust thou art, and unto dust shalt thou return. And Adam called his wife's name Eve; because she was the mother of all living. Unto Adam also and to his wife did the LORD God make coats of skins, and clothed them.

And the LORD God said, Behold, the man is become as one of us, to know good and evil; and now, lest he put forth his hand, and take also of the tree of life, and eat, and live for ever; therefore the LORD God sent him forth from the garden of Eden, to till the ground from whence he was taken. So he drove out the man; and he placed at the east of the garden of Eden Cherubims, and a flaming sword which turned every way, to keep the way of the tree of life.

CAIN AND ABEL
(*Genesis, 4*)

And Adam knew Eve his wife; and she conceived, and bare Cain, and said, I have gotten a man from the LORD. And she again bare his brother Abel. And Abel was a keeper of sheep, but Cain was a tiller of the ground. And in process of time it came to pass, that Cain brought of the fruit of the ground an offering unto the LORD. And Abel, he also brought of the firstlings of his flock and of the fat thereof. And the LORD had respect unto Abel and to his offering: but unto Cain and to his offering he had not respect. And Cain was very wroth, and his countenance fell. And the LORD said unto Cain, Why art thou wroth? and why is thy countenance fallen? If thou doest well, shalt thou not be accepted? and if thou doest not well, sin lieth at the door. And unto thee shall be his desire, and thou shalt rule over him. And Cain talked with Abel his brother; and it came to pass, when they were in the field, that Cain rose up against Abel his brother, and slew him.

And the LORD said unto Cain, Where is Abel thy brother? And he said, I know not: Am I my brother's keeper? And he said, What hast thou done? the voice of thy brother's blood crieth unto me from the ground. And now art thou cursed from the earth, which hath opened her mouth to receive thy brother's blood from thy hand. When thou tillest the ground, it shall not henceforth yield unto thee her strength; a fugitive and a vagabond shalt thou be in the earth. And Cain said unto the LORD, My punishment is greater than I can bear. Behold, thou hast driven me out this day from the face of the earth; and from thy face shall I be hid; and I shall be a fugitive and a vagabond in the earth; and it shall come to pass, that every one that findeth me shall slay me. And the LORD said unto him, Therefore whosoever slayeth Cain, vengeance shall be taken on him sevenfold. And the LORD set a mark upon Cain, lest any finding him should kill him. And Cain went out from the presence of the LORD, and dwelt in the land of Nod, on the east of Eden. . . .

THE FLOOD

(*Genesis*, 6-9)

And God saw that the wickedness of man was great in the earth, and that every imagination of the thoughts of his heart was only evil continually. And it repented the LORD that he had made man on the earth, and it grieved him at his heart. And the LORD said, I will destroy man whom I have created from the face of the earth, both man, and beast, and the creeping thing, and the fowls of the air; for it repenteth me that I have made them. But Noah found grace in the eyes of the LORD. . . .

And God said unto Noah, The end of all flesh is come before me; for the earth is filled with violence through them; and, behold, I will destroy them with the earth. Make thee an ark of gopher wood[1]; rooms shalt thou make in the ark, and shalt pitch it within and without with pitch. And this is the fashion which thou shalt make it of: The length of the ark shall be three hundred cubits,[2] the breadth of it fifty cubits, and the height of it thirty cubits. A window shalt thou make to the ark, and in a cubit shalt thou finish it above; and the door of the ark shalt thou set in the side thereof; with lower, second, and third stories shalt thou make it. And, behold, I, even I, do bring a flood of waters upon the earth, to destroy all flesh, wherein is the breath of life, from under heaven; and every thing that is in the earth shall die. But with thee will I establish my covenant; and thou shalt come into the ark, thou, and thy sons, and thy wife, and thy sons' wives with

1. *gopher wood*, apparently a species of pine or fir.
2. A cubit is about eighteen inches.

thee. And of every living thing of all flesh, two of every sort shalt thou bring into the ark, to keep them alive with thee; they shall be male and female. Of fowls after their kind, and of cattle after their kind, of every creeping thing of the earth after his kind, two of every sort shall come unto thee, to keep them alive. And take thou unto thee of all food that is eaten, and thou shalt gather it to thee; and it shall be for food for thee, and for them. Thus did Noah; according to all that God commanded him, so did he.

And the Lord said unto Noah, Come thou and all thy house into the ark; for thee have I seen righteous before me in this generation. Of every clean beast[3] thou shalt take to thee by sevens, the male and his female; and of beasts that are not clean by two, the male and his female. Of fowls also of the air by sevens, the male and the female; to keep seed alive upon the face of all the earth. For yet seven days, and I will cause it to rain upon the earth forty days and forty nights; and every living substance that I have made will I destroy from off the face of the earth. And Noah did according unto all that the Lord commanded him. . . .

In the six hundredth year of Noah's life, in the second month, the seventeenth day of the month, the same day were all the fountains of the great deep broken up, and the windows of heaven were opened. And the rain was upon the earth forty days and forty nights. In the selfsame day entered Noah, and Shem, and Ham, and Japheth, the sons of Noah, and Noah's wife, and the three wives of his sons with them, into the ark; they, and every beast after his kind, and all the cattle after their kind, and every creeping thing that creepeth upon the earth after his kind, and every fowl after his kind, every bird of every sort. And they went in unto Noah into the ark, two and two of all flesh, wherein is the breath of life. And they that went in, went in male and female of all flesh, as God had commanded him; and the Lord shut him in. And the flood was forty days upon the earth; and the waters increased, and bare up the ark, and it was lift up above the earth. And the waters prevailed, and were increased greatly upon the earth; and the ark went upon the face of the waters. And the waters prevailed exceedingly upon the earth; and all the high hills, that were under the whole heaven, were covered. Fifteen cubits upward did the waters prevail; and the mountains were covered. And all flesh died that moved upon the earth, both of fowl, and of cattle, and of beast, and of every creeping thing that creepeth upon the earth, and every man: all in

3. Certain animals were ritually clean; others, such as pigs, were unclean

whose nostrils was the breath of life, of all that was in the dry land, died. And every living substance was destroyed which was upon the face of the ground, both man, and cattle, and the creeping things, and the fowl of the heaven; and they were destroyed from the earth: and Noah only remained alive, and they that were with him in the ark. And the waters prevailed upon the earth an hundred and fifty days.

And God remembered Noah, and every living thing, and all the cattle that was with him in the ark; and God made a wind to pass over the earth, and the waters asswaged. The fountains also of the deep and the windows of heaven were stopped, and the rain from heaven was restrained; and the waters returned from off the earth continually; and after the end of the hundred and fifty days the waters were abated. And the ark rested in the seventh month, on the seventeenth day of the month, upon the mountains of Ararat.[4] And the waters decreased continually until the tenth month: in the tenth month, on the first day of the month, were the tops of the mountains seen.

And it came to pass at the end of forty days, that Noah opened the window of the ark which he had made; and he sent forth a raven, which went forth to and fro, until the waters were dried up from off the earth. Also he sent forth a dove from him, to see if the waters were abated from off the face of the ground; but the dove found no rest for the sole of her foot, and she returned unto him into the ark, for the waters were on the face of the whole earth; then he put forth his hand, and took her, and pulled her in unto him into the ark. And he stayed yet other seven days; and again he sent forth the dove out of the ark; and the dove came in to him in the evening; and, lo, in her mouth was an olive leaf pluckt off: so Noah knew that the waters were abated from off the earth. And he stayed yet other seven days, and sent forth the dove, which returned not again unto him any more.

And it came to pass in the six hundredth and first year, in the first month, the first day of the month, the waters were dried up from off the earth: and Noah removed the covering of the ark, and looked, and, behold, the face of the ground was dry. And in the second month, on the seven and twentieth day of the month, was the earth dried.

And God spake unto Noah, saying, Go forth of the ark, thou, and thy wife, and thy sons, and thy sons' wives with thee. Bring forth with thee every living thing that is with thee, of all flesh, both of fowl, and of cattle, and of every creeping thing that creepeth upon the

4. *Ararat*, a district on the eastern border of Turkey.

earth; that they may breed abundantly in the earth, and be fruitful, and multiply upon the earth. . . .

And God spake unto Noah, and to his sons with him, saying, And I, behold, I establish my covenant with you, and with your seed after you; and with every living creature that is with you, of the fowl, of the cattle, and of every beast of the earth with you; from all that go out of the ark, to every beast of the earth. And I will establish my covenant with you; neither shall all flesh be cut off any more by the waters of a flood; neither shall there any more be a flood to destroy the earth. And God said, This is the token of the covenant which I make between me and you and every living creature that is with you, for perpetual generations: I do set my bow in the cloud, and it shall be for a token of a covenant between me and the earth. And it shall come to pass, when I bring a cloud over the earth, that the bow shall be seen in the cloud; and I will remember my covenant, which is between me and you and every living creature of all flesh; and the waters shall no more become a flood to destroy all flesh.

ABRAHAM AND ISAAC
(*Genesis, 22*)

And it came to pass after these things, that God did tempt Abraham, and said unto him, Abraham; and he said, Behold, here I am. And he said, Take now thy son, thine only son Isaac, whom thou lovest, and get thee into the land of Moriah; and offer him there for a burnt offering upon one of the mountains which I will tell thee of.

And Abraham rose up early in the morning, and saddled his ass, and took two of his young men with him, and Isaac his son, and clave the wood for the burnt offering, and rose up, and went unto the place of which God had told him. Then on the third day Abraham lifted up his eyes, and saw the place afar off. And Abraham said unto his young men, Abide ye here with the ass; and I and the lad will go yonder and worship, and come again to you. And Abraham took the wood of the burnt offering, and laid it upon Isaac his son; and he took the fire in his hand, and a knife; and they went both of them together. And Isaac spake unto Abraham his father, and said, My father; and he said, Here am I, my son. And he said, Behold the fire and the wood; but where is the lamb for a burnt offering? And Abraham said, My son, God will provide himself a lamb for a burnt offering; so they went both of them together. And they came to the place which God had told him of; and Abraham built an altar there, and laid the wood in order, and bound Isaac his son, and laid him on the altar upon the wood. And Abraham stretched forth his hand, and took the knife to slay his son. And the angel of the LORD called unto him out of heaven, and said, Abraham, Abraham; and he said, Here am I. And he said, Lay not thine hand upon the lad, neither do thou any thing unto him; for now I know that thou fearest God, seeing thou hast not withheld thy son, thine only son from me. And Abraham lifted up his eyes, and looked, and behold behind him a ram caught in a thicket by his horns: and Abraham went and took the ram, and offered him up for a burnt offering in the stead of his son. . . .

And the angel of the LORD called unto Abraham out of heaven the second time, and said, By myself have I sworn, saith the LORD, for because thou hast done this thing, and hast not withheld thy son, thine only son, that in blessing I will bless thee, and in multiplying I will multiply thy seed as the stars of the heaven, and as the sand which is upon the sea shore; and thy seed shall possess the gate of his enemies; and in thy seed shall all the nations of the earth be blessed; because thou hast obeyed my voice. So Abraham returned unto his young men, and they rose up and went together to Beer-sheba; and Abraham dwelt at Beer-sheba.

MOSES
(Exodus, 1-3, 13, 14, 19, 20; Joshua, 34)

Now there arose up a new king over Egypt, which knew not Joseph.[1] And he said unto his people, Behold, the people of the children of Israel are more and mightier than we: come on, let us deal wisely with them; lest they multiply, and it come to pass, that, when there falleth out any war, they join also unto our enemies, and fight against us, and so get them up out of the land. Therefore they did set over them taskmasters to afflict them with their burdens. And they built for Pharaoh treasure cities, Pithom and Raamses. But the more they afflicted them, the more they multiplied and grew. And they were grieved because of the children of Israel. And the Egyptians made the children of Israel to serve with rigour; and they made their lives bitter with hard bondage, in morter, and in brick, and in all manner

1. Joseph had been sold into slavery in Egypt, but had risen to a position second only to the king. A famine had reunited him with his family, and he had brought them to Egypt, as well as other Hebrews.

of service in the field; all their service, wherein they made them serve, was with rigour. . . .

And Pharaoh charged all his people, saying, Every son that is born ye shall cast into the river, and every daughter ye shall save alive.

And there went a man of the house of Levi, and took to wife a daughter of Levi. And the woman conceived, and bare a son; and when she saw him that he was a goodly child, she hid him three months. And when she could not longer hide him, she took for him an ark of bulrushes, and daubed it with slime and with pitch, and put the child therein; and she laid it in the flags by the river's brink. And his sister stood afar off, to wit what would be done to him.

And the daughter of Pharaoh came down to wash herself at the river; and her maidens walked along by the river's side; and when she saw the ark among the flags, she sent her maid to fetch it. And when she had opened it, she saw the child; and, behold, the babe wept. And she had compassion on him, and said, This is one of the Hebrews' children. Then said his sister to Pharaoh's daughter, Shall I go and call to thee a nurse of the Hebrew women, that she may nurse the child for thee? And Pharaoh's daughter said to her, Go. And the maid went and called the child's mother. And Pharaoh's daughter said unto her, Take this child away, and nurse it for me, and I will give thee thy wages. And the woman took the child, and nursed it. And the child grew, and she brought him unto Pharaoh's daughter, and he became her son. And she called his name Moses. . . .

[Moses killed an Egyptian whom he found beating a Hebrew. Finding that this act was known, he fled Egypt, and married one of the daughters of Jethro.]

Now Moses kept the flock of Jethro his father in law, the priest of Midian; and he led the flock to the backside of the desert, and came to the mountain of God, even to Horeb.[2] And the angel of the LORD appeared unto him in a flame of fire out of the midst of a bush; and he looked, and, behold, the bush burned with fire, and the bush was not consumed. And Moses said, I will now turn aside, and see this great sight, why the bush is not burnt. And when the LORD saw that he turned aside to see, God called unto him out of the midst of the bush, and said, Moses, Moses. And he said, Here am I. And he said, Draw not nigh hither; put off thy shoes from off thy feet, for the place whereon thou standest is holy ground. Moreover he said, I am the God

2. Horeb and Sinai are the same mountain. Its exact location is uncertain.

of thy father, the God of Abraham, the God of Isaac, and the God of Jacob. And Moses hid his face; for he was afraid to look upon God.

And the LORD said, I have surely seen the affliction of my people which are in Egypt, and have heard their cry by reason of their task-masters; for I know their sorrows. And I am come down to deliver them out of the hand of the Egyptians, and to bring them up out of that land unto a good land and a large, unto a land flowing with milk and honey; unto the place of the Canaanites, and the Hittites, and the Amorites, and the Perizzites, and the Hivites, and the Jebusites. Now therefore, behold, the cry of the children of Israel is come unto me; and I have also seen the oppression wherewith the Egyptians oppress them. Come now therefore, and I will send thee unto Pharaoh, that thou mayest bring forth my people the children of Israel out of Egypt.

And Moses said unto God, Who am I, that I should go unto Pharaoh, and that I should bring forth the children of Israel out of Egypt? And he said, Certainly I will be with thee; and this shall be a token unto thee, that I have sent thee: when thou hast brought forth the people out of Egypt, ye shall serve God upon this mountain. And Moses said unto God, Behold, when I come unto the children of Israel, and shall say unto them, The God of your fathers hath sent me unto you; and they shall say to me, What is his name? what shall I say unto them? And God said unto Moses, I AM THAT I AM; and he said, Thus shalt thou say unto the children of Israel, I AM hath sent me unto you. And God said moreover unto Moses, Thus shalt thou say unto the children of Israel, The LORD God of your fathers, the God of Abraham, the God of Isaac, and the God of Jacob, hath sent me unto you: this is my name for ever, and this is my memorial unto all generations. . . .

And I am sure that the king of Egypt will not let you go, no, not by a mighty hand. And I will stretch out my hand, and smite Egypt with all my wonders which I will do in the midst thereof; and after that he will let you go. And I will give this people favour in the sight of the Egyptians; and it shall come to pass, that, when ye go, ye shall not go empty; but every woman shall borrow of her neighbour, and of her that sojourneth in her house, jewels of silver, and jewels of gold, and raiment: and ye shall put them upon your sons, and upon your daughters; and ye shall spoil the Egyptians. . . .

[By sending various plagues on the Egyptians, God finally enabled Moses to arrange the flight of the children of Israel.]

And it came to pass, when Pharaoh had let the people go, that God led them not through the way of the land of the Philistines, although that was near; for God said, Lest peradventure the people repent when they see war, and they return to Egypt; but God led the people about, through the way of the wilderness of the Red Sea. And the LORD went before them by day in a pillar of a cloud, to lead them the way; and by night in a pillar of fire, to give them light; to go by day and night: he took not away the pillar of the cloud by day, nor the pillar of fire by night, from before the people. . . .

And it was told the king of Egypt that the people fled: and the heart of Pharaoh and of his servants was turned against the people, and they said, Why have we done this, that we have let Israel go from serving us? And he made ready his chariot, and took his people with him; and he took six hundred chosen chariots, and all the chariots of Egypt, and captains over every one of them. And the LORD hardened the heart of Pharaoh king of Egypt, and he pursued after the children of Israel; and the children of Israel went out with an high hand. But the Egyptians pursued after them, all the horses and chariots of Pharaoh, and his horsemen, and his army, and overtook them encamping by the sea.

And when Pharaoh drew nigh, the children of Israel lifted up their eyes, and, behold, the Egyptians marched after them; and they were sore afraid; and the children of Israel cried out unto the LORD. And they said unto Moses, Because there were no graves in Egypt, hast thou taken us away to die in the wilderness? Wherefore hast thou dealt thus with us, to carry us forth out of Egypt? Is not this the word that we did tell thee in Egypt, saying, Let us alone, that we may serve the Egyptians? For it had been better for us to serve the Egyptians, than that we should die in the wilderness.

And Moses said unto the people, Fear ye not, stand still, and see the salvation of the LORD, which he will shew to you to day; for the Egyptians whom ye have seen to day, ye shall see them again no more for ever. The LORD shall fight for you, and ye shall hold your peace.

And the LORD said unto Moses, Wherefore criest thou unto me? Speak unto the children of Israel, that they go forward; but lift thou up thy rod, and stretch out thine hand over the sea, and divide it; and the children of Israel shall go on dry ground through the midst of the sea. And I, behold, I will harden the hearts of the Egyptians, and they shall follow them; and I will get me honour upon Pharaoh, and upon all his host, upon his chariots, and upon his horsemen. And the

Egyptians shall know that I am the LORD, when I have gotten me honour upon Pharaoh, upon his chariots, and upon his horsemen. . . .

And Moses stretched out his hand over the sea; and the Lord caused the sea to go back by a strong east wind all that night, and made the sea dry land, and the waters were divided. And the children of Israel went into the midst of the sea upon the dry ground; and the waters were a wall unto them on their right hand, and on their left.

And the Egyptians pursued, and went in after them to the midst of the sea, even all Pharaoh's horses, his chariots, and his horsemen. And it came to pass, that in the morning watch the LORD looked unto the host of the Egyptians, and troubled the host of the Egyptians, and took off their chariot wheels, that they drave them heavily; so that the Egyptians said, Let us flee from the face of Israel; for the LORD fighteth for them against the Egyptians.

And the LORD said unto Moses, Stretch out thine hand over the sea, that the waters may come again upon the Egyptians, upon their chariots, and upon their horsemen. And Moses stretched forth his hand over the sea, and the sea returned to his strength when the morning appeared; and the Egyptians fled against it; and the LORD overthrew the Egyptians in the midst of the sea. And the waters returned, and covered the chariots, and the horsemen, and all the host of Pharaoh that came into the sea after them; there remained not so much as one of them. But the children of Israel walked upon dry land in the midst of the sea; and the waters were a wall unto them on their right hand, and on their left. Thus the LORD saved Israel that day out of the hand of the Egyptians; and Israel saw the Egyptians dead upon the sea shore.

In the third month, when the children of Israel were gone forth out of the land of Egypt, the same day came they into the wilderness of Sinai. For they were departed from Rephidim, and were come to the desert of Sinai, and had pitched in the wilderness; and there Israel camped before the mount. And Moses went up unto God, and the LORD called unto him out of the mountain, saying, Thus shalt thou say to the house of Jacob, and tell the children of Israel; ye have seen what I did unto the Egyptians, and how I bare you on eagles' wings, and brought you unto myself. Now therefore, if ye will obey my voice indeed, and keep my covenant, then ye shall be a peculiar treasure unto me above all people, for all the earth is mine; and ye shall be unto me a kingdom of priests, and an holy nation. These are the words which thou shalt speak unto the children of Israel.

And Moses came and called for the elders of the people, and laid before their faces all these words which the LORD commanded him. . . .

And the LORD said unto Moses, Go unto the people, and sanctify them to day and to morrow, and let them wash their clothes, and be ready against the third day; for the third day the LORD will come down in the sight of all the people upon mount Sinai. . . .

And Moses went down from the mount unto the people, and sanctified the people; and they washed their clothes. And he said unto the people, Be ready against the third day; come not at your wives.

And it came to pass on the third day in the morning, that there were thunders and lightnings, and a thick cloud upon the mount, and the voice of the trumpet exceeding loud; so that all the people that was in the camp trembled. And Moses brought forth the people out of the camp to meet with God; and they stood at the nether part of the mount. And mount Sinai was altogether on a smoke, because the LORD descended upon it in fire; and the smoke thereof ascended as the smoke of a furnace, and the whole mount quaked greatly. And when the voice of the trumpet sounded long, and waxed louder and louder, Moses spake, and God answered him by a voice. And the LORD came down upon mount Sinai, on the top of the mount: and the LORD called Moses up to the top of the mount; and Moses went up. . . .

And God spake all these words, saying, I am the LORD thy God, which have brought thee out of the land of Egypt, out of the house of bondage. Thou shalt have no other gods before me. Thou shalt not make unto thee any graven image, or any likeness of any thing that is in heaven above, or that is in the earth beneath, or that is in the water under the earth; thou shalt not bow down thyself to them, nor serve them; for I the LORD thy God am a jealous God, visiting the iniquity of the fathers upon the children unto the third and fourth generation of them that hate me, and shewing mercy unto thousands of them that love me, and keep my commandments. Thou shalt not take the name of the LORD thy God in vain; for the LORD will not hold him guiltless that taketh his name in vain. Remember the sabbath day, to keep it holy. Six days shalt thou labour, and do all thy work; but the seventh day is the sabbath of the LORD thy God; in it thou shalt not do any work, thou, nor thy son, nor thy daughter, thy manservant, nor thy maidservant, nor thy cattle, nor thy stranger that is within thy gates: for in six days the LORD made heaven and earth, the sea, and all that in them is, and rested the seventh day; wherefore the LORD blessed the sabbath day, and hallowed it.

Honour thy father and thy mother, that thy days may be long upon the land which the LORD thy God giveth thee. Thou shalt not kill. Thou shalt not commit adultery. Thou shalt not steal. Thou shalt not bear false witness against thy neighbour. Thou shalt not covet thy neighbour's house, thou shalt not covet thy neighbour's wife, nor his manservant, nor his maidservant, nor his ox, nor his ass, nor any thing that is thy neighbour's.

And all the people saw the thunderings, and the lightnings, and the noise of the trumpet, and the mountain smoking: and when the people saw it, they removed, and stood afar off. And they said unto Moses, Speak thou with us, and we will hear; but let not God speak with us, lest we die. And Moses said unto the people, Fear not; for God is come to prove you, and that his fear may be before your faces, that ye sin not. . . .

[Moses led his people for a generation of residence and wandering in the wilderness. During this time he organized their government and religious system, put down idolatry and insurrection, and sought the land which God had promised to his people.]

And Moses went up from the plains of Moab unto the mountain of Nebo, to the top of Pisgah, that is over against Jericho. And the LORD shewed him all the land of Gilead, unto Dan, and all Naphtali, and the land of Ephraim, and Manasseh, and all the land of Judah, unto the utmost sea, and the south, and the plain of the valley of Jericho, the city of palm trees, unto Zoar. And the LORD said unto him, This is the land which I sware unto Abraham, unto Isaac, and unto Jacob, saying, I will give it unto thy seed; I have caused thee to see it with thine eyes, but thou shalt not go over thither.

So Moses the servant of the LORD died there in the land of Moab, according to the word of the LORD. And he buried him in a valley in the land of Moab, over against Bethpeor, but no man knoweth of his sepulchre unto this day.

And Moses was an hundred and twenty years old when he died; his eye was not dim, nor his natural force abated.

And the children of Israel wept for Moses in the plains of Moab thirty days; so the days of weeping and mourning for Moses were ended.

And Joshua the son of Nun was full of the spirit of wisdom, for

Moses had laid his hands upon him; and the children of Israel hearkened unto him, and did as the LORD commanded Moses.

And there arose not a prophet since in Israel like unto Moses, whom the LORD knew face to face, in all the signs and the wonders, which the LORD sent him to do in the land of Egypt to Pharaoh, and to all his servants, and to all his land, and in all that mighty hand, and in all the great terror which Moses shewed in the sight of all Israel.

RUTH

Now it came to pass in the days when the judges ruled, that there was a famine in the land. And a certain man of Beth-lehem-judah went to sojourn in the country of Moab, he, and his wife, and his two sons. And the name of the man was Elimelech, and the name of his wife Naomi, and the name of his two sons Mahlon and Chilion, Ephrathites of Beth-lehem-judah. And they came into the country of Moab, and continued there. And Elimelech, Naomi's husband, died; and she was left, and her two sons. And they took them wives of the women of Moab; the name of the one was Orpah, and the name of the other Ruth; and they dwelled there about ten years. And Mahlon and Chilion died also both of them; and the woman was left of her two sons and her husband.

Then she arose with her daughters in law, that she might return from the country of Moab, for she had heard in the country of Moab how that the LORD had visited his people in giving them bread. Wherefore she went forth out of the place where she was, and her two daughters in law with her; and they went on the way to return unto the land of Judah. And Naomi said unto her two daughters in law, Go, return each to her mother's house; the LORD deal kindly with you, as ye have dealt with the dead, and with me. The LORD grant you that ye may find rest, each of you in the house of her husband. Then she kissed them; and they lifted up their voice, and wept. And they said unto her, Surely we will return with thee unto thy people. And Naomi said, Turn again, my daughters; why will ye go with me? are there yet any more sons in my womb, that they may be your husbands? Turn again, my daughters, go your way; for I am too old to have an husband. If I should say, I have hope, if I should have an husband also to night, and should also bear sons, would ye tarry for them till they were grown? Would ye stay for them from having husbands? Nay, my daughters; for it grieveth me much for your sakes that the hand of the LORD is gone out against me. And they lifted up their voice, and wept again; and Orpah kissed her mother in law, but Ruth clave unto her. And she said, Behold, thy sister in law is gone back unto her people, and unto her gods; return thou after thy sister in law. And Ruth said, Intreat me not to leave thee, or to return from following after thee: for whither thou goest, I will go; and where thou lodgest, I will lodge; thy people shall be my people, and thy God my God; where thou diest, will I die, and there will I be buried; the LORD do so to me, and more also, if ought but death part thee and me. When she saw that she was stedfastly minded to go with her, then she left speaking unto her.

So they two went until they came to Beth-lehem. And it came to pass, when they were come to Beth-lehem, that all the city was moved about them, and they said, Is this Naomi? And she said unto them, Call me not Naomi, call me Mara[1]; for the Almighty hath dealt very bitterly with me. I went out full, and the LORD hath brought me home again empty; why then call ye me Naomi, seeing the LORD hath testified against me, and the Almighty hath afflicted me? So Naomi returned, and Ruth the Moabitess, her daughter in law, with her, which returned out of the country of Moab; and they came to Beth-lehem in the beginning of barley harvest.

And Naomi had a kinsman of her husband's, a mighty man of wealth, of the family of Elimelech; and his name was Boaz. And Ruth the Moabitess said unto Naomi, Let me now go to the field, and glean ears of corn after him in whose sight I shall find grace. And she said unto her, Go, my daughter. And she went, and came, and gleaned in the field after the reapers; and her hap was to light on a part of the field belonging unto Boaz, who was of the kindred of Elimelech.

And, behold, Boaz came from Beth-lehem, and said unto the reapers, The LORD be with you. And they answered him, The LORD bless thee. Then said Boaz unto his servant that was set over the reapers, Whose damsel is this? And the servant that was set over the reapers answered and said, It is the Moabitish damsel that came back with Naomi out of the country of Moab; and she said, I pray you, let me glean and gather after the reapers among the sheaves; so she came, and hath continued even from the morning until now, that she tarried a little in the house. Then said Boaz unto Ruth, Hearest thou not, my daughter? Go not to glean in another field, neither go from hence, but abide here fast by my maidens; let thine eyes be on the field that they

1. *Mara* means "bitter."

do reap, and go thou after them; have I not charged the young men
that they shall not touch thee? And when thou art athirst, go unto the
vessels, and drink of that which the young men have drawn. Then she
fell on her face, and bowed herself to the ground, and said unto him,
Why have I found grace in thine eyes, that thou shouldest take
knowledge of me, seeing I am a stranger? And Boaz answered and
said unto her, It hath fully been shewed me, all that thou hast done
unto thy mother in law since the death of thine husband, and how
thou hast left thy father and thy mother, and the land of thy nativity,
and art come unto a people which thou knewest not heretofore. The
LORD recompense thy work, and a full reward be given thee of the LORD
God of Israel, under whose wings thou art come to trust. Then she
said, Let me find favour in thy sight, my Lord; for that thou hast comforted me, and for that thou hast spoken friendly unto thine handmaid,
though I be not like unto one of thine handmaidens. And Boaz said
unto her, At mealtime come thou hither, and eat of the bread, and dip
thy morsel in the vinegar. And she sat beside the reapers; and he
reached her parched corn, and she did eat, and was sufficed, and left.
And when she was risen up to glean, Boaz commanded his young
men, saying, Let her glean even among the sheaves, and reproach her
not; and let fall also some of the handfuls of purpose for her, and leave
them, that she may glean them, and rebuke her not. So she gleaned in
the field until even, and beat out that she had gleaned; and it was about
an ephah² of barley.

And she took it up, and went into the city, and her mother in law
saw what she had gleaned; and she brought forth, and gave to her that
she had reserved after she was sufficed. And her mother in law said
unto her, Where hast thou gleaned to day? and where wroughtest
thou? Blessed be he that did take knowledge of thee. And she shewed
her mother in law with whom she had wrought, and said, The man's
name with whom I wrought to day is Boaz. And Naomi said unto her
daughter in law, Blessed be he of the LORD, who hath not left off his
kindness to the living and to the dead. And Naomi said unto her, The
man is near of kin unto us, one of our next kinsmen. And Ruth the
Moabitess said, He said unto me also, Thou shalt keep fast by my young
men, until they have ended all my harvest. And Naomi said unto Ruth
her daughter in law, It is good, my daughter, that thou go out with
his maidens, that they meet thee not in any other field. So she kept fast

2. *ephah*, about 1⅓ bushels.

by the maidens of Boaz to glean unto the end of barley harvest and of wheat harvest, and dwelt with her mother in law.

Then Naomi her mother in law said unto her, My daughter, shall I not seek rest for thee, that it may be well with thee? And now is not Boaz of our kindred, with whose maidens thou wast? Behold, he winnoweth barley to night in the threshingfloor. Wash thyself therefore, and anoint thee, and put thy raiment upon thee, and get thee down to the floor; but make not thyself known unto the man, until he shall have done eating and drinking. And it shall be, when he lieth down, that thou shalt mark the place where he shall lie, and thou shalt go in, and uncover his feet, and lay thee down; and he will tell thee what thou shalt do. And she said unto her, All that thou sayest unto me I will do.

And she went down unto the floor, and did according to all that her mother in law bade her. And when Boaz had eaten and drunk, and his heart was merry, he went to lie down at the end of the heap of corn; and she came softly, and uncovered his feet, and laid her down.

And it came to pass at midnight, that the man was afraid, and turned himself; and, behold, a woman lay at his feet. And he said, Who art thou? And she answered, I am Ruth thine handmaid; spread therefore thy skirt over thine handmaid, for thou art a near kinsman. And he said, Blessed be thou of the LORD, my daughter, for thou hast shewed more kindness in the latter end than at the beginning, inasmuch as thou followedst not young men, whether poor or rich. And now, my daughter, fear not; I will do to thee all that thou requirest: for all the city of my people doth know that thou art a virtuous woman. And now it is true that I am thy near kinsman; howbeit there is a kinsman nearer than I. Tarry this night, and it shall be in the morning, that if he will perform unto thee the part of a kinsman, well; let him do the kinsman's part; but if he will not do the part of a kinsman to thee, then will I do the part of a kinsman to thee, as the LORD liveth; lie down until the morning.

And she lay at his feet until the morning; and she rose up before one could know another. And he said, Let it not be known that a woman came into the floor. Also he said, Bring the vail that thou hast upon thee, and hold it. And when she held it, he measured six measures of barley, and laid it on her; and she went into the city. And when she came to her mother in law, she said, Who art thou, my daughter? And she told her all that the man had done to her. And she said, These six measures of barley gave he me; for he said to me, Go not empty unto thy mother in law. Then said she, Sit still, my daughter, until thou know how the matter will fall; for the man will not be in rest, until he have finished the thing this day.

Then went Boaz up to the gate, and sat him down there, and, behold, the kinsman of whom Boaz spake came by; unto whom he said, Ho, such a one! turn aside, sit down here. And he turned aside, and sat down. And he took ten men of the elders of the city, and said, Sit ye down here. And they sat down. And he said unto the kinsman, Naomi, that is come again out of the country of Moab, selleth a parcel of land, which was our brother Elimelech's; And I thought to advertise thee, saying, Buy it before the inhabitants, and before the elders of my people. If thou wilt redeem it, redeem it; but if thou wilt not redeem it, then tell me, that I may know, for there is none to redeem it beside thee, and I am after thee. And he said, I will redeem it. Then said Boaz, What day thou buyest the field of the hand of Naomi, thou must buy it also of Ruth the Moabitess, the wife of the dead, to raise up the name of the dead upon his inheritance.

And the kinsman said, I cannot redeem it for myself, lest I mar mine own inheritance; redeem thou my right to thyself, for I cannot redeem it. Now this was the manner in former time in Israel concerning redeeming and concerning changing, for to confirm all things: a man plucked off his shoe, and gave it to his neighbour, and this was a testimony in Israel. Therefore the kinsman said unto Boaz, Buy it for thee. So he drew off his shoe.

And Boaz said unto the elders, and unto all the people, Ye are witnesses this day, that I have bought all that was Elimelech's and all that was Chilion's and Mahlon's, of the hand of Naomi. Moreover Ruth the Moabitess, the wife of Mahlon, have I purchased to be my wife, to raise up the name of the dead upon his inheritance, that the name of the dead be not cut off from among his brethren, and from the gate of his place: ye are witnesses this day. And all the people that were in the gate, and the elders, said, We are witnesses. . . .

So Boaz took Ruth, and she was his wife; and when he went in unto her, the LORD gave her conception, and she bare a son. And the women said unto Naomi, Blessed be the LORD, which hath not left thee this day without a kinsman, that his name may be famous in Israel. And he shall be unto thee a restorer of thy life, and a nourisher of thine old age, for thy daughter in law, which loveth thee, which is better to thee than seven sons, hath born him. And Naomi took the child, and laid it in her bosom, and became nurse unto it. And the women her neighbours gave it a name, saying, There is a son born to Naomi; and they called his name Obed; he is the father of Jesse, the father of David. . . .

JOB

There was a man in the land of Uz,[1] whose name was Job; and that man was perfect and upright, and one that feared God, and eschewed evil. And there were born unto him seven sons and three daughters. His substance also was seven thousand sheep, and three thousand camels, and five hundred yoke of oxen, and five hundred she asses, and a very great household; so that this man was the greatest of all the men of the east. And his sons went and feasted in their houses, every one his day, and sent and called for their three sisters to eat and to drink with them. And it was so, when the days of their feasting were gone about, that Job sent and sanctified them, and rose up early in the morning, and offered burnt offerings according to the number of them all; for Job said, It may be that my sons have sinned, and cursed God in their hearts. Thus did Job continually.

Now there was a day when the sons of God came to present themselves before the LORD, and Satan came also among them. And the LORD said unto Satan, Whence comest thou? Then Satan answered the LORD, and said, From going to and fro in the earth, and from walking up and down in it. And the LORD said unto Satan, Hast thou considered my servant Job, that there is none like him in the earth, a perfect and an upright man, one that feareth God, and escheweth evil? Then Satan answered the LORD, and said, Doth Job fear God for nought? Hast not thou made an hedge about him, and about his house, and about all that he hath on every side? thou hast blessed the work of his hands, and his substance is increased in the land. But put forth thine hand now, and touch all that he hath, and he will curse thee to thy face. And the LORD said unto Satan, Behold, all that he hath is in thy power; only upon himself put not forth thine hand. So Satan went forth from the presence of the LORD.

And there was a day when his sons and his daughters were eating and drinking wine in their eldest brother's house; and there came a messenger unto Job, and said, The oxen were plowing, and the asses feeding beside them; and the Sabeans[2] fell upon them, and took them

1. The land of Uz seems to have been somewhere on the edge of the Arabian Desert.
2. The Sabeans are not positively identified.

away; yea, they have slain the servants with the edge of the sword; and I only am escaped alone to tell thee. While he was yet speaking, there came also another, and said, The fire of God is fallen from heaven, and hath burned up the sheep, and the servants, and consumed them; and I only am escaped alone to tell thee. While he was yet speaking, there came also another, and said, The Chaldeans[3] made out three bands, and fell upon the camels, and have carried them away, yea, and slain the servants with the edge of the sword; and I only am escaped alone to tell thee. While he was yet speaking, there came also another, and said, Thy sons and thy daughters were eating and drinking wine in their eldest brother's house: and, behold, there came a great wind from the wilderness, and smote the four corners of the house, and it fell upon the young men, and they are dead; and I only am escaped alone to tell thee. Then Job arose, and rent his mantle, and shaved his head, and fell down upon the ground, and worshipped, and said, Naked came I out of my mother's womb, and naked shall I return thither: the LORD gave, and the LORD hath taken away; blessed be the name of the LORD. In all this Job sinned not, nor charged God foolishly.

Again there was a day when the sons of God came to present themselves before the LORD, and Satan came also among them to present himself before the LORD. And the LORD said unto Satan, From whence comest thou? And Satan answered the LORD, and said, From going to and fro in the earth, and from walking up and down in it. And the LORD said unto Satan, Hast thou considered my servant Job, that there is none like him in the earth, a perfect and an upright man, one that feareth God, and escheweth evil? and still he holdeth fast his integrity, although thou movedst me against him, to destroy him without cause. And Satan answered the LORD, and said, Skin for skin, yea, all that a man hath will he give for his life. But put forth thine hand now, and touch his bone and his flesh, and he will curse thee to thy face. And the LORD said unto Satan, Behold, he is in thine hand; but save his life.

So went Satan forth from the presence of the LORD, and smote Job with sore boils from the sole of his foot unto his crown. And he took him a potsherd to scrape himself withal; and he sat down among the ashes.

Then said his wife unto him, Dost thou still retain thine integrity? curse God, and die. But he said unto her, Thou speakest as one of the foolish women speaketh. What? shall we receive good at the hand of

3. *Chaldeans*, a Semitic race, long a part of the Babylonian Empire.

God, and shall we not receive evil? In all this did not Job sin with his lips.

Now when Job's three friends heard of all this evil that was come upon him, they came every one from his own place; Eliphaz the Temanite, and Bildad the Shuhite, and Zophar the Naamathite: for they had made an appointment together to come to mourn with him and to comfort him. And when they lifted up their eyes afar off, and knew him not, they lifted up their voice, and wept; and they rent every one his mantle, and sprinkled dust upon their heads toward heaven. So they sat down with him upon the ground seven days and seven nights, and none spake a word unto him: for they saw that his grief was very great.

After this opened Job his mouth, and cursed his day. And Job spake, and said, Let the day perish wherein I was born, and the night in which it was said, There is a man child conceived. Let that day be darkness; let not God regard it from above, neither let the light shine upon it. Let darkness and the shadow of death stain it; let a cloud dwell upon it; let the blackness of the day terrify it. As for that night, let darkness seize upon it; let it not be joined unto the days of the year; let it not come into the number of the months. Lo, let that night be solitary, let no joyful voice come therein. Let them curse it that curse the day, who are ready to raise up their mourning. Let the stars of the twilight thereof be dark; let it look for light, but have none; neither let it see the dawning of the day: because it shut not up the doors of my mother's womb, nor hid sorrow from mine eyes. Why died I not from the womb? why did I not give up the ghost when I came out of the belly? Why did the knees prevent me? or why the breasts that I should suck? For now should I have lain still and been quiet, I should have slept; then had I been at rest, with kings and counsellors of the earth, which built desolate places for themselves; or with princes that had gold, who filled their houses with silver; or as an hidden untimely birth I had not been, as infants which never saw light. There the wicked cease from troubling, and there the weary be at rest. There the prisoners rest together; they hear not the voice of the oppressor. The small and great are there, and the servant is free from his master. Wherefore is light given to him that is in misery, and life unto the bitter in soul, which long for death, but it cometh not, and dig for it more than for hid treasures; which rejoice exceedingly, and are glad, when they can find the grave? Why is light given to a man whose way is hid, and whom God hath hedged in? For my sighing cometh before I eat, and my roarings are poured out like the waters. For the thing which I greatly feared is come upon me, and that which I was afraid of is come unto me. I was not in safety, neither had I rest, neither was I quiet; yet trouble came.

[Job's three friends—who have given us the term "Job's comforters"—argue with him, beginning mildly, but finally insisting that he must in some way deserve everything that has happened to him. Job replies to them, lamenting his life and longing for some peace before death.]

Then answered Zophar the Naamathite, and said, Should not the multitude of words be answered? and should a man full of talk be justified? Should thy lies make men hold their peace? and when thou mockest, shall no man make thee ashamed? For thou hast said, My doctrine is pure, and I am clean in thine eyes. But oh that God would speak, and open his lips against thee; and that he would shew thee the secrets of wisdom, that they are double to that which is! Know therefore that God exacteth of thee less than thine iniquity deserveth. Canst thou by searching find out God? canst thou find out the Almighty unto perfection? It is as high as heaven; what canst thou do? deeper than hell; what canst thou know? The measure thereof is longer than the earth, and broader than the sea. If he cut off, and shut up, or gather together, then who can hinder him? For he knoweth vain men; he seeth wickedness also; will he not then consider it? For vain man would be wise, though man be born like a wild ass's colt. If thou prepare thine heart, and stretch out thine hands toward him; if iniquity be in thine hand, put it far away, and let not wickedness dwell in thy tabernacles. For then shalt thou lift up thy face without spot; yea, thou shalt be stedfast, and shalt not fear, because thou shalt forget thy misery, and remember it as waters that pass away. And thine age shall be clearer than the noonday; thou shalt shine forth, thou shalt be as the morning. And thou shalt be secure, because there is hope; yea, thou shalt dig about thee, and thou shalt take thy rest in safety. Also thou shalt lie down, and none shall make thee afraid; yea, many shall make suit unto thee. But the eyes of the wicked shall fail, and they shall not escape, and their hope shall be as the giving up of the ghost.

And Job answered and said, No doubt but ye are the people, and wisdom shall die with you. But I have understanding as well as you; I am not inferior to you: yea, who knoweth not such things as these?

I am as one mocked of his neighbour, who calleth upon God, and he
answereth him; the just upright man is laughed to scorn. He that is
ready to slip with his feet is as a lamp despised in the thought of him
that is at ease. The tabernacles of robbers prosper, and they that provoke God are secure, into whose hand God bringeth abundantly. But
ask now the beasts, and they shall teach thee, and the fowls of the air,
and they shall tell thee; or speak to the earth, and it shall teach thee,
and the fishes of the sea shall declare unto thee. Who knoweth not in
all these that the hand of the Lord hath wrought this? in whose hand
is the soul of every living thing, and the breath of all mankind. Doth
not the ear try words? and the mouth taste his meat? With the ancient
is wisdom; and in length of days understanding. With him is wisdom
and strength, he hath counsel and understanding. Behold, he breaketh
down, and it cannot be built again; he shutteth up a man, and there
can be no opening. Behold, he withholdeth the waters, and they dry
up; also he sendeth them out, and they overturn the earth. With him
is strength and wisdom; the deceived and the deceiver are his. He
leadeth counsellors away spoiled, and maketh the judges fools. . . . He
removeth away the speech of the trusty, and taketh away the understanding of the aged. He poureth contempt upon princes, and weak-
eneth the strength of the mighty. He discovereth deep things out of
darkness, and bringeth out to light the shadow of death. He increaseth the nations, and destroyeth them; he enlargeth the nations,
and straiteneth them again. He taketh away the heart of the chief of
the people of the earth, and causeth them to wander in a wilderness
where there is no way. They grope in the dark without light, and he
maketh them to stagger like a drunken man.

Lo, mine eye hath seen all this; mine ear hath heard and understood it. What ye know, the same do I know also: I am not inferior
unto you. Surely I would speak to the Almighty, and I desire to reason
with God. But ye are forgers of lies; ye are all physicians of no value.
O that ye would altogether hold your peace! and it should be your
wisdom. Hear now my reasoning, and hearken to the pleadings of my
lips. Will ye speak wickedly for God, and talk deceitfully for him?
Will ye accept his person? will ye contend for God? Is it good that he
should search you out? or as one man mocketh another, do ye so
mock him? He will surely reprove you, if ye do secretly accept persons.
Shall not his excellency make you afraid? and his dread fall upon you?
Your remembrances are like unto ashes, your bodies to bodies of clay.
Hold your peace, let me alone, that I may speak, and let come on me

what will. Wherefore do I take my flesh in my teeth, and put my life in mine hand? Though he slay me, yet will I trust in him; but I will maintain mine own ways before him. He also shall be my salvation, for an hypocrite shall not come before him. Hear diligently my speech, and my declaration with your ears. Behold now, I have ordered my cause; I know that I shall be justified. Who is he that will plead with me? for now, if I hold my tongue, I shall give up the ghost. Only do not two things unto me; then will I not hide myself from thee. Withdraw thine hand far from me, and let not thy dread make me afraid. Then call thou, and I will answer, or let me speak, and answer thou me. How many are mine iniquities and sins? make me to know my transgression and my sin. Wherefore hidest thou thy face, and holdest me for thine enemy? Wilt thou break a leaf driven to and fro? and wilt thou pursue the dry stubble? For thou writest bitter things against me, and makest me to possess the iniquities of my youth. Thou puttest my feet also in the stocks, and lookest narrowly unto all my paths; thou settest a print upon the heels of my feet. And he, as a rotten thing, consumeth, as a garment that is moth-eaten.

Man that is born of a woman is of few days, and full of trouble. He cometh forth like a flower, and is cut down; he fleeth also as a shadow, and continueth not. And dost thou open thine eyes upon such an one, and bringest me into judgment with thee? Who can bring a clean thing out of an unclean? Not one. Seeing his days are determined, the number of his months are with thee, thou hast appointed his bounds that he cannot pass; turn from him, that he may rest, till he shall accomplish, as an hireling, his day. For there is hope of a tree, if it be cut down, that it will sprout again, and that the tender branch thereof will not cease. Though the root thereof wax old in the earth, and the stock thereof die in the ground; yet through the scent of water it will bud, and bring forth boughs like a plant. But man dieth, and wasteth away; yea, man giveth up the ghost, and where is he? As the waters fail from the sea, and the flood decayeth and drieth up, so man lieth down, and riseth not; till the heavens be no more, they shall not awake, nor be raised out of their sleep. O that thou wouldest hide me in the grave, that thou wouldest keep me secret, until thy wrath be past, that thou wouldest appoint me a set time, and remember me! If a man die, shall he live again? all the days of my appointed time will I wait, till my change come. Thou shalt call, and I will answer thee; thou wilt have a desire to the work of thine hands. For now thou numberest my steps; dost thou not watch over my sin? My transgression is sealed up in a bag, and thou sewest up mine iniquity. And surely the mountain falling cometh to nought, and the rock is removed out of his place. The waters wear the stones: thou washest away the things which grow out of the dust of the earth; and thou destroyest the hope of man. Thou prevailest for ever against him, and he passeth; thou changest his countenance, and sendest him away. His sons come to honour, and he knoweth it not; and they are brought low, but he perceiveth it not of them. But his flesh upon him shall have pain, and his soul within him shall mourn.

[Eliphaz says that it is wicked for Job to try to justify himself. In reply, Job appeals from men to God, and says that his hope lies in death. Bildad calls this appeal presumptuous, and insists that it is the wicked who are overtaken by calamities.]

Then Job answered and said, How long will ye vex my soul, and break me in pieces with words? These ten times have ye reproached me; ye are not ashamed that ye make yourselves strange to me. And be it indeed that I have erred, mine error remaineth with myself. If indeed ye will magnify yourselves against me, and plead against me my reproach; know now that God hath overthrown me, and hath compassed me with his net. Behold, I cry out of wrong, but I am not heard; I cry aloud, but there is no judgment. He hath fenced up my way that I cannot pass, and he hath set darkness in my paths. He hath stripped me of my glory, and taken the crown from my head. He hath destroyed me on every side, and I am gone; and mine hope hath he removed like a tree. He hath also kindled his wrath against me, and he counteth me unto him as one of his enemies. His troops come together, and raise up their way against me, and encamp round about my tabernacle. He hath put my brethren far from me, and mine acquaintance are verily estranged from me. My kinsfolk have failed, and my familiar friends have forgotten me. They that dwell in mine house, and my maids, count me for a stranger: I am an alien in their sight. I called my servant, and he gave me no answer; I intreated him with my mouth. My breath is strange to my wife, though I intreated for the children's sake of mine own body. Yea, young children despised me; I arose, and they spake against me. All my inward friends abhorred me, and they whom I loved are turned against me. My bone cleaveth to my skin and to my flesh, and I am escaped with the skin of my teeth. Have pity upon me, have pity upon me, O ye my friends, for the hand of God hath touched me. Why do ye persecute me as God, and are not satisfied with my flesh? Oh that my words were now written! oh that they were printed in a book! That they were graven with an iron pen and lead in the rock for ever! For I know that my redeemer liveth, and that he shall stand at the latter day upon the earth; and though after my skin worms destroy this body, yet in my flesh shall I see God, whom I shall see for myself, and mine eyes shall behold, and not another, though my reins be consumed within me. But ye should say, Why persecute we him, seeing the root of the matter is found in me? Be ye afraid of the sword, for wrath bringeth the punishments of the sword, that ye may know there is a judgment.

Then answered Zophar the Naamathite, and said, Therefore do my thoughts cause me to answer, and for this I make haste. I have heard the check of my reproach, and the spirit of my understanding causeth me to answer. Knowest thou not this of old, since man was placed upon earth, that the triumphing of the wicked is short, and the joy of the hypocrite but for a moment? Though his excellency mount up to the heavens, and his head reach unto the clouds, yet he shall perish for ever like his own dung; they which have seen him shall say, Where is he? He shall fly away as a dream, and shall not be found; yea, he shall be chased away as a vision of the night. The eye also which saw him shall see him no more; neither shall his place any more behold him. His children shall seek to please the poor, and his hands shall restore their goods. His bones are full of the sin of his youth, which shall lie down with him in the dust. Though wickedness be sweet in his mouth, though he hide it under his tongue; though he spare it, and forsake it not, but keep it still within his mouth; yet his meat in his bowels is turned; it is the gall of asps within him. He hath swallowed down riches, and he shall vomit them up again; God shall cast them out of his belly. He shall suck the poison of asps; the viper's tongue shall slay him. . . . The heaven shall reveal his iniquity; and the earth shall rise up against him. The increase of his house shall depart, and his goods shall flow away in the day of his wrath. This is the portion of a wicked man from God, and the heritage appointed unto him by God.

But Job answered and said, Hear diligently my speech, and let this be your consolations. Suffer me that I may speak; and after that I have spoken, mock on. As for me, is my complaint to man? and if it were so, why should not my spirit be troubled? Mark me, and be astonished, and lay your hand upon your mouth. Even when I re-member I am afraid, and trembling taketh hold on my flesh. Wherefore do the wicked live, become old, yea, are mighty in power? Their seed is established in their sight with them, and their offspring before their eyes. Their houses are safe from fear, neither is the rod of God upon them. Their bull gendereth, and faileth not; their cow calveth, and casteth not her calf. They send forth their little ones like a flock, and their children dance. They take the timbrel and harp, and rejoice at the sound of the organ. They spend their days in wealth, and in a moment go down to the grave. Therefore they say unto God, Depart from us, for we desire not the knowledge of thy ways. What is the Almighty, that we should serve him? and what profit should we have, if we pray unto him? Lo, their good is not in their hand; the counsel of the wicked is far from me. How oft is the candle of the wicked put out! and how oft cometh their destruction upon them! God distributeth sorrows in his anger. They are as stubble before the wind, and as chaff that the storm carrieth away. God layeth up his iniquity for his children; he rewardeth him, and he shall know it. His eyes shall see his destruction, and he shall drink of the wrath of the Almighty. For what pleasure hath he in his house after him, when the number of his months is cut off in the midst? Shall any teach God knowledge? seeing he judgeth those that are high. One dieth in his full strength, being wholly at ease and quiet. His breasts are full of milk, and his bones are moistened with marrow. And another dieth in the bitterness of his soul, and never eateth with pleasure. They shall lie down alike in the dust, and the worms shall cover them. Behold, I know your thoughts, and the devices which ye wrongfully imagine against me. For ye say, Where is the house of the prince? and where are the dwelling places of the wicked? Have ye not asked them that go by the way? and do ye not know their tokens, that the wicked is reserved to the day of destruction? they shall be brought forth to the day of wrath. Who shall declare his way to his face? and who shall repay him what he hath done? Yet shall he be brought to the grave, and shall remain in the tomb. The clods of the valley shall be sweet unto him, and every man shall draw after him, as there are innumerable before him. How then comfort ye me in vain, seeing in your answers there remaineth falsehood?

Then Eliphaz the Temanite answered and said, Can a man be profitable unto God, as he that is wise may be profitable unto himself? Is it any pleasure to the Almighty, that thou art righteous? or is it gain to him, that thou makest thy ways perfect? Will he reprove thee for fear of thee? will he enter with thee into judgment? Is not thy wicked-

ness great? and thine iniquities infinite? For thou hast taken a pledge
from thy brother for nought, and stripped the naked of their clothing.
Thou hast not given water to the weary to drink, and thou hast withholden bread from the hungry. But as for the mighty man, he had the
earth; and the honourable man dwelt in it. Thou hast sent widows
away empty, and the arms of the fatherless have been broken. Therefore snares are round about thee, and sudden fear troubleth thee, or
darkness, that thou canst not see; and abundance of waters cover thee.
Is not God in the height of heaven? and behold the height of the stars,
how high they are! And thou sayest, How doth God know? can he
judge through the dark cloud? Thick clouds are a covering to him,
that he seeth not; and he walketh in the circuit of heaven. Hast thou
marked the old way which wicked men have trodden? which were cut
down out of time, whose foundation was overflown with a flood;
which said unto God, Depart from us: and what can the Almighty do
for them? Yet he filled their houses with good things; but the counsel
of the wicked is far from me. The righteous see it, and are glad; and
the innocent laugh them to scorn. Whereas our substance is not cut
down, but the remnant of them the fire consumeth. Acquaint now
thyself with him, and be at peace; thereby good shall come unto thee.
Receive, I pray thee, the law from his mouth, and lay up his words in
thine heart. If thou return to the Almighty, thou shalt be built up;
thou shalt put away iniquity far from thy tabernacles. Then shalt thou
lay up gold as dust, and the gold of Ophir as the stones of the brooks.
Yea, the Almighty shall be thy defence, and thou shalt have plenty of
silver. For then shalt thou have thy delight in the Almighty, and shalt
lift up thy face unto God. Thou shalt make thy prayer unto him, and
he shall hear thee, and thou shalt pay thy vows. Thou shalt also decree
a thing, and it shall be established unto thee; and the light shall shine
upon thy ways. When men are cast down, then thou shalt say, There
is lifting up; and he shall save the humble person. He shall deliver the
island of the innocent; and it is delivered by the pureness of thine
hands.

Then Job answered and said, Even to day is my complaint bitter;
my stroke is heavier than my groaning. Oh that I knew where I might
find him! that I might come even to his seat! I would order my cause
before him, and fill my mouth with arguments. I would know the
words which he would answer me, and understand what he would
say unto me. Will he plead against me with his great power? No; but
he would put strength in me. There the righteous might dispute with

him; so should I be delivered for ever from my judge. Behold, I go forward, but he is not there; and backward, but I cannot perceive him; on the left hand, where he doth work, but I cannot behold him; he hideth himself on the right hand, that I cannot see him: but he knoweth the way that I take; when he hath tried me, I shall come forth as gold. My foot hath held his steps; his way have I kept, and not declined. Neither have I gone back from the commandment of his lips; I have esteemed the words of his mouth more than my necessary food. But he is in one mind, and who can turn him? and what his soul desireth, even that he doeth. For he performeth the thing that is appointed for me, and many such things are with him. Therefore am I troubled at his presence; when I consider, I am afraid of him. For God maketh my heart soft, and the Almighty troubleth me, because I was not cut off before the darkness, neither hath he covered the darkness from my face.

Why, seeing times are not hidden from the Almighty, do they that know him not see his days? Some remove the landmarks; they violently take away flocks, and feed thereof. They drive away the ass of the fatherless; they take the widow's ox for a pledge. They turn the needy out of the way; the poor of the earth hide themselves together. Behold, as wild asses in the desert, go they forth to their work, rising betimes for a prey; the wilderness yieldeth food for them and for their children. They reap every one his corn in the field; and they gather the vintage of the wicked. They cause the naked to lodge without clothing, that they have no covering in the cold. They are wet with the showers of the mountains, and embrace the rock for want of a shelter. They pluck the fatherless from the breast, and take a pledge of the poor. . . . They are of those that rebel against the light; they know not the ways thereof, nor abide in the paths thereof. The murderer rising with the light killeth the poor and needy, and in the night is as a thief. The eye also of the adulterer waiteth for the twilight, saying, No eye shall see me; and disguiseth his face. In the dark they dig through houses, which they had marked for themselves in the daytime: they know not the light. For the morning is to them even as the shadow of death: if one know them, they are in the terrors of the shadow of death. He is swift as the waters; their portion is cursed in the earth; he beholdeth not the way of the vineyards. Drought and heat consume the snow waters; so doth the grave those which have sinned. The womb shall forget him; the worm shall feed sweetly on him; he shall be no more remembered; and wickedness shall be broken as a tree.

He evil entreateth the barren that beareth not; and doeth not good to
the widow. He draweth also the mighty with his power; he riseth
up, and no man is sure of life. Though it be given him to be in safety,
whereon he resteth, yet his eyes are upon their ways. They are exalted
for a little while, but are gone and brought low; they are taken out
of the way as all other, and cut off as the tops of the ears of corn. And
if it be not so now, who will make me a liar, and make my speech
nothing worth?

[Bildad argues that no man can be considered sinless before God,
and Job, while resenting this uncharitable attitude, admits that the
power of God is beyond human comprehension.]

Moreover Job continued his parable, and said, As God liveth, who
hath taken away my judgment; and the Almighty, who hath vexed
my soul; all the while my breath is in me, and the spirit of God is
in my nostrils, my lips shall not speak wickedness, nor my tongue utter
deceit. God forbid that I should justify you; till I die I will not remove
mine integrity from me. My righteousness I hold fast, and will not let
it go; my heart shall not reproach me so long as I live. Let mine enemy
be as the wicked, and he that riseth up against me as the unrighteous.
For what is the hope of the hypocrite, though he hath gained, when
God taketh away his soul? Will God hear his cry when trouble cometh
upon him? Will he delight himself in the Almighty? will he always
call upon God? I will teach you by the hand of God; that which is
with the Almighty will I not conceal. Behold, all ye yourselves have
seen it; why then are ye thus altogether vain? This is the portion of
a wicked man with God, and the heritage of oppressors, which they
shall receive of the Almighty. If his children be multiplied, it is for
the sword: and his offspring shall not be satisfied with bread. Those
that remain of him shall be buried in death; and his widows shall not
weep. Though he heap up silver as the dust, and prepare raiment as
the clay, he may prepare it, but the just shall put it on, and the innocent
shall divide the silver. He buildeth his house as a moth, and as a
booth that the keeper maketh. The rich man shall lie down, but he
shall not be gathered; he openeth his eyes, and he is not. Terrors take
hold on him as waters, a tempest stealeth him away in the night. The
east wind carrieth him away, and he departeth; and as a storm hurleth
him out of his place. For God shall cast upon him, and not spare; he

would fain flee out of his hand. Men shall clap their hands at him, and shall hiss him out of his place.

Surely there is a vein for the silver, and a place for gold where they fine it. Iron is taken out of the earth, and brass is molten out of the stone. . . . There is a path which no fowl knoweth, and which the vulture's eye hath not seen; the lion's whelps have not trodden it, nor the fierce lion passed by it. . . . But where shall wisdom be found? and where is the place of understanding? Man knoweth not the price thereof; neither is it found in the land of the living. The depth saith, It is not in me; and the sea saith, It is not with me. It cannot be gotten for gold, neither shall silver be weighed for the price thereof. It cannot be valued with the gold of Ophir, with the precious onyx, or the sapphire. The gold and the crystal cannot equal it; and the exchange of it shall not be for jewels of fine gold. . . . Whence then cometh wisdom? and where is the place of understanding? seeing it is hid from the eyes of all living, and kept close from the fowls of the air. Destruction and death say, We have heard the fame thereof with our ears. God understandeth the way thereof, and he knoweth the place thereof. For he looketh to the ends of the earth, and seeth under the whole heaven to make the weight for the winds; and he weigheth the waters by measure. When he made a decree for the rain, and a way for the lightning of the thunder, then did he see it, and declare it; he prepared it, yea, and searched it out. And unto man he said, Behold, the fear of the Lord, that is wisdom; and to depart from evil is understanding.

[Job describes his former prosperity and honor, and contrasts them with the calamity and contempt which are now his lot.]

I made a covenant with mine eyes; why then should I think upon a maid? For what portion of God is there from above? and what inheritance of the Almighty from on high? Is not destruction to the wicked? and a strange punishment to the workers of iniquity? Doth not he see my ways, and count all my steps? If I have walked with vanity, or if my foot hath hasted to deceit, let me be weighed in an even balance, that God may know mine integrity. If my step hath turned out of the way, and mine heart walked after mine eyes, and if any blot hath cleaved to mine hands, then let me sow, and let another eat; yea, let my offspring be rooted out. If mine heart have been deceived by a woman, or if I have laid wait at my neighbour's door, then let my wife grind unto another, and let others bow down upon her. For this is an heinous crime; yea, it is an iniquity to be punished by the judges. For it is a fire that consumeth to destruction, and would root out all mine increase. If I did despise the cause of my manservant or of my maidservant, when they contended with me, what then shall I do when God riseth up? and when he visiteth, what shall I answer him? Did not he that made me in the womb make him? and did not one fashion us in the womb? If I have withheld the poor from their desire, or have caused the eyes of the widow to fail; or have eaten my morsel myself alone, and the fatherless hath not eaten thereof (for from my youth he was brought up with me, as with a father, and I have guided her from my mother's womb)—if I have seen any perish for want of clothing, or any poor without covering; if his loins have not blessed me, and if he were not warmed with the fleece of my sheep —if I have lifted up my hand against the fatherless, when I saw my help in the gate: then let mine arm fall from my shoulder blade, and mine arm be broken from the bone, for destruction from God was a terror to me, and by reason of his highness I could not endure. If I have made gold my hope, or have said to the fine gold, Thou art my confidence—if I rejoiced because my wealth was great, and because mine hand had gotten much—if I beheld the sun when it shined, or the moon walking in brightness, and my heart hath been secretly enticed, or my mouth hath kissed my hand: this also were an iniquity to be punished by the judge, for I should have denied the God that is above. If I rejoiced at the destruction of him that hated me, or lifted up myself when evil found him, neither have I suffered my mouth to sin by wishing a curse to his soul. . . . Oh that one would hear me! behold, my desire is, that the Almighty would answer me, and that mine adversary had written a book. Surely I would take it upon my shoulder, and bind it as a crown to me. I would declare unto him the number of my steps; as a prince would I go near unto him. If my land cry against me, or that the furrows likewise thereof complain, if I have eaten the fruits thereof without money, or have caused the owners thereof to lose their life: let thistles grow instead of wheat, and cockle instead of barley. The words of Job are ended.

[At this point one Elihu the Buzite, not previously mentioned, delivers a long harangue in which he seeks to improve on the other three comforters' answers to Job. Since most biblical scholars regard Elihu's speech as an inferior interpolation, it is entirely omitted here.]

Then the LORD answered Job out of the whirlwind, and said, Who is this that darkeneth counsel by words without knowledge? Gird up now thy loins like a man; for I will demand of thee, and answer thou me. Where wast thou when I laid the foundations of the earth? declare, if thou hast understanding. Who hath laid the measures thereof, if thou knowest? or who hath stretched the line upon it? Whereupon are the foundations thereof fastened? or who laid the corner stone thereof; when the morning stars sang together, and all the sons of God shouted for joy? Or who shut up the sea with doors, when it brake forth, as if it had issued out of the womb? when I made the cloud the garment thereof, and thick darkness a swaddlingband for it, and brake up for it my decreed place, and set bars and doors, and said, Hitherto shalt thou come, but no further: and here shall thy proud waves be stayed? . . .

Wilt thou hunt the prey for the lion? or fill the appetite of the young lions, when they couch in their dens, and abide in the covert to lie in wait? Who provideth for the raven his food? When his young ones cry unto God, they wander for lack of meat.

Knowest thou the time when the wild goats of the rock bring forth? or canst thou mark when the hinds do calve? Canst thou number the months that they fulfil? or knowest thou the time when they bring forth? They bow themselves, they bring forth their young ones, they cast out their sorrows. Their young ones are in good liking, they grow up with corn; they go forth, and return not unto them. Who hath sent out the wild ass free? or who hath loosed the bands of the wild ass, whose house I have made the wilderness, and the barren land his dwellings. He scorneth the multitude of the city, neither regardeth he the crying of the driver. The range of the mountains is his pasture, and he searcheth after every green thing. Will the unicorn[4] be willing to serve thee, or abide by thy crib? Canst thou bind the unicorn with his band in the furrow? or will he harrow the valleys after thee? Wilt thou trust him, because his strength is great? or wilt thou leave thy labour to him? Wilt thou believe him, that he will bring home thy seed, and gather it into thy barn? Gavest thou the goodly wings unto the peacocks? or wings and feathers unto the ostrich, which leaveth her eggs in the earth, and warmeth them in dust, and forgetteth that the foot may crush them, or that the wild beast may break them. She is hardened against her young ones, as though they were not hers; her labour is in vain without fear, because

4. *unicorn*, the wild ox, or aurochs.

God hath deprived her of wisdom, neither hath he imparted to her understanding. What time she lifteth up herself on high, she scorneth the horse and his rider. Hast thou given the horse strength? hast thou clothed his neck with thunder? Canst thou make him afraid as a grass-hopper? The glory of his nostrils is terrible. He paweth in the valley, and rejoiceth in his strength; he goeth on to meet the armed men. He mocketh at fear, and is not affrighted; neither turneth he back from the sword. The quiver rattleth against him, the glittering spear and the shield. He swalloweth the ground with fierceness and rage; neither believeth he that it is the sound of the trumpet. He saith among the trumpets, Ha, ha; and he smelleth the battle afar off, the thunder of the captains, and the shouting. Doth the hawk fly by thy wisdom, and stretch her wings toward the south? Doth the eagle mount up at thy command, and make her nest on high? She dwelleth and abideth on the rock, upon the crag of the rock, and the strong place. From thence she seeketh the prey, and her eyes behold afar off. Her young ones also suck up blood; and where the slain are, there is she.

Moreover the Lord answered Job, and said, Shall he that con-tendeth with the Almighty instruct him? He that reproveth God, let him answer it.

Then Job answered the Lord, and said, Behold, I am vile; what shall I answer thee? I will lay mine hand upon my mouth. Once have I spoken; but I will not answer: yea, twice; but I will proceed no further.

Then answered the Lord unto Job out of the whirlwind, and said, Gird up thy loins now like a man; I will demand of thee, and declare thou unto me. Wilt thou also disannul my judgment? Wilt thou con-demn me, that thou mayest be righteous? Hast thou an arm like God? or canst thou thunder with a voice like him? Deck thyself now with majesty and excellency; and array thyself with glory and beauty. Cast abroad the rage of thy wrath, and behold every one that is proud, and abase him. Look on every one that is proud, and bring him low; and tread down the wicked in their place. Hide them in the dust together, and bind their faces in secret. Then will I also confess unto thee that thine own right hand can save thee.

Behold now behemoth,[5] which I made with thee; he eateth grass as an ox. Lo now, his strength is in his loins, and his force is in the navel of his belly. He moveth his tail like a cedar: the sinews of his stones are wrapped together. His bones are as strong pieces of brass;

5. *behemoth,* probably the hippopotamus.

his bones are like bars of iron. He is the chief of the ways of God; he that made him can make his sword to approach unto him. Surely the mountains bring him forth food, where all the beasts of the field play. He lieth under the shady trees, in the covert of the reed, and fens. The shady trees cover him with their shadow; the willows of the brook compass him about. Behold, he drinketh up a river, and hasteth not; he trusteth that he can draw up Jordan into his mouth. He taketh it with his eyes; his nose pierceth through snares.

Canst thou draw out leviathan[6] with an hook? or his tongue with a cord which thou lettest down? Canst thou put an hook into his nose? or bore his jaw through with a thorn? Will he make many supplications unto thee? Will he speak soft words unto thee? Will he make a covenant with thee? Wilt thou take him for a servant for ever? Wilt thou play with him as with a bird? or wilt thou bind him for thy maidens? Shall the companions make a banquet of him? Shall they part him among the merchants? Canst thou fill his skin with barbed irons? or his head with fish spears? Lay thine hand upon him, remember the battle, do no more. Behold, the hope of him is in vain; shall not one be cast down even at the sight of him? None is so fierce that dare stir him up; who then is able to stand before me? Who hath prevented me, that I should repay him? Whatsoever is under the whole heaven is mine. I will not conceal his parts, nor his power, nor his comely proportion. Who can discover the face of his garment? or who can come to him with his double bridle? Who can open the doors of his face? His teeth are terrible round about. His scales are his pride, shut up together as with a close seal. One is so near to another that no air can come between them. They are joined one to another; they stick together, that they cannot be sundered. . . . In his neck remaineth strength, and sorrow is turned into joy before him. The flakes of his flesh are joined together: they are firm in themselves; they cannot be moved. His heart is as firm as a stone; yea, as hard as a piece of the nether millstone. When he raiseth up himself, the mighty are afraid; by reason of breakings they purify themselves. The sword of him that layeth at him cannot hold; the spear, the dart, nor the habergeon.[7] He esteemeth iron as straw, and brass as rotten wood. The arrow cannot make him flee; slingstones are turned with him into stubble. Darts are counted as stubble; he laugheth at the shaking of

6. *leviathan*, the crocodile.
7. *Habergeon* (coat of mail) is a mistranslation; the Revised Version has *pointed shaft.*

a spear. Sharp stones are under him; he spreadeth sharp pointed things upon the mire. He maketh the deep to boil like a pot; he maketh the sea like a pot of ointment. He maketh a path to shine after him; one would think the deep to be hoary. Upon earth there is not his like, who is made without fear. He beholdeth all high things; he is a king over all the children of pride.

Then Job answered the LORD, and said, I know that thou canst do everything, and that no thought can be withholden from thee. Who is he that hideth counsel without knowledge? Therefore have I uttered that I understood not; things too wonderful for me, which I knew not. Hear, I beseech thee, and I will speak; I will demand of thee, and declare thou unto me. I have heard of thee by the hearing of the ear, but now mine eye seeth thee. Wherefore I abhor myself, and repent in dust and ashes.

And it was so, that after the LORD had spoken these words unto Job, the LORD said to Eliphaz the Temanite, My wrath is kindled against thee, and against thy two friends; for ye have not spoken of me the thing that is right, as my servant Job hath. Therefore take unto you now seven bullocks and seven rams, and go to my servant Job, and offer up for yourselves a burnt offering; and my servant Job shall pray for you, for him will I accept; lest I deal with you after your folly, in that ye have not spoken of me the thing which is right, like my servant Job. So Eliphaz the Temanite and Bildad the Shuhite and Zophar the Naamathite went, and did according as the LORD commanded them. The LORD also accepted Job.

And the LORD turned the captivity of Job, when he prayed for his friends; also the LORD gave Job twice as much as he had before. Then came there unto him all his brethren, and all his sisters, and all they that had been of his acquaintance before, and did eat bread with him in his house; and they bemoaned him, and comforted him over all the evil that the LORD had brought upon him. Every man also gave him a piece of money, and every one an earring of gold. So the LORD blessed the latter end of Job more than his beginning, for he had fourteen thousand sheep, and six thousand camels, and a thousand yoke of oxen, and a thousand she asses. He had also seven sons and three daughters. And in all the land were no women found so fair as the daughters of Job; and their father gave them inheritance among their brethren.

After this lived Job an hundred and forty years, and saw his sons, and his sons' sons, even four generations. So Job died, being old and full of days.

PSALMS

Psalm 1

Blessed is the man that walketh not in the counsel of the ungodly, nor standeth in the way of sinners, nor sitteth in the seat of the scornful.

But his delight is in the law of the Lord; and in his law doth he meditate day and night.

And he shall be like a tree planted by the rivers of water, that bringeth forth his fruit in his season; his leaf also shall not wither; and whatsoever he doeth shall prosper.

The ungodly are not so, but are like the chaff which the wind driveth away.

Therefore the ungodly shall not stand in the judgment, nor sinners in the congregation of the righteous.

For the Lord knoweth the way of the righteous; but the way of the ungodly shall perish.

Psalm 8

O Lord our Lord, how excellent is thy name in all the earth! who hast set thy glory above the heavens.

Out of the mouth of babes and sucklings hast thou ordained strength because of thine enemies, that thou mightest still the enemy and the avenger.

When I consider thy heavens, the work of thy fingers, the moon and the stars, which thou hast ordained;

What is man, that thou art mindful of him? and the son of man, that thou visitest him?

For thou hast made him a little lower than the angels, and hast crowned him with glory and honour.

Thou madest him to have dominion over the works of thy hands; thou hast put all things under his feet:

All sheep and oxen, yea, and the beasts of the field;

The fowl of the air, and the fish of the sea, and whatsoever passeth through the paths of the seas.

O Lord our Lord, how excellent is thy name in all the earth!

Psalm 19

The heavens declare the glory of God; and the firmament sheweth his handywork.

Day unto day uttereth speech, and night unto night sheweth knowledge.

There is no speech nor language, where their voice is not heard.

Their line is gone out through all the earth, and their words to the end of the world. In them hath he set a tabernacle for the sun,

Which is as a bridegroom coming out of his chamber, and rejoiceth as a strong man to run a race.

His going forth is from the end of the heaven, and his circuit unto the ends of it: and there is nothing hid from the heat thereof.

The law of the LORD is perfect, converting the soul; the testimony of the LORD is sure, making wise the simple.

The statutes of the LORD are right, rejoicing the heart; the commandment of the LORD is pure, enlightening the eyes.

The fear of the LORD is clean, enduring for ever; the judgments of the LORD are true and righteous altogether.

More to be desired are they than gold, yea, than much fine gold; sweeter also than honey and the honeycomb.

Moreover by them is thy servant warned, and in keeping of them there is great reward.

Who can understand his errors? Cleanse thou me from secret faults.

Keep back thy servant also from presumptuous sins; let them not have dominion over me: then shall I be upright, and I shall be innocent from the great transgression.

Let the words of my mouth, and the meditation of my heart, be acceptable in thy sight, O LORD, my strength, and my redeemer.

Psalm 23

The LORD is my shepherd; I shall not want.

He maketh me to lie down in green pastures: he leadeth me beside the still waters.

He restoreth my soul: he leadeth me in the paths of righteousness for his name's sake.

Yea, though I walk through the valley of the shadow of death, I will fear no evil: for thou art with me; thy rod and thy staff they comfort me.

Thou preparest a table before me in the presence of mine enemies: thou anointest my head with oil; my cup runneth over.

Surely goodness and mercy shall follow me all the days of my life: and I will dwell in the house of the Lord for ever.

Psalm 46

God is our refuge and strength, a very present help in trouble.

Therefore will not we fear, though the earth be removed, and though the mountains be carried into the midst of the sea;

Though the waters thereof roar and be troubled, though the mountains shake with the swelling thereof. Selah.[1]

There is a river, the streams whereof shall make glad the city of God, the holy place of the tabernacles of the most High.

God is in the midst of her; she shall not be moved: God shall help her, and that right early.

The heathen raged, the kingdoms were moved: he uttered his voice, the earth melted.

The Lord of hosts is with us; the God of Jacob is our refuge. Selah.

Come, behold the works of the Lord, what desolations he hath made in the earth.

He maketh wars to cease unto the end of the earth; he breaketh the bow, and cutteth the spear in sunder; he burneth the chariot in the fire.

Be still, and know that I am God: I will be exalted among the heathen, I will be exalted in the earth.

The Lord of hosts is with us; the God of Jacob is our refuge. Selah.

Psalm 90

Lord, thou hast been our dwelling place in all generations.

Before the mountains were brought forth, or ever thou hadst formed the earth and the world, even from everlasting to everlasting, thou art God.

Thou turnest man to destruction; and sayest, Return, ye children of men.

For a thousand years in thy sight are but as yesterday when it is past, and as a watch in the night.

1. This word occurs frequently in the Psalms, and occasionally elsewhere. It is not a part of the text, and may possibly have been some kind of musical direction. Many different explanations of it have been advanced, none of them conclusive.

Thou carriest them away as with a flood; they are as a sleep: in the morning they are like grass which groweth up.

In the morning it flourisheth, and groweth up; in the evening it is cut down, and withereth.

For we are consumed by thine anger, and by thy wrath are we troubled.

Thou hast set our iniquities before thee, our secret sins in the light of thy countenance.

For all our days are passed away in thy wrath: we spend our years as a tale that is told.

The days of our years are threescore years and ten; and if by reason of strength they be fourscore years, yet is their strength labour and sorrow; for it is soon cut off, and we fly away.

Who knoweth the power of thine anger? even according to thy fear, so is thy wrath.

So teach us to number our days, that we may apply our hearts unto wisdom.

Return, O Lord, how long? and let it repent thee concerning thy servants.

O satisfy us early with thy mercy; that we may rejoice and be glad all our days.

Make us glad according to the days wherein thou hast afflicted us, and the years wherein we have seen evil.

Let thy work appear unto thy servants, and thy glory unto their children.

And let the beauty of the Lord our God be upon us: and establish thou the work of our hands upon us; yea, the work of our hands establish thou it.

Psalm 91

He that dwelleth in the secret place of the most High shall abide under the shadow of the Almighty.

I will say of the Lord, He is my refuge and my fortress: my God; in him will I trust.

Surely he shall deliver thee from the snare of the fowler, and from the noisome pestilence.

He shall cover thee with his feathers, and under his wings shalt thou trust: his truth shall be thy shield and buckler.

Thou shalt not be afraid for the terror by night; nor for the arrow that flieth by day;

Nor for the pestilence that walketh in darkness; nor for the destruction that wasteth at noonday.

A thousand shall fall at thy side, and ten thousand at thy right hand; but it shall not come nigh thee.

Only with thine eyes shalt thou behold and see the reward of the wicked.

Because thou hast made the LORD, which is my refuge, even the most High, thy habitation;

There shall no evil befall thee, neither shall any plague come nigh thy dwelling.

For he shall give his angels charge over thee, to keep thee in all thy ways.

They shall bear thee up in their hands, lest thou dash thy foot against a stone.

Thou shalt tread upon the lion and adder: the young lion and the dragon shalt thou trample under feet.

Because he hath set his love upon me, therefore will I deliver him: I will set him on high, because he hath known my name.

He shall call upon me, and I will answer him: I will be with him in trouble; I will deliver him, and honour him.

With long life will I satisfy him, and shew him my salvation.

Psalm 121

I will lift up mine eyes unto the hills, from whence cometh my help.

My help cometh from the LORD, which made heaven and earth.

He will not suffer thy foot to be moved: he that keepeth thee will not slumber.

Behold, he that keepeth Israel shall neither slumber nor sleep.

The LORD is thy keeper: the LORD is thy shade upon thy right hand.

The sun shall not smite thee by day, nor the moon by night.

The LORD shall preserve thee from all evil: he shall preserve thy soul.

The LORD shall preserve thy going out and thy coming in from this time forth, and even for evermore.

Psalm 137

By the rivers of Babylon, there we sat down, yea, we wept, when we remembered Zion.[2]

2. *Zion*, a hill in Jerusalem. This psalm refers to the period of exile, or "Babylonian captivity" of the Children of Israel (586-538 B.C.).

We hanged our harps upon the willows in the midst thereof.

For there they that carried us away captive required of us a song; and they that wasted us required of us mirth, saying, Sing us one of the songs of Zion.

How shall we sing the LORD's song in a strange land?

If I forget thee, O Jerusalem, let my right hand forget her cunning.

If I do not remember thee, let my tongue cleave to the roof of my mouth; if I prefer not Jerusalem above my chief joy.

Remember, O LORD, the children of Edom in the day of Jerusalem; who said, Rase it, rase it, even to the foundation thereof.

O daughter of Babylon, who art to be destroyed; happy shall he be, that rewardeth thee as thou hast served us.

Happy shall he be, that taketh and dasheth thy little ones against the stones.

THE NEW TESTAMENT

THE BIRTH OF CHRIST
(Matthew, 1-2)

Now the birth of Jesus Christ was on this wise: When as his mother Mary was espoused to Joseph, before they came together, she was found with child of the Holy Ghost. Then Joseph, her husband, being a just man, and not willing to make her a publick example, was minded to put her away privily. But while he thought on these things, behold, the angel of the Lord appeared unto him in a dream, saying, Joseph, thou son of David,[1] fear not to take unto thee Mary thy wife, for that which is conceived in her is of the Holy Ghost. And she shall bring forth a son, and thou shalt call his name JESUS, for he shall save his people from their sins.[2] . . . Then Joseph, being raised from sleep, did as the angel of the Lord had bidden him, and took unto him his wife, and knew her not till she had brought forth her firstborn son; and he called his name JESUS.

Now when Jesus was born in Bethlehem of Judæa in the days of Herod the king, behold, there came wise men from the east to Jerusalem, saying, Where is he that is born King of the Jews? for we have

1. Joseph was a descendant of David.
2. *Jesus* is the Greek form of the Hebrew name *Joshua*, meaning "salvation."

seen his star in the east, and are come to worship him. When Herod
the king had heard these things, he was troubled, and all Jerusalem
with him. And when he had gathered all the chief priests and scribes
of the people together, he demanded of them where Christ should be
born. And they said unto him, In Bethlehem of Judæa: for thus it is
written by the prophet:[3] And thou Bethlehem, in the land of Juda, art
not the least among the princes of Juda: for out of thee shall come a
Governor, that shall rule my people Israel. Then Herod, when he had
privily called the wise men, enquired of them diligently what time the
star appeared. And he sent them to Bethlehem, and said, Go and search
diligently for the young child; and when ye have found him, bring
me word again, that I may come and worship him also. When they
had heard the king, they departed; and, lo, the star, which they saw in
the east, went before them, till it came and stood over where the young
child was. When they saw the star, they rejoiced with exceeding great
joy.

And when they were come into the house, they saw the young
child with Mary his mother, and fell down, and worshipped him; and
when they had opened their treasures, they presented unto him gifts,
gold, and frankincense, and myrrh. And being warned of God in a
dream that they should not return to Herod, they departed into their
own country another way. And when they were departed, behold, the
angel of the Lord appeareth to Joseph in a dream, saying, Arise, and
take the young child and his mother, and flee into Egypt, and be thou
there until I bring thee word; for Herod will seek the young child to
destroy him. When he arose, he took the young child and his mother
by night, and departed into Egypt. . . .

Then Herod, when he saw that he was mocked of the wise men,
was exceeding wroth, and sent forth, and slew all the children that
were in Bethlehem, and in all the coasts thereof, from two years old
and under, according to the time which he had diligently enquired of
the wise men. . . .

But when Herod was dead, behold, an angel of the Lord appeareth in a dream to Joseph in Egypt, saying, Arise, and take the
young child and his mother, and go into the land of Israel, for they
are dead which sought the young child's life. And he arose, and took
the young child and his mother, and came into the land of Israel. But
when he heard that Archelaus did reign in Judæa in the room of his
father Herod, he was afraid to go thither; notwithstanding, being

3. *Micah*, 5, 2. Micah is one of the Old Testament prophets

warned of God in a dream, he turned aside into the parts of Galilee; and he came and dwelt in a city called Nazareth: that it might be fulfilled which was spoken by the prophets,[4] He shall be called a Nazarene.

JOHN THE BAPTIST
(*Matthew, 3*)

In those days came John the Baptist, preaching in the wilderness of Judæa, and saying, Repent ye: for the kingdom of heaven is at hand. . . . And the same John had his raiment of camel's hair, and a leathern girdle about his loins; and his meat was locusts and wild honey. Then went out to him Jerusalem, and all Judæa, and all the region round about Jordan, and were baptized of him in Jordan, confessing their sins. . . .

Then cometh Jesus from Galilee to Jordan unto John, to be baptized of him. But John forbad him, saying, I have need to be baptized of thee, and comest thou to me? And Jesus answering said unto him, Suffer it to be so now, for thus it becometh us to fulfil all righteousness. Then he suffered him. And Jesus, when he was baptized, went up straightway out of the water; and, lo, the heavens were opened unto him, and he saw the Spirit of God descending like a dove, and lighting upon him; and lo a voice from heaven, saying, This is my beloved Son, in whom I am well pleased.

THE TEMPTATION
(*Matthew, 4*)

Then was Jesus led up of the Spirit into the wilderness to be tempted of the devil. And when he had fasted forty days and forty nights, he was afterward an hungred. And when the tempter came to him, he said, If thou be the Son of God, command that these stones be made bread. But he answered and said, It is written, Man shall not live by bread alone, but by every word that proceedeth out of the mouth of God. Then the devil taketh him up into the holy city, and setteth him on a pinnacle of the temple, and saith unto him, If thou be the Son of God, cast thyself down; for it is written, He shall give his angels charge concerning thee; and in their hands they shall bear thee up, lest at any time thou dash thy foot against a stone. Jesus said

4. *Judges*, 13, 5.

unto him, It is written again, Thou shalt not tempt the Lord thy God. Again, the devil taketh him up into an exceeding high mountain, and sheweth him all the kingdoms of the world, and the glory of them, and saith unto him, All these things will I give thee, if thou wilt fall down and worship me. Then saith Jesus unto him, Get thee hence, Satan: for it is written, Thou shalt worship the Lord thy God, and him only shalt thou serve. Then the devil leaveth him, and, behold, angels came and ministered unto him. . . .

From that time Jesus began to preach, and to say, Repent: for the kingdom of heaven is at hand.

And Jesus, walking by the sea of Galilee, saw two brethren, Simon called Peter, and Andrew his brother, casting a net into the sea, for they were fishers. And he saith unto them, Follow me, and I will make you fishers of men. And they straightway left their nets, and followed him. And going on from thence, he saw other two brethren, James the son of Zebedee, and John his brother, in a ship with Zebedee their father, mending their nets; and he called them. And they immediately left the ship and their father, and followed him.

And Jesus went about all Galilee, teaching in their synagogues, and preaching the gospel of the kingdom, and healing all manner of sickness and all manner of disease among the people. And his fame went throughout all Syria; and they brought unto him all sick people that were taken with divers diseases and torments, and those which were possessed with devils, and those which were lunatick, and those that had the palsy; and he healed them. And there followed him great multitudes of people from Galilee, and from Decapolis, and from Jerusalem, and from Judæa, and from beyond Jordan.

THE SERMON ON THE MOUNT
(Matthew, 5-7)

And seeing the multitudes, he went up into a mountain, and when he was set, his disciples came unto him; and he opened his mouth, and taught them, saying: Blessed are the poor in spirit: for theirs is the kingdom of heaven. Blessed are they that mourn: for they shall be comforted. Blessed are the meek: for they shall inherit the earth. Blessed are they which do hunger and thirst after righteousness: for they shall be filled. Blessed are the merciful: for they shall obtain mercy. Blessed are the pure in heart: for they shall see God. Blessed are the peacemakers: for they shall be called the children of God. Blessed are they which are persecuted for righteousness' sake: for theirs is the kingdom of heaven. Blessed are ye, when men shall revile you, and persecute you, and shall say all manner of evil against you falsely, for my sake. Rejoice, and be exceeding glad, for great is your reward in heaven, for so persecuted they the prophets which were before you.

Ye are the salt of the earth; but if the salt have lost his savour, wherewith shall it be salted? It is thenceforth good for nothing, but to be cast out, and to be trodden under foot of men. Ye are the light of the world. A city that is set on an hill cannot be hid. Neither do men light a candle, and put it under a bushel, but on a candlestick; and it giveth light unto all that are in the house. Let your light so shine before men, that they may see your good works, and glorify your Father which is in heaven.

Think not that I am come to destroy the law, or the prophets: I am not come to destroy, but to fulfil. For verily I say unto you, Till heaven and earth pass, one jot or one tittle shall in no wise pass from the law, till all be fulfilled. Whosoever therefore shall break one of these least commandments, and shall teach men so, he shall be called the least in the kindom of heaven; but whosoever shall do and teach them, the same shall be called great in the kingdom of heaven. For I say unto you, That except your righteousness shall exceed the righteousness of the scribes and Pharisees,[1] ye shall in no case enter into the kingdom of heaven.

Ye have heard that it was said by them of old time, Thou shalt not kill; and whosoever shall kill shall be in danger of the judgment; but I say unto you, That whosoever is angry with his brother without a cause shall be in danger of the judgment: and whosoever shall say to his brother, Raca,[2] shall be in danger of the council; but whosoever shall say, Thou fool, shall be in danger of hell fire. Therefore if thou bring thy gift to the altar, and there rememberest that thy brother hath ought against thee, leave there thy gift before the altar, and go thy way; first be reconciled to thy brother, and then come and offer thy gift. Agree with thine adversary quickly, whiles thou art in the way with him; lest at any time the adversary deliver thee to the judge,

1. The scribes were experts in minute points of the law, and the Pharisees were a sect placing great emphasis on the minute observance of tradition and ritual. Christ frequently condemns the scribes and Pharisees together because their basic idea is to observe the letter of the law because of fear rather than to observe its spirit with love.
2. *Raca*, "empty(head)." The exact strength of this insult is debatable, but it is obviously weaker than, "Thou fool!"

and the judge deliver thee to the officer, and thou be cast into prison. Verily I say unto thee, Thou shalt by no means come out thence, till thou hast paid the uttermost farthing.

Ye have heard that it was said by them of old time, Thou shalt not commit adultery; but I say unto you, That whosoever looketh on a woman to lust after her hath committed adultery with her already in his heart. And if thy right eye offend thee, pluck it out, and cast it from thee; for it is profitable for thee that one of thy members should perish, and not that thy whole body should be cast into hell. And if thy right hand offend thee, cut it off, and cast it from thee; for it is profitable for thee that one of thy members should perish, and not that thy whole body should be cast into hell. It hath been said, Whosoever shall put away his wife, let him give her a writing of divorcement; but I say unto you, That whosoever shall put away his wife, saving for the cause of fornication, causeth her to commit adultery; and whosoever shall marry her that is divorced committeth adultery.

Again, ye have heard that it hath been said by them of old time, Thou shalt not forswear thyself, but shalt perform unto the Lord thine oaths; but I say unto you, Swear not at all; neither by heaven, for it is God's throne; nor by the earth, for it is his footstool; neither by Jerusalem, for it is the city of the great King. Neither shalt thou swear by thy head, because thou canst not make one hair white or black. But let your communication be, Yea, yea; Nay, nay: for whatsoever is more than these cometh of evil.

Ye have heard that it hath been said, An eye for an eye, and a tooth for a tooth[3]; but I say unto you, That ye resist not evil; but whosoever shall smite thee on thy right cheek, turn to him the other also. And if any man will sue thee at the law, and take away thy coat, let him have thy cloke also. And whosoever shall compel thee to go a mile, go with him twain. Give to him that asketh thee, and from him that would borrow of thee turn not thou away.

Ye have heard that it hath been said, Thou shalt love thy neighbour, and hate thine enemy. But I say unto you, Love your enemies, bless them that curse you, do good to them that hate you, and pray for them which despitefully use you, and persecute you, that ye may be the children of your Father which is in heaven, for he maketh his

3. This is from the laws given by God to Moses on Mt. Sinai (*Exodus*, 21, 23-25): "And if any mischief follow, then thou shalt give life for life, eye for eye, tooth for tooth, hand for hand, foot for foot, burning for burning, wound for wound, stripe for stripe."

sun to rise on the evil and on the good, and sendeth rain on the just and on the unjust. For if ye love them which love you, what reward have ye? Do not even the publicans the same? And if ye salute your brethren only, what do ye more than others? Do not even the publicans so? Be ye therefore perfect, even as your Father which is in heaven is perfect.

Take heed that ye do not your alms before men, to be seen of them: otherwise ye have no reward of your Father which is in heaven. Therefore when thou doest thine alms, do not sound a trumpet before thee, as the hypocrites do in the synagogues and in the streets, that they may have glory of men. Verily I say unto you, They have their reward. But when thou doest alms, let not thy left hand know what thy right hand doeth, that thine alms may be in secret; and thy Father, which seeth in secret, himself shall reward thee openly.

And when thou prayest, thou shalt not be as the hypocrites are, for they love to pray standing in the synagogues and in the corners of the streets, that they may be seen of men. Verily I say unto you, They have their reward. But thou, when thou prayest, enter into thy closet, and when thou hast shut thy door, pray to thy Father which is in secret; and thy Father which seeth in secret shall reward thee openly. But when ye pray, use not vain repetitions, as the heathen do; for they think that they shall be heard for their much speaking. Be not ye therefore like unto them, for your Father knoweth what things ye have need of, before ye ask him. After this manner therefore pray ye: Our Father which art in heaven, Hallowed be thy name. Thy kingdom come. Thy will be done in earth, as it is in heaven. Give us this day our daily bread. And forgive us our debts, as we forgive our debtors. And lead us not into temptation, but deliver us from evil, for thine is the kingdom, and the power, and the glory, for ever. Amen. For if ye forgive men their trespasses, your heavenly Father will also forgive you; but if ye forgive not men their trespasses, neither will your Father forgive your trespasses.

Moreover when ye fast, be not, as the hypocrites, of a sad countenance, for they disfigure their faces, that they may appear unto men to fast. Verily I say unto you, They have their reward. But thou, when thou fastest, anoint thine head, and wash thy face, that thou appear not unto men to fast, but unto thy Father which is in secret; and thy Father, which seeth in secret, shall reward thee openly.

Lay not up for yourselves treasures upon earth, where moth and rust doth corrupt, and where thieves break through and steal; but lay up for yourselves treasures in heaven, where neither moth nor rust doth corrupt, and where thieves do not break through nor steal, for where your treasure is, there will your heart be also. The light of the body is the eye; if therefore thine eye be single, thy whole body shall be full of light. But if thine eye be evil, thy whole body shall be full of darkness. If therefore the light that is in thee be darkness, how great is that darkness!

No man can serve two masters: for either he will hate the one, and love the other; or else he will hold to the one, and despise the other. Ye cannot serve God and mammon. Therefore I say unto you, Take no thought for your life, what ye shall eat, or what ye shall drink; nor yet for your body, what ye shall put on. Is not the life more than meat, and the body than raiment? Behold the fowls of the air; for they sow not, neither do they reap, nor gather into barns; yet your heavenly Father feedeth them. Are ye not much better than they? Which of you by taking thought can add one cubit unto his stature? And why take ye thought for raiment? Consider the lilies of the field, how they grow; they toil not, neither do they spin; and yet I say unto you, That even Solomon in all his glory was not arrayed like one of these. Wherefore, if God so clothe the grass of the field, which to day is, and to morrow is cast into the oven, shall he not much more clothe you, O ye of little faith? Therefore take no thought, saying, What shall we eat? or, What shall we drink? or, Wherewithal shall we be clothed? (For after all these things do the Gentiles seek) for your heavenly Father knoweth that ye have need of all these things. But seek ye first the kingdom of God, and his righteousness; and all these things shall be added unto you. Take therefore no thought for the morrow; for the morrow shall take thought for the things of itself. Sufficient unto the day is the evil thereof.

Judge not, that ye be not judged. For with what judgment ye judge, ye shall be judged; and with what measure ye mete, it shall be measured to you again. And why beholdest thou the mote that is in thy brother's eye, but considerest not the beam that is in thine own eye? Or how wilt thou say to thy brother, Let me pull out the mote out of thine eye; and, behold, a beam is in thine own eye? Thou hypocrite, first cast out the beam out of thine own eye; and then shalt thou see clearly to cast out the mote out of thy brother's eye.

Give not that which is holy unto the dogs, neither cast ye your pearls before swine, lest they trample them under their feet, and turn again and rend you.

Ask, and it shall be given you; seek, and ye shall find; knock, and it shall be opened unto you: for every one that asketh receiveth; and he that seeketh findeth; and to him that knocketh it shall be opened. Or what man is there of you, whom if his son ask bread, will he give him a stone? Or if he ask a fish, will he give him a serpent? If ye then, being evil, know how to give good gifts unto your children, how much more shall your Father which is in heaven give good things to them that ask him? Therefore all things whatsoever ye would that men should do to you, do ye even so to them, for this is the law and the prophets.

Enter ye in at the strait gate; for wide is the gate, and broad is the way, that leadeth to destruction, and many there be which go in thereat; because strait is the gate, and narrow is the way, which leadeth unto life, and few there be that find it.

Beware of false prophets, which come to you in sheep's clothing, but inwardly they are ravening wolves. Ye shall know them by their fruits. Do men gather grapes of thorns, or figs of thistles? Even so every good tree bringeth forth good fruit; but a corrupt tree bringeth forth evil fruit. A good tree cannot bring forth evil fruit, neither can a corrupt tree bring forth good fruit. Every tree that bringeth not forth good fruit is hewn down, and cast into the fire. Wherefore by their fruits ye shall know them.

Not every one that saith unto me, Lord, Lord, shall enter into the kingdom of heaven; but he that doeth the will of my Father which is in heaven. Many will say to me in that day, Lord, Lord, have we not prophesied in thy name? and in thy name have cast out devils? and in thy name done many wonderful works? And then will I profess unto them, I never knew you; depart from me, ye that work iniquity.

Therefore whosoever heareth these sayings of mine, and doeth them, I will liken him unto a wise man, which built his house upon a rock; and the rain descended, and the floods came, and the winds blew, and beat upon that house; and it fell not: for it was founded upon a rock. And every one that heareth these sayings of mine, and doeth them not, shall be likened unto a foolish man, which built his house upon the sand; and the rain descended, and the floods came, and the winds blew, and beat upon that house; and it fell: and great was the fall of it.

And it came to pass, when Jesus had ended these sayings, the people were astonished at his doctrine: for he taught them as one having authority, and not as the scribes.

THE PARABLE OF THE SOWER
(*Matthew, 13*)

The same day went Jesus out of the house, and sat by the sea side. And great multitudes were gathered together unto him, so that he went into a ship, and sat; and the whole multitude stood on the shore. And he spake many things unto them in parables, saying, Behold, a sower went forth to sow; and when he sowed, some seeds fell by the way side, and the fowls came and devoured them up; some fell upon stony places, where they had not much earth; and forthwith they sprung up, because they had no deepness of earth; and when the sun was up, they were scorched; and because they had no root, they withered away. And some fell among thorns; and the thorns sprung up, and choked them. But other fell into good ground, and brought forth fruit, some an hundredfold, some sixtyfold, some thirtyfold. Who hath ears to hear, let him hear. And the disciples came, and said unto him, Why speakest thou unto them in parables? He answered and said unto them, Because it is given unto you to know the mysteries of the kingdom of heaven, but to them it is not given. For whosoever hath, to him shall be given, and he shall have more abundance; but whosoever hath not, from him shall be taken away even that he hath. Therefore speak I to them in parables: because they seeing see not; and hearing they hear not, neither do they understand. . . . For this people's heart is waxed gross, and their ears are dull of hearing, and their eyes they have closed; lest at any time they should see with their eyes, and hear with their ears, and should understand with their heart, and should be converted, and I should heal them. But blessed are your eyes, for they see; and your ears, for they hear. For verily I say unto you, That many prophets and righteous men have desired to see those things which ye see, and have not seen them; and to hear those things which ye hear, and have not heard them.

Hear ye therefore the parable of the sower. When any one heareth the word of the kingdom, and understandeth it not, then cometh the wicked one, and catcheth away that which was sown in his heart. This is he which received seed by the way side. But he that received the seed into stony places, the same is he that heareth the word, and anon with joy receiveth it; yet hath he not root in himself, but dureth for a while, for when tribulation or persecution ariseth because of the word, by and by he is offended. He also that received seed among the thorns is he that heareth the word; and the care of this world, and the deceitfulness of riches, choke the word, and he becometh unfruitful. But he that received seed into the good ground is he that heareth the word, and understandeth it; which also beareth fruit, and bringeth forth, some an hundredfold, some sixty, some thirty.

LITTLE CHILDREN, AND THE RICH
(*Matthew, 19*)

Then were there brought unto him little children, that he should put his hands on them, and pray; and the disciples rebuked them. But Jesus said, Suffer little children, and forbid them not, to come unto me, for of such is the kingdom of heaven. And he laid his hands on them, and departed thence.

And, behold, one came and said unto him, Good Master, what good thing shall I do, that I may have eternal life? And he said unto him, Why callest thou me good? there is none good but one, that is, God; but if thou wilt enter into life, keep the commandments. He saith unto him, Which? Jesus said, Thou shalt do no murder, Thou shalt not commit adultery, Thou shalt not steal, Thou shalt not bear false witness, Honour thy father and thy mother; and, Thou shalt love thy neighbour as thyself. The young man saith unto him, All these things have I kept from my youth up; what lack I yet? Jesus said unto him, If thou wilt be perfect, go and sell that thou hast, and give to the poor, and thou shalt have treasure in heaven; and come and follow me. But when the young man heard that saying, he went away sorrowful: for he had great possessions.

Then said Jesus unto his disciples, Verily I say unto you, That a rich man shall hardly enter into the kingdom of heaven. And again I say unto you, It is easier for a camel to go through the eye of a needle, than for a rich man to enter into the kingdom of God. When his disciples heard it, they were exceedingly amazed, saying, Who then can be saved? But Jesus beheld them, and said unto them, With men this is impossible; but with God all things are possible.

THE SCRIBES AND PHARISEES
(*Matthew, 23*)

Then spake Jesus to the multitude, and to his disciples, saying, The scribes and the Pharisees sit in Moses' seat: all therefore whatsoever they bid you observe, that observe and do; but do not ye after their works, for they say, and do not. For they bind heavy burdens and grievous to be borne, and lay them on men's shoulders; but they themselves will not move them with one of their fingers. But all their works they do for to be seen of men; they make broad their phylacteries,[1] and enlarge the borders of their garments, and love the uppermost rooms at feasts, and the chief seats in the synagogues, and greetings in the markets, and to be called of men, Rabbi, Rabbi. But be not ye called Rabbi: for one is your Master, even Christ; and all ye are brethren. And call no man your father upon the earth, for one is your Father, which is in heaven. Neither be ye called masters, for one is your Master, even Christ. But he that is greatest among you shall be your servant. And whosoever shall exalt himself shall be abased; and he that shall humble himself shall be exalted.

But woe unto you, scribes and Pharisees, hypocrites! for ye shut up the kingdom of heaven against men; for ye neither go in yourselves, neither suffer ye them that are entering to go in. Woe unto you, scribes and Pharisees, hypocrites! for ye devour widows' houses, and for a pretence make long prayer; therefore ye shall receive the greater damnation. Woe unto you, scribes and Pharisees, hypocrites! for ye compass sea and land to make one proselyte, and when he is made, ye make him twofold more the child of hell than yourselves. Woe unto you, ye blind guides, which say, Whosoever shall swear by the temple, it is nothing; but whosoever shall swear by the gold of the temple, he is a debtor! Ye fools and blind; for whether is greater, the gold, or the temple that sanctifieth the gold? And, Whosoever shall swear by the altar, it is nothing; but whosoever sweareth by the gift that is upon it, he is guilty. Ye fools and blind: for whether is greater, the gift, or the altar that sanctifieth the gift? Whoso therefore shall swear by the altar, sweareth by it, and by all things thereon. And whoso shall swear by the temple, sweareth by it, and by him that dwelleth therein. And he that shall swear by heaven, sweareth by the throne of God, and by him that sitteth thereon. Woe unto you, scribes and Pharisees, hypocrites! for ye pay tithe of mint and anise and cummin, and have omitted the weightier matters of the law, judgment, mercy, and faith; these ought ye to have done, and not to leave the other undone. Ye blind guides, which strain at a gnat, and swallow a camel. Woe unto you, scribes and Pharisees, hypocrites! for ye make

---

1. *phylacteries*, bands worn by all orthodox Jews of Christ's time, to which were attached leather pouches containing four texts of the Law. Making these bands broad, then, amounts to ostentatious piety.

clean the outside of the cup and of the platter, but within they are full of extortion and excess. Thou blind Pharisee, cleanse first that which is within the cup and platter, that the outside of them may be clean also. Woe unto you, scribes and Pharisees, hypocrites! for ye are like unto whited sepulchres, which indeed appear beautiful outward, but are within full of dead men's bones, and of all uncleanness. Even so ye also outwardly appear righteous unto men, but within ye are full of hypocrisy and iniquity. Woe unto you, scribes and Pharisees, hypocrites! because ye build the tombs of the prophets, and garnish the sepulchres of the righteous, and say, If we had been in the days of our fathers, we would not have been partakers with them in the blood of the prophets. Wherefore ye be witnesses unto yourselves, that ye are the children of them which killed the prophets. Fill ye up then the measure of your fathers. Ye serpents, ye generation of vipers, how can ye escape the damnation of hell?

Wherefore, behold, I send unto you prophets, and wise men, and scribes; and some of them ye shall kill and crucify; and some of them shall ye scourge in your synagogues, and persecute them from city to city, that upon you may come all the righteous blood shed upon the earth, from the blood of righteous Abel unto the blood of Zacharias son of Barachias, whom ye slew between the temple and the altar. Verily I say unto you, All these things shall come upon this generation. O Jerusalem, Jerusalem, thou that killest the prophets, and stonest them which are sent unto thee, how often would I have gathered thy children together, even as a hen gathereth her chickens under her wings, and ye would not! Behold, your house is left unto you desolate. For I say unto you, Ye shall not see me henceforth, till ye shall say, Blessed is he that cometh in the name of the Lord.

EPISODES FROM THE MINISTRY OF JESUS
(*Luke, 15; John, 2; Mark, 12; Luke, 7*)

Then drew near unto him all the publicans and sinners for to hear him. And the Pharisees and scribes murmured, saying, This man receiveth sinners, and eateth with them.

And he spake this parable unto them, saying, What man of you, having an hundred sheep, if he lose one of them, doth not leave the ninety and nine in the wilderness, and go after that which is lost, until he find it? And when he hath found it, he layeth it on his shoulders, rejoicing. And when he cometh home, he calleth together his friends and neighbours, saying unto them, Rejoice with me, for I have found my sheep which was lost. I say unto you, that likewise joy shall be in heaven over one sinner that repenteth, more than over ninety and nine just persons, which need no repentance. . . .

And he said, A certain man had two sons; and the younger of them said to his father, Father, give me the portion of goods that falleth to me. And he divided unto them his living. And not many days after the younger son gathered all together, and took his journey into a far country, and there wasted his substance with riotous living. And when he had spent all, there arose a mighty famine in that land; and he began to be in want. And he went and joined himself to a citizen of that country; and he sent him into his fields to feed swine. And he would fain have filled his belly with the husks that the swine did eat; and no man gave unto him. And when he came to himself, he said, How many hired servants of my father's have bread enough and to spare, and I perish with hunger! I will arise and go to my father, and will say unto him, Father, I have sinned against heaven, and before thee, and am no more worthy to be called thy son; make me as one of thy hired servants. And he arose, and came to his father. But when he was yet a great way off, his father saw him, and had compassion, and ran, and fell on his neck, and kissed him. And the son said unto him, Father, I have sinned against heaven, and in thy sight, and am no more worthy to be called thy son. But the father said to his servants, Bring forth the best robe, and put it on him; and put a ring on his hand, and shoes on his feet; and bring hither the fatted calf, and kill it; and let us eat, and be merry: for this my son was dead, and is alive again; he was lost, and is found. And they began to be merry. Now his elder son was in the field; and as he came and drew nigh to the house, he heard musick and dancing. And he called one of the servants, and asked what these things meant. And he said unto him, Thy brother is come; and thy father hath killed the fatted calf, because he hath received him safe and sound. And he was angry, and would not go in; therefore came his father out, and intreated him. And he answering said to his father, Lo, these many years do I serve thee, neither transgressed I at any time thy commandment; and yet thou never gavest me a kid, that I might make merry with my friends. But as soon as this thy son was come, which hath devoured thy living with harlots, thou hast killed for him the fatted calf. And he said unto him, Son, thou art ever with me, and all that I have is thine. It was meet that we should make merry, and be glad:

for this thy brother was dead, and is alive again; and was lost, and is found. . . .

And the Jews' passover was at hand, and Jesus went up to Jerusalem, and found in the temple those that sold oxen and sheep and doves, and the changers of money sitting. And when he had made a scourge of small cords, he drove them all out of the temple, and the sheep, and the oxen; and poured out the changers' money, and overthrew the tables; and said unto them that sold doves, Take these things hence; make not my Father's house an house of merchandise. And his disciples remembered that it was written, The zeal of thine house hath eaten me up. . . .

And they send unto him certain of the Pharisees and of the Herodians,[1] to catch him in his words. And when they were come, they say unto him, Master, we know that thou art true, and carest for no man; for thou regardest not the person of men, but teachest the way of God in truth: Is it lawful to give tribute to Cæsar, or not? Shall we give, or shall we not give? But he, knowing their hypocrisy, said unto them, Why tempt ye me? Bring me a penny, that I may see it. And they brought it. And he saith unto them, Whose is this image and superscription? And they said unto him, Cæsar's. And Jesus answering said unto them, Render to Cæsar the things that are Cæsar's, and to God the things that are God's. . . .

And one of the Pharisees desired him that he would eat with him. And he went into the Pharisee's house, and sat down to meat. And, behold, a woman[2] in the city, which was a sinner, when she knew that Jesus sat at meat in the Pharisee's house, brought an alabaster box of ointment, and stood at his feet behind him weeping, and began to wash his feet with tears, and did wipe them with the hairs of her head, and kissed his feet, and anointed them with the ointment. Now when the Pharisee which had bidden him saw it, he spake within himself, saying, This man, if he were a prophet, would have known who and what manner of woman this is that toucheth him, for she is a sinner. And Jesus answering said unto him, Simon, I have somewhat to say unto thee. And he said, Master say on. There was a certain creditor

---

1. *Herodians*, partisans of the Herod dynasty. They did not object to Roman domination, and made common cause with the Pharisees against Christ.

2. This repentant sinner is the Mary Magdalene of literature, art, and popular legend, though biblical scholars question the identification.

which had two debtors; the one owed five hundred pence, and the other fifty. And when they had nothing to pay, he frankly forgave them both. Tell me therefore, which of them will love him most? Simon answered and said, I suppose that he, to whom he forgave most. And he said unto him, Thou hast rightly judged. And he turned to the woman, and said unto Simon, Seest thou this woman? I entered into thine house, thou gavest me no water for my feet; but she hath washed my feet with tears, and wiped them with the hairs of her head. Thou gavest me no kiss; but this woman since the time I came in hath not ceased to kiss my feet. My head with oil thou didst not anoint; but this woman hath anointed my feet with ointment. Wherefore I say unto thee, Her sins, which are many, are forgiven, for she loved much; but to whom little is forgiven, the same loveth little. And he said unto her, Thy sins are forgiven. And they that sat at meat with him began to say within themselves, Who is this that forgiveth sins also? And he said to the woman, Thy faith hath saved thee; go in peace.

PARABLES OF THE VIRGINS AND THE TALENTS
(*Matthew, 25*)

Then shall the kingdom of heaven be likened unto ten virgins, which took their lamps, and went forth to meet the bridegroom. And five of them were wise, and five were foolish. They that were foolish took their lamps, and took no oil with them; but the wise took oil in their vessels with their lamps. While the bridegroom tarried, they all slumbered and slept. And at midnight there was a cry made, Behold, the bridegroom cometh; go ye out to meet him. Then all those virgins arose, and trimmed their lamps. And the foolish said unto the wise, Give us of your oil, for our lamps are gone out. But the wise answered, saying, Not so, lest there be not enough for us and you; but go ye rather to them that sell, and buy for yourselves. And while they went to buy, the bridegroom came, and they that were ready went in with him to the marriage; and the door was shut. Afterward came also the other virgins, saying, Lord, Lord, open to us. But he answered and said, Verily I say unto you, I know you not. Watch therefore, for ye know neither the day nor the hour wherein the Son of man cometh.

For the kingdom of heaven is as a man travelling into a far country, who called his own servants, and delivered unto them his goods. And unto one he gave five talents, to another two, and to another one, to every man according to his several ability, and straightway took his journey. Then he that had received the five talents went and traded with the same, and made them other five talents. And likewise he that had received two, he also gained other two. But he that had received one went and digged in the earth, and hid his lord's money. After a long time the lord of those servants cometh, and reckoneth with them. And so he that had received five talents came and brought other five talents, saying, Lord, thou deliveredst unto me five talents; behold, I have gained beside them five talents more. His lord said unto him, Well done, thou good and faithful servant; thou hast been faithful over a few things, I will make thee ruler over many things; enter thou into the joy of thy lord. He also that had received two talents came and said, Lord, thou deliveredst unto me two talents; behold, I have gained two other talents beside them. His lord said unto him, Well done, good and faithful servant; thou hast been faithful over a few things, I will make thee ruler over many things; enter thou into the joy of thy lord. Then he which had received the one talent came and said, Lord, I knew thee that thou art an hard man, reaping where thou hast not sown, and gathering where thou hast not strawed; and I was afraid, and went and hid thy talent in the earth; lo, there thou hast that is thine. His lord answered and said unto him, Thou wicked and slothful servant, thou knewest that I reap where I sowed not, and gather where I have not strawed. Thou oughtest therefore to have put my money to the exchangers, and then at my coming I should have received mine own with usury. Take therefore the talent from him, and give it unto him which hath ten talents. For unto every one that hath shall be given, and he shall have abundance; but from him that hath not shall be taken away even that which he hath. And cast ye the unprofitable servant into outer darkness; there shall be weeping and gnashing of teeth.

When the Son of man shall come in his glory, and all the holy angels with him, then shall he sit upon the throne of his glory; and before him shall be gathered all nations; and he shall separate them one from another, as a shepherd divideth his sheep from the goats; and he shall set the sheep on his right hand, but the goats on the left. Then shall the King say unto them on his right hand, Come, ye blessed of my Father, inherit the kingdom prepared for you from the foundation of the world: for I was an hungred, and ye gave me meat; I was thirsty, and ye gave me drink; I was a stranger, and ye took me in; naked, and ye clothed me; I was sick, and ye visited me; I was in prison, and ye came unto me. Then shall the righteous answer him, saying, Lord, when saw we thee an hungred, and fed thee? or thirsty, and gave thee drink? When saw we thee a stranger, and took thee in? or naked, and clothed thee? Or when saw we thee sick, or in prison, and came unto thee? And the King shall answer and say unto them, Verily I say unto you, Inasmuch as ye have done it unto one of the least of these my brethren, ye have done it unto me. . . .

THE LAST SUPPER AND THE BETRAYAL
(Matthew, 26)

And it came to pass, when Jesus had finished all these sayings, he said unto his disciples, Ye know that after two days is the feast of the passover, and the Son of man is betrayed to be crucified.

Then assembled together the chief priests, and the scribes, and the elders of the people, unto the palace of the high priest, who was called Caiaphas, and consulted that they might take Jesus by subtilty, and kill him. But they said, Not on the feast day, lest there be an uproar among the people. . . .

Then one of the twelve, called Judas Iscariot, went unto the chief priests and said unto them, What will ye give me, and I will deliver him unto you? And they covenanted with him for thirty pieces of silver. And from that time he sought opportunity to betray him.

Now the first day of the feast of unleavened bread the disciples came to Jesus, saying unto him, Where wilt thou that we prepare for thee to eat the passover? And he said, Go into the city to such a man, and say unto him, The Master saith, My time is at hand; I will keep the passover at thy house with my disciples. And the disciples did as Jesus had appointed them; and they made ready the passover. Now when the even was come, he sat down with the twelve. And as they did eat, he said, Verily I say unto you, that one of you shall betray me. And they were exceeding sorrowful, and began every one of them to say unto him, Lord, is it I? And he answered and said, He that dippeth his hand with me in the dish, the same shall betray me. The Son of man goeth as it is written of him; but woe unto that man by whom the Son of man is betrayed! It had been good for that man if he had not been born. Then Judas, which betrayed him, answered and said, Master, is it I? He said unto him, Thou hast said.

And as they were eating, Jesus took bread, and blessed it, and brake it, and gave it to the disciples, and said, Take, eat; this is my

body. And he took the cup, and gave thanks, and gave it to them, saying, Drink ye all of it, for this is my blood of the new testament, which
is shed for many for the remission of sins. But I say unto you, I will not
drink henceforth of this fruit of the vine, until that day when I drink
it new with you in my Father's kingdom. And when they had sung an
hymn, they went out into the mount of Olives. Then saith Jesus unto
them, All ye shall be offended because of me this night, for it is
written, I will smite the shepherd, and the sheep of the flock shall be
scattered abroad. But after I am risen again, I will go before you into
Galilee. Peter answered and said unto him, Though all men shall be
offended because of thee, yet will I never be offended. Jesus said unto
him, Verily I say unto thee, That this night, before the cock crow, thou
shalt deny me thrice. Peter said unto him, Though I should die with
thee, yet will I not deny thee. Likewise also said all the disciples.

Then cometh Jesus with them unto a place called Gethsemane, and
saith unto the disciples, Sit ye here, while I go and pray yonder. And he
took with him Peter and the two sons of Zebedee, and began to be sorrowful and very heavy. Then saith he unto them, My soul is exceeding
sorrowful, even unto death; tarry ye here, and watch with me. And he
went a little farther, and fell on his face, and prayed, saying, O my
Father, if it be possible, let this cup pass from me; nevertheless not as
I will, but as thou wilt. And he cometh unto the disciples, and findeth
them asleep, and saith unto Peter, What, could ye not watch with me
one hour? Watch and pray, that ye enter not into temptation; the
spirit indeed is willing, but the flesh is weak. He went away again the
second time, and prayed, saying, O my Father, if this cup may not pass
away from me, except I drink it, thy will be done. And he came and
found them asleep again, for their eyes were heavy. And he left them,
and went away again, and prayed the third time, saying the same
words. Then cometh he to his disciples, and saith unto them, Sleep on
now, and take your rest; behold, the hour is at hand, and the Son of
man is betrayed into the hands of sinners. Rise, let us be going; behold,
he is at hand that doth betray me.

And while he yet spake, lo, Judas, one of the twelve, came, and
with him a great multitude with swords and staves, from the chief
priests and elders of the people. Now he that betrayed him gave them a
sign, saying, Whomsoever I shall kiss, that same is he; hold him fast.
And forthwith he came to Jesus, and said, Hail, master; and kissed
him. And Jesus said unto him, Friend, wherefore art thou come? Then
came they, and laid hands on Jesus, and took him. And, behold, one of

them[1] which were with Jesus stretched out his hand, and drew his sword, and struck a servant of the high priest's, and smote off his ear. Then said Jesus unto him, Put up again thy sword into his place, for all they that take the sword shall perish with the sword. Thinkest thou that I cannot now pray to my Father, and he shall presently give me more than twelve legions of angels? But how then shall the scriptures be fulfilled, that thus it must be? In that same hour said Jesus to the multitudes, Are ye come out as against a thief with swords and staves for to take me? I sat daily with you teaching in the temple, and ye laid no hold on me. But all this was done, that the scriptures of the prophets might be fulfilled. Then all the disciples forsook him, and fled.

And they that had laid hold on Jesus led him away to Caiaphas, the high priest, where the scribes and the elders were assembled. But Peter followed him afar off unto the high priest's palace, and went in, and sat with the servants, to see the end. Now the chief priests, and elders, and all the council, sought false witness against Jesus, to put him to death, but found none; yea, though many false witnesses came, yet found they none. At the last came two false witnesses, and said, This fellow said, I am able to destroy the temple of God, and to build it in three days. And the high priest arose, and said unto him, Answerest thou nothing? What is it which these witness against thee? But Jesus held his peace. And the high priest answered and said unto him, I adjure thee by the living God, that thou tell us whether thou be the Christ, the Son of God. Jesus saith unto him, Thou hast said; nevertheless I say unto you, Hereafter shall ye see the Son of man sitting on the right hand of power, and coming in the clouds of heaven. Then the high priest rent his clothes, saying, He hath spoken blasphemy; what further need have we of witnesses? Behold, now ye have heard his blasphemy. What think ye? They answered and said, He is guilty of death. Then did they spit in his face, and buffeted him; and others smote him with the palms of their hands, saying, Prophesy unto us, thou Christ, Who is he that smote thee?

Now Peter sat without in the palace: and a damsel came unto him, saying, Thou also wast with Jesus of Galilee. But he denied before them all, saying, I know not what thou sayest. And when he was gone out into the porch, another maid saw him, and said unto them that were there, This fellow was also with Jesus of Nazareth. And again he denied with an oath, I do not know the man. And after a while came unto him they that stood by, and said to Peter, Surely thou also art

1. Peter.

one of them, for thy speech bewrayeth thee. Then began he to curse and to swear, saying, I know not the man. And immediately the cock crew. And Peter remembered the word of Jesus, which said unto him, Before the cock crow, thou shalt deny me thrice. And he went out, and wept bitterly.

THE TRIAL AND CRUCIFIXION
(Matthew, 27)

When the morning was come, all the chief priests and elders of the people took counsel against Jesus to put him to death; and when they had bound him, they led him away, and delivered him to Pontius Pilate the governor.

Then Judas, which had betrayed him, when he saw that he was condemned, repented himself, and brought again the thirty pieces of silver to the chief priests and elders, saying, I have sinned in that I have betrayed the innocent blood. And they said, What is that to us? See thou to that. And he cast down the pieces of silver in the temple, and departed, and went and hanged himself. . . .

And Jesus stood before the governor; and the governor asked him, saying, Art thou the King of the Jews? And Jesus said unto him, Thou sayest.[1] And when he was accused of the chief priests and elders, he answered nothing. Then said Pilate unto him, Hearest thou not how many things they witness against thee? And he answered him to never a word; insomuch that the governor marveled greatly. Now at that feast the governor was wont to release unto the people a prisoner, whom they would. And they had then a notable prisoner, called Barabbas.[2] Therefore when they were gathered together, Pilate said unto them, Whom will ye that I release unto you? Barabbas, or Jesus which is called Christ?[3] For he knew that for envy they had delivered him.

When he was set down on the judgment seat, his wife sent unto

1. At this point in the account of the trial in *John* (18, 37-38) the following passage occurs: "Pilate therefore said unto him, Art thou a king then? Jesus answered, Thou sayest that I am a king. To this end was I born, and for this cause came I into the world, that I should bear witness unto the truth. Every one that is of the truth heareth my voice. Pilate said unto him, What is truth? And when he had said this, he went out again unto the Jews and saith unto them, I find in him no fault at all."

2. Barabbas was in prison for robbery, sedition, and murder.

3. *Christ* is a Greek term meaning "the (Lord's) Annointed," and is regularly used as the name of the Messiah who had been promised to the Hebrews.

him, saying, Have thou nothing to do with that just man, for I have suffered many things this day in a dream because of him. But the chief priests and elders persuaded the multitude that they should ask Barabbas, and destroy Jesus. The governor answered and said unto them, Whether of the twain will ye that I release unto you? They said, Barabbas. Pilate saith unto them, What shall I do then with Jesus which is called Christ? They all say unto him, Let him be crucified. And the governor said, Why, what evil hath he done? But they cried out the more, saying, Let him be crucified.

When Pilate saw that he could prevail nothing, but that rather a tumult was made, he took water, and washed his hands before the multitude, saying, I am innocent of the blood of this just person; see ye to it. Then answered all the people, and said, His blood be on us, and on our children.

Then released he Barabbas unto them; and when he had scourged Jesus, he delivered him to be crucified. Then the soldiers of the governor took Jesus into the common hall, and gathered unto him the whole band of soldiers. And they stripped him, and put on him a scarlet robe.

And when they had platted a crown of thorns, they put it upon his head, and a reed in his right hand: and they bowed the knee before him, and mocked him, saying, Hail, King of the Jews! And they spit upon him, and took the reed, and smote him on the head. And after that they had mocked him, they took the robe off from him, and put his own raiment on him, and led him away to crucify him. And as they came out, they found a man of Cyrene, Simon by name; him they compelled to bear his cross.

And when they were come unto a place called Golgotha, that is to say, a place of a skull, they gave him vinegar to drink mingled with gall;[4] and when he had tasted thereof, he would not drink. And they crucified him, and parted his garments, casting lots. . . . And sitting down they watched him there, and set up over his head his accusation written, THIS IS JESUS THE KING OF THE JEWS. Then were there two thieves crucified with him, one on the right hand, and another on the left.

And they that passed by reviled him, wagging their heads, and saying, Thou that destroyest the temple, and buildest it in three days, save thyself. If thou be the Son of God, come down from the cross.

---

4. This drink was something of a narcotic; hence the offering of it was an act of mercy.

Likewise also the chief priests mocking him, with the scribes and elders, said, He saved others; himself he cannot save. If he be the King of Israel, let him now come down from the cross, and we will believe him. He trusted in God; let him deliver him now, if he will have him, for he said, I am the Son of God. The thieves also, which were crucified with him, cast the same in his teeth. Now from the sixth hour there was darkness over all the land unto the ninth hour. And about the ninth hour Jesus cried with a loud voice, saying, Eli, Eli, lama sabachthani? that is to say, My God, my God, why hast thou forsaken me? Some of them that stood there, when they heard that, said, This man calleth for Elias.[5] And straightway one of them ran, and took a spunge, and filled it with vinegar, and put it on a reed, and gave him to drink. The rest said, Let be, let us see whether Elias will come to save him.

Jesus, when he had cried again with a loud voice, yielded up the ghost. And, behold, the veil of the temple was rent in twain from the top to the bottom; and the earth did quake, and the rocks rent; and the graves were opened; and many bodies of the saints which slept arose, and came out of the graves after his resurrection, and went into the holy city, and appeared unto many. Now when the centurion, and they that were with him, watching Jesus, saw the earthquake, and those things that were done, they feared greatly, saying, Truly this was the Son of God. And many women were there beholding afar off, which followed Jesus from Galilee, ministering unto him, among which was Mary Magdalene, and Mary the mother of James and Joses, and the mother of Zebedee's children. When the even was come, there came a rich man of Arimathæa, named Joseph, who also himself was Jesus' disciple; he went to Pilate, and begged the body of Jesus. Then Pilate commanded the body to be delivered. And when Joseph had taken the body, he wrapped it in a clean linen cloth, and laid it in his own new tomb, which he had hewn out in the rock; and he rolled a great stone to the door of the sepulchre, and departed. And there was Mary Magdalene, and the other Mary, sitting over against the sepulchre.

Now the next day, that followed the day of the preparation, the chief priests and Pharisees came together unto Pilate, saying, Sir, we remember that that deceiver said, while he was yet alive, After three days I will rise again. Command therefore that the sepulchre be made sure until the third day, lest his disciples come by night, and steal him away, and say unto the people, He is risen from the dead; so the last

5. *Elias,* Elijah.

error shall be worse than the first. Pilate said unto them, Ye have a watch; go your way, make it as sure as ye can. So they went, and made the sepulchre sure, sealing the stone, and setting a watch.

THE RESURRECTION
(Matthew, 28)

In the end of the sabbath, as it began to dawn toward the first day of the week, came Mary Magdalene and the other Mary to see the sepulchre. And, behold, there was a great earthquake; for the angel of the Lord descended from heaven, and came and rolled back the stone from the door, and sat upon it. His countenance was like lightning, and his raiment white as snow; and for fear of him the keepers did shake, and became as dead men. And the angel answered and said unto the women, Fear not ye; for I know that ye seek Jesus, which was crucified. He is not here; for he is risen, as he said. Come, see the place where the Lord lay. And go quickly, and tell his disciples that he is risen from the dead; and, behold, he goeth before you into Galilee; there shall ye see him; lo, I have told you. And they departed quickly from the sepulchre with fear and great joy; and did run to bring his disciples word.

And as they went to tell his disciples, behold, Jesus met them, saying, All hail. And they came and held him by the feet, and worshipped him. Then said Jesus unto them, Be not afraid: go tell my brethren that they go into Galilee, and there shall they see me.

Now when they were going, behold, some of the watch came into the city, and shewed unto the chief priests all the things that were done. And when they were assembled with the elders, and had taken counsel, they gave large money unto the soldiers, saying, Say ye, His disciples came by night, and stole him away while we slept. And if this come to the governor's ears, we will persuade him, and secure you. So they took the money, and did as they were taught; and this saying is commonly reported among the Jews until this day.

Then the eleven disciples went away into Galilee, into a mountain where Jesus had appointed them. And when they saw him, they worshipped him; but some doubted. And Jesus came and spake unto them, saying, All power is given unto me in heaven and in earth.

Go ye therefore, and teach all nations, baptizing them in the name of the Father, and of the Son, and of the Holy Ghost, teaching them to observe all things whatsoever I have commanded you; and, lo, I am with you alway, even unto the end of the world. Amen.

THE

RENAISSANCE

THE RENAISSANCE

LIKE MOST GREAT historical movements, the Renaissance cannot be said to have begun at any specific moment, or to have been confined to any one department of human activity. *Renaissance* means literally "rebirth," and the name refers to the rebirth of classical, especially Greek, learning, after centuries of comparative neglect. But this revived interest is only part of a larger change in point of view. It is related to a questioning of tradition, the rise of a scientific spirit, emphasis on the complete development of the individual, and a concentration of attention on this present world rather than the next.

During the Middle Ages only a handful of men in Western Europe had known Greek, and little Greek literature had been available to them. Whatever they knew about Greek civilization came through the medium of summaries, quotations, or occasional translations, usually through Latin, but sometimes by much more devious routes. The only available version of Aristotle's *Poetics,* for example, had come through Asia Minor and North Africa into Spain, and was actually a Latin translation of an Arabic abridgement of an Arabic translation of a Syriac translation of the Greek text. Other works were more fortunate. There were adequate Latin translations of many of Aristotle's works and of some others, but many Greek writers were untranslated and many Latin writers forgotten. During the Middle Ages, Homer was little more than a reputation, and Greek tragedy, Lucretius, and Catullus were hardly that.

Throughout these centuries Constantinople, the capital of the Eastern Roman Empire, was the treasury of Greek manuscripts and scholarship. By the latter part of the fourteenth century some men, especially in Italy, began to grow curious about these matters, and Boccaccio and Petrarch devoted a considerable part of their lives to classical scholarship and the search for forgotten manuscripts. Also, a few teachers of Greek traveled to Italy from Constantinople. Thus the movement for a revival of learning was already considerably advanced by the middle of the fifteenth century. Then came an event of great importance. On May 29, 1453, the Turks stormed Constantinople and the Eastern Empire fell. Many scholars became refugees, and their only avenue of escape lay westward; hence they carried their learning and their manuscripts into Europe, and particularly to an Italy which was now ready to welcome and encourage them. So great was the influence of this event that people who insist on having their history tidy often consider 1453 as the beginning of the Renaissance.

Under medieval conditions the revival of classical learning would have been very slow, for manuscripts had to be copied by hand and were consequently both expensive and relatively scarce. A few years before the fall of Constantinople, however, someone in northern Europe had invented the process of printing from movable type. (The Chinese had invented it earlier, but their knowledge had not spread to Europe.) The result of this new process is almost beyond the imagination of the modern reader. Books became available to the average man instead of remaining the luxury of a few. Printing made popular education both practicable and advantageous: a man cannot learn to read without books, and there would be no point in his doing it even if he could. The extensive publication during the Renaissance of chapbooks and broadsides addressed to readers with no intellectual pretensions is in itself evidence of the rapid increase in literacy after the invention of printing from movable type.

Another great movement of this period, the Reformation, owed at least a part of its success to printing, for it was necessary that the reformers of an established institution like the Roman Catholic Church be able to get their views before the populace rapidly and thus establish a following too large to be easily crushed. During the latter part of the fourteenth century such men as Wyclif in England and John Huss in Bohemia had led dissenting movements which had much in common with the later Protestants. But the time was not yet ripe and the movements failed: Wyclif's translation of the *Bible* was publicly burned, and Huss himself met the same end. In the Renaissance, however, the spirit of the age was more favorable. A general atmosphere of individualism and self-reliance reinforced the proposition that a man is responsible directly to his God, without the necessary mediation of an ecclesiastical hierarchy, and that he is entitled to have the *Bible* available in his own tongue so that he can make his own interpretations of the will of God rather than accept a series of official dogmas.

The opposition to attempts at reform was so determined that the reformers soon found themselves forced to make a clean break with the Church and a new beginning of their own. In 1517 Martin Luther nailed to the church-door in Wittenberg ninety-five theses against indulgences—that is, against pardons like those sold by Chaucer's Pardoner. As the quarrel with the Church increased, he went on to demand the abolition of monasteries (he had been a monk), the *Bible* as the one religious authority, the abolition of worship of saints and of inquisitions against heretics, and a system of education independent of the Church. And the press was his most formidable weapon. He was not alone. During the same century Melancthon in Bohemia, Calvin in Switzerland, and Knox in Scotland led similar movements; and since that time Christianity has been divided into Catholics and Protestants.

It is interesting to notice that the Renaissance and the Reformation were really two different manifestations of the same spirit, and that no country felt both in their full force. Italy and Spain were affected primarily by the Renaissance; Germany by the Reformation, and England and France by both, but by neither in its full strength. Both movements were basically a rejection of authority and tradition in favor of individual initiative and responsibility. The same spirit is visible in all branches of human activity, from the human dissections of Leonardo da Vinci and Rabelais and Bacon's insistence on empirical science to the voyages of Columbus, Vasco da Gama, and Magellan, and the colonization of the Western Hemisphere.

In everyday life, the great ideal of the Renaissance was the well-rounded man—a concept almost diametrically opposed to our present worship of the specialist. Castiglione's *The Courtier* established this ideal of a man who should be able to handle a pen and a rapier with equal dexterity, to lead an expedition or to make a graceful compliment, to sing his part in a complicated madrigal at sight, to ride any horse over any terrain, to speak and write several languages fluently, and to play chess well, but not too well. If such an ambition seems unattainable, we should remember that such men as Leonardo da Vinci, Michelangelo, Sir Walter Raleigh, and Sir Philip Sidney actually did attain to it.

So did the best writing of the period. With respect to literature, the Renaissance definitely began in Italy and gradually spread over the rest of Europe. This "cultural lag" explains why Petrarch is considered a poet of the Renaissance, whereas Chaucer, who outlived him by a quarter of a century, is clearly a medieval writer. But the new spirit ultimately swept the whole of Europe, and wherever it came it brought with it a boundless intellectual curiosity, a combination of verve and scholarship, and a tumultuous joy in life unmatched in any other period of human history.

Rabelais

Gargantua

NOT LONG BEFORE the end of the fifteenth century, François Rabelais (*c.* 1490-1553) was born in the little town of Chinon, in the Touraine district of France, which was at that time the seat of the French monarchy. Neither the exact year nor the exact place of his birth is known, and it would probably delight this devotee of the extravagant to know that, by virtue of rival claims, he is now supposed to have been born in two different houses several blocks apart. Nothing whatsoever is known of his childhood, but one wonders whether the vast fortress of Chinon, which overhangs the town with sheer walls of masonry ten feet thick, may have led him to people his imaginary world with giants.

The Church seemed the obvious career for a youth bent on study, and Rabelais entered a Franciscan monastery where he learned and read Greek at a time when few Frenchmen knew it. However, an attempt of the authorities to dissuade the brethren from their passion for learning discouraged him, and he joined the Benedictines. About 1530 he left them as well. The specific reasons are unknown, but he had evidently made a definite decision that monastic life was not for him, for he left by the simple process of absconding; and it was some five

years before he could get a papal bull of absolution for this act. Shortly
after leaving the Benedictines he went to the University of Montpellier
as a student of medicine. He was appointed physician to the Hôtel
Dieu in Lyons, where we find him editing earlier medical works and
—while respectfully working on these authorities—pioneering in medicine by giving lectures on human anatomy based on and illustrated by
his own dissections.

At this period he ran across a crude satire which suggested the
characters and tone of his main work, and in 1532, under the pseudonym of Alcofribas Nasier (an anagram of François Rabelais), he
published *Pantagruel*. This book, which formed Book II of the finished
work, was followed by *Gargantua* (Book I) two years later, under the
same pseudonym. The concealment of the author's identity seems to
have been a matter of simple prudence, for though the satire on certain
aspects of religion was probably not particularly dangerous, ridicule
of the Sorbonne was at this time tantamount to heresy. In later life
Rabelais gained such powerful friends that concealment was no longer
necessary. He thrice accompanied Cardinal du Bellay to Rome, and he
had specific royal protection for his later work. Thus it was possible
for him to publish Book III (1546) and Book IV (1552) under his own
name, though even so he spent one short period in Metz waiting to be
sure of the favor of a new king. The fifth and final book of *Gargantua
and Pantagruel* was posthumously published in 1564, and its authorship has been seriously questioned. It probably represents some work
by Rabelais together with a good deal of padding and eking out by
an unknown hand.

Rabelais has always been something of a puzzle to critics, who
have tended to make him something more or less than he actually
was. The principal difficulty lies in keeping the elements of his character in balance. He was an insatiable student and a man of vast
learning, yet he threw his erudition casually into a fantastic tale full
of obscenity and absurdity. We think of him as a writer, yet his only
literary production of any size or consequence was twenty years in the
writing, and works out at an average of about two pages a month:
probably his statement that he devoted only an occasional few minutes
after dinner to it can be taken at face value. He was a deeply religious
man who mercilessly satirized almost every institution of his church,
but the Protestants who had begun to count on him as an ally against
Rome were soon disabused by his reference to Calvin as the "impostor
of Geneva." His preface announces that he will enunciate profound

truths in an absurd form, and at the same time cautions us against making any such interpretations. But the truths are there, and they are not far to seek in Picrochole's plan of world-conquest; in the judge who, after allowing his cases to ripen through the usual course of pleadings and delays, decides them by a throw of dice; or in the oration of the pedant from the Sorbonne.

Many of the apparent contradictions are resolved by a French critic who sees in Rabelais a temperament of the Middle Ages combined with an intellect of the Renaissance. Certainly his casualness about literary form, his satirical yarns of the *fabliau* type, his fondness for the absurd and illogical seem to belong to an age earlier than his own. Yet the ever-enquiring intellect, the distrust of superstition (most of Book III is devoted to ridiculing attempts to foretell the future by various occult means), the insistence of his giants on plain human common-sense, and the utter devotion to this life and this world show the first real impact of the Renaissance on France.

Above all, however, Rabelais is himself and is unique. Others have matched him in satire, common-sense, and narrative skill; a few have equalled him in making writing sound like particularly lively and effective impromptu speech; but in all literature there is no one who can rival him in sheer verve, exuberance, and joy of life. Many writers have learned from him, but few have dared imitate him, and they have failed. The realists have adopted a good deal of his directness and plain speech, but their somber sociological theses are far below the level of Pantagruel's benevolence. In recent years it has become fashionable to misuse his name, and when a publisher nowadays describes a work as "Rabelaisian" he is merely trying to make a potential buyer hope that it is obscene. Usually it is, for though obscenity is only an incidental characteristic of Rabelais, it is the only one that any fool can imitate.

GARGANTUA

THE AUTHOR'S PROLOGUE

Most Noble and Illustrious Drinkers, and you thrice precious Pockified blades, (for to you, and none else do I dedicate my writings) Alcibiades, in that Dialogue of Plato's, which is entitled *The Banquet*, whil'st he was setting forth the praises of his Schoolmaster Socrates (without all question the Prince of Philosophers) amongst other discourses to that purpose said, that he resembled the Silenes. Silenes of old were little boxes, like those we now may see in the shops of Apothecaries, painted on the outside with wanton toyish figures, as Harpyes, Satyrs, bridled Geese, horned Hares, saddled Ducks, flying Goats, Thiller Harts, and other suchlike counterfeted pictures at discretion, to excite people unto laughter, as Silenus himself, who was the foster-father of good Bacchus, was wont to do; but within those capricious caskets were carefully preserved and kept many rich jewels, and fine drugs, such as Balme, Ambergreece, Amamon, Musk, Civet, with several kindes of precious stones, and other things of great price. Just such another thing was Socrates; for to have eyed his outside, and esteemed of him by his exterior appearance, you would not have given the peel of an Oinion for him, so deformed he was in body, and ridiculous in his gesture: he had a sharp pointed nose, with the look of a Bull, and countenance of a foole: he was in his carriage simple, boorish in his apparel, in fortune poore, unhappy in his wives, unfit for all offices in the Common-wealth, alwayes laughing, tipling, and merrily carousing to every one, with continual gybes and jeeres, the better by those meanes to conceale his divine knowledge: now opening this boxe you would have found within it a heavenly and inestimable drug, a more than humane understanding, an admirable vertue, matchlesse learning, invincible courage, unimitable sobriety, certaine contentment of minde, perfect assurance, and an incredible misregard of all that, for which men commonly do so much watch, run, saile, fight, travel, toyle and turmoile themselves.

Whereunto (in your opinion) doth this little flourish of a preamble tend? For so much as you, my good disciples, and some other jolly fooles of ease and leasure, reading the pleasant titles of some books of our invention, as Gargantua, Pantagruel, Whippot, the dignity of Cod-peeces, of Pease and Bacon with a Commentary, etc., are too ready to judge, that there is nothing in them but jests, mockeries, lascivious discourse, and recreative lies; because the outside (which is the title) is usually (without any farther enquiry) entertained with scoffing and derision: but truly it is very unbeseeming to make so light account of the works of men, seeing your selves avouch that it is not the habit makes the Monk, many being Monasterially accoutred, who inwardly are nothing lesse than monachal, and that there are of those that weare Spanish caps, who have but little of the valour of Spaniards in them. Therefore is it, that you must open the book, and seriously consider of the matter treated in it, then shall you finde that it containeth things of farre higher value then the boxe did promise; that is to say, that the subject thereof is not so foolish, as by the Title at the first sight it would appear to be.

And put the case that in the literal sense, you meet with purposes merry and solacious enough, and consequently very correspondent to their inscriptions, yet must not you stop there as at the melody of the charming Sirens, but endeavour to interpret that in a sublimer sense, which possibly you intended to have spoken in the jollitie of your heart; did you ever pick the lock of a cupboard to steal a bottle of wine out of it? Tell me truly, and if you did call to minde the countenance which then you had? or, did you ever see a Dog with a marrow-bone in his mouth, (the beast of all other, saies Plato, lib. 2, *de Republica*, the most Philosophical)? If you have seene him, you might have remarked with what devotion and circumspectnesse he wards and watcheth it; with what care he keeps it: how fervently he holds it: how prudently he gobbets it: with what affection he breaks it: and with what diligence he sucks it: To what end all this? what moveth him to take all these paines? what are the hopes of his labour? what doth he expect to reap thereby? nothing but a little marrow: True it is, that this little is more savoury and delicious than the great quantities of other sorts of meat, because the marrow (as Galen testifieth, 3. *facult, nat.* and 11. *de usu partium*) is a nourishment most perfectly elaboured by nature.

In imitation of this Dog, it becomes you to be wise, to smell, feele and have in estimation these faire goodly books, stuffed with high conceptions, which though seemingly easie in the pursuit, are in the cope and encounter somewhat difficult; and then like him you must, by a sedulous Lecture, and frequent meditation break the bone, and suck out the marrow; that is, my allegorical sense, or the things

I to my self propose to be signified by these Pythagorical Symbols, with assured hope, that in so doing, you will at last attaine to be both well-advised and valiant by the reading of them: for in the perusal of this Treatise, you shall finde another kinde of taste, and a doctrine of a more profound and abstruse consideration, which will disclose unto you the most glorious Sacraments, and dreadful mysteries, as well in what concerneth your Religion, as matters of the publike State, and Life œconomical.

Do you beleeve upon your conscience, that Homer whil'st he was a couching his *Iliads* and *Odysses*, had any thought upon those Allegories, which Plutarch, Heraclides Ponticus, Fristatius, Cornutus squeesed out of him, and which Politian filched againe from them: if you trust it, with neither hand nor foot do you come neare to my opinion, which judgeth them to have beene as little dreamed of by Homer, as the Gospel-sacraments were by Ovid in his *Metamorphoses*, though a certaine gulligut Fryer and true bacon-picker would have undertaken to prove it, if perhaps he had met with as very fools as himself, (and as the Proverb saies) a lid worthy of such a kettle: if you give no credit thereto, why do not you the same in these jovial new chronicles of mine; albeit when I did dictate them, I thought upon no more then you, who possibly were drinking (the whil'st) as I was; for in the composing of this lordly book, I never lost nor bestowed any more, nor any other time then what was appointed to serve me for taking of my bodily refection, that is, whil'st I was eating and drinking. And indeed that is the fittest, and most proper hour, wherein to write these high matters and deep Sciences: as Homer knew very well, the Paragon of all Philologues and Ennius, the father of the Latine Poets (as Horace calls him) although a certain sneaking jobernol[1] alledged that his Verses smelled more of the wine then oile.

So saith a Turlupin or a new start-up grub of my books, but a turd for him. The fragrant odour of the wine; O how much more dainty, pleasant, laughing, celestial and delicious it is, then that smell of oile! And I will glory as much when it is said of me, that I have spent more on wine then oile, as did Demosthenes, when it was told him, that his expense on oile was greater than on wine; I truly hold it for

---

1. *jobernol*, blockhead. Rabelais' terms of abuse (and Urquhart's translations of them) are very rich and varied. Many of them have no meaning more precise than a general sense of abuse or contempt. For the most part they require no explanation.

an honour and praise to be called and reputed a Frolick Gualter, and
a Robin goodfellow; for under this name am I welcome in all choise
companies of Pantagruelists: it was upbraided to Demosthenes by an
envious surly knave, that his Orations did smell like the sarpler or
wrapper of a foul and filthy oile-vessel; for this cause interpret you all
my deeds and sayings in the perfectest sense; reverence the cheese-like
brain that feeds you with these faire billevezees,[2] and trifling jollities,
and do what lies in you to keep me always merry. Be frolick now
my lads, cheer up your hearts, and joyfully read the rest, with all
the ease of your body and profit of your reines; but hearken joltheads,
you viedazes, or dickens take ye, remember to drink a health to me
for the like favour again, and I will pledge you instantly, *Tout
aresmetys.*[3]

THE FIRST BOOK

I must referre you to the great Chronicle of Pantagruel for the
knowledge of that Genealogy, and Antiquity of race by which Gargantua is come unto us; in it you may understand more at large how
the Giants were born in this world, and how from them by a direct
line issued Gargantua the father of Pantagruel: and do not take it
ill, if for this time I passe by it, although the subject be such, that the
oftener it were remembered, the more it would please your worshipful
Seniorias; according to which you have the authority of Plato in
Philebo and Gorgias; and of Flaccus, who saies that there are some
kindes of purposes (such as these are without doubt) which the fre-
quentlier they be repeated, still prove the more delectable.

Would to God every one had as certaine knowledge of his Genealogy since the time of the Arke of Noah untill this age. I think many
are at this day Emperours, Kings, Dukes, Princes, and Popes on the
earth, whose extraction is from some porters, and pardon-pedlars, as
on the contrary, many are now poor wandring beggars, wretched
and miserable, who are descended of the blood and lineage of great
Kings and Emperours, occasioned (as I conceive it) by the transport
and revolution of Kingdomes and Empires, from the Assyrians to the
Medes, from the Medes to the Persians, from the Persians to the
Macedonians, from the Macedonians to the Romans, from the Romans
to the Greeks, from the Greeks to the French, etc.

2. *billevezees,* idle tales.
3. *Tout aresmetys,* immediately.

And to give you some hint concerning my self, who speaks unto you, I cannot think but I am come of the race of some rich King or Prince in former times, for never yet saw you any man that had a greater desire to be a King, and to be rich, then I have, and that onely that I may make good chear, do nothing, nor care for any thing, and plentifully enrich my friends, and all honest and learned men: but herein do I comfort myself, that in the other world I shall be so, yea and greater too then at this present I dare wish: as for you, with the same or a better conceit consolate your selves in your distresses, and drink fresh if you can come by it.

To returne to our weathers, I say, that by the sovereign gift of heaven, the Antiquity and Genealogy of Gargantua hath been reserved for our use more full and perfect then any other except that of the Messias, whereof I mean not to speak; for it belongs not unto my purpose, and the Devils (that is to say) the false accusers, and dissembled gospellers will therein oppose me. This Genealogy was found by John Andrew in a meadow, which he had near the Pole-arch, under the Olive-tree, as you go to Marsay: where, as he was making cast up some ditches, the diggers with their mattocks struck against a great brazen tomb, and unmeasurably long, for they could never finde the end thereof, by reason that it entered too farre within the Sluces of Vienne; opening this Tomb in a certain place thereof, sealed on the top with the mark of a goblet, about which was written in Hetrurian letters HIC BIBITUR; they found nine Flaggons, of which that which was placed in the middle, had under it a big, fat, great, gray, pretty, small, mouldy, little pamphlet, smelling stronger, but no better than roses. In that book the said Genealogy was found written all at length in a Chancery hand, not in paper, nor in parchment, nor in wax, but in the bark of an elme-tree, yet so worne with the long tract of time, that hardly could three letters together be there perfectly discerned.

I (though unworthy) was sent for thither, and with much help of those Spectacles, whereby the art of reading dim writings, and letters that do not clearly appear to the sight, is practised, as Aristotle teacheth it, did translate the book as you may see in your pantagruelising, that is to say, in drinking stiffly to your own hearts desire.

Grangousier was a good fellow in his time, and notable jester; he loved to drink neat, as much as any man that then was in the world, and would willingly eate salt meat: to this intent he was ordinarily well furnished with gammons of Bacon, both of Westphalia, Mayence and Bayone; with store of dried Neats tongues, plenty of Links, Chitterlings and Puddings in their season; together with salt Beef and mustard, a good deale of hard rows of powdered mullet called Botargos, great provision of Sauciges, not of Bolonia but of Bigorre, Longaulnay, Brene, and Rouargue. In the vigor of his age he married Gargamelle, daughter to the King of the Parpaillons, a jolly pug, and well mouthed wench. At last she became great with childe of a faire sonne, and went with him unto the eleventh moneth.

As soone as the childe was borne, he cried not as other babes use to do, *miez, miez, miez, miez*, but with a high, sturdy, and big voice shouted aloud, Some drink, some drink, some drink, as inviting all the world to drink with him; the noise hereof was so extremely great, that it was heard in both the Countreys at once, of Beauce and Bibarois.

The good man Grangousier drinking and making merry with the rest, heard the horrible noise which his sonne had made as he entered into the light of his world; whereupon he said in French, *Que grand tu as et souple le gousier*, that is to say, How great and nimble a throat thou hast; which the company hearing said, that verily the childe ought to be called Gargantua; because it was the first word that after his birth his father had spoke in imitation, and at the example, of the ancient Hebrewes, whereunto he condescended, and his mother was very well pleased therewith; in the meanwhile to quiete the childe, they gave him to drink a tirelaregot,[4] that is, till his throat was like to crack with it; then was he carried to the Font, and there baptized, according to the manner of good Christians.

Immediately thereafter were appointed for him seventeen thousand, nine hundred, and thirteen Cowes of the townes of Pautille and Breemond to furnish him with milk in ordinary, for it was impossible to finde a nurse sufficient for him in all the Countrey, considering the great quantity of milk that was requisite for his nourishment. Thus was he handled for one yeare and ten months, after which time by the advice of Physicians, they began to carry him, and then was made for him a fine little cart drawn with Oxen, wherein they led him hither and thither with great joy, and he was worth the seeing; for he was a fine boy, had a burly physnomie, and almost ten chins. He cried very little. Yet without a cause did not he sup one drop; for if he happened to be vexed, angry, displeased, or sorry; if he did fret, if

4. *tirelaregot*, enormous drink.

he did weep, if he did cry, in bringing him some drink, he would be instantly pacified, reseated in his own temper, in a good humour againe, and as still and quiet as ever. One of his governesses told me how he was so accustomed to this kinde of way, that, at the sound of pintes and flaggons, he would on a sudden fall into an extasie, as if he had then tasted of the joyes of Paradise: so that they upon consideration of this his divine complexion, would every morning, to cheare him up, play with a knife upon the glasses, on the bottles with their stopples, and on the pottle-pots with their lids and covers, at the sound whereof he became gay, did leap for joy, would loll and rock himself in the cradle, then nod with his head, monocording with his fingers, and barytonising with his taile.

Being of this age, his father ordained to have clothes made to him in his owne livery, which was white and blew. To work then went the Tailors, and with great expedition were those clothes made, cut, and sewed, according to the fashion.

For his breeches were taken up eleven hundred and five ells, and a third of white broad cloth; they were cut in forme of pillars, chamfered, channel'd and pinked behinde, that they might not over-heat his reines: and were within the panes, puffed out with the lining of as much blew damask as was needful: and remark, that he had very good Leg-harnish, proportionable to the rest of his stature.

For his shoes, were taken up foure hundred and six elles of blew Crimson-velvet, and were very neatly cut by parallel lines, joyned in uniforme cylindres: for the soling of them were made use of eleven hundred Hides of brown Cowes.

For his coate were taken up eighteen hundred elles of blew velvet, died in grain, embroidered in its borders with faire Gilliflowers, in the middle decked with silver purle, intermixed with plates of gold, and store of pearles, hereby shewing, that in his time he would prove an especial good fellow, and singular whip-can.

His girdle was made of three hundred elles and a halfe of silken serge, halfe white and halfe blew, if I mistake it not. His sword was not of Valentia, nor his dagger of Saragosa, for his father could not endure these *hidalgos borrachos maranisados como diablos*:[5] but he had a faire sword made of wood, and the dagger of leather, as well painted and guilded as any man could wish.

His purse was made of the cod of an Elephant, which was given him by Herre Præcontal, Proconsul of Lybia.

5. sottish gentlemen, curst as devils.

For his Gown were employed nine thousand six hundred elles, wanting two thirds, of blew velvet, as before, all so diagonally purled, that by true perspective issued thence an unnamed colour, like that you see in the necks of Turtle-doves or Turkie-cocks.

Gargantua from three yeares upwards unto five, was brought up and instructed in all convenient discipline, by the commandment of his father; and spent that time like the other little children of the countrey, that is, in drinking, eating and sleeping: in eating, sleeping and drinking: and in sleeping, drinking and eating: still he wallowed and rowled up and down himself in the mire and dirt: he blurred and sullied his nose with filth: he blotted and smutch't his face with any kinde of scurvie stuffe, he trode down his shoes in the heele: At the flies he did oftentimes yawn, and ran very heartily after the Butterflies.

Afterwards, that he might be all his lifetime a good Rider, they made to him a faire great horse of wood, which he did make leap, curvete, yerk out behinde, and skip forward, all at a time: to pace, trot, rack, gallop, amble, to play the hobbie, the hackney-guelding: go the gate of the camel, and of the wilde asse. Himself of an huge big post made a hunting nag; and another for daily service, of the beam of a Vinepress: and of a great Oak made up a mule.

[As Gargantua grew older, his nurses were supplanted by male tutors. These teachers did him more harm than good. They filled his mind with much useless lumber, and although the boy spent all his time at study, it was clear that he was learning nothing of any value. At last in disgust, Grangousier dismissed the tutors and employed a young man named Ponocrates, who undertook to rid Gargantua's mind of the mess of medieval rubbish it contained and induct him into the gracious new learning of the Renaissance.

Grown a young man, Gargantua, accompanied by Ponocrates and other instructors, was sent to Paris to study. His appearance there was sensational.]

Some few dayes after that they had refresh't themselves, he went to see the city, and was beheld of every body with great admiration; for the People of Paris are so sottish, so foolish and fond by nature, that a jugler, a carrier of indulgences, a sumpter-horse, or mule with cymbals, or tinkling bells, a blinde fidler in the middle of a crosse lane, shall draw a greater confluence of people together, then an

Evangelical Preacher: and they prest so hard upon him, that he was constrained to rest himself upon the towers of our Ladies Church. He considered the great bells, which were in the said tours, and made them sound very harmoniously, which whilest he was doing, it came into his minde, that they would serve very well for tingling Tantans, and ringing Campanels, to hang about his mares neck, when she should be sent back to his father, (as he intended to do) loaded with Brie cheese, and fresh herring; and indeed he forthwith carried them to his lodging. All the city was risen up in sedition, they being upon any slight occasion, so ready to uproars and insurrections, that forreign nations wonder at the patience of the Kings of France. The place wherein the people gathered together was called Nesle. There was the case proposed, and the inconvenience shewed of the transporting of the bells: After they had well ergoted pro and con, they concluded in Baralipton,[6] that they should send the oldest and most sufficient of the facultie unto Gargantua, to signifie unto him the great and horrible prejudice they sustain by the want of those bells. There was chosen for this purpose our Master Janotus de Bragmardo.

Master Janotus, with his haire cut round like a dish *à la cæsarine*, in his most antick accoustrement Liripipionated with a graduates hood, and, having sufficiently antidoted his stomach with Oven-marmalades, that is, bread and holy water of the Cellar, transported himself to the lodging of Gargantua, driving before him three red muzled beadles, and dragging after him five or six artlesse masters, all throughly bedaggled with the mire of the streets. At their entry Ponocrates met them, who was afraid, seeing them so disguised, and thought they had been some maskers out of their wits, which moved him to enquire of one of the said artlesse masters of the company, what this mummery meant? It was answered him, that they desired to have their bells restored to them. As soon as Ponocrates heard that, he ran in all haste to carry the newes unto Gargantua, that he might be ready to answer them, and speedily resolve what was to be done. Gargantua being advertised hereof, called apart his Schoolmaster Ponocrates, Philotimus Steward of his house, Gymnastes his Esquire, and Eudemon, and very summarily conferred with them, both of what he should do, and what answer he should give. They were all of opinion that they should bring them unto the goblet-office, which is the Buttery, and there make them drink like Roysters, and line their

6. *Baralipton*, a type of proof in logic.

jackets soundly: and that this cougher might not be puft up with
vain-glory, by thinking the bells were restored at his request, they
sent, (whilest he was chopining and plying the pot,) for the Major
of the City, the Rector of the facultie, and the Vicar of the Church,
unto whom they resolved to deliver the bells, before the Sophister
had propounded his commission; after that, in their hearing, he should
pronounce his gallant Oration, which was done, and they being come,
the Sophister was brought into a full hall, and began as followeth, in
coughing.

Hem, hem, Gudday, Sirs, Gudday, *et vobis*, my masters, it were
but reason that you should restore to us our bells; for we have great
need of them. Hem, hem, aihfuhash, we have often-times heretofore
refused good money for them of those of London in Cahors, yea and
of those of Bourdeaux in Brie, who would have bought them for
the substantifick quality of the elementary complexion, which is in-
tronificated in the terrestreity of their quidditative nature, to extraneize
the blasting mists, and whirlwindes upon our Vines. If you restore
them unto us at my request, I shall gaine by it six basketfuls of sauciges, and a fine paire of breeches, which will do my legs a great deal
of good, or else they will not keep their promise to me. Ho by gob,
domine, a paire of breeches is good, *et vir sapiens non abhorrebit eam.*[7]
Ha, ha, a paire of breeches is not so easily got, I have experience of it
my self. Consider, *Domine*, I have been these eighteen dayes in mata-
grabolising this brave speech *Reddite quæ sunt Cæsaris, Cæsari, et quæ
sunt Dei, Deo. Ibi jacet lepus*, by my faith, *Domine*, if you will sup
with me in *cameris*, by cox body, *charitatis, nos faciemus bonum
cherubin; ego occidit unum purcum, et ego habet bonum vino;* but
of good wine we cannot make bad Latine. Well, *de parte Dei date
nobis bellas nostras;* Hold, I give you in the name of the facultie a
Sermones de utino, that *utinam* you would give us our bells. They
are useful to every body, if they fit your mare well, so do they do
our facultie; *quæ comparata est jumentis insipientibus, et similis facta
est eis, Psalmo nescio quo;* yet did I quote in my notebook, *et est
unum bonum* Achilles, a good defending argument, hem, hem, hem,
haikhash; for I prove unto you that you should give me them. *Ego
sic argumentor, Omnis bella bellabilis in Bellerio bellando, bellans
bellative, bellare facit, bellabiliter bellantes: parisius habet bellas; ergo
gluc.* Ha, ha, ha, this is spoken to some purpose; it is *in tertio primæ,*

7. It is sufficient to indicate that the Latin used by this great scholar of the
Sorbonne is silly, pretentious, and often wrong.

in *Darii*, or elsewhere. By my soul, I have seen the time that I could play the devil in arguing, but now I am much failed, and henceforward want nothing but a cup of good wine, a good bed, my back to the fire, my belly to the table, and a good deep dish. Hei *domine*, I beseech you, *in nomine Patris, Filii, et Spiritûs sancti, Amen*, to restore unto us our bells.

The Sophister had no sooner ended, but Ponocrates and Eudemon burst out into a laughing so heartily, that they had almost split with it, and given up the ghost, in rendering their souls to God. Together with them Master Janotus fell a laughing too as fast as he could, in which mood of laughing they continued so long, that their eyes did water by the vehement concussion of the substance of the braine, by which these lachrymal humidities, being prest out, glided through the optick nerves.

[The matter of the bells having been settled, Gargantua applied himself with vigor to a prodigious program of study and exercise.]

He put himself into such a way of studying, that he lost not any one houre in the day, but employed all his time in learning, and honest knowledge. Gargantua awaked about foure a clock in the morning: whilest they were in rubbing of him, there was read unto him some chapter of the holy Scripture aloud and clearly, with a pronunciation fit for the matter, and hereunto was appointed a young page, named Anagnostes. According to the purpose and argument of that lesson, he oftentimes gave himself to worship, adore, pray, and send up his supplications to that good God, whose Word did shew his majesty and marvellous judgement. Then went he into the secret places to make excretion of his natural digestions: there his master repeated what had been read, expounding unto him the most obscure and difficult points; in returning, they considered the face of the sky, if it was such as they had observed it the night before, and into what signes the Sun was entering, as also the Moon for that day. This done, he was apparelled, combed, curled, trimmed and perfumed, during which time they repeated to him the lessons of the day before: he himself said them by heart, and upon them would ground some practical cases concerning the estate of man, which he would prosecute sometimes two or three houres, but ordinarily they ceased as soon as he was fully clothed. Then for three good houres he had a lecture read unto him. This done, they went forth, still conferring of the

substance of the lecture, either unto a field near the University called
the Brack, or unto the medowes where they played at the ball, the
long-tennis, and at the Piletrigone, (which is a play wherein we
throw a triangular piece of iron at a ring), most gallantly exercising
their bodies, as formerly they had done their mindes. All their play
was but in liberty, for they left off when they pleased, and that was
commonly when they did sweat over all their body, or were otherwayes weary. Then were they very well wiped and rubbed, shifted
their shirts, and, walking soberly, went to see if dinner was ready.
Whilest they stayed for that, they did clearly and eloquently pronounce some sentences that they had retained of the lecture. In the
mean time Master Appetite came, and then very orderly sate they
down at table; at the beginning of the meale, there was read some
pleasant history of the warlike actions of former times, until he had
taken a glasse of wine. Then, (if they thought good,) they continued
reading, or began to discourse merrily together; speaking first of the
vertue, propriety, efficacy and nature of all that was served in at the
table; of bread, of wine, of water, of salt, of fleshes, fishes, fruits,
herbs, roots, and of their dressing, by meanes whereof, he learned in
a little time all the passages competent for this, that were to be found
in Plinie, Athenæus, Dioscorides, Julius Pollux, Galen, Porphirie,
Oppian, Polybius, Heliodore, Aristotle, Elian, and others. Whilest
they talked of these things, many times to be the more certain, they
caused the very books to be brought to the table, and so well and
perfectly did he in his memory retain the things above said, that in
that time there was not a Physician that knew half so much as he
did. Afterwards they conferred of the lessons read in the morning,
and ending their repast with some conserve or marmalade of quinces:
he pick't his teeth with mastick tooth-pickers, wash't his hands and
eyes with faire fresh water, and gave thanks unto God in some fine
Canticks, made in praise of the divine bounty and munificence. This
done, they brought in cards, not to play, but to learn a thousand
pretty tricks, and new inventions, which were all grounded upon
Arithmetick: by this means he fell in love with that numerical science,
and every day after dinner and supper he past his time in it as pleasantly, as he was wont to do at cardes and dice: so that at last he
understood so well both the Theory and Practical part thereof, that
Tunstal the Englishman, who had written very largely of that
purpose, confessed that verily in comparison of him he had no skill
at all. And not only in that, but in the other Mathematical Sciences,

as Geometrie, Astronomie, Musick, etc. For in waiting on the con-
coction, and attending the digestion of his food, they made a thousand
pretty instruments and Geometrical figures, and did in some measure practise the Astronomical canons.

After this they recreated themselves with singing musically, in
foure or five parts, or upon a set theme or ground at random, as it
best pleased them; in matter of musical instruments, he learned to
play upon the Lute, the Virginals, the Harp, the Allman Flute with
nine holes, the Viol, and the Sackbut. This houre thus spent, and
digestion finished, he did purge his body of natural excrements, then
betook himself to his principal study for three houres, together, or
more, as well to repeat his matutinal lectures, as to proceed in the book
wherein he was, as also to write handsomly, to draw and forme the
Romane letters. This being done, they went out of their house, and
with them a young gentleman of Touraine, named the Esquire Gymnast, who taught him the Art of Riding; changing then his clothes,
he rode a Naples courser, a Dutch roussin, a Spanish gennet, a barbed
or trapped steed, then a light fleet horse, unto whom he gave a hundred carieres, made him go the high saults, bounding in the aire, free
the ditch with a skip, leap over a stile or pale, turne short in a ring
both to the right and left hand. There he broke not his lance; for
it is the greatest foolery in the world, to say, I have broken ten lances
at tilt or in fight, a Carpenter can do even as much; but it is a glorious
and praise-worthy action, with one lance to break and overthrow ten
enemies: therefore with a sharp, stiffe, strong and well-steeled lance,
would he usually force up a door, pierce a harnesse, beat down a tree,
carry away the ring, lift up a cuirasier saddle, with the male-coat and
gantlet; all this he did in compleat armes from head to foot. He was
singularly skilful in leaping nimbly from one horse to another, without putting foot to ground: he could likewise from either side, with a
lance in his hand, leap on horseback without stirrups, and rule the
horse at his pleasure without a bridle, for such things are useful in
military engagements. Another day he exercised the battel-axe, which
he dextrously wielded, both in the nimble, strong and smooth management of that weapon, and in all the feats practiseable by it.

Then tost he the pike, played with the two-handed sword, with
the back-sword, with the Spanish tuck, the dagger, poiniard, armed,
unarmed, with a buckler, with a cloak, with a targuet. Then would
he hunt the hart, the roebuck, the Beare, the fallow Deer, the wilde
Boare, the Hare, the Phesant, the Partridge and the Bustard. He

played at the baloon, and made it bound in the aire, both with fist and foot. He wrestled, ran, jumped, not at three steps and a leap, but at one leap he would skip over a ditch, spring over a hedge, mount six paces upon a wall, ramp and grapple after this fashion up against a window, of the full height of a lance. He did swim in deep waters on his belly, on his back, sidewise, with all his body, with his feet only, with one hand in the air, wherein he held a book, crossing thus the bredth of the river of Seine, without wetting it, and dragged along his cloak with his teeth, as did Julius Cæsar; then with the help of one hand he entred forcibly into a boat, from whence he cast himself again headlong into the water, sounded the depths, and plunged into the pits and gulphs. Then turned he the boat about, governed it, led it swiftly or slowly with the stream and against the stream, stopped it in his course, guided it with one hand, and with the other laid hard about him with a huge great Oare, hoised the saile, hied up along the mast by the shrouds, ran upon the edge of the decks, set the compasse in order, and steer'd the helme. Coming out of the water, he ran furiously up against a hill, and with the same alacrity and swiftnesse ran down again; he climbed up at trees like a cat, and leaped from the one to the other like a squirrel; he did pull down the great boughs and branches, like another Milo; then with two sharp well-steeled daggers, and two tried bodkins, would he run up by the wall to the very top of a house like a cat; then suddenly came down from the top to the bottom, with such an even composition of members, that by the fall he would catch no harme.

He did cast the dart, throw the barre, put the stone, practise the javelin, the boar-spear, and the halbard; he broke the strongest bowes in drawing, bended against his breast the greatest crosse-bowes of steele, took his aime by the eye with the hand-gun, and shot well, traversed and planted the canon, shot at butmarks, at the papgay from below upwards, or to a height from above downwards, or to a descent; then before him, sidewise, and behinde him, like the Parthians. They tied a cable-rope to the top of a high Tower, by one end whereof hanging near the ground, he wrought himself with his hands to the very top: Then upon the same tract came down so sturdily and firme that you could not on a plaine meadow have run with more assurance. They set up a great pole fixed upon two trees, there would he hang by his hands, and with them alone, his feet touching at nothing, would go back and fore along the foresaid rope with so great swiftnesse, that hardly could one overtake him with running; and then to exercise his breast and lungs, he would shout like all the Devils in hell. Stentor had never such a voyce at the siege of Troy. Then for the strengthening of his nerves or sinewes, they made him two great sows of lead, each of them weighing eight thousand and seven hundred kintals; those he took up from the ground, in each hand one, then lifted them up over his head, and held them so without stirring three quarters of an hour and more, which was an inimitable force; he fought at Barriers with the stoutest and most vigorous Champions; and when it came to the cope, he stood so sturdily on his feet, that he abandoned himself unto the strongest, in case they could remove him from his place, as Milo was wont to do of old; in whose imitation like wise he held a Pomgranat in his hand, to give it unto him that could take it from him: The time being thus bestowed, and himself rubbed, cleansed, wiped, and refresht with other clothes, he returned fair and softly; and passing through certain meadows, or other grassie places, beheld the trees and plants, comparing them with what is written of them in the books of the Ancients, and carried home to the house great handfuls of them.

Being come to their lodging, whilest supper was making ready, they repeated certain passages of that which hath been read, and sate down at table. Here remark, that his dinner was sober and thrifty, for he did then eat only to prevent the gnawings of his stomack. During that repast was continued the lesson read at dinner as long as they thought good: the rest was spent in good discourse, learned and profitable. After that they had given thanks, he set himself to sing vocally, and play upon harmonious instruments, or otherwayes passed his time at some pretty sports, made with cards or dice, or in practising the feats of Legerdemain, with cups and balls. There they stayed some nights in frolicking thus, and making themselves merrie till it was time to go to bed.

Then prayed they unto God the Creator, in falling down before him, and strengthening their faith towards him, and glorifying him for his boundlesse bounty, and, giving thanks unto him for the time that was past, they recommended themselves to his divine clemency for the future, which being done, they went to bed, and betook themselves to their repose and rest.

[While Gargantua, with his staff of instructors and trainers, thus passed his time profitably in Paris, a situation arose at home which caused his father great perplexity and distress and which at last made it necessary for Gargantua to return.

The kingdom next to Grangousier's was governed by one Picrochole, a rash and silly monarch. Surrounded by a group of advisers as rash and silly as himself, he was ripe for any folly that might come to hand. An "incident" offered itself when a group of truculent bakers from Lerne, Picrochole's capital, peddling their wares along a highroad through Grangousier's domain, fell into a trivial squabble with some of the natives.]

At that time, which was the season of Vintage, in the beginning of Harvest, when the countrey shepherds were set to keep the Vines, and hinder the Starlings from eating up the grapes; as some cakebakers of Lerne happened to passe along in the broad high way, driving unto the City ten or twelve horses loaded with cakes, the said shepherds courteously intreated them to give them some for their money, as the price then ruled in the market; for here it is to be remarked, that it is a celestial food to eate for breakfast hot fresh cakes with grapes, especially the frail clusters, the great red grapes, the muscadine, the verjuice grape and the luskard. The Bunsellers or Cake-makers were in nothing inclinable to their request; but (which was worse) did injure them most outrageously, calling them pratling gablers, lickorous gluttons, freckled bittors, mangie rascals, shiteabed-scoundrels, drunken roysters, slie knaves, drowsie loiterers, slapsauce fellows, slabberdegullion druggels, lubbardly lowts, cosening foxes, ruffian rogues, paultrie customers, sycophant-varlets, drawlatch hoydons, flouting milksops, jeering companions, staring clowns, forlorn snakes, ninnie lobcocks, scurvie sneaksbies, fondling fops, base lowns, sawcie coxcombs, idle lusks, scoffing Braggards, noddie meacocks, blockish grutnols, doddi-pol-jolt-heads, jobernol goosecaps, foolish loggerheads, slutch calf-lollies, grouthead gnat-snappers, lob-dotterels, gaping changelings, codshead loobies, woodcock slangams, ninnie-hammer flycatchers, noddiepeak simpletons, turdie gut, shitten shepherds, and other such like defamatory epithetes, saying further, that it was not for them to eate of these dainty cakes, but might very well content themselves with course bread, or to eat of the great brown houshold loaf. To which provoking words, one amongst them, called Forgier, (an honest fellow of his person, and a notable springal,[8]) made answer very calmly thus: How long is it since you have got hornes,

8. *springal*, young fellow.

that you are become so proud? indeed formerly you were wont to give us some freely, and will you not now let us have any for our money? This is not the part of good neighbours. Then Marquet, a prime man in the confraternity of the cake-bakers, said unto him, Yea Sir, thou art pretty well crest-risen this morning, thou didst eat yesternight too much millet and bolymoug, come hither, Sirrah, come hither, I will give thee some cakes: whereupon Forgier dreading no harm, in all simplicity went towards him, and drew a sixpence out of his leather sachel, thinking that Marquet would have sold him some of his cakes; but, in stead of cakes, he gave him with his whip such a rude lash overthwart the legs, that the marks of the whipcord knots were apparent in them; then would have fled away, but Forgier cried out as loud as he could, O murther, murther, help, help, help, and in the mean time threw a great cudgel after him, which he carried under his arme, wherewith he hit him in the coronal joynt of his head, upon the crotaphick arterie of the right side thereof, so forcibly, that Marquet fell down from his mare, more like a dead then living man. Meanwhile the farmers and countrey-swaines, that were watching their walnuts near to that place, came running with their great poles and long staves, and laid such load on these cake-bakers, as if they had been to thresh upon green rie. The other shepherds and shepherdesses, hearing the lamentable shout of Forgier, came with their slings and slackies following them, and throwing great stones at them, as thick as if it had been haile. At last they overtook them, and took from them about foure or five dosen of their cakes; neverthelesse they payed for them the ordinary price, and gave them over and above one hundred egges, and three baskets of mulberries. Then did the cake-bakers help to get up to his mare Marquet, who was most shrewdly wounded, and forthwith returned to Lerne. This done, the shepherds and shepherdesses made merry with these cakes and fine grapes, and sported themselves together at the sound of the pretty small pipe, scoffing and laughing at those vainglorious cake-bakers, who had that day met with a mischief for want of crossing themselves with a good hand in the morning. Nor did they forget to apply to Forgiers leg some faire great red medicinal grapes, and so handsomely drest it and bound it up, that he was quickly cured.

The Cake-bakers, being returned to Lerne, went presently, before they did either eat or drink, to the Capitol, and there before their King called Picrochole, the third of that name, made their complaint, shewing their paniers broken, their caps all crumpled, their coats

torn, their cakes taken away, but, above all Marquet most enormously
wounded, saying, that all that mischief was done by the shepherds
and herdsmen of Grangousier, near the broad high way beyond Sevile:
Picrochole incontinent grew angry and furious; and without asking
any further what, how, why or wherefore, commanded the ban and
arriere ban to be sounded throughout all his countrey, that all his
vassals of what condition soever, should upon paine of the halter
come in the best armes they could, unto the great place before the
Castle, at the houre of noone, and, the better to strengthen his designe,
he caused the drum to be beat about the town. Himself, whilest his
dinner was making ready, went to see his artillery mounted upon the
carriage, to display his colours, and set up the great royal standard,
and loaded waines with store of ammunition both for the field and
the belly, armes and victuals: at dinner he dispatch't his commissions,
and by his expresse Edict my Lord Shagrag was appointed to command the Vanguard, wherein were numbered sixteen thousand and
fourteen harquebusiers or fire-locks, together with thirty thousand
and eleven Voluntier-adventurers. The great Touquedillion, Master
of the horse, had the charge of the ordnance, wherein were reckoned
nine hundred and fourteen brazen pieces, in cannons, double cannons, basilisks, serpentines, culverins, bombards or murtherers, falcons,
bases or passevolans, spiroles and other sorts of great guns. The Reer-
guard was committed to the Duke of Scrapegood: In the maine battel
was the King, and the Princes of his Kingdome. Thus being hastily
furnished, before they would set forward, they sent three hundred
light horsemen under the conduct of Captain Swillwind, to discover
the countrey, clear the avenues, and see whether there was any ambush
laid for them: but, after they had made diligent search, they found
all the land round about in peace and quiet, without any meeting or
convention at all; which Picrochole understanding, commanded that
every one should march speedily under his colours: then immediately
in all disorder, without keeping either rank or file, they took the fields
one amongst another, wasting, spoiling, destroying and making havock
of all wherever they went, not sparing poor nor rich, priviledged nor
unpriviledged places, Church nor laity, drove away oxen and cowes,
bulls, caves, heifers, wethers, ewes, lambs, goats, kids, hens, capons,
chickens, geese, ganders, goslings, hogs, swine, pigs and such like.
Beating down the walnuts, plucking the grapes, tearing the hedges,
shaking the fruit-trees, and committing such incomparable abuses, that
the like abomination was never heard of. Neverthelesse, they met with

none to resist them, for every one submitted to their mercy, beseeching them, that they might be dealt with courteously, in regard that they had always carried themselves, as became good and loving neighbours, and that they had never been guilty of any wrong or outrage done upon them, to be thus suddenly surprised, troubled and disquieted, and that if they would not desist, God would punish them very shortly; to which expostulations and remonstrances no other answer was made, but that they would teach them to eat cakes.

So much they did, and so farre they went pillaging and stealing, that at last they came to Sevile, where they robbed both men and women, and took all they could catch. The town being thus pillaged, they went unto the Abbey with a horrible noise and tumult, but they found it shut and made fast against them. Two hundred lanciers broke down the walls of the Closse, to waste, spoile and make havock of all the Vines and Vintage within that place. The Monks (poor devils) knew not in that extremity to which of all their Sancts they should vow themselves; neverthelesse, at all adventures they rang the bells; there it was decreed, that they should make a faire Procession, stuffed with good lectures, prayers and letanies.

There was then in the Abbey a Monk, called Freer Jhon, young, gallant, frisk, lustie, nimble, quick, active, bold, adventurous, resolute, tall, lean, wide-mouthed, long-nosed, a faire dispatcher of morning prayers, unbridler of masses, and runner over of vigils; and to conclude summarily in a word, a right Monk, if ever there was any, since the Monking world monked a Monkerie. This Monk hearing the noise that the enemy made within the inclosure of the Vineyard, went out to see what they were doing; and perceiving that they were cutting and gathering the grapes, whereon was grounded the foundation of all their next yeares wine, returned unto the quire of the Church where the other Monks were, all amazed and astonished like so many Bell-melters, whom when he heard sing, im, nim, pe, ne, ne, ne, ne, nene, tum, ne, num, num, ini, imi, co, o, no, o, o, neno, ne, no, no, no, rum, nenum, num: It is well sung, (said he). By the vertue of God, why do not you sing Paniers farewell, Vintage is done; The devil snatch me, if they be not already within the middle of our Closse, and cut so well both Vines and Grapes, that by cods body, there will not be found for these four yeares to come so much as a gleaning in it. By the belly of Sanct James, what shall we (poor devils) drink the while? Lord God! *da mihi potum.*

As he spake this, he threw off his great Monks habit, and laid

hold upon the staffe of the crosse, which was made of the heart of a
sorbaple-tree, it being of the length of a lance, round, of a full gripe,
and a little poudred with lilies called flower de luce, the workmanship
whereof was almost all defaced and worn out. Thus went he out in a
faire long-skirted jacket, putting his frock scarfewayes athwart his
breast, and in this equipage, with his staffe, shaft or truncheon of the
crosse, laid on so lustily, brisk and fiercely upon his enemies, who
without any order, or ensigne, or trumpet, or drum, were busied in
gathering the grapes of the Vineyard. For the Cornets, Guidons, and
Ensigne-bearers, had laid down their standards, banners, and colours
by the wallsides: the Drummers had knockt out the heads of their
Drums on one end, to fill them with grapes: the Trumpeters were
loaded with great bundles of bunches, and huge knots of clusters:
In summe, every one of them was out of aray, and all in disorder. He
hurried therefore upon them so rudely, without crying gare or beware,
that he overthrew them like hogs, tumbled them over like swine,
striking athwart and alongst, and by one means or other laid so about
him, after the old fashion of fencing, that to some he beat out their
braines, to others he crushed their armes, battered their legs, and
bethwacked their sides till their ribs cracked with it; to others again
he unjoynted the spondyles or knuckles of the neck, disfigured their
chaps, gashed their faces, made their cheeks hang flapping on their
chin, and so swinged and belammed them, that they fell down before
him like hay before a Mower: to some others he spoiled the frame of
their kidneys, marred their backs, broke their thigh-bones, pash't in
their noses, poached out their eyes, cleft their mandibules, tore their
jaws, dung in their teeth into their throat, shook asunder their omo-
plates or shoulderblades, sphacelated their shins, mortified their shanks,
inflamed their ankles, heaved off of the hinges their ishies, their sciatica
or hip-gout, dislocated the joints of their knees, squattered into pieces
the boughts or pestles of their thighs, and so thumped, mawled and
belaboured them every where, that never was corne so thick and
threefold thresht upon by Plowmens flailes, as were the pitifully dis-
joynted members of their mangled bodies, under the mercilesse baton
of the crosse.

   Thus by his prowesse and valour were discomfited all those of
the army that entred into the Closse of the Abbey, unto the number
of thirteen thousand, six hundred, twenty and two, besides the women
and little children, which is alwayes to be understood. Never did
Maugis the Hermite bear himself more valiantly with his bourdon or

Pilgrims staffe against the Saracens then did this Monk against his enemies with the staffe of the Crosse.

Whilest the Monk did thus skirmish, as we have said, against those which were entered within the Closse; Picrochole in great haste passed the ford of Vede, (a very special passe,) with all his souldierie, and set upon the rock Clermond, where there was made him no resistance at all: and, because it was already night, he resolved to quarter himself and his army in that town, and to refresh himself of his pugnative choler. In the morning he stormed and took the Bulwarks and Castle, which afterwards he fortified with rampiers, and furnished with all ammunition requisite, intending to make his retreat there, if he should happen to be otherwise worsted; for it was a strong place, both by Art and Nature, in regard of the stance and situation of it. But let us leave them there, and return to our good Gargantua, who is at Paris very assiduous and earnest at the study of good letters, and athletical exercitations, and to the good old man Grangousier his father, who after supper warmeth his ballocks by a good, clear, great fire, and, waiting upon the broyling of some chestnuts, is very serious in drawing scratches on the hearth, with a stick burnt at the one end, wherewith they did stirre up the firre, telling to his wife and the rest of the family pleasant old stories and tales of former times. Whilest he was thus employed, one of the shepherds which did keep the Vines, (named Pillot) came towards him, and to the full related the enormous abuses which were committed, and the excessive spoil that was made by Picrochole, King of Lerne, upon his lands and territories, and how he had pillaged, wasted and ransacked all the countrey, except the inclosure at Sevile, which Friar Jhon to his great honour had preserved: and that at the same present time the said King was in the rock Clermond; and there with great industry and circumspection, was strengthening himself and his whole army. Halas, halas, alas, (said Grangousier,) what is this good people? do I dream, or is it true that they tell me? Picrochole my ancient friend of old time, of my own kinred and alliance, comes he to invade me? what moves him? what provokes him? what sets him on? what drives him to it? who hath given him this counsel? Ho, ho, ho, ho, ho, my God, my Saviour, help me, inspire me, and advise me what I shall do. I protest, I swear before thee, so be thou favourable to me, if ever I did him or his subjects any damage or displeasure, or committed any the least robbery in his countrey; but on the contrary I have succoured and supplied him with men, money, friendship and counsel upon

any occasion, wherein I could be steadable for the improvement of his
good; that he hath therefore at this nick of time so outraged and
wronged me, it cannot be but by the malevolent and wicked spirit.
Good God, thou knowest my courage, for nothing can be hidden
from thee; if perhaps he be grown mad, and that thou hast sent him
hither to me for the better recovery and re-establishment of his brain;
grant me power and wisdome to bring him to the yoke of thy holy
will by good discipline. Ho, ho, ho, ho, my good people, my friends
and my faithful servants, must I hinder you from helping me? alas,
my old age required henceforward nothing else but rest, and all the
dayes of my life I have laboured for nothing so much as peace: but
now I must (I see it well) load with armes my poor, weary and
feeble shoulders; and take in my trembling hand the lance and horsemans mace, to succour and protect my honest subjects: reason will
have it so; for by their labour am I entertained, and with their sweat
am I nourished, I, my children and my family. This notwithstanding,
I will not undertake warre, until I have first tried all the wayes and
means of peace, that I resolve upon.

[Grangousier sends a letter to Gargantua asking him to come
home and help protect his people.
   He also tries to talk reason with Picrochole, and when this embassy fails he tries to avert war by direct appeasement: he sends
Picrochole a cart-load of cakes for each dozen originally taken, and
adds a large sum of money to this gift.]

The carts being unloaded, and the money and cakes secured,
there came before Picrochole the Duke of Smalltrash, the Earle Swashbuckler, and Captain Durtaille, who said unto him, Sir, this day we
make you the happiest, the most warlike and chivalrous Prince that
ever was since the death of Alexander of Macedonia. Be covered, be
covered, (said Picrochole.) Grammercie (said they) we do but
our duty: The manner is thus, you shall leave some Captain here to
have the charge of this Garrison, with a Party competent for keeping of the place, which besides its natural strength, is made stronger
by the rampiers and fortresses of your devising. Your Army you are
to divide into two parts, as you know very well how to do. One part
thereof shall fall upon Grangousier and his forces, by it shall he be
easily at the very first shock routed, and then shall you get money
by heaps, for the Clown hath store of ready coine: Clown we call

him, because a noble and generous Prince hath never a penny, and that to hoard up treasure is but a clownish trick. The other part of the Army in the mean time shall draw towards Onys, Xaintonge, Angoulesme and Gascony: then march to Perigourt, Medos, and Elanes, taking whereever you come without resistance, townes, castles, and forts: Afterwards to Bayonne, St. Jhon de Luz, to Fuentarabia, where you shall seize upon all the ships, and coasting along Galicia and Portugal, shall pillage all the maritime places, even unto Lisbone, where you shall be supplied with all necessaries befitting a Conquerour. By copsodie[9] Spain will yield, for they are but a race of Loobies: then are you to passe by the streights of Gibraltar, where you shall erect two pillars more stately than those of Hercules, to the perpetual memory of your name, and the narrow entrance there shall be called the Picrocholinal sea.

Having past the Picrocholinal sea, behold, Barbarossa yields himself your slave: I will (said Picrochole) give him faire quarter and spare his life. Yea, (said they) so that he be content to be christened. And you shall conquer the Kingdomes of Tunes, of Hippos, Argier, Bomine, Corode, yea all Barbary. Furthermore, you shall take into your hands Majorca, Minorca, Sardinia, Corsica, with the other Islands of the Ligustick and Balearian seas. Going alongst on the left hand, you shall rule all Gallia Narbonensis, Provence, the Allobrogians, Genua, Florence, Luca, and then God bi wy Rome; By my faith (said Picrochole,) I will not then kisse his pantuffle.[10]

Italy being thus taken, behold, Naples, Calabria, Apulia and Sicilie all ransacked, and Malta too. I wish the pleasant Knights of the Rhodes heretofore would but come to resist you, that we might see their urine. I would (said Picrochole) very willingly go to Loretta. No, no, (said they) that shall be at our return; from thence we will saile Eastwards, and take Candia, Cyprus, Rhodes, and the Cyclade Islands, and set upon Morea. It is ours by St. Trenian, the Lord preserve Jerusalem; for the great Soldan is not comparable to you in power. I will then (said he) cause Solomons Temple to be built. No, (said they) not yet, have a little patience, stay a while, be never too sudden in your enterprises. Can you tell what Octavian Augustus said? *Festina lentè.* It is requisite that you first have the lesser Asia, Caria, Lycia, Pamphilia, Cilicia, Lydia, Phrygia, Mysia, Bithynia, Carazia, Satalia, Samagaria, Castamena, Luga, Sanasta, even unto Euphrates.

9. *copsodie*, God's body.
10. *pantuffle*, slipper.

Shall we see, (said Picrochole,) Babylon and Mount Sinai? There is no need (said they) at this time; have we not hurried up and down, travelled and toyled enough, in having transfreted and past over the Hircanian sea, marched alongst the two Armenias and the three Arabias? By my faith (said he) we have played the fooles, and are undone: Ha, poor soules! What's the matter, said they? What shall we have (said he) to drink in these deserts? For Julian Augustus, with his whole Army died there for thirst, as they say. We have already (said they), given order for that. In the Siriack sea you have nine thousand and fourteen great ships laden with the best wines in the world: they arrived at Port Joppa, there they found two and twenty thousand Camels, and sixteen hundred Elephants, which you shall have taken at one hunting about Sigelmes, when you entered into Lybia: and, besides this, you had all the Mecca Caravane. Did not they furnish you sufficiently with wine? Yes, but (said he) we did not drink it fresh. By the vertue, (said they) not of a fish, a valiant man, a Conquerour, who pretends and aspires to the Monarchy of the world, cannot alwayes have his ease. God be thanked, that you and your men are come safe and sound unto the banks of the river Tigris. But (said he) what doth that part of our Army in the mean time, which overthrows that unworthy Swill-pot Grangousier? They are not idle (said they) we shall meet with them by and by, they shall have won you Britany, Normandy, Flanders, Haynault, Brabant, Artois, Holland, Zealand; they have past the Rhine over the bellies of the Switsers and Lanskenets, and a Party of these hath subdued Luxemburg, Lorrain, Champaigne, and Savoy, even to Lions, in which place they have met with your forces, returning from the naval Conquests of the Mediterranean sea: and have rallied again in Bohemia, after they had plundered and sacked Suevia, Wittemberg, Bavaria, Austria, Moravia, and Styria. Then they set fiercely together upon Lubeck, Norway, Swedeland, Rie, Denmark, Gitland, Greenland, the Sterlins, even unto the frozen sea: this done, they conquered the iles of Orkney, and subdued Scotland, England, and Ireland. From thence sailing through the sandie sea, and by the Sarmates, they have vanquished and overcome Prussia, Poland, Lituania, Russia, Walachia, Transilvania, Hungarie, Bulgaria, Turquieland, and are now at Constantinople. Come (said Picrochole), let us go joyn with them quickly, for I will be Emperour of Trebezonde also: shall we not kill all these dogs, Turks and Mahumetans? What a devil should we do else, said they: and you shall give their goods and lands to such as shall have served you honestly. Reason (said he) will have it so, that is but just, I give unto you the Caramania, Surie, and all the Palestine. Ha, Sir (said they) it is out of your goodnesse: Grammercie, we thank you, God grant you may always prosper. There was there present at that time an old Gentleman well experienced in the warres, a sterne souldier, and who had been in many great hazards, named Echephron, who hearing this discourse, said, I do greatly doubt that all this enterprise will be like the tale or interlude of the pitcher full of milk, wherewith a Shoemaker made himself rich in conceit: but, when the pitcher was broken, he had not whereupon to dine: what do you pretend by these large Conquests? what shall be the end of so many labours and crosses? Thus it shall be (said Picrochole) that when we are returned, we shall sit down, rest and be merry. But (said Echephron,) if by chance you should never come back, for the voyage is long and dangerous, were it not better for us to take our rest now, then unnecessarily to expose our selves to so many dangers? O (said Swashbuckler,) by G—, here is a good dotard, come, let us go hide our selves in the corner of a chimney, and there spend the whole time of our life amongst ladies, in threading of pearles, or spinning like Sardanapalus: He that nothing ventures, hath neither horse nor mule, (sayes Solomon). He who adventureth too much (said Echephron) loseth both horse and mule, answered Malchon. Enough (said Picrochole,) go forward: I feare nothing, but that these devillish legions of Grangousier, whilest we are in Mesopotamia, will come on our backs, and charge up our reer, what course shall we then take? what shall be our remedy? A very good one (said Durtaille), a pretty little commission, which you must send unto the Muscoviters, shall bring you into the field in an instant foure hundred and fifty thousand choice men of warre. O that you would but make me your Lieutenant General, I should for the lightest faults of any inflict great punishments. I fret, I charge, I strike, I take, I kill, I slay, I play the devil. On, on, (said Picrochole) make haste, my lads, and let him that loves me, follow me.

[With a small party of friends, Gargantua hurries home. He first encounters and defeats a body of the enemy at a castle at the Ford of Vede.]

Then Gargantua mounted his great Mare, accompanied as we have said before, and finding in his way a high and great tree, (which

commonly was called by the name of St. Martins tree, because heretofore St. Martin planted a pilgrims staffe there, which in tract of
time grew to that height and greatnesse,) said, This is that which
I lacked; this tree shall serve me both for a staffe and lance: with
that he pulled it up easily, plucked off the boughs, and trimmed it at
his pleasure. Gargantua, being come to the place of the wood of Vede,
was informed by Eudemon, that there was some of the enemy within
the Castle, which to know, Gargantua cried out as loud as he was
able, Are you there, or are you not there? if you be there, be there
no more; and if you are not there, I have no more to say. But a
ruffian gunner, whose charge was to attend the Portcullis over the
gate, let flie a cannon-ball at him, and hit him with that shot most
furiously on the right temple of his head, yet did him no more hurt,
then if he had but cast a prune or kernel of a wine-grape at him:
What is this? (said Gargantua) do you throw at us grape-kernels
here? the vintage shall cost you dear, thinking indeed that the bullet
had been the kernel of a grape, or raisin-kernel.

Those who were within the Castle, when they heard this noise,
ran to the towers and fortresses, from whence they shot at him above
nine thousand and five and twenty falconshot and harcabusades,
aiming all at his head, and so thick did they shoot at him, that he
cried out, Ponocrates my friend, these flies here are like to put out
mine eyes, give me a branch of those willow-trees to drive them away,
thinking that the bullets and stones shot out of the great ordnance
had been but flies. Ponocrates looked and saw that there were no flies,
but great shot which they had shot from the Castle. Then was it that
he rusht with his great tree against the Castle, and with mighty blowes
overthrew both towers and fortresses, and laid all level with the
ground, by which means all that were within were slaine and broken
in pieces. Going from thence, they came to the bridge at the Mill.
There they were at a stand, consulting how they might passe. But
Gymnast said, if the devils have past there, I will passe well enough.
The devils have past there (said Eudemon,) to carry away the
damned soules. By St. Rhenian (said Ponocrates) then by necessary
consequence he shall passe there. Yes, yes, (said Gymnastes) or I
shall stick in the way: then setting spurs to his horse, he past through
freely. The other three followed him very close, except Eudemon only,
whose horses foreright or far forefoot sank up to the knee in the
paunch of a great fat chuffe, who lay there upon his back drowned,
and could not get it out: there was he pestered, until Gargantua with

the end of his staffe thrust down the rest of the villains tripes into the water, whilest the horse pulled out his foot; and the said horse was throughly cured of a ringbone which he had in that foot, by this touch of the burst guts of that great loobie.

Being come out of the river of Vede, they came very shortly after to Grangousiers Castle, who waited for them with great longing; at their coming they were entertained with many congies, and cherished with embraces, never was seen a more joyful company. The truth was, that Gargantua, in shifting his clothes, and combing his head with a combe, which was nine hundred foot long and whereof the teeth were great tusts of Elephants, whole and entire, he made fall at every rake above seven balls of bullets, at a dozen the ball, that stuck in his haire, at the razing of the Castle of the wood of Vede, which his father Grangousier seeing, thought they had been lice, and said unto him, What, my dear sonne, hast thou brought us this farre some short-winged hawkes of the Colledge of Mountague? I did not mean that thou shouldest reside there. Then answered Ponocrates, My sovereign Lord, think not that I have placed him in that lowsie Colledge, which they call Montague; I had rather have put him amongst the gravediggers of Sanct Innocent. Then, taking up one of these bullets, he said, These are cannon-shot, which your sonne Gargantua hath lately received by the treachery of your enemies, as he was passing before the Wood of Vede.

But they have been so rewarded, that they are all destroyed in the ruine of the Castle, as were the Philistines by the policy of Samson, and those whom the tower of Silohim slew, as it is written in the thirteenth of Luke. My opinion is, that we pursue them whilest the luck is on our side, for occasion hath all her haire on her forehead, when she is past, you may not recal her, she hath no tuft whereby you can lay hold on her, for she is bald in the hind-part of her head, and never returneth again. Truly (said Grangousier,) it shall not be at this time; for I will make you a feast this night, and bid you welcome.

This said, they made ready supper, and of extraordinary besides his daily fare, were rosted sixteen oxen, three heifers, two and thirty calves, threescore and three fat kids, fourscore and fifteen wethers, three hundred farrow pigs or sheats sowced in sweet wine or must, eleven score partridges, seven hundred snites and woodcocks, foure hundred Loudun and Cornwal-capons, six thousand pullets, and as many pigeons, six hundred crammed hens, fourteen hundred leverets, or young hares and rabbets, three hundred and three buzzards, and one thousand and seven hundred cockrels. For venison, they could not so suddenly come by it, only eleven wilde bores, which the Abbot of Turpenay sent, and eighteen fallow deer which the Lord of Gramount bestowed; together with seven score phesants, which were sent by the Lord of Essars; and some dozens of queests, coushots, ringdoves, and woodculvers; Riverfowl, teales and awteals, bitterns, courtes, plovers, francolins, briganders, tyrasons, young lapwings, tame ducks, shovelers, woodlanders, herons, moore-hens, criels, storks, canepetiers, oranges, flamans, which are phænicopters, or crimson-winged sea-fowles, terrigoles, turkies, arbens, coots, solingeese, curlews, termagants and waterwagtails, with a great deal of cream, curds and fresh cheese, and store of soupe, pottages, and brewis with great variety. Without doubt there was meat enough, and it was handsomly drest by Snapsauce, Hotchpot and Brayverjuice, Grangousiers Cooks. Jenkin Trudg-apace and Cleanglasse were very careful to fill them drink.

The story requireth, that we relate that which happened unto six Pilgrims, who came from Sebastian near to Nantes: and who for shelter that night, being afraid of the enemy, had hid themselves in the garden among the cabbages and lettices. Gargantua finding himself somewhat dry, asked whether they could get any lettice to make him a sallet; and hearing that there were the greatest and fairest in the countrey (for they were as great as plum-trees, or as walnut-trees,) he would go thither himself, and brought thence in his hand what he thought good, and withal carried away the six Pilgrims who were in so great feare, that they did not dare to speak nor cough.

Washing them therefore first at the fountain, the Pilgrims said one to another softly, What shall we do? we are almost drowned here amongst these lettice, shall we speak? but if we speak, he will kill us for spies: and, as they were thus deliberating what to do, Gargantua put them with the lettice into a platter of the house, as large as the huge tun of the White Friars of the Cistertian order, which done, with oile, vinegar and salt he ate them up, to refresh himself a little before supper: and had already swallowed up five of the Pilgrims, the six being in the platter, totally hid under a lettice, except his bourdon or staffe that appeared, and nothing else. Which Grangousier seeing, said to Gargantua, I think that is the horne of a shell-snail, do not eat it. Why not, (said Gargantua) they are good all this moneth, which he no sooner said, but, drawing up the staffe, and therewith taking up the Pilgrim, he ate him very well, then drank a terrible draught of excellent white wine. The

Pilgrims, thus devoured, made shift to save themselves as well as they could, by withdrawing their bodies out of the reach of the grinders of his teeth, but could not escape from thinking they had been put in the lowest dungeon of a prison. And when Gargantua whiffed the great draught, they thought to have been drowned in his mouth, and the flood of wine had almost carried them away into the gulf of his stomack. Neverthelesse skipping with their bourdons, as St. Michaels Palmers use to do, they sheltered themselves from the danger of that inundation under the banks of his teeth. But one of them by chance, groping or sounding the countrey with his staffe, to try whether they were in safety or no, struck hard against the cleft of a hollow tooth, and hit the mandibulary sinew, or nerve of the jaw, which put Gargantua to very great pain, so that he began to cry for the rage that he felt; to ease himself therefore of his smarting ache, he called for his toothpicker, and rubbing towards a young walnut-tree, where they lay skulking, unnestled you my Gentlemen Pilgrims.

For he caught one by the legs, another by the scrip, another by the pocket, another by the scarf, another by the band of the breeches, and the poor fellow that had hurt him with the bourdon, him he hooked to him by the Codpiece, which snatch neverthelesse did him a great deal of good, for it pierced unto him a pockie botch he had in the groine, which grievously tormented him. The Pilgrims thus dislodged ran away athwart the Plain a pretty fast pace, and the paine ceased, even just at the time when by Eudemon he was called to supper, for all was ready.

When Gargantua was set down at table, after all of them had somewhat stayed their stomacks by a snatch or two of the first bits eaten heartily; Grangousier began to relate the source and cause of the warre, raised between him and Picrochole: and came to tell how Friar Jhon had triumphed at the defence of the close of the Abbey, and extolled him for his valour. Then Gargantua desired that he might be presently sent for, to the end that with him they might consult of what was to be done; whereupon, by a joynt consent, his steward went for him, and brought him along merrily, with his staffe of the Crosse, upon Grangousiers mule: when he was come, a thousand huggings, a thousand embracements, a thousand good dayes were given: Ha, Friar Jhon, my friend, Friar Jhon, my brave cousin, Friar Jhon from the devil: let me clip thee (my heart) about the neck, to me an armesful; I must gripe thee (my ballock), till thy back crack with it, Come (my cod) let me coll thee till I kill thee. And Friar Jhon, the gladdest man in the world, never was man made welcomer, never was any more courteously and graciously received then Friar Jhon. Come, come, (said Gargantua,) a stool here close by me at this end. I am content, (said the Monk), seeing you will have it so. Some water (page); fill, my boy, fill, it is to refresh my liver; give me some, (childe) to gargle my throat withal. *Deposita cappa,* (said Gymnast), let us pull off this frock. Ho, by G—, Gentleman (said the Monk) there is a chapter *in statutis ordinis,* which opposeth my laying of it down. Pish (said Gymnast) a fig for your chapter, this frock breaks both your shoulders, put it off. My friend (said the Monk) let me alone with it; for by G—, I'le drink the better that it is on: It makes all my body jocund; if I should lay it aside, the waggish Pages would cut to themselves garters out of it, as I was once served at Coulaines; and, which is worse, I shall lose my appetite: but if in this habit I sit down at table, I will drink by G—, both to thee and to thy horse, and so courage, frolick, God save the company: I have already sup't, yet will I eat never a whit the lesse for that; for I have a stomack as hollow as a But of malvoisie. And lustie my lads, some bousing liquour, Page! so: Crack, crack, crack. O how good is God that gives us of this excellent juice! I call him to witnesse, if I had been in the time of Jesus Christ, I would have kept him from being taken by the Jewes in the garden of Olivet: and the devil faile me, if I should have failed to cut off the hams of these Gentlemen Apostles, who ran away so basely after they had well supped, and left their good Master in the lurch. I hate that man worse than poison that offers to run away, when he should fight and lay stoutly about him. Oh that I were but King of France for forescore or a hundred years! By G— I should whip like curtail-dogs these runawayes of Pavie: A plague take them, why did they not chuse rather to die there, then to leave their good Prince in that pinch and necessity? Is it not better and more honourable to perish in fighting valiantly, then to live in disgrace by a cowardly running away? We are like to eate no great store of goslings this yeare, therefore, friend, reach me some of that rosted pig there.

Thus went out those valiant champions on their adventure, in full resolution, to know what enterprise they should undertake, and what to take heed of, and look well to, in the day of the great and horrible battel. And the Monk encouraged them, saying, My children, do not feare nor doubt, I will conduct you safely; God and Sanct Benedict be with us. If I had strength answerable to my courage, by Sdeath, I would plume them for you like ducks. I feare nothing but the great ordnance; yet I know of a charm by way of Prayer, which the sub-sexton of our Abbey taught me, that will preserve a man from the violence of guns, and all manner of fire-weapons and engines, but it will do me no good, because I do not believe it. Neverthelesse, I hope my staffe of the crosse shall this day play devillish pranks amongst them; by G— whoever of our Party shall offer to play the duck, and shrink when blowes are a dealing, I give myself to the devil, if I do not make a Monk of him in my stead, and hamper him within my frock, which is a sovereign cure against cowardise. Did you never heare of my Lord Meurles his grey-hound, which was not worth a straw in the fields; he put a frock about his neck; by the body of G—, there was neither hare nor fox that could escape him. The Monk uttering these words in choler, as he past under a walnut-tree, in his way toward the Causey, he broached the vizor of his helmet, on the stump of a great branch of the said tree: nevertheless, he met his spurres so fiercely to the horse, who was full of mettal, and quick on the spurre, that he bounded forwards, and the Monk, going about to ungrapple his vizor, let go his hold of the bridle, and so hanged by his hand upon the bough, whilest his horse stole away from under him. By this meanes was the Monk left, hanging on the walnut-tree, and crying for help, murther, murther, swearing also that he was betrayed: Eudemon perceived him first, and calling Gargantua said, Sir, come and see Absalom hanging. Gargantua being come, considered the countenance of the Monk, and in what posture he hanged; wherefore he said to Eudemon, You were mistaken in comparing him to Absalom; for Absalom hung by his haire, but this shaveling Monk hangeth by the eares. Help me (said the Monk) in the devils name, is this a time for you to prate? you seem to me to be like the decretalist preachers, who say, that whosoever shall see his neighbour in the danger of death, ought upon pain of excommunication, rather choose to admonish him to make his Confession to a Priest, and put his conscience in the state of Peace, then otherwise to help and relieve him.

And therefore when I shall see them fallen into a river, and ready to be drowned, I shall make them a faire long sermon *de contemptu mundi, et fuga seculi;* and when they are stark dead, shall then go to their aid and succour in fishing after them: Be quiet (said Gymnast,) and stirre not my minion; I am now coming to unhang thee, and to set thee at freedome, for thou art a pretty little gentle Monachus. I have seen above five hundred hanged, but I never saw any have a better countenance in his dangling and pendilatory swagging;

truly, if I had so good a one, I would willingly hang thus all my lifetime. What? (said the Monk) have you almost done preaching: help
me, in the name of God, seeing you will not in the name of the other
spirit, or by the habit which I wear you shall repent it.

Then Gymnast alighted from his horse and, climbing up the
walnut-tree, lifted up the Monk with one hand, by the gushets of his
armour under the arm-pits, and with the other undid his vizor from
the stump of the broken branch, which done, he let him fall to the
ground and himself after. As soon as the Monk was down, he put off
all his armour, and threw away one piece after another about the field,
and taking to him again his staffe of the Crosse, remounted up to his
horse, which Eudemon had caught. Then went they on merrily, riding
along on the high way.

Meanwhile Picrochole sent under the command and conduct of
the Count Draw-forth the number of sixteen hundred horsemen. Being
come down towards Seville, they were heard by Gargantua, who said
then unto those that were with him, Camerades and fellow souldiers,
we have here met with an encounter, and they are ten times in number
more than we: shall we charge them or no? What a devil (said the
Monk), shall we do else? Do you esteem men by their number, rather
then by their valour and prowes? With this he cried out, Charge,
devils, charge; which when the enemies heard, they thought certainly
that they had been very devils, and therefore even then began all of
them to run away as hard as they could drive, Draw-forth only excepted,
who immediately settled his lance on its rest, and therewith hit the
Monk with all his force on the very middle of his breast, but, coming
against his horrifick frock, the point of the iron, being with the blow
either broke off or blunted, it was in matter of execution, as if you
had struck against an Anvil with a little wax-candle.

Then did the Monk, with his staffe of the Crosse, give him such
a sturdie thump and whirret betwixt his neck and shoulders, upon the
Acromion bone, that he made him lose both sense and motion, and
fall down stone dead at his horses feet.

Then ran he after them at a swift and full gallup, till he overtook
the reere, and felled them down like tree-leaves, striking athwart
and alongst and every way, charging all he overtook, and giving
quarter to none, until he met with a trouper, who carried behinde him
one of the poor pilgrims, and there would have rifled him. The Pilgrim, in hope of relief at the sight of the Monk, cried out, Ha, my Lord
Prior, my good friend, my Lord Prior, save me, I beseech you, save

me; which words being heard by those that rode in the van, they instantly faced about, and seeing there was no body but the Monk that made this great havock and slaughter among them, they loded him with blows as thick as they use to do an Asse with wood: but of all this he felt nothing, especially when they struck upon his frock, his skin was so hard. Then they committed him to two of the Marshals men to keep, and looking about, saw nobody coming against them, whereupon they thought that Gargantua and his Party were fled: then was it that they rode as hard as they could towards the walnut-trees to meet with them, and left the Monk there all alone, with his two foresaid men to guard him. Gargantua heard the noise and neighing of the horses, and said to his men, Camerades, I hear the track and beating of the enemies horse-feet, and withall perceive that some of them come in a troupe and full body against us; let us rallie and close here, then set forward in order, and by this means we shall be able to receive their charge, to their losse and our honour.

The Monk seeing them break off thus without order, conjectured that they were to set upon Gargantua and those that were with him, and was wonderfully grieved that he could not succour them; then considered he the countenance of the two keepers in whose custody he was, who would have willingly runne after the troops to get some booty and plunder, and were alwayes looking towards the valley unto which they were going; farther, he syllogized, saying, These men are but badly skilled in matters of warre, for they have not required my paroll, neither have they taken my sword from me; suddenly hereafter he drew his brackmard or horsemans sword, wherewith he gave the keeper which held him, on the right side such a sound slash, that he cut clean thorough the jugularie veins, and the sphagitid or transparent arteries of the neck, with the fore-part of the throat called the gargareon; and redoubling the blow, he opened the spinal marrow betwixt the second and third verteber; there fell down that keeper stark dead to the ground. Then the Monk, reining his horse to the left, ranne upon the other, who seeing his fellow dead, and the Monk to have the advantage of him, cried with a loud voice, Ha, my Lord Prior, quarter, I yeeld, my Lord Prior, quarter, quarter, my good friend, my Lord Prior: and the Monk cried likewise, my Lord Posterior, my friend, my Lord Posterior, you shall have it upon your posteriorums. Ha, said the keeper, my Lord Prior, my Minion, my Gentile Lord Prior, I pray God make you an Abbot. By the habit (said the Monk), which I weare, I will here make you a Cardinal; you shall therefore have by and by a red hat of my giving: and the fellow cried, Ha, my Lord Prior, my Lord Prior, my Lord Abbot that shall be, my Lord Cardinal, my Lord all, ha, ha, hes, no my Lord Prior, my good little Lord the Prior, I yeeld, render and deliver my self up to you: and I deliver thee (said the Monk), to all the Devils in hell; then at one stroak he cut off his head, cutting his scalp upon the temple-bones, and lifting up in the upper part of the scul the two triangularie bones called sincipital, or the two bones bregmatis, together with the sagittal commissure or dart-like seame which distinguisheth the right side of the head from the left, as also a great part of the coronal or forehead-bone, by which terrible blow likewise he cut the two meninges or filmes which inwrap the braine, and made a deep wound in the braine's two posterior ventricles, and the cranium or skull abode hanging upon his shoulders by the skin of the pericranium behinde, in forme of a Doctors bonnet, black without and red within. Thus fell he down also to the ground stark dead.

And presently the Monk gave his horse the spurre, and kept the way that the enemy held, who had met with Gargantua and his companions in the broad highway, and were so diminished of their number, for the enormous slaughter that Gargantua had made with his great tree amongst them, as also Gymnast, Ponocrates, Eudemon, and the rest, that they began to retreat disorderly and in great haste. The Monk, perceiving that their whole intent was to betake themselves to their heels, alighted from his horse, and got upon a big large rock, which was in the way, and with his great Brackmard sword laid such load upon those runawayes, and with maine strength fetching a compasse with his arme without feigning or sparing, slew and overthrew so many, that his sword broke in two pieces. Then thought he within himself that he had slaine and killed sufficiently.

[After these doughty deeds, the Monk, feeling a little weary and furiously hungry and thirsty, rejoins Gargantua, Eudemon, and the others, and the whole party retires to Grangousier's castle, where a mighty breakfast awaits the warriors. After breakfast a council of war is held, at which it is decided that the Gargantuists shall assault Picrochole and his main army where they have established themselves in the city of Clermond, situated almost impregnably on top of a precipitous and rocky hill.]

Gargantua had the charge of the whole Army. Having thus set forward, as soon as they had gained the Passe at the Ford of Vede, with boats and bridges speedily made they past over in a trice, then considering the situation of the town, which was on a high and advantageous place, Gargantua thought fit to call his counsel, and passe that night in deliberation upon what was to be done: But Gymnast said unto him, My sovereign Lord, such is the nature and complexion of the Frenches, that they are worth nothing, but at the first push, then are they more fierce than devils; but if they linger a little, and be wearied with delays, they'll prove more faint and remisse than women: my opinion is therefore, that now presently after your men have taken breath, and some small refection, you give order for a resolute assault, and that we storme them instantly. His advice was found very good, and for effectuating thereof, he brought forth his army into the plain field, and placed the reserves on the skirt or rising of a little hill. The Monk took along with him six companies of foot, and two hundred horsemen well armed, and with great diligence crossed the marish, and valiantly got up on the top of the green hillock, even unto the high-way which leads to Loudin. Whilest the assault was thus begun, Picrocholes men could not tell well what was best, to issue out and receive the Assailants, or keep within the town and not to stirre: Himself in the mean time, without deliberation, sallied forth in a rage with the cavalry of his guard, who were forthwith received, and royally entertained with great cannon-shot, that fell upon them like haile from the high grounds, on which the Artillery was planted; whereupon the Gargantuists betook themselves unto the valleys, to give the ordnance leave to play, and range with the larger scope.

Those of the town defended themselves as well as they could, but their shot past over us, without doing us any hurt at all: Some of Picrocholes men, that had escaped our Artillery, set most fiercely upon our souldiers, but prevailed little; for they were all let in betwixt the files, and there knock't down to the ground, which their fellow-souldiers seeing, they would have retreated, but the Monk having seised upon the Passe, by the which they were to return, they ran away and fled in all the disorder and confusion that could be imagined.

Some would have pursued after them, and followed the chase, but the Monk withheld them, apprehending that in their pursuit the Pursuers might lose their ranks, and so give occasion to the besieged to sallie out of the town upon them. Then staying there some space, and none coming against them, he sent the Duke Phrontist, to advise Gargantua to advance towards the hill up on the left hand, to hinder Picrocholes retreat at that gate, which Gargantua did with all expedition, and sent thither foure brigades under the conduct of Sebast, which had no sooner reach't the top of the hill, but they met Picrochole in the teeth, and those that were with him scattered.

Then charged they upon them stoutly, yet were they much in-damaged by those that were upon the walles, who galled them with all manner of shot, both from the great ordnance, small guns and bowes. Which Gargantua perceiving, he went with a strong Partie to their relief, and with his Artillery began to thunder so terribly upon that canton of the wall, and so long, that all the strength within the town, to maintain and fill up the breach, was drawn thither. The Monk, seeing that quarter which he kept besieged, void of men and competent guards, and in a manner altogether naked and abandoned, did most magnanimously on a sudden lead up his men towards the fort, and never left it till he had got up upon it.

Neverthelesse he gave no alarm till all his souldiers had got within the wall, except the two hundred horsemen, whom he left without to secure his entry, then did he give a most horrible shout, so did all these who were with him, and immediately thereafter without resist-ance, putting to the edge of the sword the guard that was at that gate, they opened it to the horsemen, with whom most furiously they altogether ran towards the East-gate, where all the hurlie burlie was, and coming close upon them in the reer, overthrew all their forces. The besieged seeing that the Gargantuists had won the town upon them, and that they were like to be secure in no corner of it, sub-mitted themselves unto the mercy of the Monk, and asked for quarter, which the Monk very nobly granted to them, yet made them lay down their armes; then shutting them up within Churches, gave order to seise upon all the staves of the Crosses, and placed men at the doores to keep them from coming forth; then opening that East-gate, he issued out to succour and assist Gargantua; but Picrochole, thinking it had been some relief coming to him from the towne, ad-ventured more forwardly then before, and was upon the giving of a most desperate home-charge, when Gargantua cried out, Ha, Friar Jhon, my friend, Friar Jhon, you are come in a good houre; which unexpected accident so affrighted Picrochole and his men, that giving all for lost, they betook themselves to their heels, and fled on all hands. Gargantua chased them till they came near to Vaugaudry, killing and slaying all the way, and then sounded the retreat.

Picrochole thus in despaire, fled towards the Bouchard Island, and in the way to Riveere his horse stumbled and fell down, whereat he on a sudden was so incensed, that he with his sword without more ado killed him in his choler; then not finding any that would remount him, he was about to have taken an Asse at the Mill that was thereby: but the Millers men did so baste his bones, and so soundly bethwack him, that they made him both black and blew with strokes; then, stripping him of all his clothes, gave him a scurvie old canvas jacket wherewith to cover his nakednesse. Thus went along this poor cholerick wretch. What is become of him since we cannot certainly tell. The first thing Gargantua did after his return into the town was to call the Muster-roll of his men, which when he had done, he found that there were very few either killed or wounded. Then he caused them all at and in their several posts and divisions to take a little refreshment, which was very plenteously provided for them in the best drink and victuals that could be had for money, and gave order to the Treasurers and Commissaries of the Army, to pay for and defray that repast, and that there should be no outrage at all, nor abuse committed in the town, seeing it was his own. And furthermore commanded, that immediately after the souldiers had done with eating and drinking for that time sufficiently, and to their own hearts desire, a gathering should be beaten for bringing them altogether, to be drawn up on the Piazza before the Castle, there to receive six moneths pay compleatly, all which was done. After this by his direction, were brought before him in the said place, all those that remained of Picrocholes party, unto whom in the presence of the Princes, Nobles, and Officers of his Court and Army, he spoke as followeth.

Our forefathers and Ancestors of all times, have been of this nature and disposition, that, upon the winning of a battel, they have chosen rather for a signe and memorial of their triumphs and victories, to erect trophies and monuments in the hearts of the vanquished by clemencie, then by architecture in the lands which they had conquered; for they did hold in greater estimation, the lively remembrance of men purchased by liberality, then the dumb inscription of arches, pillars and pyramides, subject to the injury of stormes and tempests, and to the envie of every one. All this hemisphere of the world was filled with the praises and congratulations which your selves and your fathers made, when Alpharbal King of Canarre, not satisfied with his own fortunes, did most furiously invade the land of Onyx, and with cruel Piracies molest all the Armorick islands, and confine regions of Britanie; yet was he in a set naval fight justly taken and vanquished by my father, whom God preserve and protect. But what? whereas other Kings and Emperours, yea those who entitle themselves Catholiques, would have dealt roughly with him, kept him a close prisoner, and put him to an extream high ransom: he intreated him very courteously, lodged him kindly with himself in his own Palace, and out of his incredible mildnesse and gentle disposition sent him back with a safe conduct, loaden with gifts, loaden with favours, loaden with all offices of friendship: what fell out upon it? Being returned into his countrey, he called a Parliament, where all the Princes and States of his Kingdom being assembled, he shewed them the humanity which he had found in us, and therefore wished them to take such course by way of compensation therein, as that the whole world might be edified by the example, as well of their honest graciousnesse to us, as of our gracious honesty towards them. The result hereof was, that it was voted and decreed by an unanimous consent, that they should offer up entirely their Lands, Dominions and Kingdomes, to be disposed of by us according to our pleasure.

Alpharbal in his own person, presently returned with nine thousand and thirty eight great ships of burden, bringing with him the treasures, not only of his house and royal lineage, but almost of all the countrey besides.

Being safely arrived, he came to my said father, and would have kist his feet: that action was found too submissively low, and therefore was not permitted, but in exchange he was most cordially embraced: he offered his presents, they were not received, because they were too excessive: he yielded himself voluntarily a servant and vassal, and was content his whole posterity should be liable to the same bondage; this was not accepted of, because it seemed not equitable: he surrendered by vertue of the decree of his great Parliamentarie councel, his whole Countreys and Kingdomes to him, offering the Deed and Conveyance, signed, sealed and ratified by all those that were concerned in it; this was altogether refused, and the parchments cast into the fire. In end, this free good will, and simple meaning of the Canarriens wrought such tendernesse in my fathers heart, that he could not abstain from shedding teares, and wept most profusely: then, by choise words very congrously adapted, strove in what he could to diminish the estimation of the good offices which he had

done them. But so much the more did Alpharbal augment the repute
thereof. What was the issue? They made themselves perpetual tribu-
taries, and obliged to give us every year two millions of gold at foure
and twenty carats fine. The first year we received the whole sum of
two millions: the second yeare of their own accord they payed freely
to us three and twenty hundred thousand crowns: the third year six
and twenty hundred thousand; the fourth year, three millions, and
do so increase it alwayes out of their own good will, that we shall be
constrained to forbid them to bring us any more. This is the nature
of gratitude and true thankfulnesse. For time, which gnawes and
diminisheth all things else, augments and increaseth benefits; because
a noble action of liberality, done to a man of reason, doth grow continually, by his generous thinking of it, and remembring it.

Being unwilling therefore any way to degenerate from the hereditary mildnesse and clemencie of my Parents, I do now forgive you,
deliver you from all fines and imprisonments, fully release you, set
you at liberty, and every way make you as frank and free as ever
you were before. Moreover, at your going out of the gate, you shall
have every one of you three moneths pay to bring you home into your
houses and families. God be with you. I am sorry from my heart that
Picrochole is not here; for I would have given him to understand,
that this warre was undertaken against my will, and without any hope
to increase either my goods or renown: but seeing he is lost, it is my
will that his Kingdome remain entire to his sonne; who, because he
is too young, (he not being yet full five yeares old,) shall be brought
up and instructed by the ancient Princes, and learned men of the
Kingdom. And because a Realm thus desolate, may easily come to
ruine; if the covetousnesse and avarice of those, who by their places
are obliged to administer justice in it, be not curbed and restrained:
I ordain and will have it so, that Ponocrates be overseer and super-
intendent above all his governours, with whatever power and authority
is requisite thereto, and that he be continually with the childe, until
he finde him able and capable to rule and govern by himself.

Now I must tell you, that you are to understand how a too feeble
and dissolute facility in pardoning evil-doers, giveth them occasion
to commit wickednesse afterwards more readily, upon this pernicious
confidence of receiving favour. It is my will and pleasure, that you
deliver over unto me, before you depart hence, first, that fine fellow
Marquet, who was the prime cause, origin and ground-work of this
warre, by his vain presumption and overweening: secondly, his fellow

cake-bakers, who were neglective in checking and reprehending his idle haire-brain'd humour in the instant time: and lastly, all the Councillors, Captains, Officers and Domesticks of Picrochole, who had been incendiaries or fomenters of the warre, by provoking, praising or counselling him to come out of his limits thus to trouble us.

[As a reward for the Monk's services Grangousier endowed and built for him the abbey of Theleme. Here he established his own monastic order, which was the direct opposite of those in existence: both men and women were admitted, anyone was free to leave at any time, and there was, in fact, only one rule—"Do what thou wilt."

Book II relates the birth and upbringing of Gargantua's son Pantagruel, particularly his escapades with his droll friend Panurge, a confirmed practical joker. There is also a war with the kingdom of the Dipsodes, in which the Pantagruelians are victorious.

In Book III Panurge considers marriage and, wondering how it would turn out, visits every sort of soothsayer, conjuror, and oracle. Finally, he sets out on a long expedition by sea to visit the Oracle of Bacbuc, the Holy Bottle.

In Books IV and V the travels of this expedition are told. Many strange islands are visited, each of which gives Rabelais his chance to satirize some particular folly or institution. After many adventures, the group reaches the Oracle of the Bottle. At the end of long and intricate ceremonies, Panurge at last stands before the Bottle himself, ready to hear the word of final wisdom. And he hears exactly one word—"Drink!"]

MONTAIGNE

Essays

MICHEL EYQUEM DE MONTAIGNE (1533-1592) was born in his father's château near Bordeaux, and was carefully educated in the manner described in one of the following selections. At the age of six he went to a "college" at Bordeaux, where he completed his studies seven years later. After devoting some years to the study of law, he became a person of some importance. In 1557 he served as a Councillor in the Parliament of Bordeaux, and soon thereafter he began to receive marks of royal favor culminating in the highest honor possible to the nobility of France, admission to the Order of St. Michael. The diplomatic missions with which he was entrusted and his surviving correspondence with kings show that he was a man of real importance to the French monarchy.

At the age of thirty-seven, however, he withdrew from a promising career and retired to his own château to devote himself to the reading and reflection which produced his *Essays*. The first two books of these were published in 1580, towards the end of this first period of retirement. After eight years of this life he set out for Italy in search of mineral waters that were expected to improve his health. He was still there when he received the news that he had been named Mayor of Bordeaux. Having no desire for the position, he said as much, but the insistence of the city was reinforced by a letter from Henry III saying, "It is my desire, and I specifically require and command you to proceed without delay to assume the duties to which you have been so legitimately summoned." Montaigne had no choice: he served one two-year term, and was the third mayor in the city's history to be re-elected for a second term. Having thus done his duty, he again retired to his estate, and his last years, though interrupted occasionally by public duties, were largely devoted to enlarging and revising the *Essays*.

Montaigne was essentially a thoughtful spectator of life. He was well equipped to shine in the game, but actual participation deprived him of the serenity and the disinterested point of view necessary for understanding it, and that was his chief interest. Hence he repeatedly reaffirmed his choice of meditation in preference to action. During his later years he enjoyed the confidence of those two arch-enemies in politics and religion, Henry of Navarre (soon to become Henry IV) and the Duke of Guise. At one time he was called on to negotiate between them. Clearly, a brilliant political career was his for the asking, but he preferred to go back to his château—and write the essay "On the Inconvenience of Greatness."

In the *Essays,* Montaigne considers almost every kind of subject, always with interest and wisdom. In spite of his learning, it is this quality of human wisdom that has preserved his writings for nearly four centuries. He is often referred to as a philosopher, but the term cannot be applied to him in the same sense as to the builders of logical systems, for what he created for himself was not a philosophical system, but a philosophy of life. The difference is clearly seen in his skepticism. He adopted the motto "What do I know?" not as an abstract thinker who had proved the fallibility of human thought, but as a man who had noticed, both in history and life, how often people were mistaken. Above all, he saw the people of France cutting each other's throats over religious differences. "Since a wise man may be wrong, or a hundred men, or several nations, and since even human nature (as we think) goes wrong for several centuries on this matter or on that, how can we be certain that it occasionally stops going wrong, and that in this century it is not mistaken?" If Montaigne's contemporaries could have grasped such a practical skepticism, a generation of bloodshed would have been avoided.

Since the beginning of the seventeenth century, the *Essays* have been an essential part of the world's thought. Eleven years after Montaigne's death, John Florio published an English translation (1603) which became one of the most widely read of all Elizabethan books. The list of English writers influenced by these *Essays* begins immediately with Bacon and Shakespeare, and comes down to the present. The ideas of Montaigne have gained wide currency, but in the last analysis he is read more for himself than for his thoughts. He allows the reader to overhear the casual meditations of an experienced and learned man who viewed everything, including himself, with a tolerant understanding. But on this personal aspect of the book the best introduction is that written by Montaigne himself for the first edition of the *Essays*:

"Reader, here is an honest book. It warns you at the beginning that my only purpose has been domestic and private: I have given no consideration to your profit or to my reputation, for my powers are not equal to such an undertaking. I have dedicated it to the special convenience of my relatives and friends, so that, having lost me (as they must soon do), they will here be able to retrieve some traits of my character and moods, and that thus they may keep their knowledge of me more complete and alive. If I had sought the favor of the world, I would have adorned myself with borrowed beauties; but I wish to be seen in my simple, natural, everyday manner, without study or artifice, for it is myself that I am drawing. Here my defects can be seen to the life, with my imperfections and my natural form, as far as public respect has permitted it. For if I had been among those nations which are said still to live under the sweet liberty of the original laws of nature, I assure you that I would most gladly have painted myself at full length and naked. Thus, reader, I myself am the subject of my book. There is no reason for you to spend your leisure on such a slight and vain subject. Farewell, then."

ESSAYS

OF THE EDUCATION OF CHILDREN

...A friend of mine, then, having read the preceding chapter,[1] the other day told me, that I should a little farther have extended my discourse on the education of children. Now, madam, if I had any sufficiency in this subject, I could not possibly better employ it, than to present my best instructions to the little gentleman that threatens you shortly with a happy birth (for you are too generous to begin otherwise than with a male); for having had so great a hand in the treaty of your marriage, I have a certain particular right and interest in the greatness and prosperity of the issue that shall spring from it; besides that, your having had the best of my services so long in possession, sufficiently obliges me to desire the honour and advantage of all wherein you shall be concerned. But, in truth, all I understand as to that particular is only this, that the greatest and most important difficulty of human science is the education of children. For as in agriculture, the husbandry that is to precede planting, as also planting itself, is certain, plain, and well known; but after that which is planted comes to life, there is a great deal more to be done, more art to be used, more care to be taken, and much more difficulty to cultivate and bring it to perfection: so it is with men; it is no hard matter to get children; but after they are born, then begins the trouble, solicitude, and care rightly to train, principle, and bring them up. The symptoms of their inclinations in that tender age are so obscure, and the promises so uncertain and fallacious, that it is very hard to establish any solid judgment or conjecture upon them. Cubs of bears and puppies readily discover their natural inclination; but men, so soon as ever they are grown up, applying themselves to certain habits, engaging themselves in certain opinions, and conforming themselves to particular laws and customs, easily alter, or at least disguise, their true and real disposition; and yet it is hard to force the propension of nature. Whence it comes to pass, that for not having chosen the right course, we often take very great pains, and consume a good part of our time in training up children to things, for which, by their natural constitution, they are totally unfit. In this difficulty, nevertheless, I am clearly of opinion, that they ought

1. "Of Pedantry."

804

to be elemented in the best and most advantageous studies, without taking too much notice of, or being too superstitious in those light prognostics they give of themselves in their tender years, and to which Plato, in his Republic, gives, methinks, too much authority.

Madam, science[2] is a very great ornament, and a thing of marvellous use, especially in persons raised to that degree of fortune in which you are. And, in truth, in persons of mean and low condition, it cannot perform its true and genuine office, being naturally more prompt to assist in the conduct of war, in the government of peoples, in negotiating the leagues and friendships of princes and foreign nations, than in forming a syllogism in logic, in pleading a process in law, or in prescribing a dose of pills in physic. Wherefore, madam, believing you will not omit this so necessary feature in the education of your children, who yourself have tasted its sweetness, and are of a learned extraction, I will, upon this occasion, presume to acquaint your ladyship with one particular fancy of my own, contrary to the common method, which is all I am able to contribute to your service in this affair.

For a boy of quality then, who pretends to letters not upon the account of profit (for so mean an object as that is unworthy of the grace and favour of the Muses, and moreover, in it a man directs his service to and depends upon others), nor so much for outward ornament, as for his own proper and peculiar use, and to furnish and enrich himself within, having rather a desire to come out an accomplished cavalier than a mere scholar or learned man; for such a one, I say, I would, also, have his friends solicitous to find him out a tutor, who has rather a well-made than a well-filled head; seeking, indeed, both the one and the other, but rather of the two to prefer manners and judgment to mere learning, and that this man should exercise his charge after a new method.

'Tis the custom of pedagogues to be eternally thundering in their pupil's ears, as they were pouring into a funnel, whilst the business of the pupil is only to repeat what the others have said: now I would have a tutor to correct this error, and, that at the very first, he should, according to the capacity he has to deal with, put it to the test, permitting his pupil himself to taste things, and of himself to discern and choose them, sometimes opening the way to him, and sometimes leaving him to open it for himself; that is, I would not have him alone to invent and speak, but that he should also hear his pupil speak in turn. Socrates, and since

2. *science*, liberal knowledge.

him Arcesilaus,[3] made first their scholars speak, and then they spoke to them. "Obest plerumque iis, qui discere volunt, auctoritas eorum, qui docent."[4] It is good to make him, like a young horse, trot before him, that he may judge of his going, and how much he is to abate of his own speed, to accommodate himself to the vigour and capacity of the other. For want of which due proportion we spoil all; which also to know how to adjust, and to keep within an exact and due measure, is one of the hardest things I know, and 'tis the effect of a high and well-tempered soul, to know how to condescend to such puerile motions and to govern and direct them. I walk firmer and more secure up hill than down.

Such as, according to our common way of teaching, undertake, with one and the same lesson, and the same measure of direction, to instruct several boys of differing and unequal capacities, are infinitely mistaken; and 'tis no wonder, if in a whole multitude of scholars, there are not found above two or three who bring away any good account of their time and discipline. Let the master not only examine him about the grammatical construction of the bare words of his lesson, but about the sense and substance of them, and let him judge of the profit he has made, not by the testimony of his memory, but by that of his life. Let him make him put what he has learned into a hundred several forms, and accommodate it to so many several subjects, to see if he yet rightly comprehends it, and has made it his own, taking instruction of his progress by the pedagogic institutions of Plato.[5] 'Tis a sign of crudity and indigestion to disgorge what we eat in the same condition it was swallowed; the stomach has not performed its office unless it have altered the form and condition of what was committed to it to concoct. Our minds work only upon trust, when bound and compelled to follow the appetite of another's fancy, enslaved and captivated under the authority of another's instruction; we have been so subjected to the trammel, that we have no free, nor natural pace of our own; our own vigour and liberty are extinct and gone. . . .

Let him make him examine and thoroughly sift everything he reads, and lodge nothing in his fancy upon simple authority and upon trust. Aristotle's principles will then be no more principles to him, than

3. Greek philosopher and teacher, *c.* 250 B.C.
4. "The authority of teachers is very often an obstacle to those who wish to learn" (Cicero).
5. *the pedagogic institutions of Plato*, the Socratic method, as shown in Plato's dialogues.

those of Epicurus and the Stoics: let this diversity of opinions be propounded to, and laid before him; he will himself choose, if he be able; if not, he will remain in doubt.

"Che, non men che saper, dubbiar m' aggrata,"[6]

for, if he embrace the opinions of Xenophon and Plato, by his own reason, they will no more be theirs, but become his own. Who follows another, follows nothing, finds nothing, nay, is inquisitive after nothing. Let him, at least, know that he knows. It will be necessary that he imbibe their knowledge, not that he be corrupted with their precepts; and no matter if he forget where he had his learning, provided he know how to apply it to his own use. Truth and reason are common to every one, and are no more his who spake them first, than his who speaks them after: 'tis no more according to Plato, than according to me, since both he and I equally see and understand them. Bees cull their several sweets from this flower and that blossom, here and there where they find them, but themselves afterwards make the honey, which is all and purely their own, and no more thyme and marjoram: so the several fragments he borrows from others, he will transform and shuffle together to compile a work that shall be absolutely his own; that is to say, his judgment: his instruction, labour and study, tend to nothing else but to form that. He is not obliged to discover whence he got the materials that have assisted him, but only to produce what he has himself done with them. Men that live upon pillage and borrowing, expose their purchases and buildings to every one's view: but do not proclaim how they came by the money. No man divulges his revenue; or at least, which way it comes in: but every one publishes his acquisitions. The advantages of our study are to become better and more wise. 'Tis, says Epicharmus,[7] the understanding that sees and hears, 'tis the understanding that improves everything, that orders everything, and that acts, rules, and reigns: all other faculties are blind, and deaf, and without soul. And certainly we render it timorous and servile, in not allowing it the liberty and privilege to do anything of itself. Whoever asked his pupil what he thought of grammar and rhetoric, or of such and such a sentence of Cicero? Our masters stick them, full feathered, in our memories, and there establish them like oracles, of which the letters and syllables are of the substance

6. "To doubt is as pleasing to me as to know" (Dante).
7. Greek tragic poet, *fl.* 500 B.C.

of the thing. To know by rote, is no knowledge, and signifies no more but only to retain what one has intrusted to our memory. That which a man rightly knows and understands, he is the free disposer of at his own full liberty, without any regard to the author from whence he had it or fumbling over the leaves of his book. A mere bookish learning is a poor, paltry learning; it may serve for ornament, but there is yet no foundation for any superstructure to be built upon it, according to the opinion of Plato, who says, that constancy, faith, and sincerity, are the true philosophy, and the other sciences, that are directed to other ends, mere adulterate paint. I could wish that Paluel or Pompey, those two noted dancers of my time, could have taught us to cut capers, by only seeing them do it, without stirring from our places, as these men pretend to inform the understanding, without ever setting it to work; or that we could learn to ride, handle a pike, touch a lute, or sing, without the trouble of practice, as these attempt to make us judge and speak well, without exercising us in judging or speaking. Now in this initiation of our studies and in their progress, whatsoever presents itself before us is book sufficient; a roguish trick of a page, a sottish mistake of a servant, a jest at the table, are so many new subjects.

And for this reason, conversation with men is of very great use and travel into foreign countries; not to bring back (as most of our young monsieurs do) and account only of how many paces Santa Rotonda[8] is in circuit; or of the richness of Signora Livia's petticoats; or, as some others, how much Nero's face, in a statue in such an old ruin, is longer and broader than that made for him on some medal; but to be able chiefly to give an account of the humours, manners, customs, and laws of those nations where he has been, and that we may whet and sharpen our wits by rubbing them against those of others. I would that a boy should be sent abroad very young, and first, so as to kill two birds with one stone, into those neighbouring nations whose language is most differing from our own, and to which, if it be not formed betimes, the tongue will grow too stiff to bend.

And also 'tis the general opinion of all, that a child should not be brought up in his mother's lap. Mothers are too tender, and their natural affection is apt to make the most discreet of them all so overfond, that they can neither find in their hearts to give them due correction for the faults they commit, nor suffer them to be inured to hardships and hazards, as they ought to be. They will not endure to see them return all dust and sweat from their exercise, to drink cold drink when they

8. The Pantheon of Agrippa.

are hot, nor see them mount an unruly horse, nor take a foil in hand against a rude fencer, or so much as to discharge a carbine. And yet there is no remedy; whoever will breed a boy to be good for anything when he comes to be a man, must by no means spare him when young, and must very often transgress the rules of physic. It is not enough to fortify his soul; you are also to make his sinews strong; for the soul will be oppressed if not assisted by the members, and would have too hard a task to discharge two offices alone. I know very well, to my cost, how much mine groans under the burden, from being accommodated with a body so tender and indisposed, as eternally leans and presses upon her; and often in my reading perceive that our masters, in their writings, make examples pass for magnanimity and fortitude of mind, which really are rather toughness of skin and hardness of bones; for I have seen men, women, and children, naturally born of so hard and insensible a constitution of body, that a sound cudgelling has been less to them than a flirt with a finger would have been to me, and that would neither cry out, wince, nor shrink, for a good swinging beating; and when wrestlers counterfeit the philosophers in patience, 'tis rather strength of nerves than stoutness of heart. Now to be inured to undergo labour, is to be accustomed to endure pain: "labor callum obducit dolori."[9] A boy is to be broken in to the toil and roughness of exercise, so as to be trained up to the pain and suffering of dislocations, cholics, cauteries, and even imprisonment and the rack itself; for he may come, by misfortune, to be reduced to the worst of these, which (as this world goes) is sometimes inflicted on the good as well as the bad. As for proof, in our present civil war whoever draws his sword against the laws, threatens the honestest men with the whip and the halter.[10]

And, moreover, by living at home, the authority of this governor, which ought to be sovereign over the boy he has received into his charge, is often checked and hindered by the presence of parents; to which may also be added, that the respect the whole family pay him, as their master's son, and the knowledge he has of the estate and greatness he is heir to, are, in my opinion, no small inconveniences in these tender years.

And yet, even in this conversing with men I spoke of but now, I have observed this vice, that instead of gathering observations from

9. "Labor hardens against pain" (Cicero).
10. From 1562 to 1589, France was in a state of continual religious civil war. Both Catholics and Protestants were merciless wherever and whenever they were in power.

others, we make it our whole business to lay ourselves upon them, and are more concerned how to expose and set out our own commodities, than how to increase our stock by acquiring new. Silence, therefore, and modesty are very advantageous qualities in conversation. One should, therefore, train up this boy to be sparing and a husband of his knowledge when he has acquired it; and to forbear taking exceptions at or reproving every idle saying or ridiculous story that is said or told in his presence; for it is a very unbecoming rudeness to carp at everything that is not agreeable to our own palate. Let him be satisfied with correcting himself, and not seem to condemn everything in another he would not do himself, nor dispute it as against common customs. "Licet sapere sine pompa, sine invidia."[11] Let him avoid these vain and uncivil images of authority, this childish ambition of coveting to appear better bred and more accomplished, than he really will, by such carriage, discover himself to be. Let him be instructed not to engage in discourse or dispute but with a champion worthy of him, and, even there, not to make use of all the little subtleties that may seem pat for his purpose, but only such arguments as may best serve him. Let him be taught to be curious in the election and choice of his reasons, to abominate impertinence, and, consequently, to affect brevity; but, above all, let him be lessoned to acquiesce and submit to truth so soon as ever he shall discover it, whether in his opponent's argument, or upon better consideration of his own; for he shall never be preferred to the chair for a mere clatter of words and syllogisms, and is no further engaged to any argument whatever, than as he shall in his own judgment approve it: nor yet is arguing a trade, where the liberty of recantation and getting off upon better thoughts, are to be sold for ready money.

If his governor be of my humour, he will form his will to be a very good and loyal subject to his prince, very affectionate to his person, and very stout in his quarrel; but withal he will cool in him the desire of having any other tie to his service than public duty. Besides several other inconveniences that are inconsistent with the liberty every honest man ought to have, a man's judgment, being bribed and prepossessed by these particular obligations, is either blinded and less free to exercise its function, or is blemished with ingratitude and indiscretion. A man that is purely a courtier, can neither have power nor will to speak or think otherwise than favourably and well of a master, who, amongst so many millions of other subjects, has picked out him with his own hand

11. "Let him be wise without ostentation, without envy" (Seneca).

to nourish and advance; this favour, and the profit flowing from it, must needs, and not without some show of reason, corrupt his freedom and dazzle him; and we commonly see these people speak in another kind of phrase than is ordinarily spoken by others of the same nation, though what they say in that courtly language is not much to be believed.

Let his conscience and virtue be eminently manifest in his speaking, and have only reason for their guide. Make him understand, that to acknowledge the error he shall discover in his own argument, though only found out by himself, is an effect of judgment and sincerity, which are the principal things he is to seek after; that obstinacy and contention are common qualities, most appearing in mean souls; that to revise and correct himself, to forsake an unjust argument in the height and heat of dispute, are rare, great, and philosophical qualities. Let him be advised, being in company, to have his eye and ear in every corner; for I find that the places of greatest honour are commonly seized upon by men that have least in them, and that the greatest fortunes are seldom accompanied with the ablest parts. I have been present when, whilst they at the upper end of the chamber have been only commending the beauty of the arras, or the flavour of the wine, many things that have been very finely said at the lower end of the table have been lost and thrown away. Let him examine every man's talent; a peasant, a bricklayer, a passenger: one may learn something from every one of these in their several capacities, and something will be picked out of their discourse whereof some use may be made at one time or another; nay, even the folly and impertinence of others will contribute to his instruction. By observing the graces and manners of all he sees, he will create to himself an emulation of the good, and a contempt of the bad.

Let an honest curiosity be suggested to his fancy of being inquisitive after everything; whatever there is singular and rare near the place where he is, let him go and see it; a fine house, a noble fountain, an eminent man, the place where a battle has been anciently fought, the passages of Cæsar and Charlemagne.

Let him inquire into the manners, revenues, and alliances of princes, things in themselves very pleasant to learn, and very useful to know.

In this conversing with men, I mean also, and principally, those who only live in the records of history; he shall, by reading those books, converse with the great and heroic souls of the best ages. 'Tis an idle and vain study to those who make it so by doing it after a negligent manner, but to those who do it with care and observation, 'tis a study of inestimable fruit and value; and the only study, as Plato reports, that the Lacedæmonians reserved to themselves. What profit shall he not reap as to the business of men, by reading the lives of Plutarch? But, withal, let my governor remember to what end his instructions are principally directed, and that he do not so much imprint in his pupil's memory the date of the ruin of Carthage, as the manners of Hannibal and Scipio;[12] nor so much where Marcellus died, as why it was unworthy of his duty that he died there.[13] Let him not teach him so much the narrative parts of history as to judge them; the reading of them, in my opinion, is a thing that of all others we apply ourselves unto with the most differing measure. I have read a hundred things in Livy that another has not, or not taken notice of at least; and Plutarch has read a hundred more there than ever I could find, or than, peradventure, that author ever wrote; to some it is merely a grammar study, to others the very anatomy of philosophy, by which the most abstruse parts of our human nature penetrate. There are in Plutarch many long discourses very worthy to be carefully read and observed, for he is, in my opinion, of all others the greatest master in that kind of writing; but there are a thousand others which he has only touched and glanced upon, where he only points with his finger to direct us which way we may go if we will, and contents himself sometimes with giving only one brisk hit in the nicest article of the question, whence we are to grope out the rest. As, for example, where he says that the inhabitants of Asia came to be vassals to one only, for not having been able to pronounce one syllable, which is No. Only to see him pick out a light action in a man's life, or a mere word that does not seem to amount even to that, is itself a whole discourse. 'Tis to our prejudice that men of understanding should so immoderately affect brevity; no doubt their reputation is the better by it, but in the meantime we are the worse. Plutarch had rather we should applaud his judgment than commend his knowledge, and had rather leave us with

12. *Hannibal and Scipio*, Carthaginian and Roman generals, respectively, in the Second Punic War (218-201 B.C.).

13. Marcellus, one of the great Roman generals of the Second Punic War, was killed by an ambush. Hannibal concealed soldiers in the woods on top of a steep hill, thinking that it would attract the Romans as a good camp-site. Marcellus went with a small force to reconnoiter it, and was killed. Plutarch makes the point that it was the duty of a man who had been five times consul, and on whom the fate of Rome largely depended, not to expose himself by acting as "a mere scout."

an appetite to read more, than glutted with that we have already read.
He knew very well, that a man may say too much even upon the best
subjects, and that Alexandridas justly reproached him who made very
good but too long speeches to the Ephori,[14] when he said: "O stranger!
thou speakest the things thou shouldst speak, but not as thou shouldst
speak them." Such as have lean and spare bodies stuff themselves out
with clothes; so they who are defective in matter, endeavour to make
amends with words.

Human understanding is marvellously enlightened by daily conversation with men, for we are, otherwise, compressed and heaped up
in ourselves, and have our sight limited to the length of our own
noses. One asking Socrates of what country he was, he did not make
answer, of Athens, but of the world; he whose imagination was fuller
and wider, embraced the whole world for his country, and extended
his society and friendship to all mankind; not as we do, who look no
further than our feet. When the vines of my village are nipped with
the frost, my parish priest presently concludes, that the indignation of
God is gone out against all the human race, and that the cannibals have
already got the pip. Who is it, that seeing the havoc of these civil wars
of ours, does not cry out, that the machine of the world is near dissolution, and that the day of judgment is at hand; without considering, that
many worse things have been seen, and that, in the meantime, people
are very merry in a thousand other parts of the earth for all this? For
my part, considering the licence and impunity that always attend such
commotions, I wonder they are so moderate, and that there is no more
mischief done. To him who feels the hailstones patter about his ears,
the whole hemisphere appears to be in storm and tempest; like the
ridiculous Savoyard, who said very gravely, that if that simple king of
France could have managed his fortune as he should have done, he
might in time have come to have been steward of the household to the
duke his master: the fellow could not, in his shallow imagination, conceive that there could be anything greater than a Duke of Savoy. And,
in truth, we are all of us, insensibly, in this error, an error of a very
great weight and very pernicious consequence. But whoever shall represent to his fancy, as in a picture, that great image of our mother
Nature, in her full majesty and lustre, whoever in her face shall read
so general and so constant a variety, whoever shall observe himself in
that figure, and not himself but a whole kingdom, no bigger than the
least touch or prick of a pencil in comparison of the whole, that man

14. Magistrates (of Sparta).

alone is able to value things according to their true estimate and grandeur.

This great world which some do yet multiply as several species under one genus, is the mirror wherein we are to behold ourselves, to be able to know ourselves as we ought to do in the true bias. In short, I would have this to be the book my young gentleman should study with the most attention. So many humours, so many sects, so many judg-ments, opinions, laws, and customs, teach us to judge aright of our own, and inform our understanding to discover its imperfection and natural infirmity, which is no trivial speculation. So many mutations of states and kingdoms, and so many turns and revolutions of public fortune, will make us wise enough to make no great wonder of our own. So many great names, so many famous victories and conquests drowned and swallowed in oblivion, render our hopes ridiculous of eternising our names by the taking of half-a-score of light horse, or a henroost, which only derives its memory from its ruin. The pride and arrogance of so many foreign pomps and ceremonies, the tumorous majesty of so many courts and grandeurs, accustom and fortify our sight without astonishment or winking to behold the lustre of our own; so many millions of men, buried before us, encourage us not to fear to go seek such good company in the other world: and so of all the rest. Pythagoras was wont to say, that our life resembles the great and populous assembly of the Olympic games, wherein some exercise the body, that they may carry away the glory of the prize, others bring mer-chandise to sell for profit; there are also some (and those none of the worst sort) who pursue no other advantage than only to look on, and consider how and why everything is done, and to be spectators of the lives of other men, thereby the better to judge of and regulate their own.

To examples may fitly be applied all the profitable discourses of philosophy, to which all human actions, as to their best rule, ought to be especially directed: a scholar shall be taught to know what it is to know, and what to be ignorant; what ought to be the end and design of study; what valour, temperance, and justice are; the difference betwixt ambition and avarice, servitude and subjection, licence and liberty; by what token a man may know true and solid contentment; how far death, affliction, and disgrace are to be apprehended:

"Et quo quemque modo fugiatque feratque laborem;"[15]

15. "And how he may avoid or bear every hardship" (Virgil).

by what secret springs we move, and the reason of our various agitations and irresolutions. . . . If we are once able to restrain the offices of
human life within their just and natural limits, we shall find that most
of the sciences in use are of no great use to us, and even in those that
are, that there are many very unnecessary cavities and dilatations which
we had better let alone, and following Socrates' direction, limit the
course of our studies to those things only where is a true and real
utility.

'Tis a great foolery to teach our children the knowledge of the stars
and the motion of the eighth sphere, before their own. . . .

After having taught him what will make him more wise and
good, you may then entertain him with the elements of logic, physics,
geometry, rhetoric, and the science which he shall then himself most
incline to, his judgment being beforehand formed and fit to choose, he
will quickly make his own. The way of instructing him ought to be
sometimes by discourse, and sometimes by reading; sometimes his
governor shall put the author himself, which he shall think most
proper for him, into his hands, and sometimes only the marrow and
substance of it; and if himself be not conversant enough in books to
turn to all the fine discourses the books contain for his purpose, there
may some man of learning be joined to him, that upon every occasion
shall supply him with what he stands in need of, to furnish it to his
pupil. . . .

'Tis a thousand pities that matters should be at such a pass in this
age of ours, that philosophy, even with men of understanding, should
be looked upon as a vain and fantastic name, a thing of no use, no
value, either in opinion or effect, of which I think those ergotisms[16]
and petty sophistries, by prepossessing the avenues to it, are the cause.
And people are much to blame to represent it to children for a thing
of so difficult access, and with such a frowning, grim, and formidable
aspect. Who is it that has disguised it thus, with this false, pale, and
ghostly countenance? There is nothing more airy, more gay, more
frolic, and I had like to have said, more wanton. She preaches nothing
but feasting and jollity; a melancholic anxious look shows that she
does not inhabit there. . . .

The soul that lodges philosophy, ought to be of such a constitution
of health, as to render the body in like manner healthful too; she ought
to make her tranquillity and satisfaction shine so as to appear without,
and her contentment ought to fashion the outward behaviour to her

16. *ergotisms*, formal logical inferences.

own mould, and consequently to fortify it with a graceful confidence, an active and joyous carriage, and a serene and contented countenance. The most manifest sign of wisdom is a continual cheerfulness; her state is like that of things in the regions above the moon, always clear and serene. . . .

If this pupil shall happen to be of so contrary a disposition, that he had rather hear a tale of a tub than the true narrative of some noble expedition or some wise and learned discourse; who at the beat of drum, that excites the youthful ardour of his companions, leaves that to follow another that calls to a morris or the bears;[17] who would not wish, and find it more delightful and more excellent, to return all dust and sweat victorious from a battle, than from tennis or from a ball, with the prize of those exercises; I see no other remedy, but that he be bound prentice in some good town to learn to make minced pies, though he were the son of a duke; according to Plato's precept, that children are to be placed out and disposed of, not according to the wealth, qualities, or condition of the father, but according to the faculties and the capacity of their own souls.

Since philosophy is that which instructs us to live, and that infancy has there its lessons as well as other ages, why is it not communicated to children betimes?

They begin to teach us to live when we have almost done living. A hundred students have got the pox before they have come to read Aristotle's lecture on temperance. Cicero said, that though he should live two men's ages, he should never find leisure to study the lyric poets; and I find these sophisters yet more deplorably unprofitable. The boy we would breed has a great deal less time to spare; he owes but the first fifteen or sixteen years of his life to education; the remainder is due to action. Let us, therefore, employ that short time in necessary instruction. Away with the thorny subtleties of dialectics, they are abuses, things by which our lives can never be amended: take the plain philosophical discourses, learn how rightly to choose, and then rightly to apply them; they are more easy to be understood than one of Boccaccio's novels; a child from nurse is much more capable of them, than of learning to read or to write. Philosophy has discourses proper for childhood, as well as for the decrepit age of men.

I am of Plutarch's mind, that Aristotle did not so much trouble his great disciple with the knack of forming syllogisms, or with the elements of geometry, as with infusing into him good precepts con-

17. *a morris or the bears*, a morris-dance or a bear-baiting.

cerning valour, prowess, magnanimity, temperance, and the contempt
of fear; and with this ammunition, sent him, whilst yet a boy, with
no more than thirty thousand foot, four thousand horse, and but
forty-two thousand crowns, to subjugate the empire of the whole
earth. For the other arts and sciences, he says, Alexander highly indeed
commended their excellence and charm, and had them in very great
honour and esteem, but not ravished with them to that degree, as to be
tempted to affect the practice of them in his own person.

Epicurus, in the beginning of his letter to Meniceus, says, "That
neither the youngest should refuse to philosophise, nor the oldest grow
weary of it." Who does otherwise, seems tacitly to imply, that either
the time of living happily is not yet come, or that it is already past. And
yet, for all that, I would not have this pupil of ours imprisoned and
made a slave to his book; nor would I have him given up to the
morosity and melancholic humour of a sour, ill-natured pedant; I
would not have his spirit cowed and subdued, by applying him to the
rack, and tormenting him, as some do, fourteen or fifteen hours a day,
and so make a pack-horse of him. Neither should I think it good,
when, by reason of a solitary and melancholic complexion, he is discovered to be overmuch addicted to his book, to nourish that
humour in him; for that renders him unfit for civil conversation, and
diverts him from better employments. And how many have I seen in
my time totally brutified by an immoderate thirst after knowledge?
Neither would I have his generous manners spoiled and corrupted by
the incivility and barbarism of those of another. The French wisdom
was anciently turned into proverb: "early, but of no continuance." And,
in truth, we yet see, that nothing can be more ingenious and pleasing
than the children of France; but they ordinarily deceive the hope and
expectation that have been conceived of them; and grown up to be
men, have nothing extraordinary or worth taking notice of: I have
heard men of good understanding say, these colleges of ours to which
we send our young people (and of which we have but too many) make
them such animals as they are.

But to our little monsieur, a closet, a garden, the table, his bed,
solitude and company, morning and evening, all hours shall be the
same, and all places to him a study; for philosophy, who, as the forma-
trix of judgment and manners, shall be his principal lesson, has that
privilege to have a hand in everything. The orator Isocrates, being at a
feast entreated to speak of his art, all the company were satisfied with
and commended his answer: "It is not now a time," said he, "to do

what I can do; and that which it is now time to do, I cannot do." For
to make orations and rhetorical disputes in a company met together to
laugh and make good cheer, had been very unseasonable and improper,
and as much might have been said of all the other sciences. But as to
what concerns philosophy, that part of it at least that treats of man, and
of his offices and duties, it has been the common opinion of all wise
men, that, out of respect to the sweetness of her conversation, she is
ever to be admitted in all sports and entertainments. . . . But as the
steps we take in walking to and fro in a gallery, though three times as
many, do not tire a man so much as those we employ in a formal
journey, so our lesson, as it were accidentally occurring, without any
set obligation of time or place, and falling naturally into every action,
will insensibly insinuate itself. By which means our very exercises and
recreations, running, wrestling, music, dancing, hunting, riding, and
fencing, will prove to be a good part of our study. I would have his
outward fashion and mien, and the disposition of his limbs, formed at
the same time with his mind. 'Tis not a soul, 'tis not a body that we are
training up, but a man, and we ought not to divide him. And, as Plato
says, we are not to fashion one without the other, but make them draw
together like two horses harnessed to a coach. By which saying of his,
does he not seem to allow more time for, and to take more care of,
exercises for the body, and to hold that the mind, in a good proportion,
does her business at the same time too?

As to the rest, this method of education ought to be carried on
with a severe sweetness, quite contrary to the practice of our pedants,
who, instead of tempting and alluring children to letters by apt and
gentle ways, do in truth present nothing before them but rods and
ferules, horror and cruelty. Away with this violence! away with this
compulsion! than which, I certainly believe nothing more dulls and
degenerates a well-descended nature. If you would have him apprehend shame and chastisement, do not harden him to them: inure him
to heat and cold, to wind and sun, and to dangers that he ought to
despise; wean him from all effeminacy and delicacy in clothes and
lodging, eating and drinking; accustom him to everything, that he may
not be a Sir Paris, a carpet-knight, but a sinewy, hardy, and vigorous
young man. I have ever from a child to the age wherein I now am,
been of this opinion, and am still constant to it. But amongst other
things, the strict government of most of our colleges has evermore displeased me; peradventure, they might have erred less perniciously on
the indulgent side. 'Tis a real house of correction of imprisoned youth.

They are made debauched, by being punished before they are so. Do but come in when they are about their lesson, and you shall hear nothing but the outcries of boys under execution, with the thundering noise of their pedagogues drunk with fury. A very pretty way this, to tempt these tender and timorous souls to love their book, with a furious countenance, and a rod in hand! A cursed and pernicious way of proceeding! . . . Where their profit is, let them there have their pleasure too. Such viands as are proper and wholesome for children, should be sweetened with sugar, and such as are dangerous to them, embittered with gall. 'Tis marvellous to see how solicitous Plato is in his Laws concerning the gaiety and diversion of the youth of his city, and how much and often he enlarges upon their races, sports, songs, leaps, and dances: of which, he says, that antiquity has given the ordering and patronage particularly to the gods themselves, to Apollo, Minerva, and the Muses. He insists long upon, and is very particular in, giving innumerable precepts for exercises; but as to the lettered sciences, says very little, and only seems particularly to recommend poetry upon the account of music. . . .

Young bodies are supple; one should, therefore, in that age bend and ply them to all fashions and customs: and provided a man can contain the appetite and the will within their due limits, let a young man, in God's name, be rendered fit for all nations and all companies, even to debauchery and excess, if need be; that is, where he shall do it out of complacency to the customs of the place. Let him be able to do everything, but love to do nothing but what is good. The philosophers themselves do not justify Callisthenes for forfeiting the favour of his master Alexander the Great, by refusing to pledge him a cup of wine. Let him laugh, play, wench, with his prince: nay, I would have him, even in his debauches, too hard for the rest of the company, and to excel his companions in ability and vigour, and that he may not give over doing it, either through defect of power or knowledge how to do it, but for want of will. "Multum interest, utrum peccare aliquis nolit, an nesciat."[18] I thought I passed a compliment upon a lord, as free from those excesses as any man in France, by asking him before a great deal of very good company, how many times in his life he had been drunk in Germany, in the time of his being there about his majesty's affairs; which he also took as it was intended, and made answer, "Three times"; and withal, told us the whole story of his

18. "It makes a great difference whether a person doesn't want to sin, or doesn't know how" (Seneca).

debauches. I know some, who for want of this faculty, have found a great inconvenience in negotiating with that nation. . . .

The lad will not so much get his lesson by heart as he will practise it: he will repeat it in his actions. We shall discover if there be prudence in his exercises, if there be sincerity and justice in his deport-ment, if there be grace and judgment in his speaking; if there be constancy in his sickness; if there be modesty in his mirth, temperance in his pleasures, order in his domestic economy, indifference in his palate, whether what he eats or drinks be flesh or fish, wine or water. . . . With such a one, after fifteen or sixteen years' study, compare one of our college Latinists, who has thrown away so much time in nothing but learning to speak. The world is nothing but babble; and I hardly ever yet saw that man who did not rather prate too much, than speak too little. . . . Let but our pupil be well furnished with things, words will follow but too fast; he will pull them after him if they do not voluntarily follow. I have observed some to make excuses, that they cannot express themselves, and pretend to have their fancies full of a great many very fine things, which yet, for want of eloquence, they cannot utter; 'tis a mere shift, and nothing else. Will you know what I think of it? I think they are nothing but shadows of some imperfect images and conceptions that they know not what to make of within, nor consequently bring out: they do not yet themselves understand what they would be at, and if you but observe how they haggle and stammer upon the point of parturition, you will soon conclude, that their labour is not to delivery, but about conception, and that they are but licking their formless embryo. For my part, I hold, and Socrates commands it, that whoever has in his mind a sprightly and clear imagination, he will express it well enough in one kind of tongue or another, and, if he be dumb, by signs

"Verbaque prævisam rem non invita sequentur."[19]

And as another as poetically says in his prose, "Quum res animum occupavere, verba ambiunt": and this other, "Ipsæ res verba rapiunt." He knows nothing of ablative, conjunctive, substantive, or grammar, no more than his lackey, or a fishwife of the Petit Pont; and yet these will give you a bellyful of talk, if you will hear them, and peradventure shall trip as little in their language as the best masters of art in

19. "Once a thing is conceived in the mind, the words to express it soon present themselves" (Horace). The next two quotations, from Seneca and Cicero, say substantially the same thing.

France. He knows no rhetoric, nor how in a preface to bribe the
benevolence of the courteous reader; neither does he care to know it.
Indeed all this fine decoration of painting is easily effaced by the lustre
of a simple and blunt truth: these fine flourishes serve only to amuse
the vulgar, of themselves incapable of more solid and nutritive diet.
The ambassadors of Samos, prepared with a long and elegant oration,
came to Cleomenes, King of Sparta, to incite him to a war against the
tyrant Polycrates; who, after he had heard their harangue with great
gravity and patience, gave them this answer: "As to the exordium,[20]
I remember it not, nor consequently the middle of your speech; and
for what concerns your conclusion, I will not do what you desire": a
very pretty answer this, methinks, and a pack of learned orators most
sweetly gravelled. And what did the other man say? The Athenians
were to choose one of two architects for a very great building they had
designed; of these, the first, a pert affected fellow, offered his service
in a long premeditated discourse upon the subject of the work in hand,
and by his oratory inclined the voices of the people in his favour; but
the other in three words; "O, Athenians, what this man says, I will
do." Let it go before, or come after, a good sentence or a thing well
said, is always in season; if it neither suit well with what went before,
nor has much coherence with what follows after, it is good in itself. I
am none of those who think that good rhyme makes a good poem. Let
him make short long, and long short if he will, 'tis no great matter;
if there be invention, and that the wit and judgment have well performed their offices, I will say, here's a good poet, but an ill rhymer.
Let a man, says Horace, divest his work of all method and measure,
he will never the more lose himself for that; the very pieces will be
fine by themselves. Menander's[21] answer had this meaning, who being
reproved by a friend, the time drawing on at which he had promised
a comedy, that he had not yet fallen in hand with it; "It is made, and
ready," said he, "all but the verses." Having contrived the subject, and
disposed the scenes in his fancy, he took little care for the rest. Since
Ronsard and Du Bellay[22] have given reputation to our French poesy,
every little dabbler, for aught I see, swells his words as high, and
makes his cadences very near as harmonious as they. "Plus sonat, quam
valet."[23] For the vulgar, there were never so many poetasters as now;

20. *exordium*, formal introduction to an oration.
21. *Menander*, Greek comic poet (342-291 B.C.).
22. *Ronsard and Du Bellay*, members of the *Pléiade*, a group of seven poets
who succeeded in reforming French poetry in the middle of the 16th century.
23. "It sounds better than it is" (Seneca).

but though they find it no hard matter to imitate their rhyme, they yet fall infinitely short of imitating the rich descriptions of the one, and the delicate invention of the other of these masters. . . .

No doubt but Greek and Latin are very great ornaments, and of very great use, but we buy them too dear. I will here discover one way, which has been experimented in my own person, by which they are to be had better cheap, and such may make use of it as will. My late father having made the most precise inquiry that any man could possibly make amongst men of the greatest learning and judgment, of an exact method of education, was by them cautioned of this inconvenience then in use, and made to believe, that the tedious time we applied to the learning of the tongues of them who had them for nothing, was the sole cause we could not arrive to the grandeur of soul and perfection of knowledge, of the ancient Greeks and Romans. I do not, however, believe that to be the only cause. However, the expedient my father found out for this was, that in my infancy, and before I began to speak, he committed me to the care of a German, who since died a famous physician in France, totally ignorant of our language, but very fluent, and a great critic in Latin. This man, whom he had fetched out of his own country, and whom he entertained with a very great salary for this only end, had me continually with him: to him there were also joined two others, of inferior learning, to attend me, and to relieve him; who all of them spoke to me in no other language but Latin. As to the rest of his family, it was an inviolable rule, that neither himself, nor my mother, man nor maid, should speak anything in my company, but such Latin words as every one had learned only to gabble with me. It is not to be imagined how great an advantage this proved to the whole family; my father and my mother by this means learned Latin enough to understand it perfectly well, and to speak it to such a degree as was sufficient for any necessary use; as also those of the servants did who were most frequently with me. In short, we Latined it at such a rate, that it overflowed to all the neighbouring villages, where there yet remain, that have established themselves by custom, several Latin appellations of artisans and their tools. As for what concerns myself, I was above six years of age before I understood either French or Perigordin,[24] any more than Arabic; and without art, book, grammar, or precept, whipping, or the expense of a tear, I had, by that time, learned to speak as pure Latin

24. Montaigne's local dialect.

as my master himself, for I had no means of mixing it up with any other. . . .

As to Greek, of which I have but a mere smattering, my father also designed to have it taught me by a device, but a new one, and by way of sport; tossing our declensions to and fro, after the manner of those who, by certain games at tables and chess, learn geometry and arithmetic. For he, amongst other rules, had been advised to make me relish science and duty by an unforced will, and of my own voluntary motion, and to educate my soul in all liberty and delight, without any severity or constraint; which he was an observer of to such a degree, even of superstition, if I may say so, that some being of opinion that it troubles and disturbs the brains of children suddenly to wake them in the morning, and to snatch them violently and over-hastily from sleep (wherein they are much more profoundly involved than we), he caused me to be wakened by the sound of some musical instrument, and was never unprovided of a musician for that purpose. By this example you may judge of the rest, this alone being sufficient to recommend both the prudence and the affection of so good a father, who is not to be blamed if he did not reap fruits answerable to so exquisite a culture. Of this, two things were the cause: first, a sterile and improper soil; for, though I was of a strong and healthful constitution, and of a disposition tolerably sweet and tractable, yet I was, withal, so heavy, idle, and indisposed, that they could not rouse me from my sloth, not even to get me out to play. What I saw, I saw clearly enough, and under this heavy complexion nourished a bold imagination, and opinions above my age. I had a slow wit, that would go no faster than it was led; a tardy understanding, a languishing invention, and above all, incredible defect of memory; so that, it is no wonder, if from all these nothing considerable could be extracted. Secondly, like those, who, impatient of a long and steady cure, submit to all sorts of prescriptions and recipes, the good man being extremely timorous of any way failing in a thing he had so wholly set his heart upon, suffered himself at last to be overruled by the common opinions, which always follow their leader as a flight of cranes, and complying with the method of the time, having no more those persons he had brought out of Italy, and who had given him the first model of education, about him, he sent me at six years of age to the College of Guienne, at that time the best and most flourishing in France. And there it was not possible to add anything to the care he had to provide me the most able tutors, with all other circumstances of education, reserving also several particular rules contrary to the college practice; but so it was, that with all these precautions it was a college still. My Latin immediately grew corrupt, of which also by discontinuance I have since lost all manner of use; so that this new way of education served me to no other end, than only at my first coming to prefer me to the first forms; for at thirteen years old, that I came out of the college, I had run through my whole course (as they call it), and, in truth, without any manner of advantage, that I can honestly brag of, in all this time.

The first thing that gave me any taste for books, was the pleasure I took in reading the fables of Ovid's Metamorphoses, and with them I was so taken, that being but seven or eight years old, I would steal from all other diversions to read them, both by reason that this was my own natural language, the easiest book that I·was acquainted with, and for the subject, the most accommodated to the capacity of my age: for as for Lancelot of the Lake, Amadis of Gaul, Huon of Bordeaux,[25] and such trumpery, which children are most delighted with, I had never so much as heard their names, no more than I yet know what they contain; so exact was the discipline wherein I was brought up. But this was enough to make me neglect the other lessons that were prescribed me; and here it was infinitely to my advantage, to have to do with an understanding tutor, who very well knew discreetly to connive at this and other truantries of the same nature; for by this means I ran through Virgil's Æneid, and then Terence, and then Plautus, and then some Italian comedies, allured by the sweetness of the subject; whereas had he been so foolish as to have taken me off this diversion, I do really believe, I had brought nothing away from the college but a hatred of books, as almost all our young gentlemen do. But he carried himself very discreetly in that business, seeming to take no notice, and allowing me only such time as I could steal from my other regular studies, which whetted my appetite to devour those books. For the chief things my father expected from their endeavours to whom he had delivered me for education, were affability and good humour; and, to say the truth, my manners had no other vice but sloth and want of mettle. The fear was not that I should do ill, but that I should do nothing; nobody prognosticated that I should be wicked, but only useless; they foresaw idleness, but no malice; and I find it falls out accordingly. . . .

Yet for all this heavy disposition of mine, my mind, when retired into itself, was not altogether without strong movements, solid and

25. Romances of chivalry.

clear judgments about those objects it could comprehend, and could also, without any helps, digest them; but, amongst other things, I do really believe, it had been totally impossible to have made it to submit by violence and force. Shall I here acquaint you with one faculty of my youth? I had great assurance of countenance, and flexibility of voice and gesture, in applying myself to any part I undertook to act: for before—

"Alter ab undecimo tum me vix ceperat annus,"[26]

I played the chief parts in the Latin tragedies of Buchanan, Guerente, and Muret,[27] that were presented in our college of Guienne with great dignity, and I was looked upon as one of the best actors. 'Tis an exercise that I do not disapprove in young people of condition; and I have since seen our princes, after the example of some of the ancients, in person handsomely and commendably perform these exercises; it was even allowed to persons of quality to make a profession of it in Greece. Nay, I have always taxed those with impertinence who condemn these entertainments, and with injustice those who refuse to admit such comedians as are worth seeing into our good towns, and grudge the people that public diversion. Well-governed corporations take care to assemble their citizens, not only to the solemn duties of devotion, but also to sports and spectacles. They find society and friendship augmented by it; and, besides, can there possibly be allowed a more orderly and regular diversion than what is performed in the sight of every one, and, very often, in the presence of the supreme magistrate himself? And I, for my part, should think it reasonable, that the prince should sometimes gratify his people at his own expense, out of paternal goodness and affection; and that in populous cities there should be theatres erected for such entertainments, if but to divert them from worse and private actions.

To return to my subject, there is nothing like alluring the appetite and affections; otherwise you make nothing but so many asses laden with books; by dint of the lash, you give them their pocketful of learning to keep; whereas, to do well, you should not only lodge it with them, but make them espouse it.

26. "I had just entered upon my twelfth year" (Virgil).
27. Renaissance scholars who composed Latin tragedies in imitation of those of Seneca.

OF THE INCONVENIENCE OF GREATNESS

Since we cannot attain unto it, let us revenge ourselves by railing at it; and yet it is not absolutely railing against anything, to proclaim its defects, because they are in all things to be found, how beautiful or how much to be coveted soever. Greatness has, in general, this manifest advantage, that it can lower itself when it pleases, and has, very near, the choice of both the one and the other condition; for a man does not fall from all heights; there are several from which one may descend without falling down. It does, indeed, appear to me that we value it at too high a rate, and also overvalue the resolution of those whom we have either seen, or heard, have contemned it, or displaced themselves of their own accord: its essence is not so evidently commodious that a man may not, without a miracle, refuse it. I find it a very hard thing to undergo misfortunes, but to be content with a moderate measure of fortune, and to avoid greatness I think a very easy matter. 'Tis, methinks, a virtue to which I, who am no conjuror, could without any great endeavour arrive. What, then, is to be expected from them that would yet put into consideration the glory attending this refusal, wherein there may lurk worse ambition than even in the desire itself, and fruition of greatness? Forasmuch as ambition never comports itself better, according to itself, than when it proceeds by obscure and unfrequented ways.

I incite my courage to patience, but I rein it as much as I can towards desire. I have as much to wish for as another, and allow my wishes as much liberty and indiscretion; but, yet it never befel me to wish for either empire or royalty, or the eminency of those high and commanding fortunes: I do not aim that way; I love myself too well. When I think to grow greater 'tis but very moderately, and by a compelled and timorous advancement, such as is proper for me in resolution, in prudence, in health, in beauty, and even in riches too; but this supreme reputation, this mighty authority, oppress my imagination; and, quite contrary to that other,[1] I should, peradventure, rather choose to be the second or third in Perigord, than the first at Paris: at least, without lying, rather the third at Paris than the first. I would neither dispute, a miserable unknown, with a nobleman's porter, nor make crowds open in adoration as I pass. I am trained up to a moderate condition, as well by my choice as fortune; and have made it appear, in the whole conduct of my life and enterprises, that I have rather

1. Julius Caesar.

avoided than otherwise the climbing above the degree of fortune wherein God has placed me by my birth: all natural constitution is equally just and easy. My soul is so sneaking that I measure not good fortune by the height, but by the facility.

But if my heart be not great enough, 'tis open enough to make amends, at any one's request, freely to lay open its weakness. Should any one put me upon comparing the life of L. Thorius Balbus, a brave man, handsome, learned, healthful, understanding, and abounding in all sorts of conveniences and pleasures, leading a quiet life, and all his own, his mind well prepared against death, superstition, pain, and other incumbrances of human necessity, dying, at last, in battle, with his sword in his hand, for the defence of his country, on the one part; and on the other part, the life of M. Regulus, so great and high as is known to every one, and his end admirable[2]—the one without name and without dignity, the other exemplary, and glorious to wonder—I should doubtless say as Cicero did,[3] could I speak as well as he. But if I was to compare them with my own, I should then also say that the first is as much according to my capacity, and from desire, which I conform to my capacity, as the second is far beyond it; that I could not approach the last but with veneration, the other I could readily attain by use.

But let us return to our temporal greatness, from which we are digressed. I disrelish all dominion, whether active or passive. Otanes, one of the seven who had right to pretend to the kingdom of Persia, did, as I should willingly have done, which was, that he gave up to his concurrents his right of being promoted to it, either by election or by lot, provided that he and his might live in the empire out of all authority and subjection, those of the ancient laws excepted, and might enjoy all liberty that was not prejudicial to these, being as impatient of commanding as of being commanded.

The most painful and difficult employment in the world, in my opinion, is worthily to discharge the office of a king. I excuse more of their mistakes than men commonly do, in consideration of the intolerable weight of their function, which astounds me. 'Tis hard to

2. Regulus won notable victories as a general against the Carthaginians, but they eventually captured him. After keeping him a prisoner for five years, they allowed him to return to Rome with their envoys, who were to propose a truce; but he had to promise that he would return if their terms were rejected. In the Senate in Rome he spoke against the truce and defeated it; then he kept his word and returned to Carthage to be tortured to death.

3. Cicero declared Regulus to be the happier man.

keep measure in so immeasurable a power; yet so it is, that it is, even
to those who are not of the best nature, a singular incitement to virtue,
to be seated in a place where you cannot do the least good that shall
not be put upon record; and where the least benefit redounds to so
many men, and where your talent of administration, like that of
preachers, principally addresses itself to the people, no very exact judge,
easy to deceive, and easily content. There are few things wherein we
can give a sincere judgment, by reason that there are few wherein we
have not, in some sort, a private interest. Superiority and inferiority,
dominion and subjection, are bound to a natural envy and contest, and
must of necessity perpetually intrench upon one another. I believe
neither the one nor the other touching the rights of the other party;
let reason therefore, which is inflexible and without passion, determine
when we can avail ourselves of it. 'Tis not above a month ago that I
read over two Scotch authors contending upon this subject, of whom
he who stands for the people makes kings to be in a worse condition
than a carter; and he who writes for monarchy places them some
degrees above God Almighty in power and sovereignty.

Now, the inconveniency of greatness that I have made choice of to
consider in this place, upon some occasion that has lately put it into
my head, is this: there is not, peradventure, anything more pleasant in
the commerce of men than the trials that we make against one another,
out of emulation of honour and worth, whether in the exercises of the
body or in those of the mind, wherein sovereign greatness can have no
true part. And, in earnest, I have often thought that by force of
respect itself men use princes disdainfully and injuriously in that particular; for the thing I was infinitely offended at in my childhood, that
they who exercised with me forbore to do their best because they found
me unworthy of their utmost endeavour, is what we see happen to
them daily, every one finding himself unworthy to contend with them.
If we discover that they have the least desire to get the better of us,
there is no one who will not make it his business to give it them, and
who will not rather betray his own glory than offend theirs; and will,
therein, employ so much force only as is necessary to save their honour.
What share have they, then, in the engagement, where every one is on
their side? Methinks I see those Paladins of ancient times presenting
themselves to jousts and battle with enchanted arms and bodies.
Brisson,[4] running against Alexander, purposely missed his blow, and

4. Most of the characters and examples in this essay are taken from Plutarch
and are sufficiently explained in the text.

made a fault in his career; Alexander chid him for it, but he ought to have had him whipped. Upon this consideration Carneades said, that "the sons of princes learned nothing right but to ride; by reason that, in all their other exercises, every one bends and yields to them; but a horse, that is neither a flatterer nor a courtier, throws the son of a king with no more ceremony than he would throw that of a porter." . . .

Who does not participate in the hazard and difficulty can claim no interest in the honour and pleasure that are the consequents of hazardous actions. 'Tis pity a man should be so potent that all things must give way to him; fortune therein sets you too remote from society, and places you in too great a solitude. This easiness and mean facility of making all things bow under you is an enemy to all sorts of pleasure: 'tis to slide, not to go; 'tis to sleep, and not to live. Conceive man accompanied with omnipotence: you overwhelm him; he must beg disturbance and opposition as an alms: his being and his good are in indigence.

Their good qualities are dead and lost; for they can only be perceived by comparison, and we put them out of this: they have little knowledge of true praise, having their ears deafened with so continual and uniform an approbation. Have they to do with the stupidest of all their subjects? they have no means to take any advantage of him; if he but say: " 'Tis because he is my king," he thinks he has said enough to express, that he, therefore, suffered himself to be overcome. This quality stifles and consumes the other true and essential qualities: they are sunk in the royalty; and leave them nothing to recommend themselves with but actions that directly concern and serve the function of their place; 'tis so much to be a king, that this alone remains to them. The outer glare that environs him conceals and shrouds him from us; our sight is there repelled and dissipated, being filled and stopped by this prevailing light. The senate awarded the prize of eloquence to Tiberius[5]; he refused it, esteeming that though it had been just, he could derive no advantage from a judgment so partial, and that was so little free to judge.

As we give them all advantages of honour, so do we soothe and authorize all their vices and defects, not only by approbation, but by imitation also. Every one of Alexander's followers carried his head on one side, as he did; and the flatterers of Dionysius[6] ran against one another in his presence, and stumbled at and overturned whatever was

5. A Roman Emperor.
6. See the last note on this essay.

under foot, to show they were as purblind as he. Hernia itself has also served to recommend a man to favour; I have seen deafness affected; and because the master hated his wife, Plutarch has seen his courtiers repudiate theirs, whom they loved: and, which is yet more, uncleanliness and all manner of dissolution have so been in fashion; as also disloyalty, blasphemy, cruelty, heresy, superstition, irreligion, effeminacy, and worse, if worse there be; and by an example yet more dangerous than that of Mithridates' flatterers who, as their master pretended to the honour of a good physician, came to him to have incisions and cauteries made in their limbs; for these others suffered the soul, a more delicate and noble part, to be cauterised.

But to end where I began: the Emperor Adrian, disputing with the philosopher Favorinus about the interpretation of some word, Favorinus soon yielded him the victory; for which his friend rebuking him; "You talk simply," said he, "would you not have him wiser than I, who commands thirty legions?" Augustus wrote verses against Asinius Pollio,[7] and "I," said Pollio, "say nothing, for it is not prudence to write in contest with him who has power to proscribe"; and he had reason; for Dionysius,[8] because he could not equal Philoxenus in poesy and Plato in discourse, condemned the one to the quarries, and sent the other to be sold for a slave into the island of Ægina.

THAT THE PROFIT OF ONE MAN IS THE DAMAGE OF ANOTHER

Demades the Athenian condemned one of his city, whose trade it was to sell the necessaries for funeral ceremonies, upon pretence that he demanded unreasonable profit, and that that profit could not accrue to him but by the death of a great number of people. A judgment that appears to be ill grounded, forasmuch as no profit whatever can possibly be made but at the expense of another, and that by the same rule he should condemn all gain of what kind soever. The mer-

7. None of Pollio's poetry has survived, but such contemporaries of his as Virgil, Horace, and Cicero thought well of it.

8. Dionysius, Tyrant of Syracuse (430-367 B.C.) got all Sicily and part of Italy under his control. He was one of the most powerful and ruthless Greek rulers, as well as an amateur poet and philosopher. When he asked the poet Philoxenus to revise one of his poems for him, the latter replied that the only possible way to correct it was to draw a heavy black line through the whole thing. The result on the critic is given above. Plato visited the court of Dionysius, and there is a story (of questionable authenticity) that he sold Plato into slavery after a quarrel, but the philosopher was soon released—though not by Dionysius.

chant only thrives by the debauchery of youth; the husbandman by
the dearness of grain; the architect by the ruin of buildings; lawyers,
and officers of justice, by the suits and contentions of men; nay, even
the honour and office of divines are derived from our death and vices.
A physician takes no pleasure in the health even of his friends, says
the ancient Greek comic writer, nor a soldier in the peace of his
country, and so of the rest. And, which is yet worse, let every one but
dive into his own bosom, and he will find his private wishes spring
and his secret hopes grow up at another's expense. Upon which consideration it comes into my head, that Nature does not in this swerve
from her general polity; for physicians hold, that the birth, nourishment, and increase of everything is the dissolution and corruption of
another:—

> "Nam quodcumque suis mutatum finibus exit,
> Continuo hoc mors est illius, quod fuit ante."[1]

1. "For whatever passes, changed, beyond its own limits, this is immediately
the death of that which preceded it" (Lucretius).

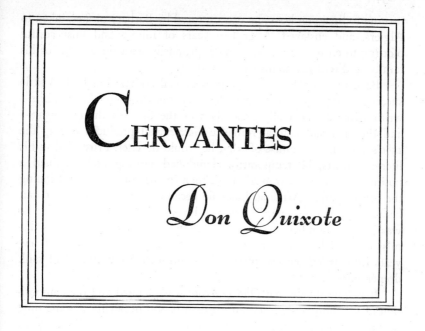

CERVANTES
Don Quixote

POPULARLY ACCLAIMED TODAY as the greatest of Spanish writers, Cervantes (1547-1616) in his own time endured hardship, misadventure, and poverty and gained due recognition of his genius only in the last years of his life. After his death, it is said that seven different cities, repeating the pattern of an earlier mystery, contended for the honor of being his birthplace.

Miguel de Cervantes Saavedra, son of an apothecary, was born in Alcalá de Henares in New Castile in 1547 and during his boyhood and youth probably lived in Valladolid, Madrid, and Seville. Very little is known of his education, but he began writing poetry very early and then at the age of twenty-one set out for Rome with an ecclesiastical delegation. In that city he was for a while in the service of a Spanish cardinal, but soon he enlisted with the Spanish troops that were part of the allied forces of Christendom assembled against the threat of Turkish invasion. He distinguished himself in the epochal naval battle of Lepanto in 1571, but he was severely wounded, and his left hand permanently maimed.

Cervantes continued in military service until 1575, when, upon returning to Spain on leave, he was captured by Barbary pirates, taken to Algiers, and enslaved. After five years of misery and unsuccessful plotting to escape he was ransomed, primarily with the savings of his family, and returned to his native land.

Back in Spain he became a professional author; but he had little success, and the slight poems, the very numerous mediocre plays— written just as the really great days of the Spanish theater began— and the artificial pastoral romance *Galatea,* all produced during the 1580's, gave little promise of what he would do later. Frustrated in his literary efforts, he temporarily abandoned writing and obtained a position in the naval commissariat, then in the course of provisioning the great Spanish Armada. Later he became a royal tax collector, but because of his unbusinesslike habits, he was constantly in trouble; he was jailed a number of times, and around the year 1597 he was dismissed from the government service. Of his life during the next few years little is known except that he continued his writing and sank deeper into poverty.

It is quite likely that *Don Quixote* was planned and the composition of it begun while Cervantes was in prison in Seville at some time between 1597 and 1602. The first mention of the book is in 1604, an entirely uncomplimentary passage in a letter of Lope de Vega, the great Spanish dramatist with whom Cervantes had formerly been on friendly terms. "No poet," wrote Lope, "is as bad as Cervantes, nor so foolish as to praise *Don Quixote.*" The first part of the work appeared in 1605, and despite Lope's strictures, its popularity was immediate and lasting and as wide as Western culture; but the book did not bring its author a great deal of money. Cervantes continued to publish poetry, dramas, and stories, and to promise a second part of *Don Quixote.* In 1613 he completed the publication of his collection of stories called *Exemplary Tales;* and then, nettled by the appearance of a spurious sequel to the first part of *Don Quixote,* he drove himself to the completion of this work. *Don Quixote,* Part II, appeared in 1615 and equalled if it did not surpass Part I in its discerning and philosophic humor.

Admired now by his countrymen, translated in other lands, and relieved finally from the poverty and distress that he had suffered for years, Cervantes had reached the heights of literary success. In the early part of 1616 he completed his romance *Persiles and Sigismunda,* but he did not live to see the work published. Suffering from dropsy, he died in Madrid on April 23, 1616, the very same day on which William Shakespeare died in England.

Although Cervantes made no sound reputation as a poet, he did produce a number of successful plays in an age of flourishing drama; but it was as a story teller that he rose to greatness. His *Exemplary Tales* alone would have given him a high place among Spanish novelists; his *Galatea* was his favorite among his own works; but *Don Quixote* was the book that insured his lasting fame. About this work he himself wrote: "Children handle it, youngsters read it, grown men understand it, and old people applaud it. In short, it is universally so thumbed, so gleaned, so studied, and so known that if the people but see a lean horse, they presently cry, 'There goes Rozinante!'"

The narrative of *Don Quixote* is ostensibly told by an Arabian author, "Cid Hamet Benengeli," as a satire on the innumerable, drearily discursive, and run-to-seed romances—degenerated from the early romances of chivalry like those of Charlemagne and Arthur—which had infatuated late medieval Europe. But the vogue for these tales was already in its last stage when Cervantes assailed them; and his protest against them was ultimately the protest of reason against vagueness, misproportion, and impulse—against those qualities that Cervantes thought were weakening his countrymen and his country. In this regard *Don Quixote* is the commentary of the superbly distinguished mind of its author upon the antic performance that most other minds exhibit without reference to date or place.

But the greatness of *Don Quixote* lies in more positive virtues than are found in the spirit of protest, however practical and worthwhile that spirit may be. Its greatness lies in its comprehensive view of sixteenth-century Spain, in the breadth and depth of its humanity, and in the stature of its central character. Don Quixote de la Mancha, for all his absurdities, is essentially right—just as his squire Sancho Panza is right. The generosity, courage, and idealism of Don Quixote, wrongheaded as he may seem, are complementary to the realism of Sancho; and the virtues of both characters are essential to the whole man. In his large implications Cervantes seems to make plain that the business of humanity in this world is largely furthered by both sun-dazzled nobility and earth-bound commonplace—however absurd either one, at times, may seem to be.

DON QUIXOTE

PART THE FIRST

CHAPTER I

The quality and way of living of Don Quixote

In a certain village in La Mancha, of which I cannot remember the name, there lived not long ago one of those old-fashioned gentlemen, who are never without a lance upon a rack, an old target, a lean horse, and a greyhound. His diet consisted more of beef than mutton; and, with minced meat on most nights, lentils on Fridays, and a pigeon extraordinary on Sundays, he consumed three-quarters of his revenue; the rest was laid out in a plush coat, velvet breeches, with slippers of the same, for holidays; and a suit of the very best homespun cloth, which he bestowed on himself for working-days. His whole family was a housekeeper something turned of forty, a niece not twenty, and a man that served in the house and in the field, and could saddle a horse, and handle the pruning-hook. The master himself was nigh fifty years of age, of a hale and strong complexion, lean-bodied and thin-faced, an early riser, and a lover of hunting. Some say his surname was Quixada, or Quesada (for authors differ in this particular); however, we may reasonably conjecture, he was called Quixada (*i.e.,* lantern-jaws), though this concerns us but little, provided we keep strictly to the truth in every point of this history.

Be it known, then, that when our gentleman had nothing to do (which was almost all the year round), he passed his time in reading books of knight-errantry, which he did with such application and delight, that at last he in a manner wholly left off his country sports, and even the care of his estate; nay, he grew so strangely enamoured of these amusements, that he sold many acres of land to purchase books of that kind, by which means he collected as many of them as he could. . . .

He would often dispute with the curate of the parish, a man of learning, that had taken his degrees at Giguenza, as to which was the better knight, Palmerin of England, or Amadis de Gaul[1]; but Master

1. Heroes of two of the best known romances of chivalry: *Palmerin of England*, a 16th century work of Spanish or Portuguese authorship, and *Amadis of Gaul*, composed in its present form by Garcia de Montalvo in the 15th century.

Nicholas, the barber of the same town, would say, that none of them could compare with the Knight of the Sun; and that if any one came near him, it was certainly Don Galaor, the brother of Amadis de Gaul; for he was a man of a most commodious temper, neither was he so finical, nor such a whining lover, as his brother; and as for courage, he was not a jot behind him.

In fine, he gave himself up so wholly to the reading of romances, that at night he would pore on until it was day, and would read on all day until it was night; and thus a world of extraordinary notions, picked out of his books, crowded into his imagination; now his head was full of nothing but enchantments, quarrels, battles, challenges, wounds, complaints, love-passages, torments, and abundance of absurd impossibilities; insomuch that all the fables and fantastical tales which he read seemed to him now as true as the most authentic histories. . . .

Having thus confused his understanding, he unluckily stumbled upon the oddest fancy that ever entered into a madman's brain; for now he thought it convenient and necessary, as well for the increase of his own honour, as the service of the public, to turn knight-errant, and roam through the whole world, armed cap-à-pie, and mounted on his steed, in quest of adventures; that thus imitating those knights-errant of whom he had read, and following their course of life, redressing all manner of grievances, and exposing himself to danger on all occasions, at last, after a happy conclusion of his enterprises, he might purchase everlasting honour and renown.

The first thing he did was to scour a suit of armour that had belonged to his great grandfather, and had lain time out of mind carelessly rusting in a corner; but when he had cleaned and repaired it as well as he could, he perceived there was a material piece wanting; for, instead of a complete helmet, there was only a single head-piece. However, his industry supplied that defect; for with some pasteboard he made a kind of half-beaver, or vizor, which, being fitted to the head-piece, made it look like an entire helmet. Then, to know whether it were cutlass-proof, he drew his sword, and tried its edge upon the pasteboard vizor; but with the very first stroke he unluckily undid in a moment what he had been a whole week in doing. He did not like its being broke with so much ease, and therefore, to secure it from the like accident, he made it anew, and fenced it with thin plates of iron, which he fixed on the inside of it so artificially, that at last he had reason to be satisfied with the solidity of the work; and so, without any farther experiment, he resolved it should pass to all intents and purposes for a full and sufficient helmet.

The next moment he went to view his horse, whose bones stuck out like the corners of a Spanish real,[2] being a worse jade than Gonela's *qui tantum pellis et ossa fuit*[3]*;* however, his master thought that neither Alexander's Bucephalus,[4] nor the Cid's Babieca,[5] could be compared with him. He was four days considering what name to give him; for, as he argued with himself, there was no reason that a horse bestrid by so famous a knight, and withal so excellent in himself, should not be distinguished by a particular name; so, after many names which he devised, rejected, changed, liked, disliked, and pitched upon again, he concluded to call him Rozinante.[6]

Having thus given his horse a name, he thought of choosing one for himself; and having seriously pondered on the matter eight whole days more, at last he determined to call himself Don Quixote.[7] Whence the author of this history draws this inference, that his right name was Quixada, and not Quesada, as others obstinately pretend. And observing, that the valiant Amadis, not satisfied with the bare appellation of Amadis, added to it the name of his country, that it might grow more famous by his exploits, and so styled himself Amadis de Gaul; so he, like a true lover of his native soil, resolved to call himself Don Quixote de la Mancha; which addition, to his thinking, denoted very plainly his parentage and country, and consequently would fix a lasting honour on that part of the world.

And now, his armour being scoured, his head-piece improved to a helmet, his horse and himself new-named, he perceived he wanted nothing but a lady, on whom he might bestow the empire of his heart; for he was sensible that a knight-errant without a mistress was a tree without either fruit or leaves, and a body without a soul. "Should I," said he to himself, "by good or ill fortune, chance to encounter some giant, as it is common in knight-errantry, and happen to lay him prostrate on the ground, transfixed with my lance, or cleft in two, or, in short, overcome him, and have him at my mercy, would it not be

2. A coin of irregular shape.
3. "Who was so much skin and bone." Gonela was a jester in the service of one of the dukes of Ferrara in Italy.
4. The horse of Alexander the Great.
5. The horse of the Spanish hero of the 11th century, the Cid Rodrigo Diaz.
6. From *Rozin*, a common work-horse, and *ante*, formerly.
7. Spanish *quixote* is the same as English *cuisse*, armor for the thigh.

proper to have some lady to whom I may send him as a trophy of my valour? Then when he comes into her presence, throwing himself at her feet, he may thus make his humble submission: 'Lady, I am the giant Caraculiambro, lord of the island of Malindrania, vanquished in single combat by that never-deservedly-enough-extolled knight-errant Don Quixote de la Mancha, who has commanded me to cast myself most humbly at your feet, that it may please your honour to dispose of me according to your will.'" Near the place where he lived dwelt a good-looking country girl, for whom he had formerly had a sort of an inclination, though, it is believed, she never heard of it, nor regarded it in the least. Her name was Aldonza Lorenzo, and this was she whom he thought he might entitle to the sovereignty of his heart; upon which he studied to find her out a new name, that might have some affinity with her old one, and yet at the same time sound somewhat like that of a princess, or lady of quality; so at last he resolved to call her Dulcinea, with addition of del Toboso, from the place where she was born; a name, in his opinion, sweet, harmonious, and dignified, like the others which he had devised.

CHAPTER II

Which treats of Don Quixote's first sally

These preparations being made, he found his designs ripe for action, and thought it now a crime to deny himself any longer to the injured world that wanted such a deliverer; the more when he considered what grievances he was to redress, what wrongs and injuries to remove, what abuses to correct, and what duties to discharge. So one morning before day, in the greatest heat of July, without acquainting any one with his design, with all the secrecy imaginable, he armed himself cap-à-pie, laced on his ill-contrived helmet, braced on his target, grasped his lance, mounted Rozinante, and at the private door of his back-yard sallied out into the fields, wonderfully pleased to see with how much ease he had succeeded in the beginning of his enterprise. But he had not gone far ere a terrible thought alarmed him; a thought that had like to have made him renounce his great undertaking; for now it came into his mind, that the honour of knighthood had not yet been conferred upon him, and therefore, according to the laws of chivalry, he neither could nor ought to appear in arms against any

professed knight; nay, he also considered, that though he were already
knighted, it would become him to wear white armour, and not to
adorn his shield with any device, until he had deserved one by some
extraordinary demonstration of his valour.

These thoughts staggered his resolution; but his frenzy prevailing
more than reason, he resolved to be dubbed a knight by the first he
should meet, after the example of several others, who, as the romances
informed him, had formerly done the like. As for the other difficulty
about wearing white armour, he proposed to overcome it, by scouring
his own at leisure until it should look whiter than ermine. And having
thus dismissed these scruples, he rode calmly on, leaving it to his horse
to go which way he pleased; firmly believing, that in this consisted
the very essence of adventures. And as he thus went on, "no doubt,"
said he to himself, "that when the history of my famous achievements
shall be given to the world, the learned author will begin it in this very
manner, when he comes to give an account of this my setting out:
'Scarce had the ruddy Phœbus begun to spread the golden tresses of his
lovely hair over the vast surface of the earthly globe, and scarce had
those feathered poets of the grove, the pretty painted birds, tuned their
little pipes, to sing their early welcomes in soft melodious strains to the
beautiful Aurora, displaying her rosy graces to mortal eyes from the
gates and balconies of the Manchegan horizon,—when the renowned
knight Don Quixote de la Mancha, disdaining soft repose, forsook the
voluptuous down, and mounting his famous steed Rozinante, entered
the ancient and celebrated plains of Montiel.' "[8] . . . To these extravagant conceits, he added a world of others, all in imitation, and in
the very style of those which the reading of romances had furnished
him with; and all this while he rode so softly, and the sun's heat increased so fast, and was so violent, that it would have been sufficient to
have melted his brains, had he had any left.

He travelled almost all that day without meeting any adventure
worth the trouble of relating, which put him into a kind of despair;
for he desired nothing more than to encounter immediately some person on whom he might try the vigour of his arm.

Towards the evening, he and his horse being heartily tired and
almost famished, Don Quixote looked about him, in hopes to discover
some castle, or at least some shepherd's cottage, there to repose and refresh himself; and at last near the road which he kept, he espied an
inn, a most welcome sight to his longing eyes. Hastening towards it

8. In La Mancha, scene of a battle in 1369.

with all the speed he could, he got thither just at the close of the evening. There stood by chance at the inn-door two young female adventurers, who were going to Seville with some carriers that happened to take up their lodging there that very evening; and as whatever our knight-errant saw, thought, or imagined, was all of a romantic cast, and appeared to him altogether after the manner of his favourite books, he no sooner saw the inn but he fancied it to be a castle fenced with four towers, and lofty pinnacles glittering with silver, together with a deep moat, drawbridge, and all those other appurtenances peculiar to such kind of places.

When he came near it, he stopped awhile at a distance from the gate, expecting that some dwarf would appear on the battlements, and sound his trumpet to give notice of the arrival of a knight; but finding that nobody came, and that Rozinante was for making the best of his way to the stable, he advanced to the inn-door, saw there the two country girls, who appeared to him to be beautiful damsels, or lovely dames, taking their pleasure at the castle-gate.

It happened just at this time, that a swineherd, who in a stubble hard by was tending a drove of hogs, blew his horn, as was his custom, to call them together; and instantly Don Quixote's imagination represented to him that a dwarf gave the signal of his arrival. With great satisfaction, therefore, he rode up to the inn. The women, perceiving a man armed with lance and buckler, were frightened, and about to retreat into the house. But Don Quixote, guessing at their fear by their flight, lifted up his pasteboard vizor, and discovering his withered and dusty visage, with gentle voice and respectful demeanour thus accosted them.

"Fly not, ladies, nor fear any discourtesy; for the order of knighthood, which I profess, forbids my offering injury to any one, much less to damsels of such exalted rank as your presence denotes you to be." The women stared at him with all their eyes, endeavouring to find out his face, which the sorry beaver almost covered, and could not help laughing so loudly that Don Quixote was offended, and said to them: "Modesty is becoming in beauty, and excessive laughter, proceeding from a slight cause, is folly. This I mention not as a reproach, by which I may incur your resentment: on the contrary, I have no wish but to do you service."

This language, which they did not understand, and the extraordinary appearance of the knight, increased their laughter, which also increased his displeasure, and he would probably have shown it in a less civil way, but for the timely arrival of the innkeeper. He was a man whose burden of fat inclined him to peace and quietness, yet when he observed such a strange disguise of human shape in his old armour and equipage, he could hardly forbear laughter; but having the fear of such a warlike appearance before his eyes, he resolved to give him good words, and therefore accosted him civilly.

"Sir Knight," said he, "if your worship be disposed to alight, you will fail of nothing here but of a bed; as for all other accommodations, you may be supplied to your mind."

Don Quixote observing the humility of the governor of the castle (for such the innkeeper and inn seemed to him), "Signor Castellano," said he, "the least thing in the world suffices me; for arms are the only things I value, and combat is my bed of repose." The host thought from Don Quixote calling him Castellano[9] that he took him for an honest Castilian, while he was really an Andalusian, and as full of fun and mischief as a schoolboy or a page. He answered:

"At this rate, Sir Knight, you may safely alight, and I dare assure you, you can hardly miss being kept awake all the year long in this house, much less one single night."

With that he went and held Don Quixote's stirrup, who having ate nothing all that day, dismounted with no small trouble and difficulty. He immediately desired the governor (that is, the innkeeper) to have special care of his steed, assuring him that there was not a better in the universe; upon which the innkeeper viewed him narrowly, but could not think him to be half so good as Don Quixote said. However, having put him in the stable, he came back to the knight to see if he wanted anything.

He found the damsels, already reconciled to his guest, unarming him. They had disencumbered him of the back and breast-pieces of his armour, but could not find out how to unlace his gorget, or take off the counterfeit beaver, which he had fastened with ribbons, in such a manner, that, as there was no possibility of untying them, they must of necessity be cut. To this, however, the knight would by no means consent, and he therefore remained all night with his helmet on; the strangest and most ridiculous figure imaginable.

While the women, whom he still imagined to be of the first quality and ladies of the castle, were thus aiding him, he addressed them, with much self-satisfaction and perfect courtesy.

"Never was knight so nobly served as Don Quixote, after his de-

9. The word means both Castilian and governor of a castle.

parture from his village. Damsels waited upon him; princesses cared for his steed. O Rozinante! That, dear ladies, is my horse's name, and Don Quixote de la Mancha my own; though I had no intention to discover myself, till deeds achieved for your service and benefit should have proclaimed me; but the necessity of accommodating the old romance of Sir Launcelot to my present situation has occasioned your knowing my name before the proper season. The time, however, will come when your highnesses shall command and I obey, and the valour of my arm shall make manifest the desire I have to be your slave."

The girls, unaccustomed to such rhetorical flourishes, made no reply to them, but simply asked the knight whether he would be pleased to eat anything.

"Most willingly," answered he; "anything eatable I feel would come very seasonably." . . .

Thereupon they laid the cloth at the inn-door for the benefit of the fresh air, and the landlord brought him a piece of salt fish, but ill-watered and as ill-dressed; and as for the bread, it was as mouldy and brown as the knight's armour.

It was a source of great mirth to see him eat; for his hands being occupied in keeping his helmet on and the beaver up, he had no means of feeding himself, and the office was performed by one of the ladies. To give him drink would have been utterly impossible, had not the innkeeper bored a reed, and, putting one end to the knight's mouth, poured in the wine leisurely at the other; but all this Don Quixote patiently endured, rather than cut the lacings of his helmet.

While he was at supper, a pig-driver happened to sound his cane-trumpet, or whistle of reeds, four or five times as he came near the inn, which made Don Quixote the more positive that he was in a famous castle, where he was entertained with music at supper, that the country girls were great ladies, and the innkeeper the governor of the castle, which made him applaud himself for his resolution, and his setting out on such an account. The only thing that vexed him was, that he was not yet dubbed a knight; for he fancied he could not lawfully undertake any adventure till he had received the order of knight-hood.

CHAPTER III

An account of the pleasant method taken by Don Quixote to be dubbed a knight

Don Quixote's mind being disturbed with that thought, he abridged even his short supper; and as soon as he had done, he called his host; then shut him and himself up in the stable, and falling at his feet, "I will never rise from this place," cried he, "most valorous knight, till you have graciously vouchsafed to grant me a boon, which I will now beg of you, and which will redound to your honour and the good of mankind."

The innkeeper, strangely at a loss to find his guest at his feet, and talking at this rate, endeavoured to make him rise; but all in vain, till he had promised to grant him what he asked.

"I expected no less from your great magnificence, noble sir," replied Don Quixote; "and therefore I make bold to tell you, that the boon which I beg, and you generously condescend to grant me, is, that to-morrow you will be pleased to bestow the honour of knighthood upon me. This night I will watch my armour in the chapel of your castle, and then in the morning you shall gratify me, that I may be duly qualified to seek out adventures in every corner of the universe, to relieve the distressed, according to the laws of chivalry and the inclinations of knights-errant like myself."

The innkeeper, who, as I said, was an arch fellow, and had already a shrewd suspicion of his guest's disorder, was fully convinced of it when he heard him talk in this manner; and to make sport he resolved to humour him, telling him he was much to be commended for his choice of such an employment, which was altogether worthy a knight of the first order, such as his gallant deportment discovered him to be: that he himself had in his youth followed that profession, ranging through many parts of the world in search of adventures, till at length he retired to this castle, where he lived on his own estate and those of others, entertaining all knights-errant of what quality or condition soever, purely for the great affection he bore them, and to partake of what they might share with him in return. He added, that his castle at present had no chapel where the knight might keep the vigil of his arms, it being pulled down in order to be new built; but that he knew they might lawfully be watched in any other place in a case of necessity, and therefore he might do it that night in the courtyard of the castle; and in the morning all the necessary ceremonies should be performed, so that he might assure himself he should be dubbed a knight, nay, as much a knight as any one in the world could be. He then asked Don Quixote whether he had any money?

"Not a cross," replied the knight, "for I never read in any history of chivalry that any knight-errant ever carried money about him."

"You are mistaken," cried the innkeeper; "for admit the histories are silent in this matter, the authors thinking it needless to mention things so evidently necessary as money and clean shirts, yet there is no reason to believe the knights went without either; and you may rest assured, that all the knights-errant, of whom so many histories are full, had their purses well lined to supply themselves with necessaries, and carried also with them some shirts, and a small box of salves to heal their wounds; for they had not the conveniency of surgeons to cure them every time they fought in fields and deserts, unless they were so happy as to have some sage or magician for their friend to give them present assistance, sending them some damsel or dwarf through the air in a cloud, with a small bottle of water of so great a virtue, that they no sooner tasted a drop of it, but their wounds were as perfectly cured as if they had never received any. But when they wanted such a friend in former ages, the knights thought themselves obliged to take care that their squires should be provided with money and other necessaries; and if those knights ever happened to have no squires, which was but very seldom, then they carried those things behind them in a little bag. I must therefore advise you," continued he, "never from this time forwards to ride without money, nor without the other necessaries of which I spoke to you, which you will find very beneficial when you least expect it."

Don Quixote promised to perform all his injunctions; and so they disposed everything in order to his watching his arms in the great yard. To which purpose the knight, having got them all together, laid them in a horse-trough close by a well; then bracing his target, and grasping his lance, just as it grew dark, he began to walk about by the horse-trough with a graceful deportment. In the meanwhile, the innkeeper acquainted all those that were in the house with the extravagances of his guest, his watching his arms, and his hopes of being made a knight. They all marvelled very much at so strange a kind of folly, and went on to observe him at a distance; where, they saw him sometimes walk about with a great deal of gravity, and sometimes lean on his lance, with his eyes all the while fixed upon his arms. It was now undoubted night, but yet the moon did shine with such a brightness, as might almost have vied with that of the luminary which lent it her; so that the knight was wholly exposed to the spectators' view. While he was thus employed, one of the carriers who lodged in the inn came out to water his mules, which he could not do without removing the arms out of the trough. With that, Don Quixote, who saw him make towards them, cried out to him aloud, "O thou, whoever thou art, rash knight, that prepares to lay thy hands on the arms of the most valorous knight-errant that ever wore a sword, take heed; do not audaciously attempt to profane them with a touch, lest instant death be the too sure reward of thy temerity." But the carrier regarded not these threats; and laying hold of the armour without any more ado, threw it a good way from him; though it had been better for him to have let it alone; for Don Quixote no sooner saw this, but lifting up his eyes to heaven, and thus addressing his thoughts, as it seemed, to his lady Dulcinea: "Assist me, lady," cried he, "in the first opportunity that offers itself to your faithful slave; nor let your favour and protection be denied me in this first trial of my valour!"

Repeating such-like ejaculations, he let slip his target, and lifting up his lance with both his hands, he gave the carrier such a terrible knock on his inconsiderate head with his lance, that he laid him at his feet in a woful condition; and had he backed that blow with another, the fellow would certainly have had no need of a surgeon. This done, Don Quixote took up his armour, laid it again in the horse-trough, and then walked on backwards and forwards with as great unconcern as he did at first.

Soon after another carrier, not knowing what had happened, came also to water his mules, while the first yet lay on the ground in a trance; but as he offered to clear the trough of the armour, Don Quixote, without speaking a word, or imploring any one's assistance, once more dropped his target, lifted up his lance, and then let it fall so heavily on the fellow's pate, that without damaging his lance, he broke the carrier's head in three or four places. His outcry soon alarmed and brought thither all the people in the inn, and the landlord among the rest: which Don Quixote perceiving, "Thou Queen of Beauty," cried he, bracing on his shield, and drawing his sword, "thou courage and vigour of my weakened heart, now is the time when thou must enliven thy adventurous slave with the beams of thy greatness, while this moment he is engaging in so terrible an adventure!"

With this, in his opinion, he found himself supplied with such an addition of courage, that had all the carriers in the world at once attacked him, he would undoubtedly have faced them all. On the other side, the carriers, enraged to see their comrades thus used, though they were afraid to come near, gave the knight such a volley of stones, that he was forced to shelter himself as well as he could under the covert of his target, without daring to go far from the horse-trough, lest he should seem to abandon his arms. The innkeeper called to the carriers as loud as he could to let him alone; that he had told them already he was mad, and consequently the law would acquit him, though he should kill them. Don Quixote also made yet more noise, calling them false and treacherous villains, and the lord of the castle base and inhospitable, and a discourteous knight, for suffering a knight-errant to be so abused.

"I would make thee know," cried he, "what a perfidious wretch thou art, had I but received the order of knighthood; but for you, base, ignominious rabble, fling on, do your worst; come on, draw nearer if you dare, and receive the reward of your indiscretion and insolence."

This he spoke with so much spirit and undauntedness, that he struck a terror into all his assailants; so that, partly through fear, and partly through the innkeeper's persuasions, they gave over flinging stones at him; and he, on his side, permitted the enemy to carry off their wounded, and then returned to the guard of his arms as calm and composed as before.

The innkeeper, who began somewhat to disrelish these mad tricks of his guest, resolved to despatch him forthwith, and bestow on him that unlucky knighthood, to prevent further mischief; so coming to him, he excused himself for the insolence of those base scoundrels, as being done without his privity or consent; but their audaciousness, he said, was sufficiently punished. He added, that he had already told him there was no chapel in his castle; and that indeed there was no need of one to finish the rest of the ceremony of knighthood, which consisted only in the application of the sword to the neck and shoulders, as he had read in the register of the ceremonies of the order; and that this might be performed as well in a field as anywhere else: that he had already fulfilled the obligation of watching his arms, which required no more than two hours' watch, whereas he had been four hours upon the guard. Don Quixote, who easily believed him, told him he was ready to obey him, and desired him to make an end of the business as soon as possible; for if he were but knighted, and should see himself once attacked, he believed he should not leave a man alive in the castle, except those whom he should desire him to spare for his sake.

Upon this, the innkeeper, lest the knight should proceed to such extremities, fetched the book in which he used to set down the carriers' accounts for straw and barley; and having brought with him the two kind females already mentioned, and a boy that held a piece of lighted candle in his hand, he ordered Don Quixote to kneel: then reading in his manual, as if he had been repeating some pious oration, in the midst of his devotion he lifted up his hand, and gave him a good blow on the neck, and then a gentle slap on the back with the flat of his sword, still mumbling some words between his teeth in the tone of a prayer. After this he ordered one of the ladies to gird the sword about the knight's waist: which she did with much solemnity, and, I may add, discretion, considering how hard a thing it was to forbear laughing at every circumstance of the ceremony: it is true, the thoughts of the knight's late prowess did not a little contribute to the suppression of her mirth. As she girded on his sword, "Heaven," cried the kind lady, "make your worship a lucky knight, and prosper you wherever you go." Don Quixote desired to know her name, that he might understand to whom he was indebted for the favour she had bestowed upon him, and also make her partaker of the honour he was to acquire by the strength of his arm. To which the lady answered with all humility, that her name was Tolosa, a cobbler's daughter, that kept a stall among the little shops of Sanchobinaya at Toledo; and that whenever he pleased to command her, she would be his humble servant. Don Quixote begged of her to do him the favour to add hereafter the title of lady to her name, and for his sake to be called from that time Donna Tolosa; which she promised to do. Her companion having buckled on his spurs, occasioned a like conference between them; and when he had asked her name, she told him she went by the name of Molivera, being the daughter of an honest miller of Antequera. Our new knight entreated her also to style herself the Donna Molivera, making her new offers of service. These extraordinary ceremonies (the like never seen before) being thus hurried over in a kind of post-haste, Don Quixote could not rest till he had taken the field in quest of adventures; therefore, having immediately saddled his Rozinante, and being mounted, he embraced the innkeeper, and returned him so many thanks at so extravagant a rate, for the obligation he had laid upon him in dubbing him a knight, that it is impossible to give a true relation of them all:

to which the innkeeper, in haste to get rid of him, returned as rhetorical, though shorter answers; and, without stopping his horse for the reckoning, was glad with all his heart to see him go.

CHAPTER IV

What befel the Knight after he had left the inn

Aurora began to usher in the morn, when Don Quixote sallied out of the inn, so overjoyed to find himself knighted, that he infused the same satisfaction into his horse, who seemed ready to burst his girths for joy. But calling to mind the admonitions which the innkeeper had given him, concerning the provision of necessary accommodation in his travels, particularly money and clean shirts, he resolved to return home to furnish himself with them, and likewise get him a squire, designing to entertain as such a labouring man, his neighbour, who was poor and had a number of children, but yet very fit for the office. With this resolution he took the road which led to his own village. . . .

Don Quixote had not gone above two miles when he discovered a company of people riding towards him, who proved to be merchants of Toledo, going to buy silks in Murcia. They were six in all, every one screened with an umbrella, besides four servants on horseback, and three muleteers on foot. The knight no sooner perceived them but he imagined this to be some new adventure; so, fixing himself in his stirrups, couching his lance, and covering his breast with his target, he posted himself in the middle of the road, expecting the coming up of the supposed knights-errant. As soon as they came within hearing, with a loud voice and haughty tone, "Hold," cried he; "let no man hope to pass further, unless he acknowledge and confess that there is not in the universe a more beautiful damsel than the empress of La Mancha, the peerless Dulcinea del Toboso."

At those words the merchants made a halt, to view the unaccountable figure of their opponent; and conjecturing, both by his expression and disguise, that the poor gentleman had lost his senses, they were willing to understand the meaning of that strange confession which he would force from them; and therefore one of the company, who loved raillery, and had discretion to manage it, undertook to talk to him.

"Signor Cavalier," cried he, "we do not know this worthy lady you talk of; but be pleased to let us see her, and then if we find her possessed of those matchless charms, of which you assert her to be the mistress, we will freely, and without the least compulsion, own the truth which you would extort from us."

"Had I once shown you that beauty," replied Don Quixote, "what wonder would it be to acknowledge so notorious a truth? the importance of the thing lies in obliging you to believe it, confess it, affirm it, swear it, and maintain it, without seeing her; and therefore make this acknowledgment this very moment, or know that with me you must join in battle, ye proud and unreasonable mortals! Come one by one, as the laws of chivalry require, or all at once, according to the dishonourable practice of men of your stamp; here I expect[10] you all my single self, and will stand the encounter, confiding in the justice of my cause."

"Sir Knight," replied the merchant, "I beseech you, that for the discharge of our consciences, which will not permit us to affirm a thing we never heard or saw, your worship will vouchsafe to let us see some portraiture of that lady, though it were no bigger than a grain of wheat; for by a small sample we may judge of the whole piece, and by that means rest secure and satisfied, and you contented and appeased. Nay, I verily believe, that we all find ourselves already so inclinable to comply with you, that though her picture should represent her to be blind of one eye, and distilling vermilion and brimstone at the other, yet, to oblige you, we shall be ready to say in her favour whatever your worship desires."

"Distil, ye infamous scoundrels," replied Don Quixote in a burning rage, "distil, say you? know, that nothing distils from her but amber and civet; neither is she defective in her make or shape, but more straight than a Guadaramian Spindle.[11] But you shall all severely pay for the blasphemy which thou hast uttered against the transcendent beauty of my incomparable lady."

Saying this, with his lance couched, he ran so furiously at the merchant who thus provoked him, that had not good fortune so ordered it that Rozinante should stumble and fall in the midst of his career, the audacious trifler had paid dear for his raillery: but as Rozinante fell, he threw down his master, who rolled and tumbled a good way on the ground without being able to get upon his legs, though he used all his skill and strength to effect it, so encumbered

10. Await.
11. Near Guadarama there was a formation of perpendicular rocks called the Spindles.

he was with his lance, target, spurs, helmet, and the weight of his rusty armour. However, in this helpless condition he played the hero with his tongue; "Stay," cried he; "cowards, rascals, do not fly! it is not through my fault that I lie here, but through that of my horse, ye poltroons!"

One of the muleteers, who was none of the best-natured creatures, hearing the overthrown knight thus insolently treat his master, could not bear it without returning him an answer on his ribs; and therefore coming up to him as he lay wallowing, he snatched his lance, and having broke it to pieces, so belaboured Don Quixote's sides with one of them, that in spite of his arms, he thrashed him like a wheatsheaf. His master indeed called to him not to lay on him so vigorously, and to let him alone; but the fellow, whose hand was in, would not give over till he had tired out his passion and himself; and therefore running to the other pieces of the broken lance, he fell to it again without ceasing, till he had splintered them all on the knight's iron enclosure. At last the mule-driver was tired, and the merchants pursued their journey, sufficiently furnished with matter of discourse at the poor knight's expense. When he found himself alone, he tried once more to get on his feet; but if he could not do it when he had the use of his limbs, how should he do it now, bruised and battered as he was? But yet for all this, he esteemed himself a happy man, being still persuaded that his misfortune was one of those accidents common in knight-errantry, and such a one as he could wholly attribute to the falling of his horse.

[A poor peasant, a neighbor of Don Quixote, comes upon him and takes him home. His friends the priest and the barber have in the meantime come to his house and learned of his wild sally. With Don Quixote's niece and his housekeeper they decide to burn his books of knight-errantry. They save *Amadis of Gaul* and *Palmerin of England,* but most of the rest they toss into the yard.]

CHAPTER VII

Don Quixote's second sally in quest of adventures

... The night was no sooner set in, than the housekeeper kindled a fire, and burned all the books that were either in the yard, or the house; and some must have perished that deserved to be treasured up in perpetual archives; but their fate, and the laziness of the scrutineers, would not permit it: and in them was fulfilled the saying, "that a saint may sometimes suffer for a sinner."

Another remedy, which the priest and barber prescribed for their friend's malady, was, to alter his apartment, and wall up the closet in which the books had been kept, in the hope that upon his getting up, and not finding them, the cause being removed, the effect might cease; and it was agreed they should pretend, that an enchanter had carried them away, room and all; which things were done accordingly within the two days that Don Quixote was confined to his bed. When he rose, the first thing he did was to visit, as had been supposed, his study; and, not finding the room where he left it, he went up and down looking for it: coming to the place where the door used to be, he felt with his hands, and stared about in every direction, without speaking a word; at last he asked the housekeeper where the room stood, in which his books were. She, who was already well tutored what to answer, said to him—

"What room, or what nothing, does your worship look for? there is neither room nor books in this house; for the devil himself has carried all away."

"It was not the devil," said the niece, "but an enchanter, who came one night, after your departure hence, upon a cloud, and, alighting from a serpent on which he rode, entered into the room. I know not what he did there, but after a short time out he came, flying through the roof, and left the house full of smoke; and when we went to see what he had been doing, we could find neither books nor room; only we very well remember, both I and mistress housekeeper here, that when the old thief went away, he said with a gruff voice, that for a secret enmity he bore to the owner of those books and of the room, he had done a mischief, which would soon be manifest. He told us also, that he was the sage Munniaton."

"Freston,[12] he meant to say," quoth Don Quixote.

"I know not," answered the housekeeper, "whether his name be Freston or Friton; all I know is, that it ended in ton."

"It doth so," replied Don Quixote; "he is a wise enchanter, a great enemy of mine, and bears me a grudge, because by the mystery of his art he knows, that, in process of time, I shall engage in single combat

12. A necromancer in one of Don Quixote's favorite books, *Don Belianis of Greece.*

with a knight whom he favours, and shall vanquish him, without his being able to prevent it: and for this reason he endeavours to do me all the discourtesy he can: but let him know from me, it will be difficult for him to withstand or avoid what is decreed by Heaven." . . .

He stayed after this fifteen days at home, very composed, without discovering any symptom of relapse, or inclination to repeat his late frolics; in which time there passed many very pleasant discourses between him and his two gossiping friends, the priest and the barber; he affirming, that the world stood in need of nothing so much as knights-errant, and the revival of chivalry; and the priest sometimes contradicting him, and at other times acquiescing; for without this artifice, there would have been no means left to bring him to reason.

In the meantime, Don Quixote tampered with a neighbouring labourer, an honest man, but of a very shallow brain; to whom he said so much, used so many arguments, and made so many fair promises, that at last the poor silly clown consented to go with him, and be his squire. Among other inducements to entice him to do it willingly, Don Quixote failed not to tell him, that it was likely such an adventure would present itself, as might secure him the conquest of some island in the time that he might be picking up a straw or two, and then the squire might promise himself to be made governor of the place. Allured with these large promises, and many others, Sancho Panza (for that was the name of the fellow) forsook his wife and children to be his neighbour's squire.

This done, Don Quixote made it his business to furnish himself with money; to which purpose, selling one house, mortgaging another, and losing by all, he at last got a pretty good sum together. He also borrowed a target of a friend; and having patched up his head-piece and beaver as well as he could, he gave his squire notice of the day and hour when he intended to set out, that he also might furnish himself with what he thought necessary; but, above all, he charged him to provide himself with a wallet; which Sancho promised to do, telling him he would also take his ass along with him, which being a very good one, might be a great ease to him, for he was not used to travel much a-foot. The mentioning of the ass made the noble knight pause awhile; he mused and pondered whether he had ever read of any knight-errant, whose squire used to ride upon an ass; but he could not remember any precedent for it: however, he gave him leave at last to bring his ass, hoping to mount him more honourably with the first opportunity, by unhorsing the next discourteous knight he should meet.

He also furnished himself with linen, and as many other necessaries as he could conveniently carry, according to the innkeeper's advice. Which being done, Sancho Panza, without bidding either his wife or children good-bye, and Don Quixote, without taking any more notice of his housekeeper or of his niece, stole out of the village one night, not so much as suspected by anybody, and made such haste, that by break of day they thought themselves out of reach, should they happen to be pursued. As for Sancho Panza, he rode like a patriarch, with his canvas knapsack, or wallet, and his leathern bottle; having a huge desire to see himself governor of the island, which his master had promised him. . . .

CHAPTER VIII

Of the good success which the valorous Don Quixote had in the most terrifying and incredible adventure of the Windmills, with other transactions worthy to be transmitted to posterity

As they were thus discoursing, they discovered some thirty or forty windmills, in the plain; and as soon as the knight had spied them, "Fortune," cried he, "directs our affairs better than we could have wished; look yonder, Sancho, there are at least thirty outrageous giants, whom I intend to encounter; and having deprived them of life, we will begin to enrich ourselves with their spoils: for they are lawful prize; and the extirpation of that cursed brood will be an acceptable service to heaven."

"What giants?" quoth Sancho Panza.

"Those whom thou seest yonder," answered Don Quixote, "with their long extended arms; some of that detested race have arms of so immense a size that sometimes they reach two leagues in length."

"Pray look better, sir," quoth Sancho; "those things yonder are not giants, but windmills, and the arms are their sails, which being whirled about by the wind, make the mill go."

" 'Tis a sign," cried Don Quixote, "thou art but little acquainted with adventures! I tell thee, they are giants; and therefore if thou art afraid, go aside and say thy prayers, for I am resolved to engage in combat with them all."

This said, he clapped spurs to his horse, without giving ear to his squire, who bawled out to him, and assured him that they were windmills, and no giants. But he was so fully possessed with a strong conceit of the contrary, that he did not so much as hear his squire, nor was he sensible of what they were, although he was already very near them.

"Stand, cowards!" cried he as loud as he could; "stand your ground, ignoble creatures, and fly not basely from a single knight, who dares encounter you all."

At the same time the wind rising, the mill-sails began to move, which, when Don Quixote spied, "Base miscreants," cried he, "though you move more arms than the giant Briareus,[13] you shall pay for your arrogance."

He most devoutly recommended himself to his Lady Dulcinea, imploring her assistance in this perilous adventure; and so covering himself with his shield, and couching his lance, he rushed with Rozinante's utmost speed upon the first windmill he could come at, and running his lance into the sail, the wind whirled it about with such swiftness, that the rapidity of the motion presently broke the lance into shivers, and hurled away both knight and horse along with it, till down he fell, rolling a good way off in the field. Sancho Panza ran as fast as his ass could drive to help his master, whom he found lying, and not able to stir.

"Did not I give your worship fair warning?" cried he; "did not I tell you they were windmills, and that nobody could think otherwise, unless he had also windmills in his head?"

"Peace, friend Sancho," replied Don Quixote; "there is nothing so subject to the inconstancy of fortune as war. I am verily persuaded, that cursed necromancer Freston, who carried away my study and my books, has transformed these giants into windmills, to deprive me of the honour of the victory; such is his inveterate malice against me: but in the end, all his pernicious wiles and stratagems shall prove ineffectual against the prevailing edge of my sword."

"So let it be," replied Sancho.

And heaving him up again upon his legs, once more the knight mounted poor Rozinante, who was half disjointed with his fall. . . .

Sancho desired him now to consider that it was high time to go to dinner; but his master answered him, that he might eat whenever he pleased; as for himself, he was not yet disposed to do so. Sancho having obtained leave, fixed himself as orderly as he could upon his ass; and taking some victuals out of his wallet, fell to munching lustily; and ever and anon he lifted his bottle to his nose, and fetched such hearty

13. In Greek mythology a giant with fifty heads and a hundred arms.

pulls, that it would have made the best-pampered vintner in Malaga dry to have seen him.

In fine, they passed that night under some trees; from one of which Don Quixote tore a withered branch, which in some sort was able to serve him for a lance, and to this he fixed the head or spear of his broken lance. But he did not sleep all that night, keeping his thoughts intent on his dear Dulcinea, in imitation of what he had read in books of chivalry, where the knights pass their time, without sleep, in forests and deserts, wholly taken up with entertaining thoughts of their absent ladies. The next day they went on directly towards the pass of Lapice, which they discovered about three o'clock. When they came near it:

"Here it is, brother Sancho," said Don Quixote, "that we may, as it were, thrust our arms up to the very elbows in that which we call adventures. But let me give thee one necessary caution; know, that though thou shouldst see me in the greatest extremity of danger, thou must not offer to draw thy sword in my defence, unless thou findest me assaulted by base plebeians and vile scoundrels; for in such a case thou mayest assist thy master; but if those with whom I am fighting are knights, thou must not do it, for the laws of chivalry do not allow thee to encounter a knight till thou art one thyself."

"Never fear," quoth Sancho; "I'll be sure to obey your worship in that, I'll warrant you; for I have ever loved peace and quietness, and never cared to thrust myself into frays and quarrels."

As they were talking, they spied coming towards them two monks of the order of St. Benedict mounted on two dromedaries, for the mules on which they rode were so high and stately, that they seemed little less. After them came a coach, with four or five men on horseback, and two muleteers on foot. There proved to be in the coach a Biscayan lady, who was going to Seville to meet her husband, that was there in order to embark for the Indies, to take possession of a considerable post. Scarce had the Don perceived the monks, who were not of the same company, though they went the same way, but he cried to his squire, "Either I am deceived, or this will prove the most famous adventure that ever was known; for without all question those two black things that move towards us must be necromancers, that are carrying away by force some princess in that coach; and 'tis my duty to prevent so great an injury."

"I fear me this will prove a worse job than the windmills," quoth Sancho. "These are Benedictine monks, and the coach must belong to some traveller. Take warning, sir, and do not be led away a second time."

"I have already told thee, Sancho," replied Don Quixote, "thou art miserably ignorant in matters of adventures: what I say is true, and thou shalt find it so presently."

This said, he spurred on his horse, and posted himself just in the midst of the road where the monks were to pass. And when they came within hearing, he immediately cried out in a loud and haughty tone, "Release those high-born princesses whom you are violently conveying away in the coach, or else prepare to meet with instant death, as the just punishment of your deeds."

The monks stopped, no less astonished at the figure than at the expressions of the speaker. "Sir Knight," cried they, "we are no such persons as you are pleased to term us, but religious men of the order of St. Benedict, that travel about our affairs, and are wholly ignorant whether or no there are any princesses carried away by force in that coach."

"I am not to be deceived," replied Don Quixote; "I know you well enough, perfidious caitiffs:" and immediately, without waiting their reply, he set spurs to Rozinante, and ran so furiously, with his lance couched, against the first monk, that if he had not prudently flung himself to the ground, the knight would certainly have laid him either dead, or grievously wounded. The other observing this, clapped his heels to his mule's flanks, and scoured over the plain as if he had been running a race with the wind. Sancho no sooner saw the monk fall, but he leapt off his ass, and running to him, began to strip him immediately; but the two muleteers, who waited on the monks, came up to him, and asked why he offered to strip him. Sancho told them that this belonged to him as lawful plunder, being the spoils won in battle by his lord and master Don Quixote. The fellows, with whom there was no jesting, not knowing what he meant by his spoils and battle, and seeing Don Quixote at a good distance in deep discourse by the side of the coach, fell both upon poor Sancho, threw him down, tore his beard from his chin, trampled on him, and there left him lying without breath or motion. In the meanwhile the monk, scared out of his wits and as pale as a ghost, got upon his mule again as fast as he could, and spurred after his friend, who stayed for him at a distance, expecting the issue of this strange adventure; but being unwilling to stay to see the end of it, they made the best of their way, making more signs of the cross than if the devil had been posting after them.

Don Quixote was all this while engaged with the lady in the coach.

"Lady," cried he, "your discretion is now at liberty to dispose of your beautiful self as you please; for the presumptuous arrogance of those who attempted to enslave your person lies prostrate in the dust, overthrown by this arm: and that you may not be at a loss for the name of your deliverer, know I am called Don Quixote de la Mancha, by profession a knight-errant and adventurer, captive to that peerless beauty Donna Dulcinea del Toboso: nor do I desire any other recompense for the service I have done you, but that you return to Toboso to present yourself to that lady, and let her know what I have done to purchase your deliverance."

All that Don Quixote said was overheard by a certain squire, who accompanied the coach, a Biscayner, who, finding he would not let it go on, but insisted upon its immediately returning to Toboso, flew at Don Quixote, and, taking hold of his lance, addressed him, in bad Castilian, and worse Biscayan, after this manner:

"Get thee gone, cavalier; I swear if thou dost not quit the coach, thou shalt forfeit thy life, as I am a Biscayner."

Our knight, who understood him very well, with great calmness answered, "Wert thou a gentleman, as thou art not, I would before now have chastised thy folly and presumption, thou pitiful slave."

To which the Biscayner replied, "I no gentleman! I swear thou liest, as I am a Christian; if thou wilt throw away thy lance, and draw thy sword, thou shalt see I will make no more of thee than a cat does of a mouse: Biscayner by land, gentleman by sea, gentleman for the devil, and thou liest: look then if thou hast anything else to say."

"Thou shalt see that presently," answered Don Quixote; and throwing down his lance, he drew his sword, and grasping his buckler, set upon the Biscayner, with a determined resolution to put him to death. The Biscayner, seeing him come on in that manner, would fain have alighted from his mule, which, being but a sorry hack, was not to be depended upon, but had only time to draw: it, however, fortunately happened that he was close to the coach, out of which he snatched a cushion, to serve him for a shield; and immediately they began to fight, as if they had been mortal enemies. The rest of the company would fain have made peace between them, but could not succeed; for the Biscayner swore in his gibberish, that, if they would not let him finish the combat, he would kill his mistress, and everybody that offered to oppose it. The lady, amazed and terrified at what she saw, ordered the coachman to drive a little out of the way, and she sat at a distance, beholding the conflict; in the progress of which, the Biscayner bestowed on one of the shoulders of Don Quixote, and above his buckler, so mighty a stroke, that had it not been for his coat of mail, he would have been cleft to the very girdle. Don Quixote, feeling the weight of this terrific blow, ejaculated in a loud and pious tone, "O Dulcinea, lady of my soul, flower of all beauty, now aid thy knight, who for the satisfaction of thy great goodness, exposes himself to this great peril."

The ejaculation, the drawing the sword, the covering himself with his buckler, and attacking the Biscayner, were the business of a moment, for he resolved to venture all on the fortune of a single effort. The Biscayner, who saw him coming thus upon him, and perceived his bravery by his resolution, resolved to imitate his example, and accordingly waited for him, shielding himself with his cushion; but he was not able to turn his mule either to the right or the left, for she was already so jaded, and so little used to such sport, that she would not stir a step.

Don Quixote, then, as we have said, advanced against the wary Biscayner, with his lifted sword, fully determined to cleave him asunder; and the Biscayner expected him, with his sword also lifted up, and guarded by his cushion. All the bystanders trembled, and were in breathless suspense, at what might be the event of the prodigious blows with which they threatened each other; and the lady in the coach, and her waiting-women, put up a thousand prayers to heaven, and vowed an offering to every image and place of devotion in Spain, if God would deliver them and their squire from the great peril they were in. But the misfortune is, that in this very critical minute, the author of the history leaves the battle unfinished, excusing himself, that he could find no farther account of these exploits of Don Quixote than what he has already related.[14] It is true, indeed, that the second undertaker of this work[15] would not believe that so curious a history could be lost in oblivion, or that the wits of La Mancha should have so little curiosity, as not to preserve in their archives, or their cabinets, some papers relating to this famous knight; and upon that presumption he did not despair to find the conclusion of this delectable history; in which, Heaven favouring his search, he at last succeeded, as shall faithfully be recounted.

14. Cervantes breaks off his narrative in this fashion in imitation of a common device of the chivalric romances.
15. Cervantes himself, who pretends to be following an original history by the Arabic Cid Hamet Benengeli.

CHAPTER IX

Wherein is concluded the stupendous battle between the vigorous
Biscayner and the valiant Manchegan

... As I was walking one day on the exchange of Toledo, a boy
offered for sale some bundles of old papers to a mercer; and as I am
fond of reading, though it be torn scraps thrown about the streets, led
by this my natural inclination, I took a parcel of those which the boy
was selling, and perceived that the characters in which they were
written were Arabic. As I could not read the language, though I knew
the letters, I looked about for some Moorish sage, to read them for me.
In short, I met with one; and acquainting him with my desire, I put
the book into his hands, and he opened it towards the middle, and,
having read a little, began to laugh. I asked him what he laughed at:
and he replied, at something which he found written in the margin, by
way of annotation. I desired him to tell me what it was; and, still
laughing, he said, there was written in the margin of one of the leaves
as follows: "This Dulcinea del Toboso, so often mentioned in this
history, is said to have the best hand at salting pork of any woman in
all La Mancha." When I heard the name of Dulcinea del Toboso, I
stood amazed and confounded: for I instantly fancied to myself, that
the bundles of paper contained the whole history of Don Quixote.

With this thought, I pressed him to turn to the beginning; which
he did, and, rendering extempore the Arabic into Castilian, said that
it began thus: "The history of Don Quixote de la Mancha, written by
Cid Hamet Benengeli, Arabian historiographer." Much discretion was
necessary to dissemble the joy I felt at hearing the title of the book; and
snatching what was in the hands of the mercer, I bought the whole
bundle of papers from the boy for half a real. I posted away immediately with the Morisco, through the cloister of the great church, and
desired him to translate for me, into the Castilian tongue, all the papers
that treated of Don Quixote, without taking away or adding a syllable,
offering to pay him for his trouble whatever he should demand. But I,
to make the business more sure, and not let so valuable a prize slip
through my fingers, took him home to my own house, where, in little
more than six weeks, he translated the whole, in the manner you have
it here related.

In the first sheet was drawn, in a most lively manner, Don

Quixote's combat with the Biscayner, in the very attitude in which the history sets it forth; their swords lifted up, the one covered with his buckler, the other with his cushion. . . . In short, the second part, according to the translation, began in this manner:—

The trenchant blades of the two valorous and enraged combatants, being brandished aloft, seemed to threaten heaven, earth, and the deep abyss; such was the courage and gallantry of those who wielded them. The first who discharged his blow was the choleric Biscayner, and it fell with such force and fury, that, if the edge of the weapon had not turned aslant by the way, that single blow had been enough to have put an end to this cruel conflict, and to all the adventures of our knight: but good fortune, that preserved him for greater things, so twisted his adversary's sword, that, though it alighted on the left shoulder, it did him no other hurt than to disarm that side, carrying off by the way a great part of his helmet, with half an ear; all which, with hideous ruin, fell to the ground, leaving him in a piteous plight.

Who is he that can worthily recount the rage that entered into the breast of our Manchegan, at seeing himself so roughly handled? Let it suffice to say, it was such, that he raised himself afresh in his stirrups, and grasping his sword faster in both hands, struck with such fury at the Biscayner, taking him full upon the cushion, and upon the head, which he could not defend, that, as if a mountain had fallen upon him, the blood began to gush out at his nostrils, his mouth, and his ears; and he seemed as if he was just falling from his mule, which doubtless he must have done, had he not laid fast hold of her neck; but presently, losing his stirrups, he let go his hold; and the mule, frightened by the terrible stroke, galloped about the field, and, after two or three plunges, laid her master flat upon the ground. Don Quixote had looked on with great calmness, but when he saw him fall, he leaped from his horse, and with much agility ran up to him, and, directing the point of his sword to his eyes, bid him yield, on pain of having his head cut off. The Biscayner was so stunned, that he could not answer a word: and it had gone hard with him, so blinded with rage was Don Quixote, if the ladies of the coach, who had hitherto in great dismay beheld the conflict, had not approached, and earnestly besought that he would do them the great kindness and favour to spare the life of their squire. Don Quixote answered with solemn gravity, "Assuredly, fair ladies, I am very willing to grant your request, but it must be upon a certain condition and compact; which is, that this knight shall promise to repair to the town of Toboso, and present himself, as from me, before the peerless Dulcinea, that she may dispose of him according to her good pleasure."

The terrified and disconsolate lady, without considering what was demanded, and without inquiring who Dulcinea was, promised that her squire should perform everything he enjoined him. "Upon the faith of your word then," said Don Quixote, "I will do him no farther hurt, though he has richly deserved it at my hands."

[Don Quixote and Sancho Panza are entertained by some goat-herds, who offer them food and who bind up Don Quixote's injured ear. Knight and squire then proceed to an inn—another castle, as Don Quixote conceives it—where they are involved in a brawl precipitated by the serving-girl Maritornes when she mistakes the bed of Don Quixote for that of her lover. Don Quixote concludes that the castle is enchanted.

The next day, when the knight refuses to pay for his lodging, some frolicsome people of the inn set upon Sancho and toss him in a blanket. Numerous adventures follow, the most remarkable being Don Quixote's assault upon two flocks of sheep that he takes for two armies in combat, and his setting free a company of galley slaves on their way to the coast. In the mountains of Sierra Morena, Don Quixote des-patches Sancho to Dulcinea with a letter, which, of course, the squire never delivers though later he pretends to have done so.

Meanwhile Don Quixote's old friends, the priest and the barber, have engaged the help of a young girl named Dorothea in a plan to return the mad knight to his home. Dorothea pretends to be the Princess Micomicona of Micomicon in Ethiopia, dispossessed of her kingdom by a wicked giant. She begs Don Quixote's aid. Not unac-countably the road to Ethiopia leads through La Mancha, and on the way the company stops at the inn where Don Quixote and Sancho have lodged before. The weary knight takes to his bed, but the priest entertains the company by reading to them "The Novel of the Curious Impertinent."]

CHAPTER XXIX

The dreadful battle Don Quixote fought with certain wine-skins

There remained but little more of the novel to be read when
Sancho Panza came running out of Don Quixote's chamber in a terrible fright, crying out, "Help, help, good people! help my master! He
is just now at it tooth and nail with that same giant, the Princess
Micomicona's foe; I never saw a more dreadful battle in my born days.
He has lent him such a blow, that whip off went the giant's head, as
round as a turnip."

"You are mad, Sancho," said the curate, starting up astonished; "is
thy master such a wonderful hero as to fight a giant at two thousand
leagues distance?"

Upon this they presently heard a noise and bustle in the chamber,
and Don Quixote bawling out, "Stay, villain! robber, stay! since I have
thee here, thy scimitar shall but little avail thee!" and with this they
heard him strike with his sword with all his force against the walls.

"Good folks," said Sancho, "my master does not want your
hearkening; why do not you run in and help him? though I believe
it is after-meat mustard; for sure the giant is dead by this time, and
giving an account of his ill life; for I saw his blood run all about the
house, and his head sailing in the middle on it; but such a head! it is
bigger than any wine-skin in Spain."

"Mercy on me!" cried the innkeeper, "I will be cut like a cucumber,
if this Don Quixote, or Don Devil, has not been hacking my wine-
skins that stood filled at his bed's head, and this coxcomb has taken the
spilt liquor for blood."

Then running with the whole company into the room, they found
the poor knight in the most comical posture imaginable.

He wore on his head a little red greasy nightcap of the innkeeper's; he had wrapped one of the best blankets about his left arm
for a shield; and wielded his drawn sword in the right, laying about
him pell-mell; with now and then a start of some military expression,
as if he had been really engaged with some giant. But the best jest of
all, he was all this time fast asleep; for the thoughts of the adventure
he had undertaken had so wrought on his imagination that his depraved fancy had in his sleep represented to him the kingdom of
Micomicon and the giant; and dreaming that he was then fighting

him, he assaulted the wine-skins so desperately that he set the whole chamber afloat with good wine. The innkeeper, enraged to see the havoc, flew at Don Quixote with his fists; and had not the curate taken him off, he had proved a giant indeed against the knight. All this could not wake the poor Don, till the barber, throwing a bucket of cold water on him, wakened him from his sleep, though not from his dream.

Sancho ran up and down the room searching for the giant's head, till, finding his labour fruitless, "Well, well," said he, "now I see plainly that this house is haunted; for now the giant's head that I saw cut off with these eyes is vanished, and I am sure I saw the body spout blood like a pump."

"What prating and nonsense!" said the innkeeper; "I tell you, rascal, it is my wine-skins that are slashed, and my wine that runs about the floor here."

"Well, well," said Sancho, "do not trouble me; I only tell you that I cannot find the giant's head, and my earldom is gone after it; and so I am undone, like salt in water."

And truly Sancho's waking dream was as pleasant as his master's when asleep. The innkeeper was almost mad to see the foolish squire harp so on the same string with his frantic master, and swore they should not come off now as before; that their chivalry should be no satisfaction for his wine, but that they should pay him sauce for the damage, and for the very leathern patches which the wounded wine-skins would want.

Don Quixote in the meanwhile, believing he had finished his adventure, and mistaking the curate, that held him by the arms, for the Princess Micomicona, fell on his knees before him, and with a respect due to a royal presence, "Now may your highness," said he, "great and illustrious princess, live secure, free from any further apprehensions from your conquered enemy; and now I am acquitted of my engagement, since, by the assistance of Heaven, and the influence of her favour by whom I live and conquer, your adventure is so happily achieved."

"Did not I tell you so, gentlefolks?" said Sancho; "who is drunk or mad now? See if my master has not already put the giant in pickle?"

The whole company (except the unfortunate innkeeper) were highly diverted at the extravagances of both. At last, the barber, and the curate, having with much ado got Don Quixote to bed, he presently fell asleep, being heartily tired; and then they left him to comfort Sancho Panza for the loss of the giant's head; but it was no easy matter to appease the innkeeper, who was at his wit's end for the unexpected and sudden fate of his wine-skins.

The hostess in the meantime ran up and down the house crying and roaring: "In an ill hour," said she, "did this unlucky knight-errant come into my house; I wish, for my part, I had never seen him, for he has been a dear guest to me. He and his man, his horse and his ass, went away last time without paying me a cross for their supper, their bed, their litter, and provender; and all, forsooth, because he was seeking adventures. What, in the wide world, have we to do with his statutes of chivalry? If they oblige him not to pay, they should oblige him not to eat neither. . . . But I will be paid, so I will, to the last maravedis,[16] or I will disown my name, and forswear my mother." Her honest maid Maritornes seconded her fury; but Master Curate stopped their mouths by promising that he would see them satisfied for their wine and their skins. Dorothea comforted Sancho, assuring him that whenever it appeared that his master had killed the giant, and restored her to her dominions, he should be sure of the best earldom in her disposal. With this he buckled up again, and vowed "that he himself had seen the giant's head, by the same token that it had a beard that reached down to his middle; and if it could not be found, it must be hid by witchcraft, for everything went by enchantment in that house, as he had found to his cost when he was there before." . . .

[At the inn various new characters are introduced and various stories told. Finally Don Quixote is threatened with arrest for his part in the affair of the galley slaves and barely escapes the officers when the priest convinces them that the knight is insane. With elaborate hocus-pocus and show of enchantments the friends of Don Quixote take him from his room in a wooden cage. In this cage, enchanted, upon a wagon drawn by oxen, Don Quixote leaves the inn.

On the way the knight and his party fall in with a canon and with a goatherd named Eugenio. They stop together to rest, the enchanted knight is released from his cage on parole, and Eugenio entertains the group with a tale.]

16. A Spanish coin of low value.

CHAPTER XLI

*Of the quarrel between Don Quixote and the Goatherd, with the rare
adventure of the Disciplinants*

The goatherd's tale amused all his auditors, especially the canon,
who was struck by his manner of telling it, which was more like that
of a scholar and a gentleman than an unpolished goatherd; and he was
convinced that the priest was perfectly right when he affirmed that men
of letters were often produced among mountains. They all offered their
service to Eugenio; but the most liberal in his offers was Don Quixote,
who said to him, "In truth, brother goatherd, were I in a situation to
undertake any new adventure, I would immediately engage myself in
your service. . . ."

The goatherd stared at Don Quixote, and observing his odd appearance, he whispered to the barber who sat next to him, "Pray, sir,
who is that man that looks and talks so strangely?"

"Who should it be," answered the barber, "but the famous Don
Quixote de la Mancha, the redresser of injuries, the righter of wrongs,
the protector of maidens, the dread of giants, and the conqueror of
armies?"

"Why this is like what we hear in the stories of knights-errant,"
said the goatherd; "but I take it either your worship is in jest, or the
apartments in this gentleman's skull are unfurnished."

"You are a very great blockhead," exclaimed the knight; "it is
yourself who are empty-skulled and shallow-brained;" and as he spoke,
he snatched up a loaf that was near him, and threw it at the goatherd's
face with so much fury that he laid his nose flat. The goatherd did not
much relish the jest, so, without any respect to the tablecloth or to the
company present, he leaped upon Don Quixote, and seizing him by the
throat with both hands, would doubtless have strangled him, had not
Sancho Panza, who came up at that moment, taken him by the shoulders and thrown him back on the tablecloth, demolishing dishes and
platters, and spilling and overturning all that was upon it. Don
Quixote, finding himself free, turned again upon the goatherd, who,
being kicked and trampled upon by Sancho, was feeling about upon
all fours for some knife or weapon to take revenge withal; but the
canon and the priest prevented him. The barber, however, maliciously
contrived that the goatherd should get Don Quixote under him, whom

he buffeted so unmercifully that he had ample retaliation for his own sufferings. This ludicrous encounter overcame the gravity of both the churchmen; while the troopers of the holy brotherhood, enjoying the conflict, stood urging on the combatants, as if it had been a dog-fight. Sancho struggled in vain to release himself from one of the canon's servants, who prevented him from going to assist his master. In the midst of this sport a trumpet was suddenly heard sounding so dismally that every face was instantly turned in the direction whence the sound proceeded. Don Quixote's attention was particularly excited, though he still lay under the goatherd in a bruised and battered condition.

"Thou demon," he said to him, "for such thou must be to have this power over me, I beg that thou wilt grant a truce for one hour, as the solemn sound of that trumpet seems to call me to some new adventure."

The goatherd, whose revenge was by this time sated, immediately let him go; and Don Quixote, having got upon his legs again, presently saw several people descending from a rising ground, arrayed in white, after the manner of disciplinants.

That year the heavens having failed to refresh the earth with seasonable showers, throughout all the villages of that district, processions, disciplines, and public prayers were ordered, beseeching God to show His mercy by sending them rain. For this purpose the people of a neighbouring village were coming in procession to a holy hermitage built upon the side of a hill not far from that spot. The strange attire of the disciplinants struck Don Quixote, who, not recollecting what he must often have seen before, imagined it to be some adventure which, as a knight-errant, was reserved for him alone; and he was confirmed in his opinion on seeing an image clothed in black that they carried with them, and which he doubted not was some illustrious lady, forcibly borne away by ruffians and miscreants. With all the expedition in his power, he therefore went up to Rozinante, and taking the bridle and buckler from the pommel of the saddle, he bridled him in a trice; and calling to Sancho for his sword, he mounted, braced his target, and, in a loud voice said to all that were present, "Now, my worthy companions, ye shall see how important to the world is the profession of chivalry; now shall ye see, in the restoration of that captive lady to liberty, whether knights-errant are to be valued or not."

So saying, he clapped heels to Rozinante (for spurs he had none); and on a hand-gallop (for we nowhere read, in all this faithful history, that Rozinante ever went full speed), he advanced to encounter the disciplinants. The priest, the canon, and the barber, in vain endeavoured to stop him; and in vain did Sancho cry out, "Whither go you, Signor Don Quixote? what possesses you to assault the catholic faith? Evil befal me! do but look—it is a procession of disciplinants, and the lady carried upon the bier is the blessed image of our Holy Virgin; take heed, for this once I am sure you know not what you are about."

Sancho wearied himself to no purpose; for his master was so bent upon an encounter, that he heard not a word; nor would he have turned back though the king himself had commanded him.

Having reached the procession, he checked Rozinante, who already wanted to rest a little, and in a hoarse and agitated voice cried out, "Stop there, ye who cover your faces—for an evil purpose, I doubt not—stop and listen to me!"

The bearers of the image stood still; and one of the four ecclesiastics, who sung the litanies, observing the strange figure of Don Quixote, the leanness of Rozinante, and other ludicrous circumstances attending the knight, replied, "Friend, if you have anything to say to us, say it quickly; for these our brethren are scourging their flesh, and we cannot stay to hear anything that may not be said in two words."

"I will say it in one," replied Don Quixote; "you must immediately release that fair lady, whose tears and sorrowful countenance clearly prove that she is carried away against her will, and that you have done her some atrocious injury. I, who was born to redress such wrongs, command you, therefore, not to proceed one step further until you have given her the liberty she desires and deserves."

By these expressions they concluded that Don Quixote must be some whimsical madman, and only laughed at him; which enraged him to such a degree, that, without saying another word, he drew his sword and attacked the bearers, one of whom, leaving the burden to his comrades, stepped forward brandishing the pole on which the bier had been supported; but it was quickly broken in two by a powerful stroke aimed by the knight, who, however, received instantly such a blow on the shoulder of his sword-arm, that, his buckler being of no avail against rustic strength, he was felled to the ground. Sancho, who had followed him, now called out to the man not to strike again, for he was a poor enchanted knight, who had never done anybody harm in all his life. The peasant forbore, it is true, though not on account of Sancho's appeal, but because he saw his opponent without motion, and thinking he had killed him, he hastily tucked up his vest under his girdle, and fled like a deer over the field.

By this time all Don Quixote's party had come up; and those in the procession began to be alarmed, and drew up in a circle round the image; then lifting up their hoods, and grasping their whips, and the ecclesiastics their tapers, they waited the assault, determined to defend themselves, or, if possible, offend their aggressors; while Sancho threw himself on the body of his master, and believing him to be really dead, poured forth the most dolorous lamentation. Sancho's cries roused Don Quixote, who finally said, "He who lives absent from thee, sweetest Dulcinea, endures far greater miseries than this!—Help, friend Sancho, to place me upon the enchanted car; I am no longer in a condition to press the saddle of Rozinante for this shoulder is broken to pieces."

"That I will do with all my heart, dear sir," answered Sancho; "and let us return to our homes with these gentlemen, who wish you well; and there we can prepare for another sally that may turn out more profitable."

"Thou sayest well, Sancho," answered Don Quixote; "and it will be highly prudent in us to wait until the evil influence of the star which now reigns is passed over."

The canon, the priest, and the barber told him they approved his resolution; and the knight being now placed in the waggon as before, they prepared to depart. The goatherd took his leave. The canon also separated from them, having first obtained a promise from the priest that he would acquaint him with the future fate of Don Quixote. Thus the party now consisted only of the priest, the barber, Don Quixote, and Sancho, with good Rozinante, who bore all accidents as patiently as his master. The waggoner yoked his oxen, and having accommodated Don Quixote with a truss of hay, they jogged on in the way the priest directed, and at the end of six days reached Don Quixote's village. It was about noon when they made their entrance, and it being a holiday, all the people were standing about the market-place through which the waggon passed. Everybody ran to see who was in it, and were not a little surprised when they recognised their townsman; and a boy ran off at full speed with tidings to the housekeeper that he was coming home, lean and pale, stretched out at length in a waggon drawn by oxen. On hearing this, the two good women made the most pathetic lamentations, and renewed their curses against books of chivalry, especially when they saw the poor knight entering at the gate.

Upon the news of Don Quixote's arrival, Sancho Panza's wife repaired thither; and, on meeting him, her first inquiry was, whether the ass had come home well. Sancho told her that he was in a better condition than his master.

"Heaven be praised," replied she, "for so great a mercy to me! But tell me, husband, what good have you got by your squireship? Have you brought a petticoat home for me, and shoes for your children?"

"I have brought you nothing of that sort, dear wife," quoth Sancho; "but I have got other things of greater consequence."

"I am very glad of that," answered the wife; "pray show me your things of greater consequence, friend; for I would fain see them to gladden my heart, which has been so sad all the long time you have been away."

"You shall see them at home, wife," quoth Sancho, "so be satisfied at present; for if it please God that we make another sally in quest of adventures, you will soon see me an earl or governor of an island, and no common one neither, but one of the best that is to be had."

"Grant Heaven it may be so, husband," quoth the wife; "for we have need enough of it. But pray tell me what you mean by islands, for I do not understand you."

"Honey is not for the mouth of an ass," answered Sancho; "in good time, wife, you shall see, yea and admire to hear yourself styled ladyship by all your vassals."

"What do you mean, Sancho, by ladyship, islands, and vassals?" answered Teresa Panza; for that was the name of Sancho's wife, though they were not of kin, but because it was the custom of La Mancha for the wife to take the husband's name.

"Do not be in so much haste, Teresa," said Sancho; "it is enough that I tell you what is true, so lock up your mouth; only take this by the way, that there is nothing in the world so pleasant as to be an honourable esquire to a knight-errant and seeker of adventures. . . ."

While this discourse was passing between Sancho Panza and his wife Teresa, the housekeeper and the niece received Don Quixote, and they laid him in his old bed, whence he looked at them with eyes askance, not knowing perfectly where he was. Often did the women raise their voices in abuse of all books of chivalry, overwhelming their authors with the bitterest maledictions. His niece was charged by the priest to take great care of him, and to keep a watchful eye that he did not again make his escape, after taking so much pains to get him home. Yet they were full of apprehensions lest they should lose him again as soon as he found himself a little better; and, indeed, the event proved that their fears were not groundless.

PART II

[After a month the priest and the barber visit Don Quixote, only to learn that although he seems entirely sane on most subjects he is as insane as ever on the subject of knight-errantry. Sancho visits his master and tells him of a certain bachelor Samson Carrasco, a university graduate, who has read their history and who is greatly interested in their affairs. When Samson is introduced to the knight he advises him to journey to Saragossa, where a great tournament is to be held. To the despair of his housekeeper and his niece, Don Quixote and Sancho again take to the road, but the knight is intent first of all upon seeking out Dulcinea in Toboso.]

CHAPTER XLVIII

That gives an account of things which you will know when you have read it

The sable night had spun out half her course, when Don Quixote and Sancho entered Toboso. A profound silence reigned over all the town, and the inhabitants were fast asleep, and stretched out at their ease. Nothing disturbed the general tranquillity but now and then the barking of dogs, that wounded Don Quixote's ears, but more poor Sancho's heart. Sometimes an ass brayed, hogs grunted, cats mewed; which jarring mixture of sounds was not a little augmented by the stillness and serenity of the night, and filled the enamoured champion's head with a thousand inauspicious chimeras. Nevertheless he said, "Sancho, lead on to Dulcinea's palace; it is possible we may find her awake."

"To what palace?" answered Sancho; "that in which I saw her highness was but a little mean house."

"It was, I suppose, some small apartment of her castle which she had retired to," said the knight, "to amuse herself with her damsels as is usual with great ladies and princesses."

"Since your worship," quoth Sancho, "will needs have my Lady Dulcinea's house to be a castle, is this an hour to find the gates open?"

"First, however, let us find this castle," replied Don Quixote, "and then I will tell thee how to act;—but look, my eyes deceive me, or that huge dark pile yonder must be Dulcinea's palace."

"Then lead on, sir," said Sancho; "it may be so; though if I were to see it with my eyes, I will believe it just as much as that it is now day."

The Don led the way, and having gone about two hundred paces, he came up to the edifice which cast the dark shade; and perceiving a large tower, he soon found that the building was no palace, but the principal church of the place; whereupon he said, "We are come to the church, Sancho."

"I see we are," answered Sancho; "and pray God we be not come to our graves; for it is no good sign to be rambling about churchyards at such hours, and especially since I have already told your worship that this same lady's house stands in a blind alley."

"Blockhead!" said the knight; "where hast thou ever found castles and royal palaces built in blind alleys?"

"Sir," said Sancho, "each country has its customs; so perhaps it is the fashion here to build your palaces in alleys; and so I beseech your worship to let me look among these lanes and alleys just before me; and perhaps I may pop upon this same palace, which I wish I may see devoured by dogs for bewildering us at this rate."

"Speak with more respect, Sancho, of what regards my lady," said Don Quixote; "let us keep our holidays in peace, and not throw the rope after the bucket."

"I will curb myself," answered Sancho; "but I cannot think that though I have seen the house but once, your worship will needs have me find it at midnight, when you cannot find it yourself, though you must have seen it thousands of times."

"Thou wilt make me desperate, Sancho," quoth Don Quixote; "come hither, heretic; have I not told thee a thousand times that I never saw the peerless Dulcinea in my life, nor ever stepped over the threshold of her palace, and that I am enamoured by report alone, and the great fame of her wit and beauty?"

"I hear it now," said Sancho; "and to tell the truth, I have seen her just as much as your worship."

"How can that be?" cried Don Quixote; "didst thou not tell me that thou sawest her winnowing wheat?"

"Take no heed of that, sir," replied the squire; "for the fact is, her message, and the sight of her too, were both by hearsay, and I can no more tell who the Lady Dulcinea is than I can buffet the moon."

"Sancho, Sancho," answered Don Quixote, "there is a time to jest, and a time when jests are unseasonable. What! because I say that I never saw nor spoke to the mistress of my soul, must thou say so likewise, when thou knowest it to be untrue?"

They were here interrupted by the approach of a man with two mules; and by the sound of a ploughshare, our travellers rightly guessed that he was a husbandman. The country fellow having now come up to them, Don Quixote said to him, "Good morrow, honest friend; canst thou direct me to the palace of the peerless princess, Donna Dulcinea del Toboso?"

"Sir," answered the fellow, "I am a stranger here; for I have been but a few days in the service of a farmer of this town. But the parish priest, or the sexton across the road, can give your worship an account of that same lady princess; for they keep a register of all the inhabitants of Toboso; not that I think there is any princess living here, though there are several great ladies that may every one be a princess in her own house."

"Among those, friend," said the Don, "may be her for whom I am inquiring."

"Not unlikely," said the ploughman, "and so God speed you; for it will soon be daybreak."

Then pricking on his mules, he waited for no more questions.

Sancho seeing his master perplexed, said to him, "Sir, the day comes on apace, and we shall soon have the sun upon us; so I think we had better get out of this place, and, while your worship takes shelter in some wood, I will leave not a corner unsearched for this house, castle, or palace of my lady; and it shall go hard with me but I find it; and as soon as I have done so, I will speak to her ladyship, and tell her where your worship is waiting her orders and directions how you may see her without damage to her honour and reputation."

"Sancho," quoth Don Quixote, "thou hast uttered a thousand sentences in a few words. Thy counsel I relish much, and shall most willingly follow it. Come on, and let us seek for some shelter: then shalt thou return and seek out my lady, from whose discretion and courtesy I expect more than miraculous favours."

Sancho was impatient till he got his master out of the town, lest his tricks should be detected; he therefore hastened on, and when they had gone about two miles, the knight retired to a shady grove, while

the squire returned in quest of the Lady Dulcinea; on which embassy
things occurred well worthy of credit and renewed attention.

CHAPTER XLIX

Wherein is related the stratagem practised by Sancho, of enchanting
the Lady Dulcinea; with other events no less ludicrous than true

The knight's frenzy appears now to be carried to an excess beyond
all conception. Having retired into a grove near the city of Toboso, he
despatched Sancho with orders not to return into his presence till he
had spoken to his lady, beseeching her that she would be pleased to
grant her captive knight permission to wait upon her, and that she
would deign to bestow on him her benediction, whereby he might
secure complete success in all his encounters and arduous enterprises.
Sancho promised to return with an answer no less favourable than
that which he had formerly brought him.

"Go then, son," replied Don Quixote, "and be not in confusion
when thou standest in the blaze of that sun of beauty. Happy thou
above all the squires in the world! . . . Go friend, and be thou more
successful than my anxious heart will bode during the painful period
of thy absence."

"I will go, and return quickly," quoth Sancho. "In the meantime,
good sir, cheer up, and remember the saying, that 'A good heart breaks
bad luck;' and 'If there is no hook, there is no bacon;' and 'Where we
least expect it, the hare starts:' this I say, because though we could not
find the castle or palace of my Lady Dulcinea in the dark, now that it
is daylight I reckon I shall soon find it, and then—let me alone to deal
with her."

"Verily, Sancho," quoth Don Quixote, "thou dost apply thy proverbs most happily: yet Heaven grant me better luck in the attainment
of my hopes!"

Sancho now switched his Dapple[17] and set off, leaving Don
Quixote on horseback, resting on his stirrups and leaning on his lance,
full of melancholy and confused fancies, where we will leave him and
attend Sancho Panza, who departed no less perplexed and thoughtful;
insomuch that, after he had got out of the grove, and looked behind
him to ascertain that his master was out of sight, he alighted, and, sit-

17. The name of Sancho's ass.

ting down at the foot of a tree, he began to hold a parley with himself.

"Tell me now, brother Sancho," quoth he, "whither is your worship going? Are you going to seek some ass that is lost?" "No, verily." "Then what are you going to seek?" "Why, I go to look for a thing of nothing—a princess, the sun of beauty, and all heaven together!" "Well, Sancho, and where think you to find all this?" "Where? In the great city of Toboso." "Very well; and pray who sent you on this errand?" "Why, the renowned knight Don Quixote de la Mancha, who redresses wrongs, and gives drink to the hungry and meat to the thirsty." "All this is mighty well; and do you know her house, Sancho?" "My master says it must be some royal palace or stately castle." "And have you ever seen her?" "Neither I nor my master have ever seen her!—Well," continued he, "there is a remedy for everything but death, who, in spite of our teeth, will have us in his clutches. This master of mine, I can plainly see, is mad enough for a strait waistcoat; and, in truth, I am not much better; nay; I am worse, in following and serving him, if there is any truth in the proverb, 'Show me who thou art with, and I will tell thee what thou art;' or in the other, 'Not with whom thou wert bred, but with whom thou art fed.' He then being in truth a madman, and so mad as frequently to mistake one thing for another, and not know black from white; this being the case, I say, it will not be very difficult to make him believe that a country girl (the first I light upon) is the Lady Dulcinea; and, should he not believe it, I will swear to it; and if he swears, I will outswear him; and if he persists, I will persist the more: so that mine shall still be uppermost, come what will of it. By this plan I may perhaps tire him of sending me on such errands; or he may take it into his head that some wicked enchanter has changed his lady's form, out of pure spite."

This project set Sancho's spirit at rest, and he reckoned his business as good as half done: so he stayed where he was till towards evening, that Don Quixote might suppose him travelling on his mission. Fortunately for him, just as he was going to mount his Dapple, he espied three country girls coming from Toboso, each mounted on a young ass. Sancho no sooner got sight of them than he rode back at a good pace to seek his master Don Quixote, whom he found breathing a thousand sighs and amorous lamentations. When Don Quixote saw him, he said, "Well, Sancho, am I to mark this day with a white or a black stone?"

"Your worship," answered Sancho, "had better mark it with red ochre, as they do the inscriptions on professors' chairs, to be the more easily read by the lookers-on."

"Thou bringest me good news, then?" cried Don Quixote.

"So good," answered Sancho, "that your worship has only to clap spurs to Rozinante, and get out upon the plain to see the lady Dulcinea del Toboso, who, with a couple of her damsels is coming to pay your worship a visit."

"Gracious Heaven!" exclaimed Don Quixote, "what dost thou say? Take care that thou beguilest not my real sorrow by a counterfeit joy."

"What should I get," answered Sancho, "by deceiving your worship, only to be found out the next moment? Come, sir, put on, and you will see the princess, our mistress, all arrayed and adorned—in short, like herself. She and her damsels are one blaze of flaming gold; all strings of pearls, all diamonds, all rubies, all cloth of tissue above ten hands deep; their hair loose about their shoulders, like so many sunbeams blowing about in the wind; and, what is more, they come mounted upon three pied belfreys, the finest you ever laid eyes on."

"Palfreys, thou wouldst say, Sancho," quoth Don Quixote.

"Well, well," answered Sancho, "belfreys and palfreys are much the same thing; but let them be mounted how they will, they are sure the finest creatures one would wish to see, especially my mistress the princess Dulcinea, who dazzles one's senses."

"Let us go, son Sancho," answered Don Quixote; "and, as a reward for this welcome news, I bequeath to thee the choicest spoils I shall gain in my next adventure."

They were now got out of the wood, and saw the three girls very near. Don Quixote looked eagerly along the road towards Toboso, and seeing nobody but the three girls, he asked Sancho, in much agitation, whether they were out of the city when he left them.

"Out of the city!" answered Sancho; "are your worship's eyes in the nape of your neck that you do not see them now before you, shining like the sun at noonday?"

"I see only three country girls," answered Don Quixote, "on three asses."

"Now keep me from mischief!" answered Sancho; "is it possible that three belfreys, or how do you call them, white as the driven snow, should look to you like asses? As I am alive, you shall pluck off this beard of mine if it be so."

"I tell thee, friend Sancho," answered Don Quixote, "that it is as certain they are asses as that I am Don Quixote and thou Sancho Panza; at least so they seem to me."

"Sir," quoth Sancho, "say not such a thing; but snuff those eyes of yours, and come and pay reverence to the mistress of your soul."

So saying he advanced forward to meet the peasant girls; and, alighting from Dapple, he laid hold of one of their asses by the halter, and, bending both knees to the ground, said to the girl, "Queen, princess, and duchess of beauty, let your haughtiness and greatness be pleased to receive into your grace and good-liking your captive knight, who stands there turned into stone, all disorder and without any pulse, to find himself before your magnificent presence. I am Sancho Panza, his squire, and he is that wayworn knight Don Quixote de la Mancha, otherwise called the Knight of the Rueful Countenance."

Don Quixote had now placed himself on his knees by Sancho, and with wild and staring eyes surveyed her whom Sancho called his queen, and seeing nothing but a peasant girl, with a broad face, flat nose, coarse and homely, he was so confounded that he could not open his lips. The girls were also surprised to find themselves stopped by two men so different in aspect, and both on their knees; but the lady who was stopped, breaking silence, said in an angry tone, "Get out of the road, plague on ye! and let us pass by, for we are in haste."

"O princess and universal lady of Toboso!" cried Sancho, "is not your magnificent heart melting to see, on his knees before your sub-limated presence, the pillar and prop of knight-errantry?"

"Heyday! what's here to do?" cried another of the girls; "look how your small gentry come to jeer us poor country girls, as if we could not give them as good as they bring. Go, get off about your business, and let us mind ours, and so speed you well."

"Rise, Sancho," said Don Quixote, on hearing this; "for I now perceive that fortune, not yet satisfied with persecuting me, has barred every avenue whereby relief might come to this wretched soul I bear about me. And thou, O extreme of all that is valuable, summit of human perfection, thou sole balm to this disconsolate heart that adores thee, though now some wicked enchanter spreads clouds and cataracts over my eyes, changing, and to them only, thy peerless beauty into that of a poor rustic; if he has not converted mine also into that of some goblin, to render it horrible to thy view, bestow on me one kind look, and let this submissive posture, these bended knees, before thy dis-guised beauty, declare the humility with which my soul adores thee."

"Marry come up," quoth the girl, "with your idle gibberish! get on with you, and let us go, and we shall take it kindly."

Sancho now let go the halter; delighted that he had come off so well with his contrivance. The imaginary Dulcinea was no sooner at liberty than, pricking her beast with a sharp-pointed stick which she held in her hand, she scoured along the field; but the ass, smarting more than usual under the goad, began to kick and wince in such a manner that down came the Lady Dulcinea to the ground. Don Quixote was proceeding to raise his enchanted mistress, but the lady saved him that trouble; for immediately upon getting up from the ground she retired three or four steps back, took a little run, then, clapping both hands upon the ass's crupper, jumped into the saddle lighter than a falcon, and seated herself astride like a man.

"By Saint Roque!" cried Sancho, "our lady mistress is lighter than a bird, and could teach the nimblest Cordovan or Mexican how to mount. She springs into the saddle at a jump, and without the help of spurs makes her palfrey run like a wild ass; and her damsels are not a whit short of her, for they all fly like the wind!"

And this was the truth; for, Dulcinea being remounted, the other two made after her at full speed, without looking behind them, for above half a league.

Don Quixote followed them with his eyes as far as he was able; and when they were out of sight, turning to Sancho, he said, "What dost thou think now, Sancho? See how I am persecuted by enchanters! Mark how far their malice extends, even to depriving me of the pleasure of seeing my mistress in her own proper form! Surely I was born to be an example of wretchedness, and the butt and mark at which all the arrows of ill-fortune are aimed! And thou must have observed, too, Sancho, that these traitors were not contented with changing and transforming the countenance of my Dulcinea, but they must give her the base and uncouth figure of a country wench. But tell me, Sancho, that which to me appeared to be a pannel, was it a side-saddle or a pillion?"

"It was a side-saddle," answered Sancho, "with a field covering, worth half a kingdom for the richness of it."

"And that I should not see all this!" exclaimed Don Quixote. "Again I say, and a thousand times will I repeat it, I am the most unfortunate of men!"

The sly rogue Sancho had much difficulty to forbear laughing to think how finely his master was gulled. After more dialogue of the

same kind, they mounted their beasts again, and followed the road to
Saragossa, still intending to be present at a solemn festival annually
held in that city. But before they reached it, events befel them which
for their importance, variety, and novelty, well deserve to be recorded
and read.

[Famous adventures follow but none more glorious than the
contest with the Knight of the Mirrors, who claims to have defeated
the renowned Don Quixote de la Mancha. The two knights fight, Don
Quixote triumphs, and the Knight of the Mirrors proves to be the
bachelor Samson Carrasco, who has practised his deception hoping to
defeat Don Quixote and to force him to return home.

Proceeding, Don Quixote and Sancho are joined by a gentleman
in a green riding coat, one Don Diego de Miranda, with whom Don
Quixote discourses upon morals and letters. Not interested in their
discussion, Sancho seeks to buy milk from some shepherds. Presently
Don Quixote sees a wagon upon the road, feels that an adventure is
toward, and calls upon Sancho for his helmet.]

CHAPTER LVI

*Wherein is set forth the last and highest point at which the unheard-
of courage of Don Quixote ever did, or could, arrive; with the happy
conclusion of the adventure of the lions*

The history relates that, when Don Quixote called out to Sancho to
bring him his helmet, he was buying some curds of the shepherds; and,
being hurried by the violent haste of his master, he knew not what to
do with them, nor how to bestow them; and that he might not lose
them, now they were paid for, he bethought himself of clapping them
into his master's helmet; and with this excellent shift, back he came to
learn the commands of his lord; who said to him, "Friend, give me the
helmet; for either I know little of adventures, or that, which I descry
yonder, is one that does and will oblige me to have recourse to arms."

He in the green riding-coat, hearing this, cast his eyes as far as he
could in every direction, but could discover nothing, except a car
coming towards them, with two or three small flags flying; by which
he conjectured that it was loaded with money for the royal treasury,
and he said so to Don Quixote; but the knight believed him not,

always imagining that everything that befel him must be an adventure, adventure upon adventure, in an endless series; and therefore he thus replied: "Preparation is half the battle, and nothing is lost by being upon one's guard; I know by experience that I have enemies both visible and invisible, but am ignorant when, from what quarter, at what time, or in what shape, they will encounter me;" and turning, he again demanded his helmet of Sancho, who, not having time to take out the curds, was forced to give it him as it was. Don Quixote took it, and, without minding whether anything was in it, instantly put it upon his head; and as the curds were squeezed and pressed, the whey began to run down the face and beard of our hero; at which he was so startled that he said to Sancho, "What can this mean, Sancho? surely my skull is softening, or my brain melting. If thou hast anything with which to wipe off this copious excretion, give it me quickly, for my eyes are quite blinded."

Sancho said nothing, but gave him a cloth, and at the same time thanked God that his master had not found out the truth. Don Quixote having wiped himself, took off his helmet, to see what it was that so over-cooled his head; and, observing some white lumps, he put them to his nose, and smelling them said, "By the life of my lady Dulcinea del Toboso, thou hast put curds into my helmet, vile traitor and inconsiderate squire!"

To which Sancho answered, with great phlegm and dissimulation, "If they are curds, give me them to eat. What! I offer to make your worship's helmet dirty? In faith, sir, I perceive that I too have my enchanters, who persecute me, as a creature and member of your worship, and, I warrant, they have put the curds there to stir your patience to wrath against me, and provoke you to anoint my sides as you used to do. But truly this bout they have missed their aim; for I trust to the candid judgment of my master, who will consider that I have neither curds, nor cream, nor anything like it; and that, if I had, I should sooner have put them into my mouth, than into your honour's helmet."

"It may be so," quoth Don Quixote, perfectly satisfied.

All this the gentleman saw, and saw with admiration, which was raised still higher when Don Quixote, after having wiped his head, face, beard, and helmet, again put it on, and fixing himself firm in his stirrups, trying the easy drawing of his sword, and grasping his lance, said, "Now come what will; for here I am prepared to encounter Satan himself in person."

By this time the car with the flags was come up, attended only by a driver, who rode upon one of the mules that drew it, and a man who sat upon the fore-part. Don Quixote planted himself in the middle of the way, and said, "Whither go ye, brethren? what car is this? and what have you in it? and what banners are those?"

"The waggon is mine," answered the waggoner: "I have there two brave lions, which the general of Oran is sending to the king, and these colours are to let the people understand that what goes here belongs to him."

"Are the lions large?"

"Very large," answered the man in the fore-part of the waggon; "bigger never came from Africa. I am their keeper, and have had charge of several others, but I never saw the like of these before. In the foremost cage is a lion, and in the other a lioness. By this time they are cruelly hungry, for they have not eaten to-day; therefore, pray, good sir, ride out of the way, for we must make haste to get to the place where we are to feed them."

"What!" said Don Quixote, with a scornful smile; "lion-whelps against me! And at this time of day? Well, I will make those gentlemen that sent their lions this way, know whether I am a man to be scared with lions. Get off, honest fellow; and since you are the keeper, open their cages and let them both out; for, in despite of those enchanters that have sent them to try me, I will make the creatures know, in the midst of this very field, who Don Quixote de la Mancha is."

While he was making this speech Sancho came up to Don Diego, and begged him to dissuade his master from his rash attempt.

"Oh, good dear sir!" cried he, "for pity's sake hinder my master from falling upon these lions by all means, or we shall be torn in pieces."

"Why," said the gentleman, "is your master so arrant a madman, then, that you should fear he would set upon such furious beasts?"

"Ah, sir!" said Sancho, "he is not mad, but terribly venturesome."

"Well," replied the gentleman, "I will take care there shall be no harm done;" and with that, coming up to the Don, who was urging the lion-keeper to open the cage, "Sir," said he, "knights-errant ought to engage in adventures from which there may be some hope of coming off with safety, but not in such as are altogether desperate; for courage which borders on temerity is more like madness than true fortitude. Besides, these lions are not come against you, but sent as a present to the king; and therefore it is not your duty to detain them, or stop the waggon."

"Pray, sweet sir," replied Don Quixote, "go and amuse yourself with your tame partridges and your ferrets, and leave every one to his own business. This is mine, and I know best whether these worthy lions are sent against me or no."

Then turning about to the keeper, "Sirrah!" said he, "open your cages immediately, or I will certainly pin thee to the waggon with this lance."

"Good sir," cried the waggoner, seeing this strange apparition in armour so resolute, "for mercy's sake, do but let me take out our mules first, and get out of harm's way with them as fast as I can, before the lions get out; for if they should once set upon the poor beasts, I should be undone for ever; for, alas! that cart and they are all I have in the world to get a living with."

"Thou man of small faith," said Don Quixote, "take them out quickly then, and go with them where thou wilt; though thou shalt presently see that thy precaution was needless, and thou mightest have spared thy pains."

The waggoner on this made all the haste he could to take out his mules, while the keeper cried out, "Bear witness, all ye that are here present, that it is against my will that I open the cages and let loose the lions; and that I protest to this gentleman here, that he shall be answerable for all the mischief they may do; together with the loss of my salary and fees. And now, sirs, shift for yourselves as fast as you can, before I open the cages; for, as for myself, I know the lions will do me no harm."

Once more the gentleman tried to dissuade Don Quixote from doing so mad a thing; telling him, that he tempted Heaven in exposing himself without reason to so great a danger. To this Don Quixote made no other answer but that he knew what he had to do.

"Consider, however, what you do," replied the gentleman; "for it is most certain that you are mistaken."

"Well, sir," said Don Quixote, "if you care not to be spectator of an action which you think is likely to be a tragedy, put spurs to your mare and provide for your safety."

Sancho, hearing this, came up to his master with tears in his eyes, and begged him not to go about this fearful undertaking, to which the adventure of the windmills and all the brunts he had ever borne in his life, were but children's play.

"Good, your worship," cried he, "do but mind; here is no enchantment in the case, nor any thing like it. Alack-a-day, sir, I peeped even now through the grates of the cage, and I am sure I saw the claw of a true lion, and such a claw as makes me think the lion that owns it must be as big as a mountain."

"Alas, poor fellow!" said Don Quixote, "thy fear will make him as big as half the world. Retire, Sancho, and leave me, and if I chance to fall here, thou knowest our old agreement; repair to Dulcinea—I say no more."

To this he added some expressions which cut off all hopes of his giving over his mad design.

The gentleman in green would have opposed him; but considering the other much better armed, and that it was not prudence to encounter a madman, he even took the opportunity, while Don Quixote was storming at the keeper, to march off with his mare, as Sancho did with Dapple, and the carter with his mules, every one making the best of his way to get as far as he could from the waggon before the lions were let loose. Poor Sancho at the same time made sad lamentations for his master's death; for he gave him up for lost, not doubting but that the lions had already got him into their clutches. He cursed his ill-fortune, and the hour he came again to his service; but for all his wailing and lamenting, he urged on poor Dapple, to get as far as he could from the lions. The keeper, perceiving the persons who fled to be at a good distance, fell to arguing and entreating Don Quixote as he had done before. But the knight told him again that all his reasons and entreaties were but in vain, and bid him say no more, but immediately despatch.

Now while the keeper took time to open the foremost cage, Don Quixote stood debating with himself whether he had best make his attack on foot or on horseback; and upon mature deliberation he resolved to do it on foot, lest Rozinante, not used to lions, should be put into disorder. Accordingly, he quitted his horse, threw aside his lance, grasped his shield, and drew his sword; then advancing with a deliberate motion, and an undaunted heart, he posted himself just before the door of the cage, commending himself to Heaven, and afterwards to his lady.

The keeper observing that it was not possible for him to prevent letting out the lions without incurring the resentment of the desperate knight, set the door of the foremost cage wide open, where, as I have said, the lion lay, who appeared of a monstrous size and of a frightful aspect. The first thing he did was to turn himself round in his cage; in the next place he stretched out one of his paws, put forth his claws, and roused himself. After that he gaped and yawned for a good while, and showed his dreadful fangs, and then thrust out half a yard of tongue, and with it licked the dust from his face. Having done this, he thrust his head quite out of the cage, and stared about with his eyes that looked like two live coals of fire; a sight and motion enough to have struck terror into temerity itself. But Don Quixote only regarded it with attention, wishing his grim adversary would leap out of his hold, and come within his reach, that he might exercise his valour, and cut the monster piecemeal. To this height of extravagance had his folly transported him; but the generous lion, more gentle than arrogant, taking no notice of his vapouring and bravados, after he had looked about him awhile, turned his back upon the knight, and very contentedly lay down again in his apartment.

Don Quixote, seeing this, commanded the keeper to rouse him with his pole, and force him out whether he would or no.

"Not I, indeed, sir," answered the keeper; "I dare not do it for my life; for if I provoke him, I am sure to be the first he will tear to pieces. Let me advise you, sir, to be satisfied with your day's work. 'Tis as much as the bravest that wears a head can pretend to do. Then pray go no farther, I beseech you; the door stands open, the lion is at his choice whether he will come out or no. You have waited for him; you see he does not care to look you in the face; and since he did not come out at the first, I dare engage he will not stir out this day. You have shown enough the greatness of your courage; the scandal is his, the honour the challenger's."

"'Tis true," replied Don Quixote. "Come, shut the cage-door, honest friend, and give me a certificate under thy hand, in the amplest form thou canst devise, of what thou hast seen me perform; while I make signs to those that ran away from us, and get them to come back, that they may have an account of this exploit from thy own mouth."

The keeper obeyed: and Don Quixote, clapping a handkerchief on the point of his lance, waved it in the air, and called as loud as he was able to the fugitives, who fled nevertheless, looking behind them all the way, and trooped on in a body with the gentleman in green at the head of them.

At last Sancho observed the signal, and called out, "Hold! my master calls; I will be hanged, if he has not got the better of the lions!"

At this they all faced about, and perceived Don Quixote flourish-

ing his ensign; whereupon recovering a little from their fright, they
leisurely rode back till they could plainly distinguish his voice. As soon
as they were got near the waggon, "Come on, friend," said he to the
carter; "put-to thy mules again, and pursue thy journey; and, Sancho,
do thou give him two ducats for the lion-keeper and himself, to make
them amends for the time I have detained them."

"Ay, that I will with all my heart," quoth Sancho; "but what is
become of the lions? Are they dead or alive?"

Then the keeper very formally related the whole action, not failing
to exaggerate, to the best of his skill, Don Quixote's courage; how, at
his sight alone, the lion was so terrified, that he neither would nor
durst quit his stronghold, though for that end his cage-door was kept
open for a considerable time; and how at length, upon his remonstrat-
ing with the knight, who would have had the lion forced out, that it
was presuming too much upon Heaven, he had permitted, though
with great reluctance, that the lion should be shut up again.

"Well, Sancho," said Don Quixote to his squire, "what dost thou
think of this? Can enchantment prevail over true fortitude? No; these
magicians may rob me of success, but never of my invincible greatness
of mind."

Sancho gave the waggoner and the keeper the two pieces. The first
harnessed his mules, and the last thanked Don Quixote for his bounty,
and promised to acquaint the king himself with his heroic action
when he went to court.

"Well," said Don Quixote, "if his majesty should chance to inquire
who the person was that did this thing, tell him it was the Knight of
the Lions; a name I intend henceforth to take up, in place of that
which I have hitherto borne; in which proceeding I do but conform to
the ancient custom of knights-errant, who changed their names as
often as they pleased, or as it suited with their advantage." . . .

[After many adventures, including the daring descent into the
cave of Montesinos and the experience with the fortune-telling ape,
Don Quixote and his squire come to the castle of a duke who is well
acquainted with their exploits. This whimsical nobleman and his
duchess fall in with the knight's many vagaries and indulge and hoax
him without limit. Through their devices a means is discovered to
disenchant Dulcinea: to that end Sancho must receive thirty-three
hundred lashes. And through their bounty Sancho finally obtains the
governorship of an island, which he rules for ten days and abandons in

frustration. Don Quixote and Sancho finally leave this luxurious existence and come to Barcelona, where they are entertained by the exalted Don Antonia Moreno, who, like everyone else now, knows of their fame. In Barcelona they make the acquaintance of the viceroy and other nobility of the city.]

CHAPTER XCIV

Treating of the adventure which gave Don Quixote more sorrow than any which had hitherto befallen him

. . . Don Quixote, riding out one morning to take the air on the strand, armed at all points, as usual, for, as he was wont to say, his arms were his splendour, and fighting his recreation, he perceived advancing toward him a knight, armed in like manner, with a bright moon blazoned on his shield, who, coming within hearing, called out to him, "Illustrious Don Quixote de la Mancha, I am the Knight of the White Moon, whose incredible achievements perhaps have reached thy ears. Lo! I am come to enter into combat with thee, and to compel thee, by dint of sword, to own and acknowledge my mistress, by whatever name and dignity she be distinguished, to be, without any degree of comparison, more beautiful than thy Dulcinea del Toboso. Now if thou wilt fairly confess this truth, thou freest thyself from certain death, and me from the trouble of taking or giving thee thy life. If not, the conditions of our combat are these: If victory be on my side, thou shalt be obliged immediately to forsake thy arms and the quest of adventures, and to return to thy own house, where thou shalt engage to live quietly and peaceably for the space of one whole year, without laying hand on thy sword, to the improvement of thy estate, and the salvation of thy soul. But, if thou comest off conqueror, my life is at thy mercy, my horse and arms shall be thy trophy, and the fame of all my former exploits, by the lineal descent of conquest, be vested in thee as victor. Consider what thou hast to do, and let thy answer be quick, for my despatch is limited to this very day."

Don Quixote was amazed and surprised, as much at the arrogance of the Knight of the White Moon's challenge, as at the subject of it; so, with a composed and solemn address, he replied, "Knight of the White Moon, whose achievements have as yet been kept from my knowledge, it is more than probable that you have never seen the illustrious Dulcinea; for had you viewed her perfections, you had found arguments enough to convince you, that no beauty, past, present, or to come, can parallel hers; and therefore I tell you, knight, you are mistaken; and this position I will maintain, by accepting your challenge on your own conditions, except that article of your exploits descending to me; for, not knowing what character your actions bear, I shall rest satisfied with the fame of my own, by which, such as they are, I am willing to abide. And since your time is so limited, choose your ground, and begin your career as soon as you will, and expect a fair field and no favour."

While the two knights were adjusting the preliminaries of combat, the viceroy, who had been informed of the Knight of the White Moon's appearance near the city walls, and his parleying with Don Quixote, hastened to the scene of battle. Several gentlemen, and Don Antonio among the rest, accompanied him thither. They arrived just as Don Quixote was wheeling Rozinante to fetch his career, and seeing them both ready for the onset, he interposed, desiring to know the cause of the sudden combat. The Knight of the White Moon told him there was a lady in the case; and briefly repeated to his excellency what passed between him and Don Quixote. The viceroy whispered Don Antonio, and asked him whether he knew that Knight of the White Moon, and whether their combat was not some jocular device to impose upon Don Quixote? Don Antonio answered positively, that he neither knew the knight, nor whether the combat were in jest or earnest. This put the viceroy to some doubt whether he should not prevent their engagement; but being at last persuaded that it must be a jest at the bottom, he withdrew.

"Valorous knights," said he, "if there be no medium between confession and death, but Don Quixote be still resolved to deny, and you, the Knight of the White Moon, as obstinately to urge, I have no more to say; the field is free, and so proceed."

The knights made their compliments to the viceroy; and Don Quixote, making some short ejaculations to Heaven and his lady, as he always used upon these occasions, began his career, without either sound of trumpet or any other signal. His adversary was no less forward; for setting spurs to his horse, which was much the swifter he met Don Quixote so forcibly, before he had run half his career, that without making use of his lance, which it is thought he lifted up on purpose, he overthrew the Knight of La Mancha and Rozinante, both coming to the ground with a terrible fall.

The Knight of the White Moon got immediately upon him; and clapping the point of his lance to his face: "Knight," cried he, "you are vanquished and a dead man, unless you immediately fulfil the conditions of your combat."

Don Quixote, bruised and stunned with his fall, without lifting up his beaver, answered in a faint hollow voice, as if he had spoken out of a tomb, "Dulcinea del Toboso is the most beautiful woman in the world, and I the most unfortunate knight upon the earth. It were unjust that such perfection should suffer through my weakness. No, pierce my body with thy lance, knight, and let my life expire with my honour."

"Not so rigorous neither," replied the conqueror; "let the fame of the Lady Dulcinea remain entire and unblemished; provided the great Don Quixote return home for a year, as we agreed before the combat, I am satisfied."

The viceroy and Don Antonio, with many other gentlemen, were witnesses to all these passages, and particularly to this proposal; to which Don Quixote answered, that upon condition he should be enjoined nothing to the prejudice of Dulcinea, he would, upon the faith of a true knight, be punctual in the performance of everything else. This acknowledgment being made, the Knight of the White Moon turned about his horse, and saluting the viceroy, rode at a hand-gallop into the city, whither Don Antonio followed him, at the viceroy's request, to find out who he was, if possible.

Don Quixote was lifted up, and, upon taking off his helmet, they found him pale, and in a cold sweat. As for Rozinante, he was in so sad a plight, that he could not stir for the present. Then, as for Sancho, he was in so heavy a taking, that he knew not what to do, nor what to say: he was sometimes persuaded he was in a dream, sometimes he fancied this rueful adventure was all witchcraft and enchantment. In short, he found his master discomfited in the face of the world, and bound to good behaviour and to lay aside his arms for a whole year. Now he thought his glory eclipsed, his hopes of greatness vanished into smoke, and his master's promises, like his bones, put out of joint by that terrible fall, which he was afraid had at once crippled Rozinante and his master. At last, the vanquished knight was put into a chair, which the viceroy had sent for that purpose, and they carried him into town, accompanied likewise by the viceroy, who had a great curiosity to know who this Knight of the White Moon was, that had left Don Quixote in so sad a condition.

CHAPTER XCV

*Wherein is given an account of the Knight of the White Moon;
with other matters*

Don Antonio Moreno followed the Knight of the White Moon to
his inn, whither he was attended by a rabble of boys. The knight being
got to his chamber, where his squire waited to take off his armour,
Don Antonio came in, declaring he would not be shaken off till he had
discovered who he was. The knight finding that the gentleman would
not leave him, "Sir," said he, "since I lie under no obligation of concealing myself, if you please, while my man disarms me, you shall
hear the whole truth of the story.

"You must know, sir, I am called the Bachelor Carrasco: I live in
the same town with this Don Quixote, whose unaccountable frenzy
has moved all his neighbours, and me among the rest, to endeavour by
some means to cure his madness; in order to which, believing that rest
and ease would prove the surest remedy, I bethought myself of this
present stratagem; and, about three months ago, in the equipage of a
knight-errant, under the title of the Knight of the Mirrors, I met him
on the road, fixed a quarrel upon him, and the conditions of our combat were as you have heard already. But fortune then declared for him,
for he unhorsed and vanquished me; and so I was disappointed: he
prosecuted his adventures, and I returned home very much hurt with
my fall. But willing to retrieve my credit, I have made this second attempt, and now have succeeded; for I know him to be so nicely
punctual in whatever his word and honour is engaged for, that he will
undoubtedly perform his promise. This, sir, is the sum of the whole
story; and I beg the favour of you to conceal me from Don Quixote,
that my project may not be ruined a second time, and that the honest
gentleman, who is naturally a man of good parts, may recover his understanding."

"Oh, sir," replied Don Antonio, "what have you to answer for, in
robbing the world of the most diverting folly that ever was exposed
among mankind! Consider, sir, that his cure can never benefit the
public half so much as his distemper. But I am apt to believe, Sir
Bachelor, that his madness is too firmly fixed for your art to remove;
and, indeed, I cannot forbear wishing it may be so; for by Don
Quixote's cure, we not only lose his good company, but the drolleries

and comical humours of Sancho Panza too, which are enough to cure melancholy itself of the spleen. However, I promise to say nothing of the matter; though I confidently believe, sir, your pains will be to no purpose."

Carrasco told him, that having succeeded so far, he was obliged to cherish better hopes; and asking Don Antonio if he had any farther service to command him, he took his leave; and packing up his armour on a carriage-mule, presently mounted his charging horse, and leaving the city that very day, posted homewards, meeting no adventure on the road worthy a place in this faithful history.

Don Antonio gave an account of the discourse he had had with Carrasco to the viceroy, who was vexed to think that so much pleasant diversion was like to be lost to all those that were acquainted with the Don's exploits.

Six days did Don Quixote keep his bed, very dejected, and full of severe and dismal reflections on his fatal overthrow. Sancho was his comforter; and among his other crumbs of comfort, "My dear master," quoth he, "cheer up; come, pluck up a good heart, and be thankful for coming off no worse. Why, a man has broken his neck with a less fall, and you have not so much as a broken rib. Consider, sir, that they that game must sometimes lose; we must not always look for bacon where we see the hooks. Come, sir, cry a fig for the doctor, since you will not need him this bout; let us jog home fair and softly, without thinking any more of sauntering up and down, nobody knows whither, in quest of adventures and bloody noses. Why, sir, I am the greatest loser, if you go to that, though it is you that are in the worst pickle. It is true, I was weary of being a governor, and gave over all thoughts that way; but yet I never parted with my inclination of being an earl; and now, if you miss being a king, by casting off your knight-errantry, poor I may go whistle for my earldom."

"No more of that, Sancho," said Don Quixote; "I shall only retire for a year, and then reassume my honourable profession, which will undoubtedly secure me a kingdom, and thee an earldom."

"Heaven grant it may," quoth Sancho, "and no mischief betide us; hope well and have well, says the proverb." . . .

In leaving Barcelona, Don Quixote could not help turning round to survey the spot, which had been the unfortunate scene of his overthrow, and as he did it, he exclaimed: "There stood Troy! there my evil destiny, not my cowardice, despoiled me of my glory: there fortune in her fickleness deserted me; there was the lustre of my exploits obscured; and lastly, there fell my happiness, never to rise again!"

Which Sancho hearing, he said: "It is as much the part of valiant minds, dear sir, to be patient under misfortunes as to rejoice in prosperity; and this I judge by myself; for as, when a governor, I was merry, now that I am a squire on foot, I am not sad. Besides I have often heard, that the dame called Fortune is a capricious jade, and so blind withal, that she does not see what she is about, does not know whom she casts down, or whom she exalts."

"Thou art much of a philosopher, Sancho," answered Don Quixote, "and hast spoken discreetly: though I know not how thy discretion has been acquired. I must however set thee right in one point, which is, that there is no such thing in the world as Fortune, nor do the events which happen in it, be they good or bad, happen by chance, but by the particular appointment of Heaven; and hence the saying, that every man is the maker of his own fortune. I have been so of mine, but not with all the necessary prudence; and my presumption has been punished accordingly: for I ought to have considered, that Rozinante's feebleness was no match for the ponderous bulk of the steed bestrode by the Knight of the White Moon. In short, I adventured; I did my best; I was overthrown, and thereby lost my honour: but I neither did nor could lose my integrity. When I was a knighterrant, daring and valiant, by my deeds I gained credit to my exploits; and, now that I am reduced to a mere walking squire, I will gain reputation to my words, by faithfully performing my promise. March on, therefore, friend Sancho, and let us pass at home in quiet the year of our novitiate; a retreat by which we shall acquire fresh vigour, to return to the never-by-me-to-be-forgotten exercise of arms." . . .

[Don Quixote agrees to spend in La Mancha his year of inaction, and after another visit to the castle of the duke and duchess he and Sancho come home. The knight tells his friends the sad tale of his defeat and declares his intention of living the life of a shepherd. He invites all his companions to join him in this new existence. But at this latest eccentricity his housekeeper and his niece are filled with alarm and wait upon him with unusual care.]

CHAPTER C

How Don Quixote fell sick, made his last will, and died

As all human things, especially the lives of men, are transitory, their very beginnings being but steps to their dissolution; so Don Quixote, who was no way exempted from the common fate, was snatched away by death when he least expected it. He was seized with a violent fever that confined him to his bed for six days, during all which time his good friends, the curate, bachelor, and barber, came often to see him, and his trusty squire Sancho Panza never stirred from his bedside.

They conjectured that his sickness proceeded only from the regret of his defeat, and his being disappointed of Dulcinea's disenchantment; and accordingly they left nothing unessayed to divert him. The bachelor begged him to pluck up a good heart and rise, that they might begin their pastoral life; telling him, that he had already written an eclogue to that purpose, not inferior to those of Sanazaro; and that he had bought, with his own money, of a shepherd of Quintanar, two famous dogs to watch their flock, the one called Barcino, and the other Butron; but this had no effect on Don Quixote, for he still continued dejected. A physician was sent for, who, upon feeling his pulse, did not very well like it; and therefore desired him of all things to provide for his soul's health, for that of his body was in a dangerous condition. Don Quixote heard this much more calmly than those about him; for his niece, his housekeeper, and his squire, fell a-weeping as bitterly as if he had been laid out already. The physician was of opinion that mere melancholy and vexation had brought him to his approaching end. Don Quixote desired them to leave him a little, because he found himself inclined to rest; they retired, and he had a hearty sleep of about six hours which the maid and niece were afraid would have been his last.

At length he awaked, and with a loud voice, "Praised be the Almighty," cried he, "for this great benefit he has vouchsafed to me!"

The niece, hearkening very attentively to these words of her uncle, and finding more sense in them than there was in his usual talk, at least since he had fallen ill: "What do you say, sir?" said she; "has anything extraordinary happened? What mercies are these you mention?"

"Mercies," answered he, "that Heaven has this moment vouchsafed to show me, in spite of all my iniquities. My judgment is returned, clear and undisturbed, and that cloud of ignorance is now removed which the continual reading of those books of knight-errantry had cast over my understanding. I am only sorry the discovery happens so late, when I want time to make amends by those studies that should enlighten my soul, and prepare me for futurity. I find, niece, my end approaches; but I would have it such, that though my life has got me the character of a madman, I may deserve a better at my death. Dear child," continued he, "send for my honest friend the curate, the bachelor Carrasco, and Master Nicholas, the barber; for I intend to make my confession and my will."

His niece was saved the trouble of sending, for presently they all three came in; which Don Quixote perceiving, "My good friends," said he, "I have happy news to tell you; I am no longer Don Quixote de la Mancha, but Alonzo Quixano, the same whom the world, for his fair behaviour, has been formerly pleased to call *The Good*. I now declare myself an enemy to Amadis de Gaul, and his whole generation; all foolish stories of knight-errantry I detest. I have a true sense of the danger of reading them, and of all my past follies; and, through Heaven's mercy and my own experience, I abhor them."

His three friends were not a little surprised to hear him talk at this rate, and concluded some new frenzy had possessed him.

"What now?" said Samson to him: "what is all this to the purpose, Signor Don Quixote? We have just had the news that the lady Dulcinea is disenchanted; and now we are upon the point of turning shepherds, to sing, and live like princes, you are dwindled down to a hermit!"

"No more of that, I beeseech you," replied Don Quixote; "all the use I shall make of these follies at present is to heighten my repentance; and though they have hitherto proved prejudicial, yet, by the assistance of Heaven, they may turn to my advantage at my death: I find it comes fast upon me; therefore pray, gentlemen, let us be serious. I want a priest to receive my confession, and a scrivener to draw up my will. There is no trifling at a time like this; and therefore, pray let the scrivener be sent for, while Mr. Curate prepares me by confession."

Don Quixote's words put them all into such wonder, that they stood gazing upon one another; they thought they had reason to doubt of the return of his understanding, and yet they could not help believing him. They were also apprehensive he was near the point of death, considering the sudden recovery of his intellects; and he delivered himself after that with so much sense, discretion, and piety, and showed himself so resigned to the will of Heaven, that they made no scruple to believe him restored to his perfect judgment at last. The curate thereupon cleared the room of all the company but himself and Don Quixote, and then confessed him. In the meantime the bachelor ran for the scrivener, and presently brought him with him; and Sancho Panza, being informed by the bachelor how ill his master was, and finding his niece and housekeeper all in tears, began to make a sad face and fall a-crying. The curate, having heard the sick man's confession, came out and told them that the good Alonzo Quixano was very near his end, and certainly in his senses; and therefore they had best go in that he might make his will. These dismal tidings opened the sluices of the housekeeper's, the niece's, and the good squire's swollen eyes, so that a whole inundation of tears burst out of those floodgates, and a thousand sighs from their hearts; for indeed, either as Alonzo Quixano, or as Don Quixote de la Mancha, as it has been observed, the sick gentleman had always showed himself such a good-natured man, and of so agreeable a behaviour, that he was not only beloved by his family, but by every one that knew him.

The scrivener, with the rest of the company, then went into the chamber; and the preamble and former part of the will being drawn, and the testator having recommended his soul to Heaven, and bequeathed his body to the earth, according to custom, he came to the legacies, as follows:—

"Item, I give and bequeath to Sancho Panza, whom in my madness I made my squire, whatever money he has or may have of mine in his hands: and whereas there are reckonings and accounts to be adjusted between us, for what he has received and disbursed, my will and pleasure is, that whatever may remain due to me, which can be but small, be enjoyed by him as my free gift, without any let or molestation; and much good may it do him. And as he was, through my means, made governor of an island, I would now, in my right senses, give him the government of a kingdom, were it in my power, in consideration of his integrity and faithfulness. And now, my friend," said he, turning to Sancho, "pardon me that I have brought upon thee, as well as myself, the scandal of madness, by drawing thee into my own errors, and persuading thee that there have been, and still are, knights-errant in the world."

"Woe's me, my dear master's worship!" cried Sancho, all in tears, "do not die this time, but even take my counsel, and live on many years. For shame, sir, do not give way to sluggishness, but get out of your doleful dumps, and rise. Is this a time to lie groaning a-bed, when we should be in the fields, in our shepherd's clothing, as we had resolved? Ten to one but behind some bush, or under some hedge, we may find the Lady Madam Dulcinea stripped of her enchanted rags, and as fine as a queen. Mayhaps you take it to heart that you were unhorsed and a little scratched the other day; but if that be all, lay the blame upon me, and say it was my fault in not girthing Rozinante tight enough. You know, too, there is nothing more common in your errantry-books than for the knights to be every foot jostled out of the saddle. There is nothing but ups and downs in this world, and he that is down to-day may be up to-morrow."

"Even so," said Samson; "honest Sancho has a right notion of the matter."

"Soft and fair, gentlemen," replied Don Quixote; "never look for birds of this year in the nests of the last. I was mad, but now I am in my right senses; I was once Don Quixote de la Mancha, but I am now (as I said before) the plain Alonzo Quixano; and I hope the sincerity of my words, and my repentance, may restore me to the same esteem you have had for me before; and so, Mr. Scrivener, pray go on."

"Item, I constitute and appoint Antonia Quixano, my niece here present, sole heiress of all my estate, real and personal, after all my just debts and legacies, bequeathed by these presents, shall have been paid, satisfied, and deducted out of the best of my goods and chattels; and the first of that kind to be discharged shall be the salary due to my housekeeper, together with twenty ducats over and above her wages, which said sum I leave and bequeath her to buy her mourning.

"Item, I appoint Mr. Curate, and Mr. Samson Carrasco, the bachelor, here present, to be the executors of this my last will and testament.

"Item, It is my will, that if my niece Antonia Quixano be inclinable to marry, it be with none but a person who, upon strict inquiry, shall be found never to have read a book of knight-errantry in his life; and in case it appears that he has been conversant in such books, and that she persists in her resolution to marry him, she is then to forfeit all right and title to my bequest, which, in such case, my executors are hereby empowered to dispose of to pious uses, as they shall think most proper."

Having finished the will, he fell into a swooning fit. All the company were troubled and alarmed, and ran to his assistance. However he came to himself at last, but relapsed into the like fits almost every hour, for the space of three days that he lived after he had made his will.

In short, Don Quixote's last day came, after he had made those preparations for death which good Christians ought to do; and by many fresh and weighty arguments, showed his abhorrence of books of knight-errantry. The scrivener, who was by, protested he had never read in any books of that kind of any knight-errant who ever died in his bed so quietly, and like a good Christian, as Don Quixote did. When the curate perceived that he was dead, he desired the scrivener to give him a certificate how Alonzo Quixano, commonly called *The Good,* and sometimes known by the name of Don Quixote de la Mancha, was departed out of this life into another, and died a natural death. This he desired, lest any other author but Cid Hamet Benengeli should take occasion to raise him from the dead, and presume to write endless histories of his pretended adventures.

Thus died that ingenious gentleman, Don Quixote de la Mancha whose native place Cid Hamet has not thought fit directly to mention, with design that all the towns and villages in La Mancha should contend for the honour of giving him birth, as the seven cities of Greece did for Homer. We shall omit Sancho's lamentations, and those of the niece and the housekeeper, as also several epitaphs that were made for his tomb, and will only give you this which the bachelor Carrasco caused to be put over it—

> "The body of a knight lies here,
>   So brave that, to his latest breath,
> Immortal glory was his care,
>   And made him triumph over death.

> "Nor has his death the world deceived
>   Less than his wondrous life surprised;
> For if he like a madman lived,
>   At least he like a wise one died."

A NOTE ON TYPOGRAPHY

The text of this book has been set on
the Linotype in Granjon 11 point, with one
point leading. The rectangles enclosing the
titles of each selection were drawn by hand, and
the names of authors and works were hand-set in
Bernhard Modern Roman Bold and Bernhard Cursive
Bold. Monotype Garamont and Deepdene appear
in the table of contents and title-page. The
words "Masterworks of World Literature"
on the backbone and title page
were hand-lettered.